Fodor's

GREECE

Portions of this book appear in *Fodor's Greek Islands*.

WELCOME TO GREECE

A visit to the land of Homer, Aristotle, and Sophocles is a journey to the dawn of classical civilization, with archaeological splendors from Athens to Crete. The towering monasteries of Meteora and soaring Mt. Olympus inspire awe, while relaxing islands like Corfu and Santorini invite simple pleasures and a taste of the good life on the Aegean Sea. The Greek countryside presents the perfect coda with idyllic landscapes of cypress groves, vineyards, and olive trees, as well as dramatic coves with sparkling white sand and rugged mountains that plunge into the sea.

TOP REASONS TO GO

★ **Athens.** Spread out below the towering Acropolis, Greece's capital pulses with excitement.

★ **Islands.** Spiritual Patmos, peaceful Naxos, medieval Rhodes, sylvan Skopelos, and more.

★ **Stunning Beaches.** Some 9,000 miles of shoreline mean a beach for every interest.

★ **Ancient Splendors.** Sacred Delphi, ancient Olympia, and the Minoan palaces of Crete.

★ **Food and Drink.** Succulent lamb, freshly grilled fish, fiery ouzo, and flavorful wines.

★ **Nightlife.** The world parties at the beaches of Mykonos and seaside clubs of Glyfada.

Fodor's GREECE

Publisher: Amanda D'Acierno, *Senior Vice President*

Editorial: Arabella Bowen, *Editor in Chief*; Linda Cabasin, *Editorial Director*

Design: Tina Malaney, *Associate Art Director*; Chie Ushio, *Senior Designer*; Ann McBride, *Production Designer*

Photography: Jennifer Arnow, *Senior Photo Editor*; Mary Robnett, *Photo Researcher*; Jennifer Romains, *Photo Researcher*

Production: Linda Schmidt, *Managing Editor*; Evangelos Vasilakis, *Associate Managing Editor*; Angela L. McLean, *Senior Production Manager*

Maps: Rebecca Baer, *Senior Map Editor*; Mark Stroud and Henry Colomb (Moon Street Cartography), David Lindroth, Inc., *Cartographers*

Sales: Jacqueline Lebow, *Sales Director*

Marketing & Publicity: Heather Dalton, *Marketing Director*; Katherine Punia, *Publicity Director*

Business & Operations: Susan Livingston, *Vice President, Strategic Business Planning*; Sue Daulton, *Vice President, Operations*

Fodors.com: Megan Bell, *Executive Director, Revenue & Business Development*; Yasmin Marinaro, *Senior Director, Marketing & Partnerships*

Copyright © 2015 by Fodor's Travel, a division of Random House LLC

Writers: Alexia Amvrazi, Stephen Brewer, Natasha Giannousi-Varney, Hilary Whitton Paipeti, Marissa Tejada, Adrian Vrettos

Editorial Contributor: Linda Coffman

Editors: Douglas Stallings *(lead editor)*, Alexis Crisman Kelly, Denise Leto, Megan Wood

Production Editor: Carolyn Roth

11th Edition

ISBN 978-1-101-87809-5

ISSN 0071-6413

SPECIAL SALES

This book is available at special discounts for bulk purchases for sales promotions or premiums. For more information, e-mail specialmarkets@penguinrandomhouse.com

PRINTED IN THE UNITED STATES OF AMERICA

10 9 8 7 6 5 4 3 2 1

CONTENTS

Fodor's Features

MAPS

ABOUT THIS GUIDE

Fodor's Recommendations

Everything in this guide is worth doing—we don't cover what isn't—but exceptional sights, hotels, and restaurants are recognized with additional accolades. Fodor's Choice★ indicates our top recommendations; and **Best Bets** call attention to notable hotels and restaurants in various categories. Care to nominate a new place? Visit Fodors.com/contact-us.

Trip Costs

We list prices wherever possible to help you budget well. Hotel and restaurant price categories from **$** to **$$$$** are noted alongside each recommendation. For hotels, we include the lowest cost of a standard double room in high season. For restaurants, we cite the average price of a main course at dinner or, if dinner isn't served, at lunch. For attractions, we always list adult admission fees; discounts are usually available for children, students, and senior citizens.

Hotels

Our local writers vet every hotel to recommend the best overnights in each price category, from budget to expensive. Unless otherwise specified, you can expect private bath, phone, and TV in your room. For expanded hotel reviews, facilities, and deals visit Fodors.com.

Top Picks	Hotels &
★ Fodor's Choice	**Restaurants**
	🏨 Hotel
Listings	⇗ Number of
✉ Address	rooms
✉ Branch address	⦿ Meal plans
☎ Telephone	✕ Restaurant
🖷 Fax	⌲ Reservations
⊕ Website	🏛 Dress code
✉ E-mail	▭ No credit cards
🎫 Admission fee	$ Price
⊗ Open/closed	
times	**Other**
Ⓜ Subway	⇨ See also
✛ Directions or	☞ Take note
Map coordinates	⅃ Golf facilities

Restaurants

Unless we state otherwise, restaurants are open for lunch and dinner daily. We mention dress code only when there's a specific requirement and reservations only when they're essential or not accepted. To make restaurant reservations, visit Fodors.com.

Credit Cards

The hotels and restaurants in this guide typically accept credit cards. If not, we'll say so.

EUGENE FODOR

Hungarian-born Eugene Fodor (1905–91) began his travel career as an interpreter on a French cruise ship. The experience inspired him to write *On the Continent* (1936), the first guidebook to receive annual updates and discuss a country's way of life as well as its sights. Fodor later joined the U.S. Army and worked for the OSS in World War II. After the war, he kept up his intelligence work while expanding his guidebook series. During the Cold War, many guides were written by fellow agents who understood the value of insider information. Today's guides continue Fodor's legacy by providing travelers with timely coverage, insider tips, and cultural context.

EXPERIENCE GREECE

WHAT'S NEW

Responding to Crisis

It doesn't take someone with a job on the Athens Stock Exchange to tell you that times are tough in the cradle of democracy—but don't be spooked by the headlines. The Acropolis isn't for sale, and all the natural beauty and updated tourism and cultural sites are still open. Life goes on—in colorful Greek style— but the country's changing finances have brought other changes to Greek society.

Greece became synonymous with the words "economic crisis" when its public debt topped €350 billion. The dire situation caused by overspending on infrastructure, services, and public-sector wages worsened further thanks to rampant tax dodging. Although the roots of the country's financial crisis were decades in the making, the response by the financial markets was not. Large financial institutions were suddenly reluctant to invest further in Greece until the country got its financial house in better order. As a result, the country's borrowing costs skyrocketed, and by 2010, Greece found itself in need of a bailout.

The European Union, International Monetary Fund and European Central Bank—collectively known as "the troika"—agreed to help Greece in its hour of need, but this financial rescue came with significant strings attached. While Greece was offered huge loans to bridge its budgetary chasm, EU authorities required the country to implement stringent austerity measures to cut down on government spending. The Greeks did not like these measures at all and showed their frustration. Protests, strikes, and even some violent riots hit the capital as the government slashed pay and benefits for state employees, reduced incomes, and raised taxes. Unemployment soared, and hundreds of thousands working in the private sector didn't see paychecks for months at a time.

In response to the uncertain economic and social climate, Greek leadership changed hands. In 2012, Andreas Papandreou's Panhellenic Socialist Movement (PASOK) collapsed. Antonis Samaras, the president of New Democracy, became the new Prime Minister. Unexpectedly, a new, controversial far-right political party, Golden Dawn, gained seats in parliament. Golden Dawn's members had been accused of violent attacks against immigrants and are said to follow neo-Nazi philosophies. But the situation is not entirely grim.

Family and Forward Thinking

While the bleak economy and high unemployment have meant that some Greeks have left their homeland for better opportunities abroad, a strong sense of family has allowed others to weather this storm. Families worked together to provide childcare and help to their elders. With less income, trips abroad became a dream. However, for Greeks, summer vacations are considered a birthright, so in tough times many tap their family networks to head out to a cousin's cottage by the sea. Greeks are strongly connected to their roots and enjoy spending holidays at traditional village homes, away from the city.

In fact, many Greeks began to look at their villages in a new way. They have learned that local agricultural products, which provide cheap, healthy, and delicious sustenance for Greeks at home, can also be marketed with success abroad. While Greece remains the world's top olive oil consumer, they have fallen behind competing producers, Spain and Italy. Instead of packaging their oil in bulk, producers

have begun to bottle and market their quality extra virgin olive oil abroad for the first time. This move has spurred new entrepreneurship in one of the oldest and largest agriculture markets of the country.

Starting Up

Greece has always shown strong entrepreneurship, but the country has remained mostly unproductive and associated with corruption. While most ventures still follow the failed principles of the past, there are a few high-impact start-ups that have succeeded, and these have had an impact in tourism.

Mobile apps like TaxiBeat, Bug Sense, and Pinnatta and high-tech companies like Workable are setting a high bar. Meanwhile, the eco-minded furniture company Coco-Mat and successful cosmetics companies like Apivita and Korres continue to establish their worldwide presence, setting the bar for success. Agribusiness and tourism, Greece's most promising sectors, continue to move forward with companies like Fage, mastihashop, and Hotelbrain.

A Bright Light for Tourism?

Despite the vast political and socioeconomic upheaval, Greeks remain optimistic by nature and remain hospitable hosts. No matter what challenges they face as a country, they're a proud, warm-hearted, and outgoing people that continue to be as welcoming as ever. One-fifth of the population of Greece works in tourism, and more than 18 million tourists visit Greece annually. Greeks are moving forward with innovative ideas to showcase the country's beautiful landscape and islands.

The Annual Spetses Mini-Marathon has gathered a considerable following since it started in 2010, and other islands have begun to offer sporting events, spurning new waves of island sport tourism. And in 2014, after years of unveiled—then failed—plans for a seaplane network between the islands, Hellenic Seaplanes plans for service to begin by early 2015. These flights will not only bring tourists to the islands but also connect communities. The company hopes to provide service to more than 100 islands, many of which have no airport.

Back in the capital, Greeks are going back to their roots to survive the downturn. In the center of Athens, restaurant, bar, and café owners are bringing new life to once-abandoned squares and streets in the commercial center, including Platia Agia Irini. Steady as ever above the modern city built around it, the Acropolis continues to welcome tourists daily as it undergoes a seemingly endless renovation plan. Nearby, the Acropolis Museum elegantly showcases its ancient wares.

By night, there is no sign of crisis as the country's nightlife remains as vibrant as ever. Traditional and often pricey Greek music clubs called *bouzoukia* pump with live music that inspires flower-throwing and tabletop dancing into the early morning hours. For the first time, Greek pop music bands are headlining on its raised stages to attract a wider audience. In the summer, outdoor clubs that hug the coastline of the Athens Riviera open up for the summer with refurbished, glamorous seaside balconies welcoming posh Greek clubbers who still prefer to smoke and stare, rather than dance.

And while some businesses struggle, new hotels and business open all over Greece, including on the islands.

WHAT'S WHERE

Numbers correspond to chapters.

3 Athens. The capital has greeted the new millennium with a sleek subway and other spiffy municipal makeovers. But for five-million Athenians, it's still the tried-and-true pleasures that put the spin on urban life here: the endless parade of cafés, the charming Plaka district, and, most of all, the glorious remnants of one of the greatest civilizations the West ever produced, such as the Acropolis.

4 Attica. Some of the most important remains of ancient Greece are only an hour away from Athens. Delphi was center of the universe for the ancients; at Marathon, the Athenians defeated the Persians; and the Temple of Poseidon hovers between sea and sky at Sounion.

5 The Saronic Gulf Islands. When Athenians want a break, they often make a quick crossing to the idyllic islands of the Saronic Gulf. You're well-advised to follow suit. The most popular of these destinations are Aegina, Hydra, and Spetses.

6 The Sporades. The northern Sporades deliver quintessential Greek-island pleasures: villages spilling down hillsides like giant sugar cubes, Byzantine monasteries, and ageless paths, where the tinkle of goat bells may be the only sound for miles. Weekenders savor Skiathos, but Skopelos has great beaches and Skyros is washed by some of the clearest waters in Greece.

7 Epirus and Thessaly. Less visited than other parts of Greece and none the worse for it, Epirus is a land of stark mountains and swift rivers, where Ali Pasha ruled an 18th-century kingdom from the handsome lakeside city of Ioannina. The route east to Thessaly leads into the Meteora—the name derives from "to hang in midair," which is what the region's mountain-top Byzantine monasteries spectacularly do.

8 Thessaloniki and Central Macedonia. This northern region shelters two of Greece's most sacred places, Mount Olympus, the stormy heights where Zeus reigned, and Mount Athos, a male-only sanctuary dedicated, ironically, to the Virgin Mary. The hub of the region is Thessoloniki, Greece's second-largest city—a cosmo-politan crossroads leading to Pella and Vergina, remnants of Alexander the Great's Macedo-nian empire.

9 Corfu. Temperate, multi-hued Corfu—of turquoise waters lapping rocky coves, and jacaranda spread over

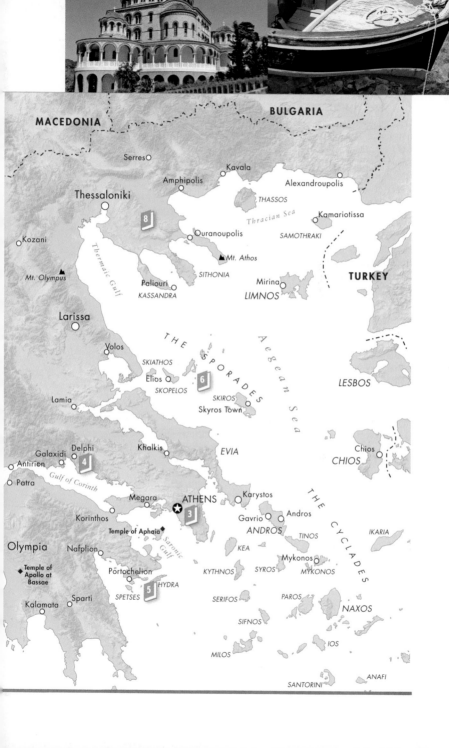

WHAT'S WHERE

cottages—could have inspired Impressionism. The island has a history equally as colorful, reflecting the commingling of Venetians, French, and British. First stop, of course, is Corfu town—a stage set for a Verdi opera.

10 The Peloponnese. The veritable birthplace of Greece, the rugged mountains that loom here cradle some of Greece's most important ancient sites—Olympia, Corinth, Mycenae, and Ancient Messene. Gorgeous Nafplion is the work of later empire builders—Byzantines, Venetians, and Turks—and is as mellow as wines from the region's vineyards. Southward lies rugged Sparta and the often inhospitable but hauntingly beautiful Mani peninsula.

11 The Cyclades. The ultimate Mediterranean archipelago, the Cyclades easily conjure up the magical words "Greek islands." Santorini, with its ravishing caldera, is the most picturesque; Mykonos, with its sexy jet-set lifestyle, takes the prize for hedonism. Mountainous Folegandros, verdant Naxos, idyllic Sifnos, church-studded Tinos, and Brad Pitt–discovered Antiparos have their own distinct charms, and all center on ancient Delos, birthplace of Apollo.

12 Crete. Crete is Greece's southernmost and largest island, and the claims to superlatives don't stop there. Here, too, are some of Greece's tallest mountains, its deepest gorge, many of its best beaches, and a wealth of Venetian and Byzantine wonders. Treasure of treasures is the Palace of Knossos— the high point of Minoan civilization.

13 Rhodes and the Dodecanese. Wrapped enticingly around the shores of Turkey, the Dodecanese ("Twelve Islands") have attracted some notable visitors. St. John the Divine received his *Revelation* on Patmos, Hippocrates established a healing center on Kos, and the Crusader Knights of St. John lavished their wealth on palaces in Rhodes, still famed for its glitzy resorts.

14 Northern Aegean Islands. Flung like puzzle pieces into the Aegean, each of these green and gold islands is distinct: Chios retains an eerie beauty amid its fortified villages and Byzantine monasteries; Lesbos is a getaway favored by artists and writers; and lush, mountainous Samos whispers of the classical wonders of antiquity.

Larissa

Volos

Elio

Lamia

Delphi

Khalkis

Galaxidi

Gulf of Corinth

Megara

Korinthos

Temple of Aphaia

Nafplion

10

Portochelion

HYD

Sparti

Kalamata

MEDITERRANEAN SEA

KITHIRA

0   40 mi

0   40 km

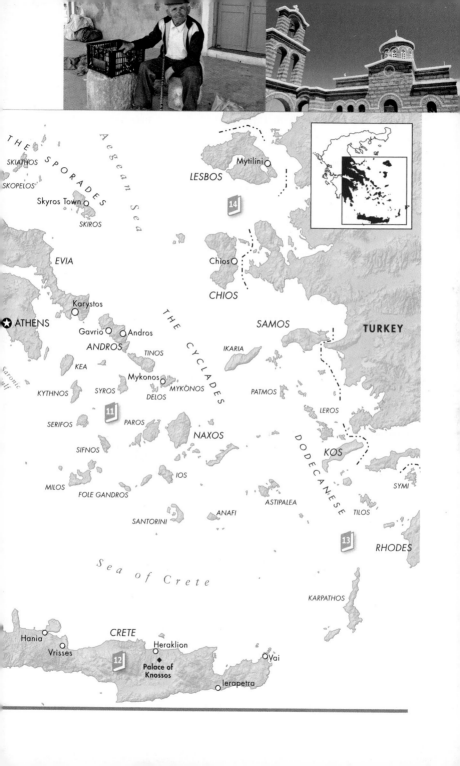

NEED TO KNOW

AT A GLANCE

Capital: Athens

Population: 10,815,197

Currency: Euro

Money: ATMs are common, but some smaller places don't take credit cards

Language: Greek

Country Code: ☎ 30

Emergencies: ☎ 166

Driving: On the right

Electricity: 200v/50 cycles; electrical plugs have two round prongs

Time: Six hours ahead of New York

Documents: Up to 90 days with valid passport; Schengen rules apply

Mobile Phones: GSM (900 and 1800 bands)

Major Mobile Companies: Cosmote, Vodafone, Wind

WEBSITES

Greece: ⊕ www.visitgreece.gr

Athens: ⊕ www. breathtakingathens.com

Greek Ministry of Culture: ⊕ www.culture.gr

GETTING AROUND

✈ **Air Travel:** Most flights are to Athens (or Thessaloniki). Crete, Mykonos, and Santorini also have international airports.

🚌 **Bus Travel:** There is an extensive network of inexpensive, orange KTEL buses that are fairly modern and depart from Athens for major sites such as Sounion, Delphi, and Olympia.

🚗 **Car Travel:** If you want to explore at your own pace on the mainland or islands, a car is a good idea.

🚆 **Train Travel:** Except for the Athens metro, trains in Greece are limited and unreliable.

PLAN YOUR BUDGET

	HOTEL ROOM	MEAL	ATTRACTIONS
Low Budget	€80	€10	90-minute Athens metro ticket, €1.40
Mid Budget	€120	€25	Ticket for the Athens Concert Hall (Megaron Mousikis), €25
High Budget	€400	€120	Night out at a Greek music club (*bouzoukia*), €100

WAYS TO SAVE

Share a platter of *mezedes*. Typical small plates with a bit of wine make a great meal.

Visit the local farmers' market. Weekly farmers' markets sell fresh ingredients for a home-cooked Greek meal.

Take advantage of air ticket offers. Even with the merger of Aegean and Olympic Air, there are still frequent sales on domestic flights.

Unification of Archaeological Sites ticket. The combined ticket (€12) includes a week of access to major sights in Athens.

Hassle Factor	Medium. Flights to Athens are frequent, but most require a change in Europe; in the summer, cheaper charter flights go directly to the islands.
3 days	Visit Athens and venture out to watch the sun set over the Temple of Poseidon at Sounion, or you can do a short island escape.
1 week	Combine a short trip to Athens with an island stay and perhaps an overnight at Delphi.
2 weeks	You can visit two or three islands of your choice, before heading back to Athens to visit the Acropolis and its museum.

WHEN TO GO

High Season: June through August is the most expensive and popular time to visit Greece. Athens is fairly empty in August, except for the mobs of tourists.

Low Season: Most island hotels are closed in the low season, from mid-October to the end of April, although this is the perfect time to discover the mountainous regions of the mainland, including the ski resorts not too far from Delphi. Athens is cold and humid.

Value Season: May and September offer the best combination of mild Mediterranean weather and value. The Aegean may still be too cold for swimming in May, but things get better in early June, when you are still beating the crowds. Some island hotels are open until the start of November; others close in early October. An Athenian city break is a good, affordable option all year round.

BIG EVENTS

April/May: Greek Easter is a movable feast: a traditional highlight is lamb roasting on the spit.

August: The Assumption of Mary on August 15 marks summer vacation for Greeks.

November: Run in the Athens Classic Marathon ⊕ www.athensauthenticmarathon.gr.

May to October: The Athens and Epidavros Festival invites global artists to perform in magnificent surroundings ⊕ www.greekfestival.gr.

READ THIS

■ *Eurydice Street: A Place in Athens,* Sofka Zinovieff. The author adapts to life in Athens.

■ *Murder in Mykonos,* Jeffrey Siger. Big-time detective from Athens needs to prove himself fast.

■ *Sunlight in the Wine,* Robert Leigh. An Englishman moves to the island of Andros for a simpler life.

WATCH THIS

■ *Mamma Mia!* A feel-good Abba musical.

■ *Captain Corelli's Mandolin.* A WWII Italian officer falls in love on Cephallonia.

■ *Zorba the Greek.* Anthony Quinn brings the Greek spirit to life.

EAT THIS

■ **Feta cheese:** crumbly aged sheep or goat cheese

■ **Greek salad:** country salad with feta and seasoning

■ **Moussaka:** layered eggplant, potato, and ground meat, topped with béchamel

■ **Fava:** a traditional Santorini dip made of pureed yellow split peas

■ **Pita me gyro:** spit-roasted meat, wrapped in pita with tomatoes, onions, and tzatziki

■ **Lamb kleftiko:** slow-roasted leg of lamb wrapped in baking paper

ISLAND FINDER

Not sure which Greek island is your kind of paradise? Use this chart to compare how each island measures up to your vacation dreams.

	Aegina	Hydra	Spetses	Corfu	Skiathos	Skopelos	Skyros	Crete	Mykonos	Tinos	Naxos
Tops for Hotels	○	●	◐	●	●	◐	◐	●	●	◐	◑
Tops for Beauty	○	●	◐	●	●	●	●	●	○	○	○
Tops for Food	◐	●	○	◐	●	◐	◐	●	●	●	◑
White-Cube Houses	○	○	○	○	○	○	○	○	○	○	◑
Charming Harbors	○	●	●	◐	◐	●	●	●	◐	●	◑
Deserted Beaches	●	◐	○	○	○	●	◐	●	○	◐	○
Beaches for Activities	●	○	◐	◐	●	◐	○	●	●	●	◑
Gorgeous Beaches	●	○	◐	◐	◐	●	◐	●	○	◐	○
Authentically Greek	○	●	◐	○	◐	●	●	●	○	●	◑
Picturesque Villages	○	●	◐	◐	○	◐	●	●	◐	○	○
Archaeological Sites	●	◐	○	○	○	○	○	●	●	◐	○
Medieval and Byzantine Sites	◐	●	○	○	◐	◐	◐	●	○	○	◑
Good for Families	●	○	◐	●	◐	●	◐	●	○	◐	○
For Partygoers	○	◐	◐	◐	○	○		◐	●	●	◑
Folkloric Shopping	○	●	◐	○	○	◐	●	●	○	●	◑
Historic Homes/Museums	○	●	●	●	●	◐	●	●	○	◐	○
Crowds	○	●	◐	●	●	◐	○	●	●	○	◑
Postcard Churches	◐	●	○	○	◐	●	◐	◐	●	○	○
For Romantics	○	●	◐	◐	○	●	●	○	●	◐	○
Good Bus System	●	○	○	◐	◐	◐	◐	●	●	◐	○
Good Walks	◐	●	○	○	◐	●	◐	◐	◐	◐	○
Natural Wonders	◐	●	○	○	○	◐	◐	◐	○	○	○
Blue Sea Vistas	●	◐	○	●	◐	●	●	●	○	○	○
For Culture Lovers	◐	●	◐	◐	○	◐	◐	◐	◐	●	◑

KEY: ○ few or none ◑ moderate ● noteworthy

Paros	Santorini	Folegandros	Sifnos	Rhodes	Symi	Kos	Patmos	Lesbos	Chios	Samos
◐	●	○	○	◐	○	◐	◐	◐	◐	●
◐	●	●	●	◐	●	◐	●	●	●	◐
◐	●	○	○	○	○	○	◐	●	●	◑
◐	●	●	◐	○	○	○	○	○	○	○
◐	◐	◐	◐	○	●	○	○	○	○	●
○	○	◐	○	◐	●	◐	●	◐	◐	◑
◐	◐	○	○	●	○	●	◐	◐	◐	●
○	○	○	◐	◐	◐	◐	●	●	●	●
◐	○	●	●	◐	●	○	●	●	●	●
◐	●	●	◐	◐	◐	○	◐	◐	●	●
◐	●	○	○	◐	○	◐	○	◐	◐	●
○	◐	○	●	◐	◐	○	●	●	●	●
○	○	○	○	●	◐	●	◐	●	●	●
○	●	○	○	◐	○	●	○	◐	○	●
◐	◐	○	◐	◐	◐	◐	◐	○	◐	◑
◐	◐	○	◐	●	◐	○	○	●	●	◑
◐	●	○	○	●	○	●	○	○	○	◑
○	●	●	◐	◐	●	◐	●	◐	●	●
○	●	●	○	○	●	○	●	◐	●	●
○	◐	●	◐	●	○	●	●	◐	◐	◑
◐	●	◐	◐	◐	●	◐	●	●	●	◑
◐	●	◐	◐	◐	●	◐	●	●	●	●
◐	●	●	○	●	●	●	●	◐	◐	●
○	○	○	○	◐	○	◐	◐	●	●	●

GREECE
TOP ATTRACTIONS

The Acropolis

(A) The great emblem of classical Greece has loomed above Athens (whose harbor of Piraeus is gateway to all the Greek Islands) for 2,500 years. Even from afar, the sight of the Parthenon—the great marble temple that the 5th century BC statesmen Pericles conceived to crown the site—stirs strong feelings about the achievements and failings of Western Civilization.

Corfu

(B) More than a million visitors a year answer the call of the island that inspired the landscapes of Shakespeare's *The Tempest*. Historically, these admirers are in good company—Normans, Venetians, Turks, Napoléon Bonaparte, and the British have all occupied Corfu, leaving fortresses, seaside villas, and an unforgettable patina of cosmopolitan elegance.

Delphi

(C) On Greece's most sacred ground, follow in the footsteps of the ancients and step into the temple of Apollo, where the Pythian oracle may or may not present a garbled answer to your questions. Even if the oracle doesn't send you into a spell, the spectacle of the sanctuary, theater, and treasure-filled museum will.

Knossos

(D) Crete will introduce you to the marvels of the Minoans, the first great European civilization that flourished around 1500 BC. First stop is Knossos, the massive palace complex of King Minos, then it's on to the nearby archaeological museum in Heraklion, where the playful frescoes that once lined the royal chambers show just how urbane these early forbearers were.

Meteora

(E) Getting closer to God, being halfway to Heaven . . . however you choose to describe the experience, ascending to these Byzantine monasteries perched atop 1,000-foot-high peaks is a most unearthly experience. With worldly diversions so far below, the religious visions lavishly pictured in frescoes and mosaics are all the more transcendent.

Mykonos

(F) Backpackers and jet-setters alike share the beautiful beaches and the Dionysian nightlife—this island is not called the St-Tropez of the Aegean without reason—but the old ways of life continue undisturbed in fishing ports and along mazelike town streets. Not only are the hotels and cafés picture-perfect, the famous windmills actually seem to be posing for your camera.

Olympia

(G) The games that still hold all the world in their thrall were first staged here in the pine-scented stadium and hippodrome, arranged around a sacred zone of temples, in 776 BC. Natives of Greek city-states called a temporary truce and suspended all warfare to compete peacefully in their chariot races, boxing matches, and pentathlons, a tradition we moderns would be wise to follow.

Santorini

(H) One of the world's most picturesque islands cradles the sunken caldera of a volcano that last erupted around 1600 BC. To merely link the phenomenon to the Atlantis myth and the Minoan collapse misses the point—what matters is the ravishing sight of the multicolor cliffs rising 1,100 feet out of sparkling blue waters, a visual treat that makes the heart skip a beat or two.

IF YOU LIKE

Ancient Splendors

The sight greets you time and again in Greece—a line of solid, sun-bleached masonry silhouetted against a clear blue sky. If you're lucky, a cypress waves gently to one side. What makes the scene all the more fulfilling is the realization that a kindred spirit looked up and saw the same temple or theater some 2,000 or more years ago. Temples, theaters, statues, a stray Doric column or two, the fragment of a Corinthian capital: these traces of the ancients are thick on the ground in Greece, from the more than 3,000-year-old **Minoan Palace of Knossos** on the island of Crete to such relatively "new" monuments as the **Parthenon.** You can prepare yourself by reading up on mythology, history, and architecture, but get used to the fact that coming upon these magnificent remnants of ancient civilizations is likely to send a chill up your spine every time you see them.

Temple of Poseidon, Sounion, Attica. Set over the sea and showstopper of the Apollo Coast, the extant columns of this great temple are one of the icons of ancient Greece, hallowed by King Aegeus and visited by Lord Byron.

Delphi, west of Attica. Set in a spectacular vale, this was the ancient site of the most venerated and consulted Greek oracle. The site is breathtaking, and the remnant artworks, such as the fabled *Charioteer,* even more so.

Mycenae, Northern Peloponnese. Haunted by the legendary spirits of Agamennon and Clytemnestra, this royal town of the 13th century BC conjures up the days of Homer, thanks to such staggering relics as the Lion Gate.

Majestic Monasteries

A legacy of the great Byzantine era, and often aligned with great historic churches of the Greek Orthodox Church, the monasteries of Greece seem as spiritual and peaceful as when St. John walked the land. A religious mystique hangs over these island retreats, infusing them with a sense of calm that you will appreciate even more when escaping from party-central towns or overcrowded beaches. The natural beauty and calm of many of these places heal your body and soul, revitalizing you for the rest of your trip.

Monastery of St. John the Theologian, Patmos. On the hill overlooking Hora is this retreat built to commemorate St. John in the 11th century—not far away is the cave where he experienced his *Revelation,* near the Monastery of the Apocalypse.

Nea Moni, Chios, the Northern Aegean Islands. The island of Chios has an array of stunningly perched monasteries, including this one, whose interior blazes with color, marble slabs, and mosaics of Christ's life. Built by an 11th-century emperor, it has a rare octagonal Katholikon church.

Monastery of Taxiarchis Michael Panormitis, Symi, the Dodecanese. Dedicated to Symi's patron saint, the protector of sailors, this magnificently frescoed monastery—landmarked by its elaborate bell tower—makes a great day trip from Symi, but why not make a night of it by booking one of its 60 guest rooms?

Evangelistria, Skiathos, the Sporades. Sitting on Skiathos's highest point, not far from the town of Lalaria, is this late-18th-century jewel, looming above a gorge and set with a magnificent church with three domes.

Natural Wonders

Some countries have serene pastures and unobtrusive lakes, environments beautiful in a subtle way. Not Greece. Its landscapes seem put on Earth to astound outright, and often the intertwined history and spiritual culture are equally powerful. This vibrant modern nation is a land of majestic mountains whose slopes housed the ancient gods long before they nestled Byzantine monasteries or ski resorts. The country's sapphire-rimmed islands served as a cradle of great civilizations before they became playgrounds for sailors and beach lovers. If there are no temples to the ancient gods on many of the mountains on the Greek islands, the looming summits that seem to reach into the heavens, impressive from any perspective, inspired the Greeks to worship natural forces. Many islands have ancient goat and donkey trails that are sublime hikes; prime walking months are April, May, and September, when temperatures are reasonable, wildflowers seem to cover every surface, and birds are on their migratory wing.

Samaria Gorge, Hania, Crete. From Omalos, a zigzag path descends steeply 2,500 feet into the tremendous Samaria gorge that splits the cliffs here for 13 km (8 miles) down to Ayia Roumeli on the Libyan Sea. Catch views of the Cretan *kri-kri* goat near the famous "Iron Gates" stone passageway.

The flooded caldera, Santorini, the Cyclades. What may be the most beautiful settlements in the Cyclades straddle the wondrous crescent of cliffs, striated in black, pink, brown, white, and pale green, rising 1,100 feet over the haunting, wine-color Aegean Sea.

The Most Beautiful Towns and Villages

Historic, simple, famous, nondescript, or perfectly preserved: almost any Greek village seems to possess that certain balance of charm and mystique that takes your breath away. The sight of miragelike white clusters of houses appearing alongside blue waters or tumbling down cliffs and hillsides is one of the top allures of any trip here. Villages are awash in cubical, whitewashed houses—often built atop one another along mazelike streets (designed to confound invaders). Add in distinctive architectural landmarks—a Byzantine cathedral, a Venetian 16th-century *kastro* (fortress), and monasteries that seem sculpted of zabaglione custard—and these villages and towns often look like unframed paintings.

Rethymnon, Crete. A Venetian *fortessa* rests on a hill above this city, where cobblestone alleyways squirm their way through Turkish and Italianate houses. Bypass the newer parts of town to stroll through the Venetian harbor, packed solid with atmospheric cafés and shops.

Ia, Santorini, the Cyclades. Here you can find the cubical white houses you've dreamed of and a sunset that is unsurpassed.

Hydra, the Saronic Gulf Islands. The chico-scenti steal away to this harbor beauty, set with crumbling 19th-century merchant's mansions, joyously festive waterside cafés, art galleries, and some Hollywood pixie dust (Sophia Loren filmed *Boy on a Dolphin* here).

Corfu town, Corfu. A little beauty of a city, Corfu town retains evocative traces of its Venetian, French, and British occupiers. It is a grand gateway to one of the greenest and perhaps prettiest islands in all Greece.

GREAT ITINERARIES

CLASSICAL SITES

Lovers of art, antiquity, and mythology journey to Greece to make a pilgrimage to its great archaeological sites. Here, at Delphi, Olympia, and Epidauros, the gods of Olympus were revered, Euripides's plays were first presented, and some of the greatest temples ever built still evoke the genial atmosphere of Greece's golden age (in spite of 2,500 years of wear and tear). Take this tour and you'll learn that it's not necessary to be a scholar of history to feel the proximity of ancient Greece.

2 Days: Athens

Begin at the beginning—the Acropolis plateau—where you can explore the greatest temple of Periclean Greece, the Parthenon, while drinking in heart-stopping views over the modern metropolis. After touring the ancient Agora, the Monument of Lysikrates, and the Odeon of Herod Atticus, finish up at the National Archaeological Museum (check opening hours). ⇨ *Chapter 3.*

Logistics: *Your Acropolis ticket also gets you into the other archaeological sites in Athens. Use the efficient Metro to avoid constant traffic slowdowns.*

1 Day: Sounion

Sun, sand, art, and antiquity all lie southeast of Athens in Sounion. Here, the spectacular Temple of Poseidon sits atop a cliff 195 feet over the Saronic Gulf. Pay your own respects to the god of the sea at the beach directly below or enjoy the coves of the Apollo Coast as you head back west to the seaside resort of Vouliagmeni for an overnight. ⇨ *Attica in Chapter 4.*

Logistics: *If you don't want to go on your own, most travel agencies offer tours to Sounion, and then you can spend another night in Athens.*

1 Day: Eleusis and Corinth

Heading west of Athens, make a stop at Eleusis, home of the Sanctuary of Demeter and the haunted grotto of Hades, god of the Underworld. Past the Isthmus of Corinth—gateway to the Peloponnese—Ancient Corinth and its sublime Temple of Apollo beckon. Head south to the coast and Nafplion; en route, stop at a roadside stand for some tasty Nemean wine. ⇨ *Attica in Chapter 4 and Argolid and Corinthiad in Chapter 10.*

Logistics: *Stopping briefly at Eleusis is easier if you have a car. Otherwise, you are at the mercy of bus schedules.*

2 Days: Nafplion, Tiryns, Mycenae, Epidauros

Nafplion is a stage set of Venetian fortresses, Greek churches, and neoclassical mansions, and you can explore the mysteries of forgotten civilizations in nearby Tiryns, Mycenae, and Epidauros. North is Tiryns, where Bronze Age ramparts bear witness to Homer's "well-girt city." Farther north is Agamemnon's blood-soaked realm, the royal citadel of Mycenae, destroyed in 468 BC. Then take a day trip east to the famous ancient Theater at Epidauros, where a summer drama festival still presents the great tragedies of Euripides. ⇨ *Argolid and Corinthiad in Chapter 10.*

Logistics: *Set up base in Nafplion and visit the nearby sights at your leisure. It's obviously easier to do this if you have a car.*

2 Days: Olympia and Bassae

After your third overnight in Nafplion, head west to Olympia—holiest site of the ancient Greek religion, home to the Sanctuary of Zeus, and birthplace of the Olympics. Walk through the olive groves of the sacred precinct; then get acquainted with Praxiteles' *Hermes* in the museum.

Overnight here and then make a trip south to the remote Temple of Apollo at Bassae. ⇨ *Argolid/Corinthiad and Arcadia in Chapter 10.*

Logistics: *From Nafplion, you can get to Olympia via Argos by train or Tripoli by car (on the E65).*

1 Day: Delphi

Set aside a day to discover Delphi, whose noble dust and ancient ruins are theatrically set amid cliffs. Despite the tour buses, it is still possible to imagine the power of the most famous oracle of antiquity. From here, head back to Athens. ⇨ *In Delphi and Environs in Chapter 4.*

Logistics: *From Olympia, head north through verdant forests of the Elis region to Patras or nearby Rion for the ferry or bridge across the Corinthian Gulf; travel east along the coast and overnight in chic Galaxidi, with its elegant stone seafarers' mansions.*

TIPS

KTEL buses leave from Platia Aigyptou, Liossion, and Odos Kifissou terminals in downtown Athens and connect to most of the major sites: southeast to Sounion along the coast, northwest to Delphi, and west to the Peloponnese. In some cases you will need to take the bus to the provincial capital (Corinth, Argos, Tripoli), then change to a local bus.

Daily trains connect Athens's Peloponnisou station to Corinth and Argos, with bus connections to Nafplion and Olympia.

These are popular destinations and can also be seen on guided tours arranged through almost any travel agent in Athens.

GREAT ITINERARIES

MARVELS OF CENTRAL GREECE

With a rich wilderness of mountains, rocky gorges, and white-water rivers crossed by stone-arch bridges, Epirus is the antithesis of what most people think about Greece. Take a tour of the region that sweeps down from the borders of Albania, and drive south into Central Greece almost to the Gulf of Corinth to discover a stunning landscape that shows off Greece's mountainous character at its best.

1 Day: Ioannina

Ioannina, which was a crossroads of trading, is the handsome capital of Epirus and reflects its Balkan, Ottoman, and Byzantine roots that are preserved in its Old Town. You can soak in the panoramic view of the city from its castle walls that date back to AD 528 and visit the city's Byzantine Museum within the city's citadel. Take a boat ride and glide to the city's landmark, Lake Pamvotis, for a stop at Nissi Island. Visit the little village on Nissi, which is free of most vehicular traffic, then head to the museum that unveils the historical details of enigmatic Ottoman ruler, Ali Pasha, during his dramatic reign of the region from 1788 until he was deposed by the Turks in 1821. It's housed in the 16th-century era Pandelimonos Monastery, where Ali Pasha lived until he was killed. ⇨ *Chapter 7.*

Logistics: *A bus from Athens to Ioannina can take 7 hours; it's much easier to fly.*

1 Day: Zagorohoria

In the Zagorohoria region north of Ioannina, numerous traditional villages defined by stone, wood, and slate rock hug the mountain slopes. Admire the handicrafts in Monodendri village,

altitude 3,400 feet, where you can also enter the depths of the Vikos Gorge, the deepest in the world, and walk the cobblestone trail to the 15th-century Aghia Paraskevi Monastery. ⇨ *Chapter 7.*

Logistics: *Drive from Ioannina to Zagorohoria (1 hour), or take a bus. There are just a few places to stay in Zagorohoria, so you may want to remain for a second night in Ioannina and visit on a day-trip, especially if you have a car. The area can be especially busy during summer weekends in July and August, so plan ahead if visiting during that time.*

1 Day: Metsovo

Metsovo is a traditional village cascading down a mountainside in the heart of the Pindos mountain range (below the Katara pass marking the highest point in Greece and the border between Epirus and Thessaly), where outdoor aficionados can hike and raft. Even during the summer, the temperatures at this altitude will be considerably cooler than in other parts of Greece, with highs in the 70s F. Wind down in the village and walk through its stone-paved streets. Be sure to see the Tositsa Museum, the home of one of the village's most prominent families. Stop to sample local wines and cheeses; the Katogi-Averoff Winery is an important regional winery and produces fine red wines. ⇨ *Chapter 7.*

Logistics: *Metsovo is another 1½ hours from Zagorohoria; drive to Kalambaka (1 hour farther), just outside Meteora, for an overnight stay.*

1 Day: Meteora

Wake up ready to spend the day exploring Meteora's sky-high monasteries built on seemingly inaccessible sandstone peaks. In an awe-inspiring effort, Byzantine emperors funded the construction of these

aeries, and monks settled on these rock towers from the 11th century onwards. At one point there were 16 monasteries. Today only six remain, and they are on the UNESCO World Heritage list. ⇨ *Chapter 7.*

Logistics: *Two or three monasteries are usually enough for anyone. After your visit, drive to the next stop, Delphi (3½ hours), in the early afternoon.*

2 Days: Delphi and Environs

Wake up in the land that was once regarded as the center of the world by Ancient Greeks. Spend the day touring the archeological site of Delphi. Positioned on the slopes of Mt. Parnassos the site housed the ancients' most famous oracle. Next, visit Arachova, also perched on the slopes of Mt. Parnassos, and stop at the monastic complex of Osios Loukas before returning to either Delphi or Arachova for the night. ⇨ *Chapter 4.*

Logistics: *It's three to four hours back to Athens by car, longer if you are going by bus.*

TIPS

■ Points in Epirus may be quite high in altitude, and those who are sensitive to heights may be affected. Mountain roads may have numerous blind curves and they can be steep. Drive with caution.

■ The preferred route back to Athens takes you back through Levadia; if you want a short detour, follow the signs for the ancient springs of Lethe and Mnemosyne.

■ Guided tours can get you to Delphi and back, but to do this full itinerary, you will need to rent a car or take multiple buses.

GREAT ITINERARIES

GREECE'S GREAT NORTH

Northern Greece sparkles with the sights, sounds, and aromas of a melting-pot history and crossroads geography. The region's seaside capital, Thessaloniki, impresses with its young, hip nightlife, diverse culture, and easy-going nature. Just east of the metropolis is the trident-shaped arch of Halkidiki, the summer playground for northern Greeks and southeastern Europeans. The landmass juts out into the Aegean, offering spectacular beaches lined with aquamarine waters and green rolling hills and mountains. The Sporadic Island chain including its southernmost island, Skyros, matches that nature with the same loveliness with the charm only a Greek Island can offer. To get the most out of your trip around Northern Greece's coast and on Skyros island, plan your flights in advance and consider the drive times between each destination.

3 Days: Skyros

Fly from Athens directly to Skyros. Once your flight gets in, rent a car and get settled in. Time your next few days to explore the sights of this island of the Sporades chain that resembles a Cycladic Island due its whitewashed architecture, and a Dodecanese Island due to its rugged landscape. Its main town was built like an amphitheater around a Byzantine-era Monastery of St. George, where an ancient acropolis remains on the highest point of the Old Town. Weave in through its alleyways, where much of the island's population lives, and be sure to visit the outstanding Faltaits Historical and Folklore Museum. Choose one of the golden sandy beaches, typically surrounded by the green hills covered by lush pine trees. Take a day-trip to the tiny Sarakino Island

and feel calmly isolated on its white-sand beach, Glyfada. ⇨ *Chapter 6.*

Logistics: *If you don't want to fly, you can get a ferry to Skyros from Evia, but that requires a bus ride from Athens.*

2 Days: Thessaloniki

Wake up early and take a flight to Greece's second-largest city, Thessaloniki. Walk around the port where the icon of the city, a 15th-century White Tower stands by the sea. Stop at the city's grand monuments including the 5th-century Church of Agios Dimitrios, the impressive Roman Rotunda, and the 3rd-century palace ruins of Roman emperor Galerius. Much of the city's charm lies in its ever-changing character, since it's been conquered and rebuilt so many times of the year; its modern appeal lies in part in its warmth, accessibility, and languid pace; an opportunity to slow down and relax for a couple of days. By night, enjoy the city's vibrant nightlife and great restaurants. ⇨ *Chapter 8.*

Logistics: *You'll need to fly from Skyros to Thessaloniki; there's just no other way to do the trip in a reasonable amount of time.*

1 Day: Alexander the Great Country

After enjoying Greece's second city, rent a car and explore some of the fascinating sights in Central Macedonia. These include Pella, Alexander the Great's birthplace; the royal tombs of Vergina, where his father was buried after his assassination; and Dion at the base of Mount Olympus, an underrated temple city named after Zeus that is not widely visited. ⇨ *Chapter 8.*

Logistics: *If you want to see everything here, you must have a car. If you want to rely on buses, choose either Vergina or Dion, but not both, but keep your hotel*

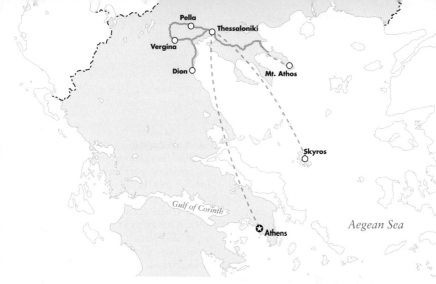

base in Thessaloniki; there are not very many places to stay in this area.

2 Days: Halkidiki and Mt. Athos

Reserve some time to explore Halkidiki's third leg, Mt. Athos. Drive from Thessaloniki to Ouranoupolis, which will be your base, and give yourself some time to simply wind down. That's why the Greeks come here. The village, which is on the final point of land that separates the secular world from the sacred sanctuaries of Mt. Athos, is noted for its tapestry and rug weaving. On the second day, the men in your group can make a pilgrimage to the monastery of Mt. Athos, which is only open to men who seek advance permission to enter. But anyone can enjoy a scenic boat ride around the peninsula, which is like no other in the world. All boats depart from the docks in Ouranoupolis. ⇨ Chapter 8.

Logistics: *Drive back to Thessaloniki (2 hours) in the afternoon, and take a one-hour flight back to Athens.*

TIPS

Athens to Skyros flights leave at least three times per week and more frequently during peak season on Aegean Airlines. Skyros to Thessaloniki flights depart two or three times per week on Aegean Airlines and Sky Express.

There are an abundance of flights leaving daily between Athens and Thessaloniki on Aegean Airlines and Ryanair.

Also note that the Thessaloniki Airport is not within Thessaloniki city center limits. Schedule 30-minute drive time from the airport to and from the Thessaloniki city center.

GREAT ITINERARIES

WONDERS OF THE PELOPONNESE COAST

The Peloponnese remains generally unknown to most Americans, but for those that take the leap to explore it the rewards are great. The coastline is divine, showcasing the natural and rural beauty of Greece from rugged cliffs that meet the sparkling seas swirling in bright shades of turquoise. Peloponnese port cities also give off a special Greek island–like charm with their small village atmosphere, beautiful architecture, and expansive views of the sea. If you have time, an excursion here will be well rewarded.

1 Day: Epidauros

Epidauros has Greece's best-preserved ancient theater, which still amazes audiences with its perfect acoustics. You can literally hear a pin drop on the stage from 55 rows up. Seating 14,000 people, with a breathtaking view of the mountains and valleys directly behind its stage, the venue gets packed each summer (June through August) for the Athens Epidauros Festival, which features notable actors from all over the world. Also visit the Sanctuary of Asklepios, the supposed birthplace of Apollo's son, the world's greatest healer, which has been a major place of healing dating since the 4th century. Take a break by the port with an orange juice, freshly squeezed from oranges grown in the area's famous orange groves. ⇨ *Chapter 10.*

Logistics: *This itinerary really needs to be done by car; it's 1½ hours from Athens to Epidauros. However, during the festival buses run to and from Nafplion especially for the performances, and that's where you should base yourself for the night.*

1 Day: Nafplion

The first capital of Greece is often described as the most cultural, historic, and romantic port city in the country. Discover its Old Town, a peninsula that juts out into the Gulf of Argos and where Greek, Venetian, and Turkish architecture melds in harmony in its little streets and tree-shaded plazas. It deserves at least a day of your undivided attention, but you could certainly spend more time if you have it. ⇨ *Chapter 10.*

Logistics: *The drive from Epidauros to Nafplion is just 40 minutes, but if you are staying the night, you'll likely want to start this itinerary in Nafplion, which is 2 hours from Athens by toll road.*

1 Day: Monemvasia

From afar it's incredible to think people live in the massive rock, towering at 1,148 feet, just ahead of you. One narrow bridge connects the Peloponnese landmass to Monemvasia, where a little walled community has thrived since AD 600. Its name translates as *one entrance,* and it's a perfectly preserved medieval town filled with shops, small hotels, and restaurants. Its alleyways lined with traditional homes are a delight to explore with viewing spots, including at Agia Sofia Church, that offer sweeping views of both the town and sea. ⇨ *Chapter 10.*

Logistics: *An overnight here allows you to enjoy this strange place when the tour groups have departed. Just be aware that cars are not allowed, so you will have to carry your luggage in (have your hotel meet you to help).*

1 Day: Mystras and Sparta

Although not on the coast, Mystras are not to be missed. While modern Sparta may be disappointing to many because of its paucity of ruins, not so for Mystras,

which has the most impressive ruins in the Pelopponese, albeit from the 14th century rather than from ancient times. The abandoned palaces, churches, and monasteries are well worth the detour. ⇨ *Chapter 10.*

Logistics: *The Kinsterna Hotel & Spa in Agios Stefanos is one of the most distinctive hotels in Greece, but there are less expensive options near Mystras.*

2 Days: Mani

Mani is one of the most unique areas of Greece. Byzantine chapels, towered houses, and stories of lawless locals are connected with a rocky, wild, dry yet strikingly handsome landscape. Walk to the mythical gate to the end of the world and the southernmost point of mainland Greece, Cape Tenaro. Then, explore seaside villages of Gerolimenas and Areopolis, trying Mani's famous local olive oils and honey along the way. ⇨ *Chapter 10.*

Logistics: *You can stay in a distinctive property in either Areopolis or Gerolimenas. It's a three-hour drive back to Athens from here.*

TIPS

Driving through the Peloponnese is pleasant, scenic and easy. Roads are typically traffic-free, safe and exits are marked with the Latin alphabet.

An overnight stay at one of the small hotels situated within "the rock" of Monemvasia is a unique experience, but you have to carry your luggage into town, which is not accessible to cars.

If you are up for a scenic, rocky but easy-to-follow hike head toward the lighthouse at the tip of Cape Tenaro. The amazing views from the very tip of mainland Greece will be your reward.

ISLAND-HOPPING: CYCLADES TO CRETE

There is no bad itinerary for the Greek islands. Whether you choose the Sporades, the Dodecanese, or any of those other getaways floating in the Aegean, the leading isles in Greece differ remarkably, and they are all beautiful. But the needle flies off the beauty-measuring gauge when it comes to the Cyclades. It might be possible to "see" any of these famous islands in a day: the "must-see" sights—monasteries or ancient temples—are often few. Still, it is best to take a slower pace and enjoy a sumptuous, idyllic 14-day tour. Planning the details of this trip depends on your sense of inclusiveness, your restlessness, your energy, *and* your ability to accommodate changing boat schedules. Just be warned: the danger of sailing through the Cyclades is that you will never want to leave them. From these suggested landfalls, some of the most justly famous, you can set off to find other idyllic retreats on your own.

2 Days: Mykonos

Jewel of the Cyclades, this island manages to retain its seductive charm. Spend the first day and evening enjoying appealing Mykonos town, where a maze of beautiful streets is lined with shops, bars, restaurants, and discos; spend time on one of the splendid beaches; and, if you want to indulge in some hedonism, partake of the wild nightlife. The next morning take the local boat to nearby Delos for one of the great classical sites in the Aegean. ⇨ *Mykonos in Chapter 11.*

Logistics: *Mykonos is one of the main transport hubs of the Greek islands, with many ferries, boats, and planes connecting to Athens and its port of Piraeus. For a short stay like this, it's best to be in or near Mykonos Town.*

2 Days: Naxos

Sail south to Naxos, arriving from Mykonos in the late afternoon or evening, and begin with a pre-dinner stroll around Naxos town, visiting the Portara (an ancient landmark), the castle, and other sights in the old quarter. The next morning, visit the Archaeological Museum; then drive through the island's mountainous center for spectacular views. Along the way, visit such sights as the Panayia Drosiani, a church near Moni noted for 7th-century frescoes; the marble-paved village of Apeiranthos; and the Temple of Demeter. If you have time, stop for a swim at one of the beaches facing Paros, say Mikri Vigla. ⇨ *Naxos in Chapter 11.*

Logistics: *During high season in summer, there are many ferries to Naxos from Mykonos, but there are many fewer in the off-season. The fast-ferry trip takes less than an hour.*

3 Days: Paros

Go west, young man, to Paros, where the large spaces provide peace and quiet. Paros town has delights profane—buzzing bars—and sacred, such as the legendary Hundred Doors Church. But the highlight will be a meal in the impossibly pretty little fishing harbor of Naousa or, on a morning drive around the island, a visit to the lovely mountain village of Lefkes. Then spend an extra night of magic on the neighboring isle of Antiparos, where off-duty Hollywood celebs bliss out with all the white sands, pink bougainvillea, and blue seas. ⇨ *Paros in Chapter 11.*

Logistics: *It's a very short hop from Naxos to Paros.*

2 Days: Folegandros

This smaller isle is not only beautiful but, rarer in these parts, authentic. It boasts one of the most stunning Chora towns;

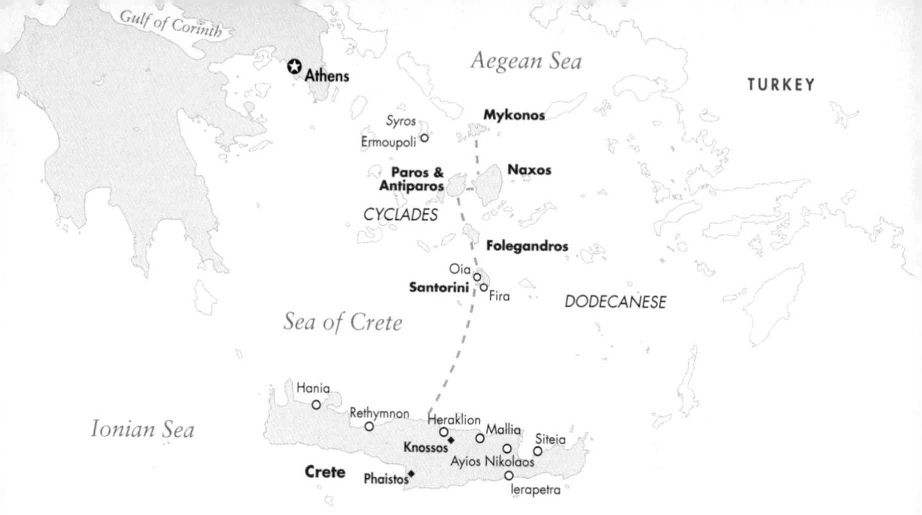

Gulf of Corinth
Athens
Aegean Sea
TURKEY
Syros
Ermoupoli
Mykonos
Paros &
Antiparos
Naxos
CYCLADES
Folegandros
Oia
Santorini
Fira
DODECANESE
Sea of Crete
Hania
Rethymnon
Heraklion
Mallia
Siteia
Knossos
Ayios Nikolaos
Ionian Sea
Crete
Phaistos
Ierapetra

deliberately downplayed touristic development; several good beaches; quiet evenings; traditional local food; and respectful visitors. The high point, literally and figuratively, is the siting of the main town—on a towering cliff over the sea, its perch almost rivals that of Santorini. ⇨ *Folegandros in Chapter 11.*

3 Days: Santorini

Take a ferry from Folegandros south to the spectacle of all spectacles. Yes, in summer the crowds will remind you of the running of the bulls in Pamplona but even they won't stop you from gasping at the vistas, the seaside cliffs, and stunning Cycladic cubist architecture. Once you've settled in, have a sunset drink on a terrace overlooking the volcanic caldera. You can also find many view-providing watering holes in Fira, the capital, or Ia, Greece's most-photographed village. The next day, visit the Museum of Prehistoric Thera; then enjoy a third day just swimming one of the black-sand beaches at Kamari or Perissa. ⇨ *Santorini in Chapter 11.*

2 Days: Crete

Despite the attractions of sea and mountains, it is still the mystery surrounding Europe's first civilization and empire that draws many travelers to Crete. Like them, you can discover stunning testimony to the island's mysterious Minoan civilization, particularly at the legendary Palace of Knossos. Along these shores are blissful beaches as well as the enchanting Venetian-Turkish city of Hania. From Heraklion, Crete's main port, there are frequent flights and ferries back to Piraeus, Athens, and reality. ⇨ *Crete in Chapter 12.*

TIPS

- High-speed catamarans have halved travel time between Piraeus and Santorini. If you have more time, you can take a slower car ferry all the way to Crete and work your way back to Athens on quicker, high-speed ferries.
- In summer, when ferries and boats run frequently, you should have little trouble moving from any of these islands to another, but be sure to make advance reservations. During the high season, ferries sell out.
- All islands are served by air if you would prefer flying, but not all of these islands have airports.

WHEN TO GO

The best time to visit Greece is late spring and early fall. In May and June the days are warm, even hot, but dry, and the seawater has been warmed by the sun. For sightseeing or hitting the beach, this is the time. Greece is relatively tourist-free in spring, so if the beach and swimming aren't critical, April and early May are good; the local wildflowers are at their loveliest, too. Carnival, usually in February just before Lent, and Greek Easter are seasonal highlights. July and August (most locals vacation in August) are always busy—especially on the islands. If you visit during this peak, plan ahead and be prepared to fight the crowds. September and October are a good alternative to spring and early summer, especially in the cities where bars and cultural institutions reopen. Elsewhere, things begin to shut down in November. Transportation to the islands is limited in winter, and many hotels outside large cities are closed until April.

Climate

Greece has a typical Mediterranean climate: hot, dry summers and cool, wet winters. Chilliness and rain begin in November, the start of Greece's deceptive winters. Any given day may not be cold—except in the mountains, snow is uncommon in Athens and to the south. But the cold is persistent, and many places are not well-heated. Spring and fall are perfect, with warm days and balmy evenings. In the south a hot wind may blow across the Mediterranean from Africa. The average high and low temperatures for Athens and Heraklion and the average temperature for Thessaloniki are presented here.

Forecasts National Observatory of Athens ⊕ *www.noa.gr.* **Weather Channel Connection**

☎ *900/932–8437 95¢ per minute from a touch-tone phone* ⊕ *www.weather.com.*

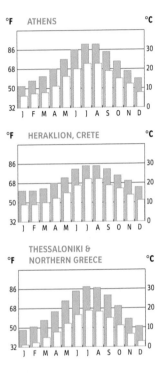

ON THE CALENDAR

1

	Many celebrations throughout the year revolve around Greek Orthodox holidays and saint days. But Greeks also love any good excuse to dance and feast, and they love to celebrate the arts, including film, dance, and drama.
JANUARY	**Epiphany, January 6.** To commemorate the day of Christ's baptism, a sizeable gathering in Athens takes place at the Port of Piraeus. A priest throws a large crucifix into the water, and young men brave the cold to recover it. The finder is awarded with a blessing.
FEBRUARY	**Apokries.** Thousands take to the streets of Greece, prancing and dancing in costume, drinking, and just being merry during the country's three-week pre-Lenten Carnival season. The islands of Skyros and Crete attract some of the largest crowds, but the Greek carnival capital is Patras in the northern Peloponnese. ⊕ *carnival-in-rethymnon-crete-greece.com* or ⊕ *carnivalpatras.gr.*
MARCH	**Thessaloniki International Documentary Festival.** Documentary filmmakers from all over the world screen their work at this March festival that's gaining a name for itself in the industry. ⊕ *tdf.filmfestival.gr.* **Greek Independence Day, March 25.** A military parade that commemorates the start of the War of Greek Independence of 1821 is held with pomp and circumstance. It marches straight through the heart of Athens in Syntagma Square. **Feast of the Annunciation, March 25.** While Greece celebrates its independence, the islands of Tinos and Hydra hold special religious festivities to honor the news that Mary would be the mother of Christ.
APRIL–MAY	**Holy Easter Week Celebrations, April or May.** Throughout the country, church services and processions are scheduled during the most important holiday in Greece. On Easter midnight families gather at local churches, candles in hand. The rest of the day is dedicated to feasting on roasted lamb and other traditional food. On Holy Thursday, "The Last Supper" is reenacted at the Monastery of St. John the Divine on the island of Patmos. **Art-Athina Festival.** One of the longest-lasting contemporary art fairs in Europe takes place in Athens each May. International artists gather to collaborate and present their work to

more than 30,000 visitors over a four-day period. ⊕ *www. art-athina.gr.*

JUNE	**Athens and Epidavrus Festival, June to October.** A full schedule of classical Greek dramas, opera, orchestra, and dance performances fills venues across Athens, including the ancient Odeon of Herodes Atticus next to the Acropolis. Over the years a roster of famous actors including Helen Mirren, Ethan Hawke, and Kevin Spacey have graced the stage at the magnificent ancient Theatre of Epidauros in the Peloponnese. ⊕ *www.greekfestival.gr.* **Nafplion Festival.** Established as one of the most successful classical music events in Greece, the festival is set in various venues in the beautiful seaside Peloponnese city and attracts the brightest ensembles and artists from around the world. ⊕ *www.nafplionfestival.gr.*
JULY	**International Puppet Festival.** The International Puppet Festival draws talented puppeteers from around the world, who perform their interpretation of famous fables and plays on the pretty little island of Hydra. **Medieval Rose Festival.** The gorgeous medieval town of Rhodes is the perfect backdrop for well-rehearsed reenactments from Byzantine and Medieval times. Musical and art events add to the program with the aim to educate and entertain. ⊕ *www. medievalfestival.gr.* **Festival of the Aegean.** Hundreds of singers and dancers from all over the world, including more than a dozen choirs, gather in Syros, the capital of the Cyclades, each summer. Their inspiring performances pack audiences at beautiful venues including the elegant Apollo Theatre and St. Nicholas Church. ⊕ *www.festivaloftheaegean.com.*
AUGUST	**Feast of the Assumption of the Virgin, August 15.** On this national holiday, thousands of pilgrims crowd Tinos to ask for a special blessing or a miracle. In crowds, they crawl on their hands and knees to the cathedral of Panagia Evangelistria. **Sani Festival.** Coined as "Jazz on the Hill," the fun music fest gathers significant artists from around the world for a jam-packed program of concerts in the Halkidi region of northern Greece. Performances take place at various venues, including Sani Hill, a small islet surrounded by the lapping waves of the Aegean. ⊕ *sanifestival.gr.*

Renaissance Festival at Rethymnon. In a celebration of art, theater, and music, hundreds of artists from around the globe act, sing, and dance in venues throughout the most picturesque Cretan town in performances that begin in August and continue through September. Each performance aims to honor of the spirit of the Renaissance era. ⊕ *www.rfr.gr.*

SEPTEMBER

Aegina Pistachio Festival. Go dance, sing, and enjoy your share of delicious pistachio products as you learn about the Aegina's appreciation for the nut that has helped their island thrive. ⊕ *www.aeginafistikifest.gr.*

Dionysia Wine Festival. One of Naxos Island's key events, with music, theater, and art exhibitions, celebrates the island's ties to the Ancient Greek God of Wine, Dionysus, during the first week of September.

OCTOBER

Spetses Mini Marathon. The biggest island sporting event in Greece features running and swimming races and a children's run. Social events are also open for those who want to feel the energetic vibe of the island during the action-packed weekend. Get a welcoming taste of the savory homemade pies baked and handed out by local women. ⊕ *spetsesmarathon.com.*

NOVEMBER

Thessaloniki International Film Festival. For more than 50 years, the sophisticated city has hosted independent filmmakers from all over the world, who compete for the event's highest award, The Golden Alexander. ⊕ *www.filmfestival.gr.*

Athens Marathon. Tens of thousands of runners head to Greece in early November to run the course based on the original marathon from Ancient Greek times. The 26.2-mile course begins in Marathon and finishes at the grand, marble Panathinaiko Stadium in Athens. ⊕ *www.athensauthenticmarathon.gr.*

November 17th. The widely observed anniversary commemorates the 1973 uprising by Athens Polytechnic University students, who were killed for protesting the Greek military junta. Metro stations close down, and protests typically take to the streets, making it a difficult day for travel and sightseeing.

DECEMBER

Christmas. Athens gets festive, especially for kids. The National Gardens are transformed into a Christmas village, where activities are scheduled during school vacation. Additional city venues and public spaces hold events as well. ⊕ *www.cityofathens.gr.*

GREECE
THE GREAT BEACH QUEST

Computed by the acres of sun-tanned flesh exposed along 9,000 miles of shoreline, Greece's beaches are to Europeans what Florida's are to Americans. But there are so many fabulous beaches that choosing the right one is a task of almost Herculean proportions. To help you decide, here's a look at Greece's best—the most beautiful, the liveliest, the quietest, the most active, the best for kids, and others to suit every taste.

LIFE'S A BEACH

For us *xènos* (foreigners), Greek beaches are paradises around the corner—sandy playgrounds that live up to their promise of sun, sand, and azure seas. But from May through October, when seas are warm and sunshine can be taken for granted, the beach also becomes the center of Greek social life, an extension of the *platia* (square) or the *kafenion* (café). Let Americans seek out patches of sand as far from the crowds as possible; for the locals, the beach is another place to gather, gossip, catch up on local news, argue about politics, play a game of tavli, and keep an eye on the neighbors.

Happily, as the song says, the best things in life are free: all Greek beaches are freely accessible to the public—even if rented beach lounges line the sands, you can always find a place to plop down on a towel. And when night falls, the gear gets put away and the Versace sandals come out. At island hot-spots like Mykonos, Aegean style nightlife takes over. There, the dance-til-sunrise party scene ends with the promise that dawn will bring another flawless day on the beach.

LICENSE TO CHILL

But is every trip "a day at the beach"? No, not when the famed *meltemi*, the dry northwesterly winds, usually hit in August. These summer bummers can be both a curse and a blessing for beachgoers. Scorching temperatures drop when the winds pick up, but waters on north-facing beaches can become dangerous churns for swimmers and gusts kick sand into the faces of 90-pound weaklings and muscle men alike. Beachgoers in the know often make a beeline for south-facing strands, where the meltemi usually, but not always, packs a less powerful punch.

Lemonakia beach, Kokkari, Samos

SHORE TO PLEASE: GREECE'S BEST BEACHES

When Greece starts to sizzle, there's no better way to beat the heat than to hit the beach. So keep your cool and make a splash by savoring these top beaches—Greece has no greater liquid assets.

GOOD BEACHES FOR KIDS

Santa Maria, Paros, Cyclades Windsurfers love the winds here, and parents will welcome the warm, shallow waters and those beautiful dunes that are irresistible to the sandbox set.

Ayia Marina, Aegina, Saronic Gulf Shallow waters, paddle-boat rentals, and other amenities make this beach outside Aegina town especially popular with Athenian families.

Elafonisi, Crete Turquoise waters, pure-white sandbars, with a sea shallow enough to create a beautiful wading pool for youngsters. Young explorers love to wade across the "bathtub" to Elafonisi islet.

BEST PARTY BEACH SCENES

Super Paradise Beach and Paradise Beach, Mykonos, Cyclades Greece's celebrated party island lives up to its reputa-

Elafonisi, Crete

tion at a string of bars that line these soft sands, where an international crowd lingers until dawn.

Aegina town, Saronic Gulf Islands A party scene prevails at a parade of bars on the coast just outside of town, where a spectacular sunset kicks off a night of cocktails and notched-up music.

Skiathos town, Sporades For those who prefer drinking and dancing next to the sea, come evening the lively harbor front becomes a big party, one long row of hopping clubs and bars.

OUT-OF-THE-WAY BEACHES

Ayios Georgios, Rhodes, Dodecanese Shaded with heavenly scented cedars, this pristine strand is the loveliest beach on Rhodes and well worth the harrowing, four-wheel drive down a cypress-lined track.

Psili Amos, Patmos, Dodecanese A caïque ride or half-hour hike are the ways to reach the island's most beautiful stretch of sand.

Red Beach, Matala, Crete A beautiful hike from Matala allows you to plunge in the surf at this delightfully isolated strand. Nearby caves have sheltered everyone from prehistoric nomads to hippies.

Golden Beach, Paros

BEACHES WITH A PAST

Olous, Elounda Peninsula, Crete Strap on a snorkel mask, dive into the crystal clear waters, and regard the Roman settlement on the sandy seafloor—finds from this seafloor are on view at the nearby archaeological museum in Agios Nikolas.

Kommos Beach, Matala, Crete This mile-plus-long strand of golden sand is justifiably popular with sunbathers, who would be humbled to know ancient Minoans once inhabited this now-being-excavated spot.

PRIME SPOTS FOR WATER SPORTS

Chrissi Akti (Golden Beach), Paros, Cyclades The long stretch of golden sand is Greece's windsurfing capital, hosting the International Windsurfing World Cup every August.

Vai, Crete

Paradise Beach, Mykonos, Cyclades

Mykonos is considered to be the diving center of the Aegean, and Mykonos Diving Center is the place for serious instruction and rewarding dives.

Paleokastritsa, Corfu

This stretch of sand-rimmed coves and seaside grottoes rewards divers and snorkelers with crystal clear waters. Korfu Diving and other outfitters provide all the necessary equipment for underwater fun.

THE MOST BEAUTIFUL BEACHES

Plaka, Naxos, Cyclades

The most beautiful beach of all on an island of beautiful beaches is backed by sand dunes and bamboo groves, an exotic setting enhanced by a predictably spectacular sunset almost every evening.

Vai, Crete A grove of palm trees provides an MGM-worthy backdrop to a beach that even the ancients raved about.

Mavra Volia, Chios, Northern Islands A "wine-dark sea" washes the black volcanic shores of a cove nestled between sheltering cliffs—little wonder the hauntingly appealing place is aptly called "Black Pebbles."

Kolimbithres, Paros, Cyclades Smooth boulders whimsically shaped by the wind create a string of coves backed by golden sands. The calm, warm waters are ideal for swimming.

Myrtidiotissa, Corfu Sheer cliffs shelter soft sands backed by olive groves; Lawrence Durrell was not exaggerating when, in *Prospero's Cell*, he described this spot as "perhaps the loveliest beach in the world."

Lemonakia, Kokkari, Samos Beauty and the Beach describes this winner, with its perfect half-moon crescent magnificently framed by rocky promontories green with pine trees.

Paleokastritsa, Corfu

GOOD TO KNOW

Skiathos

WHAT SHOULD I WEAR?

Although on Mykonos you may encounter some of those multi-hundred-dollar designer straps of cloth that never come into contact with the water, for the most part Greek beach wear is decidedly casual and non-fussy. In addition to a swimming suit, you will want to bring the following: a tee-shirt or other cover-up for the strong sun; a hat; Jellies or other water-ready sandals for walking on hot sand and over pebbles; a pair of shorts or a cover-up to slip on for walks through a town or for a taverna meal. Remember, bathing suits are not acceptable street wear in many places in Greece. "No Nudity" signs are posted on many Greek beaches, especially those close to towns. Even if no sign is present, be discreet—find a spot removed from attired Greek beachgoers, many of whom find the notion of baring it all to be a distinctly foreign habit.

Boat in sunny waters
at Elafonisi beach

BEACH TALK

- **Paralia** means "beach."

- **Amos** means "sand."

- **Thalassa** means "sea."

- **Petseta** means "towel."

- **Is the water warm?**
  To nero ineh zesto?

- **Pou tha noikiaso?**
  Where do I rent...

- **...an umbrella**
  obrella

- **...a beach lounge**
  xsaplosra

Relaxing under parasol, beach on Skiathos island

HOW DO I GET THERE?

Many, but certainly not all, beaches on most resort islands are served by public buses running on a fairly limited schedule—drop off in the morning, pick up in the afternoon (tourist offices and major hotels can provide schedules). However, the only way to reach some beaches—including many of the prettiest and least crowded—is by car; parking is almost always free, though it can be scarce in high season. On Patmos and other islands another option is a caïque, a motor launch that usually leaves from the main port in the morning for remote beaches and returns in the afternoon; expect to pay about €15 for this pleasant mode of transport.

WHAT SHOULD I BRING?

Consider a towel and beach mat or blanket; a large bottle of water; plenty of sunscreen; and an umbrella for shade (these are not always available for rental). Your own snorkel gear is another option. Umbrella rentals, along with shade, are a rare commodity at many beaches and the sun can be fierce. You can usually buy one for about €10 in shops in beach towns.

WHAT SHOULD I EXPECT?

Activities and Rentals: In some of the major getaways—Kos, Paros, Mykonos, the north coast of Crete—you'll come upon every water sport under the sun, and sailboats, jet skis, and snorkeling and diving gear are often available from outfits operating out of large resorts. If your exertions in these places are going to be no more strenuous than lounging, you can usually rent a beach lounge and umbrella for about €12 a day.

Eating and Drinking: Some of the more popular beaches on resort islands are backed by tavernas and bars; these are usually casual, outdoor places that are open seasonally and serve sandwiches or such basic but delicious Greek grub as grilled octopus or lamb kebabs. At some beaches, a snack wagon (cantina) will dispense cold drinks, ice cream, and snacks. Many beaches, however, offer nothing in the line of food, so come prepared. Lunch at a beachside taverna is a Greek tradition, especially popular on Sunday. Expect to find yourself surrounded by families, many dressed in their Sunday best.

Facilities: Lifeguards are on duty at very few Greek beaches, and most beaches lack any kind of public facilities. A few have port-a-potties, but in many places beachside bars or tavernas fill the gap; out of courtesy order something if you use the facilities.

WHAT SHOULD I WATCH OUT FOR?

Grecian seas are gentle, with few hazards from undertows or strong waves which can strike the southern coast of Crete. Some underwater hazards to keep an eye out for are sharp rocks, sea urchins (*achinos*, which live on rocks and whose quills can inflict a sharp sting), and the now-rare jellyfish (medusa).

LOOK FOR THE BLUE FLAGS

The Blue Flags that fly above 425 Greek beaches mean they have met the standards set by the nonprofit Foundation for Environmental Education for water cleanliness, garbage disposal, overall safety, and other criteria. You will find a listing of Greece's Blue Flag beaches at ⊕ www.blueflag.org.

WATER WORLDS

Greece entertains its young visitors and their adult companions with a growing number of water parks. While none offer a particularly Greek experience, your kids won't mind—they'll love the pools, slides, and concessions. Two of Greece's largest and most popular are Aqua Paros Waterpark (Kolimbithres, Paros, Cyclades) and Acquaplus Waterpark (Hersonissos, Crete).

Local flags at Elafonisi beach, Crete

CRUISING
IN GREECE

Updated
by Marissa
Tejada and
Linda Coffman

Travelers have been sailing Greek waters ever since 3,500 BCC (before Chris-Crafts). The good news is that today's visitor will have a much, much easier time of it than Odysseus, the world's first tourist and hero of Homer's *Odyssey*. Back in his day, exploring the Greek islands—1,425 geological jewels thickly scattered over the Aegean sea like stepping-stones between East and West—was a fairly daunting assignment. Zeus would often set the schedule (during the idyllic days in midwinter the master of Mt. Olympus forbade the winds to blow during the mating season of the halcyon or kingfisher); waterlogged wooden craft could be tossed about in summer, when the *meltemi,* the north wind, would be a regular visitor to these waters; and pine-prow triremes often embarked with a scramble of 170 oarsmen, not all of them pulling in the right direction.

Now travelers can sail those same blue highways in effortless fashion. A flotilla of—often—spectacularly outfitted cruise ships helps banish many typical landlubbers' irritations: ferry schedules, hotel reservations, luggage porterage, to name a few. When you add in 21st-century allurements—pulling into Santorini after a deck-side luncheon created by the gastronomic wizardry at Nobu; a game of golf in Mykonos via your onboard 18-hole miniature-golf course; a renowned archaeologist illuminating the fascinating history of Rhodes, your next stop—you can see why a vacation aboard one of these gleaming white islands has become one of the most popular travel choices available.

Cruises have always had a magical quality, even without dramatic views of whitewashed Cycladic villages and ancient ruins anchored for eternity above a sheer drop *(for a rundown of the ABCs, see the Cruise Basics at the end of this chapter)*. Sailing into a harbor has a grand ceremonial feel lacking in air travel arrivals, and Greece, the eastern Mediterranean's showcase, is an ideal cruise destination for travelers with limited time who wish to combine sightseeing with relaxation. This is especially true in spring and autumn, when milder Aegean and Ionian climates are better suited than the sweltering summer months to, for example, explore those hilltop ancient ruins.

Although cruises have historically attracted an older group of travelers, more and more young people and family groups are setting sail in Europe. With the peak season conveniently falling during school's summer hiatus, cruise lines have responded to multigenerational travel with expanded children's programs and discounted shore excursions for youngsters under age 12. Shore excursions have become more varied, too, often incorporating activities that families can enjoy together, such as biking and hiking. Cruise lines now offer more programs than ever before for adults as well, including pre- or post-cruise land tours as options, plus extensive onboard entertainment and learning programs. Some lines increasingly hire expert speakers to lead discussions based on local cultures.

Cruise ships may idyllically appear to be floating resorts, but keep in mind that if you decide you don't like your ship, you can't check out and move somewhere else. Whichever one you choose will be your home for seven days, or more in some cases. The chosen ship will determine the type of accommodations you'll enjoy, the kind of food you'll eat, the entertainment program, and even the destinations you'll visit. That is why the most important endeavor you can undertake when planning a cruise is evaluating the proposed itinerary, the cruise line, and the particular ship.

CHOOSING YOUR CRUISE

Greece is a place where dramatic landscapes unfold before you. The beautiful beaches, ancient history, charming villages, and scenic islands all become within reach when you are aboard a ship.

After giving some thought to your itinerary and where in Greece you might wish to go, the ship you select is the most vital factor. Cruises in Greece set sail with all types of ships including mainstream ships that carry over 1,500 passengers, midsize ships that carry between 500 and 1,500 passengers, and small cruise lines that carry less than 500. Big ships offer a variety of activities and facilities. Small ships feel more intimate—like a private club. For every big-ship fan there is someone who would never set foot aboard a "floating resort." Examine your lifestyle to see which kind of ship best meets your needs. But realize also that the size of your ship will also impact which ports you visit as well as how you see them.

The big mainstream cruise ships take you to the busiest ports enabling you to explore the most visited attractions—check everything from the Acropolis of Athens to the whitewashed island of Santorini off your

bucket list. Greece may also be a stop on a longer tour that features ports of call in neighboring European countries. Meanwhile, small and midsize ships can visit smaller Greek ports with itineraries that are more off the beaten path including Hydra and its picturesque little harbor; the Ionian resort of Parga and its pastel-hued Venetian homes; and the impressive natural rock fortress of Monemvasia on the coast of the Peloponnese. Where to go to satisfy your inner explorer is a highly personal decision, and one of the first you must make.

Meanwhile, you can opt for cruises that suit your interests, whether it's discovering Greece's archaeology, history, or religious relevance. Thousands of years of history can come to life through a combination of onboard lectures and well-planned excursions. Other itineraries focus on island-hopping, bringing you to some of the most idyllic beaches in the world. Today's Greek islands cruises can also be featured on larger itineraries that cover wider swaths of the Mediterranean, extending from Rome to Alexandria, but this has been the Greek way of seafaring for more than 3,000 years. In ancient times, the Aegean and the Mediterranean were propitious for coastal trade, and it was by sea that the Greek way was spread. Greek ships colonized the whole Mediterranean coast to such an extent that for a thousand years the Mediterranean was known as a veritable Greek lake.

ITINERARIES

Cruise ships typically follow one of two itinerary types in the eastern Mediterranean: round-trip loops that start and finish in the same port city, and one-way cruises that pick you up in one port and drop you off at another for the flight home. Itineraries are usually 7 to 10 days, though some lines offer longer sailings covering a larger geographic span. Some cruises concentrate on covering an area that includes the Greek islands, Turkish coast, Cyprus, Israel, and Egypt, while others reach from Gibraltar to the Ionian isles, the western Peloponnese, and Athens.

For an overview of Greece's top sights, choose an itinerary that includes port calls in Piraeus for a shore excursion to the Acropolis and other sights in Athens; Mykonos, a sparkling Cycladic isle with a warren of whitewashed passages, followed by neighboring Delos, with its Pompeii-like ruins; Santorini, a stunning harbor that's actually a partially submerged volcano; Rhodes, where the Knights of St. John built their first walled city before being forced to retreat to Malta; and Heraklion, Crete, where you'll be whisked through a medieval harbor to the reconstructed Bronze Age palace at Knossos. Port calls at Katakolon and Itea mean excursions to Olympia and the Temple of Apollo at Delphi. Some cruises call at Epidaurus and Nafplion, offering an opportunity for visits to the ancient theater and the citadel of Mycenae, or at Monemvasia or Patmos, the island where St. John wrote the book of *Revelation*.

If you'd rather relax by the pool than trek through temples, opt for a cruise with more time at sea and fewer or shorter port calls. If you'd like time to explore each island destination, you'll want to choose a cruise where the ship spends the entire day in port and travels at night.

Alternately, if the number of places you visit is more important than the time you spend in each one, book a cruise with a full itinerary and one or two port calls a day.

A cruise spares the planning headaches of solitary island-hopping and the inconvenience of carting luggage from one destination to the next, and, for budget-conscious travelers, cruises offer the advantage of controlled expenses. Nevertheless, because one disadvantage is that port calls may be long enough only to allow time for a quick visit to one or two main attractions, cruises may be best for an overview, useful for planning a return trip to the more appealing island stops.

MAJOR PORTS IN GREECE

The cruise ports of Greece vary in size and popularity, not to mention what you'll find once you get off the cruise ship. Some ports can get extremely crowded, and there may be wait times for your ship to even dock. Depending on the ship you are sailing, you may need to take a smaller tender to go ashore. Once there, there may be other types of excursions worth checking out that require an hour of drive time so plan your day appropriately. At every port listed a beach stop can be found nearby if you prefer to relax by the sea instead of exploring a village or archeological site.

Ayios Nikolaos, Crete. A charming and animated port town, Ayios Nikolaos is a dramatic composition of bare mountains, islets, and deep blue sea. Its hilly streets offer fantastic views over Mirabello bay, and the "bottomless" lake Voulismeni remains its core. There aren't any significant beaches in the town but a few nice bays. Its streets are lined with simple tavernas, and its architecture reflects the Venetian and Byzantine influences that followed the Minoan civilization.

Chania, Crete. This elegant city of eucalyptus-lined avenues features miles of waterfront promenades and shady, cobbled alleyways lined with Venetian and Ottoman homes. There's a lighthouse at sea, and the waterfront Firka Fortress, once a Turkish prison, is now a maritime museum. A converted Turkish mosque now hosts art exhibitions. You can tour several monasteries on Agia Triada, an area that extends into the sea from the east side of Chania. A short walk west of the harbor takes you to Chania's main beach. Buses and tours depart for Samaria, protected as a national park, known for its deep, breathtaking gorge that cuts through Crete's mountains.

Corfu. Stroll through the narrow, winding streets and steep stairways that make up the Campiello, the traffic-free medieval area. Head to the center of town, known as the Spianada, where seven- and eight-story Venetian and English Georgian houses line the way. Wander through the maze inside the New Fort, which was built by the Venetians. There's also the Old Fort to discover, built in the 15th century. Other highlights include the Church of St. George, built like an ancient Doric temple; St. Spyridon Cathedral, with its high bell tower; and Antivouniotissa church, which dates back to the 15th century. The archeological museum houses collections from Kanoni, the site of Corfu's ancient capital.

Delos. During a stop in the jet-set whitewashed island of Mykonos, a short boat ride takes you to the tiny uninhabited island of Delos, a well-preserved archaeological site that was once a holy sanctuary for a thousand years. It's the fabled birthplace of Apollo and Artemis, and the ruins that remain give visitors a glimpse of the prosperous life during ancient Greece. Walk through formerly luxurious villas including the House of Cleopatra and the House of Dionysus to see 2,500-year-old mosaic floors and remnants of magnificent marble sculptures. Other highlights include the Sacred Way, the Temple of Apollo, and the marbled and imposing Avenue of Lions. Smaller cruise ships can anchor offshore and tender their passengers ashore.

Heraklion, Crete. This port gives you access to visit the Palace of Knossos 3 km (2 miles) away. It was the Minoan king's residence as well as the religious center for the whole region. Right in the center of the Heraklion, near the main Eleftherias Platia, you can find the Archeological Museum of Heraklion, which displays artifacts from Minoan culture discovered during the excavations of Knossos. The streets of the capital are lined with Venetian buildings, promenades and outdoor cafés. In the port's inner harbor you'll find Koules, the massive fortress.

Katakolon. This small port is known as "the door to Olympia" since it is the closest port to the Greek city known for the most important sanctuaries of ancient Greece, the birthplace of the ancient Olympic Games. The ancient site includes the remains of the original 20,000-spectator stadium, and its archaeological museum houses prehistoric, archaic, and classical statues from ancient times. If you don't want to make the trip to Olympia, then Katakolon is an ideal place for a leisurely Greek lunch while you watch the fishermen mend their nets.

Kos. Ships dock in Kos town, putting you within walking distance to the main sights of this Dodecanese island known as the birthplace of Hippocrates, father of modern medicine. You can stop by the archeological museum located in the central Eleftherios Square and explore the impressive Castle of Neratzia (Knight's castle), which dates back to the 15th century. You may also want to see Hippocrates's Tree, a plane tree situated next to the entrance of the castle, where the ancient Greek physician lectured his students in its shade. In wooded foothills 3½ km (2 miles) west of Kos town you can discover the ruins of the ancient Greek hospital of Asklepieion.

Mytilini, Lesvos. Mytilini, or Lesvos, is Greece's third-largest island known as the birthplace of ancient Greek poet Sappho. It's also known for its landscapes that produce fine olive oil and ouzo. Once your cruise boat docks in harbor you'll be right near Mytilini town, where you'll find waterfront mansions and bustling streets lined with shops, taverns, and good ouzeries serving up local ouzo. A 15-minute walk up a pine-clad hill stands one of the largest castles in the Mediterranean, the Fortress of Mytilini. The Archaeological Museum of Mytilene, housed in a 1912 neoclassical mansion, is located behind the ferry dock.

Monemvasia. Cruise ships tender you close to this unique medieval island town, which is actually a natural rock fortress that has been inhabited since AD 583. A narrow road connects you to the town, and from that point on you must travel by foot or donkey. Once inside, explore the nooks, grottoes, tiny alleys, and homes carved into the rock. In Lower Town you'll find Elkomenos Square, where the medieval Elkomenos Christos church and a small museum stand. Follow the remains of the medieval fortress to Upper Town to stand at the top of the rock. There you'll bask in memorable sea views right where Agia Sophia church is located.

Mykonos. Cruise ships drop anchor at Tourlos, where a small boat shuttles you to the island's main town called Mykonos town, a well-preserved whitewashed Cycladic village comprised of a maze of narrow, small, and winding streets lined with shops, restaurants, bars and cafés. Other ships dock in the modern cruise port and shuttle passengers into Mykonos town by bus. Once in town, you'll be within walking distance of several highlights, including one of the most photographed churches in the world, Panagia Paraportiani, as well as the town's picturesque waterfront district called Little Venice. At night, Mykonos town comes alive as a cosmopolitan nightlife and dining destination.

Nafplion. Ships anchor off the coast of Nafplion and shuttle you to the main village, where you'll pass the picturesque Bourtzi Islet, where a tower fortress seems to stand in the center of the sea. The top attraction of Nafplion is the Palamidi Fortress built by the Venetians in 1711. Getting to it requires a climb up 899 stairs to the entrance, where you'll have fantastic views of the region. The village itself is a picturesque maze of Venetian and Byzantine architecture lined with colorful bougainvillea, sidewalk cafés, tavernas and shops. In the center of it all is Syntagma Square where you'll find a beautiful 18th-century Venetian arsenal and the archeological museum.

Patmos. Smaller ships can dock in pretty, mountainous Patmos. At the port of Skala you can venture on a scenic 20-minute hike up to Kastelli hill to the town's 6th- to 4th-century BC stone remains. A quick taxi or bus ride 4 km (2½ miles) away takes you to neighboring Patmos town, where you'll discover the religious significance of the island; it was where St. John the Divine was once exiled and where he wrote the Book of Revelation. Traditional whitewashed homes surround the bottom of the exterior walls of the Monastery of St. John the Divine, dating back to 1088. It's also where the Sacred Grotto is found, the sacred place where St. John received his visions that he recorded in the Book of the Revelation.

Piraeus. The port of Piraeus is located 11 km (7 miles) southwest of Central Athens. You can easily catch the metro or a taxi to reach the worthy sites of the city, including the Acropolis, the ancient core of the modern capital. On its southwest slope you'll see the Odeon of Herodes Atticus, an ancient and impressive stone theater. Within the perimeter you'll find yourself in the heart of Old Athens and can easily stroll through Plaka and visit the bazaars of Monastiraki. The birthplace of democracy called the ancient Agora is at the northern edge of the Plaka. In the city, you can browse the impressive collections at the Acropolis Museum, the Benaki Museum, and the National Archaeological Museum. In central Syntagma Square you'll find parliament, formerly King Otto's royal palace, and have the opportunity to watch the Changing of the Evzone Guards at the Tomb of the Unknown Soldier.

Rhodes. Ships dock at the cruise port east of St. Catherine's Gate, bringing you close to the island's historical center. For two centuries Rhodes town was ruled by the Knights of St. John. The monuments of that era are the island's highlights, including its 4-km (2½-mile) fortress walls; Palace of the Grand Master of the Knights of Rhodes; and the Mosque of Suleiman, dedicated to a Turkish sultan, that dates back to the 1522. You'll also discover where the ancient wonder called the Colossus once towered above the harbor in 280 BC. A 48-km (30-mile) trip away from Rhodes town leads to the whitewashed medieval village of Lindos known for its grand hilltop acropolis.

Santorini. Cruise ships anchor near the cliffs of Fira, offering memorable views of the whitewashed mountaintop villages of Santorini. Once a tender shuttles you to the Old Port, you'll find a picturesque, romantic village with whitewashed homes and churches topped with bright blue roofs. The Museum of Prehistoric Fira gives insight into the island's prehistoric and archaeological history. If you want to venture 11 km (7 miles) farther into the island you'll find yourself taking in the view in Ia, another beautiful village that's built on a steep slope of the island's impressive cliffs. The remains of Akrotiri, destroyed millennia ago by a massive volcanic eruption, are on the island's southeastern tip.

Gythion. This small port located right on the southernmost peninsula in the Peloponnese is in a unique geographical and cultural area called the Mani. Gythion is known for its seaside cafés, restaurants, and beaches. The Diros caves, accessible by underground boat tours, are located 37 km (22 miles) southwest. Tours also head out to other Peloponnese towns popular for their beauty and history including Mystras, Sparta, and Monemvasia.

FERRY TRAVEL IN GREECE

Greece has a comprehensive ferry network connecting the islands to major ports. While it's difficult to plan an island-hopping trip months in advance, the system is extensive. Sites like ⊕ *www.ferries.gr* and ⊕ *www.greekferries.gr* list what information is available at any given time and enable travelers to view schedules as available including a means to pay for tickets in advance. Nevertheless, if you want to guarantee seeing a specific island within a set period of time—and on your schedule—it's recommended to contact a Greece-based travel agent to get you where you want to be. If you prefer to explore on your own, your best bet is departing from the easily accessible main port of Athens in Piraeus. You can even catch a ferry at the last minute if you simply want to visit any Greek island. *See Travel Agents in Travel Smart for more information.* The Saronic islands are the closest to the capital, so they remain popular weekend getaways for Athenians. Located about an hour away via fast ferry, the islands of Spetses, Hydra, Poros, Aegina, and Agistri are worth a day's visit or an overnight stay. A one-way ticket is relatively inexpensive, between €10 and €20. Depending on the season, ferries offer connections between the islands, or tiny water taxis offer a quick way to travel between those that are very close together like Agistri and Aegina. Several small cruise boats that take up to 50 passengers per day offer day tours that may visit up to three of the islands for less than €100 per person. Leaving Piraeus in the morning, the boat stops for an hour or two at each island port while providing a meal or refreshments on board as well as options for tours on each island at an extra cost.

Within three to five hours via ferry from Pireaus, you can also reach the Cycladic islands. Naxos, Tinos, Syros, Sifnos, Paros, and Mykonos are a few that are known the world over for their whitewashed architecture, picturesque villages, and pristine beaches. During peak tourist months there are ferries that run between the islands of the Cyclades, making rounds each day and enabling you to island-hop on your own—provided you have reserved a place to stay, which can be difficult to find in the high season. By utilizing the services of Greek travel agencies on each island to help you synchronize your ferry schedules and tickets, you can usually plan your journey on the fly, especially in the less busy shoulder-season months of May and September.

WHEN TO GO

When to go is as important as where to go. The Greek cruising season is lengthy, starting in March and ending in November. In July or August, the islands are crowded with Greek and foreign vacationers, so expect sights, beaches, and shops to be crowded. High temperatures could also limit time spent on deck. May, June, September, and October are the best months—warm enough for sunbathing and swimming, yet not so uncomfortably hot as to make you regret the trek up Lindos. Cruising in the low seasons provides plenty of advantages besides discounted fares. Availability of ships and particular cabins is greater in the low and shoulder seasons, and the ports are almost completely free of tourists.

CRUISE COSTS

Average cruise fares vary considerably by itinerary and season, as well as by the category of accommodations you select. Published rates are highest for the most unusual and desirable itineraries, as well as for cruises during peak summer months, when most North Americans plan for vacations in Europe. Europeans are known to prefer late-summer holidays, with August being the busiest month. Typical daily per diems on a luxury line such as Silversea or Seabourn can be as much as three times or more the cost of a cruise on a mainstream line such as Royal Caribbean or even a premium Celebrity Cruises ship. It goes without saying that longer cruises are naturally more expensive.

Solo travelers should be aware that single cabins have virtually disappeared from cruise ships, although they are available on P&O's *Azura*, Norwegian Cruise Line's *Norwegian Epic* (in a particularly successful format), and a few older vessels. Taking a double cabin can cost up to twice the advertised per-person rates (which are based on double occupancy). Some cruise lines will find same-sex roommates for singles; each then pays the per-person, double-occupancy rate.

2

Although the overall price you pay for your cruise is always a consideration, don't think of the bottom line in terms of the fare alone. You also have to figure in the cost of other shipboard charges beyond the basic fare. However, the ultimate cost isn't computed only in dollars spent; it is in what you get for your money. The real bottom line is value. Many cruise passengers don't mind spending a bit more to get the vacation they really want.

TIPPING

One of the most delicate—yet frequently debated—topics of conversation among cruise passengers involves the matter of tipping. Who do you tip? How much? What's "customary" and "recommended?" Should parents tip the full amount for children or is just half adequate? Why do you have to tip at all?

When transfers to and from your ship are a part of your air-and-sea program, gratuities are generally included for luggage handling. In that case, do not worry about the interim tipping. But if you take a taxi to the pier and hand over your bags to a stevedore, be sure to tip him. Treat him with respect and pass along the equivalent of at least $5.

During your cruise, room-service waiters generally receive a cash tip of $1 to $3 per delivery. A 15% to 18% gratuity will automatically be added to each bar bill during the cruise. If you use salon and spa services, a similar percentage might be added to the bills there as well. If you dine in a specialty restaurant, you may be asked to provide a one-time gratuity for the service staff.

There will be a "disembarkation talk" on the last day of the cruise that explains tipping procedures. If you are expected to tip in cash, small white "tip" envelopes will appear in your stateroom that day. If you tip in cash, you usually give the tip envelope directly to each person on the last night of the cruise. Tips generally add up to about $11.50 to $14 per person per day. You tip the same amount for each person who shares the cabin, including children, unless otherwise indicated.

Most cruise lines now either automatically add gratuities to passengers' onboard charge accounts or offer the option. If that suits you, then do nothing further. But you are certainly free to adjust the amounts up or down to more appropriate levels or ask that the charge be removed altogether if you prefer distributing cash gratuities.

EXTRAS

In addition to the cost of your cruise, there are further expenses to consider.

AIR TRAVEL TO EUROPE

Almost every cruise passenger will have to purchase airfare to the port of embarkation (for most cruises in Greece, this would be either Barcelona, Rome, Venice, Athens, or Istanbul, though some cruises embark in Malta). These days virtually all cruise lines offer air add-ons, which are sometimes—but not always—less expensive than the lowest available airline fare. Airfares to Europe can be considerably more expensive from May through September than during the rest of year.

SHORE EXCURSIONS

Shore excursions can also be a substantial expense on any cruise; the best are not cheap. But if you skimp too much on your excursion budget, you'll deprive yourself of an important part of the Greek cruising experience. They are worth it if you want to venture to attractions that are located far from the pier, such as the major sights in Athens. But if all you want to do is walk around town, shop, or visit the beach, it could be much cheaper and less time-consuming to get a map and go it on your own.

The top shore excursions in Greece revolve around the country's ancient archeological sites. The Acropolis of Athens, a grand and imposing ancient site crowned by the Parthenon is one that can hardly be missed. As dramatic as it can be when seen from a distance, it is even better up close. You know you are walking in the same space as many famed ancient Greeks—and the view from the Acropolis is equally extraordinary. An organized shore excursion can help you negotiate the substantial crowds during the high season. Other popular excursions include Olympia (the birthplace of the first Olympic Games), and the various museums of Greece (including the archeological museum and the highly acclaimed Acropolis museums in Athens). In Mykonos, a popular and worthy shore excursion is to the uninhabited island of Delos via a small boat. Being guided through these historic sights gives you the perfect overview of Greek art, sculpture, and history you may have always wanted to learn about up close.

If archaeology and mythology aren't of interest—or if you are on a return trip to Greece and have already seen these major sights—you can seek out shore excursions that take you deeper into modern-day Greek culture. Smaller cruise ships often specialize in this since they can slide easily into the ports of Greek cities, villages, and islands that are less traveled. As a result, you can participate in events that showcase Greek gastronomy, religion, traditional dance, and more. Some ships stay in port in the evening, encouraging passengers to return at midnight for a chance to dine among locals or experience the nightlife of a Greek destination.

You don't necessarily have to take the tour offered by your ship. Although there's a distinct advantage these days to having your shore excursions priced in dollars rather than euros, you can still have a high-quality (though perhaps not cheaper) experience by banding together with a group of like-minded travelers to arrange a private tour rather than relying on the ship's big-bus experience. Or if you are more intrepid, you can simply hop in a taxi or onto public transportation and do some independent exploring. Whether you choose to take ship-sponsored tours or go it alone, you do need to budget for off-ship touring because that's the reason you came to Europe in the first place.

ONBOARD EXTRAS

Finally, there will be many extras added to your shipboard account during the cruise, including drinks (both alcoholic and nonalcoholic), activity fees (you pay to use that golf simulator), dining in specialty restaurants, spa services, gratuities, and even cappuccino and espresso on most ships.

BOOKING YOUR CRUISE

As a rule, the majority of cruisers plan their trips four to six months ahead of time. It follows, then, that a four- to six-month window should give you the pick of sailing dates, ships, itineraries, cabins, and flights to the port city. If you're looking for a standard itinerary and aren't choosy about the vessel or dates, you could wait for a last-minute discount, but they are becoming harder to find.

If particular shore excursions are important to you, consider booking them when you book your cruise to avoid disappointment later.

USING A TRAVEL AGENT

The most important steps in cruise-travel planning are research, research, and more research; your best friend in booking a cruise is a knowledgeable travel agent. It's a complex process, and it's seldom wise to try to go it alone, particularly the first time. The last thing you want when considering a costly cruise vacation is an agent who has never been on a cruise, calls a cruise ship "the boat," or—worse still—quotes brochure rates. So how do you find a cruise travel agent you can trust?

The most experienced and reliable agent will be certified as an Accredited Cruise Counselor (ACC), Master Cruise Counselor (MCC), or Elite Cruise Counselor (ECC) by CLIA (the Cruise Lines International Association). These agents have completed demanding training programs, including touring or sailing on a specific number of ships. Your agent should also belong to a professional trade organization. In North America, membership in the American Society of Travel Agents (ASTA) indicates that an agency has pledged to follow the code of ethics set forth by the world's largest association for travel professionals. In the best of all worlds, your travel agent is affiliated with both ASTA and CLIA.

Contrary to what conventional wisdom might suggest, cutting out the travel agent and booking directly with a cruise line won't necessarily get you the lowest price. Approximately 90% of all cruise bookings are still handled through travel agents. In fact, cruise-line reservation systems simply are not capable of dealing with tens of thousands of direct calls from potential passengers. Without an agent working on your behalf, you're on your own. Do not rely solely on Internet message boards for authoritative responses to your questions—that is a service more accurately provided by your travel agent.

Travel Agent Professional Organization American Society of Travel Agents *ASTA* ☎ *703/739–2782, 800/965–2782 24-hr hotline* ⊕ *www.travelsense.org.*

Cruise Line Organizations Cruise Lines International Association *CLIA* ☎ *754/224–2200* ⊕ *www.cruising.org.*

BOOKING YOUR CRUISE ONLINE

In addition to local travel agencies, there are many hardworking, dedicated travel professionals working for websites. Both big-name travel sellers and mom-and-pop agencies compete for the attention of cyber-savvy clients, and it never hurts to compare prices from a variety of these sources. Some cruise lines even allow you to book directly with them through their websites.

As a rule, Web-based and toll-free brokers will do a decent job for you. They often offer discounted fares, though not always the lowest, so it pays to check around. If you know precisely what you want and how much you should pay to get a real bargain—and you don't mind dealing with an anonymous voice on the phone—by all means make your reservation when the price is right. Just don't expect the personal service you get from an agent you know. Also, be prepared to spend a lot of time and effort on the phone if something goes wrong.

BEFORE YOU GO

To expedite your preboarding paperwork, some cruise lines have convenient forms on their websites. As long as you have your reservation number, you can provide the required immigration information (usually your citizenship information and passport number), reserve shore excursions, and even indicate any special requests from the comfort of your home. Less-wired cruise lines might mail preboarding paperwork to you or your travel agent for completion after you make your final payment and request that you return the forms by mail or fax. No matter how you submit them, be sure to make hard copies of any forms you fill out and bring them with you to the pier to smooth the embarkation process.

DOCUMENTS

It is every passenger's responsibility to have proper identification. If you arrive at the airport without it, you will not be allowed to board your plane. Should that happen, the cruise line will not issue a fare refund. Most travel agents know the requirements and can guide you to the proper agency to obtain what you need if you don't have it.

Everyone must have a valid passport to travel to Europe. Additionally, some countries to which cruise ships call require visas, though it's also true that tourist visas are sometimes not required for cruise passengers, even if they are generally required to visit a particular country. If your itinerary requires a visa of *all* passengers prior to boarding, you should receive an information letter from your cruise line with instructions and, possibly, application forms. It is your responsibility to obtain all necessary visas. Visa information and applications may also be obtained through the local embassy or consulate of the country you will be visiting. Although you can obtain visas yourself, a more hassle-free route is to use a visa service, such as Visa Central or Travisa, that specializes in the process. ■ TIP→ **If you arrive at the pier without a required visa, you will not be allowed to board your ship, and the cruise line will not issue a fare refund.**

CLOSE UP

Before You Book

If you've decided to use a travel agent, ask yourself these 10 simple questions, and you'll be better prepared to help the agent do his or her job.

1. Who will be going on the cruise?

2. What can you afford to spend for the entire trip?

3. Where would you like to go?

4. How much vacation time do you have?

5. When can you get away?

6. What are your interests?

7. Do you prefer a casual or structured vacation?

8. What kind of accommodations do you want?

9. What are your dining preferences?

10. How will you get to the embarkation port?

2

Contacts Travisa ⊕ *www.travisa.com.* **Visa Central** ⊕ *www.visacentral.com.*

Children under the age of 18—when they are not traveling with *both* parents—almost always require a letter of permission from the absent parent(s). Airlines, cruise lines, and immigration agents can deny children initial boarding or entry to foreign countries without proper proof of identification and citizenship *and* a notarized permission letter from absent or noncustodial parents. Your travel agent or cruise line can help with the wording of such a letter.

GETTING OR RENEWING A PASSPORT

In light of changing government regulations, you should apply for a passport as far in advance of your cruise as possible. In normal times, the process usually takes at least six weeks, but it can take as long as 12 weeks during busy periods. You can expedite your passport application if you are traveling within two weeks by paying an additional fee of $60 (in addition to the regular passport fee) and appearing in person at a regional passport office. Also, several passport expediting services will handle your application for you (for a hefty fee, of course) and can get you a passport in as few as 48 hours. If you are a U.S. citizen, you can read all about the passport application process at the website of the U.S. Department of State; a passport costs $140 if you are 16 or older and is valid for 10 years, $110 if you are under 16, when it is only valid for five years.

If you have left your passport renewal to the last minute, you can call on a company like A. Briggs Passport & Visa Expeditors to help you get a renewal, sometimes in as little as 48 hours. Most visa expeditors can also help you expedite a passport renewal.

Contacts A. Briggs Passport & Visa Expeditors ☏ *800/806–0581 or 202/464–3000* ⊕ *www.abriggs.com.* **U.S. Department of State** ⊕ *travel.state.gov/passport.*

SAMPLE PERMISSION LETTER

Here's the text you might use for a typical letter of permission. You should type this up yourself, putting in all the specific details of your trip in place of the blanks.

CONSENT FOR MINOR CHILDREN TO TRAVEL

Date: _____

I (we): _____

authorize my/our minor child(ren): _____

to travel to: _____ on _____

aboard Airline/Flight Number: _____

and/or Cruise Ship: _____

with _____.

Their expected date of return is: _____.

    In addition, I (we) authorize: _____ to consent to any necessary routine or emergency medical treatment during the aforementioned trip.

Signed: _____(Parent)

Signed: _____(Parent)

Address: _____

    _____

    _____

Telephone: _____.

Sworn to and signed before me, a Notary Public,

this _____ day of _____, 20_____

_____

Notary Public Signature and Seal

WHAT TO PACK

Be sure to pack your necessary travel documents. Failure to have the right travel documents including your passport, cruise tickets, and vouchers may make it difficult to embark your ship. And you'll need your passport to exchange currency. Greece is picturesque, so bring a camera or video camera. Also, remember over-the-counter medications you may need can be packed along with any prescription medications just in case.

WHAT TO WEAR

July and August are the hottest months in Greece; May and September are also prime cruising months and are also warm. The Greek sun can be brilliant yet intense, so the best clothing items to pack should be loose, light-colored, and lightweight. Remember to bring along a sun hat and sunglasses. Even in the hotter months, you may want to pack a sweater or pullover (or a wrap for ladies). Greek summer nights, especially around the islands, can get windy. Early spring or fall nights can get quite cool even if temps remain high during the day. Cover-ups will also come in handy for the cruise ship's summertime air-conditioning.

If you plan to take shore excursions, make sure to pack good walking shoes. You'll find yourself among archaeological sites or areas that are paved in stone or marble, and some areas can be slippery. Keep in mind that some tours focus on religious sites where it's forbidden to wear shorts or to show one's shoulders, back, or legs, so trousers or tops to significantly cover up may be necessary. The cruise line should advise and remind you of such requirements before you go. A bathing suit, flip-flops, or sandals are also ideal for any Greek beach visits.

Other essentials include a good bottle of sunscreen, which can be very expensive in Greece, and remember a small umbrella, just in case it should rain. Special clothing to consider includes cocktail dresses for women and jacket and tie for men during cocktail or gala evenings. Some cruises feature theme nights as well, so you might want to join in and dress up accordingly. Greek nights often encourage guests to wear the national colors of blue and white. Ships often have gyms, so workout gear may be on your packing list if you plan to make use of the facilities on board. Electrical devices like hair dryers, electric shavers, and curling irons may require an adapter so it's best to check beforehand.

INSURANCE

It's a good idea to purchase travel insurance, which covers a variety of possible hazards and mishaps, when you book a cruise. Any policy should insure you for travel and luggage delays. A travel policy will ensure that you can get to the next port of call should you miss your ship, or replace delayed necessities secure in the knowledge that you will be reimbursed for those unexpected expenditures. Save your receipts for all out-of-pocket expenses to file your claim, and be sure to get an incident report from the airline at fault.

Insurance should also cover you for unexpected injuries and illnesses. The medical insurance program you depend on at home might not extend coverage beyond the borders of the United States. Medicare assuredly will not cover you if you are hurt or sick while abroad. It is worth noting that all ships of foreign registry are considered to be "outside the United States" by Medicare.

Nearly all cruise lines offer their own line of insurance. Compare the coverage and rates to determine which is best for you. Keep in mind that insurance purchased from an independent carrier is more likely to include coverage if the cruise line goes out of business before or during your cruise. Although it is a rare and unlikely occurrence, you do want to be insured in the event that it happens.

MONEY

On board your ship you won't have any worries about money, but you will need cash while ashore. If you have not arranged for transfers from the airport to the ship, you will need taxi fare in the local currency, which is the euro. Currency exchange is almost always more costly in your home country than at your foreign destination, but many banks, as well as the American Automobile Association (AAA), American Express, and Travelex bureaus offer the service. In addition, you will find currency exchange booths in the international terminal at your departure and arrival airport.

If you are looking to exchange money inside a Greek bank, note that typical banking hours are 8 am to 2 pm on weekdays. There are exceptions on the larger islands and cities like Athens and Thessaloniki. ATMs are available for use all the time and are the simplest—and usually least expensive—method of obtaining local currency. Visa and MasterCard debit and credit cards are widely accepted at ATMs in Greece. Keep in mind that fees are usually imposed for international withdrawals. Before leaving home, make sure you have a four-digit numerical PIN (personal identification number) for your card and understand any fees associated with its use. Also, notify the credit card company that you will be using your card overseas so they don't refuse your charges when they notice its repeated use in foreign locales.

For days in port you will also want some cash on hand for beverages, snacks, and souvenir purchases. Your cruise ship may offer a foreign currency exchange service onboard, but, like hotels, the exchange rate is not always the most favorable. We suggest that instead of carrying large amounts of cash when ashore, you use a credit card for major purchases.

Contacts American Automobile Association *AAA* ☎ *315/797–5000* ⊕ *www.aaa.com.* **American Express** ☎ *888/412–6945 in U.S., 801/945–9450 collect outside U.S. to add value or speak to customer service* ⊕ *www.americanexpress.com.* **Travelex** ⊕ *www.travelex.com.*

CUSTOMS AND DUTIES

TAXES

If you are not a European Union citizen and make large purchases while in Greece, you can check for merchants that offer tax-free refunds—not all stores do, nor are they required to. If they are a participating retailer you can ask for a V.A.T. refund form. In Greece it is called FPA and is noted as **ΦΠΑ** in Greek letters on a receipt with a percentage. The minimum purchase to be eligible for a V.A.T. refund in Greece at the time of publication is $120.

To get a V.A.T. refund in Greece, keep an eye out for the "V.A.T. Refund" or "Tax Free Shopping Network" signs in store windows. You should have your passport on you to make the purchase; copies are usually not accepted. Ask for the V.A.T. refund form when you are given your receipt. If the merchant participates in the refund program, he is required to have it at the shop and will give it to you at the time of purchase.

If you're visiting several E.U. countries, have the form stamped like any customs form by customs officials when you leave the country or when you leave the European Union. This has to be done at the airport on the day you are flying home. After you're through passport control, take the form to a refund-service counter for an on-the-spot refund (which is usually the quickest and easiest option), or mail it to the address on the form (or the envelope with it) after you arrive home. You receive the total refund stated on the form, but the processing time can be long, especially if you request a credit-card adjustment.

In the Athens International Airport, bring your form and item to the V.A.T. refund desk. Global Blue and Premier Tax Free is located at the Eurochange currency exchange kiosks that are located at the departures level in the Non Schengen Area and at the departures level Schengen Area, which is accessible to all passengers. If you need to repack the item, do this step before checking in your suitcases.

Global Blue (formerly known as Global Refund) is a Europe-wide service with 225,000 affiliated stores and more than 700 refund counters at major airports and border crossings. Its refund form, called a Tax Free Check, is the most common across the European continent. The service issues refunds in the form of cash, check, or credit-card adjustment. *See Travel Smart for more information.*

U.S. CUSTOMS

Each individual or family returning to the United States must fill out a customs declaration form, which will be provided before your plane lands. If you owe any duties, you will have to pay them directly to the customs inspector, with cash or check. Be sure to keep receipts for all purchases; and you may be asked to show officials what you've bought. If your cruise is a transatlantic crossing, U.S. Customs clears ships sailing into arrival ports. After showing your passport to immigration officials, you must collect your luggage from the dock, then stand in line to pass through the inspection point. This can take up to an hour.

ALLOWANCES

You're always allowed to bring goods of a certain value back home without having to pay any duty or import tax. But there's a limit on the amount of tobacco and liquor you can bring back duty-free. The values of so-called duty-free goods are included in these amounts. When you shop abroad, save all your receipts, as customs inspectors may ask to see them as well as the items you purchased. If the total value of your goods is more than the duty-free limit, you'll have to pay a tax (most often a flat percentage) on the value of everything beyond that limit. For U.S. citizens who have been in Europe for at least 48 hours, the duty-free exemption is $800. But the duty-free exemption includes 800 cigarettes or 200 cigars or 400 cigarillos or 1 kg of tobacco. There's a limit of 10L of spirits (over 22%), 20L of spirits (under 22%), 90L of wine and 110L of beer. If you purchase above these amounts listed, you have to pay duties, even if you didn't spend more than the $800.

Contacts **U.S. Customs and Border Protection** ⊕ *www.cbp.gov.*

SENDING PACKAGES HOME

Although you probably won't want to spend your time looking for a post office, you can send packages home duty-free, with a limit of one parcel per addressee per day (except alcohol or tobacco products or perfume worth more than $5). You can mail up to $200 worth of goods to yourself, or $100 worth of goods to a friend or relative; label the package "personal use" or "unsolicited gift" (depending on which is the case) and attach a list of the contents and their retail value. If the package contains your used personal belongings, mark it "personal goods returned" to avoid paying duty on your laundry. You do not need to declare items that were sent home on your declaration forms for U.S. Customs.

CRUISE LINES

Just as trends and fashion evolve over time, cruise lines embrace the ebb and flow of change. To keep pace with today's lifestyles, some cruise lines strive to include something that will appeal to everyone on their ships. Others focus on narrower elements and are more traditional. Today's passengers have higher expectations and they sail on ships that are far superior to their predecessors—and they often do so at a much lower comparable fare than in the past.

So which cruise line is best? Only you can determine which is best for you. You won't find ratings by Fodor's—either quality stars or value scores. Why? Ratings are personal and heavily weighted to the reviewer's opinion. Your responsibility is to select the right cruise for you—no one knows your expectations better than you. It's your time, money, and vacation that are at stake. No matter how knowledgeable your travel agent is, how sincere your friends are, or what any expert can tell you, you are the only one who really knows what you like. The short wait for a table might not bother you because you would prefer a casual atmosphere with open seating; however, some people want the security of a set time at an assigned table served by a waiter who gets to know their preferences. You know what you are willing to trade off in order to get what you want.

TYPES OF CRUISE LINES

MAINSTREAM CRUISE LINES

The mainstream lines are the ones most often associated with modern cruising. They offer the advantage of something for everyone and nearly every available sports facility imaginable. Some ships even have ice-skating rinks, 18-hole miniature golf courses, bowling alleys, and rock-climbing walls.

Generally speaking, the mainstream lines have two basic ship sizes—large cruise ships and megaships—in their fleets. These vessels have plentiful outdoor deck space, and many have a wraparound outdoor promenade deck that allows you to stroll or jog the ship's perimeter. In the newest vessels, traditional meets trendy. You'll find atrium lobbies and expansive sun and sports decks, picture windows instead of portholes, and cabins that open onto private verandas. For all their resort-style innovations, they still feature cruise-ship classics—afternoon tea, complimentary room service, and lavish pampering. The smallest ships carry 1,000 passengers or fewer, while the largest accommodate more than 5,000 passengers and are filled with diversions.

These ships tend to be big and boxy. Picture windows are standard equipment, and cabins in the top categories have private verandas. From their casinos and discos to their fitness centers, everything is bigger and more extravagant than on other ships. You'll pay for many extras on the mainstream ships, from drinks at the bar to that cup of cappuccino, to a spa treatments, to a game of bowling, to dinner in a specialty restaurant. You may want to rethink a cruise aboard one of these ships if you want a little downtime, since you'll be joined by thousands of fellow passengers.

PREMIUM CRUISE LINES

Premium cruise lines have a lot in common with the mainstream cruise lines, but with a little more of everything. The atmosphere is more refined, surroundings more gracious, and service more polished and attentive. There are still activities like pool games, although they aren't quite the high jinks typical of mainstream ships. In addition to traditional cruise activities, onboard lectures are common. Production shows are somewhat more sophisticated than on mainstream lines.

Ships tend to be newer midsize to large vessels that carry fewer passengers than mainstream ships and have a more spacious feel. Decor is usually more glamorous and subtle, with toned-down colors and extensive original art. Staterooms range from inside cabins for three or four to outside cabins with or without balconies to suites with numerous amenities, including butlers on some lines.

Most premium ships offer traditional assigned seatings for dinner. High marks are afforded the quality cuisine and presentation. Many ships have upscale bistros or specialty restaurants, which usually require reservations and command an additional charge. Although premium lines usually have as many extra charges as mainstream lines, the overall quality of what you receive is higher.

LUXURY CRUISE LINES

Comprising only 5% of the market, the exclusive luxury cruise lines, such as Crystal, Cunard, Oceania, Regent Seven Seas, Seabourn, SeaDream, and Silversea offer high staff-to-guest ratios for personal service, superior cuisine in a single seating (except Crystal, with two assigned seatings, and Cunard, with dual-class dining assignments), and a highly inclusive product with few onboard charges. These small and midsize ships offer much more space per passenger than you will find on the mainstream lines' vessels. Lines differ in what they emphasize, with some touting luxurious accommodations and entertainment and others focusing on exotic destinations and onboard enrichment.

If you consider travel a necessity rather than a luxury and frequent posh resorts, then you will appreciate the extra attention and the higher level of comfort that luxury cruise lines offer. Itineraries on these ships often include the marquee ports, but luxury ships also visit some of the more uncommon destinations.

EUROPEAN CRUISE LINES

With more similarities to American-owned cruise lines than differences, these European-owned-and-operated cruise lines compare favorably to the mainstream cruise lines of a decade ago. Many lines have embarked upon shipbuilding programs that rival the most ambitious in the cruise industry, but some European fleets still consist of older and smaller, yet well-maintained vessels. These cruises cater to Europeans—announcements may be broadcast in as many as five languages—and Americans are generally in the minority. English is widely spoken by the crew, however.

OTHER CRUISE LINES

A few small cruise lines sail through Europe and offer boutique to nearly bed-and-breakfast experiences. Notably, Star Clippers, Lindblad Expeditions, and Hurtigruten appeal to passengers who eschew mainstream cruises. Most of these niche vessels accommodate 200 or fewer passengers, and their focus is on soft adventure; Hurtigruten's ships and itineraries are perfectly suited for scenic coastal cruising and have few other onboard amenities. Other lines cruise between nearby ports and drop anchor so passengers can swim and snorkel directly from the ship (as on Star Clippers), and they have itineraries that usually leave plenty of time for exploring and other activities on- or offshore. Many of these cruises schedule casual enrichment talks that often continue on decks, at meals, and during trips ashore.

MAJOR CRUISE LINES

Azamara Club Cruises. Designed to offer exotic destination-driven itineraries, Azamara Club Cruises presents an intimate onboard experience while allowing access to the less traveled ports of call experienced travelers want to visit. Its two ships, *Azamara Journey* and *Azamara Quest*, offer not quite luxury but more than premium cruising, a deluxe cruise with concierge-style amenities for which you'd have to upgrade to a suite on other cruise lines. In addition, since its launch Azamara Club Cruises has added a number of more inclusive amenities to passengers' fares, with no charge for a specific brand of bottled water, specialty coffees and teas; shuttle bus service to/from port communities, where available; standard spirits, wines, and international beers throughout the ships during bar hours; and complimentary self-service laundry.

Your Shipmates: Azamara is designed to appeal to discerning travelers, primarily American couples of any age who appreciate a high level of service in a nonstructured atmosphere.

Dress Code: While passengers are welcome to wear formal attire, there are no scheduled formal nights. The nightly dress code is simply "sophisticated" casual—a jacket and tie are never required, but men who are accustomed to wearing them will do so anyway.

Tipping: Housekeeping and dining gratuities are included in the fare. A standard 18% is added to beverage charges. It is recommended that a $5-per-person gratuity be extended when dining in the specialty restaurants. ☎ 877/999–9553 ⊕ *www.azamaraclubcruises.com* ☞ *Cruise Style: Premium.*

Carnival Cruise Lines. The world's largest cruise line originated the Fun Ship concept in 1972. Sporting red-white-and-blue flared funnels, which are easily recognized from afar, new ships are continuously added to the fleet and rarely deviate from a successful pattern. If you find something you like on one vessel, you're likely to find something similar on another. Each vessel features themed public rooms, ranging from ancient Egypt to futuristic motifs, although many of those elements are being replaced with a more tropical decor as older ships are upgraded. Carnival is also introducing features either branded by the line itself, such as the poolside Blue Iguana Tequila Bar with an adjacent burrito cantina and the Red Frog Rum Bar that also serves Carnival's own brand of Thirsty Frog Red beer, or in partnership with well-known brands, such as EA SPORTS, Food Network star Guy Fieri, and Hasbro. Implementation of the new features is scheduled for completion in 2015.

Your Shipmates: Carnival's passengers are predominantly active Americans, mostly couples in their midthirties to midfifties. Many families enjoy Carnival cruises in the Caribbean year-round.

Dress Code: Two "cruise elegant" nights are standard on seven-night cruises; one is the norm on shorter sailings. Although men should feel free to wear tuxedos, dark suits (or sport coats) and ties are more prevalent. All other evenings are "cruise casual," with jeans and dress shorts permitted in the dining rooms. All ships request that no short-shorts or cutoffs be worn after 6 pm, but that policy is often ignored.

Tipping: A gratuity of $11.50 per passenger per day is automatically added to passenger accounts, and gratuities are distributed to stewards and waitstaff. Passengers may adjust the amount based on the level of service experienced. All beverage tabs at bars get an automatic 15% addition. ☎ 305/599–2600 or 800/227–6482 ⊕ *www.carnival.com* ☞ *Cruise Style: Mainstream.*

Celebrity Cruises. The Chandris Group, owners of budget Fantasy Cruises, founded Celebrity in 1989. Celebrity gained a reputation for professional service and fine food despite the shabby-chic vessel on which it was elegantly served. The cruise line eventually built premium sophisticated cruise ships. Signature amenities followed, including large standard staterooms with generous storage, fully equipped spas, and butler service. Valuable art collections grace the fleet. Although spacious accommodations in every category are a Celebrity standard, Concierge-class, an upscale element on all ships, makes certain premium ocean-view and balcony staterooms almost the equivalent of suites in terms of service.

Your Shipmates: Celebrity caters to American cruise passengers, primarily couples from their midthirties to midfifties. Many families enjoy cruising on Celebrity's fleet during summer months and holiday periods, particularly in the Caribbean. Lengthier cruises and exotic itineraries attract passengers in the over-sixty age group.

Dress Code: Two formal nights are standard on seven-night cruises, and men are encouraged to wear tuxedos. Other evenings are designated "smart casual and above." Although jeans are discouraged in formal restaurants, they are appropriate for casual dining venues after 6 pm. Most people observe the dress code of the evening, unlike on some other cruise lines.

Tipping: Gratuities are automatically added daily to onboard accounts in the following amounts (which may be adjusted at your discretion): $11.50 per person per day for passengers in stateroom categories; $12 per person per day for Concierge-class and Aqua-class staterooms; and $15 per person per day for Suites. An automatic gratuity of 15% is added to all beverage tabs. ☎ *800/647–2251* ⊕ *www.celebritycruises. com* ☞ *Cruise Style: Premium.*

Costa Cruises. Europe's number-one cruise line combines a Continental experience, enticing itineraries, and Italy's classical design and style with relaxing days and romantic nights at sea. Genoa-based Costa Crociere, parent company of Costa Cruise Lines, was bought by Airtours and Carnival Corporation in 1997. In 2000 Carnival completed a buyout of the Costa line and began expanding the fleet with larger and more dynamic ships. An ongoing shipbuilding program has brought Costa ships into the 21st century with innovative large-ship designs that reflect their Italian heritage and style without overlooking the amenities expected by modern cruisers. Acknowledging changing habits (even among Europeans), Costa Cruises has eliminated smoking entirely in dining rooms and show lounges. Nevertheless, smokers are permitted to light up in designated areas in other public rooms, as well as on the pool deck.

Your Shipmates: Couples in the 35- to 55-year-old range are attracted to Costa Cruises; on most itineraries, up to 80% of passengers are European, and many of them are of Italian descent. An international air prevails on board, and announcements are often made in a variety of languages. The vibe on Costa's newest megaships is most likely to appeal to American tastes and expectations.

Dress Code: Two formal nights are standard on seven-night cruises. Men are encouraged to wear tuxedos, but dark suits or sport coats and ties are appropriate and more common than black tie. All other evenings are resort casual, although jeans are discouraged in restaurants. It's requested that no shorts be worn in public areas after 6 pm.

Tipping: A standard gratuity of €7 per adult per day for cruises up to eight nights or €6 per adult per day on longer cruises is automatically added to shipboard accounts and distributed to cabin stewards and dining-room staff. The applicable charge for teens between the ages of 14 and 17 is 50% of those amounts; there is no charge for children under the age of 14. Passengers may adjust the amount based on the level of service experienced. An automatic 15% gratuity is added to all beverage tabs, as well as to checks for spa treatments and salon services. ☎ 954/266–5600 or 800/462–6782 ⊕ www.costacruise.com ☞ Cruise Style: Mainstream.

Crystal Cruises. Winner of accolades and too many hospitality industry awards to count, Crystal Cruises offers a taste of the grandeur of the past along with all the modern touches discerning passengers demand today. Crystal ships, unlike other luxury vessels, are large, carrying upward of 900 passengers. What makes them distinctive are superior service, a variety of dining options, spacious accommodations, and some of the highest ratios of space per passenger of any cruise ship and Asian-inspired design.

Your Shipmates: Affluent, well-traveled couples, from their late thirties and up, are attracted to Crystal's destination-rich itineraries, shipboard enrichment programs, and elegant ambience. The average age of passengers is noticeably higher on longer itineraries.

Dress Code: Formal attire is required on at least two designated evenings, depending on the length of the cruise. Men are encouraged to wear tuxedos, and many do, although dark suits are also acceptable. Other evenings are informal or resort casual; the number of each is based on the number of sea days. The line requests that dress codes be observed in public areas after 6 pm, and few, if any, passengers disregard the suggestion. Most, in fact, dress up just a notch from guidelines.

Tipping: Housekeeping and dining gratuities are included in the fare. A 15% gratuity is suggested for spa and salon services. ☎ 888/799–4625 or 310/785–9300 ⊕ www.crystalcruises.com ☞ Cruise Style: Luxury.

Cruise and Maritime Voyages. Founded in 2009, U.K.-based Cruise and Maritime Voyages specializes in adults-only cruises for travelers over 60 who seek a low-key, traditional British experience. Two refurbished 800-passenger ships, *Marco Polo* and *Discovery,* offer classic cruising itineraries from 2-night mini-excursions to 44-night cruises and are designed to maximize time in ports of call. With departure from six U.K. cities, afternoon tea service, an English-speaking staff, and pounds sterling as onboard currency, the cruise line attracts a predominantly unpretentious, British crowd.

Your Shipmates: Expect an older crowd on all CMV cruises, with the minimum age in the midfifties. While the staff and entertainers are a multicultural blend of British and international citizens, the cruise line attracts primarily British travelers since all points of departure are located in the United Kingdom.

Dress Code: Ships have traditional formal, informal, and casual nights. On most evenings, informal attire applies, making ties optional (but not jackets) for men. On casual evenings, passengers can choose what they want to wear. On formal nights, black tie or dinner jackets are suggested for men, cocktail dresses for women. Casual nights occur on evenings in port or during special events such as deck parties.

Tipping: An automatic tipping charge of £5 per person per night is added to onboard customer accounts (£4 per person per night for cruises lasting more than 16 days). At the end of the cruise, passengers can adjust the charged amount to reflect personal satisfaction levels. ☎ *0845/430–0274 in the U.K.* ⊕ *www.cruiseandmaritime.com* ☞ *Cruise Style: Mainstream*

Cunard Line. One of the world's most distinguished names in ocean travel since 1840, the Cunard Line has a long history of deluxe transatlantic crossings and worldwide cruising. The line's ships are legendary for their comfortable accommodations, excellent cuisine, and personal service. After a series of owners tried with little success to revive the company's flagging passenger-shipping business, Carnival Corporation offered an infusion of ready cash and the know-how to turn the line around in 1998. Exciting new ships have followed. Delightful daily events include afternoon tea and the maritime tradition of sounding the ship's bell at noon. The line offers North Atlantic crossings and seasonal shorter cruises, including Northern European and Mediterranean itineraries.

Your Shipmates: Discerning, well-traveled American and British couples from their late thirties to retirees are drawn to Cunard's traditional style and the notion of a cruise aboard an ocean liner. The availability of spacious accommodations and complimentary self-service laundry facilities makes Cunard liners a good option for families, although there may be fewer children on board than on similar size ships.

Dress Code: Glamorous evenings are typical of Cunard cruises, and specified attire includes formal, informal, and casual. Although resort casual clothing prevails throughout the day, Cunard vessels are ocean liners at heart and, as expected, are dressier than most cruise ships at night. To maintain their high standards, the cruise line requests passengers to dress as they would for dining in fine restaurants.

Tipping: Suggested gratuities of $13 per person per day (for Grill Restaurant accommodations) or $11 per person per day (all other accommodations) are automatically charged to shipboard accounts for distribution to stewards and waitstaff. An automatic 15% gratuity is added to beverage tabs for bar service. Passengers can still tip individual crew members directly in cash for any special services. ☎ *661/753–1000 or 800/728–6273* ⊕ *www.cunard.com* ☞ *Cruise Style: Luxury.*

Disney Cruise Line. With the launch of Disney Cruise Line in 1998, families were offered yet another reason to take a cruise. The magic of a Walt Disney resort vacation plus the romance of a sea voyage are a tempting combination, especially for adults who discovered Disney movies and the Mickey Mouse Club as children. Mixed with traditional shipboard activities, who can resist scheduled opportunities for the young and young-at-heart to interact with their favorite Disney characters? Although Disney

Cruise Line voyages stuck to tried-and-true Bahamas and Caribbean itineraries in their formative years, and sailed exclusively from Port Canaveral, Florida, where a terminal was designed especially for Disney ships, the line has branched out to other regions, including Europe.

Your Shipmates: Disney Cruises appeal to kids of all ages—the young and not so young, singles, couples, and families. Multigenerational family groups are the core audience for these ships, and the facilities are ideal for family gatherings. What you might not have expected are the numerous newlywed couples celebrating their honeymoons on board.

Dress Code: One-week cruises schedule a semiformal evening and a formal night, during which men are encouraged to wear tuxedos, but dark suits or sport coats and ties are acceptable for both. Resort casual is the evening dress code for dinner in the more laid-back dining rooms. A sport coat is appropriate for the restaurants designated as fancier, as well as the adults-only specialty restaurants; however, you won't be turned away and could probably get by without the sport coat.

Tipping: Suggested gratuity amounts are calculated on a per-person, per-cruise rather than per-night basis and can be added to onboard accounts or offered in cash on the last night of the cruise. Guidelines include gratuities for your dining-room server, assistant server, head server, and stateroom host–hostess for the following amounts: $36 for three-night cruises, $48 for four-night cruises, and $84 for seven-night cruises. Tips for room-service delivery, spa services, and the dining manager are at the passenger's discretion. An automatic 15% gratuity is added to all bar tabs. ☎ *407/566–3500 or 888/325–2500* ⊕ *www. disneycruise.com* ☞ *Cruise Style: Mainstream.*

Fred. Olsen Cruise Lines. With its Norwegian heritage of seamanship spanning over 150 years, family-owned Fred. Olsen Cruise Lines has built a solid reputation of reliability and comfort for its U.K.-based fleet of smaller ships. Major refitting and refurbishment of old and recently acquired ships since 2008 have earned the company high industry accolades. Shipboard ambience is friendly, relaxed, and unabashedly British. As Fred. Olsen Cruise Lines expands, the line takes pride in maintaining the consistency their passengers prefer and expect, both on board—in the self-described "British country house" atmosphere—and ashore. Activities and entertainment are traditional cruise-ship fare with a laid-back tempo, albeit on a much smaller scale compared to a typical American megaship. British pounds are used for all transactions on board. Although the line is destination-focused—itineraries are seldom repeated within any cruise season—itinerary planning is versatile.

Your Shipmates: Well-traveled, mature British passengers who enjoy the time-honored shipboard environment with a formal style make up the majority on board Fred. Olsen sailings. Children's programs are offered only during summer months and school holiday breaks.

Dress Code: Requested attire is appropriately casual during the day and consists of three types of traditional shipboard evening dress—formal, informal, and casual. Most passengers still "dress" for dinner, which includes black tie on formal nights and a regular jacket and tie for men on informal evenings.

Tipping: Recommended gratuities, which are added to your onboard account, are £4 per passenger per day for your cabin steward and dining room waiter. ☎ *01473/742–424 in the U.K.* ⊕ *www.fredolsencruises. com* ☞ *Cruise Style: Mainstream.*

Holland America. Holland America Line has enjoyed a distinguished record of traditional cruises, world exploration, and transatlantic crossings since 1873—all facets of its history are reflected in the fleet's multimillion-dollar shipboard art and antiques collections. Noted for focusing on passenger comfort, Holland America Line cruises are classic in design and style, and with an infusion of younger adults and families on board, they remain refined without being stuffy or stodgy. Following a basic design theme, returning passengers feel as at home on the newest Holland America vessels as they do on older ones.

Your Shipmates: No longer just your grandparents' cruise line, today's Holland America sailings attract families and discerning couples, mostly from their late thirties on up. Holidays and summer months are peak periods when you'll find more children in the mix. Comfortable retirees are often still in the majority, particularly on longer cruises.

Dress Code: Evenings on Holland America Line cruises fall into two categories: smart casual and formal. For the two formal nights standard on seven-night cruises, men are encouraged to wear tuxedos, but dark suits or sport coats and ties are acceptable, and you'll certainly see them. On smart-casual nights, expect the type of attire you'd see at a country club or upscale resort. It's requested that no T-shirts, jeans, swimsuits, tank tops, or shorts be worn in public areas after 6 pm.

Tipping: Gratuities of $11.50 per passenger per day are automatically added to shipboard accounts, and distributed to stewards and wait-staff. Passengers may adjust the amount based on the level of service experienced. Room-service tips are usually given in cash (it's at the passenger's discretion here). Gratuities for spa and salon services can be added to the bill or offered in cash. An automatic 15% gratuity is added to bar-service tabs. ☎ *206/281–3535 or 800/577–1728* ⊕ *www. hollandamerica.com* ☞ *Cruise Style: Premium.*

Lindblad Expeditions. Every Lindblad cruise is educational, focusing on soft adventure and environmentally conscientious travel. Since 2004 the line has partnered with *National Geographic* to enhance the cruise experience by including experts and photographers on board to lead discussions and hold workshops and help balance "must-see" destinations and less-traveled spots. The ships of Lindblad Expeditions spend time looking for wildlife, exploring out-of-the-way inlets, and making Zodiac landings at isolated beaches. Each ship has a fleet of kayaks as well as a video-microphone: a hydrophone (underwater microphone) is combined with an underwater camera so passengers can listen to whale songs and watch live video of what's going on beneath the waves. All activities and shore excursions, from guided walks and hikes to museum entrance fees to water activities like kayaking and snorkeling, are included in the cost of every Lindblad Expedition. Guests always have the freedom to pick and choose activities as the day unfolds.

Your Shipmates: Lindblad attracts active, adventurous, well-traveled over-forties, and quite a few singles, as the line charges one of the industry's lowest single supplements. But the line is making a push to be more family-friendly by adding cruises aimed specifically at families and children.

Dress Code: Casual and comfortable attire is always appropriate. Recommendations are based on practicality and the likely weather conditions in the region you're exploring. Good walking shoes are essential.

Tipping: Although gratuities are at your discretion, tips of $12–$15 per person per day are suggested; these are pooled among the crew at journey's end. Tip the massage therapist individually following a treatment. ☎ *212/765–7740 or 800/397–3348 ⊕ www.expeditions.com ☞ Cruise Style: Small-ship.*

Louis Cruises. Louis Cruises was established in 1986, with a fleet of refurbished, well-maintained ships. Today, the value-oriented line has six ships, two of which are chartered by and sail under the Thomson brand (⇨ *see Thomson Cruises*). Ships vary in size, age, and available amenities, but all the ships' cabins and facilities are well maintained and clean. Lacking luxury appointments and the accompanying prices and pretension, a cruise on any of the four Louis Cruises vessels concentrates more on destination than the actual shipboard experience. Some Louis ships may not meet the high expectations of well-heeled globe-trotters, but the itineraries can be outstanding.

Your Shipmates: A wide range of ages and nationalities embark on Louis Cruise voyages. While crew and staff are all local Greeks, Cypriots, and other Eastern Europeans, clientele are usually British, French, German, and a variety of northern Europeans, with a growing number of Americans and Canadians as passengers.

Dress Code: Casual attire is common by day, and the evening dress code is country club casual, with more formalwear visible during special dinners. Women tend to wear long trousers or cocktail dresses. Men wear a jacket and tie. "Greek Night" suggests attire in blue and white, the colors of Greece.

Tipping: Tipping is expected. The line will debit shipboard accounts €8 per person per day for adults over 16 and €4 per person per day for children ages 6–16. Amounts can be adjusted by speaking with the staff at reception. ☎ *(44) 0800/0183883 in the U.K.; (30) 210/4583400 in Greece ⊕ www.louiscruises.com ☞ Cruise Style: Mainstream.*

MSC Cruises. More widely known as one of the world's largest cargo shipping companies, MSC has operated cruises with an eclectic fleet since the late 1980s. This line is growing into a major player in both Europe and the Caribbean. MSC blankets the Mediterranean nearly year-round with a dizzying selection of cruise itineraries that allow a lot of time in ports of call and include few if any sea days. In summer months, several ships sail off to northern Europe to ply the Baltic. Itineraries planned for repositioning sailings visit some intriguing, off-the-beaten-track ports of call that other cruise lines bypass. No glitz, no clutter—just elegant simplicity—is the standard of MSC's seaworthy interior decor. Extensive use of marble, brass, and wood reflects the best of Italian styling and design; clean lines and bold colors set their modern sophisticated tone. MSC adopts some activities that appeal to American passengers without abandoning those preferred by Europeans; however, regardless of the itinerary, be prepared for an Italian-influenced experience.

Your Shipmates: Most passengers are couples in the 35- to 55-year-old range, as well as some family groups who prefer the international atmosphere prevalent on board. Although more than half the passengers on Caribbean itineraries are North Americans, expect a more international mix on European cruises, with North Americans in the minority.

Dress Code: Two formal nights are standard on seven-night cruises, and three may be scheduled on longer sailings. Men are encouraged to wear dark suits, but sport coats and ties are appropriate. All other evenings are casual, although jeans are discouraged in restaurants. It's requested that no shorts be worn in public areas after 6 pm.

Tipping: For cruises of eight nights or less, customary gratuities are added to your shipboard account in the amount of €7 per person per day for adults and half that amount for children; for longer cruises, the customary daily amount is €6. You can always adjust these amounts at the reception desk or even pay in cash, if you prefer. Automatic 15% gratuities are incorporated into all bar purchases. You may also reward staff in the spa and casino for exceptional service. ☎ *800/666–9333* ⊕ *www.msccruisesusa.com* ☞ *Cruise Style: Premium.*

Norwegian Cruise Line. Norwegian Cruise Line (originally known as Norwegian Caribbean Line) set sail in 1966 with an entirely new concept: regularly scheduled Caribbean cruises from the then-obscure port of Miami. Good food and friendly service combined with value fares established Norwegian as a winner for active adults and families. Innovative and forward-looking, Norwegian has been a cruise-industry leader for four decades, and is as much at home in Europe as it is in the Caribbean.

Noted for top-quality, high-energy entertainment and emphasis on fitness facilities and programs, Norwegian combines action, activities, and a variety of dining options in a casual, free-flowing atmosphere. Freestyle cruising signaled an end to rigid dining schedules and dress codes. Norwegian ships now offer a host of flexible dining options that allow passengers to eat in the main dining rooms or any of a number of à la carte and specialty restaurants at any time and with whom they please. Now co-owned by Genting Hong Kong Limited and Apollo Management, a private equity company, Norwegian continues to be an industry innovator.

Your Shipmates: Norwegian's mostly American cruise passengers are active couples ranging from their midthirties to midfifties. Many families enjoy cruising on Norwegian ships during holidays and summer months. Longer cruises and more exotic itineraries attract passengers in the over-55 age group.

Dress Code: Resort casual attire is appropriate at all times; the option of one formal evening is available on all cruises of seven nights and longer. Most passengers actually raise the casual dress code a notch to what could be called casual-chic attire.

Tipping: A fixed service charge of $12 per person per day is added to shipboard accounts. An automatic 15% gratuity is added to bar tabs. Staff members may also accept cash gratuities. Passengers in suites who have access to concierge and butler services are asked to offer a cash gratuity at their own discretion. ☎ *305/436–4000 or 800/327–7030* ⊕ *www.ncl.com* ☞ *Cruise Style: Mainstream.*

Oceania Cruises. This distinctive cruise line was founded by Frank Del Rio and Joe Watters, cruise-industry veterans with the know-how to satisfy the wants of inquisitive passengers. By offering itineraries to interesting ports of call and upscale touches—all for fares much lower than you would expect—they are succeeding quite nicely. Intimate and cozy public spaces reflect the importance of socializing on Oceania ships. Waiters are on standby to offer chilled towels or serve passengers with beverages or snacks, whether they are on deck or in a lounge. In addition, you can request a spa service in your cabana. Varied, destination-rich itineraries are an important characteristic of Oceania Cruises, and most sailings are in the 10- to 12-night range.

Your Shipmates: Oceania Cruises appeal to singles and couples from their late thirties to well-traveled retirees who have the time for and prefer longer cruises. Most are American couples attracted to the casually sophisticated atmosphere, creative cuisine, and high level of service.

Dress Code: Leave the formal wear at home—attire on Oceania ships is country-club casual every evening, although some guests can't help dressing up to dine in the beautifully appointed restaurants. A jacket and tie are never required for dinner, but many men wear sport jackets, as they would to dine in an upscale restaurant ashore. Jeans, shorts, T-shirts, and tennis shoes are discouraged after 6 pm in public rooms.

Tipping: Gratuities of $14.50 per person per day are added to shipboard accounts for distribution to stewards and waitstaff; an additional $6 per person per day is added for occupants of suites with butler service. Passengers may adjust the amount based on the level of service experienced. An automatic 18% gratuity is added to all bar tabs for bartenders and drink servers and to all bills for salon and spa services. ☎ *305/514–2300 or 800/531–5658* ⊕ *www.oceaniacruises.com* ☞ *Cruise Style: Premium.*

P&O Cruises. P&O Cruises is the oldest cruise in the world and remains Britain's leading cruise line, sailing the United Kingdom's largest and most modern fleet. The ships are equipped with every traditional big-ship amenity, including swimming pools, stylish restaurants, spas, bars, casinos, theaters, and showrooms. Seven ships in the P&O fleet offer a diverse range of venues for relaxation and entertainment, including cocktail bars, nightclubs, cinemas, games rooms, and cabaret lounges. To offer passengers a variety of choices, P&O has adapted their fleet to match the preferences of their primary markets. Although most of the ships cater to families as well as couples and singles of all ages, *Arcadia*, *Adonia*, and *Oriana* are adults-only ships. The *Aurora*, *Azura*, *Oceana*, and *Ventura* complete the P&O armada and welcome both adults and children. Following customer feedback, P&O announced major refurbishments for the *Ventura*, *Oceana*, and *Arcadia* in 2013.

Your Shipmates: Count on fellow passengers to be predominantly British singles, couples, and families. Depending on which ship you are sailing on, the age demographic and passenger profile will vary; you may find Scandinavians, Americans, Australians, and other Europeans on board for some sailings in addition to the primarily British clientele. Passengers must be 18 or older to sail aboard the all-adult ships.

Dress Code: Daytime attire is appropriately casual; evening wear falls into three traditional categories: formal, informal, and smart casual. Formal is either a tuxedo or dark suit for men, and informal generally requires men to wear a jacket to dinner. For women, cocktail dresses or elegant ensembles are the norm. Check P&O's website for specific theme-night dress codes for each ship and itinerary.

Tipping: A daily amount of £3.10 per person over the age of 12 is added automatically to passengers' onboard accounts and is shared among the waitstaff and cabin stewards. Prepayment is not possible. Should you wish to amend this amount, you can do so by visiting Reception during your cruise. ☎ *0845/374–0111* ⊕ *www.pocruises.com* ☞ *Cruise Style: Mainstream.*

Paul Gauguin Cruises. With one ship built specifically to sail the waters of Tahiti, French Polynesia, and the South Pacific and synonymous with luxury and exotic destinations, Paul Gauguin Cruises remains a top choice for discerning travelers and honeymooners. Paul Gauguin Cruises was acquired in 2010 by Pacific Beachcomber SC, the largest luxury hotel and cruise operator in French Polynesia. In order to offer similarly luxurious cruises in other regions—Europe in summer months and the Caribbean during the winter season—the line introduced a second vessel, MV *Tere Moana* in 2012. Intimate and luxurious, Paul Gauguin ships offer a cruise experience tailored to the regions in which they sail. A relaxed atmosphere prevails throughout both vessels, but the cruise line definitely has a split personality, with voyages on MS *Paul Gauguin* limited to the South Pacific and those of MV *Tere Moana* as varied as the Caribbean and Europe.

Your Shipmates: Paul Gauguin Cruises attracts passengers of all ages, and on *Paul Gauguin* especially you'll see young honeymooners mingling with mature well-traveled couples. Most enjoy the relaxed atmosphere on board in addition to the exotic ports and unique experiences ashore.

Dress Code: Elegant resort-casual attire is appropriate at all times. Slacks and a golf or sport shirt for men and sporty dresses or skirts or pants with a sweater or blouse for women are suggested for evening. Jackets are not required, but many men bring along a sport coat for the Captain's Welcome Reception.

Tipping: Tipping is neither required nor expected. ☎ *800/848–6172* ⊕ *www.pgcruises.com* ☞ *Cruise Style: Luxury.*

Princess Cruises. Princess Cruises may be best known for introducing cruise travel to millions of viewers, when its flagship became the setting for *The Love Boat* television series in 1977. Since that heady time of small-screen stardom, the Princess fleet has grown both in the number and size of ships. Although most are large in scale, Princess vessels manage to create the illusion of intimacy through the use of color and decor in understated yet lovely public rooms graced by multimillion-dollar art collections. Princess has also become more flexible; Personal Choice Cruising offers alternatives for open-seating dining (when you wish and with whom you please) and entertainment options as diverse as those found in resorts ashore.

Your Shipmates: Princess Cruises attract mostly American passengers, ranging from their midthirties to midfifties. Families enjoy cruising together on the Princess fleet, particularly during holiday seasons and in summer months, when many children are on board. Longer cruises appeal to well-traveled retirees and couples who have the time.

Dress Code: Two formal nights are standard on seven-night cruises; an additional formal night may be scheduled on longer sailings. Men are encouraged to wear tuxedos, but dark suits are appropriate. All other evenings are casual, although jeans are discouraged, and it's requested that no shorts be worn in public areas after 6 pm.

Tipping: A gratuity of $11.50 per person per day ($12 for passengers in suites and minisuites) is added to shipboard accounts for distribution to stewards and waitstaff. Passengers may adjust the amount based on the level of service experienced. An automatic 15% is added to all bar tabs for bartenders and drink servers; gratuities to other staff members may be extended at passengers' discretion. ☎ 661/753–0000 or 800/774–6237 ⊕ www.princess.com ☞ Cruise Style: Premium.

Regent Seven Seas Cruises. The 1994 merger of Radisson Diamond Cruises and Seven Seas Cruise Line launched Radisson Seven Seas Cruises with an eclectic fleet of vessels that offers a nearly all-inclusive cruise experience in sumptuous, contemporary surroundings. The line was rebranded as Regent Seven Seas Cruises in 2006, and ownership passed to Prestige Cruise Holdings (which also owns Oceania Cruises) in 2008. Even more inclusive than in the past, the line has maintained its traditional tried-and-true formula—delightful ships offering exquisite service, generous staterooms with abundant amenities, a variety of dining options, and superior lecture and enrichment programs. Guests are greeted with champagne on boarding and find an all-inclusive beverage policy that offers not only soft drinks and bottled water, but also cocktails and select wines at all bars and restaurants throughout the ships. Some shore excursions are included in the cruise fare.

Your Shipmates: Regent Seven Seas Cruises are inviting to active, affluent, well-traveled couples ranging from their late thirties to retirees who enjoy the ship's chic ambience and destination-rich itineraries. Longer cruises attract veteran passengers in the over-sixty age group.

Dress Code: Elegant casual is the dress code for most nights; formal and semiformal attire is optional on sailings of 16 nights or longer, but it's no longer required. It's requested that dress codes be observed in public areas after 6 pm.

Tipping: Gratuities are included in the fare, and none are expected. To show their appreciation, passengers may elect to make a contribution to a crew welfare fund that benefits the ship's staff. ☎ 877/505–5370 ⊕ www.rssc.com ☞ Cruise Style: Luxury.

Royal Caribbean International. Big, bigger, biggest! In the early 1990s, Royal Caribbean launched Sovereign-class ships, the first of the modern megacruise liners, which continue to be the all-around favorite of passengers who enjoy traditional cruising ambience with a touch of daring and whimsy. Plunging into the 21st century, each ship in the current fleet carries more passengers than the entire Royal Caribbean fleet of the 1970s, and has amenities—such as new surfing pools—that were unheard of in the past. All Royal Caribbean ships are topped by the company's distinctive signature Viking Crown Lounge, a place to watch the seascape by day and dance at night. Expansive multideck atriums and promenades, as well as the generous use of brass and floor-to-ceiling glass windows, give each vessel a sense of spaciousness and style. The action is nonstop in casinos and dance clubs after dark, while daytime hours are filled with poolside games and traditional cruise activities.

Your Shipmates: Royal Caribbean cruises have a broad appeal for active couples and singles, mostly in their thirties to fifties. Families are partial to the newer vessels that have larger staterooms, huge facilities for children and teens, and seemingly endless choices of activities and dining options.

Dress Code: Two formal nights are standard on seven-night cruises; one formal night is the norm on shorter sailings. Men are encouraged to wear tuxedos, but dark suits or sport coats and ties are more prevalent. All other evenings are casual, although jeans are discouraged in restaurants. It's requested that no shorts be worn in public areas after 6 pm, although there are passengers who can't wait to change into them after dinner.

Tipping: Tips can be prepaid when the cruise is booked, added on to shipboard accounts, or given in cash on the last night of the cruise. Suggested gratuities per passenger per day are $5 for the cabin steward ($7.25 for suites), $3.75 for the waiter, $2.15 for the assistant waiter, and $0.75 for the headwaiter. A 15% gratuity is automatically added to all bar tabs and spa and salon services. ☎ *305/539–6000 or 800/327– 6700 ⊕ www.royalcaribbean.com ⚲ Cruise Style: Mainstream.*

Saga Cruises. Saga Cruises purchased its first ship in 1996. Itineraries brim with longer sailings to far-flung corners of the globe, making Saga voyages destination-oriented. Classic cruisers in every sense of the word, Saga's passengers are travelers who expect inspiring itineraries coupled with traditional onboard amenities and comfortable surroundings. In the style of Saga Holidays' land-based tours, Saga Cruises takes care of the details that discerning passengers don't wish to leave to chance— from providing insurance and arranging visas to placing fruit and water in every cabin. Ships have card rooms, but you won't find casinos. With numerous accommodations designed for solo cruisers, Saga Cruises are particularly friendly for senior singles. Especially convenient on lengthy sailings, each ship features complimentary self-service launderettes and ironing facilities. In port, the line offers complimentary shuttle transfers to the town center from the cruise pier.

Your Shipmates: Saga Cruises are exclusively for passengers age 50 and older; the minimum age for traveling companions is 40. On a typical cruise—particularly one of the longer itineraries—the average age of passengers may be quite a bit higher than 50. The overwhelming majority of passengers are from Great Britain, with a sprinkling of North Americans in the mix.

Dress Code: Dress on Saga ships is very traditional. While the requested attire on board is generally casual during the day, including sea days, by night there are three dress codes—formal, informal, and smart casual.

Tipping: Gratuities are included in the fare, and additional tipping is not expected. ☏ *0800/096–0079 or (44) 1303/771–111* ⊕ *www.saga. co.U.K.* ☞ *Cruise Style: Premium.*

Seabourn Cruise Line. Seabourn was founded on the principle that dedication to personal service in elegant surroundings would appeal to sophisticated, independent-minded passengers whose lifestyles demand the best. Lovingly maintained since their introduction in 1987—and routinely updated with new features—the original megayachts of Seabourn and their new fleetmates have proved to be a smashing success over the years. They remain favorites with people who can take care of themselves but would rather do so aboard a ship that caters to their individual preferences. Recognized as a leader in small-ship, luxury cruising, Seabourn delivers all the expected extras—complimentary wines and spirits, a stocked minibar in all suites, and elegant amenities. Expect the unexpected as well—from exclusive travel-document portfolios and luggage tags to the pleasure of a complimentary mini-massage while lounging at the pool. If you don't want to lift a finger, Seabourn will even arrange to have your luggage picked up at home and delivered directly to your suite—for a price. Peace and tranquility reign on these ships, so the daily roster of events is somewhat thin. Although the trio of original Seabourn ships has been upgraded over the years, the line launched a newer set of larger, even more luxurious triplets that were introduced in 2009 (*Seabourn Odyssey*), 2010 (*Seabourn Sojourn*), and 2011 (*Seabourn Quest*).

Your Shipmates: Seabourn's yacht-like vessels appeal to well-traveled, affluent couples of all ages who enjoy destination-intense itineraries, a subdued atmosphere, and exclusive service. Passengers tend to be fifty-plus and retired couples who are accustomed to evening formality.

Dress Code: At least one formal night is standard on seven-night cruises and three to four nights, depending on the itinerary, on two- to three-week cruises. Men are required to wear tuxedos or dark suits after 6 pm, and the majority prefers black tie. All other evenings are elegant casual, and slacks with a jacket over a sweater or shirt for men and a sundress or skirt or pants with a sweater or blouse for women are suggested.

Tipping: Tipping is neither required nor expected. ☏ *800/929–9391* ⊕ *www.seabourn.com* ☞ *Cruise Style: Luxury.*

SeaDream Yacht Club. SeaDream yachts began sailing in 1984 beneath the Sea Goddess banner, and after a couple of changes of ownership and total renovations, they have evolved into the ultimate boutique ships. A voyage on one of these sleek megayachts is all about personal choice. Passengers enjoy an unstructured holiday at sea doing what they please, making it easy to imagine the diminutive vessel really is a private yacht. The ambience is refined and elegantly casual. Fine dining and socializing with fellow passengers and the ships' captains and officers are preferred yachting pastimes.

The weekly picnic on a private beach is considered by many passengers as their most memorable experience ashore during a SeaDream cruise. SeaDream yachts are often chartered by families, corporations, and other affinity groups, but the company does not charter both ships at the same time.

Your Shipmates: SeaDream yachts attract energetic, affluent travelers of all ages, as well as groups. Passengers tend to be couples in their mid-forties up to retirees who enjoy the unstructured informality, subdued ambience, and utterly exclusive service.

These ships are not recommended for passengers who use wheelchairs. Although there's one accessible stateroom, public facilities have thresholds and the elevator doesn't reach the uppermost deck. Tide conditions can cause the gangway to be steep when docked, and negotiating shore tenders would be impossible.

Dress Code: Leave the formal duds at home—every night is yacht casual on SeaDream. Men wear open-collar shirts and slacks; sport coats are preferred but not required. A tie is never necessary. For women, sundresses, dressy casual skirts and sweaters, or pants and tops are the norm.

Tipping: Tipping is neither required nor expected. ☏ *305/631–6100 or 800/707–4911* ⊕ *www.seadream.com* ☞ *Cruise Style: Luxury.*

Silversea Cruises. Silversea Cruises was launched in 1994 by the former owners of Sitmar Cruises, the Lefebvre family of Rome, whose concept for the new cruise line was to build and sail the highest-quality luxury ships at sea. Intimate ships, paired with exclusive amenities and unparalleled hospitality, are the hallmarks of Silversea cruises. All-inclusive air-and-sea fares can be customized to include not just round-trip airfare but all transfers, porterage, and deluxe precruise accommodations as well. Personalization is a Silversea maxim. Their ships offer more activities than other comparably sized luxury vessels. Take part in those that interest you, or opt instead for a good book and any number of quiet spots to read or snooze in the shade. Silversea's third generation of ships introduced even more luxurious features when the 36,000-ton *Silver Spirit* launched late in 2009. Silversea's *Silver Explorer* is the top choice for luxurious, soft-adventure, expedition cruising, and in 2013 Silversea will add a second exploration ship that will sail exclusively in the Galapagos Islands.

Your Shipmates: Silversea Cruises appeal to sophisticated, affluent couples who enjoy the country club–like atmosphere, exquisite cuisine, and polished service on board, not to mention the exotic ports and unique experiences ashore.

Dress Code: Two formal nights are standard on seven-night cruises and three to four nights, depending on the itinerary, on longer sailings. Men are required to wear tuxedos or dark suits after 6 pm. All other evenings are either informal, when a jacket is called for (a tie is optional, but most men wear them), or casual, when slacks with a jacket over an open-collar shirt for men and sporty dresses or skirts or pants with a sweater or blouse for women are suggested.

Tipping: Tipping is neither required nor expected. ☎ *954/522–2299 or 877/276–6816* ⊕ *www.silversea.com* ☞ *Cruise Style: Luxury.*

Star Clippers. Star Clippers vessels are four- and five-masted sailing beauties—the world's largest barkentine and full-rigged sailing ships. Filled with modern, high-tech equipment as well as the amenities of private yachts, the ships rely on sail power while at sea unless conditions require the assistance of the engines. Minimal heeling, usually less than 6%, is achieved through judicious control of the sails. A lack of rigid scheduling is one of Star Clippers' most appealing attractions. As attractive as the ships' interiors are, the focal point of Star Clippers cruises is the outdoors. Plan to spend a lot of time on deck soaking in the sun, sea, and sky. Although the Star Clippers ships are motorized, their engines are shut down whenever crews unfurl the sails (36,000 square feet on *Star Clipper* and *Star Flyer*, and 56,000 square feet on *Royal Clipper*) to capture the wind. On a typical cruise, the ships rely exclusively on sail power any time favorable conditions prevail.

Your Shipmates: Star Clippers cruises draw active, upscale American and European couples in their thirties and up, who enjoy sailing but in a casually sophisticated atmosphere with modern conveniences. Many sailings are equally divided between North Americans and Europeans. This is not a cruise line for the physically challenged: there are no elevators or ramps, nor are staterooms or bathrooms wheelchair-accessible. Gangways and shore launches can also be difficult to negotiate.

Dress Code: All evenings are elegant casual, so slacks and open-collar shirts are fine for men, and sundresses, skirts, or pants with a sweater or blouse are suggested for women. Coats and ties are never required. Shorts and T-shirts are not allowed in the dining room at dinner.

Tipping: Gratuities are not included in the cruise fare and are extended at the sole discretion of passengers. The recommended amount is €8 per person per day. Tips are pooled and shared; individual tipping is discouraged. You can either put cash in the tip envelope provided and drop it at the Purser's Office or charge gratuities to your shipboard account. An automatic 15% gratuity is added to each passenger's bar bill. ☎ *305/442–0550 or 800/442–0551* ⊕ *www.starclippers.com* ☞ *Cruise Style: Small Ship.*

Windstar Cruises. Since 1986, these masted sailing yachts have filled an upscale niche. They often visit ports of call inaccessible to huge, traditional cruise ships and offer a unique perspective of any cruising region. Though Windstar ships seldom depend on wind alone to sail, if you're fortunate and conditions are perfect, as they sometimes are, the complete silence of pure sailing is heavenly. Stabilizers and computer-controlled ballast systems ensure no more than a mere few degrees of lean. Onboard diversions are for the most part social, laid-back, and impromptu. Multimillion-dollar upgrades in 2012 enhanced each ship from stern to stern with chic new decor that mimics the colors of the sky and sandy beaches. In addition, all accommodations and bathrooms have been remodeled with updated materials; new weights and televisions were added to the gym; a couples massage room enhances the *Wind Surf* spa; the casual Veranda was expanded; the decks now have Balinese sun beds; and cooling mist sprayers are near the pools.

Your Shipmates: Windstar Cruises appeal to upscale professional couples in their late thirties to sixties who enjoy the unpretentious, yet casually sophisticated atmosphere, creative cuisine, and refined service. Nevertheless, Windstar's ships were not designed for accessibility, and are not a good choice for the physically challenged.

Dress Code: All evenings are country-club casual, and slacks with a jacket over a sweater or shirt for men, and sundresses, skirts, or pants with a sweater or blouse for women are suggested. Coats and ties for men are not necessary, but some male passengers prefer to wear a jacket with open-collar shirt to dinner.

Tipping: A service charge of $12 per guest per day (including children) is added to each shipboard account. A 15% service charge is added to all bar bills. All these proceeds are paid directly to the crew. ☎ *206/292–9606 or 800/258–7245* ⊕ *www.windstarcruises.com* ☞ *Cruise Style: Luxury.*

3

ATHENS

Visit Fodors.com for advice, updates, and bookings

WELCOME TO ATHENS

TOP REASONS TO GO

★ **The Acropolis:** A beacon of bygone glory rising above Athens's smog, this iconic citadel represents everything the Athenians were and still aspire to be.

★ **Evzones on Syntagma Square:** Unmistakable in tasseled hats and pom-pom shoes, Evzones act out a traditional changing of the guard that falls somewhere between discipline and comedy.

★ **The Ancient Agora and Monastiraki:** Socrates and Plato once discoursed at the Agora, and today you can do the same at the nearby Monastiraki marketplace.

★ **Opa!:** Whether jamming to post-Grunge in Gazi-Kerameikos—Athens's Greenwich Village—or dirty dancing on the tables at live *bouzoukia* clubs, the Athenians party like no one else.

★ **Benaki Bounty:** Housed in a neoclassic mansion, the Benaki Museum—Greece's oldest private collection—has everything from ancient sculpture to modern art.

1 Acropolis. This massive citadel and its magnificent buildings stand on a plateau above the city.

2 Makriyianni. The neighborhood at the foot of the Acropolis.

3 Koukaki. The few restored neoclassical homes here are reminders of 19th-century Athens.

4 Plaka. The quiet maze of streets is dotted by Byzantine churches, age-old schools, and ancient monuments.

5 Anafiotika. Up the Acropolis slope is an oasis of serenity and calmness.

6 Monastiraki. Adjacent to the ancient Agora is Athens's Central Market.

7 Thissio. Lined with pretty cafés and galleries.

8 Syntagma. The heart of modern Athens.

9 Psirri. South of the Central Market lies this diverse area of low-key eateries, traditional grocery shops, and artisanal workshops.

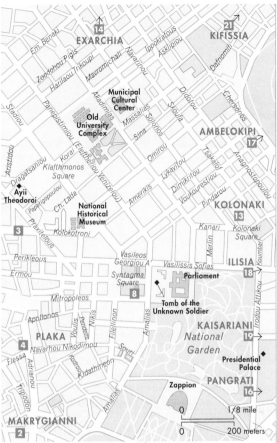

GETTING ORIENTED

3

Athens's main grid consists of three parallel streets—Stadiou, Eleftheriou Venizelou (widely called—and known—as Panepistimiou by natives), and Akadimias—that link two main squares, Syntagma and Omonia. Although the modern city sprawls in almost every direction, most of the finest Greek, Roman, and Byzantine landmarks are concentrated around the city center.

18 Ilisia. A bit off the beaten track, Ilisia is home to the Athens Concert Hall.

19 Kaisariani. North of Pangrati this neighborhood is known for its fish tavernas.

20 Neos Kosmos. The Onassis Cultural Centre has breathed new life into this residential neighborhood with some Bauhaus-style apartment blocks.

21 Kifissia. This wealthy, tree-lined residential area was once a summer resort. It is now a major shopping destination.

22 Piraeus. Athens's busy port also has some recommendable restaurants.

10 Gazi-Kerameikos. Once the city's gas works; now an up-and-coming arts and nightlife district.

11 Rouf. An industrial neighborhood now has an annex of the Benaki Museum.

12 Metaxourgeio. Artists have started to move into this run-down and at times still sketchy neighborhood.

13 Kolonaki. East of Syntagma Square lies this fashionable residential area loaded with cafés and museums.

14 Exarchia. In the northern reaches of the city, this somewhat run-down area is home to the famed National Archaeological Museum.

15 Omonia Square. The second major Athens square is an important transport hub.

16 Pangrati. This mostly residential neighborhood was home to the first modern Olympic Games.

17 Ambelokipi. This area's lively nightlife scene is focused around Mavili Square.

Updated by Natasha Giannousi-Varney

It's no wonder that all roads lead to the fascinating and maddening metropolis of Athens. Lift your eyes 200 feet above the city to the Parthenon, its honey-colored marble columns rising from a massive limestone base, and you'll behold architectural perfection that has not been surpassed in 2,500 years. Today, this shrine of classical form dominates a 21st-century boomtown.

Athens is home to 4.5 million souls, many of whom spend the day discussing the city's faults: the lack of city funding, the murky pollution cloud known as the *nefos*, the overcrowding, the traffic jams with their hellish din, the transport strikes, and the characterless cement apartment blocks. Romantic travelers, nurtured on the truth and beauty of Keats's Grecian urn, are dismayed to find that much of Athens has succumbed to that red tubular glare that owes only its name, neon, to the Greeks. But while Athens is a difficult city to love, its concentration of culture and lively spirit make it impossible to ignore.

To experience Athens—Athìna in Greek—fully is to understand the essence of Greece: ancient monuments surviving in a sea of cement, startling beauty amid the squalor, tradition juxtaposed with modernity—a smartly dressed lawyer chatting on her cell phone as she maneuvers around a priest in flowing robes heading for the sleek, space-age metro. Locals depend on humor and flexibility to deal with the chaos and, lately, the raging economic crisis; you should do the same. The rewards are immense. To appreciate Athens is to appreciate life with all its surprises and complexities.

THE NEW ATHENS

Those rewards are even greater now thanks to the many splendid features created for the city's 2004 Olympics. In 2000, Athens opened its still-expanding metro, many of whose gleaming stations function as minimuseums, displaying ancient artifacts found on-site (the new trains have blissfully cut down the effects of Athens's notorious gridlock and pollution). About a decade ago, the city unveiled Eleftherios

Venizelos International Airport, high-tech and efficient (affectionately called by many locals "El.Vel."). New infrastructure blessings include a tram line running from the city center to the south-coast beaches; an express train running to the airport and far-flung suburbs; and a ring-road beltway and the repaving and expansion of most of the city's potholed highways.

Within the city, beautification projects took priority. The most successful has been the completion of Athens's Archaeological Park, which links the capital's ancient sites in a pedestrian network. The stone-paved, tree-lined walkway allows you to stroll through the city center undisturbed by traffic from the Panathenaic stadium, home of the first modern Olympics in 1896, past the Temple of Olympian Zeus, the Acropolis, Filopappou hill, the ancient Greek and Roman agoras, Hadrian's Library, and Kerameikos, the city's ancient cemetery. Cars have also been banned or reduced in other streets in the historical center thanks to the introduction of odd/even plate-numbers traffic restrictions.

While various museums have received renovations, such as the National Archaeological Museum and the Benaki Museum, one museum garnered headlines around the world when it finally opened in June 2009: the Acropolis Museum, a spectacularly modern showcase for some of the most venerated ancient statues in the world. And the invigorating buzz that seized Athens pre-2004 has also helped newly transform entire neighborhoods like Gazi-Kerameikos, Thissio, Metaxourgeio, Kerameikos, and Psirri from industrial warehouse districts to hot spots of hip restaurants and happening nightclubs.

THE AGELESS CITY

Happily, you can still wander into less-touristy areas to discover pockets of timeless charm. Here, in the lovelier Athenian neighborhoods, you can delight in the pleasures of strolling—*Peripatos,* the Athenians call it, and it's as old as Aristotle, whose students learned as they roamed about in his Peripatetic school. This ancient practice survives in the modern custom of the evening *volta,* or stroll, taken along the pedestrianized Dionyssiou Areopagitou street skirting the base of the Acropolis.

Along your way, be sure to stop in a taverna to observe Athenians in their element. They are lively and expressive, their hands fiddling with worry beads or gesturing excitedly. Although often expansively friendly, they are aggressive and stubborn when they feel threatened, and they're also insatiably curious.

Amid the ancient treasures and the 19th-century delights of neighborhoods such as Anafiotika and Plaka, the pickax, pneumatic drill, and cement mixer have given birth to countless office buildings and modern apartments. Hardly a monument of importance attests to the city's history between the completion of the Temple of Olympian Zeus 19 centuries ago and the present day. That is the tragedy of Athens: the long vacuum in its history, the centuries of decay, neglect, and even oblivion. But within the last 150 years the Greeks have created a modern capital out of a village centered on a group of ruined marble columns. And since the late 1990s, inspired by the 2004 Olympics, they have gone far in transforming Athens into a sparkling modern metropolis that the ancients would strain to recognize but would heartily endorse. Its joyous spirit remains unscathed even in the face of financial adversity and shrinking public coffers.

PLANNING

WHEN TO GO

Athens often feels like a furnace in summer, due to the capital's lack of parks and millions of circulating cars. Mornings between 7 am and 9 am or evenings after 5 pm are often pleasant but temperatures can still hover in the 90s during heat waves. The capital is far more pleasant in spring and fall. The sunlight is bright but bearable, the air feels crisp and invigorating, and even the famously surly Athenians are friendlier. Winters are mild here, just as they are in all of Greece: it rains but rarely snows, so a light coat is all that is needed.

PLANNING YOUR TIME

Although still an agelessly beautiful city, the post-Olympic "European" Athens is burgeoning with energy, life, and wonders. And the only way you'll be able to see most of them is if you have a planned itinerary to guide you through this most challenging of cities.

IF YOU HAVE ONE DAY: ATHENS 101

Early in the morning, pay homage to Athens's most impressive legacy, the Acropolis, and stop by the glowing Acropolis Museum. Then descend through Anafiotika, the closest thing you'll find to an island village. Explore the 19th-century quarter of Plaka, with its neoclassical houses framed by hanging bougainvillea, and stop for lunch at one of its many tavernas. Do a little bargaining with the merchants in the old bazaar around Monastiraki Square. Spend a couple of hours in the afternoon marveling at the stunning collection of antiquities in the National Archaeological Museum; then pass by Syntagma Square to watch the changing of the costumed Evzones guards in front of the Tomb of the Unknown Soldier. You can then window-shop or people-watch in the tony neighborhood of Kolonaki. Nearby, take the funicular up to Mt. Lycabettus for the sunset before enjoying a performance at the Roman theater of Herod Atticus, followed by dinner in the newly revived district of Psirri.

IF YOU HAVE THREE DAYS

After a morning tour of the Acropolis, with a stop at the Acropolis Museum to view sculptures found on the site, pause on your descent at Areopagus, the site of the ancient Supreme Court; the view is excellent. Continue through Anafiotika and Plaka, making sure to stop at the Greek Folk Art Museum; the Roman Agora, with its Tower of the Winds, an enchanting water clock from the 1st century BC; and the Little Mitropolis Church on the outskirts of the quarter. After a late lunch, detour to Hadrian's Arch and the Temple of Olympian Zeus,

Athens's most important Roman monuments. In Syntagma Square, watch the changing of the Evzones guards, and then head to Kolonaki, followed by a *kafedaki* on the slopes of Mt. Lycabettus at the café-restaurant that graces the peak, with its splendid panorama of the Acropolis and the sea. Dine in a local taverna, perhaps in Pangrati, the neighborhood near the Panathenaic Stadium, which is lit at night. This Roman arena was reconstructed for the first modern Olympics in 1896.

On day two, visit the cradle of democracy, the fabled ancient Agora, with Greece's best-preserved temple, the Hephaistion. Explore the Monastiraki area, including the tiny Byzantine chapel of Kapnikarea, which stands in the middle of the street. In Monastiraki you can snack on the city's best souvlaki, but leave room for your night of nights: In the evening, splurge at stunning new/old, hot/cool Kuzina, and then dance the *tsifteteli* (the Greek version of a belly dance) to Asia Minor blues in a *rembetika* club, or, if it's summer and you're the hardy sort, visit the coastal stretch toward the airport, where the irrepressible bars stay open until dawn.

On the third day, start early for the legendary National Archaeological Museum, crammed with many of ancient Greece's most spectacular sculptures, breaking for lunch in one of the city's *mezedopoleio* (places that sell *mezedes*). Swing through the city center, past the Old University complex, a vestige of King Otto's reign, to the Cycladic Museum in Kolonaki, with the curious minimalist figurines that inspired artists such as Modigliani and Picasso. Stroll through the lovely National Gardens, and have a coffee in the romantic setting of the popular café by the grandiose Zappeion Hall. Complete the evening with a ballet performance or pop music show at Herod Atticus, a movie at a *therino* (open-air cinema), or, in winter, a concert at the Megaron Concert Hall.

DISCOUNTS AND DEALS

Athens's best deal is the €12 ticket that allows one week's admission to all the sites and corresponding museums along the Unification of Archaeological Sites walkway. You can buy the ticket at any of the sites, which include the Acropolis, ancient Agora, Areopagus, Roman Agora, Temple of Olympian Zeus, Kerameikos and its museum, and Hadrian's Library. Entrance is usually free every day for European Union students, half off for students from other countries, and about a third off for senior citizens.

GETTING HERE AND AROUND

Many major sights, as well as hotels, cafés, and restaurants, are within a fairly small central area of Athens. It's easy to walk everywhere, though sidewalks are often obstructed by parked cars. Most far-flung sights, such as beaches, are reachable by metro, bus, and tram.

AIR TRAVEL

The opening of Athens's sleek Eleftherios Venizelos International Airport has made air travel around the country much more pleasant and efficient. Greece is so small that few in-country flights take more than an hour or cost more than €200 round-trip.

Aegean Airlines and Olympic Airways have regular flights between Athens, Thessaloniki, and most major cities and islands in Greece. *For further information, see Air Travel in the Travel Smart chapter.*

AIRPORT TRANSFERS

The best way to get to the airport from downtown Athens is by metro or light-rail. Single tickets cost €8 and include transfers within 90 minutes of the ticket's initial validation to bus, trolley, or tram. Combined tickets for two (€14) and three (€20) passengers are also available; if you're just making a stopover in Athens, opt for a round-trip ticket (€20), valid for trips to and from the airport made during a single 48-hour period.

In Athens four reliable express buses connect the airport with the metro (Nomismatokopeio, Ethniki Amyna, and Dafni station), Syntagma Square, Kifissos Bus Station, and Piraeus. Express buses leave the arrivals level of the airport every 15 minutes and operate 24 hours a day. Bus X95 will take you to Syntagma Square (Amalias avenue); Bus X96 takes the Vari–Koropi Road inland and links with the coastal road, passing through Voula, Glyfada, and Alimos; it then goes on to Piraeus (opposite Karaiskaki Square). Bus X97 goes to the Dafni metro stop, while X93 brings voyagers to the dusty Kifissos intercity bus station. The Attiki Odos ring road and the expansion of the city's network of bus lanes have made travel times more predictable.

Bus tickets to and from the airport cost €5 and are valid on all forms of transportation in Athens for 24 hours from the time of validation. Purchase tickets (and get bus schedules) from the airport terminal, kiosks, metro stations, or even on the express buses.

Taxis are readily available at the arrivals level of the Athens airport; it costs an average of €35 to get into downtown Athens. (If you fear you have been overcharged, insist on a receipt with the driver's details and contact the tourist police.) Limousine Service and Royal Prestige Limousine Service provide service; an evening surcharge of up to 50% often applies, and you should call in advance. Prices start at around €80 for a one-way transfer from the airport to a central hotel for four people.

Contacts Limousine Service Travel ☎ 210/973–0730 ⊕ www.limousine-service.gr. **Royal Prestige Limousine Service** ☎ 6944/305000 ⊕ www.limousine-services.gr.

BOAT AND FERRY TRAVEL

Boat travel in Greece is common and relatively inexpensive. Every weekend thousands of Athenians set off on one- and two-hour trips to islands like Aegina, Hydra, and Andros, while in summer ferries are weighed down with merrymakers on their way to Mykonos, Rhodes, and Santorini. Cruise ships, ferries, and hydrofoils from the Aegean and most other Greek islands dock and depart every day from Athens's main port, Piraeus, 10 km (6 miles) southwest of Central Athens. Ships for

Corfu sail from ports nearer to it, such as Patras and Igoumenitsa. Connections from Piraeus to the main island groups are good, while connections from main islands to smaller ones within a group are less so.

Travel agents and ship offices in Athens and Piraeus have details. Boat schedules are published in *Kathimerini,* an insert in the *International New York Times.* Also check the useful travel website ⊕ *www.openseas. gr.* You can also call a daily Greek recording for ferry departure times. Timetables change according to seasonal demand, and boats may be delayed by weather conditions, so your plans should be flexible. Buy your tickets at least two or three days in advance, especially if you are traveling in summer or taking a car. Reserve your return journey or continuation soon after you arrive. *For further information, see Boat Travel in Travel Smart.*

GETTING TO AND FROM PIRAEUS AND RAFINA

To get to and from Piraeus harbor, you can take the Green Line metro (Line 1) from Central Athens directly to the station at the main port. The trip takes 25 to 30 minutes. A taxi can take longer because of traffic and costs around €15–€18. Express bus line X80 links the OLP cruise terminal to the Acropolis and Syntagma Square in the center of Athens and runs daily every 30 minutes from 7 am until 9:30 pm.

Athens's other main port is Rafina, which serves some of the closer Cyclades and Evia. KTEL buses run every 45 minutes between the port and the Mavromateon terminal in Central Athens, from 5:40 am until 10:30 pm, and cost €2.40 (⇨ *Bus and Tram Travel).* At Rafina, the buses leave from an area slightly uphill from the port. The trip takes about one hour depending on traffic.

Contacts Piraeus boat departures/arrivals ☎ *14541, 14944.* **Piraeus Port Authority** ⊠ *Piraeus Port Authority, Akti Miaouli 10, Piraeus* ☎ *210/455–0000 through 210/455–0100* ⊕ *www.olp.gr.* **Rafina KTEL Buses** ☎ *22940/23440 bus terminal* ⊕ *www.ktelattikis.gr.*

BUS AND TRAM TRAVEL

Athens and its suburbs are covered by a good network of buses, with express buses running between Central Athens and major neighborhoods, including nearby beaches.

During the day, buses tend to run every 15 to 30 minutes, with reduced service at night and on weekends. Buses run daily from about 5 am to midnight.

Main bus stations are at Akadimias and Sina and at Kaningos Square. Bus and trolley tickets cost €1.20 for one ride. The slightly more expensive €1.40 ticket is valid for a duration of 90 minutes and can be used for all modes of public transport (bus, trolley, tram, and metro). Remember to validate the ticket (insert it in the ticket machine on the platform or on the train or bus to get it stamped with the date) when you begin your journey and keep it until you've exited the bus or tram. Day passes for €4, weekly passes for €14, and monthly passes for all means of transport for €50 are sold at special booths at the main terminals. The three-day tourist pass costs €20.

Passes are not valid for travel to the airport or on the E22 Saronida Express.

Maps of bus routes (in Greek only) are available at terminal booths or from EOT. The website of the Organization for Urban Public Transportation (OASA) has a helpful English-language section (⊕ *www.oasa. gr*). Orange-and-white KTEL buses provide efficient service throughout the Attica basin. Most buses to the east Attica coast, including those for Sounion (€5.70 for inland route and €6.30 on coastal road) and Marathon (€3.70), leave from the KTEL terminal in Pedion Areos.

A tram link between downtown Athens and the coastal suburbs features two main lines.

Line A runs from Syntagma to Glyfada; Line B traces the shoreline from Glyfada to the Peace & Friendship Stadium on the outskirts of Piraeus. Single tickets cost €1.40 and are sold at machines on the tram platforms.

Contacts City tram ⊕ *www.stasy.gr.* **KTEL Buses - Attica** ✉ *Aigyptou Sq. at corner of Mavromateon and Leoforos Alexandras near Pedion Areos park, Pedion Areos* ☎ *210/880–8080 departure info for Lavrio and Sounion, 210/880–80117 departure info for Marathon and Rafina* ⊕ *www.ktelattikis.org.* **Organization for Urban Public Transportation (OASA)** ☎ *11 185 info line* ⊕ *www.oasa.gr.*

BUS TRAVEL TO AND FROM ATHENS

Travel around Greece by bus is inexpensive and usually comfortable (though a lot depends on your driver and the condition of the bus). The journey from Athens to Thessaloniki takes roughly the same time as the regular train, though the InterCity Express train covers the distance 1¼ hours faster.

To reach the Peloponnese, buses are speedier than trains, though Proastiakos, the high-speed rail to Corinth and beyond (to Kiato) is slowly changing this. Information and timetables are available at tourist information offices and metro stations.

Make reservations at least one day before your planned trip, earlier for holiday weekends.

Terminal A—aka Kifissos Station—is the arrival and departure point for bus lines that serve parts of northern Greece, including Thessaloniki, and the Peloponnese destinations of Epidauros, Mycenae, Nafplion, Olympia, and Corinth. Terminal B serves Evia, most of Thrace, and central Greece, including Delphi. Tickets for these buses are sold only at this terminal, so you should call to book seats well in advance in high season or holidays. *For more detailed bus information, see Bus Travel in Travel Smart.*

CAR TRAVEL IN ATHENS

Driving in Athens is not recommended unless you have nerves of steel; it can be unpleasant and even unsafe. Traffic tends toward gridlock or heart-stopping speeding and parking in most parts of the city could qualify as an Olympic sport. Locals are quick to point out that it is fairly easy to get around the city with a combination of public transportation and taxis, so why not save car rentals for excursions out of town? Driving is on the right, and although the vehicle on the right has the right-of-way, don't expect this to be obeyed.

The speed limit is 50 kph (31 mph) in town. Seat belts are compulsory, as are helmets for motorcyclists, though many ignore the laws. In the downtown sectors of the city do not drive in the bus lanes marked by a yellow divider; if caught, you may be fined. You're better off leaving your car in the hotel garage and walking or taking a cab. Gas pumps and service stations are everywhere, but be aware that all-night stations are few and far between.

CAR TRAVEL OUTSIDE ATHENS

Greece's main highways to the north and the south link up in Athens; both are called Ethniki Odos (National Road). Take the Attiki Odos, a beltway around Athens that also accesses Eleftherios Venizelos International Airport, to speed your travel time entering and exiting the city. The toll is €2.80 for cars, payable upon entering this privately owned highway. At the city limits, signs in English clearly mark the way to both Syntagma Square and Omonia Square in the city center. Leaving Athens, routes to the highways and Attiki Odos are well marked; green signs usually name Lamia for points north, and Corinth or Patras for points southwest. From Athens to Thessaloniki, the distance is 515 km (319 miles); to Kalamata, 257 km (159 miles); to Corinth, 84 km (52 miles); to Patras, 218 km (135 miles); to Igoumenitsa, 472 km (293 miles).

Most car rental offices are around Syngrou and Syntagma Square in Central Athens but note it can be cheaper to book from your home country; small-car rentals start at around €20/day. *For more information, see Car Rental in the Travel Smart chapter.*

CRUISE TRAVEL

Piraeus is the port of Athens, 11 km (7 miles) southwest of the city center, and is itself the third-largest city in Greece, with a population of about 500,000. In anticipation of a flood of visitors during the 2004 Olympics, the harbor district was given a general sprucing up. The cruise port has 12 berths, and the cruise terminal has duty-free shops, information, and refreshments.

The fastest and cheapest way to get to Athens from Piraeus is to take the metro. Line 1 (Green Line) reaches the downtown Athens stops most useful to tourists, including Platia Victorias, near the National Archaeological Museum; Omonia Square; Monastiraki, in the old Turkish bazaar; and Thission, near the ancient Agora. The trip takes 25 to 30 minutes. The Piraeus metro station for Line 1 (Piraeus-Kifissia) is off Akti Kallimasioti on the main harbor, a 20-minute walk from the cruise port, and you must walk all the way around the harbor to reach these piers.

You can also take the express X80 bus line, leaving the OLP cruise terminal for Acropolis and Syntagma Square (for info, ⊕ *www.oasa.gr*).

Taxis wait outside the terminal entrance. Taxis into the city are not necessarily quicker than public transport because of traffic, and cost around €12–€15. Athens taxi drivers have a reputation for overcharging passengers, so make sure the meter is switched on. It is common practice for drivers to pick up other passengers if there is room in the cab. These extra passengers will also pay the full fare for the trip. Radio taxis also have an additional charge of €3 to €5 for the pickup. Taxis are also readily available at the port to get you to the airport for around €45.

METRO (SUBWAY) TRAVEL

The best magic carpet ride in town is the metro. Cars are not worth the stress and road rage and, happily, the metro is fast, cheap, and convenient; its three lines go to all the major spots in Athens. Line 1, or the Green Line, of the city's metro system is often called the *elektrikos* (or the electrical train) and runs from Piraeus to the northern suburb of Kifissia, with several downtown stops (including Victoria Square, near the National Archaeological Museum; Omonia Square; Monastiraki, in the old Turkish bazaar; Thissio, near Kerameikos; the ancient Agora; and the nightlife districts of Psirri, Gazi-Kerameikos and Thissio).

In 2000, the city opened Lines 2 and 3 of the metro, many of whose gleaming gray-marble stations function as minimuseums, displaying ancient artifacts found on-site. These lines are safe and fast but cover limited (but expanding) territory. Line 2, or the Red Line, cuts northwest across the city, starting from suburban Anthoupoli and passing through such useful stops as Syntagma Square, opposite the Greek Parliament; Panepistimiou (near the Old University complex and the Numismatic Museum); Omonia Square; Metaxourgeio; the Stathmos Larissis stop next to Athens's central train station; Acropolis, at the foot of the famous site; and finishing off at the south suburb of Elliniko.

Line 3, or the Blue Line, runs from the suburb of Ayia Varvara (the Ayia Marina terminal station) through Kerameikos (the stop for bustling Gazi-Kerameikos) and Monastiraki; some trains on this line go all the way to the airport, but they only pass about every half hour and require a special ticket. The stops of most interest for visitors are Evangelismos, near the Byzantine and Christian Museum, Hilton Hotel, and National Gallery of Art, and Megaron Mousikis, next to the U.S. Embassy and the concert hall. The fare is €1.40, except for tickets to the airport, which are €8. A 24-hour travel pass, valid for use on all forms of public transportation, is €4. You must validate all tickets at the machines in metro stations before you board (if you're caught without a valid ticket you will be fined, so retain your ticket until you reach your final destination). Trains run between 5:30 am and 1 am. Maps of the metro are available in stations. There is no phone number for information about the system, so check the website (⊕ *www.stasy.gr*).

TAXI TRAVEL

Most drivers in Athens speak basic English. Although you can find an empty taxi on the street, it's often faster to call out your destination to one carrying passengers; if the taxi is going in that direction, the driver will pick you up. Likewise, don't be alarmed if your driver picks up other passengers (although he should ask your permission first). Each passenger pays full fare for the distance he or she has traveled. Make sure the driver turns on the meter and that the rate listed in the lower corner is 1, the normal rate before midnight; after midnight, the rate listed is 2.

Taxi drivers know the major central hotels, but if your hotel is less well known, show the driver the address written in Greek and make note of the hotel's phone number and, if possible, a nearby landmark. If all else fails, the driver can call the hotel from his mobile phone or a kiosk. Athens has thousands of short side streets, and few taxi drivers have maps, although newer taxis have GPS installed. Neither tipping nor bargaining is generally practiced; if your driver has gone out of the way for you, a small gratuity (10% or less) is appreciated.

The Athens taximeter starts at €1.19 and, even if you join other passengers, you must add this amount to your final charge. The minimum fare is €3.16. The basic charge is €0.68 per kilometer (½ mile); this increases to €1.19 between midnight and 5 am or if you go outside city limits. There are surcharges for holidays (€1), trips to and from the airport (€3.84), and rides to (but not from) the port, train stations, and bus terminals (€1.07). There is also a €0.40 charge for each suitcase over 10 kilos (22 pounds), but drivers expect €0.40 for each bag anyway. Waiting time is €10.85 per hour. Radio taxis charge an additional €2 to €5.65 for the pickup, depending on time of day requested.

Contacts Athens 1 Intertaxi ☎ *210/921–2800* ⊕ *www.athens1.gr.* **Ermis Taxi Service** ☎ *210/411–5200.* **Radio Taxi Hellas** ☎ *210/645–7000, 181 80* ⊕ *www.radiotaxihellas.gr.* **Parthenon Radio Taxi** ☎ *210/532–3300* ⊕ *www.radiotaxi-parthenon.gr.*

TRAIN TRAVEL

The *Proastiakos* ("suburban"), a light-rail network offering travelers a direct link from Athens Eleftherios Venizelos Airport to Kiato (en route to Patras for €12), has introduced Athenians to the concept of commuting. The trains now serve the city's northern and eastern suburbs as well as western Attica. The Athens-to-Corinth fare is €9; lower fares apply for points in between. If you plan on taking the train while in Athens, call the Greek Railway Organization (OSE) to find out which station your train leaves from, and how to get there. Trains from the north and international trains arrive at, and depart from, Stathmos Larissis, which is connected to the metro. If you want to buy tickets ahead of time, it's easier to visit a downtown railway office. *For further information, see Train Travel in the Travel Smart chapter.*

Contacts Stathmos Larissis Train Station ☎ *210/524–0601, 210/524–0646.*

VISITOR INFORMATION

Greek National Tourism Organization has a new information center in Central Athens near the Acropolis Museum.

The website of the city of Athens has a growing section in English. The English-speaking tourist police can handle complaints, steer you to an open pharmacy or doctor, and locate phone numbers of hotels and restaurants.

Contacts City of Athens ⊕ *www.thisisathens.org.* **Greek National Tourism Organisation** ✉ *Dionysiou Areopagitou 18-20, Plaka* ☎ *210/331–0347.*

TOUR OPTIONS

Most travel agencies offer excursions at about the same prices, but CHAT is reputed to have the best service and guides. You can take traditional day or night tours of Athens by bus and be picked up at your hotel. Full- and half-day tours go to many destinations in Attica, including Sounion, Corinth, Delphi; longer tours go to Meteora, Nafpilion, and the Peloponnese. It's best to reserve a few days in advance. *For a full list of agencies that offer tours—including CHAT—see Travel Agencies in Travel Smart.*

SIGHTSEEING HOP-ON, HOP-OFF TOUR BUSES

The best way to get quickly acquainted with Athens is to opt for a ride on the "Athens City Sightseeing Bus," a typical tourist double-decker with open top floors, which stops at all the city's main sights. Those buses run by City Sightseeing run every 15 minutes and tickets cost €18. The full tour takes 90 minutes, but you can hop on and off as you please at one of the 18 stops (including Syntagma Square) all through the day. There is also a new combined tour of Piraeus and Athens, lasting 70 minutes, and departing from the harbor terminal in Akti Miaouli.

Contacts City Sightseeing ⊕ *www.city-sightseeing.com.*

PRIVATE SIGHTSEEING GUIDES

It's easy to arrange for a private or small-group tour in Athens.

Contacts Athens Walking Tours. The 13 certified guides of the Athens Walking Tours company offer walking tours of the Acropolis, as well as a culinary Food Tour around the city's central food market to celebrate both traditional and modern Greek cuisines. ☎ *210/884–7269, 69458/59662* ⊕ *www.athenswalkingtours.gr.* **Union of Certified Guides.** The Union of Official Guides provides licensed guides for individual or group tours, starting at about €100, including taxes, for a four-hour tour of the Acropolis and its museum. ☎ *210/322–9705, 210/322–0090* 🖷 *210/323–9200* ⊕ *www.tourist-guides.gr.*

EXPLORING

Although Athens covers a huge area, the major landmarks of the ancient Greek, Roman, and Byzantine periods are close to the modern city center. You can easily walk from the Acropolis to many other key sites, taking time to browse in shops and relax in cafés and tavernas along the way. From many quarters of the city you can glimpse "the glory that was Greece" in the form of the Acropolis looming above the horizon, but only by actually climbing that rocky precipice can you feel the impact of the ancient settlement. The Acropolis and Filopappou, two craggy hills sitting side by side; the ancient Agora (marketplace); and Kerameikos, the first cemetery, form the core of ancient and Roman Athens. Along the Unification of Archaeological Sites promenade, you can follow stone-paved, tree-lined walkways from site to site, undisturbed by traffic. Cars have also been banned or reduced in other streets in the historical center. In the National Archaeological Museum, vast numbers of artifacts illustrate the many millennia of Greek civilization; smaller museums such as the Goulandris Museum of Cycladic Art Museum and the Byzantine and Christian Museum illuminate the history of particular regions or periods.

Athens may seem like one huge city, but it is really a conglomeration of neighborhoods with distinctive characters. The Eastern influences that prevailed during the 400-year rule of the Ottoman Empire are still evident in Monastiraki, the bazaar area near the foot of the Acropolis. On the northern slope of the Acropolis, stroll through Plaka (if possible by moonlight), an area of tranquil streets lined with renovated mansions, to get the flavor of the 19th century's gracious lifestyle. The narrow lanes of Anafiotika, a section of Plaka, thread past tiny churches and small, color-washed houses with wooden upper stories, recalling a Cycladic island village. In this maze of winding streets, vestiges of the older city are everywhere: crumbling stairways lined with festive tavernas; dank cellars filled with wine vats; occasionally a court or diminutive garden, enclosed within high walls and filled with magnolia trees and the flaming trumpet-shaped flowers of hibiscus bushes.

Makriyianni and Koukaki are prime real estate land. Formerly rundown old quarters, such as Kerameikos, Gazi-Kerameikos, and Psirri, popular nightlife areas filled with bars and *mezedopoleio* (similar to tapas bars), are now in the process of gentrification, although they still retain much of their original charm. The area around Syntagma Square, including the café scene at Ayias Irinis Square, and Omonia Square, form the commercial heart of the city. Athens is distinctly European, having been designed by the court architects of King Otto, a Bavarian, in the 19th century. The chic shops and bistros of ritzy Kolonaki nestle at the foot of Mt. Lycabettus, Athens's highest hill (909 feet). Each of the city's outlying suburbs has a distinctive character: Pangrati, Ambelokipi, and Ilisia are more residential in nature, densely populated, with some lively nightlife spots and star attractions like the Panathenaic Stadium and the Athens Concert Hall (Megaron Mousikis).

In Kaisariani and Neos Kosmos, you can still see some old refugee apartment blocks next to gleaming modernist buildings like the Onassis Culture Centre.

Farther out, in the north, is wealthy, tree-lined Kifissia, once a summer resort for aristocratic Athenians. Just beyond the southern edge of the city is Piraeus, a bustling port city of waterside fish tavernas and Saronic gulf views that is still connected to Central Athens by metro. And beyond Athens proper, in Attica to the south and southeast, lie Glyfada, Voula, and Vouliagmeni, with their sandy beaches, seaside bars, and lively summer nightlife.

THE ACROPOLIS ΑΚΡΟΠΟΛΗ

Although Athens, together with its suburbs and port, sprawls across the plain for more than 240 square km (150 square miles), most of its ancient monuments cluster around the Acropolis, which rises like a massive sentinel, white and beautiful, out of the center of the city. In mountainous Greece, most ancient towns were backed up by an acropolis, an easily defensible upper town (which is what the word means), but when spelled with a capital "A" it can only refer to antiquity's most splendid group of buildings—the Acropolis of Athens.

Continued on page 108

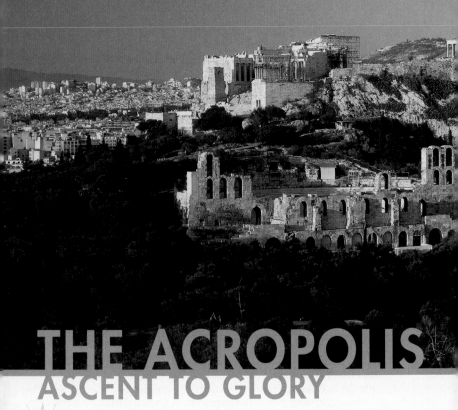

THE ACROPOLIS
ASCENT TO GLORY

One of the wonders of the world, the Acropolis symbolizes Greece's Golden Age. Its stunning centerpiece, the Parthenon, was commissioned in the 5th century BC by the great Athenian leader Pericles as part of an elaborate building program designed to epitomize the apex of an iconic culture. Thousands of years later, the Acropolis pulls the patriotic heartstrings of modern Greeks and lulls millions of annual visitors back to an ancient time.

You don't have to look far in Athens to encounter perfection. Towering above all—both physically and spiritually—is the Acropolis, the ancient city of upper Athens and womb of Western civilization. Raising your eyes to the crest of this *ieros vrachos* (sacred rock), the sight of the Parthenon will stop you in your tracks. The term Akropolis (to use the Greek spelling) means "High City," and today's traveler who climbs this table-like hill is paying tribute to the prime source of civilization as we know it.

A TITANIC TEMPLE

Described by the 19th-century French poet Alphonse de Lamartine as "the most perfect poem in stone," the Acropolis is a true testament to the Golden Age of Greece. While archaeological evidence has shown that the flat-top limestone outcrop, 512 feet high, attracted settlers as early as Neolithic times, most of its most imposing structures were built from 461 to 429 BC, when the intellectual and artistic life of Athens flowered under the influence of the Athenian statesman, Pericles. Even

in its bleached and silent state, the Parthenon—the Panathenaic temple that crowns the rise—has the power to stir the heart as few other ancient relics do.

PERICLES TO POLLUTION

Since the Periclean Age, the buildings of the Acropolis have been inflicted with the damages of war, as well as unscrupulous transformations into, at various times, a Florentine palace, an Islamic mosque, a Turkish harem, and a World War II sentry. Since then, a more insidious enemy—pollution—has emerged. The site is presently undergoing conservation measures as part of an ambitious rescue plan. Today, the Erechtheion temple and Temple of Athena Nike have been completely restored, and work on the Parthenon and the Propylaea is due for completion by the end of 2014. A final phase, involving massive landscaping works, will last through 2020. Despite the ongoing restoration work, a visit to the Acropolis today can evoke the spirit of the ancient heroes and gods who were once worshiped here.

THE PARTHENON

PINNACLE OF THE PERICLEAN AGE

DEDICATED TO ATHENA

At the loftiest point of the Acropolis stands the Parthenon, the architectural masterpiece conceived by Pericles and executed between 447 and 438 BC by the brilliant sculptor Pheidias, who supervised the architects Iktinos and Kallikrates in its construction. It not only raised the bar in terms of sheer size, but also in the perfection of its proportions.

Dedicated to the goddess Athena (the name Parthenon comes from the Athena Parthenos, or the virgin Athena) and inaugurated at the Panathenaic Festival of 438 BC, the Parthenon served primarily as the treasury of the Delian League, an ancient alliance of cities formed to defeat the Persian incursion. In fact, the Parthenon was built as much to honor the city's power as to venerate Athena. Its foundations, laid after the victory at Marathon in 490 BC, were destroyed by the Persian army in 480–479 BC. In turn, the city-state of Athens banded together with Sparta to rout the Persians by 449 BC.

To proclaim its hegemony over all Greece, Athens envisioned a grand new Acropolis. After a 30-year building moratorium, the titanic-scale project of reconstructing the temple was initiated by Pericles around 448 BC.

490 BC
Foundation for Acropolis laid

447–438 BC
The Parthenon is constructed

420 BC
Temple of Athena Nike is complete

TIMELINE

EDIFICE REX: PERICLES

His name means "surrounded by glory." Some scholars consider this extraordinary, enigmatic Athenian general to be the architect of the destiny of Greece at its height, while others consider him a megalomaniac who bankrupted the coffers of an empire and an elitist who catered to the privileged few at the expense of the masses.

Indeed, Pericles (460–429 BC) plundered the treasury of the Athenian alliance for the Acropolis building program. One academic has even called the Periclean building program the largest embezzlement in human history.

MYTH IN MARBLE

But Pericles's masterstroke becomes more comprehensible when studied against the conundrum that was Athenian democracy.

In truth an aristocracy that was the watchdog of private property and public order, this political system financed athletic games and drama festivals; it constructed exquisite buildings. Its motto was not only to live, but to live well. Surrounded by barbarians, the Age of Pericles was the more striking for its high level of civilization, its qualities of proportion, reason, clarity, and harmony, all of which are epitomized nowhere else as beautifully as in the Parthenon.

To their credit, the Athenians rallied around Pericles' vision: the respect for the individualistic character of men and women could be revealed through art and architecture.

Even jaded Athenians, when overwhelmed by the city, feel renewed when they lift their eyes to this great monument.

TRICK OF THE TRADE

One of the Parthenon's features, or "refinements," is the way it uses meiosis (tapering of columns) and entasis (a slight swelling so that the column can hold the weight of the entablature), deviations from strict mathematics that breathed movement into the rigid marble. Architects knew that a straight line looks curved, and vice versa, so they cleverly built the temple with all the horizontal lines somewhat curved. The columns, it has been calculated, lean toward the center of the temple; if they were to continue into space, they would eventually converge to create a huge pyramid.

1456
Converted to mosque by occupying Turks

September 26, 1687
The Parthenon, used for gunpowder storage, explodes after being hit by a mortar shell

The Acropolis in Pericles's Time

RAISING A HUE

"Just my color—beige!" So proclaimed Elsie de Wolfe, celebrated decorator to J. Pierpont Morgan, when she first saw the Parthenon. As it turns out, the original Parthenon was anything but beige. Especially ornate, it had been covered with a tile roof, decorated with statuary and marble friezes, adorned with gilded wooden doors and ceilings, and walls and columns so brightly hued that the people protested, "We are adorning our city like a wanton woman" (Plutarch). The finishing touch was provided by the legendary sculptor Pheidias, who created some of the sculpted friezes—these were also brightly colored.

THE ERECHTHEION

PARTHENON

ATHENA PROMACHOS
Pheidias's colossal bronze statue of Athena Promachos, one of the largest of antiquity at 30′ (9 m) high, could be seen from the sea. It was destroyed after being moved to Constantinople in 1203.

THE PROPYLAEA

TOURING THE ACROPOLIS

Most people take the metro to the Acropolis station, where the New Acropolis Museum opened in 2009. They then follow the pedestrianized street Dionyssiou Areopagitou, which traces the foothill of the Acropolis to its entrance at the Beulé Gate. Another entrance is along the rock's northern face via the Peripatos, a paved path from the Plaka district.

THE BEULÉ GATE

You enter the Acropolis complex through this late-Roman structure named for the French archaeologist Ernest Beulé, who discovered the gate in 1852. Made of marble fragments from the destroyed monument of Nikias on the south slope of the Acropolis, it has an inscription above the lintel dated 320 BC, dedicated by "Nikias son of Nikodemos of Xypete." Before Roman times, the entrance to the Acropolis was a steep processional ramp below the Temple of Athena Nike. This Sacred Way was used every fourth year for the Panathenaic procession, a spectacle that honored Athena's remarkable birth (she sprang from the head of her father, Zeus).

THE PROPYLAEA

This imposing structure was designed to instill the proper reverence in worshipers as they crossed from the temporal world into the spiritual world of the sanctuary, for this was the main function of the Acropolis. Conceived by Pericles, the Propylaea was the masterwork of the architect Mnesicles. Conceived to be the same size as the Parthenon, it was to have been the grandest secular building in Greece. Construction was suspended during the

TEMPLE OF
ATHENA NIKE

THE BEULÉ GATE

Peloponnesian War, and it was never finished. The structure shows the first use of both Doric and Ionic columns together, a style that can be called Attic. Six of the sturdier fluted Doric columns, made from Pendelic marble, correspond with the gateways of the portal. Processions with priests, chariots, and sacrificial animals entered via a marble ramp in the center (now protected by a wooden stairway), while ordinary visitors on foot entered via the side doors. The slender Ionic columns had elegant capitals, some of which have been restored along with a section of the famed paneled ceiling, originally decorated with gold eight-pointed stars on a blue background. Adjacent to the Pinakotheke, or art gallery (with paintings of scenes from Homer's epics and mythological tableaux), the south wing is a decorative portico. The view from the inner porch of the Propylaea is stunning: the Parthenon is suddenly revealed in its full glory, framed by the columns.

THE TEMPLE OF ATHENA NIKE

The 2nd-century traveler Pausanias referred to this fabled temple as the Temple of Nike Apteros, or Wingless Victory, for "in Athens they believe Victory will stay forever because she has no wings." Designed by Kallikrates, the mini-temple was built in 427–424 BC to celebrate peace with Persia. The bas-reliefs on the surrounding parapet depicting the Victories leading heifers to be sacrificed must have been of exceptional quality, judging from the section called "Nike Unfastening Her Sandal" in the New Acropolis Museum. In 1998, Greek archaeologists began dismantling the entire temple for conservation. After laser-cleaning the marble to remove generations of soot, the team reconstructed the temple on its original site.

THE ERECHTHEION

If the Parthenon is the masterpiece of Doric architecture, the Erechtheion is undoubtedly the prime exemplar of the more graceful Ionic order. A considerably smaller structure than the Parthenon, it outmatches, for sheer refinement of design and execution, all other buildings of the Greco-Roman world.

For the populace, the much smaller temple—*not* the Parthenon—remained Athena's holiest shrine: legend has it that on this spot Poseidon plunged his trident into the rock, dramatically producing a spring of water, whereas Athena created a simple olive tree, whose fruit remains a main staple of Greek society. A panel of judges declared her the winner, and the city was named Athens. A gnarled olive tree still grows outside the Erechtheion's west wall, where Athena's once grew, and marks said to be from Poseidon's trident can be seen on a rock wedged in a hole near the north porch.

Completed in 406 BC, the Erechtheion was divided into two Ionic sanctuaries. The most delightful feature is the Caryatid Porch, supported on the heads of six strapping but shapely maidens (caryatids) wearing delicately draped Ionian garments, their folds perfectly aligned to resemble flutes on columns.

Now replaced by casts, the originals of the Erechtheion's famous Caryatid maidens are in the New Acropolis Museum.

PLANNING YOUR VISIT

When exploring the Acropolis, keep the below pointers in mind. As the hill's stones are slippery and steep, it is best to wear rubber-soled shoes.

What Are the Best Times to Go? Such is the beauty of the Acropolis and the grandeur of the setting that a visit in all seasons and at all hours is rewarding. In general, the earlier you start out the better. In summer, by noon the heat is blistering and the reflection of the light thrown back by the rock and the marble ruins is almost blinding. An alternative, in summer, is to visit after 5 PM, when the light is best for taking photographs. In any season the ideal time might be the two hours before sunset, when occasionally the fabled violet light spreads from the crest of Mt. Hymettus (which the ancients called "violet-crowned") and gradually embraces the Acropolis. After dark the hill is spectacularly floodlighted, creating a scene visible from many parts of the capital. A moonlight visit—sometimes scheduled by the authorities during full moons in summer—is highly evocative. In winter, if there are clouds trailing across the mountains, and shafts of sun lighting up the marble columns, the setting takes on an even more dramatic quality.

How Long Does a Visit Usually Run? Depending on the crowds, the walk takes about three hours, plus several more spent in the nearby Acropolis Museum.

Are Tour Guides Available? The Union of Official Guides (Apollonos 9A, Syntagma, 210/322-9705, 210/322-0090) offers licensed guides for tours of archaeological sites within Athens. However, most tour companies and travel agents can set up group or private tours. Guides will also help kids understand the site better.

What's the Handiest Place to Refuel? The Tourist Pavilion (Filoppapou Hill), a landscaped, tree-shaded spot soundtracked by chirping birds is just outside the Beulé Gate. It serves drinks, snacks, and a few hot dishes.

Dionysiou Areopagitou, Acropolis

☎ 210/321-4172 or 210/321-0219

🌐 www.culture.gr

✉ Joint ticket for all Unification of Archaeological Sites €12. Good for five days—and for free admission—to the Ancient Agora, Theatre of Dionysus, Kerameikos cemetery, Temple of Olympian Zeus, and the Roman Forum.

🕙 Apr.–Oct., daily 8–6:30; Nov.–Mar., daily 8–3

Ⓜ Acropolis

DON'T FORGET:

■ If it's hot, remember to bring water, sunscreen, and a hat to protect yourself from the sun.

■ Get a free bilingual pamphlet guide (in English and Greek) at the entrance gate. It is packed with information, but staffers usually don't bother to give it out unless asked.

■ An elevator now ascends to the summit of the Acropolis, once inaccessible to people with disabilities.

■ All large bags, backpacks, and shopping bags will have to be checked in the site cloakroom.

Temple of Olympian Zeus

3

IN FOCUS THE ACROPOLIS: ASCENT TO GLORY

HAS GREECE LOST
ITS MARBLES?

Sleek, state-of-the-art, and sumptuous, the Acropolis Museum has thrown down a gauntlet of sorts by challenging the venerable British claim that Greece has never provided a suitable home for the Parthenon treasures. Ever since the early 19th century, when Lord Elgin removed half of the Parthenon Marbles to England for "safekeeping," Greece has been fighting to have these masterworks of 5th-century BC art returned to their homeland. Now that Athens has created a magnificent home for these sculptures, the debate has become even more heated.

Back in Pericles's day, the Parthenon was most famous for two colossal (now vanished) statues fashioned by Pheidias: a tall bronze statue of Athena inside the temple, and one of Athena the Champion (Promachos), which faced anyone climbing the great hill. Today, all attention is focused on the "missing" marbles—the statues from the temple frieze and pediments that were shipped to England by Lord Elgin between 1801 and 1805. At that time, during the rule of the Ottoman Empire, Elgin, as British ambassador in Constantinople, was given permission by the Sultan Selim III to remove stones with inscriptions from the Acropolis; he took this as permission to dismantle shiploads of sculptures.

Some historians say Elgin was neither ethical nor delicate in removing two-thirds of the famous Parthenon friezes and half the marbles, causing irreparable damage to both the marbles and the Parthenon by hacking or sawing the sculptures into pieces to extricate them. On the other side, many argue that the marbles would have been destroyed if left on site. About 50 of the best-preserved pieces of the Panathenaian procession, called the Parthenon Marbles by Greeks but known as the Elgin Marbles by others, are in the British Museum; some can be

Dull is the eye that will not weep to see / Thy walls defaced, thy mouldering shrines removed / By British hands, which it had best behoved / To guard those relics ne'er to be restored.

—From the poem "Childe Harolde's Pilgrimage" by the philhellene Lord Byron, published between 1812–18.

IN THIS CORNER: LORD ELGIN

The British nobleman and future diplomat Thomas Bruce, the seventh Earl of Elgin, became Britain's ambassador to the Ottoman Empire in 1799. His years in Constantinople were not happy: he suffered from what was very likely syphilis (the disease ate away his nose), and his wife soon took off with her personal escort. But Lord Elgin found purpose in "saving" priceless antiquities ignored by the ruling Turks and shipping them to Britain at enormous personal expense. Today, some consider him "a prince among thieves."

seen in the Acropolis Museum, while a few remain on the temple itself.

GREECE VS. BRITAIN

The minuets of museum politics become fully apparent when one enters the top-floor Parthenon Gallery of the Acropolis Museum. The Parthenon Marbles still in London are replaced here by replicas, instantly and provokingly apparent when their whiter tone is compared to the creamy stone hue of the original sculptures on view right alongside them. This gallery was designed—as Greek officials have made clear—to hold the Parthenon Marbles in their *entirety*. Their spirited long-term campaign aims to have them returned to Greece, to be appreciated in their original context, thanks to the spectacular Acropolis Museum.

IN THIS CORNER: MELINA MERCOURI

She was so beloved as an actress and singer that people called her only by her first name. But behind the smoky eyes and husky voice that lit up the film *Never On Sunday* (1960) lay the heart of a fierce activist. As the country's first female culture minister, Melina led the fight to reclaim the Parthenon Marbles from Britain—"In the world over, the very name of our country is immediately associated with the Parthenon," she proclaimed. After she passed away, in 1994, a bust of her likeness was placed in the Dionysiou Areopagitou pedestrian walkway, in the shadow of the Acropolis.

(Above): Scenes from the Parthenon Frieze (447- 432 BC) preserved at the British Museum in London; reconstruction of Parthenon interior, showing statue of Athena.

Towering over the modern metropolis of 4.5 million as it once stood over the ancient capital of 50,000, it has remained Athens's most spectacular attraction ever since its first settlement around 5000 BC. It had been a religious center long before Athens became a major city-state in the 6th century BC. It has been associated with Athena ever since the city's mythical founding, but virtually all of the city's other religious cults had temples or shrines here as well. As Athens became the dominant city-state in the 5th century BC, Pericles led the city in making the Acropolis the crowning symbol of Athenian power and successful democracy.

After the Acropolis all will at first seem to be an anticlimax. But there is much more that is still well worth seeing on the citadel's periphery, including the Acropolis Museum, the neoclassic buildings lining Dionyssiou Areopagitou, the centuries-old Odeon of Herodes Atticus, and Filopappou, the pine-clad summit that has the city's best view of the Acropolis.

TOP ATTRACTIONS

Fodor's Choice ★ **Acropolis.** Towering over a modern city of 4.5 million inhabitants much as it stood over the ancient capital of 50,000, the Acropolis (literally "high town") continues to be Athens's most spectacular, photogenic, and visited attraction despite hundreds of years of renovations, bombings, and artistic lootings. The buildings, constructed under the direction of Pericles during the city's golden age in the 5th century BC, were designed to be as visually harmonious as they were enormous, and they stand today in a perfect balance of stubborn immortality and elegant fragmentation. ⇨ *For an in-depth look at this emblem of the glories of classical Greek civilization, and the adjacent, headline-making New Acropolis Museum, see our photo-feature, "The Acropolis: Ascent to Glory," in this chapter.* ⊠ *Dionyssiou Areopagitou, Acropolis* ☎ *210/321–4172, 210/321–0219* ⊕ *www.culture.gr* ⌸ *€12 joint ticket for all Unification of Archaeological Sites* ☉ *Apr.–Oct., daily 8–6:30 (last entry); Nov.–Mar., daily 8–3* Ⓜ *Acropolis.*

Fodor's Choice ★ **Acropolis Museum.** Designed by the celebrated Swiss architect Bernard Tschumi in collaboration with Greek architect Michalis Fotiadis, the Acropolis Museum made world headlines when it opened in June 2009. If some buildings define an entire city in a particular era, Athens's newest museum boldly sets the tone of Greece's modern era. Occupying a large plot of the city's most prized real estate, the Acropolis Museum nods to the fabled ancient hill above it but speaks—thanks to a spectacular building—in a contemporary architectural language.

The museum drew 90,000 visitors in its first month and proved it is spacious enough to accommodate such crowds (happily, as a whopping six and a half million visitors had entered the doors of the ingenious, airy structure by June 2014). Unlike its cramped, dusty predecessor, there is lots of elbow room, from the museum's olive tree–dotted grounds to its prized, top-floor Parthenon Gallery.

Regal glass walkways, very high ceilings, and panoramic views are all part of the experience. In the five-level museum, every shade of marble is on display and bathed in abundant, UV-safe natural light. Visitors pass into the museum through a broad entrance and move ever upwards.

The ground floor exhibit, *The Acropolis Slopes*, features objects found in the sanctuaries and settlements around the Acropolis—a highlight is the collection of theatrical masks and vases from the sanctuary of the matrimonial deity Nymphe. The next floor is devoted to the Archaic period (650 BC–480 BC), with rows of precious statues mounted for 360-degree viewing. The floor includes sculptural figures from the Hekatompedon—the temple that may have predated the classical Parthenon—such as the noted group of stone lions gorging a bull from 570 BC. The legendary five Caryatids (or Korai)—the female figures supporting the Acropolis's Erectheion building—symbolically leave a space for their sister, who resides in London's British Museum.

The second floor is devoted to the terrace and restaurant/coffee shop with a wonderful view of the Acropolis, which starts by serving a traditional Greek breakfast every day except Monday, before moving on to more delicious Greek dishes (every Friday the restaurant remains open until midnight).

Drifting into the top-floor atrium, the visitor can watch a video on the Parthenon before entering the star gallery devoted to the temple's Pentelic marble decorations, many of which depict a grand procession in the goddess Athena's honor. Frieze pieces (originals and copies), metopes, and pediments are all laid out in their original orientation. This is made remarkably apparent because the gallery consists of a magnificent, rectangle-shaped room tilted to align with the Parthenon itself. Floor-to-ceiling windows provide magnificent vistas of the temple just a few hundred feet away.

Museum politics are unavoidable here. This gallery was designed—as Greek officials have made obvious—to hold the Parthenon Marbles in their *entirety*. This includes the sculptures Lord Elgin brought to London two centuries ago. Currently, 50 meters of the frieze are in Athens, 80 meters in London's British Museum, and another 30 meters scattered in museums around the world. The spectacular and sumptuous new museum challenges the British claim that there is no suitable home for the Parthenon treasures in Greece. Pointedly, the museum avoids replicas, as the top-floor gallery makes a point of highlighting the abundant missing original pieces.

Elsewhere on view are other fabled works of art, including the *Rampin Horseman* and the compelling *Hound*, both by the sculptor Phaidimos; the noted pediment sculpted into a calf being devoured by a lioness—a 6th-century BC treasure that brings to mind Picasso's *Guernica*; striking pedimental figures from the Old Temple of Athena (525 BC) depicting the battle between *Athena and the Giants*; and the great *Nike Unfastening Her Sandal*, taken from the parapet of the Acropolis's famous Temple of Athena Nike. ⊠ *Dionyssiou Areopagitou 15, Acropolis* ☎ *210/900–0900* ⊕ *www.theacropolismuseum.gr* ⌨ €5 ⊗ *Apr.–Oct., Tues.–Sun. 8–8, Fri. 8–10, Nov.–Mar., Tues.–Thurs. 9–5, Fri. 9–10, Sat.–Sun. 9–8* Ⓜ *Acropolis.*

Odeon of Herodes Atticus. Hauntingly beautiful, this ancient theater was built in AD 160 by the affluent Herodes Atticus in memory of his wife, Regilla. Known as the Irodion by Athenians, it is nestled Greek-style

CLOSE UP

Grand Promenade

One of the most popular features created in Athens for the 2004 Olympics was the Grand Promenade, a pedestrian walkway meant to beautify some of the traffic-choked streets much favored by tourists. Part of the city's Archaeological Unification Project, the promenade connects fabled ancient sites along a landscaped walkway paved with gneiss cobblestones from Naxos and marble slabs from Tinos. It stretches through several neighborhoods but is often accessed near the Acropolis since its pedestrian ribbon includes the roads around its southern end.

Start out at the Acropolis metro stop, surface and walk north, and then left, to find Dionyssiou Areopagitou, the famed road running below the hill. You'll first pass the Acropolis Museum on your left and the Theater of Dionysus and Odeon of Herodes Atticus on your right. You can begin your climb here up to the Beulé Gate entrance to the Acropolis but, instead, take the marble walkway up Filopappou Hill—its summit flaunts Cinerama views of the Acropolis. Head back down to Apostolou Pavlou to find some of the best café real estate in the world: pull up a seat and enjoy a meal with the Acropolis looming above you.

Farther up the road is the Thissio metro station, Ayion Asomaton Square, and Melidoni street, which heads to the great ancient cemetery of Kerameikos. Here, Ermou street connects with Piraeus street, which leads to Technopolis and the Gazi-Kerameikos district, Athens at its 21st-century hipster best.

Keep the following restaurants and cafés in mind if you want to enjoy food-with-a-view, and not just any old view, but the Acropolis itself: Dionysos Zonars (built almost inside the archaeological site); Filistron mezedopoleio-restaurant (especially the rooftop on summer nights); Strofi restaurant (perfect for a summer post-performance dinner at the ancient Odeon of Herodes Atticus); Kuzina (for a wonderful view from its rooftop); and Orizontes (seen from another angle, this one from Lycabettus Hill). Last but not least, the café and restaurant of the Acropolis Museum, with its huge glass windows and extensive verandas, is a definite must for spectacular photo ops of the ancient landmark. Some hotels in the area, for example Herodion and Hera, also have rooftop restaurants with mouthwatering views.

into the hillside, but with typically Roman arches in its three-story stage building and barrel-vaulted entrances. The circular orchestra has now become a semicircle, and the long-vanished cedar roof probably covered only the stage and dressing rooms, not the 34 rows of seats. The theater, which holds 5,000, was restored and reopened in 1955 for the Athens and Epidaurus Festival. To enter you must hold a ticket to one of the summer performances, which range from the Royal Ballet to ancient tragedies usually performed in modern Greek. Contact the festival's box office for ticket information. Children under 6 are not allowed except at some special performances. ✉ *Dionyssiou Areopagitou, near Propylaion, Acropolis* ☎ *210/324–1807* ⊕ *www.greekfestival. gr* ☉ *Open only during performances* Ⓜ *Acropolis.*

WORTH NOTING

Filopappou. This summit includes **Lofos Mousson** (Hill of the Muses), whose peak offers the city's best view of the Parthenon, which appears almost at eye level. Also there is the **Monument of Filopappus,** depicting a Syrian prince who was such a generous benefactor that the people accepted him as a distinguished Athenian. The marble monument is a tomb decorated by a frieze showing Filopappus driving his chariot. In 294 BC a fort strategic to Athens's defense was built here, overlooking the road to the sea. On the hill of the **Pnyx** (meaning "crowded"), the all-male general assembly (Ecclesia) met during the time of Pericles. Originally, citizens of the Ecclesia faced the Acropolis while listening to speeches, but they tended to lose their concentration as they gazed upon the monuments, so the positions of the speaker and the audience were reversed. The speaker's platform is still visible on the semicircular terrace; from here, Themistocles persuaded Athenians to fortify the city and Pericles argued for the construction of the Parthenon. Farther north is the **Hill of the Nymphs,** with a 19th-century observatory designed by Theophilos Hansen, responsible for many of the capital's grander edifices. He was so satisfied with his work, he had "servare intaminatum" ("to remain intact") inscribed over the entrance. ⊠ *Acropolis* ✛ *Enter from Dionyssiou Areopagitou or Apostolou Pavlou* Ⓜ *Acropolis.*

Theater of Dionysus. It was on this spot in the 6th century BC that the Dionyssia festivals took place; a century later, dramas such as Sophocles's *Oedipus Rex* and Euripides's *Medea* were performed for the entire population of the city. Visible are foundations of a stage dating from about 330 BC, when it was built for 15,000 spectators as well as the assemblies formerly held on Pnyx. In the middle of the orchestra stood the altar to Dionysus. Most of the upper rows of seats have been destroyed, but the lower levels, with labeled chairs for priests and dignitaries, remain. The fantastic throne in the center was reserved for the priest of Dionysus: regal lions' paws adorn it, and the back is carved with reliefs of satyrs and griffins. On the hillside above the theater stand two columns, vestiges of the little temple erected in the 4th century BC by Thrasyllus the Choragus (the ancient counterpart of a modern impresario). ⊠ *Dionyssiou Areopagitou, across from Mitsaion street, Acropolis* ☎ *210/322–4625* ⊡ *€2; €12 joint ticket under the Unification of Archaeological Sites* ⊗ *May–Oct., daily 8–8 (last entry 7:30); Nov.–Apr., daily 8–5 (last entry 4:30)* Ⓜ *Acropolis.*

MAKRIYIANNI ΜΑΚΡΥΓΙΑΝΝΗ

A quiet neighborhood on the foothills of the Acropolis, Makriyianni was really put on the map by the opening of the nearby Acropolis Museum, which contains thousands of artifacts unearthed during the lengthy excavations on the Sacred Rock. This is "old Athens" at its best, so take a relaxing stroll along the pedestrianized Stratigou Makriyianni street (by the Acropolis metro station) and its side streets to discover—behind the leafy plane trees—some beautiful neoclassical houses that have survived the passage of time and the violent urbanization and demolition wave of the 1960s. One of them has been transformed into the Ilias Lalaounis Jewelry Museum. Many Makriyianni restaurants attract both locals and visitors. Strofi is a popular choice as it enjoys spectacular Acropolis views (especially from the rooftop), while ManiMani offers delicious regional cuisine from Mani, in the Peloponnese.

TOP ATTRACTIONS

Hadrian's Arch. One of the most important Roman monuments surviving in Athens, Hadrian's Arch has become, for many, one of the city's most iconic landmarks. This marble gateway, built in AD 131 with Corinthian details, was intended both to honor the Hellenophile emperor Hadrian and to separate the ancient and imperial sections of Athens. On the side facing the Acropolis an inscription reads "this is athens, the ancient city of theseus", but the side facing the Temple of Olympian Zeus proclaims "this is the city of hadrian and not of theseus." ⊠ *Vasilissis Amalias at Dionyssiou Areopagitou, Makriyianni* ⌸ *Free* ☉ *Daily* Ⓜ *Acropolis.*

Fodor's Choice
★

Ilias Lalaounis Jewelry Museum. Housing the creations of internationally renowned artist-jeweler Ilias Lalaounis, this private foundation also operates as an international center for the study of decorative arts. The fifty collections include 4,000 pieces inspired by subjects as diverse as the Treasure of Priam of Troy to the wildflowers of Greece; many of the works are eye-catching, especially the massive necklaces evoking the Minoan and Byzantine periods. Besides the well-made videos that explain jewelry making, craftspeople in the workshop demonstrate ancient and modern techniques, such as chain weaving and hammering. During the academic year the museum can arrange educational programs in English for groups of children. The founder also has several stores in Athens. The museum has a calendar of fascinating temporary exhibitions, usually focusing on the relation between Greek life and jewelry. ⊠ *Kallisperi 12, at Karyatidon, Makriyianni* ☏ *210/922–1044* ⊕ *www.lalaounis-jewelrymuseum.gr* ⌸ *€5* ☉ *Tues.– Sat. 9–3, Sun. 11–4* Ⓜ *Acropolis.*

Temple of Olympian Zeus. Begun in the 6th century BC, this gigantic temple was completed in AD 132 by Hadrian, who also commissioned a huge gold-and-ivory statue of Zeus for the inner chamber and another, only slightly smaller, of himself. Only 15 of the original Corinthian columns remain, but standing next to them may inspire a sense of awe at their bulk, which is softened by the graceful carving on the acanthus-leaf capitals. The clearly defined segments of a column blown down in 1852 give you an idea of the method used in its construction. The site is floodlighted on summer evenings, creating a majestic scene when you turn round the bend from Syngrou avenue. On the outskirts of the site to the north are remains of Roman houses, the city walls, and a Roman bath. Hellenic "neopagans" also use the site for ceremonies. Hadrian's Arch lies just outside the enclosed archaeological site. ⊠ *Vasilissis Olgas 1, Makriyianni* ☏ *210/922–6330* ⌸ *€2; €12 joint ticket for all Unification of Archaeological Sites* ☉ *Tues.–Sun. 8:30–3, 8-8 during the summer months* Ⓜ *Acropolis.*

KOUKAKI ΚΟΥΚΑΚΙ

This mostly transient neighborhood, from tourist-central Plaka to more residential districts of Athens, like Neos Kosmos and Petralona, was named after a pre-World War II bed-manufacturing factory that was owned by a businessman named Koukakis. Serviced by two metro stations, Acropolis and Fix, this is one of the most sought-after residential areas of Athens, due to its proximity to the Acropolis. A resurgence of the area has followed the pedestrianization of G. Olympiou street (on Koukaki Square). Faliron Square is also popular, and its many alternative bars and cozy eateries are attracting hip young things from all over the city.

PLAKA ΠΛΑΚΑ

Fanning north from the slopes of the Acropolis, picturesque Plaka is the last corner of 19th-century Athens. Set with Byzantine accents provided by churches, the Old Town district extends north to Ermou street and eastward to the Leofóros Amalias. During the 1950s and '60s, the area became garish with neon as nightclubs moved in and residents moved out, but locals, architects, and academicians joined forces in the early 1980s to transform a decaying neighborhood. Noisy discos and tacky pensions were closed, streets were changed into pedestrian zones, and old buildings were restored. At night merrymakers crowd the old tavernas, which feature traditional music and dancing; many have rooftops facing the Acropolis.

TOP ATTRACTIONS

FAMILY **Greek Folk Art Museum.** Run by the Ministry of Culture, the museum encompasses four buildings and focuses on folk art from 1650 to the present, with especially interesting embroideries, stone and wood carvings, Carnival costumes, and *Karaghiozis* (shadow player figures). In recent years, the museum has undergone an impressive expansion and now incorporates the beautiful 19th-century neoclassical Bathhouse of the Winds in Kyrristou street, a spectacularly vast mosque (now deconsecrated and given over to museum displays) located in Areos street, and exhibitions at nearby Panos 22, which handles the vast overflow of objects on view. Everyday tools—stamps for communion bread, spinning shuttles, *raki* flasks—attest to the imagination with which Greeks have traditionally embellished the most utilitarian objects. Don't miss the room of uniquely fanciful landscapes and historical portraits by beloved Greek folk painter Theophilos Hatzimichalis, from Mytilini. ⊠ *Main building, Kidathineon 17, Plaka* 🕾 *210/322–9031* ⊕ *www.melt.gr* 🎫 *€2, valid for each of the 4 buildings* 🕙 *Tues.–Sun. 9–2:30* Ⓜ *Acropolis.*

Kanellopoulos Museum. The stately Michaleas Mansion, built in 1884, now showcases the Kanellopoulos family collection. It spans Athens's history from the 3rd century BC to the 19th century, with an emphasis on Byzantine icons, jewelry, and Mycenaean and Geometric vases and bronzes. Note the painted ceiling gracing the first floor. ⊠ *Theorias 12 and Panos, Plaka* 🕾 *210/321–8873, 210/321–2313* ⊕ *www. pakanellopoulosfoundation.org* 🎫 *Free* 🕙 *Tues.–Sun. 8:30–2:30* Ⓜ *Monastiraki.*

NEED A
BREAK?

Cafe Oionos. Stop for an ice-cold frappé (Nescafé instant coffee frothed with sugar and condensed milk) and a game of backgammon at Cafe Oionos. You can also try their freshly made salads, pasta dishes, pizzas, and sandwiches, served throughout the day. ✉ *Kydathinaion and Geronta 7, Plaka* ☎ *210/322–3139.* ⊕ *www.oionos-cafe.gr*

Melina Cafe. If you're craving a good dessert (try the pecan pie) combined with some Greek cinematic history, go to the lovely nearby café-bistrot Melina, dedicated to famous Greek actress-turned-politician, Melina Mercouri. The walls are loaded with memorabilia from her life and distinguished career. ✉ *Lysiou 22, Plaka* ☎ *210/324–6501.*

Little Mitropolis. This church snuggles up to the pompous Mitropolis (on the northern edge of Plaka), the ornate Cathedral of Athens. Also called Panayia Gorgoepikoos ("the virgin who answers prayers quickly"), the chapel dates to the 12th century; its most interesting features are its outer walls, covered with reliefs of animals and allegorical figures dating from the classical to the Byzantine period. Look for the ancient frieze with zodiac signs and a calendar of festivals in Attica. Most of the paintings inside were destroyed, but the famous 13th- to 14th-century Virgin, said to perform miracles, remains. If you would like to follow Greek custom and light an amber beeswax candle for yourself and someone you love, drop the price of the candle in the slot. ✉ *Mitropolis Sq., Plaka* ⊙ *Hrs depend on services, but usually daily 8–1* Ⓜ *Syntagma.*

Monument of Lysikrates. Located on one of the ancient city's grandest avenues (which once linked the Theater of Dionysus with the Agora), this tempietto-like monument is a delightfully elegant jewel of the Corinthian style. It was originally built (335–334 BC) by a *choregos* (theatrical producer) as the support for the tripod (a three-footed vessel used as a prize) he won for sponsoring the best play at the nearby Theater of Dionysus. Six of the earliest Corinthian columns are arranged in a circle on a square base, topped by a marble dome from which rise acanthus leaves. In the 17th century the exceedingly picturesque monument was incorporated into a Capuchin monastery where Byron stayed while writing part of *Childe Harold.* The monument was once known as the Lantern of Diogenis because it was incorrectly believed to be where the famous orator practiced speaking with pebbles in his mouth in an effort to overcome his stutter. A fresh-looking dirt track at the monument's base is a section of the ancient street of the Tripods (now called Tripodon), where sponsors installed prizes awarded for various athletic or artistic competitions. ✉ *Lysikratous and Herefondos, Plaka* ⊙ *Daily 8:30–3* Ⓜ *Acropolis.*

Roman Agora. The city's commercial center from the 1st century BC to the 4th century AD, the Roman Market was a large rectangular courtyard with a peristyle that provided shade for the arcades of shops. Its most notable feature is the west entrance's Bazaar Gate, or **Gate of Athena Archegetis,** completed around AD 2; the inscription records that it was erected with funds from Julius Caesar and Augustus.

STEP-BY-STEP: A WALK THROUGH PLAKA

Begin your stroll at the ancient, jewel-like **Monument of Lysikrates,** one of the few remaining supports (334 BC) for tripods (vessels that served as prizes) awarded to the producer of the best play in the ancient Dionyssia festival. Take Herefondos to Plaka's central square, Filomoussou Eterias (or Kidathineon Square), a great place to people-watch.

Up Kidathineon Square is the small but worthy **Greek Folk Art Museum,** with a rich collection, including works by the beloved native artist Theophilos Hatzimichalis. Across from the museum is the 11th- to 12th-century church of Metamorfosi Sotira Tou Kottaki, in a tidy garden with a fountain that was the main source of water for the neighborhood until sometime after Turkish rule. Down the block and around the corner on Angelikis Hatzimichali is the **Center of Folk Art and Tradition.** Continue west to the end of that street, crossing Adrianou to Hill, then right on Epimarchou to the striking Church House (on the corner of Scholeiou), once a Turkish police post and home to Richard Church, who led Greek forces in the War of Independence.

At the top of Epimarchou is Ayios Nikolaos Rangavas, an 11th-century church built with fragments of ancient columns. The church marks the edge of the **Anafiotika** quarter, a village smack-dab in the middle of the metropolis: its main street, Stratonos, is lined with cottages, occasional murals painted on the stones, and a few shops. Wind your way through the narrow lanes off Stratonos, visiting the churches Ayios Georgios tou Vrachou, Ayios Simeon, and Metamorphosis Sotiros. Another interesting church is 8th-century Ayioi Anargyroi, at the top of Erechtheos. From the church, make your way to Theorias, which parallels the ancient *peripatos* (public roadway) that ran around the Acropolis. The collection at the **Kanellopoulos Museum** spans Athens's history; nearby on Panos you'll pass the Athens University Museum (Old University, otherwise known as the Kleanthis Residence), the city's first higher-learning institution. Walk down Panos to the **Roman Agora,** which includes the Tower of the Winds and the Fethiye Mosque. Nearby visit the engaging **Museum of Greek Popular Musical Instruments,** where recordings will take you back to the age of *rembetika* (Greek blues). Also next to the Agora is Athens's only remaining Turkish bathhouse, providing a glimpse into a daily social ritual of Ottoman times. On your way back to Syntagma Square, cut across Mitropoleos Square to the impressive 12th-century church of **Little Mitropolis.**

Halfway up one solitary square pillar behind the gate's north side, an edict inscribed by Hadrian regulates the sale of oil, a reminder that this was the site of the annual bazaar where wheat, salt, and oil were sold. On the north side of the Roman Agora stands one of the few remains of the Turkish occupation, the **Fethiye (Victory) Mosque.** The eerily beautiful mosque was built in the late 15th century on the site of a Christian church to celebrate the Turkish conquest of Athens and to honor Mehmet II (the Conqueror). During the few months

of Venetian rule in the 17th century, the mosque was converted to a Roman Catholic church; now used as a storehouse, it is closed to the public. Three steps in the right-hand corner of the porch lead to the base of the minaret, the rest of which no longer exists. ⊠ *Pelopidas and Aiolou, Plaka* ☎ *210/321–6690* ⊕ *www.culture.gr* 🎟 *€2; €12 joint ticket for all Unification of Archaeological Sites* ⊗ *Daily 8–3 (last entry 2:45)* Ⓜ *Monastiraki*

Tower of the Winds (*Aerides*). Surrounded by a cluster of old houses on the western slope of the Acropolis, the world-famous Tower of the Winds (Aerides), located inside the Roman Agora, is the most appealing and well preserved of the Roman monuments of Ath-

---

AN ATHENS HAMMAM

During Ottoman times, every neighborhood in Athens had a hammam, or public bathhouse, where men and women met to socialize among the steam rooms and take massages on marble platforms. If you want to see Athens's last remaining example, head to Kyrrestou 8 in Plaka. Sunlight streaming through holes cut on the domed roofs of the Bathhouse of the Winds and playing on the colorful tiled floors created a languorous atmosphere here. The pretty 15th-century building now functions as part of the Greek Folk Art Museum.

---

ens, keeping time since the 1st century BC. It was originally a sundial, water clock, and weather vane topped by a bronze Triton with a metal rod in his hand, which followed the direction of the wind. Its eight sides face the direction of the eight winds into which the compass was divided; expressive reliefs around the tower personify these eight winds, called *I Aerides* (the Windy Ones) by Athenians. Note the north wind, Boreas, blowing on a conch, and the beneficent west wind, Zephyros, scattering blossoms. ⊠ *Roman Agora, Kyrristou* ☎ *210/321–6690* 🎟 *€2; €12 joint ticket under the Unification of Archaeological Sites* ⊗ *Daily 8–3 (last entry 2:45).*

WORTH NOTING

Center of Folk Art and Tradition. Exhibits in the neoclassical family mansion of folklorist Angeliki Hatzimichali (1895–1965) include detailed costumes, ceramic plates from Skyros, handwoven fabrics and embroideries, and family portraits. ⊠ *6 Angelikis Hatzimichali, Plaka* ☎ *210/324–3972* 🎟 *Free* ⊗ *Tues.–Fri. 9–7, Sat.–Sun. 9–3* Ⓜ *Syntagma.*

NEED A BREAK?

Vyzantino. Vyzantino is directly on Plaka's main square—great for a good, reasonably priced bite to eat in the center of all the action. Try the *lahanodolmades (*stuffed cabbage leaves in egg and lemon sauce), the roast potatoes, or the stuffed oven chicken. ⊠ *Kidathineon 18, Plaka* ☎ *210/322-7368* ⊕ *www.vyzantinorestaurant.gr* Ⓜ *Acropolis.*

O Glikis. Traditional-looking Glikis and its shady, far-from-the-madding-crowd courtyard are perfect for a Greek coffee or ouzo and a *mikri pikilia* (a small plate of appetizers, including cheese, sausage, olives, and dips). ⊠ *Aggelou Geronta 2 and Angelikis Hatzimichali, Plaka* ☎ *210/322-3925.*

FAMILY **Museum of Greek Popular Musical Instruments.** An entertaining crash course in the development of Greek music, from regional *dimotika* (folk) to *rembetika* (blues), this museum has three floors of instruments. Headphones are available so you can appreciate the sounds made by such unusual delights as goatskin bagpipes and discern the differences in tone between the Pontian lyra and Cretan lyra, string instruments often featured on world-music compilations. The museum, which is housed in the historic Lassanis mansion and has a pretty shaded courtyard, is home to the Fivos Anoyiannakis Center of Ethnomusicology. ⊠ *Diogenous 1–3, Plaka* ☎ *210/325–0198* ⊕ *www. instruments-museum.gr* 🎫 *Free* ⊙ *Tues. and Thurs.–Sun. 10–2, Wed. noon–6* Ⓜ *Monastiraki.*

ANAFIOTIKA ΑΝΑΦΙΩΤΙΚΑ

Fodor'sChoice
★
Set in the shadow of the Acropolis and often compared to the whitewashed villages of the rural Greek islands, the Anafiotika quarter is populated by many descendants of the Anafi stonemasons who arrived from that small island in the 19th century to work in the expanding capital. It remains an enchanting area of simple stone houses, many nestled right into the bedrock, most little changed over the years, others stunningly restored. Cascades of bougainvillea and pots of geraniums and marigolds enliven the balconies and rooftops, and the prevailing serenity is in blissful contrast to the cacophony of modern Athens. In classical times, this district was abandoned because the Delphic Oracle claimed it as sacred ground. The buildings here were constructed by masons from Anafi island, who came to find work in the rapidly expanding Athens of the 1840s and 1850s. They took over this area, whose rocky terrain was similar to Anafi's, hastily erecting homes overnight and taking advantage of an Ottoman law that decreed that if you could put up a structure between sunset and sunrise, the property was yours. Ethiopians, imported as slaves by the Turks during the Ottoman period, stayed on after independence and lived higher up, in caves, on the northern slopes of the Acropolis.

Today, the residents are seldom seen—only a line of wash hung out to dry, the lace curtains on the tiny houses, or the curl of smoke from a wood-burning fireplace indicates human presence. Perched on the bedrock of the Acropolis is **Ayios Georgios tou Vrachou** (St. George of the Rock), which marks the southeast edge of the district. One of the most beautiful churches of Athens, it is still in use today. **Ayios Simeon,** a neoclassical church built in 1847 by the settlers, marks the western boundary and contains a copy of a famous miracle-working icon from Anafi, Our Lady of the Reeds. The **Church of the Metamorphosis Sotiros** (Transfiguration), a high-dome 14th-century stone chapel, has a rear grotto carved right into the Acropolis. For those with children, there is a small playground at Stratonos and Vironos.

MONASTIRAKI ΜΟΝΑΣΤΗΡΑΚΙ

The Times Square, Piccadilly Circus, and St. Basil's Square of ancient Athens, the Agora was once the focal point of urban life. All the principal urban roads and country highways traversed it; the procession of the great Panathenaea Festival, composed of chariots, magistrates, virgins, priests, and sacrificial animals, crossed it on the way to the Acropolis; the Assembly met here first, before moving to the Pnyx; it was where merchants squabbled over the price of olive oil; the forum where Socrates met with his students; and centuries later, where St. Paul went about his missionary task. Lying just under the citadel of the Acropolis, it was indeed the heart of the ancient city and a general meeting place, where news was exchanged and bargains transacted, alive with all the rumors and gossip of the marketplace. The Agora became important under Solon (6th century BC), founder of Athenian democracy; construction continued for almost a millennium. Today, the site's sprawling confusion of stones, slabs, and foundations is dominated by the best-preserved Doric temple in Greece, the Hephaistion, built during the 5th century BC, and the impressive reconstructed Stoa of Attalos II, which houses the Museum of the Agora Excavations.

You can still experience the sights and sounds of the marketplace in Monastiraki, the former Turkish bazaar area, which retains vestiges of the 400-year period when Greece was subject to the Ottoman Empire.

The Varvakeios Agora (Central Market) around Athinas avenue sells fish, meat, and produce from all over Greece and is the major supplier for the city—and even serves as an indicator for the country's economic health. It is a bustling and colorful complex of both indoor and outdoor stalls and shops scattered around the back streets. Lovers of flea markets will also love this area. Street vendors loudly advertise their stock, trying to lure customers to buy all sorts of bric-a-brac, spices, sausages, fresh vegetables, tools, and household goods.

Inside the covered market there are also a couple of age-old tavernas where you can taste traditional *patsas* (tripe soup) alongside the traders who come to have a rest from the day's trade. The rembetika joint Stoa Athanaton is also housed in the Varvakeios, but is accessible only from Sofokleous, one of the side streets.

TOP ATTRACTIONS

Fodor's Choice ★ **Ancient Agora.** The commercial hub of ancient Athens, the Agora was once lined with statues and expensive shops, the favorite strolling ground of fashionable Athenians as well as a mecca for merchants and students. The long colonnades offered shade in summer and protection from rain in winter to the throng of people who transacted the day-to-day business of the city, and, under their arches, Socrates discussed matters with Plato and Zeno expounded the philosophy of the Stoics (whose name comes from the six *stoes,* or colonnades of the Agora). Besides administrative buildings, it was surrounded by the schools, theaters, workshops, houses, stores, and market stalls of a thriving town. The foundations of some of the main buildings that may be most easily distinguished include the circular Tholos, the principal seat of executive power in the city; the Mitroon, shrine to

Rhea, the mother of gods, which included the vast state archives and registry office (*mitroon* is still used today to mean registry); the Vouleuterion, where the council met; the Monument of Epony-mous Heroes, the Agora's informa-tion center, where announcements such as the list of military recruits were hung; and the Sanctuary of the Twelve Gods, a shelter for refu-gees and the point from which all distances were measured.

The Agora's showpiece was the **Stoa of Attalos II,** where Socrates once lectured and incited the youth of Athens to adopt his progressive ideas on mortality and moral-ity. Today the Museum of Agora Excavations, this two-story build-ing was first designed as a retail complex and erected in the 2nd century BC by Attalos, a king of Pergamum. The reconstruction in 1953–56 used Pendelic marble and creamy limestone from the original structure. The colonnade, designed for promenades, is protected from the blistering sun and cooled by breezes. The most notable sculptures, of historical and mythological figures from the 3rd and 4th centuries BC, are at ground level outside the museum.

> **IN AND AROUND THE AGORA**
>
> After browsing through the market stalls, enter the ancient Agora at the corner of Kinetou and Adrianou (the latter runs parallel to Ifestou). Be sure to visit the site's Museum of Agora Excava-tions, which offers a fascinat-ing glimpse of everyday life in the ancient city. Exit at the site's opposite end onto Dionys-siou Areopagitou, crossing the boulevard to the Thissio quarter, a lively area with neoclassic homes overlooking trendy cafés and home to the Melina Mercouri Cultural Center, where exhibits re-create the streets of Athens during different epochs.

Take a walk around the site and speculate on the location of Simon the Cobbler's house and shop, which was a meeting place for Socrates and his pupils. The carefully landscaped grounds display a number of plants known in antiquity, such as almond, myrtle, and pomegranate. By standing in the center, you have a glorious view up to the Acropolis. **Ayii Apostoloi** is the only one of the Agora's nine churches to survive, saved because of its location and beauty.

On the low hill called Kolonos Agoraios in the Agora's northwest corner stands the best-preserved Doric temple in all Greece, the **Hep-haistion,** sometimes called the Thission because of its friezes showing the exploits of Theseus. Like the other monuments, it is roped off, but you can walk around it to admire its preservation. A little older than the Parthenon, it is surrounded by 34 columns and is 104 feet in length, and was once filled with sculptures (the only remnant of which is the mutilated frieze, once brightly colored). It never quite makes the impact of the Parthenon, in large part due to the fact that it lacks a noble site and can never be seen from below, its sun-matured columns towering heavenward. The Hephaistion was originally dedi-cated to Hephaistos, god of metalworkers, and it is interesting to note that metal workshops still exist in this area near Ifestou street. Behind the temple, paths cross the northwest slope past archaeological ruins

One of the hearts of the center city, Monastiraki Square is presided over by the 18th century Tzistarakis Mosque.

half hidden in deep undergrowth. Here you can sit on a bench and contemplate the same scene that Englishman Edward Dodwell saw in the early 19th century, when he came to sketch antiquities. ✉ *Three entrances: from Monastiraki on Adrianou; from Thission on Apostolou Pavlou; and descending from Acropolis on Polygnotou street (near the church of Ayii Apostoloi), Monastiraki* ☎ *210/321–0185* 🌐 *www.culture.gr* 📧 *€4; €12 joint ticket for holders of the Acropolis (Unification of Archaeological Sites) ticket* ☉ *Daily 8–8 (last entry 7:45)* Ⓜ *Thissio.*

Varvakeios Agora (*Central Market*). Athens's Central Market runs along Athinas Street: on one side are open-air stalls selling fruit and vegetables at the best prices in town, although wily merchants may slip overripe items into your bag. At the corner of Armodiou, shops stock live poultry and countless varieties of olives. Across the street, in the huge neoclassical covered market built between 1870 and 1884 (and renovated in 1996), the surrealistic composition of suspended carcasses and shimmering fish on marble counters emits a pungent odor that is overwhelming on hot days. The shops at the north end of the market, to the right on Sofokleous, sell the best cheese, olives, halvah, bread, spices and cold cuts, including *pastourma* (spicy cured beef), available in Athens. Small restaurants serving *patsa* (tripe soup), dot the market; these stay open until almost dawn and are popular stops with weary clubbers trying to ease their hangovers. ✉ *Athinas street, Monastiraki* ☉ *Mon.–Sat. 8–6* Ⓜ *Monastiraki.*

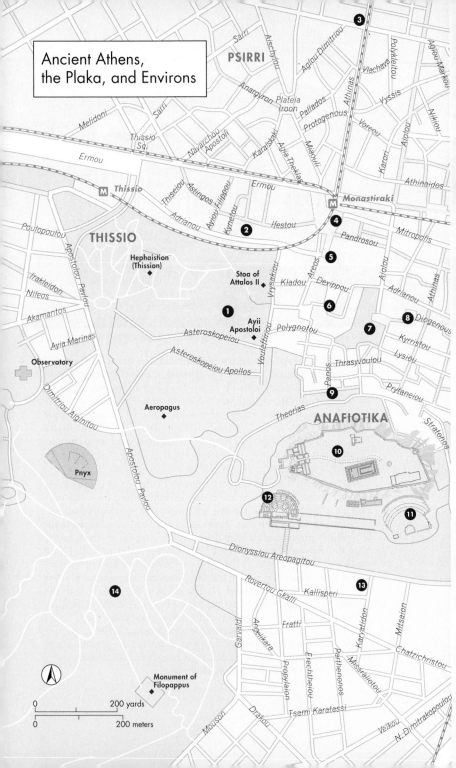

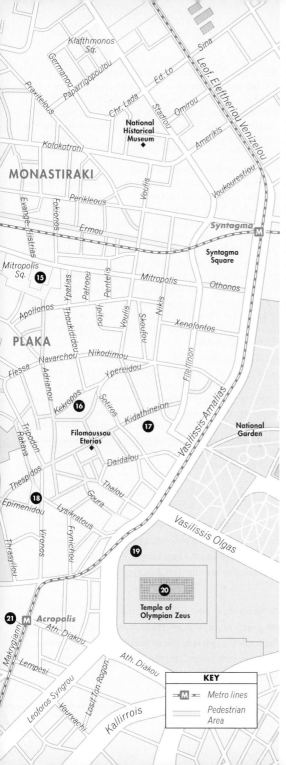

WORTH NOTING

Flea Market. Here is where the chaos, spirit, and charm of Athens turn into a feast for the senses. The Sunday-morning market has combined sight, sound, and scent into a strangely alluring little world where everything is for sale: 1950s-era scuba masks, old tea sets, antique sewing machines, old tobacco tins, gramophone needles, old matchboxes, army uniforms, and lacquered eggs. Haggle, no matter how low the price. ⊠ *Along Ifestou, Kynetou, and Adrianou street, Monastiraki* Ⓜ *Monastiraki.*

Monastiraki Square. One of Athens's most popular meeting places, the square has recently been renovated and much of it now glitters thanks to a pavement of golden mosaic pieces. Look for the special glassed-in view revealing the ancient Iridanos riverbed. The square takes its name from the small Panayia Pantanassa Church, commonly called Monastiraki ("Little Monastery"). It once flourished as an extensive convent, perhaps dating to the 10th century, which stretched from Athinas to Aiolou. The nuns took in poor people, who earned their keep weaving the thick textiles known as *abas*. The buildings were destroyed during excavations and the train (and later metro) line construction that started in 1896. The convent's basic basilica form, now recessed a few steps below street level, was altered through a poor restoration in 1911, when the bell tower was added. ⊠ *South of Ermou and Athinas junction, Monastiraki* Ⓜ *Monastiraki.*

Tzistarakis Mosque. The square's focal point, the 18th-century Tzistarakis Mosque, is now one of the four branches of the Greek Folk Art Museum. It houses a beautifully designed ceramics collection, with the exhibits handsomely lighted and labeled. The mosque's creator, Tzistarakis, a then newly appointed Turkish civil governor, knocked down a column from the Temple of Olympian Zeus to make lime for the mosque. Punished by the sultan for his audacity, he was also blamed by Athenians for an ensuing plague; it was believed the toppling of a column released epidemics and disasters from below Earth. The ticket here ensures entry to all four branches of the Greek Folk Art Museum. ⊠ *Areos 1, Monastiraki* ☎ *210/324–2066* ⊕ *www.melt.gr* 🎫 *€2* ⊙ *Wed.–Mon. 8–3* Ⓜ *Monastiraki.*

NEED A BREAK?

On Mitropoleos off Monastiraki Square are a handful of counter-front places selling souvlaki—grilled meat rolled in a pita with onions, *tzatziki* (yogurt-garlic dip), and tomatoes—the best bargain in Athens. Make sure you specify either a "souvlaki me pita" (sandwich) or a "souvlaki plate," an entire meal.

Thanasis. With the hands-down best kebab (especially the traditional *yiaourtlou*, i.e. with yogurt sauce) in town, Thanasis is always crowded with hungry Greeks who crave the specially spiced ground meat, along with a nicely oiled pita bread, yogurt, onions, and tomatoes. ⊠ *Mitropoleos 69, Monastiraki* ☎ *210/324–4705.*

THISSIO ΘΗΣΕΙΟ

On the opposite side of the Agora is another meeting place of sorts: Thissio, a former red-light district that has been one of the most sought-after residential neighborhoods since about 1990. Easily accessible by metro and offering a lovely view of the Acropolis, it has become one of the liveliest café and restaurant districts in Athens. The area has excellent *rakadika* and *ouzeri*—pub-like eateries that offer plates of appetizers to go with *raki*, a fiery spirit made from grape must; *rakomelo*, a mix of raki and honey heated to boiling; the ever-appealing ouzo; as well as barrels of homemade wine. The main strip is the Nileos pedestrian zone across from the ancient Agora entrance, lined with cafés that are cozy in winter and have outdoor tables in summer. The rest of the neighborhood is quiet, an odd mix of mom-and-pop stores and dilapidated houses that are slowly being renovated; take a brief stroll along Akamantos (which becomes Galatias) around the intersections of Dimofontos or Aginoros, or down Iraklidon, to get a feel for the quarter's past.

TOP ATTRACTIONS

NEED A BREAK?

Athinaion Politeia. For a fancy coffee (think espresso mixed with sambuca), sweet crêpes (such as banana and chocolate hazelnut) and impromptu lunches (thanks to a wide selection of salads and hot and cold dishes), stop at Athinaion Politeia, a restored neoclassical-style mansion and watch the crowds on Apostolou Pavlou. Thirtysomething hipsters hold court here, telling raucous stories that spill into laughter, making you feel like you're in the middle of the best party in town. ⊠ *Akamantos 1 and Apostolou Pavlou 33, Thissio* ☎ *210/341–3795* ⊕ *www.athinaionpoliteia.gr.*

SYNTAGMA ΠΛΑΤΕΙΑ ΣΥΝΤΑΓΜΑΤΟΣ

From the Tomb of the Unknown Soldier to Queen Amalia's National Garden, to the top of Mt. Lycabettus (three times the height of the Acropolis), this center-city sector is packed with marvels and wonders. Sooner or later, everyone passes through its heart, the spacious Syntagma Square (Constitution Square), which is surrounded by sights that span Athens's history from the days of the Roman emperors to King Otto's reign after the 1821 War of Independence. Some may have likened his palace (now the Parliament) to a barracks but they shouldn't complain: it was paid for by Otto's father, King Ludwig I of Bavaria, who luckily vetoed the plans for a royal residence atop the Acropolis itself, using one end of the Parthenon as the entrance and blowing up the rest. The palace was finished just in time for Otto to grant the constitution of 1843, which gave the square its name. Neighboring Kolonaki—the chic shopping district and one of the most fashionable residential areas—occupies the lower slopes of Mt. Lycabettus. Besides visiting its several museums, you can spend time window-shopping and people-watching, since cafés are busy from early morning to dawn. Nursing a single coffee for hours remains not only socially acceptable—but a vital survival tactic in frequently stressful modern Greek life.

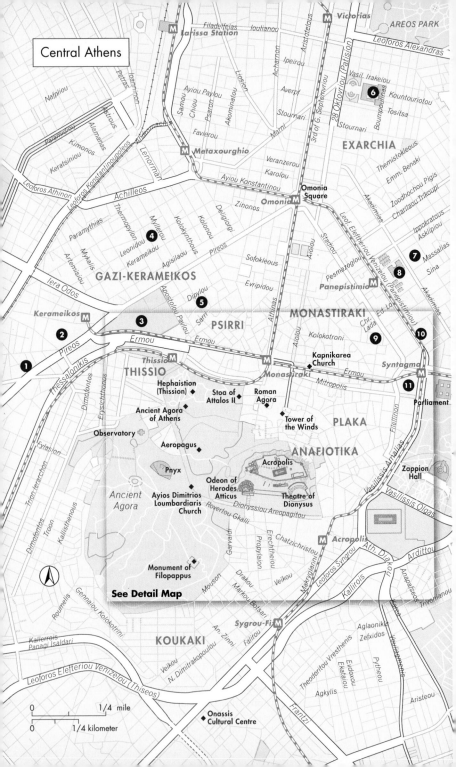

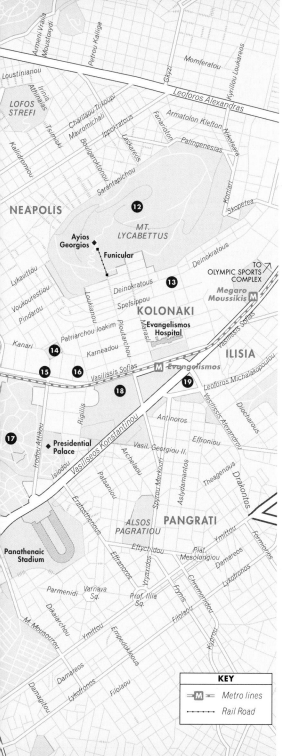

TOP ATTRACTIONS

National Historical Museum. After making the rounds of the ancient sites, you might think that Greek history ground to a halt when the Byzantine Empire collapsed. A visit to this gem of a museum, housed in the spectacularly majestic Old Parliament mansion (used by parliamentarians from 1875 to 1932), will fill in the gaps, often vividly, as with Lazaros Koyevina's copy of Eugene Delacroix's *Massacre of Chios*, to name but one example. Paintings, costumes, and assorted artifacts from small arms to flags and ships' figureheads are arranged in a chronological display tracing Greek history from the mid-16th century and the Battle of Lepanto through World War II and the Battle of Crete. A small gift shop near the main entrance—framed by a very grand neoclassical portico of columns—has unusual souvenirs, like a deck of cards featuring Greece's revolutionary heroes. ⊠ *Stadiou 13, Syntagma* ☎ *210/323–7617* ⊕ *www.nhmuseum.gr* ⌑ *€3* ⊗ *Tues.– Sun. 8:30–2:30* Ⓜ *Syntagma.*

> ### CHANGING OF THE GUARDS
>
> Near the Parliament, you can watch the **Changing of the Evzones Guards** at the Tomb of the Unknown Soldier—in front of Parliament on a lower level—which takes place at intervals throughout the day. On Sunday the honor guard of tall young men don a dress costume—a short white and very heavy *foustanella* (kilt) with 400 neat pleats, one for each year of the Ottoman occupation, and red shoes with pom-poms—and still manage to look brawny rather than silly. A band accompanies them: they all arrive by 11:15 am in front of Parliament.

FAMILY **National Garden.** When you can't take the city noise anymore, step into this oasis completed in 1860 as part of King Otto and Queen Amalia's royal holdings. Here old men on the benches argue politics, police officers take their coffee breaks, runners count early-morning jog laps, and animal lovers feed the stray cats that roam among the more than 500 species of trees and plants, many labeled. At the east end is the neoclassic **Zappeion Hall,** built in 1888 as an Olympic building (with funds from Greek benefactor Evangelos Zappas). Since then it has been used for major political and cultural events: it was here that Greece signed its accession to what was then the European Community. Next door, a leafy café and open-air cinema attract Athenians all year-round. Cross the road to the nearby Panathenaic Stadium, which was built on the very site of an ancient stadium for the revived Olympic Games in 1896. You can look at the stadium only from the outside, but there is an elevated dirt running track behind it (free entrance through a big gate on Archimidous street, which runs directly behind the stadium). The tree-lined track area and adjacent Ardittos hill constitute one of the most pleasant, quiet public spaces in the city—they also offer some stunning vantage points.

Children appreciate the playgrounds, duck pond, and small zoo at the east end of the National Garden. ⊠ *Syntagma* ☎ *210/323–7830* ⊕ *www. zappeion.gr* Ⓜ *Syntagma.*

For patriotic Greeks, the Changing of the Guard in front of the Tomb of the Unknown Soldier is always a heart-stirring ceremony.

NEED A BREAK? **Aeglí Zappiou.** Visit the elegant Aeglí Zappiou, an excellent spot for a classic Greek coffee experience. Nestled among fountains and flowering trees next to the Zappeion Exhibition Hall in the National Garden, it's an ideal spot to sample a fresh dessert or some haute cuisine, or watch a movie at the open-air Cine Aegli next door! Adjacent to this café is the noted Cibus restaurant, which offers a special *degustation* menu of modern Greek cuisine every Wednesday evening (reservations recommended). ✉ *Zappio Megaro, Syntagma* ☎ *210/336–9300* ⊕ *www.aeglizappiou.gr.*

Fodor's Choice
★

Numismatic Museum Iliou Melathron. Even those uninterested in coins might want to visit this museum for a glimpse of the former home of Heinrich Schliemann, who famously excavated Troy and Mycenae in the 19th century. Built by the Bavarian architect Ernst Ziller for the archaeologist's family and baptized the "Iliou Melathron" (or Palace of Troy), it flaunts an imposing neo-Venetian facade. Inside are some spectacular rooms, including the vast and floridly decorated Hesperides Hall, ashimmer with colored marbles and neo-Pompeian wall paintings. Today, in this exquisite neoclassic mansion, seemingly haunted by the spirit of the great historian, you can see more than 600,000 coins; displays range from the archaeologist's own coin collection to 4th-century BC measures employed against forgers to coins grouped according to what they depict—animals, plants, myths, and famous buildings like the Lighthouse of Alexandria. Instead of trying to absorb everything, concentrate on a few cases—perhaps a pile of coins dug up on a Greek road, believed to be used by Alexander the Great to pay off local mercenaries. To relax, head to the museum's peaceful garden café—a cozy oasis just a few feet away from Pan-epistimiou avenue's hustle and bustle. ⊠ *Panepistimiou 12, Syntagma* ☎ *210/363–2057, 210/361–2834* ⊕ *www.nma.gr* 🎫 *€3; €12 for unified museum ticket (includes National Archaeological Museum, Epigraphical Museum, Byzantine & Christian Museum)* ☉ *Tues.–Sun. 8–5, Mon. 1–8* Ⓜ *Syntagma or Panepistimiou.*

Syntagma (Constitution) Square. At the top of the city's main square stands the Greek **Parliament,** formerly King Otto's (Othon's in Greek) royal palace, completed in 1838 for the new monarchy. It seems a bit austere and heavy for a southern landscape, but it was proof of progress, the symbol of the new ruling power. The building's saving grace is the stone's magical change of color from off-white to gold to rosy mauve as the day progresses. Here you can watch the **Changing of the Evzones Guards** at the **Tomb of the Unknown Soldier**—in front of Parliament on a lower level—which takes place at intervals throughout the day. On a wall behind the Tomb of the Unknown Soldier, the bas-relief of a dying soldier is modeled after a sculpture on the Temple of Aphaia in Aegina; the text is from the funeral oration said to have been given by Pericles. In recent years the square has become the new frontline of mass protests against harsh austerity measures and the ongoing economic crisis in Greece, as well as the base for the citizen movement of the "Indignants."

Pop into the gleaming Syntagma metro station to examine artfully displayed artifacts uncovered during subway excavations. A floor-to-ceiling cross section of earth behind glass shows finds in chronological layers, ranging from a skeleton in its ancient grave to traces of the 4th-century BC road to Mesogeia to an Ottoman cistern. The 21st century arrived here in 2006 when the first public wireless network with free access to the Internet was set up in Syntagma Square. (Note that this station is the first one to shut its doors for security reasons when a demonstration takes place outside in Syntagma Square.) ⊠ *Vasilissis Amalias and Vasilissis Sofias, Syntagma* Ⓜ *Syntagma.*

NEED A BREAK?

Ethnikon. Lovely cafés like Ethnikon have opened in the square as a result of the city's 2004 Olympic remodeling. This café-brasserie is shady, atmospheric, and has an excellent selection of desserts, including chocolate cake and homemade spoon sweets, or *glyka tou koutaliou.* ⊠ *Syntagma Sq., Vas. Georgiou 2, Syntagma* ☎ *210/331–0676.*

Café Voulis. On Voulis street, the tiny pedestrian road just behind Syntagma Square, you can stop for a swift espresso coffee break. Café Voulis has been voted one of the Top 10 espresso bars in the country, but its aficionados also swear by the fresh sandwiches and salads for an easy lunch break. It is also remarkably cool in summer. ⊠ *Voulis 17 and Ermou, Syntagma* ☎ *210/323-4333.*

PSIRRI ΨΥΡΗ

During his stint in Athens, Lord Byron stayed in Psirri, and this is where he supposedly met Thiresia-Tereza Makri, who inspired him to write "The Maid of Athens." His romance was not meant to be, but the romance of the Athenians with the gentrified neighborhood of Psirri is getting stronger and stronger, despite some lurking signs of the economic crisis (a few shops have closed in recent years), though an influx of artists, designers, bakers, and organic grocers seems to be taking advantage of the available rental opportunities.

Defined by Ermou, Kerameikou, Athinas, Evripidou, Epikourou, and Pireos streets, Psirri has many buildings older than those in picturesque Plaka. A plethora of tavernas, *mezedopoleio* (Greek tapas bars), nightspots, and cafés, as well as a small number of hotels, including the O & B Hotel, can be found in the area. Peek over the wrought-iron gates of the old houses on the narrow side streets between Ermou and Kerameikou to see the pretty courtyards bordered by long, low buildings, whose many small rooms were rented out to different families. In the Square of the Heroes, revolutionary fighters once met to plot against the Ottoman occupation. Linger on into the evening if you want to dance on tabletops to live Greek music, sing along with a soulful accordion player, hear salsa in a Cuban club, or watch hoi polloi go by as you snack on updated or traditional *mezedes* (small plates).

The classic old Athens eatery Diporto is well hidden in the corner basement of an olive shop (with no sign) on Platia Theatrou. The regulars know where it is and that's good enough (you can ask). On Evripidou street you can find spice and herb shops. Tasting the olives from all over Greece, and buying spices and herbs collected on the hills of Attica are some of the must-do things around here.

GAZI-KERAMEIKOS ΓΚΑΖΙ-ΚΕΡΑΜΕΙΚΟΣ

Gazi-Kerameikos takes its name from the industrial gas works that even today dominate the neighborhood's landscape. The plant that used to provide gas for lighting and power throughout the city (called Technopolis) is now a cultural center offering festivals, temporary exhibitions, and open-air concerts. A slew of bars, clubs, and restaurants are spearheading the revival of the neighborhood and are served by the sleek Kerameikos metro station.

TOP ATTRACTIONS

Kerameikos Cemetery. At the western edge of the Gazi district lies the wide, green expanse of Kerameikos, the main cemetery in ancient Athens until Sulla destroyed the city in 86 BC. The name is associated with the modern word "ceramic": in the 12th century BC the district was populated by potters who used the abundant clay from the languid Eridanos river to make funerary urns and grave decorations. From the 7th century BC onward, Kerameikos was the fashionable cemetery of ancient Athens. During succeeding ages cemeteries were superimposed on the ancient one until the latter was discovered in 1861. From the main entrance, you can still see remains of the **Makra Teixi** (Long

Walls) of Themistocles, which ran to Piraeus, and the largest gate in the ancient world, the **Dipylon Gate,** where visitors entered Athens. The walls rise to 10 feet, a fraction of their original height (up to 45 feet). Here was also the **Sacred Gate,** used by pilgrims headed to the mysterious rites in Eleusis and by those who participated in the Panathenaic procession, which followed the Sacred Way. Between the two gates are the foundations of the **Pompeion,** the starting point of the Panathenaic procession. It is said the courtyard was large enough to fit the ship used in the procession. On the **Street of Tombs,** which branches off the Sacred Way, plots were reserved for affluent Athenians. A number of the distinctive *stelae* (funerary monuments) remain, including a replica of the marble relief of Dexilios, a knight who died in the war against Corinth (394 BC); he is shown on horseback preparing to spear a fallen foe. To the left of the site's entrance is the **Oberlaender Museum,** also known as the Kerameikos Museum, whose displays include sculpture, terra-cotta figures, and some striking red-and-black-figured pottery. The extensive grounds of Kerameikos are marshy in some spots; in spring, frogs exuberantly croak their mating songs near magnificent stands of lilies. ⊠ *Ermou 148, Gazi-Kerameikos* ☎ *210/346–3552* 🎫 *€2 site and museum; €12 joint ticket for all Unification of Archaeological Sites* ⊙ *Daily 8–8* Ⓜ *Kerameikos.*

WORTH NOTING

Benaki Museum of Islamic Art. Housed in a gleaming white neoclassical mansion with a sweeping view of the Kerameikos cemetary, this newest annex of the Benaki Museum provides a welcoming home to its extensive Islamic art collection (which is considered amongst the most important in the world). More than 8,000 pieces of art hail from regions as widely spread geographically as North Africa, India, Persia, Asia Minor, Arabia, Mesopotamia, and even Sicily and Spain. Among the ceramics, gold, metalwork, textiles, glass, funerary steles, and weaponry on display, a couple of exhibits really stand out: a set of carved wooden memorial door panels from 8th-century Mesopotamia, and the marble-faced interior of a reception room from a 17th-century Cairo mansion. ⊠ *Dipilou 12, at Ag. Asomaton 22, Gazi-Kerameikos* ☎ *210/325–1311* ⊕ *www.benaki.gr* 🎫 *€7* ⊙ *Thurs.–Sun. 9–5.*

FAMILY **Technopolis.** Gazi, the neighborhood surrounding this former 19th-century gasworks–turned–arts complex, takes its name from the toxic gas fumes that used to spew from the factory's smokestacks. Today Gazi is synonymous with the hippest restaurants, edgiest galleries, and trendiest nightclubs in town. The smokestacks now glow crimson with colored lights, anchoring a burgeoning stretch that runs from the central neighborhood of Kerameikos to the once-decrepit neighborhood of Rouf. The city of Athens bought the disused gasworks in the late 1990s and helped convert it into Technopolis, a city of arts and culture, which since 2013 also houses the Industrial Gas Museum. The transformation preserved all the original architecture and stonework, and includes exhibition spaces dedicated to preserving the gasworks heritage and a large courtyard with a coffeeshop open to the public. The spaces regularly host shows on a range of topics—war photography, open-air jazz, comic-book art, rock and theater performances, rave nights, and parties. ⊠ *Pireos 100, Gazi-Kerameikos* ☎ *210/346–1589* ⊕ *www.technopolis-athens.com* ✉ *Technopolis free; Gas Museum €1* ⊘ *Tues.–Sun., 9–9 during exhibition;, Gas Museum Tues.–Sun. 10–6* Ⓜ *Kerameikos.*

ROUF ΡΟΥΦ

In mid-19th century, Bavarian aristocrat Ludwig Rouf, who had arrived in Athens with King Otto, owned significant land in the Athenian neighborhood that now bears his name. Southwest of Omonia Square, between Pireos avenue (south of Gazi-Kerameikos) and Petrou Ralli avenue, Rouf was a mostly industrial/manufacturing district in the 1960s. But the factories have now mostly departed, leaving behind large, abandoned warehouses, empty plants, and cheap rents, which help explain the influx of artists, galleries, clubs, and even restaurants. A new annex for the Benaki Museum can be found here, on Pireos avenue, as well as a couple of interesting theaters.

Benaki Museum Pireos Street Annexe. The eye-knocking Benaki Museum Annexe is located at one of the busiest and most industrially developed points in the city. The minimalist exterior is covered in smooth pink stone—a kind of beacon of modernity—with creatively designed clean lines on the dusty, loud avenue. Inside, all is high-ceilinged atriums, walkway ascents, and multiple levels, a dramatic setting for the museum's temporary exhibitions (many of which are more avant-garde in character than those housed in the main building). The Annexe is closed in August. ⊠ *138 Pireos street, at Andronikou street, Rouf* ☎ *210/345–3111* ⊕ *www.benaki.gr* ✉ *€4–€6 (varies by special exhibit)* ⊘ *Sept.–Jul., Thurs. and Sun. 10–6, Fri. and Sat. 10–10* Ⓜ *Kerameikos.*

METAXOURGEIO ΜΕΤΑΞΟΥΡΓΕΙΟ

Once ignored as simply a transient neighborhood, Metaxourgeio has acquired its own character as an emerging artist hub. The Municipal Gallery of Athens set up shop here. The surrounding urban grid is an assorted collection of crumbling buildings and renovated houses that pays equal tribute to the glorious past and the hopeful future. But this is definitely a transitional neighborhood filled with recent immigrants (a small Chinatown of grocery and clothing shops is located between Kolonou and Kolokynthous streets), so always be mindful of your surroundings. You may wish to admire the Metaxourgeio metro station even if you don't have to go anywhere in particular, if only to admire the wall mural "The myth of my neighborhood" by renowned Greek painter Yiannis Moralis. Just up the road from traffic-ladden Metaxourgeio Square, on Ayiou Konstantinou street, is the headquarters of the Greek National Theatre.

TOP ATTRACTIONS

New Municipal Gallery of Athens. One of Athens's oldest neoclassical buildings—an architectural jewel set in the rapidly regaining-its-former-glory Metaxourgeio neighborhood—became the new home of the city's Municipal Art Collection in 2010. The former silk factory, designed in

1833 by Danish architect Hans Christian Hansen, now houses almost 3,000 important art works from leading 19th- and 20th-century Greek artists (most of the works were acquired during the 1930s and '40s). The renovated building was inaugurated with a major showing of the Economou Collection (he's a well-known Greek businessman and art collector) and will continue hosting its municipal permanent collection as well as an evolving calendar of temporary exhibitions and events. ⊠ *Leonidou and Myllerou, Metaxourgeio* 🕾 *210/323–1841* 🗊 *Free* ☽ *Tues. 10–9, Wed.–Sat. 10–7, Sun. 10–3.*

KOLONAKI ΚΟΛΩΝΑΚΙ

Kolonaki was named after a marble column dating from the Middle Ages, probably a memento of a religious procession, that was discovered in Dexameni Square, on the foot of Mt. Lycabettus. On its southwestern edge is Syntagma Square and the Parliament building; the neighborhood extends all the way to Lycabettus and beyond. It is a posh neighborhood with lots of upmarket boutiques, Italian-style cafés, and museums. In front of the Hilton hotel, you can pay homage to the power of movement and clean lines of the impressive *Runner*, a glass sculpture of impressive proportions by local artist Kostas Varotsos. If you want to use this district as a base to explore the rest of Athens, the Hilton and the Hotel Periscope are a couple of excellent options. There are also nearby recommendable restaurants.

TOP ATTRACTIONS

Fodor'sChoice
★

Benaki Museum. Greece's oldest private museum received a spectacular addition in 2004, just before the Athens Olympics, with a hypermodern new branch that looks like it was airlifted in from New York City. Located on the gentrifying Pireos Street, the new annex is all the more striking when compared to the main museum, set in an imposing neoclassic mansion in the posh Kolonaki neighbourhood. Established in 1926 by an illustrious Athenian family, the Benaki was one of the first to place emphasis on Greece's later heritage at a time when many archaeologists were destroying Byzantine artifacts to access ancient objects. The permanent collection (more than 20,000 items are on display in 36 rooms, and that's only a sample of the holdings) moves chronologically from the ground floor upward, from prehistory to the formation of the modern Greek state. You might see anything from a 5,000-year-old hammered gold bowl to an austere Byzantine icon of the Virgin Mary to Lord Byron's pistols to the Nobel medals awarded to poets George Seferis and Odysseus Elytis. Some exhibits are just plain fun—the re-creation of a Kozani (Macedonian town) living room; a tableau of costumed mannequins; a Karaghiozi shadow puppet piloting a toy plane—all contrasted against the marble and crystal-chandelier grandeur of the Benaki home. The mansion that serves as the main building of the museum was designed by Anastassios Metaxas, the architect who helped restore the Panathenaic Stadium. The Benaki's gift shop, a destination in itself, tempts with exquisitely reproduced ceramics and jewelry. The second-floor café serves coffee and snacks, with a few daily specials, on a generous veranda overlooking the National Garden.

Try to catch the purple glow of sundown from atop Mt. Lycabettus, Athens's highest hill.

The annexe displays avant-garde temporary exhibitions at 138 Pireos Street in the Rouf neighborhood. Topping the complex off is a state-of-the-art amphitheater. Latest addition to the Benaki Museum is the Benaki Museum of Islamic Art, which is housed in a beautifully restored neoclassical mansion behind the Kerameikos cemetery. ⊠ *Koumbari 1, Kolonaki* ☎ *210/367–1000* ⊕ *www.benaki.gr* ✉ *€7 (free Thurs.)* ☉ *Wed. and Fri. 9–5, Thurs. and Sat. 9 am–midnight, Sun. 9–3* Ⓜ *Syntagma or Evangelismos, Kerameikos for the New Wing on Pireos.*

FAMILY
Fodor's Choice
★

Mt. Lycabettus. Myth claims that Athens's highest hill came into existence when Athena removed a piece of Mt. Pendeli, intending to boost the height of her temple on the Acropolis. While she was en route, a crone brought her bad tidings, and the flustered goddess dropped the rock in the middle of the city. Kids love the ride up the steeply inclined *teleferique* (funicular) to the summit (one ride every 30 minutes), crowned by whitewashed **Ayios Georgios** chapel with a bell tower donated by Queen Olga. On a clear day, you can see Aegina island, with or without the aid of coin-operated telescopes. Built into a cave on the side of the hill, near the spot where the I Prasini Tenta café used to be, is a small shrine to **Ayios Isidoros.** In 1859 students prayed here for those fighting against the Austrians, French, and Sardinians with whom King Otto had allied. From Mt. Lycabettus you can watch the sunset and then turn about to watch the moon rise over "violet-crowned" Hymettus as the lights of Athens blink on all over the city. Refreshments are available from the modest kiosk popular with concertgoers who flock to events at the hill's open-air theater during summer months. Diners should also note that Lycabettus is home to Orizontes Lykavittou, an excellent fish restaurant (by day this establishment also houses the relaxing Café Lycabettus). ⊠ *Kolonaki* ⊕ *The base is a 15-min walk northeast of Syntagma Sq.; funicular runs every 30 mins (10 mins during rush hour) from corner of Ploutarchou and Aristippou (take Minibus 060 from Kanari or Kolonaki Sq.)* ☎ *210/721–0701 Funicular information* ⊕ *www.orizonteslycabettus.gr* ⊠ *Funicular €7 (round-trip)* ☉ *Funicular daily 9 am–2:30 am.*

FAMILY
Fodor's Choice
★

Museum of Cycladic Art. Also known as the Nicholas P. and Dolly Goulandris Foundation, and funded by one of Greece's richest families, this museum has an outstanding collection of 350 Cycladic artifacts dating from the Bronze Age, including many of the enigmatic marble figurines whose slender shapes fascinated such artists as Picasso, Modigliani, and Brancusi. The main building is an imposing glass-and-steel design dating from 1985 and built to convey "the sense of austerity and the diffusion of refracted light that predominate in the Cycladic landscape," as the museum puts it. Along with Cycladic masterpieces, a wide array from other eras is also on view, ranging from the Bronze Age through the 6th century AD. The third floor is devoted to Cypriot art while the fourth floor showcases a fascinating exhibition on "scenes from daily life in antiquity." To handle the overflow, a new wing opened in 2005. A glass corridor connects the main building to the gorgeous 19th-century neoclassic Stathatos Mansion, where temporary exhibits are mounted. There is also a lovely skylit café in a courtyard centered around a Cycladic-inspired fountain, a charming art shop, and many children-oriented activities all year-round. ⊠ *Neofitou Douka 4, Kolonaki* ☎ *210/722–8321 through 210/722–8323* ⊕ *www.cycladic. gr* ⊠ *€7 (half-price Mon.)* ☉ *Mon., Wed., Fri., Sat. 10–5, Thurs. 10–8, Sun. 11–5* Ⓜ *Evangelismos.*

NEED A BREAK?

Clemente VIII. One of the toniest pedestrian malls in Athens is Voukourestiou, where you will find the one of the hippest cafés in the city, Clemente VIII. With the best espresso and cappuccino (both hot and iced) in town and a fresh daily platter of sandwiches and sweets, this Italianate-style café (named after the 16th-century pope who gave his blessing to the then exotic coffee bean) is a favorite of the Armani-clad business lunch crowd. ⊠ *City Link Mall, Voukourestiou 3, Kolonaki* ☎ *210/321–9340.*

Zonar's Café d'Athenes. Clemente VIII no longer basks in its glory alone, for 100 feet away sits Zonar's Café d'Athenes. After a heartbreaking closure and more than six years of renovation, this is back with a vengeance. Despite hefty prices, the sleek "moderne" decor of this very exclusive café triumphantly looks better than ever while the mouthwatering pastry corner attracts the attention of old and young alike. ⊠ *Attica Department Store, Panepistimiou and Voukourestiou, Kolonaki* ☎ *210/321–1158* ☉ *9 am–1am.*

WORTH NOTING

B&M Theocharakis Foundation. Founded in 2004, this private non-profit foundation focuses on the visual arts and music, with a special interest in modernism. The driving force behind the imposing cultural center, housed in a neoclassical building opposite the Greek Parliament, is Basil Theocharakis, a prominent businessman who is also an avid and talented painter, and his wife Marina. Temporary exhibitions, classical concerts, and workshops are held here on a regular basis (check the foundation's website or local listings for the current offerings), while Cafe Merlin, the elegant first-floor café, offers a welcome respite from the city's hustle and bustle. ⊠ *9 Vassilissis Sofias avenue, at 1 Merlin street, Kolonaki* ☎ *210/361–1206* ⊕ *www.thf.gr.*

Byzantine & Christian Museum. One of the few museums in Europe focusing exclusively on Byzantine art displays an outstanding collection of icons, mosaics, tapestries, and sculptural fragments (the latter provides an excellent introduction to Byzantine architecture). The permanent collection is divided in two main parts: the first is devoted to Byzantium (4th through 15th century AD) and contains 1,200 artifacts while the second is entitled *From Byzantium to the Modern Era* and presents 1,500 artworks dating from the 15th to the 21st century. ⊠ *Vasilissis Sofias 22, Kolonaki* ☎ *213/213–9572, 213/723–9511* ⊕ *www. byzantinemuseum.gr* 🎟 *€4; €12 for unified museum ticket (includes National Archaeological Museum, Epigraphical Museum, Numismatic Museum)* ☉ *Tues.–Sun. 8–8* Ⓜ *Evangelismos.*

Gennadius Library. Book lovers who ascend the grand staircase into the hallowed aura of the Reading Room may have difficulty tearing themselves away from this superb collection of material on Greek subjects, from first editions of Greek classics to the papers of Nobel Laureate poets George Seferis and Odysseus Elytis. The library's collection includes Lord Byron's memorabilia (including a lock of his hair); Heinrich Schliemann's diaries, notebooks, and letters; impressionistic watercolors of Greece by Edward Lear; and the first edition printed in Greek of Homer's *Iliad* and *Odyssey*. The Gennadius is not a lending library (first-time users, usually scholars, must apply for a library card), but the temporary exhibitions (curated by internationally renowned figures) are always worth a visit. ⊠ *Souidias 61, Kolonaki* ☎ *210/721–0536* ⊕ *www.ascsa.edu.gr* ☉ *Sept.–June, Mon.–Wed. and Fri. 9–5, Thurs. 9–8, Sat. 9–2; check with reception for special hours during July and Aug.* Ⓜ *Evangelismos.*

Kolonaki Square. To see and be seen, Athenians gather not on Kolonaki Square—hub of the chic Kolonaki district—but at the cafés on its periphery and along the Tsakalof and Milioni pedestrian zones. Clothespin-thin models, slick talk-show hosts, middle-aged executives, elegant pensioners, university students, and expatriate teen queens all congregate on the square (officially known as Filikis Eterias) for a coffee before work, a lunchtime gossip session, a drink after a hard day of shopping, or an afternoon of sipping iced cappuccinos while reading a stack of foreign newspapers and magazines purchased from the all-night kiosk. ⊠ *Intersection of Patriarchou Ioakeim and Kanari, Kolonaki* Ⓜ *Syntagma or Evangelismos, then 10- to 15-min walk.*

NEED A
BREAK?

Caffe Da Capo. Enjoy a cappuccino and an Italian dolce standing inside Caffe Da Capo or, if you have more time, try to find a table. This place is usually packed with young trendsetters and stern policy makers; people-watching is part of the pleasure. ⊠ *Tsakalof 1, Kolonaki* ☎ *210/360–2497.*

Old University complex. In the sea of concrete that is Central Athens, this imposing group of marble buildings conjures up an illusion of classical antiquity. The three dramatic buildings belonging to the University of Athens were designed by the Hansen brothers in the period after independence in the 19th century and are built of white Pendelic marble, with tall columns and decorative friezes. In the center is the **Senate House** of the university. To the right is the **Academy**, flanked by two slim columns topped by statues of Athena and Apollo; paid for by the Austro-Greek Baron Sina, it is a copy of the Parliament in Vienna. Frescoes in the reception hall depict the myth of Prometheus. At the left end of the complex is a griffin-flanked staircase leading to the **National Library**, containing more than 2 million Greek and foreign-language volumes and now undergoing the daunting task of modernization. The university complex, as well as Syntagma Square, often serves as the meeting point for protest groups before their marches through the city center, so don't be surprised if city traffic come to a halt when marchers stride by (during certain times of the year, there are at least one or two marches a week, much to the chagrin of Athenians). ⊠ *Panepistimiou between Ippokratous and Sina, Kolonaki* ☎ *210/368–9765 Senate, 210/366–4700 Academy, 210/360–8185 Library* ⊕ *www.nlg.gr* ☉ *National library Sept.–July, Mon.–Thurs. 9–8, Fri.–Sat. 9–2* Ⓜ *Panepistimiou.*

EXARCHIA ΕΞΑΡΧΕΙΑ

The neighborhood of Exarchia is full of life and largely student-central, as the National Technical University of Athens (Polytechneio) is located just a few hundred yards away from Exarchia Square down tech-friendly Stournari street. The area is also infamous for the anarchist groups that use it as a base for their demonstrations, although in recent years peace and quiet have largely prevailed. The National Archaeological Museum (the neighborhood's biggest draw) is next to the Polytechnic, where the historic student uprising of 1973, which led to the ousting of the junta, took place. Look for the "Blue" building in Exarchia Square, which is a prime example of the modernist movement in Greek architecture. Rembetika music clubs, record shops, comic-book shops, quaint little bars, traditional tavernas, and cheap souvlaki corners all coexist in the area, which is always buzzing with creative—one might dare say revolutionary—energy.

TOP ATTRACTIONS

Fodor's Choice
★

National Archaeological Museum. Many of the greatest achievements in ancient Greek sculpture and painting are housed here in the most important museum in Greece. Artistic highlights from every period of its ancient civilization, from Neolithic to Roman times, make this a treasure trove beyond compare. With a massive renovation completed, works (more than 11,000 of them) that have languished in storage for decades are now on view, reorganized displays are accompanied by enriched English-language information, and the panoply of ancient Greek art appears more spectacular than ever.

Although the classic culture that was the grandeur of the Greek world no longer exists—it died, for civilizations are mortal—it left indelible markers in all domains, most particularly in art, and many of its masterpieces are on show here. The museum's most celebrated display is the **Mycenaean Antiquities.** Here are the stunning gold treasures from Heinrich Schliemann's 1876 excavations of Mycenae's royal tombs: the funeral mask of a bearded king, once thought to be the image of Agamemnon but now believed to be much older, from about the 15th century BC; a splendid silver bull's-head libation cup; and the 15th-century BC Vapheio Goblets, masterworks in embossed gold. Mycenaeans were famed for their carving in miniature, and an exquisite example is the ivory statuette of two curvaceous mother goddesses, each with a child nestled on her lap.

Withheld from the public since they were damaged in the 1999 earthquakes, but not to be missed, are the beautifully restored **frescoes from Santorini,** delightful murals depicting daily life in Minoan Santorini. Along with the treasures from Mycenae, these wall paintings are part of the museum's Prehistoric Collection.

Other stars of the museum include the works of Geometric and Archaic art (10th to 6th century BC), and **kouroi** and **funerary stelae** (8th to 5th century BC), among them the stelae of the warrior Aristion signed by Aristokles, and the unusual *Running Hoplite* (a hoplite was a Greek infantry soldier). The collection of classical art (5th to 3rd century BC) contains some of the most renowned surviving ancient statues: the bareback *Jockey of Artemision,* a 2nd-century BC Hellenistic bronze salvaged from the sea; from the same excavation, the bronze *Artemision Poseidon* (some say Zeus), poised and ready to fling a trident (or thunderbolt?); and the *Varvakios Athena,* a half-size marble version of the gigantic gold-and-ivory cult statue that Pheidias erected in the Parthenon.

Light refreshments are served in a lower ground-floor café, which opens out to a patio and sculpture garden. Don't forget to also check the museum's temporary exhibitions. ⊠ *28 Oktovriou (Patission) 44, Exarchia* ☎ *213/214–4800, 213/214–4891* ⊕ *www.namuseum.gr* ✆ *€7; €12 for unified museum ticket (includes Byzantine & Christian Museum, Epigraphical Museum, Numismatic Museum)* ⊗ *Mon.–Sun. 8–8* Ⓜ *Victoria, then 10-min walk.*

OMONIA (CONCORD) SQUARE ΠΛΑΤΕΙΑ ΟΜΟΝΟΙΑΣ

Omonia is the meeting point of several vital avenues: Stadiou, Panepistimiou, Ayiou Konstantinou, 3rd September, Pireos, and Athinas. The commercial hot spots of the pedestrianized Aiolou street and Patission avenue are also within walking distance. It's a major transport hub, the meeting place of lines 1 (from Kifissia to Piraeus) and 2 (the red metro line). Omonia Square was built at the request of King Otto in 1846, and it quickly became one of the busiest meeting points in the young capital. Soon, however, the low and elegant neoclassical buildings gave way to the grey concrete blocks that dominate the urban horizon today.

In recent years, the economic crisis has meant that the once-lively commercial square (a symbol of the economic development of the 1960s) is struggling to find its character after the dramatic influx of illegal immigrants and rise in petty crime rates.

In Kotzia Square, one can admire the imposing Old Town Hall (now the city's registry office), an ongoing archaeological excavation in the middle of the square and some lovely neoclassical buildings scattered around (one of them is the National Bank of Greece's Cultural Centre). The Gregotel Pallas Athena hotel is right here, and Omonia Square is just a couple of hundred yards away.

NEED A BREAK?

Aegaion. *Loukoumades* (deep-fried dough soaked in honey with cinnamon) are making a comeback in Athenian culinary preferences, and this traditional pastry shop has been making them since 1926. ✉ *Panepistimiou 46 and Harilaou Trikoupi, Omonia Sq.* ☎ *210/381-4621* ⊕ *www.loukoumades-aigaion.gr.*

Krinos. For a true taste of bygone Athens, don't miss Krinos, an endearingly old-timey café that serves Athens's best *loukoumades*—irresistible, doughnutlike fritters sprinkled with cinnamon and drizzled with a honeyed syrup based on a Smyrna recipe. Krinos has been serving the treat since it opened its doors in the 1920s and also makes excellent *boughatsa* (cream pies), *rizogalo* (rice pudding), and kaymak-flavored ice cream, an eastern version of vanilla; it is closed Sunday. Squeeze into one of the many tables and enjoy your treat with the old gents and ladies who have been regulars for decades. ✉ *Aiolou 87, Omonia Sq.* ☎ *210/321-6852.*

PANGRATI ΠΑΓΚΡΑΤΙ

Just behind the marble Panathenaic Stadium, which hosted the first Olympic Games of modern times in 1896, Pangrati is filled with concrete apartment blocks as well as such leafy squares as Platia Proskopon and Platia Varnava. Unfortunately, only a few neoclassical buildings from the turn of the 20th century survived the building boom of the 1960s. This is a safe and quiet neighborhood, with Central Athens a comfortable half-hour walk (there is also good bus service). The First Cemetery of Athens is located in Pangrati, and notable politicians and personalities in recent Greek history are buried here. The neighborhood also has a few noteworthy tavernas and restaurants.

AMBELOKIPI ΑΜΠΕΛΟΚΗΠΟΙ

This mostly residential neighborhood that is bounded by Kifissias, Vassilissis Sofias, and Alexandras avenues, Ambelokipi has the dubious honor of being the second most densely populated district (after Kypseli) in Athens. The United States Embassy is here, while trendy Mavili Square comes alive on hot summer nights as people from the nearby bars come out—with drinks in hand—looking for a cool breeze by the square's water fountain.

ILISIA ΙΛΙΣΙΑ

On the outskirts of Central Athens, this densely populated neighborhood takes its name from the river Ilisos, which once flowed here (between the streets Michalakopoulou and Kalirrois) before it was drained in the 1960s to create space for the construction of apartment blocks and the expansion of the city's road network. It is also known for its many hospitals built early in the 20th century. It is still within easy reach of the main sights (via Megaron Mousikis metro station) and a bit closer to the Eleftherios Venizelos Airport than more central neighborhoods like Monastiraki and Plaka, and offers some excellent accommodation and dining options.

KAISARIANI ΚΑΙΣΑΡΙΑΝΗ

Kaisariani is north of Pangrati, on the foot of Mt. Hymettus, about 3 km (2 miles) away from Central Athens. It is mostly known as one of the residential suburbs that welcomed thousands of Greek refugees from Asia Minor after the Smyrna catastrophe of 1922. Kaisariani Square has traditionally housed a plethora of fish tavernas.

NEOS KOSMOS ΝΕΟΣ ΚΟΣΜΟΣ

Not too far from Athens's historic center lies another neighborhood, which was created in order to accommodate Greek refugees who arrived by the thousands after the Smyrna catastrophe of 1922. Its name means "New World" in Greek. Opposite the main entrance of the Athenaeum Intercontinental Hotel, it is still possible to see today some of the original surviving refugee buildings. They are bare, simple, and functional, built in the Bauhaus style of the 1930s—and still occupied today by immigrants, the Dougrouti, who moved into the area in the 1980s. The recent arrival of the Onassis Cultural Centre, together with its award-winning restaurant, has added to the artistic flair of Neos Kosmos.

KIFISSIA ΚΗΦΙΣΙΑ

One of the wealthiest suburbs of Athens, leafy Kifissia used to be an aristocratic resort and was also linked to powerful political families that influenced Greece's turbulent history. Some of the impressive mansions still remain scattered around the terminal train station (Line 1, which continues to the port of Piraeus). But most people come here today for the shopping and entertainment options.

WHERE TO EAT

Doesn't anybody eat at home anymore? When you're on vacation, travelers don't have much choice in the matter, but these days—even in the throes of the current economic crisis—Athenians are going out to restaurants (many of which have lowered their prices accordingly) in record numbers. And it's easy for visitors to the capital to become a part of the clatter, chatter, and song, especially at the city's neighborhood tavernas.

These Athenian landmarks were famous for their wicker chairs that inevitably pinched your bottom, checkered tablecloths covered with butcher paper, wobbly tables that needed coins under one leg, and wine drawn from the barrel and served in small metal carafes. Today, some of their clientele has moved up to a popular new restaurant hybrid: the "neo-taverna," which serves traditional fare in surroundings that are more stylish than the usual tavern decor of island posters and wooden figurines; most are located in the up-and-coming industrial-cum-arty districts of Central Athens, such as Gazi-Kerameikos and Metaxourgeio. At the same time, enduring in popularity are the traditional *magereika* ("cookeries"): humble, no-frills eateries where the food, usually displayed behind glass windows, is cooked Grandma's style—it's simple, honest, time-tested, filling comfort (note that some noteworthy new magereika, like Mother's Kitchen and Melilotos, are located around the bustling Ayias Irinis Square and may even be open for dinner). Even local fast-food chain Goody's has been influenced by this style of cooking and offers a seasonal selection of dishes and salads that emulate home cooking.

Trends? Athens's got 'em. On the one hand, there is a marked return to Greek regional cooking, especially Cretan cuisine, widely regarded as one of the healthiest versions of the olive oil–rich Mediterranean diet. On the other hand, Athenians are increasingly eager to explore international flavors. With many groundbreaking chefs obsessed with modern nouveau cuisine, there was, for a while, a real danger of some loss of tradition. Since then, things have stabilized. What saved the day were Greek ingredients: fresh out of the garden and right off the boat, they inspired chefs to get reacquainted with their culinary roots. A whole constellation of hip, all-in-one bar-restaurants have emerged, revolving around star chefs and glitterati customers. Sleek interior designs, very late-night hours, dedicated DJs, and adjoining lounges full of beautiful people have become Athenian recipes for success.

But some things remain eternal. Athenian dining is seasonal. In August, when residents scatter to the hills and seaside, many restaurants and tavernas close, with the hippest bar-restaurants reopening at choice seaside positions. And visitors remain shocked by how late Greeks dine. It's normal (even on a weekday) to show up for a meal at 9 or 10 and to leave long after midnight, only to head off for drinks. Hotel restaurants, seafood places, and Plaka tavernas keep very late hours. Most places serve lunch from about noon to 4 (and sometimes as late as 6) and dinner from about 8 or 9 until at least midnight. When in Athens, don't hesitate to adopt this Zorbaesque lifestyle. Eat, drink, party, and enjoy life—knowing full well that, as a traveler, there can always be a siesta the next day.

CLOSE UP

The Greek Fish Taverna

Enjoying the bounty of the seas that wash against Greek shores can be a fishy business. The waters have been overfished for decades and much "Greek" fish served today is often frozen from other waters. Take heart, though. You can still feast on delicious fish in Greece—it's just a question of what you order, and where.

Patrons of fish restaurants are usually greeted with iced displays of the catch of the day. Proprietors will often spout some mumbo-jumbo about the fish being caught only an hour earlier—allow the shills some poetic license and go for the operative word here: *fresco,* fresh, as opposed to *katepsigmeno,* frozen.

The fish you choose will be sold by the portion, *merida,* and priced by the kilo. Expect to pay at least €55 a kilo for such popular fish as *xifia,* swordfish; *lavraki,* sea bass; *tsipoura,* sea bream; and *barbounia,* red mullet.

Yes, fish is expensive in Greece, but remember: that price is per kilo, and the portion you order may well weigh, and cost, less.

WHAT TO ORDER
Garides, shrimp, are often served deliciously as *saganaki,* baked with fresh tomatoes and feta cheese and brought to the table sizzling.

Sardelles, sardines, are grilled, fried, or eaten raw and marinated. *Papalina*

are small sardines, and *atherina* are very small sardines.

Gavros, anchovies, are almost always fried and served with lemon and vinegar.

Kalamari, squid, are often fried. A far more satisfying treat is whole kalamari, grilled or stuffed with rice and herbs and baked. A tasty relative is the *soupia,* cuttlefish, usually baked in tomato sauce.

Htapodi, octopus, is grilled, marinated in vinegar and oil, or stewed with tomatoes and onions.

Mydia, mussels, are usually steamed, and are often taken out of their shells and served in risotto, seafood pasta, or salads.

OLD-TIME FAVORITES
In addition to fresh fish, keep an eye out for these old standards. *Taramasalata,* fish roe salad, is a tasty spread, a poor man's caviar made from carp eggs, blended with olive oil, lemon juice, and garlic.

Kakavia and *psarosoupa* are variations of fish soup, usually made from pieces of whatever fish is available, simmered in broth with vegetables, and always embellished with the special flourishes of the individual cook.

Bakaliaros, cod, is often served as *bakaliaros skordalia,* dipped in batter and deep-fried.

3

DINING, ATHENS STYLE
Taverna culture is all about sharing. People often order their own main meat, fish, or vegetable courses, but often share these, salads, and appetizers with the entire dinner party. It's a nice alternative to being stuck with just one choice. Vegetarians will find some of their best options in the appetizers, though they'd be wise to avoid grill restaurants, where fried potatoes may be their only option. Tipping is less strict than in

many countries. There is a service charge on the bill, but it doesn't necessarily go to the staff, so Athenians often leave a tip of 10%. Feel free to request tap water in a pitcher (it's good in Athens) as opposed to bottled water, which may be brought automatically to your table without your request. As in most other cosmopolitan cities, dress varies from casual to fancy, according to the establishment. Although Athens is informal and none of the restaurants listed here requires a jacket or tie, locals make an effort to look their best when out on the town, so you may feel more comfortable dressing up a bit, especially at more-expensive places. After years of swallowing secondhand smoke, the scales are tilting in nonsmokers' favor. Smoking is no longer permitted inside bars and restaurants (though some still allow smoking in their outside areas). Some larger establishments, however, are allowed to have special smoking sections. It's best to check a restaurant's smoking policy by phone first. Children are welcome in most places, but it's best to check in advance for upscale establishments.

Use the coordinate (⊕ B2) at the end of each listing to locate a site on the corresponding map.

DINING PRICES IN EUROS

	$	$$	$$$	$$$$
Restaurants	Under €16	€16–€25	€26–€40	Over €40

Restaurant prices are the average cost of a main course at dinner or, if dinner is not served, at lunch.

MAKRIYIANNI ΜΑΚΡΥΓΙΑΝΝΗ

Makriyianni eateries have the distinct advantage of a prestigious location and unbeatable views of the Acropolis; the food is also highly recommended by the locals.

$$$ MEDITERRANEAN Fodor's Choice ★ 🍴 **Dionysos Zonars.** Location, location, location used to be the catchphrase that best summed up the raison d'être of this famously historic restaurant. It just happened to be the spot where movies were always filmed (those window views!), political treaties were signed, and tourists rested their feet after their heated Acropolis climbs. But a change of management and renovation work have lifted this legendary high-end restaurant up another notch. It now serves high-quality, traditional Greek and international dishes with a creative twist, such as *arnaki ambelourgou* (lamb wrapped in vine leaves, with melted cheese and vegetables) and *kritharoto me garides* (Greek pasta in tomato sauce with shrimp). The traditional syrupy *baklava* dessert is also exceptional. Extending all the good vibes, the adjoining café now serves breakfast and stays open until after midnight. [$] *Average main: €30* ✉ *Robertou Galli 43, Makriyianni* ☎ *210/923–3182* 🌐 *www.dionysoszonars.gr* ✍ *Reservations essential* ⊕ *C5.*

$$ GREEK Fodor's Choice ★ 🍴 **Manimani.** Featuring inspired recipes—and many ingredients—from the southern Peloponnese's Mani region, Manimani strikes the perfect balance between sophistication and heartiness. Located in a converted neoclassic residence, the decor has the relaxed precision of an upscale home-decor catalog (a gauzy drape or rag rug here, a

beautiful glass vase there), but the food and extensive regional wine list quickly take center stage. It's comfort food that sweetly screams "village"—from the *kayiana* omelet with citrus-flavored sausage to the regional noodles and rich salads. The chef adds delicate new fruity or spicy touches to dishes and embraces organic products at this spot just around the corner from the Acropolis metro. It's also open for late lunch (kitchen opens at 2:30), which makes it the perfect pit-stop after visiting the Acropolis and its museum. [$] *Average main: €18* ✉ *Falirou 10, Makriyianni* ☎ *210/921–8180* 🌐 *www.manimani.com.gr* ✍ *Reservations essential* ✣ *D5.*

$$ GREEK Fodor's Choice ★ 🍴 **Strofi.** Walls lined with autographed photos of actors from the nearby Odeon of Herodes Atticus attest to Strofi's success with the after-theater crowd that flocks to the Greek festival. Despite the strong following among tourists, the renovated rooftop garden with dramatic views of the lighted Acropolis still attracts locals who have been coming here for decades. In fact, the amazing views come close to stealing the show, although the cuisine comes a very close second. Start with some *mezedes,* including the smoked eggplant salad or a velvety tzatziki, which perfectly complements the baked zucchini. For the main course, choose roast lamb wrapped in vine leaves and stuffed with cheese, the rooster in wine sauce served with Greek pasta, or a variety platter of specially grilled meats. Reservations are essential for the rooftop garden with the famed Acropolis view. [$] *Average main: €25* ✉ *Rovertou Galli 25, Makriyianni* ☎ *210/921–4130* 🌐 *www.strofi.gr* ✍ *Reservations essential* 🕓 *Closed Mon.* ✣ *C5.*

PLAKA ΠΛΑΚΑ

Popular Plaka delights in its traditional homes, winding alleys, and bustling cafés and gift shops.

$$$ GREEK 🍴 **Daphne's.** The refined Mediterranean and Greek dishes (such as pork with celery and egg lemon sauce, fricassee of melt-off-the-bone lamb with greens, rabbit in Mavrodaphne wine sauce and the traditional *moussaka*) help make Daphne's one of the most exclusive (and at times pricey) destinations in Plaka. The Pompeian frescoes on the walls, the fragments of an ancient Greek building in the garden, and the tasteful restoration of the neoclassic building in terra-cotta and ochre hues also contribute to a pleasant and romantic evening. [$] *Average main: €35* ✉ *Lysikratous 4, Plaka* ☎ *210/322–7991* 🌐 *www.daphnesrestaurant.gr* ✣ *D5.*

$$ SEAFOOD 🍴 **I Palia Taverna tou Psarra.** Founded way back in 1898, this is one of the few remaining Plaka tavernas serving reliably good food as well as having the obligatory mulberry-shaded terrace (with excellent Acropolis views). The previous owners (the taverna is now run by a well-known family of Greek restaurateurs) claimed to have served Brigitte Bardot and Laurence Olivier, but it's the number of Greeks who come here that testifies to Psarra's (aka the Fisherman's Tavern) appeal. Oil-oregano marinated octopus and *gavros* (a small fish) are good appetizers. Simple, tasty entrées include rooster in wine, *arnaki pilino* (lamb baked in clay pots), and pork chops with ouzo. Can't make up your mind? Try the *ouzokatastasi* ("ouzo situation"), a plate of tidbits to nibble while you

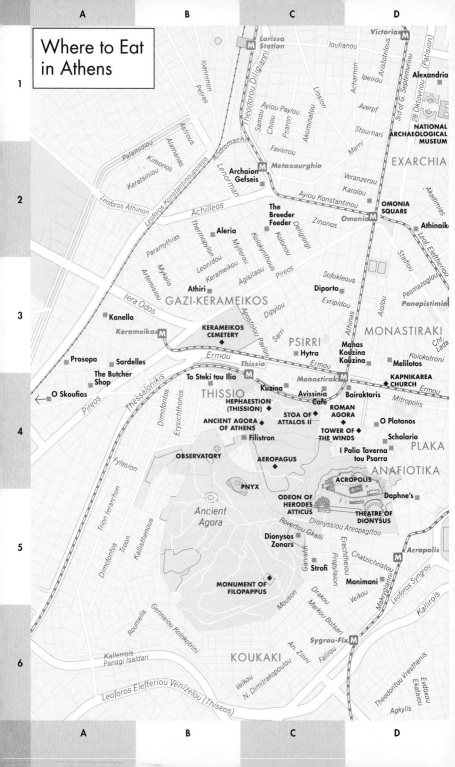

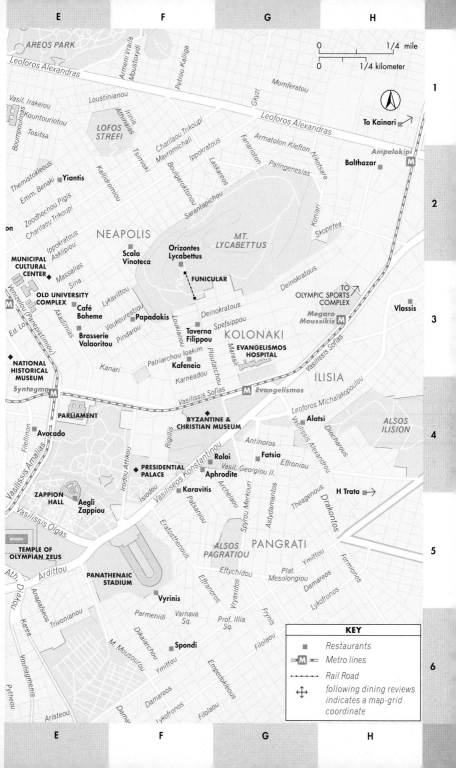

BEST BETS FOR ATHENS DINING

Fodor's Choice★

Aegli Zappiou, $$$, p. 151
Aleria, $$$, p. 154
Athiri, $$, p. 152
Café Avissinia, $$, p. 151
Dionysos Zonars, $$$, p. 144
Hytra, $$$$, p. 151
Kuzina, $$$, p. 150
Manimani, $$, p. 144
Papadakis, $$$$, p. 155
Sardelles, $$, p. 153
Spondi, $$$$, p. 158
Strofi, $$, p. 145

By Price

$

Avocado, p. 150
Bairaktaris, p. 149

$$

Athinaikon, p. 157
Café Avissinia, p. 151
Café Boheme, p. 155
Kanella, p. 152
Manimani, p. 144
O Platanos, p. 148
Sardelles, p. 153
To Steki tou Ilia, p. 150
Vlassis, p. 161
Yiantes, p. 157

$$$

Aleria, p. 154
Balthazar, p. 160
Daphne's, p. 145
Dionysos Zonars, p. 144
Kuzina, p. 150
Orizontes Lycabettus, p. 155
Prosopa, p. 153

$$$$

Hytra, p. 151
Spondi, p. 158

decide. A bit hard to find, it's definitely worth the effort. [$] *Average main: €20* ✉ *Erechtheos 16, and Erotokritou 12, Plaka* ☎ *210/321–8733* 🌐 *www.psaras-taverna.gr* ✣ *D4.*

$$ GREEK 🍴 **O Platanos.** Set on a picturesque pedestrianized square, this is one of the oldest tavernas in Plaka (established 1932); while not as good as it used to be, it's still worth a stop. It is a district landmark—set midway between the Tower of the Winds and the Museum of Greek Popular Musical Instruments. Although the rooms here are cozily adorned with old paintings and photos, most of the crowd opts to relax under the courtyard's plane trees (which give the place its name). Locals come here because the food is good Greek home cooking. Don't miss the oven-baked potatoes, lamp or veal casserole with spinach or eggplant, the stuffed squid, and the cheap but delicious barrel retsina. It's also open for lunch. [$] *Average main: €17* ✉ *Diogenous 4, Plaka* ☎ *210/322–0666* 💳 *No credit cards* 🕓 *Closed Sun. June–Aug. No dinner Sun.* ✣ *D4.*

$ GREEK 🍴 **Scholarhio.** A favorite with university students, tourists, and grizzled workers, this open-hearted ouzo taverna offers a tasty daily platter of all the best in home-cooked Greek cuisine. Waiters bring a giant tray of the day's offerings, which include such favorites as taramosalata, Smyrna-style tzatziki, cuttlefish stewed with onions, *lahanodolmades* (cabbage rolls), eggplant dip, fried calamari, moussaka, and *bekri mezedes* (wine-marinated pork cutlets). You can choose between one of 14 menus, based on the number of people dining and the number of dishes desired. Dessert (traditional Greek halva) is on the house. [$] *Average main: €14* ✉ *Tripodon 14, Plaka* ☎ *210/324–7605* 🌐 *www.scholarhio.gr* ✣ *D4.*

MONASTIRAKI ΜΟΝΑΣΤΗΡΑΚΙ

Northwest of Plaka, Monastiraki retains the gritty charm of an Anatolian bazaar to magnetize the city's hard-core café and bar crowd.

$ GREEK 🍴 **Bairaktaris.** Run by the same family since 1879, this is an almost legendary souvlaki eatery in Monastiraki Square. After admiring the painted wine barrels, the black-and-white stills of Greek film stars, and the snapshots of politicians who have held lunches here, go to the window case to view the day's *magirefta* (stove-top-cooked dish, usually made earlier)—maybe *pastitsio,* a Greek oven-baked pasta dish with minced meat and béchamel sauce. Or sit down and order the famed gyro or the kebab platter. [$] *Average main: €10* ✉ *Monastiraki Sq. 2, Monastiraki* ☎ *210/321–3036* ✥ *D4.*

$ GREEK 🍴 **Manas Kouzina Kouzina.** Homey cuisine, served at a counter (there's no table service), with prices lower than a fast food meal are the secrets that keep Mother's Kitchen successful. Every dish comes in three sizes, so you can choose based on how hungry you are. For about €6 you get a small (but still generous) main course with a side salad. Pick from six to seven daily dishes, which you can see laid out on large trays, then pick a salad and a Greek soda to drink, and sit outside at one of the long tables—or inside, where you can admire the beautiful mosaic floor and the clean, simple decor. All the ingredients are locally sourced, and you may feel as if you have just had a meal in a Greek home. Plus you are in the bustling and now very happening Ayias Irinis Square. [$] *Average main: €10* ✉ *Aiolou 27A, Monastiraki* ☎ *210/325–2335* ✥ *D3.*

$ GREEK 🍴 **Melilotos.** In the city's main shopping district, the compact but modern Melilotos offers a large variety of quick-bite options, from traditional Greek dishes (for example, veal cooked in beer with mustard and mushrooms) to a variety of pies (like the wild greens pie, *hortopita*), to freshly made sandwiches, to coffee and dessert. It's an ideal spot for a quick, refreshing stopover regardless of the time of day. [$] *Average main: €15* ✉ *Kalamiotou 19, Monastiraki* ☎ *210/322–2458* 🌐 *www.melilotos.gr* ✥ *D3.*

THISSIO ΘΗΣΕΙΟ

Thissio's pedestrianized streets are perfect meeting points for coffee lovers, but the mezedopoleio there are also of a high caliber and offer beautiful Acropolis views.

$$ GREEK 🍴 **Filistron.** In warm weather it's worth stopping by this place just to have a drink and enjoy the delightful, painterly scene from the roof garden—a sweeping view of the Acropolis and Mt. Lycabettus. In cooler weather take a seat in the sunny, cheerful dining room off a pedestrian walkway and enjoy a traditional Greek coffee prepared on hot ashes (*xovoli)* and homemade cookies. The long list of mezedes includes both classics as well as more unusual dishes: *tigania* pork bites cooked in wine sauce; traditional Cretan *bourek* with potatoes, zucchini, and soft cheese; kidneys with olive oil and oregano; and an array of regional cheeses, all washed down with a flowery white *hima* (barrel wine). The service is top-notch. [$] *Average main: €24* ✉ *Apostolou Pavlou 23,*

Thissio ☎ *210/342–2897* 🌐 *www.filistron.com* ✍ *Reservations essential* ⏲ *Closed 1 wk in Aug. No lunch weekdays* ✥ *C4.*

$$$ GREEK FUSION Fodor's Choice ★

🍴 **Kuzina.** Sleek, dazzlingly decorated, and moodily lit, this bistro attracts many style-conscious Athenians. But Kuzina isn't just a pretty face. The food—especially the inventive seafood and pasta dishes concocted by chef Aris Tsanaklides—is among the best in Athens, standing out on touristy Adrianou. Happily, the decor is almost as attractive as the reasonably priced, three-course prix-fixe menu. The main room soars skyward, glittering with birdcage chandeliers and factory ducts, with a vast lemon-yellow bar set below a spotlighted wall lined with hundreds of wine bottles. The menu showcases newfangled Greek as well as old faves, including the 12-hour slow-roasted pork with lemon and basil sauce. Whether you sit outside on the street, in the spectacular main dining room, or on the roof (the *Tarazza* offers a fantastic view of the Acropolis and some tasty cocktails), finish your meal off with a delicious dessert such as the white-chocolate mousse with strawberries and rose meringue. [$] *Average main: €27* ✉ *Adrianou 9, Thissio* ☎ *210/324–0133* 🌐 *www.kuzina.gr* ✍ *Reservations essential* ✥ *C4.*

$$ STEAKHOUSE

🍴 **To Steki tou Ilia.** Athenians who love fresh-grilled lamb chops and thick-cut fried potatoes that could have come from their *yiayia's* very kitchen flock to this classic taverna along a quiet pedestrianized street in Thissio. It's a place to relax with friends: split a giant plate of *paidakia* (lamb chops), fries, creamy tzatziki, and fava bean spread. Even the bread is prepared the Greek way: grilled and sprinkled with olive oil and oregano. The tables on the street fill rapidly so arrive early to soak in the Greek island vibe. The original old-fashioned hangout with a gated garden is on Eptahalkou, and a more recent and more modern-looking extension is a bit farther down Thessalonikis street (Thessaolonikis 7; 210/342–2407; closed Mon.; no lunch during the week). Reservations are accepted, but credit cards are not. [$] *Average main: €17* ✉ *Eptachalkou 5, Thissio* ☎ *210/345–8052* 💳 *No credit cards* ⏲ *No lunch Tues.–Fri.; no dinner Sun.* ✥ *B4.*

SYNTAGMA SQUARE ΠΛΑΤΕΙΑ ΣΥΝΤΑΓΜΑΤΟΣ

Syntagma, a bustling central square between Parliament and Ermou street, is also popular with tourists.

$ VEGETARIAN

🍴 **Avocado.** For such a tiny spot in a narrow street just off the Greek Parliament building, small but stylish Avocado has many devoted fans. And not without reason. This friendly vegetarian and vegan corner also appeals to non-vegetarians (and caters to those with celiac disease as well). Really, anyone who likes a healthy meal based on fresh produce, complemented by deliciously fresh smoothies, is attracted to the cool, green-hued interior and the few pavement tables. Big hits are the Margherita pizza, the *Atma Ham* vegetable mix with organic black rice noodles, and the forest mushroom burger. The chef's Asian origins account for the menu's tasteful leaning toward the Far East. [$] *Average main: €15* ✉ *Nikis 30, Syntagma* ☎ *210/323–7878* 🌐 *www.avocadoathens.com* ⏲ *No dinner Sun.* ✥ *E4.*

$$$
MODERN GREEK
Fodor'sChoice
★

X **Aegli Zappiou.** The lush Zappeion Gardens have always been a tranquil green oasis for stressed-out Athenians, who head here to gaze at the distant views of the Parthenon and Temple of Olympian Zeus, catch an open-air cinema showing, or chill out at the landmark café Aegli Zappiou. Sharing the same premises as the café, this chic restaurant is luring fashionables, business people, and even families. It is a must during summer with its beautiful garden—shady in daytime, beautifully lighted at night. The food has a modern Greek touch, and it offers excellent value for money. Try the take on traditional local dishes as the Greek salad, fried zucchini balls, or the kebabs. The meat platter is another excellent choice. After dinner, have a drink and listen to the latest grooves at the Aegli bar. Reservations are recommended for dinner in the summer. $ *Average main: €30* ⊠ *Zappio Megaro, Syntagma* ☎ *210/336–9364* ⊕ *www.aeglizappiou.gr* ✛ *E5.*

PSIRRI ΨΥΡΡΗ

The former warehouse district between Omonia and Monastiraki is party central for Athens.

$$
GREEK
Fodor'sChoice
★

X **Café Avissinia.** Facing hoary and merchant-packed Abyssinia Square, this timeworn but exceptional eatery—the Greek version of a French bistro—is popular with locals who want home-cooked traditional food with a heavy Asia Minor culinary influence and endless servings of the excellent barrel wine and local ouzo. Diners love to nestle within the elegant glass-and-wood interior as they sample the mussels and rice pilaf, the wine-marinated octopus with pasta, the fresh garden salad, or any of the dips (including the spicy eggplant-and-garlic spread). Little wonder so many head here to relax after a day of shopping at the nearby flea market. Another plus: music is often in the air—on weekend afternoons, you can enjoy accordion music (and the waiters' impromptu piano accompaniment!). $ *Average main: €18* ⊠ *Abyssinia Sq., Kinetou 7, Psirri* ☎ *210/321–7047* ⊕ *www.avissinia.gr* ⊘ *Tues.–Sat. 11–1, Sun. 11–7* ⊘ *Closed Mon.* ✛ *C4.*

$$$$
CONTEMPORARY
Fodor'sChoice
★

X **Hytra.** The Onassis Cultural Centre is the perfect new home for Hytra, one of the city's most fashionable eateries, which has been awarded a second Michelin star for its avant-garde molecular cuisine. Young Greek chef Nikos Karathanos has created the adventurous menu, which is enthusiastically explained to the uninitiated by the knowledgable staff. If you find it hard to choose, sample the degustation menu, with such noteworthy creations as "dirt" made from porcini mushrooms, potato foam, and edible foil paper decorating a not-so-traditional version of moussaka. For those with more mainstream tastes, Simply Hytra bistro is next door, where fellow chef Chrisanthos Karamolengos offers mainly Greek finger food with a modern twist: hummus served with sausages from the city of Drama; burgers with *graviera* cheese, pine nuts, and pomegranate; and a winning and very homey chicken soup. Every summer Hytra's faithful clientele move up to the 7th floor, where the bar and restaurant offer spectacular views of the Acropolis. Or they pick up and move from the restaurant's post-industrial city setting to a completely different seasonal home ever nearer to the sea; check the

website for details of the latest venue of *Galazia Hytra.* $ *Average main:*
€60 ⊠ *Onassis Cultural Centre, 107–109 Andrea Syngrou avenue, 6th*
floor, Neos Kosmos ☏ *210/331–6767* ⊕ *www.hytra.gr* ⌖ *Reservations*
essential ⊙ *Closed Wed. and Thurs. No lunch* ⊹ *C3.*

GAZI-KERAMEIKOS ΓΚΑΖΙ

West of Psirri, Gazi-Kerameikos has turned into the city's hottest art,
culture, and nightlife zone. The new Kerameikos metro station has also
made it ultraconvenient.

$$ ⨯ **Athiri.** Once you step into the lush and peaceful urban garden of
MODERN GREEK this popular restaurant (now with a Michelin star), you'll relax imme-
Fodor'sChoice diately. This food star, which has very user-friendly prices, is located
★   on a backstreet of Kerameikos, a formerly run-down neighborhood
that is undergoing a rejuvenation, and its presence is a big plus for the
area. The casual elegance of the setting is perfectly matched by the cre-
ative Greek cuisine on the menu: smoked aubergine salad with spring
onion, parsley, and roasted red peppers is a perfect starter; the salt cod
"doughnut" with beetroot salad, capers, and cold fish sauce, and the
veal with spinach are firm favorites among the main courses. There is
a useful play area for the children, and on cold nights, you will find the
interior of the old building cozy and warm. On Sunday Athiri is open
only for lunch. $ *Average main: €25* ⊠ *Plateon 15, Gazi-Kerameikos*
☏ *210/346-2983* ⊕ *www.athirirestaurant.gr* ⌖ *Reservations essential*
⊙ *Closed Mon. No lunch Tues.–Sat. No dinner Sun.* ⊹ *B3.*

$$ ⨯ **The Butcher Shop.** A carnivore's paradise, this simple taverna does its
STEAKHOUSE meats superbly. Try the steaks, sausages, and the juicy, gigantic hamburg-
ers. Don't miss the crispy home fries, specialty cheeses, and cold cuts from
around Greece. For sides, go for a plate of fresh, vinegary beets or the
seasonal salads. The menu also offers an eclectic selection of local wines.
The lemon pie and the rice pudding feature prominently on the dessert
menu, while the complimentary *mastiha,* or mastic-flavored liqueur, from
Chios, served at the end leaves you with a sweet taste. The owners of this
heart-warming eatery with tables out on the pavements when the weather
allows are the same people behind another success story, the Sardelles fish
restaurant right next door. In both places, you can order half portions,
in order to sample as many different dishes as possible. $ *Average main:*
€20 ⊠ *Persefonis 19, Gazi-Kerameikos* ☏ *210/341–3440* ⊹ *A4.*

$$ ⨯ **Kanella.** Housed in a cool, airy building with modern and traditional
MODERN GREEK touches, this lively example of a neo-taverna is infused with Gazi's cre-
ative energy. The excellent home cooking includes the simmered pork
with mushrooms and mashed potatoes; the spaghetti Bolognese (con-
sidered one of the best in Athens); the grilled-chicken mille-feuille with
roasted *manouri* (goat cheese), tomato, and fresh basil sauce; the fried
zucchini balls; and a tasty salad with boiled zucchini, sliced avocado, and
grated *graviera* cheese. Wine comes in beautifully designed glass carafes.
Warning: when the neutral-tone interior gets busy, it gets almost psy-
chedelically loud. Thankfully, there are outside pavement tables in good
weather. $ *Average main: €20* ⊠ *Konstantinoupoleos 70 and Evmolpi-*
don, Gazi-Kerameikos ☏ *210/347–6320* ⊕ *www.kanellagazi.gr* ⊹ *A3.*

$$ SEAFOOD Fodor's Choice ★ 🍴 **Sardelles.** If you love seafood and don't want to pay a fortune for it, don't miss this trendy (and by now classic) eatery in the heart of party-loving Gazi. The simple lines of Greek island decor are evident in *kafeneio* (coffeehouse) tables and 1950s-style metal-frame garden chairs picked up at auctions and painted dazzling white. Try the cod cutlets, the grilled fish drizzled with mastic-flavored sauce, and the house specialty sardines ("sardelles")—either the classic recipe or the "hot and spicy" in rock salt. Also recommended are any of the house salads, especially the mixed greens with goat cheese and pomegranate seeds, and the potato-and-zucchini salad with spearmint. Top it off with a free hot *mastiha* drink and a slice of lemon or chocolate tart. In the summer the tables extend out to the busy street bustling with nightlife. Sardelles offers consistently high value for money; the fish is guaranteed for its freshness. [$] *Average main: €20* ✉ *Persofonis 15, Gazi-Kerameikos* ☎ *210/347–8050* ✢ *A3.*

ROUF ΡΟΥΦ

The industrial neighborhood of Rouf offers some unexpectedly excellent dining options, even if a bit off the beaten track.

$$ GREEK 🍴 **O Skoufias.** This pretty neo-taverna has some of the best food in town—and at reasonable prices. Menus are the royal-blue lined notebooks used by Greek schoolchildren; the proprietors have handwritten the Cretan-inspired offerings on the pages. Enjoy Skoufias's signature (and wildly popular and excellently priced at €8) honey-roasted pork shank, or Sfakian (i.e., from the town of Sfakia) lamb with manouri cheese, which is so tender it just falls off the bone, at one of the tables outside. Other excellent choices include braised beef with eggplant purée (*hunikiar beyianti,* as it is called), *dolmadakia* (stuffed wine leaves) with pine nuts, potato salad with orange peels and herbs, and syrupy *ravani* cake with mastic-flavor *kaïmaki* ice cream. On weekends O Skoufias is open for both lunch and dinner. [$] *Average main: €16* ✉ *Troon 69, Petralona* ☎ *210/341–2252* 💳 *No credit cards* 🕓 *No lunch weekdays* ✢ *A4.*

$$$ GREEK FUSION 🍴 **Prosopa.** Despite the regular influx of local celebrities, this modern, industrial looking bar-restaurant near the train tracks has never lost its friendly, down-to-earth face (after all, *prosopa* means "faces" in Greek). Service is impeccable —expect to be treated "on the house" with a plate of appetizers upon arrival, as well as with dessert and liqueurs upon departure. Menu faves include shrimp wrapped in spaghetti of potato with mango sauce; vegetable salad with hot goat cheese, pistachio, and apple vinagrette; or the rump steak with espresso sauce and figs. Food and wine are of exceptional quality, music is played at the right level, the waiting staff is attentive and helpful: this hip eaterie is definitely worth the short taxi ride to its slightly off-the-beaten-track location (where it moved from its previous home in 2009). On Sunday lunch is also available. [$] *Average main: €26* ✉ *Meg. Vasileiou 52 and Konstantinoupoleos 4, Rouf* ☎ *210/341–3433* 🌐 *www.prosopa.gr* ✍ *Reservations essential* 🕓 *No lunch Mon.–Sat.* ✢ *A3.*

METAXOURGEIO ΜΕΤΑΞΟΥΡΓΕΙΟ

This former red-light district gets the green light when it comes to award-winning and avant-garde dining.

$$$ MEDITERRANEAN Fodor's Choice ★

🍴 **Aleria.** Athenian trend-watchers are so enthusiastic about the gritty-cool neighborhood of Metaxourgeio that they say it will soon be like Paris's boho-chic Marais district. Restaurants, including this award-winning gem of neoclassic design and inventive Mediterranean cuisine, are one reason the area's star is rising. Chef Gikas Xenakis's cooking is a serious candidate for future notoriety, while young restaurateur Nikoforos Kehayiadakis will be the perfect host for your evening. Try the seafood orzo risotto with grilled peppers, salami, and basil, or the slow-cooked pork belly with celery root purée, coriander sauce, and onion pickles. Wine Wednesday is extremely popular and provides a perfect introduction to small Greek wine producers, combined with eclectic tastes from the menu (at an extremely affordable fixed price). You'll undoubtedly agree that the restaurant is stylish yet scrumptious. [$] *Average main: €32* ✉ *Meg. Alexandrou 57, Metaxourgeio* ☎ *210/522–2633* 🌐 *www.aleria.gr* ✍ *Reservations essential* 🕒 *Closed Sun. No lunch* ✣ *B2.*

$$$ GREEK

🍴 **Archaion Gefseis.** The epicurean owners of "Ancient Flavors" combed through texts and archaeological records in an effort to recreate foods eaten in antiquity—not to mention how they were eaten, with spoon and knife only. Dishes like pancetta seasoned with thyme, stuffed suckling pig (which must be specially ordered two days in advance), and squid cooked in its ink prove, if anything, the continuity between ancient and modern Greek cuisine. There's an undeniable kitsch factor in the setting, but it is a unique experience to enjoy at least once. [$] *Average main: €27* ✉ *Karaiskaki Sq., Kodratou 22, Metaxourgeio* ☎ *210/523–9661* 🌐 *www.archeon-gefseis.gr* 🕒 *No lunch* ✣ *C2.*

$$$ ECLECTIC

🍴 **The Breeder Feeder.** You wouldn't think Athens is on the bleeding edge of the restaurant scene but what can top this? This contemporary art space, housed in a masterfully converted old ice-cream factory in the hot Metaxourgeio neighborhood, is now also an experimental, rotating restaurant, which invites different teams of chefs to cook for its eclectic crowd (in a concept not unlike the rotating exhibitions regularly held in the gallery's 1,000 feet of exhibition space). The compact 45-seater eaterie has been tastefully decorated with traditional Greek rugs and cushions, cleverly contrasting with the stark white furniture. Check the restaurant's blog, thebreederfeeder.blogspot.com, for upcoming guest chef appearances and its "opening days" (usually Tuesdays, Thursdays, and Fridays). [$] *Average main: €30* ✉ *Iasonos 45, Metaxourgeio* ☎ *210/331–7527* 🌐 *www.thebreedersystem.com* ✍ *Reservations essential* ✣ *C2.*

KOLONAKI ΚΟΛΩΝΑΚΙ

Located east of Plaka, Kolonaki is an old-money neighborhood that's a haunt for politicians, expats, and high-maintenance ladies who lunch (and shop).

$$$ MEDITERRANEAN

🍴 **Brasserie Valaoritou.** This cosmopolitan-yet-homey brasserie draws a varied crowd, from high-flying businessmen to politicians to theater buffs, who come here to enjoy a delicious cappuccino or, at lunchtime, a generous and delicious salad, or a late dinner after an evening at the theater. The menu includes a range of pasta dishes as well as traditional Greek fare like juicy lemon-oregano chicken breast and succulent lamb chops. But save room for the fabulous desserts, especially the lemon pie and the amazing *galaktoboureko* (custard in phyllo) made with Camembert cheese instead of the traditional custard. [$] *Average main: €26* ✉ *Valaoritou 15, Kolonaki* ☎ *210/361–1993* 🌐 *www.brasserie.gr* ✥ *E3.*

$$ ECLECTIC 🍴 **Café Boheme.** Comfort food and splashy cocktails abound at this petite hangout situated on the cusp of Kolonaki and the city center. The international ownership is reflected in its Mediterranean-meets-U.K. culinary style. Try the aromatic risotto with mint, beetroot, and walnuts, or the grilled seafood. And don't miss out on the mouthwatering desserts and cocktails dreamed up by Cassie (especially the mangotini). [$] *Average main: €22* ✉ *Omirou 36, Kolonaki* ☎ *210/360–8018* 🌐 *www.cafeboheme.gr* ⏲ *No lunch* ✥ *E3.*

$$ GREEK 🍴 **Kafeneio.** A Kolonaki institution, this urban-style *ouzeri* reminiscent of an old-fashioned French bistro is slightly fancier than the normal mezedopoleio, with cloth napkins, candles on the tables, and a handsome dark-wood interior, serving politicians on their lunch break from the Greek Parliament nearby. The menu offers imaginative twists on Greek classic dishes. For the freshest dishes, ask the waiter for the day's specials, which include traditional fare such as *kolokithokeftedes* (fried zucchini balls), marinated octopus, and roast suckling pig, as well as more-modern creations, such as Kafeneio's mixed greens salad with pomegranate. [$] *Average main: €25* ✉ *Loukianou 26, Kolonaki* ☎ *210/722–9056* ⏲ *Closed Sun. and 3 wks in Aug.* ✥ *F3.*

$$$ SEAFOOD 🍴 **Orizontes Lycabettus.** Have a seat on the terrace atop Mt. Lycabettus: the Acropolis glitters below, and beyond Athens unfolds like a map out to the Saronic gulf. It's tough for the dining experience to compete with such a view, although this mostly seafood restaurant has a decent kitchen and better than decent service. Best bets include the chicken with artichokes and mushrooms in a lime sauce, or the grouper cheeks with risotto in a lemon sauce. For dessert, try the Greek version of walnut pie, *karydopita*. Remember that no road goes this high: the restaurant is reached by cable car (the ticket price of €7 is deductible from your restaurant bill). A very reasonable prix-fixe option (including wine) attracts many diners. [$] *Average main: €35* ✉ *Mt. Lycabettus, Kolonaki* ☎ *210/722–7065* 🌐 *www.orizonteslycabettus.gr* ✍ *Reservations essential* ✥ *F2.*

$$$$ SEAFOOD Fodor's Choice ★ 🍴 **Papadakis.** The arrival of Greek TV chef Argiro Barbarigou has brought a breath of fresh air to this well-established seafood restaurant in Kolonaki. After a day of shopping, the elegant white tablecloths, the cool green walls and the fresh flowers on the tables of the basement eatery create a pleasant dining oasis. Or you can sit outside, in the narrow lane and under the orange trees, to watch the busy Kolonaki life. The menu is almost entirely focused on seafood although Argiro does throw some non-fish options in the mix. The Paros salad with capers, cherry tomatoes, and *xinomizithra* (sour white cheese), the shrimp with chili peppers and feta, and the crawfish with orzo in a light tomato sauce are not to be missed. The traditional fish recipes with a twist are perfectly

accompanied by sweet Vinsanto wine from Santorini. $ *Average main:* €45 ✉ *Voukourestiou 47, at Fokylidou 15, Kolonaki* 🕾 *210/360–8621* ⌂ *Reservations essential* ✛ *F3.*

$$$ ✕ **Scala Vinoteca.** Brainchild of renowned Greek chef Christoforos Pes-
WINE BAR kias, this urban wine-restaurant divides its menu into four main price ranges, with dishes priced at €6, €8, €12, and €16—the result is a flexible and budget-friendly dining option. Delicious dishes include asparagus in Mastello (sweet Santorini wine) sauce, beef tartare with marinated swedes (rutabagas), or the ravioli with shrimp and crab in a bisque seafood sauce. More than 100 wine labels are on offer, while many wines are also served by the glass. The chic, downtown location is a hidden Athenian gem, an additional bonus being that the warm mini-malist interiors have been designed by Benaki Museum Annexe archi-tects Maria Kokkinou and Andreas Kourkoulas. $ *Average main: €27* ✉ *Sina 50 and Anagnostopoulou, Kolonaki* 🕾 *210/361–0041* ⊕ *www. scalavinoteca.com* ⌂ *Reservations essential* ⊘ *Closed Sun.* ✛ *F2.*

$$ ✕ **Taverna Filippou.** This unassuming urban taverna is hardly the sort
GREEK of place you'd expect to find in chic Kolonaki, yet its devotees (since 1923) have included cabinet ministers, diplomats, actresses, and film directors. The appeal is simple: well-prepared Greek classics, mostly *ladera* (vegetable or meat casseroles cooked in an olive-oil–and–tomato sauce), *moussaka* (a baked dish of sliced eggplant layered with ground beef and smothered in a thin white sauce), and *pastitsio* (baked pasta with minced meat and a béchamel topping). Everything's home-cooked, so the menu adapts to what's fresh at the open-air produce market. In summer and on balmy spring or autumn evenings, choose a table on the pavement under the ivy; in winter, seating is in a cozy dining room a few steps below street level. $ *Average main: €20* ✉ *Xenokratous 19, Kolonaki* 🕾 *210/721–6390* ⊘ *Closed Sun. and mid-Aug. No din-ner Sat.* ✛ *F3.*

EXARCHIA ΕΞΑΡΧΕΙΑ

The student district of Exarchia offers some casual and more adventur-ous dining options.

$ ✕ **Alexandria.** Egyptian spice infuses Greek cuisine with an exotic, eclec-
GREEK FUSION tic, and dynamic menu at this popular restaurant in a restored neoclas-sical building, making for a spot that Lawrence Durrell would truly relish. The choices include simple but stunning fare such as a tomato salad with thick yogurt and caramelized onions as well as a tender lamb cooked with dried plums and apricots, and veal with vegetables and couscous. If you're an adventurous foodie, don't miss Alexandria's signature dish: tender, wine-simmered baby octopus on a creamy bed of fava. The wine list is extensive and well priced; the Om Ali dessert with warm chocolate and nuts is a dream come true; and the service is happy and welcoming. The relaxing, clean-white interior design recalls the cosmopolitan flair of the Egyptian Greeks. $ *Average main: €15* ✉ *Metsovou 13 and Rethymnou, behind Park Hotel, near Archaeologi-cal Museum, Exarchia* 🕾 *210/821–0004* ⊕ *www.alexandrianet.gr* ▤ *No credit cards* ⊘ *Closed Mon. No dinner Sun.* ✛ *D1.*

$$ 🍴 **Yiantes.** In a flower-filled courtyard—fashionably green and framed by wisteria and jasmine—you peruse a menu that, despite some modern influences, reads like an honest culinary journey through the far reaches of Greece. Although a little pricier than the norm, this neo-taverna attracts intellectuals, students, lawyers, actors, and health buffs, partly because it is co-owned by two of Greece's foremost organic farmers. Almost everything is fresh and delicious, as the chef estimates that about 90% of the ingredients he uses are organic, including the house wine. Perennial favorites on the menu include the fresh grilled cuttlefish with spinach salad, the grilled liver with caramelized onions, and the couscous with smoked pancetta, cherry tomatoes, fresh thyme, and parmesan. The bargain prix-fixe menu offers excellent value for money, [$] *Average main: €20* ✉ *Valtetsiou 44, Exarchia* ☎ *210/330–1369* 🌐 *www.yiantes.gr* ⏲ *Mon. and 1st 2 wks in Aug.* ✥ *E2.*

MEDITERRANEAN

OMONIA SQUARE ΠΛΑΤΕΙΑ ΟΜΟΝΟΙΑΣ

North of Monastiraki, Omonia, the city's main square, is busy by day and seedy by night, but it bursts with cultural diversity and the kaleidoscopic Varvakeios Agora, Athens's Central Market.

$$ 🍴 **Athinaikon.** Choose among classic specialties at this old-fashioned mezedopoleio founded in 1932: grilled octopus, shrimp croquettes with white sauce, broad beans simmered in thick tomato sauce, fresh grilled calamari, and *ameletita* (sautéed lamb testicles). All goes well with the light barrel red or ouzo. The decor is no-nonsense ouzeri, with marble tables, dark wood, and framed memorabilia. It's a favorite of attorneys, politicians, and local office workers. A new branch of this eaterie has recently opened at Mitropoleos 34, in Central Athens, with the same menu but a more modern interior. [$] *Average main: €20* ✉ *Themistokleous 2, Omonia Sq.* ☎ *210/383–8485, 210/383–5905* 🌐 *www.athinaikon.gr* ⏲ *Closed Sun. and Aug.* ✥ *D2.*

GREEK

$ 🍴 **Diporto.** It's the savvy local's treasured secret. Through the years, everyone wandering around Omonia Square has come here for lunch—butchers from the Central Market, suit-clad businessmen and lawyers, artists, migrants, and even bejeweled ladies who lunch (and they're often sitting at the same tables when it gets crowded). Owner-chef Barba Mitsos keeps everyone happy with his handful of simple, delicious, and dirt-cheap homemade dishes. There's always an exceptional *horiatiki* (Greek salad), sometimes studded with fiery-hot green pepperoncini; other favorites are his buttery *gigantes* (large, buttery white beans cooked in tomato sauce), *vrasto* (boiled goat, pork, or beef with vegetables), and fried finger-size fish. Wine is drawn directly from the barrels lining the walls. As for decor, the feeling is authentic 1950s Athens. There is no sign on the door: just walk down the staircase of this corner neoclassical building. [$] *Average main: €10* ✉ *Platia Theatrou, Socratous 9, Omonia Sq.* ☎ *210/321–1463* 💳 *No credit cards* ⏲ *No dinner. Closed Sun.* ✥ *C3.*

GREEK

3

PANGRATI ΠΑΓΚΡΑΤΙ

Urbane without being snobby or expensive, mostly residential Pangrati is a haven for academics, artists, and expats who bask in the homey warmth of this neighborhood in the southeastern quarter of the city.

$ GREEK 🍴 **Roloi.** This mezedopoleio in the up-and-coming neighborhood of Proskopon Square has had a change of ownership, which is reflected in an updated and more affordable menu. After you have tried the day's special or a round of mezedes: roasted red peppers stuffed with goat cheese, *bekri meze* ("drunken" meat stew), the marinated anchovies, and a range of salads in season, sip a complimentary homemade *limoncello* while you enjoy dessert which is also on the house. In warm weather tables go out on the *platia* (square) under the shady trees; in winter, seating is in a split-level dining room with a chic ambience (the walls are adorned by many clocks—*roloi*—which inspired the name of the place). [$] *Average main: €15* ✉ *Ptolemeon and Amynta 6, Proskopon Sq., Pangrati* ☎ *210/724–8822* ✥ *F4.*

$$ GREEK 🍴 **Fatsio.** Don't be fooled by the Italian name: the food at this old-fashioned, family-owned restaurant is all home-style Greek, albeit with an Eastern influence. Walk past the kitchen and point at what you want before taking a seat. Favorites include a "soufflé" that is actually a variation on baked macaroni-and-cheese, with slices of beef and a topping of eggplant and tomato sauce. The flavorful pasta-based dish *pastitsio* (meat pie with macaroni and béchamel sauce) is another customer-favorite. Quick service and good value for the money are the reasons for Fatsio's enduring popularity (since 1948) among both elder Kolonaki residents and office workers seeking an alternative to fast food for their lunch. [$] *Average main: €18* ✉ *Efroniou 5–7, off Rizari, Pangrati* ☎ *210/725–0028* ⏲ *Closed 1 wk in mid-Aug.* ✥ *G4.*

$ GREEK 🍴 **Karavitis.** The winter dining room maintains its prewar ambience ("since 1926") and is insulated with huge wine casks; in summer there is garden seating in a courtyard across the street (get there early so you don't end up at the noisy sidewalk tables). The classic Greek cuisine is well prepared, including pungent *tirokafteri* (a peppery cheese dip), *bekri mezes* (lamb chunks in zesty red sauce), lamb ribs (when in season), *stamnaki* (beef baked in a clay pot), and melt-in-the-mouth meatballs, the taverna's specialty. [$] *Average main: €15* ✉ *Arktinou 35, at Pausaniou, Pangrati* ☎ *210/721–5155* 🌐 *www.karavitistavern.gr* 💳 *No credit cards* ⏲ *Closed 1 wk mid-Aug. No lunch Mon.–Sat.* ✥ *F4.*

$$$$ MODERN FRENCH Fodor's Choice ★ 🍴 **Spondi.** One of Athens's most intensely designed temples to great food is justly celebrated as a feast for both the eyes and the taste buds. One salon shimmers with arty Swarovski chandeliers, walls of hot pink and cool aubergine, and chic black leather couches; for less glamour opt for the white-linen vaulted room, a beige-on-beige sanctorum; or, in summer, chill in the vast, bougainvillea-draped courtyard. No matter where you sit, you'll be able to savor the transcendentally delicious creations of chef Michel del Burgo, who has arrived with the aim to help two-star Spondi finally win its coveted third Michelin star. Highlights of their mostly French-inspired Mediterranean menu include the pan-fried foie

CLOSE UP

Greek Fast Food

Souvlaki is the original Greek fast food: spit-roasted or grilled meat, tomatoes, onions, and garlicky tzatziki wrapped in a pita. Greeks on the go have always eaten street food, such as the endless variations of cheese pie, *koulouri* (sesame-covered bread rings), roasted chestnuts or ears of grilled corn, and palm-size paper bags of nuts. But modern lifestyles and the arrival of foreign pizza and burger chains have cultivated a taste for fast food—and spawned several local brands definitely worth checking out. **Goody's** serves burgers and spaghetti as well as some salads and sandwiches. Items like baguettes with grilled vegetables or seafood salads are seasonal additions to the menu. **Everest** is tops when it comes to *tost*—oval-shaped toasted sandwich buns with any combination of fillings, from omelets and smoked turkey breast to fries, roasted red peppers, and various spreads. It also sells sweet and savory pies, ice cream, and desserts. Its main rival is **Grigoris,** a chain of sandwich and pie shops that also serves freshly squeezed orange juice and wonderful cappuccino *freddo.* If you want to sit down while you eat your fast food, look for a **Flocafe,** where you can find great iced espresso *freddo* coffee. Along with espresso, frappé, *filtrou* (drip), and cappuccino, they also serve a selection of pastries and sandwiches, including brioche with mozzarella and pesto. The newest and currently in vogue coffee chain is Mikel Coffee Company; with branches open from 5 am it's an essential stopover for sleepy Athenians on their way to work.

gras with rice popcorn, date, and vanilla; the scallops with edamame and wasabi ice cream; and the duck with turnip, bok choy, and cocoa. Or you can try the five-course "Discovery" tasting menu accompanied by selected Greek wines. For dessert, try the Alpaco chocolate from Equador. You may wish to opt for a taxi ride out to Pangrati—but isn't one of the best meals in all of Greece worth it? [$] *Average main: €60* ✉ *Pirronos 5, Varnava Sq., Pangrati* ☎ *210/756–4021* 🌐 *www.spondi.gr* ✍ *Reservations essential* ⏲ *No lunch* ✥ *F6.*

$$ GREEK 🍴 **Vyrinis.** Huge wine barrels line one wall—and white Christmas lights cover the other—in this always busy neighborhood neo-taverna located just behind the Panathenaic Stadium. In summer, couples and groups of all ages find refuge in its adjacent open-air garden and enjoy its mellow social effervescence. Choose pork stew, rabbit in lemon sauce, lamb with fries, oven-cooked perch, or go for standard nibbles like fava, grilled cheese saganaki, or the tomato-based eggplant stew. With lots of students, local celebs and staff from the nearby international schools, this tavern, run by the third generation of the same family, sees a lot of red house wine flowing with every meal. [$] *Average main: €20* ✉ *Archimidou 11, Pangrati* ☎ *210/701–2153* ⏲ *No dinner Sun.* ✥ *F5.*

AMBELOKIPI ΑΜΠΕΛΟΚΗΠΟΙ

This residential neighborhood is home to some upmarket, and very popular with chic Athenians, bar-restaurants.

$$$ CONTEMPORARY 🍴 **Balthazar.** In an airy neoclassical mansion with a leafy, minimalist courtyard—paved with original painted tiles, canopied by huge date palms, and illuminated by colored lanterns—Balthazar truly feels like a summer oasis in the middle of Athens. The crowd is fun and hip, moneyed, cosmopolitan, and beautiful, so you might wish to come for dinner, then stay to mingle and taste the cocktails (like the passion-fruit martini) as the DJ picks up the beat. Chef Savvas Konstantinides keeps the quality and flavor high on the up-to-the-minute Mediterranean menu. Opt for any of the creative appetizers (especially the grilled octopus with fava, truffle oil, and caramelized onions); the tasty main dishes (such as the sea bass with black-eyed peas salad and fennel seed lemon-oil sauce, as well as the barley risotto with red shrimps from Mani); and the homemade desserts, especially the "Fresh Passion" (with a soft chocolate biscuit, yogurt honey *namelaka*, caramelized hazelnuts, praline ice cream, and framboise sauce). Though it's been around since the late 1990s, this place has miraculously managed to remain as fresh and trendy today as when it first opened. [$] *Average main: €40* ✉ *Tsoha 27, at Vournazou, Ambelokipi* ☎ *210/641–2300* 🌐 *www.balthazar.gr* ✍ *Reservations essential* 🕒 *Closed Sun.–Mon. No lunch* ✥ *H2.*

$ GREEK 🍴 **To Kainari.** Handwoven throws and an odd collection of photographs and mementos adorn the walls of this cozy neighborhood taverna, where you'll rub elbows—literally—with businessmen, doctors, students, and other regulars. But what it lacks in space, it makes up for with an extensive menu combining daily specials (ask the fishmonger sipping ouzo at the next table) and favorites, like *bouyiourdi* (spicy sausage, peppers, feta cheese, and tomato sauce), the calamari stuffed with feta cheese, or the lamb with hand-cut fries cooked in olive oil. On cold winter nights, this cozy place warms the body and soul. There's also live Greek music on Friday and Saturday evenings, and Sunday at lunchtime. [$] *Average main: €14* ✉ *Xiromerou 20, behind the Errikos Dynan Hospital, Ambelokipi* ☎ *210/698–3011* 💳 *No credit cards* 🕒 *Closed Aug. No dinner Sun.* ✥ *H1.*

ILISIA ΙΛΙΣΙΑ

Ilisia is close to the center and its open spaces are an excellent base for some easily accessible restaurants offering tastes of Greek regional cuisine.

$$$ GREEK 🍴 **Alatsi.** A few years ago, journalist-turned-politician Stavros Theodorakis decided to bring the culinary traditions of his Cretan hometown of Chania to Athens. Located behind the Hilton hotel, his restaurant immediately became a success with the crème-de-la-crème of the city. Alatsi (which means natural sea salt on his native island) serves Cretan delicacies such as *kaltsounia* (small pies) with wild greens, lemon-braised goat shoulder with *stamnagathi* wild greens, and Cretan *gamopilafo* (traditional wedding pilaf boiled in goat meat). For dessert, there is *Iordani's bougatsa,* a sweet and savory cheese pie that

comes straight from Chania. The complimentary glass of raki at the end of your meal is ideal for digestion. $ *Average main: €27* ✉ *Vrasida 13, Ilisia* ☎ *210/721–0501* ⊕ *www.alatsi.gr* ⚑ *Reservations essential* ☾ *Closed Sun. and mid-Aug.* ✛ *G4.*

$$ **╳ Vlassis.** Relying on traditional recipes from northern Greece and the
GREEK islands, the chefs here whip up some noteworthy home-style cooking in the heart of the city. There's no menu in this modern Greek bistro with huge glass windows, adorned with authentic works of art by well-known Greek painters. Just start by picking from the tray of 20 or so small dishes brought to your table: they're all good, but best bets include the fried eggplant with yogurt and tomato, *lahanodolmades* (stuffed cabbage leaves), fried red mullets, *katsiki ladorigani* (goat with oil and oregano), and the octopus *stifado* (a stew of octopus, onions, and tomatoes), which is tender and sweet. For dessert, order the halvah or a huge slice of *galaktoboureko.* For your main course, just follow the waiter's lead, but don't forget to ask for the daily specials. $ *Average main: €20* ✉ *Maiandrou 15, Ilisia* ☎ *210/646–3060, 210/725–6335* ⊕ *www. vlassisrestaurant.gr* ▭ *No credit cards* ☾ *Closed Aug.–mid-Sept. No dinner Sun.* ✛ *H3.*

KAISARIANI ΚΑΙΣΑΡΙΑΝΗ

Like Pangrati, Kaisariani is a predominately residential neighborhood with some good restaurants.

$$$ **╳ H Trata.** The owner of this popular fish taverna on the historical Kai-
SEAFOOD sariani square works directly with fishermen, guaranteeing that the freshest catch comes to the table. Just point to your preference, and it will soon arrive in the way Greeks insist upon: grilled with exactitude, coated in the thinnest layer of olive oil to seal in juices, and accompanied by lots of lemon. The deep-fried calamari and buttered prawns are house specialties. Even those who scrunch up their nose at fish soup will be converted by this version of the dense yet delicate *kakkavia.* H Trata is also one of the few remaining places you can get real homemade taramosalata. Avoid the lively square during Sunday lunch unless you want to squeeze in with the entire city. Parking is available. $ *Average main: €28* ✉ *Anagenisseos Sq. 7–9, off Ethnikis Antistaseos, Kaisariani* ☎ *210/729–1533* ⊕ *www.tratakaisariani.gr* ☾ *Closed 10 days for Orthodox Easter* ✛ *H5.*

WHERE TO STAY

Greeks pride themselves for their *philoxenia,* or hospitality. Even in antiquity, many of them referred to Zeus as Xenios Zeus—the God in charge of protecting travelers. Today, Greek philoxenia is alive and well in the capital city, whether displayed in the kindness of strangers you ask for directions or in the thoroughness of your hotel receptionist's care. With 20% of the small country's GDP derived from tourism, philoxenia isn't optional.

The city is full of hotels, many of which were built in Greek tourism's heyday in the 1960s and 1970s. In the years prior to the 2004

Athens Olympic Games, financial incentives were provided to hoteliers to upgrade and renovate their facilities, to the effect that many hotels—such as the Athens Hilton—completely renovated themselves inside and out as they increased their range of services.

But while prices have increased since the Olympics, accommodations are still available at all price levels. In Athens you can find everything from boutique hotels dreamed up by prestigious designers and decorated by well-known artists to no-fuss youth hostels that for decades have served the backpacking crowds on their way to Mykonos and Santorini. Athens's budget hotels—once little better than dorms—now almost always have air-conditioning and TV, along with prettier public spaces and possibly even Wi-Fi. In the post-Olympics years, there was a notable increase in the number of good-quality, middle-rank family hotels. At the same time, the city's classic luxury hotels, such as the Grande Bretagne and the King George, introduced modern perks like modern spas.

The most convenient hotels for travelers are in the heart of the city center. Some of the older hotels in Plaka and near Omonia Square are comfortable and clean, their charm inherent in their age. But along with charm may come leaking plumbing, sagging mattresses, or other lapses in the details—take a good look at the room before you register. The thick stone walls of neoclassical buildings keep them cool in summer, but few of the budget hotels have central heating, and Athens can be devilishly cold in winter.

PRICES

Along with higher quality have come higher hotel prices: room rates in Athens are not much less than in many European cities. Still, there are bargains to be had. It's also a good idea to bargain in person at smaller hotels, especially off-season. When negotiating a rate, bear in mind that the longer the stay, the lower the nightly rate, so it may be less expensive to spend six consecutive nights in Athens than to stay two or three nights at either end of your trip through Greece.

Bear in mind that usually hotels will charge extra for a view of the Acropolis, and that breakfast is not always included. It is sometimes best to book through an agent for better bulk rates (this can lead to cost savings of up to 20%). Often it is also worth checking the websites of hotels for special seasonal offers or bargain packages. In the off-season months (October to April) it is possible to negotiate for, and achieve, better rates.

Use the coordinate (✛ B2) at the end of each listing to locate a site on the corresponding map.

PRICES IN EUROS			
$	**$$**	**$$$**	**$$$$**
Hotels	Under €126	€126–€225	€226–€275	Over €275

Hotel prices are the lowest cost of a standard double room in high season.

MAKRYGIANNI ΜΑΚΡΥΓΙΑΝΝΗ

$ **Hera Hotel.** Attention to elegant detail—the lobby's marble floors, HOTEL wood paneling, and leather sofas—reigns at this small and elegant hotel, a good value that is perfectly located across the street from the Acropolis Museum. **Pros:** unbeatable location; the Acropolis view from the dreamy roof garden; cleanliness and service; friendly staff. **Cons:** smallish rooms; rooms at the back have no views; lofty restaurant prices; breakfast not included in the price (€15). $ *Rooms from: €111* ✉ *Falirou 9, Makrygianni* ☎ *210/322–5891* ⊕ *www.herahotel.gr* ⤢ *38 rooms, 3 suites* ⦿ *No meals* ✛ *D5.*

$ **Philippos Hotel.** Just around the corner from its sister hotel, the Hero-HOTEL dion, the Philippos shares its sister property's best qualities, namely a quiet location convenient to the Acropolis and friendly, efficient service. **Pros:** clean rooms; excellent location; free Wi-Fi with some travel packages. **Cons:** smallish rooms; some in need of updating; no restaurant or swimming pool. $ *Rooms from: €110* ✉ *Mitseon 3, Makrygianni* ☎ *210/922–3611* ⊕ *www.philipposhotel.gr* ⤢ *46 rooms, 4 suites* ⦿ *Breakfast* ✛ *D5.*

KOUKAKI ΚΟΥΚΑΚΙ

$ **Acropolis Select.** For about €10 more per night than many basic budget HOTEL options, you get to stay in a slick-looking hotel with a lobby full of designer furniture in the residential neighborhood of Koukaki, south of Filopappou Hill, a 10-minute walk from the Acropolis and literally around the corner from the Acropolis Museum. **Pros:** comfortable rooms; friendly staff; located in a pretty, low-key neighborhood; good value for money. **Cons:** no free Wi-Fi in the rooms; small elevator; some noise from the street at night. $ *Rooms from: €75* ✉ *Falirou 37–39, Koukaki* ☎ *210/921–1610* ⊕ *www.acropoliselect.gr* ⤢ *72 rooms* ⦿ *No meals* ✛ *D5.*

$ **Art Gallery Pension.** A handsome house on a pretty residential street, B&B/INN this pension is comfortably old-fashioned, with family paintings on the muted white walls, comfortable beds, hardwood floors, ceiling fans, and balconies in many guest rooms that offer views of Filopappou or the Acropolis—though the residential neighborhood (a 10-minute walk south of the Acropolis) lacks the charm of Plaka, it has many fewer tourists, and the metro offers easy access to many of the city's sights. **Pros:** clean, comfy rooms; free Wi-Fi in every room; lounge with Acropolis view. **Cons:** basic rooms; small showers; no credit cards. $ *Rooms from: €80* ✉ *Erechthiou 5, Koukaki* ☎ *210/923–8376, 210/923–1933* ⊕ *www.artgalleryhotel.gr* ⤢ *21 rooms* ▭ *No credit cards* ⦿ *Multiple meal plans* ✛ *C5.*

$$ **Herodion Hotel.** A good compromise between the area's budget ven-HOTEL ues and deluxe digs, this hospitable hotel is down the street from the Odeon of Herodes Atticus, where Athens Festival performances are held, and a few minutes from the Acropolis. **Pros:** tastefully designed rooms; knowledgeable and polite staff; great Acropolis views from some rooms; wide choice at buffet breakfast. **Cons:** rooms a bit small; no free Wi-Fi in rooms. $ *Rooms from: €130* ✉ *Rovertou Galli 4, Makriyanni* ☎ *210/923–6832 through 210/923–6836* ⊕ *www.herodion.gr* ⤢ *86 rooms, 4 suites* ⦿ *Breakfast* ✛ *D5.*

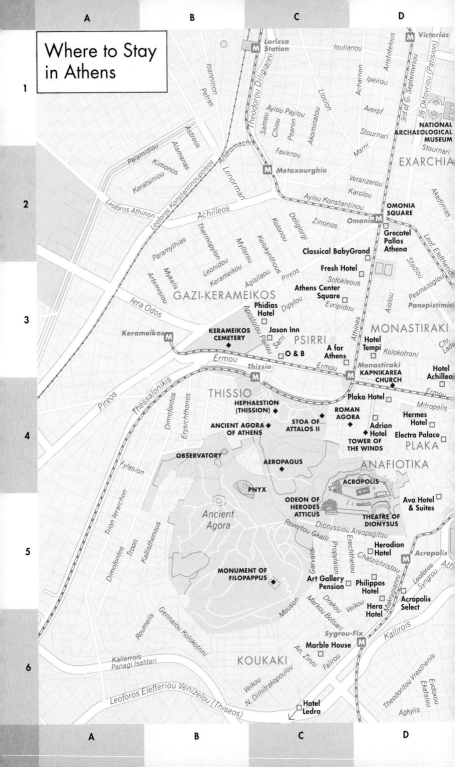

Where to Stay in Athens

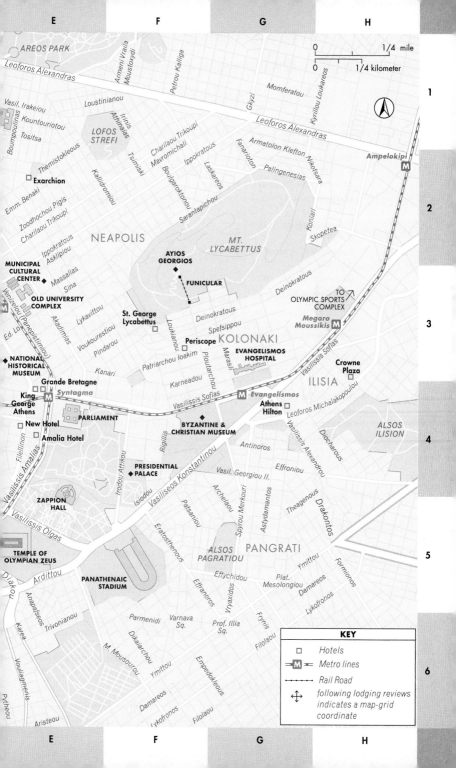

BEST BETS FOR ATHENS LODGING

Fodor's Choice★	The New Hotel, $$, p. 169	$$
A for Athens, $, p. 167	O&B, $$$, p. 170	Amalia Hotel, p. 168
Athens Center Square, $, p. 169	Periscope, $$, p. 170	Athens Hilton, p. 171
Athens Hilton, $$, p. 171		Electra Palace, p. 167
Electra Palace, $$, p. 167	**By Price**	Herodion Hotel, p. 163
Grande Bretagne, $$$$, p. 169		The New Hotel, p. 169
	$	Periscope, p. 170
Grecotel Pallas Athena, $, p. 170	Acropolis Select, p. 163	$$$
Hermes Hotel, $, p. 167	Grecotel Pallas Athena, p. 170	King George Athens, p. 169
King George Athens, $$$, p. 169	Hera Hotel, p. 163	O&B, p. 170
	Plaka Hotel, p. 167	$$$$
		Grande Bretagne, p. 169

$ **Marble House.** This welcoming guesthouse has a steady clientele who
B&B/INN don't mind the basic accomodation and facilities in return for gracious,
welcoming service, a convenient location, and unbeatable prices. **Pros:**
unbeatable price for the budget traveler; quiet neighborhood ideally
located for sight-seeing; friendly staff. **Cons:** a bit outdated interiors;
breakfast an extra charge. *$ Rooms from: €45 ⊠ Anastassiou Zinni
35, Koukaki ☎ 210/923–4058, 210/922–8294 ⊕ www.marblehouse.
gr ⇥ 16 rooms, 11 with bath* ⊙| *No meals ✛ C6.*

PLAKA ΠΛΑΚΑ

$ **Adrian Hotel.** This comfortable pension offers friendly service and an
HOTEL excellent location in the heart of Plaka—incurable romantics should
ask for one of just three rooms looking toward the Acropolis. **Pros:**
great central location; friendly staff; excellent value for money; free
Wi-Fi. **Cons:** Adrianou street can be noisy during the summer months;
smallish rooms; bathroom and some interior details (i.e., carpets) need
updating. *$ Rooms from: €93 ⊠ Adrianou 74, Plaka ☎ 210/325–
0454 ⊕ www.douros-hotels.com ⇥ 22 rooms* ⊙| *Breakfast ✛ D4.*

$$$ **AVA Hotel & Suites.** On a quiet sidestreet in the Plaka, this lovely small
HOTEL hotel is ideally located for all the major Athens attractions and has
become a firm favorite among leisure and business travelers alike.
Pros: spacious rooms; elegant furnishings; impeccable service; amaz-
ing views. **Cons:** lacks big-hotel amenities and a restaurant; small eleva-
tor. *$ Rooms from: €230 ⊠ Lyssicratous 9-11, Plaka ☎ 210/325–9000
⊕ www.avahotel.gr ⇥ 16 rooms* ⊙| *Breakfast ✛ D5.*

$$ ⊞ **Electra Palace.** If you want simple elegance, good service, and a great
HOTEL location, this is the hotel for you—rooms from the fifth floor up have
Fodor'sChoice a view of the Acropolis—and in summer you can bask in the sunshine
★ at the outdoor swimming pool as you take in the view of Athens's
greatest monument or catch the sunset from the rooftop garden. **Pros:**
gorgeous rooms; great location; shady garden and large rooftop pool;
early check-in available. **Cons:** a/c can be problematic; free Wi-Fi for
only the first half-hour. $ *Rooms from: €200 ⊠ Nikodimou 18–20,
Plaka* ☎ *210/337–0000* ⊕ *www.electrahotels.gr* ⤳ *135 rooms, 20 suites*
Breakfast ✚ *D4.*

$ ⊞ **Hermes Hotel.** Athens's small, modestly priced establishments have
HOTEL generally relied on little more than convenient central locations to
FAMILY draw visitors, but the Hermes goes further, with sunny guest rooms
Fodor'sChoice with brightly colored decorative details and marble bathrooms that
★ feel warm and welcoming. **Pros:** great staff; sleak, clean decor; central
location; free Wi-Fi; free tea and coffee available for guests until 7 pm.
Cons: some smallish rooms, some without a balcony (check availabil-
ity). $ *Rooms from: €125 ⊠ Apollonos 19, Plaka* ☎ *210/323–5514*
⊕ *www.hermeshotel.gr* ⤳ *45 rooms* *Breakfast* ✚ *D4.*

$ ⊞ **Plaka Hotel.** The guest rooms in this charming, centrally located hotel
HOTEL offer a comfortable place to rest your head while in the heart of old Ath-
ens. **Pros:** excellent location; diligent staff; good breakfast and lounge
areas; view of the Acropolis from the roof garden; free tea and cof-
fee every afternoon. **Cons:** small and sometimes stuffy rooms; no pets
allowed; Wi-Fi has a small cost. $ *Rooms from: €115 ⊠ Kapnikareas
7 and Mitropoleos, Plaka* ☎ *210/322–2706* ⊕ *www.plakahotel.gr* ⤳ *67
rooms* *Breakfast* ✚ *D4.*

MONASTIRAKI ΜΟΝΑΣΤΗΡΑΚΙ

$ ⊞ **A for Athens.** One of Athens's newest hotels is as fresh a concept as
HOTEL its name, a restored 1960s building with minimalist rooms with wood
Fodor'sChoice floors and all the modern amenities (including both air-conditioning and
★ free Wi-Fi). **Pros:** perfect location next to a convenient metro stop; com-
fortable rooms with a contemporary design; breathtaking views. **Cons:**
some noise from the street and the bar; no gym or swimming pool.
$ *Rooms from: €75 ⊠ Miaouli 2-4, Monastiraki* ☎ *210/324–4244*
⊕ *www.aforathens.com* ⤳ *35 rooms* *Breakfast* ✚ *C3.*

$ ⊞ **Hotel Tempi.** It's all about location for this bare-bones budget hotel
B&B/INN ideal for budget travelers on a quick Athens stopover who still want
a convenient location, just a short, pleasant stroll from Plaka, the
Roman Agora, and right on the happening Ayias Irinis Square. **Pros:**
friendly staff; nice roof terrace; central location; good a/c; free Wi-Fi;
some rooms have Acropolis views. **Cons:** smallish, basic rooms; hostel-
like vibe; no elevator for the top three floors, just a steep staircase;
some noise from nearby clubs and restaurants; no breakfast option.
$ *Rooms from: €50 ⊠ Aiolou 29, Monastiraki* ☎ *210/321–3175*
⊕ *www.tempihotel.gr* ⤳ *24 rooms, 12 with bath* *No meals* ✚ *D3.*

For food-with-a-view, the Plaka district is famed for its lovely garden restaurants with front-row seats to the Acropolis Hill.

THISSIO ΘΗΣΕΙΟ

$ HOTEL **Jason Inn.** Though it's on a run-down, seemingly out-of-the-way little corner, the modern Jason Inn is steps away from the buzzing nightlife districts of Psirri and Thissio, not to mention the ancient Agora and the Acropolis farther up the pedestrianized street. **Pros:** strategic location; reasonable price, including breakfast. **Cons:** run-down neighborhood; rooms feel dated, and the building, too. [$] *Rooms from: €60* ✉ *Ayion Assomaton 12, Thissio* ☎ *210/520–2491, 210/523–4721* 🌐 *www.douros-hotels.com* 🛏 *57 rooms* 🍴 *Breakfast* ✣ *C3.*

$ HOTEL **Phidias Hotel.** Stay here, and you may develop the impression that Athens is all fun and not a car-packed, frantic metropolis—simply put, there's no better spot to stay, location-wise, on Athens's most beautiful pedestrian walkway. **Pros:** good location with proximity to metro and shopping; quiet; pets OK; a particularly good value. **Cons:** public and private spaces could use a makeover; old elevator; dated bathrooms; sometimes the nearby Thissio partying is loud; parking difficult. [$] *Rooms from: €70* ✉ *Apostolou Pavlou 39, Thissio* ☎ *210/345–9511* 🌐 *www.phidias.gr* 🛏 *15 rooms* ✣ *C3.*

SYNTAGMA SQUARE ΠΛΑΤΕΙΑ ΣΥΝΤΑΓΜΑΤΟΣ

$$ HOTEL **Amalia Hotel.** The central location and competitive prices are the main attractions here for most visitors, with a location right on one of Athens's biggest, busiest streets, directly across from Parliament, but double-glazed windows (fortunately) and a view to the pretty National Garden keep things peaceful inside. **Pros:** perfect central location; easy

access to transport, to Plaka, and the pretty National Garden; free Wi-Fi. **Cons:** on a busy thoroughfare; no restaurant at the hotel, just a snack bar; front rooms can be a bit noisy. [$] *Rooms from: €130* ✉ *Amalias 10, Syntagma* ☎ *210/323–7300* 🌐 *www.amalia.gr* 🛏 *98 rooms, 1 suite* 🍴 *Breakfast* ✥ *E4.*

$$$$ HOTEL Fodor's Choice ★ 🏨 **Grande Bretagne.** With a guest list that includes more than a century's worth of royals, rock stars, and heads of state, the landmark Grande Bretagne remains the most exclusive hotel in Athens. **Pros:** all-out luxury; beautiful rooms; excellent café, spa, and pool lounge; central location. **Cons:** pricey; no free Wi-Fi; demonstrations sometimes take place right in front of the hotel. [$] *Rooms from: €320* ✉ *Vasileos Georgiou A'1 at Syntagma Sq., Syntagma* ☎ *210/333–0000, 210/331–5555 through 210/331–5559 reservations* 🌐 *www.grandebretagne.gr* 🛏 *321 rooms, 56 suites* 🍴 *Breakfast* ✥ *E4.*

$$ HOTEL 🏨 **Hotel Achilleas.** This hotel combines modern amenities and a central location with the personal service that comes from being family-run—and a price at the lower end of its category. **Pros:** excellent location; free use of Internet in the lobby; plentiful breakfast. **Cons:** somewhat basic rooms; perhaps just a bit pricey for what it offers; small elevator; front rooms can be a bit noisy. [$] *Rooms from: €130* ✉ *Lekka 21, Syntagma* ☎ *210/322–5826* 🌐 *www.achilleashotel.gr* 🛏 *34 rooms* 🍴 *Breakfast* ✥ *D4.*

$$$ HOTEL Fodor's Choice ★ 🏨 **King George Athens.** One of the most historic and luxurious hotels in Athens, the King George is probably the best hotel in town. **Pros:** beautiful design; luxurious rooms; attentive service; outstanding food; 24-hour business center. **Cons:** slow elevators; thin walls in rooms; in-room Wi-Fi at a charge. [$] *Rooms from: €260* ✉ *2 Vasileos Georgiou A, Syntagma* ☎ *210/322–2210* 🌐 *www.kinggeorgeathens.com* 🛏 *77 rooms, 25 suites* 🍴 *No meals* ✥ *E4.*

$$ HOTEL Fodor's Choice ★ 🏨 **The New Hotel.** Years in the making, the cutting-edge New Hotel was heralded as an aesthetic triumph in the inner city's ever-changing landscape when it opened in 2011, and it has maintained its edge, all for the better. **Pros:** sleek, quirky, unique design; helpful staff; free Wi-Fi in public areas; sumptuous breakfasts; central location. **Cons:** pricey pay-per-view TV; front-facing rooms can be noisy (small church with loud bell in the square across the street). [$] *Rooms from: €160* ✉ *Filellinon 16, Syntagma* ☎ *210/628–4800* 🌐 *www.yeshotels.gr* 🛏 *79 rooms and suites* 🍴 *Multiple meal plans* ✥ *E4.*

PSIRRI ΨΥΡΡΗ

$ HOTEL Fodor's Choice ★ 🏨 **Athens Center Square.** This surprisingly peaceful, modern hotel nevertheless blends nicely into the iconic, bustling landscape of the Athens Central Market. **Pros:** knowledgable, friendly staff; rooftop with Acropolis views; excellent price-to-quality ratio. **Cons:** a safe, albeit inner-city, location that may not be to everyone's taste; free Wi-Fi can be slow in rooms. [$] *Rooms from: €100* ✉ *Aristogeitonos 15, at Athinas, Psirri* ☎ *210/321–1770* 🌐 *www.athenscentersquarehotel.gr* 🛏 *54 rooms* 🍴 *Breakfast* ✥ *C3.*

$$$ HOTEL Fodor's Choice ★ **O&B.** Each room in this elegant boutique hotel with a sleek design and an outstanding restaurant-bar is a little haven of urban cool, thanks to flat-screen TVs, personal stereo/DVD systems, Moulton Brown bath products, high-drama high-design color schemes, black minimalistic headboards, and soft white Egyptian cotton sheets. **Pros:** beautiful rooms; excellent food; personalized service; informed and multilingual staff; relaxed and stylish atmosphere. **Cons:** all rooms but the penthouse have limited views; street not very attractive; pricey. [$] *Rooms from: €230* ✉ *Leokoriou 7, Psirri* ☎ *210/331–2950* 🌐 *www.oandbhotel.com* 🛏 *22 rooms, 5 suites* 🍴 *Breakfast* ✥ *C3.*

KOLONAKI ΚΟΛΩΝΑΚΙ

$$ HOTEL Fodor's Choice ★ **Periscope.** This sleek concept hotel combines minimalist urban-chic design, amenity-filled rooms, and exceptional service for a truly relaxing experience. **Pros:** great locale; eatery (PBox) created by award-winning chef; great breakfast; outstanding service. **Cons:** rooms are a bit on the small side and have limited views; only suites have balconies: no parking. [$] *Rooms from: €155* ✉ *Haritos 22, Kolonaki* ☎ *210/729–7200* 🌐 *www.yeshotels.gr* 🛏 *17 rooms, 4 suites* 🍴 *Breakfast* ✥ *F3.*

$ HOTEL **St. George Lycabettus.** This upscale hotel on the forested slopes of Mt. Lycabettus, in happening Kolonaki, is steps from Athens's museum row and designer shops. **Pros:** nice location; excellent rooftop restaurant combines views and good food. **Cons:** blah views from some rooms; this 1970s hotel is beginning to look a bit dated; Wi-Fi in rooms available for a charge. [$] *Rooms from: €115* ✉ *Kleomenous 2, Kolonaki* ☎ *210/729–0711 through 210/729–0719* 🌐 *www.sglycabettus.gr* 🛏 *153 rooms, 5 suites* 🍴 *No meals* ✥ *F3.*

OMONIA SQUARE ΠΛΑΤΕΙΑ ΟΜΟΝΟΙΑΣ

$ HOTEL Fodor's Choice ★ **Grecotel Pallas Athena.** Fun yet posh, this dream pad for the young and the young-at-heart is a crazy/cool boutique art hotel (fully refurbished in 2013). **Pros:** beautiful rooms; great staff; excellent in-house food; reliable free Wi-Fi. **Cons:** many rooms have poor views; neighborhood a little run-down (but location excellent for sightseeing). [$] *Rooms from: €120* ✉ *Athinas 65, at Lykourgou, Omonia Sq.* ☎ *210/325–0900* 🌐 *www.grecotelpallasathena.com* 🛏 *76 rooms, 11 suites* 🍴 *Breakfast* ✥ *D2.*

$$ HOTEL **Fresh Hotel.** Reveling in minimalist glam, this attractive boutique hotel has relaxing and expertly decorated rooms, a plugged-in staff, and two restaurants that feature nouvelle-Mediterranean cuisine—in a centrally located, albeit somewhat dodgy neighborhood (by night, at least). **Pros:** Air Lounge Bar restaurant has great food and atmosphere; central location; plugged-in staff. **Cons:** surrounding neighborhood is a bit unattractive and dodgy at night. [$] *Rooms from: €130* ✉ *Sofokleous 26, Omonia Sq.* ☎ *210/524–8511* 🌐 *www.freshhotel.gr* 🛏 *133 rooms* 🍴 *Breakfast* ✥ *D3.*

EXARCHIA ΕΞΑΡΧΕΙΑ

$
B&B/INN
Exarchion. Smack in the center of a lively bohemian bar and café district, this basic hotel has been a fixture on the international backpacking circuit for years. **Pros:** unbeatable price; clean and comfortable; free Wi-Fi. **Cons:** musty rooms; the location might not be to everyone's taste, especially families; can be noisy as near to bars and restaurants (pick a room on the higher floors if possible). *$ Rooms from: €35 ⊠ Themistokleous 55, Exarchia* ☎ *210/380–0731* ⊕ *www.exarchion.com* ↝ *49 rooms* ⎟○⎟ *No meals* ⊹ *E2.*

ILISIA ΙΛΙΣΙΑ

$$
HOTEL
Fodor's Choice
★
Athens Hilton. While the impressive Hilton is one of the city's venerable architectural landmarks, it's also been kept up to date with modern, clean-lined, and minimalist design. **Pros:** outstanding service; beautiful rooms; great Acropolis and city view from rooftop; excellent buffet breakfast; huge pool. **Cons:** very expensive; extra fee to use the pool, spa, and gym, unless you are staying in one of the suites; high extra charge for Internet access for most room deals; 1% bill surcharge if paying by credit card. *$ Rooms from: €150 ⊠ Vasilissis Sofias 46, Ilisia* ☎ *210/728–1000, 210/728–1100 reservations* ⊕ *www.athens.hilton. com* ↝ *498 rooms, 19 suites* ⎟○⎟ *Multiple meal plans* ⊹ *G4.*

$
HOTEL
Crowne Plaza Athens City Centre. On the site of the city's former Holiday Inn (it opened its doors in mid-2008), this may be one of the most technology-friendly Athens hotels. **Pros:** high-tech infrastructure; outdoor swimming pool (closes at 7 pm); spacious rooms and bathrooms; extra comfortable beds; free Wi-Fi. **Cons:** costly breakfast; a bit off-center; the pool is on the small side. *$ Rooms from: €106 ⊠ 50 Michalakopoulou avenue, Ilisia* ☎ *210/727–8000* ⊕ *www.cpathens. com* ↝ *186 rooms, 7 suites* ⎟○⎟ *No meals* ⊹ *H3.*

NEOS KOSMOS ΝΕΟΣ ΚΟΣΜΟΣ

$
HOTEL
Hotel Ledra. The Ledra's main calling cards are its high-performance staff, high style, and dining comfort: the lobby piano bar sits below a spectacular 1,000-crystal chandelier. **Pros:** modern-chic rooms; relaxed and jazzy atmosphere in bar; great breakfast choice; excellent service. **Cons:** Syngrou is an ugly and busy street; a long walk or short taxi ride to the city center (though there is an hourly shuttle for a small fee). *$ Rooms from: €100 ⊠ Syngrou 115, Neos Kosmos* ☎ *210/930–0000* ⊕ *www.athensledrahotel.com* ↝ *308 rooms, 6 suites* ⊹ *C6.*

NIGHTLIFE AND PERFORMING ARTS

From ancient Greek tragedies in quarried amphitheaters to the chicest dance clubs, Athens rocks at night. Several of the former industrial districts are enjoying a renaissance, and large spaces have filled up with galleries, restaurants, and theaters—providing one-stop shopping for an evening's entertainment. The Greek weekly *Athinorama* covers current performances, gallery openings, and films, as does

English-language *Kathimerini,* inserted in the *International New York Times* (available Monday through Saturday). The monthly English-language magazine *Insider* has features and listings on entertainment in Athens, with a focus on the arts. *Odyssey,* a glossy bimonthly magazine, also publishes an annual summer guide in late June, sold at newsstands around Athens with the season's top performances and exhibitions. You can also "tune in" to the regular English reports on municipal station Athens International Web Radio for what's happening around town; click for Athens International Radio on their website (⊕ *www.athina984.gr*).

NIGHTLIFE

Athens's heady nightlife starts late. Most bars and clubs don't get hopping until midnight and they stay open at the very least until 3 am. Drink prices can be rather steep (about €7–€13), but the pours are generous. Often there is a cover charge on weekends at the most popular clubs, which also have bouncers (aptly called "face-control" by Greeks because they tend to let only the "lookers" in). For a uniquely Greek evening, visit a club featuring rembetika music, a type of blues, or the popular *bouzoukia* (clubs with live bouzouki, a stringed instrument, music). Few clubs take credit cards for drinks.

Nightclubs in Greece migrate with the seasons. From October through May, they're in vast, throbbing venues in Central Athens and the northern suburbs; from June through September, many relocate to luxurious digs on the south coast. The same spaces are used from year to year, but owners and names tend to bounce around. Before heading out, check local listings or talk to your hotel concierge, especially during the summer. One way to avoid both lines and cover charges—since partying doesn't get going until after 1 am—is to make an earlier dinner reservation at one of the many clubs that have restaurants as well.

BOUZOUKIA

Many tourists think Greek social life centers on large clubs where live bouzouki music plays while patrons smash up the plates. Plate-smashing is now prohibited, but plates of flowers (at high prices) are sold for scattering over the performer or your companions when they take to the dance floor. Upscale bouzoukia clubs line the middle section of Pireos avenue and stretch out to the south coast, where top entertainers command top prices. Be aware that bouzoukia food is overpriced and often second-rate. There is a per-person minimum (around €25) or a prix-fixe menu; a bottle of whiskey may cost around €100. For those who choose to stand at the bar, a drink runs about €15 to €20 at a good bouzoukia place.

REMBETIKA

The Greek equivalent of the urban blues, rembetika music is rooted in the traditions of Asia Minor and was brought to Greece by refugees from Smyrna in the 1920s. It filtered up from the lowest economic levels to become one of the most enduring genres of Greek popular music, still enthralling club goers today. At these thriving clubs, you can catch a glimpse of Greek social life and even join the dances (but remember, it's considered extremely rude to interrupt a solo dance). The two most common dances are the *zeimbekiko,* in which the man improvises in circular movements that become ever more complicated, and the belly dance–like *tsifteteli.* Most of the clubs are closed in summer; call in advance. Drink prices range from €10 to €15, a bottle of whiskey from €70 to €90, and the food is often expensive and unexceptional; it's wisest to order a fruit platter or a bottle of wine.

PLAKA
BARS
Brettos. With walls adorned by brightly lit bottles in all colors of the spectrum, Brettos is a favorite hangout of many locals who come here to relish the memories of the oldest distillery in town (going strong since 1909) and the second-oldest bar in the whole of Europe. The huge barrels store spirits produced on the premises even today—ouzo, cognac, liqueurs (like top picks cinnamon or mango), Tsipouro, and more. Order a Greek *mezedes* platter to accompany your beverage of choice. ⊠ *Kydathinaion 41, Plaka* ☎ *210/323–2110* ⊕ *www.brettosplaka.com.*

TAVERNAS WITH MUSIC
Neos Rigas. At this traditional music taverna you can get a taste of folk dances and costumes from throughout Greece. At the end of the night the music turns more "Eastern," and everybody is invited to show off their own dance moves (if you don't want to dance, pick your seat accordingly). The price of this slice of old-style Greek entertainment is reasonable; the prix-fixe menu costs €35 euros (plus the cost of drinks); a bottle of wine costs around €18. ⊠ *Adrianou and Agg. Hatzimihali 13, Plaka* ☎ *210/324–0830* ⊕ *www.newrigas.gr.*

Palia Taverna (*Old Tavern of Stamatopoulos*). This taverna has everything: good food, barrel wine, an acoustic duo with guitar and bouzouki playing old Athenian songs in an 1882 house. In summer the show moves to the garden. Whatever the season, Greeks will often get up and dance, beckoning you to join them (don't be shy). Live music starts at about 8:30 and goes on until 1 am. ⊠ *Lysiou 26, Plaka* ☎ *210/322–8722* ⊕ *www.stamatopoulostavern.gr.*

KOLONAKI
CLUBS
Rock n' Roll. This legendary bar from the 1980s and '90s, Rock n' Roll has reopened its doors a couple hundred meters from its original location, right in the heart of fashionable Kolonaki Square. And—no surprise here—it is as popular as ever, especially in winter. Athens's party crowd comes to this club/restaurant to groove mostly to rock music (with some dance and Greek pop hits subtly making their way into the playlist). Saturday is very busy, so your best bet is to book a table and enjoy the Mediterranean menu (try the mushroom risotto or a pizza if you want to keep things simple) before moving on to cocktails and a bit of dancing. From May to September, Rock n' Roll goes on holiday. ⊠ *Kolonaki Sq. (Filikis Etairias) 14, Kolonaki* ☎ *210/722–0649* ⊕ *www.rocknroll.gr.*

MONASTIRAKI

BARS

Osterman. Atmospheric, ultrapopular Osterman is housed in an old textile shop and has impossibly high ceilings and wonderful mosaic floors on lively and fashionable Ayia Irinis Square. The dark mahogany wood, the long bar, the cream leather sofas work together to create a cinematic effect: is this modern Athens or a film noir set from the 1950s? Though mostly a cocktail bar (bartender Yiannis Korovesis is rumored to make the best Bloody Mary in town), it also draws a young, trendy, and artsy crowd who comes here for the food (especially dishes like the tuna with caramelized onions and the lamb burger). There is also a more affordable lunch menu option until 5 pm (expect to pay around €17 for a main). At night it can get very busy, so make sure you have a reservation. This is a smoke-friendly place so come prepared. ⊠ *Ayia Irinis Square 10, Monastiraki* ☎ *210/324-3331* ⊕ *www.osterman.gr.*

360 Cocktail Bar. With a menu of more than 70 cocktails (especially good are the Gspiced, the Baby Oak, and the Negroni) and an extensive wine list, there is something for everyone at this rooftop bar in the heart of lively Monastiraki Square. An unexpected bonus is the magical view of the Acropolis. The bar occupies the 3rd floor and the rooftop (in summer), while there is also an excellent, industrial-styled restaurant on the second floor. ⊠ *Ifaistou 2, Monastiraki Square, Monastiraki* ☎ *210/321–0006* ⊕ *www.three-sixty.gr.*

REMBETIKA

Kapnikarea Cafe. The ideal refreshing lunchtime spot to relax at after shopping on busy Ermou street, Kapnikarea is named after the sunken Byzantine church that's next to it. Take in live rembetika music as you sip ouzo and savor traditional specialties and ethnic dishes inspired from owner Dimitris's world travels. Music usually starts at 2:30 and continues until 11 pm. ⊠ *Hristopoulou 2 and Ermou 57, Monastiraki* ☎ *210/322–7394.*

Stoa Athanaton. "Arcade of the Immortals" has been around since 1930, housed in a converted warehouse in the meat-market area. Not much has changed since then. The music is enhanced by an infectious, devil-may-care mood and the enthusiastic participation of the audience, especially during the best-of rembetika afternoons (3:30–7:30). The small dance floor is always jammed. Food here is delicious and very reasonably priced, but liquor is expensive (although the affordable house wine is good and a bargain at €6 per kilo). Make reservations for the performances, when the orchestra is led by old-time rembetika greats. Open Friday and Saturday evening and Sunday afternoon, this landmark is closed in the summer months, so always call before visiting. ⊠ *Sofokleous 19, Monastiraki* ☎ *210/321–4362.*

THISSIO

BARS

Stavlos. All ages feel comfortable at the bar in what used to be the Royal Stables. Sit in the courtyard or in the brick-wall restaurant for a snack like Cretan *kaltsounia* (similar to a calzone), or dance in the long bar. Stavlos often hosts art and jewelry exhibits, film screenings, mini-concerts, and other "happenings," as the Greeks call them, throughout the week. ⊠ *Irakleidon 10, Thissio* ☎ *210/345–2502, 210/346–7206* ⊕ *www.stavlos.gr.*

SYNTAGMA SQUARE

BARS

Heteroclito. This small and elegant wine bar focuses exclusively on Greek wines, and has knowledgable owners who will help you navigate their extensive wine list. ⊠ *Fokionos 2, at Petraki 30, Syntagma* ☎ *210/323–9406* ⊕ *www.heteroclito.gr.*

CLUBS

Booze Cooperativa. Laptops, coffee mugs, and chess sets cover the long wooden tables in this Central Athens joint by day. By night, chatty partygoers squeeze—booze in hand—into any spot they can find at this bar, which remains as cool as when it first opened in the 1990s. It often feels like a laid-back party, as DJs navigate through rock, pop, and dance tunes and the multitasking bar hosts art exhibits, dance performances, and theater. Wood details and wax artworks give a warm feel to the high-ceilinged space. ⊠ *Kolokotroni 57, Syntagma* ☎ *210/324–0944* ⊕ *www.boozecooperativa.com.*

PSIRRI

CLUBS

Venti. This successful Psirri club-restaurant is also now open in summer, one of the few in the city center to do so. Its open-air style (due to a retractable roof when weather allows) comes complete with a canopy of olive and palm trees while the crowd dances to a furious beat of Greek pop music. The restaurant opens at 9 pm and then stays open late for the dancing. ⊠ *Lepeniotou 20, Psirri* ☎ *210/325–4504* ⊕ *www.venti.gr.*

TAVERNAS WITH MUSIC

Klimataria. In the evenings, a rembetika band plays sing-along favorites much appreciated by the largely Greek crowd. The price of the old-style Greek entertainment at this century-old taverna is surprisingly reasonable. Meanwhile, the food is displayed on big trays, which allows you to choose the dish of your choice with help from owners Mario and Pericles (who is also a noted rembetika singer). Klimataria is also open for lunch. Don't miss the Friday evening jazz—adapted for bouzouki—performances (starting at around 10 pm), with the lovely voice of Eva Kesserling. ⊠ *Platia Theatrou 2, Psirri* ☎ *210/321–6629* ⊕ *www. klimataria.gr* ▭ *No credit cards.*

GAZI-KERAMEIKOS

BARS

Fodor'sChoice
★
Aliarman. Hidden in one of the tiny backstreets of the popular district of Gazi is this cozy treasure. The converted workers' house has a fairy-tale vibe, with impressive floor mosaics, floral frescoes, and atmospheric lighting. Colorful cocktails include the apple martini, strawberry daiquiri, mai tai, and you can also grab a bite to eat in the shabby chic garden. ⊠ *Sofroniou 2, Gazi-Kerameikos* ☎ *210/342–6322* ⊕ *www.aliarman.gr.*

Sodade2. This gay-friendly bar-club-lounge attracts a standing-room-only crowd every weekend. The draw is the great music, the joyous vibe, and the very fact that it's in Gazi, the hottest place in Central Athens. ✉ *Triptolemou 10, Gazi-Kerameikos* ☎ *210/346–8657.*

BOUZOUKIA

Iera Odos. Local pop and bouzouki stars regularly appear at this popular nightspot delivering all the joyous frenzy expected of a Greek-style night out. The club (open Friday and Saturday) gets packed as Athenians flock there to sing along with popular and traditional Greek music hits as well as some international tunes. ✉ *Iera Odos 18–20, Gazi-Kerameikos* ☎ *210/342–8272* ⊕ *www.ieraodos.gr.*

CLUBS

Bios. Cool architects and graphic designers, arty students and intellectuals, revolutionaries and experimental philosophers: they all hang out in the cavernous basement of this Bauhaus building in the Kerameikos neighborhood, part of the greater Gazi district. Expect to hear the best electronica music in town. In summer, relish the view of the Acropolis from the postmodern, neon-lighted roof terrace. A handful of "multispace" imitators have emerged, offering offbeat film/video and music events in painfully hip industrial spaces—but Bios remains the standard. ✉ *Pireos 84, Gazi-Kerameikos* ☎ *210/342–5335* ⊕ *www.bios.gr.*

Maze. On hot summer nights, clubbers can groove under the stars in this open-air dance club right in the center of industrial Athens. Maze is located in the backyard of industrial complex "Area 19" in Votanikos. Underground house and techno music lovers flock here for the warehouse parties hosted by Athenian and international guest DJs. ✉ *Area 19, Orfeos 182, Gazi-Kerameikos* ☎ *69430/74329.*

EXARCHIA
REMBETIKA

Boemissa. Usually crowded and pleasantly raucous, Boemissa attracts a young crowd, especially university students, who quickly start gyrating in various forms of the *tsifteteli.* Doors are open Thursday through Sunday (closed June through September) and the music starts at 10 pm. A meal platter and unlimited wine will set you back just €15. ✉ *Solomou 13–15, Exarchia* ☎ *210/384–3836, 210/333–8803* ⊕ *www.boemissa.gr.*

Rembetiki Istoria. The oldest rembetika music hangout in Athens is open every night of the week, and the live performance starts at 10 pm (11 pm on Friday). Musician-owner Pavlos Vasileiou has gathered an expert group of rembetika musicians. A drink is €7.50, a bottle of whisky €90. Reservations are required. ✉ *181 Ippokratous street, Exarchia* ☎ *210/642–4937* ⊕ *www.rebetikiistoria.com.*

Taximi. At one time or other, most of Greece's greatest rembetika musicians have played at this old-time live venue housed in an elegant neoclassic building (closed in summer); many of their black-and-white portraits and photos are on the smoke-stained walls. Not to be missed: the *Smyrnaika* music night every Tuesday, with old rembetika songs from Asia Minor. ✉ *Isavron 29C, at 110 Harilaou Trikoupi, Exarchia* ☎ *210/363–9919.*

OMONIA SQUARE

BOUZOUKIA

Rex Music Theatre. Over-the-top is the way to describe a performance at Rex Music Theater—it's a laser-light show, multicostume-change extravaganza, with headlining pop and bouzouki stars. Programs and performances change every season, so do check out the local press for the most current listings. ⊠ *Panepistimiou 48, Omonia Sq.* ☎ *210/381–4591, 211/850–1100.*

AMBELOKIPI

BARS

Balthazar. Athenians of all ages come to escape the summer heat at this stylish, upscale bar-restaurant in a neoclassical house with a lush garden courtyard and subdued music. Reservations are essential for the popular restaurant. ⊠ *Tsoha 27, at Vournazou, Ambelokipi* ☎ *210/641–2300* ⊕ *www.balthazar.gr.*

Baraonda. Beautiful people, breakneck music, and a VIP vibe have made this club-restaurant a perennial city favorite all year-round. The food here is also top-line and there's a beautiful garden when you need a breather. Reservations are highly recommended for both the club and the restaurant. ⊠ *Tsoha 43, Ambelokipi* ☎ *210/644–4308 Restaurant, 210/645–8406 Club* ⊕ *www.baraonda.gr.*

ILISIA

BARS

Briki. On hot summer nights, the fountain in Mavili Square (a five-minute walk from the Athens Hilton and next to the U.S. Embassy), spreads coolness over the tables of café-bars like this one, enjoyed by many urban night owls until the morning's wee hours. Funk and jazz music is usually on the playlist. In the morning Briki—really anyplace in Mavili Square—is ideal for a coffee break. ⊠ *Dorilaiou 6, Ilisia* ☎ *210/645–2380.*

Fodor'sChoice ★ **To Parko Eleftherias.** With low-key music and a romantic setting, Parko is located in the greenery next to the Megaron Mousikis concert hall (and the U.S. Embassy) and is a summer favorite for snacks, food and drink, day and night. ⊠ *Eleftherias Park, Ilisia* ☎ *210/722–3784* ⊕ *www.toparko.gr.*

NEOS KOSMOS

BOUZOUKIA

Fever. One of Athens's most popular bouzoukia clubs showcases the most popular singers of the day, including Yiannis Parios, Sakis Rouvas, and Stamatis Gonidis. It's open Friday and Saturday, from September to June. ⊠ *Syngrou avenue and Lagoumitzi 25, near Fix, Neos Kosmos* ☎ *210/921–7331* ⊕ *www.fever.gr.*

PERFORMING ARTS

Athens's energetic year-round performing arts scene kicks into a higher gear from June through September, when numerous stunning outdoor theaters host everything from classical Greek drama (in both Greek and English), opera, symphony, and ballet, to rock, pop, and hip-hop concerts. In general, dress for summer performances is fairly casual, though the city's glitterati get decked out for events such as a world premiere opera at the Odeon of Herodes Atticus. From October through May, when the arts move indoors, the Megaron Mousikis/Athens Concert Hall is the biggest venue. Performances at outdoor summer venues, stadiums, and the Megaron tend to be priced between €15 to €120 for tickets, depending on the location of seats and popularity of performers.

FESTIVALS

Every summer, the city center is covered with posters for a host of big-name music festivals.

Fodor'sChoice **Athens and Epidaurus Festival.** The city's primary artistic event (formerly
★ known as the Hellenic Festival) runs from June through August at a dozen venues, including the ancient Odeon of Herodes Atticus in the Acropolis. The festival has showcased performers such as Norah Jones, Dame Kiri Te Kanawa, Luciano Pavarotti, and Diana Ross; such dance troupes as the Royal London Ballet, the Joaquin Cortes Ballet, and Maurice Béjart; symphony orchestras; and local groups performing ancient Greek drama. Usually a major world premiere is staged during the festival. Starting in 2006, creative director Yiorgos Loukos rejuvenated the festival, adding more youthful venues and bringing a wider gamut of performances, including world musicians, modern dance, and multimedia artists. The Odeon theater makes a delightful backdrop, with the floodlighted Acropolis looming behind the audience and the Roman arches behind the performers. The upper-level seats have no cushions, so bring something to sit on, and wear low shoes, since the marble steps are steep. For viewing most performances, the *Gamma* zone is the best seat choice. Tickets go on sale three weeks before performances but sell out quickly for popular shows; they are available from the festival box office in Syntagma Square, at the box office outside the Odeon theater, and at major bookshops in Athens (for a full list, check the website). Prices range from €15 to as high as €120 for the big names; student and youth discounts are available. ☎ 210/928–2900 *General Information* ⊕ *www.greekfestival.gr.*

Ejekt Festival. The Ejekt Festival, which brings together pop, rock and electronica bands, usually takes place every July in one of the Olympic venues in Faliro. ⊕ *www.ejekt.gr.*

Festival Vrahon "In the Shadow of the Rocks". Performances by well-known Greek performer Haroula Alexiou, international acts such as the Beijing Opera and James, and ancient Greek theater classics are staged in an attractively remodeled old quarry, now known as the Theatro Vrahon *Melina Merkouri* (and its sister stage nearby, the *Anna Synodinou*). The festival begins in early June and lasts until the end of September every year; most performances start at 9 pm. Buy tickets (€20–€100) at the theater before the show. ☎ 210/762–6438, 210/760–9340 ⊕ www.festivalvraxon.gr.

ARTS PERFORMANCES

Two Athens 2004 Olympic venues located about 20 to 30 minutes from the city center by taxi or public transportation host the biggest concerts. Madonna, Jennifer Lopez, and U2 have performed at the open-air Athens Olympic Sports Complex (OAKA), while Brazilian star Caetano Veloso and the international *West Side Story* troupe have appeared inside the Badminton Theater. There are other important performing arts venues around town.

TICKETS

It's easiest to buy tickets through ticket vendors like Ticket House or at Public (an electronics store that sells music CDs).

Public. You can buy tickets for popular concerts and performing arts events at this electronics store with a convenient location in Central Athens. ⊠ *Karageorgi Servias 1, Syntagma* ☎ 80111/40000 ⊕ *www.public.gr.*

Ticket House. Like Ticketmaster in the United States, Ticket House sells all sorts of performing arts and popular music concert tickets. ⊠ *Panepistimiou 42, Kolonaki* ☎ 210/360–8366 ⊕ *www.tickethouse.gr.*

PERFORMANCE VENUES

Athens Olympic Sports Complex (OAKA). Big acts fill the main Athens 2004 Games arena with music—as many as 75,000 people jammed the place when U2 appeared during their 2010 "360" tour. Lady Gaga, the Rolling Stones, and Madonna have also performed here—the latter actually holds the arena record, with 75,637 people attending her 2008 show. ⊠ *OAKA complex, off Kifissias avenue 37, Maroussi* ☎ 210/683–4060 ⊕ *www.oaka.com.gr.*

Badminton Theater. This state-of-the-art performance center specializes in slick song-and-dance acts, occasionally geared towards children. ⊠ *Goudi Military Park, off Mesogeion or Katehaki avenue, Goudi* ☎ 210/884–0600 ⊕ *www.badmintontheater.gr.*

Fodor's Choice ★ **Dora Stratou Theater.** The country's leading folk dance company performs exhilarating and sublime Greek folk dances (from all regions), as well as from Cyprus, in eye-catching authentic costumes in programs that change every two weeks. Performances are held Wednesday through Sunday from the end of May through September. Show times are at 9:30 pm, with shows on Saturday and Sunday at 8:15 pm. Tickets cost €15, and they can be purchased at the box office before the show (each performance lasts 90 minutes, with no intermission). ⊠ *Arakinthou and*

FULL MOON FESTIVALS IN ATHENS

Many years, on the night of the full moon in August (believed to be the brightest moon of the year), the Ministry of Culture holds a celebration of the August Full Moon in Athens and other sites around the country. In the past, venues including the Acropolis, Roman Agora, and the Odeon of Herodes Atticus have been open for free, with performances of opera, Greek dance, and classical music amid the ancient columns by moonlight. Check the ministry's site (⊕ *www.culture.gr*) and local English-language publications to see if you're lucky enough to be there in a year when this must-see is happening.

Voutie, Filopappou ☎ *210/921–4650 theater, 210/324–4395 troupe's office* ⊕ *www.grdance.org.*

Lycabettus Theater. The specialty of this theater (capacity: 5,000), set on a pinnacle of Mt. Lycabettus, is popular concerts; past performers have included Bryan Ferry, Marianne Faithful, Pink Martini, and Cesaria Evora. Since buses travel only as far as the bottom of the hill, either take a taxi, or buy a one-way ticket on the funicular and then walk about 10 minutes to the theater. Check local listings for scheduled concerts during the summer months. ⊠ *At top of Mt. Lycabettus, Kolonaki* ☎ *210/322–7200, 210/722–7209 theater box office.*

Megaron Mousikis/Athens Concert Hall. World-class Greek and international artists take the stage at the Megaron Mousikis to perform in concerts and opera from September through June. Information and tickets are available weekdays 10–6 and Saturday 10–2. Prices range from €10 to €90; there's a substantial discount for students and those 8 to 18 years old. Tickets go on sale a few weeks in advance, and many events sell out within hours. On the first day of sales, tickets can be purchased by cash or credit card only in person at the Athens Concert Hall. From the second day on, remaining tickets may be purchased by phone, in person from the downtown box office (Omirou 8, Kolonaki, weekdays 10–4), at Public stores all over Athens, and online. ⊠ *Vasilissis Sofias and Kokkali, Ilisia* ☎ *210/728–2333* ⊕ *www.megaron.gr* Ⓜ *Megaro.*

Onassis Cultural Centre. Athens's impressive cultural space, the Onassis Cultural Centre, hosts events from across the whole spectrum of the arts, from theater, dance, and music to the written word. Its construction was exclusively funded by the Onassis Foundation, in memory of the legendary Greek tycoon, and the architecturally noteworthy building now occupies an entire block along one of Athens's main busy thoroughfares. Inside the airy rectangular shell, contructed in a design composed of white marble bands (which reflect the sun by day) and encompassing the lit interiors at night, the center is home to two amphitheaters, a Greek bistro (Hytra Apla), an award-winning restaurant (*Hytra, reviewed in Where to Eat*), a rooftop bar (in summer) and exhibition spaces that occupy more than 18,000 square meters and can be seen bustling with activity from October to June. The emphasis here is on contemporary artistic expression—to that effect, an ongoing calendar of exhibitions and art programs showcase and assist contemporary Greek artists. ⊠ *107–109 Syngrou avenue, Neos Kosmos* ☎ *210/900–5800* ⊕ *www.sgt.gr.*

Philippos Nakas Conservatory. Inexpensive classical or jazz music concerts are held throughout the year at this conservatory. Tickets cost about €10. ⊠ *Ippokratous 41, Exarchia* ☎ *210/363–4000* ⊕ *www.nakas.gr.*

Romantso. An alternative cultural center located in a 1960s concrete block that used to be a printing plant for popular magazine *Romantso*. Come here for a drink at the post-industrial minimalist bar, to attend a yoga session, a talk, or to watch a film at the auditorium (check the listings). Upstairs are "incubators" of emerging companies/start-ups. ⊠ *Anaxagora 3-5, Omonia Sq.* ☎ *216/700-3325* ⊕ *www.romantso.gr.*

FILM

Films are shown in original-language versions with Greek subtitles (except for major animated films), a definite boon for foreigners. Downtown theaters have the most advanced technology and most comfortable seats. Tickets run about €9. Check the *Kathimerini* in the *International New York Times* for programs, schedules, and addresses and phone numbers of theaters, including outdoor theaters. Unless old cinema theaters have air-conditioning, they close from June through September, making way for *therina* (open-air theaters), an enchanting, uniquely Greek entertainment that offers instant escapism under a starry sky.

Cine Paris. Kitschy posters of old Greek movies are for sale in the lobby of this rooftop-garden movie theater (first opened in 1920). It's close to many hotels and tavernas, on Plaka's main walkway, and boasts Dolby Digital sound. It is open from May to October. ⊠ *Kidathineon 22, Plaka* ☎ *210/322–2071* ⊕ *www.cineparis.gr.*

Elli Filmcenter. Frequent Elli for independent and art films that don't make it to Greece's more-mainstream cinemas. This movie theater closes during the summer months. ⊠ *Akadimias 64, Syntagma* ☎ *210/363–2789* ⊗ *Closed Jun.–Aug.*

Fodor's Choice ★ **Cine Thisio.** Films at this open-air theater, the oldest in Athens (1935), compete with a view of the Acropolis. It's on the Unification of Archaeological Sites walkway and conveniently boasts tables among the seating. The owners offer homemade sour cherry juice or Tsipouro accompanied with fish roe, a Messolonghi delicacy from their hometown. ⊠ *Apostolou Pavlou 7, Thissio* ☎ *210/342–0864, 210/347–0980* ⊕ *www.cinethisio.gr* ⊗ *Nightly Apr.–Oct.*

SHOPPING

For serious retail therapy, most Athenians head to the shopping streets that branch off central Syntagma and Kolonaki squares. Syntagma is the starting point for popular Ermou, a pedestrian zone where large, international chains like Zara, Sephora, H&M, Massimo Dutti, Mothercare, Replay, Nike, Accessorize, and Marks & Spencer have edged out small, independent retailers. You'll find local shops on streets parallel and perpendicular to Ermou: Mitropoleos, Voulis, Nikis, Perikleous, and Praxitelous among them. Poke around here for real bargains, like strings of freshwater pearls, loose semiprecious stones, or made-to-fit hats. Much ritzier is the Kolonaki quarter, with boutiques and designer shops on fashionable streets like Anagnostopoulou, Tsakalof, Skoufa, Solonos, and Kanari. Voukourestiou, the link between Kolonaki and Syntagma, is where you'll find Louis Vuitton, Hermes, Polo Ralph Lauren, and similar brands. In Monastiraki, coppersmiths have their shops on Ifestou. You can pick up copper wine jugs, candlesticks, cookware, and more for next to nothing.

Many stores in Athens are open until only 3 or 4 on Monday, Wednesday, and Saturday, but they may be open later (until 7 or 8) on Tuesday, Thursday, and Friday.

The flea market centered on Pandrossou and Ifestou operates on Sunday morning and has practically everything, from secondhand guitars to Russian vodka. Keep one rule in mind: always bargain!

WHAT TO BUY

Antiques are in vogue now, so the prices of these items have soared. Shops on Pandrossou sell small antiques and icons; always check for authenticity. You must have government permission to export genuine objects from the ancient Greek, Roman, or Byzantine periods.

Greece is known for its well-made shoes (most shops are clustered around the Ermou pedestrian zone and in Kolonaki), its furs (Mitropoleos near Syntagma), its jewelry (Voukourestiou and Panepistimiou), and its durable leather items (Pandrossou in Monastiraki). In Plaka shops you can find sandals (currently making a fashionable comeback), fishermen's caps—always a good present—and the hand-knit sweaters worn by fishermen; across the United States these have surfaced at triple the Athens price. Greek skincare ranges like Korres and Apivita are also much more affordable in Athens than abroad.

Discover touristy treasures in the numerous souvenir shops along the streets of Plaka and Monastiraki—in particular, look for them in the Monastiraki flea market and the shops along Adrianou street, behind the Monastiraki train station.

Prices are much lower for gold and silver in Greece than in many Western countries, and the jewelry is of high quality. Many shops in Plaka carry original pieces available at a good price. For those with more expensive tastes, the Voukourestiou pedestrian mall off Syntagma Square has a number of the city's leading jewelry shops.

If you're looking for a cheap and iconic gift to take back home, pick up a string of *komboloi* (worry beads) in plastic, wood, or stone. You can pick them up very cheaply in Monastiraki or look in antiques shops for more-expensive versions, with amber, silver, or black onyx beads. Another popular gift option is *matia*, the good-luck charms (usually turquoise) that ward off the evil eye. Reasonably priced natural sponges also make good presents. Look for those that are unbleached, since the lighter ones tend to fall apart quickly.

MAKRIYIANNI

JEWELRY

Andronikos Sagiannos. For five generations, the Sagiannos family's creations have adorned the fingers, necks, and ears of stylish Athenian matrons. The tradition continues in this shop/gallery, but with more-modern, one-of-a-kind pieces inspired by ordinary objects like bar codes and buttons. The contemporary space often hosts the work of young and progressive jewelry designers and offers many pieces at affordable prices. ⊠ *Makriyianni 3, Makriyianni* ☎ *210/924–7323.*

PLAKA

ANTIQUES AND ICONS

Elliniko Spiti. Art restorer Dimitris Koutelieris is inspired by his home island of Naxos. He salvages most of his materials from houses under restoration, then fashions them into picture frames, little wooden boats, small chairs, and other decorative objects. In his hands objects like cabin doors or window shutters gain a magical second life. ⊠ *Kekropos 14, Plaka* ☎ *210/323–5924.*

FOOD

Taste of Greece. This ethnic grocery store is a treasure trove of traditional delicacies from all over Greece—from the unique-tasting *mastiha* liqueur from the island of Chios to truffle-flavored extra virgin olive oil from Kalamata. The friendly owner is eager to offer little tastes of everything and chat about the provenance of all the products he has painstakingly picked for his quaint little shop. ⊠ *Adrianou 67, Plaka* ☎ *210/321–0550.*

GIFTS

Fine Wine. Elegant wine gift packs are available at this old-fashioned wine shop, where you can browse a broad selection of Greek wines and liqueurs. The couple who own this place are veritable wine lovers themselves and will be eager to offer any advice you need. ⊠ *Lysikratous 3, Plaka* ☎ *210/323–0350* ⊕ *www.finewine.gr.*

Fodor's Choice ★

Forget Me Not. This inspirational "cultural goods" shop already has faithful customers, even though it only opened its doors in April 2014. You can buy gifts with a contemporary Greek design twist and a sense of humor, created by local designers Greece is for Lovers, Beetroot, Yiorgos Drakos, Studiolav, AC Design, and more. From Idisti's beach towels with printed good luck charms to a copy of the classic Hermes of Praxitelous sporting sunglasses (by design team Greece is for Lovers) and the scarves by The Greek.Flag.Project, this is Greek design at its best. ⊠ *Adrianou 100, Plaka* ☎ *210/325–3740* ⊕ *www.forgetmenot-athens.gr.*

HANDICRAFTS

Amorgos. Wood furniture and ceramics, all hand-carved and hand-painted by the shop's owners—a creative couple specializing in antique furniture restoration and interior design—beautifully feature motifs from regional Greek designs. Needlework, hanging ceiling lamps, shadow puppets, and other decorative accessories like cushions, fabrics, wooden carved chests, and traditional low tables called *sofras,* are also for sale. ⊠ *Kodrou 3, Plaka* ☎ *210/324–3836* ⊕ *www.amorgosart.gr.*

The Olive Tree Store. This unique shop sells items made exclusively of olive wood, such as salad bowls and tongs, wall clocks, jewelry, and even backgammon sets. Alas, the beautiful, specially made, olive wood Gibson-style guitar is not for sale. ⊠ *Adrianou 67, Plaka* ☎ *210/322–2922.*

MONASTIRAKI

ANTIQUES AND ICONS

Old Market. Old coins, from Greece and around the world, are for sale at this antiques shop, along with stamps, engravings, antique toys and radios, musical instruments, and medals. ⊠ *Normanou 7, Monastiraki* ☎ *210/331–1638* ⊕ *www.oldmarket.gr.*

CLOTHING

Pantelis Melissinos. Pantelis follows in the steps of his father Stavros, a poetic figure, gentle soul, and longtime fixture of the Monastiraki scene, as well as artist shoemaker, whose shop was once visited by the Beatles and Jackie O. Pantelis also writes poetry but his main claim to fame remains the handmade sandals that continue to delight countless tourists and celebrities. ⊠ *Ayias Theklas 2, Monastiraki* ☎ *210/321–9247* ⊕ *www.melissinos-art.com.*

HANDICRAFTS

Center of Hellenic Tradition. The center is an outlet for quality handicrafts—ceramics, weavings, sheep bells, wood carvings, prints, and old paintings. Take a break from shopping in the center's quiet and quaint I Oraia Ellas café, to enjoy a salad or mezedes in clear view of the Parthenon. Upstairs is an art gallery hosting temporary exhibitions of Greek art. ⊠ *Mitropoleos 59 and Pandrossou 36, Monastiraki* ☎ *210/321–3023, 210/321–3842 café* ⊕ *www.kelp.gr.*

THISSIO

SPAS

Fodor'sChoice ★ **Hammam Baths.** For a modern Hammam experience head to Hammam Baths, a gorgeous neoclassic house that has been converted into a full-amenities day spa with Eastern decorative undertones and excellent service. ⊠ *Ayion Asomaton 17, Thissio* ☎ *210/322–3073* ⊕ *www.hammam.gr.*

SYNTAGMA

ANTIQUES AND ICONS

Pylarinos. Stamp and coin collectors love this packed shop, which also has a good selection of 19th-century engravings. ⊠ *Panepistimiou 18, inside arcade, Syntagma* ☎ *210/363–0688.*

CLOTHING

Kaplan Furs. Despite animal-rights campaigns, Mitropoleos is lined with fur shops. Kaplan has everything from pieced-together stoles to fluffy purple handbags and full-length minks (which often hail from the northern city of Kastoria). ⊠ *Mitropoleos 22–24, Syntagma* ☎ *210/322–2226.*

GIFTS

Fodor'sChoice ★ **Diplous Pelekys.** A large variety of handwoven articles, genuine folk art, ceramics from all over Greece, and traditional and modern jewelry all on show here make excellent, and affordable, gifts. The cozy and tasteful shop is run by third-generation weavers and is the oldest folk art shop in Athens (established 1925). ⊠ *Bolani Arcade, Voulis 7 and Kolokotroni 3, Syntagma* ☎ *210/322–3783* ⊕ *www.diplouspelekys.gr.*

Fresh Line. Among the solid shampoo cakes, body oils, and face packs sold here are a tremendous number of organic Greek-made soaps, most sliced from big blocks or wheels (as though they were cheese)—you pay by weight. Best bets are the cinnamon-and-jasmine soap, "Cybele," which contains organic moisturizers and the "Orpheus and Eurydice" soap for sensitive skin—it's made with vanilla, milk, and rice, just like Greek *rizogalo* (rice pudding). Try also the new "Galatea" range. The scents are uplifting and sensuous. ⊠ *Ermou 30, Syntagma* ☎ *210/324–6500* ⊕ *www.freshline.gr.*

Korres. The flagship store of this comestics line sells only the company's namesake cosmetics, not the full range of drugs and medications that are available at the original pharmacy in the Pangrati neighborhood. ⊠ *Ermou 4, Syntagma* ☎ *210/321-0054.*

Mastiha Shop. Medical research lauding the healing properties of gum mastic, a resin from trees only found on the Greek island of Chios, has spawned a range of exciting wellness products, from chewing gum and cookies to liqueurs and cosmetics. ✉ *Panepistimiou 6, at Kriezotou, Syntagma* ☎ *210/363–2750.*

Tanagrea. Hand-painted ceramic pomegranates—a symbol of fertility and good fortune—are one of the most popular items in one of the city's oldest gift shops. ✉ *Petraki 3, enter from Ermou 11, Syntagma* ☎ *210/321–6783.*

JEWELRY

Fodor'sChoice ★ **Lalaounis.** This world-famous Greek jewelry house experiments with its designs, taking ideas from nature, biology, African art, and ancient Greek pieces—the last are sometimes so close to the original that they're mistaken for museum artifacts. The pieces are mainly in gold, some in silver—look out for the decorative objects inspired by ancient Greek houseware. The famed tradition here started with Ilias Lalaounis (also founder of the Lalaounis Jewelry Museum) and is now proudly continued by his four daughters and grandchildren. There's also a branch at Papadiamandi 7 (☎ *210/623–1900*) in the leafy Kifissia neighborhood of north Athens. ✉ *Panepistimiou 6, at Voukourestiou, Syntagma* ☎ *210/361–1371* ⊕ *www.lalaounis.gr.*

PSIRRI

CLOTHING

Occhi Concept Store. Art and the latest clothes, jewelry, and accessories by progressive Greek designers are displayed side-by-side in this gallery-style shop, where you can also find some hip souvenirs. ✉ *Ipitou 5 and Voulis 40, Syntagma* ☎ *211/184–5416* ⊕ *www.occhi.biz.*

KOLONAKI

ANTIQUES AND ICONS

Fodor'sChoice ★ **Martinos.** Antiques collectors should head here to look for items such as exquisite dowry chests, old swords, precious fabrics, and Venetian glass. You will certainly discover something you like in the four floors of this renovated antiques shop that has been an Athens landmark over the past 100 years. There's another branch in the Kolonaki neighborhood at Pindarou 24 (☎ *210/360–9449*). ✉ *Pandrossou 50, Monastiraki* ☎ *210/321–3110* ⊕ *www.martinosart.gr.*

ART GALLERIES

Zoumboulakis Art-Design-Antiques. The art shop of this respected private art gallery stocks some beautiful, limited edition silkscreens by famous Greek painters Yiannis Moralis, Nikos Xatzikyriakos-Gikas, Yiannis Tsarouchis, and many more. It's usually open until at least 3 or 4 (until 8 on Tuesday, Thursday, and Friday) and closed Sunday. ✉ *Kriezotou 6, Kolonaki* ☎ *210/363–4454* ⊕ *www.zoumboulakis.gr.*

CLOTHING

Koukoutsi. Urban design hipsters will love this T-shirt shop. It has a collection humorously and lovingly "commemorating" living in Athens in the years of the economic crisis, with such classic print logos as "Ich bin ein Athener, Athens needs love" and "Eat more feta to reduce greek debt." ✉ *Skoufa 81, Kolonaki* ☎ *210/361–4060* ⊕ *www.koukoutsi.net.*

Parthenis. Fashion designer Dimitris Parthenis opened his first boutique in 1970. Today his daughter Orsalia Parthenis continues the family tradition of creating urban chic fashion with a Bohemian hint. Natural fibers, such as wool, silk, and cotton are used to create relaxed, body-hugging silhouettes. There is an eyewear line and a wedding collection, too. ⊠ *Dimokritou 20 and Tsakalof, Kolonaki* ☎ *210/363–3158* ⊕ *www.orsalia-parthenis.gr.*

GIFTS

Fodor's Choice ★ **Benaki Museum Gift Shop.** The airy museum shop has excellent copies of Greek icons, jewelry, and folk art—at fair prices. You will also find embroideries, ceramics, stationery, art books, small reliefs, and sculpture pieces. The new Benaki Museum Annexe on Pireos Street has its own shop with an interesting collection of modern Greek jewelry. The gift shop is also open on Monday (even though museum is closed). ⊠ *Benaki Museum, Koumbari 1, at Vasilissis Sofias, Kolonaki* ☎ *210/362–7367* ⊕ *www.benaki.gr.*

Fodor's Choice ★ **Kombologadiko.** From pinhead-size "evil eyes" to 2-inch-diameter wood, sugarcane, or shell beads, you'll find a dizzying selection of beads here to string your own *komboloi* (worry beads). You'll admire the variety of this unique Greek version of a rosary, which can be made from traditional amber, but also from coral root, camel bone, semi-precious stones, and many more materials. ⊠ *Amerikis 9, Kolonaki* ☎ *212/700–0500* ⊕ *www.kombologadiko.gr.*

Thiamis. Talented iconographer Aristides Makos creates beautiful hand-painted, gold-leaf icons on wood and stone. His slightly cluttered shop also sells beautiful handmade model ships and made-to-order items. Check out the website for some very traditional (and amazing) Greek artwork and style. ⊠ *Asklipiou 71, Kolonaki* ☎ *210/363–7993* ⊕ *www.thiamis.com.*

JEWELRY

Elena Votsi. Elena Votsi designed jewelry for Gucci and Ralph Lauren before opening her own boutiques, where she sells exquisite, larger than life creations in coral, amethyst, aquamarine, and turquoise. In 2003 she designed the Athens 2004 Olympic Games gold medal; in 2009 her handmade 18-karat gold ring with diamonds won a Couture Design Award in the "Best-to-Couture" category in Las Vegas. Brava! ⊠ *Xanthou 7, Kolonaki* ☎ *210/360–0936* ⊕ *www.elenavotsi.com.*

Fanourakis. Original gold masterpieces can be had at these shops, where Athenian masters, prompted by jewelry designer Lina Fanouraki, use gold almost like a fabric—creasing, scoring, and fluting it. There's another branch at Panagitsas 6 (☎ *210/623–2334*) in the Kifissia neighborhood. ⊠ *Patriarchou Ioakeim 23, Kolonaki* ☎ *210/721–1762* ⊕ *www.fanourakis.gr.*

Museum of Cycladic Art Shop. Exceptional modern versions of ancient jewelry designs are available in the gift shop of this museum, where you can also find museum replicas and inspired ceramics. ⊠ *Museum of Cycladic Art, Neofitou Douka 4, Kolonaki* ☎ *210/722–8321* ⊕ *www.cycladic.gr.*

Continued on page 190

GREEK BY DESIGN

Shopping is now considered an Olympic sport in Greece. Many get the urge to splurge in the chic shops of Mykonos, Rhodes, and Crete, the islands that launched a thousand gifts. But if you really want to bag the best in Greek style, Athens is where to get the goods.

The Greeks had a word for it: *tropos*. Style. You would expect nothing less from the folks who gave us the Venus de Milo, the Doric column, and the lyre-back chair. To say that they have had a long tradition as artisans and craftsmen is, of course, an understatement. Even back in ancient Rome, Greece was the word. The Romans may have engineered the stone vault and perfected the toilet, but when it came to style and culture, they were perfectly content to knock off Grecian dress, sculpture, décor, and architecture, then considered the height of fashion. Fast-forward 2,500 years and little has changed. Many works of modern art were conceived as an Aegean paean, including the statues of Brancusi and Le Corbusier's minimalistic skyscrapers—both art-

ists were deeply influenced by ancient Cycladic art. Today, the goddess dress struts the runways of Michael Kors and Valentino while Homer has made the leap to Hollywood in such box-office blockbusters as *300* and *Troy*.

Speaking of which, those ancient Trojans may have once tut-tutted about Greeks bearing gifts but would have second thoughts these days. Aunt Ethel has now traded in those plastic souvenir models of the Parthenon for a new Athenian bounty: pieces of Byzantine-style gold jewelry; hand-woven bedspreads from Hydra; strands of amber *komboloi* worry beads; and reproductions of red-figure ceramic vases. These are gifts you cannot resist and will be forever be glad you didn't.

(above) Byzantine design jewelry

BEARING GIFTS?

Seeing some of the glories of Aegean craftsmanship is probably one of the reasons you've come to Greece. The eggshell-thin pottery Minoans were fashioning more than 3,500 years ago, Byzantine jewelry and icons, colorful rugs that were woven in front of the fire as part of a dowry, not to mention all those bits of ancient masonry—these comprise a magnificent legacy of arts and crafts.

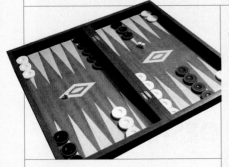

LEATHER SANDALS

Ancient Greek women with means and a sense of style wore sandals with straps that wrapped around the ankles—what today's fashion mags call "strappy sandals," proof that some classics are always in vogue. The most legendary maker is Athens's very own Stavros Melissinos, whose creations were once sported by the Beatles and Sophia Loren. He has been crafting sandals for more than 50 years.

TAVLÍ BOARDS

No matter where you are in Greece, follow the sound of clicking dice and you'll probably find yourself in a kafenion. There, enthusiasts will be huddled over Greece's favorite game, a close cousin to backgammon. Tavlí boards are sold everywhere in Greece, but the most magnificent board you'll ever see is not for sale—a marble square inlaid with gold and ivory, crafted sometime before 1500 BC for the amusement of Minoan kings and now on display at the archaeological museum in Heraklion, Crete.

WORRY BEADS

Feeling fidgety? Partake of a Greek custom and fiddle with your worry beads, or komboloi. The amber or coral beads are loosely strung on a long strand and look like prayer beads, yet they have no religious significance. Even so, on a stressful day the relaxing effect can seem like divine intervention. Particularly potent are beads painted with the "evil eye."

ICONS

Icon painting flourished in Greece as the Renaissance took hold of Western Europe, and panels of saints and other heavenly creatures are among the country's greatest artistic treasures. Some, like many of those in the 799 churches on the island of Tinos, are said to possess miraculous healing powers, attracting thousands of cure-seeking believers each year. Icons attract art buyers too, but if you can easily afford one, it's almost certainly a modern reproduction.

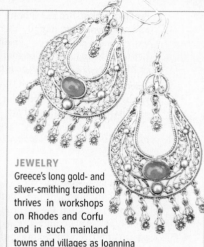

JEWELRY

Greece's long gold- and silver-smithing tradition thrives in workshops on Rhodes and Corfu and in such mainland towns and villages as Ioannina and Stemnitsa. Many artisans turn to the past for inspiration—Bronze Age cruciform figures, gold necklaces from the Hellenistic period dangling with pomegranates, Byzantine-style pendants—while others tap out distinctly modern creations using age-old techniques.

WEAVING

Even goddesses spent their idle hours weaving (remember Arachne, so proud of her skills at the loom that Athena turned her into a spider?). From the mountains of Arcadia to such worldly enclaves as Mykonos, mortals sit behind handlooms to clack out folkloric rugs, bedspreads, and tablecloths.

CERAMICS

Ancient Greek pottery was a black-and-red medium: the Spartans and Corinthians painted glossy black figures on a reddish-orange background; later ceramists switched the effect with stunning results, reddish-hued figures on a black background. Artisans still create both, and potters on Crete and elsewhere in Greece throw huge terracotta storage jars, pithoi, that are appealing, if no longer practical, additions to any household.

BARGAINING FOR BEGINNERS

In Greece there is often the "first price" and the "last price." Bargaining is still par for the course (except in the fanciest stores). And if you're planning a shopping day, leave those Versace shoes at home—shopkeepers often decide on a price after sizing up the prospective buyer's income bracket.

Pentheroudakis. Browse among the classic designs in gold, diamond, and gemstones but, happily, there are less expensive trinkets, like silver worry beads that can be personalized with cubed letters in Greek or Latin and with the stone of your choice. ⊠ *Voukourestiou 19, Kolonaki* ☎ *210/361–3187* ⊕ *www.pentheroudakis.com.*

Zolotas. Since 1895, this jeweler, Lalaounis's main competitor in the status sweepstakes, is noted for its superb museum copies in gold and also its exquisite objets d'art. There's another branch at Stadiou 9 (☎ *210/322–1212*), near Syntagma Square. ⊠ *Panepistimiou 10, Kolonaki* ☎ *210/360–1272* ⊕ *www.zolotas.gr.*

EXARCHIA
GIFTS

Greece is for Lovers. The showroom of this daring Greek design team is open by appointment only, but it is certainly worth the effort to call ahead. Traditional Greek products like sandals, the humble donkey saddle, and clay decanters get a contemporary face-lift here, often with a splash of bittersweet humor and irony. It is a luxe aesthetic that borders on kitsch. You can also buy the company's designs at Forget Me Not in the Plaka neighborhood. ⊠ *Valtetsiou 50–52, Exarchia* ☎ *210/924–5064* ⊕ *www.greeceisforlovers.com.*

PANGRATI
GIFTS

Fodor'sChoice
★

Korres Pharmacy. Natural beauty products blended in traditional recipes using Greek herbs and flowers have graced the bathroom shelves of celebrities like Rihanna and Angelina Jolie but in Athens they are available at most pharmacies for regular-folk prices. For the largest selection of basil-lemon shower gel, coriander body lotion, olive-stone face scrub, and wild-rose eye cream, go to the flagship store on Ermou street or the original Korres pharmacy (behind the Panathenaic Stadium). Not surprisingly, Korres also maintains a traditional laboratory for herbal preparations such as tinctures, oils, capsules, and teas. ⊠ *Eratosthenous 8 and Ivikou, Pangrati* ☎ *210/722–2774* ⊕ *www.korres.com.*

4

ATTICA AND DELPHI

Visit Fodors.com for advice, updates, and bookings

WELCOME TO ATTICA AND DELPHI

TOP REASONS TO GO

★ **Delphi, "Navel of the World":** Delphi's Sanctuary of Apollo invites you to imagine a time of oracles, enigmatic prophecies, and mystical emanations.

★ **Sunset at Sounion:** Perched over the water, the spectacular Temple of Poseidon still summons strong emotions in this land of seafarers.

★ **Mighty Marathon:** Dare you retrace Pheidippides's first marathon when he ran 26 hilly miles from this town to Athens in 490 BC?

★ **Cape Vouliagmeni:** Enjoy a sun-kissed day on the beach at the heart of the eternally glamorous Athens Riviera.

★ **Naval Galaxidi:** The town the shipbuilders built back in the 18th century today oozes old-world charm and quaint character.

1 Attica. Head for the rolling hills (and a few mountains) for a welcome change from the capital's hectic pace. Explore the archaeological sites, secluded beaches, small vineyards, riding clubs, serene monasteries, and hot nightlife at the seaside resorts of Vouliagmeni and Kavouri. Top sights here include ancient treasures like the Temple of Poseidon at Sounion, the Marathon Tomb, and Eleusis's Sanctuary of Demeter, plus the Byzantine monastery of Kaisariani and the trails of Mount Hymettos.

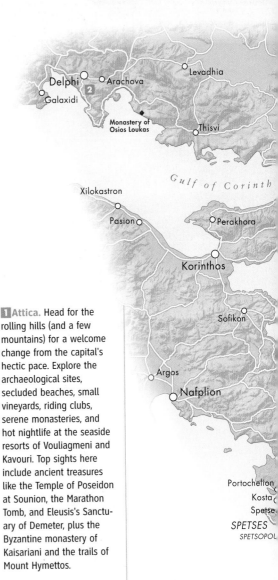

2 **Delphi and Environs.**
Not far from Athens, Delphi's ancient rocks signal a time of ancient worship and secret ritual. Steeped in history, this region is today popular not only with tourists who flock to the sublime Sanctuary of Apollo, its renovated museum, and the nearby monastery of Osios Loukas, but also with skiers, who have turned Arachova into the most cosmopolitan ski resort in the country.

GETTING ORIENTED

Attica, the southeastern tip of central Greece, is much more than the home of Athens—it is also a fertile land, with fabled temples and beautiful Byzantine monasteries. Bordered by three mountain masses—Mt. Hymettos to the east, Mt. Aigaleo and Mt. Parnitha to the west, and Mt. Pendeli to the north—Attica mainly lies east and north of the Athens basin. A tramline from Glyfada to downtown Athens allows travelers to easily enjoy the famed Athens Riviera and the Apollo Coast, with its Temple of Sounion and luxurious resorts. Cradled in the mountains, the Delphi region is set around Mt. Parnassus and Arachova.

4

Updated
by Natasha
Giannousi

If anything was ever truly "classical," it is the landscape of Attica. Attikí is a mountainous region, bounded on three sides by the sea and an indented coastline fringed with innumerable beaches. On stony foothills pungently aromatic shrubs grow: thyme, myrtle, and lentisk. Higher up, the feathery Aleppo pine of Attica becomes supplanted by dark firs. Inland, gently undulating hills are laced with vineyards and, over all, hangs the famed light, the purest of lights sharply delineating a majestic land.

It is the proper setting for a region immensely rich in mythological and historical allusions. In fact, recorded history began here, in the towns of the Boeotian plain, although where legend leaves off and fact begins is often a matter of conjecture (witness Thebes, home to the luckless Oedipus). However, the story of Attica has been almost inextricably bound to that of Athens, the most powerful of the villages that lay scattered over the peninsula. By force and persuasion Athens brought these towns together, creating a unit that by the 5th century BC had become the center of an empire.

The heart of the region was the sacred precinct of Delphi. For the ancient Greeks, this site was the center of the universe, home to Apollo and the most sacred oracle, and, today, its archaeological site remains a principal place of pilgrimage.

For more worldly pleasures, travelers head to the sun-gilt sea bordering the Athens Riviera and the "Apollo Coast"—home to the famed Temple to Poseidon atop Cape Sounion.

PLANNING

WHEN TO GO

June and September offer the benefits of summer without the July and August crowds. Athens's nightlife shifts to the southern coast July through August. Après-ski town Arachova is the place to be in winter (though expensive), but it's only a stepping stone to Delphi in summer. Attica's northeastern coast is beautiful anytime, though in the winter things can feel dead. In Delphi, be prepared to go head-to-head with the crowds and the heat in summer. The beaches, of course, are most enjoyable in full summer, but even chic and pricey Astir beach gets engulfed by a rising tide of tourists. A much better time to visit is April to June, when wildflowers carpet the arid hillsides of Attica and the Marathon plain. September and October is another beautiful stretch since the sea remains warm, with temperatures that are still ideal for swimming.

PLANNING YOUR TIME

A week in this region would allow plenty of time for exploring, letting you hit the major archaeological sites of Delphi and Sounion as well as traverse Marathon at less than breakneck speed. Short on time? In two to three days, you can explore Attica's coasts and visit a few key sites. The ancient Greeks believed Delphi was the center of the world, so you could do worse than making it the focus of a trip. With stunning mountain scenery, a world-famous archaeological site, and an excellent museum, touring it can easily take up two days. (Note: While it's possible to drive from Athens to Delphi and back in a day, we don't recommend it. A night in the crisp mountain air is a pleasant alternative to falling asleep behind the wheel.) If you do need to see Delphi in a day, however, be sure to leave Athens early (it's a three- to four-hour trip). A second day could be spent hiking around the mountain village of Arachova, or even skiing (in season). Or head to the pretty port town of Galaxidi.

GETTING HERE AND AROUND

Athens and Attica system buses (and trams) run from Athens's center to the southern and northeastern coast, and points from Marathon to Eleusis. Taking a bus to Arachova, Delphi, and Galaxidi may help you avoid road fatigue. Attica's public bus service is extensive, though buses can be infrequent so, for ambitious exploring in the area, a car is invaluable. The roads to Arachova, Mt. Parnassus, and Galaxidi are decent, but include hairpin turns and can get icy in winter.

BUS TRAVEL

Places close to Athens can be reached with the blue city bus lines (€1.40): Bus A16 from Koumoundourou Square for Daphni and Eleusina via Iera Odos; Bus 224 from Vassilisis Sofias or Akadimias, coupled with a 25-minute walk, for Kaisariani; Bus A2, A3, or B3 from Syntagma Square for Glyfada; Bus A2 to Voula; Bus A2 to Glyfada, then connect with Bus 114, or 116 to Vouliagmeni; Bus A2 or A3 to Glyfada, then connect with Bus 116, or 149 for Varkiza. For the rest of the destinations, if you don't rent a car, the next most efficient mode of travel is the regional KTEL bus system in combination with taxis.

The extensive network serves all points in Attica from Athens, and local buses connect the smaller towns and villages at least daily. KTEL buses for eastern Attica leave hourly from their main station in downtown Athens (Aigyptou Square at the corner of Mavromateon and Leoforos Alexandras). KTEL buses depart regularly for Marathon (€3.70), Ayia Marina (stopping at Rhamnous on the way; €5.20), and Sounion (€6.30).

The Greek National Tourism Organization (EOT) distributes a list of bus schedules, as does the Attica KTEL terminal in Aigyptou Square. KTEL buses servicing Delphi, Arachova, Osios Loukas, and Galaxidi depart from Terminal B in Athens. To Delphi (via Arachova), there are four departures (eight on Friday and Sunday), beginning at 7:30 am. The journey takes about three hours and costs €15.10. Three buses daily (four on Sunday) make the four-hour trip to Galaxidi, starting at 7:30 am; the fare is €18.60. Buses depart hourly from 6:30 am to 8:30 pm for Livadeia near Osios Loukas; the journey takes 2½ hours and costs €12.40. From there, you can take the local bus to Osios Loukas, for an additional €3.50. For more information on this journey, call KTEL buses in Athens (☎ *210/831–7173*) and in Livadeia (☎ *22610/28336*). Note that the prices above are one-way fares. To get to Terminal B from downtown Athens, catch Bus 24 on Amalias in front of the National Garden. Tickets for these buses are sold only at this terminal. *For more detailed contact information, see Bus Travel in Travel Smart.*

CAR TRAVEL

Points in Attica and Delphi can be reached from the main Thessaloniki–Athens and Athens–Patras highways, with the National Road (Ethniki Odos) the most popular route, now connecting to the Athens ring road (*Attiki Odos*; toll €2.85).

From the Peloponnese, drive east via Corinth to Athens, or from Patras, cross the Rio–Antirrio bridge to visit Delphi. Most roads off these highways are two-lane secondary arteries. Several of these—notably from Athens to Delphi and Itea and from Athens to Sounion—are spectacularly scenic.

Local and international car rental agencies have offices in downtown Athens—most are on Syngrou avenue—as well as at the arrivals level at "Eleftherios Venizelos" Athens International Airport, in Spata.

TAXI TRAVEL

You will find "Piatsa" taxi ranks next to all the airports, and taxis will be lined up even late at night if there is a boat or flight coming in. On the other hand, your hotel can usually arrange a taxi for you, but if you need one in the wee hours of the morning make sure you book it in advance.

HOTELS

The standards are high at the hotels along Attica's much-traversed coast, and they fit roughly into three groups: those catering to families on a budget, those aimed at corporate travelers, and those servicing luxury lovers. It's no surprise why corporate moguls from all over the world often rent over-the-top bungalows at some of these resorts for the whole season, with their stunning seaside views, state-of-the-art spas, and dazzling public spaces. But no matter how many face-lifts they endure, Attica's luxury hotels cannot remove their predominant mid-20th-century "shipping-tycoon" style. Conversely, in Delphi and Arachova, accommodations tend to be homey, chalet-style. In some places, you may even have the sensation of being part of a family, as rooms are decorated with personal heirlooms, and breakfast includes homemade goodies. You may spend some time in your room, as it may be your refuge from the mountain elements outside. In Delphi and Arachova, peak demand is during ski season and Easter (many places close for summer in Arachova).

RESTAURANTS

The cuisine of Attica resembles that of Athens, central Greece, and the Peloponnese. Local ingredients dominate, with fresh fish perhaps the greatest (and most expensive) delicacy. Since much of Attica's vegetation used to support herds of grazing sheep and the omnivorous goat, the meat of both animals is also a staple in many country tavernas. Although it is becoming increasingly difficult to find the traditional Greek taverna with large stewpots full of the day's hot meal, or big *tapsi* (pans) of *pastitsio* (layers of pasta, meat, and cheese laced with cinnamon) or *papoutsakia* (eggplant slices filled with minced meat), market towns and villages in Attica still harbor the occasional rustic haunt, offering tasty, inexpensive meals. Always ask to see the *kouzina* (kitchen) to look at the day's offerings, or even to peer inside the pots. Regional cuisine in Delphi and Arachova relies heavily on meats, including game, while in the coastal town of Galaxidi, fresh fish and seafood courses dominate. Informal dress is appropriate at all but the very fanciest of restaurants, and unless noted, reservations are not necessary.

DINING AND LODGING PRICES IN EUROS			
	$	**$$**	**$$$**	**$$$$**
Restaurants	under €16	€16–€25	€26–€40	over €40
Hotels	under €126	€126–€225	€226–€275	over €275

Restaurant prices are the average cost of a main course at dinner or, if dinner is not served, at lunch. Hotel prices are the lowest cost of a standard double room in high season.

VISITOR INFORMATION

See the main offices listed under "Visitor Information" in the larger towns in this chapter. Also note the tour outfitters that are found under Tours, below.

TOURS

Most agencies run tour excursions at about the same prices, but CHAT and Key Tours have the best service and guides, plus comfortable air-conditioned buses. Taking a half-day trip from Athens to the breathtaking Temple of Poseidon at Sounion (€43) avoids the hassle of dealing with the crowded public buses or paying a great deal more for a taxi. A one-day tour to Delphi with lunch costs €98, but the two-day tour (€132, including half-board in first-class hotels) gives you more time to explore this wonder. Full-service travel agencies, like Dolphin Hellas, handle hotel reservations, transportation tickets, and tours.

RECOMMENDED OPERATORS

CHAT. Based in Athens, CHAT offers good tours and employs informed guides. If you're in Athens and want to explore Attica, it's a good choice. ☎ *210/322–3137* ⊕ *www.chatours.gr* ✉ *From €43.*

Dolphin Hellas. With headquarters within walking distance of the Acropolis, Dolphin Hellas provides a range of services for individual and group travelers: hotel accommodations, villa rentals, ferry tickets, air tickets, organized coach tours, car rentals, fly and drive programs, transfer and guide services. The company's website lists ferry schedules in the reservations section. ⊠ *Syngrou Ave. 16, Makriyianni, Athens* ☎ *210/922–7772* ⊕ *www.dolphin-hellas.gr.*

Key Tours. Key Tours has been showing travelers around Greece since 1963. Its offerings range from one-day cruises of the Saronic Islands to more personalized services like helicopter tours and regional Greek winery visits. More than 20 different scheduled excursions are among its offerings. ⊠ *Athanasiou Diakou 26, Athens* ☎ *210/923–3166* ⊕ *www. keytours.gr* ✉ *From €43.*

Winemakers' Association of Attica Vineyards. The Winemakers' Association of Attica Vineyards has a comprehensive Internet site with plenty of information about the history of wine-making in the Attica region and potential wine tour routes encompassing its active members. ☎ *210/603–8019* ⊕ *www.enoaa.gr.*

ATTICA ΑΤΤΙΚΗ

Want to escape from the cacophony of Athens? Head for the interior of Attica, with its rustic inns, local wineries, small towns, and rolling hills.

Northeast of Mt. Pendeli, between the slopes and the sea, lies the fabled plain of Marathon, its flat expanse now dotted with small agricultural communities and seaside resorts, where many Athenians have summer homes. Attica includes such sites as the Temple of Poseidon, spectacularly perched on Cape Sounion, the famed Sanctuary of Demeter at Eleusis, and the Monastery of Daphni.

It is in the small towns of the interior of Attica that the soul of Attica lies. This once quiet and undulating landscape has changed significantly since the construction of the "Eleftherios Venizelos" Athens International Airport in Spata. The many olive groves and vineyards once gracing this region made way for increased development (including big shopping malls and company headquarters), as new highways give these once-remote towns almost immediate access to Athens.

GLYFADA ΓΛΥΦΑΔΑ

17 km (10½ miles) southeast of Athens.

Gateway to the Athens Riviera and the "Apollo coast"—which stretches from Pireaus to Cape Sounion's famed temple to Poseidon—Glyfada is

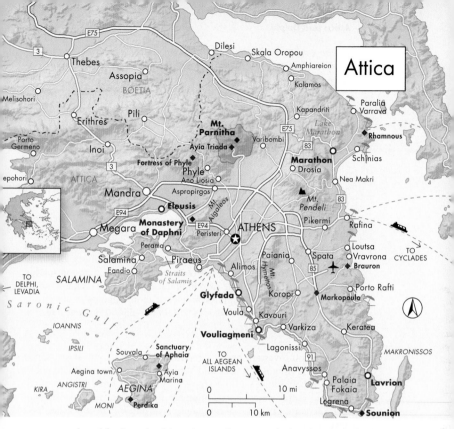

loved for its palm-fringed coastal promenade, lined with parks, beautiful villas, golf courses, shopping, dance clubs, and seaside dining spots.

GETTING HERE AND AROUND

Buses A2, A3, and B3 leave Athens's center (Akadimia and Syntagma Square) and stop at Glyfada's main square. The buses (€1.40) run regularly (two to five an hour) in both directions until midnight. The ride can take an hour or more. Express Bus E22 (Akadimia–Saronida) also stops in Glyfada. And on summer weekends only OASA bus line 790 operates through the night (12 to 4:30 am) to serve clubbers who come to party and escape the Athens heat; it leaves from Glyfada Square and heads into Peristeri through the center of Athens.

The tram offers a more scenic, if often slower, route. Take the Asklipeio Voulas tram from Syntagma Square; it passes through the Zappion park and endless city blocks before it reaches Palio Faliro, where it curves to the left, following Poseidonos avenue along the sea to Glyfada. Most trams run until 1 am daily, except for Friday and Saturday, when they run until 2:30 am (and a couple even later than that, but be sure to check the timetable before you depart). The Athens metro has also recently arrived at nearby suburb Elliniko, making it even more accessible from the metropolitan center. *For more information on Athens*

*public transportation options, including all relevant contact informa-
tion, see "Getting Here and Around" in Athens.*

EXPLORING

Since the old international airport here closed, Glyfada is much quieter
and less touristy. Athenians come to swim, stroll, shop, and spend quiet
moments gazing at the sea. At night, however, the area transforms itself
into a pulsing dance club scene. A large expat community seeks out
exquisite local cuisine and ample international offerings in Glyfada's
center. Trams to downtown Athens and Piraeus (change at Neo Faliro)
have eased traffic. Glyfada has several fine hotels and, with Athens city
center just a tram ride away, makes a good base for travelers who prefer
being near the beach.

FAMILY **Sea Turtle Rescue Center.** Since 1983, the primary objective of Archelon,
the Sea Turtle Protection society of Greece, has been to protect the sea
turtles and their habitats in Greece. At the Glyfada rescue center, housed
in five disused train wagons donated by the Greek Railway Organisation (OSE), you can watch the team of volunteers in action (caring
for turtles at the last stage of rehabilitation), lend a helping hand by
bringing much needed supplies, and learn about ongoing rescue efforts
throughout Greece. ⊠ *3rd Marina* ☎ *210/898–26000* ⊕ *www.archelon.
gr* ☉ *Sept.–July, weekends 11–5.*

BEACHES

Attica's southwestern coast is mainly rock, with some short, sandy
stretches in Alimos, Glyfada, and Voula that have been made into public
pay beaches. Along with beach bars, changing rooms, beach umbrellas, and rental water-sport equipment for windsurfing and waterskiing, there are gardens, parking, and playgrounds. These beaches have
received Blue Flags for cleanliness from the European Union despite
their proximity to Athens. Most are open from 8 am to 8 pm in summer,
and entry fees are generally from €4 to €15. At some beaches, fees go up
on weekends, and at others you may have to pay extra for a lounge chair
or parking. In July and August, when temperatures climb past 100°F
(38°C), public beaches often stay open until midnight. Farther south or
east along the coast, accessible by tram, there are open or free beaches
from Flisvos up to Glyfada's Asteria, and beyond towards Voula.

Alimos Beach (*Akti tou Iliou*). The town of Alimos has the nearest developed—and clean—beach to Athens. The so-called "Beach of the Sun"
extends over 60,000 square meters and has umbrellas and lounge chairs
for rent, three beach bars, a couple of tavernas, and one minimarket.
Expect it to be packed over the hot summer months. There is an entry
fee (€5 on weekdays, €6 on weekends); expect to be charged extra for
the sun beds during weekends as well. **Amenities:** food and drink; lifeguards; showers; toilets; parking. **Best for:** swimming; walking. ⊠ *Poseidonos avenue, opposite no. 62, Kalamaki, Alimos* ✛ *10 km (6 miles)
south of Athens, 5 km (3 miles) north of Glyfada* ☎ *210/985–5169*
⊕ *www.aktitouiliou.gr.*

Asteras Beach. This sprawling, upmarket complex really stands out in
Glyfada, drawing a hip young crowd as well as families with children, who enjoy different sides of the beach. Built around a fine sand

In the summer, many of Athens's trendiest clubs and restaurants relocate to be closer to Glyfada's popular beaches, many of which have received a coveted Blue Flag for cleanliness.

beach and landscaped grounds shaded by elegant pergolas, Asteras offers lounge chairs, umbrellas, pools, lockers, changing rooms, showers, trampolines, a playground, a self-service restaurant, three bars, and water sports—all for an entry fee of €5. You can keep going all day and night at the youthful Balux poolside café-club, where you can cool off on abundant pillows with a chilled coffee in hand or sip a cocktail long after sundown. **Amenities:** food and drink; parking; showers; toilets; water sports. **Best for:** partiers; swimming; walking; windsurfing. ✉ *58 Poseidonos avenue* ✣ *15 km (9 miles) south of Athens* ☎ *210/894–1620, 210/894–41189* 🌐 *www.asterascomplex.com.*

WHERE TO EAT

$$$ MEDITERRANEAN 🍴 **Akanthus Beachside Summer Escape.** Although mostly known for its lively open-air club, this restaurant within the Akti tou Iliou (Costa del Sol) beach complex offers a separate dining area as well as the golden opportunity to hang out with Athens's most beautiful people. Chef Nikos Kontomakros prepares a selection of Mediterranean dishes in the restaurant section, while the adjoining, fashionable Nalu Cafe is a popular all-day bar and café option right on the beach (you can even take a refreshing dip in the sea from the club's private beach). Even better: the dance floor is right there so your fun can continue uninterrupted after dinner. Live music performances are held on Thursday, Greek music parties on Friday, mainstream sound parties on Saturday. During the winter months Akanthus moves closer to the center of Athens, in the happening neighborhood of Gazi. [$] *Average main: €40* ✉ *Akti tou Iliou (Costa del Sol) Beach Complex, Poseidonos avenue, Alimos* ☎ *210/968–08000* 🌐 *www.akanthus.gr* ✍ *Reservations essential.*

$ STEAKHOUSE

🍴 **George's Steak House.** When all you really want is a burger, head to George's, a classic destination since the late 1980s in the heart of Glyfada's "Burger Town" district. This spot (affectionately called *Biftekakia* or "burger joint" by the locals) started out as the local butcher shop in 1951. It is little wonder that the menu is limited to grilled meats, like steaks (George learned how to carve a T-bone from a visiting American) and *biftekia* (thick, grilled, hamburger-like patties of ground beef and pork served without a bun), plus a limited selection of side dishes like fries, tzatziki, seasonal boiled greens, and Greek salad. The service is fast, so don't be disappointed if all the tables are taken when you arrive; there's a continuous stream of diners coming and going. You get great value for your money, whether you choose a tender beefsteak or a succulent hamburger, but this is an old-fashioned, no-frills taverna after all, and it operates on a strictly cash-only basis. [$] *Average main: €15* ✉ *Konstantinoupoleos 4–6* ☎ *210/894–2041, 210/894–6020* 🌐 *www.georgessteakhouse.gr* 💳 *No credit cards.*

$$ MODERN GREEK Fodor's Choice ★

🍴 **Mentzelo's Slow Food and Drinks.** Greek chef Mentzelos Drosopoulos is an ardent proponent of the so-called "slow food" movement and wants his customers at this colorful Glyfada eatery (where a long bookcase painted in intense Aegean blue hues dominates the interior) to share his enthusiasm for locally sourced products, which are prepared as responsibly and as naturally as possible. The menu focuses on classic Greek dishes that are always cooked with a modern twist. So enjoy stuffed octopus, beef cooked in a caper and lemon sauce with fresh gnocchi, and rooster marinated in piri-piri sauce and coriander. Mentzelos and his staff are always at hand to help you navigate the extensive menu, while the daily specials promise even more culinary surprises. [$] *Average main: €25* ✉ *Pandoras street 16* ☎ *210/894–1071* ✍ *Reservations essential.*

WHERE TO STAY

$$ HOTEL

🏨 **Blazer Suites.** This all-suites hotel may be sparkling and clean, but it's aimed at more than executives: late breakfast and a clublike panache, coupled with friendly and personal service, make it an appealing choice for vacationers. **Pros:** good price-quality ratio; five-minute walk from cosmopolitan Glyfada center; free Wi-Fi. **Cons:** located on a busy six-lane avenue, which can get noisy during rush hour. [$] *Rooms from: €130* ✉ *Karamanli Ave. 1, Voula* ☎ *210/965–8801* 🌐 *www.blazersuites.gr* 🛏 *28 suites* 🍽 *Breakfast.*

$$ RENTAL Fodor's Choice ★

🏨 **Brasil Suites Hotel Apartments.** Here's a serene and inviting all-suites alternative for visitors who want to see the sights of Athens but stay away from the bustling city center, closer to the lively suburb of Glyfada and its beaches. **Pros:** spacious, modern and comfortable; excellent accommodation option for families; on-site restaurant for lunch. **Cons:** a bit of a journey to reach major tourist sites in downtown Athens; it's a walk to the beach from here. [$] *Rooms from: €200* ✉ *Eleftherias street 4* ☎ *210/894–2124* 🌐 *www.brasilhotel.gr* 🛏 *15 suites* 🍽 *Breakfast.*

$ HOTEL FAMILY

🏨 **Emmantina Hotel.** Although the decor here could use a little updating, this hotel is a reasonably priced option with consistently clean rooms and a friendly staff, close to trams into Athens. **Pros:** reasonable prices; free Wi-Fi; the center of Glyfada just 10 minutes away on foot.

Cons: busy and noisy six-lane avenue just outside the door with narrow sidewalks; a bit "tired" looking; Athens center 45 minutes away on the tram. [$] *Rooms from: €75* ✉ *Poseidonos Ave. 33* ☎ *210/898–0683* 🌐 *www.emmantina.gr* 🛏 *80 rooms* 🍴 *Breakfast.*

NIGHTLIFE

Glyfada is renowned as a summer party spot, since some of Athens's most popular clubs close up shop downtown and move here in summer. Places seem to change their name and style each season to keep up with trends; ask at your hotel for the latest information. Most clubs have a cover charge that includes a drink (€10–€25); if you're a large party, take a tip from the Greeks and share a bottle (whiskey, vodka) to save on the cost of ordering single drinks. It is sensible to make a reservation for a table beforehand.

4

Akrotiri Club Restaurant. Easygoing music gives way to lively post-midnight clubbing at the seaside Akrotiri Club. One of Glyfada's hottest nightspots, it is attached to a ritzy restaurant, and even has an outdoor bar area around a huge swimming pool with a huge disco ball. The club is open nightly, but during high season, from April to October, reservations for both the club section and the restaurant section are essential well in advance. ✉ *Vas. Georgiou II 5, Agios Kosmas* ☎ *210/985–9147* 🌐 *www.akrotirilounge.gr.*

Fodor's Choice ★ **Balux Cafe—The House Project.** A must-visit destination club within the Asteras seaside complex, this stylish café is creatively designed as an open-plan house, complete with playroom and pool area, to create a feeling of "home away from home." By day, Balux Cafe offers affordable—and good quality—sushi in addition to a contemporary Greek menu. But once the sun sets, it becomes the perfect spot to slowly sip your cocktail right on the beachfront, enjoying one of the bands performing live (usually on Thursday), or the dance music played by top local DJs. And it's open year-round. ✉ *Poseidonos avenue 58* ☎ *210/898–3577* 🌐 *www.baluxcafe.com.*

The Beachhouse. Have a drink by the sea at this trendy spot, which draws crowds of all ages to its beachside location for the all-white, sailing-inspired decor, mainstream fusion dance tunes, open-air bar, and Mediterranean menu of mainly finger food, pasta, and seafood. It is open from early morning, for a refreshing fruit juice or frappé (cold shaken coffee), until well after midnight. ✉ *A' Voula Beach, Karamanli avenue 4, Voula* ☎ *210/347–7330.*

Noa Bay Club. This open-air club (ex-Eirinikos) is a new arrival on the summer clubbing scene. It has a dance stage, four bars, an additional cocktail bar, a balcony with beach access, impressive sound and light installations, and a VIP area. ✉ *A' Beach Voula, Karamanli Ave. 4, opposite Asklipieion Hospital, Voula* ☎ *21300/08790.*

Ocean Poolside All-Day Resto Club. The action at the new and impressive Ocean Poolside is of course centered around the pool! The club offers Ibiza-inspired house music parties (with famous guest DJs like David Morales), and Greek nights as well. During the day, snacks and drinks are served poolside to a hip, young crowd. ✉ *Paralia Agiou Kosma, Hellenikon, next to the kart racing* ☎ *21303/25571.*

Sideradiko Summer. This huge dance club is dedicated primarily to contemporary Greek sounds (also look out for house, R&B, and mainstream parties every Sunday). ⊠ *Poseidonos Ave., Agios Kosmas* ☎ *210/701–8700* ⊕ *www.sideradiko.gr.*

Thalassa People's Stage. Right next to Balux Cafe—and also inside the Asteras beach complex—Thalassa, which offers one of the hottest live stages in Glyfada for *bouzoukia,* the traditional Greek music style and a true favorite of local performers and celebrities. ⊠ *Vas. Georgiou B' Ave. 58* ☎ *210/898–2979, 210/894–1620* ⊕ *www.asterascomplex.com.*

SHOPPING

Boutique 52. The boutique sells bohemian-chic fashions, including flowing sun dresses and Grecian-style evening gowns, by such international and Greek designers as the up and coming Stelios Koudounaris. The store is closed on Sunday. ⊠ *Kyprou street 52* ☎ *210/894–4250* ⊕ *www. boutique52.gr.*

SPORTS AND THE OUTDOORS

BOATING AND SAILING

Yachts can be rented year-round, but May, June, September, and October are less expensive than summer, and, even better, the *meltemi* (brisk northern winds) are not blowing then. Many yacht brokers charter boats and organize scuba tours and flotilla cruises in small, rented sailboats around the islands.

Vernicos Yachts. Headquartered in a seaside suburb between Glyfada and Athens, Vernicos Yachts hosts weeklong cruises and also charters boats. Offering both bareboat and crewed yacht charters (not to mention a brokerage and new yacht sales), the company also operates a marina and even manages hotels. This is the best place to go near Athens if you want to rent a boat to sail down to the islands. The business is run by the same family that established the maritime firm in Constantinople in the 1850s. ⊠ *Poseidonos Ave. 11, Alimos* ☎ *210/989–6000, 210/985–0129* ⊕ *www.vernicos.com.*

GOLF

Konstantinos Karamanlis Glyfada Golf Course. With many distinguished politicians (including the legendary Greek politician it is named after), businessmen, and members of the diplomatic community on its roster, this green oasis of rolling hills is lovingly landscaped with tall trees and shrubbery. You need to make reservations for the weekend by Wednesday, while the greens are open Tuesday–Sunday from 7:30 am until sunset and Monday 1 pm (noon in winter) until sunset. ⊕ *Off Saki Karagiorga and end of Pronois St., between Leoforos Poseidonos and Vouliagmenis* ☎ *210/894–6820* ⊕ *www.golfglyfada.gr* 🖃 *€62 for 18 holes, €50 for 9 holes* ⅄ *18 holes. 6847 yards. par 72.*

SCUBA DIVING

Athina Diving. Take lessons or go on scheduled dives with the experienced instructors of Athina Diving, located on the 38th km of the coastal Athina–Sounio road. Not to be missed: the night diving available upon request, either from shore or by boat. Equipment rentals are also available. ⊠ *Athina–Sounio Rd., Km 38, Lagonissi* ☎ *22910/25434* ⊕ *www. athinadiving.gr.*

VOULIAGMENI ΒΟΥΛΙΑΓΜΕΝΗ

8 km (5 miles) southwest of Glyfada, 25 km (16 miles) south of Athens.

A classy seaside residential suburb, Vouliagmeni is the most prestigious address for an Athenian's summer home or business.

GETTING HERE AND AROUND

Express Bus E22 is the easiest way to get to Vouliagmeni from Athens. It runs two to three times an hour, but only until 10 pm. (The last bus returning to Athens leaves at 9:45 pm.) Several buses, including 114, 115, and 170, originate in Glyfada and pass through Vouliagmeni on the way to Athens. Bus 114 stops outside the Astir Hotel Complex (with a good 15-minute walk to the front gate), but only runs until 7:10 pm, with just one bus an hour. Bus 115 does very few runs but caters to night owls, between 9:30 pm and midnight. *For more information, see Bus and Tram Travel in Athens.*

EXPLORING

Vouliagmeni is coveted for the large yacht harbor (including the exclusive Nautical Club that caters to water-sports lovers) and the scenic promontory, Laimos Vouliagmenis, which is covered with umbrella pines and includes an area called Kavouri, where there are several seaside fish tavernas. Much like Glyfada, Vouliagmeni can serve as a convenient base from which to explore Attica, but it is far less crowded and more exclusive.

BEACHES

Here, beaches are quieter, and even cleaner, than the beaches farther north toward Athens.

FAMILY **Akti Vouliagmenis.** For the reasonable fee of €4 per person, Akti Vouliagmenis provides elegant wooden lounge chairs, white umbrellas, and access to shiny beach bars. Also on-site at this public beach are basketball, volleyball, and tennis courts as well as a playground for pre- or post-swimming fun. There's also Wi-Fi and a first-aid station during the summer. **Amenities:** food and drink; lifeguards; parking (free); toilets. **Best for:** swimming; walking. ⊠ *Poseidonos Ave. 2, at Apollonos* ☏ *210/896–0697* ⊕ *www.vouliagmeni-akti.gr* ⊙ *May–Sept., daily 8:30–8; Oct.–Apr., daily 8:30–4:30 pm.*

FAMILY **Anavyssos Beach.** The broad, sandy beach at Anavyssos, just 47 km (30 miles) from the center of Athens, is very popular with windsurfers (especially the stretch of beach called Alykes). There's a children's playground and beach volleyball courts, as well as sun beds and umbrellas for hire. **Amenities:** food and drink; showers; toilets; water sports. **Best for:** solitude; swimming; windsurfing. ⊠ *Sounion* ✛ *13 km (8 miles) northwest of Sounion.*

Astir Beach. The upscale beach club on the Laimos Vouliagmenis promontory, Astir beach is on the premises of the Arion Resort & Spa of the Astir Hotel Complex, but is open to the public daily from 8 am to 9 pm. Its more exclusive location has always commanded a hefty entry fee (€15 on weekdays, €25 on weekends, significantly reduced during the low season), which means the green lawns and sandy stretch are usually not so crowded. Sand sports are played on the beach, including at two beach volleyball courts. A range of services (including shopping, dining, water sports, and yoga on the beach) are offered at an extra cost. **Amenities:** food and drinks; water sports. **Best for:** swimming; walking. ✉ *Apollonos 40* ☎ *210/890–1619* 🌐 *astir-beach.com.*

Kavouri Beach. The free beach Kavouri extends south from Voula to Vouliagmeni. It is about 16 km (9 miles) southeast of Athens, making it one of the most easily accessible public free beaches with fine golden sand near the city and a good one for families. There are a few modest cafés along the beach as well as some shops, while umbrellas and sun beds are available for rent (around €4). **Amenities:** food and drink; parking (free); showers; toilets. **Best for:** swimming; walking. ✉ *Western shore of Vouliagmeni headland.*

Vouliagmeni Lake. The part-salt, part spring-fed warm waters of Vouliagmeni lake are reputed to have curative powers, and thus are popular with older Greeks. The lake, with a dramatic rocky backdrop that makes it one of the most exotic places in Attica, is open daily from 7 am to 7:30 pm during high season. You can rent umbrellas, and there are showers, as well as a pleasant and popular café-restaurant open until much later (1:30 am). Most of the lake has a gradual slope and sandy bottom (although caution is recommended, as it deepens suddenly in parts). **Amenities:** food and drink; showers. **Best for:** sunset; swimming; walking. ✉ *2 km (1 mile) southeast of Vouliagmeni* ☎ *210/896–2237* 🌐 *www.limnivouliagmenis.gr* 🎟 *€8.*

FAMILY **YaBanaki Beach Varkiza.** With a range of fees (starting at €5 for adult entry on weekdays), Yabanaki has beach-club amenities—umbrellas and sun beds for rent, water sports, bars, restaurants (including a popular souvlaki eatery), a children's water park, and cabins where you can change—spread across 25 acres. Varkiza's sandy beach park is open daily from 8 am to 7 pm during the summer months. Varkiza is popular with windsurfers and waterskiers. **Amenities:** food and drink; lifeguards; water sports. **Best for:** walking; windsurfing. ✉ *Varkiza* ✣ *5 km (3 miles) east of Vouliagmeni* ☎ *210/897–2414* 🌐 *www.yabanaki.com.*

WHERE TO EAT

$$$ SEAFOOD 🍴 **Garbi.** Athenians flock year-round to share a seafood platter and bottle of white wine or feast on a fisherman's version of bouillabaisse made up of *kakavia* fish (when available). There's meat on the menu, too, but most opt for the fresh grilled fish that is brought daily from Kalimnos, Patmos, and Leros islands and a selection of appetizers with subtle influences from the cuisine of Istanbul Greeks. Oysters and prawns are also a specialty. But it's not just the food that attracts locals to this family-run restaurant: there are also elegant wood-beamed ceilings (the ceiling is partly retractable, so on a good night you can dine under the stars) and a superb view of the coast, all just 30 minutes from downtown Athens. Reservations are essential during weekends. [$] *Average main: €35* ✉ *Iliou 21 and Selinis, Kavouri* ✣ *3 km (2 miles) west of Vouliagmeni* ☎ *210/896–3480, 210/896–3460* ✍ *Reservations essential* ⏲ *No lunch.*

$$$$ MEDITERRANEAN Fodor's Choice ★ 🍴 **Island.** Claim a place at the bar of this sophisticated and pricey beachside restaurant, which is now also open for brunch, and observe the fashionable exchange air kisses while casting an eye around to see who's watching. People come in waves, either by car or yacht: some early for

drinks, some late for dancing, and some flowing from the bar to the restaurant to the disco in this complex. Palm trees, bamboo, flowering shrubs, and staggered terraces create an elegant and slightly exotic backdrop for one of the city's hottest summer hangouts; inside, it is all white sofas and billowing drapes, outside the main terrace's gigantic red awnings excite the eye. Experienced chef Nikos Skliras oversees the restaurant's creative Mediterranean cuisine, utilizing ingredients such as saffron and feta. His fine cuisine comes at a price, but you can sample some of these flavors at the bar for less. While there, get started with the simply exquisite tapas. $ *Average main: €50* ✉ *Sounio Ave., Varkiza* ✛ *3 km (2 miles) southeast of Vouliagmeni* ☎ *210/965–3563* ⊕ *www. islandclubrestaurant.gr* ⌂ *Reservations essential.*

$$$ ✕ **Lambros.** Perched next to the waters of scenic Lake Vouliagmeni,
SEAFOOD this traditional fish taverna has been serving the best of Greek fishermen's catches since 1889. Despite a renovation, the restaurant still exudes the aura of its golden years, when it was the leading star in the galaxy of Attica seaside entertainment spots dubbed the "Athenian Riviera." Located on the seafront, with wonderful views of crystalline, aquamarine waters, Lambros remains legendary for its mussel rice (*mydopilafo*), its seafood pasta, and its grilled fresh fish (with prices ranging from €50–€70 per kilo) that arrives daily from all parts of Greece. $ *Average main: €35* ✉ *Poseidonos Ave. 20* ☎ *210/896–0144* ⊗ *Closed Mon.*

$$$ ✕ **Mojito Bay.** Named after the Cuban cocktail, this is one of the most
CUBAN happening—albeit a bit pricey—restaurant/club/beach bars on the Athenian Riviera. You can relax on the rejuvenated Lombarda beach (newly decked out with sun-loungers), nibble on select tapas, and enjoy the summer party events that last until sunrise. Many of the younger, shirtless, Facebook generation that flock here like to do exactly that. $ *Average main: €30* ✉ *Athens–Sounion Ave., Km 33, Lombarda beach, Ayia Marina* ☎ *22910/78950.*

$$$ ✕ **Moorings Vouliagmeni.** With wonderful views over the best of the
MODERN GREEK Athenian Riviera, the Vouliagmeni marina, and a small church shrine added to the mix, Moorings can make for an unforgettably romantic evening. The hip lounge atmosphere of this seafront café-restaurant is complemented by the Nouveau Greek menu created by chef Andreas Sxinas, with the healthy seafood and Mediterranean options standing out from the rest. $ *Average main: €40* ✉ *Marina Vouliagmenis* ☎ *210/967–0659, 210/896–0310* ⊕ *www.moorings.gr* ⌂ *Reservations essential.*

$$ ✕ **Remezzo Vouliagmeni.** You may feel as if you are dining on a sail-
MEDITERRANEAN boat, but in reality, you are just happily sitting on the wooden deck of Remezzo. Dinner begins nightly at 9:30, though drinks and snacks are available throughout the day, so you can enjoy the sea views and shady pine trees. If you're in the mood for a summery cocktail, try the eponymous Remezzo with vodka and melon juice—it sums up all the fun and élan of this place. $ *Average main: €25* ✉ *Ermou 1* ☎ *210/896–4310* ⊗ *No lunch.*

$$ ✕ **Remvi.** The last of the traditional fish tavernas lining the coastal
SEAFOOD road in Palaia Fokaia, this is the smallest, the cheapest, and the most

romantic. *Remvi* means "daydreaming," which is easy to do as you sit at little tables with checkered tablecloths sipping potent barreled wine and gazing out to sea. The family-run place keeps expanding its delicious menu—the fish soup *sinagrida*, made with the freshest bream, sweet onions, carrots, and potatoes, is worth the wait. As for mains, the seafood pasta, served al dente with fresh seafood and tomato sauce, is a must. $ *Average main: €20* ⊠ *Souniou Ave. 14, at Galinis, Palaia Fokaia* ✛ *52-km (32-mile) point on Athens–Sounion coastal road, 34 km (21 miles) south of Vouliagmeni* ☎ *22910/36236.*

WHERE TO STAY

$$$$
RESORT
Fodor's Choice
★

Arion: A Luxury Collection Resort & Spa. A Westin resort since 2006, Vouliagmeni's 80-acre prestigious Astir Palace complex on the scenic peninsula that once made waves may be a bit dated and tired now, but in general the hotel is well-maintained and still worth considering. **Pros:** best-of-the-best luxury; relaxing setting; wide range of modern facilities on offer. **Cons:** high prices for food and drink; high-speed internet in rooms costs €15 per day (free Wi-Fi in the lobby, though); far from Athens, and the free shuttle doesn't run very often; daily use of spa pool is also charged extra. $ *Rooms from: €350* ⊠ *Apollonos 40* ☎ *210/890–2000* ⊕ *www.astir-palace.com* ⇄ *153 rooms, 76 bungalows, 9 suites* ¶◎¶ *Breakfast.*

$$$$
RESORT
FAMILY

Grand Resort Lagonissi. With its own beaches, nine restaurants (ranging from Greek to Lebanese to Polynesian, but only two of them open in the low season), three bars, two nightclubs, an open-air cinema and a sports center, you may have little need to stray from these hotel grounds. **Pros:** incredible sea views; excellent spa; gourmet dining; good for romantic getaways. **Cons:** prices are not only expensive but border on ridiculous; far from Athens sightseeing and airport; slow room service; generally, guest reports on service are mixed. $ *Rooms from: €320* ⊠ *Lagonissi* ✛ *Km 40 on Athens–Sounio road* ☎ *22910/76010* ⊕ *www.lagonissiresort.gr* ⇄ *267 rooms, 75 bungalows, 49 suites, 46 villas* ¶◎¶ *No meals.*

$$
RESORT
FAMILY

Plaza Resort Hotel. This resort offers spacious rooms right next to Anavyssos beach and is a good alternative if you are looking for a weekend getaway from Athens or are on your way to the islands and would like to avoid the Athens center. **Pros:** impressive lobby; free Wi-Fi; private sandy beach with pool. **Cons:** nearby town a bit dull; worn carpets; high restaurant and beach bar prices. $ *Rooms from: €160* ⊠ *Athens–Souniou Ave. Km 52, Palea Fokaia, Anavyssos* ☎ *22910/75000* ⊕ *www. plaza-resort.com* ⇄ *135 rooms* ¶◎¶ *Breakfast.*

$$
HOTEL
Fodor's Choice
★

The Margi. A sculptural stone fireplace in the lobby, a rich brown leather headboard in one guest room, an antique dressing table in another: no detail escapes notice at Margi, an upscale boutique hotel whose Malabar pool and handsome guest rooms attract young and trendy Athenians. **Pros:** romantic atmosphere; nicely decorated pool area; cool vibe. **Cons:** smallish rooms; not beachfront; some furniture getting a bit tired. $ *Rooms from: €200* ⊠ *Litous 11* ☎ *210/892–9000* ⊕ *www.themargi.gr* ⇄ *89 rooms, 7 suites* ¶◎¶ *Breakfast.*

$ **Stefanakis Hotel and Apartments.** If you can sacrifice style for value,
HOTEL you can get a good location, balconies, cleanliness, basic amenities,
FAMILY and a breakfast buffet, along with Varkiza's wonderful sandy beach
and café-lined waterfront just a short walk away. **Pros:** good location
near the airport and ideal for exploring Attica; 100 feet from the beach;
nice pool and outdoor areas; family-run hotel. **Cons:** basic amenities;
limited breakfast options; a bit tired 1970s-style decor. $ *Rooms from:*
€90 ⌦ *Aphroditis 17, Varkiza* ✛ *3 km (2 miles) east of Vouliagmeni*
☎ *210/897-0528* ⊕ *www.stefanakishotel.gr* ↪ *40 rooms, 12 apart-*
ments ⊘ *Closed Nov.–Mar.* ❙⃝❙ *Breakfast.*

SHOPPING

Georgiadou Bakery. Stop here to pick up a snack. Athenians flock here for
the *piroshki*, a Russian turnover filled with spicy ground meat, but leave
carrying bags filled with all types of baked goods, from baguettes and
hearty peasant loaves to honey-drenched cakes. A branch of this historic
bakery (founded in 1910) recently opened right in the center of Athens,
on Ermou street, a few yards away from the Greek Parliament. ⌦ *Vas.*
Konstantinou 98, at Afroditis 2, Varkiza ✛ *5 km (3 miles) southeast of*
Vouliagmeni ☎ *210/897-5602* ⊕ *www.georgiadou.gr.*

SPORTS AND THE OUTDOORS

Kouros Surf Club. On Anavyssos's Alykes beach, the Kouros Surf Club
offers beginner and advanced windsurfing, kitesurfing, wakeboard-
ing, stand-up paddling, and sailing lessons, a pro shop, and a relaxed
beach bar/restaurant. ⌦ *Athens–Sounion Ave., Km 50, Anavyssos*
☎ *22910/40804* ⊕ *www.kourosclub.gr.*

EN
ROUTE   South of Vouliagmeni the road threads along a rocky and heavily developed coastline dotted with inlets where intrepid bathers swim off the
rocks, after leaving their cars in the roadside parking areas and scrambling down to the inviting *limanakia* (coves) below. (If you're not driving, you can take the urban E22 Saronida Express from the Akadimias
terminal in central Athens to Saronida or a KTEL bus from various
points in Athens.) If you are a good swimmer and want to join them,
take along your snorkel, fins, and mask so you can enjoy the underwater scenery, but avoid the stinging sea urchins (you won't have to be
reminded a second time) clustered on rocks.

SOUNION ΣΟΥΝΙΟ

50 km (31 miles) southeast of Vouliagmeni, 70 km (44 miles) southeast
of Athens.

Poised at the edge of a rugged 195-foot cliff, the Temple of Poseidon
hovers between sea and sky, its "marble steep, where nothing save the
waves and I may hear mutual murmurs sweep" unchanged in the centuries since Lord Byron penned these lines. Today the archaeological
site at Sounion is one of the most photographed in Greece. The coast's
raw, natural beauty has attracted affluent Athenians, whose splendid
summer villas dot the shoreline around the temple. There is a tourist
café–restaurant by the temple, and a few minimarts on the road, but
no village proper. Arrange your visit so that you enjoy the panorama

of sea and islands from this airy platform either early in the morning, before the summer haze clouds visibility and the tour groups arrive, or at dusk, when the promontory has one of the most spectacular sunset vantage points in Attica. Be prepared, however, to be shuttled out quickly by guards.

In antiquity, the view from the cliff was matched emotion for emotion by the sight of the cape (called the "sacred headland" by Homer) and its mighty temple when viewed from the sea—a sight that brought joy to sailors, knowing upon spotting the massive temple that they were close to home. Aegeus, the legendary king of Athens, threw himself off the cliff when he saw his son's ship approaching flying a black flag. The king's death was a Greek tragedy born of misunderstanding: Theseus had forgotten to change his ship's sails from black to white—the signal that his mission had succeeded. So the king thought his son had been killed by the Minotaur. To honor Aegeus, the Greeks named their sea, the Aegean, after him.

GETTING HERE AND AROUND

Orange KTEL buses leave from Aigyptou Square, off Pedion Areos park, for Sounion (also spelled Sounio). It's a two-hour journey on modern buses from Athens that follow either an inland (€5.70) or seaside (€6.30) route. The inland buses run daily, about an hour apart, from 5:45 am to 8:30 pm, passing through points including Koropi, Markopoulo, and Lavrio. Coastal buses (every two hours) run between 6:30 am and 6 pm daily, hitting spots including Varkiza, Anavyssos, and Legrena. Unfortunately for sunset-gazers, there aren't buses returning from the site later than 7:30 or 8 pm (in summer). *For more information on Athens buses and bus stations, see Bus and Train Travel in Athens.*

EXPLORING

Fodor's Choice ★ **Temple of Poseidon.** Although the columns at the Temple of Poseidon appear to be gleaming white from a distance in the full sun, when you get closer you can see that they are made of gray-veined marble, quarried from the Agrileza valley 2 km (1 mile) north of the cape, and have 16 flutings rather than the usual 20. Climb the rocky path that roughly follows the ancient route, and beyond the scanty remains of an ancient *propylon* (gateway), you enter the temple compound. On your left is the *temenos* (precinct) of Poseidon, on your right, a *stoa* (arcade) and rooms. The temple itself (now roped off) was commissioned by Pericles, the famous leader of Greece's golden age. It was probably designed by Ictinus, the same architect who helped design the Temple of Hephaistos in the ancient Agora of Athens, and was built between 444 and 440 BC. The people here were considered Athenian citizens, the sanctuary was Athenian, and Poseidon occupied a position second only to Athena herself. The badly preserved frieze on the temple's east side is thought to have depicted the fight between the two gods to become patron of Athens.

The temple was built on the site of an earlier cult to Poseidon; two colossal statues of youths, carved more than a century before the temple's construction (perhaps votives to the god), were discovered in early excavations. Both now reside at the National Archaeological Museum

DID YOU KNOW?

A sighting of the Temple of Sounion always brought cheer to the heart of ancient Greek sailors—perched atop the southernmost cape of Attica, the temple was a sign that Athens was near.

in Athens. The 15 Doric columns that remain stand sentinel over the Aegean, visible from miles away. Lord Byron had a penchant for carving his name on ancient monuments, and you can see it and other graffiti on the right corner pillar of the portico. The view from the summit is breathtaking. In the slanting light of the late-afternoon sun, the landmasses to the west stand out in sharp profile: the bulk of Aegina backed by the mountains of the Peloponnese. To the east, on a clear day, one can spot the Cycladic islands of Kea, Kythnos, and Serifos. On the land side, the slopes of the acropolis retain traces of the fortification walls. ✉ *Cape Sounion* ☎ *22920/39363* 🌐 *www.culture.gr* 🎟 *€4* 🕘 *Apr.–Oct., daily 8–8.*

BY THE LIGHT OF THE SILVERY MOON

On summer full-moon nights, the Temple of Poseidon opens free of charge to the public.

BEACHES

Sounion Beach. If you are spending the morning visiting the temple of Poseidon, you might also want to take a swim on the free public beach just below it. Of course, this sandy strip—known locally as Kavokolones—becomes uncomfortably crowded in summer. **Amenities:** none. **Best for:** sunset; swimming. ✉ *Athens–Sounion Ave., Km 68.*

Legrena Beach. On your approach to the Temple of Poseidon, there is a decent sandy beach at Legrena. The fine golden sand is reminiscent of the Cycladic islands, while an added bonus is the usual lack of crowds. A few miles before you arrive (from Athens), look for the sight of the small island of Patroklos. It is uninhabited today, has ancient fortress ruins, and is said to belong to a wealthy Greek family. **Amenities:** food and drink. **Best for:** solitude; swimming; walking. ✉ *Legrena* ✥ *4 km (2½ miles) north of Sounion, before the turnoff for Haraka.*

WHERE TO EAT

$$ SEAFOOD 🍴 **O Ilias.** Every table at this restaurant founded in 1944 by Ilias Georgiou (uncle of owner Vassili Kampiti) has a view of the Temple of Poseidon. The fish taverna's traditional menu remains centered around *psari* (fish), from "small frys" like marida, atherina, and anchovy to large ones by the kilo. Try the homemade french fries or fried peppers to start with, or perhaps have a fresh salad. Top off a meal with refreshing, seasonal fruit, or—if there's a piece left in the large pan it was baked in—some *ravani* (a traditional Greek honey-covered cake). [$] *Average main: €20* ✉ *On beach below Temple of Poseidon* ☎ *22920/39114, 69368/11616* 🕘 *No dinner weekdays Nov.–Mar.*

$$ GREEK 🍴 **Syrtaki.** A spotless taverna with a good reputation for solid fare sits among the pines and with a view of the sea. Try the traditional *pites* (homemade pastry pies, these with cheese-and-spinach filling); the green salad sprinkled with pomegranate seeds, seed cones, and baby tomatoes; the fava; and, of course, the fresh fish. Grilled meats are also excellent here. [$] *Average main: €20* ✉ *Athens–Sounion Ave., Km 69* ✥ *4 km (2½ miles) north of Sounion* ☎ *22920/39125.*

$$ SEAFOOD
🍴 **Theodoros-Eleni.** Just off the narrow road leading into Legrena village and a few miles before Sounio, this reasonably priced fish restaurant is open for lunch and dinner. More than two-thirds of the diners here are returning customers, which says a lot about this taverna run by a Greek-British husband-and-wife team. The menu is built around huge portions of fresh fish and seafood, like the steamed mussels with feta in wine cheese sauce or the seafood pasta, with marvelous additions like boiled or fresh mixed salads in season. At the end of the dinner, the plate of seasonal fruit or the homemade chocolate *kormos* (log-shaped) cake is on the house. Beware of busy summer weekends, when reservations are strongly advised. [$] *Average main: €25* ✉ *Off Athens–Sounion Ave., Legrena* ✣ *3 km (2 miles) south of Sounion* ☎ *22920/51936, 22920/51810* ⊗ *Closed Nov.–Mar.*

WHERE TO STAY

$$ HOTEL
🏨 **Aegeon Beach Hotel.** Nothing can beat this hotel's location—much objected to by environmentalists and archaeologists—*on* the beach at the foot of the peninsula whose lofty prow holds the Temple of Poseidon, above the very harbor where ancient ships once navigated. **Pros:** unbeatable view lets you enjoy one of the best sunsets in the world; very comfortable beds; free Wi-Fi in rooms and public areas. **Cons:** beach especially crowded with Athenians during summer weekends. [$] *Rooms from: €150* ✉ *Athens–Sounion Ave., Km 68* ☎ *22920/39200* 🌐 *www.aegeon-hotel.com* 🛏 *39 rooms, 6 suites* 🍴 *Multiple meal plans.*

$$$$ HOTEL FAMILY Fodor's Choice ★
🏨 **Grecotel Cape Sounio.** One of the most elaborate hotels in Greece, this showpiece—looking a bit like a Greek temple left over from a spectacular Cecil B. DeMille movie set—perches amid the verdant pine forest of Sounion National Park: the stunning bay view includes a picture-perfect castle-fort and the Temple of Sounion itself. **Pros:** grandiose architecture; family-friendly; immaculate service; many loyal customer privileges. **Cons:** still a bit pricey even though it has recently adjusted prices downwards; food very good but pricey; no pets. [$] *Rooms from: €350* ✉ *Athens–Sounion Ave., Km 67* ☎ *22920/69700* 🌐 *www.capesounio.com* 🛏 *153 bungalows* ⊗ *Closed Nov.–Apr.* 🍴 *Breakfast.*

LAVRION ΛΑΥΡΙΟ

10 km (6 miles) north of Sounion, 80 km (50 miles) southeast of Athens.

After Sounion, the road twists and turns along the coast, winding past holiday homes, before hitting a rather dreary stretch by Lavrion's boatyard, where there always seems to be marina construction work underway. There is increasing activity in the post of Lavrion during the summer, as many boats for nearby Cycladic islands (Kythnos, Kea [Tzia], etc.) depart from here, and an increasing number of cruise ships also stop here for easy access to the Temple of Poseidon at Sounion. Lavrion, an industrial town with a few remnants of belle epoque architecture, was celebrated in antiquity for its silver mines. Several thousand ancient shafts have been discovered in the area—devoid of the riches they once yielded. Themistocles could not have built the fleet that saved Greece from the Persians, nor Pericles the monuments on the Acropolis, without the area's riches. Easy access to the airport at Spata via the

Markopoulou highway has begun to attract investment, including a joint public-private venture to create a technological and cultural park on the grounds of the now-defunct mining company (worth a visit if only for its architectural value).

EXPLORING

Lavrion Mineralogical Museum. Not only geology buffs can fully appreciate the small mineralogical museum, whose 700 exhibits—including several rare and beautiful specimens such as laurionite and azurite—are housed in a charming late-19th-century building then used by the French Mining Company to wash minerals. Lavrio is an old mining town, whose rich deposits were known to the ancient Greeks who mined here the silver used in some coins (also exhibited here). Exactly opposite the Mineralogical Museum is the tiny Archeological Museum, also worth a visit. ✉ *Iroon Polytechniou Sq.* ☎ *22920/25295* 🎫 *€2* 🕓 *Daily 8:30–3.*

WHERE TO EAT

$ GREEK ✕ **To Petrino.** Known by locals as *o stathmos* (the station), To Petrino is based in a cute stone house right in front of the small yacht marina in Lavrion and used to hold patrons waiting for a train instead of a meal. Whether it's lunch or dinner, you're assured simple but fresh taverna fare—start with the lightly fried calamari or *htapodaki xidato* (small pieces of boiled octopus drizzled with oil and vinegar) and don't forget the ouzo. The generous seafood plate *poikilia* is ideal for sharing. [$] *Average main: €15* ✉ *Akti Kountourioti 4* ☎ *22920/25297.*

WHERE TO STAY

$ HOTEL **Hotel Saron.** The most moderately priced hotel near Sounio, well worth it if you are on a tight budget, the Hotel Saron is found on a short drive north of Cape Sounion, and about 4 km (2½ miles) from the port of Lavrion. **Pros:** family-oriented holidays on a budget; friendly owners; good value for money; open year-round. **Cons:** retro decor in need of renovation; rather basic amenities. [$] *Rooms from: €75* ✉ *Leof. Lavriou-Souniou 46* ✥ *Sounion–Lavrion coastal road, at Km 60, 10 km (6 miles) north of Sounion* ☎ *22920/39144* 🌐 *www.saronhotel.gr* *52 rooms* 🍽 *Breakfast.*

MARATHON ΜΑΡΑΘΩΝΑΣ

165 km (102 miles) northwest of Sounion, 42 km (26 miles) northeast of Athens.

Today Athenians enter the fabled plain of Marathon to enjoy a break from the capital, visiting the freshwater lake created by the dam, or sunning at the area's beaches. The beauty of the region endures, though the ecosystem is still recovering from large-scale fires in the summer of 2009. When the Athenian *hoplites* (foot soldiers), assisted by the Plataians, entered the plain in 490 BC, it was to crush a numerically superior Persian force. Some 6,400 invaders were killed fleeing to their ships, while the Athenians lost 192 warriors. This, their proudest victory, became the stuff of Athenian legend; the hero Theseus was said to have appeared himself in aid of the Greeks, along with the god Pan. The Athenian commander Miltiades sent a messenger, Pheidippides, to

Athens with glad tidings of the victory; it's said he ran the 42 km (26 miles) hardly taking a breath, shouted *Nenikikamen!* ("We won!"), then dropped dead of fatigue (more probably of a heart attack)—the inspiration for the marathon race in today's Olympics. To the west of the Marathon plain are the quarries of Mt. Pendeli, the seemingly inexhaustible source for a special marble that weathers to a warm golden tint. The hillside vistas across the bay and to the island of Euboia are exceptional.

GETTING HERE AND AROUND

Head to the outdoors Attica KTEL bus terminal in Aigyptou Square in Athens to check routes and plan your Marathon trip. The journey takes about 1½ hours (depending on the traffic along the busy Mesogeion and Marathonos avenues) and a ticket costs €3.70. Buses depart approximately every half-hour, starting at 5:30 am. *For more information on Athens buses and bus stations, see Bus and Train Travel in Athens.*

EXPLORING

FAMILY **Attica Zoological Park.** Youngsters tired of trekking through museums may appreciate the distraction of the Attica Zoological Park. Spread across 32 acres, the zoo is home to more than 2,000 animals, 46 mammal species, 30 types of reptiles, and 238 species of birds, from a jaguar and wallaby to a brown bear, African penguin, and snowy owl. Take the Spata exit if you're coming from the airport, or the Rafina exit if you're coming from the direction of Eleusis. ⊠ *Yalou region, Spata* ☎ *210/663–4724* ⊕ *www.atticapark.com* ⊠ *€15* ☉ *Daily 9–dusk.*

Lake Marathon. Lake Marathon, the huge man-made reservoir formed by the Marathon Dam (built by an American company in 1925–31), used to enjoy unparalleled physical beauty as the sight of the water contrasted with the startling green of the surrounding pine forest. Although the devastating fires of 2009 eroded some of this beauty, the lake is still worth a visit if only to see the only dam in the world said to be faced with real marble. At the downstream side is a marble replica of the Athenian Treasury of Delphi. This is a main source of water for Athens, supplemented with water from Parnitha and the Boeotia region. If you are looking for a drink or snack (pasta dishes and pies with phyllo pastry are the chef's specialty), stop at the café-restaurant Fragma (⊕ *www. fragma.gr*) on the east side of the dam. Wonderful views glimpsed from the tall front windows help make this a perfect and refreshing stop on your way back to Athens from Sxinias beach. ⊠ *8 km (5 miles) west of Marathon, down side road from village of Ayios Stefanos.*

Fodor's Choice **Marathon Archaeological Museum.** About 1½ km (1 mile) north of the
★ Marathon Tomb in the Vranas area of the Marathon municipality is the smaller burial mound of the Plataians killed in the same battle, as well as the Archaeological Museum, which was fully renovated in 2004. Five rooms contain very well-preserved objects from excavations in the area, ranging from neolithic pottery from the cave of Pan to Hellenistic and Roman inscriptions and statues (labeled in English and Greek). Eight larger-than-life sculptures came from the gates of a nearby sanctuary of the Egyptian gods and goddesses. In the center of one of the rooms stands part of the Marathon victory trophy—an Ionic column that the

Athenians erected in the valley of Marathon after defeating the Persians. Next to the museum, the Middle Hellenic cemetery is well-sheltered from the forces of nature and very visitor-friendly. ⊠ *Plataion 114 ✛ approximately 6 km (4 miles) southwest of Marathon* ☎ *22940/55155* ⌨ *Combined ticket with Marathon Tomb €3* ⊗ *Tues.–Sun. 8:30–3.*

Marathon Run Museum. A permanent Olympic Marathon exhibit is housed near the start of the Athens Authentic Marathon (where the Olympic marathon also started in 2004) in the historic town of Marathon, where courier Pheidipiddes is said to have set off on his impressive feat of running 26 miles to Athens to bring home the news of victory over the Persians in 490 BC. ⊠ *Marathonos Ave. and 25th Martiou street* ☎ *22940/67617* ⊕ *www.marathonrunmuseum.com* ⌨ *€2* ⊗ *Tues.–Fri. 9–3 pm, weekends 10–2.*

Marathon Tomb. The 30-foot-high Marathon Tomb is built over the graves of the 192 Athenians who died in the 490 BC battle against Persian forces. At the base, the original gravestone depicts the Soldier of Marathon, a hoplite, which has been reproduced here (the original is in the National Archaeological Museum in Athens). This collective tomb, which contains the cremated remains of the national heroes, was built to honor them. The battle is plotted on illustrated panels, supplemented by a three-dimensional map of local landmarks. ✛ *5 km (3 miles) south of Marathon* ☎ *22940/55462* ⌨ *Combined ticket with Archaeological Museum €3* ⊗ *Tues.–Sun. 8:30–3.*

Rhamnous. The archaeological site at Rhamnous, an isolated, romantic spot on a small promontory, which was saved at the last minute from the devastating 2009 fires, overlooks the sea between continental Greece and the island of Euboia. It is a bit off the beaten track but if you want to escape the crowds of Athens and make it a day trip together with a swim at nearby Sxinias, it is definitely worth the drive (especially if you have your own vehicle). From at least the Archaic period, Rhamnous was known for the worship of Nemesis, the great leveler, who brought down the proud and punished the arrogant. The scenic site, excavated during many years, preserves traces of temples from the 6th and 5th centuries BC. The smaller temple from the 6th century BC was dedicated to Themis, goddess of Justice. The later temple housed the cult statue of Nemesis, envisioned as a woman, the only cult statue remaining from the high classical period. Many fragments have turned up, including the head, in the British Museum. The acropolis stood on the headland, where ruins of a fortress (5th and 4th centuries BC) are visible. As you wander over this usually serene, and always evocative, site you discover at its edge little coves where you can enjoy a swim. For those going by public transportation, take a KTEL bus from Athens toward the Ayia Marina port, get off at the Ayia Marina and Rhamnous crossroads, and follow the signs, about 3 km (2 miles) down the road. Or take a taxi from Marathon village. ⊠ *Ayia Marina ✛ 15 km (9 miles) northeast of Marathon* ☎ *22940/63477* ⌨ *€3* ⊗ *Tues.–Sun. 8–3.*

BEACHES

Rhamnous Beach. The coves at Rhamnous, about 2,000 feet from the approach and not far from the archaeological site, are cozy and remote. These are favorite swimming spots of nudists and free campers, although this is technically forbidden. Beware of spiny sea urchins when swimming off the rocks from this pebbly beach. **Amenities:** parking (free). **Best for:** solitude; nudists; walking. ✉ *Ayia Marina* ✣ *8 km (5 miles) northeast of Marathon.*

FAMILY **Schinias Beach.** The best beach in the north of Attica, just a couple of miles away from the historic town of Marathon, is the long, sandy, pine-backed stretch called Schinias. It's crowded with Athenians on the weekend, has a few simple tavernas along the sand and quite a lot of beach bars, and is frequently struck by strong winds that windsurfers love in summer. Campers like to settle in the Schinias forest during the summer, taking care not to disturb its precious natural habitat, which is environmentally protected. **Amenities:** food and drink; lifeguards; parking (free); showers; toilets; water sports. **Best for:** sunset; swimming; walking; windsurfing. ✉ *Schinias* ✣ *10 km (6 miles) southeast of Marathon.*

Sessi Beach. Sessi beach, near Grammatikon village, is probably the cleanest and most remote in the Attica region. The smaller Sessi beach on the left is about 400 meters long and has a small canteen, while the main pebble beach with its crystal clear waters has a couple of tavernas and a beach bar. There are also a few smaller stretches of sand accessible on foot that are fairly private. Bring your own sun beds and umbrellas because there's nothing for rent here. **Amenities:** food and drink. **Best for:** solitude; swimming. ✉ *Grammatiko* ✣ *6 km (4 miles) northeast of Marathon.*

Varnavas Beach. Less crowded than Schinias, fine-pebbled Varnavas beach is reached from Varnavas village. There is a lifeguard here during the summer months and a few tavernas nearby where you can enjoy a post-swim snack. It's a popular spear-fishing spot. **Amenities:** food and drink; lifeguards; parking (free). **Best for:** swimming; snorkeling. ✉ *Varnavas* ✣ *10 km (6 miles) northeast of Marathon.*

WHERE TO EAT

$$ ARGENTINE 🍴 **Argentina.** While living in South America, owner Nikos Milonas learned how to carve beef, how high to fire up the grill, and exactly how to time a perfect medium-rare steak (size XXL!). The meat-loving population of Greece has been benefiting from his expertise ever since. Salad and home fries round out both the luncheon and dinner menus. On a clear day you get a peek at the sea from the large veranda. The decor is simple, without frills, just like the menu. It is advised to call in and order meat in advance (or as soon as you sit down), as grilling takes at least an hour. [$] *Average main: €25* ✉ *Bitakou 3, About 1½ km (1 mile) after dam crossing, Kalentzi* ☎ *22940/66476* ✍ *Reservations essential* ⏲ *Closed Mon. and 2 wks. in Aug. No dinner Sun.*

$$ MEDITERRANEAN 🍴 **Cavo Seaside Bar & Restaurant.** Enjoy delicious dishes and frozen cocktails (try the amazing caipirinha) at one of the most popular seaside spots in Attica, under the pine trees and right next to the beach. After

its 2010 renovation, Cavo Seaside has been attracting an ever-increasing clientele, who come here to savor such creative Mediterranean delights as the smoked salmon with mango salad, the octopus cannelloni, and the risotto mojito (with chicken and lime sauce). The owners have a good sense of humor, too: they never neglect to send over shots (of a drink) to the newlyweds getting married in the church next door. [$] *Average main: €25* ✉ *Poseidonos Ave. 105, Mati* ☎ *22940/39018* 🌐 *www.cavo.gr.*

$$ SEAFOOD 🍴 **Isidora Fish Tavern.** Do as the Greeks do, and finish off a long day at the beach (or a visit to the Marathon Tomb and Museum) by heading to a traditional beachfront taverna to enjoy the sunset and regional cuisine. Isidora's front tables are nearly immersed in the sea, and the rest of this eatery is bordered by a Mediterranean garden. Proud family matriarch Isidora is behind the relaxed atmosphere and the delicious homemade dishes. Head into the kitchen to have a look at the fresh fish of the day, and choose some sea bream, which the chef will grill especially for you. It all begins with rich seasonal salads and fresh village bread and ends with either a halvah dessert or a plate of fresh fruit that's on the house. Just remember: it's cash only. [$] *Average main: €20* ✉ *Perikleous St. 5, 1000 feet down from the Golden Coast hotel* ☎ *22940/56467* 🌐 *www.isidora.com.gr* 💳 *No credit cards* 🕒 *Closed weekdays Nov.–Apr.*

$ BARBECUE 🍴 **Ta Patitiria tou Mpairaktari.** This traditional, well-preserved taverna is located on the major throughway Marathonos avenue, but the renovated former wine-press (*patitiri*) stone building is surrounded in its own greenery, maintaining coolness and serenity. Owner Stefanos Mpairaktaris, a skilled craftsman and culinary fan, took a hands-on approach to shifting the decades-old (since 1948) family focus on wine toward food. In the taverna with white embroidered curtains and a stone fireplace, he's worked on details including the vine motif painted onto wood chairs and branch candleholders. Try the stuffed potato *tis Yiayias* (Granny's), the spicy pork with peppers, the lamb cooked in a clay pot, and game (during hunting season). [$] *Average main: €15* ✉ *Marathonos Ave. 285* ✥ *3 km (2 miles) south of Marathon* ☎ *22940/55261.*

WHERE TO STAY

$ RESORT 🏨 **Aquis Aquamarina.** Some 26 km (16 miles) north of Athens and 4 km (2½ miles) from the port of Rafina, this hotel is perfect for a stopover as it offers an ideal combination of modern conveniences and seaside relaxation. **Pros:** spacious rooms; beautiful bay view; rich breakfast; free spa facilities. **Cons:** about 45-minute drive from the center of Athens; some rooms look a bit "tired"; need to hire a car to tour the area or get to the airport; children under 12 not allowed in the indoor pool. [$] *Rooms from: €75* ✉ *Poseidonos Ave. 55–57, Mati* ☎ *22940/77555, 210/362–0662 Athens office* 🌐 *www.aquamarina.gr* 🛏 *130 rooms* 🍽 *Breakfast.*

$ HOTEL 🏨 **Cabo Verde.** Small enough to provide personal service but large enough to have a pool, spa with sauna, and the Italian-style Regal restaurant on the premises, Cabo Verde offers spacious guest rooms with delightful sea views that include Evia island's profile directly across the strait and the small marina of Mati. **Pros:** relaxing views of the small harbor; 20 minutes from Athens International Airport so good for overnights and short stays; free Wi-Fi in rooms. **Cons:** somewhat far from Athens city center; in a summer resort crowded with Athenians; one needs a car or taxi to get there. $ *Rooms from: €75* ⊠ *Poseidonos 41, Mati* ✛ *7 km (4½ miles) south of Marathon* ☎ *22940/33111, 22940/33113 restaurant reservations* ⊕ *www.caboverde.gr* ↰ *34 rooms, 4 suites* ⊚⊚ *Breakfast.*

$
RESORT
ALL-INCLUSIVE
⊞ **Golden Coast Hotel & Bungalows.** A former Club Med, this beachfront resort was acquired in 2010 by Xenotel group, a Greek hotel chain determined to restore its former glow and island village feel. **Pros:** relaxing family atmosphere; excellent pool area; nice entertainment. **Cons:** hotel in the process of gradual renovation/rejuvenation; beds a bit on the hard side; although free in public areas, Wi-Fi use costs €5 in rooms. $ *Rooms from: €100* ⊠ *Marathon beach* ☎ *22941/13000* ⊕ *www.goldencoast.gr* ↰ *540 rooms* ⊚⊚ *All-inclusive.*

SPORTS AND THE OUTDOORS

RUNNING

Fodor's Choice
★
Athens Authentic Marathon. Every year in early November, the Athens Authentic Marathon is run over roughly the same course taken in 490 BC by the courier Pheidippides, when he carried to Athens the news of victory over the Persians. The 42-km (26-mile) race—organized by SEGAS, the Athens-based Hellenic Association of Amateur Athletics—is open to men and women of all ages, starts in Marathon, and finishes at the Panathenaic Stadium in Athens. In recent years, the event has been updated to include pasta parties, an expo, and other events for runners. If following in all of Pheidippides's footsteps is too much for you, the 5-km (3-mile), 10-km (6-mile), or power walking races are good options. You can apply and pay your entry fee either online or by mail. Even if you don't have the stamina for the race, cheer on the runners at the end of the route in Athens—they represent many ages, nationalities, and physiques. Those who finish the course sprint triumphantly into the marble stadium, where the first modern Olympics were held in 1896.

A permanent "Olympic Marathon" exhibit is housed at the Museum of the Marathon Run in the historic town of Marathon. ⊠ *Marathonos Ave. at 25th Martiou St.* ☎ *22940/67617* ⊕ *www. athensauthenticmarathon.gr.*

WATER SPORTS

Moraitis Sports Center. This part of Attica is ideal for all kinds of water sports. If you want to get a taste of windsurfing, drive to nearby Schinias for your first lesson with the excellent accredited instructors of Moraitis Sports Center, which also boasts a popular beach bar that's open until sunset in summer. The beach volleyball tournament is also popular with local players, while many triathletes use the center as a basis for their year-round training. ⊠ *Schinias* ☎ *22940/55965* ⊕ *www. moraitis-sports.gr.*

4

MT. PARNITHA ΠΑΡΝΗΘΑ

62 km (38 miles) west of Marathon, 33 km (20½ miles) northwest of Athens.

The summit of Mt. Parnitha, Attica's highest mountain, has a splendid view of the plain of Athens cradled by Mt. Pendeli and Mt. Hymettos. Tragically, large swaths of the mountain's protected national park, particularly its western side, were destroyed in a 2007 fire. However, lovely nature walks threading through the Mt. Parnitha massif are still possible. Visitors are discouraged from passing through the charred area until the forest regenerates. In April and May the forest blooms with wildflowers, red poppies, white crocuses, purple irises, and numerous species of orchid. Many Athenians come year-round, especially on Sunday, to enjoy the clean air, mountain bike, or picnic, but some are equally attracted by the gaming tables at the nearby casino.

EXPLORING

Regency Casino Mont Parnes. This popular casino welcomes visitors while in the process of a gradual renovation. The scenic ascent in the funicular is free of charge, while the casino can also be reached by car. ⊠ *Mount Parnitha, Acharnes* ☎ *210/242–1234* ⊕ *www.regencycasinos.gr.*

WHERE TO EAT

$$
GREEK
FAMILY
✕ **Leonidas.** You're invited to visit the kitchen and peer into the pots of *ladera* (vegetables in season), such as okra or fresh green beans, cooked in an olive-oil-and-tomato sauce. You might also see pans of *yemista* (tomatoes and peppers stuffed with rice and pine nuts or rice and ground beef). The house specialty is pork, served with applesauce, roasted slowly to drain its fat but retain the juices. Two large reception areas often fill with up to 400 wedding guests and other revelers each. Children can move around freely in the playground. $ *Average main: €20* ⊠ *Tatoiou Ave., at the end, Varimbombi* ✚ *23 km (14 miles) north of Athens, 20 km (12 miles) west of Phyle, off Athens–Lamia highway* ☎ *210/816–9391* ⊕ *www.leonidas-estiatorio.gr.*

$
STEAKHOUSE
✕ **O Kakias.** O Kakias is one of the better-known traditional meat tavernas in Hasia, on the feet of Mt. Parnitha, serving great, inexpensive lamb, goat, ewe, sausages and other grilled meats, potatoes, and wild herb salads. On cold days, cozy up to the fireplace; on warm days, bask in the sun on the outdoor terrace that's within a pine forest. The taverna opens early on weekends for lunch but is only open for dinner on weekdays. No credit cards. $ *Average main: €15* ⊠ *Phylis Ave. 100, Hasia, Ano Liosia* ☎ *210/241–1734* ▭ *No credit cards* ⊘ *No lunch weekdays.*

$$
BARBECUE
Fodor'sChoice
★
✕ **Pappas.** This family-run taverna is popular for its mountain views and cozy fireplace in the winter, as well as for its serene garden with tall plane trees providing a much-needed respite from the summer heat. The menu is built around grilled meat, mostly ribs and chops, served by the kilo on heaping platters. Accompaniments include lightly fried zucchini, eggplant chips for dipping in the yogurt-garlic *tzatziki*, and delicious pies of wild greens wrapped in thick, hand-rolled phyllo. $ *Average main: €20* ⊠ *Thessalonikis 2, off Attiki Odos, Acharnes* ☎ *210/243–1232* ⊕ *www.pappas-taverna.gr.*

SPORTS AND THE OUTDOORS
HIKING
There are 12 marked hiking trails, with varying degrees of difficulty, on
Mt. Parnitha—the EOS Athinon Alpine Club reports that though the
view is beautiful at Pan's cave, en route you pass through the devastat-
ing fire of 2007 area. So it's still not recommended for hikers, except
for the northeastern part of the mountain. The area between Bafi and
Flambouri remains unchanged.

Bafi Refuge. A 2.2-km (1.4-mile) ascent from the church of Ayia Triada
(takes approximately 40 minutes) leads to the Bafi Refuge, run by the
EOS Athinon (Hiking Club of Athens), where basic board and lodging
are available. The refuge has a fireplace and kitchen; water is piped in
from a nearby spring. The refuge remains open all year long. ⊠ *Mt.
Parnitha, Parnithos Rd., Acharavi* ☎ *210/240–3566* ⊕ *www.mpafi.gr.*

Church of Ayios Petros. One of the milder, and most pleasant, hikes on
Mt. Parnitha follows a marked trail from the church of Ayia Triada
through the national park to the church of Ayios Petros at Mola forest. The path leads past the Skipiza spring, providing spectacular views
of western Attica and the town of Thebes along the way. The 6-km
(4-mile) walk takes about two hours, and you might even spot deer
darting among the trees. ⊠ *Mola forest, Parnithos Rd., Mt. Parnitha,
Acharnes* ☎ *210/246–1528* ⊕ *www.eosacharnon.gr.*

EOS Athinon Alpine Club. The Hiking Club of Athens runs huts where you
can spend the night in the Bafi refuge, and the organization can also give
you information on the trails. In most cases, when you call you'll be
able to find someone who speaks English. ☎ *210/321–2355 in Athens.*

EOS Axarnon Alpine Club. The Axarnon Hiking Club in Acharnes can give
you information on the trails in the Flambouri Refuge, where the club
maintains and rents out huts. ☎ *210/383–3168 in Acharnes.*

Flambouri Refuge. From Bafi, one trail turns south, tracing the fir and pine
woods along the Houni ravine, skirting the craggy Flambouri peak—a
favorite nesting place of the park's raptors. This trail intersects with
another path leading to the Flambouri Refuge, a basic hikers' hut run
by EOS Acharnon Hiking Club. You can stay the night or enjoy their
views of Mt. Parnitha and hearty food, before exploring more trails.
⊠ *Parnithos Ave., Acharnes* ☎ *210/246–4666* ⊕ *www.flabouri.gr.*

MONASTERY OF DAPHNI ΜΟΝΗ ΔΑΦΝΙΟΥ

*61 km (38 miles) southwest of Mt. Parnitha, 11 km (7 miles) west of
Athens.*

Daphni means "laurel tree," which was sacred to Apollo, whose sanctuary once occupied this site. The original temple was destroyed in AD
395 after the anti-pagan edicts of the emperor Theodosius, and the
Orthodox monastery that stands here now was probably established
in the 6th century, incorporating materials of Apollo's sanctuary in the
church and walls. Reoccupied by Orthodox monks only in the 16th
century, the Daphni neighborhood has since been host to a barracks and

mental institution. The monastery, a UNESCO World Heritage Site, is once again open to the public even though restoration work is ongoing.

Fodor's Choice ★ **Monastery of Daphni.** Sacked by Crusaders, inhabited by Cistercian monks, and desecrated by Turks, the Monastery of Daphni remains one of the most splendid Byzantine monuments in Greece. Dating from the 11th century, the golden age of Byzantine art, the church contains a series of miraculously preserved mosaics without parallel in the legacy of Byzantium: powerful portraits of figures from the Old and New Testaments, images of Christ and the Virgin Mary in the *Presentation of the Virgin,* and, in the golden dome, a stern *Pantokrator* ("ruler of all") surrounded by 16 Old Testament prophets who predicted his coming. The mosaics, made of chips of four different types of marble, are set against gold.

There is free entrance to the monastery, which is a UNESCO World Heritage Site. An ongoing long-term restoration project makes it hard to see some of the mosaics, but this doesn't take away much of the awe inspired by the craftmanship of the Byzantine masters. ✉ *Iera Odos at Athinon Ave., Haidari* ☎ *210/581–1558* ⊕ *www.culture.gr* ✉ *Free* ☉ *Tues.–Sun. 8–3.*

ELEUSIS ΕΛΕΥΣΙΝΑ

11 km (7 miles) west of the Monastery of Daphni, 22 km (14 miles) west of Athens.

The growing city of Athens co-opted the land around Eleusis, placing shipyards in the pristine gulf and steel mills and petrochemical plants along its shores. It is hard to imagine that there once stretched in every direction fields of corn and barley sacred to the goddess Demeter, whose realm was symbolized by the sheaf and sickle.

EXPLORING

Sanctuary of Demeter. The Sanctuary of Demeter lies on an eastern slope, at the foot of the ancient acropolis protecting the settlement of Eleusis, hardly visible amid the modern buildings of the main square of Elefsina (or Eleusis, as it was called in the ancient Greek world). The legend of Demeter and her daughter Persephone explained for the ancients the cause of the seasons and the origins of agriculture.

It was to Eleusis that Demeter traveled in search of Persephone after the girl had been kidnapped by Hades, god of the underworld. Zeus himself interceded to restore her to the distraught Demeter but succeeded only partially, giving mother and daughter just half a year together.

Nevertheless, in gratitude to King Keleos of Eleusis, who had given her refuge in her time of need, Demeter presented his son Triptolemos with wheat seeds, the knowledge of agriculture, and a winged chariot so he could spread them to mankind. Keleos built a *megaron* (large hall) in Demeter's honor, the first Eleusinian sanctuary.

The worship of Demeter took the form of mysterious rites, part purification and part drama, and both the Lesser and the Greater Eleusinian rituals closely linked Athens with the sanctuary. The procession for the

Greater Eleusinia began and ended there, following the route of the Sacred Way (along the avenue still called Iera Odos today).

Much of what you see now in the sanctuary is of Roman construction or repair, although physical remains on the site date back to the Mycenaean period. Follow the old Sacred Way to the great *propylaea* (gates) and continue on to the Precinct of Demeter, which was strictly off-limits on pain of death to any but the initiated. The *Telesterion* (Temple of Demeter), now a vast open space surrounded by battered tiers of seats, dates to 600 BC, when it was the hall of initiation. It had a roof supported by six rows of seven columns, presumably so the mysteries would be obscured, and it could accommodate 3,000 people.

The museum, just beyond, contains pottery and sculpture, particularly of the Roman period. Although the site is closed at night, you can see the sacred court and propylaea from a distance thanks to special lighting by Pierre Bideau, the French expert who also designed the lighting for the Acropolis in Athens. ⊠ *Gkioka 1, Eleusis (Elefsina)* ☎ *210/554–6019* ⊕ *www.visit-ancient-greece.com/eleusis.html* 🎫 *€3* ⊙ *Tues.–Sun. 8–3.*

WHERE TO STAY

$ | **Elefsina Hotel.** An easy getaway to the Peloponnese—that's what HOTEL western Attica's most up-to-date hotel offers. **Pros:** modern and simple Fodor'sChoice decor; free Wi-Fi; very comfortable rooms; free room service. **Cons:** ★ location in a suburban neighborhood might be hard to find; narrow ramp for otherwise free parking. $ *Rooms from: €70* ⊠ *Dimitros 55 and Riga Feraiou Sts., Eleusis (Elefsina)* ☎ *210/558–9700* ⊕ *www. elefsinahotel.gr* 🛏 *83 rooms* ⊙ *Breakfast.*

DELPHI AND ENVIRONS ΔΕΛΦΟΙ

The world-famous region of Delphi is steeped in history: it was in Thebes, according to legend, and so described by Sophocles in *Oedipus Rex,* that the infant Oedipus was left by his father, Laius, on a mountainside to die after an oracle predicted he would murder his father and marry his mother. Some shepherds, ignorant of the curse, rescued him, and he was raised by the king of Corinth. The saga unfolded when, as a young man, Oedipus was walking from Delphi and met his father, Laius, king of Thebes, near the Triple Way. The latter, having struck Oedipus with his whip in order to make room for his chariot to pass, was in turn attacked and accidentally killed by the young man, who did not recognize his father, not having seen his parents since his birth. Journeying to Thebes, he solved the riddle of the terrible Sphinx and, as a reward, was offered the throne and the hand of Jocasta (who was, unbeknownst to him, his mother). When they discovered what had happened, Oedipus blinded himself and Jocasta hanged herself.

The preferred route from Athens follows the National Road to the Thebes turnoff, at 74 km (46 miles). Take the secondary road south past Thebes and continue west through the fertile plain—now planted with cotton, potatoes, and tobacco—to busy Levadia, capital of the province of Boeotia. If you detour in Levadia by following the signs for the *piges*

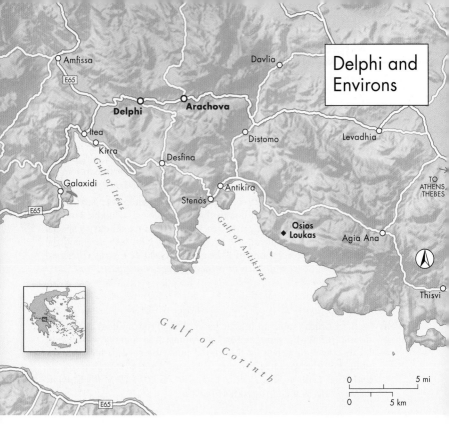

(hot springs), you come to the banks of the ancient springs of Lethe and Mnemosyne, or Oblivion and Remembrance (these springs are about a 10-minute walk from the main square); in antiquity the Erkinas (Hercyne) gorge was believed to be the entrance to the underworld. Today, the plane- and maple-tree-shaded river is spanned by an old stone arch bridge built in Ottoman times. Almost halfway between Levadia and Delphi, the Triple Way (where the roads from Delphi, Daulis, and Levadia meet) is where Oedipus fatefully met his father.

If you turn south toward Distomo at the junction, you can visit the monastic complex at Osios Loukas and its Byzantine architecture. The National Road continues to Mt. Parnassus, where the formerly quiet mountain village of Arachova is now a successful confluence of traditional Greek mountain village and Athenian-style, fashionable cafés, thanks to the proximity of ski lifts. The sublime ruins at Delphi are captivating whether you have little knowledge of ancient Greece or have long awaited a chance to see where the Pythian priestesses uttered their cryptic prophecies. After the Acropolis of Athens, Delphi is the most powerful ancient site in Greece. Its history reaches back at least as far as the Mycenaean period; in Homer's *Iliad* it is referred to as Pytho. Southwest of the Delphi ruins on the coast, picturesque Galaxidi now caters to wealthy Athenians who have restored many of the mansions once owned by shipbuilders.

OSIOS LOUKAS ΟΣΙΟΣ ΛΟΥΚΑΣ

150 km (93 miles) northwest of Athens.

The monastic complex at Osios Loukas, still inhabited by a few monks, is notable for its exquisite mosaics and its dramatic location, looming on a prominent rise with a sweeping view of the Elikonas peaks and the sparsely inhabited but fertile valley. The outside of the buildings is typically Byzantine, with rough stonework interspersed with an arched brick pattern. It is especially beautiful in February when the almond branches explode with a profusion of delicate oval pinkish-white blooms.

GETTING HERE AND AROUND

Osios Loukas is located near the town of Distomo in the Voiotia prefecture, about 160 km (99 miles) north of Athens. Driving is easiest, but there are also buses. Take one of the KTEL buses that depart daily from bus Terminal B in Athens for Livadeia. The one-way journey takes 2½ hours and costs €12.40. From there, you can take the local bus to Osios Loukas, for an additional €3.50. *For more information on Athens buses and bus stations, see Bus and Train Travel in Athens.*

EXPLORING

Osios Loukas. Luke (Loukas) the Hermit—not the evangelist who wrote a book of the New Testament—was a medieval oracle who founded a church at this site and lived here until his death in AD 953. He was probably born in Delphi, after his family fled from Aegina during a raid of Saracen pirates. This important monastery was founded by the emperor Romanos II in AD 961, in recognition of the accuracy of Loukas's prophecy that Crete would be liberated by an emperor named Romanos. The katholikon, a masterpiece of Byzantine architecture, was built in the 11th century over the tomb of Luke. It follows to perfection the Byzantine cross-in-a-square plan under a central dome and was inspired by Ayia Sophia in Constantinople; in turn, it was used as a model for both the Monastery of Daphni and Mystra churches. Impressive mosaics in the narthex and in portions of the domed nave are set against a rich gold background and done in the somber but expressive 11th-century hieratic style by artists from Thessaloniki and Constantinople. Particularly interesting are the reactions evident on the faces of the apostles, which range from passivity to surprise as Christ washes their feet in the mosaic of *Niptir,* to the far left of the narthex.

In the second niche of the entrance is a mosaic showing Loukas sporting a helmet and beard, with his arms raised. The engaging *Nativity, Presentation in the Temple,* and the *Baptism of Christ* mosaics are on the curved arches that support the dome. Two priceless icons from the late 16th century, *Daniel in the Lion's Den* and *Shadrach, Meshach, and Abednego in the Flames of the Furnace,* by Damaskinos, a teacher of El Greco, were stolen a few years back from the white marble iconostasis in the little apse and have been replaced with copies. The tomb of Osios Loukas is in the crypt of the katholikon; his relics, formerly in the Vatican, were moved here in 1987, making the monastery an official shrine. A highlight of the complex is the Theotokos (Mother of God), a small communal church dedicated to the Virgin Mary, on the left as you enter. On the periphery are the monks' cells and a refectory, now restored, which has been used as a sculpture museum since 1993. To visit you must wear either long pants or a skirt. Bring a small flashlight to help see some of the frescoes. ⊠ *On rise above valley of Mt. Elikon, Osios Loukas* ☎ *22670/22797* 🖃 *€3* ⊙ *Mon. closed, Tue.–Sun. 9–5.*

ARACHOVA ΑΡΑΧΩΒΑ

24 km (16 miles) northwest of Osios Loukas, 157 km (97 miles) northwest of Athens.

Arachova's gray-stone houses with red-tile roofs cling to the steep slopes of Mt. Parnassus, the highest mountain in Greece after Mt. Olympus. The 1980s brought a boom to this once-quiet region, which in winter is transformed into a busy ski resort. Weekends bring sophisticated Athenians heading for the slopes: hotel prices soar and rooms are snapped up; cobblestone streets fill with SUVs carrying skis aloft; and village taverns get crowded after dark as people warm their weary bones before the fires. Unlike other Greek destinations, in summer there are hardly any Greek tourists in Arachova and not everything may be open.

GETTING HERE AND AROUND

KTEL buses servicing Arachova depart from the Terminal B bus station in Athens. The journey takes about three hours and costs €15.10. It is the same regional bus that continues on to Delphi and there are five daily departures, beginning at 7:30 am. Tickets for the KTEL buses to Arachova are sold only at Terminal B, so you should call to book seats well in advance during high season or holidays. *For more information on Athens buses and bus stations, see Bus and Train Travel in Athens.*

EXPLORING

St. George's Day. If you're lucky enough to be in Arachova for the festival on St. George's Day—April 23 (or the Monday after Easter if April 23 falls during Lent)—you're in for the time of your life. St. George, the dragon slayer, is the patron saint of Arachova, and the largest church on the top of the highest hill in town is dedicated to him. So, naturally, the festival here lasts three days and nights, starting with a procession behind the generations-old silver icon from the church, in which the villagers don the local costumes, most of them ornately embroidered silken and brocaded heirlooms that testify to the rich cultural heritage of the town. The festival is kicked off in fine form with the race of the *yeroi,* the old men of the town, who are astonishingly agile as they clamber up the hill above the church without so much as a gasp for air. The following days are filled with athletic contests, cooking competitions, and, at night, passionate dancing in the tavernas until long after the goats go home. Visitors are welcome to partake of a feast held outside St. George (Ayios Yiorgios) church that features Mt. Parnassus's legendary roast lamb and feta cheese and a steady flow of Arachova wine. ☎ *22670/31241 Ayioa Yiorgios church* ⊕ *www.panigiraki.gr.*

For Byzantine splendor, look no further than the paintings covering the Crypt of the great monastery at Osios Loukas.

WHERE TO EAT

$$ GREEK 🍴 **Dasargiris.** Arachova's oldest taverna (more that a hundred years old) still draws gargantuan crowds—causing occasional staff surliness—simply because of the amazing food. Lamb with oregano, and beef in a red sauce are both served with *hilopites*, the thin egg noodles cut into thousands of tiny squares, for which the area is known. Sample the fried *formaella* (a mild local sheep's-milk cheese); the *hortopites* (pastries filled with mountain greens); grilled beef patties stuffed with formaella or Gouda cheese *(bourekakia)*; or the *kokoretsi* (a tasty mix of various lamb organs), which Greek customers swear by. At Easter the cook makes an unforgettable roast lamb and egg-lemon soup. Try the brusco red wine straight from the barrel. [$] *Average main: €18* ✉ *Delfon 56* ☎ *22670/31291* 💳 *No credit cards* 🕒 *Closed Aug.*

$$$ GREEK 🍴 **Panagiota.** It is well worth climbing the 263 steps leading from the main road up to the church of Ayios Georgios. Behind the churchyard, the lovely smells from this hilltop restaurant's kitchen will prepare you for a tasty meal. The restaurant dates back to the 1930s and has served many a Greek politician and poet. Start with local specialty *opsimotyri* (tart yogurt dip) and the house salad of shredded red cabbage, carrot, and grilled mushrooms. Then, dig into a plump *bifteki* (ground meat) flavored with parsley, or *dolmades* (stuffed vine leaves) with a creamy lemon sauce. The lamb stewed on vine leaves is also a favorite with regular clients. Reservations are essential during winter weekends, when there is Greek live music and the impromptu party continues until the early morning hours. [$] *Average main: €28* ✉ *Ano Arachova, behind Ayios Giorgios* ☎ *22670/32735* ✍ *Reservations essential* 🕒 *Closed Mon.–Wed. in June–Aug.*

$$ ✕**Taverna To Agnandio.** In the winter you can warm yourself at your
GREEK   choice of several fireplaces in this old stone house that's been deemed a
historic building by the state, and look out at the excellent views of the
mountains. *Tirokafteri*, a piquant cheese spread, is the perfect accompa-
niment to the stone-ground country bread to start. Follow with a sam-
pling of the large purplish Amphissa olives, *fava* (mashed yellow split
peas, lemon, and raw onions), or the potent skordalia. Meat dominates
the mains: rooster with *xylopites* (tiny pasta squares) in tomato sauce,
and stuffed lamb shank, for example. $ *Average main: €18* ⊠ *Delfon,
next to town hall and clock tower* ☎ *22670/32114* ☾ *Closed June–Aug.*

WHERE TO STAY

$ ⌂**Guesthouse Maria.** Simple and affordable, this family-run rustic inn
B&B/INN   is housed in a restored 19th-century building on a quiet lane off the
main road. **Pros:** ample-size rooms; charming ski-lodge feeling; close
to town center; free Wi-Fi. **Cons:** no parking; no elevator; basic break-
fast; no views. $ *Rooms from: €75* ⊠ *Off Delfon, near village center*
☎ *22670/31803* ⊕ *www.mariarooms.com* ⤳ *4 rooms, 3 studios* ⊟ *No
credit cards* ⼂⃝| *Breakfast.*

$$ ⌂**Skamnos.** Part ski hotel, part mountain lodge, this cozy retreat offers
HOTEL   some of the best views plus such luxurious perks as a heated indoor
Fodor's Choice   pool, outdoor Jacuzzi, and a spa. **Pros:** incredible mountain views,
★   perfect for relaxation; relatively good value for money. **Cons:** some
smallish rooms; a bit of a drive to Arachova for nightlife and food.
$ *Rooms from: €135* ⊠ *On road between Arachova and Parnassus Ski
Center, Voiotia* ☎ *22670/31927* ⊕ *www.skamnos.com* ⤳ *15 rooms, 7
suites* ⼂⃝| *Breakfast.*

NIGHTLIFE

On winter weekends Arachova streets are jammed with Athenians who
come almost as much for the nightlife as for the skiing. Clubs change
frequently, but favorites remain.

Aquarella Restaurant Bar. Greek music—sometimes live—sets the tone
at warm Aquarella: drop by for a drink or tuck into a large gourmet
menu of meaty offerings Friday and Saturday nights. Later at night,
you can still get finger food, and some center tables might be removed
to make room for dancing, and even better, for some legendary "flower
wars" among happy club-goers. Smart dress is strongly recommended.
⊠ *Lakka Sq.* ☎ *22670/32660.*

Café Bonjour. Catch a coffee or freshly squeezed mixed fruit juice by day
or a drink by night at Café Bonjour in tree-covered Lakka Square—and
don't forget their croissants: the best in town! ⊠ *Delfon, Lakka Sq.*
☎ *22670/32330* ⊕ *www.cafebonjour.gr.*

FAMILY   **Emboriko Tsitsi.** Emboriko Tsitsi is where an up-and-coming crowd of
Fodor's Choice   politicians, journalists, and artists mingle anonymously. The charming
★   gathering spot is housed in a beautiful mountain chalet in the Livadi
area (just outside Arachova). It's especially popular later in the evening,
when there are tasty cocktails offered at the bar and occasional live
performances. Throughout the day, Emboriko also draws for pre- and
post-skiing food; it also offers organized Segway and bike rides and sells

delicious homemade sweets and wine. There's ample parking. ⊠ *Livadi* ☎ *22670/31218* ⊕ *www.tsitsi.gr.*

Flox All-Day Bar Restaurant. Located off of the Ayios Giorgos steps, trendy Flox is a restaurant-bar, open from October through March, that is transformed into a club after midnight. Red wine flows on chilly nights within the carefully lighted rock-wall interior. ⊠ *Ayios Giorgos* ☎ *22670/31007.*

Isidora Gallery. Don't be misled by the name. This is actually a wine bar, not a gallery (although temporary exhibitions of up-and-coming Greek artists are often shown here). Isadora Gallery combines the traditional village aura of this old mansion (built in 1760) with a monk-like austerity accentuated by some interesting details like the wooden table, the tall candles, and the minimalist mirror on the wall. A selection of excellent Greek wine is on offer, or you can opt for one of the cocktails. The cheese platters are an ideal accompaniment to your drink, while the jazzy notes in the background will not obstruct your conversation. It opens nightly at 7. ⊠ *Odyssea Androutsou 297* ☎ *6980/195968.*

Red Six Bar. The rowdy Red Six Bar is a split-level club with mainstream music, young things dancing on the bar, and a doorman to keep out the unhip. It is still as popular with après-skiers as it was 25 years ago when it first opened its doors. ⊠ *Lakka Sq.* ☎ *6940/777444.*

SPORTS AND THE OUTDOORS
HIKING
Arachova and its environs are made for exploring on foot, either by simply walking a country lane to see where it leads or picking up one of the hiking trails like the E4 through Parnassus National Park or the ancient footpath down the mountain. The 8,061-foot summit of Mt. Parnassus is now easily accessible, thanks to roads opened up for the ski areas. The less hardy can drive almost up to the summit.

Arachova Hiking and Skiing Club. The local Arachova Hiking and Skiing Club organizes regular group hiking outings; give them a call to join the next one. ☎ *22670/311118* ⊕ *www.shoarahovas.com.*

Fodor'sChoice
★ **M. Defner Sarandari Refuge.** You can motor up to the small M. Defner Sarandari Refuge, run by the ski shop company Klaoudatos, 6,201 feet up on the slopes of Mt. Parnassus. It accommodates up to 20 people, and you can spend the night, enjoy the breathtaking views (and homemade meals), and then walk to the summit in time to catch the sunrise—the best time to be on this legendary mountain. The refuge is just 500 m away from the Gerontovraxos ski center. ☎ *6936/861064* ⊕ *www.klaoudatos-ski.gr.*

SKIING
Parnassos Ski Center. Rental ski equipment is available at local shops in Arachova and at the Parnassos Ski Center, just 40 minutes from Arachova. The Fterolakka area has a good restaurant and several more-challenging runs. The Kelaria area is good for beginners. A daily ski pass costs about €30 on weekends, €15 weekdays. Perks include night ski parties. ⊠ *Kelaria* ✛ *25 km (17 miles) north of Arachova* ☎ *22340/22700* ⊕ *www.parnassos-ski.gr.*

SHOPPING

Arachova was known even in pre-ski days as a place to shop for wool, with stores selling rugs and weavings lining the main street. The modern mass-produced bedspreads, *flokates* (woolen rugs, sometimes dyed vivid colors), and kilim-style carpets sold today are reasonably priced. If you poke into dark corners in the stores, you still might turn up something made of local wool; anything that claims to be antique bears a higher price. Also look for local foodstuffs like the delicious Parnassus honey, the local cheese formaella (often served warm), and the fiery hot *rakomelo* (a combination of anise liqueur and honey), which is served in most of the bars and cafés to warm those who've been outside all day on a cold winter's night.

Klaoudatos Ski Shop. Klaoudatos is a well-known outdoor-sports goods retailer that caters to all levels, from beginners to pros; it also runs ski bus tours, two mountain refuges, and organizes ski camps. ⊠ *Distomo-Arachova intersection* ☎ *22670/31457* ⊕ *www.klaoudatos-ski.gr.*

Pappos-Baldoumis Snow Republic Ski Shop and Ski School. The biggest ski school in Greece, Pappos-Baldoumis Ski Shop and Ski School operates a couple of well-equipped ski shops, including one in Arachova's main square and a second one along the main road, going towards Athens. ⊠ *Lakka Sq.* ☎ *22670/31552* ⊕ *www.skischool.gr.*

DELPHI ΔΕΛΦΟΙ

10 km (6 miles) west of Arachova, 189 km (118 miles) northwest of Athens.

Nestled in the mountain cliffs, modern Delphi is perched dramatically on the edge of a grove leading to the sea, west of an extraordinary ancient site. A stay in town can prove most memorable—especially if you come at *Pascha* (Easter). The hospitable people of modern Delphi take great pride in their town. They maintain a tradition of comfortable, small hotels and a main street thick with restaurants and souvenir shops. Ancient Delphi, the home of a famous oracle in antiquity, can be seen from the town's hotels or terraced village houses. It's easily reached from almost any point in the central town, at most a 10- to 15-minute walk. When the archaeological site is first seen from the road, it would appear that there is hardly anything left to attest to the existence of the ancient religious city. Only the Treasury of the Athenians and a few other columns are left standing, but once you are within the precincts, the plan becomes clearer and the layout is revealed in such detail that it is possible to conjure up a vision of what the scene must have once been when Delphi was the holiest place in all Greece.

GETTING HERE AND AROUND

Surprisingly, there are no trains to Delphi, just buses. In fact, the same KTEL buses from Athens that go to Arachova continue on to Delphi, for the same cost of €15.10. The journey lasts 3½ hours. The first KTEL bus leaves Athens Terminal B at 7:30 am; the last one at 8 pm. *For more information on Athens buses and bus stations, see Bus and Train Travel in Athens.*

EXPLORING

At first the settlement probably was sacred to Gaia, the mother goddess; toward the end of the Greek Dark Ages (circa 1100–800 BC), the site incorporated the cult of Apollo. According to Plutarch, who was a priest of Apollo at Delphi, the oracle was discovered by chance, when a shepherd noticed that his flock went into a frenzy when it came near a certain chasm in the rock. When he approached, he also came under a spell and began to utter prophecies, as did his fellow villagers. Eventually a *Pythia*, an anointed woman over 50 who lived in seclusion, was the one who sat on the three-footed stool and interpreted the prophecy.

On oracle day, the seventh of the month, the Pythia prepared herself by washing in the Castalian Fountain and undergoing a purification involving barley smoke and laurel leaves. If the male priests of Apollo determined the day was propitious for prophesying, she entered the Temple of Apollo, where she drank the Castalian water, chewed laurel leaves, and presumably sank into a trance. Questions presented to her received strange and garbled answers, which were then translated into verse by the priests. A number of the lead tablets on which questions were inscribed have been uncovered, but the official answers were inscribed only in the memories of questioners and priests. Those that have survived, from various sources, suggest the equivocal nature of these sibylline emanations: perhaps the most famous is the answer given to King Croesus of Lydia, who asked if he should attack the Persians. "Croesus, having crossed the Halys River, will destroy a great realm," said the Pythia. Thus encouraged, he crossed it, only to find his *own* empire destroyed.

During the 8th and 7th centuries BC, the oracle's advice played a significant role in the colonization of southern Italy and Sicily (Magna Graecia) by Greece's Amphictyonic League. By 582 BC the Pythian Games had become a quadrennial festival similar to those held at Olympia. Increasingly an international center, Delphi attracted supplicants from beyond the Greek mainland, including such valued clients as King Midas and King Croesus, both hailing from wealthy kingdoms in Asia Minor. During this period of prosperity many cities built treasure houses at Delphi. The sanctuary was threatened during the Persian War but never attacked, and it continued to prosper in spite of the fact that Athens and Sparta, two of its most powerful patrons, were locked in war.

Delphi came under the influence first of Macedonia and then of the Aetolian League (290–190 BC) before yielding to the Romans in 189 BC. Although the Roman general Sulla plundered Delphi in 86 BC, there were at least 500 bronze statues left to be collected by Nero in AD 66, and the site was still full of fine works of art when Pausanias visited and described it a century later. The emperor Hadrian restored many sanctuaries in Greece, including Delphi's, but within a century or two the oracle was silent. In AD 385 Theodosius abolished the oracle. Only in the late 19th century did French excavators begin to uncover the site of Apollo.

Fodor'sChoice ★ **Ancient Delphi.** After a square surrounded by late-Roman porticoes, pass through the main gate to Ancient Delphi and continue on to the **Sacred Way,** the approach to the Altar of Apollo. Walk between building foundations and bases for votive dedications, stripped now of ornament and statue, mere scraps of what was one of the richest collections of art and treasures in antiquity. Thanks to the 2nd-century AD writings of Pausanias, archaeologists have identified treasuries built by the Thebans, the Corinthians, the Syracusans, and others—a roster of 6th- and 5th-century BC powers. The **Treasury of the Athenians,** on your left as you turn right, was built with money from the victory over the Persians at Marathon. The **Stoa of the Athenians,** northeast of the treasury, housed, among other objects, an immense cable with which the Persian king Xerxes roped together a pontoon bridge for his army to cross the Hellespont from Asia to Europe.

The **Temple of Apollo** visible today (there were three successive temples built on the site) is from the 4th century BC. Although ancient sources speak of a chasm within, there is no trace of that opening in the earth from which emanated trance-inducing vapors. Above the temple is the well-preserved **theater,** which seated 5,000. It was built in the 4th century BC, restored in about 160 BC, and later was restored again by the Romans. From a sun-warmed seat on the last tier, you see a panoramic bird's-eye view of the sanctuary and the convulsed landscape that encloses it. Also worth the climb is the view from the **stadium** still farther up the mountain, at the highest point of the ancient town. Built and restored in various periods and cut partially from the living rock, the stadium underwent a final transformation under Herodes Atticus, the Athenian benefactor of the 2nd century AD. It lies cradled in a grove of pine trees, a quiet refuge removed from the sanctuary below and backed by the sheer, majestic rise of the mountain. Markers for the starting line inspire many to race the length of the stadium. ⊠ *Road to Arachova, immediately east of modern Delphi* ☎ *22650/82312* ⊕ *www. culture.gr* 🖾 *€6; €9 combined ticket of Delphi site and museum* ☉ *Daily 8–8 (last entry 7:30 pm).*

Fodor'sChoice ★ **Delphi Museum.** Visiting this museum is essential to understanding the site and sanctuary's importance to the ancient Greek world, which considered Delphi its center (literally—look for the copy of the *omphalos,* or Earth's navel, a sacred stone from the adytum of Apollo's temple). The museum is home to a wonderful collection of art and architectural sculpture, principally from the Sanctuaries of Apollo and Athena Pronoia. Curators have used an additional 15,000 square feet of museum space, opened in 2004, to create contextual, cohesive exhibits. You can now view all the pediments from Apollo's temple together and new exhibits include a fascinating collection of 5th-century BC votives.

One of the greatest surviving ancient bronzes on display commands a prime position in a spacious hall, set off to advantage by special lighting: the *Charioteer* is a sculpture so delicate in size (but said to be scaled to life) it is surprising when you see it in person for the first time. Created in about 470 BC, the human figure is believed to have stood on a terrace wall above the Temple of Apollo, near which it was found in 1896. It was part of a larger piece, which included a four-horse chariot. Scholars

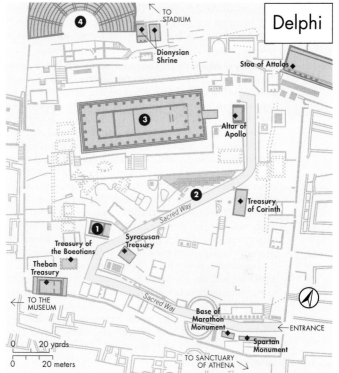

do not agree on who executed the work, although Pythagoras of Samos is sometimes mentioned as a possibility. The donor is supposed to have been a well-known patron of chariot racing, Polyzalos, the Tyrant of Gela in Sicily. Historians now believe that a sculpted likeness of Polyzalos was originally standing next to the charioteer figure. The statue commemorates a victory in the Pythian Games at the beginning of the 5th century BC. Note the eyes, inlaid with a white substance resembling enamel, the pupils consisting of two concentric onyx rings of different colors. The sculpture of the feet and of the hair clinging to the nape of the neck is perfect in detail.

Two life-size Ionian *chryselephantine* (ivory heads with gold head-dresses) from the Archaic period are probably from statues of Apollo and his sister Artemis (she has a sly smirk on her face). Both gods also figure prominently in a frieze depicting the Gigantomachy, the gods' battle with the giants. These exquisitely detailed marble scenes, dated to the 6th century BC, are from the Treasury of the Siphnians. The *caryatids* (supporting columns in a female form) from the treasury's entrance have been repositioned to offer a more accurate picture of the building's size and depth. The museum's expansion also allowed curators to give more space to the *metopes,* marble sculptures depicting the feats of Greece's two greatest heroes, Heracles and Theseus, from the

Treasury of the Athenians. The museum also has a pleasant outdoor café (weather permitting). ✉ *East of Ancient Delphi* ☎ *22650/82313* 🌐 *www.culture.gr* 🎫 *€6; €9 Ancient Delphi site and museum* 🕒 *Daily 8–8 (last entry 7:30 pm).*

Fodor's Choice ★ **Sanctuary of Athena.** Start your tour of the old Delphi in the same way the ancients did, with a visit to the Sanctuary of Athena. Pilgrims who arrived on the shores of the bay of Itea proceeded up to the sanctuary, where they paused before going on to the Ancient Delphi site. The most notable among the numerous remains on this terrace is the **Tholos** (Round Building), a graceful 4th-century BC ruin of Pendelic marble, the purpose and dedication of which are unknown, although round templelike buildings were almost always dedicated to a goddess. By the 2nd millennium BC, the site was already a place of worship of the earth goddess Gaia and her daughter Themis, one of the Titans. The gods expressed themselves through the murmuring of water flooding from the fault, from the rustle of leaves, and from the booming of earth tremors. The Tholos remains one of the purest and most exquisite monuments of antiquity. Theodoros, its architect, wrote a treatise on his work: an indication in itself of the exceptional architectural quality of the monument. Beneath the Phaedriades, in the cleft between the rocks, a path leads to the **Castalian Fountain,** a spring where pilgrims bathed to purify themselves before continuing. (Access to the font is prohibited because of the danger of falling rocks.) On the main road, beyond the Castalian Fountain, is the modern entrance to the sanctuary. ✉ *Below road to Arachova, before Phaedriades* 🎫 *€6 for all Delphi sites, €9 for Delphi sites and Delphi museum* 🕒 *Daily 8–8 (last entry 7:30 pm).*

WHERE TO EAT

$$ GREEK 🍴 **Epikouros.** Nothing in the simple restaurant design detracts from the view of the beautiful Itea gorge from the large, open veranda. Even in the colder months, a glass canopy protects the seating area and allows diners to look out year-round. Start with rooster soup and peppers stuffed with melted cheese. The house specialty is a must: the wild boar *stifado* is cooked with plenty of baby onions and fresh tomato sauce. You can also try deer or hare variations, while chicken in tomato sauce with eggplant and feta is an interesting alternative for timid palates. The chef has been trained in France and likes to add tasteful twists in traditional Greek recipes. The restaurant is a favorite with tourist groups, so it can get quite lively all of a sudden. [$] *Average main: €20* ✉ *Karamanlis 33(formerly Vas. Pavlou & Freiderikis)* ☎ *22650/83250* 🌐 *www.epikouros.net.*

$$ GREEK 🍴 **Iniohos.** Local specialties and small dishes, such as zucchini croquettes, grilled mushrooms, and the *bekri* ("drunk's") *meze*—a meat appetizer meant to be consumed slowly with the region's red brusco wine—are served at this hotel restaurant, which you'll find next to the King Iniohos hotel. Residents stop by late at night to have a nightcap or a snack—fried formaella cheese, *sfongato* (country vegetable omelet), or a sweet baklava. In winter, warm yourself at the fireplace with a vegetable soup; in summer eat on the enormous veranda overlooking the valley of Delphi. Set menus cost as little as €15. [$] *Average main: €20*

✉ *Karamanli 19(formerly Vas. Pavlou & Freiderikis)* ☎ *22650/83101* 🌐 *www.delphi-hotel-iniohos.gr.*

$$ GREEK 🍴 **To Patriko Mas.** A traditional stone house built in 1850 in the center of Delphi houses this taverna, which offers hearty lunches and dinners—no wonder this place has long been a favorite with meat-loving skiers. In winter, dine near the fireplace and relish hot soups, homemade pies with wild greens, and zucchini balls (kolokythokeftedes). The region's red wine perfectly accompanies seasonal game dishes. In summer you can enjoy the scenic view, while opting for lighter dishes, such as several generous Greek salads. Service can be a bit slow on busy days. [$] *Average main: €20* ✉ *69 Karamanli St. (formerly Vas. Pavlou & Freiderikis), opposite the gas station* ☎ *22650/82150* 🌐 *www.topatrikomas.gr.*

$$ GREEK Fodor's Choice ★ 🍴 **Taverna Vakchos.** Owner Ilias Theorodakis, his wife, and their two sons keep a watchful eye on the kitchen and on the happiness of their customers. Choose to eat in the spacious dining room or out on the large sheltered veranda with vines growing across the balcony rail, a Bacchus-theme wall painting, and a stunning valley view. The menu is heavy on meat dishes, either grilled, boiled, or simmered in the oven, but vegetarians can put together a small feast from boiled greens and other homemade meatless Greek classics, like sweet peas in tomato sauce and stuffed cabbage leaves. Seasonal dishes in the winter season include game such as hare and, if you're really lucky, venison. Service is especially efficient and friendly, as are prices. Dessert is on the house. [$] *Average main: €16* ✉ *Apollonos 31* ☎ *22650/83186* 🌐 *www.vakhos.com.*

WHERE TO STAY

$ HOTEL 🏨 **Acropole.** Feel completely secluded, though you're in the heart of Delphi town's action, as you look out over an awesome view of a sea of olive trees and the Itea gorge (just make sure you ask for a room with a view of the Corinthian gulf). **Pros:** charming family-run hotel; awesome views of the gorge; ample-sized triple rooms. **Cons:** compact bathrooms with shower only; no parking; a bit dated decor. [$] *Rooms from: €65* ✉ *Filellinon 13* ☎ *22650/82675* 🌐 *www.delphi.com.gr* 🛏 *42 rooms* 🍽 *Breakfast.*

$ HOTEL Fodor's Choice ★ 🏨 **Amalia Hotel Delphi.** Clean-cut retro chic predominates at this 1965 landmark built by well-known Greek architect Nikos Valsamakis as a part of one of the country's oldest hotel chains—one look reveals the sleek, modern, low-lying hotel blending seamlessly with 35 acres of hotel gardens which spread down the mountainside to the olive groves and pines of surrounding Delphi with, in the distance, a breathtaking vista of Itea port and the Corinthian bay. **Pros:** great vintage architecture and decoration; charming gardens and public areas; nice variety of breakfast buffet options; free Wi-Fi in the lobby. **Cons:** a bit off-center of town compared to other hotels; caters mostly to tour groups; slightly impersonal service. [$] *Rooms from: €80* ✉ *Apollonos 1 and Osiou Louka 47* ☎ *22650/82101, 210/607–2000 in Athens* 🌐 *www.amaliahoteldelphi.gr* 🛏 *184 rooms* 🍽 *Breakfast.*

$ B&B/INN 🏨 **Fedriades.** This hotel in the center of Delphi was purchased by the family that runs all the hotels Epikouros and Acropole, and their renovation work has created a simple, functional look accented by warm colors and a touch of Greek mountain style, while avoiding the "ancient kitsch" of other nearby hotels. **Pros:** spic-and-span cleanliness; convenient location for sightseeing; free Wi-Fi. **Cons:** smallish rooms; can be noisy due to traffic on the main street; somewhat dated furniture. $ *Rooms from: €70* ✉ *Karamanli 46* ☎ *22650/82370* ⊕ *www. fedriades.com* ⌨ *21 rooms, 3 suites* ❍⬤ *Breakfast.*

FESTIVALS

Fodor'sChoice **Delphi Summer Arts Festival.** Sit in the ancient stadium of Delphi or at
★ the Frynichos theater under the stars and watch everything from the National Beijing Opera Theater's *The Bacchae* to the tragedies of Aeschylus and Euripides, and even folk and traditional music improvisations at the Summer Arts Festival, organized by the European Cultural Centre of Delphi. All performances, which begin around 8:30 pm, are open to the public and charge a small fee. ✉ *Ancient Delphi site* ☎ *22650/82731* ⊕ *www.eccd.gr.*

GALAXIDI ΓΑΛΑΞΕΙΔΙ

35 km (22 miles) southwest of Delphi.

Sea captains' homes with classic masonry and an idyllic seaside location reminiscent of an island have steadily attracted outsiders recognizing Galaxidi's potential. The heyday of the harbor town was in the 19th century—thanks to shipbuilding and a thriving mercantile economy—but after the invention of steamships it slipped into decline. Today the Old Town is classified a historical monument and undergoes continual renovation and restoration.

GETTING HERE AND AROUND

Three buses daily make the four-hour trip from Athens to Galaxidi (four on Sunday), starting at 7:30 am; the fare is €18.60 one-way. KTEL buses servicing Galaxidi depart from Terminal B in Athens. This is the same bus that also reaches Delphi and Arachova, with a vehicle change in the city of Itea. *For more information on Athens buses and bus stations, see Bus and Tram Travel in Athens.*

FESTIVALS

Kathara Deftera (*Clean Monday*). If you happen to be in Galaxidi at the start of Greek Orthodox Lent, Kathara Deftera, duck. Locals observe the holiday with flour fights in the town's streets, a custom dating back to the 18th century. The common baking flour is tinted with food dye and by the end of the day everyone and everything in sight—buildings, cars, shrubs—is dusted with a rainbow of colors that match spring's bright palette. The custom has pagan roots: every year the dead were thought to be allowed to leave Hades for a day and return to Earth; if they had a good time, a good crop was assured. Remember to wear your old, unwanted T-shirt and jeans for the day—nobody will ask for your permission before they throw!

EXPLORING

If you are a shore person rather than a mountain person, Galaxidi is a good alternative to Delphi as a base for the region. Stroll Galaxidi's narrow streets with their elegant stone mansions and squares with

CLOSE UP

Easter Week in Delphi

Orthodox Easter Week is the most important holiday in Greece, and Delphians celebrate it with true passion. The solemn Good Friday service in Ayios Nikolaos church and the candlelight procession following it, accompanied by the singing of haunting hymns, is one of the most moving rituals in all of Greece. By Saturday evening, the mood is one of eager anticipation as the townspeople are decked out in their nicest finery and the earnest children are carrying *lambades,* beautifully decorated white Easter candles. At midnight the lights of the cathedral are extinguished, and the priest rushes into the sanctuary shouting *Christos anesti!* (Christ is risen!). He lights one of the parishioner's candles with his own and the flame is passed on, one to the other, until the entire church is illuminated with candlelight, which is reflected in the radiant faces of the congregation. Firecrackers are set off by the village schoolboys outside to punctuate the exuberance of the moment. After the liturgy is finished, each person tries to get his or her candle home while still lighted, a sign of good luck for the following year, whereupon the sign of the cross is burned over the door. Then the Easter fast is broken, usually with *mayiritsa* (Easter soup made with lamb) and brilliantly red-dyed hard-boiled eggs. On Easter Sunday, the entire village works together to roast dozens of whole lambs on the spit. It is a joyous day, devoted to feasting with family and friends, but you are welcome and may be offered slices of roast lamb and glasses of the potent dark red local wine. In the early evening, a folk-dance performance is held in front of the town-hall square, followed by communal dancing and free food and drink.

geraniums and palm trees, and then take a late-afternoon swim in one of the pebbly coves around the headland to the north, dine along the waterfront, and enjoy the stunning mountain backdrop over the sea. If you walk to the far side of the sheltered harbor, Galaxidi appears, reflected in the still waters.

Ayios Nikolaos. Peek into Ayios Nikolaos. The cathedral, named after the patron saint of sailors (Nicholas), possesses a beautiful carved 19th-century altar screen. ✉ *Old Town* 🕒 *Daily 8–3.*

Nautical and Ethnological Museum. Housed in an 1868 neoclassical building, this little museum has a collection of paintings with nautical themes and many local artifacts from Greek ships and from old sea captains' houses. It is also the home of a small archaelogical collection. ✉ *Mouseiou 4* ☎ *22650/41558* 🎟 *€5* 🕒 *Tues.–Sun. 7:30–3.*

WHERE TO EAT

$ GREEK 🍴 **Albatros.** This tiny and cozy taverna in one of the inland streets feels like a home away from home. Eleni, the owner, cooks traditional Greek fare like stuffed tomatoes with rice, fried eggplant, and chicken in lemon sauce with thick-cut chips. [$] *Average main: €15* ✉ *Kon. Satha 36* ☎ *22650/42333.*

$$ GREEK Fodor's Choice ★ 🍴 **O Bebelis.** The wine barrel by the front door is the first hint that this cozy *ouzeri*, tucked into a side street off the harbor, is a place for the *meraklides*, people who savor life's every moment. Sit back, order the house wine, and taste the little treats laid before you, like home-cured olives, steamed mussels, and other seasonal small dishes prepared and served by the genial owner. The stuffed onions and the pork with plums come highly recommended. Beware, though, this restaurant is closed in the summer months. [$] *Average main: €18* ✉ *Nikolaou Mama, near start of harbor* ☎ *22650/41677* ✍ *Reservations essential* 💳 *No credit cards* ⏲ *Closed Jun.–Aug.*

$$ SEAFOOD 🍴 **O Tassos.** Locals and tourists pack O Tassos's waterfront terrace, the first you see as you approach from the center; they're drawn in year-round by the quality of the seafood in this basic taverna with reasonable prices. Farm-raised crawfish (*karavides*) are simply boiled and sprinkled with lemon—a true delicacy. Crispy fried calamari and shrimp, tender grilled octopus, and whole fish such as char-grilled snapper are fresh as can be. Complete the feast with boiled greens, grilled eggplant salad, a large village salad, and a carafe of local wine. [$] *Average main: €24* ✉ *Akti Ianthis 69, at far end of harbor on waterfront* ☎ *22650/41291.*

$$ VEGETARIAN 🍴 **Porto.** Located on the edge of the picturesque port, this quaint little taverna has some tasteful antique decorative touches. It is a popular choice for its warm atmosphere and local specialties, especially its spinach pie and grilled meats and fish. There is something for everyone here, and if you are a vegan or vegetarian the owner will be more than happy to accommodate your dining preferences. [$] *Average main: €20* ✉ *Akti Oianthis* ☎ *22650/41182.*

$$$ SEAFOOD 🍴 **To Barko tis Maritsas.** Inside a captains' *kafeneio* (coffeehouse) from 1850, this waterfront restaurant, probably the most popular of the scenic port town, is elegantly decorated in a nautical theme with classic Chesterfield sofas. Fresh fish is always plentiful, but mussels are what Galaxidi is known for—here they're served in a saganaki, steamed, and in a pilaf. There's also seafood risotto and lobster pasta, as well as traditional non-seafood dishes such as the homemade pies. Homemade sweets include walnut paste with *kaymak* (very heavily creamed) vanilla ice cream. Service is a bit on the slow side, but the flavors are impeccable. [$] *Average main: €35* ✉ *Akti Ianthis 34, on waterfront* ☎ *22650/41059* ✍ *Reservations essential* ⏲ *Closed weekdays Nov.–Apr.*

WHERE TO STAY

$ B&B/INN 🏨 **Archodiko Art Hotel.** Yiannis Schizas, who established this homey and comforting hotel with his wife Argyroula, has a knack for collecting odd items, and each guest room is decorated differently (and tastefully) with his finds. **Pros:** cute little bed-and-breakfast; lovely home-away-from-home feeling; nice garden. **Cons:** may be a bit hard to find so be sure to consult the map on the website. [$] *Rooms from: €60* ✉ *Parodos, Eleftherias 80* ☎ *22650/42292* 🌐 *www.archodikoarthotel.gr* 🛏 *8 rooms* 💳 *No credit cards* 🍽 *Breakfast.*

$ B&B/INN 🏨 **Hotel Ganimede.** Elegant spaces take full advantage of the 19th-century sea captain's house in a lush garden, making this a good destination if you are looking for a homey little hotel. **Pros:** Chysoula's award-winning home-baked breakfast served in luscious garden (purchase some of the homemade jams and chutneys); the hospitality; welcome drinks served in the garden. **Cons:** no elevator; small bathrooms; somewhat hard beds. [$] *Rooms from: €70* ✉ *N. Gourgouris 20* ☎ *22650/41328* 🌐 *www.ganimede.gr* 🛏 *5 rooms, 1 studio, 1 suite* 🍴 *No meals.*

$ B&B/INN 🏨 **Villa Oianthia.** Superb hospitality is the main reason you won't want to leave Villa Oianthia after you're welcomed into the neoclassical-style reception room that's warmed up by an Italianate *tapeto marmo* (marble carpet) or savor your sunsetter drink in a reception room graced by a stained-glass window. **Pros:** sensible prices; special offers for honeymooners; romantic atmosphere. **Cons:** few vegetarian choices at breakfast; beds a bit on the hard side. [$] *Rooms from: €90* ✉ *Anexartisias 1 and Tsalagkira, opposite town hall* ☎ *22650/42433* 🌐 *www.villaoianthia.com* 🛏 *10 rooms, 2 suites* 🍴 *Breakfast.*

SHOPPING

Avra Grocery. A traditional grocery shop on the waterfront that not only stocks all the essentials, most of them locally sourced, but also transports you back in time with its old-fashioned, romantic decor. It has been lovingly created by the owners of the Archontiko Art Hotel. ✉ *Oianthis St. 95* ☎ *22650/42295.*

Nikotakis. A traditional pastry shop in the heart of town, where you'll taste local sweet delicacies like syrupy sponge cake with rice, almond paste, and the fresh cream pastry, *galaktoboureko.* ✉ *28 Nik. Mama* ☎ *22650/42001* 🌐 *www.nikotakis.com.*

Fodor's Choice ★ **Ostria.** Clearly, artists are behind the dazzling selection of gift items at Ostria. Beautifully displayed items include nautical items like brass compasses and model ships, but also an array of toys, clocks, icons, and jewelry. There's also a huge selection of ceramics, some by owner Petros Skourtis. He and co-owner Katie Kapi, who is a painter, also invite customers to visit their nearby workshop, where they can even take a pottery course. ✉ *Akti Ianthis 101, on the waterfront* ☎ *22650/41206.*

THE SARONIC
GULF ISLANDS

WELCOME TO
THE SARONIC GULF ISLANDS

TOP REASONS
TO GO

★ **Handsome Hydra:**
The place for the jet-setter who appreciates walking more than showing off new wheels, Hydra offers both tranquility and sociability—a bustling main town and abundant walking trails. What's here (stone houses set above a welcoming harbor) and what's not (cars) provide a relaxing retreat.

★ **Ship-Shape Spetses:** A fine jumping-off point for the Peloponnesian shore, cosmopolitan Spetses is famed for its Spetsiot seafaring tradition—not surprisingly, the Old Town harbor is car-free and picture-perfect.

★ **Ancient Aegina:** Not far from this vast island's medieval Paliachora—with nearly 20 churches—is the Temple of Aphaia, one of Greece's best-preserved Archaic sites. Aegina's isle is the closest Saronic island to Athens's port of Piraeus.

★ **Pistachio Perfection:** You can already taste them—salty, sweet, mellow—and the best pistachio nuts anywhere may come from Aegina.

1 **Aegina.** The largest of Saronic islands, Aegina is a land of contrasts—from its crowded beach towns to its isolated, rugged mountain peaks, scattered ruins, and forgotten monasteries. Take in the main town's famous fish market, visit the pre-Hellenic Temple of Aphaia, then explore the ghost town of Paliachora, still spirit-warm thanks to its 20 chapels.

2 **Hydra.** Noted for its 19th-century *archontika* (mansions), its crescent-shape waterfront, and fashionable boutiques, Hydra has been catnip to writers and artists for decades—visit the isle's galleries or bring along your easel and let your own creative juices flow. For Hydriot splendor in excelsis, visit the 1780 Lazaros Koundouriotis Mansion or buy a glittering jewel or two at Elena Votsi's harbor-front jewelry shop.

ATTICA · Avlon · Mt. Parnitha · Marathon · Eleusis · Monasteries of Daphni · Monasteries of Kaisariani · Sanctuary of Brauron · Megara · ATHENS · Paiania · Piraeus · Glyfada · Markopoulon · *Saronic* · Vouliagmeni · *Gulf* · Temple of Aphaia · FLEVES · Aegina · 1 AEGINA · ANGISTRI · Palaiachora · Sounion · Makrilongos · METHANON · POROS · Poros · Troezen · AGIOS GEORGIOS · Hydra · 2 HYDRA

0 — 50 mi
0 — 50 km

GETTING ORIENTED

Bounded on three sides by sea, Attikí (Attica) has an indented, sun-gilded coastline fringed with innumerable sandy beaches and rocky inlets. Just to the south of Athens, straddling the gulf between its bustling port of Piraeus and the Peloponnese, are the Saronic gulf islands, the aristocracy of the Greek isles. Riddled with coves and natural harbors ideal for seafaring, the islands of Aegina, Hydra, and Spetses are enveloped in a patrician aura that is the combined result of history and their more recent cachet as the playgrounds of wealthy Athenians. Owing to their proximity and beauty, they can get swamped with vacationers during the summer, yet they retain their distinct cultural traditions, perhaps best appreciated out of season.

5

3 Spetses. The island, with regular boat service to pine-lined beaches, is perfect for beach hopping. It's also top contender for the most dining and nightlife offerings of the Saronic isles. As for sights, Bouboulina Museum in the main town offers fascinating details about the island's storied history.

Updated by Natasha Gian-nousi-Varney

Only have a few days in Greece but need to taste island life? One of the Saronic isles offers the perfect solution. Called the "offshore islands" by day-tripping Athenians, they are treasured for their proximity to the burly city. Just south of hectic Piraeus, Aegina still feels like another world. Heading southward you'll find chic and cosmopolitan Hydra, a fitting stage for one of Sophia Loren's first forays into Hollywood. Finally, there is splendid Spetses, anchored off mainland Kosta—a playground prized by carefree vacationing Greeks.

The Saronic gulf islands, whose ancient city-states rivaled Athens, are now virtually a part of the capital. Aegina, one of the most-visited islands in Greece because of its proximity to the capital, is 30 minutes from Piraeus by hydrofoil, while Spetses, the most "remote" and the greenest of the Saronic islands, is 120 minutes away. South of the Argolid, the peninsula that divides the Saronic gulf from the gulf of Argolis, rests Hydra, poor in beaches but rich in charm.

Aegina's pretty country villas have drawn shipping executives, who often commute daily from the island to their offices in Piraeus. Here pine forests mix with groves of pistachio trees, a product for which Aegina is justly famous. Hydra and Spetses are farther south and both ban automobiles. Hydra's stately mansions, restaurants, and boutiques cater to the sophisticated traveler and art lover. Spetses has both broad forests and regal, neoclassical buildings. Rather than being spoiled by tourism, all four islands have managed to preserve their laid-back attitude, well suited to the hedonistic lifestyle of weekend pleasure-seekers arriving by yacht and hydrofoil.

PLANNING

WHEN TO GO

The weather on the islands tends to be the same as in Athens, though the heat can feel more intense on the arid peaks of Aegina and Hydra. The island breeze—felt on all the Saronic isles, particularly later in the day—makes these vacation destinations more refreshing than the mainland on summer evenings (and in winter, more bitter, due to the colder humidity). Due to the risk of summer fires, do not wander into forested areas in the hot-weather months. Check the forecast before heading to Aegina, Hydra, or Spetses at any time of year—bad weather in the off-season or strong August winds (*meltemia*) may strand you on the island you only intended to visit briefly.

PLANNING YOUR TIME

The Saronic isles make fabulous day trips, though an overnight stay—or hop to a second isle—is recommended if you have the time. To ease into the pace of island life probably requires at least two days per island; however, you can visit all the islands in as few as four days. Aegina—the closest to Piraeus—is the easiest to do in a day since it has the most regular traffic to and fro, especially if your time is very limited. Although all the Saronic islands have swimming beaches, Spetses's are the best, so you may want to linger. In three days you can explore most of Hydra or Spetses, or really get to know Aegina. Is island-hopping on your agenda? Devote the first two days to Spetses's small main town and beautiful beaches. In the next two, wander Hydra's port town, and if you're ambitious (and in shape), hike to a monastery. Then give Aegina its day's due. One no-sweat tip to keep in mind: In July and August visit Saronic island archaeological sites like the Temple of Aphaia as early in the day as possible. There is little shade at such sites, and the midday heat can be withering. And, of course, an early start may help you avoid crowds.

GETTING HERE AND AROUND

A car is only truly useful on Aegina, as cars are prohibited on the islands of Hydra and (except by special permit) Spetses. Renting scooters, mopeds, and bicycles is popular with tourists on Aegina and Spetses. But extreme caution is advised: the equipment may not be in good condition, roads can be narrow and treacherous, and many drivers are scornful of your safety. Wear a helmet. If braving the road isn't part of your plan, never fear: on Aegina, there is regular bus service between towns and beaches. But on Hydra, you can famously travel only by water taxi, mule, bike, horse, or donkey—no cars or buses allowed! On Spetses, get around by buggy, scooter, boat, and two buses. But, as with any personal transportation in Greece, it's best to confirm prices first, so you don't get taken for a different kind of ride.

BOAT AND FERRY TRAVEL

Spetses is so close to the Peloponnese mainland that you can drive there from Athens, park, and ferry across the channel in any of a number of caïques (price negotiable) at the ports, but to get to any of the other Saronic gulf islands, you must take to the sea in a ferry. You can get a weekly boat schedule from the Greek National Tourism Organization

(⊕ *www.visitgreece.gr*). You can get detailed info about ferry schedules at ⊕ *www.ferries.gr or* ⊕ *www.directferries.gr*, and you can also reserve through a travel agent. Large ferries are the leisurely and least expensive way to travel; however, most people prefer the speedier passenger-only and "flying dolphins" (and be aware that there's also a ferry company called "Aegean Flying Dolphins") and hydrofoils.

Hellenic Seaways, ANES Ferries, and Nova Ferries will carry you and your car from the main port in Piraeus (Gate E8), about a thousand feet from the Metro, to Aegina (1 hour). There are approximately a half-dozen daily departures, and boat fares begin at about €7 per person for Aegina, triple or quadruple that for cars (there are no slow ferries to Hydra or Spetses). Speedier Hellenic Seaways and Aegean Flying Dolphins ferries and hydrofoils also depart from Piraeus (Gate E8 or E9). These faster ferries can get you to Aegina in 40 minutes (€13), to Hydra in 90 minutes (€25.50), and to Spetses in just under two hours (€35). There are about a half-dozen departures daily to each island, but make reservations ahead of time—boats fill quickly.

What about boats and ferries between the various Saronic gulf islands? Hellenic Seaways fast- ferry routes connect Piraeus to Hydra and Spetses year-round. There are about five daily round-trips from October to April, more the rest of the year. In summer, Saronic Ferries offers daily service that connects Aegina with the tiny islands of Angistri, Poros, and Methana. But plan your Argo-Saronic island-hopping carefully in the off-season. During that time, boats between the islands are much less frequent, and you may have to combine several ferries to reach your destination, some fast and some slow. And connecting service is not available every day; on some days (and in some seasons), you will have to backtrack to the main port at Piraeus to catch another boat. *For information regarding specific ferry companies, see Boat and Ferry Travel in Travel Smart.*

ANES Ferries ⊠ *Ioulias Katsa 6, Aegina town* ☎ *210/422–5625 in Piraeus, 22970/25625 in Aegina* ⊕ *www.anes.gr.* **Hellenic Seaways** ⊠ *Astiggos 6, Karaiskaki Sq., Piraeus* ☎ *210/419–9000 Ticket information, 210/419–9100 Central office* ⊕ *www.hellenicseaways.gr.* **Nova Ferries** ⊠ *L. Dimokratias 1, Aegina town* ☎ *22970/24200 in Aegina, 210/412–6181 in Piraeus* ⊕ *www.saronicferries.gr.*

CAR TRAVEL

On Aegina, there is a good network of mostly narrow rural roads (two lanes at best). Drivers should be prepared for occasional abrupt turns; major towns and sites are well marked. Cars are not allowed on Hydra. Unlike on Hydra, cars are not banned outright on Spetses: residents are permitted to ferry their autos to the island. Sadly, the presence of cars seems to be getting more pronounced every year, despite the wishes of many inhabitants. Karagiannis Klimi Travel, on Aegina, rents both cars and motorcycles. *(See Tour Options, below.)*

Contacts Karagiannis Klimi Travel. This full-service travel agency on Aegina can find you accommodations, help you book ferry tickets, and rent you a car or motorcycle for use on the island. ⊠ *Panayi Irioti 44, Aegina town, Aegina* ☎ *22970/25664, 22970/28780* ✉ *nklimi@otenet.gr.*

HOTELS

Accommodations on the Saronic gulf islands range from elegant 19th-century mansions—usually labeled as "traditional settlements"—to boutique-style hotels to spare rental rooms overlooking a noisy waterfront. Rented rooms can be less expensive than hotels and offer an easy option for fly-by-the-seaters: just follow signs, or solicitors who show up when boats come in. (And note that it's okay to check out the room before committing.) From June to September, book far in advance. Off-season (October–April), you'll have fewer hotels to choose from, as many close during the colder months. Souvala and Ayia Marina are suitable lodging alternatives to Aegina's main town, but on the other islands, if you'd like choices when it comes to eating and nightlife, make sure to stay in the main port. If you want to plan a great off-season trip with minimum hassle, putting your itinerary in the hands of a professional is your best bet. On Aegina we recommend Karagiannis Klimi Travel *(see Tour Options, below)*. Also note that during certain times of the year (most notably summer) you may get better deals on weekdays than on Athenian-heavy weekends.

RESTAURANTS

The cuisine of the Saronic islands resembles that of Athens, Attica, and the Peloponnese. Local ingredients predominate, with fresh fish perhaps the greatest (and most expensive) delicacy. Because much of Attica's vegetation is used to support herds of grazing sheep and the omnivorous goat, the meat of both animals is also a staple in many country tavernas. Although it is becoming increasingly difficult to find the traditional Greek taverna with large stewpots full of the day's hot meal, or big *tapsi* (pans) of *pastitsio* (layers of pasta, meat, and cheese laced with cinnamon) or *papoutsakia* (eggplant slices filled with minced meat), market towns still harbor the occasional rustic haunt, offering tasty, inexpensive meals. Always ask to see the *kouzina* (kitchen) to look at the day's offerings, or to even peer inside the pots. Informal dress is appropriate at all but the very fanciest restaurants and, unless noted, reservations are not necessary.

WHAT IT COSTS IN EUROS			
	$	**$$**	**$$$**	**$$$$**
Restaurants	Under €16	€16–€25	€26–€40	Over €40
Hotels	Under €126	€126–€225	€226–€275	Over €275

Restaurant prices are the average cost of a main course at dinner or, if dinner is not served, at lunch. Hotel prices are the lowest cost of a standard double room in high season.

VISITOR INFORMATION

There are few main official tourist offices for the Saronic gulf islands, though you'll find an information center on Aegina that is operated by the Aegina Municipality. Keep in mind that in lieu of official agencies, there is an array of private travel agencies (usually based in offices near each island's harbor port), and these offer myriad services, tickets, car rentals, and guided tours. Top agencies include CHAT and Key Tours, both based in Athens, Karagiannis Klimi Travel on Aegina, and Hydreoniki Travel on Hydra *(see Tour Optionss, below, for contact information)*.

TOUR OPTIONS

Most agencies run tour excursions at about the same prices, but CHAT and Key Tours have the best service and guides. A full-day cruise from Piraeus, with either CHAT or Key Tours, visits Aegina, Poros, and Hydra, and costs around €98 (including buffet lunch on the ship). Karagiannis Klimi Travel on Aegina and Hydreoniki Travel on Hydra also offer local tours.

Contacts CHAT. Based in Athens, CHAT offers good tours and employs informed guides. If you're in Athens and want to explore Attica, it's a good choice. ☎ 210/322–3137 ⊕ *www.chatours.gr* ✉ *From €43.* **Key Tours.** Key Tours has been showing travelers around Greece since 1963. Its offerings range from one-day cruises of the Saronic islands to more personalized services like helicopter tours and regional Greek winery visits. More than 20 different scheduled excursions are included among its offerings. ✉ *Athanasiou Diakou 26, Athens* ☎ *210/923–3166* ⊕ *www.keytours.gr* ✉ *From €43.* **Hydreoniki Travel.** Hydreoniki Travel is open year-round and provides tourism and travel services. Located just opposite the main port, this is the main island agent for Hellenic Seaways, whose high-speed catamarans connect Hydra with Piraeus. ✉ *Hydra Port, Hydra town, Hydra* ☎ *22980/54007, 22980/53812* ⊕ *www.hydreoniki.gr.* **Karagiannis Klimi Travel.** This full-service travel agency on Aegina can find you accommodations, help you book ferry tickets, and rent you a car or motorcycle for use on the island. ✉ *Panayi Irioti 44, Aegina town, Aegina* ☎ *22970/25664, 22970/28780* ✐ *nklimi@otenet.gr.*

AEGINA ΑΙΓΙΝΑ

30 km (19 miles) south of Piraeus by ferry.

The eastern side of Aegina is rugged and sparsely inhabited today, except for Ayia Marina, a former fishing hamlet now studded with hotels. The western side of the island, where Aegina town lies, is more fertile and less mountainous than the east; fields are blessed with grapes, olives, figs, almonds, and, above all, the treasured pistachio trees. Idyllic seascapes, quaint backstreets, and a number of beautiful courtyard gardens make Aegina town attractive.

Although it may seem hard to imagine, by the Archaic period (7th to 6th centuries BC), Aegina was a mighty maritime power. It introduced the first silver coinage (marked with a tortoise) and established colonies in the Mediterranean. By the 6th century BC, Egina—to use its alternative spelling—had become a major art center, known in particular for its bronze foundries (worked by such sculptors as Kallon, Onatas, and Anaxagoras) and its ceramics, which were exported throughout the Mediterranean. Testimony to its great glory is the Temple of Aphaia, one of the most extant of the great Greek temples and famed for its spectacular array of Doric columns.

As it turns out, this powerful island, lying so close to the Attica coast, could not fail to come into conflict with Athens. As Athens's imperial ambitions grew, Aegina became a thorn in its side. In 458 BC Athens laid siege to the city, eventually conquering the island. In 455 BC the islanders were forced to migrate, and Aegina never again regained its former power.

From the 13th to the 19th century, Aegina ping-ponged between nations. A personal fiefdom of Venice and Spain after 1204, it was fully claimed by Venice in 1451. Less than a century later, in 1537, it was devastated and captured by the pirate Barbarossa and repopulated with Albanians. Morosini recaptured Aegina for Venice in 1654, but Italian dominance was short-lived: the island was ceded to Turkey in 1718. Its Greek roots were brushed off in the early 19th century, when it experienced a rebirth as an important base in the 1821 War of Independence, briefly holding the fledgling Greek nation's government (1826–28). The first modern Greek coins were minted here. At this time many people from the Peloponnese, plus refugees from Chios and Psara, immigrated to Aegina, and many of the present-day inhabitants are descended from them.

GETTING HERE AND AROUND

Aegina is so close to the port of Piraeus (less than an hour) that some Athenians live on the island and commute. Two well-known companies that offer boat service to Aegina are Hellenic Seaways and Aegean Flying Dolphins.

To get around while in Aegina, use the KTEL buses that leave from the main bus station on Ethneyersias Square (⊠ *Platia Ethneyersias* ☎ *22970/22787*), just left of the main port; purchase tickets here, not on the bus. Routes stop at many spots, including Ayia Marina and Perdika; a popular destination is the Temple of Aphaia, with nearly hourly departures in summer (€2.50). Service on the island becomes infrequent from late October to early May.

VISITOR INFORMATION

Contacts Aegina Municipality ⊠ *Town hall, Xristou Lada 1, Aegina town* ☎ *22973/20026* ⊕ *www.discoveraegina.gr.*

AEGINA TOWN ΑΙΓΙΝΑ ΠΟΛΗ

84 km (52 miles) southwest of Piraeus by ferry.

As you approach from the sea, your first view of Aegina town takes in the sweep of the harbor, punctuated by the tiny white chapel of Ayios Nikolaos. A large population of fishermen adds character to the many waterfront café-taverna hybrids serving ouzo and beer with pieces of grilled octopus, home-cured olives, and other *mezedes* (appetizers).

Much of the ancient city lies under the modern, although the world-famous ancient Temple of Aphaia looms over the entire island from its hilltop perch. Although some unattractive contemporary buildings (and some less well-preserved older ones) mar the harborscape, a number of well-preserved neoclassic buildings and village houses are found on the backstreets.

EXPLORING

Aegina Archaeological Museum. This small but choice collection of archaeological artifacts was the first ever to be established in Greece (1829). Finds from the famed Temple of Aphaia and excavations throughout the island, including early and middle Bronze Age pottery, are on display. Among the Archaic and classical works of art is the distinctive Ram Jug, which depicts Odysseus and his crew fleeing the Cyclops, and a 5th-century BC sphinx, a votive monument with the head of a woman and a body that is half-eagle, half-lion.

Aegina was one of the best schools of pottery and sculpture in antiquity and the exhibits here prove it. Just above the Archaeological Museum is the ancient site of the **Acropolis of Aegina**, the island's religious and political center. The settlement was first established in the Copper Age, and was renamed Kolona, or "column," in the Venetian era, after the only remaining pillar of the Temple of Apollo that once stood there. Although in great disarray—11 successive cities once stood here—it remains a true treat for those into archaeology. Examine ruins and walls dating back to 1600–1300 BC, as well as Byzantine-era buildings. ⊠ *Harbor front, 350 feet from ferry dock, Aegina town* ☎ *22970/22248* ⊠ *€3* ☉ *Tues.–Sun. 8:30–3.*

FAMILY **Aegina Museum of History and Folklore.** Housed in an 1828 neoclassical house endowed to the municipality of Aegina, this museum colorfully allows you to experience home and work life in a traditional Aegina house. On the second floor discover exhibits of authentic old furniture, paintings, costumes, lace in a typical island setting. On the ground floor, the Fisherman's house features fishery and sponge fishing equipment, while the Cottage house hosts farm tools of the old days. The ground floor hall regularly hosts temporary exhibitions. ⊠ *16 Spyrou Rodi, behind the harbor road, Aegina town* ☎ *22970/26401* ⊕ *laografiko.gr* ⊠ *Free* ☉ *Wed.–Thurs. 8:30–2:30, Fri. 8:30–2:30 and 4:30–7:30, Sat. 10–1 and 4:30–7:30, Sun. 10–1.*

Ayios Nikolaos. As you approach from the sea, your first view of Aegina town takes in the sweep of the harbor, with quaint neoclassic buildings in the background, the lovely vista punctuated by the gleaming white chapel of Ayios Nikolaos Thalassinos (St. Nicholas the Seafarer). ⊠ *Harbor front, Aegina town.*

Markelon Tower. During the negotiations for Greece during the War of Independence, Ioannis Kapodistrias, the first president of the country, conducted meetings in the Markelon Tower, dating back to the late 17th century. Today, the pink- and ochre-hued tower is being looked after by the municipality and occasionally houses cultural events and exhibitions. ⊠ *Corner of Thomaidou and Pileos, Aegina town.*

Psaragora. A trip to (not to mention a bite to eat at) the covered fish market is a must in Aegina town. A small dish of grilled octopus at the World War II–era Taverna Agora is perfect with an ouzo—if you aren't averse to the smell of raw fish wafting over. Fishermen gather midafternoon and early evening in the pedestrianized street, worrying their beads while seated beside glistening octopus hung up to dry—as close to a scene from the film *Zorba the Greek* as you are likely to see in modern Greece. ⊠ *Panayi Irioti, Aegina town* ☎ *22970/27308.*

An often overlooked wonder of ancient Greece, Aegina's Temple of Aphaia boasts more than 25 of its original 32 columns and spectacularly perches atop a promontory.

BEACHES

Kolona Beach. Aegina town's beaches, notably the pine-surrounded Kolona, are pleasant enough with their shallow waters—and crowds—for a refreshing dip after a hot day. This largely undeveloped beach is within easy walking distance to a few tavernas and the archaeological site of Kolona (hotel Rastoni is also not too far away); you can find some precious shade in the adjacent pine forest. **Amenities:** none. **Best for:** swimming. ⊠ *Near Kolona site.*

WHERE TO EAT

$$ ✕ **O Skotadis.** At the front of the harbor, opposite the fishing boats and
SEAFOOD the floating fruit market, O Skotadis serves (since 1945) a large selection of *mezedes* for starters and then mostly fresh fish dishes, usually to be accompanied by ouzo, the classic Greek anise drink. Don't forget to try the large fresh salad with caper leaves. Also try to bag a table on the second-floor terrace with its panoramic view of Aegina's harbor. $ *Average main: €20* ⊠ *Dimokratias avenue, Aegina town* ☎ *22970/24014* ⊕ *www.skotadis.com.*

$ ✕ **Tsias.** For a light bite, try this harborside *ouzeri* (bar serving mezedes)
SEAFOOD restaurant that's a hangout for locals as well as tourists passing through. Except for the 30 varieties of ouzo, everything is homemade in this small establishment whose warm yellow walls are decorated with stencils. Vouta Vouta (Dip Dip), a shrimp-and-pink-spicy-sauce concoction, is a palate pleaser, but the real don't-miss dishes are baked apple in cognac and the custom omelets for breakfast. Reservations are recommended at night during the summer months. $ *Average main: €15* ⊠ *47 Dimocratias avenue, Aegina town* ☎ *22970/23529.*

$$ | **GREEK** | **Fodor's Choice** | ★

✕**Vatzoulias.** Ask a local to name the best restaurant in Aegina, and the response is invariably Vatzoulias. In summer the garden is a pleasant oasis, scented with jasmine and honeysuckle; in winter, nestle inside the cozy dining room. Eggplant in garlic sauce, and zucchini croquettes are can't-go-wrong starters. Continue with taverna classics such as veal in red sauce; thick, juicy grilled pork chops; or moussaka, oven-baked eggplant and potatoes with minced meat enlivened with cinnamon and a wonderfully fluffy béchamel. In winter try the hare stew. A 10-minute walk from Aegina town center gets you to this rustic taverna where only dinner is served, please note, only three evenings a week. $ *Average main: €20* ⊠ *Aphaias 75, Ayioi Asomatoi, Aegina town* ☎ *22970/22711* ⚜ *Reservations essential* ▭ *No credit cards* ⊗ *Closed Mon., Tues., Thurs., and Fri.*

> ### BEACH BUMMED?
>
> If Aegina's beaches don't wow you, climb aboard one of the many daily boats from Aegina's harbor to the smaller nearby isle of **Angistri**. Without cars, but with food, drink, and small coves to swim in, Angistri has a relaxed, out-of-the-way feel, and more than its share of lovely beaches. A closer alternative is the tiny **Moni island,** which can be reached in less than 10 minutes from the fishing village of Perdika.

WHERE TO STAY

$ | **B&B/INN**

⌂ **Aeginitiko Archontiko.** Staying at this small bed and breakfast within a neoclassic house from the 1700s feels like a crash course in Greek history: it's easy to imagine what living in Aegina in 1827 was like, when it became the first capital of the newborn nation and shipping minister Admiral Kountouriotis lived in this house; or later, at the beginning of the 1920s, when poet Kostas Varnalis resided here for two years and was visited by author Nikos Kazantzakis; and, today, when the historical roots of the terra-cotta-hue house come alive in the breathtaking murals of rooms on the first floor and in select antique furniture carefully placed in the public salons, the shady internal garden, and in the guest rooms. **Pros:** homey feeling; historic mansion; bright, feel-good colors; central location in town. **Cons:** no sea view; small basic rooms; bathrooms look tired and could do with a makeover. $ *Rooms from: €65* ⊠ *Ayiou Nikolaou, Thomaidou and Liakou 1, Aegina town* ☎ *22970/24968* ⊕ *www.aeginitikoarchontiko.gr* ⇥ *12 rooms* ⎮⊙⎮ *Breakfast.*

$ | **B&B/INN** | **Fodor's Choice** | ★

⌂ **Rastoni.** Quiet and secluded, this boutique hotel's peaceful quality is heightened by the landscaped mature Mediterranean garden, which has pistachio trees, wood pergolas and benches, and rattan armchairs where you can curl up with a book or just spend the day staring out at sea. **Pros:** oh, those verandas with panoramic views; beautiful four-poster beds; fabulous Mediterranean garden, ideal for relaxing. **Cons:** few hotel facilities. $ *Rooms from: €90* ⊠ *Dimitriou Petriti 31, Aegina town* ☎ *22970/27039* ⊕ *www.rastoni.gr* ⇥ *12 rooms* ⎮⊙⎮ *Breakfast.*

NIGHTLIFE

Greek bars and clubs frequently change names, so it's sometimes hard to keep up with the trends.

Aqua Loca. An Aegina mainstay since 1996, beach bar Aqua Loca promises delicious cocktails (ask for the house special), relaxing music, and magical sunsets. Consider nibbling on a *poikilia mezedon,* an hors d'oeuvre assortment, served until 7 pm. ⊠ *Ayios Vasileios Beach, Ayios Vasileios ✛ 1½ km (1 mile) north of Aegina town, on road toward Perdika* ☎ *6942/696709.*

Avli. The ever-popular Avli serves delicious appetizers in a small courtyard, crowned by an impressively tall palm tree, that goes from café-bistro by day to bar (playing Latin rhythms) by night. Free Wi-Fi is available. ⊠ *Panayi Irioti 17, Aegina town* ☎ *22970/26438.*

Fodor's Choice

★ **Inn on the Beach.** On the outskirts of Aegina town, the multileveled Inn on the Beach draws an early crowd with its sunset seafront cocktails and chill-out music, before notching up the music to a beach-party tempo. ⊠ *Akti Toti Hazi, Aegina town* ☎ *22970/25116* ⊕ *www. innonthebeach.gr.*

SHOPPING

Aegina's famous pistachios, much coveted by Greeks, can be bought from stands along the town harbor. They make welcome snacks and gifts. A treat found at some of the Aegean town bakeries behind the harbor is *amigdalota,* rich almond macaroons sprinkled with orange flower water and powdered sugar. If you want to have a picnic lunch on the island or on the ferryboat while en route to another Saronic island, check out the luscious fruit displayed on several boats that double as picturesque floating groceries, in the center of the harbor.

Animal Respect. Cheap secondhand items from lamps to undergarments can be found at the Animal Respect charity shop and information centre. Run by the nonprofit organization *Animal Protection Aegina-Angistri* (FAZA) that cares for stray animals on the islands, the shop also sells fashionable pet accessories. ⊠ *Panayi Irioti 67, behind town hall, Aegina town* ☎ *22970/27049* ☉ *10–1:30* ☉ *Closed Sundays.*

Ceramics Art Workshop. Sisters Martha and Maria Kottaki are talented examples of the new generation of Aegina potters (following on the footsteps of their equally talented mother, Triantafyllia). They create useful and elegant household items such as colorful salad bowls and country-chic fruit platters. ⊠ *33 Spyrou Rodi, Aegina town* ☎ *22970 shop, 22970 workshop.*

EGINAAIGINA. Naif paintings by local artists, monochromatic ceramics, and minimalist sculptures can be found in this petite yet refined art gallery. It generally closes from 1:30 to 6:30. ⊠ *23 Aiakou street, Aegina town* ☎ *22970/23967.*

Fistiki. Flip-flops, shoes, bikinis, jewelry, papier-mâché figures, dangling Turkish charms, and kitchenware form the rainbow of items available at Fistiki. The shop's small entrance opens into a maze of boxy rooms filled with everything you could possibly need to stay stylish on your trip. ⊠ *Panayi Irioti 15, Aegina town* ☎ *22970/28327.*

SPORTS AND THE OUTDOORS

BOATING AND SAILING

Aegean Sailing School. Learn to sail a yacht, try power boating, or join this lively international group of sailors on one of their day trips to nearby islands of Moni and Angistri. ✉ *Neoptolemou 8, Aegina town* ☎ *22970/32265* 🌐 *www.aegeansailingschool.com.*

SOUVALA ΣΟΥΒΑΛΑ

10 km (6 miles) northeast of Aegina town.

Souvala is a sleepy fishing village that comes to life in summer, as it is a favorite resort of many Athenians. The tamarisks and pine trees offer natural shade on the beach, or you can head to the Vagia beach 3 km (2 miles) farther down the seaside road.

BEACHES

FAMILY **Souvala.** The sandy and pebbled beach of Souvala is one the nicest on the island and used to be famous for its therapeutic hot and cold springs (which closed five years ago). Located close to the Souvala village, it offers umbrellas, sun beds, and the Banio Banio beach bar. Elsewhere along the coastline here are many other spots where you can sunbathe and swim off the rocks. There's windsurfing available near the hotel Irides. **Amenities:** food and drink; lifeguards; showers; water sports. **Best for:** swimming; windsurfing. ✉ *Souvala, Aegina* ☎ *22970/54140* 🌐 *www.baniobanio.gr.*

Vagia Beach. This is a sandy beach next to a picturesque little harbor. The quaint beachfront taverna O Thisavros tis Vagias looks after the beach, renting sun beds and umbrellas, and serves coffee, drinks, and food all day long. A few pine trees provide much-needed shade, and there's easy parking nearby. The taverna is also open during winter weekends, with lunch and dinner served by a fireplace. Look for an even quieter stretch of beach at the right side of the little harbor. **Amenities:** food and drink. **Best for:** solitude; walking; swimming. ✉ *Vagia* ✥ *13 km (8 miles) northeast of Aegina town* ☎ *22970/71191 O Thisavros tis Vagias.*

WHERE TO STAY

$ B&B/INN 🏨 **Ethrio Guesthouse.** About 9 km (5½ miles) from Aegina town, at the small port of Souvala, this modern bed-and-breakfast operates year-round and is popular with Athenians seeking relaxing weekends away from the city. **Pros:** direct boat from Piraeus to Souvala; homey ambience; clean and modern; free Wi-Fi in the lobby and breakfast area. **Cons:** few hotel-type facilities; no credit cards accepted. [$] *Rooms from: €60* ✉ *Souvala beach, Alipranti 154* ☎ *22970/52030* 🌐 *www.ethrio.gr* 🛏 *12 rooms* 💳 *No credit cards* 🕒 *Open year-round.* 🍴 *Breakfast.*

$ B&B/INN 🏨 **Irides Studios & Apartments.** It all started a few years ago, when a derelict house around 5 km (3 miles) to the east of the port of Souvala was rebuilt into a friendly hotel by the same family that operates the Rastoni hotel in Aegina town; then, in 2009, Irides Luxury Studios expanded into a brand new building, just 30 yards away from the seafront, so all guest rooms and studios here enjoy a sea view. **Pros:** great for families;

all those great group activities; friendly owners; disabled access; free Wi-Fi. **Cons:** rocky beach; somewhat isolated; extra breakfast charge if you are staying for less than two nights. $ *Rooms from: €80* ✉ *Agii* ☎ *22970/52215, 22970/52183* ⊕ *www.irides.gr* ➳ *18 rooms, 7 studios* ⊗ *Closed Dec.–Feb.*

FESTIVALS

Panayia Chrysoleontissa. On the Assumption of the Virgin Mary, August 15th—the biggest holiday of the Christian summer throughout Europe—a celebration is held at Panayia Chrysoleontissa, a mountain monastery built between 1403 and 1614. ✉ *Aegina* ⊹ *6 km (4 miles) east of Aegina town.*

Ayios Nektarios Monastery. Two of the most important festivals held at Ayios Nektarios Monastery are Whitmonday, or the day after Pentecost (the seventh Sunday after Easter), and the November 9th Saint's nameday, when the remains of Ayios Nektarios are brought down from the monastery and carried in a procession through the streets of town, which are covered in carpets and strewn with flowers. ✉ *Kontos* ⊹ *7 km (4½ miles) southeast of Aegina town* ☎ *22970/53806 monastery.*

AYIA MARINA ΑΓΙΑ ΜΑΡΙΝΑ

13 km (8 miles) east of Aegina town, via small paved road below Temple of Aphaia.

The small, somewhat-overrun port of Ayia Marina has many hotels, cafés, restaurants, and a family-friendly beach with shallow waters. On the opposite side of the Ayia Marina harbor, you'll find small bays with deeper waters, ideal for diving. Ayia Marina is easily accessible by regular KTEL bus service from Aegina town (about a 25-minute trip).

EXPLORING

Fodor'sChoice   **Temple of Aphaia.** One of the great glories of ancient Greek art, the
★   Temple of Aphaia is among the most extant examples of classical Doric architecture. Once adorned with an exquisite group of pedimental sculptures (now in the Munich Glyptothek), it still proudly bears 25 of its original 32 columns, which were either left standing or have been reconstructed. The structure is perched on a pine-clad promontory, offering superb views of Athens and Piraeus across the water—with binoculars you can see both the Parthenon and the Temple of Poseidon at Sounion. The saying goes that the ancient Greeks built the Temple of Aphaia in Aegina, the Parthenon in Athens, and the Temple of Poseidon at Sounion as the tips of a perfect equidistant triangle (called Antiquity's Perfect Triangle). This site has been occupied by many sanctuaries to Aphaia; the ruins visible today are those of the temple built in the early 5th century BC. Aphaia was apparently a pre-Hellenic deity, whose worship eventually converged with that of Athena.

You can visit the museum for no extra fee. The exhibit has a reconstructed section of the pediment of the temple, many fragments from the once brilliantly colored temple interior and the votive tablet (560 BC) on which is written that the temple is dedicated to the goddess Aphaia. From Aegina town, catch the KTEL bus for Ayia Marina on

Be at the regal Ayios Nektarios Monastery on November 9 to see the saint's day celebration, when the streets are covered with carpets and strewn with flowers.

Ethneyersias Square, the main Aegina town bus station; ask the driver to let you off at the temple. A gift and snack bar across the road is a comfortable place to have a drink and wait for the return bus to Aegina town or for the bus bound for Ayia Marina and its pebbled beach. ✉ *Ayia Marina, Aegina* ✢ *15 km (9 miles) east of Aegina town* ☎ *22970/32398* 🌐 *www.culture.gr* 🎟 *€4* 🕒 *Temple: Apr.–Nov., daily 9:30–4:30; Dec.–Mar., daily 9:30–4:30. Museum: Tues.–Sun. 10:30–1:30.*

BEACHES

FAMILY **Ayia Marina Beach.** Ayia Marina beach is popular with the parenting set, as the shallow water is ideal for playing children. A more rocky beach lies to the north of the marina that is good for diving and snorkeling. There are plenty of tavernas and cafés along the bay, while hotel Apollo is not too far away. This is the best sandy beach on the island. **Amenities:** food and drink; lifeguards; toilets; water sports. **Best for:** snorkeling; swimming; walking. ✉ *Ayia Marina, Aegina.*

WHERE TO EAT

$$ GREEK 🍴 **Kyriakakis.** This taverna is the oldest and the most established one in Ayia Marina. In fact it has been here since 1950, when Kyriakos Haldaios brought out a gas stove and started frying fish and fries under the pine trees for local sunbathers. Today, the seafront taverna is owned by his grandson, also named Kyriakos, and offers traditional Greek specialties, like *moussaka,* the famous dish of layered eggplant and ground meat, and plenty of fresh fish, especially gilthead and sea bass. In the summer these are served in the spacious veranda overlooking the crystal blue waters. [$] *Average main: €18* ✉ *Ayia Marina, Aegina* ☎ *22970/32165* 🌐 *www.kyriakakis-aegina.gr.*

$$ GREEK 🍴 **O Kostas.** Hollowed-out wine barrels used for decorative purposes are more kitsch than antique, but they match the lightheartedness of this country tavern. Cooks showily prepare *saganaki* over live flames by the table as waiters pull wine (red and retsina) from the barrels lining the walls. The menu is solid Greek fare, slightly tweaked for non-Greek palates in search of a "genuine" taverna experience, all to be enjoyed under the mulberry trees in the summer. Yes, it's touristy, but it's also fun and tasty. [$] *Average main: €18* ✉ *Aegina–Alones Rd.* ☎ *22970/32424* 🌐 *www.alones.gr.*

WHERE TO STAY

$ HOTEL Fodor'sChoice ★ 🏨 **Hotel Apollo.** Take advantage of this hotel's beautiful hillside location over a beach by relaxing on the restaurant terrace or renting a boat to water-ski in the clear blue waters; not surprisingly, guest rooms at this gracefully aging, white, block-shaped hotel, built in a typical 1970s style, have balconies and most of them sea views. **Pros:** panoramic views of the Saronic gulf; pool with saltwater; crystal sea waters set against a dramatic volcanic backdrop. **Cons:** room decor a bit on the spartan side; rocky beach. [$] *Rooms from: €80* ✉ *Ayia Marina beach* ☎ *22970/32271, 210/323–4292 winter in Athens* 🌐 *www.apollohotel aegina.gr* 🛏 *107 rooms* 🕒 *Closed Nov.–Mar.* 🍽 *Breakfast.*

PALIACHORA ΠΑΛΑΙΟΧΩΡΑ

7 km (4½ miles) south of Aegina town center.

Fodor'sChoice ★ The haunting remains of Aegina's medieval Paliachora (Old Town), built in the 9th century by islanders whose seaside town was the constant prey of pirates, are found on the rocky, barren hill above the monastery. Capital of the island until 1826, Paliachora has the romantic aura of a mysterious ghost town, a miniature Mistras that still has more than 30 churches (out of the original 365). They are mostly from the 13th century, and a number of them have been restored and are still in use. They sit amid the ruins of the community's houses, abandoned in the early 19th century. **Episkopi** (often closed), **Ayios Giorgios,** and **Metamorphosi** have lovely but faded (by dampness) frescoes. The frescoes of the church of **Ayioi Anargyroi** are especially fascinating because they are of pagan subjects, such as the mother goddess, Gaia, on horseback and Alexander the Great. The view from the hilltop castle to the beach of Souvala, on the other side of the island, is impressive.

The massive **Ayios Nektarios Monastery** (☎ *22970/53802*), 1 km (½ miles) west of Paliachora, is one of the largest in the Balkans. The memory of its saint is celebrated every year on his name day, November 9th.

BEACHES

Aiginitissa Beach. After Marathonas, Aiginitissa is a small, sandy bay with crystalline green waters surrounded by huge eucalyptus trees. The shallow water makes its accessible to beginner swimmers. There's a bar, beach volleyball court, and umbrellas and lounge chairs are available for rent. **Amenities:** food and drink; showers; water sports. **Best for:** swimming; sunset. ✉ *Paliachora, Aegina* ✣ *7 km (4½ miles) south of Aegina town.*

MARATHONAS ΜΑΡΑΘΩΝΑΣ

6 km (4 miles) south of Aegina town.

This small village a few miles south of Aegina town is reachable by bicycle or bus. The beach is just beyond.

BEACHES

FAMILY **Marathonas Beach.** There's a good swimming spot at the sandy Marathonas A beach on the west side of the island, with sun beds and umbrellas available for hire at either Ammos or Ostria restaurants, both of which are right on the beach. Beyond the village lies another nice beach, Marathonas B. These two beaches get very busy during the summer months, so be sure to arrive early if you want to beat the crowds (and pick the perfect spot!). Sun beds and umbrellas are available for rent, as are canoes. **Amenities:** food and drink; lifeguards. **Best for:** sunset; swimming. ⊠ *Marathonas, Aegina* ☎ *22970/28160 Ammos, 22970/27677 Ostria.*

PERDIKA ΠΕΡΔΙΚΑ

FAMILY *9 km (5½ miles) south of Aegina town.*

Fodor's Choice
★

Follow the lead of the locals and visiting Athenians, and, for an excursion, take a bus (a 25-minute ride from Ethneyersias Square) to the pretty port village of Perdika to unwind and eat lunch at a seaside taverna. Places to eat in Perdika have multiplied over the years but are still low-key and have a strong island flavor, transporting you light-years away from the bustle of much of modern Greece. Try O Nontas, the first fish taverna after the bus station, for a meal on the canopied terrace overlooking the little bay, the sailing boats, and the islet of Moni. Antonis, the famous fish tavern, draws big-name Athenians year-round. Across the bay, and only a short walk away, stands the sole modern building of a camera obscura. Inside, the cylindrical chamber allows the light to enter and projects an inverted image of the landscape outside—a technique that is now thought to have been used by many celebrated artists, including Leonardo and Vermeer. It is definitely worth a visit.

EXPLORING

FAMILY **Hellenic Wildlife Hospital** (*EKPAZ*). Located at the foot of Mount Oros, half a mile south east of the village of Pachia Rachi, the Hellenic Wildlife Hospital (EKPAZ) is a non-profit institution, the oldest and largest wildlife rehabilitation center in Greece and southern Europe. It treats 3,000 to 4,500 wild animals from all over Greece every year. You can visit the sanctuary and adopt a wild animal, such as Miko the raccoon (an American species that was imported illegally to Greece and cannot be returned back), or the Grand-dad, a monkey from the Amazon who is more than 25 years old, for €50 per year. ⊠ *Mount Oros, Pachia Rachi* ☎ *22970/31338* ⊕ *www.ekpazp.gr.*

BEACHES

Klima. A semi-secluded sandy beach, Klima, which is just south of Perdika, has a finely pebbled bay of crystal clear waters. To reach it, turn left at the intersection towards Sfentouri before entering Perdika; then, go right at the crossroads and keep going until you reach Klima. It is also a popular destination for yachts. There's a beach bar that rents sun

5

beds and umbrellas during the summer months. **Amenities:** food and drink. **Best for:** swimming; snorkeling. ✉ *Perdika, Aegina* ✣ *10 km (6 miles) south of Aegina town.*

Fodor's Choice ★ **Moni Beach.** In summer, caïques make frequent trips of 10 minutes (to cover a distance of 5 nautical km [3 nautical miles]) from the fishing port of Perdika to Moni, a real heaven-on-earth inhabited only by peacocks, wild deer, relocated *kri-kri* (Cretan goats), and some remains of a campsite dating back to the 1960s. Shadowed by pine trees, hiking trails wind their way through the little island's pristine landscape. Once the property of the Monastery of Chrysoleontissa, it is now a nature preserve. After your hike, take a most refreshing swim off the little sandy beach in the marvelously clear green waters by the quay. Note that the boatmen come back every hour, allowing you to leave whenever you wish (the return-trip ticket to and from Perdika costs €5). A small beach bar operates in summer, offering cool drinks and toasted sandwiches, but if you plan to spend the day here, you would be better off bringing a full picnic lunch. In crowded Attica, Moni is a lovely way to escape the madding crowds. **Amenities:** food and drink. **Best for:** swimming; walking. ✉ *Moni.*

WHERE TO EAT

$ SEAFOOD Fodor's Choice ★ 🍴 **Antonis.** Seafood is the word at this famed taverna run by Antonis and his sons. The octopus grilled in front of the establishment lures bathers and other visitors who tuck into options ranging from teeny fried smelt to enormous lobsters. People-watching is as much of a draw as the food, since the tables afford a view of all the comings and goings of the harbor's small boats as well as some sleek yachts. Other than splurging on the bouillabaisse here (expect to pay around €50 euros per kilo for sole, mullet, grouper—you name it), most dishes here, such as the veal and onions or "vegetables in the oven *(briam)*" rarely exceeds more than €10. [$] *Average main: €15* ✉ *Waterfront* ☎ *22970/61443* 🌐 *www.antonisperdika.gr.*

FESTIVALS

Ayios Sostis. On September 6th and 7th, the feast of the martyr Sozon is observed with a two-day *paniyiri* (saint's day festival), celebrated at the church of Ayios Sostis in Perdika. ✉ *Perdika, Aegina* ✣ *9 km (5½ miles) south of Aegina town.*

NIGHTLIFE

Muzik Café Bar. In Perdika, Muzik Café Bar is popular with the yachting crowd, who appreciate the food and relaxed atmosphere, as well as the great music and cocktails (try the lemon mojito) served until late at night. ✉ *Waterfront* ☎ *22970/29888* 🌐 *www.cafemuzik.gr.*

HYDRA ΥΔΡΑ

139 km (86 miles) south of Aegina by ferry.

As the full length of Hydra stretches before you when you round the easternmost finger of the northern Peloponnese, your first reaction might not, in fact, be a joyful one. Gray, mountainous, and barren, Idra (to use its alternative spelling) has the gaunt look of a saintly figure in a Byzantine icon. But as the island's curved harbor—one of the most picturesque in all of Greece—comes into view, delight will no doubt take over. Because of the nearly round harbor, the town is only visible from a perpendicular angle, a quirk in the island's geography that often saved the island from attack, since passing ships completely missed the port. Although there are traces of an ancient settlement, the island was sparsely inhabited until the Ottoman period. Hydra took part in the Greek War of Independence, begun in 1821, by which time the island had developed an impressive merchant fleet, creating a surge in wealth and exposing traders to foreign cultures. Their trade routes stretched from the mainland to Asia Minor and even America.

In the middle of the 20th century the island became a haven for artists and writers like Arthur Miller, Canadian singer-songwriter Leonard Cohen, and the Norwegian novelist Axel Jensen. In the early 1960s, an Italian starlet named Sophia Loren emerged from Hydra's harbor waters in the Hollywood flick *Boy on a Dolphin*. The site of an annex of Athens's Fine Arts School, today Hydra remains a favorite haunt of new and established artists.

The arrival of world-famous contemporary art collector Dakis Ioannou (who set up an exhibition space at the island's former Slaughterhouse in 2009 for his Deste Foundation) means that Hydra is now a magnet for today's chic art crowd. Every summer, the opening night of the Slaughterhouse is one of the art world's most coveted invitations; modern art lovers flock here to catch a glimpse of the most avantgarde artworks, refreshed by the fresh Hydriot breeze. In summer there are ongoing art exhibitions in many venues around the island, from the town's schools (where curator Dimitris Antonitsis organizes his annual collaborative Hydra School Projects) to the Melina Mercouri exhibition space right by the Hydra harbor, opposite the hydrofoil dock. The Hydra Workshop is a waterfront art space that puts together an annual exhibition inspired by the collection of London-based art patron Pauline Karpidas.

There are many reasons to love Hydra, not the least of which is the fact that all motor traffic is banned from the island (except for several rather noisy garbage trucks). After the racket of inner Athens and ear-splitting assaults on the eardrums by motorbikes in Aegina and Spetses, Hydra's blissful tranquility, especially off-season, is a cause for rejoicing.

GETTING HERE AND AROUND

At this writing the only ferry company that travels to Hydra is Hellenic Seaways. Due to high-season demand, it is essential to make reservations for boat tickets on weekends. It takes about 90 minutes to get to Hydra. These depart from Gate E8 or E9 in the port of Piraeus. There are eight departures per day during high season. Scheduled itineraries become scarcer during the winter months. The price of the ticket starts at €25.50 for economy class. You can get detailed information about departures on the websites ⊕ *www.hellenicseaways.gr* or *www.ferries.gr*.

Famously, cars are not allowed on Hydra—and that means there are no public buses either! Mule transport is the time-honored and most practical mode of transport up to the crest; you may see mules patiently hauling anything from armchairs and building materials to cases of beer. When you arrive, mule tenders in the port will rent you one of their fleet to carry your baggage—or better yet, you—to your hotel, for around €10 (make sure to agree on a price before you leave).

Other modes of transportation include water taxis and bikes for rent—hotel concierges can give you information.

VISITOR INFORMATION

Contacts Hydra Tourist Information ⊠ *Town Hall, Hydra Harbor, Hydra* ☎ *22980/53003, 22980/52210* ⊕ *www.hydra.gr.*

HYDRA TOWN ΥΔΡΑ ΠΟΛΗ

Even though Hydra's beautiful harbor is flush with bars and boutiques, Hydra town seems as fresh and innocent as when it was "discovered." The two- and three-story gray and white houses with red tile roofs, many built from 1770 to 1821, climb the steep slopes around Hydra town harbor. The noble port and houses have been rescued and placed on the Council of Europe's list of protected monuments, with strict ordinances regulating construction and renovation. Although Hydra has a landmass twice the size of Spetses, only a fraction is habitable, and after a day or so on the island, faces begin to look familiar—and not just because you saw them in last month's *Vanity Fair.*

EXPLORING

Church of the Dormition. Founded in 1643 as a monastery, the Church of the Dormition has since been dissolved and the monks' cells are now used to house municipal offices and the small ecclesiastical museum, Ayios Makarios Notaras. The church's most noticeable feature is an ornate, triple-tier bell tower made of Tinos marble, likely carved in the early 19th century by traveling artisans. There's also an exquisite marble iconostasis. ⊠ *Along central section of harbor front, Hydra town* ☎ *22980/54071 museum* ⊕ *www.imhydra.gr* ⊠ *Church free (donations accepted), museum €2* ⊗ *Church: daily 10–2 and 5–8. Museum: Apr.–Nov. 15, Tues.–Sun.10–5.*

Fodor's Choice　**Hydra Historical Archives and Museum.** Housed in an impressive mansion,
★　this collection of historical artifacts and paintings has exhibits that date back to the 18th century. Heirlooms from the Balkan wars as well as from World War I and II are exhibited in the ground-floor lobby. A small first-floor room contains figureheads from ships that fought in the 1821 War of Independence. There are old pistols and navigation aids, as well as portraits of the island's heroes and a section devoted to traditional local costume, including the dark *karamani* pantaloons worn by Hydriot men. There are also temporary art exhibits showcased from time to time. ⊠ *On east end of harbor, Hydra town* ☎ *22980/52355* ⊕ *www.iamy.gr* ⊠ *€5* ⊗ *Daily 9–4 and 7:30–9:30.*

Lazaros Koundouriotis Mansion. Impressed by the architecture they saw abroad, shipowners incorporated many of the foreign influences into their *archontika,* old, gray-stone mansions facing the harbor. The forbidding, fortresslike exteriors are deliberately austere, the combined result of the steeply angled terrain and the need for buildings to blend into the gray landscape. One of the finest examples of this Hydriot architecture is the Lazaros Koundouriotis Mansion, built in 1780 and beautifully restored in the 1990s as a branch of Greece's National Historical Museum. The interior is lavish, with hand-painted ceiling borders, gilt moldings, marquetry, and floors of black-and-white marble tiles. Some rooms have pieces that belonged to the Koundouriotis family, who played an important role in the War of Independence; other rooms have exhibits of costumes, jewelry, wood carvings, and pottery from the National Museum of Folk History. The basement level has three rooms full of paintings by Periklis Vyzantinos and his son, friends of the Koundouriotis family. ⊠ *On a graded slope above the port, on west headland, Hydra town* ☎ *22980/52421* ⊕ *www. nhmuseum.gr* ⊠ *€4* ⊙ *Mar.–Oct., Tues.–Sun.10–2 and 5:30–8:30.*

> ### HYDRA'S TASTE TREAT
>
> Before departing Hydra, be sure to enjoy some *amygdalota*, the island's famed sweet almond macaroons. They can be purchased in many bakeries and sweet shops on the island. Especially scrumptious are the amygdalota from Tsangaris, a sweet shop near the port (☎ *22980/52314*).

Slaughterhouse/DESTE Foundation Project Space. Internationally renowned modern art collector Dakis Ioannou acquired this former Hydra slaughterhouse, located a leisurely 10-minute walk from the town (towards Mandraki), in 2009 to host artistic events and projects organized by his budding Deste Foundation. Surprisingly, this is not what one might expect a chic and modern art gallery to look like: housed in an unassuming small building on a cliff by the sea, it is difficult to miss if you don't actively look for it. But perhaps that is exactly the point that Ioannou wanted to make with the Slaughterhouse, which has already acquired a leading role in Hydra's cultural life. Starting with the 2009 multimedia project *Blood of Two* by Matthew Barney and Elizabeth Peyton (which paid homage to the space's morbid past), every summer the space is now assigned to a different artist who is invited to stage a site-specific exhibition. In 2014, Pawel Althamer explored the secret of the Phaistos disc. ⊠ *10-minute walk east of the port, towards Mandraki, Hydra town* ⊕ *www.deste.gr* ⊠ *Free* ⊙ *Wed.–Mon. 11–1 and 7–10.*

BEACHES

Beaches are not the island's main attraction; the only sandy beach on Hydra is at Mandraki, east of Hydra town. There are small, shallow coves at Kamini and Vlichos, both west of the harbor. And a few mostly pebble beaches are found on the southern coast, also reachable by water taxi.

At Hydroneta beach bar and café, located just underneath the Hydriot cannons, the gray crags have been blasted and laid with cement to form sundecks. Sunbathing, socializing at the cocktail bar, and the views of the harbor may take priority over swimming, but old-timers can attest to the fact that diving off the rocks into the deep water is truly exhilarating, and it's the closest spot to Hydra town where you can take a refreshing dip.

SEEING HYDRA'S MONASTERIES

If you're staying for more than a day, you have time to explore Hydra's monasteries. Hire a mule (the donkey rank is located just outside the Alpha Bank in the western corner of Hydra's harbor; be sure to check prices with the muleteers first, as these can soar to more than €70 for some routes) for the ascent up Mt. Klimaki, where you can visit the **Profitis Ilias Monastery** (about two hours by mule from Hydra town) and view the embroidery work of an inhabitant of the nearby nunnery of **Ayia Efpraxia.** Experienced hikers might be tempted to set off for the **Zourvas Monastery** at Hydra's tip. It's a long and difficult hike, but compensation comes in the form of spectacular views and a secluded cove for a refreshing dip. An alternative: hire a water taxi to Zourvas.

The convent of **Ayios Nikolaos Monastery** is to the southeast of Hydra town, after you pass between the monasteries of Ayios Triadas and Ayias Matronis (the latter can be visited). Stop here for a drink and a sweet (a donation is appropriate), and to see the beautiful 16th-century icons and frescoes in the sanctuary. When hiking, wear sturdy walking shoes, and in summer start out early in the morning—even when traveling by mule—to minimize exposure to the midday sun. Your reward: stunning vistas over the island (resplendent with wildflowers and herbs in spring), the western and eastern coasts, and nearby islets on the way to area monasteries.

Ayios Nikolaos. Boats ferry bathers from Hydra town harbor near the Mitropolis church to pebble beaches on the island's southern coast, the best of which is Ayios Nikolaos, where there are sun beds and umbrellas for a charge (starting at €3) and you can also rent canoes. Ayios Nikolaos is located on the back side of the island, facing the Aegean sea, and it is the largest organized beach on the island. It is mostly pebbled with some small sandy stretches that are ideal for children's play. The large boats heading to and from here have set fees (e.g., €7.50 to Ayios Nikolaos from Hydra town); water taxis, whose rates you should negotiate in advance, start at €12. **Amenities:** food and drink; water sports. **Best for:** swimming; snorkeling. ✉ *Ayios Nikolaos.*

WHERE TO EAT

$$$ MEDITERRANEAN Fodor's Choice ★ 🍴 **Omilos.** The spot where Aristotle Onassis and Maria Callas once danced is now a vision in minimalist island white, reopened in 2007 by one of Enalion's owners. Tables nestle in the small, high-ceiling Hydra Nautical Club and wind around the deck outside, which affords an exquisite sea view. The setting is romantic at this pricey gourmet bar restaurant offering an extensive salad and pasta menu and tempting starters such as Greek caviar with fava bean mash and caramelized onions. Try the extremely moist grilled salmon with wild rice and vegetables or select from six different sauces for your grilled meats. After dinner, the owners will treat you to a glass of limoncello, or you can try the strawberry daquiri and mojito at the lively bar. [$] *Average main: €35* ✉ *Hydra port, on the way to Hydronetta, Hydra harbor*

Hydra is a shore thing—who needs a beach when you have waters as electric-blue as this?

☎ 22980/53800 ⊕ *www.omilos-hydra.com* ⚲ *Reservations essential* ⊘ *Closed Mon.–Thurs. Oct.–Apr.*

$$ ✕ **To Geitoniko.** Christina and her husband, Manolis, cook home-style
GREEK Greek dishes in a typical old Hydriot house with stone floors and
wooden ceilings, where time seems to have been standing still since
the 1950s. Try the octopus *stifado* (stew) with pearl onions; beef with
quince; or eggplant stuffed with ground meat. Grilled meats and fresh
fish, including the island's own calamari, are also available. Scrumptious
desserts include baklava and two types of halvah. It's a good idea to
arrive before 9 pm for dinner; there are only 20 tables under the open-
air vine-covered pergola upstairs, and they fill up quickly. $ *Average
main: €22* ⊠ *Spiliou Harami, opposite Pension Antonis, Hydra town*
☎ 22980/53615 ▭ *No credit cards* ⊘ *Closed Dec.–Feb.*

WHERE TO STAY

$ 🛏 **Angelica Hotel.** A three-minute walk from Hydra's bustling port, this
HOTEL alluring place is composed of two island villas in Hydra stone, garden
areas, and red barrel-tile roofs; happily, the main villa has been restored
to bring it up to the high standards of its fully renovated VIP Villa sister,
where streamlined wood furniture and soft neutral colors predominate
in eight spacious guest rooms with names like Sappho and Amazon,
each with unique decor. **Pros:** the Jacuzzi on the veranda (free use for
VIP Villa rooms); generously sized rooms; friendly owners. **Cons:** no
elevator; limited variety of breakfast options; slow Wi-Fi. $ *Rooms
from: €110* ⊠ *Andrea Miaouli 43, Hydra town* ☎ 22980/53202,
22980/53264 ⊕ *www.angelica.gr* ⤳ *21 rooms* ⊙| *Breakfast.*

Continued on page 270

EAT LIKE A GREEK

Hailed for its healthfulness, heartiness, and eclectic spicing, Greek cuisine remains one of the country's greatest gifts to visitors. From gyros to galaktoboureko, moussaka to myzthira, and soutzoukakia to snails, food in Greece is rich, exotic, and revelatory.

To really enjoy communal meals of fresh fish, mama's casseroles, flavorful salads, house wine, and great conversation, keep two ground rules in mind.

ORDER LIKE A NATIVE
Go for *tis oras* (grilled fish and meat "of the hour") or *piato tis imeras* (or "plate of the day," often stews, casseroles, and pastas). Remember that fish is always expensive, but avoid frozen selections and go for the freshest variety by asking the waitstaff

what the day's catch is (you can often inspect it in the kitchen). Note that waiters in Greece tend to be impatient—so don't waffle while you're ordering.

DINE LIKE A FAMILY
Greeks share big plates of food, often piling bites of *mezedes*, salads, and main dishes on small dishes. It's okay to stick your fork into communal platters but not in each other's personal dishes (unless you're family or dear friends).

(top) lunching alfresco; (bottom) Kadalee with cinnamon

GRECIAN BOUNTY

Can't understand the menu? Just point!

Greece is a country of serious eaters, which is why there are so many different kinds of eateries here. Here is a list of types to seek out.

Estiatorio: You'll often find fine tablecloths, carefully placed silverware, candles, and multipage menus at an *estiatorio*, or restaurant; menus range from traditional to nouvelle.

Oinomageirio: Now enjoying a retro resurgence, these simple eateries were often packed with blue-collar workers filling up on casseroles and listening to *rembetika*, Greece's version of the blues.

Taverna: This is vintage Greece—family-style eateries noted for great spreads of grilled meat *tis oras* (of the hour), thick-cut fried potatoes, dips, salads, and wine—all shared around a big table and with a soundtrack of *bouzouki* music.

Psarotaverna: Every bit like a regular taverna, except the star of the menu is fresh fish. Remember that fish usually comes whole; if you want it filleted, ask "*Mporo na exo fileto?*" Typical fish varieties include *barbounia* (red mullet), *perka* (perch), *sardella* (sardine), *bakaliaros* (cod), *lavraki* (sea bass), and *tsipoura* (sea bream).

Mezedopoleia: In this Greek version of tapas bars, you can graze on a limited menu of dips, salads, and hot and cold mezedes. Wildly popular with the pre-nightclub crowd.

Ouzeri and Rakadiko: *Ouzo* and the Cretan firewater *raki* (also known as *tsikoudia*) are the main attractions here, but there's always a generous plate of hot or cold mezedes to go with the spirits. A mix of oldtimers and young scenesters make for great people-watching.

Kafeneio (café): Coffee rules here—but the food menu is usually limited to sandwiches, crepes, *tiropites* (cheese pies), and *spanakopites* (spinach pies).

Zacharoplasteio (patisserie): Most dessert shops are "to go," but some old-style spots have a small klatch of tables to enjoy coffee and that fresh slice of *galaktoboureko* (custard in phyllo dough).

FOR THOSE ON THE GO

Greeks are increasingly eating on the run, since they're working longer (right through the afternoon siesta that used to be a mainstay) and happy that eateries have adapted to this lifestyle change. *Psitopoleia* (grill shops) have the most popular takeaway food: the wrapped-in-pita *souvlaki* (pork, lamb, or chicken chunks), *gyros* (slow-roasted slabs of pork and lamb, or chicken), or *kebabs* (spiced, grilled ground meat). Tzatziki, onions, tomatoes, and fried potatoes are also tucked into the pita. Toasted sandwiches and tasty hot dogs are other satisfying options.

Gyros: a take-away treat

ON THE GREEK TABLE

Mezedes Μεζέδες (appetizers): Eaten either as a first course or as full meals, they can be hot (pickled octopus, chickpea fritters, dolmades, fried squid) or cold (dips like *tzatziki*; *taramosalata*, puree of salted mullet roe and potato; or the spicy whipped feta called *htipiti*). Start with two or three, then keep ordering to your heart's content.

Tzatziki (cucumber in yogurt)

Salata Σαλάτα (salad): No one skips salads here since the vegetables burst with flavor, texture, and aroma. The most popular is the *horiatiki*, or what the rest of the world calls a "Greek salad"—this country-style salad has tomato, onion, cucumber, feta, and Kalamata olives. Other popular combos include *maroulosalata* (lettuce tossed with fresh dill and fennel) and the Cretan *dakos* (bread rusks topped with minced tomato, feta, and onion).

Horiatiki (Greek salad)

Kyrios Piato Κύριο Πιάτο (main course): Main dishes were once served family-style, like mezedes, but the plates are now offered as single servings at many restaurants. Some places serve the dishes as they are ready while more Westernized eateries bring all the plates out together. Order all your food at the same time, but be sure to tell the waiter if you want your main dishes to come after the salads and mezedes. Most grilled meat dishes come with a side of thick-cut fried potatoes, while seafood and casseroles such as *moussaka* are served alone. *Horta*, or boiled greens, drenched in lemon, are the ideal side for grilled or fried fish.

Sardines with rice, potatoes, and salad

Epidorpio Επιδόρπιο (dessert): Most restaurants give diners who have finished their meals a free plate of fresh seasonal fruit or some homemade *halva* (a cinnamony semolina pudding-cake with raisins).

Krassi Κρασί (wine): Greeks almost always have wine with a meal, usually sharing a carafe or two of *hima* (barrel or house wine) with friends. Bitter resinated wine, or *retsina*, has become less common in restaurants. Instead, the choice is often a dry Greek white wine that goes well with seafood or poultry.

Moussaka

Psomi Ψωμί (bread): Bread, often pita-fashion, always comes with a meal and usually costs 1 to 2 euros—a *kouver* (cover) charge—regardless of whether you eat it.

Nero Νερό (water): If you ask for water, waitstaff will usually bring you a big bottle of it—and charge you, of course. If you simply want tap water (free and safe to drink) ask for a *kanata*—or a pitcher.

Galaktoboureko (custard-filled phyllo pastry)

LIKE MAMA USED TO MAKE

Nearly all Greek restaurants have the same homey dishes that have graced family dinner tables here for years. However, some of these dishes are hardly ever ordered by locals, who prefer to eat them at home—most Greeks just avoid moussaka and pastitsio unless they're made fresh that day. So if you order the following foods at restaurants, make sure to ask if they're fresh ("*tis imeras*").

■ **DOLMADES**—grape leaves stuffed with rice and herbs

■ **KOTOPOULO LEMONATO**—whole chicken roasted with thickly sliced potatoes, lemon, and oregano

■ **MOUSSAKA**—a casserole of eggplant and spiced beef topped with béchamel

■ **PASTITSIO**—tube-shaped pasta baked with spiced beef, béchamel, and cheese

Best bet: Grape leaves

■ **PSARI PLAKI**—whole fish baked with tomato, onions, garlic, and olive oil

■ **SOUPA AVGOLEMONO**—an egg-lemon soup with a chicken stock base

COFFEE CULTURE

Greek coffee: tiny but strong

A *kafeneio* coffeehouse

Frappé

Greeks go out for coffee not because of caffeine addiction but because they like to spend at least two hours mulling the world with their friends. *Kafeneia*, or old-style coffeehouses, are usually full of courtly old men playing backgammon and sipping tiny but strong cups of *elliniko* (Greek coffee). Modern cafés (*kafeterias*) are more chic, packed with frappé-loving office workers, freddo-swilling college students, and arty hipsters nursing espressos. Order your coffee *sketos* (without sugar), *metrios* (medium sweet), or *glykos* (sweet).

■ **Frappé**—a frothy blend of instant coffee (always Nescafé), cold water, sugar, and evaporated milk

■ **Elliniko**—the strong traditional coffee made from Brazilian beans ground into a fine powder

■ **Freddo**—an iced cappuccino or espresso

■ **Nes**—instant coffee, often served with froth

$$ HOTEL **Bratsera Hotel.** An 1860 sponge factory was transformed into this charming character hotel (doors made out of old packing crates still bearing the "Piraeus sponge" stamp, etc.), **Pros:** helpful staff; the relaxing-by-the-pool experience; free Wi-Fi. **Cons:** some basic, tired rooms; some small dark bathrooms; hard beds. [$] *Rooms from: €180* ✉ *On left leaving port, Hydra town* ☎ *22980/53971, 22980/52794 restaurant* 🌐 *www.bratserahotel.com* 🛏 *17 rooms, 8 suites* 🕓 *Closed mid-Oct.–Mar.* 🍴 *Breakfast.*

$$ B&B/INN Fodor'sChoice ★ **Cotommatae 1810 Guesthouse.** This old mansion has been refurbished by a descendant of the original owners, a wealthy and well-known Hydriot shipping family, without losing its original charm. **Pros:** relaxing, elegant atmosphere; easy walking distance from the port; welcoming staff. **Cons:** no swimming pool, just a small plunge pool in the garden; no sea views; Jacuzzi at extra cost for all suites except Pigeon house. [$] *Rooms from: €200* ✉ *Votsi street, Hydra town* ☎ *22980/53873* 🌐 *www.cotommatae.gr* 🛏 *7 rooms* 🍴 *Breakfast.*

$$ HOTEL **Hotel Hydra.** Situated in an idyllic setting, this boutique hotel with eight relaxing, modern, and beautifully decorated guest suites offers panoramic views of the port and separate living and bedroom areas (as well as a small kitchenette). **Pros:** suites feel more like small apartments rather than rooms; friendly host; free Wi-Fi. **Cons:** must climb about 150 stairs to get to the hotel from the port; not all rooms have great panoramic views of the harbor, so make sure you ask in advance if that is what you want. [$] *Rooms from: €160* ✉ *Petrou Voulgari 8, close to the Lazaros Koundouriotis mansion, Hydra town* ☎ *22980/53420* 🌐 *www.hydra-hotel.gr* 🛏 *8 suites* 🕓 *Closed Nov.–late Mar.* 🍴 *Breakfast.*

$$ HOTEL **Hotel Leto Hydra.** Right in the middle of Hydra town, this small upscale hotel has a sparkling interior with an elegant "old Greece" touch provided by an array of antique Hydriot rugs, mirrors, and lanterns—and some modern artworks by well-known Greek painters (Papanikolaou and Akrithakis to name two) thrown in to liven things up. **Pros:** the distinguished feel of an old mansion; spacious, shady rooms; marble bathrooms. **Cons:** a bit pricey; no views and no significant outside spaces; can be difficult to find on your own (ask for directions at the harbor port). [$] *Rooms from: €150* ✉ *Town center, Hydra town* ☎ *22980/53385* 🌐 *www.letohydra.gr* 🛏 *30 rooms* 🕓 *Closed Nov.–mid-Mar.* 🍴 *Breakfast.*

$$ B&B/INN **Miranda Hotel.** Antiques lovers might feel right at home among the 18th- and 19th-century furniture and decor (Oriental rugs, wooden chests, nautical engravings, ceilings painted in detailed Venetian motifs) decorating this traditional Hydriot home, now a gracious small hotel. **Pros:** peaceful garden; precious artworks on display. **Cons:** somewhat dated and smallish rooms; thin doors do not provide enough sound insulation. [$] *Rooms from: €140* ✉ *Miaouli, 2 blocks inland from port center, Hydra town* ☎ *22980/52230* 🌐 *www.mirandahotel.gr* 🛏 *12 rooms, 2 suites* 🕓 *Closed Nov.–Feb.* 🍴 *Breakfast.*

$$ B&B/INN Fodor'sChoice ★ **Orloff Boutique Hotel.** Commissioned in 1796 by Catherine the Great for her lover Count Orloff—who came to Greece with a Russian fleet to try to dislodge the Turks—this *archontiko* mansion retains its splendor now that it has been turned into a small boutique hotel. **Pros:**

homey feeling; friendly owners; refurbished bathrooms in 2013; lovely decor. **Cons:** a bit noisy air-conditioning; no balconies. $ *Rooms from: €165* ✉ *Rafalia 9 and Votsi, 350 feet from the port, Hydra town* ☎ *22980/52564* ⊕ *www.orloff.gr* ⊃ *5 rooms, 4 suites* ⊙ *Closed Nov.– Mar.* ✵ *Breakfast.*

FESTIVALS

Its image as a weekend destination has made Hydra a popular venue for all sorts of events, from trail races and art exhibitions to sailing events and regattas. Exhibitions, concerts, and performances are usually held from June through August to coincide with the busy summer season. The International Rembetika music festival takes place here in October. Plus the new and ever-growing contemporary art scene here is sure to be highlighted with happenings that will draw an international art crowd.

FAMILY
Fodor'sChoice
★
Hydra's Trail Event. During one long weekend in April the whole of Hydra lives and breathes trail running. The locals have embraced the vertical trail race that sees runners starting at the top of the mountain by the monastery of Profitis Hlias (individual starts every minute ensure their safety) and finishing after a steep downhill 3.2 km (2 miles) later, in the heart of the harbor. Other trail races and plenty of side activities take place, too, most of them good for kids. ✉ *Hydra town* ⊕ *www.hydrastrail.gr.*

Fodor'sChoice
★
Miaoulia. The island celebrates its crucial role in the War of Independence with the Miaoulia, which takes place the last weekend of June. At around 10 o'clock on Saturday night, Hydra's small port goes dark, and a journey into history commences as the day's festivities culminate in a reenactment of the night Admiral Miaoulis loaded a vessel with explosives and sent it upwind to the Turkish fleet back in 1821. Naturally, the model enemy's ship goes down in flames. Fireworks, music, traditional dancing, treasure hunts, and sports competitions all accompany the burning of the fleet, a glorious part of Hydra's Naval Week.

NIGHTLIFE

Bars often change names, ownership, and music—if not location—so check with your hotel for what's in vogue.

Amalour. On the ground floor of an early-19th-century mansion, Amalour attracts a thirtysomething crowd who sip expertly made cocktails (especially the exquisite daquiris) and listen to ethnic, jazz, soul, and funk music. ✉ *Tombazi street, behind the port, Hydra town* ☎ *22980/29680.*

Andy's Bar. Andy's bar hosts Greek music jam sessions. ✉ *West of harbor, Hydra town* ☎ *6944/543174.*

Beach Club Spilia. Tucked into the seaside rocks just below the Hydroneta bar, recently renovated Spilia provides a nice escape from the midday sun and is a popular nocturnal haunt, too. The view towards the port is impressive and the deck chairs are comfortable. Spilia offers both coffee and drinks; the daiquiris are excellent. There are also salads and snacks on offer. The steps to the refreshing sea are especially inviting on hot summer days, which means you can end up spending a whole day here without realizing it. ✉ *After Omilos, on the way to the Cannons, Hydra town* ☎ *22980/54166* ⊕ *www.spiliacafe.com.*

5

Hydroneta. The minuscule Hydroneta bar-restaurant has an enchanting view from its perch above the harbor. Embraced by rocks and surrounded by water, it is jam-packed during the day and it is *the* place to enjoy a glass of chilled beer or fruity long drink at sunset. Hydroneta's trademark events are its "Full Moon" parties, fun-filled events under Hydra's starlit skies. ⊠ *Hydroneta beach, west of Hydra town, on the way to Kamini, past the Canons* ☎ *22980/54160.*

Papagalos. On the western tip of the harbor towards Mandraki, where the first disco club of the island used to be, newcomer Papagalos is a cocktail and tapas bar (created by the owners of locally renowned Amalour) with a panoramic view of the harbor action. Rock music is a staple on the decks, while live gigs are held here on a regular basis. Free Wi-Fi is available. ⊠ *Harbor front, Hydra town* ☎ *22980/52626.*

Fodor'sChoice ★ **The Pirate Bar.** Café-bar Pirate has been a fixture of the island's nightlife since the late 1970s. Over the years, it's gotten face-lifts, added some mainstream dance hits to its rock music–only playlist, and remains popular and raucous. The spot is actually open all day with delicious home-cooked dishes (burgers, salads, and lemon pies) but it is at night that the fun really takes off, often with the help of one of the popular house drinks, such as the fruity Tropical Sun. ⊠ *South end of harbor, Hydra town* ☎ *22980/52711.*

SHOPPING

A number of elegant shops (some of them offshoots of Athens stores) sell fashionable and amusing clothing and jewelry, though you won't save much by shopping here.

Elena Votsi. Worth a visit, the stylish store of local jewelry designer Elena Votsi showcases her exquisite handmade pieces—more works of art than accessories. Her designs sell well in Europe and New York. ⊠ *Ikonomou 3, Hydra town* ☎ *22980/52637* ⊕ *www.elenavotsi.com.*

Fodor'sChoice ★ **The Hydra Trading Company & the Hydra Gallery.** On the site of the old police station, French mother-and-son team Veronique and Tom Powell (himself a talented painter) have created an eclectic boutique/gallery offering a wide selection of pure white linen, ceramics in all shades of Aegean blue, lucky charms, and household items exuding island chic and a bit of country flair. Painting exhibitions are also organized regularly in this charming second-floor shop. ⊠ *Old police station, Hydra town* ☎ *22980/29700.*

Speak Out Hydra. This boutique is so hip the owners run a way-cool art and fashion blog (⊕ speakouthydra.blogspot.com). Most of the stock is by up-and-coming Greek designers. ⊠ *Harbor front, Hydra town* ☎ *22980/52099.*

Spoiled!. Hydra's trendoisie head to Spoiled! for a top selection of glamorous evening togs in the latest fashion. ⊠ *Tombazi street, Hydra town* ☎ *22980/52363* ⊕ *www.spoiled.gr.*

Studio Hydra. Not simply your typical tourist gift shop, this is a treasure trove full of stylish fashion finds, chic mementos, and even dreamy Hydra watercolors. ⊠ *Harbor front, Hydra town* ☎ *22980/52132.*

Fodor's Choice
★ **Tsagkaris Hydriot Macaroons.** Don't leave Hydra without some traditional almond macaroons in your suitcase. The Tsagkaris family, led
by 85-year-old matriarch Anna Tsagkari, have been lovingly making
them in their workshop for more than 60 years. ⊠ *Miaouli street, 30
meters from the harbor front, Hydra town* ☎ *22980/52314.*

SPORTS AND THE OUTDOORS

HORSEBACK RIDING

Harriet's Horses. Discover Hydra by riding one of Harriet's lovely horses;
the friendly Hydra native leads treks to the island's mountains, monasteries, and beaches. Prices start at €20 (+V.A.T.) for a 90-minute ride
to Kaminia village, suitable for all levels. ⊠ *Harborfront, Hydra town*
☎ *6980/323347.*

SCUBA DIVING

Hydra Diving Center. For those who love the great outdoors, snorkeling
and scuba-diving (scuba lessons are available for first-time divers, too)
in the rocky seabeds of Hydra (especially around the bay of Bisti) could
be a highlight of a Greek vacation. The center is located at the back
of taverna Enalion, in Vlichos, as it is its enthusiastic owner Yiannis
Kitsos that runs both. His boat can also pick up divers from Hydra's
port. ⊠ *Taverna Enalion, Hydra town* ☎ *6977/792493* ⊕ *www.hydra.
com.gr/diving-center.*

KAMINIA KAMINIA

1 km (½ mile) west of Hydra town.

A small fishing hamlet built around a shallow inlet, Kamini has much
of Hydra town's charm but none of its bustle—except on Orthodox
Good Friday, when the entire island gathers here to follow the funerary
procession of Christ. On a clear day, the Peloponnese coast is plainly
visible across the water, and spectacular at sunset. Take the 20-minute
stroll from Hydra town west; a paved coastal track gives way to a staggered, white path lined with fish tavernas; Kamini's small beach also
has restaurants nearby, which you can spot arriving by boat or sea taxi.

BEACHES

FAMILY **Mikro Kamini.** Kamini's small gray-pebbled beach, known as Mikro
Kamini, is about 300 meters beyond the sleepy fishing port, just in
front of the Castello Bar & Restaurant, where you can rent sun beds and
umbrellas. There are more tavernas nearby, from where you can spot
arriving boats and water taxis. The water here is calm and shallow, so
the beach is good for families with small children. **Amenities:** food and
drink. **Best for:** swimming; walking. ⊠ *Kamini, Kamini.*

WHERE TO EAT

$$$ ✕ **Castello Bar and Restaurant.** Set right on Kamini beach, this fully reno-
MEDITERRANEAN vated 18th-century fortress is a popular bar-restaurant. Its multilevel
Fodor's Choice café serves breakfast, coffee, drinks, and snacks and is the ideal spot for
★ enjoying Hydra sunsets. Just a leisurely 15-minute walk from the port
(or 5 minutes by mule or 1 minute by water taxi), the reward is some
of the most fortifying dining on the island. Castello is the only place
where you can find sushi on the island, or if you are craving a snack,

try the whole-meal pizza with pesto sauce. You can come in early and have breakfast, or you can try the best apple martini on the island later. Hiring a sun bed for the day right in front of Castello will set you back €5. $ *Average main: €27* ⊠ *Mikro Kamini* ☎ *22980/54101* ⊕ *www. castellohydra.gr* ⌖ *Reservations essential* ⊙ *Closed Dec.–Feb.*

$$$ ✕ **Kodylenia's Taverna.** Fantasy: a whitewashed fisherman's cottage on a
SEAFOOD promontory overlooking the little harbor of Kaminia, with a veranda terrace charmingly set with folkloric pennants and communal tables—the perfect perch to catch some sublime sunsets. Reality: Kodylenia's, an irresistibly alluring (if a little pricey) place that has enraptured town folk and off-duty billionaires alike. Talk a look at the website's slide-show to see what all the fuss is about (get set for a 2-minute Greek vacation). When there, peek into the kitchen below the terrace to see what's cooking: a whole fish may be char-grilling and, when available, order *kritamos* (rock samphire, a vegetation which grows on the island's rocky coast), the urchin salad, or share an order of fresh-caught grilled squid in tomato sauce. $ *Average main: €26* ⊠ *On the headland above the harbor* ☎ *22980/53520* ⊕ *www.hydra-kodylenia.gr* ▭ *No credit cards* ⊙ *Closed Nov.–Mar. No lunch.*

$$ ✕ **Pirofani.** The half-Greek, half-Danish host of this taverna in Kamini,
MEDITERRANEAN the second-largest village in Hydra, likes to cook for and entertain all his visitors himself. Being the life of the party that he is, by the time you leave after a heartening dinner, you will feel as if you've made a new friend. Theo cooks Greek and international dishes with a twist, as evidenced by the chicken souvlaki marinated in lemon and sage, and the pork fillet with Roquefort cheese sauce. $ *Average main: €25* ⊠ *Ka-minia, Hydra* ☎ *22980/53175* ⊕ *www.pirofani.com* ⌖ *Reservations essential* ⊙ *Closed Mon. and Tues. and Oct.–Apr. No lunch.*

VLICHOS ΒΛΥΧΟΣ

6 km (4 miles) west of Hydra town.

From Kamini, the coastal track continues to Vlichos, another pretty village with tavernas, a historic bridge, and a gray-pebbled beach on a bay. It's a 5-minute water-taxi ride from the Hydra town port or a 40-minute walk (25 minutes past Kamini).

BEACHES

FAMILY **Vlichos Beach.** This scenic little gray-pebble beach west of Kamini is a good dive destination (ask at Enalion taverna) as well as a nice swim-ming spot for families due to its shallow waters. Sun beds and umbrellas can be rented from the beachfront tavernas. **Amenities:** food and drink. **Best for:** swimming; walking. ⊠ *Vlichos, Hydra.*

WHERE TO EAT

$$ ✕ **Enalion.** The charming young trio of owners—Yiannis, Kostas and
MEDITERRANEAN Alexandros—have imbued this beach taverna next to Vlichos beach
Fodor'sChoice with energy and attentive service. The all-white surroundings (with
★ cool blue undertones) contrast gloriously with the injection of color from the surrounding pink bougainvillea. The traditional taverna fare includes favorite Greek dishes like fried tomato balls, beet salad, fried calamari, and stuffed tomatoes and peppers. All go perfectly with a glass

of house wine and the accompanying relaxing tunes. At the back of the taverna you will find the headquarters of the Hydra Diving Center. ⓢ *Average main: €18* ✉ *100 feet from beach* ☎ *22980/53455* ⊕ *www. enalion-hydra.gr* ⊗ *Closed Dec.–Mar.*

WHERE TO STAY

$$ ⊡ **Four Seasons Luxury Suites.** No, this is not one of the famous chain's
HOTEL hotels but rather a tiny (6-room) hotel inspired by the magical colors of the four seasons (the Sun Suite is the cream of the crop) sweetly set in an atmospheric, fully-renovated 150-year-old stone mansion in Vlichos. **Pros:** alluring interiors; next to the beach; homey feeling. **Cons:** challenging distance from town; pricey. ⓢ *Rooms from: €220* ✉ *Vlichos beach* ☎ *22980/53698* ⊕ *www.fourseasonshydra.gr* ⇄ *6 suites* ⊗ *Closed Nov.–late Mar.* �ⓞ *Breakfast.*

MANDRAKI ΜΑΝΔΡΑΚΙ

4 km (1½ miles) east of Hydra town.

The only sandy beach on Hydra is an activity-centered beach by the Mira Mare hotel, near Mandraki, which is currently closed and under renovation (but you can still visit the beach with one of the boats or water taxis that regularly depart from Hydra town; the nearby taverna is also open).

BEACHES

Mandraki Beach. One of the few sandy beaches of Hydra, Mandraki is a leisurely 2-km (1-mile) walk west of the town, but you can also come here by small boat or water taxi from the main port. The hotel right on the beach (hotel Miramare) is under renovation at this writing, but you can still enjoy the fine sand and the sun beds. More amenities (such as water sports) should be available once the hotel reopens. **Amenities:** food and drink. **Best for:** swimming; walking. ✉ *Mandraki, Hydra town.*

SPETSES ΣΠΕΤΣΕΣ

24 km (15 miles) southwest of Hydra.

Spetses shows evidence of continuous habitation through all of antiquity. From the 16th century, settlers came over from the mainland and, as on Hydra, they soon began to look to the sea, building their own boats. They became master sailors, successful merchants, and, later, in the Napoleonic Wars, skilled blockade runners, earning fortunes that they poured into building larger boats and grander houses. With the outbreak of the War of Independence in 1821, the Spetsiots dedicated their best ships and brave men (and women) to the cause.

In the years leading up to the revolution, Hydra's great rival and ally was the island of Spetses. Lying at the entrance to the Argolic gulf, off the mainland, Spetses was known even in antiquity for its hospitable soil and verdant pine tree–covered slopes. The pines on the island today, however, were planted by a Spetsiot philanthropist dedicated to restoring the beauty stripped by the shipbuilding industry in the 18th and 19th centuries. There are far fewer trees than there were in antiquity, but the island is still well watered, and the many prosperous Athenians who have made Spetses their second home compete to have the prettiest gardens and terraces. Today's visitor can enjoy spotting this verdant beauty all over the island.

GETTING HERE AND AROUND

Hellenic Seaways' Flying Dolphins hydrofoils and catamarans travel regularly, year-round, from Piraeus (Gate E8 or E9) to Spetses (usually stopping at Poros and Hydra as well). There are half a dozen such daily rounds from April to October, and fewer the rest of the year. You can get to Spetses (€35 economy) in just under two hours. Make reservations ahead of time—boats fill quickly. You can get detailed info about departure times on ⊕ *www.hellenicseaways.gr.*

The island of Spetses is so close to the Peloponnese mainland that you also can drive to the small port of Costa (200 km [124 miles] from Athens), park your car, and ferry across the channel in any of a number of caïques (price at around €5 per person, but you have to wait for the boat to fill up before it leaves for the 20-minute crossing). You can also take a water taxi on demand (price negotiable; expect to pay around €30 in total for a 5-minute crossing). For water taxi information, call ☎ 22980/72072.

Only homeowners are usually allowed to bring cars on the island. Visitors must hire bikes, scooters, mopeds, water taxis, carriages, or use one of the two high-season-only (Easter–September) municipal buses: one bus line goes from Ayios Mamas beach to Ayioi Anargyri and Ayia Paraskevi; the other, with nearly hourly departures during the day, from Poseidonion Grand Hotel to Ligoneri and Vrellos beach. Tickets range from €1 to €3. For bus schedule information you can contact the two bus drivers directly on their mobile phones (for Ayios Mamas and Ayioi Anargyroi, call Anargyros Kotzias at ☎ 69/4480–2536; for Ligoneri and Vrellos, call Konstantinos Mouratis at ☎ 69/7894–9722). It is worth going on one of the buses if only for the scenic route.

VISITOR INFORMATION

Contacts Spetses Tourist Information ⊠ *Town hall, Spetses town* ☎ *22980/72255, 22983/20010 info line (daily 8–3)* ⊕ *www.spetses.gr.*

SPETSES TOWN ΣΠΕΤΣΕΣ ΠΟΛΗ

91 km (56 miles) southwest of Hydra.

By most visitors' standards, Spetses town is small—no larger than most city neighborhoods—yet it's nevertheless divided into districts. You will arrive in Dapia, the modern harbor. Kastelli, the oldest quarter, extends toward Profitis Ilias and is marked by the 18th-century Ayia Triada Church, the town's highest point. The area along the coast to the north is known as Kounoupitsa, a residential district of pretty cottages and gardens with pebble mosaics in mostly nautical motifs. A water-taxi ride here from Costa, across the channel on the mainland, takes about 15 minutes.

EXPLORING

Anargyrios and Korgialenios School. Known as the inspiration for the school in John Fowles's *The Magus*, this institution was established in 1927 as an English-style boarding school for the children of Greece's Anglophilic upper class. Up until 2010, tourism management students studied amid the elegant amphitheaters, black-and-white-tile floors, and huge windows. Today, the tourism students have relocated to Piraeus, and the buildings are used for private seminars and summer schools. Nevertheless, visitors can still take a peek (free) inside the school and stroll around the fabulous gardens throughout the year. ⊠ *Spetses town* ⊕ ½ *km (¼ mile) west of Dapia* ☎ *22980/74306* ⊕ *www.akss.gr.*

Ayios Mamas. The town's stone promontory is the site of the little 19th-century church, Ayios Mamas—take your photos from a distance as the church is privately owned and often locked. ⊠ *Above the harbor, Spetses town.*

Fodor's Choice ★ **Bouboulina Museum.** In front of a small park is Bouboulina's House, now a museum, where you can take a 45-minute guided tour (available in English) and learn about this interesting heroine's life. Laskarina Bouboulina was the bravest of all Spetsiot revolutionaries, the daughter of a Hydriot sea captain, and the wife—then widow—of two more sea captains. Left with a considerable inheritance and nine children, she dedicated herself to increasing her already substantial fleet and fortune. On her flagship, the *Agamemnon,* the largest in the Greek fleet at the time, she sailed into war against the Ottomans at the head of the Spetsiot ships. Her fiery temper led to her death in a family feud many years later. It's worth visiting the mansion, which is run by her fourth-generation grandson, just for the architectural details, like the carved-wood Florentine ceiling in the main salon. Tour times (in groups of up of 35 visitors) are posted on the museum website, in front of the museum, and on announcement boards at the port of Dapia. The museum closes for maintentance during winter. ⊠ *Behind Dapia, Spetses town* ☎ *22980/72416* ⊕ *www.bouboulinamuseum-spetses.gr* 🎫 *€6* ⊙ *Late Mar.–Oct., daily 9:45–2:15 and 3:45–8:15.*

Dapia. Ships dock at the modern harbor, Dapia, in Spetses town. This is where the island's seafaring chieftains met in the 1820s to plot their revolt against the Ottoman Turks. A protective jetty is still fortified with cannons dating from the War of Independence. Today, the town's waterfront strip is packed with cafés, and the navy-blue-and-white color scheme adopted by Dapia's merchants hints of former maritime glory. The harbormaster's offices, to the right as you face the sea, occupy a building designed in the simple two-story, center-hall architecture typical of the period and this place. ⊠ *Dapia, Spetses town.*

Ekklisia Ayios Nikolaos. On the headland sits Ayios Nikolaos, the current cathedral of Spetses, and a former fortified abbey. Its lacy white-marble bell tower recalls that of Hydra's port monastery. It was here that the islanders first raised their flag of independence. ⊠ *On road southeast on waterfront, Spetses town* ☎ *22980/72423.*

Palio Limani (*Balitiza*). Spetses actually has two harbors. The new harbor, Dapia, is busy while the old harbor, Palio Limani—also known as

5

Baltiza—slumbers in obscurity. As you stroll the waterfront, you might imagine it as it was in its 18th- and 19th-century heyday: the walls of the mansions resounding with the noise of shipbuilding and the streets humming with discreet whisperings of revolution and piracy. Today, the wood keels in the few remaining boatyards are the backdrop for cosmopolitan bars, cafés, and restaurants; the sailing boats linger lazily in the bay. Walk up the hill to the ochre-hued chapel of Panayia Armata for unforgettable sunset views. ⊠ *Spetses town* ✚ *Waterfront, 1½ km (1 mile) southeast of Dapia.*

Poseidonion Grand Hotel. This waterfront 1914 landmark was the scene of glamorous Athenian society parties and balls in the era between the two world wars. It was once the largest resort in the Balkans and southeastern Europe. The hotel was the brainchild of Sotirios Anargyros, a visionary benefactor who was responsible for much of the development of Spetses. It reopened in the summer of 2009—after extensive renovations—to recapture its former glory and has quickly regained its position as a Spetsiot landmark. (*See also our hotel review, below*) ⊠ *West side of Dapia, Spetses town* ☎ *22980/74553* ⊕ *www.poseidonion.com.*

Fodor's Choice ★ **Spetses Museum.** A fine late-18th-century impressive *archontiko* owned by the locally renown Hatziyianni-Mexi family and built in a style that might be termed Turko-Venetian, contains the town's municipal museum. It holds articles from the period of Spetses's greatness during the War of Independence, including the bones of the town's heroine, Bouboulina, and a revolutionary flag. A small collection of ancient artifacts consists mostly of ceramics and coins. Also on display are representative pieces of furniture and household items from the period of the Greek revolution. ⊠ *Archontiko Hatziyianni-Mexi, 600 ft. south of harbor, Spetses town* ☎ *22980/72994* 🖅 *€3* ☉ *Tues.–Sun. 8:30–2:30.*

BEACHES

Spetses's best beaches are on the west side of the island, and most easily reached by water taxi or the daily boats from Spetses town. You can ask for caïque information directly at the port. Water taxis at Dapia (the New Port) make scheduled runs to the most popular outlying beaches but can also be hired for trips to more remote coves. The rides can be pricey, ranging from €7 to go from Dapia to the Old Port, up to €30 to the Ayia Paraskevi beach, and €60 for a tour of the island—but the experience is unique. There are currently seven water taxis serving Spetses.

Kaiki. Trendy Kaiki beach (otherwise known as Scholes or College beach due to its proximity to the Anargyros School) is a triangular patch of sandy beach that draws a young crowd with its beach volleyball court, water-sport activities (about €40 for 20 minutes of jet skiing), and the Kaiki beach bars (yes, there are two of them!) and restaurant, the hippest one on the beach in Spetses. It will cost you about €10 for a huge umbrella, two bamboo sun beds, two beach towels, and a bottle of water for a relaxing day on the beach. You can even rent an iPad (€5 per 20 minutes) or get a beach massage. **Amenities:** food and drink; lifeguards; toilets; water sports. **Best for:** swimming; walking. ⊠ *Opposite Anargyrios and Korgialenios School, Spetses town* ☎ *22980/74507 Kaiki Beach Bar Restaurant.*

WHERE TO EAT

$$ SEAFOOD
🍴 **Exedra.** Called Sioras or Giorgos by locals (all three names are on the sign), this traditional waterside taverna, whose terrace overlooks the water, lets you ogle mooring yachts while digging into a well-prepared and thoroughly Greek meal—not to mention reasonably priced as well. Mussels *saganaki* (fried) and a dish called *Argo* (shrimp and lobster baked with feta) are among the specialties. This is also the ultimate place in Spetses to try fish *á la Spetsiota,* the local specialty of broiled fish-and-tomato casserole. [$] *Average main: €20* ✉ *At edge of the Palio Limani, Spetses town* ☎ *22980/73497* ⏲ *Closed Nov.–Feb.*

$$ GREEK
🍴 **Lazaros.** A boisterous local crowd fills the small tables—which spill onto the street in summer—and old family photos, potted ivy, and barrels of retsina line the walls. A small selection of well-prepared dishes includes some daily specials, such as goat in lemon sauce, chicken *kokkinisto* (slow-cooked with orzo and tomato sauce), *spetsofai* (tender pieces of pork with piccante peppers), and, occasionally, fresh fish at good prices. Tasty appetizers include homemade *tzatziki* (cucumber-yogurt dip), *taramosalata* (fish roe dip), *mavromatika* (black-eyed pea salad), and tender beets with *skordalia* (galic-potato dip). Order the barrel retsina, priced by the kilo. [$] *Average main: €18* ✉ *Kastelli, 600m uphill from the harbor, Spetses town* ☎ *22980/72600* ⏲ *Closed mid-Nov.–mid-Mar. No lunch.*

$$$ MEDITERRANEAN
Fodor's Choice ★
🍴 **Liotrivi Restaurant.** A former olive oil mill dating back to the 1800s, this fashionable bar-restaurant by the pier offers upscale Mediterranean dishes, such as fresh ravioli stuffed with lobster, crab salad, and *mayiatiko à la spetsiota,* a variation of the local fish specialty made with yellowtail. In summer, you can enjoy the live Latin music from the beachfront tables. At sunset, the candlelit tables and the boats moored nearby create a dreamy experience. Later the place turns into a popular hangout. [$] *Average main: €35* ✉ *Palio Limani, Spetses town* ☎ *22980/72269* 🌐 *www.liotrivirestaurant.gr* ✍ *Reservations essential* ⏲ *Closed Nov.–Mar.*

$$ MEDITERRANEAN
🍴 **Mourayo.** This restaurant and music club is located right on the water in Dapia and is *the* all-time classic bar and night club of Spetses (running since 1975). The food in the restaurant is pretty decent, too, and it's probably one of the better choices on the island. Lounge in the veranda's comfy armchairs surrounded by maritime antiques and enjoy the predominantly Mediterranean cuisine (or an excellent cheeseburger) and cool cocktails while enjoying a romantic view of the yachts moored in the quaint little port. [$] *Average main: €22* ✉ *Palio Limani, Spetses town* ☎ *22980/73700* 🌐 *www.mourayospetses.gr.*

$$ SEAFOOD
Fodor's Choice ★
🍴 **Patralis.** Sit on the seaside veranda and savor seafood mezedes and fresh fish right from the sea in one of the more affordable restaurants on this sometimes overpriced island. As the very friendly waiters will tell you, the house specialties are the fish soup, *astakomakaronada* (lobster with spaghetti), and a kind of paella with mussels, shrimp, and crayfish. *Magirefta* (oven-baked dishes) include stuffed aubergines; oven-baked lamb; and roast scarpine fish with tomato and garlic. Expect to pay around €50 per kilo for the fresh grilled fish (compared to €60 in other fish tavernas). The chef makes a mean baked apple for dessert,

but before you order, know that mini-portions of baklava, *karydopita*, and spoon sweets with yogurt are on the house. [$] *Average main: €25 ⊠ Kounoupitsa, near Spetses Hotel, Spetses town* ☎ *22980/72134* ⊕ *www.patralis.gr* ⊗ *Closed Nov. and Dec.*

$
GREEK
✕ **Stelios Restaurant.** Swift service and good value for your money more than make up for a lack of ambience at this little restaurant. Pass up the grilled dishes for the *magirefta* (baked dishes), like goat slowly cooked in a clay pot and oven-roasted potatoes lightly flavored with lemon and oregano. Not to be missed: the small homemade cheese pies for starters and the seafood pasta. [$] *Average main: €15 ⊠ Dapia, Spetses town* ☎ *22980/73748* ▭ *No credit cards* ⊗ *Closed mid-Nov.–mid-Mar.*

$$$$
ECLECTIC
✕ **Tole.** On the sight of legendary Figaro nightclub, Yiannis Morakis, one of the best-known Greek restaurateurs, has created an eatery that is attracting the younger generation of Greek politicians and entrepreneurs. Chef Nikos Contomarkos offers eclectic Mediterrannean dishes, such as linguini with smoked salmon and tuna tartare, with a view of the sailing boats of the Old Port behind the palm trees and the huge design lights. [$] *Average main: €45 ⊠ Palio Limani, Spetses town* ☎ *22980/74110* ⊕ *www.tole.gr* ⚲ *Reservations essential.*

WHERE TO STAY

$
B&B/INN
Fodor'sChoice
★
🛏 **Archontiko Economou.** Captain Mihail Economou's heirs have converted his 1851 stone mansion into a beautiful seaside hotel, perfect for romantic getaways, with the atmosphere heightened by the pebbled gardens, home to a small, pretty swimming pool and a handful of live tortoises. **Pros:** relaxing atmosphere; car transport to the port; lovely renovation. **Cons:** some noise coming from the main street; 10-minute walk from the old or new harbor; late breakfast start at 9:30 am. [$] *Rooms from: €100 ⊠ Harbor Rd., near Town Hall, Spetses town* ☎ *22980/73400* ⊕ *www.economouspetses.gr* ⇱ *6 rooms, 2 suites* ⊙⃒ *Breakfast.*

$
B&B/INN
🛏 **Niriides Apartments.** With cheerful, renovated exteriors surrounded by myriad flowers, these four-bed apartments a short walk from the main harbor are a good value, especially in the off-season. **Pros:** on a centrally located, quiet side street; hospitable owners; nice breakfast served in pretty, cool courtyard. **Cons:** bathrooms a bit on the small side; aside from breakfast, offers few hotel-style amenities. [$] *Rooms from: €110 ⊠ Dapia, near the clock tower square, Spetses town* ☎ *22980/73392* ⊕ *www.niriides-spetses.gr* ⇱ *7 apartments* ⊙⃒ *Breakfast.*

$$$
HOTEL
Fodor'sChoice
★
🛏 **Poseidonion Grand Hotel.** Set with fin-de-siècle cupolas, imposing mansard roof, and elegant neoclassical facade, this landmark mansion was acclaimed as the Saronic gulf's own Hotel Negrescu in 1914—like that Nice landmark, this hotel was built to attract the cosmopolitan ocean-liner set and, today, after reopening its doors in 2009 after an extensive five-year refurbishment, the Poseidonion has been hailed as the most elegant hotel in all the Greek islands. **Pros:** an unforgettable experience, say many; deluxe and tasteful renovation; beautiful landmark buiding; impeccable service; simple but elegant guest rooms with high ceilings; you really do get a lot for your money. **Cons:** historic patina suffers a bit amidst modern decor; free Wi-Fi only in lobby not in rooms. [$] *Rooms from: €240 ⊠ Dapia, Spetses town* ☎ *22980/74553* ⊕ *www.poseidonion.com* ⇱ *45 rooms, 7 suites* ⊙⃒ *Breakfast.*

Spetses is studded with extravagant mansions, such as this one, built for Sotirios Anargyros, owner of the famed Poseidonion Grand Hotel.

$$ HOTEL **Spetses Hotel.** Enjoy both privacy—surrounded by greenery, beach, and water—and proximity (about 15 minutes walk) to town at this spot, which dates back to the 1970s. **Pros:** free Wi-Fi in common areas; nice café on the beach; excellent location and view of the harbor. **Cons:** rooms basic and a bit small and need to be refurbished; charge for Wi-Fi access in rooms. [$] *Rooms from: €130* ✉ *Kounoupitsa beachfront, 1 km (½ mile) west of Dapia, Spetses town* ☎ *22980/72602, 22980/72603, 22980/72604* 🌐 *www.spetses-hotel.gr* 🛏 *77 rooms* ⏲ *Closed Nov.–Mar.* 🍴 *Breakfast.*

FESTIVALS

Fodor's Choice ★ **Armata Festival.** Thousands flock in from all over Greece to attend the Armata festival celebrations on Spetses, held in honor of Panayia Armata (Virgin Mary of the Arms), in what is probably the most glorious weekend on the island's calendar. Spetses mounts an enormous harbor-front reenactment of a War of Independence naval battle during the second week of September (the epic battle took place on September 8, 1822), complete with costumed fighters and burning ships. Book your hotel well in advance if you wish to see this popular event, popularly known as the Armata. There are also concerts and exhibitions the week leading up to it.

Saronic Chamber Festival. The Saronic Chamber Music Festival, home of the Leondari Ensemble, opens on the island of Spetses in August (performances take place at the Poseidonion Grand Hotel), before moving on to Hydra and then Poros. All concerts start at 9pm. ✉ *Poseidonian Grand Hotel, Spetses town* 🌐 *www.saronicfestival.com.*

NIGHTLIFE

For the newest "in" bars, ask at your hotel or just stroll down to the Old Harbor, which has the highest concentration of clubs.

Adore. On the site of the late Brachera, one of the most historic bars of Spetses, the newest arrival on the island's nightlife is Adore. Already popular with the in crowd, the club really comes alive later at night with dance tunes selected by special guest DJs. ⊠ *Palio Limani waterfront, Spetses town* 🕾 *69/4714–1928.*

Bikini Cocktails & Snacks. This bar in a typical neoclassical building stands out for its romantic ambience. Enjoy the atmosphere as you sip one of the imaginative cocktails with names like Oki Monkey and Inferno while sitting at a candlelit table right by the water. Things get more lively later in the evening as this is one of *the* happening places on the island. ⊠ *Palio Limani, Spetses town* 🕾 *22980/74888.*

Spetsa Bar. The island's all-time-classic hangout, where Kostas likes to play music from the 1960s and '70s. It's a perfect choice for a pre-dinner drink (bar opens at 8 pm). ⊠ *Ag. Mama Sq., Spetses town* 🕾 *22980/74131* ⊕ *www.barspetsa.org* ⊗ *Closed Nov.–Mar.*

Stavento Club. Popular since the late 1990s, Stavento allows you to enjoy your drink on a veranda while taking in a picturesque view of the Palio Limani (Old Harbor) before going back inside to resume a night of dancing to popular Greek and international hits. ⊠ *Palio Limani waterfront, Spetses town* 🕾 *22980/75245* ⊕ *www.clubstavento.com.*

Votsalo. Tiny, cozy, and cute, Votsalo is a great meeting point for breakfast (it serves excellent espresso), but is equally popular after sunset, when you can order dreamy cocktails and listen to cool acid jazz tunes. ⊠ *Stavrou Niarchou 79, Dapia, Spetses town* 🕾 *22980/073031.*

SHOPPING

Fodor'sChoice ★ **Isola di Spezzie.** At this traditional Greek grocery, you can find aromatic herbs and spices, homemade jams, dried pasta, sumptuous olives, and other local delicacies that you can taste on the spot before taking home with you. ⊠ *Roloi Sq., Dapia, Spetses town* 🕾 *22980/073982.*

Rota. Locally sourced objects, from silver jewelry and kitchen bowls to souvenirs and decorative gifts, some of them handmade by the owner himself, are showcased here. ⊠ *High street, Dapia, Spetses town* 🕾 *22980/74013* ⊗ *10:30–3 and 5:30–9:30.*

White Spetses. For a healthy dose of retail therapy, head to this clothing boutique, which offers a wide selection of caftans, bikinis, sandals, and other casual-chic clothing. ⊠ *Dapia, Spetses town* 🕾 *22980/073308.*

SPORTS AND THE OUTDOORS

BIKING

The lack of cars and the predominantly level roads make Spetses ideal for cycling. One good trip is along the coastal road that circles the island, going from the main town to Ayia Paraskevi beach.

Ilias Rent-A-Bike. Head here to rent well-maintained mountain bikes (about €7 per day), motorbikes, and other equipment. A handy drop-off and pickup service is available. ⊠ *Ayia Marina Rd., near Analipsis Sq., Spetses town* 🕾 *6973/86407.*

Ayia Marina beach is one of the sizzling reasons why people love Spetses.

BOATING

Spetses Classic Yacht Race. For a long weekend in June, Spetses fills with skippers and sailors who participate in this popular regatta celebrating the island's seafaring tradition. ☎ *210/422–0506 Race organizers, in Piraeus* ⊕ *www.classicyachtrace.com.*

AYIA MARINA ΑΓΙΑ ΜΑΡΙΝΑ

2 km (1½ miles) southeast of Spetses town.

Ayia Marina is the most cosmopolitan beach on the island, so head here if you want to see and be seen.

BEACHES

Ayia Marina. Favored by fashionable Greek socialites, the mostly sandy beach at Ayia Marina is the home of the elegant Paradise Beach Bar, tavernas, and many water sport activities. Sun beds and umbrellas are available for a fee. You can hire a horse-drawn buggy from town to arrive in style, or you can come by caïque. Warning: this beach can get pretty busy during the summer months with a younger, party-loving crowd. **Amenities:** food and drink; showers; toilets; water sports. **Best for:** partiers; swimming; walking. ⊠ *Ayia Marina, Spetses* ☎ *22980/72195 Paradise Beach Bar.*

AYIOI ANARGYROI ΑΓΙΟΙ ΑΝΑΡΓΥΡΟΙ

6 km (4 miles) west of Spetses town.

With plenty of water sports options, this popular beach is set against a luscious green backdrop, offering the added prospect of exploring the nearby Bekiris cave at your own pace.

BEACHES

Ayioi Anargyroi. A clean and cosmopolitan beach, Ayioi Anargyroi has a gently sloped seabed with deep waters suitable for snorkeling, water-skiing, and other water sports (rentals are available on-site). It is the island's best-known beach, 6 km (4 miles) away from town. You can also swim (or take a path) to beautiful Bekiris Cave, a famous historical spot, as Greek revolutionaries used it as a hiding place during the 1821 revolution. Look for the taverna Manolis by the beach; nearby you can hire two sun beds and an umbrella for about €8 a day. There is also a pretty hotel (hotel Acrogiali) right on the beach. **Amenities:** showers; lifeguards; water sports. **Best for:** swimming; walking; snorkeling; windsurfing. ⊠ *Ayioi Anargyroi.*

ZOGERIA ΖΩΓΕΡΙΑ

7½ km (4¾ miles) west of Spetses town.

BEACHES

Zogeria. This little beach offers a day of relaxation away from the cosmopolitan crowds, with few amenities other than the beautiful water. You can rent sun beds and umbrellas from Taverna Loula. On a clear day you can see all the way to Nafplio. **Amenities:** food and drink. **Best for:** solitude; swimming. ⊠ *Zogeria* ☎ *69446/27851 Taverna Loula.*

AYIA PARASKEVI ΑΓΙΑ ΠΑΡΑΣΚΕΥΗ

10 km (6 miles) west of Spetses town.

Located in a sheltered cove and easily accessible by bus or water taxi, this is a favorite with locals and visitors alike. In the height of summer the pine trees offer some much needed natural shade.

BEACHES

Ayia Paraskevi. Pine trees, a canteen, sun beds, and umbrellas line Ayia Paraskevi, a sheltered and popular beach with a mostly sandy shore (and coarse pebbles in other parts). Look for the cubic Ayia Paraskevi chapel at the back—it has given its name to the bay. Many locals consider this beach the most beautiful on the island; it can be reached either via road or with a caïque. The beach gets fairly busy during the summer months, then it's a great spot for people-watching. **Amenities:** food and drink. **Best for:** walking; swimming; snorkeling. ⊠ *Ayia Paraskevi, Spetses.*

THE SPORADES

Skiathos, Skopelos, and Skyros

WELCOME TO THE SPORADES

TOP REASONS TO GO

★ **Sun-and-Fun Skiathos:** Thousands of international sunseekers head here to enjoy famous beaches and then work on their neon tans in the buzzing nightclubs.

★ **Skyros's Style:** Set against a dramatic rock, the main town of Skyros is a showstopper of Cycladic houses colorfully set with folk wood carvings and embroideries.

★ **Sylvan Skopelos:** Not far from the verdant forests lie 40 picturesque monasteries and Skopelos town, which may remind some of Positano.

★ **Golden Sands:** The beaches are best on Skiathos, the star location being Koukounaries, whose luscious sands are famous throughout Greece.

★ **"Forever England":** The grave of Edwardian poet Rupert Brooke draws pilgrims to Vouno on Skyros.

1 Skiathos. The 3,900 residents are eclipsed by the 50,000 visitors who come here each year for clear blue waters and scores of beaches, including the world-famous Koukounaries. Close to the mainland, this island has some of the aura of the Pelion peninsula, with red-roof villages and picturesque hills. Beauty spots include the monastery of Evangelistria and Lalaria beach.

2 Skopelos. Second largest of the Sporades, this island is lushly forested and more prized by ecologists than fun-seekers. The steep streets of Skopelos town need mountain-goat negotiating skills, but the charming alleys are irresistible, as are the island's monasteries, the famous cheese pies, and the traditional *kalivia* farmhouses around Panormos bay.

GETTING ORIENTED

This small cluster of islands off the coast of central Greece is just a short hop from the mainland and, consequently, often overrun in high season. Obviously, the Cyclades aren't the only Greek islands that serve up a cup of culture and a gallon of hedonism to travelers looking for that perfect tan. Each of the Sporades is very individual in character. Due east of tourism-oriented Skiathos are lesser visited eco-blessed Skopelos and folk-craft-famous Skyros.

6

○ PSATHOURA

GIOURA

PIPERI

PELAGOS

Aegean Sea

SKANTZOURA

SPORADES

SKYROS

Atsitsa

3

Skyros Town

SKYROPOULA   Linaria   Vouno

ERINIA

VALAXA

SARAKINA

3 Skyros. Located at the virtual center of the Aegean Sea, this Sporades Shangri-la is the southernmost of the island group. The top half is covered with pine forests and is home to Skyros town, a Cycladic cubic masterpiece, which climbs a spectacular rock peak and is a tangle of lanes, whitewashed houses, and Byzantine churches. The arid southern half is the site of noted Edwardian poet Rupert Brooke's grave, at Vouno.

Updated
by Alexia
Amvrazi

Little mentioned in mythology or history, the Sporades confidently rely on their great natural beauty and cultural history to attract visitors. Some locals poetically claim them to be the handful of colored pebbles the gods were left with after creating the world, and as an afterthought, they flung them over the northwestern Aegean.

Bustling with tourists, Skiathos sits closest to the mainland; it has a pretty harbor area and the noisiest nightlife, international restaurants and pubs, and resort hotels. Due east is Skopelos, covered with dense, fragrant pines, where you can visit scenic villages, hundreds of churches, and lush beaches. The least contemporary of the islands, it is the most naturally beautiful and has a fascinating old hill town.

Then there is traditional Skyros. Some visitors return year after year to this mythical isle, southeast of the other islands, for its quiet fishing villages, expansive beaches, and stunning cubist eagles-nest of a town that seems to spill down a hill. As a current citadel of Greek defense, Skyros also has the bonus of an airport.

Like emerald beads scattered on sapphire satin, the aptly named Sporades ("scattered ones") are resplendent with pines, ripe fruit, and olive trees. The lush countryside, marked with sloping slate roofs and wooden balconies, reflects the aura of the neighboring, hauntingly beautiful Pelion peninsula, to which the islands were once attached. Only on Skyros, farther out in the Aegean, will you see a windswept, treeless landscape with steep cobbled slopes, or the cubist architecture of the Cyclades. Sitting by itself, Skyros is neither geographically nor historically related to the other Sporades.

The Sporades have changed hands constantly throughout history, and wars, plunder, and earthquakes have eliminated all but the strongest ancient walls. A few castles and monasteries remain, but these islands are better suited for having fun than for sightseeing. Skiathos is the most touristy, in some cases to the point of overkill, while less-developed Skopelos has fewer (but purer) beaches and a far less contrived nightlife, but has a main town that is said to be the most beautiful in the Sporades. Late to attract tourists, Skyros is the least traveled of the Sporades (probably because it is hardest to reach). It's also the quirkiest, with well-preserved traditions.

Quintessential Greek-island delights beckon on all three islands: sun, sand, and surf, along with starlit dinners. Almost all restaurants have outside seating, often under cooling trees, where you can watch the passing classically Greek, ubiquitous dramas of daily life: lovers arm-in-arm, stealing a kiss; children running free through village squares; sizzling arguments that end in friendship; fishermen cleaning their bright yellow nets and exchanging banter as they work. Relax and immerse yourself in the blue-and-green watercolor of it all.

PLANNING

WHEN TO GO
Winter is least desirable, as the weather turns cold and rainy; most hotels, rooms, and restaurants are closed, and ferry service is minimal. If you do go from November through April, book in advance and leave nothing to chance. The same advice applies to July and August peak season, when everything is open but overcrowded, except on Skyros. The *meltemi*, the brisk north-easterly summer wind of the Aegean, keeps things cooler than on the mainland even on the hottest days. Late spring and early summer are ideal, as most hotels are open, crowds have not arrived, the air is warm, and the roadsides and fields of flowers are incredible; September is also mild.

If you want to catch one of the Sporades' famous religious and cultural festivals on your visit, keep the following dates in mind. The lively Carnival (February) traditions of Skopelos, although not as exotic as those of Skyros, parody the expulsion of the once-terrifying Barbary pirates. August 15 is the day of the Panayia (Festival of the Virgin), celebrated on Skyros at Magazia Beach and on Skopelos in the main town; cultural events there continue to late August. Skiathos hosts several cultural events in summer, including a dance festival in July. Feast days? Skiathos: July 26, for St. Paraskevi; Skopelos: February 25, for St. Riginosi.

PLANNING YOUR TIME
Inveterate island hoppers might spend one night on each island, although your trip might be more comfortable if you plant yourself on one. There are regular cruises that travel around the Sporades in three to four days, but as each of the islands are so very varied, it's worth spending at least two days on each. That noted, you can get around Skiathos and Skopelos in a total of two days, since there are daily ferry connections between them and they are relatively near each other. Traveling between these islands and Skyros, however, requires advance planning, since ferries and flights to Skyros are much less frequent. Also, make sure that you are arriving and leaving from the correct harbor: some islands, such as Skopelos, have more than one from which to depart. Five days can be just enough for touching each island in summer; off-season you need more days to accommodate the ferry schedule.

How to choose if you're only visiting one of the Sporades? If you're the can't-sit-still type and think crowds add to the fun, Skiathos is your island. By day you can take in the beautiful, thronged beaches and Evangelistria Monastery or the fortress-turned-cultural-center, and at night stroll the port to find the most hopping nightclub. Day people with a historical bent should explore Skopelos's many monasteries and churches and its 18th-century Folk Art Museum. Skyros should be at the top of your list if you're a handicraft collector, as the island's furniture, embroidery, and pottery are admired throughout the country and can be bought and sent abroad from several shops.

GETTING HERE AND AROUND

AIR TRAVEL

During the summer Olympic Air flies almost daily—or even twice a day, depending on the period—to Skiathos from Athens International Airport at varying times. The trip takes 45 minutes. In summer there are also weekly flights from Athens and Thessaloniki to Skyros Airport. Aegean Air flies from Athens; the flight takes 40 minutes. Olympic Air flies from Thessaloniki; the flight takes 40 minutes. Fares vary dramatically depending on how far in advance you book.

Skiathos Airport also has direct charter flights from many European cities.

BOAT AND FERRY TRAVEL

Ferry travel to Skiathos and Skopelos requires that you drive or take a bus to Agios Konstantinos, located 2½ hours north of Athens; if arriving from central or northern Greece, however, you may wish to board a ferry at the big port of Volos or Thessaloniki. For all ferries, it's best to call a travel agency ahead of time to check schedules and prices and to book your ferry in advance—especially if you are bringing a car—as boat times change seasonally. Tickets are also available from several travel agents on the dock. Madro is recommended for advance bookings (⇨ *Travel Agencies*).

Altogether, there are at least three to four ferries per day in the summer from Agios Konstantinos to Skiathos (these may be regular ferries or the so-called "Flying Dolphin" and "Flyingcat" ferries, which are smaller, faster, and more expensive but do not take cars). There are significantly fewer departures in winter.

Fast ferries from Agios Konstantinos to Skiathos take approximately 90 minutes and cost €32–€37; ferries continue to Skopelos in another 60 minutes and cost €40–€49.50. Regular ferries from Agois Konstantinos to Skiathos take about 3 hours and cost €30.50; ferries continue to Skopelos in another hour and 45 minutes and cost €38. From Volos, the travel time is slightly less and has similar pricing.

Getting to Skyros is trickier. You must drive or take a bus to Kimi—on the giant island of Evia—and then catch one of the two daily ferries (or the weekly hydrofoil) to Skyros. You can buy ferry tickets at the Kimi dock when you get off the bus; the trip to Skyros takes two hours and costs €9. Should you choose to book your return when you get to Skyros, note that Skyros Travel (⇨ *Travel Agencies*) has a virtual monopoly on hydrofoil tickets.

Regular ferries also connect Skiathos and Skopelos. From Skopelos to Skyros there are two ferries weekly, and the ticket price is €21. The once-per-week Flying Dolphin hydrofoil that travels from Kimi, on the large nearby island of Evia, to all the Sporades is by far the quicker, more reliable way to travel between the islands. Because schedules change frequently, check the timetables listed outside travel agencies in each of the port towns; the agents sell tickets. Connecting through Kimi is the easiest way to get between Skyros and the other islands (the alternative is to fly from Athens). *For information on ferry companies, see Boat and Ferry Travel in Travel Smart.*

Contacts Port Authority ☏ *223/5031759 in Agios Konstantinos, 222/2022606 in Kimi, 242/7022017 in Skiathos town, 242/4022180 in Skopelos town, 222/2091475 in Skyros town.*

BUS TRAVEL

From Central Athens, buses leave every hour to Agios Konstantinos, the main port for the Sporades (except Skyros, for which ferries leave from Kimi on the island of Evia). Fares are about €15.70, and travel time is about 2½ hours. Buses from Athens to Kimi, on Evia island (the only port from which boats depart for Skyros) cost €15.30 and take 2½ hours. The trip between Agios Konstantinos and Halkidha, on Evia island, costs €8 and takes 90 minutes. Both schedules and fares change, so be sure to verify them with KTEL or a travel agent.

Bus service is available throughout the Sporades, although on some islands buses run more frequently than on others.

Contacts Athens to Agios Konstantinos ☏ *22/3102–2802 for reservations, 210/831–7147 in Athens* ⊕ *www.ktelfthiotidos.gr.* **Athens to Skyros** ☏ *210/8317163 in Athens.*

CAR TRAVEL

To get to Skiathos and Skopelos by car, you must drive to the port of Agios Konstantinos (Agios), and from there, take the ferry. The drive to Agios from Athens takes about two hours. For high-season travel you might have to reserve a place on the car ferry a day ahead. For Skyros you must leave from the port of Kimi on the big island of Evia. From Athens, take the Athens–Lamia National Road to Skala Oropou, and make the 30-minute ferry crossing to Eretria on Evia (every half-hour in the daytime). No reservations are needed. Because it is so close to the mainland, you can skip the ferry system and drive directly to Evia over a short land bridge connecting Agios Minas on the mainland with Halkidha. From Athens, about 80 km (50 miles) away, take the National Road 1 to the Schimatari exit, and then follow the signs to Halkidha. Beware that weekend crowds can slow traffic across the bridge.

The best way to get around is by renting a car (ideally with four-wheel drive), but be warned: in the busy summer months, parking is hard to come by in the main towns and villages. Using public transport or a scooter can work as well, though scooters are best for experienced riders. A lot of hotels now provide shuttle services in and out of town. Car rentals cost €30–€70 per day, while scooters cost €14–€30 (with insurance). Scooters are ubiquitous, but if you rent a scooter, be extra cautious: some of those for hire are in poor condition. The locals are not used to the heavy summer traffic on their narrow roads, and accidents provide the island clinics with 80% of their summer business. Check with local travel agencies for rental information.

On Skiathos, car-rental companies include Aivaliotis Rental, Avis, and The First. On Skopelos, there's Alamo/National. On Skyros, companies include Martina's and Pegasus. See the individual island sections for detailed contact information.

TAXI TRAVEL

Taxis throughout the Sporades are unmetered, so be sure to negotiate your fare in advance or (better) check with your hotel for correct fares. You will find "Piatsa" taxi ranks next to all the harbor ports and airports, and taxis will be lined up even late at night if there is a boat or flight coming in. On the other hand, your hotel can usually arrange a taxi for you, but if you need one in the wee hours of the morning make sure you book it in advance. The prices on the islands are not cheap (compared to Athens or Thessaloniki), and can be as much as €10 to €20 for a 10-minute drive.

HOTELS

Accommodations reflect the pace of tourism on each particular island: Skopelos has a fair number of hotels, Skiathos a huge number, and there are far fewer on Skyros. Most hotels close from October or November to April or May. Reservations are a good idea, though you may learn about rooms in pensions and private homes when you arrive at the airport or ferry landing. The best bet, especially for those on a budget, is to rent a converted room in a private house—look for the Greek National Tourism Organization (EOT or GNTO) license displayed in windows. Owners meet incoming ferries to tout their location, offer rooms, and negotiate the price. In Skyros most people take lodgings in town or along the beach at Magazia and Molos: you must choose between being near the sea or the town's bars and eateries. Accommodations are basic, and not generally equipped with television sets. Always negotiate rates off-season.

RESTAURANTS

In the Sporades, most tavernas are opened from midday until just past midnight, and welcome guests to stay as long as they like. Unless you are looking for a gourmet experience you can't go wrong with a salad and fish, or a home-cooked moussaka. Be sure to ask the waiter what fresh fish they serve and what are the dishes of the day, and don't hesitate to go inside and see the food for yourself before ordering. As with everywhere in Greece, the *hima* (homemade) house wine is usually good enough, sometimes excellent; the waiter will not mind if you order a taste before deciding.

As for your food, traditional recipes such as *mageirefta* (home-cooked) dishes based on local meat and vegetables, and a variety of fresh fish, reign supreme in the Sporades, but the rendition you taste can be a hit-or-miss experience—that is, if you are looking for truly succulent, fresh, and authentic food with an imaginative twist. To better your chance, dining where the locals dine is always a good idea, as is exploring past the harbor fronts and seeking out smaller tavernas often hidden along the side streets. Look for local specialties such as the *Skopelitiki tiropita*, or cheese pie (a spiral of tubed phyllo pastry filled with creamy white feta and fried to a crispy texture), or the fluffy *avgato* yellow plums in light syrup that can be savored as a dressing for fresh yogurt or on a small plate as *glyko koutaliou* (spoon sweet).

DINING AND LODGING PRICES IN EUROS			
	$	$$	$$$	$$$$
Restaurants	Under €16	€16–€25	€26–€40	Over €40
Hotels	Under €126	€126–€225	€226–€275	Over €275

Restaurant prices are the average cost of a main course at dinner, or if dinner is not served at lunch. Hotel prices are the lowest price for a standard double room in high season.

VISITOR INFORMATION

There are few main official tourist offices for the Sporades. The closest you'll come is the Skiathos Municipality agency. In lieu of official agencies, however, there are an array of private travel agencies, and these offer myriad services, tickets, car rentals, and guided tours. See the individual islands sections for specific recommendations.

SKIATHOS ΣΚΙΑΘΟΣ

Part sacred (scores of churches), part profane (active nightlife), the hilly, wooded island of Skiathos is the closest of the Sporades to the Pelion peninsula. It covers an area of only 42 square km (16 square miles), but it has some 70 beaches and sandy coves. A jet-set island 25 years ago, today it teems with European—mostly British—tourists on package deals promising sun, sea, and late-night revelry. Higher prices and a bit of Mykonos's attitude are part of the deal, too.

In winter most of the island's 5,000 or so inhabitants live in its main city, Skiathos town, built after the War of Independence on the site of the colony founded in the 8th century BC by the Euboean city-state of Chalkis. Like Skopelos and Alonissos, Skiathos was on good terms with the Athenians, prized by the Macedonians, and treated gently by the Romans. Saracen and Slav raids left it virtually deserted during the early Middle Ages, but it started to prosper during the later Byzantine years.

When the Crusaders deposed their fellow Christians from the throne of Constantinople in 1204, Skiathos and the other Sporades became the fief of the Ghisi, knights of Venice. One of their first acts was to fortify the hills on the islet separating the two bays of Skiathos harbor. Now connected to the shore, this former islet, the Bourtzi, still has a few stout walls and buttresses shaded by some graceful pine trees.

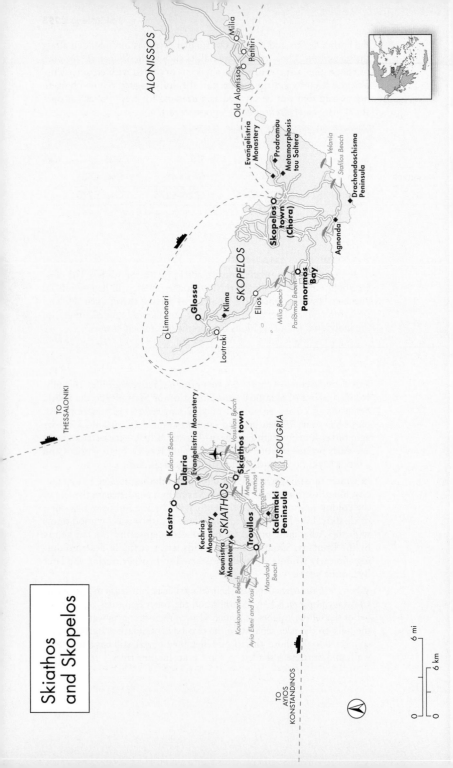

GETTING HERE AND AROUND

AIR TRAVEL

The island airport is located 1 km (½ miles) northeast of Skiathos town; buses to town are very infrequent so plan on jumping in a taxi to get to your hotel.

Contacts Skiathos Airport ⊠ *1 km (½ mile) northeast of Skiathos town* ☎ *24/2702–9100, 24/2702–9101.*

BOAT TRAVEL

Ferries run regularly to Skiathos from both Agios Konstantinos and Volos, and these generally continue to Skopelos. There is also a daily hydrofoil to Thessaloniki as well as weekly ferry service to Santorini (13 hours). There are only a couple of boats that connect Skiathos with Skyros weekly so it is advisable only if you have plenty of time at your disposal or you are well organized.

Caïques leave from the main port for the most popular beaches, and interisland excursions are also made between Skiathos and Skopelos. You can also head to the harbor and look around for a caïque (haggle over the price) or a sailboat with skipper to hire and tour around the islands; they are generally the preferred way to get around by day. For popular routes, captains have signs of their destinations and departure times posted.

BUS TRAVEL

The main bus route on Skiathos connects Skiathos town with the famed beach at Koukounaries (Maratha), a 30-minute ride. With half-hour departures in high season, the route has 20 other stops, mostly along the southern coast of the island. Fares are €1.50 to €3, with service from 7:30 am to 1 am in high season. The main taxi stand is near the ferry pier.

CAR TRAVEL

Several companies, including Aivaliotis Rental, Avis, and The First operate on Skiathos. *For information on international car-rental firms, see Car Travel in Travel Smart.*

Contacts Aivaliotis Rental ⊠ *Port of Skiathos, Skiathos town* ☎ *242/7021246* ⊕ *www.skiathoscheapcarrental.gr.* **The First** ⊠ *Papadiamantis street, Skiathos town* ☎ *24/2702–2810, 69/4244–3165 mobile* ⊕ *www.skiathoshire.com.*

TAXI TRAVEL

Arrange taxis through your hotel, or you can call operators directly.

Contacts Skiathos Taxi Rank (*Skiathos Piasta*). ⊠ *Port of Skiathos, Skiathos town* ☎ *24/2702–4461.*

TRAVEL AGENCIES

Contacts Dolphin of Skiathos. This travel agency offers a wide range of services, from booking ferry tickets and accommodation to leading excursions around Skiathos and the rest of the Sporades. ⊠ *Parodos Evaggelistrias, Skiathos town* ☎ *24270/21910* ⊕ *www.dolphin-skiathos.gr.*

VISITOR INFORMATION

Contacts Skiathos Municipality ⊠ *Nikotsara street 12, Skiathos town* ☎ *242/7022022* ⊕ *www.skiathos.gr.*

SKIATHOS TOWN ΣΚΙΑΘΟΣ (ΠΟΛΗ)

2½ hours by ferry from Agios Konstantinos.

Though the harbor is picturesque from a distance—especially from a ferry docking at sunset, when a violet-orange light casts a soft glow and the lights on the hills behind the quay start twinkling like faint stars—Skiathos town close-up has few buildings of any distinction. Many traditional houses were burned by the Germans in 1944, and postwar development has pushed up cement apartments between the pleasant, squat, red-roof older houses. Magenta bougainvillea, sweet jasmine, and the casual charm of brightly painted balconies and shutters camouflage most of the eyesores as you wander through the narrow lanes and climb up the steep steps that serve as streets. Activity centers on the waterfront or on Papadiamantis, the main drag, with banks, travel agents, telephones, post offices, police and tourist police stations, plus myriad cafés, fast-food joints, postcard stands, tacky souvenir shops, tasteful jewelry stores, and car- and bike-rental establishments. Shops, bars, and restaurants line the cobbled side streets, where you can also spot the occasional modest hotel and rooms-to-rent signs. The east side of the port (more commonly known as the New Port), where the larger boats and Flying Dolphin hydrofoils dock, is not as interesting. The little church and clock tower of Ayios Nikolaos watch over it from a hill reached by steps so steep they're almost perpendicular to the earth.

EXPLORING

Bourtzi. A lovely physical feature of Skiathos harbor—standing on a small, piney peninsula that divides the main port—the Bourtzi was a fortress built in 1207 by the Venetian Gyzi brothers to protect Skiathos from pirate attacks. Not much remains of the original building, also called "the castle of St. George," yet the cultural center here hosts wonderful events every summer, particularly in July and August, when art and antiquities exhibitions and open-air performances entertain tourists and locals alike. It's well worth taking in the view of the harbor from the tranquil, refreshing spots found here; west of the waterfront you'll see the fishing port where caïques come and go. The sidewalk is increasingly filled with cafés and *ouzeris* (ouzo bars) and, at the far end of the port beginning at the square and set around the 1846 church of Trion Hierarchon, more elegant restaurants spread out under awnings. There is also a café-bar at the Bourtzi itself. ⊠ *End of causeway extending from port.*

Papadiamantis Museum. The House of Papadiamantis is a tribute to one of Greece's finest writers, Alexandros Papadiamantis (1851–1911), lauded by some as "the Greek Dostoyevsky." His native Skiathos played a prominent role in his essays, short stories, and novels, as did plots strongly inspired by the human condition, war, pirate invasions, the Greek Orthodox faith, captivity, and simple rural life. Several of his novels have been translated into English, including the internationally acclaimed *The Murderess*. The exhibits here deal with the author's daily life, ranging from his furniture and personal belongings to vintage photographs. ⊠ *Right off Papadiamanti street at fork* ☎ *242/7023843* 🎫 *€1.50* ⊙ *July and Aug., daily 9:30–1:30 and 5:30–8:30; Sept.–June, daily 9:30–1:30 and 5:30–8:30; Closed Mon.*

On Skiathos, the coast is always clear.

BEACHES

Skiathos is known for its beaches, but as has happened so many times before throughout Greece, unchecked popularity has a way of spoiling special places. Since the arrival of mainly English expatriates in the early 1960s, the beautiful, piney 14-km (9-miles) stretch of coast running south of the town to the famed, gold-sand Koukounaries beach has become an almost continuous array of villas, hotels, and tavernas. One beach succeeds another, and in summer the asphalted coastal road carries a constant torrent of cars, buses, motorbikes, and pedestrians buzzing from beach to beach like frenzied bees sampling pollen-laden flowers. To access most beaches, you must take little, usually unpaved, lanes down to the sea. Along this coast, the beaches—**Megali Ammos, Vassilias, Achladia, Tzaneria, Vromolimnos,** and **Platania**—all offer water sports, umbrellas, lounge chairs, and plenty of company.

Megali Ammos. Walking distance from Skiathos town, the sandy stretch of Megali Ammos is an easy option for many. The bars and eating options lining the back of the beach have sun loungers reaching down to the water's edge, and many of the bars offer a free drink when you rent one for the day. There is a water-sports school on the busier right side of the beach where you can enjoy white-knuckle rides on giant inflatable bananas and doughnuts pulled at high speeds by little motorboats. **Amenities:** food and drink; lifeguard; showers; toilets; water sports. **Best for:** swimming. ⊹ *Walk west over the hill then on the coastal road past the Eye Q Resort and Megali Ammos Guesthouse.*

Vassilias Beach. One of the better beaches close to Skiathos town, parts of Vassilias beach have qualities of some of the more distant unspoiled shore lines. Pine trees lean thirstily toward the shallow seashore lending themselves as shade to those who wish to rest under their aromatic branches. A rustic canteen serves up refreshments that can be enjoyed while lazing on lounge chairs and gazing at the splendor of the Old Town beyond the twinkling waters. On the right side of the beach, where some hotels spill down the hillside, there are places to eat like Vassilias Beach Hotel's restaurant Ta Nissia, while Stefanos Ski School offers all sorts of sea-based adventures. There are rows of shaded sun loungers on this stretch of beach but some are reserved for hotel guests so to be sure ask an attendant first. **Amenities:** food and drink; parking (free); showers; toilets; water sports. **Best for:** snorkeling; swimming; walking. ✉ *2 km (1 mile) from Old Town.*

YOUR OWN PRIVATE ISLAND

Nine idyllic islets lush with pines and olive groves surround Skiathos, and two lie across the main harbor, with safe anchorage and a small marina. You can sail over, or hire a caïque, to swim and sun on the isolated beaches.

Vromolimnos. One of the most popular and therefore busiest beaches on Skiathos, Vromolimnos has a beach bar and café that blasts music all day long creating the party vibe. On this luxuriously sandy beach you can also partake in water sports such as waterskiing, which is especially good in the afternoon when the sea usually calms to a lake-like smoothness. On the opposite end of the beach, just far enough away from the pulsating tunes and rumbling boat engines, there's space to lie out a towel and soak up the sun. There's also a decent little taverna. **Amenities:** food and drink; lifeguard; parking (free); showers; toilets; water sports. **Best for:** partiers; sunset; swimming. ✉ *Kolios* ✣ *8 km (5 miles) south west of Skiathos town.*

WHERE TO EAT

$ INTERNATIONAL

🍴 **Amphiliki.** Set on a balcony overlooking Siferi bay, this restaurant, open throughout the day, pairs an inviting ozonic breeze with one of the most sprawling views in town. The menu is focused on fresh local fish, and the latest additions to the menu are an entrée of fresh tuna fillet sautéed with onion and lemon and "Chef" mussels cooked in a mustard and feta sauce. Owner Christos takes pride in the organic vegetables he serves, which are all sourced from his own garden. Service is attentive and the white house wine crisp and refreshing. Leave space for the feather-light traditional *ekmek* (custard cake) with mastic ice cream or try the restaurant's cheesecake if you prefer a more Western dessert. [$] *Average main: €15* ✉ *Agia Triada, opposite health center* ☎ *242/7022839* 🌐 *www.amfiliki.gr* ✍ *Reservations essential* ⏲ *Closed Oct.–May.*

$ TAPAS

🍴 **Don Quijote Tapas Bar Restaurant.** The tapas bar, a rare type of restaurant to find not only on Skiathos but in the country overall, will provide you with a pleasant change of flavor and scene. Its colorful selection of hot and cold tapas includes classic Spanish eats such as paella and *jamon* (Spanish crude ham) as well as Greek-inspired appetizers, to be savored with a local or Spanish wine, or a refreshing mojito. Try also the tuna tartare, made with fresh local tuna and seasoned with a zingy lime and coriander dressing. The Catalan *cream* (a Spanish version of crème brûlée) or the chocolate soufflé make for two sweet finales. A friendly waitstaff is happy to advise you on dishes as you take in the expansive harbor view, intoxicated by the lively atmosphere—but not the noise—of the main town below. $ *Average main: €15* ⊠ *East harbor* ☎ 242/7021600 ⚷ *Reservations essential.*

$$
CONTEMPORARY
Fodor'sChoice
★

✕ **The Final Step.** Atop the hill in Skiathos town, enjoy spectacular views of the new harbor while dining on some familiar "modern" dishes that artfully borrow Mediterranean and Asian flavors. Each dessert is better than the next, and you can try them all by ordering the medley for two—a sampling of each and every one! The climb to reach the restaurant is short but vigorous; however, the food and ambience will have you clambering back up again for more. $ *Average main: €17* ⊠ *Ayios Nikolaos Sq.* ☎ 24270/21877, 69/7188–4249 ⊕ *www. finalsteprestaurant.com* ⚷ *Reservations essential.*

$
SEAFOOD

✕ **Ta Psarädika.** You can't get any closer to the fish market than this family-run taverna, and the fresh seafood dishes (served grilled or fried) prove it. Sit outside facing the sea and sip an icy ouzo while sampling a variety of *mezedes* (appetizers), or if you prefer a heartier meal, try some of the finny creatures: mussels steamed in wine, or the taverna's specialty of fresh swordfish with a rosemary, garlic, raisin, and honey sauce, or a seafood pasta with tomato sauce. Psaradika also serves fresh and boiled salads, grilled meats, and a few traditional home-style dishes like the oil-based *ladera* stuffed tomatoes and creamy moussaka. $ *Average main: €12* ⊠ *Far end of Old Port* ☎ 242/7023412.

$$
INTERNATIONAL

✕ **The Windmill.** Escape the buzz of Skopelos town by climbing up the hill above Ayios Nikolaos to dine at this well-restored 1880s mill–turned– unpretentiously elegant restaurant. Run by Scottish Karen McCann, the Windmill offers the town's most awesome views of the moonlit harbor accompanied by a gourmet rendition of British pub dishes with a breezy Mediterranean and Southeast Asian twist. Start with the calamari with Parmesan crumb, chili, and ginger dip, then sample the popular chargrilled fillet of beef (with a choice of sauces such as peppercorn or mushroom and bacon) before ending with a rich dessert. The Windmill has a little balcony that seats two, which places diners at the highest spot above the town; if you'd like to dine at new heights, book this coveted perch way in advance. $ *Average main: €17* ⊠ *Above clock tower, Kotronia* ☎ 242/7024550 ⊕ *www.skiathoswindmill.gr* ⚷ *Reservations essential* ⊘ *No lunch.*

WHERE TO STAY

$
RESORT

⌂ **Alkyon.** Don't be put off by the boxy exterior and the lack of architectural embellishments—this discreet, light-filled hotel has many rooms offering lovely views of the new harbor—be sure to specify that you want a room with a sea view when booking. **Pros:** comfortable, sunny rooms all come with private balconies; inviting lounge areas. **Cons:** hotel location is near nightlife district so get a room looking at the sea rather than the town (unless you enjoy the noise or merriment); not wheelchair-accessible. $ *Rooms from: €90* ⊠ *New Port* ☎ 242/7022981 ⊕ *www.alkyon-skiathos.gr* ⇗ *90 rooms* ⊘ *Closed Nov.–Mar.* ⎮⊙⎮ *Breakfast.*

$$$
HOTEL
Fodor's Choice
★

⊡ Bourtzi Boutique Hotel. Run by brothers Dimitris and Stanis, this stylish, contemporary hotel has received beaming reviews for its efficient staff and relaxing, luxurious ambience—the simple yet elegant exterior doesn't divulge the far sparklier plushness of the lobby and or the cream-and-gold bar, which is a popular hot spot for chic socializing over cocktails and snacks while watching the world go by on the main street. **Pros:** a great option for travelers seeking a more sophisticated stay; there is an elevator and ramps. **Cons:** no rooms that accommodate large families. $ *Rooms from: €240* ⊠ *Moraitou 8* ☎ *242/7021304* ⊕ *www.hotelbourtzi.gr* ⊃ *38 rooms* ⁺◯⁺ *Breakfast.*

$
B&B/INN

⊡ Fresh Studios. Owners Astergios and Spyros can be counted on to entertain when imparting their in-depth knowledge of the island if you are a guest at their hotel, which is mostly comprised of simple studios with basic modern furnishings complete with kitchenettes. **Pros:** relatively low prices given the nice view, location, and decor; Wi-Fi available in all the rooms. **Cons:** quite a few steps leading up to some of the rooms. $ *Rooms from: €50* ⊠ *New Port* ☎ *24270/21998* ⊕ *www. myskiathosrooms.com* ⊃ *7 rooms* ⁺◯⁺ *Breakfast.*

$
HOTEL

⊡ Mouria Hotel and Taverna. Located in the heart of the main town and a quality choice for budget travelers, this family-run hotel and restaurant—managed by Greek-American Harriet Ioannou and her husband, Yiannis—offers clean, cool, and cheerful guest rooms ideal for pairs (or families: some can accommodate up to six people and have access to kitchen and laundry facilities). **Pros:** very cozy and friendly; affordable. **Cons:** rooms overlooking Papadiamantis street can be noisy during high season. $ *Rooms from: €50* ⊠ *Behind National Bank, Papadiamantis street* ☎ *242/7023069* ⊕ *www.mouriahotel.com* ⊃ *12 rooms* ⊘ *Closed Oct.–May* ⁺◯⁺ *Breakfast.*

$
HOTEL

⊡ Villa Ariadni. Uniquely located near the beautiful lake of Agios Georgios and a beach—while being only a 15-minute walk from the main town—Villa Ariadni offers simply furnished, newly renovated island-style studios and apartments (for up to six guests), all of which overlook the sea or lake. **Pros:** self-sufficiency; disability-friendly. **Cons:** out of town, and close to the airport. $ *Rooms from: €75* ⊠ *Agios Georgios* ☎ *242/7022931* ⊕ *www.ariadnivilla.gr* ⊃ *11 rooms* ⁺◯⁺ *Breakfast.*

NIGHTLIFE

Skiathos is filled with night owls, and for good reason. Bars for all tastes line main and side streets, from pubs run by Brits to quintessential Greek bouzouki joints in beach tavernas. Most of the nightlife in Skiathos town is centered along the waterfront and on Papadiamantis, Politechniou, and Evangelistrias streets.

CINEMAS

Cinema Attikon. To enjoy the silver screen under the summer stars spend a few hours at Attikon Cinema, which screens three different films per week and often two English-language films per night (with a regular tribute to *Mamma Mia!*), from 9 pm on. ⊠ *Papadiamantis street* ☎ *242/7022352.*

MUSIC AND NIGHTCLUBS

Bourtzi Café. For a real change of pace take a gentle stroll to a lesser-known café/bar at the tip of the Bourtzi fortress's promontory. Here, like the locals, you can enjoy an affordable seaside drink away from the madding crowds. ⊠ *Bourtzi.*

Kahlua. For late-night action along a row of hopping clubs, head to Kahlua, which has indoor and outdoor dancing and is open in summer. Doors open 10:30—the action doesn't usually get going tilt after midnight—and it goes until at least 3 am. ⊠ *Tasos Antonaros (New Port)* ☎ *242/7023205* ⊕ *www.kahluaclub.com* ☉ *Closed Sept.–June.*

Kentavros Bar. This popular bar entertains a young professional crowd with rhythm and blues, funk, soul, and classic rock starting at 9:30 pm. ⊠ *Papadiamantis Sq.* ☎ *242/7022980* ☉ *Closed Oct.–Apr.*

Rock 'n' Roll Bar. Situated by the Old Port, Rock 'n' Roll is one of the crop of lounge bars to have made its home on the large cobbled steps leading away from the waterfront. The outdoor spaces are lit with twinkling candles and adorned with comfy low couches and giant cushions. And, as the night wears on and temperatures cool, the atmosphere and music heat up. Happy hour is 7–9 pm every night when the colorful cocktails are half price. ⊠ *Old Port* ☎ *24270/22944.*

Slip Inn. Popular during the day for its good coffee, the Slip Inn transforms into a funky lounge at night where passion-fruit margaritas are best enjoyed resting on one elbow, Dionysian style, on multicolor floor cushions. ⊠ *Old Port, Antoniou Riga bay* ☎ *24270/21006* ☉ *Closed Oct.–Apr.*

SPORTS AND THE OUTDOORS

SAILING

Active Yachts. For multiday charters with or without crew, contact Active Yachts; weekly charter rates start at €2,499. They also rent out motorboats by the day. ⊠ *Portside* ☎ *69/7224–5391, 24270/29028* ⊕ *activeyachts.gr* ☉ *Closed Oct.–Apr.*

SCUBA DIVING

Dolphin Diving Center. Skiathos is the only Sporades island with scuba-diving schools, and its popular beaches often have diving-equipment rentals and instructors on hand. Dolphin Diving Center, the first in operation, offers single or multiple dives, as well as full-certification programs. Prices for diving courses start at €50. ⊠ *Hotel Nostos, Tzaneria Beach, Kalamaki peninsula* ☎ *24270/21599, 69/4499–9181* ⊕ *www.ddiving.gr* ☉ *Closed Nov.–Apr.*

SHOPPING

ANTIQUES AND CRAFTS

Galerie Varsakis. Kilims, embroideries, jewelry, icons, and hundreds of antiques from around the world are available here, all set off by proprietor Charalambos Varsaki's impressive surrealistic paintings and prints. Also noteworthy is his collection of guns and swords dating to 1780–1820 and used in the Greek War of Independence. ⊠ *Trion Hierarchon Sq.* ☎ *242/7022255* ⊕ *www.varsakis.com* ☉ *Closed 2–6 pm.*

JEWELRY

Phaedra. Celebrating jewelry making with an artsy twist, Phaedra showcases silver and gold pieces that are part of collections by noteworthy Greek designers. ✉ *Papadiamantis 23* ☎ *242/7921233.*

Seraïna. Greek jewelry, original-looking glass lampshades, and a variety of ceramic plates are among the wares here. ✉ *Papadiamantis 13* ☎ *242/7022039.*

Simos. Jewelry in 14-karat and 18-karat yellow and white gold, and more recently in silver, are Simos specialties, from simple designs to classical Greece-inspired baubles encrusted with precious stones. The shop is open daily from 9 am–11 pm. ✉ *Papadiamantis 29* ☎ *242/7023232.*

KALAMAKI PENINSULA ΚΑΛΑΜΑΚΙ (ΧΕΡΣΟΝΗΣΟΣ)

6 km (4 miles) south of Skiathos town.

The less-developed area on the south coast of Skiathos is the Kalamaki peninsula, where the British built their first villas. Some are available for rent in summer, many above tiny, unfrequented coves. Access here is by boat only, so you can usually find your own private beach. Motor launches run at regular intervals to the most popular beaches from Skiathos town, and you can always hire a boat for a private journey.

WHERE TO STAY

$$ RESORT FAMILY Fodor's Choice ★

🏨 **Skiathos Princess.** Understated glamour and polished island chic rule at Skiathos Princess, which stretches over the whole of the blue flag–designated Ayia Paraskevi beach—as expected, it offers all the expected amenities of an exclusive luxury resort (guest rooms that look lifted from a glossy magazine, an absolute "wow" of a pool area, three restaurants) with polite, professional service to match. **Pros:** lullingly luxurious; wonderful views; airport shuttle. **Cons:** pricey (but worth it). [$] *Rooms from: €221* ✉ *8 km (5 miles) from Skiathos town, Ayia Paraskevi* ☎ *242/7049731* 🌐 *www.skiathosprincess.com* 🛏 *131 rooms, 25 suites, 2 apartments* ⏲ *Closed Nov.–Apr.* 🍴 *Multiple meal plans.*

TROULLOS ΤΡΟΥΛΛΟΣ

4 km (2½ miles) west of Kalamaki peninsula, 8 km (5 miles) west of Skiathos town.

On the coast road west of Kalamaki peninsula lies Troullos bay, a resort area. Continue west and you come to Koukounaries beach—famous, beautiful, and overcrowded.

EXPLORING

Kounistra Monastery. The dirt road north of Troullos leads to beaches and to the small, now deserted, Kounistra Monastery. It was built in 1655 on the spot where a monk discovered an icon of the Virgin miraculously dangling from a pine tree. The icon spends most of the year in the church of Trion Hierarchon, in town, but on November 20 the townspeople parade it to its former home for the celebration of the Presentation of the Virgin the following day. You can enter the deserted monastery church any time, though its interior has been blackened by fire and its 18th-century frescoes are difficult to see. ⊠ *4 km (2½ miles) north of Troullos.*

BEACHES

Fodor'sChoice **Koukounaries.** If what you are looking for is the ideal combination of ★ a scenic landscape with facilities like water sports, nice refreshments and light meals, and sun beds and umbrellas, then the world-renowned, picture-perfect beach of Koukounaries is the place for you. Some call it "Golden Coast," after its fine, sparkling golden sand, but in high season, when boatloads of tourists land there you'll be lucky to find a free patch to sit on. This beautiful beach owes its name to the interesting surrounding forest of umbrella pines, which are almost watered by the waves. Enjoy a leisurely stroll behind the beach to Strofilia Lake, an impressive biotope where rare species of birds find shelter. **Amenities:** food and drink; lifeguard; parking (free); showers; toilets; water sports. **Best for:** partiers; snorkeling; sunrise; swimming; walking. ⊹ *4 km [2½ miles] northwest of Troullos, 12 km [8 miles] west of Skiathos town.*

Ayia Eleni and Krasa. Around the island's western tip are Ayia Eleni and Krasa, facing the nearby Pelion peninsula. The beaches are also known as Big and Little Banana, perhaps because sun worshippers—mainly gay men on Little Banana—often peel their clothes off. Rocky coves provide some privacy. **Amenities:** food and drink; parking (free); showers; toilets; water sports. **Best for:** partiers; nudists; sunset; swimming. ⊠ *1 km [½ mile] west of Koukounaries beach, 13 km [8 miles] west of Skiathos town.*

Mandraki Beach. A good 2½ km (1½ miles) from the main road—but now accessible with a 4x4—the sandy beach of Mandraki offers a sense of peace and privacy. Sometimes called Xerxes's harbor, this is where the notorious Persian king stopped on his way to ultimate defeat at the battles of Artemisium and Salamis. The reefs opposite are the site of a monument Xerxes allegedly erected as a warning to ships, the first such marker known in history. **Amenities:** food and drink; parking (free); toilets. **Best for:** nudists; snorkeling; swimming; walking; solitude. ⊹ *5 km (3 miles) northwest of Troullos bay, 12 km (7½ miles) west of Skiathos town.*

Fodor'sChoice **Megalos Aselinos and Mikros Aselinos.** The expansive and laid-back Mega-★ los Aselinos is a favorite of locals and tourists visiting on boat trips, while Mikros Aselinos, where you'll find a charming little beach taverna, is quieter and can be reached by car or bike. **Amenities:** food and drink; parking (free); toilets. **Best for:** solitude; snorkeling; sunset; swimming. ⊠ *Troullos Bay ⊹ 7 km [4½ miles] north of Troullos, 12 km [7 miles] west of Skiathos town.*

WHERE TO EAT

$$ ✕ **Elia's.** Located at the Mandraki Village boutique hotel but popu-MEDITERRANEAN lar among nonguests, Elia's has received rave reviews from some of Fodor'sChoice Greece's leading food critics and keeps visitors coming back for more. ★ White, deep red, and shocking magenta are the theme colors at this airy, colonial-style restaurant with high-backed, material-covered chairs, soft, radiant lighting, and a sophisticated allure. The chef combines

mainly seasonal, locally sourced ingredients with creative, contemporary Franco-Mediterranean flair and few will be able to resist the aubergine and goat's cheese mille-feuille with pear, the octopus carpaccio, the fisherman's pasta with prawns and shellfish, or the divine homemade crème brûlée. [$] *Average main: €20* ✉ *Koukounaries* ☎ *242/70493014* 🌐 *www.mandraki-skiathos.gr.*

$ GREEK 🍴 **Ratatouille Taverna-Grill House.** This popular, no-frills taverna offers traditional Greek food; it's a great fill-up point after a lazy day on Troullos beach. As the establishment's name suggests, the succulent char-grilled meats and *briam* (a Greek version of ratatouille) are the specialties. During peak summer months it can get busy, so for dinner make sure to book in advance to avoid disappointment. [$] *Average main: €10* ✉ *Morfia Hotel* ✣ *200 meters on the right off main road Skiathos-Koukouniaries just before Troullos beach* ☎ *242/7049367* 🌐 *www.hotelmorfia.gr* ✍ *Reservations essential.*

WHERE TO STAY

$$$$ RESORT 🏨 **Aegean Suites.** In a league of its own on Skiathos, this luxurious boutique hotel pampers eclectic and demanding guests ages 18 and up in what resembles a Mediterranean grand villa. **Pros:** outstanding service; as-luxurious-as-it-gets amenities (Champagne bar, yacht cruises, helicopter transfer, and dinners served in your balcony Jacuzzi). **Cons:** no elevator; can be challenging for some to climb from the lobby to the highest suite. [$] *Rooms from: €350* ✉ *Megali Ammos beach* ☎ *242/7024069* 🌐 *www.aegeansuites.com* 🛏 *20 suites* ⏲ *Closed Nov.–Apr.* 🍽 *Breakfast.*

$$ HOTEL FAMILY Fodor's Choice ★ 🏨 **Mandraki Village.** Lovingly renovated by well-known architect Dimitris Tsitsos in 2007 and transformed into a top-class boutique hotel, Mandraki Village offers a gratifyingly familial holiday ambience in a setting of easy luxury and designer charm. **Pros:** three tempting restaurants, including top-rated Elia's; out-and-out gorgeous, some designers would say; high sophistication factor; in-house spa and beauty treatments. **Cons:** leaving. [$] *Rooms from: €161* ✉ *Koukounaries* ☎ *242/7049301, 242/7049302* 🌐 *www.mandraki-skiathos.gr* 🛏 *38 rooms* 🍽 *Breakfast.*

$ HOTEL FAMILY 🏨 **Troulos Bay Hotel.** A great place to stay if you desire a restful time by the sea, this hotel is decorated in a clean, minimalist, and modern style, with guest rooms that look out to the pretty beach. **Pros:** affordable; great location; good restaurant. **Cons:** a little too sedate for some tastes. [$] *Rooms from: €110* ✉ *Troullos bay* ☎ *24270/49390, 24270/49391* 🌐 *www.troulosbayhotel.gr* 🛏 *43 rooms* ⏲ *Closed Nov.–Apr.* 🍽 *Breakfast.*

KASTRO ΚΑΣΤΡΟ

13 km (8 miles) northeast of Troullos, 9 km (5½ miles) northeast of Skiathos town.

Also known as the Old Town, Kastro perches on a forbidding promontory high above the water, accessible only by steps. Skiathians founded this former capital in the 16th century when they fled from the pirates and the turmoil on the coast to the security of this remote cliff—staying until 1829. Its landward side was additionally protected by a moat and drawbridge, and inside the stout walls they erected 300 houses and 22 churches, of which only two remain. The little Church of the Nativity has some icons and must have heard many prayers for deliverance from the sieges that left the Skiathians close to starvation.

You can drive or take a taxi or bus to within 325 feet of the Old Town, or wear comfortable shoes for a walk that's mostly uphill. Better, take the downhill walk back to Skiathos town; the trek takes about three hours and goes through orchards, fields, and forests on the well-marked paths of the interior.

Kechrias Monastery. Southwest of Kastro is the deserted Kechrias monastery, an 18th-century church embellished with frescoes and surrounded by olive and pine trees. Be warned: the road to Kechria from Skiathos town and to the beach below is tough going; stick to a four-wheel-drive vehicle or a sturdy motorbike. ⊠ *Kechria ✢ 4 km (2½ miles) southwest of Kastro.*

LALARIA ΛΑΛΑΡΙΑ

2 km (1 miles) east of Kastro, 7 km (4½ miles) north of Skiathos town.

Fodor's Choice ★ The much-photographed, lovely Lalaria beach, on the north coast, is flanked by a majestic, arched limestone promontory. The polished limestone and marble add extra sparkle to the already shimmering Aegean. There's no lodging here, and you can only reach Lalaria by taking a boat from the Old Port in Skiathos town, where taxi and tourist boats are readily available. In the same area lie **Skoteini (Dark) cave, Galazia (Azure) cave,** and **Halkini (Copper) cave.** If taking a tour boat, you can stop for an hour or two here to swim and frolic. Bring along a flashlight to turn the water inside these grottoes an incandescent blue.

Evangelistria. The island's best-known and most beautiful monastery, Evangelistria, sits on Skiathos's highest point and was dedicated in the late 18th century to the Annunciation of the Virgin by the monks of Mt. Athos. It encouraged education and gave a base to revolutionaries, who pledged an oath to freedom and first hoisted the flag of Greece here in 1807. Looming above a gorge, and surrounded by fragrant pines and cypresses, the monastery has a high wall that once kept pirates out; today it encloses a ruined refectory kitchen, the cells, a small museum library, and a magnificent church with three domes. A gift shop sells the monastery's own Alypiakos wine, olive oil, locally made preserves, and Orthodox icons. It's near to Lalaria, and about a 10-minute drive, or an hour's walk, from Skiathos town. ⊠ *2 km (1 mile) south of Lalaria, 5 km (3 miles) north of Skiathos town* 🖾 *Donations accepted* ☉ *Daily 9–7.*

SKOPELOS ΣΚΟΠΕΛΟΣ

This triangular island's name means "a sharp rock" or "a reef"—a fitting description for the terrain on its northern shore. It's an hour away from Skiathos by hydrofoil and is the second largest of the Sporades. Most of its 122 square km (47 square miles), up to its highest peak on Mt. Delfi, are covered with dense pine forests, olive groves, and orchards. On the south coast, villages overlook the shores, and pines line the pebbly beaches, casting jade shadows on turquoise water.

Legend has it that Skopelos was settled by Peparethos and Staphylos, colonists from Minoan Crete, said to be the sons of Dionysus and Ariadne, King Minos's daughter. They brought with them the lore of the grape and the olive. The island was called Peparethos until Hellenistic times, and its most popular beach still bears the name Stafilos. In the 1930s a tomb believed to be Staphylos's was unearthed, filled with weapons and golden treasures (now in the Volos museum on the Pelion peninsula).

The Byzantines were exiled here, and the Venetians ruled for 300 years, until 1204. In times past, Skopelos was known for its wine, but today its plums and almonds are eaten rather than drunk, and incorporated into the simple cuisine. Many artists and photographers have settled on the island and throughout summer are part of an extensive cultural program. Little by little, Skopelos is cementing an image as a green and artsy island, still unspoiled by success.

Although this is the most populated island of the Sporades, with two major towns, Skopelos remains peaceful and absorbs tourists into its life rather than giving itself up to their sun-and-fun desires. It's not surprising that ecologists claim it's the greenest island in the region.

GETTING HERE AND AROUND

AIR TRAVEL

There is no airport on Skopelos but you can take an Athens–Skiathos Olympic Airlines flight mid-June to mid-September, then taxi to Skiathos town port, and from there take a hydrofoil to Skopelos.

BOAT AND FERRY TRAVEL

Ferries from the mainland leave from Agios Konstantinos or Volos, and ferries back to the mainland stop in Skiathos. Skopelos has two main ports: Skopelos town and, at the northwestern end of the island, Loutraki (near the town of Glossa).

Caïques leave from the main port for the most popular beaches, and interisland excursions are also made between Skiathos and Skopelos. You can also head to the harbor and look around for a caïque (haggle over the price) or a sailboat with skipper to hire and tour around the islands; they are generally the preferred way to get around by day. For popular routes, captains have their destinations and departure times posted.

BUS TRAVEL

The main bus station on Skopelos is located in front of a large church at a junction for Agiou Riginou and Loutraki. The last stop on the island-wide route is Glossa (€3.50, 1 hour), with stops along the way including Panormos and Elios.

CAR TRAVEL

Alamo/National is a reliable car-rental company on Skopelos. *For contact information, see Car Travel in Travel Smart.*

Alamo/National ⊠ *Paralia Skopelou, Skopelos town* ☎ *24/2402–3033.*

TAXI TRAVEL

Taxis can be arranged through your hotel, or you can call operators directly.

Contacts Mr. G. Stamoulos ☎ *69/7242–9568 mobile.*
Mr. Z. Stamoulis ☎ *69/7284–1329 mobile.*

TOURS

Skopelos Walks. To gain a unique perspective on Skopelos town take one of the walking tours offered by Heather Parsons. She offers half- and full-day walking tours of the town and the island in May, June, September, and October lasting between 3 and 5 hours (longer tours have a lunchtime picnic stop). Most tours cost between €10 and €25. Advance reservations online or by phone are required. ⊠ *Skopelos town* ☎ *69452/49328* ⊕ *skopelos-walks.com.*

TRAVEL AGENCIES

Madro Travel. Because of owners Mahi and George Drossou's inviting personalities and impressively extensive knowledge of the island, this is the kind of travel agency most people wish existed on *every* island. Both with deep roots in Skopelos's own history, these two charismatic travel agents can offer quality suggestions for what to do—or avoid doing— during your time here. Local boat trips, ferry and hydrofoil tickets, exciting drives, and on-target tips on sites, restaurants, and memorable walks can be found at Madro, while their son Vaggelis can offer insights on the island's nightlife and more youth-oriented excursions. ⊠ *Old Harbor (next to Platanos Jazz Club), Skopelos town* ☎ *242/4022145* 🖷 *242/4022941* ⊕ *www.madrotravel.com.*

Thalpos Holidays. Apart from the standard travel services, Thalpos can also arrange hiking, biking, cooking lessons, and other more person- alized and alternative activities. ⊠ *Paralia Skopelou, Skopelos town* ☎ *24240/29036* ⊕ *www.holidayislands.com.*

VISITOR INFORMATION

Contacts Skopelos Municipality ⊠ *Waterfront, Skopelos town* ☎ *242/4022205* ⊕ *www.skopelosweb.gr.*

SKOPELOS TOWN ΣΚΟΠΕΛΟΣ (ΠΟΛΗ)

3 hrs from Agios Konstantinos, ½ hr from Skiathos town by ferry.

Pretty Skopelos town, the administrative center of the Sporades, over- looks a bay on the north coast. On a steep hill below, scant vestiges of the ancient acropolis and medieval castle remain. The town works hard to stay charming—building permits are difficult to obtain, signs must be in native style, pebbles are embedded in the walkways. Three- and four-story houses rise virtually straight up the hillside, reached by flagstone steps. The whitewashed houses look prosperous (18th-century Skopelos society was highly cultured and influential) and cared for, their facades enlivened by brightly painted or brown timber balconies, doors, and shutters. Flamboyant vines and potted plants complete the picture. Interspersed among the red-tile roofs are several with traditional gray fish-scale slate—too heavy and expensive to be used much nowadays.

Off the waterfront, prepare for a breath-snatching climb up the almost perpendicular steps in Skopelos town, starting at the seawall. You will encounter many churches as you go—the island has more than 300. The uppermost, located near the castle and said to be situated on the ruins of the ancient temple of Minerva, is the 11th-century Ayios Athanasios with a typically whitewashed exterior and an interior that includes 17th-century Byzantine murals. At the stairs' summit you're standing within the walls of the 13th-century castle erected by the Venetian Ghisi lords who held all the Sporades as their fief. It in turn rests on polygonal masonry of the 5th century BC, as this was the site of one of the island's three ancient acropoli. Once you've admired the view and the stamina of the old women negotiating the steps like mountain goats, wind your way back down the seawall steps by any route you choose. Wherever you turn, you may spy a church: Skopelos claims some 360, of which 123 are in the town proper. Curiously, most of them seem to be locked, but the exteriors are striking—some incorporating ancient artifacts, Byzantine plates or early Christian elements, and slate-capped domes. To gain a unique perspective on Skopelos town, take one of the walking tours offered by Heather Parsons (⊕ *www.skopelos-walks.com*).

EXPLORING

Evangelistria Monastery. Perched on Palouki mountain and overlooking the sea and Skopelos's Chora, the impressive Evangelistria Monastery was founded in 1676 and completely rebuilt in 1712 by Ioannis Grammatikos, who believed he was saved from execution by an 11th-century icon of the Virgin. It contains no frescoes but has an intricately carved iconostasis and the miraculous icon. ⊠ *On mountainside opposite Skopelos town, 1½ km (1 mile) to northeast* ☎ 24/2402-3230 ⊑ *Free* ⊙ *Daily 9–1 and 3–5.*

Folk Art Museum. For an impression of the interior of how an upper-class Skopelan house looked 200 years ago, visit the Folk Art Museum, an 18th-century mansion (1795) with hand-carved period furniture, decorative items, paintings and embroideries. Don't miss the display of the elaborately sewn wedding dress in the bridal chamber. ⊠ *Hatzistamati* ☎ 24/2402–3494 ⊑ *€3* ⊙ *June–Sept., Mon.–Sat., 10 am–noon and 5–10 pm, Sun. 7–10 pm; Oct.–May, weekdays 9 am–3 pm.*

Metamorphosis tou Sotera. The oldest monastery on the island (circa 1600) features iconography in the old basilica that was painted by renowned Byzantine painter Agorastos. The monastery has its feast day on August 6 and is occupied by a sole monk. ✠ *Follow signs east of Skopelos town, past Ayia Varvara* ⊙ *Daily Apr.–Nov.*

Prodromou (*Forerunner*). Dedicated to St. John the Baptist, Prodromou now operates as a convent. Besides being unusual in design, its church contains some outstanding 14th-century triptychs, an enamel tile floor, and an iconostasis spanning four centuries (half carved in the 14th century, half in the 18th century). The nuns sell elaborate woven and embroidered handiwork. Opening days and hours vary. ⊠ *2½ km (1½ mile) east of Skopelos town.*

The Ayia Varvara Monastery is just one of the 40 medieval beauties set on Skopelos. Some are open to visitors: wear suitable dress (no bare arms or short skirts are allowed for women).

Vakratsa. Skopelos was once a hub for a well-travelled, politically influential, and highly cultured society, and a fascinating peek into that world is offered by a visit to this 19th-century mansion. Furnishings, precious icons, and quotidian antiques made locally as well as from around the world make this a fine showcase of the life and traditions of a local family of high standing, namely that of Andigoni Vakratsa. She, along with her father, was a doctor who offered free medical services to the poor. Head upstairs to view the living room (used only for very special occasions) where you can admire a traditional island engagement dress with its 4,000-pleat skirt. ⊠ *A short walk up from Ambrosia sweet shop* 🎫 *€3* 🕑 *Daily, 10–2 and 7–10.*

Drachondoschisma peninsula. The road from the beach at Stafilos runs southwest through the rounded Drachondoschisma peninsula, where, legend has it, the island's patron St. Reginos slaughtered a dragon that was creating havoc on the island. ⊠ *5 km (3 miles) south of Skopelos town.*

BEACHES

Velania. Velania takes its name from the *valanium* (Roman bath) that once stood here. The bath has long since disintegrated under the waves, but the fresh spring water used for the baths still trickles out from a cave at the far end of the beach. To get here, follow the footpath that starts at Stafilos beach over the forested hill. This extra hike is seemingly off-putting to many beachgoers, keeping Velania isolated and quiet. Today it's broadly favored by nudists. **Amenities:** none. **Best for:** solitude; nudists; snorkeling; sunrise; swimming; walking. ⊠ *1 km (½ mile) east of Stafilos beach.*

WHERE TO EAT

MAMMA MIA!

The 2008 movie *Mamma Mia!* used a lot of Skopelos as its dreamy setting, something many locals take great pride in; sadly, a lot of these once-pure spots are now tainted by tourism. Film locations included the tiny Kastani bay—where they constructed Meryl Streep's taverna and then dismantled it after the film—Milia beach, and the breathtaking (literally) hilltop Ayios Ioannis Monastery overlooking Glossa.

$ GREEK 🍴 **Alexander Garden Restaurant.** If you've had enough of the waterfront, follow the signs up to this little garden restaurant in the hills for a homemade traditional meal. Especially recommended are appetizers such as eggplant or bell peppers stuffed with cheese, garlic, and tomato, and the restaurant's *keftedakia* meatballs made with a secret recipe, which alone is worth the amble up the hill. A 200-year-old well in the center of the elegant, leafy terrace produces its own natural spring water, which you can enjoy while dining. [$] *Average main: €10* ✉ *Manolaki street* ✥ *Turn inland after the corner shop Armoloi* ☎ *242/4022324* ⏲ *Closed Nov.–Mar. No lunch.*

$ SEAFOOD 🍴 **Klimataria.** The blackfish *stifado* (stew) with onions is so delicious here you may find yourself doing the quintessentially Greek *papara*—sponging the plate clean with a piece of bread. Patrons come to Klimataria for flavorsome local specialties such as the pork cooked in a sauce of red wine, honey, and prunes (the sweet and sour fruit was once the island's star export); succulent fresh fish; and a pleasant view of the moonlit sea. [$] *Average main: €10* ✉ *Waterfront* ☎ *242/4022273* ⏲ *Closed mid-Oct.–mid-Dec.*

$ GREEK 🍴 **Mihalis.** Come here for the delicious *Skopelitiki tiropita* (Skopelos cheese pie), or splurge on *rizogalo* (rice pudding). Bougainvillea lines the walls of the courtyard, where you hear the warble of canaries. Opposite stands a barbershop that embodies the charm of another era. [$] *Average main: €8* ✉ *East side of port, 3 blocks inland from National Bank* ☎ *242/4022014* ▭ *No credit cards.*

$ GREEK Fodor's Choice ★ 🍴 **Molos.** A favorite amongst the cluster of tavernas near the far end at the Old Port, Molos serves quality *magirefta* (dishes cooked ahead in the oven), a broad choice of pasta dishes with fresh seafood, local goat cooked in a rich tomato sauce, stuffed courgette flowers (a Skopelos specialty) and fluffy *taramosalata* fish roe dip. Although most of the courses here are traditional Greek, chef/owner Panayiotis knows how to add his signature style, and his charisma extends to musical talents that he sometimes shares with clients in live performances. [$] *Average main: €11* ✉ *Waterfront* ☎ *242/4022551* ⏲ *Closed Nov.–Mar.*

$ GREEK 🍴 **The Muses.** A romantic beachfront restaurant, The Muses serves elevated traditional Greek fare like fish grilled with a blend of herbs and meat dishes such as a delicious rabbit *stifado* (stewed with shallots, tomatoes, and cinnamon) and succulent lamb *lemonato* (slow-roasted with garlic, salt, and lemon) that falls off the bone. Its location on the quiet edge of Skopelos town provides super views of the bustling port and open sea, whose waters caress the beach a few feet from the lantern-lit tables. Family run, the service is attentive and the owners go that extra mile to make your dining experience noteworthy. ■**TIP→ Make sure you visit early on in your stay as you will want to return.** [$] *Average main: €12* ⊠ *Skopelos beach* ✛ *Southeast of the port, 100 meters along the beach road* ☎ 24240/24414.

$ ✕**Ta Kymata.** Spirited brothers Andreas, Riginos, and Christophoros
GREEK   enthusiastically run the seafront taverna that has belonged to their family since 1896, serving a gratifying lunch and dinner menu based on traditional Skopelos recipes. Try their wonderful summery salad of lettuce, sweet corn, artichokes, sundried tomatoes, capers, and *kefalotyri* cheese; for a main course choose the lamb cooked with plums or the delicious *pepperonata* stew. The signature dish is *Tis Maharas*, an intense, pungent, yet surprisingly light dish of vegetables and cheeses with a creamy sauce, dedicated to the brothers' grandmother, who's name *Mahi* means battle and whose physical strength and towering height was said to ensure there was never any trouble at the taverna. [$] *Average main: €10* ⊠ *North end of the harbor* ☎ 242/4022381 ▭ *No credit cards.*

$ ✕**To Perivoli.** The chef/owner of *To Perivoli* (garden) prides himself on
MODERN GREEK   the fact that the restaurant's menu has not changed at all in the last 20 years—the return of patrons year after year is living proof of its success. Indeed, the food and wine, charmingly served on a patio beside an herb and flower garden, is colorful and inventive enough to suit all tastes. Start with a salad with purslane, goat's cheese, and black sesame or the filo pouches stuffed with mushrooms and smoky *metsovone* cheese and then opt for the tender lamb cutlet with yogurt-mint sauce and wild rice. Leave room for the local specialty of *amygdalopitta* (almond cake) with ice cream. [$] *Average main: €12* ⊠ *Off Platanos Sq., close to waterfront* ☎ 242/4023758 ⚑ *Reservations essential* ⊘ *Closed Oct.– May. No lunch.*

WHERE TO STAY

$ ⛱ **Alkistis.** An ideal place for enjoying a sense of privacy and restfulness,
RESORT   Alkistis is made up of very simple apartments that offer a feeling of stay-
FAMILY   ing at a friend's summer house. **Pros:** harmonious atmosphere; nearby supermarket; friendly staff. **Cons:** isolated, although the hotel mini-bus takes guests to town; generic room decor. [$] *Rooms from: €115* ⊠ *2 km (1 mile) southeast of town on road to Stafilos* ☎ 242/4023006 ⊕ *www. alkistis-skopelos.gr* ⇴ *25 apartments* ⊘ *Closed Oct.–May* ⏀ *Breakfast.*

$ ⛱ **Pension Sotos.** This cozy, restored, old Skopelete house on the water-
HOTEL   front is inexpensive and casual, with tiny rooms looking onto one of the hotel's two courtyard terraces. **Pros:** low prices. **Cons:** no breakfast. [$] *Rooms from: €35* ⊠ *Waterfront* ☎ 242/4022549 ⇴ *12 rooms* ⏀ *No meals.*

$$ ⛱ **Skopelos Village.** A chic, contemporary take on traditional Greek
RESORT   island charm defines the design of the hotel, which is themed on breezy
FAMILY   peacefulness, understated luxury, and the comfort of a delightful villa. **Pros:** wonderful area; great views; steps away from the beach. **Cons:** a 10-minute walk from the town center. [$] *Rooms from: €210* ⊠ *1 km (½ mile) east of the town center* ☎ 242/4023011, 242/4022517 ⊕ *www. skopelosvillage.gr* ⇴ *35 suites* ⊘ *Closed Nov.–Apr.* ⏀ *Breakfast.*

Forget all those worries back home with one delicious dinner on the town square in Skopelos town.

$ HOTEL Fodor's Choice ★ **Thea Home.** A wonderful choice for budget travelers, the very clean, cozy, graceful, and family-run Kali Thea studios and maisonettes are a short walk from the harbor and offer a beautiful vista of the town from Thea's large terrace (where guests can use free Wi-Fi and have a home-made snack or light meal). **Pros:** every image on the absolutely gorgeous slide show at this hotel's website is a "pro"! **Cons:** steep uphill trek to reach the property. [$] *Rooms from: €60* ✉ *Ring Road, 10-minute walk up from harbor,* ☎ *24/2402–2859* 📠 *24/2402–3556* 🌐 *www.theahomehotel.com* 🛏 *13 rooms* 🍴 *Breakfast.*

NIGHTLIFE

Nightlife on Skopelos is more relaxed than it is on Skiathos. There's a smattering of cozy bars playing music of all kinds, and each summer at least one nightclub operates; look for advertisements. The *kefi* (good mood) is to be found at the western end of the waterfront, where a string of bar-nightclubs comes to life after midnight. Take an evening *volta* (stroll); most bars have tables outside, so you really can't miss them.

MUSIC CLUBS

Anatoli. At Anatoli, a converted barn perched at the highest point of the town by the Old Kastro, tap into a truly Greek vein with proprietor Giorgo Xithari. Sometimes accompanied by local musicians and friends, he strums up a storm on his bouzouki and sings *rembetika,* traditional Greek acoustic blues. With an ouzo or two, the atmosphere can get heady, and soon you may discover new dancing talents inspired by old classics. ✉ *Old Kastro* ☎ *24/2402–2851.*

Anemos. Without a doubt the best cocktail bar on the island, laid-back and casual Anemos serves impeccably mixed cocktails not often found anywhere else; try the fragrantly sophisticated Paris Martini or ask the barman to create one of his inspired concoctions to suit—or perfectly alter—your mood, as you enjoy the DJ's eclectic mix of cool grooves on the large stone terrace. The place opens at 8 am for coffee and snacks. ⊠ *Skopelos harbor front* ☎ *24/2402–3564.*

Mercurius. Perched just above the waterfront, Mercurius is ideal for a leisurely breakfast or invigorating sunset drinks with a stunning view and a soundtrack of world music. ■TIP→ **Check out the fine art exhibitions by local and visiting artists in the bar's gallery, which opened in 2012.** ⊠ *5 mins walk up from the harbor* ☎ *24/2402–4593* ⊕ *www. mercurius.gr.*

SHOPPING

FOOD SPECIALTIES

Kyria Leni. Skopelos is well known for its almonds and plums, and at this dignified, classic store you will find a grand variety of delectable, locally sourced, and homemade goods to savor. Don't miss out on the fluffy *avgato* prunes in syrup, an island specialty best eaten as a *glyko koutaliou* (eaten with a spoon and often accompanied by strong Greek coffee to contrast its sweetness). ⊠ *Waterfront* ☎ *24/2403–3688, 24/2403–3115.*

LOCAL CRAFTS

Archipelago. Head here for modern ceramics and crafts, great jewelry, handbags, and a wonderful selection of pricey antiques. Operating since 1973, it's the oldest craft shop on the island. ⊠ *Waterfront* ☎ *24/2402–3127.*

Armoloi. For 35 years Armoloi has been creating exquisite ceramic crockery, inspired Greek-style jewelry, and colorful decor items. The shop is also a wonderful spot for buying traditional-style pottery, handmade leather handbags, and crafts by artists from around the country. ⊠ *Waterfront* ☎ *24/2402–2707.*

Ploumisti. Kilims, bags, hand-painted T-shirts, ceramics, and jewelry are among the antique and new wares at Ploumisti. ⊠ *Opposite National Bank, Paralia street* ☎ *24/2402–2059.*

Yiousouri. Fans here love its decorative ceramics. ⊠ *Waterfront, near the Folklore Museum* ☎ *24/2402–3983.*

SPORTS AND THE OUTDOORS

BOATING AND SAILING

Fodor'sChoice ★ **Aegeo Sailing.** A wonderful way to explore Skopelos by sea is to hop onto "Captain" Vasilis's sailing boat, which seats up to 10 people, and travel where the winds will take you. The skipper's knowledge of the island, its waters and whimsical winds, as well as about surrounding islets and islands such as the gorgeous Alonissos wildlife preserve, offers a fantastic break from land-leg reality. Customers are shown sailing tricks, stunning out-of-the-way beaches, delectable cuisine in the form of a fish lunch in Alonissos's mini-harbor of Steni Vala, and if they're lucky, dolphins. In other words: a great way to relax, open your eyes and nostrils to the pure open sea, and learn a thing or two. Make sure you book your place in advance for a day trip (you can even charter the boat for a longer sojourn) on the sea. ⊠ *On the harbor on the*

6

waterfront road leading to main port, close to Skopelos Port Author-ity, Skopelos town ☏ *23/1095–3773, 69/7473–6333 mobile* ⊕ *www.aegeo-sailing.gr.*

AGNONDA ΑΓΝΩΝΤΑ

5 km (3 miles) south of Skopelos town.

Used as an alternative port by hydrofoils and ferryboats during bad weather, Agnonda has numerous tavernas along its pebbled beach. It is named after a local boy who returned here victorious from Olympia in 569 BC brandishing the victor's wreath.

BEACHES

FAMILY **Agnonda Beach.** Agnonda has numerous tavernas along its pebbled beach serving up fresh seafood. In 2014 it was awarded the blue flag for its clean waters. Agnonda is named after a local boy who returned here victorious from Olympia in 569 BC brandishing the victor's wreath. **Amenities:** food and drink; parking (free); showers; toilets; water sports. **Best for:** solitude; snorkeling; swimming.

Stafilos Beach. Scattered farms and two tavernas, small houses with rooms for rent, and one or two pleasant hotels line the road to the seaside, where fragrant pines meet the cool, crystal clear, calm waters. There's a simple canteen that serves snacks and refreshments (and even mojitos at sunset), and a lifeguard stand. Nearby, prehistoric walls, a watchtower, and an unplundered grave suggest that this was the site of an important prehistoric settlement. **Amenities:** food and drink; life-guard, parking (free); showers. **Best for:** snorkeling; sunrise; swimming; walking. ⊠ *Stafilos* ✛ *3.5 km (2 miles) southeast of Agnonda.*

PANORMOS BAY ΟΡΜΟΣ ΠΑΝΟΡΜΟΥ

6 km (4 miles) west of Skopelos town, 4 km (2½ miles) northwest of Agnonda.

Due northwest of Agnonda is Panormos Bay, the smallest of the ancient towns of Peparethos, founded in the 8th century BC by colonists from Chalkis. A few well-concealed walls are visible among the pinewoods on the acropolis above the bay. With its long beach and its sheltered inner cove ideal for yachts, this is fast becoming a holiday village, although so far it retains its quiet charm. Inland, the interior of Skopelos is green and lush, and not far from Panormos Bay traditional farmhouses called *kalivia* stand in plum orchards. Some are occupied; others have been turned into overnight stops or are used only for feast-day celebrations. Look for the outdoor ovens, which baked the fresh plums when Skope-los was turning out prunes galore. This rural area is charming, but the lack of signposts makes it easy to get lost, so pay attention.

BEACHES

Adrina Beach. Next to Milia, Adrina beach has crystal turquoise water and small pebbles, sun beds, umbrellas, and a feeling of seclusion. Das-sia, the thickly forested islet across the bay, was named after a female pirate who (legend has it) was drowned there—but not before hiding her treasure. ■ TIP→ **Access to the beach is somewhat difficult since you now have to go through the new resort to get to the shore.** **Amenities:** food and drink; showers; toilets; water sports. **Best for:** snorkeling; sunset; swimming. ✉ *Near Milia beach, Adrina.*

Fodor's Choice ★ **Milia Beach.** Skopelos's longest beach, Milia is considered by many to be its best. Though still secluded, the bay is up and coming—parasols and recliners are lined halfway across the beach and there's a large taverna serving average food, thankfully ensconced by pine trees. No matter: Milia is breathtaking, thanks to its white sands, clear turquoise waters, and vibrant green trees. If you'd like to live this aquatic romance, locate the owner of one of the villas for rent that are set right on the beach—well-tended, they are but a few short strides from the water's edge. **Amenities:** food and drink; parking (free); showers; toilets. **Best for:** snorkeling; sunset; swimming; walking; windsurfing. ✉ *Milia* ✣ *2 km (1 mile) north of Panormos Bay.*

WHERE TO STAY

$ HOTEL FAMILY 🏨 **Afrodite.** Less than five minutes walk from beautiful Panormos bay and ten minutes from Adrina beach stands this friendly, relaxing B-grade hotel—surrounded by lush mountains and with a good enough view of the sea, it offers a coveted sense of getting away from it all, yet is also located near enough to all the essentials one may want on a laid-back holiday: a lovely beach, where a handful of quality tavernas can be found, and two mini-markets. **Pros:** friendly; well-situated. **Cons:** Wi-Fi doesn't reach all the rooms. [$] *Rooms from: €85* ☎ *24/2402–3150* 📠 *24/2402–3152* 🌐 *www.afroditehotel.gr* 🛏 *38 rooms* 🍴 *Breakfast.*

$ RESORT FAMILY 🏨 **Delphi Hotel.** The garden filled with magnolia, cherry, plum, pear, and lemon trees, with lovely white oleander and herb bushes that frame the pool and patio, is one good reason to stay here; the well-spaced, clean, and self-sufficient apartments and maisonettes are another. **Pros:** great location thanks to backdrop of beautiful pine forest; just a few minutes walk to beach. **Cons:** rooms are pretty basic; breakfast is an added €5 per person. [$] *Rooms from: €70* ✉ *Elios, Neo Klima* ☎ *24/2403–3788, 24/2403–3172* 🌐 *www.hotel-skopelos.gr* 🛏 *40 apartments, 7 maisonettes* 🍴 *No meals.*

$ HOTEL 🏨 **Panormos Beach Hotel.** The owner's attention to detail shows in the beautifully tended flower garden, the immaculate rooms with pine furniture and handwoven linens, the country dining room, and the entrance case displaying his grandmother's elaborate clothes. **Pros:** friendly, homelike environment; hospitality plus—with sweet offerings of homegrown fruit, wine, and sweets. **Cons:** not all rooms have sea views; no elevator. [$] *Rooms from: €80* ✉ *1 block from beachfront* ☎ *24/2402–2711* 🌐 *www.panormos-beach.com* 🛏 *34 rooms* 🕒 *Closed Nov.–Apr.* 🍴 *Breakfast.*

EN ROUTE **Loutraki.** Loutraki is the tiny port village where the ferries and hydrofoils stop to and from Skiathos, and it is not very charming. Around 300 yards from the port are the remains of the Acropolis of Selinous, the island's third ancient city. Unfortunately, everything lies buried except the walls. ■ TIP→ **There is a little beach on the outer edge of the harbor wall.**

6

GLOSSA ΓΛΩΣΣΑ

38 km (23 miles) northwest of Skopelos town, 24 km (14 miles) northwest of Panormos Bay, 3 km (1½ miles) northwest of Klima.

Delightful Glossa is the island's second-largest settlement, where white-washed, red-roof houses are clustered on the steep hillside above the harbor of Loutraki. Venetian towers and traces of Turkish influence remain; the center is closed to traffic. This is a place to relax, dine, and enjoy the quieter beaches. Just to the east, have a look at Ayios Ioannis Monastery, dramatically perched above a pretty beach. There's no need to tackle the series of extremely steep steps to the monastery, as it is not open to visitors.

WHERE TO EAT

$$

MODERN GREEK

Fodor's Choice

★

× **Restaurant Agnanti.** Located in the picturesque village of Glossa, this long-established landmark today entices with its playful and innovative take on classic Greek dishes. Instead of resting assured that the restaurant's awe-inspiring panoramic vista of the Aegean sea is enough to please customers, owner Nikos Stamatakis and his chef father Stamatis keep upping the bar of the menu's wow factor. Just try the vine leaf–wrapped chicken dressed in a rich lemon geranium sauce (a play on the traditional dolma), or the creamy moussaka, which is blended with tuna instead of minced beef, or the fragrant herbed fritters, and you'll agree. The ambience? Laid-back yet elegant enough for a special occasion. $ *Average main: €17* ✉ *Next to Glossa community, Louki* ☎ *24/2403–3306* ⊕ *agnanti.com.gr* ⌂ *Reservations essential* ☽ *Closed Nov.–Apr.*

SKYROS ΣΚΥΡΟΣ

Even among these unique isles, Skyros stands out. Its rugged terrain looks like a Dodecanese island, and its spectacularly sited main town—occupied on and off for the last 3,300 years and haunted by mythical ghosts—looks Cycladic. It has military bases, and an airport with periodic connections to Athens, yet it remains the most difficult ferry connection in the Sporades. With nothing between it and Lesvos, off the coast of Turkey, its nearest neighbor is the town of Kimi, on the east coast of Evia.

Surprisingly beguiling, this southernmost of the Sporades is the largest (209 square km [81 square miles]). A narrow, flat isthmus connects Skyros's two almost-equal parts, whose names reflect their characters—*Meri* or *Imero* ("tame") for the north, and *Vouno* (literally, "mountain," meaning tough or stony) for the south. The heavily populated north is virtually all farmland and forests. The southern half of the island is forbidding, barren, and mountainous, with Mt. Kochilas its highest peak (2,598 feet). Its western coast is outlined with coves and deep bays dotted with a series of islets.

Until Greece won independence in 1831, the population of Skyros squeezed sardine-fashion into the area under the castle on the inland face of the rock. Not a single house was visible from the sea. Though

Meryl Streep's most unforgettable star turn in *Mamma Mia!* was filmed with Glossa's church of Ayios Ioannis as her beautiful backdrop.

the islanders could survey any movement in the Aegean for miles, they kept a low profile, living in dread of the pirates based at Treis Boukes bay on Vouno.

Strangely enough, although Skyros is adrift in the Aegean, the Skyrians have not had a seafaring tradition, and have looked to the land for their living. Their isolation has brought about notable cultural differences from the other Greek islands, such as pre-Christian Carnival rituals. Today there are more than 300 churches on the island, many of them private and owned by local families. An almost-extinct breed of pony resides on Skyros, and exceptional crafts—carpentry, pottery, embroidery—are practiced by dedicated artisans whose creations include unique furniture and decorative linens. There are no luxury accommodations or swank restaurants: this idiosyncratic island makes no provisions for mass tourism, but if you've a taste for the offbeat, you may feel right at home.

GETTING HERE AND AROUND

AIR TRAVEL

You can get to Skyros from Athens by air on Aegean Airlines in about 40 minutes. The airport is on the north of the island 15 km (9 miles) from Skyros town, but a shuttle bus always meets the plane. Tickets on the shuttle cost €3 to €6; the trip takes 20 minutes.

Contacts Skyros Airport ⊠ *11 km (7 miles) northwest of Skyros town* ☎ *222/2209–1684.*

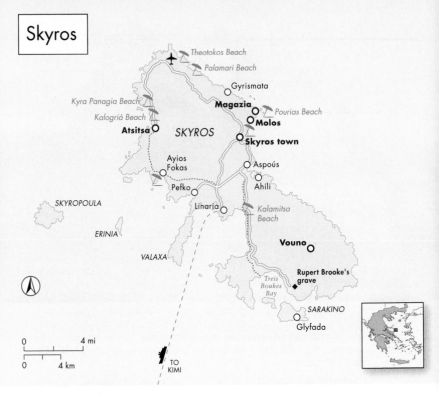

BOAT TRAVEL

Ferries to Skyros leave from Kimi on Evia (the largest of the Sporades islands) and take 2½ hours; there are several ferries on weekends, but perhaps only one during the week. All boats dock at Linaria, far from Skyros town. A shuttle bus, however, always meets the boat; bus tickets cost €2 to €3. Taxis are another option, but settle the fee before setting out. There are only a couple of boats that connect Skyros with Skiathos weekly so it is only advisable if you have plenty of time at your disposal and you plan at the beginning of your vacation.

CAR TRAVEL

Martina's and Pegasus rent cars on Skyros.

Contacts Martina's ✉ *Maheras, Skyros town* ☎ *22/2209–2022* ⊕ *www.web-greece.gr/rentacar/martinas/.* **Pegasus** ✉ *Skyros town* ⊕ *On the right of the road leading up to the Old Town* ☎ *22/2209–1600* ⊕ *www.skyrosrentacar.com.*

TAXI TRAVEL

Arrange taxis through your hotel, or call operators directly.

Contacts Mr. Kourogenis ☎ *69/7289–4088 mobile.* **Mr. Pergamalis** ☎ *69/7366–5480 mobile.* **Mr. Traxanas** ☎ *69/7836–1325 mobile.*

FESTIVALS

Apokries. The Apokries pre-Lenten Carnival revelry on Skyros relates to pre-Christian Dyonisian fertility rites and is famous throughout Greece. Young men dressed as old men, maidens, or "Europeans" roam the streets teasing and tormenting onlookers with ribald songs and clanging bells. The "old men" wear elaborate shepherd's outfits, with masks made of baby-goat hides and belts dangling with as many as 40 sheep bells.

TRAVEL AGENCIES

Contacts Skyros Travel. This friendly and professional local tour operator specializes in all things to do with Skyros: finding last-minute accommodations, car rentals, and ferry tickets, and flights to and from the island. ⊠ *Agora, Skyros town* ☎ *22220/91123, 22220/91600* ⊕ *www.skyrostravel.com.*

VISITOR INFORMATION

Contacts Greek National Tourism Organization (GNTO or EOT) ⊕ *www. visitgreece.gr.* **Skyros official website** ☎ *22/2235–0300* ⊕ *www.skyros.gr.*

SKYROS TOWN ΣΚΥΡΟΣ (ΧΩΡΙΟ)

Fodor's Choice ★ *1 hour and 40 minutes from Kimi to Linaria by boat, 30 minutes from Linaria by car.*

As you drive south from the airport, past brown, desolate outcroppings with only an occasional goat as a sign of life, Skyros town suddenly looms around a bend. Blazing white, cubist, dense, and otherworldly, clinging, precariously it seems, to the precipitous rock beneath it and topped gloriously by a fortress-monastery, this town more closely resembles a village in the Cyclades than any other you'll find in the Sporades.

Called *Horio, Hora,* and *Chora* ("village") by the locals, Skyros town is home to 90% of the island's 3,000 inhabitants. The impression as you get closer is of stark, simple buildings creeping up the hillside, with a tangle of labyrinthine lanes steeply winding up, down, and around the tiny houses, Byzantine churches, and big squares. As you stroll down from the ruins and churches of the Kastro area, or explore the alleyways off the main drag, try to peek discreetly into the houses. Skyrians are house-proud and often leave their windows and doors open to show off. In fact, since the houses all have the same exteriors, the only way for families to distinguish themselves has been through interior design. Walls and conical mantelpieces are richly decorated with European- and Asian-style porcelain, copper cooking utensils, wood carvings, and embroideries. Wealthy families originally obtained much of the porcelain from the pirates in exchange for grain and food, and its possession was a measure of social standing. Then enterprising potters started making exact copies, along with the traditional local ware, leading to the unique Skyrian style of pottery. The furniture is equally beautiful, and often miniature in order to conserve interior space.

Farther up the hill, the summit is crowned with three tiny cube-like churches with blue and pink interiors, and the ruined Venetian cistern, once used as a dungeon. From there you have a spectacular view of the town and surrounding hills. The roofs are flat, the older ones covered with a dark gray shale that has splendid insulating properties. The house walls and roofs are interconnected, forming a pattern that from above looks like a magnified form of cuneiform writing. Here and there the shield-like roof of a church stands out from the cubist composition of white houses that fills the hillside—with not an inch to spare.

EXPLORING

Most commercial activity takes place in or near the agora (the market street), familiarly known as Sisifos, as in the myth, because of its frustrating steepness. Found here are the town's pharmacies, travel agencies, shops with wonderful Skyrian pottery, and an extraordinary number of tiny bars and tavernas, but few boutiques and even less kitsch. In the summer heat, all shops and restaurants close from 2 pm to 6 pm, but the town comes alive at night.

Archaeological Museum of Skyros. This tiny archaeological museum (on the way to Magazia beach as you begin to descend from the town) contains few but rare finds, mostly from graves dating from Neolithic to Roman times. Weapons, pottery, and jewelry are exhibited. ⊠ *Rupert Brooke Sq.* ☎ *22/2209–1327* ⊕ *odysseus.culture.gr* ✉ *€2* ⊗ *Tues.–Sun. 8–3.*

Episkopi Church. Take the vaulted passageway from St. George's Monastery courtyard to the ruined church of Episkopi, the former seat of the bishop of Skyros, built in 895 on the ruins of a temple of Athena. This was the center of Skyros's religious life from 1453 to 1837. You can continue up to the summit from here. ⊠ *Above St. George's Monastery.*

Fodor's Choice   **Faltaits Historical and Folklore Museum.** This museum showcases an out-
★   standing collection of Skyrian decorative arts. Built after Greek Independence by a wealthy family (who still owns the museum), the house is one of the most impressive in Skyros town. Just as well, as it is nearly overflowing with rare books, costumes, photographs, paintings, ceramics, local embroideries, Greek statues, and other heirlooms. Of particular note are the embroideries, which are famed for their flamboyant colors and vivacious renderings of mermaids, *hoopoes* (the Skyrians' favorite bird), and mythical human figures whose clothes and limbs sprout flowers. Top treasure among the museum's historical documents is a handwritten copy of the Proclamation of the Greek Revolution against the Ottoman Empire. The informative guided tour is well worth the extra euros. ⊠ *Rupert Brooke Sq.* ☎ *22/2209–1150, 22/2209–1232* ⊕ *www.faltaits.gr* ✉ *€2, tour €5* ⊗ *Daily 10–2 and 6–9.*

Fodor's Choice   **Monastery of St. George.** The best way to get an idea of the town and its
★   history is to follow the sinuous cobbled lanes past the mansions of the Old Town to the *Kastro*, the highest point, and the 10th-century fortified Monastery of St. George, which stands on the site of the ancient acropolis and Bronze Age settlement. Little remains of the legendary fortress of King Lykomedes, portrayed in Skyros's two most colorful myths, though lower down on the north and southwest face of the rock are the so-called Pelasgian bastions of immense rectangular fitted blocks, dated to the classical period or later. A white marble lion, which may be left over from the Venetian occupation, is in the wall above the entrance to the monastery. This classical symbol is a reminder of when Skyros was under Athenian dominion and heavily populated with Athenian settlers to keep it that way. This part of the castle was built

on ancient foundations (look right) during the early Byzantine era and reinforced in the 14th century by the Venetians.

The monastery itself was founded in 962 and radically rebuilt in 1600. Today it is inhabited by a sole monk. Unfortunately, the once splendid frescoes of the Monastery of St. George are now mostly covered by layers of whitewash, but look for the charming St. George and startled dragon outside to the left of the church door. Within, the ornate iconostasis is considered a masterpiece. The icon of St. George on the right is said to have been brought by settlers from Constantinople, who came in waves during the iconoclast controversy of the 9th century. The icon has a black face and is familiarly known as Agios Georgis o Arapis ("the Negro"); the Skyrians view him as the patron saint not only of their island but of lovers as well. ⊠ *1 km (½ mile) above waterfront.*

> **MYTHIC SKYROS**
>
> In the legends of *The Iliad*, before the Trojan War, Theseus, the deposed hero-king of Athens, sought refuge in his ancestral estate on Skyros. King Lykomedes, afraid of the power and prestige of Theseus, took him up to the acropolis one evening, pretending to show him the island, and pushed him over the cliff—an ignominious end. In ancient times, Timon of Athens unearthed what he said were Theseus's bones and sword, and placed them in the Theseion—more commonly called the Temple of Hephaistion—in Athens, in what must be one of the earliest recorded archaeological investigations.

Rupert Brooke Memorial Statue. It'd be hard to miss the classical bronze statue, *To Brooke,* an honorary tribute to the heroic Edwardian-era English poet Rupert Brooke. Every street seems to lead either to it or to the Kastro, and the statue stands alone with a 180-degree view of the sea behind it. In 1915, aged 28, Brooke was on his way to the Dardanelles to fight in World War I when he died of septicemia in a French hospital ship off Skyros. Brooke was a socialist, but he became something of a paragon for war leaders such as Winston Churchill. ⊠ *Rupert Brooke Sq.* ⊕ *www.rupertbrookeonskyros.com.*

BEACHES

Theotokos. At the northwest side of Skyros and above Ayios Petros beach, Theotokos is a relatively secluded beach reachable by dirt road followed by a little stroll down a goat path. Nearby is the off-limits military base. **Amenities:** none. **Best for:** nudists; swimming; solitude; snorkeling; windsurfing. ⊠ *15 km (9 miles) northwest of Skyros town.*

WHERE TO EAT

Skyros is especially noted for spiny lobster, almost as sweet as the North Atlantic variety.

$
GREEK
✕ **Anatolikos Anemos.** Come here to enjoy tasty *mezedes* bites and light salads while sipping ouzo or cool white wine as the twilight colors the endless Aegean. This cozy little joint has a simple homey feel of a traditional Skyrian dwelling, with intricately carved dark brown walnut furnishings and colorful handmade embroideries adding verve to the boxy, whitewashed interior spaces. It's the perfect place to unwind after

an afternoon spent exploring the Old Town. The simple food is delicious and the views are stunning. $ *Average main: €10* ⊠ *Off Rupert Brookes Square* ☎ *22220/93622* 🖃 *No credit cards.*

WHERE TO STAY

$$
HOTEL
Fodor's Choice
★

ⓘ **Nefeli.** This superb little eco hotel is decorated in Cycladic white and soft green trim, with a dazzling seawater pool and elegant bar terrace. **Pros:** chock-full of delicious goodies, including impressive wine and cigar menus; a library of more than a thousand books; a telescope by the pool; karaoke nights. **Cons:** can get booked up during high season, so make sure to make reservations in advance. $ *Rooms from: €140* ⊠ *Plageiá* ☎ *22/2209–1964, 22/2209–2060* ✉ *info@skyros-nefeli.gr* ⊕ *www.skyros-nefeli.gr* ⟿ *100 rooms* ⊙*Breakfast.*

$$
GREEK

✕ **O Papous Ki'Ego.** "My Grandfather and I," as the name translates in English, serves terrific Greek cuisine in an eclectic dining room decorated with hanging spoons, bottles of wine and ouzo, and whole heads of garlic. The proud grandson suggests that diners order a selection of mezedes and share with others at the table. The best include fried pumpkins with yogurt tzatziki, zucchini croquettes, and meatballs doused with ouzo and served flambé. If you want a single dish, the baby goat served as a casserole tastes delicious. ■ **TIP→ Due to popular demand they have also opened a second taverna in Kalamitsa with the same name.** $ *Average main: €18* ⊠ *Agora* ☎ *22/2209–3200* ⊙ *Closed Nov. and Dec. No lunch.*

NIGHTLIFE

Skyros town's bars are seasonal affairs, offering loud music in summer.

Posto. Modern Greek and foreign hits entertain a laid-back, youthful crowd here. ⊠ *Agora* ☎ *22/2209–2092.*

Rodon. Takis, the owner, is also the DJ here, and he loves spinning the best tunes in town. ⊠ *Agora.*

SHOPPING

Want to buy something really unusual for a shoe lover? Check out the multi-thong *trohadia,* worn with pantaloons by Skyrian men as part of their traditional costume. Just as unique, elaborate Skyrian pottery and furniture are famous around the country. The pottery is both utilitarian and decorative, and the distinctive wooden furniture is easily recognizable by its traditionally carved style. Although you will see it all over town, the best places to shop are all on the agora. Skyrian furniture can be shipped anywhere. Don't try to shop between 2 and 6 pm, as all stores close for siesta.

CLOTHING

Argo Shop. You can find the conversation-stopping *trohadia* footwear at the Argo Shop, which specializes in high-quality imitations of ceramics from the Faltaits Museum. ⊠ *Off Rupert Brooke Sq.* ☎ *22/2209–2158.*

FURNITURE

Lefteris Avgoklouris. The workshop of Lefteris Avgoklouris, a carpenter with flair, is open to visitors. Ask around to find other master carpenters and craftspeople who make original Skyrian furniture, famous around Greece for its intricate technique, and other artistic handicrafts.

This store also ships furniture abroad. ✉ *About 100 yards from Rupert Brooke Sq. on right side of road heading downhill* ☎ *22/2209–1106* 🌐 *augoklouris.weebly.com.*

POTTERY

Ergastiri. This is by far the best workshop and store selling beautiful and highly decorative Skyrian handmade ceramics and imports. ✉ *Magazia* ☎ *22/2209–1559, 22/2209–1887.*

MAGAZIA AND MOLOS ΜΑΓΑΖΙΑ ΚΑΙ ΜΩΛΟΣ

1 km (½ miles) northeast of Skyros town.

Coastal expansions of the main town, these two resort areas are the places to stay if you love to swim. Magazia, where the residents of Skyros town used to have their storehouses and wine presses, and Molos, a bit farther north, where the small fishing fleet anchors, are both growing fast. You can sunbathe, explore the isolated coastline, and stop at sea caves for a swim. Nearby are rooms to rent and tavernas serving the day's catch and local wine. From here, Skyros town is 15 minutes away, along the steps that lead past the archaeological museum to Rupert Brooke Square.

6

Panayia (*Festival of the Virgin*). On the major Greek Orthodox celebration of August 15 (Dormition of the Virgin) children gather at Magazia beach to race on the island's domesticated small ponies, similar to Shetland ponies.

BEACHES

From **Molos** to **Magazia** is a long, sandy beach.

Palamari Beach. North of Molos, past low hills, fertile fields, and the odd farmhouse, a dirt road leads to the historical beach at Palamari, where ruins from a Neolithic fortress and settlement were discovered. Palamari has cool, crystal waters, sandy shores and offers a sense of privacy. **Amenities:** none. **Best for:** solitude; nudists; snorkeling; sunrise; swimming; walking. ✉ *North of Skyros town.*

Pourias Beach. A short walk south of Magazia, Pourias offers good snorkeling, and nearby on the cape is a small treasure: a sea cave that has been transformed into a chapel. There may be no amenities on the beach itself, but there is a little hotel nearby where one can get refreshments. **Amenities:** none. **Best for:** solitude; snorkeling; swimming; walking. ✉ *Skyros town.*

WHERE TO STAY

$ RESORT 🏨 **Perigiali.** Unlike other options in this area, Perigiali has many of the comforts of home and a few that home may be lacking—like private terraces and a pretty, lush garden with plenty of shade, where you can relax over breakfast or drinks in summer. **Pros:** next to Magazia beach. **Cons:** no parking but free community parking two minutes walk away. [$] *Rooms from: €120* ✉ *On beachfront at foot of Skyros town* ☎ *22/2209–1889, 22/2209–2075* 🌐 *www.perigiali.com* 🛏 *11 rooms* 🍴 *Breakfast.*

$ RESORT 🏨 **Skiros Palace.** With a big pool and a gorgeous, isolated beach, this is a water lover's dream. **Pros:** great location; great views. **Cons:** somewhat overpriced given the decor and space. [$] *Rooms from: €100* ✉ *North of*

Molos, Girismata, Kambos ☎ 22/2209–1994, 22/2209–2212 ⊕ www. skiros-palace.gr ⊋ 80 rooms ⊘ Closed Oct.–May ⊠ Breakfast.

NIGHTLIFE

Skiropoula. For late-night dancing, the best club is Skiropoula. Music is Western at first and later on, Greek. A laser lighting system illuminates the rocks of the acropolis after the sun has gone down. The club can be reached from Rupert Brooke Square by descending the steps past the archaeological museum towards Magazia beach. Head here to party modern-Greek style until the early hours. ⊠ *On beach before Magazia* ⊘ *Closed Oct.–Apr.*

ATSITSA ΑΤΣΙΤΣΑ

14 km (9 miles) west of Molos.

On the northwest coast, pine forests grow down the rocky shore at Atsitsa. The beaches north of town—Kalogriá and Kyra Panayia—are sheltered from the strong northern winds called the *meltemi.*

EXPLORING

Ayios Fokas. The road south from Atsitsa deteriorates into a rutted track, nerve-wracking even for experienced motorbike riders. If you're feeling fit and the weather's good, however, consider the challenging 6 km (4-mile) trek around the headland to Ayios Fokas. There are three lovely white-pebbled beaches and a small taverna where Kyria Kali serves fresh fish caught that very same day by her fisherman husband; the fish is garnished with her own vegetables, homemade cheese, and bread. She also rents out a couple of very basic rooms without electricity or plumbing. **Amenities:** food and drink; toilets. **Best for:** solitude; snorkeling; sunset; swimming; walking. ⊠ *5 km (3 miles) south of Atsitsa.*

Skyros Centre. Skyros Centre, founded in 1978, was the first major center in Europe for holistic vacations. Participants come to Atsitsa for a two-week session, staying in straw huts or in the main building, in a peaceful environment surrounded by pines and facing the sea. Studies and courses include windsurfing, creative writing with well-known authors, art, tai chi, yoga, massage, dance, drama, and sound-healing. Courses also take place in Skyros town, where participants live in villagers' traditional houses. Skyros Centre's courses are highly reputed. Contact the London office well in advance of leaving for Greece. ⊠ *Atsitsa coast* ☎ 0044/207–267–4424 *U.K.,* 0044/198–386–5566 *U.K.* ⊕ *www.skyros.co.uk.*

BEACHES

Ayios Petros Beach. North of Atsitsa (8 km/5 miles), close to the airport, this wonderful white sand and pebble beach is surrounded by lush greenery and serenely backdropped, on the hill above it, by the little chapel of Ayios Petros. Don't be put off by the 4 km (2.5 miles) of dirt road leading to the beach, as it is definitely worth the effort. **Amenities:** none. **Best for:** snorkeling; swimming; walking; windsurfing. ⊹ *15 km (9 miles) north of Skyros town.*

VOUNO BOYNO

Via Loutro, 5 km (3 miles) northwest of Linaria; access to southern territory starts at Ahilli, 4 km (2½ miles) south of Skyros town and 25 km (15½ miles) from Atsitsa.

In the mountainous southern half of Skyros, a passable dirt road heads south at the eastern end of the isthmus, from Aspous to Ahilli. The little bay of Ahilli (from where legendary Achilles set sail with Odysseus) is a yacht marina. Some beautiful, practically untouched beaches and sea caves are well worth the trip for hard-core explorers.

Thorny bushes warped into weird shapes, oleander, and rivulets running between sharp rocks make up the landscape; only goats and Skyrian ponies can survive this desolate environment. Many scholars consider the beautifully proportioned, diminutive horses to be the same breed as the horses sculpted on the Parthenon frieze. They are, alas, an endangered species, and only about 100 survive.

Rupert Brooke's grave. Pilgrims to Rupert Brooke's grave should follow the wide dirt road through the Vouno wilderness down toward the shore. As you reach the valley, you can catch sight of the grave in an olive grove on your left. He was buried the same night he died on Skyros, and his marble grave was immortalized with his prescient words, "If I should die think only this of me:/ That there's some corner of a foreign field/ That is forever England." Restored by the British Royal Navy in 1961, the gravesite is surrounded by a stout wrought-iron and cement railing. You also can arrange for a visit by taxi or caïque in Skyros town. ✉ *Southwest end of the island* ⊕ *www.rupertbrookeonskyros.com.*

BEACHES

Kalamitsa. The windy beach of Kalamitsa is 4 km (2½ miles) along the road south from Ahilli, and popular with windsurfers for obvious reasons. Nevertheless, this also means that the clean sands can be whipped up into skin-cleansing frenzy on certain days, so whether you're a surfer or bather, check the winds first. ■ TIP➜ It's known for its clean waters. There are three decent tavernas at this old harbor. **Amenities:** food and drink; parking (free); showers; toilets; water sports. **Best for:** sunset; swimming; snorkeling; surfing; windsurfing ✉ *Kalamitsa.*

EPIRUS AND THESSALY

Ioannina, Metsovo, and the
Meteora Monasteries

WELCOME TO EPIRUS AND THESSALY

TOP REASONS TO GO

★ **Meteora Monasteries:** Even more wondrous than the Meteora's soaring rock pinnacles are the medieval monasteries perched atop them—walk, climb, or drive to these still-inhabited spots where eagles once nested.

★ **Zagorohoria Region:** Dotting the dramatic Vikos gorge are 46 traditional villages filled with picturesque Ottoman houses—this is some of the best hiking countryside in all Greece.

★ **Dodona:** Visiting the ancient site of Dodona in Epirus is a must: many mystical ceremonies took place in this ancient sanctuary of Zeus.

★ **Experience Metsovo's Traditions:** This mountain village has held on hard to its traditional character— discover its stone houses, customary foods, and winding alleyways (each with its own story).

★ **Haunts of Ali Pasha:** Even Lord Byron was drawn to Ioannina to trace the haunted spirit of the legendary pasha who once made Epirus his own personal potentate.

1 Ioannina. Strongly infused by the influences of Greeks, Jews, and Turks, Ioannina rests on the banks of lake Pamvotis. Picturesquely medieval and founded by Emperor Justinian in 527, the town is shadowed by two historic mosques, which reflect the area's marked oriental character. While it has an extensive, multi-cultural history, Ioannina also has a vibrant modern scene. To the north lies the Zagorohoria, whose combo of picturesque houses and arresting gorge landscape make this a must-do.

2 Metsovo. Studded with traditional houses filled with Epirote arts and crafts, this mountain township is famously inhabited by Vlachous who speak their distinct dialect. After visiting the noted Tositsa Museum, head to the hills for an idyllic skiing vacation, nature walks, or wine tours.

Grevena

Mt.
Karakoli

Meteora **4**

Metsovo Kastraki Kalambaka

2

P I N D O S

Neraidohori Tríkala

Pili

THESSALY

Mouzáki

Drossopigi

| 0 | | 50 mi |
| 0 | | 50 km |

GETTING ORIENTED

Travelers in search of wild and romantic country will be more than delighted with these two regions of northern Greece. In the markedly Balkan region of Epirus, the route east from Ioannina leads to the thriving traditional village of Metsovo and over the Katara pass on one of the most dramatic roads in Greece. Westward lies the fertile province of Thessaly, where spectacular rock-pinnacle monasteries are shadowed by the Pindos, Plion, and Olympus mountain ranges.

7

3 Dodona. Mentioned by Homer in the 10th book of the *Iliad*, the Dodona oracle once presided here, only eclipsed by Delphi in classical times. View the remains of the sanctuary of Zeus and the majestic ancient theater, which once held 17,000 spectators, and is still the venue of Greek drama presentations.

4 Meteora. Looming out of the edge of Thessaly's main plain, the sky-kissing medieval monasteries of Meteora seem to float in midair, built atop bizarrely shaped pinnacles that tower over the town of Kalambaka. You can enjoy relaxed, fun nights in this "town near Meteora" on its central Dimoula Square, with the Meteora rocks as a backdrop.

Updated by
Adrian Vrettos

As travelers journey through the provinces of northern Greece, they quickly realize that Epirus and Thessaly may have far fewer miles of drop-dead-gorgeous coastline than the south, but if visitors have brought their hiking boots as well as their bathing suits, the north's spectacular mountains, folkloric villages, and lush valleys more than make up for it.

The land changes abruptly from the delicately shaded green of the idyllic olive and orange groves near the shore to the tremendous solidity of the bare mountains inland. This was the splendid massive landscape that came to cast its spell over Lord Byron, who traveled here to meet tyrant Ali Pasha (1741–1822). The Epirote capital of Ioannina still bears many vestiges of this larger-than-life figure, who seems to have stepped from the pages of *The Arabian Nights*.

Going back in time, and taking an easy trip southwest of Ioannina, you can visit Dodona, the site of the oldest oracle in Greece. North of Ioannina, in the mountainous region known as Zagorohoria, or the Zagori, dozens of tiny, unspoiled villages contain remnants of the Ottoman period, and outdoor activities such as hiking are abundant. The route east from Ioannina leads to the thriving traditional village of Metsovo in the Pindos mountains and over the Katara pass on one of the most dramatic roads in Greece. It ends in the fertile province of Thessaly, where, on the edge of the plain, the Byzantine-era monasteries of Meteora seem to float in midair, built atop bizarrely shaped pinnacles that tower over the town of Kalambaka. At this spiritual center of Orthodox Greece, the quiet contemplation of generations of monks is preserved in wondrously frescoed buildings. Nearby, spectacular mountain passes reveal shepherd villages with richly costumed women speaking the Vlach vernacular.

All in all, northwestern Greece, which stretches from the northern shore of the gulf of Corinth to the Albanian frontier west of the Pindos range, was aroused from its centuries-old slumber several decades ago with the advent of the ferryboats from Italy. The nautical crossing from Corfu to Igoumenitsa, the westward gateway town to mainland Greece, is

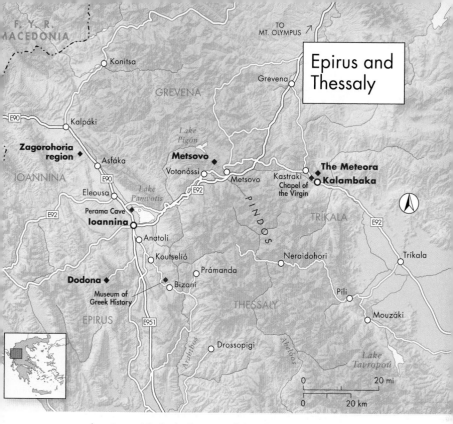

enchanting, with the lush green of the island slowly receding and the stark outlines of the mainland dramatically ahead. The bay is at its best in the early morning, but sunset will do, when the gray rocks likewise flame with deep pinks and violets in an unforgettable welcome. Igoumenitsa is generally unappealing as a port of entry, which means everyone quickly pushes on into the interior and discovers the often-overlooked wonders of Epirus and Thessaly.

PLANNING

WHEN TO GO

Ioannina is easy to visit year-round, but excursions to the countryside are best May through October, when most places are open. Winter is great for skiing and curling up by the fire, although spring, when the abundant and broadly variable natural surroundings blossom, is captivating, especially in the fabled Zagorohoria region. Metsovo can be blissfully cool even in high summer (especially at night). This helps make the town *panagyri* (saint's day festival) for Ayia Paraskevi, held July 26, quite pleasant, but the heat is oppressive elsewhere in this region at this time. The Meteora monasteries attract considerably fewer people in winter, but keep in mind the Thessalian plain can bake during summer in the vast oven formed by the surrounding high mountains. Maximum enjoyment will be obtained in the spring, especially at the Meteora monasteries. At this point, the mountains are still snow covered and blend harmoniously with the green fields, the red poppies, and the white and pink fruit trees.

In Epirus, local tourist offices and most hotels will provide information about festivals, including the famous Ioannina International Folk Festival showcasing the region's music and dancing, which takes place in July. For those seeking the haunting traditional *klarino* (clarinet) music and graceful circle dances of Epirus such as the *pogonisios* and *beratis*, this is a fascinating event. Local groups also perform eerie polyphonic singing, another unique folk tradition rooted in the region.

PLANNING YOUR TIME

Coming either from Thessaloniki, or from the Northwestern port of Igoumenitsa, it's reasonable to make the lively town of Ioannina and its glittering lake your starting point. Two nights there should be enough to get a good taste of this city, leaving ample time to take in the top attractions and regional tastes on offer. From there head to the Zagorohoria villages, a unique destination that draws visitors from around the world. Two days here will offer you a good introduction to the area, but will definitely leave you wanting more. The Vikos Gorge, the deepest in Europe, is a highlight of this stunning area.

Metsovo is the next noteworthy destination in Epirus. A couple of nights are more than enough to enjoy this unique Vlach mountain town. From Metsovo the meandering mountain roads first wind their way up out of Epirus and then down into Thessaly and the town of Kalambaka. It's next to the breathtaking Meteora monasteries perched atop giant limestone stacks, where you should linger a couple of days.

GETTING HERE AND AROUND

Although it's not a major tourist destination, Volos is the major port city of the Thessaly region and bus, train, and boat routes often use it as a base.

AIR TRAVEL

Olympic Air and Aegean Airlines are the only carriers that service this region. The Ioannina airport, the primary airport in the region, is 8 km (5 miles) north of town. *For detailed information about these airlines, see Air Travel in Travel Smart.*

Contacts Ioannina Airport ⊠ *Ethnikos Odos Ioanninon–Trikalon Rd., Km 8, Ioannina* ☎ *26510/83600, 26510/83602.*

BUS TRAVEL

About seven buses a day make the 7-hour trip from Athens's Terminal A (Kifissou) to Ioannina's main Papandreou Station. One of these takes the longer route east through Kalambaka and Trikala rather than the usual southern route to the Rion–Antirion ferry over the suspension bridge, which is the largest in Europe. From Athens's dismal Terminal B (Liossion), seven buses leave daily for the 5-hour journey to Kalambaka. Most routes require you to hop on a different bus for the final leg from Trikala, but one morning bus goes direct.

From Thessaloniki to Ioannina there are six buses a day, and thanks to the Engatia highway the trip takes a mere 3½ hours and costs €28. Thessaloniki to Kalambaka takes 2¾ hours (€20) with four buses leaving daily. Around four KTEL buses leave Ioannina daily for Metsovo (about 1 hour) and two buses for Kalambaka (2 hours); frequencies are the same in the opposite direction. Buses also head to Dodona. The several-times-weekly bus heading for Melingi village passes the ancient site. Other bus options drop you off 1 km (½ mile) or ½ km (¼ mile) from the site; ask for information based on the day you want to go. On Sunday, service is reduced for all towns. Regular bus service runs from Ioannina's main terminal to the towns in the Zagorohoria. There is also regular and frequent bus service from Athens to Volos, of little interest to travelers but a major transportation hub in the region; from Volos, you can easily connect to Thessaloniki and other destinations in the region. *For detailed information about travel by bus, see Bus Travel in Travel Smart.*

Contacts Ioannina Bus Station ✉ *Papandreou 45, Ioannina* ☎ *26510/25014, 26510/26286* ⊕ *www.ktelioannina.gr.* **Kalambaka Bus Station** ✉ *Plateia Dimarchiou, Kalambaka* ☎ *24320/22432 in Trikala.* **Papandreou Station** ✉ *Papandreou 45, Ioannina* ☎ *26510/27442, 26510/25014 for Metsovo, Kalambaka, and Dodona.*

CAR TRAVEL

This region is best explored by car, and if you plan to go beyond the main sights, your own wheels are essential. Driving to Kalambaka or Ioannina from Athens takes the greater part of a day. To reach Ioannina take the National Road west past Corinth in the Peloponnese, crossing the magnificent Rion–Antirion bridge. The total trip is 445 km (276 miles). For Kalambaka, take the National Road north past Thebes; north of Lamia there's a turnoff for Trikala and Kalambaka (a total of 330 km [204 miles]). The drive from Thessaloniki takes around 5 hours and winds you over the mountains and river valleys of Kozani and Grevena on the National Road.

The road from Ioannina to Metsovo to Kalambaka is one of the most scenic in northern Greece, but it traverses the famous Katara pass, which is curvy and can be hazardous, especially December through March (snow chains are necessary). If you are traveling with a few people, it might be more relaxing and almost as economical to hire a taxi to drive you around, at least for a day.

You can rent a car from either Budget or Hertz at the Ioannina Airport. Tomaso is a local rental agency in Ioanina with an office in town. *For information about major agencies, see Car Travel in Travel Smart.*

Contacts Tomaso ✉ *42 Dodonis, Ioannina* ☎ *26510/20000, 26510/68400* ⊕ *www.tomaso.gr.*

TAXI TRAVEL

If you see a cab along the street, step into the road and shout your destination. The driver will stop if he or she is going in your direction. You can ask your hotel reception desk to phone for a taxi and help you negotiate with a taxi driver, especially if you want a tour. You can find taxis at the local bus station and in the central square and at other spots around town. Minimum tariffs are €3.

TRAIN TRAVEL

Kalambaka is reachable by train. Locals normally prefer to travel by bus, because trains generally take longer. However, train travel makes sense on the Athens Larissis Station–Kalambaka route if you take the daily express intercity (5 hours) at 8:30 am—ironically €10 cheaper than the slow trains. It costs around the same as a bus—about €25 class A, €18.50 class B for the train and €28 for the bus. Investing in a class A seat (*proti thesi*) means more room and comfort. The nonexpress train is agonizingly slow (at least 7 hours) and requires a change at Palaiofarsalo.

There are also frequent trains between Athens and Volos (a 5-hour journey that leaves six to seven times per day and costs €35–€43) via Larissa. From Volos, buses and trains connect with Thessaloniki every 2 hours (a journey lasting around 2½ hours and costing €18.40); the train trip requires a change at Larissa. Trains to Larissa leave about every hour on the 2- to 3-hour journey; tickets cost €12 to €27.

For detailed information about taking the train, see Train Travel in Travel Smart.

Contacts Kalambaka Train Station ⊠ *Pindou, Kalambaka* ☎ *24320/22451.*

HOTELS

Rooms are usually easy to find in Ioannina and, except at the best hotels, are simply decorated. Reservations might be necessary for Kalambaka, which is packed with tour groups to the Meteora monasteries in late spring and summer, and in Metsovo during ski season or the town's July 26 festival. In these two towns, private rooms are likely to be far cheaper than comparable hotel rooms—look for advertisements as you arrive. Off-season, prices drop drastically from those listed here, and you should always try to negotiate. Ask to see the room first, and don't assume anything; if you have special requests, such as a mountain view, a *diplo drevati* (double bed) rather than a *diklino* (twin bed); a balcony; or a bathtub, speak up. In some cases, prices will skyrocket for Greek Easter and Christmas. In Epirus, most small hotels are built in the charming and traditional style—usually recognizable by the heavy use of wood and stone, most suited to the cold winter months, when these accommodations make the perfect base for skiing, hiking, and other activities.

RESTAURANTS

In all but the fanciest restaurants, check out what's cooking because menus change seasonally here. These regions, perhaps because of their dramatic winters, are known for some of the heartiest, rib-stickingest meals around Greece. Informal dress is usually appropriate. Metsovites are particularly known for their meat specialties, such as *kontosouvli* (lamb or pork kebab) and boiled goat, their *trahanas* soup (made from cracked wheat boiled in milk and dried), and their sausages or meatballs stuffed with leeks, as well as their costly but delectable smoked Metsovone cheese. *Pites* (pies, or pita) are pastry envelopes filled with local and seasonal produce, from savory meats and vegetables to sweet dairy creams and honey. Head to the lakesides, most famously those in Ioannina, to feast on aquatic delights: frogs' legs, trout, eel, and crayfish. Wherever you head, Epirote restaurants generally offer an interesting blend of Greek, Turkish, and Jewish flavors usually prepared with fresh local produce. Some of their tried-and-true recipes are *moschari kokkinisto* (a tomato-base veal stew with carrots, onions, and peas), lamb in lemon sauce, and *lathera* (stove-top vegetable stew made with artichoke hearts, beans, okra, and tomatoes). And the best wine to wash it all down with is Katogi red wine pressed from French Bordeaux grapes grown locally in Metsovo.

DINING AND LODGING PRICES IN EUROS			
	$	**$$**	**$$$**	**$$$$**
Restaurants	under €16	€16–€25	€26–€40	over €40
Hotels	under €126	€126–€225	€226–€275	over €275

Restaurant prices are for one main course at dinner, or for two mezedes (small dishes). Hotel prices are for a standard double room in high season, including taxes.

VISITOR INFORMATION

The Greek National Tourism Organization (GNTO or EOT) in Ioannina is open weekdays 7:30–2:30 and 5:30–8, Saturday 9–1 in July and August; hours vary other months. Mornings are the best time to catch someone in. In summer a tourist information booth is usually erected in the main square of Kalambaka, but it's best to visit the town hall for information.

Contacts Greek National Tourism Organization ✉ *Dodonis 39, Ioannina* ☎ *26510/41868, 26510/48442, 26510/48866* ⊕ *www.visitgreece.gr.* **Kalambaka Municipality** ✉ *Vlahava 3, Kalambaka* ☎ *24323/50200, 24323/50201.*

EPIRUS ΗΠΕΙΡΟΣ

Ipiros (Epirus) fully justifies its name, continent, by an overwhelming concentration of mountains, contrasting with the islands—Corfu, Paxi, Lefkada—strung along its littoral. The abrupt changes from the delicately shaded green of the idyllic olive groves on the coast to the tremendous solidity of the bare mountains have been faithfully depicted by that versatile Victorian, Edward Lear (of limerick fame). But few travelers would nowadays put up with the discomfort, hardship, and very real danger from bandits that Lear seems to have enjoyed. The scenery has kept its grandeur, but has become easily accessible by a good road network and plenty of hotels.

Ancient Epirus was once a huge country that stretched from modern-day Albania (an area the Greeks still call northern Epirus and one in which Greek is still spoken by large communities) to the gulf of Arta and modern Preveza. The region is bordered by the Ionian Sea to the west, the islands of Lefkada to the south, and Corfu to the north. Inland it is defined by a tangle of mountain peaks and upland plains, and the climate is markedly Balkan.

Although invaded by Normans in 1080, Epirus gained in importance after the influx of refugees from Constantinople and the Morea beginning in 1205 and was made a despotate, a principality ruled by a despot. Ioannina was subsequently made the capital of Epirus and fortified by Michalis Angelos, the first despot. After an invasion by Serbs, Ioannina surrendered to the Ottomans in 1431 and Epirus remained a part of its empire until it became part of Greece in 1913. Besides this great Turkish influence, Metsovo and the surrounding area contain the largest concentration of the non-Greek population known as the Vlachs, nomadic shepherds said to be descendants of legionnaires from garrisons on the Via Egnatia, one of the Roman Empire's main east–west routes. The Vlachs speak a Romance language related to Italian and Romanian.

IOANNINA IΩANNINA

305 km (189 miles) northwest of Athens, 204 km (126 miles) west-southwest of Thessaloniki.

On the rocky promontory of Lake Pamvotis lies Ioannina, its fortress punctuated by mosques and minarets whose reflections, along with those of the snowy peaks of the Pindos range, appear in the calm water. The lake contains tiny Nissi, or "island," where nightingales still sing and fishermen mend their nets (and now noted as the hometown of Karolos Papoulias, the current president of the Greek Republic). Although on first impression parts of the city may seem noisy and undistinguished, the Old Quarter preserves a rich heritage. Outstanding examples of folk architecture remain within the castle walls and in the neighborhoods surrounding them; Ioannina's historic mansions, folk houses, seraglios, and bazaars are a reminder of the city's illustrious past. Set at a crossroads of trading, the city is sculpted by Balkan, Ottoman, and Byzantine influences. Thanks to a resident branch of the Greek national university, today the bustling provincial capital city (population 100,000) has a thriving contemporary cultural scene (and a proliferation of good restaurants and popular bars). Things get particularly lively the first two weeks of July, when the city's International Folk Festival takes place.

The name Ioannina was first documented in 1020 and may have been taken from an older monastery of St. John. Founded by Emperor Justinian in AD 527, Ioannina suffered under many rulers: it was invaded by the Normans in 1082, made a dependency of the Serbian kingdom in 1345, and conquered by the Turks in 1431. Above all, this was Ali Pasha's city, where, during its zenith, from 1788 to 1821, the despot carved a fiefdom from much of western Greece. His territory extended from the Ionian Sea to the Pindos range and from Vaona in the north to Arta in the south. The Turks ended his rule in 1821 by using deception to capture him; Ali Pasha was then shot and decapitated by Greek monks.

GETTING HERE AND AROUND

Olympic Air offers tickets from €60 to €100 one-way from Athens. Direct charter flights from any European capital to Ioannina Airport are also available.

There is no train service to Ioannina, but it is well served by bus. Ioannina KTEL bus station (⊠ *Georgiou Papandreou 45* ☏ *26510/27442*) offers routes connecting with Konitsa (2 hours), Igoumenitsa (2½ hours), Athens (6½ hours), Thessaloniki (3½ hours), and many other towns. From Athens, buses depart weekdays every couple hours from 6:30 am to 10:30 pm, Sunday from 8:30 am until 10:30 pm; tickets are €39. Buses connect with Metsovo twice a day weekdays and once a day weekends; tickets are €5.80. Buses connect with Trikala's bus station (☏ *24310/73130*), a major hub of Thessaly, twice daily; the ride takes 2½ hours and costs €14.70.

Boats depart for Nissi island in Lake Pamvotis every hour in the winter and every 45 minutes in the summer months. The boats leave from the gate of the Kastro fortress; tickets are €1.80.

TOP ATTRACTIONS

Archaeological Museum of Ioannina. Located in the center of town, this museum is the best in the area. It houses exhibits from the greater Epirus such as Paleolithic tools, inscriptions, statues, headstones, and a collection of coins, all presented in a contemporary exhibition space with multimedia facilities. ⊠ *25th Martiou Sq.* ☏ *26510/01050* ⊕ *www. culture.gr* ⊠ *€2* ☉ *Tues.–Sun. 8–3.*

Byzantine Museum. Within the larger citadel is the fortress, called *Its Kale* by the Turks, where Ali Pasha built his palace; these days the former palace serves the city as the Byzantine Museum. The museum's small collection of artworks, actually almost all post-Byzantine, includes intricate silver manuscript Bible covers, wall murals from mansions, and carved wooden benediction crosses covered in lacy silver, gathered from all over the countryside of Epirus. It's carefully arranged in the front half of the museum with good English translations. The second half of the museum houses an important collection of icons and remarkable iconostases, painted by local masters and salvaged from 16th- and 17th-century monasteries. The most interesting section is devoted to silver works from Ali Pasha's treasury from the seraglio. Within the fortress grounds is a very pleasant little café—why not enjoy some light snacks and desserts as you take in the views of the lush gardens around the Byzantine Museum and the impressive old ruins? Nearby is the **Fethiye (Victory) Mosque,** which purports to contain Ali Pasha's tomb. ⊠ *Eastern corner of Its Kale fortress* ☏ *26510/39580* ⊠ *€3* ☉ *Tues.–Sun. 8–5.*

Kastro (*Castle*). One of Ioannina's main attractions is the Kastro, with massive, fairly intact stone walls that once dropped into the lake on three sides; Ali Pasha completely rebuilt them in 1815. The city's once-large Romaniote Jewish population, said to date from the time of Alexander the Great, lived within the walls, alongside Turks and Christians. The Jews were deported by the Nazis during World War II, to meet their deaths at extermination camps; of the 4,000-plus inhabitants around the turn of the 20th century, fewer than 100 remain today. The area inside the walls is now a quaint residential area with a few hotels, cafés, restaurants, and stores. Outside the citadel walls, near the lake, a **monument** at Karamanli and Soutsou streets commemorates the slaughter of the Jewish community. ⊠ *Lakeside end of Odhos Averoff.*

Fodor'sChoice   **Nissi Island.** Look back at the outline of the citadel and its mosques in
★   a wash of green as you take the 10-minute ride from the shore toward small Nissi Island. The whitewashed lakeside island village was founded in the late 16th century by refugees from the Mani (in the Peloponnese). No outside recreational vehicles are allowed, and without the din of motorcycles and cars, the picturesque village seems centuries away from Ioannina. Ali Pasha once kept deer here for hunting. With its neat houses and flower-trimmed courtyards, pine-edged paths, runaway chickens, and reed-filled backwater, it's the perfect place to relax, have lunch, visit some of the monasteries (dress appropriately and carry a small flashlight to make it easier to see the magnificent frescoes), and have a pleasant dinner. Frogs' legs, eel, trout, and carp (displayed live in large tanks) take center stage, although traditional fare is also served at most tavernas here. To cap off your visit, stop by quiet Aleion Square for a relaxed coffee and a leisurely game of backgammon. ⊠ *Ferry below citadel, near Mavili Sq.* 🎫 *Ferry €2* ⊗ *May–Sept., ferry daily on the hour 8 am–11 am then every ½ hr 11 am–1 pm; Oct.–Apr., daily on the hr 8 am–10 pm.*

WORTH NOTING

Agios Nikolaos ton Filanthropinon. Of Nissi's several monasteries, Agios Nikolaos ton Filanthropinon has the best frescoes. The monastery was built in the 13th century by an important Byzantine family, the Filanthropinos, and a fresco in the northern exonarthex (the outer narthex) depicts five of them kneeling before St. Nikolaos (1542). Many of the frescoes are by the Kontaris brothers, who later decorated the mighty Varlaam in Meteora. Note the similarities in the bold coloring, expressiveness, realism, and Italian influence—especially in the bloody scenes of martyrdom. Folk tradition says the corner crypts in the south chapel were the meeting places of the secret school of Hellenic culture during the Ottoman occupation. A most unusual fresco here of seven sages of antiquity, including Solon, Aristotle, and Plutarch, gives credence to this story. It is not really feasible, however, that the school would have been kept a secret from the Ottoman governors for long; more likely, the reigning Turkish pasha was one who allowed religious and cultural freedom (as long as the taxes were paid). ⊠ *On Nissi island, follow signs* 🎫 *Donations accepted* ⊗ *Daily 8–8.*

Ali Pasha Museum. The main attraction on Nissi is the 16th-century Pandelimonos Monastery, now the Ali Pasha Museum. Ali Pasha was killed here in the monks' cells on January 17, 1822, after holding out for almost two years. In the final battle, Ali ran into an upstairs cell, but the soldiers shot him through its floorboards from below. (The several "bullet" holes in the floor were drilled there when the original floor had to be replaced.) A wax version of the assassination can be seen at the Pavlos Vrellis Museum of Greek History in Bizani, south of Ioannina. A happier Ali Pasha, asleep on the lap of his wife, Vasiliki, can be seen in the museum's famous portrait. The Ali Pasha Museum also houses the crypt where Vasiliki hid, some evocative etchings and paintings of that era, an edict signed by Ali Pasha with his ring seal (he couldn't write), and his magnificent narghile (water pipe) standing on the fireplace. The community-run museum is generally open as long as boats are running; if the doors are shut, ask around to be let in. The local ticket taker will give a brief tour of the museum in Greek and broken English (supplemented by an English-language printed guide). A tour is free, but do leave a tip. ⊠ *On Nissi, take left from boat landing and follow signs* ☎ *26510/81791* 🖃 *€3* ⊗ *Daily 9–8:45.*

Kostas Frontzos Museum of Epirote Folk Art. In a finely restored Ottoman house, this small museum has a collection of richly embroidered local costumes, rare woven textiles made by the nomadic tent-dwelling Sarakatsanis, ceramics, and cooking and farm implements. ⊠ *Michail Angelou 42* ☎ *26510/23566* 🖃 *€2* ⊗ *Daily 9 am–2 pm; also Mon. and Wed. 5:30–8.*

Lake Pamvotis. Despite the fact that the water level is so low (the streams that feed it are drying up) and it has become too polluted for swimming, Lake Pamvotis remains picturesque. Still, it has the longest rowing course in Greece, and teams from all over the Balkans use it for training. The Valkaniadia rowing championships are periodically hosted here. Legend has it that the notorious Ali Pasha drowned his son's lover (after she rejected the Pasha's wishes for her to become his own mistress) in this lake along with other local women, and that their spirits haunt it to this day.

Mavili Square. This waterfront square is lined with large, noisy cafés that fill with locals and travelers waiting for the next boat to the nearby isle of Nissi. In the evening the seawall is *the* place to hang out—the youth of Ioannina while away the hours here sipping turbo-charged frappé iced coffees or aperitif drinks. The *volta* (ritual promenade) is still a favorite way of passing the time and keeping up to date with all the action and gossip, particularly at night when the town shifts into high gear.

Municipal Museum. The collections in the well-preserved Aslan Mosque, now the Municipal Museum, recall the three communities (Greek, Turkish, Jewish) that lived together inside the fortress from 1400 to 1611. The vestibule has recesses for shoes, and inscribed over the doorway is the name of Aslan Pasha and "there is only one god, Allah, and Muhammad is his prophet." The mosque retains its original decoration and *mihrab,* a niche that faces Mecca. Exhibited around the room are a walnut-and-mother-of-pearl table from Ali Pasha's period, ornate inlaid hammam (Turkish bath), shoes on tall wooden platforms, treasure chests, traditional clothing, a water pipe, and a collection of 18th- and 19th-century guns. ⊠ *North end of citadel* ☎ *26510/26356* 🖃 *€2* ⊗ *Daily 9–4:30.*

Old Bazaar. Vestiges of 19th-century Ioannina remain in the Old Bazaar. On Anexartisias are some Turkish-era structures, such as the Liabei arcade (where cool and trendy bars and clubs now dominate), across from the bustling municipal produce market and, on Filiti, a smattering of the copper-, tin-, and silversmiths who fueled the city's economy for

To assert their rule over Ioannina, the Turks built the Its Kale fortress; but it was transformed into Ali Pasha's palace in the early 19th century.

centuries. Some workshops still have wares for sale. ⊠ *Around citadel's gates at Ethnikis Antistasios and Averoff.*

NEED A BREAK?
Filistron. An intimate café on a main street near the citadel area, Filistron occupies a 200-year-old residence with a colorful folk interior including decorated ceilings. Pamper yourself with some of the most unique drinks in Greece. Try *salepi* and other Arab herbal drinks with a splash of alcohol, or stop by in the late evening for Metaxa brandy and a *visino* (a spoon sweet made up of black cherries preserved in syrup, eaten by the spoonful or added to a beverage). For breakfast, try the thick strained yogurt topped with chestnut-color honey and chopped walnuts. ⊠ *Andronikou Paleologou 20* 🕾 *26510/33131* 🕙 *Mon. 4–midnight, Tues.–Sun. noon–midnight.*

FAMILY **Pavlos Vrellis Museum of Greek History.** Want to see a tableau of Ali Pasha's legendary murder? Head to this museum to be shocked and amused, by turn, by its collection of historical Epirote waxwork figures from the past 2,500 years, all leading players in more than 30 historical "settings," including streets, mountains, caves, churches, and more. All the figures were sculpted in wax by artist Pavlos Vrellis, a local legend who embarked on this endeavor at the ripe age of 60. His studio is on the premises, a modern building that has stayed true to Eipirotic architectural style. ⊠ *12 km (7 miles) south of Ioannina, Ethnikos Odos Ioanninon–Athinon Rd., Bizani* 🕾 *26510/92128* ⊕ *www.vrellis.gr* 🖃 *€5* 🕙 *Apr.–Sept., daily 9:30–5; Oct.–Mar., daily 10–4.*

Perama Cave. The cave's passageways, discovered in the early 1940s by locals hiding from the Nazis, extend for more than 1 km (½ mile) under the hills. You learn about the high caverns and multihued limestone stalagmites during the 45-minute guided tour; one begins about every 15 minutes. Printed English-language information is available. Be prepared for the many steps you must walk up on the way out. At the information center you can see some of the paleontological finds from Perama and learn more about the geology of caves. Bus No. 8 from Ioannina's clock tower gets you here. ✉ *E92, 4 km (2½ miles) north of Ioannina* ☎ *26510/81521* 🌐 *spilaio-perama.gr* 🎫 *€7* 🕒 *May–Oct., daily 9–5.*

THE PRETTIEST WALK

Set at the lakeside end of Odhos Averoff, tree-lined Dionyssiou Skylosofou, which circles the citadel along the lake, is ideal for a late-afternoon stroll. The street was named for a defrocked Trikala bishop who led an ill-fated uprising against the Turks in 1611 (and was flayed alive as a result). A moat, now filled, ran around the southwest landward side, and today the walls divide the Old Town—with its rose-laden pastel-color houses, overhanging balconies, cobblestone streets, and birdsong—from the new.

WHERE TO EAT

$ GREEK 🍴 **Fisa Roufa.** This is best place in Ioannina to enjoy grandma's home-style cooking, such as pork and celery in a velvety egg-lemon sauce, chicken in yogurt sauce, and patsa (tripe) and beef in tomato sauce—simply head to the counter at the back of the simple, charming restaurant and point at the dishes that strike your fancy. Beer is served cold and the wine, by the kilo (half if you must). [$] *Average main: €6* ✉ *Averof 55* ☎ *26510/26262.*

$ GREEK 🍴 **Gastra.** Mr. Vassilis has run this friendly traditional taverna for more than 30 years. Here you can discover how Greek grandmothers cooked before the comforts of electricity were introduced to Epirus. The *gastra* is basically a large container with hot coals placed on the iron lid over the pot. Your meal (of lamb, chicken, or goat) roasts very slowly in its own juices, resulting in tender, juicy meat with a crispy outer skin. [$] *Average main: €11* ✉ *Opposite the Dodonis factory, 7 km (4½ miles) north of Ioannina on the way to the airport, Eleousa* ☎ *26510/61530* 🌐 *www.gastra.gr* ✍ *Reservations essential* 🕒 *Closed Mon.*

$ GREEK Fodor's Choice ★ 🍴 **Mirovolos.** One of the last in Ioannina's main and famous row of lake-side tavernas, family-run and welcoming Mirovolos serves great food. Enjoy delightful local starters, such as *melitzana bourekakia* (eggplant-stuffed phyllo sheets), *kolokithokeftedes* (zucchini and feta fritters), and the zingy cheese dip *tirokafteri* (made with feta) from nearby Dodoni, washed down with their light house white. For a main course, savor the spiced *kontosouvli* (pork tenderloin) or the Greco-Roman chicken pie with a light Parmesan sauce. Graze while you gaze at the lovely view of the miniaret of Aslan Mosque reflecting on the calm waters of Lake Pamvotis. [$] *Average main: €10* ✉ *Strat. Papagou 28* ☎ *26510/78695.*

WHERE TO STAY

$ HOTEL FAMILY 🏨 **Epirus Palace.** Indulging oneself in the city of that sybarite Ali Pasha seems entirely fitting, and you can do so in style at this stunning and lavish hotel, which was opened in 1999 by the innovative brothers Natsis. **Pros:** check for special deals that can make your five-star stay very affordable; top restaurant; lush decor; gently priced. **Cons:** 10 minutes away from Ioannina by car. $ *Rooms from: €120 ⊠ 7 km (4½ miles) south of Ioannina, Ethnikos Odos Ioanninon–Athinon ☎ 26510/93555, 26510/91072 ⊕ www.epiruspalace.gr* ❢◯❙ *Breakfast.*

$ ⚏ **Grand Serai.** If you're looking for bombastic decor and over-the-
HOTEL top plushness, this luxurious hotel is the place for you—the lobby's vast chandeliers and heavy brocaded armchairs may not be to everyone's taste, but the guest rooms are more subdued, with golden gilt wood trimmings and modern marble en suite bathrooms. **Pros:** ideal for business trips thanks to well-equipped conference facilities; atmospheric spa; central location; helpful staff. **Cons:** beware of hidden costs (like pool extras, in-room Wi-Fi). $ *Rooms from: €110 ⊠ Dodonis 33 ☎ 26510/90550, 26510/90557 ⊕ ioannina-luxuryhotelgrandserai. clickhere.gr* ❢◯❙ *Breakfast.*

$ ⚏ **Kastro Hotel.** Delightful wood beams, painted wooden ceilings, two
HOTEL fireplaces (in the sitting and breakfast rooms), and the wood-trimmed
Fodor's Choice guest rooms of this hotel—one of the few options within the walls of
★ the historic Citadel—quietly give off the stylish vibe of old aristocracy and also seem to be in the best minimalist good taste: no wonder this restored neoclassical mansion is often booked so far in advance. **Pros:** welcoming and helpful owners; delightful decor; historical location. **Cons:** can get booked up year-round. $ *Rooms from: €50 ⊠ Andronikou Paleologou 57 ☎ 26510/22866 ⊕ hotelkastro.gr* ❢◯❙ *No meals.*

$ ⚏ **Kentrikon Hotel.** Located in Ioannina's city center, this renovated man-
HOTEL sion offers modern comforts in a beautiful old building—the wood-and-stone facade, the simple but quaintly classic and traditional decor, the friendly service, and the light-filled rooms all make this a comfortable and cozy place to stay, especially when clients and visitors alike can enjoy mezedes and *tsipouro* (a liquor distilled purely from grapes) in the pretty yard in summer. **Pros:** center-city location; parking available. **Cons:** given the location it can get noisy at night. $ *Rooms from: €55 ⊠ Koletti 5A ☎ 26510/71771 ⊕ www.hotel-kentrikon.gr* ❢◯❙ *Breakfast.*

NIGHTLIFE AND PERFORMING ARTS

Even in a relatively small city like Ioannina, the *magazia* (club–cafés) are always changing names and owners; they may close for winter and open elsewhere for summer, usually under the stars. Karamanli, adjacent to the citadel, is lined with trendy *mezedopoleia* (Greek-style tapas bars) and smart pubs.

Denoar. In a creatively restored Ottoman-period marketplace, this cool bar-club is a mainstay of Ioannina nightlife. Theme nights, imaginative drinks, and a mixture of funk, rock, and dance music keep eclectic night owls flocking in. ⊠ *Anexertasias 40 ☎ 26510/69945.*

Iperokeanios. Located by the citadel near Giosif Eligia and Aetorrahis, Iperokeanios is one of the hippest coffee shops along the seawall; it serves ice cream and sweets. If it's full, try the adjacent Ploton. ⊠ *Mavili Sq. 10 ☎ 26510/33781.*

Odos Kallari. Hip bars and cafés have opened all along Kallari street, which stretches down from the walls of the castle. This old Jewish market street, which until recently was selling metal goods and wares, now seems to be the place to go for those in the know to snag a bite and a

Presiding over some of the most beautiful folkloric villages of the Zagorohoria region are grand monasteries, such as Agia Paraskevi in Monodendri.

drink. See if you can find the quirky Asteri bar—one of the cutest—tucked away in a little corner off Kallari.

Fodor's Choice ★ **Stoa Liabei.** Since 2010, this old Ottoman-era arcade has been transformed into the nightlife hub of the city. Bars and clubs, all with differing styles and music, now occupy every nook and cranny, and they have succeeded in attracting Ioannina's hip and trendy crowd. One can hop from Stoa Bar, playing deep house and funky sets, to Route 66 with its alternative, soul, and funky grooves. If it's cool yuppie vibes you're after, head to trendy Montage with its breezy uptown decor. In summer the action gets combustible, as these bars merge and mingle, since most of the action is outside. In winter they become more autonomous, shutting doors and pumping up that volume. ⊠ *Stoa Liabei, between Anexatrisias and Kannigos st.*

SHOPPING

Ioannina has long been known throughout Greece for its silver craftsmanship and for its jewelry, copper utensils, and woven items. You can find delicate jewelry on the island of Nissi, but there are also many silver shops on Odhos Averoff (the better place for larger items, like trays, glasses, and vases), near Neomartiros Georgiou Square. Avoid the shinier and brighter items in stores near the entrance to the citadel.

CRAFTS

Center of Traditional Handcraft of Ioannina (Kepavi). A silversmiths cooperative, Kepavi is set in a storefront selling the silverware and jewelry produced by 43 regional workshops. Items vary in style and technique, including many traditional Epirote pieces as well as some interesting modern ones. The prices are good and suit all pockets. ■ **TIP**➔ **You**

can also take a tour of some of the workshops and watch the smiths practicing their fine skills. ✉ *Archipiskopou 11* ✚ *on the road bordering Lake Pamvotis* ☎ *26510/27660* ☉ *Weekdays 9:30–2:30 and 6–9, Sat. 9:30–9, Sun. 10–3.*

Doublis. One of the better arts-and-crafts shops in this area, Doublis rewards the careful eye that can discern the prizes amid some typical tourist paraphernalia. ✉ *Neomartiros Georgiou Sq.* ☎ *26510/79287.*

CERAMICS

Vasilis Gatzias Ergastiri Kataskevis Kosminatos. On Nissi island you will find a handful of quaint little stores selling replicas of traditional objects such as Turkish water pipes and ornate knives, silver pillboxes encrusted with semiprecious stones, ceramic vases, and jewelry. Those interested in more-original work should head here, to the only boutique that creates unique, handmade pieces. ✉ *Nissi island* ☎ *26510/81878.*

ZAGOROHORIA REGION ΖΑΓΟΡΟΧΟΡΙΑ

40 km–60 km (25 miles–37 miles) north of Ioannina.

One of the most beguiling and untamed sections of Greece is the region of Zagorohoria (pronounced zah-go-ro-*hor*-ee-ah), also known as Zagori or Zagoria, which comprises 46 villages to the north and northwest of Ioannina. During the last decade, the Zagorohoria region has become incredibly popular among Greeks, but it's a place that only foreigners "in the know" visit. Its cultured people, stunning landscapes, cozy guesthouses, World Heritage–protected architecture, and wonderful rivers make it a unique destination.

Here you can see *arhontika* (stone mansions with walls and roofs made of gray slate from surrounding mountains), winding cobbled streets, graceful arched Turkish bridges, churches with painted interiors, *kalderimi* (old mule trails), and forests of beech, chestnut, and pine. If you have only a day to spare, rent a car or bargain with a taxi driver in Ioannina to transport you to some of the many villages connected by well-paved roads. If you opt to spend the night in one of the villages, you have the chance to truly soak up the local color, get a look at the interiors of some of the Ottoman-style living quarters, and partake of some excellent food. Wonderful hikes are another pleasure for those who choose to stay and explore awhile. Some of the villages, such as Megalo, Mikro Papingo, Monodendri, and Konitsa, are likely to be busy with travelers in July and August, particularly on weekends and major holidays. Book ahead or, better yet, stay in some of the (even) lesser-known villages, some of which have only 10 permanent residents inhabiting them.

Kipi, 40 km (25 miles) north of Ioannina in the central Zagori, is famous for its three-arch packhorse bridge, and the community runs a fascinating folklore museum. **Tsepelovo,** 5 km (3 miles) northeast of Kipi, is one of the most authentic villages. Perched on the slopes of Mt. Tymphai, at 3,960 feet, it was built using the gray-brown tile-like rock that makes up most of the surroundings. A must-see village, **Monodendri,** 44 km (27 miles) north of Ioannina, is a well-preserved settlement perched on the rim of a breathtaking gorge on the boundary of the Vikos–Aoos National Park. There's a stunning vista from the abandoned 15th-century monastery, Agia Paraskevi.

Papingo, 59 km (37 miles) north of Ioannina, has delightful architecture—many houses are still topped with the silvery blue slate that used to be so common throughout Epirus—varied scenery, and friendly locals, although it was among the first villages here "discovered" by wealthy Greeks. It's divided into two towns. **Megalo Papingo,** aka Big Papingo, is near the river Voidomatis, which has excellent rafting and canoeing. **Mikro Papingo,** aka Little Papingo, is 1½ km (1 mile) up the road from Megalo Papingo, below some limestone rocks; it's really small—the population is fewer than 100—but appealing. **Dilofo** (31 km [20 miles] from Ioannina), aka Two Hills, is one of the best preserved, quiet, and picturesque villages in the region, and among the very few where cars can park at its entrance. Your kids (and you) can run safe and free along its cobbled footpaths.

WHERE TO STAY

$
HOTEL
FAMILY

Ameliko. An imposing stone mansion lovingly restored, with a beautiful garden, Ameliko is an ideal place to stay for those exploring Zagorohoria. **Pros:** management arranges excellent tours and activities in the area; lovely garden. **Cons:** gets busy during winter breaks. $ *Rooms from: €70* ⊠ *Ano Pedina* ☎ *26530/71501* ⊕ *www.ameliko. gr* ⦿ *Breakfast.*

$
B&B/INN

Gaia. A comfortable, elegant, and well-designed guesthouse, Gaia rose from the ruins of an 1862 mansion thanks to the efforts of devoted owners, architect Yiannis Anastasakis and his wife Thomais, who literally built Gaia with their own hands after buying it on a passionate whim because they fell in love with the area on a trip. **Pros:** homey; comfortable; guides available for walks. **Cons:** few in-room facilities. $ *Rooms from: €85* ⊠ *Off main square, Dilofo* ☎ *26530/22570* ⊕ *www.gaia-dilofo.gr* ⦿ *Breakfast.*

$
HOTEL

Hotel Bourazani. The old Bourazani hunting lodge has been revamped into this accommodating hotel, one of the few places to stay in this immediate region, which has been given over to nature; the only noises to be heard at night are the distant rustling of the River Aoos and the calls of nightingales. **Pros:** owners are gold mines of info about activities in this beautiful but forgotten corner of Greece. **Cons:** access is difficult without car (call first for detailed instructions to get there). $ *Rooms from: €85* ⊠ *Bourazani* ☎ *26550/61283, 26550/61320* ⊕ *www.bourazani.gr* ⦿ *Breakfast.*

$
B&B/INN

Zarkada. Most of the guest rooms in this pension in the heart of the picturesque village of Monodendri are equipped with fireplaces—an essential luxury during the long and cold winter nights—and the inn happily comes with its own taverna, just the place to enjoy sumptuous, local savory pies and roasted meats. **Pros:** feel-good facilities; helpful service; central location. **Cons:** not all the rooms have fireplaces. $ *Rooms from: €60* ⊠ *Off main square, Monodendri* ☎ *26530/71305* ⊕ *www.monodendri.com* ⦿ *Breakfast.*

SPORTS AND THE OUTDOORS

Hiking is one of the real pleasures of the Zagorohoria region, but trails can be challenging, not to mention dangerous. Your safest bet is to go on a guided walk; a number of outfitters schedule gorge hikes (the famed Vikos is an eight-hour trek!) and other invigorating activities. Make sure you have proper footwear, hiking gear, food and water, and emergency supplies and provisions, and *never* hike in heavy rains or go far in groups of fewer than four. Staff at most hotels can provide basic maps and put you in touch with local guides or trekking clubs.

If you're a physically fit hiker, you may want to hike at least part of the steep and long **Vikos gorge**. To get to the gorge, you follow a precipitous route from the upper limestone tablelands of Monodendri down almost 3,300 feet to the clear, rushing waters of the Voidomatis trout stream (no swimming allowed) as it flows north into Albania. It's a strenuous but exhilarating eight-hour hike on which you are likely to see dramatic vistas, birds of prey, waterfalls, flowers and herbs, and hooded shepherds tending their flocks.

Metsovo Alpine Club has information on hiking trails and the nearby ski center.

MAPS

Anavasi. One of the best hiking maps of Zagori is by Anavasi. It's GPS compatible and includes shorter and longer walks in the area. ☎ *210/321–8104, 210/321–0152* ⊕ *www.mountains.gr.*

OUTFITTERS

Greek Alpine Club. Contact the Greek Alpine Club for complete walking-tour information about all of the region's celebrated hikes, including treks to the Pindos mountains. If you are an experienced hiker and intend to explore the Zagorohoria region without a guide we strongly recommend you to contact the club first to get the low down on which hikes are doable and which aren't, taking into consideration factors such as the time of year (daylight hours), weather conditions and levels of difficulty. ⊠ *October 28th 17A, Ioannina* ☎ *26510/22138 7 pm–9 pm only* ⊕ *www.orivatikos.gr.*

FAMILY
Fodor'sChoice
★

No Limits. Specialists in the Zagorohori region, No Limits tours are a fun way to see and explore this spectacular little corner of Europe. As well as rafting, rock climbing, and hiking, they also have horseback riding trips through the breathtaking Epirote countryside. ⊠ *Central square, Konitsa* ☎ *26550/23777* ⊕ *www.nolimits.com.gr* ☞ *From €45 for a two-day excursion.*

Robinson Expeditions. This Ioannina outfitter specializes in outdoor tours and can make arrangements for single travelers or groups to hike the Vikos gorge (the deepest gorge in the world); other programs are hang gliding, canyoning, rafting, mountain biking, kayaking, and nature study. The company also schedules rock-climbing excursions around the Meteora. ⊠ *Kipi (Gardens)* ☎ *26511/15502* ⊕ *www.robinson.gr* ☞ *From €33.*

Fodor'sChoice
★

Trekking Hellas. This well-established and reliable outfit offers activities and excursions throughout Greece. They use the best local experts as guides. In Zagorohoria activities range from leisurely five-hour walks up the Vikos gorge to a full eight-day expedition in the region, which includes hiking and rafting. They also lead exciting adventure tours in Meteora and Metsovo. ✉ *Spirou Labrou 7, Ioannina* ☎ *26510/71703, 69/4515–4101* ⊕ *www.trekking.gr* ✉ *From €35.*

DODONA ΔΩΔΩΝΗ

22 km (14 miles) southwest of Ioannina.

The only thing to do, or see for that matter, at the somewhat isolated Dodona are the ancient ruins. This archaeological site, steeped in history and mystery, is worthy of the time and effort it takes to visit, and dedicating a whole day is most rewarding.

Said to be the oldest oracle in Greece, the Dodona flourished for well over a millennium, from at least the 8th century BC until the 4th century AD, when Christianity succeeded the cult of Zeus. Homer, in the *Iliad,* mentions "wintry Dodona," where Zeus's pronouncements, made known through the burbling brook and the wind-rustled leaves of a sacred oak, were interpreted by priests "whose feet are unwashed and who sleep on the ground." The oak tree was central to the cult, and its image appears on the region's ancient coins. Here Odysseus sought forgiveness for slaughtering his wife's suitors, and from this oak the Argonauts took the sacred branch to mount on their ship's prow. According to one story, Apollo ordered the oracle moved here from Thessaly; Herodotus, however, writes that it was locally believed a black dove from Thebes in Egypt landed in the oak and announced, in a human voice, that the oracle of Zeus should be built.

There is a little canteen at the entrance of the site where one can get refreshments, but bringing a simple packed lunch—some bread, cheese, olives, and a tomato—is a pleasant alternative. You can sit and listen for whispers from long forgotten Zeus, father of gods.

GETTING HERE AND AROUND

The most efficient way to get here from Ioannina is with a rented car or a taxi; the driver will wait an hour or so at the site. Negotiate with one of the drivers near Ioannina's clock tower or ask your hotel to call a cab. Only on Mondays and Fridays are there buses from Ioannina's Bizaniou Station, one at 6:30 am and the other at 8:30 pm.

EXPLORING

Fodor's Choice ★ **Dodona.** Dodona has vestiges of two of Ancient Greece's important cosmological and cultural institutions, divining and drama—here you can see the space of the ancient oracle and the superbly preserved and impressive theater. As you enter the archaeological site of Dodona, you pass the **stadium** on your right, built for the Naïa games and completely overshadowed by the **theater** on your left. One of the largest and best preserved on the Greek mainland, the theater once seated 17,000; it is used for summer presentations of ancient Greek drama. Its building in the early 3rd century BC was overseen by King Pyrrhus of Epirus. The theater was destroyed, rebuilt under Philip V of Macedon in the late 3rd century, and then converted by the Romans into an arena for gladiatorial games. Its retaining wall, reinforced by bastions, is still standing.

East of the theater are the foundations of the **bouleuterion** (headquarters and council house) of the Epirote League, built by Pyrrhus, and a small rectangular temple dedicated to Aphrodite. The remains of the **acropolis** behind the theater include house foundations and a cistern that supplied water in times of siege.

The remains of the **sanctuary of Zeus Naios** include temples to Zeus, Dione (goddess of abundance), and Heracles; until the 4th century BC there was no temple. The Sacred Oak was here, surrounded by abutting cauldrons on bronze tripods. When struck, they reverberated for a long time, and the sound was interpreted by soothsayers. ⊠ *On main road Ioaninon–Dodonis, Signposted off E951, Dodoni* ☎ *26510/82287* ⊕ *odysseus.culture.gr* 🎫 *€2* ⊗ *June–Sept., daily 8–8; Oct.–May, daily 8–5.*

METSOVO ΜΕΤΣΟΒΟ

58 km (36 miles) east of Ioannina, 293 km (182 miles) northwest of Athens.

The traditional village of Metsovo cascades down a mountain at about 3,300 feet above sea level, below the 6,069-foot Katara pass, which is the highest in Greece and marks the border between Epirus and Thessaly. Even in summer, the temperatures may be in the low 20°s C (70°s F), and February's average highs are just above freezing. Early evening is a wonderful time to arrive. As you descend through the mist, dazzling lights twinkle in the ravine. Stone houses with gray slate roofs and sharply projecting wooden balconies line steep, serpentine alleys. In the square, especially after the Sunday service, old men—dressed in black flat caps, dark baggy pants, and wooden shoes with pom-poms—sit on a bench, like crows on a tree branch. Should you arrive on a religious feast day, many villagers will be decked out in traditional costume. Older women often wear dark blue or black dresses with embroidered trim every day, augmenting these with brightly colored aprons, jackets, and scarves with floral embroidery on holidays. Note that there is no EOT (tourist office) in Metsovo.

GETTING HERE AND AROUND

A bus or car from Ioannina takes about 45 minutes; bus tickets are €5.80. There is no train service to Metsovo.

EXPLORING

Although most such villages are fading away, Metsovo, designated a traditional settlement by the Greek National Tourism Organization (GNTO or EOT), has become a prosperous, self-sufficient community with a growing population. In winter it draws skiers headed for Mt. Karakoli, and in summer it is—for better or worse—a favorite destination for tourist groups. For the most part Metsovo has preserved its character despite the souvenir shops selling inauthentic "traditional handicrafts" and the slate roofs that have replaced with easy-to-maintain, cheaper tile.

The natives are descendants of nomadic Vlach shepherds, once believed to have migrated from Romania but now thought to be Greeks trained

Today the theater at Dodona—one of Greece's grandest—remains the enthralling site for summer concerts and performances.

by Romans to guard the Egnatia Highway connecting Constantinople and the Adriatic. Metsovo became an important center of finance, commerce, handicrafts, and shepherding, and the Vlachs began trading farther afield—in Constantinople, Vienna, and Venice. Ali Pasha abolished the privileges in 1795, and in 1854 the town was invaded by Ottoman troops led by Abdi Pasha. In 1912 Metsovo was freed from the Turks by the Greek army. Many important families lived here, including the Averoffs and Tositsas, who made their fortunes in Egyptian cotton. They contributed to the new Greek state's development and bequeathed large sums to restore Metsovo and finance small industries. For example, Foundation Baron Michalis Tositsa, begun in 1948 when a member of the prominent area family endowed it (although he was living in Switzerland), helped the local weaving industry get a start.

Agia Paraskevi. The freely accessible 18th-century church of Agia Paraskevi has a flamboyantly decorated altar screen that's worth a peek. Note that July 26 is its saint's day, entailing a big celebration in which the church's silver icon is carried around the town in a morning procession, followed by feasting and dancing. ⊠ *Main square.*

Averoff Museum. This fascinating museum of regional paintings and sculptures showcases the outstanding art collection amassed by politician and intellectual Evangelos Averoff (1910–90), whose effect on Matsovo is still lauded today. The 19th- and 20th-century paintings depict historical scenes, local landscapes, and daily activities. Most major Greek artists, such as Nikos Ghikas and Alekos Fassianos, are represented. One painting known to all Greeks is Nikiforos Litras's *Burning of the Turkish Flagship by Kanaris,* a scene from a decisive battle in Chios. Look on the second floor for Pericles Pantazis's *Street Urchin Eating Watermelon*, a captivating portrait of a young boy. Paris Prekas's *The Mosque of Aslan Pasha in Ioannina* depicts what Ioannina looked like in the Turkish period. ⊠ *Main Sq.* ☎ 26560/41210 ⊕ *www.averoffmuseum.gr* 🎫 €3 ⊙ *Mid-July–mid-Sept.,   Wed.–Mon. 10–6:30; mid-Sept.–mid-July, Wed.–Mon. 10–4.*

> ### NOT SO CRYSTAL CLEAR
>
> The Dodona oracle had its ups and downs. Consulted in the heroic age by Heracles, Achilles, and all the best people, it went later into a gentle decline because of its failure to equal the masterly ambiguity of Delphi.

Katogi-Averoff Winery. Enjoy a tour around this important winery and discover the wine-making process, animated with video projections and sound and art installations. The journey ends in the wine-tasting area, so just try leaving without a few bottles of the exquisite, full-bodied, musky red Katogi-Averoff wine. For those who can't seem to tear themselves away, the newly built, four-star Katogi-Averoff Hotel awaits. ⊠ *Eastern edge of village, in Upper Aoos valley* ☎ 26560/31490, 22910/41650 ⊕ *www.katogi-strofilia.gr* 🎫 *Free* ⊙ *Weekdays 10–4.*

Fodor'sChoice
★

Tositsa Museum. For generations the Tositsa family had been one of the most prominent in Metsovo, and to get a sense of how Metsovites lived (and endured the arduous winters in style), visit their home, a restored late-Ottoman-period stone-and-timber building that is now the Tositsa Museum of popular art and local Epirote crafts. Built in 1661 and renovated in 1954, this typical Metsovo mansion has carved woodwork, sumptuous textiles in rich colors on a black background, and handcrafted Vlach furniture. In the stable you'll see the gold-embroidered saddle used for special holidays and, unique to this area, a fanlight in the fireplace, ensuring that the hearth would always be illuminated. The goatskin bag on the wall was used to store cheese, one of the area's most noted products. Wait for the guard to open the door prior to the tour. Guides usually speak some English. ⊠ *Up stone stairs to right off Tositsa (main road) as you descend to main town square* ☎ 26560/41084 🎫 €3 ⊙ *By guided tour, every ½ hr May–Oct., Fri.–Wed. 8:30–1 and 4–6; Nov.–Apr., Fri.–Wed. 8:30–1:30 and 3–5.*

OFF THE
BEATEN
PATH

Ayios Nikolaos Monastery. Visit a restored 14th-century monastery, about a 30-minute walk into the valley (with the trip back up about an hour). Two images of the *Pantocrator* (Godhead), one in each dome—perhaps duplicated to give the segregated women their own view—stare down on the congregation. You can also see the monks' cells. The guided tour in English explains the 18th-century frescoes created in Epirote style. ⊠ *Down into valley via footpath (follow signs near National Bank of Greece; turn left where paving ends)* 🎫 €2 ⊙ *May–Oct., daily 9–7; Nov.–Apr., daily 9–1.*

WHERE TO EAT

$
GREEK
Fodor'sChoice
★

✕ **To Koutouki Tou Nikola.** *Koutouki* ("little box"), aptly named for its diminutive interior, is a good value, just one reason this place is so popular with the locals. All the taverna favorites are here, but order something made with the local cheese, or the amazing *hilopotes* (local pasta) cooked in a chicken broth, or the divine celery and leek beef meatballs. Anything served in this taverna is delicious and honest, and the local wine isn't bad either. *Kali Orexi!* (Good appetite!) $ *Average main: €7* ⊠ *Aghiou Georgiou, next to the post office* ☎ 26560/41732 ⊟ *No credit cards.*

$ ✕ **To Paradosiako.** The name means "traditional," and that's what this
GREEK comfortable spot decorated with colorful weavings and folk crafts is. Vasilis Bissas, the chef-owner, has revived many of the more esoteric regional specialties. Try the *fileta tou dasous* (fillet of the forest)—a choice beef fillet stuffed with cheese, ham, tomato, mushrooms, and "woodcutters' potatoes" (potato slices baked with bacon and four kinds of cheese). "Grandmothers' bread" is toasted and stuffed with cheese, bacon, tomato, peppers, and onions, then baked in the oven. Accompany your meal with the house wine, guaranteed to be a well-searched-out regional specialty, or choose the heady local red Katogi. $ *Average main: €8* ⊠ *Tositsa 44* ☎ 26560/42773 ⊟ *No credit cards.*

WHERE TO STAY

$ ⛫ **Apollon Hotel.** The family-run and centrally located Apollon looks out
HOTEL on the Pindos mountain range; topped by picturesque coves and built in traditional style, it offers comfortable, modern amenities along with old-world accents. **Pros:** friendly, obliging, family-run business; located right in the center of town; organizes excursions. **Cons:** not all rooms have good views. $ *Rooms from: €60* ⊠ *Main square* ☎ 26560/41844 ⊕ *www.metsovohotels.com* ⎮◉⎮ *Breakfast.*

$ ⛫ **Hotel Bitouni.** Local craftsmen created the elegantly carved wooden
HOTEL ceilings in this traditional-style Metsovo mansion—at its heart a large
FAMILY fireplace in the main reception room nicely warms the cozy hotel. **Pros:**
Fodor's Choice warm; cozy; atmospheric; great value. **Cons:** luxury-lovers, look else-
★ where. $ *Rooms from: €55* ⊠ *On main street leading up from central square* ☎ 26560/41217 ⊕ *www.hotelbitouni.com* ⎮◉⎮ *Breakfast.*

$ ⛫ **Hotel Galaxias Metsovo.** A great place to rest your mountain-weary
HOTEL feet, this small hotel has guest rooms designed in typical Metsovo style: simple, with a splash of color on a *kourelou*, or traditional rug. **Pros:** ideally positioned just off the main town square. **Cons:** rooms and bathrooms could do with some modernizing. $ *Rooms from: €55* ⊠ *Above main square* ☎ 26560/41202 ⊕ *www.hotel-galaxias-metsovo. gr* ⎮◉⎮ *Breakfast.*

SPORTS AND THE OUTDOORS

Metsovo is one of the few places in Greece to offer winter skiing, when the entire region is covered in snow and the area's famed Vlach shepherds even have to move their flocks from the mountains to the lowlands around Trikala.

Anilio Ski Resort. Opened in 2012, Anilio has 12 ski runs, the longest winding 1 km (½ mile) down the mountain face, and five ski lifts. A chalet serves a few bites and a good variety of soothing hot drinks. Snow cover suitable for skiing is usually from mid-November to early March. There is also an ice-skating rink nearby. ⊠ *6 km (4 miles) south of Metsovo* ⊹ *Take the E92 and then left onto the E90 following the signs for Anilio* ☎ 698/076–0850 ⊕ *www.anilio-ski.gr.*

SHOPPING

Metsovo is known for its fabrics, folk crafts, silver, and smoked cheese. Although many of the "traditional" arts and crafts here are imported low-quality imitations, with a little prowling and patience you can still make some finds, especially if you like textiles and weavings. Some are genuine antiques that cost a good deal more than the newer versions, but are far superior in quality. Everything's available on the main square.

Aris Talaris. This is actually two shops: one sells quality silver jewelry made in Talaris's own workshop, and the other displays gold pieces. The Metsovo silver-work trade is one of the oldest in the region; members of the Talaris family have been silversmiths for many generations (and now they have branched out as hoteliers, owning the hotel where their shops are). ⊠ *Hotel Egnatia, Tositsa 19* ☎ *26560/41263.*

Pigi. This colorful shop, on the left of the main thoroughfare leading to the central square, overflows with cheeses of all shapes and sizes. Metsovo is renowned for its cheese, and you will find any local vareity your heart (or palate) desires, from the smokey *metsovitico* ewe's and cow's milk cheese to the zingy *metsovela* and even a local Parmesan that rivals any from Italy. ⊠ *On main road to square* ☎ *26560/42163.*

THESSALY ΘΕΣΣΑΛΙΑ

Though Thessaly, with part of Mt. Olympus within its boundaries, is the home of the immortal gods, a Byzantine site holds pride of place: Meteora, the amazing medieval monasteries on top of inaccessible needles of rock. The monasteries' extraordinary geological setting stands in vivid contrast to the rest of Thessaly, a huge plain in central Greece, almost entirely surrounded by mountains: Pindos to the west, Pelion to the east, Othrys to the south, and the Kamvounian range to the north. It is one of the country's most fertile areas and has sizable population centers in Lamia, Larissa, Trikala, and Volos. Thessaly was not ceded to Greece until 1878, after almost five centuries of Ottoman rule; today vestiges of this period remain. Kalambaka and Meteora are in the northwest corner of the plain, before the Pindos mountains. The best time to come here, especially to the Meteora monasteries, is spring, when the mountains are still snow covered and blend harmoniously with the green fields, the red poppies, and the white and pink flowering fruit trees.

KALAMBAKA ΚΑΛΑΜΠΑΚΑ

71 km (44 miles) east of Metsovo, 154 km (95 miles) southwest of Thessaloniki.

Kalambaka may be dismissed as one more drab modern town, useful only as a base to explore the fabled Meteora complex north of town. Yet an overnight stay here, complete with a taverna dinner and a stroll in the main squares, offers a taste of everyday life in a provincial Thessalian town. This will prove quite a contrast to an afternoon spent at nearby Meteora, where you can get acquainted with the glorious history and architecture of the Greek Orthodox Church. Invariably, you return to modern Kalambaka and wind up at a poolside bar to sip ouzo and contemplate the asceticism of the Meteora monks. If you'd rather stay in a more attractive place slightly closer to the monasteries, head to Kastraki, a hamlet with some pleasing folk-style houses about 2½ km (1 mile) north of Kalambaka.

GETTING HERE AND AROUND

The famous Meteora monasteries, set just outside Kalambaka, are easily accessible by both train and slightly more expensive bus, but, as most trips, it is by far preferable to take the bus rather than the slow and creaky trains that service the area. Buses connecting Kalambaka with Trikala take 45 minutes and leave Trikala at 5 am and each hour until 1 pm, then 2:15 until 10:15 hourly; tickets are €2.10. Buses to and from Athens take 5 hours and require a change at Trikala; tickets are €29 one-way, €44 round-trip. Buses to the major port of Volos depart Kalambaka at 7 am, 11:30 am, 3 pm, and 7 pm; tickets are €15. The Kalambaka–Ioannina bus (3 hours) departs at 8:30 am and 3 pm; tickets are €15.

There are seven trains daily from Athens to Kalambaka (€18–€38). Trains often connect with Trikala (15 minutes, €1.80–€2.60), the major transportation hub of Thessaly; there are four trains daily. Kalambaka is currently the last stop on this OSE route.

EXPLORING

Dormition of the Virgin. Burned by the Germans during World War II, Kalambaka has only one building of interest, the centuries-old cathedral church of the Dormition of the Virgin. Patriarchal documents in the outer narthex indicate that it was built in the first half of the 12th century by Emperor Manuel Comnenos, but some believe it was founded as early as the 7th century, on the site of a temple of Apollo (classical drums and other fragments are incorporated into the walls, and mosaics can be glimpsed under the present floor). The latter theory explains the church's paleo-Christian features, including its center-aisle *ambo* (great marble pulpit), which is usually to the right of the sanctuary; its rare *synthronon* (four semicircular steps where the priest sat when not officiating) east of the altar; and its Roman-basilica style, originally adapted to Christian use and unusual for the 12th century. The church has vivid 16th-century frescoes, work of the Cretan monk Neophytos, son of the famous hagiographer Theophanes. The marble baldachin in the sanctuary, decorated with crosses and stylized grapes, probably predates the 11th century. ⊠ *North end of town, follow signs from Riga Fereou Sq.* ☎ *24320/22752, 24320/24962* ⊕ *odysseus.culture.gr/h/2/eh251.jsp?obj_id=1703* 🎫 *€1.50* ⊙ *Daily 7–1 and 3–9.*

WHERE TO EAT

$
GREEK

✕ **Estiatorio Meteora.** At this spot on the main square, a local favorite since 1925, the Gkertsos family serves food prepared by the matriarch, Ketty. Meteora is known for hearty main courses—try Ketty's special wine-and-pepper chicken, veal, or pork *stifado* (stew)—and some specialties from Asia Minor, including *tzoutzoukakia Smyrneika*, aromatic meatballs in a red sauce laced with cumin. The surrounding hills and

Continued on page 361

Nearer to Heaven
THE METEORA
MONASTERIES

Ayia Triada

Here in the most remote corner of Greece, landscape and legend conspire to twist reality into fantasy. Soaring skyward out of dense orchards looms a different kind of forest: gigantic rock pinnacles, the loftiest of which rises 984 feet. But even more extraordinary than these stone pillars are the monasteries that perch atop the stalagmitic skyscrapers. Funded by Byzantine emperors, run by ascetic monks, and once scaled by James Bond, these saintly castles-in-air are almost literally "out of this world."

The name Meteora comes from the Greek word *meteorizome* ("to hang in midair"). These world-famous monasteries seem to do just that. The origin of these rocks, which loom up between the Pindos range and the Thessalian plain, is an enigma. Some geologists say a lake that covered the area 30 million years ago swept away the soil and softer stone as it forced its way to the sea. Others believe the inexorable flow of the Peneus River slowly carved out the towering pillars, now greatly eroded by wind and rain. Legend created, as it often does, a more colorful story: the rock needles are meteors hurled to earth by an angry god.

THE MONASTIC BUILDERS
Man first staked claim to the Meteora peaks when the inaccessible pinnacles served as refuge to pious hermits in the turbulent 14th century. As soon as the Turkish rulers of Trikkala began warring with the Byzantine emperors of Constantinople for rights to the fertile valley, these anchorite monks were forced to retreat to the heights of the impregnable rocks. In 1336 they were joined by St. Athanasios, who hailed from fabled Mt. Athos. Notwithstanding the legend that says that the saint flew up to the rocks on the back of an eagle, Athanasios began the backbreaking task of building the Megalo Meteoro (1356–72)—the biggest of the Meteora monasteries—using pulleys and ropes to haul construction materials.

By the 16th century, 13 monasteries had been established here as bastions of Christianity. During the late-Byzantine period, they are said to have helped "save" Western civilization from the inroads of Turkish domination. In the end, however, the Meteora monasteries came to poignantly epitomize both the glory and the decline of Eastern monasticism. Once the former abodes of emperors and kings, they are now largely supported by tourism.

A VISIT TODAY
For centuries, jointed ladders and descending nets were the only way to ascend the rocky peaks. Tourists who may yearn for the days when travelers made the ascent squeezed into an outsize string-bag are cured of their nostalgia after one look at the rusty windlass, especially if accompanied by the gruesome story that the rope was only ever changed "when it broke." Today, stone bridges, rock-hewn stairs, and *monopati* (old paths) guide visitors up hundreds of steps to the heavenly monasteries.

VISITING THE MAIN MONASTERIES

Monks at Megalo Meteoro use cable cars to avoid tourist crowds on the stairs

Set atop the Meteora's "heavenly columns" are six sky-kissing monasteries. While their dizzying perch seems attributable only to divine intervention, their architecture can be dated from the 14th to 17th centuries. Restricted by space, the buildings rise from different levels. Some are whitewashed; others display the pretty Byzantine pattern of stone and brick, the multiple domes of the many churches dominating the wooden balconies that hang precariously over the frightening abysses.

NIKOLAOS ANAPAFSAS: THE ROAD LESS TRAVELED

Even though **Ayios Nikolaos Anapafsas** (Holy Monastery of St. Nicholas Anapausas) is the first monastic complex you see and is accessed by a relatively unchallenging path, many travelers hurry on to the large, Megalo Meteoro, leaving this one relatively uncrowded. Its *katholikon* (church), built 1388, faces north rather than the usual east because of the rock's peculiar shape and the rock's small area precluded the construction of a cloister, so the monks studied in the larger-than-usual narthex. While the monastery dates from the end of the 15th century, its superb frescoes are from the 16th century and the work of Theophanis Strelitzas. Though conservative, his frescoes are lively and expressive: mountains are stylized, and plants and animals are portrayed geometrically. Especially striking are the treatments of the Temptation and the scourging of Christ.

Ayios Nikolaos Anapafsas
☎ 24320/22375 🎫 €3 ⏱ Apr.–Oct., Sat.–Thurs. 9–3:30; Nov.–Mar., Sat.–Thurs. 9–1

7

VARLAAM: FABLED FRESCOES

The monastery closest to the Megalo Meteoro is the **Varlaam,** which sits atop a ravine and is reached by a bridge and a climb of 195 steps. Originally here were the Church of Three Hierarchs (14th century) and the cells of a hermitage started by St. Varlaam, who arrived shortly after St. Athanasios. Two brothers from the wealthy Aparas family of Ioannina rebuilt the church in 1518, incorporating it into a larger katholikon called Agii Pandes (All Saints). A church document relates how it was completed in 20 days, after the materials had been accumulated atop the rock over a period of 22 years. The church's main attraction, the 16th-century frescoes—including a disturbing Apocalypse with a yawning hell's mouth—completely covers the walls, beams, and pillars. The frescoes' realism, the sharp contrasts of light and dark, and the many-figured scenes show an Italian influence, though in the portrayal of single saints they follow the Orthodox tradition. Note the

Greek Icon, Meteora

Pantocrator peering down from the dome. These are the work of Frangos Katellanos of Thebes, one of the most important 16th-century hagiographers. Set around a pretty garden, other buildings include a chapel to Sts. Cosmas and Damien. By the large storerooms is an ascent tower with a net and a winch.

Varlaam ☎ 24320/22277 ✉ €3
🕙 May–Oct., Sat.–Thurs. 9–4; Nov.–Apr., Sat.–Wed. 9–3

AYIA BARBARA: GET THEE TO A NUNNERY

On the lowest rock—thought an appropriate tribute to male superiority by the early monks (who first refused to have women in the Meteora)—the compact monastery of **Ayia Barbara** (Holy Monastery of Rousanou) was the only nunnery in the complex centuries ago. With its colorful gardens in and around red- and gray-stone walls, it is a favorite for picture-taking. Set on a large mesa-like rock, the squat building was abandoned in the early 1900s and stood empty until a new order of nuns moved in some years ago and restored it. The monastery was thought to have been founded in 1288 by the monks Nicodemus and Benedict. The main church has well-preserved frescoes dating from the

mid-16th century. Most depict gory scenes of martyrdom, but one shows lions licking Daniel's feet during his imprisonment. The nunnery is accessible via steps and a new bridge.

Ayiya Barbara ☎ 24320/2269 ✉ €3
🕙 Apr–Oct., daily 9–6; Nov–Mar., daily 9–2

MEGALO METEORO: HIGHEST AND GRANDEST

Superlatives can be trotted out to describe the **Megalo Meteoro** (Church of the Metamorphosis [Transfiguration])—the loftiest, richest, biggest, and most popular of the monasteries. Founded by St. Athanasios, the monk from Athos, it was built of massive stones 1,361 feet above the valley floor and is reached by a stiff climb of more than 400 steps. As you walk toward the entrance, you see the chapel containing the cell where St. Athanasios once lived. This monastery, known as the Grand Meteoron, gained imperial prestige because it counted among Athanasius's disciples the Hermit-King Ioasaph of Serbia and John Cantacuzene, expelled by his joint emperor from the Byzantine throne. Dating from 1387—1388, the sanctuary of the present church was the chapel first built by St. Athanasios, later added to by St. Ioasaph. The rest of the church was erected in 1552 with an unusual transept built on a cross-in-square plan with lateral apses topped by

lofty domes, as in the Mt. Athos monasteries. To the right of the narthex are the tombs of Ioasaph and Athanasios; a fresco shows the austere saints holding a monastery in their hands. Also of interest are the gilded iconostasis, with plant and animal motifs of exceptional workmanship; the bishop's throne (1617), inlaid with mother-of-pearl and ivory; and the beautiful 15th-century icons in the sanctuary. In the narthex are frescoes of the Martyrdom of the Saints, gruesome scenes of persecution under the Romans. Note the kitchen, blackened by centuries of cooking, and the wine cellar, filled with massive wine barrels. The gift shop is noted for its icons and incense. From November to March the monastery may close early.

Megalo Meteoro ☎ 24320/22278
🎫 €3 ⊙ Apr.–Sept., Wed.–Mon. 9–4; Oct.–Mar., Thurs.–Mon. 9–3

AYIA TRIADA: FOR YOUR EYES ONLY?

The most spectacularly sited of all the Meteora monasteries, **Ayia Triada** (Monastery of the Holy Trinity) is shouldered high on a rock pinnacle isolated from surrounding cliffs; it is reached via rock tunnels and 130 stone-hewn steps (see opening photo). Primitive and remote, the monastery will also be strangely familiar: James Bond fans will recognize it from its starring role in the the 1981 movie *For Your Eyes Only* (the famous winch is still in place, and you may be shown it in a tour by the one monk who lives here). According to local legend, the monk Dometius was the first to arrive in 1438; the main church, dedicated to the Holy Trinity, was built in 1476, and the narthex and frescoes were added more than 200 years later. Look for the fresco with St. Sisois gazing upon the skeleton of Alexander the Great, meant to remind the viewer that power is fleeting. The apse's pseudo-trefoil window and the sawtooth decoration around it lend a measure of grace to the structure. Ayia Triada is fabled for its vistas, with Ayios Stephanos and Kalambaka in the south and Varlaam and Megalo Meteoro to the west. Conveniently, a well-traveled footpath near the entrance (red arrows) descends to Kalambaka, about 3 km (2 miles) away.

Ayia Triada ☎ 24320/22220 💳 €3 🕐 May–Sept., Fri.–Wed. 9–5; Oct.–Apr., Fri.–Tues. 10–4

AYIOS STEPHANOS: AGING GRACEFULLY

At the far end of the eastern sector of the Meteora is **Ayios Stephanos,** the oldest monastery—a permanent bridge has replaced the movable one that once connected the monastery with the hill opposite, making this perhaps the most easily accessible, with a car road passing not far below the entrance. According to an inscription that was once on the lintel, the rock was inhabited before 1200 and was the hermitage of Jeremiah. After the Byzantine emperor Andronicus Paleologos stayed here in 1333 on his way to conquer Thessaly, he made generous gifts to the monks, which funded the building of a church in 1350. Today Ayios Stephanos is an airy convent, where the nuns spend their time painting Byzantine icons, writing, or studying music; some are involved in the community as doctors and professors. The katholikon has no murals but contains a carved wooden baldachin and an iconostasis depicting the Last Supper. You can also visit the 15th-century frescoed church of Ayios Stephanos as well as a small icon museum.

Ayios Stephanos ☎ 24320/22279 💳 €3 🕐 Apr.–Oct., Tues.–Sun. 9–1:30 and 3:30–5:30; Nov.–Mar., Tues.–Sun. 9:30–1 and 3–5

PLANNING YOUR METEORA VISIT

HOW MANY MONASTERIES CAN I SEE IN A DAY? All monasteries can be visited in a single journey from Kalambaka—a 21-km (13-mile) round-trip by car—but most visitors prefer to do only two or three, especially if they are hiking along the old monopati (old paths) that connect the monasteries. Most of the stairs upwards are in fine shape but some of the paths are crumbling in places and require the skill of an inordinately sure-footed goat (no heels, please!). ■TIP→ Megalo Meteoro and Varlaam are the two most rewarding monasteries to visit if time is tight. Whatever your mode of transport, buy a map of the monasteries in Kalambaka.

WHAT IS THE GENERAL GEOGRAPHIC LAYOUT? Heading out from Kalambaka, the comfortable Patriarhou Dimitriou road serpentines past the village of Kastraki and then winds its way ingeniously through the sandstone Meteora labyrinth. The first monastery is Ayios Nikolaos Anapafsas. Beyond it lies the mammoth Megalo Meteoro and, vis-à-vis, Varlaam. Southward is Ayia Barbara and, after a major curving detour, Ayia Triada and Ayios Stephanos. Along the main road, arrowed signposts indicate the turn-offs for the various monasteries. Note, however, that you have to journey along side roads that run for at least one mile (sometimes as much as two) to get to the feet of the monasteries.

HOW CHANGEABLE ARE THE OPENING HOURS? We list official opening hours, but as these can vary depending on the season (winter hours are usually more limited), confirm the information with your hotel receptionist in Kalambaka. And leave plenty of time before setting off up

the hundreds of steps: if you don't, you may find the monastery door closed at the top once you get there!

IS THERE A DRESS CODE? When visiting you are expected to dress decorously: men must tuck up long hair and wear long pants, women's skirts (no pants allowed) should fall to the knee, and always cover shoulders. Some monasteries provide appropriate coverings at their entrances.

IS THERE ANYPLACE TO EAT? Once on the monastery circuit, there are just a few overpriced concession stands; if you plan to make a day of it, stock up on picnic goods in town.

CAN I GET TO THE MONASTERIES BY BUS? A bus leaves Kalambaka for Megalo Meteoro five times daily (once daily in winter); the bus returns to town in late afternoon.

Map labels:

0   2 mi

0   2 km

Megalo Meteoro

Varlaam

Ayios Nikolaos

Ayia Barbara

METEORA

Ayia Triada

KASTRAKI

Ayios Stefanos

KALAMBAKA

Patriarhou Dimitriou

E92

E92

mountains are noted for goat and sheep rearing, and these meats are grilled to perfection here. All customers are ushered through the kitchen to place their order. [$] *Average main: €9* ✉ *Ekonomou 4, on Dimarchiou Sq.* ☎ *24320/22316* 🌐 *meteora-restaurant.gr* 💳 *No credit cards* 🕑 *Closed Dec.–Jan. Lunch only Oct.–Nov. and Mar.–May.*

$ GREEK FUSION 🍴 **Meteoron Panorama Restaurant.** Come here just for the knockout views of Meteora and the Kalambaka plain below, and the food isn't bad either. Of course, to make sure you get a prime position on the veranda it's best to book in advance. For starters, along with typical mezes, they serve mushrooms stuffed with cheese and a deliciously rich *melitzana saganaki* (roasted eggplant) served in a clay pot with bacon. Try the beautifully prepared lamb chops or the *smirneika* meatballs, swimming in a spicy tomato sauce. For dessert don't miss out on the Ravani cake made with mastic and coated in honey. [$] *Average main: €9* ✉ *Patriarchou Dimitriou 54* ☎ *24320/78128* 🌐 *www.meteoronpanorama.gr.*

$ GREEK FAMILY 🍴 **O Kipos Tou Ilia.** Also know as Elias's Garden Restaurant, this simple taverna with a traditional Greek menu and a waterfall in the garden attracts everyone from visiting royalty to Olympic-medal winners. Kids get their own *pethika piata* (kids' plates). Unusual appetizers include spicy fried feta with peppers and grilled mushrooms. Among the main dishes are beef *stamna* (baked in a covered clay pot with herbs, potatoes, and cheese), rabbit with onions, and vegetable croquettes. [$] *Average main: €9* ✉ *Trikalon 149, at terminus of Ayia Triada, before entrance to Kalambaka* ☎ *24320/23218* 🌐 *www.gardenrestaurant.gr.*

$ GREEK 🍴 **Paradissos.** When a Greek cooks with *meraki* (good taste and mood), the world does indeed find *paradissos* (paradise). Owner Kyriakoula Fassoula serves up meat dishes cooked *tis oras* (to order), such as grilled pork and lamb chops. Vegetarians can choose from delectable eggplant *papoutsakia* ("little shoes"), fried zucchini with garlic sauce, and various boiled greens. Complimentary fruit is served for the finale, but it would be a shame to pass up the flaky baklava. [$] *Average main: €8* ✉ *On main road to Meteora across from Spania Rooms, Kastraki* ☎ *24320/22723* 🕑 *Closed Nov.*

WHERE TO STAY

$ HOTEL 🏨 **Amalia.** At this low-lying, clay-color complex just outside Kalambaka on the road to Trikala guests can relax in the sitting room with striking antiques, floral murals, and fireplace—you can also enjoy fireplaces in the bar and restaurant—or chill out at the poolside bar, with glistening blue tiles and rustic rafters. **Pros:** spacious, elegant public rooms; lush green garden setting. **Cons:** a little outside the city; no stores nearby. [$] *Rooms from: €80* ✉ *14 km (9 miles) along Ethnikos Odos Trikalon–Ioanninon road, Theopetra* ☎ *24320/72116* 🌐 *www.amaliahotelkalambaka.gr* 🍽 *Breakfast.*

$ HOTEL 🏨 **Arsenis.** The structure that stands the closest to the Meteora cliffs—located in a grove with 1,000 olive trees—is a cozy, remarkably friendly, and accommodating option. **Pros:** a perfect option—with great views—for the low-budget traveler; open year-round; great restaurant. **Cons:** no frills. [$] *Rooms from: €45* ✉ *East road of Meteora* ☎ *24320/23500, 24320/24150* 🌐 *www.arsenis-meteora.gr* 🍽 *No meals.*

$ **Divani Meteora Hotel.** A few minutes from the center of town, this
HOTEL modern hotel has optimal views of the Meteora rocks from the rooms'
balconies, and its large open spaces, quiet corners, and private garden encourage relaxation. **Pros:** book a week in advance for significantly cheaper deals; top-notch service. **Cons:** not the prettiest building
from the outside. $ *Rooms from: €100* ⊠ *Ethnikos Odos Trikalon 1*
☎ *24320/23330* ⊕ *www.divanis.com* ❖❖ *Breakfast.*

$ **Doupiani House.** Reside in a traditional stone-and-wood hotel set amid
B&B/INN vineyards in the upper reaches of the idyllic village of Kastraki. **Pros:**
the staff have excellent knowledge of the area; ideal combo of comfort
and tradition. **Cons:** not all rooms have the stunning view of the monas-
taries (request in advance). $ *Rooms from: €65* ⊠ *Kastrakiou, left off
main road to Meteora, near Cave Camping, Kastraki* ☎ *24320/75326*
⊕ *www.doupianihouse.gr* ❖❖ *Breakfast.*

NIGHTLIFE

Kalambaka isn't the most cosmopolitan city, but you may find some fun
places for ice cream or coffee along the main drag, Trikalon. Dimoula
Square is all abuzz on weekends as locals descend from the surrounding villages.

Melydron Cafe. If you're taking the bus up to Meteora, this busy café on
the square next to the Kalambaka town hall is a good spot for that extra
coffee boost, as it's right next to the bus stop. Melydron is also a decent
watering hole at night. ⊠ *Patriarchou Dimitriou 2* ☎ *24320/75003.*

Rapsodia Cafe Bar. This is Kalambaka's hot spot, with live bands and
pool tables drawing in the local youth. It's a good place to head to if
you need a break from the quiet and austerity of monastic visitations.
⊠ *Eleftheriou Venizelou 4* ☎ *24320/77741.*

THE METEORA ΜΕΤΕΩΡΑ

Fodor's Choice *3 km (2 miles) north of Kalambaka, 178 km (110 miles) southwest of*
★ *Thessaloniki.*

As you drive through the mighty Pindos range, strange rock formations rise ever higher from the plain. Just beyond the dramatic sheer
cliff that shelters the town of Kalambaka, the legendary monasteries
of the Meteora—one of the wonders of the later Middle Ages—begin
to appear along a circular road as it winds 6 km (4 miles) through an
unearthly forest of gigantic rock pillars. The ancients believed these formations to be meteors hurled by an angry god. Ascending to 1,820 feet
above sea level, these towers, in fact, owe their fantastic shapes to river
erosion. But they owe their worldwide fame (and Hollywood moment
of glory—remember the James Bond *For Your Eyes Only* climax?) to
what perches atop six of them: the impregnable monasteries built here
by pious hermits in the turbulent 14th century. *For a complete overview
of these fascinating retreats, see our special illustrated feature, "Nearer
to Heaven: The Meteora Monasteries."*

THESSALONIKI
AND CENTRAL
MACEDONIA

Visit Fodors.com for advice, updates, and bookings

WELCOME TO THESSALONIKI AND CENTRAL MACEDONIA

TOP REASONS TO GO

★ **Mt. Olympus:** Bask in a gods'-eye view from the top of Greece's highest peak, often covered in clouds and lighting as if to prove Zeus still holds sway—ascend skyward thanks to numerous enchanting trails.

★ **Thrilling Thessaloniki:** In this great commercial hub, the Armani suits and €5 coffees are in contrast to the ruins of the ancient city walls, Byzantine monuments, and the spirited bartering of the city's bazaar.

★ **Between Heaven and Earth:** Mt. Athos, pinpointed with monasteries, is Greece's most solemn precinct; off-limits to women, it is an exclusive bastion as well.

★ **Alexander the Great Sites:** The fabled ancient ruler made this region the crossroads of the ancient world—walk in his footsteps in Pella (his birthplace), and Vergina (home to the royal tomb of his father, Phillip II).

1 **Thessaloniki.** Named after Alexander the Great's stepsister, this bustling, commercial center is Greece's second city, and has always played a supporting role. Rather than wallow in this eternal bridesmaid status, Thessaloniki has excelled as a cultural and business center, with some of Greece's best food and nightlife (it is known as the country's Liverpool for the jazz and rock groups that were founded here), much of which is concentrated around its beautifully planned and architecturally rich city center.

2 **Alexander the Great Country.** Just southwest of Thessaloniki, central Macedonia dazzles with natural beauty and archaeological wonders, especially at Dion and Vergina, where Philip II of Macedonia, father of Alexander the Great, was buried.

3 **Mt. Olympus.** Don't miss an excursion to Greece's

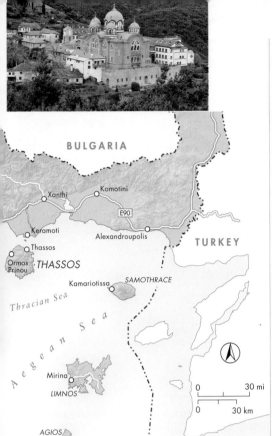

BULGARIA

Xanthi   Komotini

Keramoti   E90

Thassos   Alexandroupolis   **TURKEY**

Ormos Prinou   *THASSOS*

Kamariotissa   *SAMOTHRACE*

Thracian Sea

Aegean Sea

Mirina

LIMNOS

AGIOS

0   30 mi

0   30 km

GETTING ORIENTED

At the crossroads of East and West, Macedonia bears the traces of many civilizations: Macedonian, Hellenic, Roman, Byzantine, and Ottoman. Greece's second city, cosmopolitan Thessaloniki lies in the strategic center of Macedonia, nestled gracefully in the wide but protective arms of the Thermaic gulf and buttressed on its inland side by a low-lying mountain range around which the Axios river flows south to the Aegean. Macedonia's famed three-fingered peninsulas, tipped by famed Mt. Athos monasteries, are only a few hours away by car on good highways.

8

highest and most storied peak, which dramatically ascends from greenery to rock to cloud, with no rolling hills to muddle the effect. Look up or down at this fabled peak and you'll understand why people settled at its foot and dreamed up the 12 Greek gods believed to live in the folds of the mountain.

4 Halkidiki. East of Thessaloniki, the road leads to the three fingers of Halkidiki. Known as "Heaven's City," Ouranoupoulis is close

to several small and fetching islets on Proviakas bay. Beyond is famed Mt. Athos. Monks got to Northern Greece long before tour groups, and the sites they chose for their monasteries are truly beautiful. In this region of extraordinary Byzantine architecture, one of the most impressive monastic complexes in the world is the Ayion Oros (Holy Mountain) on Mt. Athos, a males-only community for Greek Orthodox monks.

Updated by
Adrian Vrettos
and Alexia
Amvrazi

A land shaped by gods, warriors, and ghosts, Northern Greece sparkles with the sights, sounds, scents, and colors of its melting-pot history and epic geography. Here you will find remnants of the powerful civilizations that battled each other: temples and fortifications built by Athens and Sparta, Macedonian tombs, the arches and rotundas of imperial Rome, the domes of Byzantium, and the minarets and hammams of the Ottomans. Today, these sights rank among the most splendid sightseeing delights in Greece.

Burnished by history, the area that is often called Northern Greece—the region covered in this chapter—borders Albania, the Former Yugoslav Republic of Macedonia (FYROM, often spelled Makedonia), Bulgaria, and Turkey. From north to south, this land is heritage-rich. "Even today, house-owners sometimes dream that beneath their cellars lie Turkish janissaries and Byzantine necropolises," wrote historian Mark Mazower in his 2004 book *Salonica: City of Ghosts*. "One reads stories of hidden Roman catacombs, doomed love-affairs, and the unquiet souls who haunt the decaying villas near the sea."

Around 316 BC, the Macedonian leader Cassander founded what is now the area's major city, Thessaloniki, which grew into a culturally rich and politically strategic metropolis where Christians, Muslims, and Jews lived together for hundreds of years. Today it remains the second-largest city in Greece, is an anchor for arts and culture in the Balkans, and also brims with antiquities, old-style street markets, and old-world European flavor. Beyond Thessaloniki lies central Macedonia, where you can explore ancient monasteries, admire the frescoed tomb of Philip II of Macedon, hike the bloom-filled trails leading to Mt. Olympus, commune with farmers over grilled wild mushrooms, and enjoy some of Greece's finest beaches and seaside resorts.

The region was established as the state of Macedonia in the 8th century BC, and an illustrious monarchy was ensconced by about the 7th century BC. Philip II (382–336 BC) and his son Alexander the Great conquered most of Greece—except Sparta—and all of Persia. After Alexander's death, his brother-in-law, Cassander, established Thessaloniki as the capital (316 BC), naming it for his new bride, Thessalonica, Alexander's half-sister and daughter of the much-married Philip. (Philip had named her after his famous *nike*, or "victory," in Thessaly, where her mother had been one of the prizes.) The Romans took Macedonia as Alexander's successors squabbled, and by 146 BC, the rest of Greece had fallen under Roman rule. After the assassination of Julius Caesar, Marc Anthony defeated Brutus and Cassius at the battles of Philippi in Macedonia in 42 BC. Under Pax Romana, St. Paul twice traveled through on his way to Corinth.

Greek and Macedonian culture bloomed again during the Byzantine Empire (circa AD 312–1453), when the center of Greek civilization shifted from Athens to Constantinople (modern-day Istanbul). Thessaloniki became the second-most important city in the empire, and it remained so during the Ottoman domination that lasted from the fall of Constantinople until the 1912–13 Balkan Wars. That's when Macedonia became part of Greece, and the 1923 Treaty of Lausanne established the present borders with Thrace. The collapse of Yugoslavia in the 1990s rekindled ethnic and religious animosities. Today's northern Greeks are fiercely nationalist, and they strongly oppose the Former Yugoslav Republic of Macedonia's (FYROM) insistence on calling itself "Macedonia" and using ancient Macedonian symbols such as the star of Vergina on its flag. Tempers flared again in December 2006, when FYROM announced plans to name its international airport in Skopje after Alexander the Great.

Name-game squabbling aside, Northern Greece is flourishing. It's a hub for southeast European commerce and culture, and is home to Aristotle University, Greece's largest. The area is also expected to benefit from the Egnatia Odos, a 669-km (416-mile) road project that connected the Greek–Turkish border with the western port of Igoumenitsa. An influx of immigrants, many of them from Eastern Europe and the Middle East, is once again giving a multicultural flavor to Thessaloniki.

PLANNING

WHEN TO GO

Travel throughout northern Greece is best from May through October. Fall is beautiful; the air is cool and clear and the forests are dressed in burnished hues of orange, red, and copper. Spring is also lovely, especially in Dion, with its blooming fields of wildflowers scenting the breeze. Winters are mild, though there's usually enough snow on Olympus to keep ski resorts in business. July and August are the most crowded, but best for sunning, swimming, and chatting with northern Europeans and Greek families on holiday. In summer, Thessaloniki gets hot and humid but rarely reaches the scorching temperatures that sizzle southern Greece. As a whole, Northern Greece is rainier and cooler than the rest of Greece, especially in mountainous areas.

Autumn and winter rains, besides turning some roads to mud, do not enhance the appearance of Thessaloniki, a city designed for the sun.

PLANNING YOUR TIME

Thessaloniki makes a great base for a trip to northern Greece. Most of the city's sights are concentrated within the easily walkable center, and the city is also the main hub for regional buses and rental cars. There are wonderful museums and a great counterculture vibe. You could easily spend days exploring Greece's second-largest city, especially if you're an ecclesiastical buff (the five-aisled basilica Ayios Dimitrios is Greece's largest church) or a foodie (Thessaloniki has outstanding restaurants). From Thessaloniki, go west to Pella, the birthplace of Alexander the Great. Then go south to the town of Vergina, home of the magnificent Royal Tombs, and the ancient city of Dion, tucked into the lush foothills of Mt. Olympus. You'll need at least two days to hike the great summit of the gods, including an overnight stay in the pretty village of Litochoro.

GETTING HERE AND AROUND

Thessaloniki doesn't have good public transportation, and a new metro was not open at this writing—it's scheduled to open sometime in 2015. However, getting around the city on foot is fairly easy, since most of the sights are relatively close together. Taxis are also an option, if you don't mind drivers who tend to grouse over the slightest inconvenience. If you choose to drive, know that the traffic here can be as bad as the gridlock in Athens. That changes once you get out of Thessaloniki. The national highway is easy to navigate, and the smaller roads in central Macedonia are well paved. If you wish to rent a car, there are several reliable car rental agencies in Thessaloniki. There are also buses daily that go to major sites in central Macedonia, many belonging to the giant KTEL company.

AIR TRAVEL

Thessaloniki Macedonia International Airport (SKG) is at Mikras, 13 km (8 miles) southeast of the city center on the coast; it's about a 20-minute drive. In addition to international flights from primarily European destinations, there are frequent daily flights to and from Athens; flying time is 45 minutes. Domestic carriers including Aegean Air and its subsidiary Olympic Air connect Thessaloniki with a number of other cities in mainland Greece as well as Mykonos, Santorini, Crete, Rhodes, Corfu, Limnos, Chios, and Lesvos.

Bus 78 to and from the airport originates at the KTEL bus terminal, stops at the train station, and makes a stop at Aristotle Square (along Egnatia). Taxis charge according to the meter, with a €3.20 surcharge from the airport; expect to pay around €20 to the Town Center (after midnight the charge doubles).

Contacts Thessaloniki Macedonia International Airport ⊠ *Ethnikos Odos, Thessaloniki–Perea road, Km 16, Thessaloniki* ☎ *23109/85000* ⊕ *www. thessalonikiairport.gr.*

BOAT AND FERRY TRAVEL

Hellenic Seaways, Nel, Minoan, and other sea lines connect Thessaloniki to Chios, Lesvos, Samos, Heraklion (Crete), Kos, Rhodes, Skiathos, Skopelos, Naxos, Mykonos, Paros, and Santorini. Buy tickets at the Karacharisis Travel and Shipping Agency, Zorpidis Travel Services (Sporades and Cyclades only), Alexander Travel, or another travel agency. You can connect to Piraeus from Kavala, 136 km (85 miles) east of Thessaloniki (confirm schedules with the Kavala Port Authority). In summer, you should reserve ferries a month in advance. The Greek Travel Pages (⊕ *www.gtp.gr*) list ferry schedules online.

Contacts Alexander Travel ⊠ *Egnatia 7, 1st floor, Port, Thessaloniki* ☎ *23102/29950, 23104/21160* ⊕ *alexandertravel.gr.* **Karacharisis Travel and Shipping Agency** ⊠ *Salaminas 10, Port, Thessaloniki* ☎ *23105/13005, 23105/24544* ⊕ *thesferry.gr.* **Kavala Port Authority** ⊠ *Kavala* ☎ *25102/24967, 25102/23716* ⊕ *www.portkavala.gr.* **Zorpidis Travel Services** ⊠ *Egnatia 76, Kentro, Thessaloniki* ☎ *23102/31170, 23102/44400* ⊕ *www.zorpidis.gr.*

BUS TRAVEL

The trip to Thessaloniki from Athens takes about six hours, with one rest stop. Intercity KTEL buses connect Thessaloniki with cities throughout Greece. There are small ticket-office terminals (*praktorio*) for each line and separate ticket offices and telephone numbers for each destination. You can browse the KTEL website to get an idea of timetables (it's in Greek, so use Google to translate the page), or call KTEL Thessaloniki Main Terminal, but it's best to make ticket inquiries in person. The KTEL Main Terminal is on Thessaloniki's southwestern outskirts, off the National Road (Ethnikos Odos). Buses to Halkidiki leave from another KTEL terminal. This can get confusing, so definitely confirm both the time of your bus and the terminal from where it leaves when you buy your ticket.

Contacts KTEL Main Terminal ⊠ *Giannitson 244, Thessaloniki* ☎ *23105/95400 call center, 23105/95421 reservations for buses in Thessaloniki, 23105/95444 reservations for buses to Athens, 23105/95428 reservations for buses to Litochoro, 23105/95432 reservations for buses to Veria* ⊕ *ktelmacedonia.gr.*

CAR TRAVEL

Driving to Greece through the Former Yugoslav Republic of Macedonia is possible but often time-consuming owing to many border problems. The Athens–Thessaloniki section of the Ethnikos Odos (National Road), the best in Greece, is 500 km (310 miles); the drive takes 5 to 7 hours. The roads in general are well-maintained and constantly being improved and widened throughout the region. A good four-lane highway that begins in Athens goes to the border with Turkey. Posted speed limits are up to 120 kph (75 mph). When there's traffic, vehicles regularly use the shoulder as an extra lane, even though this is illegal. Driving in Thessaloniki is not recommended because of the congestion, frequent traffic jams, and scarcity of parking. Walking and taking a local bus or taxi are much easier on the nerves.

Having a car to get out of town and explore the smaller villages is helpful. Major car-rental agencies have offices at the Thessaloniki airport (some also have in-town locations). Aeolos is a good location option.

Contacts Aeolos ✉ *Agelaki 23, Kentro, Thessaloniki* ☎ *23122/01888* ⊕ *www.e-aeolos.eu.*

TRAIN TRAVEL

Thessaloniki is the primary entry point for train travel to northern Greece. Of the seven Athens–Thessaloniki trains that run per day, six are express (taking 5½ hours). Make reservations in advance at Athens Larissis Station's (Stathmos Larissis) south office (far-left facing, not the main entrance ticket booths, which are for same-day tickets only), or in Thessaloniki. The fastest intercity train will set you back €55 for a class-A seat or €45 for class B, and it's worth paying the difference for the extra comfort. Other express trains begin at €35 for class A, €25 class B, and take seven hours. Thessaloniki Station also has a left-luggage office (€2 for 8 hours, €3 for 24 hours) where you can store your bags before checking into or after checking out of your hotel.

Contacts OSE Thessaloniki Train Station. The Central Ticket office is at Aristotelous 18 and Ermou in Kentro. ✉ *Monastiriou 28, West Thessaloniki, Thessaloniki* ☎ *1110, 23105/99068 lost and found, 23105/99421, 23105/98126 Central Ticket Office* ⊕ *www.ose.gr.*

HOTELS

In the past, Thessaloniki's hotels were nothing to write home about and were mostly geared to the needs of transient business travelers, with little emphasis on capturing the spirit-of-place so appealing to tourists. Today, there are some more fetching options out there. The selection of hotels throughout northern Greece varies from exclusive seaside resorts in Chalkidiki to modest family-managed hostels on the slopes of Mt. Olympus to luxe outposts in Thessaloniki. Throughout the countryside, hotels are usually small, somewhat spartan affairs whose charm comes mainly from their surroundings. Note that some establishments—particularly in Chalkidiki—close for the winter (we've noted when it's otherwise); it is best to make arrangements ahead.

RESTAURANTS

Traditional Thracian and Macedonian cooks adapt to the seasons: in winter, rich game such as boar and venison is served; in summer, there are mussels and other seafood from the Aegean, as well as fruits and vegetables from the fertile plains. The relatively cooler climate here is reflected in rich chicken soups, roast chicken, stuffed vegetables, and stewed lamb and pork.

Small plates (*mezedes*) are a fundamental part of the Thessaloniki dining experience. Specialties include *medhia* (mussels), which come from farms outside the bay and are served in styles that include *saganaki* (sautéed in a pan with tomatoes, peppers, and feta) and *achnista* (steamed in broth with herbs). Also look for *soutzoukakia* (Anatolian-style meatballs in tomato sauce, seasoned with cumin). *Peinerli* (an open-faced boat of bread filled with cheese and ham) is a Black Sea specialty brought here by the Pontii, Greeks who emigrated from that area.

Meals are complemented by generous amounts of wine, ouzo, and *tsipouro*, the local version of grappa. Try the excellent barrel or bottled local wines, especially reds under labels such as Naoussa or Porto

Carras or a little bottle of Malamatina retsina, considered the best bottled version in Greece. Throughout the city, little shops and cellars specialize in a Macedonian treat called a submarine (or *ipovrihio*), a spoonful of sweets such as *visino* (black) cherries in syrup, dipped in a glass of ice water. As for dinnertime, you can arrive around 8, earlier than most Greeks like to eat dinner (many places do not open before then)—but it's much more fun to come at 9 or 10 and mix with the locals.

DINING AND LODGING PRICES IN EUROS			
	$	$$	$$$	$$$$
Restaurants	under €16	€16–€25	€26–€40	over €40
Hotels	under €126	€126–€225	€226–€275	over €275

Restaurant prices are for one main course at dinner, or for two mezedes (small dishes). Hotel prices are for a standard double room in high season, including taxes.

TOURS

Dolphin Hellas. Dolphin Hellas leads organized five-day tours of northern Greece that begin in Athens and take in the ancient archaeological sites; these are offered approximately once a month. Like other agencies, the company also arranges tailored tours and books hotels and car rental. Going through an agency often nets a cheaper rate than those quoted to individual walk-ins. ☎ *210/922–7772 in Athens* ⊕ *www.dolphin-hellas.gr.*

Dopios. A super new initiative connecting locals with visitors, Dopios is a wonderful way of exploring the different facets of life and culture in Thessaloniki and its environs with a 'dopios' (local) as a guide. Check out the website to see what kind of tour may interest you, whether it be a gastro tour, bar-hopping or the more standard sightseeing. ⊕ *www. dopios.com.*

Thessaloniki Tourist Guide Association. To hire a sightseeing guide, you can contact the Thessaloniki Tourist Guide Association. Prices vary depending on the tour and the place, but count on roughly €120 for a half-day and €160 for a full-day tour in Thessaloniki itself. Note that the TTGA offices do not have regular opening hours, so leave a message or send an email and they will get back to you. ☎ *23105/46037* ✐ *guideskg@otenet.gr.*

Velas Tours. Velas Tours can set you up at a thalassotherapy spa near Thessaloniki. ⊠ *Tsimiski 33, 2nd fl., Kentro, Thessaloniki* ☎ *23105/12032, 23105/18015* ⊕ *www.velastours.gr.*

Zorpidis Travel. Many tours in the region leave from Halkidiki, but major tour operator Zorpidis runs half-day tours to Vergina–Pella from Thessaloniki, and even arranges honeymoon trips. There's another branch at Mitropoleos 24, Tel. 23102/31168. ⊠ *Egnatia 76, 1st fl., Kentro, Thessaloniki* ☎ *23102/44400* ⊕ *www.zorpidis.gr.*

8

VISITOR INFORMATION
In Thessaloniki, the Greek National Tourism Organization (GNTO or EOT) central regional office on Tsimiski is open year-round from 8:30 to 3 on weekdays, and 8:30 to 2 on Saturday. Opening hours may be longer in summer but are not guaranteed. There's also a branch at the airport.

Contacts **Greek National Tourism Organization** (*GNTO/EOT*) ⊠ *Tsimiski 136, at Dagkli, Kentro, Thessaloniki* ☎ *23102/54810, 23102/52170, 23102/54834, 23104/71170 at airport* ⊕ *www.visitgreece.gr.*

THESSALONIKI ΘΕΣΣΑΛΟΝΙΚΗ

At the crossroads of East and West, where North blends into South, Thessaloniki (accent on the "ni") has seen the rise and fall of many civilizations: Macedonian, Hellenic, Roman, Byzantine, Ottoman, and that of the Jews and the modern Greeks. Each of its successive conquerors has plundered, razed, and buried much of what went before. In 1917 a great fire destroyed much of what was left, but the colorful past can still be seen and sensed. The vibrant city with close to 1.5 million inhabitants today—also known as Thessalonike, Saloniki, Salonika, or Salonica—has a spacious, orderly layout that is partly a result of French architect Ernest Hébrard, who rebuilt the city after the fire.

Though Thessaloniki has suburbanized since the 1990s, sprawling to the east and west, the old part of the city is fairly centralized and easy to get used to. Whether you're in Ano Polis (Upper City) or along the bay, short walks here are well rewarded; you may come across parks, squares, old neighborhoods with narrow alleyways and gardens, courtyards draped with laundry, neoclassical mansions, and some of the more than 50 churches and 40 monasteries. Thessaloniki's early Christian and Byzantine monuments, with their distinctive architecture and magnificent mosaics, are UNESCO World Heritage Sites. The ever-changing nature of the city continues as neighborhoods like Ladadika, a former warehouse district (which got its name from the olives and olive oil or *ladi* stored here), have been recycled into pedestrian zones of restaurants and clubs. The neighborhood is filled with young and old, strolling by fountains, snapping fingers to the music in the air, and savoring mezedes and microbrews at tables spilling onto the stone squares.

GETTING HERE AND AROUND

You can get to Thessaloniki from Athens easily by train or bus in about 6 hours (sometimes faster by express train), or you can fly. There are also international trains daily from Thessaloniki to Istanbul, Belgrade, and Bulgaria.

Buses traveling throughout the city streets of Thessaloniki are frequent, and the routes are useful. Bus 1 goes between the train station and the KTEL Main Terminal; Bus 78 goes from the KTEL Main Terminal to the train station and the airport; Bus 36 from Voulgari and Egnatia corner (in the eastern part of the city) goes to the KTEL Halkidiki Terminal (for Ouranoupolis, etc.). Tickets cost €0.80 at bus company booths and

One of the major crossroads of Thessaloniki, Aristotelous Square is a bustling *platia* set near the sea.

at some kiosks (*periptera*) or corner stores; or €0.90 on the bus and the ticket is reusable for any trip up to 90 minutes after the initial validation. You can also buy a 24-hour ticket for €4.

Thessaloniki's official taxis are blue with white hoods, and there are plenty cruising the streets by day, though fewer at night, and they can be hailed anywhere. The Taxi sign is lit up showing the availability. The minimum fare is €3, but make sure that the meter is on (rates double after midnight). On the whole the drivers are not only honest but also helpful, and tipping, though not essential, is the norm. Despite the heavy traffic (every hour seems to be rush hour in Thessaloniki) taking a taxi is cheap in comparison to most other places in Europe and the U.S. You can also call for a pick-up or use Taxibeat, a brilliant free online service that hails the taxi of your choice in the vicinity. On Taxibeat, each taxi is rated and has useful information about the driver/taxi (e.g., languages spoken, Wi-Fi on board, pet friendly, etc.).

Bus Contacts O.A.S.T.H. For complete info, contact O.A.S.T.H., the public transport company of the city. ✉ *Papanastasiou 90, 3rd floor, West Thessaloniki* ☎ *23109/81100, 23109/81245 lost and found* ⊕ *www.oasth.gr.*

Taxi Contacts Euro ☎ *23108/66866, 23105/51525.* **Lefkos Pyrgos** (*White Tower*) ☎ *23102/14900.* **Makedonia** ☎ *23105/50500.* **Taxibeat** ⊕ *taxibeat.gr.*

EXPLORING

The appeal of Thessaloniki lies in part in its warmth, accessibility, and languid pace. The afternoon *mesimeri*, or siesta, is still sacrosanct (don't call people between 3 and 5 pm). Take your time exploring in-town archaeological sites and Byzantine treasures, making sure to stop for café-style people-watching. It's best to simply to wander through the streets responding to whatever you encounter. It is hard to get lost, since the entire city slopes downhill to the bay, where you can always align yourself with the White Tower and the city skyline.

KENTRO

The lively shopping streets, bustling markets, and cafés of the Kentro (City Center) and adjacent areas reward you with the unexpected encounters and sensual treats of a great city. A stroll along the recently developed seafront is also enjoyable and a good way to walk off a big lunch. Walking eastward along the promenade, the landscaped areas and lush gardens are found at the end towards the concert hall. If you're feeling sporty, then join the locals who come here for a jog. Exploring the area from the White Tower west along the seaside to Aristotelous Square reveals icons of the city's history: grand monuments of Emperor Galerius, artifacts from the Neolithic period through the Roman occupation housed in the Archaeological Museum, and prominent churches, as well as the city's most important landmark, the tower itself.

TOP ATTRACTIONS

Arch of Galerius. The imposing *kamára* (arch) is one of a number of monuments built by Galerius around AD 305, during his reign as co-emperor of Diocletian's divided Roman Empire. It commemorated the Roman victory over Persia in AD 297, and you can still see scenes of those battles on the badly eroded bas-reliefs. Originally, the arch had four pediments and a dome and was intended to span not only the Via Egnatia, the ancient Roman road, but also a passageway leading north to the Rotunda. Only the large arches remain. ⊠ *Sintrivaniou Sq., Egnatia, Kentro.*

Fodor's Choice
★
Archaeological Museum of Thessaloniki. The unpretentious, single-story white structure gives no hint from the outside of the treasures within. A superb collection of artifacts from Neolithic times; sculptures from the Archaic, classical, and Roman eras; and remains from the Archaic temple at Thermi all reside under this roof. Objects discovered during construction of the Egnatia and Thessaloniki–Skopje highways were added in 2005 to the collection, which is displayed in eight galleries. "Thessaloniki, the Metropolis of Macedonia" traces the city's history through artifacts and a multimedia collection. "Towards the Birth of Cities" offers remains from settlements from Kastoria to Mt. Athos that date to as early as the Iron Age. ⊠ *Manoli Andronikou 6, Kentro* ☎ *23108/30538* ⊕ *www.amth.gr* ⊠ *€6; combined ticket with Byzantine Museum €8* ☉ *Tues.–Sun. 8–8.*

Ayia Sofia. The founding date of this church, a UNESCO World Heritage Site and the focal point of the city's Easter and Christmas celebrations, has been the subject of disagreements over the centuries. Ecclesiastics think it was built after the first Council of Nicea (AD

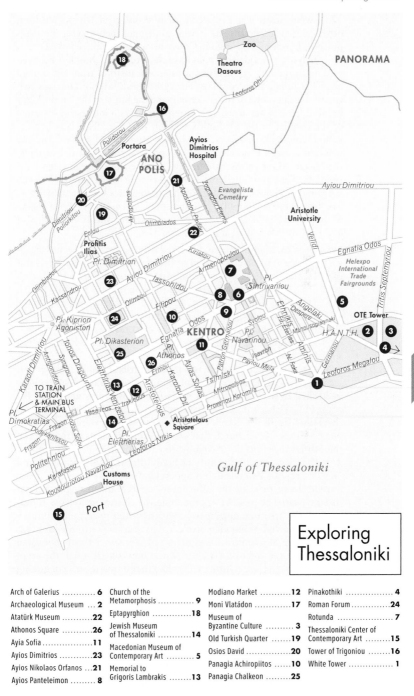

Exploring Thessaloniki

325), when Jesus was declared a manifestation of Divine Wisdom; other church historians say it was contemporaneous with the magnificent church of Ayia Sofia in Constantinople, completed in AD 537, on which it was modeled. From its architecture the church is believed to date to the late 8th century, a time of transition from the domed basilica to the cruciform plan. The rather drab interior contains two superb mosaics: one of the Ascension and the other of the Virgin Mary holding Jesus in her arms. This latter mosaic is an interesting example of the conflict in the Orthodox Church (AD 726–843) between the iconoclasts (icon smashers, which they often literally were) and the iconodules (icon venerators). At one point in this doctrinal struggle, the Virgin Mary in the mosaic was replaced by a large cross (still partly visible), and only later, after the victory of the iconodules, was it again replaced with an image of the Virgin Mary holding baby Jesus. The front gate is a popular meeting spot. ☒ *Ermou and Ayias Sofias, Kentro* ☏ *23102/70253* ⊕ *www.agiasofia.info* ⊘ *May–Oct., daily 7–1 and 6–7:30; Nov.–Apr., daily 7–1 and 5–6.*

Ayios Dimitrios. Magnificent and covered in mosaics, this five-aisle basilica is Greece's largest church and a powerful tribute to the patron saint of Thessaloniki. It was rebuilt and restored from 1926 to 1949, with attention to preserving the details of the original; the marks left by a fire can still be seen throughout. In the 4th century, during the reign of Emperor Galerius, the young, scholarly Dimitrios was preaching Christianity in the coppersmith district, in contravention of an edict. He was arrested and jailed in a room in the old Roman baths, on the site of the present church. While he was incarcerated in AD 303, Dimitrios gave a Christian blessing to a gladiator friend named Nestor, who was about to fight Galerius's champion, Lyaios. When Nestor fought and killed Lyaios, after having made Dimitrios's blessing public, the enraged Galerius had Nestor executed on the spot and had Dimitrios speared to death in his cell. His Christian brethren were said to have buried him there. A church that was built on the ruins of this bath in the 5th century was destroyed by an earthquake in the 7th century. The church was rebuilt, and gradually the story of Dimitrios and Nestor grew to be considered apocryphal until the great 1917 fire burned down most of the 7th-century church and brought to light its true past. The process of rebuilding the church uncovered rooms beneath the apse that appear to be baths; the discovery of a reliquary containing a vial of bloodstained earth gave credence to the idea that this is where St. Dimitrios was martyred. You enter through a small doorway to the right of the altar. Work your way through the crypt (which tends to close a little earlier than the church itself), containing sculpture from the 3rd to 5th century AD and Byzantine artifacts. The church's interior was plastered over when the Turks turned it into a mosque, but eight original mosaics remain on either side of the altar. ☒ *Ayiou Dimitriou 97, Kentro* ☏ *23102/70008, 23102/60915* ⊕ *www. inad.gr* ☑ *Free* ⊘ *Daily 6 am–10 pm.*

Ayios Panteleimon. A prime example of 14th-century Macedonian religious architecture, Ayios Panteleimon is an eye-catching church that draws you in to take a closer look. Restored in 1993 after an earthquake in 1978, the facade reveals the ornamental interplay of brick and stone-work, and a dome displays typically strong upward motion. ⊠ *Iasonidou and Arrianou, near Egnatia, Kentro* ☎ *23102/04150* ⊘ *Mon.–Thurs. 9–noon and 4–6, Fri. 8 pm–10:30 pm, Sat. 8:30–noon, Sun. 7:30–10 am.*

FAMILY **Museum of Byzantine Culture.** Much of the country's finest Byzantine art—priceless icons, frescoes, sculpted reliefs, jewelry, glasswork, manu-scripts, pottery, and coins—is on exhibit here. Ten rooms contain strik-ing treasures, notably an exquisite enamel-and-gold "woven" bracelet (Room 4), and an enormous altar with piratical skull-and-crossbones. A mezzanine (Room 7) shows how early pottery was made. Check the museum's website for the current temporary exhibitions. ⊠ *Leoforos Stratou 2, Kentro* ☎ *23133/06400* ⊕ *www.mbp.gr* ⊠ *€4; combined ticket with Archaeological Museum €8* ⊘ *Apr.–Oct., Tues.–Sun. 8–8; Nov.–Mar., Tues.–Sun. 8–3.*

Panagia Chalkeon. The name *Chalkeon* comes from the word for copper, and the beautiful "Virgin of the Copper Workers" stands in what is still the traditional copper-working area of Thessaloniki. Completed in 1028, this is one of the oldest churches in the city displaying the domed cruciform style and is filled with ceramic ornaments and glowing mosa-ics. Artisans and workers frequently drop by during the day to light a candle to this patron of physical laborers. Inside the sunken walls is a pretty and well-tended garden. The area around Panagia Chalkeon has many shops selling traditional copper crafts at low prices. ⊠ *Chalkeon 2, corner of Egnatia and Aristotelous, Kentro* ☎ *23102/72910* ⊘ *Sun.–Fri. 7:30–noon.*

Rotunda. Also known as Ayios Giorgios, this brickwork edifice has become a layered monument to the city's rich history. Built in AD 306, it was probably intended as Roman emperor Galerius's mausoleum. However, when he died in Bulgaria, his successor refused to have the body brought back. Under Theodosius the Great, the Byzantines con-verted the Rotunda into a church dedicated to St. George, adding the impressive 4th-century AD mosaics of early saints. The Ottomans made it a mosque (the minaret still stands). It was restored after damage suf-fered in a 1978 earthquake, and is still undergoing restoration at this writing. Once a month and on major holidays a liturgy is held here, as are occasional art exhibits and concerts. ⊠ *Platia Agiou Georgiou, Kentro* ☎ *23109/68860* ⊘ *Tues.–Sun. 8–3.*

Fodor's Choice ★ **White Tower.** The city's most famous landmark, and a symbol of Mace-donia, the White Tower is the only medieval defensive tower left stand-ing along the seafront (the other remaining tower, the Trigoniou, is in the Upper City). Now a part of the Museum of Byzantine Culture, its six floors offer a wonderful multimedia introduction to the city's history. Much of that history occurred within these walls—for cen-turies this was a prison—and *on* its walls: formerly known as "Blood Tower" it got its current name in 1896 when a convict exchanged his sentence for whitewashing the entire structure (which was removed in a 1980s renovation). The displays teach you that formidable seawalls and intermittent towers encircled the medieval city and were erected in the 15th century on the site of earlier walls. In 1866, with the threat

8

of piracy diminishing and European commerce increasingly imperative, the Ottoman Turks began demolishing them, except for the White Tower. At the top of your climb of 96 steps you are rewarded with a lovely museum café, whose rooftop setting provides sweeping vistas of the city. ⊠ *Leoforos Nikis and Pavlou Melas, Kentro* ☎ *23102/67832* ⊕ *www.lpth.gr* 🎫 *€3* ⊘ *Tues.–Sun. 8:30–3.*

WORTH NOTING

Ataturk's House. The soldier and statesman who established the Turkish republic and became its president, Ataturk (Mustafa Kemal), was born here in 1881. He participated in the city's Young Turk movement, which eventually led to the collapse of the sultanate and the formation of the modern Turkish state. About eight blocks east of the Ayios Dimitrios church, the modest pink house is decorated in Ottoman style. It has been turned into a museum, with personal items and documents of Turkey's founding father. ⊠ *Apostolou Pavlou 17 and Isaia St., at Ayiou Dimitriou, behind the Turkish Consulate, Kentro* ☎ *23102/48452* ⊘ *Daily 10–5.*

Athonos Square. A warren of side streets around a tiny square with a fountain is filled with tavernas and crafts stores. The area is frequently referred to, but it rarely appears on street maps: everyone knows where it is. ⊠ *East of Aristotelous, between Gennadiou and Karolou Dil, between Egnatia and Ermou, Kentro.*

Thessaloniki Center of Contemporary Art. This moody box of experimental and conceptual art, inside a remodeled warehouse on Thessaloniki's port, features a wide range of new-media art and video installations. It showcases some of the most exciting young Greek artists around and hosts cutting-edge, temporary exhibitions. ⊠ *Thessaloniki Port, Warehouse B1, Kentro* ☎ *23105/93270, 23105/46683* ⊕ *www.cact.gr* 🎫 *€3* ⊘ *Tues.–Sun. 10–6.*

Church of the Metamorphosis. This sunken church, part of which is (as the name would suggest) below ground level, is an example of 14th-century Macedonian ecclesiastical architecture, with a decorative mix of brick and stonework and a dome thrusting upward. Originally dedicated to the Virgin Mother, it was later dedicated to the Transfiguration of the Savior. ⊠ *Egnatia and P.P. Germanou, Kentro.*

Jewish Museum of Thessaloniki. Among the displays in this museum dedicated to the history of the local Jewish community are tombstones from the city's ancient necropolis, which was on the grounds now inhabited by Aristotle University. Also on exhibit are objects rescued from the 32

ALL ROADS LED TO THESSALONIKI

It was during the Byzantine period that Thessaloniki came into its own as a commercial crossroads, because the Via Egnatia, which already connected the city to Rome (with the help of a short boat trip across the Adriatic), was extended east to Constantinople. Today, the avenue called Egnatia Odos virtually follows the same path; it is Thessaloniki's main commercial thoroughfare (Tsimiski, which runs parallel to it two blocks to the south, is a bit more upscale).

synagogues that existed around the city, some of which were destroyed by the Nazis. The neoclassical building is one of the few Jewish structures that were spared in the great fire of 1917. ⊠ *Ayiou Mina 13, Kentro* ☎ *23102/50406* ⊕ *www.jmth.gr* 🎫 *€3* ⊘ *Tues., Fri., and Sun. 11–2; Wed. and Thurs. 11–2 and 5–8.*

Macedonian Museum of Contemporary Art. A large and expanding permanent collection of Greek and foreign works, as well as an eclectic selection of temporary shows, are on exhibit. You can unwind at the museum shop and the quirky art café. ⊠ *Egnatia 154, Helexpo, Kentro* ☎ *23102/40002, 2310/281212* ⊕ *www.mmca.org.gr* 🎫 *€4* ⊘ *Tues.–Sat. 10–6, Sun. 11–3.*

Memorial to Grigoris Lambrakis. If you've read the 1966 novel *Z* by Vassilis Vassilikos (or seen the 1969 Costas-Gavras film about the murder of Lambrakis, a leftist member of Parliament, by rightists in 1963), this monument is especially moving. The murder precipitated the events leading to the 1967–74 dictatorship of the colonels. A dramatic bronze head and arm, above which flutters a sculpted dove, marks the spot. ⊠ *Corner of Ermou and Eleftheriou Venizelou, Kentro.*

Modiano Market. Overhauled in 1922 by the Sephardic architect Eli Modiano, this old landmark is basically a rectangular building with a glass roof and pediment facade. Inside, the rich aromas of food—fish, meats, vegetables, fruits, breads, and spices—compete with music and the noisy, colorful market characters, from the market owners to the bargain hunters. In the little tavernas nearby, ouzo and mezedes are sold at all hours. It is worth a visit—as is the generally cheaper **open-air market** (on the north side of Ermou)—even if you have no intention of buying anything. ⊠ *Block bounded by Aristotelous, Ermou, Irakliou, and Komninon, Kentro* ⊘ *Mon., Wed., and Sat. 8:30–2:30; Tues., Thurs., and Fri. 8:30–1:30 and 5:30–8:30.*

Panagia Achiropiitos. The name *Achiropiitos* means "made without hands" and refers to the icon representing the Virgin that miraculously appeared in this 5th-century Byzantine church during the 12th century. An early example of the basilica form, the church has marvelous arcades, monolithic columns topped by elaborate capitals, and exquisite period mosaics of birds and flowers. It is the second-oldest church in Thessaloniki and probably the oldest in continuous use in the eastern Mediterranean. An inscription in Arabic on a column states that "Sultan Murat captured Thessaloniki in the year 1430," which was the year the church was converted temporarily into a mosque. ⊠ *Ayias Sofias 56, Kentro.*

Roman Forum. The forum in the ancient agora, or market, dates back to the end of the 2nd century AD. The small amphitheater here, which hosted public celebrations and athletic and musical contests in ancient times, is now often the site of romantic concerts on balmy summer evenings. In 2011 a new museum opened here, with items from the Hellenic area through the 4th century AD. ⊠ *Between Olimbou and Filipou, behind Dikasterion Sq., Kentro* ☎ *23102/21266* 🎫 *€3* ⊘ *Tues.–Sun. 8:30–8.*

DEPOT

The Depot neighborhood was once where the wealthy, mainly Jewish, merchants lived in impressive 19th-century villas. Very close to the port and the city center, this area was just outside the old city walls. Nowadays, the few remaining villas are mostly owned by foundations, and high-rise apartment blocks dominate the area.

TOP ATTRACTIONS

Pinakothiki (*Municipal Art Gallery*). This art gallery has a distinctive icon collection from the Byzantine and post-Byzantine periods, engravings that highlight the development of the craft of icon-making in Greece, and a representative collection of modern Greek art. One section shows the work of three generations of Thessalonian artists, documenting modern art in the city from the turn of the 20th century to 1967. The museum collection, once housed in the nearby Villa Mordoh, is now in Casa Bianca, a large three-story art nouveau villa. ⊠ *Casa Bianca, Vasilissis Olgas 180 and Them Sofouli, east of Kentro, Depot* ☎ *23104/25531* ⊕ *www.thessaloniki.gr* ⊠ *Free* ⊙ *Tues.–Fri. 10–2 and 6–9, Sat. 6–9, Sun. 10–2.*

LADAKIKA

A particularly large number of restaurants can be found in the Ladadika district in central Thessaloniki, near the port, which was named after the oil vendors who moved to the area after the great fire of 1917. Protected as a historic district from the building frenzy of the mid-1980s, the Ladadika was instead colonized by entrepreneurs who opened cheap tavernas (filling tables with inviting mezedes and carafes of ouzo) and bars in the restored old turn-of-the-20th-century buildings. Locals thronged to the lively area, and more and more establishments opened up and spilled over into the surrounding streets and alleys. Though a bit subdued after the financial crisis, the Ladadika still has buckets of charm and still hosts many of the city's best restaurants and drinking establishments.

ANO POLIS

Ano Polis, where many fortified towers once bristled along the city's upper walls, is what remains of 19th-century Thessaloniki. It's filled with timber-framed houses with their upper stories overhanging the steep streets. The views of the modern city below and the Thermaic Gulf are stunning, but other than Byzantine churches, there are few specific places of historical interest. This elevated northern area of the city gained its other name, Ta Kastra (The Castles), because of the castle of Eptapyrghion and the fortified towers that once dominated the walls. The area within and just outside the remains of the walls is like a village unto itself, a pleasing jumble of the rich, the poor, and the renovated. Rustic one-story peasant houses, many still occupied by the families that built them, sit side by side with houses newly built or restored by the wealthier class. As the area continues to be upgraded, tavernas, café-bars, and restaurants spring up to serve visitors, both Greek and foreign, who flock there for a cool evening out. It's an experience in itself to navigate the steps, past gossipy women, grandfathers playing backgammon in smoky cafés, and giggling children playing tag in tiny courtyards filled with sweet-smelling flowers, stray cats, and flapping laundry.

Getting here can be a chore, as taxi drivers often try to avoid the cramped, congested streets and fear missing a fare back down. Have your hotel find a willing driver, or take a local bus. Bus 23 leaves from the terminal at Eleftherias Square (two blocks west of Aristotelous Square, on the waterfront side) every 10 to 15 minutes and follows an interesting route through the narrow streets of Ano Polis. Or you can stroll the 30 minutes north from the White Tower, along Ethnikis Aminis, to get to Ano Polis.

TOP ATTRACTIONS

Moni Vlatádon. The Vlatades Monastery, shaded with pine and cypress, is a cruciform structure that displays a mixture of architectural additions, from Byzantine times to the present. It's known for its Ecumenical Foundation for Patriarchal Studies, the only one in the world. The small central church to the right of the apse has a tiny **chapel dedicated to Sts. Peter and Paul,** which is seldom open. It is believed to have been built on the spot where Paul first preached to the Thessalonians, in AD 49. Go through the gate entrance to get a panoramic view of the city of Thessaloniki. ⊠ *Eptapyrghiou 64, Ano Polis* ☎ *23102/09913* ⊘ *Mon.–Sat. 7:30–noon and 5:30–8, Sun. 11–2.*

Old Turkish Quarter. During the Ottoman occupation, this area, probably the most picturesque in the city, was considered the best place to live. In addition to the superb city views, it catches whatever breeze there is in summer. More recently, it was the home of some of the poorest families in Thessaloniki. Now the area is gentrifying, thanks to European Union development funds (which repaired the cobblestones), strict zoning and building codes, and the zeal of young couples with the money to restore the narrow old houses. The most notable houses are on Papadopolou, Kleious, and Dimitriou Poliorkitou streets. ⊠ *South of Dimitriou Poliorkitou, Ano Polis.*

NEED A BREAK?

Tsinari Ouzeri. A tree shades the terrace and blue, multipaned storefront of the Tsinari Ouzeri, the last remaining Turkish-style coffeehouse (opened in 1850) and the only one to have survived the fire of 1917. During the 1920s it became the social hub for the refugees from Asia Minor who lived here. Now a café and *ouzeri* (a bar where appetizers are sold), it is especially popular before siesta time (12–2 pm) and gets busy again after 9 pm. Have an ouzo and share delicious appetizers such as *melitzanonsalata* (pureed eggplant salad), octopus, or charcoal-grilled sardines. ⊠ *Papadopoulou 72, at Kleious, Ano Polis* ☎ *23102/84028.*

Fodor's Choice ★ **Osios David** (*Blessed David*). This entrancing little church with a commanding view of the city was supposedly built about AD 500 in honor of Galerius's daughter, who was secretly baptized while her father was away fighting. It was later converted into a mosque, and at some time its west wall—the traditional place of entrance (in order to look east when facing the altar)—was bricked up, so you enter Osios David from the south. No matter; this entirely suits the church's rather battered magic. You can still see the radiantly beautiful mosaic in the dome of the apse, which shows a rare beardless Jesus, as he seems to have been described in the vision of Ezekiel: Jesus is seen with a halo and is surrounded by the four symbols of the Evangelists—clockwise, from top left, are the angel, the eagle, the lion, and the calf. To the right is the prophet Ezekiel and, to the left, Habakuk. To save it from destruction, the mosaic was hidden under a layer of calfskin during the iconoclastic ravages of the 8th and 9th centuries. Plastered over while a mosque, it seems to have been forgotten until 1921, when an Orthodox monk in Egypt had a vision telling him to go to the church. On the day he arrived, March 25 (the day marking Greek independence from the Ottomans), an earthquake shattered the plaster, revealing the mosaic to the monk—who promptly died. ⊠ *Timotheou 7, near intersection of Dimitriou Poliorkitou and Ayias Sofias, Ano Polis* ☎ *23102/21506* ⊙ *Tues.–Sat. 11–5, Sun. 11–2.*

WORTH NOTING

Ayios Nikolaos Orfanos. Noted frescoes here include the unusual *Ayion Mandilion* in the apse, which shows Jesus superimposed on a veil sent to an Anatolian king, and the *Niptir,* also in the apse, in which Jesus is washing the disciples' feet. The artist is said to have depicted himself in the right-hand corner wearing a turban and riding a horse. The 14th-century church, which became a dependency of the Vlatádon Monastery in the 17th century, has an intriguing mix of Byzantine architectural styles and perhaps the most beautiful midnight Easter service in the city. ⊠ *Kallithea Sq. and Apostolou Pavlou (enter on Irodotou), Ano Polis* ☎ *23102/14497* ⊙ *Tues.–Sun. 9–2:45.*

Eptapyrghion. In modern times, this Byzantine fortress—its name means "the seven towers" even though there are ten towers—was an abysmal prison, closed only in 1988. There's not much to see here except wall ruins and a small museum that documents the building's history. The area is an untended green space, not an unpleasant place to sit and survey Thessaloniki below. The surrounding tavernas accommodate throngs of locals in the evening. ⊠ *Eptapyrghiou, Ano Polis* ☎ *23133/10400, 23103/31040* ⊙ *Tues.–Sun. 8:30–3.*

Tower of Trigoniou. From this survivor of the city walls, you can see the city spread out below you in a graceful curve around the bay, from the suburbs in the east to the modern harbor in the west and, on a clear day, even Mt. Olympus, rising near the coastline at the southwest reaches of the bay. There is, however, little of historic interest to see within the walls. ⊠ *Eptapyrghiou, Ano Polis.*

SFAGEIA

The nightlife district Sfageia is a short hike or cheap taxi ride southwest of the train station, along 26th Oktovriou street. Many of the restaurants here offer live *rembetika* (Greek blues) and other Greek music.

WHERE TO EAT

The cosmopolitan, multiracial character of Thessaloniki—building on its historic Byzantine and Ottoman influences—has created a subtly sophisticated, multifaceted cuisine; many Greeks feel Thessaloniki has the best food in the country. It is distinguished by its liberal use of fragrant Levantine spices, including sweet red peppers from Florina called *florines* and hot peppers known as *boukovo*. Thessaloniki is especially known for its *mezedes*, or small plates; every little *ouzeri* (casual bar serving ouzo and mezedes) or taverna has at least one prized house recipe. Leisurely lunches consisting of a multitude of mezedes are the focal point of a typical Thessaloniki day.

KENTRO

$ ✕**Myrovolos Smyrni.** Go to this beloved hangout—also called Tou Tha-
GREEK   nassi, after its owner, Thanassis—on a Saturday afternoon when an eclectic mix of Thessalonians fills the Modiano Market. Roaming Gypsy musicians serenade visitors with languid accordion lullabies or swooning violin ballads. The food here is equally diverting, from grilled octopus (sliced off specimens hanging nearby) and stuffed squid to *midhia saganaki* (mussels with cheese-and-tomato sauce). If you do plan to come on Saturday, make a reservation; it's the only day they are accepted. $ *Average main: €11* ✉ *Komninon 32, Modiano Market, Kentro* ☎ *23102/74170* ▭ *No credit cards* ⊘ *Closed Sun.*

$ ✕**O Loutros.** Diners at this side-street Thessaloniki institution rub
GREEK   shoulders with lawyers, students, out-of-towners, and workers from the Bezesteni market. Complete with an outside terrace, this family-run taverna sits opposite an old Turkish bath (*loutra* means "baths"). Try grilled *koutsomoura* (baby red mullets), grilled eggplant, mussels in rice pilaf, or smelt or shrimp sautéed in a casserole with cheese and peppers (*saganaki*). Do sample the owner's own retsina from the barrel and check if they have the exquisite *kazan dipi*, a marvelous flan with a slightly burned top, sweetened with a hint of rose water. For extra atmosphere, there's the bouzouki music every Friday and Saturday night. $ *Average main: €10* ✉ *M. Kountoura 5, Bezesteni, Kentro* ☎ *23102/28895.*

$ ✕**Ouzeri Aristotelous.** Behind a wrought-iron gate opening to a stoa,
GREEK   artists, scholars, couples, old friends, and businesspeople pack marble-
Fodor'sChoice   topped tables. This convivial atmospheric place epitomizes the quality
★   and spirit of Thessaloniki dining, down to the traditional spoon desserts. Once you sample the cuttlefish *gemista* (stuffed with cheese), grilled eggplant with garlic, or sautéed fillet of skate with white sauce, you'll understand why no one is in a hurry to leave. The entrance is on the east side of Aristotelous, between Irakliou and Tsimiski. ⚠ **Be warned: address numbers repeat at the square of the same name down the street, but this place is well worth the effort.** $ *Average main: €11* ✉ *Aristotelous 8, in the stoa, Kentro* ☎ *23102/30762.*

$ ✕**Ouzeri Melathron.** "Ouzo's Mansion," established as Greece's first
MEDITERRANEAN   ouzeri franchise (1993), attracts a mainly young crowd. The chefs here are trained in a style that is essentially Mediterranean, with some French and Turkish influences. Pick from irreverently named items, such as "transexual lamb" (it's chicken) or "Maria's breasts" (cones of fried phyllo filled with ground meat) on the exhaustive menu. Don't forget to order from the ecclectic choices of ouzo. $ *Average main: €10* ✉ *Eleftheriou Venizelou 23, at Ermou, in Stoa Karipi, Kentro* ☎ *23102/20043, 23102/75016* ⊕ *www.ouzoumelathron.gr.*

8

$$ ✗ **7 Thalasses.** This may be the best seafood restaurant in Thessaloniki—
SEAFOOD   it's definitely the most creative. The breezily decorated 7 Thalasses ("7
Fodor'sChoice   Seas") uses light blue and gray hues to good effect, playing them off
★   the room's exposed chrome accents and cream-color wood tables and
chairs. The cooking here maintains the delicate flavors of its ingredients,
but it also manages to add a modern twist to its dishes. For instance, the
marinated sea bass tartare, seasoned with fleur de sel, lemon, and olive
oil and then covered with a sprinkling of roe, brings to mind a wave
gently breaking against your tongue. The only thing better than the
delightfully light scallops in saffron sauce with caviar and mushrooms
may be the restaurant's signature dish, *mithopilafo* (mussels with rice),
an old favorite. As for the desserts, try its take on halva, with *loukoumi*
(Turkish delight) ice cream, toasted pine nuts, and marinated raisins.
It's a perfect way to end one of the memorable meals here. $ *Average
main: €22* ⊠ *8–10 Kalapothaki, Kentro* ☎ *2310/233173* ⊕ *7thalasses.
eu* ⌖ *Reservations essential.*

$ ✗ **Ta Nissia.** The food may be costly, but Ta Nissia doesn't seem over-
GREEK   priced thanks to the quality of ingredients and careful preparation by
owner-chef Yiannis Alexiou. You're in the city here, but the lightness
and decor of this place may make you feel as if you've been transported
to some Cycladic isle. Dishes here can be exquisite: taste sensations
include squid stuffed with cheese and herbs, veal with smoked eggplant
puree, and artichokes in saffron sauce. On the extensive wine list, check
out the very pleasing house rosé. $ *Average main: €15* ⊠ *Proxenou
Koromila 13, Kentro* ☎ *23102/24477, 23102/85991* ⊕ *www.tanisia.
com* ⌖ *Reservations essential* ⊘ *No dinner Sun. Closed July and Aug.*

$ ✗ **Vrotos.** Some of the most delicious and innovative appetizers in Thes-
GREEK   saloniki are served at this little ouzeri run by the Vrotos family. You
can sit in the noisy interior, decorated with old movie posters, or at the
tables out front, all jammed with the cognoscenti. A strong Anatolian
influence is evident in the terrific mezedes and main dishes: try the
Hunkiar Beyendi (beef with tomato sauce and eggplant puree) or the
bougiourdi (tomatoes, peppers, and feta and other cheeses baked in a
clay pot). ⚠ **For returning visitors, Vrotos has moved to a new location
nearby but worry not, the food remains top notch.** $ *Average main: €12*
⊠ *3 Skra St., Kentro* ☎ *23102/22392* ⌖ *Reservations essential* ⊟ No
credit cards ⊘ *Closed 3 wks in Aug. and Sun. June–Aug.*

$$ ✗ **Zythos Dore.** Crowded and lots of fun, Zythos Dore café/eatery has a
GREEK   good buzz inside the converted 1920s-era Viennese-style coffeehouse,
and it offers a great view of the White Tower if you choose to sit on
the terrace out front. There are plenty of choices on the menu: Decent
Greek and international dishes ranging from *pastourma* pie (with spicy
air-cured dried beef) to homemade lamb sausages. There is also a selection of European draft beers.There's another branch in Ladadika that
follows the same concept and is a fun place to hang out in the former
warehouse district. $ *Average main: €16* ⊠ *Tsiroyiannis Sq. 7, Kentro*
☎ *23102/79010* ⊕ *www.zithos.gr.*

Noted for its mosaics, the Ayios Dimitrios is Greece's largest church and is the shrine of the city's patron saint.

8

LADADIKA

$ 🍴 **Omikron.** This lovely, unpretentious new little restaurant in the trendy Ladadika district is fast becoming a local favorite. Delightful Greek-Mediterranean dishes are tastefully presented to reflect the chef-owner's culinary stint in France. As one would expect, the menu, chalked onto a blackboard at the front of house, varies according to what's been netted at the local food market. The grilled fish is succulent and well-seasoned, showing a delicate touch, and the seafood risotto with a tomato pesto is a staple that keeps people coming back again and again. In this time of crisis the great prices ensure Omicron always stays busy. [$] *Average main: €6* ✉ *Oplopoiou 3, Ladadika* ☎ *23105/32774.*

GREEK FUSION

$ 🍴 **To Full Tou Meze.** Ordering your meal at this establishment in the heart of the bustling old Turkish Quarter is quite an experience. The waiters bring their own eccentric individuality to this often mundane ritual, and the menu is printed on a "newspaper" with photos from old Greek films and articles heralding the dishes you're about to munch on. The taverna itself is done up as a deli, which gives a rough idea of the fare served. There is a wide array of cheeses, smoked meats, and fish (served either straight up or cooked in spicy sauces). It's food that goes great with a beer or an ice-filled glass of ouzo on a hot summer evening. [$] *Average main: €10* ✉ *3 Katouni, Ladadika* ☎ *23105/24700* 🌐 *www.fullmeze.gr* ✍ *Reservations not accepted.*

GREEK

Fodor's Choice ★

WHERE TO STAY

The majority of hotels are located in the Kentro (center) of Thessaloniki. There are lodgings to suit all budgets, but the area is busy and noisy all day and much of the night, so the most upscale establishments have created a quiet oasis within their walls, insulated from the chaos outside. Look to the more tranquil Faliro neighborhood for a quieter locale.

KENTRO

Stay in Kentro, and all the city action will be on your doorstep, and you'll find most attractions, shopping, and good restaurants within walking distance. More important, Kentro is close enough to the waterfront that top-floor rooms may have sea views. However, parking is difficult, and noise can be a problem, especially at cheaper hotels.

$ | **Aegeon Hotel.** Don't despair over the garish neon sign outside the
HOTEL | Aegeon—this place is actually one of the warmest and best-priced hotels along busy Egnatia street, conveniently close to the train station, port, city center, and Ladadika districts. **Pros:** double-glazing does a lot to minimize the commotion on noisy Egnatia. **Cons:** even so, it is on the busy main road. $ *Rooms from: €55* ✉ *Egnatia 19, Kentro* ☎ *23105/22921* ⊕ *www.aegeon-hotel.gr* ⦶ *Breakfast.*

$ | **Hotel Olympia.** Location counts at this boutique hotel on a corner close
HOTEL | to the flea market, copper market, Roman Forum, and Ayios Dimitrios—but there are many other pluses at this nicely stylish place, which enjoys quality service and offers an excellent, American-style breakfast. **Pros:** service is excellent; check for discounts. **Cons:** limited parking spaces for guests. $ *Rooms from: €67* ✉ *Olymbou 65, at Papageorgiou, Kentro* ☎ *23103/66466* ⊕ *www.hotelolympia.gr* ⦶ *Breakfast.*

$ | **Hotel Orestias Kastorias.** Blink and you may miss this circa-1920
HOTEL | hotel—a favorite of budget travelers—on a quiet, narrow street leading from the top corner of the Roman Forum to Ayios Dimitrios church. **Pros:** pretty good value for those on a budget; good service; views onto the Roman Forum. **Cons:** breakfast is not served (although guests can help themselves to coffee and biscuits in the reception area); very limited parking available; no elevator. $ *Rooms from: €55* ✉ *Agnostou Stratiotou 14, Kentro* ☎ *23102/76517, 23102/69815* ⊕ *www.okhotel. gr* ⦶ *No meals.*

$ | **Le Palace Art Hotel.** On one of the city's main thoroughfares, this
HOTEL | updated art deco–style hotel is popular with savvy business travel-
FAMILY | ers and Greek tourists. **Pros:** sleep like a baby on Coco-Mat luxury natural mattresses. **Cons:** can be noisy; check bill carefully for unexpected charges, such as parking. $ *Rooms from: €75* ✉ *Tsimiski 12, at Eleftheriou Venizelou, Kentro* ☎ *23102/57400* ⊕ *www.lepalace.gr* ⦶ *Breakfast.*

$ | **Tourist Hotel.** An impressively elegant, turn-of-the-20th-century build-
HOTEL | ing houses this modest family-run hotel that's very popular with regular foreign visitors—from business-trippers to families—who enjoy the guest rooms with high ceilings, plus some nifty historic touches, such as time-burnished wainscoting and an attractive 1920s-era elevator. **Pros:** the location, just west of Aristotelous Square, is prime. **Cons:** room windows are double-glazed, but ask for a room at the back if sensitive

to main-road noise; can get a little stuffy in summer. [$] *Rooms from: €60* ✉ *Mitropoleos 21, at Komninon, Kentro* ☎ *23102/70501* 🌐 *www.touristhotel.gr* 🍴 *Breakfast.*

LADADIKA

The trendy Ladadika neighborhood (very close to the Kentro) is where most of the city's tavernas and bars are located. There are only a handful of places to stay here, most in restored old buildings. These places book up quickly, so finding a room here maybe a little more challenging. The neighborhood is still very central and architecturally interesting, and it's quiet in the mornings. Views, though not expansive, are engaging. But late-night noise—especially on weekends—can be a problem, and parking is almost nonexistent (the nearest parking lots are five minutes' walk and cost at least €10/day); no hotels have parking here.

$ HOTEL Fodor's Choice ★ 🏨 **The Bristol Hotel.** An elegant retreat with a touch of history, this exquisite boutique hotel occupies one of the few buildings that survived the great fire of 1917 untouched—during Ottoman rule the structure served as the city's post office—and, today, a mixture of handmade furniture, handpicked antiques, and works of art makes this place special. **Pros:** small personal hotel; excellent location; great value for money. **Cons:** no parking. [$] *Rooms from: €125* ✉ *Oplopiou 2, at Katouni, Ladadika* ☎ *23105/06500* 🌐 *www.bristol.gr* 🍴 *Breakfast.*

$ HOTEL 🏨 **Mediterranean Palace.** From the abundance of amenities at this traditionally decorated, six-story hotel near the port and Ladadika, it's easy to see that the Mediterranean Palace caters to business travelers, who will appreciate the consistently good service and many amenities. **Pros:** top location; top-of-the-line hotel services; parking. **Cons:** rooms on the street side of hotel can be noisy; best rooms are in the front and have sea views. [$] *Rooms from: €125* ✉ *Salaminos 3, at Karatasou, Ladadika* ☎ *23105/52554* 🌐 *www.mediterranean-palace.gr* 🍴 *Breakfast.*

FALIRO

Faliro, a modern, residential area, is south of the city center and the White Tower. The hotels here are usually in large, high-rise buildings owned by trusted brands with good amenities (including swimming pools) and offering high standards of service. You're still very close to the waterfront, so it's easy to get a room with a sea view, and since there's space, hotels tend to have parking and more on-site amenities. However, you'll be slightly out of the city center (20 minutes by foot), and Faliro obviously lacks the character and sparkle of the central areas.

$ HOTEL FAMILY 🏨 **Makedonia Palace.** You might see a rock star or the president of Albania here; it's that kind of place—just note the excellent location on the waterfront, southeast of the White Tower, with stunning views of the sunset and Mt. Olympus, or the slew of amenities (mini-stereos, dual-voltage outlets, multimedia convention center) the Grecotel chain has installed behind the hotel's 1970s-era facade. **Pros:** top location right on the beachfront; discounts possible in summer. **Cons:** rooms on the lower floor might be a bit noisy from the traffic; needs some modernization; rooms can be stuffy in summer. [$] *Rooms from: €125* ✉ *Megalou Alexandrou 2, Faliro* ☎ *2310/897197* 🌐 *www.makedoniapalacehotel.com* 🍴 *Breakfast.*

NIGHTLIFE

The Thessaloniki bar-and-club scene is eclectic, dynamic, and energized. Students, academics, and artists haunt the bars on Zefxidos street near Ayia Sofia church while music-lovers crowd the stages at Mylos, a former flour mill that is now Northern Greece's most coveted arts-and-entertainment complex. In summer, most clubs close as their clients flock to the beaches of Halkidiki, which functions as an outer suburb of the city. The discos on the road to the airport go in and out of fashion and change names (and concept) from one season to the next, so ask at your hotel for the newest and best.

When you hear locals talking about Paralia, they are referring to the road that lines the city center's waterfront, Leoforos Nikis. The cafés and bars here buzz at all hours of the day and night. Walk east along Proxenou Koromila, one block up from the waterfront, to find more intimate, cool bars.

KENTRO

BARS AND CLUBS

Pastaflora Darling!. Pastaflora Darling! is a whimsically decorated hangout for students and artists philosophizing about the latest global trend. Drinks are excellent and inexpensive. It's open all day until late in the evening (or morning, rather). ⊠ *Zefxidos 6, Kentro* ☎ *23102/61518.*

Urban. Urban is a former art gallery–turned–glam bar for counterculture scenesters, young academics, and lifelong artists. The music is fantastic, as is the people-watching. The music starts kicking after 9 pm. ⊠ *Zefxidos 7, Kentro.*

Pedestrian Katouni street in Ladadika is lined with cafés and bars; this neighborhood is Thessaloniki's answer to Athens's Gazi-Kerameikos and Thission nightlife areas.

SFAGEIA

BARS AND CLUBS

Fodor'sChoice **Mylos.** Mylos, in a former mill on the southwest edge of the city, has
★ become perhaps the best venue in Greece for jazz, folk, and pop acts, both Greek and foreign. This fabulous complex of clubs, bars, and ouzeri-tavernas, as well as art galleries and a concert stage, shows how a respectful architectural conversion can become a huge success. Don't miss the Xylourgeio stage, which has some of the best alternative acts around. The lively place starts to get busy as early as 11 pm. ⊠ *Andreadou Georgiou 56, Sfageia* ☎ *23105/51836* ⊕ *www.mylos.gr.*

PERFORMING ARTS

Thessaloniki is an outstanding town for all things cultural: large orchestras and string trios, drama and comedy, and performances by international and local favorites are all part of the scene. For current happenings or information about festivals in the city or area, check with your hotel.

CONCERTS

Megaron Moussikis Thessaloniki (*Thessaloniki Concert Hall*). The Megaron Moussikis Thessaloniki is a large venue that hosts ballet, opera and other highbrow musical and cultural events. Graced by international and local orchestras (including the Municipal Orchestra of Thessaloniki) there are classical, folk, and jazz nights, as well as seminars and lectures. ✉ *Martiou 25 and Paralia, Kalamaria* ☎ *23108/95800, 23108/95938, 23108/95939 box office* ⊕ *www.tch.gr.*

FESTIVALS

Helaxpo, the large international trade fair that is held mid-September, makes hotel reservations very difficult to come by, as does the Thessaloniki Film Festival in November.

> **PLAYING WITH FIRE**
>
> *Anastanarides* (fire dancers) are a famous part of Northern Greece. Starting on the feast day of saints Constantine and Eleni, May 21, religious devotees in the villages of Langadha (25 km [15 miles] north of Thessaloniki) and Ayia Eleni (80 km [50 miles] northeast of Thessaloniki) take part in *pirovassia* (literally, "fire dancing"). During the three-day rite, participants dance unharmed on a bed of hot coals while holding the saints' icons. The rite is derived from the eastern Thracian village of Kosti, where the villagers are said to have rescued the original icons from a burning church around 1250.

☾ **Apokriés.** Apokriés—what Greeks call their Carnival celebrations—mark the period preceding Lent and ending on the night before "Clean Monday," the beginning of Lent for Eastern Orthodox and Catholics. These costume-and-parade affairs are particularly colorful (and often bawdy) in northern Greece. You are welcome to join in the fun in Thessaloniki and other towns. Sohos, 32 km (20 miles) northeast of Thessaloniki, hosts a festive event in which people cavort in animal hides with sheep bells around their waists and phallic headdresses. In Naoussa, 112 km (70 miles) west of Thessaloniki, some participants wear *foustanellas* (short, pleated white kilts), special masks, and chains of gold coins across their chests, which they shake to "awaken the Earth." The whole town dons costumes and takes to the streets behind brass marching bands, which have a tradition of playing New Orleans–style jazz.

Dimitria Festival. St. Dimitrios's feast day is celebrated on October 26. Its secular adjunct, the Dimitria Festival, has developed into a major series of cultural events that include theater, dance, art exhibits, and musical performances. They are held from September to December at venues around Thessaloniki. ☎ *23102/28414, 23102/81068* ⊕ *www.dimitriathess.gr.*

FILM

Alex. A must-do in summer, especially for film-lovers, is to see a movie at an open-air cinema. There are usually two show times (around 8 and 11 pm, the later one usually at lower volume, depending on the neighborhood). Call ahead or check the website to see what's playing—some screen oldies and foreign art films, and others run the latest from

Hollywood. Most films are subtitled, but note that animated movies are almost always dubbed. Alex is the most central theater. ⊠ *Ayias Sofias and Olympou, Kentro* ☎ *23102/69403* ⊕ *www.cine.gr/prog.asp.*

Fodor'sChoice **Thessaloniki International Film Festi-**
★ **val.** Each November, the best films by new directors from around the world are screened and awarded prizes at the Thessaloniki International Film Festival. Southeast Europe's most noted cinematic festival, it attracts well-known regional talent and some internationally acclaimed stars. Films are usually subtitled, and tickets can be hard to come by. In March, there's also an international documentary film festival. ⊠ *Olympion Bldg., Aristotelous Sq. 10, Kentro* ☎ *2310/378400* ⊕ *www.filmfestival.gr.*

> **SHOPPERS' SIESTA**
>
> The government has made efforts to make Thessaloniki's shops' opening hours consistent, but the afternoon siesta is still observed by many small establishments. Hours are generally from about 9 to 1:30 or 2; stores reopen in the evenings on Tuesday, Thursday, and Friday. Many shops close for a few weeks in July or August.

THEATER

Performances are in Greek, although there are occasional visits by English-speaking groups.

Kratiko Theatro (*State Theater*). The Kratiko Theatro presents plays, ballets, and special performances of visiting artists year-round. ⊠ *Ethnikis Aminis 2, opposite the White Tower, Kentro* ☎ *23152/00000, 23152/00200 box office* ⊕ *www.ntng.gr.*

Theatro Dasous (*Forest Theater*). Theatro Dasous stages theatrical performances in foreign languages in summer, as well as other events, such as concerts. ⊠ *In Seich-Sou forest, Oxi Ave., Ayios Pavlos* ☎ *23152/00014, 21302/88000.*

SHOPPING

ANTIQUES

Antiques shops on Mitropoleos between Ayias Sofias and the White Tower are perfect for leisurely browsing; look also on the streets around Athonos Square. But one block west of the Roman Forum, Tositsa is the best source for junk, antiques, and roaming peddlers in the city, with good finds in everything from brass beds to antique jewelry. The *paliatzidiko* (flea market) here has a marvelous jumble of fascinating, musty old shops, with the wares of itinerant junk collectors spread out on the sidewalks, intermingled with small, upscale antiques shops.

Bazaar. On Wednesday the narrow streets surrounding the Rotunda are taken over by a bazaar with knickknacks and the occasional interesting heirloom, antique, or folk art piece for sale. ⊠ *Rotunda.*

CLOTHING

Thessalonians are noted for being tastefully and stylishly dressed. Clothing here is high quality (but notice that sizes are a lot smaller than their American counterparts). The best shopping streets are Tsimiski, with its brand-name boutiques, Mitropoleos, Proxenou Koromila, Mitropolitou Iosif, Karolou Dil, and P.P. Germanou. Cheaper children's clothing (normally extortionate) can be found on Syngrou, south of Egnatia.

GREEK SOUVENIRS

Athonos Square has shops with traditional, handmade items; craftspeople themselves own many of the stores on the narrow streets between Aristotelous and Ayias Sofias. The streets around Panayia Chalkeon have shops selling copper items. Try at the Archaeological Museum for Macedonian-focused souvenirs.

Korres. Greece's leading producer of excellent natural cosmetics and beauty products, now has a shop in Thessaloniki south of the city center. Even though most pharmacies stock Korres, this shop has the full range of products. For those who want to order these and other top Greek beauty products online and have them sent to your home there are good some websites providing this service, the best of which is *www.mysecretkshopper.com.* ✉ *Agisilaou 19, Kifissia* ☎ *23103/14662.*

Mastihashop. Mastihashop carries products containing mastic—a tree resin produced on the Aegean island of Chios. The face cream, preserves, sweets, and other items come in extremely attractive, easy-to-pack tins. ✉ *Karolou Diehl 15, near Tsimiski, Kentro* ☎ *23102/50205, 23102/50206* ⊕ *www.mastihashop.com.*

SWEETS

Thessaloniki is well known for its food, including a vast array of Balkan and Eastern-oriented pastries and desserts. Sit down, sample, and decide which you think is best.

Agapitos Patisserie. With eight outlets in Thessaloniki, Agapitos Patisserie aptly translates as "loved one." The oldest son of a venerable Thessaloniki family owns this chain. ✉ *Tsimiski 10, Kentro* ☎ *23102/25950* ⊕ *www.agapitospatisserie.com.*

Averof. Averof is the only patisserie in Thessaloniki that creates kosher pastries. ✉ *Vasilissis Georgiou 11, Kentro* ☎ *23108/14284* ⊕ *www. averof.gr.*

Hatzis. Sample Thessaloniki's fabled Anatolian sweets at central Hatzis. Specialties include the buffalo milk cream-based *kazan dipi,* a kind of flan; *trigono,* a cream-filled triangle of phyllo; and *kataïfi* (logs of crushed and sugared walnuts wrapped in honey-drenched shredded phyllo) served with *kaïmaki* (mastic-flavored ice cream). Choose a beverage—like iced coffee, granita, or *boza* (a thick, sweet, millet-and-corn drink)—and people-watch from the pedestrian side street that faces the gardens of Panagia Chalkeon church. ✉ *Eleftheriou Venizelou 50, Kentro* ☎ *23102/79058* ⊕ *www.chatzis.gr.*

Terkenlis. Terkenlis serves an unforgettable *tsoureki* (sweet bread flavored with *mahlepi,* a spice made from the ground-up pits of a Persian cherry) and then filled and dipped in chocolate. This delicacy is so delicious that it disappears within hours from this extremely popular patisserie's shelves. ✉ *Tsimiski 30, Kentro* ☎ *23102/71148* ⊕ *www. terkenlis.gr.*

ALEXANDER THE GREAT COUNTRY

Makedonia, one of the less visited areas of Greece, is a region of legend and history, full of architectural treasures and remnants of the reign of Alexander the Great. Happily, many of these places are within easy reach of Thessaloniki. Few places in the world have greater ancient sites than Pella, Vergina, and Dion, which are famously connected to Alexander the Great and his father, Philip II, heroes of the ages. Even one would be worth a detour, but they are so close to Thessaloniki that it is easy to see all of them. You can rush and explore all three in a harried day trip from Thessaloniki; better would be scheduling a relaxed day for each, allowing time for contemplation, or after seeing the first two, spending the night near Dion or Mt. Olympus and visiting both of these the next day.

In the 7th century BC the Dorian Makedonoi (Macedonian) tribe moved out of the Pindos mountains (between Epirus and Macedonia), settled in the fertile plains below, and established a religious center at the sacred springs of Dion at the foot of Mt. Olympus. Perdikkas, the first king of the Macedonians, held court at a place called Aigai, now known to have been at Vergina; and in the 5th century BC, the king of that time, Archelaos (413–399), moved his capital from Aigai to Pella, which was then on a rise above a lagoon leading to the Thermaic gulf.

In 359 BC, after a succession of kings and near-anarchy exacerbated by the raids of barbarian tribes from the north, the 23-year-old Philip II was elected regent. Philip II pulled the kingdom together through diplomacy and marital alliances and then began expanding his lands, taking the gold mines of the Pangeon mountains and founding Philippi there. In 356 BC, on the day that Alexander the Great was born, Philip II was said to have simultaneously taken the strategic port of Potidea in Halkidiki, received news of his horse's triumph in the Olympic Games, and learned of a general's victory against the Illyrians. That was also the day the temple of Artemis at Ephesus was destroyed by fire, which later prompted people to say that the goddess was away on that day, tending to Alexander's birth. In 336 BC, Philip II was assassinated in Vergina at a wedding party for one of his daughters. (His tomb there was discovered in 1977 by the Greek archaeologist Manolis Andronikos.) Alexander, then 20, assumed power, and within two years he had gathered an army to be blessed at Dion, before setting off to conquer the Persians and most of the known world.

PELLA ΠΕΛΛΑ

40 km (25 miles) west of Thessaloniki.

Pella was Alexander's birthplace and the capital of the Macedonian state in the 4th century BC. The modern-day village is not the most alluring, nor is there anywhere to stay, and hides the fact that Pella was once a thriving city-state with the largest agora market of its time. It housed workshops, administrative buildings, shops, and much more. The city was built using the sophisticated Hippodamian grid plan—by none other than the great Hippodamos himself. On the hill to the north

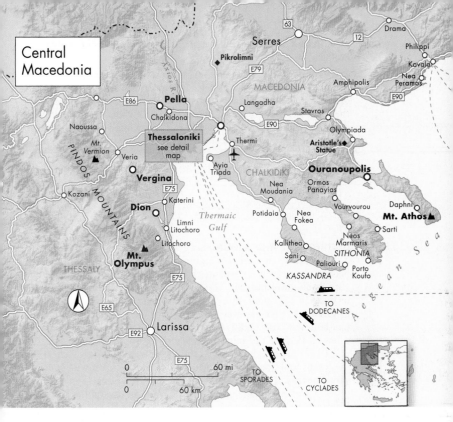

one can visit the vast palatial complex where King Philip and Alexander the Great once lived.

GETTING HERE AND AROUND

If coming by train, get off at Edessa and take the KTEL bus to the site. If coming by bus, get off the Thessaloniki–Edessa KTEL bus right at the site; there are buses every hour from 6 to 6. Zorpidis Travel, among others, arranges day-trips from Thessaloniki that cover both Pella and Vergina.

EXPLORING

Pella Archaeological Site. The ancient village ruins and its museum—both best known for their intricate, artful, beautifully preserved floor mosaics, mainly of mythological scenes—are on either side of the main road toward Edessa (where waterfalls invite a possible further trip). It's best to first get an overview at the **Archaeological Museum,** which contains a model of the 4th-century BC dwelling that stood across the road, as well as fascinating artifacts of Neolithic, Bronze, and Iron Age settlers, some as old as the 7th century BC. Note also the unique statuette of a horned Athena (apparently influenced by Minoan Crete), the statue of Alexander sprouting the horns of Pan, and the adorable sleeping Eros (Cupid), reproductions of which can be bought at the gift shop.

Descriptions are sparse, but the attendants, pointedly not experts, are happy to share what they know.

In 1914, two years after the Turks' departure, the people who lived on the land were moved to a village north of here, and excavations of the **archaeological site** began. These include portions of the walls; the sanctuaries of Aphrodite, Demeter, and Cybele; the marketplace; cemetery; and several houses. In 1987, on a small rise to the north, the remains of the **palace** came to light; at present they are still being excavated. ⊠ *Off E86, Thessaloniki–Edessa Rd.* ☎ *23820/31160* 💷 *€6* ☉ *Tues.–Sat. 8–8, Sun. 9–5.*

VERGINA ΒΕΡΓΙΝΑ

40 km (25 miles) south of Pella, 135 km (84 miles) southwest of Thessaloniki.

GETTING HERE AND AROUND

The easiest way to get to Vergina is by car. Be attentive, however, because the route is not well marked from Pella. You can also get here with public transport via Veria, 11 km (7 miles) away, using trains or buses. KTEL buses, more convenient than train services, run from Thessaloniki to Veria every hour starting early in the morning; the one-hour trip costs €6.80 one-way, €9.80 round-trip. From Veria take a bus to Vergina (20 minutes, every other hour from 6:50 am to 8 pm, €1.60). Ask to be let off at the Vergina archaeological sites. For the tombs look for a low hillock in the center of town with souvenir shops nearby. The palace and the theater are about 1 km (½ mile) southeast of the village up a low hill. Veria is also on the bus route from Athens to Naousa.

There are regular trains from Thessaloniki to Veria from 5:50 am (one hour, €5 one-way, €8 round-trip); however, the station is 3 km (2 miles) outside of Veria, so you will need to take a taxi to the bus station in the center.

EXPLORING

FAMILY
Fodor's Choice
★

Royal Tombs of Vergina. Some of antiquity's greatest treasures await you at the Royal Tombs of Vergina, opened to the public in 1993, 16 years after their discovery. Today the complex, including a museum, is a fitting shrine to the original capital of the kingdom of Macedonia, then known as Aigai. The entrance is appropriately stunning: you walk down a white sandstone ramp into the partially underground structure, roofed over by a large earth-covered dome approximately the size of the original tumulus (mounded grave). Here on display are some of the legendary artifacts from the age of Philip II of Macedonia.

For years both archaeologists and grave robbers had suspected that the large mound that stood on this site might contain something of value but, try as they might, neither of these groups was successful in penetrating its secret. Many locals still remember playing ball on the mound as children. Professor Manolis Andronikos, who discovered the tombs, theorized in his book *The Royal Tombs of Vergina* that one of Alexander's successors, wanting to protect Philip's tomb from robbers,

Burial places for famed rulers such as Philip II and Alexander IV—the father and son of Alexander the Great—the Royal Tombs of Vergina are archaeological landmarks.

had it covered with broken debris and tombstones to make it appear that the grave had already been plundered, and then built the tumulus so that Philip's tomb would be near the edge rather than the center. When Andronikos discovered it, on the final day of excavation, in 1977, he had been trying one of the last approaches, with little hope of finding anything—certainly not the tomb of Philip II, in as pristine condition as the day it was closed.

This was the first intact Macedonian tomb ever found—imposing and exquisite, with a huge frieze of a hunting scene, a masterpiece similar to those of the Italian Renaissance but 1,800 years older, along with a massive yet delicate fresco depicting the abduction of Persephone (a copy of which is displayed along one wall of the museum). Two of the few original works of great painting survive from antiquity. On the left are two tombs and one altar that had been looted and destroyed in varying degrees by the time Andronikos discovered them. Macedonian Tomb III, on the right, found intact in 1978, is believed to be that of the young Prince Alexander IV, Alexander the Great's son, who was at first kept alive by his "protectors" after Alexander's death and then poisoned (along with his mother) when he was 14. To the left of Tomb III is that of Philip II. He was assassinated in the nearby theater, a short drive away; his body was burned, his bones washed in wine, wrapped in royal purple, and put into the magnificent, solid-gold casket with the 16-point sun, which is displayed in the museum. His wife, Cleopatra (not the Egyptian queen), was later buried with him.

The tombs alone would be worth a special trip, but the golden objects and unusual artifacts that were buried within them are equally impressive. Among these finds, in excellent condition and displayed in dramatic dimmed light, are delicate ivory reliefs; elegantly wrought gold laurel wreaths; and Philip's crown, armor, and shield. Especially interesting are those items that seem most certainly Philip's: a pair of greaves (shin guards), one shorter than the other—Philip was known to have a limp. To the right of the tombs there's a gift shop that sells books and postcards; the official gift shop is outside the entrance gate (across from Philippion restaurant), on the same side of the road. Macedonian souvenirs available here are scarce elsewhere.

The winding road to the **site of Philip's assassination** goes through rolling countryside west of modern Vergina, much of it part of the vast royal burial grounds of ancient Aigai. On the way you pass three more **Macedonian tombs** of little interest, being rough-hewn stone structures in typical Macedonian style; the admission to the Royal Tombs includes these. In the field below are the remnants of the **theater,** discovered by Andronikos in 1982. It was on Philip's way here, to attend the wedding games that were to follow the marriage of his daughter to the king of Epirus, that he was murdered and where his son, Alexander the Great, was crowned. ✉ *Off E90, near Veria* ☎ *23310/92347* 🌐 *odysseus.culture.gr* 🎟 *€8* 🕒 *June–Oct., Mon. noon–8, Tues.–Sun. 8–8; Nov.–May, Tues.–Sun. 9–5.*

WHERE TO EAT

$ GREEK 🍴 **Philippion.** Choose from traditional foods such as moussaka or try the highly recommended fresh local pasta. The regional vegetables are especially delicious, and fresh frozen yogurt is made with local fruits. Self-serve cafeteria-style lunch is available, but this is also a taverna-restaurant. Reservations are not necessary, but be warned: tour buses do stop here. [$] *Average main: €11* ✉ *Outside archaeological site, Vergina* ☎ *23310/92892.*

WHERE TO STAY

$ B&B/INN FAMILY 🏨 **Archontiko Dimitra.** On a quiet street a five-minute walk from the ancient archaeological site at Vergina is this beautiful two-story hotel, built in 2003—you'll want to consider making this your base for area excursions as the hotel is designed with accents of fetching wood trim and antique brass chandeliers, with each of the eight light-filled and spacious studio suites showcasing its own classic style and private balcony. **Pros:** discounts available for extended stays. **Cons:** only eight rooms, so book early. [$] *Rooms from: €60* ✉ *Athinas 5* ☎ *23310/92900* 🌐 *www.dimitrahotel.com* 🍽 *Breakfast.*

$ B&B/INN 🏨 **Vergina Pension.** Between the modern and ancient village sits a two-story, pine-furniture-and-crisp-sheets accommodation like those found all over the country—like those, this has got all the basics covered, plus nice touches like wraparound balconies, plants in unusually wide corridors, and an on-site café-bar. **Pros:** very convenient for buses to Veria; big breakfasts. **Cons:** owners do not speak very good English. [$] *Rooms from: €40* ✉ *Aristotelous 55* ☎ *23310/92510* 💳 *No credit cards* 🍽 *Breakfast.*

DION ΔΙΟΝ

90 km (56 miles) south of Vergina, 87 km (54 miles) southwest of Thessaloniki.

At the foothills of Mt. Olympus lies ancient Dion. Even before Zeus and the Olympian gods, the mountain was home to the Muses and Orpheus, who entranced the men of the area with his mystical music. The story says that the life-giving force of Dion came from the waters in which the murderers of Orpheus (the women of Mt. Olympus, jealous for attention from their men) washed their hands on the slopes of the sacred mountain to remove the stain of their own sin. The waters entered the earth and rose, cleansed, in the holy city of Dion. (Zeus is Dias in Greek; the city was named for him.) Ancient Dion was inhabited from as early as the classical period (5th century BC) and last referred to as Dion in the 10th century AD according to the archaeological findings.

Today a feeling of tranquillity prevails at Dion, at the foot of the mountain of the gods. Few people visit this vast, underrated city site. The silence is punctuated now and then by goats, their bells tinkling so melodically you expect to spy Pan in the woods at any moment. Springs bubble up where excavators dig, and scarlet poppies bloom among the cracks—this is the essence of Greece.

GETTING HERE AND AROUND

Litochoro, an hour by KTEL bus from Thessaloniki (hourly from 7 am, €8.50 one-way, €15 round-trip), is the gateway to both Dion and Mt. Olympus *(see Mt. Olympus)*. The bus stop is in Litochoro's central *platia* (square). From Litochoro's central square, call a taxi for the 11-km (7-mile) trip, which costs €13 one-way, to the splendid archaeological park. You can also call Mr. Fotis or Mr. Vangelis, both local cabbies with good English, to come and pick you up. You take a KTEL bus from Thessaloniki to Katerini, where you can take the local "blue" bus to the Dion site (€1.20). There are buses to Katerini from Thessaloniki every half-hour.

Contacts Litochoro Taxi ✉ *Litochoro* ☎ *69773/20853 Mr. Vangelis, 69773/34188 Mr. Fotis.*

EXPLORING

FAMILY

Fodor's Choice

★

Dion Archaeological Site. At the base of sacred Olympus, Dion was a sacred city for the Macedonians, devoted primarily to Zeus and his daughters, the Muses. A city was built adjacent to the ancient city during the reign of Alexander. Unearthed ruins of various buildings include the villa of Dionysus, public baths, a stadium (the Macedonian Games were held here), shops, and workshops. The road from the museum divides the diggings at the archaeological site into two areas. On the left is the **ancient city** of Dion itself, with the juxtaposition of public toilets and several superb floor mosaics. On the right side are the **ancient theaters** and the **sanctuaries of Olympians Zeus, Demeter, and Isis.** In the latter, which is a vividly beautiful approximation of how it once looked, copies of the original statues, now in the museum, have been put in place. ⊕ *7 km (4½ miles) north* *of Litochoro off E75/1A, Thessaloniki–Athens Rd.* ☎ *23510/53206* 🌐 *www.ancientdion.org* 🎫 *€4* 🕓 *May–Oct., daily 8–7; Nov.–Apr., daily 8–3.*

Museum of Dion. The splendid museum is an important stop to help you get an idea of the history and importance of the city to the ancient Macedonians. Be sure to see the video (in English) prepared by the site's renowned archaeologist, Dimitris Pandermalis, which describes the excavations, the finds, and their significance. (His efforts to keep the artifacts in the place where they were found have established a trend for the decentralization of archaeological finds throughout Greece.) The second floor contains a topographical relief of the area and the oldest surviving pipe organ precursor—the 1st-century BC hydraulis. The basement learning area has an Alexander mosaic, a model of the city, and ancient carriage shock absorbers. ✉ *Adjacent to archaeological site* ☎ *23510/53206* 🌐 *www.ancientdion.org* 🎫 *€4* 🕓 *May–Oct., Tues.–Sun. 8–3; Nov.–Apr., Tues.–Sun. 8:30–3.*

WHERE TO EAT

$ GREEK 🍴 **Dionysos.** Excellent food and true Greek *filoxenia* (hospitality) await at the combination tourist shop, café, and three-meal-a-day restaurant. Recommended are the *loukanika* (sausages); rolled, spiced, and spit-roasted meat; and the excellent *yemista* (stuffed tomatoes and peppers) and *papoutsakia* (eggplant halves baked with cheese, spiced ground beef, and garlicky tomato sauce). If you want to try the specialty of the area, *katsikaki sti souvla* (roasted goat on a spit), order at least a day ahead. The house barrel wine, *krasi hima,* is locally produced, and the owners also serve homemade *tsipouro* (the Greek version of grappa) in a small carafe served with snacks for €6. [$] *Average main: €11* ✉ *Village center, directly opposite Museum of Dion* ☎ *23510/53276* 💳 *No credit cards.*

WHERE TO STAY

$ RENTAL FAMILY 🏨 **Safeti.** The mauve-color Safeti, opened in 2005, was a most welcome addition to Dion, offering three gorgeous, modern apartments, one of which has a hot tub (another a fireplace). **Pros:** family-run and friendly; near Olympus for winter, near sea for summer. **Cons:** only for those looking to self-cater; most of website is in Greek only. [$] *Rooms from: €70* ✉ *Opposite Museum of Dion, on main road, Olympos* ☎ *23510/46272* 🌐 *www.safetis.gr* 🍽 *No meals.*

MT. OLYMPUS ΟΡ. ΟΛΥΜΠΟΣ

17 km (10 miles) southwest of Dion, 100 km (62 miles) southwest of Thessaloniki.

To understand how the mountain must have impressed the ancient Greeks and caused them to shift their allegiance from the earth-rooted deities of the Mycenaeans to those of the airy heights of Olympus, you need to see it clearly from several different perspectives. On its northern slope, the Olympus range catches clouds in a turbulent, stormy bundle, letting fly about 12 times as many thunder-and-lightning storms as anywhere else in Greece. From the south, if there is still snow on the range, it appears as a massive, flat-topped acropolis, much like the one in Athens; its vast, snowy crest hovering in the air, seemingly capable of supporting as many gods and temples as the ancients could have imagined. As you drive from the sea to Mt. Olympus, the mountain appears as a conglomeration of thickly bunched summits rather than as a single peak. The truly awe-inspiring height is 9,570 feet.

Nearby, Litochoro is the lively town (population 7,000, plus a nearby army base) nestled at the foot of the mountain. It's the gateway to Mt. Olympus. Souvenir shops, restaurants, local-specialty bakeries (stock up before a hike), and hotels vie for customers.

GETTING HERE AND AROUND

Trains from Athens and Thessaloniki (1 hour) stop at Litochoro, but you must then take a bus into town to catch another to the site. The train station is about 5 km (3 miles) from the town, near the seaside and motorway. It is better to take the train to Katerini or to Larissa and then a bus from there, or to simply take a bus from Litchoro *(see Dion)*. Depending on which way you decide to ascend Mt. Olympus, a taxi to Prionia, a tiny settlement 18 km (11 miles) from Litochoro, will cost you approximately €20.

EXPLORING

Fodor's Choice
★

Spilios Agapitos. Mt. Olympus has some of the most beautiful nature trails in Europe. Hundreds of species of wildflowers and herbs bloom in spring, more than 85 of which are found only on this mountain. There are basically three routes to Zeus's mountaintop, all beginning in Litochoro. The most-traveled road is via Prionia; the others are by Diastavrosi (literally, "crossroads") and along the Enipeos. You can climb all the way on foot or take a car or negotiate a taxi ride to the end of the road at Prionia (there's a taverna) and trek the rest of the way (six hours or so) up to snow-clad Mytikas summit—Greece's highest peak at 9,570 feet. The climb to Prionia takes about four hours; the ride, on a bumpy gravel road with no guardrails between you and breathtakingly precipitous drops, takes little less than an hour, depending on your nerves. If you can manage to take your eyes off the road, the scenery is magnificent. The trail is snow-free from about mid-May until late October. During your Mt. Olympus hike, you could take a lunch break or stay overnight at Spilios Agapitos. The refuge is run by the daughter of Kostas Zolotas, a venerable climbing guru. To bunk down for the night costs €12 per person (€10 with an international mountaineering card); there are blankets but no sheets. Bring your own flashlight, towel, and soap. Campers can pitch tents for €4.20 per person and can use the refuge's facilities (note that cooking is not permitted in the refuge). The restaurant is open 6 am–9 pm. It's 6 km (4 miles), about 2½–3 hours, from Prionia to Refuge A. From here it's 5 km (3 miles), about 2½–3 hours, to the Throne of Zeus and the summit. The trail is easy going to Skala summit (most of the way), but the last bit is scrambling and a bit hair-raising. Some people turn back. If you plan to hike up Mt. Olympus, be sure to take a map; the best are produced by Anavasi. If you would prefer a guided hike up Mt. Olympus, the folks that administer Refuge A can arrange a guide

8

for you, and Trekking Hellas organizes treks for various-size groups. ✉ *Refuge A, Litochoro* ☎ *23520/81800* 🌐 *www.mountolympus.gr* 🕒 *Mid-May–Oct.; overnight guests must arrive by 8 pm.*

WHERE TO EAT

$$ GREEK Fodor's Choice ★

🍴 **Gastrodromio En Olympo.** Self-taught chef, Andreas Gavris, creates seasonal delights fit for the gods in his justifiably popular restaurant. Standouts include the *bourani,* a rich rice dish with nettles, wild mushrooms, and a Gruyère-like cheese from Crete; and the mountain lamb, cooked with olives and tomatoes and seasoned with rosemary. People travel from far and wide to enjoy Andreas's creations, which help make the superb location become even more enticing. The wine list has more than 500 labels on offer. [$] *Average main: €16* ✉ *Central Sq., Agios. Nikolaou 36, Litochoro* ☎ *23520/21300* 🌐 *www.gastrodromio.gr.*

$ GREEK

🍴 **To Pazari.** This homey restaurant is known for its outstanding seafood—it's always fresh, artfully prepared, and surprisingly cheap. The grilled meats are also good, as are the fresh bread and the dips—especially the *kopanisti* (spiced cheese dip with quite a kick) and the *melitzanosalata,* lovingly made from roasted eggplant and garlic. The fish soup in winter is also a specialty. Follow the signs 100 yards up past the main square and to the left around the corner. [$] *Average main: €8* ✉ *Martiou 25, Litochoro* ☎ *23520/82540.*

WHERE TO STAY

$$ RESORT FAMILY

🏨 **Dion Palace Beauty & Spa Resort.** Enjoy excellent views of the sea or the peaks at the Dion Palace, which also offers great proximity to the beach, Mt. Olympus, and the archaeological site at Dion, and let's not forget the luxury spa, as well as many activities for kids. **Pros:** enjoy the luxury of a spa while you're here. **Cons:** near the National Highway so you will need a vehicle to get around; on foot, little is close by. [$] *Rooms from: €150* ✉ *Limni Litochoro, Gritsa* ✣ *6 km (4 miles) northeast of Litochoro* ☎ *23520/61431 to 614314* 🌐 *www.dionpalace.com* 🍽 *Breakfast.*

$ B&B/INN FAMILY Fodor's Choice ★

🏨 **Ktima Faki.** This guesthouse, expanded and with a new swimming pool, is 700 meters (0.4 miles) up on the slopes of Mount Olympus, 5 km (3 miles) from Litochoro, on the road to the church of St. John (Agios Ioannis), a local landmark. **Pros:** acres of gardens for children to explore; tasteful decor. **Cons:** a car is essential. [$] *Rooms from: €70* ✉ *Road to the church of Agios Ioannis, 5 km (3 miles) from Litochoro* ☎ *23520/83750* 🌐 *www.ktimafaki.gr* 🍽 *Breakfast.*

$ HOTEL

🏨 **Olympus Mediterranean.** Pretty and friendly, this spa hotel—built in 2004—is a great value considering the quality of luxury and comfort on offer. **Pros:** welcoming, comfortable, peaceful. **Cons:** not all rooms have great views, so make sure to ask when booking if that's important to you. [$] *Rooms from: €121* ✉ *Dionyssou 5, Litochoro* ☎ *23520/81831* 🌐 *www.mediterraneanhotels.gr* 🍽 *Breakfast.*

$ B&B/INN FAMILY

🏨 **Villa Faki.** Perched at the top of Litochoro village is Villa Faki, a simple yet stylish small inn with apartment-like accommodations. **Pros:** great for families who wish to be in town. **Cons:** breakfast is not included, but can be ordered. [$] *Rooms from: €70* ✉ *Loukia, Litochoro* ☎ *23520/83750* 🌐 *www.ktimafaki.gr* 🍽 *No meals.*

$ 🏠 **Villa Pantheon.** You know you're somewhere special when you see
B&B/INN this family-run establishment at the trailhead for Mt. Olympus; views
stretch to the sea and the mountains—not surprisingly, given the location and the relatively low price for what you get here, reservations are
a must, especially on weekends and holidays. **Pros:** only a 5-minute
walk to the gorge; good value for money; nice vistas of village. **Cons:**
only the suites have a fireplace. [$] *Rooms from: €65* ✉ *Ayiou Dimitriou
terma, at the end, Litochoro* ☎ *23520/83931* ⊕ *www.villapantheon.gr*
🍴 *Breakfast.*

SPORTS AND THE OUTDOORS
Hellenic Alpine Club. The Hellenic Alpine Club can help with information on hiking Mt. Olympus. ✉ *Enipeas Gorge Entrance, Litochoro*
☎ *23520/82444, 69408/23886* ⊕ *eoslitohorou.blogspot.gr.*

Trekking Hellas. Trekking Hellas runs hiking, rafting, mountain biking, and other outdoor excursions in the region, including some great
trips up the mythical Mt. Olympus by foot (or bike) from Litochoro.
☎ *21033/10323* ⊕ *www.trekking.gr.*

HALKIDIKI ΧΑΛΚΙΔΙΚΗ

Eastern Macedonia's sandy coves and Mediterranean landscape have
had a considerably less violent history than the western end of the
realm. The birthplace of Aristotle, it now attracts visitors thanks to
profane and sacred pleasures: the region of Halkidiki, best known as
Thessaloniki's summer playground, including Ouranoupolis and its offshore islands, and the monasteries of Mt. Athos, a peninsula of natural
and spiritual beauty.

8

OURANOUPOLIS ΟΥΡΑΝΟΥΠΟΛΗ

*110 km (68 miles) east of Thessaloniki, 224 km (189 miles) north and
east of Mt. Olympus.*

Meaning "heaven's city" in Greek, Ouranoupolis (also spelled Oura-
nopolis) is an appealing cul-de-sac on the final point of land that
separates the secular world from the sacred sanctuaries of Mt. Athos.
The village, noted for its rug and tapestry weaving, is particularly
entrancing because of the bay's aquamarine waters, and the town
is full of families on holiday in summer. The narrow village beaches
can become overcrowded. There are many pensions and rooms-to-let
around town, but the hotels on an islet or slightly outside the main
town are quietest.

If you make your own way to Ouranoupolis from Thessaloniki via
Route 16, stop at Aristotle's Statue in Stagira (west of the modern village, watch for the easy-to-miss road sign), the region of this remarkable
man's birthplace. Aristotle's theories and inventions are re-created in
engaging hands-on exhibits (there's a small fee) around a grassy knoll
with a surveying view.

A thrill for many is to hike up Mt. Olympus, the legendary home of the ancient Greek gods—these are among Greece's most beautiful nature trails.

GETTING HERE AND AROUND

Ouranoupolis is reachable by KTEL bus from the Halkidiki terminal in Thessaloniki. There are six buses departing Thessaloniki daily (five on Sunday) with the first heading off at 5:30 am (6:15 on Sunday) and the last leaving at 5:45 pm. The cost is €12.40 one-way, and the trip takes 2½ hours.

Taking a taxi takes two hours but will set you back a whopping €145 from the Kentro, and €130 from Thessaloniki airport. Renting a car may be the better option as prices start from €35/day. *See Car Travel for more information on car rentals.*

TOURS

Athos Sea Cruises. Athos Sea Cruises sails for the Mt. Athos area from April to October at 10:30 am (€20), with an additional afternoon departure at 2 pm in July, August, and September; tours last three hours. There is a commentary in English, French, and German. Tickets can be bought from the Ouranoupolis central square. ⊠ *Near tower on main road, Ouranoupolis* ☎ *23770/71370, 23770/71400, 23770/21041* ⊕ *www.athos-cruises.gr.*

Tower of Prosforion. Ouranoupolis was settled by refugees from Asia Minor in 1922–23, when the Greek state expropriated the land from Vatopedi Monastery on Mt. Athos. The settlement, known as Prosforion, was until then occupied by farming monks, some of whom lived in the Byzantine Tower of Prosforion, its origins dating from the 12th century. The tower subsequently became the abode of Joice and Sydney Loch, a couple who worked with Thessaloniki's noted American Farm School to help the refugees develop their rug-weaving industry.

The tower was burned, altered, and restored through the centuries. Now it's a breezy and open place to take in the view on a sweltering day. ✉ *Main Sq., waterfront* ☎ *23770/71651* 🌐 *www.dimosaristoteli.gr* 🎫 *€2* 🕒 *Tues.–Sun. 9–5.*

OFF THE BEATEN PATH

Small Islands. Floating on the Proviakas bay's turquoise waters are tiny emerald islands that are reachable from Tripiti (6 km [4 miles] north of Ouranoupolis) via a 15-minute caïque or ferry ride that runs every half hour or so in summer—and by small outboard motorboats, which you can rent by the day. All the islets have glorious white-sand beaches, and two—**Gaidoronisi** (part of the Drenia group) and the fishing hamlet of **Amouliani town**—have places to eat.

WHERE TO EAT

$$ SEAFOOD Fodor's Choice ★

🍴 **Kritikos.** Want sublime seafood pasta? Head to a place like this one, where the owner is a local fisherman and everything served is catch-of-the-day. Here the family cooks traditional village recipes and Macedonian specialties, such as *melitzana horiatiki* (an eggplant, tomato, feta, garlic, and olive oil salad). The *kolokithokeftedes* (zucchini-and-potato croquettes) are enormous. The owner's efforts have received gourmet awards, yet the place remains unpretentious and reasonably well-priced for a seafood restaurant. They even produce their own wine and tsipouro. (Note: don't confuse this modern, cream-hued restaurant with the eponymous snack bar up the road). [$] *Average main: €22* ✉ *Main road, away from the tower* ☎ *23770/71222* 🌐 *www.okritikos.com.*

WHERE TO STAY

$ HOTEL

🏨 **Akrogiali.** Built in 1935, this was the town's first hotel, and the only one across the street from the beach—the three-story building is nothing special to look at, but the hotel was fully renovated in 2009, and the sea-view rooms are just fine for basic beach holidays. **Pros:** if you want to head out of your hotel and straight on to the beach, there's nothing closer than this. **Cons:** on a busy road. [$] *Rooms from: €60* ✉ *Beach road* ☎ *23770/71201* 💳 *No credit cards* 🍽 *No meals.*

$ B&B/INN Fodor's Choice ★

🏨 **Skités.** Find peace and privacy on a bluff off a gravel road south of town at this charming complex of garden bungalows, comprised of small and pleasant rooms, and staffed by folks that want to make you feel comfortable. **Pros:** private and peaceful; very personal service; those delicious vegetables from the owner's own plot. **Cons:** don't come here if it's buzzy nightlife you're after. [$] *Rooms from: €121* ✉ *1 km (½ mile) south of town, c/o* ✣ *If you need directions, ask for the hotel of Mrs. Pola Bohn* ☎ *23770/71140* 🌐 *www.skites.gr* 🕒 *Closed Nov.–late Apr.* 🍽 *Breakfast.*

MT. ATHOS ΟΡ. ΑΘΩΣ

50 km (31 miles) southeast of Ouranoupolis, 120 km (74 miles) southeast of Thessaloniki.

The third peninsula of Halkidiki, Mt. Athos is called *Ayion Oros* (Holy Mountain) in Greek, although it does not become a mountain until its southernmost point (6,667 feet). The peninsula is prized for its pristine

natural beauty, seclusion, and spirituality; its monasteries contain priceless illuminated books and other treasures.

The Virgin Mary, it is said, was brought to Athos by accident from Ephesus, having been blown off course by a storm, and she decreed that it be venerated as her own special place. This story has since become the rationale for keeping it off-limits to all women but the Virgin herself. Hermits began settling here and formed the first monastery in the 10th century. By the 14th century, monasteries on the 650-square-km (250-square-mile) peninsula numbered in the hundreds. In 1924 the Greek state limited the number of monasteries, including Russian, Bulgarian, and Serbian Orthodox, to 20, but a number of hermitages and separate dependencies called *skités* also exist. The semiautonomous community falls under the religious authority of the Istanbul-based Orthodox Ecumenical Patriarch.

Only men may visit the monasteries, and the numbers are strictly limited. You must apply for a permit at the Holy Executive of the Holy Mt. Athos Pilgrims' Bureau in Thessaloniki several months in advance. Mt. Athos is a place of religious pilgrimage: proper attire is long pants and shirts with sleeves at least to mid-arm; wearing hats inside the monasteries is forbidden. Video cameras and tape recorders are banned from the mountain, but taking photographs is allowed.

GETTING HERE AND AROUND

From Ouranoupolis, boats leave twice daily to Dafni (the main port on the West coast of Athos). The 6:30 am boat sails direct to Dafni, but the 9:45 am boat stops at each harbor or monastery (the trip can take as long as 90 minutes). From Dafni there's a connecting service farther south to Ayias Annas. Fares vary from €4 to €10 depending on the speed of the boat. You can also take a bus to Ierissos, from where boats leave at 8:30 am (daily in summer; Thursday–Monday from September to June) for the monastery of Iviron, which is midway down the east coast here. Boats stop at each monastery en route, with the journey taking around two hours. Make sure to double-check times and travel options at the Holy Executive of the Holy Mt. Athos Pilgrims' Bureau in Thessaloniki, or inquire at the Thessaloniki bureau of the Greek National Tourism Organization for more information.

PERMITS

Holy Executive of the Holy Mt. Athos Pilgrims' Bureau. Men who want to visit Mt. Athos should contact the Holy Executive of the Holy Mt. Athos Pilgrims' Bureau (Grafio Proskyniton Ayiou Orous) four to six months in advance of arrival. ■ TIP➔ Cancellations are quite common, and you may get a pass immediately if there has been a cancellation, so it's always worth asking if you want to go but haven't made the proper arrangements in advance. You must obtain a written permit (free) from this office, which issues 10 permits a day for non-Orthodox visitors, and 100 permits a day for Orthodox visitors (Greek or foreign). You will need to pick it up in person, presenting your passport. Inquire about making reservations for a specific monastery, which must be done in advance (some might be closed for renovations). The permits are valid for a four-day visit on specific dates, which may be extended by authorities in Karyes. When you arrive at Ouranoupolis, you also need to pick up a *diamonitirio,* or visiting permit (€30). Boats headed for the monasteries depart Ouranoupolis for Daphni on the peninsula at 9:45 am; it's a two-hour sail and costs €7.50. ■TIP➡ There are faster boats also that take 45 minutes; these leave at 8:45 am and 10:30 am and cost €12.50. You need to book a seat as soon as you receive your permit. Local transport takes you the last 13 km (8 miles) to Karyes and to monasteries beyond from there. ⊠ *Egnatia 109, Kentro, Thessaloniki* ☎ *23102/52578 for non-Greeks, 23102/52575 for Greeks* ⊕ *www.inathos.gr* ☉ *Weekdays 9–2, Sat. 10–noon.*

CORFU

9

WELCOME TO CORFU

TOP REASONS TO GO

★ **Corfu Town:** Recognized by UNESCO as a World Heritage Site, this sophisticated little gem of a city glows with a profusion of picturesque reminders of its Venetian, French, and British past.

★ **Some Enchanted Islet:** As they savor the famous panorama of Pontikonisi, from the patio of the viewpoint in suburban Kanoni, how many of today's visitors know that tiny "Mouse Island" was thought by the ancients to be Odysseus's ship turned to stone by Poseidon?

★ **Mon Repos:** Owned by the Greek royal family before they were deposed, the elegant neoclassic villa of Mon Repos, with its enchanting seaside gardens and secret beach, was originally built as a love gift from a British lord high commissioner to his wife.

★ **Homer's City of the Phaeacians:** Once extolled by Odysseus, Paleokastritsa remains a swimmable, sunable spectacle of grottoes, cliffs, white sand, and turquoise waters.

1 Corfu Town. Along the east coast mid-island, Corfu town occupies a small peninsula anchored at its eastern tip by the massive Old Fortress and to the north by the New Fortress. Between the two is the gorgeous and lively Paleopolis (Old Town) crammed with Venetian and English Georgian houses, arcaded streets, narrow alleyways, and tiny squares, the entire urban ensemble buffered by the leafy Esplanade, used as a parade ground by the British and now a popular public park.

2 South Corfu. Just south of Corfu town is a region that royals and their high-ranking officials once called home. Mon Repos, with its gorgeous seaside gardens, was the summer residence of the British lord high commissioners, later taken over by the Greek royal family, and was the birthplace of Prince Philip, Queen Elizabeth II's husband. Another 16 km (10 miles) south is Gastouri, site of the Achilleion, a late-19th-century Teutonic extravaganza built for Empress Elizabeth of Austria. To remind yourself you're really in Greece, head to Kanoni and take in the famed vista of the chapel-crowned Mouse Island.

3 West-Central Corfu. Corfu town is great for a day or three of sightseeing but you really need to head into the interior and along the western and northeastern coastlines to discover the natural beauty and charms of Corfu. Many head to Paleokastritsa, on the west side of the island, home to one of Greece's best beaches; rent a boat to visit the nearby caves.

GETTING ORIENTED

Scattered along the western coast of Greece the Ionian islands derive their name from the Ionian Greeks, their first colonizers. The proximity of these isles to Italy and their sheltered position on the East–West trade routes tempted many an occupier to the main island jewel, Corfu. Never subjected to Turkish rule, the Corfiots were greatly influenced by the urban lifestyles of Venetian settlers as well as the orderly formality of the 19th-century British protectorate. With its fairy-tale setting, Corfu (Kerkyra in Greek) basks in the clear blue-green waters of the Ionian Sea at the mouth of the Adriatic. The island is connected in high summer by ferries with Italy and Igoumenitsa on the Greek mainland. For many European travelers, Corfu is the gateway to Greece.

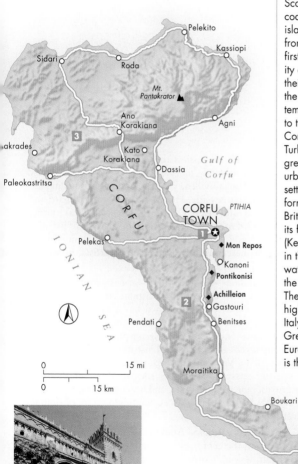

Pelekito
Kassiopi
Sidari
Roda
Mt. Pantokrator
Ano Korakiana
Agni
akrades
Kato Korakiana
Gulf of Corfu
Paleokastritsa
Dassia
CORFU TOWN
PTIHIA
Pelekas
Mon Repos
Kanoni
Pontikonisi
Achilleion
Gastouri
Pendati
Benitses
Moraitika
Boukari
Lefkimmi

C O R F U
I O N I A N   S E A

0   15 mi
0   15 km

9

Updated by
Hilary Whitton
Paipeti

Temperate, multihued Corfu—of emerald mountains; turquoise waters lapping rocky coves; ocher and pink buildings; shimmering silver olive leaves; puffed red, yellow, and orange parasails; scarlet roses, bougainvillea, and lavender wisteria and jacaranda spread over cottages—could have inspired impressionism.

Kerkyra (Corfu) is certainly the lushest and, quite possibly, the loveliest of all Greek islands. Breathlessly blue waters lap rocky, pine-rimmed coves, and plants like bougainvillea, wisteria, and sweet-smelling jasmine spread over the countryside. Homer's "well-watered gardens" and "beautiful and rich land" were Odysseus's last stop on his journey home. Corfu is also said to be the inspiration for Prospero's island in Shakespeare's *The Tempest*. This northernmost of the major Ionian islands has, through the centuries, inspired other artists, as well as conquerors, royalty, and, of course, tourists.

Today more than a million—mainly British—tourists visit every year, and in summer they crowd the evocative capital city of Corfu town (population 40,000). As a result, the town has a number of stylish restaurants and hotels and a sophisticated European ambience. The interior of Corfu, however, remains largely unspoiled, and the island has absorbed many layers of architectural history, offering an alluring mix of neoclassic villas, Venetian palazzo, pastel-painted hill towns, old farmhouses, and classy, city-sized resorts. You'll find all this, plus ancient olive groves, pine-covered cliffs, and heart-stoppingly beautiful vistas of sea and sky. Corfu remains an enchanting mixture of simplicity and sophistication.

The classical remains have suffered from the island's tempestuous history; architecture from the centuries of Venetian, French, and British rule is most evident, leaving Corfu and especially Corfu town with a pleasant combination of contrasting design elements. And although it was bombed during the Italian and Nazi occupation in World War II, the town of Corfu remains one of the most charming in all of Greece.

PLANNING

WHEN TO GO

Corfu enjoys a temperate climate, with a relatively long rainy season that lasts from late fall through early spring. Winter showers bring spring flowers, and the countryside goes into floral overdrive starting in March, when the air is perfumed with the heady fragrance of orange blossoms and jasmine and wildflowers carpet the hillsides. In May, the weather clears and starts to get warm enough for swimming. July and August are the hottest months and can also be humid. September is gloriously warm and dry, with warm evenings and the occasional cool breeze. Swimming is often possible through mid-October. Late September through late October is good for hiking and exploring the countryside, as is the spring.

PLANNING YOUR TIME

Corfu is often explored in a day—many people pass through quickly as part of a cruise of the Greek islands. Two days allows enough time to visit Corfu town and its nearby and most famous sites. With four days you can spend time exploring the island's other historic sites and natural attractions along both coasts. Six days allows you time to get a closer look at the museums, churches, and forts and perhaps even take a day trip to Albania.

Because Corfu is small, it's easy to make day trips to outlying villages and return to accommodations in or near Corfu town. Alternatively, you could spend a night at the hilltop Pelekas or farther north at the seaside Paleokastritsa. To really get off the beaten path, take the coast road northeast from Corfu town and around Daphnila bay to Agni and from there into the most mountainous part of the island, or head west from Corfu town into the mountains and ancient olive groves to stay near Kato Korakiana, home to Etrusco, the best restaurant on Corfu, and many would say Greece itself. If you're planning a visit to the northwest, avoid the tatty beach towns of Sidari and Roda: both have been ruined by overdevelopment, and neither beach is particularly clean or inviting.

As for Corfu town, where should you start upon your arrival? Catch your breath by first relaxing with a coffee or a gelato in Corfu town's shaded Liston arcade, then stroll the narrow lanes of the pedestrians-only quarter. For an overview of the immediate area, and a quick tour of Mon Repos palace, hop on the little tourist train that runs from May to September. Corfu town has a different feel at night, so book a table at one of its famed tavernas to savor Corfu's unique cuisine.

GETTING HERE AND AROUND

You don't need or want a car in Corfu town, which is compact and easily walkable. Buses run to the island's main towns and beaches, but if you want to visit some of Corfu's loveliest and most inaccessible places, all of them within an hour of Corfu town, you'll need a car. Corfu's gentle climate and rolling hills make it ideal motorbike country. You can rent cars and motorbikes at the airport or near the harbor in Corfu town. If you plan to visit only a few of the major towns, the inexpensive local bus system will do. Taxis can be hired for day trips from Corfu town.

AIR TRAVEL

Olympic Air and Aegean Airlines offer multiple daily flights from Athens to Corfu. Fares change constantly, but the hour-long flight starts at about €180 round-trip from Athens. In Greece, Astra Airlines offers five flights per week from Thessaloniki to Corfu. In the United Kingdom, easyJet has regularly scheduled flights to Corfu from Manchester, Bristol, Luton, and London's Gatwick. Monarch Airlines flies from Luton three times a week. Jet2.com operates services from Glasgow, Manchester, Leeds Bradford, Newcastle, and East Midlands airports. Ryanair flies from East Midlands, London Stansted, Manchester, Leeds Bradford, and Glasgow.

Corfu's Ioannis Kapodistrias International Airport is just south of Corfu town, about a mile from the city center. A taxi from the airport to the center costs around €10; there is no airport bus. Taxi rates are on display in the arrivals hall.

Airline Contacts **Astra Airlines** ☎ 23104/89392 ⊕ www.astra-airlines.gr. **Jet2.com** ⊕ www.jet2.com. **Monarch Airlines** ⊕ www.monarch.co.uk.

Airport Contacts **Corfu International Airport** (CFU). ☎ 26610/89600 ⊕ www.corfu-airport.com.

BUS TRAVEL

KTEL buses leave Athens Terminal A for Ignoumenitsa (11 hours, around €45 one-way, plus ferry fares), where you catch a ferry via Patras, three or four times a day.

On Corfu, bus services run from Corfu town to the main towns and villages on the island; schedules and prices can change seasonally and yearly. There are two bus lines. The Green KTEL buses leave for distant towns from the Corfu town terminal near the New Port. Blue suburban buses (with stops including Kanoni and Gastouri) leave from in and around San Rocco Square. Get timetables at both bus depots. Tickets—farthest rides are just over €4—can be bought at the depots or on the bus.

Contacts **Corfu Surburban (Blue) buses** ✉ San Rocco Sq., Corfu town, Corfu ☎ 26610/31595. **Corfu KTEL (Green) buses** ✉ Ioanni Theotoki St., Corfu town, Corfu ☎ 26610/28928.

BOAT AND FERRY TRAVEL

There are no ferries from Piraeus to Corfu. Corfu's gateway to mainland Greece is the city of Igoumenitsa, from which ferries operated by the Kerkyra-Igoumenitsa-Paxi Consortium run almost hourly to Corfu town throughout the day. Ferries three or four times daily also link Igoumenitsa with the port of Lefkimmi near Corfu's southern tip. Direct ferries from Italy (Brindisi, Bari, and Ancona) only run during July and August; outside of those months, you must change ferries in Igoumenitsa.

Most ferries dock at the New Port, in the northeast part of Corfu town; from the ferry terminal you can easily walk into town or take a cab to your hotel. You can buy ferry tickets at the ports or book in advance through the ferry lines or travel agents. For the most up-to-date information on boat schedules (which change regularly and seasonally), call the port authority in the city of departure or check the Greek ferry information website.

One-way tickets for the ferry between Igoumenitsa and Corfu town (1¼ to two hours) are about €10 per person and €40 per car.

Hydrofoils zip between Corfu and Paxos between one and three times daily. There is also a hydrofoil service to Saranda in Albania.

Contacts Greek ferry info ⊕ *www.greekferries.gr.* **Igoumenitsa Port Authority** ☏ *26650/22235.*

CAR TRAVEL

For those traveling with a car, the best route from Athens is the National Road via Corinth to Igoumenitsa (472 km [274 miles]), where you take the ferry to Corfu. As on all Greek islands, exercise caution with regard to steep, winding roads, and fellow drivers equally unfamiliar with the terrain.

Corfu town has several car-rental agencies, most of them clustered around the port, ranging from international chains to local agencies offering cheap deals; there is also an agency in Ermones. Depending on the season, prices can range from €35 a day to €230 a week for a compact, all insurance included. Chains have a bigger selection, but the locals will usually give a cheaper price. Don't be afraid to bargain, especially if you want to rent a car for several days. You can generally make arrangements to pick up your car at the airport.

A 50cc motorbike can be rented for about €15 a day or €100 a week, but you can bargain, especially if you want it for longer. Helmets are required by law. Check the lights, brakes, and other mechanics before you accept a machine.

Contacts Ansa International Rent a Car ✉ *Eleftheriou Venizelou 20, Corfu town, Corfu* ☏ *26610/21930.* **Corfu VIP Services Rent A Car** ✉ *Ermones, Corfu* ☏ *26610/71032* ⊕ *www.corfuvipservices.com.* **Ocean Car Hire** ✉ *Gouvia Marina, Gouvia, Corfu town, Corfu* ☏ *26610/44017* ⊕ *www.oceancar.gr.* **Top Cars** ✉ *Donzelot 25, Corfu town, Corfu* ☏ *26610/35237* ⊕ *www.carrentalcorfu.com.*

TAXI TRAVEL

Taxis rates are reasonable—when adhered to. If you want to hire a cab on an hourly or daily basis, negotiate the price before you travel. In Corfu town, taxis wait at San Rocco Square, the Esplanade, the airport, the Old Port Square, and the New Port. Many drivers speak English. Of course, long-distance trips on the island will pack a hefty price tag.

Contacts Radiotaxi Corfu ☏ *26610/33811.*

HOTELS

Corfu has bed-and-breakfast hotels in renovated Venetian town houses, sleek resorts with children's programs and spas, and, outside Corfu town, simple rooms and studio apartments that can be rented out on the spot. The explosion of tourism in recent years has led to prepaid, low-price package tours, and the largest hotels often cater to groups. The availability of charter flights from the United Kingdom and other European cities means there's a steady flow of tourists from spring through fall. These masses can get rowdy and overwhelm otherwise pleasant surroundings, mainly in towns along the island's southeast and northwest coast. Budget accommodation is scarce, though rooms can sometimes be found in towns and villages. Many British companies offer villas and apartments for rent—some luxurious, others more basic—by the week or month. Corfu is popular from Easter (when the island is crammed with Greek tourists) through September, and reservations are strongly recommended during that period. Many hotels and restaurants are closed from the end of October to Easter.

RESTAURANTS

Traditionally, Corfiots tend to eat their main meal at midday, with simpler food in the evening. Though meat is eaten much more frequently these days, meals at home feature casseroles bulked out with lots of vegetables, such as the winter favorite *fassoulada*, a thick bean soup. Unless they cater to the local lunchtime trade, tavernas tend not to serve these home-style dishes, but prefer generic Greek dishes like moussaka and *stifado* (beef or rabbit cooked in a spicy sauce with small onions), plus the great Sunday-lunch and holiday dishes of the island, *pastitsada* (beef or rooster in a spicy tomato sauce served with pasta) and *sofrito* (beef casserole with garlic and parsley), or the third great dish of Corfiot cooking, *bourdetto* (fish cooked in paprika, sometimes curry-hot). In the island's resorts, tavernas will also offer grills (such as pork chops and steaks), plus omelets and (invariably frozen) pizzas. Your main courses should be preceded by a variety of dips and small salads, and perhaps some *keftedes* (meatballs), which you all share.

Corfiot restaurants usually take the form of *psistaria*, or grillrooms, where all the meat is cooked on charcoal. Most of these places also run a takeaway service, so you'll eat in the company of neighborhood families waiting in line for souvlaki, whole spit-roasted chicken, or lamb chops. The most economical choice here is pita: a wrap enclosing meat, french fries, salad, *tzatziki*, and sauce. Desserts are not a strong suit on Corfu, although many love *karidopitta*—walnut cake drenched in syrup. Locals head to a *zacharoplasteio* (patisserie) for a creamy cake, some baklava or *galaktoboureko* (custard pie). In summer, the last port of call is the *gelatopoleio* (ice-cream parlor). Corfu produces wines mainly from *Skopelitiko* and *Kakotrigis* grapes, all drinkable and many excellent. Most tavernas have their own house wine, served in carafes or jugs, and usually this is a good choice. Bottled water can be bought everywhere—Corfu's salty tap water is *not* one of its pleasures. *Kali oreksi*! (Bon appetit!)

DINING AND LODGING PRICES IN EUROS				
	$	$$	$$$	$$$$
Restaurants	Under €16	€16–€25	€26–€40	Over €40
Hotels	Under €126	€126–€225	€226–€275	Over €275

Restaurant prices are the average cost of a main course at dinner or, if dinner is not served, at lunch. Hotel prices are the lowest cost of a standard double room in high season.

TOUR OPTIONS

From May through September, local travel agencies run half-day tours of Corfu's Old Town, and tour buses go daily to all the main sights on the island.

All-Ways Travel. One of the oldest travel agencies on the island, Greek- and English-run All-Ways Travel is reliable, especially helpful for any flight booking, including complicated connections. ⊠ *G. The- otoki Sq. 34, San Rocco, Corfu town, Corfu* ☎ *26610/33955* ⊕ *www. allwaystravel.gr.*

Aperghi Travel. Aperghi Travel is an expert on hiking holidays and is a designated agent for accommodation and ground arrangements along the Corfu Trail (*www.thecorfutrail.com*), a bottom-to-top-of-the-island hike that offers lovely sections easily worth an hour or two of your time. ⊠ *Dimokratias avenue and 1 Polyla street , Corfu town, Corfu* ☎ *26610/48713* ⊕ *www.aperghitravel.gr.*

Charitos Travel. Charitos Travel has more than 50 tours of the island and can create custom tours for groups of five or more. ⊠ *National Paleo- kastritsa Highway 66, Corfu town, Corfu* ☎ *26610/44611* ⊕ *www. charitostravel.gr.*

International Tours. International Tours arranges hiking, mountain bik- ing, horseback riding, Jeep trips, and other excursions around the island. ⊠ *Eth. Antistasseos 2, Corfu town, Corfu* ☎ *26610/35808, 26610/38107* ⊕ *www.internationaltours.gr.*

Ionian Cruises. Ionian Cruises offers boat day-trips to other islands in the Ionian group, to mainland Greece, and to Albania. ⊠ *Eth. Antistas- seos 4, Corfu town, Corfu* ☎ *26610/31649* ⊕ *www.ionian-cruises.com.*

CORFU TOWN ΠΟΛΗ ΤΗΣ ΚΕΡΚΥΡΑΣ

34 km (21 miles) west of Igoumenitsa, 41 km (26 miles) north of Lefkimmi.

Corfu town today is a vivid tapestry of cultures—a sophisticated weave, where charm, history, and natural beauty blend. Located about mid- way along the island's east coast, this spectacularly lively capital is the cultural heart of Corfu and has a remarkable historic center that UNESCO designated as a World Heritage Site in 2007. All ships and planes dock or land near Corfu town, which occupies a small peninsula jutting into the Ionian Sea.

Whether arriving by ferry from mainland Greece or Italy, from another island, or directly by plane, catch your breath by first relaxing with a coffee or a gelato in Corfu town's shaded Liston Arcade, then stroll the narrow lanes of its pedestrians-only quarter. For an overview of the immediate area, and a quick tour of Mon Repos palace, hop on the little tourist train that runs from May to September. Corfu town has a different feel at night, so book a table at one of its famed tavernas to savor the island's unique cuisine.

The best way to get around Corfu town is on foot. The town is small enough so that you can easily walk to every sight. There are local buses, but they do not thread their way into the streets (many now car-free) of the historic center. If you are arriving by ferry or plane, it's best to take a taxi to your hotel. Expect to pay about €10 from the airport or ferry terminal to a hotel in Corfu town. If there are no taxis waiting, you can call for one *(see Taxi Travel)*.

EXPLORING

Though beguilingly Greek, much of Corfu's Old Town displays the architectural styles of its conquerors—*molto* of Italy's Venice, a *soupçon* of France, and more than a tad of England; it may remind you of Venice or Bath. Many visitors will want to invest in the multi-attraction ticket, available at any of the sights, which includes admission to the Archaeological Museum, the Museum of Asian Art, the Byzantine Museum, and the Old Fortress.

TOP ATTRACTIONS

Antivouniotissa Museum. Panagia Antivouniotissa, an ornate church dating from the late 15th century, houses an outstanding collection of Byzantine religious art. More than 50 icons from the 13th to the 17th century hang on the walls. Look for works by the celebrated icon painters Tzanes and Damaskinos; they are perhaps the best-known artists of the Cretan style of icon painting, with unusually muscular, active depictions of saints. Their paintings more closely resemble Renaissance art—another Venetian legacy—than traditional, flat orthodox icons. ⊠ *3rd Parados Arseniou street* ☎ *26610/38313* ⊕ *www.antivouniotissamuseum.gr* ⊠ *€2* ☉ *Tues.–Sun. 8:30–3.*

Fodor's Choice ★

Campiello. This medieval quarter, part of a UNESCO-designated World Heritage Site, is an atmospheric labyrinth of narrow, winding streets, steep stairways, and secretive little squares. Laundry lines connect balconied Venetian palazzi engraved with the original occupant's coat of arms to neoclassic 19th-century buildings constructed by the British. Small cobbled squares with central wells and watched over by old churches add to the quiet, mysterious, and utterly charming urban space. If you enter, you're almost sure to get lost, but the area is small enough so that eventually you'll come out on one of Corfu town's major streets, or on the sea wall. ⊠ *West of the Esplanade, northeast of New Fortress.*

Fodor's Choice ★

Church of St. Spyridon. Built in 1596, this church is the tallest on the island, thanks to its distinctive red-dome bell tower, and is filled with silver treasures. The patron saint's remains—smuggled here after the fall of Constantinople—are contained in a silver reliquary in a small chapel; devout Corfiots visit to kiss the reliquary and pray to the saint. The silver casket is carried in procession through the town four times a year. Spyridon was not a Corfiot but a shepherd from Cyprus, who became a bishop before his death in AD 350. His miracles are said to have saved the island four times: once from famine, twice from the plague, and once from the hated Turks. During World War II, a bomb fell on this holiest place on the island but didn't explode. Maybe these events explain why it seems every other man on Corfu is named Spiros. If you keep the church tower in sight, you can wander as you wish without getting lost around this fascinating section of town. Agios Spyridonos, the street in front of the church, is crammed with shops selling religious trinkets and souvenirs. ⊠ *Agios Spyridonos.*

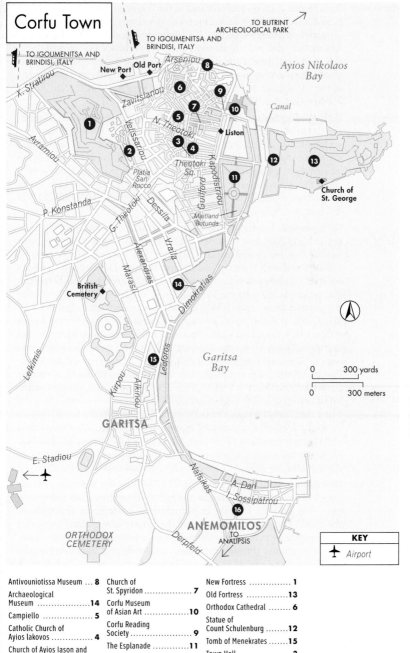

Corfu Town

TO BUTRINT
ARCHEOLOGICAL PARK

TO IGOUMENITSA AND
BRINDISI, ITALY

TO IGOUMENITSA AND
BRINDISI, ITALY

X. Stratirou

New Port   Old Port   *Arseniou*

Zavitsianou

Velissariou

Avramiou

N. Theotoki

Ayios Nikolaos Bay

Liston

Canal

1

6

5

7

3

2

4

8

9

10

12

13

Theotoki Sq.

Platia San Rocco

Kapodistriou

P. Konstanda

G. Theotoki

Dessila

11

Church of
St. George

Maitland Rotunda

Vraila

Alexandras

Marasi

British
Cemetery

Dimokratias

14

Kirpou

Sotiros

Leoforos

15

Garitsa Bay

Lefkimis

Aitinou

GARITSA

0   300 yards
0   300 meters

9

E. Stadiou

Nafsikas

ORTHODOX
CEMETERY

A. Dari
I. Sossipatrou

16

ANEMOMILOS

Derpfeld

TO
ANALIPSIS

KEY
✈ *Airport*

Fodor's Choice   **Corfu Market.** Picturesquely located in the dry-moat outer defences of the
★   New Fortress, Corfu's public market has recently been remodeled in an
attractive, traditional design. The stalls showcase local food produce,
specifically fruit and vegetables (some of it ecologically grown), fresh
fish, and local foodstuffs like olives, dry pulses, wine, and packaged
goods. Two coffee bars in the central "square" provide refreshment
at very low cost. It's a far cry from the supermarket! ⊠ *San Rocco*
⊙ *Mon.–Sat. 6:30 am–2 pm.*

Fodor's Choice   **Corfu Reading Society.** The oldest cultural institution in modern Greece,
★   the Corfu Reading Society was founded in 1836. The building, filled
with books and archives relating to the Ionian islands, stands opposite
the high commissioner's palace and has an impressive exterior staircase
leading up to a loggia. Inside is a book lover's delight, with 19th-century
decor that is evocative testimony to the "English age" that gave Corfu
so much of its character. ⊠ *Kapodistriou 120* ☎ *26610/39528* 🖥 *Free*
⊙ *Mon.–Sat. 9:30–1.*

FAMILY   **The Esplanade.** Central to the life of the town, this huge, open parade
Fodor's Choice   ground and park just west of the Old Fortress is, many say, the most
★   beautiful *spianada* (esplanade) in Greece. It is bordered on the west by
a street lined with Venetian and English Georgian houses and a famous
arcaded building called the **Liston,** built by the French under Napoleon
and meant to resemble the Rue du Rivoli in Paris. Cafés spill out onto
the passing scene, and Corfiot celebrations, games, and concerts take
place here; at night, lovers promenade and children play in this festive
public space. Sunday cricket matches, a holdover from British rule, are
occasionally played on the northern half of the Esplanade, which was
once a Venetian firing range. Standing in the center is an ornate **Victorian bandstand** and, just south of it, the **Maitland Rotunda,** a circular
Ionic memorial built in honor of Sir Thomas Maitland, the not-much-
loved first British lord high commissioner who was appointed in 1814
when the island became a protectorate of Britain. At the southernmost
tip of the Esplanade a **statue of Ioannis Kapodistrias,** a Corfu resident
and the first president of modern Greece, looks out over Garitsa bay.
Kapodistrias was also, unfortunately, the first Greek president to be
assassinated, in 1831. ⊠ *Between Old Fortress and Old Town.*

FAMILY   **New Fortress.** Built during the period 1577–78 by the Venetians, the so-
called "New" Fortress was constructed to strengthen town defenses—
only three decades after the construction of Venetian fortifications on
the "Old" Fortress. The French and the British subsequently expanded
the complex to protect Corfu town from a possible Turkish invasion.
You can wander through the maze of tunnels and fortifications; the
dry moat is the site of the town's fish-and-vegetable marketplace. A
classic British citadel stands at its heart. A coffee bar is set near the
top, from where there is a fantastic view over the rooftops of the Old
Town. ⊠ *Solomou, on promontory overlooking New Port* ☎ *No phone*
🖥 *Free* ⊙ *Daily 9am–5pm.*

FAMILY   **Old Fortress.** Corfu's entire population once lived within the walls of the
Old Fortress, or Citadel, built by the Venetians in 1546 on the site of
a Byzantine castle. Separated from the rest of the town by a moat, the

CLOSE UP

Corfu's Changing Allegiances

It may be hard to believe that an island as small as Corfu could have had such a noteworthy role in the region's history. Corfu's proximity to Europe, 72 km (45 miles) from Italy and 2 km (1 mile) or so from Albania, and its position on an ancient trade route at the mouth of the Adriatic, assured a lively series of conquests and counter-conquests. In classical times, Corinth colonized the northern Ionian islands, but Corfu, growing powerful, revolted and allied itself with Athens, a fateful move that triggered the Peloponnesian War. Subjection followed: to the tyrants of Syracuse, the kings of Epirus and of Macedonia, in the 2nd century BC to Rome, and from the 11th to the 14th century to Norman and Angevin kings. Then came the Venetians, who protected Corfu from Turkish occupation and provided a 411-year period of development. Napoléon

Bonaparte took the islands after the fall of Venice. "The greatest misfortune which could befall me is the loss of Corfu," he wrote to Talleyrand, his foreign minister. Within two years he'd lost it to a Russo-Turkish fleet.

For a short time the French regained and fortified Corfu from the Russians, and their occupation influenced the island's educational system, architecture, and cuisine. Theirs was a Greek-run republic—the first for modern Greece—which whetted local appetites for the independence that arrived later in the 19th century. In 1814 the islands came under British rule and were administered by a series of British lord high commissioners; under their watch, roads, schools, and hospitals were constructed, and commercialism developed. The fight for national independence finally prevailed, and the islands were ceded to Greece in 1864.

---

fort is on a promontory mentioned by Thucydides. Its two heights, or *korypha* ("peaks"), gave the island its name. Standing on the peaks, you have a gorgeous view west over the town and east to the mountainous coast of Albania. A statue of Count Schulenburg, an Austrian mercenary who became a local hero in 1716 when he helped to defeat the invading Turks, stands at the fort's entrance; a plaque beside the statue tells Schulenburg's story. Inside, there's an exhibition of Byzantine art and a shop with museum copies, while a second hall hosts changing events. Most of the old Venetian fortifications inside the fortress were destroyed by the British, who replaced them with their own structures. The most notable of these is the **Church of St. George,** built to look like an ancient Doric temple. Near it, overlooking Garitsa bay, there is a shaded café where you can sit and enjoy the splendid view. ⊠ *On eastern point of Corfu town peninsula* ☎ *26610/48310* ⊠ *€4* ☉ *Mon.–Sat. 8–8, Sun. 8–3.*

Fodor's Choice ★ **Corfu Museum of Asian Art.** It may seem a bit incongruous to admire Ming pottery in an ornate British colonial palace as the Ionian sea shimmers outside the windows. But this elegant, colonnaded, 19th-century Regency structure houses the Museum of Asian Art, a notable collection of Asian porcelains, Japanese *ukiyo-e* prints, Indian sculpture, and Tibetan temple art. The building was constructed as a residence for the lord high commissioner and headquarters for the order of St. Michael and St. George; it was abandoned after the British left in 1864 and renovated about a hundred years later by the British ambassador to Greece. After visiting the galleries, stop at the Art Café in the shady courtyard behind the palace, where you may have trouble tearing yourself away from the fairy-tale view of the lush islet of Vido and the mountainous coast of Albania. Don't miss the **Municipal Gallery**, accessed through a shady courtyard behind the palace, where you may have trouble tearing yourself away from the fairy-tale view of the lush islet of Vido and the mountainous coast of Albania. ⊠ *Palace of St. Michael and St. George, Palaia Anaktora, at north end of Esplanade* ☎ *26610/30443* ⊕ *www. matk.gr* ⊠ *€3* ⊗ *Tues.–Sun. 8:30–3:30.*

WORTH NOTING

Catholic Church of Ayios Iakovos. Built in 1588 and consecrated 50 years later, this elegant cathedral was erected to provide a grand place of worship for Corfu town's Catholic occupiers. If you use the Italian name, San Giacomo, locals will know it. When it was bombed by the Nazis in 1943, the cathedral's original neoclassical facade of pediments, friezes, and columns was practically destroyed; only the bell tower remained intact. It's now been restored. ⊠ *Dimarcheiou Sq., next to Town Hall.*

Church of Ayios Iason and Ayios Sosipater. The suburb of Anemomilos is crowned by the ruins of the Paleopolis church and by the 11th-century Church of Ayios Iason and Ayios Sosipater. It was named after two of St. Paul's disciples, St. Jason and St. Sosipater, who brought Christianity to the island in the 1st century. The frescoes are faded, but the icons are beautiful, and the exterior is dramatic among the unspoiled greenery. This is one of only two Byzantine churches on the island; the other is in the northern coastal village of Ayios Markos. ⊠ *Anemomilos, at south end of Garitsa bay* ⊠ *Donations accepted* ⊗ *Daily 9–2.*

Holy Trinity Church. Established in 1870 after the end of the British Protectorate (1815–1864), this Anglican church continues to serve the needs of the English-speaking community. All denominations are welcome to services and to other religious events and social activities in its sphere. ⊠ *L. Mavili 21* ☎ *26610/31467* ⊕ *www.holytrinitycorfu.net* ⊠ *Donations accepted* ⊗ *Tues.–Fri. 10–1, Sun. services at 10:30 am.*

Jewish Quarter. This maze of streets was home to the area's Jewish population from the 1600s until 1944, when the community was decimated, most sent to Auschwitz by the occupying Nazis. Fewer than 100 of 3,000 Jews survived. At the southern edge of the ghetto, a 300-year-old synagogue with an interior in Sephardic style still stands. ⊠ *Parados 4, off Velissariou, 2 blocks from New Fortress.*

Orthodox Cathedral. This small, icon-rich cathedral, called Panagia Spiliotissa, was built in 1577. It is sacred to St. Theodora, the island's second patron saint. Her headless body lies in a silver coffin by the altar; it was brought to Corfu at the same time as St. Spyridon's remains. Steps lead down to the harbor from here. ⊠ *Southwest corner of Campiello, east of St. Spyridon* ☎ *26610/39409.*

Statue of Count Schulenburg. The hero of the siege of 1716, an Austrian mercenary, is immortalized in this statue at the gate of the Old Fortress. The siege was the Turks' last (and failed) attempt to conquer Corfu. A plaque beside the statue documents his story. ⊠ *Beside entrance to Old Fortress.*

Tomb of Menekrates. Part of an ancient necropolis, this site held funerary items that are now exhibited in the Archaeological Museum. ⊠ *South around Garitsa bay, to right of obelisk dedicated to Sir Howard Douglas.*

Town Hall. The 17th-century Town Hall (now the offices of the Mayor) was originally built as a Venetian loggia and converted in 1720 into Greece's first modern theater. A second story was added by the British before it became a grand town hall early in the 20th century. Note the sculpted portraits of Venetian dignitaries over the entrance—one is actually a lion, the symbol of Venice. ⊠ *Dimarcheiou Sq.* ☎ *26610/40401* 💷 *Free* ⊗ *Weekdays 9–1.*

WHERE TO EAT

$ ✕ **Aegli.** Both local and international dishes are on the menu of this
MODERN GREEK long-established and casually elegant restaurant in the Liston arcade. Start with a plate of steamed mussels, then move on to hearty Corfiot classics such as spicy *bourdetto* (fish stewed in tomato sauce with lots of hot red pepper), or the more-unusual *arnaki kleftiko* (lamb cooked as the *kleftes,* War of Independence fighters, liked it), with onions, olives, mustard, and feta cheese. The establishment offers its own house-baked sourdough bread. Tables in front overlook the nonstop parade on the Esplanade. Aegli keeps late hours, serving drinks and sweets midnight until 2 am. $ *Average main: €12* ⊠ *Kapodistriou 23, Liston* ☎ *26610/31949* ⊕ *aeglirestaurant.com.*

$ ✕ **Avli.** Avli is a *mezedopoleio* (a restaurant serving small plates for
GREEK sharing), so instead of ordering a traditional starter and a main course each, you choose a number of small plates for the table. The young proprietors, Vasilis (front of house) and Christos (chef), source ingredients locally and combine them in inventive ways. Standard local classics include *tsigarelli* (refried greens in a hot sauce), marinated anchovies, and zucchini fritters, while the pies change daily according to what's available. Avli then goes a step further, melding purely Corfiot products with more generally available foodstuffs to create dishes exclusive to the menu. So pork fillet comes with a sauce made from Corfu-grown kumquats. And a type of fig preserve, unique to the island, serves as garnish for grilled Talagani cheese. Various seafood is always supplied, as is the establishment's own bread, baked in-house daily. $ *Average main: €12* ⊠ *Alk. Dari and Ath. Kavvada, Garitsa* ☎ *26610/31291* ⊕ *www.avlicorfu.com.*

$ ✕ **Bellissimo.** Contrary to its Italian-sounding name, this is a traditional,
GREEK family-run Greek taverna where owner Stavros invites you into the kitchen to look at what's fresh and available that day. The food here is excellent and reasonably priced, and the location, in a little square tucked off North Theotoki, adds to the cozy ambience. This is a great place to get a vegetarian meal, and two or three starters will fill you up. The spicy baked feta, fried zucchini, and spinach pie are all worth

trying. Traditional favorites such as *briam* (a mixture of eggplant, zucchini, and potatoes in olive oil and tomato sauce) are expertly prepared. Only Corfiot wine is sold, in order to keep prices affordable. $ *Average main: €10* ⊠ *Lemonia Sq., off N. Theotoki* ☎ *26610/41112* ⊙ *Closed Nov.–Easter. No lunch Sun.*

$$ ✕ **Corfu Sailing Club Restaurant.** Although the name might suggest otherwise, this classy restaurant is not exclusively for club members, and
MODERN GREEK
Fodor's Choice everyone will appreciate the spectacular location, tucked under the
★ northern wall of the Venetian Old Fortress beside the yacht club's harbor. The food is Greek but features modern twists on traditional concepts. For example, the "layered eggplant" starter brings moussaka to mind, while "cheese pie in honey" comes straight from ancient Greece. Seafood is prominent, with bass, mussels, and scallops in various combinations; the chef's signature dish is a "seafood trilogy." Meat eaters may try the location-appropriate Venetian calves liver or one of the steaks. The comprehensive wine list includes labels from all around the world. $ *Average main: €16* ⊠ *Old Fortress, Mandraki* ☎ *26610/38763* ⊕ *www.corfu-sailing-restaurant.com.*

$ ✕ **En Plo.** This appealing restaurant sits on the edge of a wave-lapped
GREEK jetty in the little waterfront Faliraki area just north of the Old Fortress. Come here for a snack, a salad, a couple of *mezedes* (small plates), or a full meal. The menu is comprehensive, the food good, and the surroundings and atmosphere wonderful. $ *Average main: €10* ⊠ *On waterfront just north of Old Fortress, Faliraki* ☎ *26610/81813* ⊕ *www.enplocorfu.com* ⊙ *Closed Jan. and Feb.*

$$ ✕ **La Cucina.** To describe a restaurant's cuisine as "international" can
INTERNATIONAL imply that it is bland, but no one would ever say that about La Cucina. Already renowned for its Italian cooking, La Cucina's menu has progressed into fusion-style dishes and now includes Thai curries, some quirky takes on Corfiot dishes, and even—with delicious, slow-roasted lamb shanks—a nod to British cooking. Naturally, the establishment maintains its Italian roots in the contemporary cuisine of the country. Carpaccio and Florentine T-bone steak fall at the classical end of the spectrum, while some of the pasta dishes (hand-rolled pasta only!) display innovation. For example, linguini is served with goat cheese, cream, mushrooms, ham, zucchini, and saffron. Tuna fillet—an Italian favorite—comes with avocado, soy sauce, and lime, a hint of the Far East that segues into full-fledged Thai with the curries. Like the pasta, pizzas are homemade, the preparation of which can be viewed through a glass wall by indoor patrons. On warm evenings, most guests choose to sit outside; the restaurant is located at the crossing place of two wide alleyways, making it a delicious spot for people-watching. While waiting for a table, the Oenus Wine Bar opposite, under the same ownership, is the place to sit and enjoy a drink accompanied by mood music. $ *Average main: €18* ⊠ *Moustoxidi 13 and Guilford* ☎ *26610/45799* ⊙ *No lunch.*

$$ ✕ **Rex.** A friendly Corfiot restaurant in a 19th-century townhouse, Rex
GREEK has been a favorite since the early 20th century, and with good rea-
Fodor's Choice son. Classic local specialties such as a hearty and meaty *pastitsada*
★ (layers of beef and pasta, called *macaronia* in Greek, cooked in a rich and spicy tomato sauce and topped off with béchamel sauce), *stifado*

9

(meat stewed with sweet onions, white wine, garlic, cinnamon, and spices), and *stamna* (lamb baked with potatoes, rice, beans, and cheese) are reliably delicious. Dishes such as rabbit stewed with fresh figs and chicken with kumquat sauce are successful twists on the regional fare. Look on the menu for the "specials of the day," which might include some other unusual dishes. Outside tables are perfect for people-watching. [$] *Average main: €16* ✉ *Kapodistriou 66, 1 block west of Liston* ☎ *26610/39649* 🌐 *www.rexrestaurant.gr.*

$ GREEK

🍴 **Rouvas.** Where do the locals eat? One frequent answer—that is, if by "locals" you are referring to discerning executives and lawyers—is Rouvas. Found near San Rocco Square and located in the center of Corfu town's commercial district, it caters (at lunch only) to natives who savor the chef's tasty yet filling traditional dishes, such as fried fish with garlic sauce, the superb *pastitsio* (baked ground meat and pasta layered with béchamel), or the rabbit *stifado* (stewed with onions, tomato, and spices), plus a seasonal dish of the day—*briam,* a delicious meld of summer vegetables cooked in oil, is a favorite. [$] *Average main: €10* ✉ *Stamatis Desyllas 13* ☎ *26610/31182* 🕒 *No dinner.*

$$ ECLECTIC

🍴 **To Dimarchio.** At the "town hall," menu items like marinated salmon with fennel, and veal carpaccio reflect the chef's classic French training. But ask the waiter what else is in the kitchen, and he may reel off a list of hearty village favorites that includes a rich *soffritto* (veal cooked in a sauce of vinegar, parsley, and plenty of garlic), pastitsada, and pork stewed with celery, leeks, and wine. In June you can sit beneath a jacaranda tree's electric-blue flowers and watch the comings and goings around the Town Hall in Dimarcheiou Square. Reservations are recommended on weekends. [$] *Average main: €20* ✉ *Dimarcheiou Sq., behind Town Hall* ☎ *26610/39031* 🌐 *www.todimarchio.com.*

$$ MEDITERRANEAN Fodor's Choice ★

🍴 **Venetian Well.** The scene is as delicious as the food in this wonderfully romantic restaurant set around a 17th-century well on the most beautiful little square in the Old Town. Expect creative Greek and Mediterranean cuisine, with a menu that changes regularly according to the availability of the always-fresh ingredients. Seafood such as king prawns and grouper may be featured, and Black Angus steak is a regular. Salads are innovative, and desserts are made in-house. Accompany your meal with one of the single-estate Greek wines—sold by the glass as well as by the bottle—or one of the selected vintages from Italy, France, or Spain. Kremasti Square is difficult to find, so be sure to get very specific directions from your hotel, or once in the Old Town ask directions from a local. [$] *Average main: €16* ✉ *Kremasti Sq., across from Panagia Spiliotissa, Campiello* ☎ *26615/50955* 🌐 *www.venetianwell.gr* ✍ *Reservations essential* 🕒 *No lunch.f*

WHERE TO STAY

$ HOTEL Fodor's Choice ★

🏨 **Cavalieri Hotel.** This hotel occupies a landmark 18th-century building with a wonderful location equidistant between the Liston and the sea; it's one of the few hotels here to remain open year-round (and therefore caters to a lot of business travelers). **Pros:** fabulous location; great views; Wi-Fi. **Cons:** service can be a bit brusque. [$] *Rooms from: €100* ✉ *Kapodistriou 4* ☎ *26610/39041* 🌐 *www.cavalieri-hotel.com* 🛏 *50 rooms* 🍽 *Breakfast.*

$$$ HOTEL 🏨 **Corfu Palace.** Built in 1950 as the island's first resort hotel—and these days showing it—the Corfu Palace is a grande dame in back need of a face-lift, albeit in an unbeatable location and with some lingering grace notes. **Pros:** very friendly service; great breakfast buffet; wonderful outdoor pool. **Cons:** decor is showing its age. [$] *Rooms from: €264* ✉ *Leoforos Dimokratias 2* ☎ *26610/39485* 🌐 *www.corfupalace.com* 🛏 *108 rooms, 5 suites* 🍴 *Multiple meal plans.*

A MUSICAL TRADITION

Corfu has a rich musical tradition, partly the result of the Italian, French, and British influences evident throughout the island. The island's numerous marching bands take part in all official ceremonies, even religious observances. Throughout summer on Sunday you can catch the local philharmonic in concert on the Esplanade in Corfu town.

$$ HOTEL 🏨 **Hotel Bella Venezia.** This elegant two-story Venetian townhouse in the center of town has been used as a hotel since the 1800s and remains one of the nicest small hotels in town. **Pros:** friendly service; Wi-Fi in rooms; modern bathrooms. **Cons:** some rooms are narrow and feel cramped; views are urban rather than maritime; decor rather generic and cold. [$] *Rooms from: €140* ✉ *Zambelli 4, behind Cavalieri Hotel* ☎ *26610/20707, 26610/44290* 🌐 *www.bellaveneziahotel.com* 🛏 *30 rooms, 1 suite* 🍴 *Breakfast.*

$ HOTEL 🏨 **Hotel Hermes.** The old, no-frills Hermes was always popular with backpackers, but since an upgrade it has more appeal for budget travelers in general. **Pros:** affordable rates; helpful staff. **Cons:** the market outside is busy early morning; breakfast is not included in the price; decor is utilitarian. [$] *Rooms from: €60* ✉ *San Rocco, G. Markora 14* ☎ *26610/39268* 🌐 *www.hermes-hotel.gr* 🛏 *30 rooms* 🍴 *No meals.*

$$ B&B/INN Fodor's Choice ★ 🏨 **Siorra Vittoria Boutique Hotel.** Right in the heart of Corfu's historic center and just a minute's walk away from the Liston, this grand mansion was built in 1823 by the aristocratic Metaxas clan and, happily, its conversion to a hotel succeeded in preserving its lovely and authentic Venetian style. **Pros:** exquisite accommodations with a real flavor of old Corfu; close to all the town's best facilities, yet tranquil; open all year. **Cons:** some rooms are small; most rooms lack balconies; not suitable for young children. [$] *Rooms from: €135* ✉ *Stefanou Padova 36* ☎ *26610/36300* 🌐 *www.siorravittoria.com* 🛏 *9 rooms* 🍴 *Breakfast.*

NIGHTLIFE AND THE ARTS

Corfu town is a late-night, café-crowded, club-happy city. During the summer months, the Greeks dine very late, often at 10 pm. The nightly *volta,* a pre- or post-dinner promenade along the Esplanade and the Liston, starts at about 9 pm. Couples stroll, families gather, kids play, and the cafés and restaurants fill up. The club and disco scene heats up much later, around midnight. Party Central lies about 2 km (1 mile) north of the town center, near the New Port, on Ethnikis Antistaseos (also known as "Bar Street"). This is where you'll find a string of plush lounge-bars (many with outdoor pools) and discos that really don't start swinging until after midnight. Clubs on Corfu come and go like tourists, with many featuring incredibly loud sound systems that throb with the latest Euro-pop and dance hits. Most clubs have a cover charge, which includes the first drink.

BARS AND CLUBS

Amaze Bar. For sunsets with your ouzo and mezedes, or a late-night cocktail with a view of the illuminated Old Fortress, try Amaze Bar on the water. ☎ 26610/22386.

Fodor's Choice ★ **Cavalieri Hotel Bar.** The rooftop bar at the Cavalieri Hotel is hard to beat for views. Hotel guests happily mingle with locals as the scene slowly enlivens from a mellow, early-evening cocktail crowd to a more-energetic partylike atmosphere. ⊠ *Kapodistriou 4* ☎ 26610/39041 ⊕ *www.cavalieri-hotel-corfu-town.com.*

Libro d'Oro. Hip but relaxed Libro d'Oro has cane chairs out on the flagstones and a good view of decked-out promenade strollers. ⊠ *Liston, south end* ☎ 26610/27279.

FILM

Finikas. Corfu town's Finikas is said to be the oldest outdoor cinema in Greece. It shows undubbed international movies in a pretty courtyard from June to September. In summer, shows generally start at 9 pm and 11 pm; selections change every two to three weeks. ⊠ *Akadimias.*

Orpheus. All year-round, you can watch movies at the indoor Orpheus. ⊠ *Aspioti* ☎ 26610/39769.

SHOPPING

Corfu town has myriad tiny shops, and half of them seem to be selling jewelry. Designer boutiques, shoe shops, and accessory stores can be found in every nook and cranny of the town. The major tourist shopping streets are Nikiphorou Theotoki (designer boutiques, jewelry) and Agios Spyridonos (local souvenirs). The local fish-and-vegetable market is open Monday through Saturday from very early in the morning until around 2 pm. For traditional goods, head for the narrow streets of the historic center, where olive wood, lace, jewelry, and wineshops abound. For perishable products such as liqueurs and candies, you may do better checking out the supermarkets than buying in the Old Town. Most of the shops listed here are in the historic center and are open May to October, from 8 am until late (whenever the last tourist leaves); they're generally closed during winter. Stores in outlying shopping areas tend to close Monday, Wednesday, and Saturday afternoons at 2:30 pm, and all day Sunday.

Ceramic Art. The award-winning ceramic artists Kostas Panaretos and Klio Brenner create beautiful and unique pieces of ceramic art using the ancient Greek technique called *Terra Sigillata.* To achieve their striking orange colors, they make glazes from Greek soil and then proceed to fire the pieces with wood, imprinting the design through the action of the smoke. In their showroom in the Jewish Quarter you'll find everything from brightly colored bowls to remarkably sophisticated plates and pieces based on ancient Greek forms. ⊠ *Ayia Sophia 23* ☎ 26610/34631 ⊙ *Daily 10—dusk.*

Fos tis Anatolis. All goods in the "Light of the East" shop—including rugs, lamps, small pieces of furniture, clay ornaments, and jewelry—have a traditional Eastern style. ⊠ *Solomou 5* ☎ 26610/45273.

Fantasy island: Legend has it that Pontikonisi—here pictured behind Vlacherena Monastery—is really Odysseus's ship turned to stone by an enraged Poseidon.

Lazari Fine Jewellers. Kostas Lazaris uses 18- and 22-carat yellow gold and white gold to encapsulate precious stones in his original designs. He will endeavor to create anything you request. ⊠ *E. Voulgareos 40* ☎ *26610/20112.*

Nikos Sculpture and Jewellery. Corfu-born Nikos Michalopoulos creates original gold and silver jewelry and sculptures in cast bronze; they're expensive, but worth it. ⊠ *Paleologou 50* ☎ *26610/31107* ⊕ *www. nikosjewellery.gr.*

Rolandos. Visit the talented artist Rolando and watch him at work on his jewelry. His mother does the paintings. ⊠ *N. Theotoki 99* ☎ *26610/45004.*

Stella. This shop sells religious icons, ceramics, religious icons, stone sculptures, and dolls in traditional costume, all handmade and sourced from Greece. ⊠ *Kapodistriou 62* ☎ *26610/24012.*

Terracotta. Contemporary Greek jewelry, ceramics, small sculptures, and one-of-a-kind art and craft objects are sold in this small, appealing shop. ⊠ *Filamonikas 2, off N. Theotoki* ☎ *26610/45260.*

Workshop ... by Tom. Located right in the heart of the Old Town, this is a genuine olive-wood workshop, where everything is made on the premises by Tom and his son. Salad servers, huge bowls, and various decorative items are among the goods on display next to the machines and tools—and outside in the tiny square. The shop is just off the main street, and you'll have to look carefully to discover it. There's also a showroom at Paleologou 58 (Jewish Quarter). ⊠ *8th Parados, N. Theotoki 3.*

SOUTH OF CORFU TOWN
ΝΟΤΙΑ ΤΗΣ ΠΟΛΗΣ ΤΗΣ ΚΕΡΚΥΡΑΣ

Outside Corfu town, near the suburb of Kanoni, are several of Corfu's most unforgettable sights, including the lovely view of the island of Pontikonisi. The nearby palace and grounds of Mon Repos were once owned by Greece's royal family and are open to the public as a museum. A few villages south of Benitses (but not including this genteel former fishing village), and some on the island's southern tip, are usually over-run with raucous package-tour groups. Avoid them unless you seek a binge-drinking, late-night, party-people scene and beaches chocka-block with shrieking crowds and tanning bodies. If you're looking for more solitary nature in the south, take a trip to Lake Korission with its juniper-covered dunes.

KANONI KANONI

5 km (3 miles) south of Corfu town.

The suburb of Kanoni was once one of the world's great beauty spots, made famous by countless pictures. Today the landscape has been engulfed by development and a coffee bar has laid claim to the best spot to take in the legendary and still-lovely view, which looks out over two beautiful islets. If you truly want to commune with nature, visit the lush and lovely seaside gardens surrounding the country palace of Mon Repos.

Kanoni's famed vistas encompass the open sea separated by a long, narrow causeway that defines the lagoon of Halikiopoulou, with the intensely green slopes of Mt. Agii Deka as a backdrop. A shorter breakwater leads to the white convent of Moni Vlaherena on a tiny islet—one of the most picturesque islets in all of Greece and the one pictured on nearly all postcards of Mouse Island. However, it is the tiny island beyond that islet—the one in the middle of the lake with the tall cypresses—that is **Pontikonisi,** or Mouse Island, a rock rising dramatically from the clear water and topped by a tiny 13th-century chapel. Legend has it that the island is really Odysseus's ship, which an enraged Poseidon turned to stone: the reason why Homer's much-traveled hero was shipwrecked on Phaeacia (Corfu) in *The Odyssey.* From June through August a boat service runs out to Pontikonisi. Keep in mind, though, that while the view *of* the islets has sold a thousand postcards, the view *from* the islets (looking back at Corfu) is that of a hilly landscape built up with resort hotels and summer homes and of the adjacent airport, where planes take off directly over the churches.

GETTING HERE AND AROUND

The local blue bus (line 2) offers frequent daily service (every 20 minutes Monday through Saturday, every 40 minutes on Sunday) to Kanoni from Plateia San Rocco in Corfu town; the fare is about €1.50. A taxi to Kanoni costs approximately €10. The islet of Pontikonisi can be reached by a short boat trip from the dock at Vlaherena, 2 km (1 mile) below Kanoni and costs €2.50 round-trip. The best way to reach Mon Repos from Corfu town is by walking; it takes about 30 minutes and you follow the seafront most of the way.

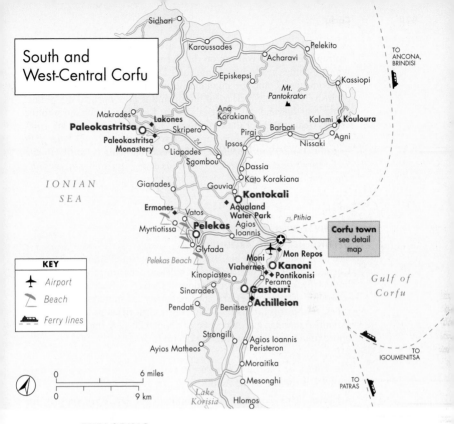

South and West-Central Corfu

KEY

✈ Airport

≥ Beach

⛴ Ferry lines

IONIAN SEA

TO ANCONA, BRINDISI

Sidhari

Karoussades

Acharavi

Pelekito

Episkepsi

Mt. Pantokrator ▲

Kassiopi

Makrades

Lakones

Paleokastritsa

Skripero

Ano Korakiana

Kalami ✦ **Kouloura**

Barbati

Paleokastritsa Monastery

Liapades

Pirgi

Agni

Ipsos

Nissaki

Sgombou

Dassia

Gianades

Gouvia

Kato Korakiana

Ermones

Vatos

Kontokali

Myrtiotissa

Pelekas

Aqualand Water Park

Ptihia

Agios Ioannis

Corfu town
see detail map

Glyfada

Moni

Mon Repos

Pelekas Beach

Viahernes

Kanoni

Kinopiastes

Pontikonisi

Gulf of Corfu

Sinarades

Perama

Gastouri

Pendati

Benitses

Achilleion

Strongili

Agios Ioannis Peristeron

Ayios Matheos

TO IGOUMENITSA

Moraitika

Mesonghi

TO PATRAS

Lake Korisia

Hlomos

0 — 6 miles
0 — 9 km

EXPLORING

FAMILY

Fodor's Choice

★

Mon Repos. The former royal palace of Mon Repos is surrounded by gorgeous English-style gardens that lend magic to an idyllic setting. The compact neoclassical palace (really a villa) was built in 1831 by Sir Frederic Adam for his wife, and it was later the summer residence of the British lord high commissioners; the architect, Sir George Whitmore, also designed the Palace of St. Michael and St. George in Corfu town. After Greece won independence from Britain in 1864, Mon Repos was used as a summer palace for the royal family of Greece. Queen Elizabeth II's husband, Prince Philip, was born here in 1921 (he was a royal prince of Greece and Denmark; the Corfiots, who have no love of royalty, call him "the penniless Greek who married a queen"). When King Constantine fled the country in 1967, the Greek government expropriated Mon Repos. Throughout the 1990s, the estate was entangled in an international legal battle over ownership; the Greek government finally paid Constantine a settlement and opened the fully restored palace as a museum dedicated to the area's archaeological history. Displays of items found in the area, as well as interpretive displays, rooms showcasing Regency design, contemporary antiques, and botanical paintings make for a truly eclectic museum collection The room where Prince Philip was born (on the kitchen table, it is said) houses a 3-D interactive map of Corfu town and its environs.

After touring the palace, wander around the extensive grounds (entrance is free, so you can do this even if you don't visit the palace), which include the elusive remains of a Doric temple from the 7th and 6th centuries BC and the small but beautiful beach that was once used exclusively by the Greek royal family and is now open to the public. Bring your suit and join the locals on the long pier jutting out into the crystal clear waters of the Ionian sea. Opposite Mon Repos are ruins of Ayia Kerkyra, the 5th-century church of the Old City. ⊠ *Paleopolis* ✛ *2 km (1 mile) south of the Old Fortress, following oceanfront walk* 🖾 *Grounds free; museum €3* ⊗ *Grounds daily 7 am–6:30 pm; museum Tues.–Sun. 8–3.*

THE ACHILLEION AND GASTOURI ΑΧΙΛΛΕΙΟΝ ΚΑΙ ΓΑΣΤΟΥΡΙ

19 km (12 miles) southwest of Corfu town.

GETTING HERE AND AROUND

The local blue bus (line No. 10) departs daily from Platia San Rocco in Corfu town for Gastouri and the Achilleion, departing about every two hours (check with the ticket window at Platia San Rocco for the exact schedule). Return times are approximately 20 minutes after arrival times; round-trip fare is €3—buy your return ticket at the same time as your outgoing one. A taxi costs about €20 (ask the driver for an approximate fare before entering the taxi).

EXPLORING

The village of Gastouri, overrun in summer by tour buses and day-trippers, is the site of the Achilleion.

Achilleion. This Teutonic palace, built in the late 19th century for Empress Elizabeth of Austria, is perhaps the most popular tourist attraction in Corfu and remains a monument of 19th-century historicism. The empress used the place as a retreat to escape court life and to ease her heartbreak over husband Franz Josef's numerous affairs and her son Archduke Rudolph's mysterious murder or suicide at Mayerling in 1889. Elizabeth named the palace after her favorite hero, Achilles, whom she inexplicably identified with Rudolph. After Elizabeth was assassinated in 1898, Kaiser Wilhelm II bought the villa and lived in it until the outbreak of World War I, during which time the Achilleion was used by French and Serbian troops as a military hospital. After the armistice, the Greek government received it as a spoil of war. During World War II, it was appropriated and used as a headquarters by the occupying Italian and German forces. In 1962 the palace was restored, leased as a gambling casino, and later used as the set for the casino scene in the James Bond film *For Your Eyes Only.* (The casino has since moved to the Corfu Holiday Palace.)

Today it's a museum, but not a terribly inspiring one. The interior is a series of rather ungainly, uninteresting rooms done in various styles (a pseudo-Byzantine chapel, a pseudo-Pompeian room, a pseudo-Renaissance dining hall), with a smattering of period furniture scattered about; the vulgar fresco called *Achilles in His Chariot,* behind a window on the upper level, tells you all you need to know about the empress's taste in pseudo-classical art. More appealing is the terrace, laid out like an

Ionic peristyle with a number of 19th-century statues, the best of which is *The Dying Achilles*. The gardens, surrounded by olive groves and with a distant view of the sea, are pretty but, all in all, the whole place looks a bit vacuous and forlorn. Still and all, lovers of period style won't want to miss this. For a website on the estate, go to the Wikipedia entry (the easiest way to access it) and then hit the link to the Achilleion site in the footnotes. ✉ *Gastouri* ☎ *26610/56210* 🎫 *€7* 🕐 *Apr.–Oct., daily 8–8; Nov.–Mar., daily 8–3.*

WHERE TO EAT

$$
GREEK
FAMILY
Fodor's Choice
★

✕ **Taverna Tripa.** This famous taverna (touristy but very quaint) in the charming hilltop village of Kinopiastes has been in business since 1936 and has had more than its share of famous visitors (snapshots of everyone from Anthony Quinn to Jimmy Carter and Jane Fonda are tacked up on the back wall). Today it's owned and operated by Spiros and Rena, the grandchildren of the original owner. The fixed-price menu begins with a series of tasty *mezedes* (small plates) followed by juicy spit-roasted lamb or beef baked in parchment and, finally, a selection of seasonal fruit and desserts, all of it washed down by unlimited quantities of the house wine. Eventually the live music begins, and locals perform Greek dances in the courtyard; patrons are encouraged to join in. This floor show takes place about five times a week, so ask about the schedule when you call to book. If you're interested, the proprietors will take you over to the town's Olive Museum, where you can see old stone olive presses. Picturesque Kinopiastes is famous for its water and people come from miles around to fill their jugs at the local fountain. 💲 *Average main: €25* ✉ *Kinopiastes* ✛ *2 km (1 mile) west of Gastouri* ☎ *26610/56333* 🌐 *www.corfu-tripas.com* 🍴 *Reservations essential* 🕐 *No lunch.*

WHERE TO STAY

$$
HOTEL
Fodor's Choice
★

🏨 **Costa Blu Hotel.** Occupying a spectacular position on a hillside directly above the sea, the Costa Blu's accommodations are all spacious and luxuriously furnished suites, so you may feel as if you are staying in a private villa instead of a hotel. **Pros:** wonderful accommodations and location; all suites have a sea view; proximity to Benitses and its yacht marina. **Cons:** no cooking facilities in rooms; the road into Benitses can be busy. 💲 *Rooms from: €160* ✉ *Benitses* ✛ *2 km (1 mile) south of Gastouri* ☎ *26610/72672* 🌐 *www.holidays-corfu.com* 🛏 *48 suites* 🕐 *Closed Nov.–Apr.* 🍽 *Multiple meal plans.*

NORTH OF CORFU TOWN
ΒΟΡΕΙΑ ΤΗΣ ΠΟΛΗΣ ΤΗΣ ΚΕΡΚΥΡΑΣ

West and north from Corfu town, sweeping roads take you across the center of the island to the rugged west coast with its dramatic sandy beaches. Approaching Paleokastritsa, the road descends in tight bends to the sea, where two headlands, 130 feet high and covered with trees and boulders, form a pair of natural harbors. The beaches on this side of Corfu are lovely, but some of them, notably around Pelekas, have stronger surf and higher waves than the more-sheltered beaches on the east side of the island. The lush and fertile Ropa valley, once Corfu's agricultural heartland, lies between the sandy beaches of the west-central coast near Ermones and the olive-blanketed low hills of the island's center, with dramatic mountains in view to the north.

PELEKAS ΠΕΛΕΚΑΣ

11 km (7 miles) northwest of Gastouri, 13 km (8 miles) west of Corfu town.

Inland from the coast at Glyfada *(see below)* is Pelekas, an attractive hilltop village that overflows with tourists because of its much-touted lookout point, called **Kaiser's Throne,** a rocky hilltop with spectacular views of the entire island and sea beyond. German Kaiser Wilhelm II enjoyed the sunset here when not relaxing at Achilleion Palace.

GETTING HERE AND AROUND

The local blue bus (line No. 11) has a regular all-day service from San Rocco Square for Pelekas, starting at €6.20, with the last bus at 10 (reduced services at weekends). In high season, the green KTEL bus has six daily departures for Glyfada, the most convenient being 9 and 11 am, from the bus terminal on Avramiou near the New Port. A taxi from Corfu town to the Kaiser's Throne costs about €30 and will save you about 20 minutes travel time.

EXPLORING

FAMILY **Aqualand Water Park.** This giant, overpriced water theme park could be viewed as yet another example of how tourist-related developments are spoiling Corfu's lovely old landscapes, or you might see it as a great place to let your kids have a few hours of fun. There are slides, rides, pools, playgrounds, restaurants and snack stands (food is mediocre in both), and stores everywhere you look, plus lots of noise. It's located mid-island, on the main road to Glyfada, near Agios Ioannis. ✉ *National Pelekas Highway, Agios Ioannis* ☎ *26610/5835* ⊕ *www. aqualand-corfu.com* 🎫 *€25* ☉ *May–Oct., daily 10–7.*

BEACHES

Glyfada Beach. Greeks have voted Glyfada beach one of the top ten in the country, and it's easy to see why when you visit this wide stretch of fine, golden sand. The central area, which is dominated by the giant Grand Glyfada Hotel, has a number of funky beach bars that are more places to be, see, and be seen. Here, the beach is highly organized, with rows of sun beds and umbrellas, sometimes rented from the nearest establishment. The northern end is more laid-back and has a small hotel, the Glyfada Beach. If you've had enough of the sun, you can find shade among the trees that back the beach. A choice of water sports is available for the active, but swimmers should be aware of the strong undertow. **Amenities:** food and drink; lifeguards; parking; showers; water sports. **Best for:** swimming; partiers. ✉ *Glyfada ✛ 3 km (2 miles) west of Pelekas.*

Myrtiotissa Beach. The writer Lawrence Durrell described Myrtiotissa as "the loveliest beach in the world." This statement may be hyperbolic, but few would argue that the strand is right up there with the best in Greece. Today, the beach is little changed from Durrell's time on Corfu in the 1930s, due to poor access keeping development at bay—there are no refreshment facilities directly on the beach, nor even organized sun bed or umbrella rentals. Most visitors park and walk down the steep road. The southern end of the beach, sheltered from view by rocks, is designated for nudists only, while at the more open northern end swimsuits are the norm. The sand is fine and golden. The sea can be rough with currents—it's only for experienced snorkelers. A small rustic restaurant stands a few minutes walk from the far end of the beach. Another minute's walk takes you to a monastery, dedicated to the Virgin of the Myrtles, hence the name. **Amenities:** none. **Best for:** snorkeling; nudists. ✛ *5 km (3 miles) north of Pelekas.*

FAMILY **Pelekas Beach.** Pelekas beach could be two separate strands, and indeed there are two access roads down the long, steep hill. The busy southern section is overlooked by the huge Aquis Pelekas Beach Hotel complex with its satellite bars and restaurants. As you walk north, the development dwindles, and at the far northern end, the beach still possesses an atmosphere of the 1970s when it was the haunt of hippies. Most amenities, such as sun beds and water sports, are clustered in the vicinity of the hotel. **Amenities:** food and drink; lifeguards; showers; water sports. **Best for:** sunset; walking.

WHERE TO EAT

$ ✕ **Jimmy's.** Only fresh ingredients and pure local olive oil are used at
GREEK this family-run restaurant serving traditional Greek food. Try *tsigareli,* a combination of green vegetables and spices, or some of Jimmy's own Corfiot meat dishes. There's a nice selection of vegetarian dishes and sweets. The place opens early in the morning for breakfast and stays open all day. $ *Average main: €9* ☎ *26610/94284* ⊕ *www. jimmyspelekas.com* ⊘ *Closed Nov.–May.*

$$ ✕ **Spiros and Vassilis.** This restaurant hidden back from the road on
FRENCH farmland belonging to the Polimeris family is something of a surprise because its menu is not Greek but classically French. The chef, born in Corfu, worked for many years in Paris restaurants. Entrecôte steak, frog's legs, and escargot are all available, and the meat is all organic and locally sourced. There are also a few simple Greek dishes. An extensive wine list and efficient, discreet service add to the pleasure of dining on one of the elegant garden terraces. $ *Average main: €18* ✉ *Agios Ioannis* ✛ *9 km (6 miles) west of Corfu town on road to Pelekas* ☎ *26610/52552, 26610/52438* ⊕ *www.spirosvasilis.com* ⌖ *Reservations essential* ⊘ *Closed Nov.–May. No lunch.*

WHERE TO STAY

$$$ ⌂ **Aquis Pelekas Beach Hotel.** Built on a steep hillside directly above Pele-
RESORT kas beach, this is one of the most attractive beach hotels on the island.
ALL-INCLUSIVE **Pros:** great sea views from many rooms; updated decor; access to beach. **Cons:** lots of tour groups; not suitable for guests with mobility problems. $ *Rooms from: €240* ✉ *Pelekas Beach* ☎ *26611/86000* ⊕ *www. aquisresorts.com* ⤳ *181 rooms* ⊘ *Closed Nov.–Apr.* ⧖ *All-inclusive.*

$ ⌂ **Levant Hotel.** Located at the top of Pelekas hill, next to the Kai-
B&B/INN ser's Throne lookout, this small hotel offers balconied guest rooms with breathtaking views (and sunsets) across silver-green olive groves

to the shimmering Ionian sea. **Pros:** great views; personable service; in-house restaurant with terrace. **Cons:** the immediate vicinity often heaves with tour groups. $ *Rooms from: €105* ✉ *Near Kaiser's Throne* ☎ *26610/94230* ⊕ *www.levanthotel.com* ⟿ *25 rooms, 1 suite* ☉ *Closed Nov.–Easter* ⍾ *Breakfast.*

$$
RENTAL
Fodor'sChoice
★

🏨 **Pelecas Country Club.** Some say this small, luxury hotel can be a bit snobbish; others insist that it lets you experience true Corfiot tradition in a unique setting: an old family mansion. **Pros:** lovely rooms and flower gardens; all rooms have a kitchen or kitchenette; free Wi-Fi throughout. **Cons:** if unmoved by fine manners and old-world style, this place is not for you. $ *Rooms from: €150* ☎ *26610/52918* ⊕ *www.country-club.gr* ⟿ *7 studios, 4 suites* ⍾ *Breakfast.*

SHOPPING

The Witch House. Harry Potter would feel right at home in The Witch House, where every single item is made by multitalented sisters Katerina and Lakshen. Artifacts range from stoneware sculptures to "Phos" jewelry, which combines crystals with precious metals, and from witch-motif key rings to hand-sculpted ceramics glazed in subtle turquoise. ✉ *Main street.*

ERMONES ΕΡΜΟΝΕΣ

8 km (5 miles) north of Pelekas.

On the coast, 8 km (5 miles) north of Pelekas lies the small, low-key resort of Ermones, with pebbly sand beaches, heavily wooded cliffs, and a backdrop of green mountains. The Ropa river, which drains the vast central plain, flows into the Ionian sea here; according to local legend, Nausicaa was rinsing her laundry at the river mouth when Odysseus came ashore, as told by Homer in *The Odyssey.* A short walk inland you find the island's only golf course; beyond that, the vast Ropa Plain extends, a paradise for hikers, bird-watchers, and botanists. Also to the rear of the resort is the mountain village of Vatos, with its stunning views and traditional, picturesque neighborhoods.

WHERE TO EAT

$ ✕ **Tristrato.** Set at a crossroads in the depths of the countryside, Tristrato
GREEK   was formerly an old wayhouse and still retains many of the building's original features; it now functions as a contemporary Greek gastropub. There's no menu: you get what's in the kitchen, generally a choice between meat meze and fish meze with the addition of salads and dips. The food is Greek but with some unusual tastes. Tables are set outside under trees, and the location at the head of two shallow valleys means there's always a cool breeze. $ *Average main: €8* ✉ *Giannades–Marmaro Crossroads, 3 km (2 miles) north of Ermones, Tristrato, Giannades* ☎ *26610/51580* ⊟ *No credit cards.*

WHERE TO STAY

$$
RESORT
Fodor'sChoice
★

🏨 **Grand Mediterraneo Resort & Spa.** Following a major face-lift and upgrade in 2010, this beachside resort is now one of the most luxurious on Corfu's west coast. **Pros:** gorgeous scenery combining mountain and sea; very spacious rooms; variety of meal plans, including all-inclusive.

Cons: the beach is not Corfu's best; the unfit and physically challenged may have difficulties with the terrain; no children under 16. [$] *Rooms from: €175* ☎ *26610/95381* 🌐 *www.atlanticahotels.com* 🛏 *235 rooms, 29 suites, 2 villas* ⏲ *Closed Nov.–Apr.* 🍴 *Multiple meal plans.*

NIGHTLIFE

Dizi Bar. With its extensive shady deck terrace, Dizi Bar is a favorite summer rendezvous for locals. Many nights feature live music or DJ-led dancing until late. Call owner Kostas to find out what's happening and when. ☎ *26610/95080.*

SPORTS AND THE OUTDOORS

Corfu Golf Club. It's been called golf's best kept secret, and, indeed, Corfu Golf Club combines a superb test of a golfer's skills with an outstanding natural environment. The course, in the delightfully rural Ropa Valley and surrounded by lushly wooded mountains, was designed in the 1970s by the famous Swiss-based architect Donald Harradine, who blended the natural features of the landscape with man-made hazards to create a course that can be enjoyed by all categories of golfers. Players enter the course on footbridges crossing the Ropa River, and walk amongst lakes and streams and between copses and avenues of indigenous trees. Nature lovers may spot otters, terrapins, wild birds such as herons and kingfishers, and other native creatures. Back at the clubhouse, attractively built of local stone, the atmosphere is laid-back and welcoming, and the pro shop well-stocked. A restaurant serves snacks and meals at reasonable prices. ☎ *26610/94220* 🌐 *www.corfugolfclub.com* 🎟 *€35 for 9 holes, €55 for 18 holes* ⛳ *18 holes. 6802 yards. Par 72.*

KONTOKALI ΚΟΝΤΟΚΑΛΙ

6 km (4 miles) north of Corfu town.

9

Kontokali is best known for providing the main entry point to Corfu's biggest marina, a delightful place to stroll and admire the yachts, especially in the evening. Behind the marina stands a large roofless structure, built by the Venetians in the early 18th century as part of their shipyards. To the south of the marina lies the island's main cricket ground, incorporating a croquet field. The northern arm of the bay comprises the promontory of Kommeno, where expensive villas and large hotels are set among the trees. Tucked in the corner of the bay, on a tiny island at the approach to Kommeno, is the church of Ipapanti, one of Corfu's most picturesque spots.

GETTING HERE AND AROUND

A few kilometers north of Corfu town, the village of Kontokali squeezes between the main road and the shoreline of Govino bay. The area is heavily commercialized, but the village, which stretches along its own road parallel with the main one, is quiet and residential.

WHERE TO EAT

$$$$ ECLECTIC Fodor's Choice ★

🍴 **Etrusco.** While this is a bit of a long drive from the Paleokastritsa region, some foodies would drive here from Athens itself: this is considered one of the best restaurants in Greece. If not, it is certainly one of the most inventive. Run by the Italian-Corfiot Botrini family, this is a showcase for their passion for both Greek and Italian cuisine, combined with flawless technique and a big blast of "molecular" creativity. You know dinner will be a marvel when you are presented with a starter of canapés, each positioned over their place of origin on a cute map of the Mediterranean. Then the marvels of chef Ettore Botrini begin and you may want to make a dinner just of the appetizers: sea urchin soup, salmon cubes with green apple sorbet, octopus carpaccio, feta cheese "snow," or shrimp risotto with Peruvian bitter cocoa powder. One winning main course is the slow-cooked pork belly with Granny Smith apple purée. Prepared by Ettore's wife, the desserts are ecstasy: will it be the chocolate soufflé with salty caramel sauce, the goat cheese ice cream with tomato marmalade and lemon sherbet, or the orange soufflé with chocolate crust? Or the "Corfu Memories," which combines chocolate and strawberry flavors in a novel way. Rounding out the experience is the cozy and modern decor, with the best tables—often booked solid with chic and wealthy Corfiots—set out in a large and charmingly antique courtyard. Just save your pennies and make your reservations now. $ *Average main: €50* ⊹ *1 km (½ mile) west of Dassia* ☎ *26610/93342* ⊕ *www.etrusco.gr* ⌕ *Reservations essential* ☾ *No lunch.*

$ ✕ **Fish Taverna Roula.** Choose from what you see—bream, snapper, squid,
SEAFOOD   sole, mullet, sardines, and whatever else is fresh that day; when the fish runs out, Roula stops serving. Sit on the waterfront terrace and watch the boats heading in and out of the bay marina. It's a bit difficult to find; pass the Kontokali Bay Hotel, then go left at every junction, keeping your eyes open for the sign to Roula. $ *Average main: €12* ☎ *26610/91832* ⊕ *taverna-roula.gr* ⌕ *Reservations not accepted.*

$$ ✕ **Gerekos.** One of the island's most famous seafood tavernas, Gerekos
SEAFOOD   pulls its catch daily from the family's own boats. The menu varies according to the season and what is available, but the friendly staff will guide your choice. For a light meze, opt for a table on the terrace and try the whitefish *me ladi* (cooked in olive oil, garlic, and pepper) with a salad and some crisp white wine. Other local fish dishes to try are *bianco* (stewed with lemon and garlic), *bourdetto* (stewed with paprika), and *marinato* (raw anchovies marinated in lemon juice). Too bad this place is located on a resort street with cars going past diners' toes. $ *Average main: €20* ☎ *26610/91281* ⌕ *Reservations not accepted.*

$ ✕ **Taverna Limeri.** This taverna, which sits in the "V" formed by the two
GREEK   streets in the village of Kora Korakiana, is where locals come to dine on wonderfully prepared local dishes. It's a good place to order several small plates and share the tastes Litsa cooks up in the kitchen. Try the *gigantes* (giant beans in red sauce), pork croquettes in cranberry sauce, the meatballs, the grilled pork souvlaki, or the steak with mushroom sauce. Ask for the daily specials not on the printed menu; you won't be disappointed. The superb red house wine is a blend of Cabernet and Merlot. On summer weekends, it is best to make a reservation. $ *Average main: €12* ⊠ *Kato Korakiana* ⊹ *1 km (½ mile) west of Dassia* ☎ *26610/97576* ☾ *No lunch.*

WHERE TO STAY

$$$$ RESORT Fodor's Choice ★ **Corfu Imperial Grecotel Exclusive Resort.** One of the most sumptuous resorts on Corfu, the Imperial complex juts into Kommeno bay atop a 14-acre peninsula and is beautiful both inside and out. **Pros:** beautifully maintained; excellent swimming; fine dining. **Cons:** so large you may feel anonymous; not in Corfu town. [$] *Rooms from: €380* ✉ *Kommeno* ✣ *10 km (6 miles) north of Corfu town* ☎ *26610/88400* 🌐 *www.grecotel.com* *136 rooms, 76 bungalows, 40 suites, 22 villas* 🕑 *Closed Nov.–Apr.* 🍴 *Multiple meal plans.*

$$$$ HOTEL **Kontokali Bay Resort and Spa.** Built the same year as the super-luxurious Corfu Imperial, this hotel-bungalow complex opened its doors in 1971 with a clean, modern look on a fantastic beach with a more-relaxed feel than its primary competitor a few miles to the north. **Pros:** great spa; lovely grounds; contemporary decor. **Cons:** not in Corfu town; large and somewhat anonymous. [$] *Rooms from: €285* ✉ *Nissi Gerekou* ☎ *26610/90500 through 26610/90509, 26610/99000 through 26610/99002* 🌐 *www.kontokalibay.com* *170 rooms, 89 bungalows* 🕑 *Closed mid-Oct.–Easter* 🍴 *Multiple meal plans.*

PALEOKASTRITSA ΠΑΛΑΙΟΚΑΣΤΡΙΤΣΑ

21 km (13 miles) north of Pelekas, 25 km (16 miles) northwest of Corfu town.

Fodor's Choice ★ To quote one recent traveler: "I'd rather go to Paleokastritsa than to Heaven." Considered by many to be the site of Homer's city of the Phaeacians, this truly spectacular territory of grottoes, cliffs, and turquoise waters has a big rock named Kolovri, which the ancient Greeks said resembled the ship that brought Ulysses home. The jaw-dropping natural beauty of Paleo, as Corfiots call it, has brought hotels, tavernas, bars, and shops to the hillsides above the bays, and the beaches swarm with hordes of people on day trips from Corfu town. You can explore the idyllic coves in peace with a pedal boat or small motorboat rented at the crowded main beach. There are also boat operators that go around to the prettiest surrounding beaches, especially those to the south, mostly inaccessible except from the sea; ask the skipper to let you off at a beach that appeals to you and to pick you up on a subsequent trip. Many visitors also enjoy a trip on the "Yellow Submarine," a glass-bottom boat that also runs night excursions (reservations are recommended).

In the Paleokastritsa region, look for La Grotta bar, built grotto-like into the rocks of a tiny cove. A mini-Acapulco, the high cliffs here tempt local youths to dive into the turquoise waters—great entertainment as you sip your cold beer or cocktail.

GETTING HERE AND AROUND

Depending on the day and the season, the green KTEL bus has four to six daily departures for Paleokastritsa from Corfu town's bus terminal on Avramiou near the New Port (the daily 9 am departure is the fastest and most convenient). The trip takes about 45 minutes. A taxi from Corfu town to Paleokastritsa costs about €40.

9

Barely changed from the days of Homer, the Paleokastritsa region of Corfu is one of the most achingly beautiful landscapes in Greece.

EXPLORING

Paleokastritsa Monastery. Paleokastritsa Monastery, a 17th-century structure, is built on the site of an earlier monastery, among terraced gardens overlooking the Ionian sea. Its treasure is a 12th-century icon of the Virgin Mary, to whom the establishment is dedicated, and there's a small museum with some other early icons. Note the Tree of Life motif on the ceiling. Be sure to visit the inner courtyard (go through the church), built on the edge of the cliff and looking down a precipitous cliff to the placid green coves and coastline to the south. There's a small gift shop on the premises. ⊠ *On northern headland* ⌦ *Donations accepted* ⊙ *Daily 7–1 and 3–8.*

Lakones. The village of Lakones, built on the steep mountain behind the Paleokastritsa Monastery, looks rather forbidding, but tourists flock there for the view. Kaiser Wilhelm was among many famous people who would make the ascent to enjoy the magnificent panorama of Paleokastritsa's coves from the cafés at Bella Vista, just beyond the village. In the village center is a small folk museum showcasing old photographs of the village. From nearby Krini you can climb up to the ruins of the 13th-century **Angelokastro**, a fortress built by a despot of Epirus during his brief rule over Corfu. On many occasions during the medieval period the fort sheltered Corfiots from attack by Turkish invaders. Look for the chapel and caves, which served as sanctuaries and hiding places. ⊠ *5 km (3 miles) northeast of Paleokastritsa.*

CLOSE UP

The Corfu Trail

The Corfu Trail is a 220-km (137-mile) trekking route that begins at the island's southern tip and takes a winding course to its northernmost point. Though a relatively small island, Corfu possesses a diversity of scenery that astounds, and the walk—which requires around ten days to complete in full—takes in many of its varied landscapes. Not only does each day offer a distinctive character, but even on a single day's walk the terrain changes constantly. At every corner, a new scene assaults the eye: a stunning view, a little church, a grove of ancient olive trees, a meadow carpeted with wild flowers. The trail takes in wild beaches, juniper-forested dunes, dense oak woodland, a karst plateau where nomad cattle roam, deep gorges, wetlands, mountain summits, and bucolic plains. The hand of modern man hardly encroaches, and only old monasteries, ruined olive presses, picturesque villages and ancient fortresses intrude on nature. On-trail accommodation and daily luggage transfer may be booked through Aperghi Travel *(⇨ tour Options)*. For more information on the trail, see 🌐 *www.thecorfutrail.com.*

WHERE TO EAT

$ CAFÉ FAMILY 🍴 **Emeral Café and Pastry Shop.** Directly on the busy National Road that connects Corfu town to Paleokastritsa, Emeral is a good spot to stop for coffee and a delicious pastry. You may have a hard time choosing a baked treat from the display cases. If you've been looking for a good cappuccino, this is the place to find it. [$] *Average main: €4* ✉ *National Paleokastritsa Rd., Km 10, Korakiana, Tzavros* ☎ *26610/91780* 💳 *No credit cards.*

$$ GREEK 🍴 **Vrahos** (*The Rock*). The stunning view from this restaurant overlooking the cliff-enclosed bay in Paleokastritsa will make you want to linger. The menu offers a bit of everything; the lobster with spaghetti is the house speciality, but it may be rather pricey for some, so you may want to content yourself with a nice Greek salad or moussaka instead. [$] *Average main: €16* ✉ *North end of Paleokastritsa beach* ☎ *26630/41233* 🌐 *www.vrachosp.gr* ⏲ *Closed Nov.–Easter.*

WHERE TO STAY

$$ HOTEL Fodor's Choice ★ 🏨 **Akrotiri Beach Hotel.** Few hotels in Corfu are so superbly positioned to take in its natural splendor the way the Akrotiri is, which lords it over a paradisical little peninsula. **Pros:** the location could not be better. **Cons:** public areas look a bit tired but are gradually being upgraded. [$] *Rooms from: €150* ☎ *26630/41237* 🌐 *www.akrotiri-beach.com* 🛏 *120 rooms, 1 suite* ⏲ *Closed Nov.–Apr.* 🍽 *Multiple meal plans.*

$ RENTAL FAMILY Fodor's Choice ★ 🏨 **Casa Lucia.** There are far grander places to stay on Corfu but few with as much quiet, unpretentious charm as Casa Lucia, where the stone buildings of an old olive press have been converted into guest cottages and smaller studios. **Pros:** rural retreat; cozy charm; family-friendly atmosphere. **Cons:** fairly basic bathrooms in studios. [$] *Rooms from: €70* ✉ *Corfu–Paleokastritsa Rd., Sgombou* ✣ *13 km (8 miles) northwest of Corfu town* ☎ *26610/91419* 🌐 *www.casa-lucia-corfu.com* 🛏 *9 cottages* ⏲ *Closed Nov.–Mar.* 🍽 *No meals.*

$ RENTAL

🏨 **Fundana Villas.** The charming suites and bungalows at this small hilltop lodging are built into and around a 17th-century stone-and-mortar Venetian storehouse; each has been turned into a comfortable hideaway. **Pros:** surrounded by lovely gardens and olive and orange groves. **Cons:** short on in-room facilities; you need transport to access restaurants and shops. [$] *Rooms from: €75* ✉ *National Paleokastritsa Rd., Km 15, Felekas* ✥ *3 km (2 miles) east of Paleokastritsa* ☎ *26630/22532* 📠 *26630/22453* 🌐 *www.fundanavillas.com* 🛏 *7 bungalows, 2 suites, 3 studios* ⏲ *Closed Nov.–Mar.* 🍴 *No meals.*

$$ B&B/INN Fodor's Choice ★

🏨 **The Merchant's House.** Owners Mark and Saskia have created their luxurious B&B from one of Perithia's former ruins with a sensitive and stylish renovation of the old stone structure. **Pros:** perfect for lovers of nature; warm and helpful personal service; combines homeliness and luxury. **Cons:** no swimming pool; the village, though isolated, can be busy with day-trippers. [$] *Rooms from: €150* ✉ *Old Perithia* ☎ *26630/98444* 🌐 *www.merchantshousecorfu.com* 🛏 *4 suites, 1 room* ⏲ *Closed Nov.–Mar.* 🍴 *Breakfast.*

THE PELOPONNESE

Monemvassia, Mycenae, Nafplion,
the Mani, and Olympia

WELCOME TO THE PELOPONNESE

TOP REASONS TO GO

★ **Ancient Ruins A to Z:** Some of Greece's greatest classical ruins, including Corinth, Mycenae, and Olympia, are packed into this region.

★ **Nafplion Grace:** The favorite Greek city of many seasoned travelers has a magnificent setting on the gulf of Argos, imposing remains, an animated waterfront, and street after street of old houses, churches, and mosques.

★ **Majestic Mani:** True connoisseurs of Greece flaunt the fact that they've traveled to this far-from-the-madding-crowds region, famed for its silent villages, stark landscapes, and feeling of mystery.

★ **High Drama:** The theater at Epidauros, the setting for a highly acclaimed drama festival, still claims acoustics so perfect that every word can be heard—even from the very last of its 55 tiers.

★ **Byzantine Glory:** Two remarkable strongholds, Mystras and Monemvasia, display the region's Byzantine legacy.

1 **Argolid and Corinthiad.** Forgotten civilizations left their mysteries here on the eastern side of the northern Peloponnese, most strikingly at the ruined city of Mycenae, with giant tombs to the heroes of Homer's *Iliad*. Nearby Nafplion, with its medieval edifices jutting into the bay of Argos, is perhaps the most beautiful city in Greece, with fabled ancient sites like Epidauros and Corinth within easy reach. To the south, beyond the mountain valleys of Elis, is famed Ancient Olympia, birthplace of the games.

2 **Arcadia.** Two of Greece's most beauteous mountain villages, Stemnitsa and Dimitsana, are here in this still somewhat remote region, as is the spectacular Temple of Apollo at Bassae.

3 **Laconia.** Surrounded on three sides by mountains and by the sea on the other, Laconia was home to the harsh Spartans and also to the civilized Byzantines, who left splendid cities at Mystras, now in ruin, and Monemvasia, an intact medieval stronghold that clings to a rock above the sea. To the south lies the hauntingly beautiful Mani peninsula, set with stark and sublime villages.

GETTING ORIENTED

The northern Peloponnese comprises the Argive peninsula, jutting into the Aegean, and runs westward past the isthmus and along the gulf of Corinth to the big transportation hub of Patras and the Adriatic coast. The oldest region is the fertile Argive plain (Argolid), the home of the heroes of Homer's *Iliad*. Heading southward, travelers love to visit beautiful Nafplion, famed for its Venetian, Ottoman, and German neoclassic houses. The southern Peloponnese's main regions—Arcadia to the north and Laconia in the southeast—are bisected with rugged mountain ranges. Arcadia is most accessible to Athens; exploring Laconia means traveling down the fingerlike peninsulas that dangle from the southernmost extremes of the Greek mainland.

10

Updated
by Stephen
Brewer

Over the millennia the rugged terrain of the Peloponnese—
a vast region that hangs like a large leaf from the stem
of the Corinthian isthmus—has nourished kingdoms and
empires. The stony achievements of these ancient achiev-
ers litter the ground liberally, from Epidaurus to Olympia
to Ancient Messe. This, indeed, is the fabulous Greece of
history and myth: if Hercules walked the earth (some historians now believe he was an actual early king of Argos
or Tiryns), his main stomping grounds—from the Argolid to
Nafplion—were here.

Traces of these lost realms—ruined Bronze Age citadels, Greek and
Roman temples and theaters, and the fortresses and settlements of the
Byzantines, Franks, Venetians, and Turks—attest to this land's historical richness. Four thousand years of history are more fully illustrated
in this region than nearly anywhere else in Europe. No wonder visitors
who spend less than a week here wind up asking themselves why they
didn't allot more time to this fascinating area of Greece, the country's
most ruin-packed terrain, ground zero for anyone even remotely interested in the ancient past—with Byzantine wonders entering the mix at
Monemvasia and Mystras. Plus, if you wish to forgo clamoring over
ruins for a day or two, it's easy to find a mountain path or isolated
stretch of sand on which to relax.

Despite the waves of invaders over the centuries this land is considered the distillation of all that is Greek, with its indulged idiosyncrasy,
intractable autonomy, and appreciation of simple pleasures. A large
portion of Greece's emigrants to the United States in the 20th century
(12%–25% of the male population) have roots in the Peloponnese (their
family names are often identified with an ending in *poulos*, meaning
"son of"); almost all dreamed of returning to their Greek villages when
they had raised their families and had accumulated a sufficient *ekono-
mies* (nest egg). Quite a number of them have done just that, so if you

find yourself unable to convey what you need through phrase-book Greek and body language in one of the remote villages here, an elderly *Helleno-Americanos* (Greek-American) may be called upon to assist. Time seems to have stood still in the smaller towns here, and even in the cities you'll encounter a lifestyle that remains more traditionally Greek than that of some of the more developed islands. The joy of exploring this region comes as much from watching life transpire in an animated square as it does from seeing the impressive ruins.

"Pelopónnisos" means "Island of Pelops," though only the narrow Corinth canal separates it from the mainland. Pelops was the son of the mythical Tantalos, whose tragic descendants dominate the half-legendary Mycenaean centuries. The myths and legends surrounding Pelops and his family—Atreus, Agamemnon, Orestes, and Electra, among others—provided the grist for poets and playwrights from Homer to Aeschylus and enshroud many of the region's sites to this day.

A walk through the Lion Gate into Mycenae, the citadel of Agamemnon, brings the Homeric epic to life, and the massive walls of nearby Tiryns glorify the age of might. Eastward lies Corinth, the economic superpower of the 7th and 6th centuries BC, and also Epidauros, the sanctuary of Asklepios, god of healing, where in summer Greek dramas are re-created in the ancient theater, one of the finest and most complete to survive.

In the western side of the Peloponnese is one of Greece's greatest ancient sites, Olympia, the sanctuary of Zeus and site of the ancient Olympic Games. Ancient Messene, with its mammoth fortifications from the 4th century BC, is on the sandy cape of Messinia, in the south of the region.

Fast forward almost two millennia. By the 13th century the armies of the Fourth Crusade (in part egged on by Venice) had conquered the Peloponnese after capturing Constantinople in 1204. But the dominion of the Franks was brief, and Byzantine authority was restored under the Palaiologos dynasty. Soon after Constantinople fell in 1453, the Turks, taking advantage of an internal rivalry, crushed the Palaiologoi and helped themselves to the Peloponnese. In the following centuries the struggle between the Venetians and the Ottoman Turks was played out in Greece. The two states alternately dominated the Peloponnese until the Ottomans ultimately prevailed as Venetian power declined in the early 1700s. The Turkish mosques and fountains and the Venetian fortifications of Nafplion recall this epic struggle. Rebellion against Turkish rule ignited in the Peloponnese, and after the Turks withdrew in 1828 in the wake of the Greek War of Independence, Nafplion was the capital of Greece from 1829 until the move to Athens in 1834.

10

PLANNING

WHEN TO GO

As in much of Greece, late April and May provide optimum conditions for exploration—hotels, restaurants, and sites have begun to extend their hours but the hordes of travelers have not yet arrived. September and October are also excellent times because the weather is warm but not oppressive, the sea is at its balmiest, and the throngs of people have gone home. In summer, morning and early-evening activity will avoid the worst of the heat, which can be a formidable obstacle. Mosquitoes are out in force around seaside villages, which are often surrounded by fields and groves, so bring repellent and, more important, seek out a hotel room with air-conditioning. Remember that snow renders many of the mountain regions hard to access in winter.

PLANNING YOUR TIME

The remains of the ancient world are what draw many visitors to the Peloponnese—Mycenae, Epidauros, and Olympia certainly top of the list of must-see sights of anyone with an interest in archaeology. Nafplion, a delightful city, with Byzantine, Venetian, and Turkish roots, makes an ideal base from which to explore these well-preserved ruins of ancient Greece. After Nafplion, don't-miss Ancient Olympia beckons the Peloponnesian traveler. Continuing southward, one enters Laconia. The rewards here include exploring the stark Mani peninsula and ancient splendors at Messene and elsewhere, and the trip down there is easy: Highway E65 allows travelers to speed from Athens to Kalamata or Sparta and Gythion in half a day or less. Resort life is relatively low-key in the southern Peloponnese; Monemvasia is a popular weekend destination for Greeks, and the narrow lanes can seem jammed. The town is much less crowded and more pleasant to visit during the week, when the medieval atmosphere regains a hold. The Mani, another favorite "remote" seaside getaway for Athenians, is rarely crowded, except on August weekends.

GETTING HERE AND AROUND

Nafplion is the major city in the east of the region, on the gulf of Argos, about 150 km (90 miles) south of Athens. Though it's possible to travel by train from Athens to the northern Peloponnesian, ongoing and often delayed improvements can make this less than a magic-carpet ride. The easiest way to get around the often-rural Peloponnese is therefore by car, on the region's well-maintained and well-marked roads. The bus network between towns is excellent, though service to smaller villages tends to be infrequent. It's easy to get to most places in the Peloponnese via the E65, a north–south highway that cuts through the region and is four lanes for much of its length, connecting Corinth, Tripoli, Sparta, and Kalamata with Athens. Another leg, E55, drops down to the western coast near Pylos. From Nafplion, an excellent base for exploring the region, you can easily reach such ancient sites as Epidauros and Mycenae.

AIR TRAVEL

The main airport in the Peloponnese is the small field 9 km (5 miles) outside Kalamata. It's not terribly well-served, though Aegean Airlines offers daily one-hour flights to and from Athens. The airport also handles charter flights to and from northern Europe in summer.

Airport Contacts Kalamata Airport ⊠ *Off Hwy. E2, 9 km (5 miles) west of city center, Kalamata* ☎ *27210/63805.*

BOAT AND FERRY TRAVEL

The big city of Patras (the tourist office is near the harbor) is the port for boats to and from Corfu and the other Ionian islands, as well as boats to and from Italy. Minoan, ANEK, and Blue Star all run boats between Patras and the Ionians, and Superfast and Minoan have the most extensive services between Patras and Ancona, Bari, and Venice in Italy. Lane Sea Lines runs once-weekly service in summer between Gythion, in the Southern Peloponnese, and Kythera and Kissamos (Kastelli), Crete; once-weekly service between Kalamata and Rethymnon, Crete; and once-weekly service between Piraeus and Monemvasia, with arrival in Monemvasia on Friday evening and returning to Piraeus on Sunday evening. The Nafplion Port Authority and Patras Port Authority can advise you about entry and exit in their ports for yachts. *For detailed information on ferry companies and port authorities, see Boat Travel in Travel Smart.*

BUS TRAVEL

Bus service between Athens and the Peloponnese is excellent—so good that you might consider taking a bus to your destination and renting a car locally, saving tolls and high fuel charges. Take advantage of the English speakers at the ticket offices to get information on traveling throughout the Peloponnese by bus—they have at their disposal a wealth of information that is otherwise hard to get. The association of regional bus companies (KTEL) no longer provides schedules on its website, only on a pay-per-minute phone line in which information is available only in Greek. Service from Athens to Corinth and Patras operates as frequently as every half hour from 6 am to late evening; it takes only an hour to Corinth and two or so to Patras. From Corinth, you can continue or connect for service to Nafplion, from where a local network serves the nearby classical sights, and to Sparta, with connections or onward service to such places as Monemvasia and the Mani. From Patras, you can make boat connections or connect to buses to Olympia and other places in the southwest Peloponnese. From Athens, direct buses also run several times daily to Gythion, Kalamata, and Tripoli and at least once a day to Andritsena, Monemvasia, and Pylos. Within the Peloponnese, bus schedules are posted at local KTEL stations, usually on the main square or main street. You will usually find English-speaking staff behind the desk in stations in the larger towns.

10

Contacts Andritsena Bus Station ✉ *Main square, Andritsena* ☎ *26260/22239.* **Corinth Bus Station** ✉ *Kolokotroni and Koilastou, Corinth* ☎ *27410/24444.* **Gythion Bus Station** ✉ *Ebrikleous, at north end of harbor, Gythion* ☎ *27330/22228.* **Kalamata Bus Station** ✉ *Artemidos 50, Kalamata* ☎ *27210/22851.* **Monemvasia Bus Station** ✉ *Off main square, Gefira, Monemvasia* ☎ *27320/61432.* **Nafplion Bus Station** ✉ *Sigrou 8, Nafplion* ☎ *27520/27323.* **Olympia Bus Station** ✉ *Outside train station, Olympia* ☎ *26102/73694.* **Patras Bus Station** ✉ *Othonos and Amalia, Patras* ☎ *26106/23886.* **Pylos Bus Station** ✉ *Trion Navarchon Sq., Pylos* ☎ *27230/22230.* **Sparta Bus Station** ✉ *Vrasidou and Paleologou, Sparta* ☎ *27310/26441.* **Tripoli Bus Station** ✉ *Kolokotronis Sq., Tripoli* ☎ *27102/24314.*

CAR TRAVEL

For pure pleasure, traveling by car through the Peloponnese really delivers. Four wheels are not only the easiest way to get around, but a car also provides a chance to enjoy dramatic scenery and get to out-of-the-way spots. The very best driving routes? Some point to the mountain roads that lead to Stemnitsa and Demitsana—on this journey, you'll encounter thick forests, stone villages clinging to steep hillsides, and brooding Frankish castles. Others tout the road from Kalamata to Mystras: this scenic route rises from the Messinia plains onto the forested flanks of the Taygettus range and the ruined city of Mystras and modern Sparta. For some, the road down the Mani peninsula can't be beat: setting out from Gythion, the landscape becomes starker the farther south you travel (on a highway that is barely more than one lane in places) until you reach cape Tenaro, the mythical entrance to the underworld.

Note that even if highways have assigned numbers, no Greek knows them by any other than their informal names, which usually refer to their destination. A toll highway, known simply as Ethnikos Odos, or National Road (officially E65), runs from Athens to the isthmus of Corinth (84 km [52 miles], 1¼ hours), and from there continues to Nafplion, Patras, and Olympia; have change ready, as a toll of about €2 is collected intermittently on parts of the system, including the segments between Athens and Patras and Athens and Nafplion.

The system is well maintained, but the highway between Corinth and Patras is two lanes for some of its length and can be extremely dangerous, with impatient drivers using the two lanes as four lanes. Slow-moving traffic is forced onto the shoulder. No speed limit is enforced, and the asphalt becomes very slippery when wet. The accident rate is high. For those traveling south from Corinth, the fastest route is the section of the E65 toll highway known as the Corinth–Kalamata road; it is four lanes to Kalamata, where you can branch off to Monemvasia, the Mani, and other places in the southern Peloponnese. Another well-maintained leg heads south from Tripoli to Sparta, from where you can head east to Monemvasia; from Corinth the trip to Kalamata takes about 2 hours and to Sparta about 3 hours.

Narrow roads cross mountainous terrain throughout the region, providing many a scenic route when not closed due to snow in winter. You'll need a good map to navigate the back roads, as well as a transliteration of the Greek alphabet—many signs on remote roads are in Greek only. A GPS device can also be a godsend when navigating the back roads. Gas stations are few and far between in some places, so top off the tank when you have the chance.

If you're renting a car in Athens, you may want to do so at the airport and drive south from there; the E94 ring road around Athens allows you to avoid the harrowing city traffic and connects with E65 south to the Peloponnese. On the other hand, bus travel into the region is so easy that you may want to travel by bus to your destination in the Peloponnese and rent a car for local exploring. You may want to rent a car in Patras if you are arriving on a boat from Italy or one of the Ionian islands. *For detailed information on renting a car, see Car Travel in Travel Smart.*

TAXI TRAVEL

If you have trouble reaching a site—for example, there is no public transportation to Ancient Messene—take a taxi from a town's main square, which is always near the bus station. In rural areas drivers don't usually speak English, though they will often find someone near the taxi stand who does to help you negotiate the ride.

In rural areas drivers may not switch on the meter if the destination has a fixed price, but make sure you agree on the cost before getting in. When leaving town limits, the driver may switch his meter to the higher rate (Tarifa 2).

TRAIN TRAVEL

The good news is that train travel from Athens to the Peloponnese is improving all the time—or, at least, is scheduled to improve. The bad news is that extensive track work is ongoing on the Peloponnesian lines, service interruptions are common, and Greece's financial woes have severely curtailed improvements. There are plans for a fast network to be running from Athens to Patras, Kalamata, and other cities in the Peloponnese, but no one is counting on such a network actually being in place soon. If you are traveling from Athens to anywhere other than Corinth and Nafplion, you will probably find bus travel to be faster, more reliable, and in many cases your only option for public transportation. The trip to Nafplion takes 3 to 4 hours using the commuter service between Athens and Corinth, with a change in Corinth to a branch line to Nafplion. Trains run to and from Corinth and Athens every hour between 8 and 8. The trip takes one hour and costs €6 to and from Athens, €8 to and from the airport. From Corinth a newly improved line runs to Nafplion, with four trains a day between the two cities. *For detailed information on traveling by train, see Train Travel in Travel Smart.*

Contacts Greek Railways Organziation (OSE) ⊕ *www.ose.gr.* **Patras railway station** ⊠ *Leoforos Othonos-Amalias 36–40, Patras* ☎ *26102/21311.*

HOTELS

Hotels in Nafplion, Sparta, and other large towns and cities tend to be open year-round. Monemvasia is a year-round getaway and hotels stay open there as well. In beach resorts, such as the Mani villages, and in Olympia, many hotels close in late October and reopen in late March or early April. In Nafplion, many old houses have been converted to pleasant small hotels and do a brisk weekend business as a getaway for Athenians, and here you'll also be likely to find the region's more luxurious and expensive lodgings. Overall, though, lodging is a good value in the Peloponnese, and even in high season you can usually manage to find a clean and pleasant room for two, with breakfast, for less than €100.

RESTAURANTS

While you can enjoy elegant and nouvelle dining in some of the finer restaurants of the Peloponnese's beauty spots, such as Nafplion and Monemvasia, one of the great pleasures of traveling in this region is enjoying a meal on a square or seaside terrace in a simple village. In fact, villages here were the source of such international favorites as avgolemono soup and lamb fricassee. There are several other local specialties to watch for: in the mountain villages near Tripoli, order *stifado* (beef with pearl onions), *arni psito* (lamb on the spit), *kokoretsi* (entrails on the spit), and thick, creamy yogurt. In Sparta, look for *bardouniotiko* (a local dish of chicken stuffed with cheese, olives, and walnuts), and, around Pylos, order fresh ocean fish (priced by the kilo). In the rest of Laconia, try *loukaniko horiatiko* (village sausage), and in the Mani ask for ham.

Vegetables are almost always locally grown and fresh in this region famous for its olives and olive oil as wells as figs, tomatoes, and other produce. Seafood is plentiful, though sometimes frozen—menus will usually indicate what's frozen and what's fresh (and frozen usually hails from beyond Greece). A fresh catch is usually available at seaside tavernas, and an octopus or two will usually be drying out front. Inland, many tavernas serve grilled pork from local farms, as well as chicken and roosters plucked that morning. As for wine, beyond those *varelisio* (from the barrel), there are great reds from the region around Nemea and a top light white from Mantinea. After dinner, try *mavrodaphne*, a heavy dessert wine, or *dendoura*, a clove liqueur, as a digestive. Dress is casual and reservations unnecessary, although you might be asked to wait for a table if you're dining with hoi polloi (the masses) at 9 pm or later.

DINING AND LODGING PRICES IN EUROS			
	$	**$$**	**$$$**	**$$$$**
Restaurants	under €16	€16–€25	€26–€40	over €40
Hotels	under €126	€126–€225	€226–€275	over €275

Restaurant prices are for one main course at dinner, or for two mezedes (small dishes). Hotel prices are for a standard double room in high season, including taxes.

TOUR OPTIONS

Many operators organize whirlwind one-day tours from Athens to Corinth, Mycenae, Epidauros, and Nafplion; the cost is about €85. These no-frills tours, aimed at those who don't expect much handholding, can be booked at travel agencies and at larger hotels. CHAT and other operators also offer a more leisurely two-day tour of Corinth, Mycenae, and Epidauros, with an overnight stay in Nafplion; cost is about €140. If you are in Nafplion, many local travel agencies can arrange day tours of the classical sites.

VISITOR INFORMATION

The Peloponnese is woefully underserved by tourist offices. Olympia has an outlet of the Greek National Tourism Organization and Nafplion has a locally run tourist office, but most towns in the region do not have tourist offices of any sort. For tourist information and general help in places without tourist offices, it's best to contact the local tourist police, who often speak English and can be extremely helpful.

ARGOLID AND CORINTHIAD
ΑΡΓΟΛΙΔΑ ΚΑΙ ΚΟΡΙΝΘΙΑ

Mycenae gazes over the plain of Argos, and nearby Epidauros hosts audiences from around the world who come to see performances in its classical theater. The city of Argos lies in the center of the plain, near the beautiful Turkish-Venetian city of Nafplion. Behind the mountains that surround the plain is the Corinthiad, a hilly region overlooked by Ancient Corinth.

ISTHMUS ΙΣΘΜΟΣ

75 km (47 miles) southwest of Athens, 7 km (4½ miles) southeast of Corinth.

More of a pit stop than a town, the isthmus is where the Peloponnese begins. Were it not for this narrow neck of land less than 7 km (4½ miles) across, the waters of the gulf of Corinth and the Saronic gulf would meet and would make the Peloponnese an island; hence the name, which means "Pelops's island."

For the ancient Greeks the isthmus was strategically important for both trade and defense; Corinth, with harbors on either side of the isthmus, grew wealthy on the lucrative east–west trade. Ships en route from Italy and the Adriatic to the Aegean had to sail around the Peloponnese, so in the 7th century BC a paved roadway called the Diolkos

THE ISTHMUS CANAL

Nero was the first to begin cutting a canal, supposedly striking the first blow, with a golden pickax, in AD 67, a task he then turned over to 6,000 Jewish prisoners. But the canal project died with Nero the following year, and the roadway was used until the 13th century. The modern canal, built 1882–93, was cut through 285 feet of rock to sea level. The impressive sight is a fleeting one if you are speeding by on the highway, so keep a sharp lookout. A well-marked turnoff leads to the tourist area, which has many restaurants (best avoided) and souvenir shops, as well as an overlook above the canal.

was constructed across the isthmus, over which ships were hauled using rollers. You can still see remnants near the bridge at the western end of the modern canal.

ANCIENT CORINTH ΑΡΧΑΙΑ ΚΟΡΙΝΘΟΣ

35 km (22 miles) northeast of Ancient Nemea, 81 km (50 miles) southwest of Athens.

West of the isthmus, the countryside opens up into a low-lying coastal plain around the head of the gulf of Corinth. Modern Corinth, near the coast about 8 km (5 miles) north of the turnoff for the ancient town, is a regional center of some 23,000 inhabitants. Concrete pier-and-slab is the preferred architectural style, and the city seems to be under a seismic curse: periodic earthquakes knock the buildings down before they have time to develop any character. Corinth was founded in 1858 after

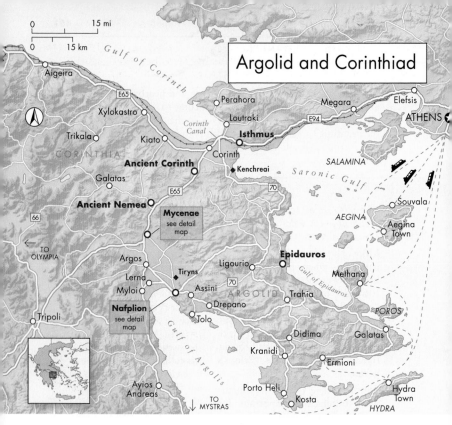

one of these quakes leveled the old village at the ancient site; another flattened the new town in 1928; and a third in 1981 destroyed many buildings. Most tourists avoid the town altogether, visiting the ruins of Ancient Corinth and moving on.

EXPLORING

Acrocorinth. Looming some 540 meters (1,772 feet) above Ancient Corinth, the Acrocorinth is one of the best naturally fortified citadels in Europe. Citizens retreated in times of invasions and earthquakes, and armies could keep an eye out for approaches by land over the isthmus and by sea from the Saronic gulf and the gulf of Corinth. The moat and three rings of wall are largely Byzantine, Frankish, Venetian, and Turkish—but the right-hand tower of the innermost of the three gates is apparently a 4th-century BC original. Corinth's famous Temple of Aphrodite, which had 1,000 prostitutes in attendance, stood here at the summit, too. On the slope of the mountain is the Sanctuary of Demeter, which you can view but not enter. Take the road next to the ticket office in Ancient Corinth; if you don't have your own car, you can hire one of the taxis that often wait for visitors for the trip up to the tourist pavilion and café (about €5 round-trip), from which it's a 10-minute walk to Acrocorinth gate. ⊠ *Off E94, 7 km (4½ miles) west of Corinth* ☎ *27410/31207* ⬚ *€6* ⊘ *Apr.–Oct., daily 8–7:30; Nov.–Mar., daily 8–5.*

Fodor's Choice ★ **Ancient Corinth.** Excavations of one of the great cities of classical and Roman Greece have gone on since 1896, exposing ruins on the slopes of Acrocorinth and northward toward the coast. In ancient times, goods and often entire ships were hauled across the isthmus on a paved road between Corinth's two ports—Lechaion on the Gulf of Corinth and Kenchreai on the Sarionic Gulf—ensuring a lively trade with colonies and empires throughout Europe and the Middle East. Most of the buildings that have been excavated are from the Roman era; only a few from before the sack of Corinth in 146 BC were rehabilitated when the city was refounded under orders of Julius Caesar.

The **Glauke Fountain** is past the parking lot on the left. According to the Greek traveler Pausanias, Glauke, Jason's second wife, also known as Creusa, threw herself into the water to obtain relief from a poisoned dress sent to her by the vengeful Medea. Beyond the fountain is the **museum,** which displays examples of the black-figure pottery—decorated with friezes of panthers, sphinxes, bulls, and warriors—for which Corinth was famous.

Seven of the original 38 columns of the **Temple of Apollo** (just above the museum) are still standing, and the structure is by far the most striking of Corinth's ancient buildings—as well as one of the oldest stone temples in Greece (mid-6th century BC). Beyond the temple are the remains of the **North Market,** a colonnaded square once surrounded by many small shops, and south of the temple is the main forum of Ancient Corinth. A row of shops bounds the forum at the far western end. East of the market is a series of small temples, and beyond is the forum's main plaza. A long line of shops runs lengthwise through the forum, dividing it into an **upper (southern)** and **lower (northern) terrace,** in the center of which is the bema (large podium), perhaps the very one where in AD 52 St. Paul delivered his defense of Christianity before the Roman proconsul Gallio.

The southern boundary of the forum was the **South Stoa,** a 4th-century-BC building, perhaps erected by Philip II of Macedonia to house delegates to his Hellenic confederacy. There were originally 33 shops across the front, and the back was altered in Roman times to accommodate such civic offices as the council hall, or *bouleuterion,* in the center. The road to Kenchreai began next to the bouleuterion and headed south. Farther along the South Stoa were the entrance to the **South Basilica** and, at the far end, the **Southeast Building,** which probably was the city archive.

In the lower forum, below the Southeast Building, was the **Julian Basilica,** a former law court. Continuing to the northeast corner of the forum, you approach the facade of the **Fountain of Peirene.** Water from a spring was gathered into four reservoirs before flowing out through the arcadelike facade into a drawing basin in front. Frescoes of swimming fish from a 2nd-century Roman refurbishment can still be seen. The Lechaion road heads out of the forum to the north. A colonnaded courtyard, the **Peribolos of Apollo,** is directly to the east of the Lechaion road, and beyond it lies a **public latrine,** with toilets in place, and the

10

remains of a **Roman-era bath,** probably the Baths of Eurykles described by Pausanias as Corinth's best known.

Along the west side of the Lechaion road is a large basilica entered from the forum through the **Captives' Facade,** named for its sculptures of captive barbarians. West of the Captives' Facade the row of **northwest shops** completes the circuit.

Northwest of the parking lot is the **odeon** (a roofed theater), cut into a natural slope, which was built during the 1st century AD, but burned around 175. Around 225 the theater was renovated and used as an arena for combats between gladiators and wild beasts. North of the odeon is the **theater** (5th century BC), one of the few Greek buildings reused by the Romans, who filled in the original seats and set in new ones at a steeper angle. By the 3rd century they had adapted it for gladiatorial contests and finally for mock naval battles.

North of the theater, inside the city wall, are the **Fountain of Lerna** and the **Asklepieion,** the sanctuary of the god of healing with a small temple (4th century BC) set in a colonnaded courtyard and a series of dining rooms in a second courtyard. Terra-cotta votive offerings representing afflicted body parts (hands, legs, breasts, genitals, and so on) were found in the excavation of the Asklepieion, and many of them are displayed at the museum. ✉ *Off E94, 7 km (4½ miles) west of Corinth* ☎ *27410/31207* ⊕ *www.culture.gr* ✂ *€6* ۞ *Apr.–Oct., daily 8–6; Nov.–Mar., daily 8–3.*

Corinth Historical and Folklore Museum. If you find yourself in the new town, it's well worth your time to step into this collection with its well-done displays of beautiful costumes, works of embroidery, and furniture from throughout Greece. ✉ *Near town wharf, Ermou 1* ☎ *27410/25352* ⊕ *www.culture.gr* ✂ *€2* ۞ *Tues.–Sun. 8:30–3.*

EPIDAUROS ΕΠΙΔΑΥΡΟΣ

62 km (38 miles) south of the isthmus, 25 km (15 miles) east of Nafplion.

What is now a pleasant little agricultural village surrounded by orange and olive groves has been on the Greek map for millennia. Epidauros was known for its theater and healing center as early as the 4th century BC. Today the beautifully preserved theater standing proud in a pine-scented glade is a magnificent sight, one of the most popular of all the ruins of ancient Greece.

EXPLORING

FAMILY **Epidauros.** The Sanctuary of Asklepios, once the most famous healing
Fodor's Choice center in the ancient world, is today best known for the **Theater at Epi-**
★ **dauros,** remarkably well preserved because it was buried at some time in antiquity and remained untouched until it was uncovered in the late 19th century. Built in the 4th century BC with 14,000 seats, the theater was never remodeled in antiquity, and because it was rather remote, the stones were never quarried for secondary building use. The extraordinary qualities of the theater were recognized even in the 2nd century AD. Pausanias of Lydia, the 2nd-century AD traveler and geographer,

wrote, "The Epidaurians have a theater in their sanctuary that seems to me particularly worth a visit. The Roman theaters have gone far beyond all the others in the world. But who can begin to rival Polykleitos for the beauty and composition of his architecture?" In addition, the acoustics of Polykleitos the Younger's theater are so perfect that even from the last of the 55 tiers every word can be heard. The theater is the setting for a highly acclaimed **summer drama festival,** with outstanding productions.

The **Sanctuary of Asklepios** is dedicated to the god of healing, the son of Apollo who was allegedly born here. The most important healing center in the ancient world drew visitors in search of a cure from throughout Greece and the colonies. The sanctuary is in the midst of a decades-long restoration project, but you can see the ruins of the Sleeping Hall, where clients slept in order to be visited by the gods in their dreams and told which cure to follow, as well as the enormous Guest House, with 160 rooms, and the Tholos, where serpents that were said to cure with a flick of the tongue were housed in a maze of labyrinths. Some copies of sculptures found among the ruins are in the **site museum** (the originals are in the National Archaeological Museum in Athens) along with ancient medical instruments, votives, and inscriptions expressing the gratitude of the cured. Heading south from the isthmus on Highway 70, don't take the turnoffs for Nea Epidauros or Palaio Epidauros; follow the signs that say "Ancient Theatre of Epidauros." ✉ *Off Hwy. 70 near Ligourio, Epidauros* ☎ *27530/23009* 🌐 *www.culture.gr* 🎫 *€6* 🕒 *May–Oct., daily 8–8; Nov.–Apr., daily 8–6.*

WHERE TO EAT

$ GREEK 🍴 **Leonidas.** Seating in a rear garden in summer and in front of a fire in winter adds to the pleasure of dining at this friendly taverna, the best dining choice in and around Epidauros. The grilled pork chops are excellent, as are the moussaka and the stuffed vine leaves in egg-lemon sauce. Dessert choices are brandy-and-cinnamon-laced *revani* (semolina cake) or luscious *kataifi* (shredded dough filled with chopped pistachio nuts) topped with *kaimaki* (clotted cream). The owner may walk you around to show off his photos of celebs who have dined here. Many actors and audience members dine here on performance nights during the summer festival, so reserve in advance on those days. [$] *Average main: €11* ✉ *Epidauros main road, Epidauros* ☎ *27530/22115.*

PERFORMING ARTS

Athens and Epidaurus Festival. In the theater at Epidauros, this festival offers memorable performances from late June through August, Friday and Saturday only, at 9 pm. All productions are of ancient Greek drama in modern Greek, many presented by the national theater troupe. Actors are so expressive (or often wear ancient masks to signal the mood) that you can enjoy the performance even if you don't know a word of Greek. Get to the site early (and bring a picnic lunch or have a drink or a light meal at the decent Xenia Café on-site), because watching the sun set behind the mountains and fields of olives and pines is unforgettable. You can buy tickets (€10–€50) through the Festival Box Office in Athens *(Panepistimiou 39, 210/928–2900)* or online, and a short time before performance days at the theater box office. Many tour operators in Athens and Nafplion offer tours that include a performance at Epidauros. On the days of performances, four or five buses run between Nafplion and the theater, and there's service back to Nafplion after the play; the cost is about €4 round-trip. Look for buses that say "theater" or "epidauros," not "nea epidauros" or "archea epidauros." Buses also run to and from Athens on days of performances for about €14 round-trip. ⊠ *Ancient theater, Epidauros* ☎ *27530/22026 theater box office* ⊕ *www.greekfestival.gr.*

NAFPLION ΝΑΥΠΛΙΟ

Fodor's Choice ★ *65 km (40½ miles) south of Corinth, 27 km (17 miles) west of Epidauros.*

Oraia (beautiful) is the word Greeks use to describe Nafplion. The town's old section, on a peninsula jutting into the gulf of Argos, mixes Greek, Venetian, and Turkish architecture; narrow streets, often just broad flights of stone stairs, climb the slopes beneath the walls of Acronafplia, the massive hilltop castle. Tree-shaded plazas surround neoclassical buildings. The Palamidi fortress—an elegant display of Venetian might from the early 1700s—guards the town. Nafplion deserves at least a leisurely day of your undivided attention, and you may want to spend several days or a week here and use the city as the base from which to explore the many surrounding ancient sights.

GETTING HERE AND AROUND

A favorite outing for Athenians is to whisk down to Nafplion on a system of toll roads. The trip takes two hours (less for some drivers). You may want to take a more leisurely trip and stop at the isthmus and Ancient Corinth *(see above)* along the way. Once in Nafplion you can usually find a space in the enormous free parking lot alongside the port next to the Old Town. From there you can walk to most Nafplion accommodations.

Travelers to Nafplion can also take advantage of the new suburban rail links between Athens and Corinth, a trip of about two hours. From there you can transfer to one of the four daily trains to Nafplion (€10 each way), for a total trip time of three to four hours, or continue to Nafplion by taxi for about €50.

Bus service, either directly from Athens or with a connection in Corinth, is good. Buses to Nafplion run about every hour, and you should allow about three hours for the trip, which costs about €12 each way and often requires a change in Corinth.

EXPLORING

Little is known about ancient Nafplion, and the town did not grow in importance until Byzantine times, when it was fought over by the Byzantines and the Frankish crusaders. Nafplion was then held by the duke of Athens, the Venetians, and the Turks; it was liberated in the War of Independence and briefly became the capital of Greece. Today Nafplion is once again just a provincial city, busy only in the tourist season and on weekends when Athenians arrive to get away from city pressures.

Surviving nearly intact from the 4th century BC, the arena at Epidauros remains the most famous ancient theater in the world.

A full exploration of this lovely town takes an entire day; a quick tour, with some omissions, could be done in three hours. Although a step-by-step itinerary can lead you to all the main sights, you can get a good sample of Nafplion just by following your nose through its winding streets and charming squares. Around Syntagma (Constitution) Square are some of Nafplion's top sights, including the Peloponnesian Folk-lore Foundation Museum, St. Spyridon Church, and the archaeological museum. The most picturesque avenue is Vasileos Konstantinou; the more-commercial Amalias is lined with shops. Westward you'll find the Church of the Virgin Mary's Birth, an elaborate post-Byzantine structure. Continuing north, you come to quayside and Philhellenes Square and St. Nicholas Church.

From St. Nicholas westward along the quayside (called Akti Miaouli) is an unbroken chain of restaurants, most just average, and, farther along, pastry shops, which are better and especially pleasant in the afternoon for postcard-writing, an iced coffee or ouzo, and conversation. From the quay, you can embark on a boat trip out to the miniature fortress of the Bourtzi in the harbor. Or you can continue walking along the waterfront promenade to the Five Brothers bastion, and then follow the winding Kostouros street up to Psaromachalas, the picturesque fishermen's quarter. Return to the Five Brothers to continue on the promenade that follows the sea along the south side of the Nafplion peninsula, or, instead, go through the tunnel that looks like a James Bond movie set from the parking lot off Kostouros street and take the elevator to the Nafplia Palace hotel and the top of the Acronafplia fortress. The hotel bar is an excellent place to enjoy a sunset. Above all looms the

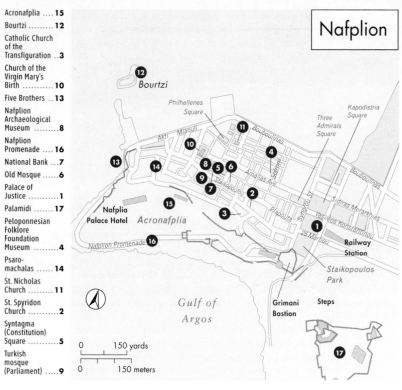

town's Venetian-era Palamidi fortress, another top sunset spot (when weekday hours permit).

TOP ATTRACTIONS

FAMILY

Fodor's Choice

★

Acronafplia. The Turks called this imposing hilltop of ruined fortifications "Its Kalé" (Inner Citadel). The heights are crowned with a series of castles: a Frankish one on the eastern end of the hill, a Byzantine one on the west, and a massive Castello del Torrione (or Toro for short), also at the eastern end, built by the Venetians around 1480. During the second Venetian occupation, the gates were strengthened and the huge Grimani bastion was added (1706) below the Toro. The Acronafplia is accessible from the west side via the elevator next to the Nafplia Palace hotel, which sits on the ruins of the Frankish fort, and from the east via Potamianou street, whose flights of steps ascend the hillside from St. Spyridon Square. Most of the remains of fortifications can be explored free of charge on overgrown paths that provide stupendous views over Nafplion and the sea.

Bourtzi. Nafplion's pocket-size fortress is a captivating presence on a speck of land in the middle of the harbor generously called St. Theodore's island. The Venetians built the Bourtzi (castle) as a single tower in 1471, and they enlarged it with a second tower and bastion when they recaptured Nafplion in 1686. Freedom fighters captured the

Bourtzi during the War of Independence in 1822 and used the island to bombard the Turks defending the town. The new Greek government retreated to the island in the unsettled times following the revolution; after 1865, the fortress was the residence of the town executioners, and from 1930 until 1970 it was run as a hotel. Boats leave on no fixed schedule from the eastern end of Akti Miaouli; the trip, including a chance to disembark at the Bourtzi, costs about €5. ⊠ *In harbor.*

Nafplion Archaeological Museum. The thick walls of this red-stone building, built in 1713 to serve as the storehouse for the Venetian fleet, ensure the coolest interior in town. The museum houses artifacts from such nearby sites as Mycenae, Tiryns, Asine, and Dendra; the loot from Mycenaean tombs is especially rich and includes wonderful masks and a suit of armor. ⊠ *West side of Syntagma Sq.* ☎ *27520/27502* ⊕ *www. culture.gr* 🖼 *€3* ⊙ *Tues.–Sun. 8–3.*

Fodor'sChoice **Nafplion Promenade.** A seaside promenade skirts the Nafplion penin-
★ sula, paved with reddish flagstones and opening every so often to terraces planted with a few rosebushes and olive and cedar trees. Along the south side of the peninsula, the promenade runs midway along a cliff—it's 100 feet up to Acronafplia, 50 feet down to the sea—and leads to Arvanitia beach, a lovely place for a dip. Here and there a flight of steps goes down to the rocky shore below. (Be careful if you go swimming here, because the rocks are covered with sea urchins, which look like purple-and-black porcupines and whose quills can inflict a painful wound.)

Palamidi. Whether in harsh sunlight or under floodlights at night, this mighty fortress is a beautiful sight, with red-stone bastions and flights of steps that zigzag down the 700-foot-tall cliff face. You can drive up the less-precipitous eastern slope, but if you are in reasonable shape and it isn't too hot, try climbing the stairs. Most guidebooks will tell you there are 999 of them, but 892 is closer to the mark. From the top you can look down on the Old Town, the bay of Argos, and the entire Argive plain.

Built in 1711–14, the Palamidi comprises three forts and a series of freestanding and connecting defensive walls. The name is taken from the son of Poseidon, Palamedes, who, legend has it, invented dice, arithmetic, and some of the Greek alphabet. Sculpted in gray stone, the lion of St. Mark looks outward from the gates. The Palamidi fell to the Turks in 1715 after only eight days, allegedly because the Venetians assumed the fortress was impregnable and saw no need to garrison a large number of troops within the walls. After the war, the fortress was used as a prison; its inmates included the revolutionary war hero Theodore Kolokotronis, whose cell is indicated by a sign. ⊠ *Above town* ☎ *27520/28036* 🖼 *€3* ⊙ *Apr.–Oct., daily 8–8; Nov.–Mar., daily 8–3.*

Peloponnesian Folklore Foundation Museum. This exemplary small museum focuses on textiles and displays outstanding costumes, handicrafts, and household furnishings. Many of the exhibits are precious heirlooms that have been donated by Peloponnesian families, and several rooms are painstaking re-creations of 19th-century Nafplion homes. The gift shop has some fascinating books and a good selection of high-quality

10

jewelry and handicrafts, such as weavings, kilims, and collector's items such as *roka* (spindles) and wooden *koboloi* (worry beads). ⊠ *Vasileos Alexandrou 1, on block immediately north of Amalias, going up Sofroni* ☎ *27520/28947* ⊕ *www.pli.gr* 🖃 *€2* ☉ *Museum: Wed.–Mon. 9–2:30; shop: Mon. and Wed.–Sat. 9–3 and 5:30–8:30.*

Syntagma (Constitution) Square. The center of the Old Town is one of Greece's prettiest *platias* (squares), distinguished by glistening, multi-color marble paving bordered by neoclassical and Ottoman-style buildings. In summer the restaurants and patisseries on the square—a focal point of Nafpliote life—are boisterous with the shouts and laughter of children and filled with diners well into the evening. ⊠ *Along Amalias and Vasileos Konstantinou.*

WORTH NOTING

Ayia Panagitsa (*All Holy Chapel*). While following the seaside promenade, before you reach the very tip of the peninsula (marked by a ship's beacon), there is a little shrine at the foot of a path leading up toward the Acronafplia walls above. The tiny church of the Little Virgin Mary, or Ayia Panagitsa, hugs the cliff on a small terrace and is decorated with icons. During the Turkish occupation the church hid one of Greece's secret schools. ⊠ *End of promenade.*

Ayios Apostoli (*Chapel of the Apostles*). This pretty, miniature white-washed chapel, perched near the top of a quiet neighborhood, has six small springs that trickle out of the side of Acronafplia. ⊠ *Off parking lot of Psaromachalas.*

Catholic Church of the Transfiguration. In the 19th century King Otho returned this 13th-century Venetian-built church, converted to a mosque under the Turks, to Nafplion's Catholics. The church is best known for the wooden arch erected inside the doorway in 1841, with the names carved on it of philhellenes (Greek admirers) who died during the War of Independence (Lord Byron is number 10). A mihrab (Muslim prayer recess) behind the altar and the amputated stub of a minaret are evidence of the church's use as a mosque. The church has a small museum and an underground crypt in which can be found sculptural work commemorating the defeat of the Turks at the hands of the Greeks and philhellenes. ⊠ *Zigomala, 2 blocks south of St. Spyridon.*

Church of the Virgin Mary's Birth. This post-Byzantine three-aisle basilica is by tradition linked to St. Anastasios, a Nafpliote painter. Anastasios was supposedly engaged to a local girl, but he abandoned her because she was immoral. Becoming despondent as a result of spells cast over him by her relatives, he converted to Islam. When the spell wore off, he cried out, "I was a Christian, I am a Christian, and I shall die a Christian." An Ottoman judge ordered that he be beheaded, but a Turkish mob stabbed Anastasios to death. His corpse was then allegedly hanged on an ancient olive tree that rises next to the church and that never again bore fruit. The basilica was the main Orthodox church during the Venetian occupation and has an elaborate wooden reredos carved in 1870. ⊠ *West of Syntagma Sq.*

Five Brothers. Above the harbor at the western edge of town are the ruins of a fortification known as the Five Brothers, the only remaining part of the lower wall built around Nafplion in 1502. The name comes from the five guns placed here by the Venetians around 1690; they remain in place, all bearing the winged lion of St. Mark. ⊠ *Near promontory of peninsula.*

NEED A
BREAK?

Beyond the Five Brothers, a few pleasant cafés and bars line the seaside promenade that follows the southern edge of the peninsula. These are good places to sit with an ouzo and watch the sun set behind the mountains across the gulf; some establishments have created little swimming areas alongside the tables, so it's not unusual to see patrons bobbing around in the water.

National Bank. This contemporary structure displays an amusing union of Mycenaean and modern Greek architectural elements fashioned with concrete. Take a look at the sculptures of a winged lion of St. Mark (which graced the main gate in the city's landward wall, long since demolished) and of Kalliope Papalexopoulou (a leader of the revolt against King Otho), whose house once stood in the vicinity. They're in the square next to the bank. ⊠ *South of Syntagma Sq.*

Old Mosque. This venerable mosque near the southeast corner of Syntagma Square has been put to various purposes since Nafplion was liberated from the Turks: as a school, a courthouse, municipal offices, and a movie theater. (The writer Henry Miller, who did not care for Nafplion, felt that the use of the building as a movie theater was an example of the city's crassness.) The landmark occasionally hosts temporary exhibits. ⊠ *Syntagma Sq.*

Palace of Justice. The gracelessness of this building is magnified by its large size, but the effect is softened by an adjacent **square** with a statue honoring Nikitaras the Turk-Eater, who directed the siege of Nafplion during the War of Independence. ⊠ *Syngrou, 2 blocks down from Kapodistria Sq.*

NEED A
BREAK?

✕ **Antica Gelateria di Roma.** The traditional Italian gelato (ice cream) at the Antica Gelateria di Roma makes a tempting excuse for a break. 💲 *Average main: €3* ⊠ *Farmakopoulou 3* ☎ *27520/23520.*

10

Psaromachalas. The fishermen's quarter is a small district of narrow lanes running between cramped little houses that huddle beneath the walls of Acronafplia. The old houses, painted in brownish yellow, green, and salmon red, are embellished with additions and overhangs in eclectic styles. The walk is enjoyable, but keep a low profile to respect the privacy of the locals. ⊠ *Along Kostouros.*

St. Nicholas Church. This church near the waterfront was built in 1713 for sailors by Augustine Sagredo, the prefect of the Venetian fleet, and is furnished with a Venetian reredos and pulpit, and a chandelier from Odessa. ⊠ *Off Philhellenes Sq.*

St. Spyridon Church. This one-aisle basilica with a dome (1702) has a special place in Greek history: it was in its doorway that the statesman Ioannis Kapodistrias, the first president of an independent Greece, was assassinated in 1831 by the Mavromichalis brothers from the Mani, the

Enjoy a boat ride out to the Bourzi fortress, built by 15th-century Venetians to protect the beautiful port town of Nafplion.

outcome of a long-running vendetta. The mark of the bullet can be seen next to the Venetian portal. On the south side of the square, opposite St. Spyridon, are two of the four Turkish fountains that remain in Nafplion. A third is a short distance east on Kapodistria street, at the steps that constitute the upper reaches of Tertsetou street. ⊠ *St. Spirdonas Sq.*

Turkish mosque. Now known as the Vouleftiko (Parliament), this former mosque was where the Greek National Assembly held its first meetings. The mosque is built of carefully dressed gray stones, and legend has it that the lintel stone from the Treasury of Atreus was used in the construction of the large, square-domed prayer hall. ⊠ *Staikopoulou, next to Nafplion Archaeological Museum and behind National Bank.*

BEACHES

Arvanitia beach. This in-town swimming spot is not really a beach but a seaside perch of smooth rocks, pebbled shoreline, and concrete platforms, all backed by fragrant pines. This is a good place for a morning wakeup swim or a refreshing plunge after a day of sightseeing. At times the popular and well-maintained spot, with a pleasant beach bar, seems as sociable as the town square, and don't be surprised to hear other bathers gossiping and exchanging recipes as they bob in the delightful water. You can walk to Arvanitia by following the seaside promenade that hugs the cliffs beneath the Acronafplia south of town. **Amenities:** food and drink; parking (no fee); showers; toilets. **Best for:** swimming. ⊠ *South side of town, below Acronafplia.*

FAMILY **Karathona.** The closest sandy beach to Nafplion, Karathona is easy to reach by road (just keep following 25 Maritou street) or a pleasant walk first along the seaside promenade and then a dirt track (you can also get there by bus in summer). The pine-backed sands are favored by Greek families with picnic baskets, and this is an ideal spot for kids, since the waters remain shallow far out into the bay. Sun loungers and umbrellas are available (about €5), though a pine grove behind the sands provides plenty of nice shady spots. Several tavernas back the beach. **Amenities:** food and drink; parking (no fee); showers; toilets; water sports. **Best for:** swimming; walking. ⊠ *About 3 km (2 miles) south of town.*

Psili Ammos. The resort town of Tolo, 12 km (7½ miles) south of Nafplion, is a short bus ride (€1.20) from Nafplion's main station or a reasonably priced taxi ride (about €17); beware, though, that in the warm months the beach of fine sand is packed solid with sunburned northern Europeans and abuzz with every water sport and beach activity ever invented, from taking in the sun in the endless rows of loungers to volleyball. A long parade of bars and tavernas backs the beach, and some tables are set right on the sands. **Amenities:** food and drink; parking (fee); showers; toilets; water sports. **Best for:** partiers; swimming; walking. ⊠ *Tolo road, Tolo.*

WHERE TO EAT

It's a Nafplion tradition to have dessert at one of the cafés on Syntagma Square or the *zacharoplasteia* (pastry shops) on the harbor. Lingering over an elaborate ice-cream concoction or after-dinner drink is a memorable way to wrap up an evening.

$ ✕ **Arapakos.** Nafplion locals are demanding when it comes to seafood,
SEAFOOD so it's a credit to this attractive, nautical-themed taverna on the waterfront that locals pack in to enjoy expert dishes made from fresh catches. The kitchen sends out such traditional accompaniments as a memorable *taramasalata* (fish roe dip) and *tzatziki* (yogurt garlic dip), as well as a few meat dishes, including exquisitely seasoned and grilled lamb chops. Ⓢ *Average main: €15* ⊠ *Bouboulinas 81* ☎ *27520/27675* ⊕ *www.arapakos.gr* ☉ *Closed Tues. in winter.*

$ ✕ **Paleo Archontiko.** Seating here is in the ground floor of an old stone
GREEK mansion or on the narrow street in front. Tassos Koliopoulos and his wife, Anya, oversee the ever-changing menu, which highlights good home cooking, such as beef *stifado* (stew slow-cooked with tomatoes and small onions) and *krassato* (rooster in wine sauce). It's not unusual for a musician to wander by and serenade the diners, another reason the place is wildly popular with locals (it's best to reserve on weekends and in high season). Ⓢ *Average main: €10* ⊠ *Siokou 7, at Ipsilantou* ☎ *27520/22449* ⌖ *Reservations essential* ☉ *No lunch weekdays and in winter.*

$ ✕ **Ta Fanaria.** Staikopoulou street is one long outdoor dining room,
GREEK with dozens of tourist-oriented tavernas serving night and day, and this popular place is leagues ahead of its neighbors. The kitchen concentrates on excellent versions of such staples as *ladera* (vegetables cooked in olive oil), charcoal-grilled lamb ribs, and *imam bayilda* (eggplant stuffed with onions), and serves them beneath a bougainvillea arbor in a quiet lane next to the restaurant. Ⓢ *Average main: €7* ⊠ *Staikopoulou 13* ☎ *27520/27141* ⊕ *www.fanaria.gr.*

$ ✕ **Taverna Byzantio.** Charcoal-grilled meats are the specialty in this snug,
GREEK FUSION high-ceilinged old room tucked away in the backstreets off the harbor.

10

The cuisine strays from Greece into the neighboring Balkans, with some wonderful schnitzels, cheese-filled pork roast, and other dishes that provide a nice change from a steady diet of Greek fare. $ *Average main: €10 ⊠ Alexandrou 15 ☎ 27520/21631 ⊕ www.taverna-byzantio. gr ⊟ No credit cards.*

WHERE TO STAY

$ **Aetoma.** A 19th-century neoclassical mansion on a quiet square has
B&B/INN been delightfully transformed, with extremely comfortable guest rooms and alluring public spaces; each room has a small balcony from which to enjoy the comings and goings below and the sight of the Palamidi above. **Pros:** friendly, attentive service; extremely well maintained; excellent bathrooms and showers; free parking nearby. **Cons:** stairs may pose an obstacle for some travelers. $ *Rooms from: €75 ⊠ Spiridomas Sq. ☎ 27520/27373 ⊕ www.nafplionhotel.gr ⧖ Breakfast.*

$$ **Amphityron.** Sea views fill every window in the airy, stylish, and con-
HOTEL temporary guest rooms here, all of which open to teakwood decks— though the old city is just a few steps away from this boutique hotel, you may feel like you're in the middle of the sea on a ship, and a pretty swanky one at that. **Pros:** at the edge of the old city and convenient to sights; extremely comfortable rooms; sea views. **Cons:** food and drink is expensive. $ *Rooms from: €170 ⊠ Spiliadou ☎ 27520/70700 ⊕ www. amphitryon.gr ⧖ Breakfast.*

$ **Byron.** A great deal of charm prevails here, from the simply but taste-
HOTEL fully decorated rooms, with Turkish carpets and the odd sloping ceiling, to the outdoor patio set atop an old Turkish hammam; the location at the top of the Old Town, up the street from the church of Ayiou Spiridona, is delightful. **Pros:** old-fashioned atmosphere; lovely patio; tucked away in the heart of Old Town; views of town and hilltop fortress. **Cons:** some rooms are cramped; views from some are limited; no public lounge; backstreet location can make for a trek with luggage (you might want to call ahead and ask for directions for the nearest parking and the easiest way to reach the hotel on foot). $ *Rooms from: €50 ⊠ Platonos 16, Kapodistria Sq. ☎ 27520/22351 ⊕ www.byronhotel. gr ⧖ No meals.*

$ **Hotel Latini.** This handsomely restored old house, just off the water-
B&B/INN front in the center of town, feels like a well-appointed private home,
Fodor's Choice and the extremely comfortable guest rooms are graciously appointed
★ and have sparkling bathrooms; all have views of the bay or a palm-filled square. **Pros:** convenient location in the Old Town near the port and parking; pleasing decor; comfortable, homelike atmosphere. **Cons:** no elevator. $ *Rooms from: €50 ⊠ Othonos 47 ☎ 27520/96470 ⊕ www. latinihotel.gr ⧖ Breakfast.*

$ **Hotel Perivoli.** Surrounded by orange groves, this hilltop retreat is just
HOTEL a few minutes outside Nafplion but provides a resortlike getaway, with
FAMILY handsome, contemporary-style rooms and large terraces overlooking
Fodor's Choice a shimmering pool and, in the near distance, the gulf of Argos. **Pros:**
★ attractive; attentive service; excellent food; one of the few Nafplion hotels with a pool. **Cons:** only reachable by car. $ *Rooms from: €110 ⊠ Pirgiotika, 8 km (5 miles) east of Nafplion ☎ 27520/47905 ⊕ hotel-perivoli.com ⧖ Breakfast.*

$ ⬚ **King Othon I.** This gracious neoclassical mansion has decorative
B&B/INN   rosette ceilings and a curving wooden staircase leading to high-ceilinged
rooms that are pleasantly decorated in a turn-of-the-20th-century style.
Pros: historic character; beautiful garden; excellent location near the
harbor. **Cons:** some rooms are small; bathrooms tend to be cramped.
Ⓢ *Rooms from: €70* ⊠ *Farmakopoulou 4* ☎ *27520/27585* ⵔ⃥ *Breakfast.*

SPORTS AND THE OUTDOORS

Captain Aris. It's easy to find Captain Aris, who, when not at sea with
an excursion, is on his deck overlooking the comings and goings on
Nafplion's seaside promenade. The captain offers daily excursions and
sailing instruction in the gulf of Argos, with a meal and several stops
for swimming included. A trip aboard his sleek sailboat is about €80
per person. ⊠ *Nafplion harbor* ☎ *69443/53200* ⊕ *www.captainaris.gr.*

NIGHTLIFE

Nafplia Palace Bar. An elevator whisks you from the Old Town up to
the extensive grounds of this rather neglected hotel perched high above
Nafplion on the ruins of the Frankish fortification atop Acronafplia.
At first glance, the 1970s-era public spaces tend to be cavernous and
austere, but the delightful pine-scented terrace hanging high above the
town and bay is a prime spot for a sunset cocktail. ⊠ *Nafplia Palace,
Acronafplia* ☎ *27520/70800.*

SHOPPING

Shopping in Nafplion is pleasant business, with a nice array of wares
filling attractive shops tucked into old houses on shady lanes. Many
shops sell clothing and decorative items geared to well-heeled Athenians
who visit Nafplion for a day or weekend, while others specialize in some
distinctly Greek goods.

Agynthes. Handwoven and naturally dyed woolens, cotton, and silks
await your own handicraft, and some have been fashioned into chic
scarves and other apparel. ⊠ *Siokou 10* ☎ *27520/21704.*

Helios. A distinctive line of stylish bric-a-brac for the home runs along
the lines of brass lanterns and candlesticks. ⊠ *Siokou 4* ☎ *27520/22329.*

10

Karonis. This family-run shop has dispensed fine wines, ouzo, and other
spirits since 1869 and offers tastings and a great deal of knowledge
about local vineyards. ⊠ *Amalias 5* ☎ *27520/24446.*

Komboloi Museum. A shop on the ground floor of this museum in an
old home sells antique and new worry beads and attractive beaded key
chains. The museum's exhibits of historic worry beads are fascinating
and provide a little insight into the national male pasttime of fiddling
with a string of them. ⊠ *Staikopoulou 25* ☎ *27520/21618* ⊕ *www.
komboloi.gr* ⬚ *Museum €2.*

Odyssey. Perched on one side of Syntagma Square, this packed little shop
is the best place in Nafplion for newspapers and books in English; the
owners are very helpful if you need advice or directions. ⊠ *Syntagma
Sq.* ☎ *27520/23430.*

Peloponnesian Folklore Foundation Museum Shop. This enticing shop on
the ground floor of the excellent museum stocks an appealing array of

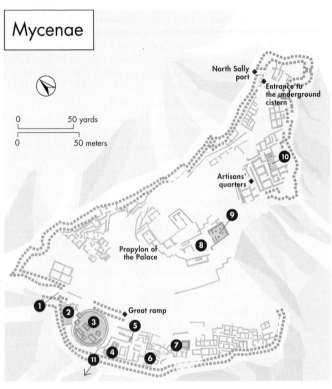

merchandise that includes jewelry, candlesticks, and other gift items.
⊠ *Vasileos Alexandrou 1* ☎ *27520/28947.*

MYCENAE ΜΥΚΗΝΕΣ

21 km (13 miles) north of Nafplion.

The ancient citadel of Mycenae, which Homer wrote was "rich in gold
and once ruled much of the Mediterranean world," stands on a low
hill, wedged between sheer, lofty peaks on the edge of two deep ravines.
The gloomy, stony ruins are hauntingly suggestive of what becomes of
might and power.

GETTING HERE AND AROUND

Once in Nafplion, you can reach Mycenae and other nearby ancient
sights via a decent local bus network; buses leave from Nafplion's Kapodistria Square. The small office is often staffed by an English speaker,
and times are usually also posted at the Municipal Tourist Office at
Martiou 25 (open only mornings and evenings and, curiously, often
staffed with only non-English speakers).

CLOSE UP

The House of Atreus

Mycenae was founded by Perseus, son of Zeus and Danae, and the Perseid dynasty provided many of its rulers. After the last of them, Eurystheus (famous for the labors he imposed on Hercules), the Mycenaeans chose Atreus, son of Pelops and Hippodamia, as their ruler. But Atreus hated his brother, Thyestes, so much that he had his children killed and served them to their father at a feast, thereby incurring the wrath of the gods. Thyestes pronounced a fearful curse on Atreus and his progeny.

Menelaus, one son of Atreus, was married to the beautiful Helen and ruled her lands. It was this Helen who was abducted by Paris, beginning the Trojan War. Atreus's heir, the renowned and energetic Agamemnon, was murdered on his return from the Trojan War by his wife, Clytemnestra, and her lover, Aegisthus (Thyestes's surviving son). Also murdered by the pair was Agamemnon's concubine, Cassandra, the mournful prophetess whom Agamemnon had brought back with him.

Orestes and his sister Electra, the children of Agamemnon, took revenge for the murder of their father, and Orestes became king of Mycenae. Another daughter of Agamemnon, Iphigenia, was brought to be sacrificed because someone—Agamemnon or one of the men in the forces of Menelaus—had offended the goddess Artemis by bragging about his hunting skills or killing a sacred animal. Various versions of Iphigenia's fate exist. During the rule of Orestes's son, Tisamenus, the descendants of Hercules returned and claimed their birthright by force, thus satisfying the wrath of the gods and the curse of Atreus.

The works of Homer and the classical plays of Aeschylus, Sophocles, and Euripides are good sources for anyone who wants to delve further into the saga of this tragic family.

EXPLORING

Fodor's Choice ★ **Mycenae.** The gloomy, gray ruins are hardly distinguishable from the rock beneath; it's hard to believe that this kingdom was once so powerful that it ruled a large portion of the Mediterranean world, from 1500 BC to 1100 BC. The major archaeological artifacts from the dig are now in the National Archaeological Museum in Athens, so seeing those first will add to your appreciation of the ruined city. The most famous object from the treasure found here is the so-called Death Mask of Agamemnon, a golden mask that 19th-century archaeologist Heinrich Schliemann found in the last grave he excavated at Mycenae. He was ecstatic, convinced this was the mask of the king of Homeric legend who launched the Trojan War with his brother, Menelaus—but it is now known that this is impossible, since the mask dates from an earlier period. The Archaeological Museum in Nafplion also houses artifacts from this once-great city.

In 1841, soon after the establishment of the Greek state, the Archaeological Society began excavations of the **ancient citadel,** and in 1874 Heinrich Schliemann began to work at the site.

10

Haunted by the spirits of Agamemnon and Clytemnestra, the royal graves of Mycenae make it one of the most brooding and memorable archaeological sites in Greece.

Today the citadel is entered from the northwest through the famous **Lion Gate**. The triangle above the lintel depicts in relief two lions, whose heads, probably of steatite, are now missing. They stand facing each other, their forepaws resting on a high pedestal representing an altar, above which stands a pillar ending in a uniquely shaped capital and abacus. Above the abacus are four sculptured discs, interpreted as representing the ends of beams that supported a roof. The gate was closed by a double wooden door sheathed in bronze. The two halves were secured by a wooden bar, which rested in cuttings in the jambs, still visible. The holes for the pivots on which it swung can still be seen in both sill and lintel.

Inside on the right stands the **Granary**, so named for the many *pithoi* (clay storage vessels) that were found inside the building, holding carbonized wheat grains.

Beyond the granary is the grave circle, made up of six **stone slabs**, encircled by a row of upright stone slabs interrupted on the northern side by the entrance. Above each grave stood a vertical stone stele. The "grave goods" buried with the dead were personal belongings including gold face masks, gold cups and jewelry, bronze swords with ivory hilts, and daggers with gold inlay, now in the National Archaeological Museum of Athens. South of the stone slabs lie the remains of the **House of the Warrior Vase**, the **Ramp House**, the **Cult Center**, and others; farther south is the **House of Tsountas** of Mycenae. The palace complex covers the summit of the hill and occupies a series of terraces; people entered through a monumental gateway in the northwest side and, proceeding to the right, beyond it, came to the **Great Courtyard** of the palace. The ground was originally covered by a plaster coating above which was a layer of painted and decorated stucco. East of the Great Courtyard is the **throne room**, which had four columns supporting the roof (the bases are still visible) and a circular hearth in the center. Remains of an **Archaic temple** and a **Hellenistic temple** can be seen north of the palace, and to the east on the right, on a lower level, are the **workshops** of the artists and craftsmen employed by the king. On the same level, adjoining the workshops to the east, is the **House of the Columns**, with a row of columns surrounding its central court. The remaining section of the east wall consists of

an addition made in around 1250 BC to ensure free communication from the citadel with the subterranean reservoir cut at the same time. ✉ *9 km (5½ miles) north of Argos* ☎ *27510/76585* ⊕ *www.culture.gr* 🎟 *Combined ticket with Treasury of Atreus and Mycenae Archaeological Museum €8* ⊗ *Apr.–Oct., daily 8–8; Nov.–Mar., daily 8–3.*

Treasury of Atreus. On the hill of Panagitsa, on the left along the road that runs to the citadel, lies this most imposing example of Mycenaean architecture. The construction of this huge *tholos* (or beehive tomb) took place around 1250 BC, contemporary with that of the Lion Gate, during the last century of Mycenaean prominence. Like other tholos tombs, it consists of a passageway cut into the hillside that was built of huge squared stones. The passage leads into a vast domed chamber. The facade of the entrance had applied decoration, but only small fragments have been preserved, and traces of bronze nails suggest that similar decoration once existed inside. The tomb was found empty, already robbed in antiquity, but it must at one time have contained rich and valuable grave goods. Pausanias wrote that the ancients considered this to be the Tomb of Agamemnon, and the Treasury is still often referred to as such. ✉ *Across from citadel of Mycenae* ☎ *27510/76585* ⊕ *www. culture.gr* 🎟 *Combined ticket with Mycenae and Mycenae Archaeological Museum €8* ⊗ *Apr.–Oct., daily 8–8; Nov.–Mar., daily 8–3.*

10

WHERE TO EAT

$ ✕ **To Mykinaiko.** At this pleasant, family-run restaurant in the modern
GREEK village, where summer seating is on the front terrace, always ask what has been cooked up as specials that day. You might try *lachanodolmades* (cabbage rolls) in a tart egg-lemon sauce, *papoutsakia* (eggplant "shoes" filled with tomatoes and garlicky ground beef, topped with béchamel), or spaghetti embellished only with tomato-meat sauce and topped with local *kefalograviera* cheese. Sample the barrel wine from the surrounding Nemea vineyards, especially the potent dark red, known to

the locals as the Blood of Hercules. $ *Average main: €8* ⊠ *Main road* ☎ *27510/76724.*

ANCIENT NEMEA ΑΡΧΑΙΑ ΝΕΜΕΑ

18 km (11 miles) north of Mycenae.

This quiet little town, surrounded by undulating vineyards, was once as famous as Olympia, site of biennial games that attracted athletes from throughout ancient Greece.

Ancient Nemea. The ancient storytellers proclaimed that it was here Hercules performed the first of the Twelve Labors set by the king of Argos in penance for killing his own children—he slew the ferocious Nemean lion living in a nearby cave. Historians are interested in Ancient Nemea as the site of a sanctuary of Zeus and the home of the biennial Nemean games, a Panhellenic competition like those at Isthmia, Delphi, and Olympia (today there is a society dedicated to reviving the games).

The main monuments at the site are the **temple of Zeus** (built about 330 BC to replace a 6th-century BC structure), the **stadium,** and an **early Christian basilica** of the 5th to 6th centuries AD. Several columns of the temple still stand. An extraordinary feature of the stadium, which dates to the last quarter of the 4th century BC, is its vaulted tunnel and entranceway. The evidence indicates that the use of the arch in building may have been brought back from India with Alexander (arches were previously believed to be a Roman invention). A spacious **museum** displays finds from the site, including pieces of athletic gear and coins of various city-states and rulers. ■**TIP➔** Around Nemea, keep an eye out for roadside stands where local growers sell the famous red Nemean wine of this region. ⊠ *North of E65 near modern village of Nemea* ☎ *27460/22739* ⊕ *odysseus.culture.gr* ▨ *Site and museum €7* ☉ *Daily 8–3.*

ARCADIA TO OLYMPIA
ΑΡΚΑΔΙΑ ΠΡΟΣ ΟΛΥΜΠΙΑ

In the relatively remote reaches of the Southern Peloponnese, ungainly yet amiable towns like Tripoli and Sparta are set amid olive groves, rugged mountains, dizzying gorges, and languorous beaches. Stone towns—like beautiful Stemnitsa and Dimitsana—and the remote Temple of Apollo in Bassae cling to the rugged hillsides of mountain ranges. Ancient ruins and historic towns and monuments pervade the landscape. Despite the waves of invaders over the centuries—Franks, Venetians, and Turks—this land is considered the distillation of all that is Greek, with its indulged idiosyncrasy, intractable autonomy, and appreciation of simple pleasures.

Arcadians are believed to be among the oldest inhabitants of the Peloponnese; this group of tribes first united when they entered the Trojan War. They later founded the powerful Arcadian League, but after Corinth fell to Rome in 146 BC, the region slipped into decline. When the Goths invaded in AD 395, Arcadia was almost entirely deserted.

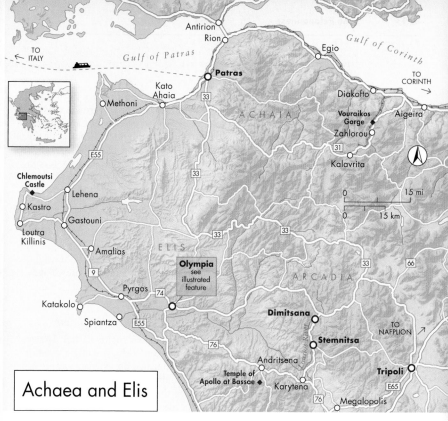

Achaea and Elis

Several centuries later the Franks conquered the area and built many castles; they were succeeded by the Byzantines and then the Turks, who ruled until the War of Independence.

No conqueror ever really dominated the Arcadians. Even when Tripoli was the Turks' administrative center, the mountain villagers lived much as they pleased, maintaining secret schools to preserve the rudiments of Greek language and religion and harassing the Turks in roaming bands. Forested mountainsides and valley farms still lend themselves to a decidedly rural way of life, and the very word "arcadia" has come to suggest the sorts of pastoral pleasures you will encounter here.

The province of Elis, farther to the south, is even more bucolic and peaceful. This is a land of hills green with forests and vegetation, and it is not surprising that the Greeks chose this region as the place in which to hold the Olympic Games. Crowning this region is the fabled archaeological site of Olympia, one of the most visited places in Greece.

TRIPOLI ΤΡΙΠΟΛΗ

150 km (93 miles) southwest of Athens, 70 km (43 miles) southwest of Corinth.

History, along with the practicalities of the road network in this part of Greece, makes it very likely that you'll at least pass through the outskirts of Tripoli when you're in the area. In the days of the Ottoman Empire, this crossroads was the capital of the Turkish pasha of the Peloponnese, and during the War of Independence it was the first target of Greek revolutionaries. They captured it in 1821 after a six-month siege, but the town went back and forth between the warring sides until 1827, when Ibrahim Pasha's retreating troops burned it to the ground.

Tripoli is a workaday town with few attractions to keep you here, although if you do hang around, you'll get an eyeful of Greek life. Its most attractive feature is the mountain scenery, with attendant hillside villages, that surrounds it; you will soon understand why this region is nicknamed the Switzerland of Greece. Unless you run out of daylight, you'll probably want to move on from Tripoli to one of these villages.

PATRAS ΠΑΤΡΑ

5 km (3 miles) west of Rion, 135 km (84 miles) west of Corinth.

Patras is the third-largest city in Greece and a major harbor. Unless you come to town to catch a ferry to Italy or Corfu, you might want to zoom right by. The municipality has launched an extensive improvement plan, paving the harbor roads and creating pedestrian zones on inner-city shopping streets. Even so, earthquakes and mindless development have laid waste to most of the elegant European-style buildings that earned Patras the nickname "Little Paris of Greece" in the 19th and early 20th centuries.

You'll pass through this city if, as many European travelers do, you arrive on a boat from Italy, or when coming to the Peloponnese from Corfu and other Ionian islands. If you're coming from Athens, you can arrive by car on the toll-road network, south to Corinth and from there west to Patras, for a total journey time of about three hours. Take note, though, that parts of the Corinth–Patras stretch, always under construction, are two lanes used as four lanes by impatient drivers. This creates one of the most dangerous stretches of roadway in Greece (and that's saying quite a bit).

GETTING HERE AND AROUND

Bus service between Athens and Patras is excellent, with buses running about every half hour to 45 minutes throughout the day. The bus station in Patras is near the port at Othonos-Amalias and is currently being reconstructed. For detailed information, see Bus Travel in Travel Smart or ask at the station or tourist information offices for schedules and other guidance.

Within the next five years direct express-train service is expected to be in operation from Athens to Patras and then down the west coast of the Peloponnese. For more information, see Train Travel in Travel Smart

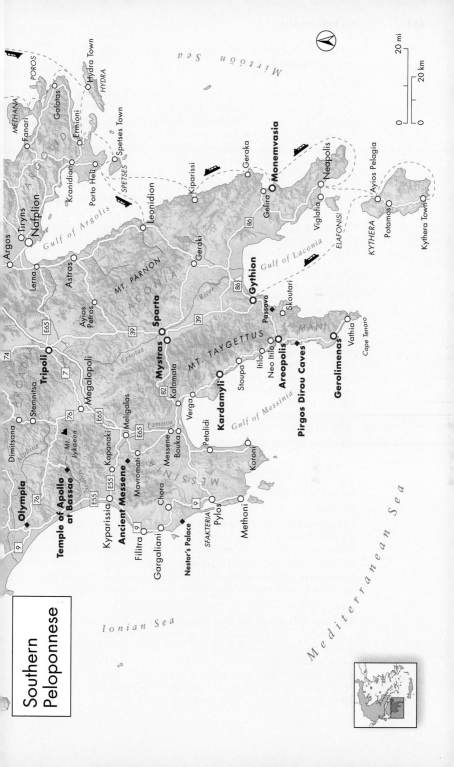

or check with a tourist office. Before the express train begins, you're better off taking the bus.

EXPLORING

Patras is Greece's major western port, and the city has the international, outward-looking feel common to port cities. The waterfront is pleasant enough. You'll find lots of mediocre restaurants, some decent hotels, the bus and train stations, and numerous travel agents (caveat emptor for those near the docks). Back from the waterfront, the town gradually rises along arcaded streets, which provide welcome shade and rain protection. Of the series of large platias, tree-shaded Queen Olga Square is the nicest. Patras is built on a grid system, and it is easy to find your way around. For a pleasant stroll, take Ayios Nikolaos street upward through the city until it comes to the long flight of steps leading to the Kastro, the medieval Venetian castle overlooking the harbor. The narrow lanes on the side of Ayios Nikolaos are whitewashed and lined with village-style houses, many of which are being restored.

Like all respectable Greek cities, Patras has an ancient history. Off the harbor in 429 BC, Corinthian and Athenian ships fought inconclusively, and in 279 BC the city helped repel an invasion of Celtic Galatians. Its acropolis was fortified under Justinian in the 6th century, and Patras withstood an attack by Slavs and Saracens in 805. Silk production, begun in the 7th century, brought renewed prosperity, but control passed successively to the Franks, the Venetians, and the Turks, until the War of Independence. Thomas Palaiologos, the last Byzantine to leave Patras before the Turks took over in 1458, carried an unusual prize with him—the skull of the apostle St. Andrew, which he gave to Pius II in exchange for an annuity. St. Andrew had been crucified in Patras and had been made the city's patron saint. In 1964 Pope Paul VI returned the head to Patras, and it now graces St. Andrew's Cathedral, seat of the Bishop of Patras.

DIMITSANA ΔΗΜΗΤΣΑΝΑ

40 km (25 miles) west of Tripoli, 40 km (25 miles) southwest of Olympia.

Leave your car at the entrance of this stone village stunningly set amid the Arcadian mountains and stroll the maze of narrow cobbled lanes. If you want to add some ancient history to your enjoyment of this romantic place, be advised that archaeologists found ruins of a cyclopean wall (irregular stones without mortar) and classical buildings near the town; the ruins belonged to the acropolis of Teuthis, an ancient city.

EXPLORING

Dimitsana Ecclesiastical Museum. Manuscripts, a 35,000-volume library, and other artifacts here are from surrounding churches, monasteries, and the School of Greek Letters that flourished in Dimitsana in the 19th century. The school educated Germanos, a bishop of Patras, and other young men who went on to become Greek scholars and church leaders. ⊠ *Off main square* ☏ *27950/31360* ⬙ *€1.50* ☾ *May–Sept., Fri.–Tues. 10–1:30 and 5–7; Oct.–Apr., weekends 9:30–1:30.*

CLOSE UP

A Little Night Music

Dance performances, accompanied by traditional music, are common in the region. In the *tsakonikos,* the dancers wheel tightly around each other and then swing into bizarre spirals; this dance resembles the sacred dance of Delos, first performed by Theseus to mime how he escaped from the Labyrinth. The popular *kalamatianos* is a circular dance from Kalamata. The *tsamikos,* from Roumeli in central Greece, is an exclusively male dance showcasing agility. You will see your fill of dancing at local festivals to celebrate a town or village's patron saint, usually in summer. Dancing is also part of a Greek wedding, and it's not entirely unlikely that you might attend one. The guest list usually includes the entire population of a village or section of town, and if you happen to be staying there at the time of a wedding, you may well be invited.

Dimitsana Town Library. The town library displays manuscripts, rare books, and memorabilia from the Greek revolutionary period, when Dimitsana was a center for revolutionary activity against the Turks. Many of the books were printed clandestinely, against Turkish law, in Greek. Also on display are household items, costumes, and other reminders of 19th-century life in Dimitsana. ✉ *Main Sq.* ☎ *27950/31219* 🎟 *Free* ⏲ *Apr.–Oct., weekdays 8–2, Sat. 8–noon.*

E2 Hiking Path. A leg of the European trail system passes through Dimitsana. You can follow the path south along the gorge of the river Lousios or east into the surrounding mountains. The trek south brings you to several small monasteries tucked into the walls of the gorge and the scanty ruins of the ancient city of Gortys.

Open Air Water Power Museum. A water mill, tannery, and gunpowder mill on the river Lousios below town provide displays and demonstrations that reveal why waterpower was the force behind the region's economy until the first part of the 20th century. Gunpowder mills like the one here operated up and down the river and helped supply the forces who successfully fought the Turks during the War of Independence in 1821. ✉ *Off main road, south of town* ☎ *27950/31630* 🌐 *odysseus.culture.gr* 🎟 *€3* ⏲ *Mar.–mid-Oct., daily 10–6; mid-Oct.–Feb., daily 10–5.*

10

WHERE TO STAY

$ HOTEL 🏨 **Hotel Dimitsana.** The lounges, restaurant, and rooms hang right over the deep gorge of the river Lousios, providing stunning views—and these vistas can be savored from guest rooms that are far more poshly decorated that you might expect in a mountain town. **Pros:** beautiful alpine setting; extremely comfortable accommodations. **Cons:** not as pleasant in winter, when rooms are expensive and hard to get and the place fills up with skiers. [$] *Rooms from: €85* ✉ *Main road, south end of town* ☎ *27950/31518 through 27950/31520* 🍴 *Breakfast.*

EN
ROUTE

The winding road between Dimitsana and Stemnitsa reveals extensive views over the forested rises and valleys of the Arcadian mountains. About halfway between the two villages you'll come to a widening in the road that's a perfect place to stop: A mountain spring supplies cool, refreshing water (make sure you have containers to fill), and a viewpoint overlooks miles of mountain scenery.

STEMNITSA ΣΤΕΜΝΙΤΣΑ

10 km (6 miles) south of Dimitsana.

Also called Ipsous, Stemnitsa is one of the most beautiful towns in southern Greece, wondrously perched 3,444 feet above sea level amid a forest of fir and chestnut trees. For centuries the stone village was one of the Balkans' best-known metalworking centers, and today a minuscule school is still staffed by local artisans. Above the lively square rises the bell tower of the church of Ayios Giorgios, and at the top of a nearby hill is the monument to fighters in the 1821 War of Independence against the Turks. Stemnitsa, in fact, claims to have been the capital of Greece for a few weeks in 1821, when it was the center for rebels who successfully routed the Turks. The views throughout the town are phenomenal, and at night the village lies beneath a canopy of bright stars.

Moni Ayiou Ioannitou. From the north side of town, a well-marked path leads through the mountains to the isolated monastery of Moni Ayiou Ioannitou, with a little chapel, covered in frescoes, that is generally open. From the monastery other paths lead through a beautiful, wooded valley to the banks of the river Lousios. Several other monasteries, closed to visitors, are nestled alongside the riverbank.

Stemnitsa Folklore Museum. This unusual collection devotes one floor to models of workshops for indigenous crafts such as candle-making and bell-casting; the other two floors house re-created traditional rooms and a charmingly haphazard collection of costumes, weapons, icons, and plates. ⊠ *Off main road* ☎ *27950/81252* ⊕ *www.culture.gr* ✉ *Free* ⊗ *Mar.–Jan., daily 8:30–3.*

OLYMPIA ΟΛΥΜΠΙΑ

112 km (69 miles) south of Patras, 85 km (53 miles) west of Stemnitsa.

Ancient Olympia, with the Sanctuary of Zeus, was famously the site of the ancient Olympic Games. Scenically located at the foot of the pine-covered Kronion hill and set in a valley near two rivers, today the ancient ruins are among the most popular attractions in Greece. Modern Olympia, an attractive mountain town surrounded by pleasant hilly countryside, has hotels and tavernas, convenient for visitors to the ancient site. *For the complete scoop on the ancient sight—one of the must-sees of any trip to Greece—see our special feature, "Ancient Olympia: Let the Games Begin!"*

GETTING HERE AND AROUND

From Athens, buses head to Olympia three times daily for a trip that takes about 6 hours; the trip sometimes requires a change in Pyrgos. The fare is about €15. From Patras, you can take one of the almost hourly

Nestled within the lofty Arcadian mountains, the stone village of Dimitsana offers amazing vistas over the valley of Megalopolis.

KTEL buses to Pyrgos, then change there for the short trip inland to Olympia; total trip time is about an hour and costs about €4.

In Pyrgos you can also hop aboard one of the trains that connect Katakolon, the cruise ship port, and Olympia. Trains run four times a day, but only when cruise ships are in port. The trip from Katakolon to Olympia with a stop in Pyrgos takes about 45 minutes and costs €10 round-trip. The website for Katalon Port has information on the train (*see Visitor Information*).

Travel directly from Athens to Olympia by car on a trip that lasts about 5 hours via toll roads to Corinth and Patras, then down the west coast to Olympia. Free parking is ample in Olympia, either on the street or in the lots near the entrance to the ancient site.

10

VISITOR INFORMATION

Contacts Katakolon Port Information ⊠ *Olympia* ⊕ *www.katakolon.org.* **Olympia Tourist Information** ⊠ *Praxitelous Kondili 75, Olympia* ☎ *26240/22262.*

EXPLORING

FAMILY **Ancient Olympia.** One of the most celebrated archaeological sites in Greece is located at the foot of the pine-covered Kronion hill and set in a valley where the Kladeos and Alpheios rivers join. Just as athletes from city-states throughout ancient Greece made the journey to compete in the ancient Olympics—the first sports competition—visitors from all over the world today make their way to the small modern Arcadian town. The Olympic Games, first staged around the 8th century BC, were played here in the stadium, hippodrome, and other venues for some 1,100 years. Today, the venerable ruins of these structures attest to the majesty and importance of the first Olympiads. Modern Olympia, an attractive mountain town surrounded by pleasant hilly countryside, has hotels and tavernas, convenient for visitors to the ancient site.

As famous as the Olympic Games were—and still are—Olympia was first and foremost a sacred place, a sanctuary honoring Zeus, king of the gods, and Hera, his wife and older sister. The sacred quarter was known as the Altis, or the Sacred Grove of Zeus, and was enclosed by a wall on three sides and the Kronion hill on the other. Inside the Altis were temples, altars, and 12 treasuries of various city-states.

> **FRANKS DOING IN THE PELOPONNESE**
>
> Franks, in the personages of itinerant French noblemen on their way to the Fourth Crusade, began settling in the Peloponnese in the early years of the 13th century. One of them, Geoffrey de Villehardouin, made landfall in Methoni and was enchanted by his surroundings. Meanwhile, his colleagues had sacked Constantinople, making it easy for Villehardouin and other nobles to take control of the Peloponnese, capturing such Byzantine strongholds as Mystras and Monemvasia.

To honor the cult of Zeus established at Olympia as early as the 10th century BC, altars were first constructed outdoors, among the pine forests that encroach upon the site. But around the turn of the 6th century BC, the earliest building at Olympia was constructed, the Temple of Hera, which originally honored Zeus and Hera jointly, until the Temple of Zeus was constructed around 470 BC. The Temple of Zeus was one of the finest temples in all of Greece. Thirteen columns flanked the sides, and its interior housed the most famous work of ancient Greece—a gold and ivory statue of Zeus. Earthquakes in 551 and 552 finished off the temple.

After the Treasuries, the Bouleuterion, and the Pelopeion were built, the 5th and 4th centuries BC—the Golden Age of the ancient games—saw a virtual building boom. The monumental Temple of Zeus, the Prytaneion, and the Metroon went up at this time. The enormous Leonidaion was built around 300 BC, and as the games continued to thrive, the Palaestra and Gymnasion were added to the complex.

The history of the Olympic Games is long and fabled. For almost 11 centuries, free-born Greeks from the various city-states gathered to participate in the games, held every four years in August or September. These games became so much a part of the culture that the four-year interval between the games became a standard unit of time, an Olympiad. An Olympic truce—the Ekecheiria—allowed safe passage for athletes from the different city-states traveling to the games, and participation in them meant allegiance to a "Panhellenic" ideal of a united Greece. The exact date of the first games is not known, but the first recorded event is a footrace, a *stade*, run in 776 BC. A longer race, a *diaulos*, was added in 724 BC, and wrestling and a pentathlon—consisting of the long jump, the javelin throw, the discus throw, a footrace, and wrestling—in 708 BC. Boxing and chariot racing were 7th-century BC additions, as was the *pankration,* a no-holds-barred match (broken limbs were frequent and strangulation sometimes the end)—Plato, the great philosopher, was a big wrestling fan. By the 5th century BC, the games featured nine events, held over four days, with the fifth day reserved for the ceremonies. Most of the participants were professional athletes, for whom winning a laurel wreath at Olympia ensured wealth and glory from the city-states that sponsored them.

Today's tranquil pine-forested valley at Olympia, set with weathered stones of peaceful dignity, belies the sweaty drama of the first sporting festivals. Stadium footraces run in the nude; *pankration* wrestling so violent today's Ultimate Fighting matches look tame; weeklong bacchanals—serviced by an army of prostitutes—held in the Olympic Village: Little wonder this ancient event is now called the "Woodstock of its day" by modern scholars (wrestlers, boxers, and discus-throwers being the rock stars of ancient Greece).

For today's sightseer, the ruins of many of Olympia's main structures are still visible. The **Altis** was the sacred quarter, also known as the Sacred Grove of Zeus. In the **Bouleuterion,** the seat of the organizers of the games, the Elean senate, athletes swore an oath of fair play. In the **Gymnasion,** athletes practiced for track and field events in an open field surrounded by porticoes. In the **Hippodrome,** horse and chariot races were run on a vast racecourse. The **House of Nero** was a lavish villa built for the emperor's visit to the games of AD 67, in which he competed. The **Leonidaion** was a luxurious hostel for distinguished visitors to the games; it later housed Roman governors. The **Metroon** was a small Doric temple dedicated to Rhea (also known as Cybele), Mother of the Gods. The **Nymphaion,** a semicircular reservoir, stored water from a spring to the east that was distributed throughout the site by a network of pipes. The **Palaestra** was a section of the gymnasium complex used for athletic training; athletes bathed and socialized in rooms around the square field. The **Pelopeion,** a shrine to Pelops, legendary king of the region now known as the Peloponnese, housed an altar in a sacred grove. **Pheidias's Workshop** was the studio of the great ancient sculptor famed for his enormous statue of Zeus, sculpted for the site's Temple of Zeus. The **Prytaneion** was a banquet room where magistrates feted the winners and a perpetual flame burned in the hearth. The **Stadium** held as many as 50,000 spectators, who crowded onto earthen embankments to watch running events. The starting and finishing lines are still in place. The **Temple of Hera,** one of the earliest monumental Greek temples, was built in the 7th century BC. The **Temple of Zeus,** a great temple and fine example of Doric architecture, housed Pheidias's enormous statue of the god, one of the seven wonders of the ancient world. The famous **Treasuries** were templelike buildings that housed valuables and equipment of 12 of the most powerful of the city-states competing in the games.

You'll need at least two hours to fully see the ruins and the Archaeological Museum of Olympia (to the north of the ancient site), and three or four hours would be better. ⊠ *Off Ethnikos Odos 74, ½ km (¼ mile) outside modern Olympia* ☎ *26240/22517* ⊕ *www.culture.gr* ✉ *€6,*

Continued on page 486

ANCIENT OLYMPIA
Let the Games Begin!

Discus-throwers, runners, and wrestlers were the rock stars of ancient Greece. Flush with the cults of beauty and physical strength, the Greeks transformed sports into a kind of religion of human vigor. While no one can trace the very beginnings of their sport mania, Greeks soon attained the heights of greatness at Olympia— the birthplace of the famed Olympic Games.

Olympia's tranquil pine-forested valley, set with weathered stones of peaceful dignity, belies the sweaty drama of the first sporting festivals. Stadium footraces run in the nude; pankration wrestling so violent that today's Ultimate Fighting matches look tame; week-long bacchanals—serviced by an army of pornoi and prostitutes—held in the Olympic Village: Little wonder this ancient event is now called the Woodstock of its day by modern scholars. Using mind over medal, today's traveler to Olympia can get an eye-opening glimpse into the ancient world.

FELLOWSHIP OF THE RINGS

For almost eleven centuries, free-born Greeks from the various city-states gathered to participate in the Olympic Games, held every four years in August or September at this town set at the foot of the tree-covered Kronion hill. These games became so much a part of the culture that the four-year interval between the games became a standard unit of time, an Olympiad. An Olympic truce—the Ekecheiria—allowed safe passage for athletes from the different city-states traveling to the games, and participation in them meant allegiance to a "pan-Hellenic" ideal of a united Greece.

The exact date of the first games is not known, but the first recorded event is a footrace, a *stade*, run in 776 BC. A longer race, a *diaulos*, was added in 724 BC, and wrestling and a pentathlon—consisting of the long jump, the javelin throw, the discus throw, a footrace, and wrestling—in 708 BC. Boxing and chariot racing were 7th-century BC additions, as was the *pankration*, a no-holds-barred match (broken limbs were frequent and strangulation sometimes the end)—Plato, the great philosopher, was a big wrestling fan.

Most of the participants were professional athletes, for whom winning a laurel wreath at Olympia ensured wealth and glory from the city-states that sponsored them. Bruce Jenner and Michael Jordan had nothing on these guys.

Large-scale building at Olympia began around the 6th century BC, with construction of a temple to Hera and Zeus. The 5th and 4th centuries BC, the Golden Age of the ancient games, saw a virtual building boom—the monumental Temple of Zeus, the Prytaneion, and the Metroon went up at this time.

THE HERCULES CONNECTION

Legend claims that Hercules founded Olympia and the games after he slew his wife and children, and in atonement for the crime, undertook twelve labors. One of these was cleaning the stables of King Augeas, a task he completed by rerouting the river Alpheios, which runs past the site. Ancient tales tell that he mapped out the outline of the vast stadium with his foot—the starting and finishing lines are still in place, 600 Olympic feet (about 630 feet) apart. The world-famous pediment sculptures of Olympia's Temple of Zeus were also devoted to Hercules's exploits.

10

Opposite page, *Discobolos* (Discus Thrower), marble, circa 450 BC; above, Rings at ancient Olympia site

IT'S A JUMBLE OUT THERE: WHAT'S WHERE

There are few extant buildings at ancient Olympia so, to make sense of the scattered stones, a handy map is needed. Map numbers mark the best route.

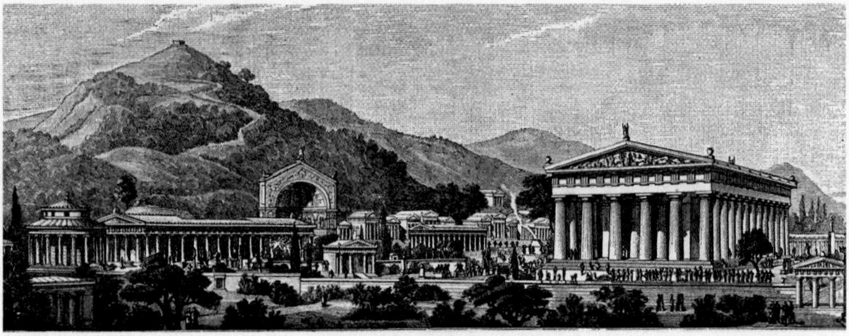

Panorama of ancient Olympia as one would have seen it from the viewpoint ✺ below.

1 Roman Baths: The earliest baths at Olympia date to the 5th century BC, though the Romans later replaced them with a more sophisticated complex.

2 Gymnasion: Athletes practiced for track and field events in an open field surrounded by porticoes.

3 Palaestra: This section of the gymnasium complex was used for athletic training; athletes bathed and socialized in rooms around the square field.

4 Pheidias's Workshop: The sculptor crafted the enormous statue of Zeus in this workshop, of the same size and orientation as the nearby Temple of Zeus.

5 Leonidaion: This luxurious hostel for distinguished visitors to the games later housed Roman governors.

6 South Hall: A vast hall surrounded by 34 Doric columns was one of the main entrances to the sanctuary.

7 Bouleuterion: Here in the seat of the organizers of the games, the Elean senate, athletes swore an oath of fair play.

8 Temple of Zeus: A great temple and fine example of Doric architecture, this housed an enormous statue of Zeus that was one of the seven wonders of the ancient world.

9 Altis: The sacred quarter was also known as the Sacred Grove of Zeus.

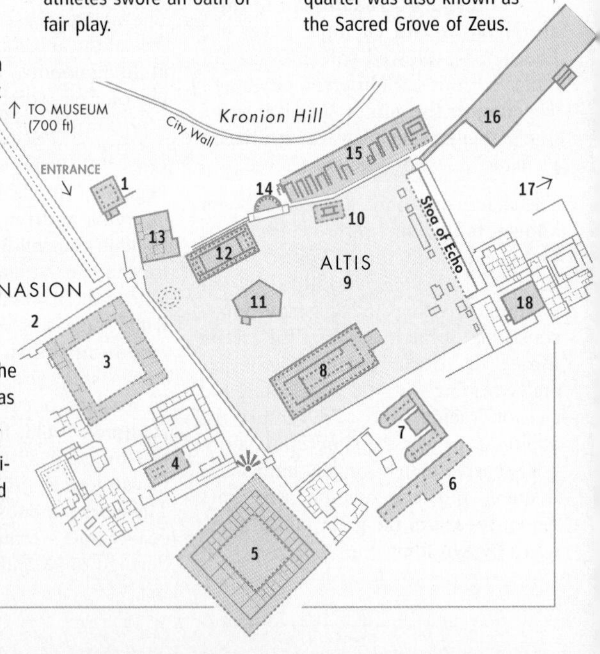

10 Metroon: A small Doric temple was dedicated to Rhea (also known as Cybele), Mother of the Gods.

11 Pelopeion: This shrine to Pelops, legendary king of the region now known as the Peloponnese, housed an altar in a sacred grove.

12 Temple of Hera: One of the earliest monumental Greek temples was built in the 7th century BC.

13 Prytaneion: Magistrates in charge of the games feted the winners here in a banquet room and a perpetual flame burned in the hearth.

14 Nymphaion: A semicircular reservoir stored water from a spring to the east, distributed throughout the site by a network of pipes.

15 Treasuries: These temple-like buildings housed valuables and equipment of twelve of the most powerful of the city-states competing in the games.

16 Stadium: As many as 50,000 spectators could crowd onto earthen embankments to watch running events. The starting and finishing lines are still in place.

17 Hippodrome: Horse and chariot races were run on this racecourse.

18 House of Nero: The lavish villa was built for the emperor's visit to the games of AD 67, in which he competed.

VISITING ANCIENT OLYMPIA

You'll need at least two hours to see the ruins and the museum, and three or four hours would be better. Ancient Olympia is located off Ethnikos Odos 74, ½ km (¼ mile) outside modern Olympia. The site is open daily year-round, with reduced hours from November through April. Modern Olympia, an attractive mountain town surrounded by pleasant hilly countryside, has hotels and tavernas convenient to the ancient site.

Spring at Olympia ruins

SACRED OLYMPIA

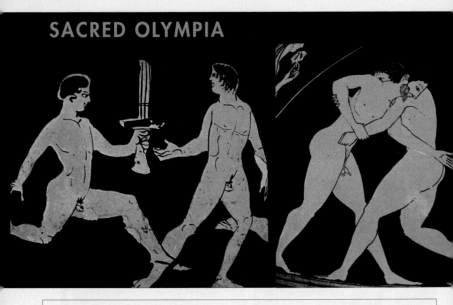

PRAISE BE TO THE GODS

As famous as the Olympic Games were—and still are—Olympia was first and foremost a sacred place, a sanctuary honoring Zeus, king of the gods, and Hera, his wife and older sister.

To honor the cult of Zeus established at Olympia as early as the 10th century BC, altars were first constructed outdoors, among the pine forests that still encroach upon the site. But around the turn of the 6th century BC, the earliest building at Olympia was constructed, the Temple of Hera, which originally honored Zeus and Hera jointly, until the Temple of Zeus was constructed around 470 BC. The Temple of Zeus was one of the finest temples in all of Greece. Thirteen columns flanked the sides and its interior housed the most famous work of ancient Greece—a gold and ivory statue of Zeus. Earthquakes in 551 and 552 finished off the temple. Two of the greatest sculptors of ancient Greece, Pheidias and Praxiteles, executed some of their best-known work for temples here.

PHEIDIAS AND PRAXITELES

Pheidias, who worked between 490-430 BC, was renowned for the enormous statue of Athena he completed for the Parthenon in 438 BC. He topped his fame at Olympia thanks to his 42-foot-high statue of Zeus for the Temple of Zeus: one of the Seven Wonders of the Ancient World, the work depicted the god sitting on a throne, holding a winged victory in one hand.

While the statue is long gone, one of the most evocative remains at Olympia are those of Pheidas's workshop—despite the ruinous state, the place looks like the sculptor might have recently stepped out and will soon return.

As for Praxiteles—who worked from around 370-330 BC and is credited with infusing Greek sculpture with unequalled grace and sensuality—the only surviving example of his work is today in the Olympia Museum, *Hermes Carrying the Infant Dionysus*, an elegant and delicate piece that once adorned the Temple of Hera.

SCANDALOUS OLYMPIA

Painted red-figures on ancient pottery (left) depict dreaded pankration matches, which mixed boxing and wrestling techniques—including choke holds and joint locks—to sometimes lethal effect. Sometimes the only form of submission was unconsciousness or death.

10

LEAVE THOSE FIG LEAVES AT HOME

While these venerated statues of gods conjure up noble scenes of raised Olympic torches and brotherhood pledges, modern scholars—most notably Tony Perrottet (in *The Naked Olympics*, Random House, 2004)—have discovered that the original Olympic Games were far from today's genteel televised spectacles.

In the hottest days of August, 50,000 spectators would have descended on Olympia—only to find no bathing facilities, no seats (many passed out from sun-stroke), open-air latrines, hoards of flies, and a sea of touts, thieves, Homer-reciters, fire-breathers, prostitutes, and sport heroes.

Long before the era of Spandex, these athletes competed in the nude, and trainers were asked to leave their clothing at the door, too—a fact that has long titillated scholars.

One theory holds that the nudity rule was imposed when a woman violated the ban on female participation at the events and disguised herself as a trainer to watch her sons compete; she revealed her gender with her screams of delight at the victory of one of her offspring and was summarily executed.

A more likely explanation is that the ancient Greeks, who found nothing shameful about nudity, simply enjoyed the display of athletic bodies. The only "outfit" was a covering of olive oil (applied by specially trained youths).

Victory processions often descended into full-scale orgies, perhaps fueled by a favored love potion for sale—a mixture of horse sweat and minced lizard.

Back on the field, bribery seems to have been the most common offense (steroids not being available).

Olympia also provides the earliest case of the sports-parent syndrome: in the 192nd Olympiad, Damonikos of Elis, whose son Polyktor was to wrestle Sosander of Smyrna, bribed the latter's father in an attempt to buy the victory for his son.

combined ticket with Archaeological Museum €9 ⊙ *May–Oct., daily 8–8; Nov.–Apr., Mon.–Sat. 8:30–5, Sun. 8:30–3.*

Archaeological Museum of Olympia. Of all the sights in ancient Olympia, some say the modern archaeological museum gets the gold. Housed in a handsome glass and marble pavilion at the edge of the ancient site, the magnificent collections include the sculptures from the Temple of Zeus and *Hermes Carrying the Infant Dionysus,* sculpted by the great Praxiteles, which was discovered in the Temple of Hera in the place noted by Pausanias. The central gallery of the museum holds one of the greatest sculptural achievements of classical antiquity: the pedimental sculptures and metopes from the Temple of Zeus, depicting Hercules's Twelve Labors. The *Hermes* was buried under the fallen clay of the temple's upper walls and is one of the best-preserved classical statues. Also on display is the famous *Nike of Paionios.* Other treasures include notable terra-cottas of Zeus and Ganymede; the head of the cult statue of Hera; sculptures of the family and imperial patrons of Herodes Atticus; and bronzes found at the site, including votive figurines, cauldrons, and armor. Of great historical interest are a helmet dedicated by Miltiades, the Athenian general who defeated the Persians at Marathon, and a cup owned by the sculptor Pheidias, which was found in his workshop on the Olympia grounds. ⊠ *Off Ethnikos Odos 74, ½ km (¼ mile) outside modern Olympia* ☎ *26240/22742* ⊕ *www.culture.gr* 🎫 *€6, combined ticket with Ancient Olympia €9* ⊙ *May–Oct., daily 8–8; Nov.–Apr., daily 8:30–3.*

WHERE TO EAT

$
GREEK
✕ **Aegean.** Don't let the garish signs depicting the menu put you off: the far-ranging offerings are excellent. You can eat lightly—a gyro or pizza—but do venture into some of the more serious fare, especially such local dishes as the fish that's been oven-baked with onion, garlic, green peppers, and parsley. The house's barrel wine is a nice accompaniment to any meal. 🅢 *Average main: €7* ⊠ *Douma, near Hotel New Olympia* ☎ *26240/22540.*

$
GREEK
✕ **Taverna Bacchus.** The best restaurants in Greece are often in small villages, and this appealing family-run taverna and inn set amid fields, a favorite among Olympians, is one such example. The poolside terrace is a lovely place to spend an afternoon or evening, though locals don't start arriving until 10 pm or so for dishes that include a delicious chicken with oregano, grilled lamb, and farm-fresh vegetables that appear in such deliciously simple preparations as baked eggplant with tomatoes and feta. 🅢 *Average main: €8* ⊠ *Ancient Pissa (Mirika)* ✛ *5 km (3 miles) west of Olympia* ☎ *26240/22298* ⊕ *www.bacchustavern. gr* ⊙ *Closed Dec.–Feb.*

$
GREEK
✕ **Taverna Thea.** Olympians flock out to the little village of Floka, about 5 km (3 miles) west of town, at dinnertime to enjoy traditional fare in this country setting. Dining is in a homey room or on the summertime terrace with wide views across the landscape, and the specialties are the expertly grilled meats. 🅢 *Average main: €9* ⊠ *Floka* ☎ *26240/23264* ▭ *No credit cards* ⊙ *No lunch Nov.–Apr.*

WHERE TO STAY

$
B&B/INN

🛏 **Bacchus Pension.** One of the region's most popular eateries *(see our restaurant review)* also provides attractive and comfortable guest rooms, all with balconies overlooking the countryside. **Pros:** great restaurant; beautiful pool and terrace area. **Cons:** outside of town, although just a short drive to ancient site. **$** *Rooms from: €65* ✉ *Ancient Pissa (Mirika)* ☎ *26240/22298* ⊕ *www.bacchustavern.gr* ☾ *Closed Dec.– Feb.* ⍥ *Breakfast.*

$
HOTEL
Fodor's Choice
★

🛏 **Hotel Europa.** White stucco, pine, and red tiles are handsome accents to gracious guest rooms that are all extremely large, with queen-size beds in many, and marble bathrooms and small terraces; most have sunken sitting areas and face either the pool, which is set in an olive-shaded garden, or the countryside. **Pros:** attractive rooms; fine restaurants; beautiful pool and garden. **Cons:** slightly out of town center and can be reached easily only by car. **$** *Rooms from: €85* ✉ *Oikismou Drouba* ☎ *26240/22650* ⊕ *www.hoteleuropa.gr* ⍥ *Breakfast.*

$
HOTEL

🛏 **Hotel Pelops.** Suzanna and Theo Spiliopoulou and their family set the gold standard for a small hotel, providing stylish and comfortable rooms that have wood floors, overlook the nearby mountains, and have small terraces—among the various delights here, Suzanna, a well-known chef, teaches cooking lessons and serves a Peloponnesian feast for the evening meal, a treat not to be missed. **Pros:** guests can use the Hotel Europa's pool; helpful hosts. **Cons:** located in town (but in a quiet and pleasant neighborhood). **$** *Rooms from: €50* ✉ *Varela 2* ☎ *26240/22543* ⊕ *www.hotelpelops.gr* ⍥ *Breakfast.*

$$$$
RESORT
Fodor's Choice
★

🛏 **Mandola Rosa.** This extremely elegant retreat, tucked into the sprawling, multihotel Olympia Riviera Resort on the coast beneath the ancient city, pampers guests with handsome and comfortable suites in a luxurious, Mediterranean-style villa and in lavish bungalows tucked into lush seaside gardens. **Pros:** an extremely attractive and comfortable place to stay; wealth of amenities; superb and friendly service. **Cons:** the cost is as high as Mt. Olympus. **$** *Rooms from: €550* ✉ *Kastro 50, 60 km (36 miles) west of Olympia, Kyllini* ☎ *26230/64400* ⊕ *www.mandolarosa.com* ⍥ *Breakfast.*

SHOPPING

Atelier Exekias. Sakis Doylas sells exquisite handmade and hand-painted ceramic bowls and urns, fashioned after finds in Ancient Olympia; the glazes and colors are beautiful. ✉ *Kondoli* ☎ *6936/314054.*

Olympia Archaeological Museum Shop. The shop of the Archaeological Museum carries an appealing line of figurines, bronzes, votives, and other replicas of objects found in the ruins. ✉ *Off Ethnikos Odos 74, north of Ancient Olympia site* ☎ *26240/22742.*

TEMPLE OF APOLLO AT BASSAE
ΝΑΟΣ ΤΟΥ ΑΠΟΛΛΩΝΑ ΣΤΙΣ ΒΑΣΣΕΣ

38 km (23 miles) southeast of Olympia, 54 km (32 miles) south of Dimitsana.

The launching point for the drive up to the Temple of Apollo is Andritsena, a pleasant collection of stone houses that cling to the side of a deep gorge. A small library in town, found 100 yards past the town square on the main road, houses 15th-century Venetian and Vatican first editions and documents relating to the War of Independence.

Temple of Apollo at Bassae. Isolated amid craggy, uncompromising scenery, the Temple of Apollo Epikourios at Bassae (also spelled Vassae) is one of the great majesties of ancient Greek architecture. Unfortunately, these days it looks more like the Sydney Opera House, thanks to a modernistic shed that has cocooned the temple in an attempt to prevent further weather damage during ongoing restoration. The covering destroys the sense of place that was so important to this temple, which sits in miles of empty, hilltop fields. For many years it was believed that this temple was designed by Iktinos, the Parthenon's architect. Although this theory has recently been disputed, Bassae remains one of the best-preserved classical temples in Greece, superseded in its state of preservation only by the Hephaistion in Athens. The residents of nearby Phygalia built it atop an older temple in 420 BC to thank Apollo for delivering them from an epidemic; *epikourios* means "helper." Made of local limestone, the temple has some unusual details: exceptional length compared to its width; a north–south orientation rather than the usual east–west (probably because of the slope of the ground); and Ionic half columns linked to the walls by flying buttresses. Here, too, were the first known Corinthian columns with the characteristic acanthus leaves— only the base remains now—and the earliest example of interior sculptured friezes illustrating the battles between the Greeks and Amazons (now in the British Museum). As for the restoration, it will be ongoing for at least another decade. ■ TIP➜ **Climb to the summit northwest of the temple for a view overlooking the Nedhas river, Mt. Lykaeon, and, on a clear day, the Ionian sea.** ⊠ *Off Rte. 76 and then up a one-lane road* ☎ *26260/22254* ⊕ *www.culture.gr* ▭ *€3* ☉ *Daily 8:30–sunset.*

ANCIENT MESSENE ΑΡΧΑΙΑ ΜΕΣΣΗΝΗ

35 km (21 miles) south of Temple of Apollo at Bassae.

The ruins of this remarkably fortified ancient city, about 20 km (12 miles) north of the modern town of the same name, are set amid a lush landscape of olive groves and pine forests on the slopes of majestic Mt. Ithomi (also known as Voulkanos).

EXPLORING

Ancient Messene. In terms of footprints, this is one of the most awe-inspiring sites of ancient Greece, thanks to mile-long bulwark walls, famed entry gates, vast theater arenas, and temples. One temple alone, the Asklepion, was thought to be an entire town by archaeologists until recently (see ⊕ *www.ancientmessene.gr* for an excellent scholarly take on the site). Epaminondas, the Theban leader, built the ancient town, which today incorporates the village of **Mavromati,** in 370–369 BC as a defense against the Spartans, whom the Messenians had battled during two Messenian Wars, in 743–724 BC and 650–620 BC.

The most striking aspect of the ruins is the city's **circuit wall,** a feat of defensive architecture that rises and dips across the hillsides for an astonishing 9 km (5½ miles). Four gates remain; the best preserved is the north or **Arcadian Gate,** a double set of gates separated by a round courtyard. On the ancient paving stone below the arch, grooves worn by chariot wheels are still visible. The heart of the walled city is now occupied by the modern village, but excavations have uncovered the most important public buildings, including a **theater,** whose seats have now been restored; the **Synedrion,** a meeting hall for representatives of independent Messene; the **Sebasteion,** dedicated to worship of a Roman emperor; the **sanctuary to the god Asklepios;** and a **temple to Artemis Orthia.** Outside the walls lie a **stadium** and a **cemetery.** The site is a bit confusing, as the ruins are spread over the hillside and approached from different paths; follow the signposts indicating the theater, gates, and other major excavations. Some of the finds are in the village's **small museum.** After exploring the ruins, enjoy a beverage in one of the tavernas that surround the main square of Mavromati. ✉ *Mavromati* ✛ *From modern town of Messene, turn north at intersection of signposted road to Mavromati* ☎ *27240/51201* ⊕ *www.culture.gr* ✉ *€4* ☼ *Apr.–Oct., daily 8–8; Nov.–Mar., daily 9–4.*

THE MANI ΜΑΝΗ

Kardamyli, the western entrance to the Mani, is about 70 km (50 miles) southeast of Ancient Messene.

Isolated and invincible, stark yet unforgettable, the Mani region may be an acquired taste, but it remains one of the must-dos of the Peloponnese for intrepid travelers. For Greeks, it has always been something of a frontier, a bit like the American West, as well as a rugged seaside getaway yet to be spoiled by large-scale development. Given its good looks, it's little wonder that the Mani is becoming increasingly popular with Athenians, who come to the region for weekends or longer getaways.

The bare mountains, rugged coastline, and simple villages suggest a different time and remind us that this was a land of bandits and blood feuds. Just look at the 19th-century stonework town of Vathia: this icon of the Mani is set over the sea and bristles with enough forbidding tower houses to look like a primeval Manhattan. The Dorians never reached this far south, Roman occupation was perfunctory, and Christianity was not established here until the 9th century. Neither the Venetians nor the Turks could quell the constant rebellions that arose when clans began building defensive tower houses (the oldest dates to the 15th century) up to four stories high and fighting for precious land in this barren landscape. The object in battle was to annihilate the enemy's tower house, as well as its entire male population. Feuds could last for years, with the women—who were safe from attack—bringing in supplies. Mani women were famous throughout Greece for their singing of the *moirologhi* (laments), like the ancient choruses in a Greek tragedy.

A temporary truce had to be called during the harvest, but a feud ended only with the complete destruction of a family or its surrender, called *psychiko* (a thing of the soul), in which losers filed out of their tower house one by one, kissing the hand of the enemy clan's parents. The victor then decided under what conditions the humbled family could

10

remain in the village. When King Otho tried to tame this incorrigible bunch in 1833, his soldiers were ambushed, stripped naked, and held for ransom. Today few people live in the Mani. If you have the good luck to share a shot of fiery raki with a Maniote, you may notice a Cretan influence in his dress—older men still wear the baggy breeches, black headbands, and decorated jackets wrapped with heavy belts.

On its western side, the Mani peninsula—the middle of the three fingers that dangle from the southern Peloponnese—stretches from Kardamyli to Cape Tenaro, the mythical entrance to the underworld, and on its eastern side from Cape Tenaro up to Gythion. The western half is the Messenian Mani, while the eastern half is the Laconian Mani.

KARDAMYLI ΚΑΡΔΑΜΥΛΙ

122 km (76 miles) southwest of Tripoli.

The gateway to the Mani on the Messenian side is Kardamyli, 31 km (19 miles) southeast of the market town of Kalamata. It is considered part of the outer Mani, an area less bleak and stark than the inner Mani, which begins at Areopolis. Here the foothills of the Taygettus range are still verdant, and the sun is more forgiving. The quiet and attractive stone town has become a tourist destination for travelers attracted to its remoteness, stark beauty, and the hiking paths that surround it. Kardamyli's most famous resident was for many years the late Patrick Leigh Fermor, an Anglo-Irish writer who wrote extensively on Greece and on the Mani in particular. The old section of Kardamyli, northwest of the modern town, is on a pine-scented hillside dotted with small clusters of tower houses, some of which are being restored; stone-paved paths cut through the enclave.

WHERE TO EAT

$

GREEK

Fodor's Choice

★

✕ **Lela's Taverna.** Mrs. Lela, once housekeeper for author Patrick Leigh Fermor, is famous these days for her simple, old-fashioned cooking using fragrant homemade olive oil and exceedingly fresh tomatoes and herbs. Her taverna is an institution in these parts, and dinner beneath the trees on the seaside terrace of an oleander-covered stone house is a high point of a visit to the Mani. Chicken with rosemary, light moussaka, and fish soup are among the dishes that Lela and her grandson, Petros, prepare daily. $ *Average main: €9* ⊠ *Seaside, above rocky beach near old soap factory* ☎ *27210/73541* ⊕ *www.lelastaverna.com* ▬ *No credit cards* ⊘ *No lunch.*

WHERE TO STAY

$

B&B/INN

☷ **Lela's.** Three basic rooms above Lela's famous taverna *(see our separate review)* have soothing sea views and plain but handsome furnishings that include traditional fabrics; all have balconies, and the terrace below is a pleasant place to lounge when the restaurant is not serving. **Pros:** beautiful seaside location; very simple but comfortable. **Cons:** few hotel services and amenities. $ *Rooms from: €50* ⊠ *Seaside, above rocky beach near old soap factory* ☎ *27210/73541* ⊕ *www.lelastaverna. com* ▬ *No credit cards* ⊙ *No meals.*

$ B&B/INN 🏨 **Notos Hotel.** These attractive apartments, scattered across hillside gardens in handsome stone houses, are furnished in bleached-wood pieces and attractive muted fabrics—each unit has a large terrace overlooking the sea; kitchens are well equipped, and baths are beautifully tiled. **Pros:** extremely attractive and well-equipped units; friendly atmosphere; just uphill from the beach. **Cons:** not in village but within walking distance. [$] *Rooms from: €80* ✉ *Above beach, about 1 km (½ mile) north of town center* ☎ *27210/73730* 🌐 *www.notoshotel.gr* 🍴 *No meals.*

BEACHES

Kardamyli's main beach, at the northern edge of town, is a long stretch of sand and pebbles backed by stands of pines. You can also swim off the dock in the clear, deep waters of the town's small harbor. Other beaches are tucked into coves as you drive south on the main road. Stoupa, about 10 km (6 miles) south of Kardamyli, is a low-key collection of seaside tavernas and rooms for rent that stretches along a beautiful sandy beach; it's a good place to come for lunch and a swim. Neo Itilo sits on a beautiful large bay with a white-pebble beach. Enjoy a swim as you watch the fishermen fixing their nets, checking their ship hulls, and talking among themselves amid the din of their portable radios.

Stoupa. This long stretch of clean sand along a curving bay is undeniably the nicest beach in the Mani, though far from the most quiet and scenic spot in this rugged region. You'll share the company of frolicking young Greeks and sun-worshipping northern Europeans, but given that this is the Mani, this is a relatively low-key beach resort, and it's quite possible to find a quiet stretch. **Amenities:** food and drink; parking (free); showers; toilets; water sports. **Best for:** partiers; snorkeling; swimming; walking. ✉ *Stoupa.*

AREOPOLIS ΑΡΕΟΠΟΛΗΣ

44 km (26 miles) southwest of Kardamyli.

In Areopolis, the typical Maniote tower houses begin to appear in earnest as spooky sentinels in the harsh landscape. The town was renamed after Ares, the god of war, because of its role in the War of Independence: Petrobey Mavromichalis, governor of the Mani, initiated the local uprising against the Turks here (his statue stands in the square, and his descendants have turned the family's seaside mansion in nearby Limeni into a stunning small hotel). Areopolis now enjoys protection as a historical monument by the government, but although the town seems medieval, most of the tower houses were built in the early 1800s. The Taxiarchis (Archangels) church, which looks as if it has 12th-century reliefs over the doors, was actually constructed in 1798. It's easy to slip vicariously into a time warp as you meander along dark cobblestone lanes past the tower houses with their enclosed courtyards and low-arched gateways.

EXPLORING

FAMILY Fodor'sChoice ★ **Pirgos Dirou Caves.** Carved out of the limestone by the slow-moving underground river Vlychada on its way to the sea, the vast Pirgos Dirou caves—actually two main caves, Glyfada and Alepotrypa—are some of

Greece's more popular natural attractions, and a visit is an entertaining and surreal experience. The eerie caverns were places of worship in Paleolithic and Neolithic times, were believed to be entrances to the underworld by the ancient Greeks, and served as hiding places millennia later for Resistance fighters during World War II.

Today you climb aboard a boat for a 25-minute tour of Glyfada's grottoes—with formations of luminous pink, white, yellow, and red stalagmites and stalactites that resemble buildings and mythical beasts. The cave system is believed to be at least 70 km (43 miles) long, with more than 2,800 waterways, perhaps extending as far as Sparta. At the end of the tour you walk for several hundred yards (about a fifth of a mile) before emerging on a path above the crashing surf. The close quarters in the passageways are not for the claustrophobic, and even in summer the caves are chilly. During high season you may wait up to two hours for a boat, so plan to arrive early. In low season you may have to wait until enough people arrive to fill up a boat. Opening hours change frequently. ✉ *Pirgos Dirou* ✣ *10 km (6 miles) southwest of Areopolis, 5 km (3 miles) west of Areopolis–Vathia Rd.* ☎ *27330/52222* 🎟 *€15* ⏲ *Nov.–Mar., daily 8:30–3; Apr.–Oct., daily 8:30–5:30.*

WHERE TO EAT

$ SEAFOOD 🍴 **Takis.** The fish and seafood, priced by the kilo and served at the water's edge, are some of the freshest in the region—and best when simply grilled, usually with mountain herbs. You may ending up dining next to the boat that brought in the fresh catch, or for that matter, near a crew cleaning the fish that will soon appear on your plate (it's much more charming than it sounds). **■ TIP→ This is an excellent stop for lunch on the drive south down the Mani peninsula.** [$] *Average main: €12* ✉ *On waterfront, Limeni* ☎ *27330/51327* 💳 *No credit cards.*

$ GREEK 🍴 **Taverna Barba Petros.** A simple, high-ceilinged room and terrace are the settings for the traditional meals here. The kitchen uses only market-fresh vegetables and locally raised meat, which appear in simple and delicious ways. Try the baked zucchini, potatoes, and grilled lamb ribs. Dessert—ask for the honey cake—is usually on the house. [$] *Average main: €9* ✉ *Main street* ☎ *27330/51026* 💳 *No credit cards.*

$ GREEK 🍴 **To Katoi.** Once used as a stable, this vaulted, stone-walled room is pleasant and welcoming and extends to a terrace on the street in good weather. The kitchen specializes in home cooking with the freshest local ingredients, including such traditional favorites as rooster roasted with potatoes and vegetables and a hearty omelet made with smoked pork. [$] *Average main: €8* ✉ *Across from Taxiarchis church* ☎ *27330/51201* 💳 *No credit cards* ⏲ *No lunch in winter.*

WHERE TO STAY

$ HOTEL 🏨 **Hotel Trapela.** In this beautiful, traditionally styled house just off the main square, large, stone-floored, stone-walled, wood-ceilinged rooms combine distinctive, traditional ambience with modern comforts. **Pros:** lovely terraces and a garden; pleasant decor; stylish and comfortable base for visiting the Mani. **Cons:** limited service; a distance from a beach. [$] *Rooms from: €70* ✉ *Near center of town* ☎ *27330/52690* 🌐 *www.trapela.gr* 🍽 *Breakfast.*

$$ B&B/INN Fodor's Choice ★ **Pirgos Mavromichali.** The fortified, seaside stronghold of the Mavromichali clan, noted for its role in Greek independence, is now an enchanting inn with 13 character-filled rooms and suites set within the walls of a centuries-old tower building and clustered around sun-drenched terraces that drop down to the turquoise waters of Limeni harbor, just north of Areopolis. **Pros:** historic setting; panoramic surroundings at the edge of the sea; extremely attentive service; an ideal base for exploring the rugged Mani landscape; family-run. **Cons:** steps may be difficult for guests with mobility issues. [$] *Rooms from: €135* ✉ *Harbor, 5 km (3 miles) north of Areopolis, Limeni* ☎ *27330/51042* 🌐 *www.pirgosmavromichali.gr* 🍴 *Breakfast.*

GEROLIMENAS ΓΕΡΟΛΙΜΕΝΑΣ

22 km (14 miles) south of Areopolis.

Located at the end of a long natural harbor, Gerolimenas was an important port in the late 19th and early 20th centuries. Sleepy as Gerolimenas now is, it's the most tourist-friendly place in this stark part of the Mani, with several hotels, tavernas, and shops and a lively town beach. About 3 km (2 miles) north of Gerolimenas is the hamlet of Stavri, from where you can make a memorable one-hour trek to the Castle of Mina, built by the Franks in 1248 into the rock face at the end of a long promontory surrounded by crashing surf. The most photogenic sight around here, however, is picture-perfect **Vathia,** 10 km (6 miles) south of Gerolimenas. Although now virtually a ghost town, its small clusters of looming tower houses perched against the sea are one of the postcard icons of Greece. The two- and three-story stone tower houses here all have small windows and tiny openings over the doors through which boiling oil was poured on the unwelcome. An effort to recolonize the village as a vast hotel several years ago failed, heightening Vathia's pervasive feeling of emptiness.

The landscape becomes more rugged and even more forbidding south of Vathia, on the way to **Cape Tenaro** at the tip of the peninsula. The road winds around the mountainsides to Porto Kayio, where a few tavernas face a lovely beach, and then to more beaches at Marmari. A narrow road leads south to barren Cape Tenaro, where the ruins of a small Roman settlement include a mosaic that is perilously open to the elements. An underwater cave here, to which you might be able to convince a boatman to take you, is one of several alleged entrances to the classical underworld. From the cape you can look out over the Mani peninsula and the gulf of Laconia and gulf of Messinia.

WHERE TO STAY

$ HOTEL Fodor's Choice ★ **Kyrimai Hotel.** The Kyrimis family have lovingly restored a welcoming assemblage of 19th-century stone warehouses into a beautiful retreat, with comfortable guest rooms furnished with antiques and a tasteful mix of traditional and contemporary pieces; many have balconies and sleeping lofts. **Pros:** atmospheric surroundings; excellent swimming from hotel jetty; pleasant seaside terraces; lavish breakfast. **Cons:** some rooms are dark and do not have views; parking can be difficult.

[$] *Rooms from: €110* ✉ *Waterfront* ☎ *27330/54288* 🌐 *www.kyrimai.gr* 🍴 *Breakfast.*

LACONIA ΛΑΚΩΝΙΑ

The Laconian plain is surrounded on three sides by mountains and on one side by the sea. Perhaps it was the fear that enemies could descend those mountains at any time that drove the Spartans to make Laconia their training ground, where they developed the finest fighting force in ancient Greece. A mighty power that controlled three-fifths of the Peloponnese, Sparta contributed to the Greek victory in the Second Persian War (5th century BC). Ultimately, Sparta's aggressiveness and jealousy of Athens brought about the Peloponnesian War, which drained the city's resources but left it victorious. The Greek world found Sparta to be an even harsher master than Athens, and this fact may have led to its losses in the Boeotian and Corinthian wars, at the Battle of Leuctra, and, in 222–221 BC, at the hands of the Achaean League, who liberated all areas Sparta had conquered. A second period of prosperity under the Romans ended with the barbarian invasions in the 3rd century AD, and Sparta declined rapidly.

Laconia can also claim two important magnificently medieval sites: Mystras and Monemvasia. The former was an intellectual and political center, the latter a sea fortress meant to ward off invaders from the east.

GYTHION ΓΥΘΕΙΟΝ

79 km (49 miles) north of Vathia, 50 km (30 miles) northeast of Gerolimenas.

At the foot of the Taygettus range on the northeastern edge of the Mani, Gythion seems terribly cosmopolitan, compared to the stark countryside that surrounds it. Graceful pastel 19th-century houses march up the steep hillside and line the busy harbor, where a fishing fleet bobs alongside ouzeri and little shops. As Laconia's main port, Gythion is the region's gateway to the Mani peninsula. It claims Hercules and Apollo as its founders, and survives today by exporting olives, oil, rice, and citrus fruits. Kranae, a tiny islet at the eastern end of the harbor, is where Paris and Helen (wife of the Mycenaean king Menelaos) allegedly consummated their love affair after escaping Sparta, provoking the Trojan War described in the *Iliad*. A causeway now joins Marathonissi to the mainland.

MONEMVASIA ΜΟΝΕΜΒΑΣΙΑ

140 km (85 miles) northeast of Gythion, at the eastern edge of the Mani.

Fodor's Choice ★ The Byzantine town of Monemvasia clings to the side of the 1,148-foot rock that was once a headland, but in AD 375 was separated from the mainland by an earthquake. The town was first settled in the 6th century AD, when Laconians sought refuge after Arab and Slav raids. Monemvasia—the name *moni emvasia* (single entrance) refers to the narrow passage to this walled community—once enjoyed enormous prosperity, and for centuries dominated the sea lanes from Western Europe to the Levant. During its golden age in the 1400s, Monemvasia was home to families made wealthy by their inland estates and the export of malmsey wine, a sweet variety of Madeira praised by Shakespeare. When the area fell to the Turks, Monemvasia was controlled first by the pope and then by the Venetians, who built the citadel and most of the fortifications. The newer settlement that has spread out along the water on the mainland is not as romantic as the Old Town, but it's pleasant and well equipped with shops and services.

Well-to-do Greeks once again live on the rock, in houses they have turned into vacation homes. Summer weekends are crowded, but off-season Monemvasia is nearly deserted. Houses are lined up along steep streets only wide enough for two people abreast, among remnants of another age—escutcheons, marble thrones, Byzantine icons. It's a delight to wander through the back lanes and along the old walls, and to find perches high above the town or the sea.

If you walk or drive from the adjoining modern town of Gefira, the rock looks uninhabited until you suddenly see castellated walls with an opening wide enough for one person. An overnight stay here allows you to enjoy this strange place when the tour groups have departed.

EXPLORING

Ayia Sofia. For solitude and a dizzying view, pass through the upper town's wooden entrance gates, complete with the original iron reinforcement. Up the hill is a rare example of a domed octagonal church, founded in the 13th century by Emperor Andronicus II and patterned after Dafni monastery in Athens. Under Venetian rule the Byzantine complex served as a convent. Follow the path to the highest point on the rock for a breathtaking view of the coast. ⊠ *At top of mountain.*

Ayios Pavlos. This humble stone structure is one of the oldest churches in Greece, dating to the 10th century. Although Ayios Pavlos was converted into a mosque under the Ottoman occupation, it was allowed to function as a church: an unusual indulgence. ⊠ *Across from Tzamiou Sq.*

Christos Elkomenos (*Christ in Chains*). The town's 13th-century cathedral is reputedly the largest medieval church in southern Greece. Carved peacocks on its portal are symbolic of the Byzantine era; the detached bell tower—like those of Italian cathedrals—is a sign of Venetian rebuilding in the 17th century. ⊠ *Tzamiou Sq., along main street.*

BEACHES

Some people swim off the rocks at the base of the Old Town and along the road leading to the main gate, but the pebble beach in the new town is safer and more appealing. For the most rewarding beach experience, head to the sandy strands at Pori, about 5 km (3 miles) northwest of Monemvasia.

WHERE TO EAT

$ ╳ **Marianthi.** You'll feel as if you're dropping into someone's home at
GREEK dinner here: family photos of stern, mustachioed ancestors hang on the walls along with local memorabilia, and the service, at tables on the

street in good weather, is just as welcoming (perhaps too much so, as cats can be as numerous as diners). A memorable meal makes the most of local ingredients—wild mountain greens, any of the fish but especially the fresh red mullet, the addictive potato salad (you may have to order two plates), and the marinated octopus sprinkled with oregano. [$] *Average main: €9* ✉ *Main street* ☎ *27320/61371* 💳 *No credit cards.*

$ GREEK 🍴 **To Kanoni.** After you roll out of bed, wander over to the Kanoni, which opens early for the day to serve breakfast on a terrace overlooking the square's *kanoni* (cannon). Choose from omelets, ham and eggs, or thick, creamy yogurt and honey, then come back at lunch or dinner for a nicely varied menu that often includes eggplant baked with other fresh vegetables and feta and *yiouvetsi* (beef baked in a clay pot with orzolike pasta). [$] *Average main: €9* ✉ *Old Town* ☎ *27320/61387* 🌐 *tokanoni.com.*

WHERE TO STAY

$ B&B/INN 🏨 **Byzantino.** All of these unusual accommodations, tucked into several stone buildings in the Old Town, are different and full of character—all are embellished with stone- and tile work and other distinctive decorations, and some are multilevel. **Pros:** character-filled accommodation in medieval houses; some units have nice terraces and sea views. **Cons:** rooms (like all those in the Old Town) are reached on foot and sometimes by stairs: if this is an issue, ask about accessibility when booking. [$] *Rooms from: €70* ✉ *Office on main street near entrance gate* ☎ *27320/61351* 🌐 *www.hotelbyzantino.com* 🍽 *No meals.*

$ HOTEL 🏨 **Hotel Pramataris.** If there's no room at the Old Town's inns, or if you don't like the idea of carting your baggage up and down narrow lanes, then this sparkling New Town choice with bright, tile-floored rooms overlooking the sea and the Gibraltar-like rock is a wonderful alternative and a real bargain. **Pros:** pleasant seaside location; very comfortable rooms; nice outdoor spaces. **Cons:** not in the atmospheric Old Town. [$] *Rooms from: €60* ✉ *New Town, on sea* ☎ *27320/61833* 🌐 *www.pramatarishotel.gr* 🍽 *Breakfast.*

$$ HOTEL Fodor's Choice ★ 🏨 **Kinsterna Hotel and Spa.** An Ottoman estate has been brought back to life as one of Greece's most distinctive hotels, where courtyards, terraces, domes, vaulted ceilings, arches, stone work, fireplaces, and other architectural elements are put to dazzling effect—the outdoor dining room overhangs a centuries-old cistern and a river-like swimming pool winds through the garden. **Pros:** architecturally distinctive surroundings; beautifully furnished and well-equipped rooms and suites; attractive pool and gardens; just 7 km (4 miles) from Monemvasia; attentive and friendly service. **Cons:** countryside setting that can only be reached by car; somewhat expensive (but many special offers are available). [$] *Rooms from: €220* ✉ *Agios Stefanos* ☎ *27320/66300* 🌐 *www.kinsternahotel.gr* 🍽 *Breakfast.*

$ B&B/INN 🏨 **Malvasia.** A complex of restored buildings at the far edge of the Old Town (reached on a trek over sometimes steep and uneven pavement) provides atmospheric and comfortable lodgings tucked into nooks and crannies under cane-and-wood or vaulted brick ceiling. **Pros:** appealing and nicely designed rooms with character; many private terraces and sea views; pleasant public indoor and outdoor spaces. **Cons:** reached via a trek through town on rough streets; another hotel with the same name is nearby, so make sure you end up in the right place. $ *Rooms from: €85* ✉ *End of Old Town* ☎ *27320/63007* ⊕ *www.malvasia-hotel. gr* ⓄⓁ *Breakfast.*

$

B&B/INN

▥ **Ta Kellia.** Accommodations in this old monastery (*kellia* means "cells") are fairly simple, but they are extremely appealing and face an airy square above the sea. **Pros:** beautiful seaside location, tucked away from the busy main street and squares; atmospheric surroundings. **Cons:** hard to find and to reach over the cobblestone streets. $ *Rooms from: €75* ✉ *On lower square opposite Church of Panagia Chrissafitissa* ☎ *27320/61520* ⊕ *www.keliamonemvasia.com* ▭ *No credit cards* ⓄⓁ *Breakfast.*

SPARTA ΣΠΑΡΤΗ

96 km (60 miles) northwest of Monemvasia.

For those who have read about ancient Sparta, the bellicose city-state that once dominated the Greek world, the modern city on the broad Eurotas river might be a disappointment, since ruins are few and far between. Given the area's earthquakes and the Spartans' tendency to live more like an army camp than a city-state, no elaborate ruins remain, a fact that so disconcerted Otto, Greece's first king, that in 1835 he ordered the modern city built on the ancient site. The modern town is not terribly attractive, but it's pleasant enough, with a lively pedestrian-only city center.

GETTING HERE AND AROUND

At least seven buses a day connect Athens and Sparta, a trip of about 5 hours that costs about €18 each way. From Sparta's bus station (☎ *27310/26441*), located downtown at the junction of Lykourgou and Dafnou, you can catch one of six daily buses to Monemvasia (about 2 hours, €5) and also continue on to the Mani region (service several times a day to Gythion and Aeropolis) and other places in the southern Peloponnese.

By car, follow the toll highway south from Athens through Corinth and Tripoli. At Tripoli the route continues in part on well-surfaced two- and three-lane roads. The trip from Athens takes about 4 to 5 hours of reasonable driving.

EXPLORING

Museum of the Olive in the Mediterranean. Olives are thick on the ground in these parts, so it's only fitting that Sparta is home to a quirky and appealing collection of apparatus and culture related to the staple of Greek economy since ancient times, housed in a stunning renovation of the city's first electricity works. ✉ *Othonos-Amalias 129* ☎ *27310/89315* ⊕ *www.oliveoilmuseums.gr* ▱ *€3* ⊗ *Mar.–mid-Oct., Wed.–Mon. 10–6; mid-Oct.–Feb., Wed.–Mon 10–5.*

Sparta Acropolis. What little remains of Ancient Sparta's acropolis is now part archaeological site, part park. Locals can be seen here strolling, along with many young couples stealing a romantic moment amid the

10

The Spartan Ethic

The Spartans' relentless militarism set them apart from other Greeks in the ancient world. They were expected to emerge victorious from a battle or not at all, and for most of its existence Sparta was without a wall, because according to Lykourgos, who wrote Sparta's constitution sometime around 600 BC, "chests, not walls, make a city." The government was an oligarchy, with two kings who also served as military leaders. Spartan society had three classes: a privileged elite involved with warfare and government; farmers, traders, and craftspeople, who paid taxes; and the numerous Helots, a serf class with few rights.

Selected boys in the reigning warrior class were taken from their parents at the age of seven and submitted to a training regimen without parallel in history for its ruthlessness. Their diet involved mostly herbs, roots, and the famous black broth, which included pork, the blood of the pig, and vinegar. Rich foods were thought to stunt growth. Forbidden to work, boys and young men trained for combat and practiced stealing, an acceptable skill—it was believed to teach caution and cunning—unless one was caught. One legend describes a Spartan youth who let a concealed fox chew out his bowels rather than reveal his theft. Girls also trained rigorously in the belief they would bear healthier offspring; for the same reason, newlyweds were forbidden to make love frequently.

The kingdom's iron coinage was not accepted outside Sparta's borders, creating a contempt for wealth and luxury (and, in turn, rapacious kings and generals). Sparta's warrior caste subjugated the native Achaean inhabitants of the region. Today all that remains of this realm founded on martial superiority is dust.

fallen limestone and shady trees. The ruins include a **theater,** a **stadium,** and a **sanctuary to Athena.** ✉ *North end of town.*

Sparta Archaeological Museum. This eclectic collection reflects Laconia's turbulent history and is worth an hour to see Neolithic pottery; jewels and tools excavated from the Alepotrypa cave; Mycenaean tomb finds; bright 4th- and 5th-century Roman mosaics; and objects from Sparta. Most characteristic of Spartan art are the bas-reliefs with deities and heroes; note the one depicting a seated couple bearing gifts who are framed by a snake (540 BC). ✉ *Ayios Nikonos, between Dafnou and Evangelistria* ☎ *27310/21516* ⊕ *www.culture.gr* ✉ *€2* ⊙ *Apr.–Oct., daily 8–4; Nov.–Mar., daily 8–3.*

Statue of Leonidas. Stop a moment and contemplate the statute of the stern Spartan leader. During the Second Persian War in the 5th century BC, with 30,000 Persians advancing on his army of 8,000, Leonidas, ordered to surrender his weapons, jeered, "Come and get them." For two days he held off the enemy, until a traitor named Efialtes (the word has since come to mean "nightmare" in Greek) showed the Persians a way to attack from the rear. When forced to retreat to a wooded knoll, he is said to have commented, "So much the better, we will fight in the shade." His entire troop was slaughtered. ✉ *End of Konstantinou.*

Temple of Artemis Orthia. At this temple outside town, young Spartan men underwent *krypteia* (initiations) that entailed severe public floggings. The altar had to be splashed with blood before the goddess was satisfied. Traces of two such altars are among sparse vestiges of the 6th-century BC temple. The larger ruins are the remains of a grandstand built in the 3rd century AD by the Romans, who revived the flogging tradition as a public spectacle. ✉ *Tripoli Rd., down path to Eurotas river.*

WHERE TO EAT

$ GREEK 🍴 **Diethnes.** Locals claim this is one of Sparta's best restaurants, but then again, most head out to village tavernas for a big meal and leave this place to the tour-bus crowd. Even so, the food is excellent, the best you're likely to find in town, and classic specialties include a fish dish made with garlic, wine, oil, and rusks; *bardouniotiko* (chicken cooked with cheese and olives); and, occasionally, sheep's heads cooked on a spit. The tree-shaded garden rounds out a perfect meal. [$] *Average main: €9* ✉ *Paleologou 105* ☎ *27310/28636* 💳 *No credit cards.*

$ GREEK 🍴 **Parthenon.** If you find yourself waiting for a bus out of Sparta at mealtime, cross the street to Parthenon for the best gyro you may ever eat. The meat, which has a local reputation for being a cut above the usual, is served in pita with the right amount of chew and generous doses of onion, tomato, and *tzatziki* (garlic and yogurt) sauce. [$] *Average main: €5* ✉ *Vrasidou 106* ☎ *27310/23767.*

WHERE TO STAY

$ HOTEL 🏨 **Menelaion Hotel.** The pool sparkling in the leafy courtyard is a welcome sight after a hot day of exploring the ruins of nearby Mystras, and the well-equipped guest rooms are quite stylish. **Pros:** attractive public areas and courtyard with pool; good in-house restaurant and bar. **Cons:** rooms are stylish but lack a little character; street noise in front-facing rooms. [$] *Rooms from: €95* ✉ *Paleologou 91* ☎ *27310/22161* 🌐 *www.menelaion.com* 🍽 *Breakfast.*

MYSTRAS ΜΥΣΤΡΑΣ

8 km (5 miles) west of Sparta, 64 km (40 miles) southwest of Tripoli.

While little remains to attest to Spartan power and might, residents of the Byzantine capital just to the west left behind a treasure trove of architectural splendors. A visit to Sparta requires a fertile imagination; in Mystras all you need is a good pair of walking shoes and some water as you scramble amid the copious remnants of the last days of the Byzantine Empire.

FAMILY Fodor's Choice ★ **Mystras Archaeological Site.** In this Byzantine city, abandoned gold and stone palaces, churches, and monasteries line serpentine paths; the scent of herbs and wildflowers permeates the air; goat bells tinkle; and silvery olive trees glisten with the slightest breeze. An intellectual and cultural center where philosophers like Chrysoloras, "the sage of Byzantium," held forth on the good and the beautiful, Mystras seems an appropriate place for the last hurrah of the Byzantine emperors in the 14th century. Today the splendid ruins are a UNESCO World Heritage Site and one

Magnificently redolent of the Byzantine era, Mystras is a town filled with churches and monasteries, many adorned with 12th-century paintings.

of the most impressive sights in the Peloponnese. A pleasant modern town adjoins the ruins.

In 1249 William Geoffrey de Villehardouin built the castle in Mystras in an attempt to control Laconia and establish Frankish supremacy over the Peloponnese. He held court here with his Greek wife, Anna Comnena, surrounded by knights of Champagne, Burgundy, and Flanders, but in 1259 he was defeated by the Byzantines. As the Byzantines built a palace and numerous churches (whose frescoes exemplified several periods of painting), the town gradually grew down the slope.

At first the seat of the Byzantine governor, Mystras later became the capital of the Despotate of Morea. It was the despots who made Mystras a cultural phenomenon, and it was the despots—specifically Emperor Constantine's brother Demetrios Palaiologos—who surrendered the city to the Turks in 1460, signaling the beginning of the end. For a while the town survived because of its silk industry, but after repeated pillaging and burning by bands of Albanians, Russians, and Ibrahim Pasha's Egyptian troops, the inhabitants gave up and moved to modern Sparta.

Among the most important buildings in the lower town (Kato Chora) is **Ayios Demetrios,** the *mitropolis* (cathedral) founded in 1291. Set in its floor is a stone with the two-headed Byzantine eagle marking the spot where Constantine XII, the last emperor of Byzantium, was consecrated. The cathedral's brilliant frescoes include a vivid depiction of the Virgin and the infant Jesus on the central apse and a wall painting in the narthex of the Second Coming, its two red-and-turquoise-winged angels sorrowful as they open the records of Good and Evil. One wing of the church houses a **museum** that holds fragments of Byzantine sculptures, later Byzantine icons, decorative metalwork, and coins.

In the Vrontokion monastery are **Ayios Theodoros** (AD 1295), the oldest church in Mystras, and the 14th-century **Church of Panagia Odegetria**, or **Afendiko**, which is decorated with remarkable murals. These include, in the narthex, scenes of the miracles of Christ: *The Healing of the Blind Man, The Samaritan at the Well*, and *The Marriage of Cana*. The fluidity of the brushstrokes, the subtle but complicated coloring, and the resonant expressions suggest the work of extremely skilled hands.

COVER YOUR HEAD AND WATCH YOUR STEP

In spring Mystras is resplendent with wildflowers and butterflies, but it can be oppressively hot in summer, so get an early start to avoid exploring the site in the midday sun. That said, it's easy to spend half a day here, so bring water, sunscreen, a hat, and sturdy shoes for traction on slippery rocks. And watch out for the occasional snake.

The **Pantanassa monastery** is a visual feast of intricate tiling, rosette-festooned loops, and myriad arches. It is the only inhabited building in Mystras; the hospitable nuns still produce embroidery that you can purchase. Step out onto the east portico for a view of the Eurotas river valley below.

Every inch of the tiny **Perivleptos monastery,** meaning "attracting attention from all sides," is covered with exceptional 14th-century illustrations from the New Testament, including *The Birth of the Virgin*, in a lush palette of reds, yellows, and oranges; *The Dormition of the Virgin* above the entrance (with Christ holding his mother's soul represented as a baby); and, immediately to the left of the entrance, the famous fresco the *Divine Liturgy.*

In the upper town (Ano Chora), where most aristocrats lived, stands a rare Byzantine civic building, the **Palace of Despots**, home of the last emperor. The older, northeastern wing contains a guardroom, a kitchen, and the residence. The three-story northwest wing contains an immense reception hall on its top floor, lighted by eight Gothic windows and heated by eight huge chimneys; the throne probably stood in the shallow alcove that's in the center of a wall.

In the palace's **Ayia Sofia chapel,** the Italian wives of emperors Constantine and Theodore Palaiologos are buried. Note the polychromatic marble floor and the frescoes that were preserved for years under whitewash, applied by the Turks when they transformed this into a mosque. Climb to the **castle** and look down into the gullies of Mt. Taygettus, where it's said the Spartans, who hated weakness, hurled their malformed babies. ⊠ *Ano Chora* ☎ *27310/23315* ⊕ *www.culture.gr* ✉ *€5* ⊗ *Apr.–Aug., Mon.–Sat. 8–8, Sun. 8–3; Sept. 1–Sept. 15, Mon.–Sat. 8–7:30, Sun. 8–3; Sept. 16–Sept. 30, Mon.–Sat. 8–6:30, Sun. 8–3; Oct., Mon.–Sat. 8–5:30, Sun. 8–3; Nov.–Mar., daily 8–3.*

10

WHERE TO EAT

$ ✕ **Stelakos.** This spot about 2 km (1 mile) east of Mystras, on the road
GREEK   to Sparta, is known for excellent chicken dishes. After a meal in the
rustic dining room or on the terrace, take a stroll around the village for
an unimpeded view of the Taygettus mountain range. You can sip an
after-dinner coffee or ouzo in one of the tavernas in the main square,
where waterfalls rush down a cliff face. $ *Average main: €9* ⊠ *Off vil-
lage square, Parori* ☎ *27310/83346* ▭ *No credit cards* ☉ *Closed Sun.*

WHERE TO STAY

$$ ⊡ **Pyrgos of Mystras.** A stone mansion set in a fragrant garden at the
B&B/INN   edge of the modern town is the setting for this stylish hotel—it comes
complete with luxurious rooms decorated with rich colors and fab-
rics and overlooks orange groves and Mt. Taygettus. **Pros:** beautiful
decor; extremely comfortable; pleasant terrace; tasty snacks available
throughout the day. **Cons:** not a full-service hotel; expensive. $ *Rooms
from: €190* ⊠ *Manousaki 3* ☎ *27310/20870* ⊕ *www.pyrgosmystra.gr*
⦿ *Breakfast.*

THE CYCLADES

Tinos, Mykonos, Delos, Syros, Naxos,
Paros, Santorini, and Folegandros

WELCOME TO
THE CYCLADES

TOP REASONS
TO GO

★ **Santorini:** Volcanic, spectacular Santorini is possibly the last remnant of the "lost continent"—the living here is as high as the towns' cliff-top perches.

★ **Naxos:** Mythic haunt of the ancient Minoan princess Ariadne, Naxos is the largest of the Cyclades and is noted for its 16th-century Venetian homes.

★ **Mykonos:** The rich arrive by yacht, the middle class by plane, the back-packers by boat—but everyone is out to enjoy the golden sands and Dionysian nightlife.

★ **Ermoupoli:** The main town of Syros (the Cycladic capital) is one of the most beautiful in the islands.

★ **Antiparos:** Hiding within the shadow of its mother island of Paros, this long-forgotten jewel has been discovered by Hollywood high-rollers like Tom Hanks and Brad Pitt.

1 Tinos. Among the most beautiful of the Cyclades, Tinos's charms remain largely unheralded but include the "Greek Lourdes"—the Panayia Evangelistria church—1,000 traditional stone dovecotes, and idyllic villages like Pirgos.

2 Syros. Elegant and beautiful, Syros is the official hub of the Cyclades, the legal and administrative capital. Through its dramatic history, both Roman Catholicism and the Greek Orthodox Church have played major roles. The main town, Ermopouli, with its ocher color, marble streets, and neoclassical grandeur, is one of the most impressive towns in the island chain.

3 Mykonos. Party Central because of its nonstop nightlife, the chief village of Mykonos, called Mykonos town, is the Cyclades' best preserved—a maze of flat-stone streets lined with white houses and flower-filled balconies.

4 Delos. A short boat ride away from Mykonos is hallowed Delos, sacred to Apollo and now a vast archaeological site.

5 Paros. West of Naxos and known for its fine beaches and fishing villages, as well as the pretty town of Naousa, Paros often takes the summer overflow crowd from Mykonos. Today, crowds head here for Paros town and its Hundred Doors Church and undeveloped beaches.

6 Naxos. Presided over by the historic castle of Naxos town, largely the creation of the Venetian dukes of the archipelago, Naxos has a landscape graced with time-stained villages like Sangri, Chalki, and Apeiranthos, many with Venetian-era towers.

7 Folegandros. Tides of travelers have yet to discover this stark island, which makes it all the more alluring to Cyclades lovers, particularly those who prize its stunning cliff scenery.

8 Santorini. Once the vast crater of a volcano, Santorini's spectacular bay is ringed by black-and-red cliffs, which rise up a thousand feet over the sea. The main towns of Fira and Ia cling inside the rim in dazzling white contrast to the somber cliffs. South lies the "Greek Pompeii" that is ancient Akrotiri.

11

GETTING ORIENTED

With their magnificent fusion of sunlight, stone, and sparking aqua sea, the Cyclades are the islands that launched a thousand trips. Set in the heart of the Grecian Mediterranean, these nearly 2,000 islands and islets are scattered like a ring (*Cyclades* is the Greek word for "circling ones") around the sacred isle of Delos, birthplace of the god Apollo. All the top spots—Santorini, Naxos, Paros, Mykonos, Tinos, Syros, and Folegandros—are beloved for their postcard-perfect olive groves, stark whitewashed cubist houses, and bays of lapis lazuli. Gateways to this Aegean archipelago include the airports on Mykonos and Santorini and the harbors of Paros and Naxos.

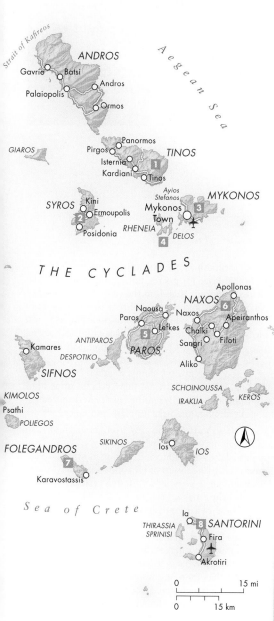

Strait of Kafireos

ANDROS
Gavrio
Batsi
Andros
Palaiopolis
Ormos

Aegean Sea

GIAROS

Panormos
Pirgos
Isternia
Kardiani
TINOS 1
Tinos

Ayios Stefanos
MYKONOS

SYROS
Kini
Ermoupolis 2
Posidonia
RHENEIA
Mykonos Town 3
DELOS 4

THE CYCLADES

Apollonas
NAXOS 6
Naousa
Paros
Naxos
Apeiranthos
Lefkes
Chalki
Paros 5
Sangri
Filoti
Kamares
ANTIPAROS
DESPOTIKO
PAROS
Aliko

SIFNOS

SCHOINOUSSA
KIMOLOS
IRAKLIA
KEROS
Psathi
POLIEGOS

SIKINOS
Ios
FOLEGANDROS
IOS 7
Karavostassis

Sea of Crete

THIRASSIA
SPRINISI
Ia
8 **SANTORINI**
Fira
Akrotiri

0 _____ 15 mi
0 _____ 15 km

Updated
by Stephen
Brewer and
Marissa
Tejada

If the words "Greek Islands" suggest blazing sun and sea, bare rock and mountains, olive trees and vineyards, white rustic architecture and ancient ruins, fresh fish and fruity oils, the Cyclades are your isles of quintessential plenty, the ultimate Mediterranean archipelago.

"The islands with their drinkable blue volcanoes," wrote Odysseus Elytis, winner of the Nobel Prize for poetry, musing on Santorini. The major stars in this constellation of islands in the central Aegean sea—Tinos, Mykonos, Naxos, Paros, and Santorini—remain the archetypes of the islands of Greece. No matter which of these islands you head for, it always seems, at least in summer, that Zeus's sky is faultlessly azure, Poseidon's sea warm, and Dionysus's nightlife swinging (especially in Mykonos's clubs). The prevailing wind is the northern *vorias*; called *meltemi* in summer, it cools the always-sunny weather. In a blazing fusion of sunlight, stone, and aqua sparkle, the Cyclades offer both culture and hedonism: ancient sites, Byzantine castles and museums, lively nightlife, shopping, dining, and beaches plain and fancy.

Each island in the Cyclades differs significantly from its neighbors, so approach your exploration according to what sort of experience you seek. The most popular islands are Santorini, with its fantastic volcanic scenery and dramatic cliff-side towns of Fira and Ia, and Mykonos, a barren island that insinuates a sexy jet-set lifestyle, flaunts some of Greece's most famous beaches, has a perfectly preserved main town, and courts celebrities. These two islands have the fanciest accommodations. Naxos has the best mountain scenery and the longest, most pristine beaches. Tinos, the least visited and most scenic of the Cyclades, is the place to explore mountain villages, hundreds of churches, and fancifully decorated dovecotes. Syros, with its aristocratic roots, is one of the smallest islands but has its own unique neoclassical elegance. Throughout the Cyclades, many shuttered houses are being authentically restored, and much traditional architecture can still be found in Ia on Santorini and Apeiranthos on Naxos—villages that are part of any deep experience of the islands.

11

These arid, mountainous islands are the peaks of a deep, submerged plateau; their composition is rocky, with few trees. They are volcanic in origin, and Santorini, southernmost of the group, actually sits on the rim of an ancient drowned volcano that exploded about 1600 BC. The dead texture of its rock is a great contrast to the living, warm limestone of most Greek islands. Santorini's basic geological colors—black, pink, brown, white, pale green—

are not in themselves beautiful; as you arrive by boat, little shows above the cliff tops but a string of white villages—like teeth on the vast lower jaw of some giant monster. Still, the island was once called Kállisti, "Loveliest," and today appreciative visitors seek its mixture of vaulted cliff-side architecture, European elegance, and stunning sunsets.

A more-idyllic rhythm prevails on many of the other Cyclades (and, of course, off-season in Santorini). In the town of Mykonos, the white-washed houses huddle together against the meltemi winds, and back-packers rub elbows with millionaires in the mazelike gray stone streets. The island's sophistication level is high, the beaches fine, and the shopping varied and upscale. It's also the jumping-off place for a mandatory visit to tiny, deserted Delos. Apollo's windswept birth islet, still watched over by a row of marble lions, was once the religious and commercial center of the eastern Mediterranean.

Tinos has stayed authentically Greek, since its heavy tourism is largely owing to its miracle-working icon, not to its beautiful villages. Naxos, greenest of the Cyclades, makes cheese and wine, raises livestock, and produces potatoes, olives, and fruit. For centuries a Venetian stronghold, it has a shrinking aristocratic Roman Catholic population, Venetian houses and fortifications, and Cycladic and Mycenaean sites. Paros, a hub of the ferry system, has reasonable prices and is a good base for trips to other islands. It's also good for lazing on white-sand beaches and for visiting fishing villages.

As reflected in its neoclassical architecture and soft ocher color, Syros stands apart. A place of religious, industrial, and aristocratic history that gave birth to the bustling port city of Ermopoulis, its strikingly beautiful capital.

Of course, throughout the Cyclades, there are countless classical sites, monasteries, churches, and villages to be explored. The best reason to visit them may be the beauty of the walk, the impressiveness of the location, and the hospitality you will likely find off the beaten track.

PLANNING

WHEN TO GO

The experience of the Cyclades is radically different in summer compared to winter. In summer all services are operating on overload, the beaches are crowded, the clubs noisy, the restaurants packed, and the scene swinging. Walkers, nature lovers, and devotees of classical and Byzantine Greece would do better to come in spring and fall, ideally in late April–June or September–October, when temperatures are lower and tourists are fewer. But off-season travel means less-frequent boat service; in fact, there is sometimes no service at all between November and mid-March, when stormy weather can make the seas too rough for sailing. In winter, many shops, hotels, and restaurants are closed, and the open cafés are full of locals recuperating from summer's intensity. The villages can feel shuttered and the nightlife evaporates. Cultural organizations, film clubs, concerts of island music, and religious festivals become more important. The temperature will often seem colder than the thermometer indicates: if it is in the low 50s, cloudy, drizzling, and windy, you will feel chilled and want to stay indoors, and these island are at their best outdoors.

PLANNING YOUR TIME

The Cyclades are more for lazing around than for book-nosed tourism. Start with the livelier islands (Mykonos, Santorini), add one or two of the larger islands (Naxos, Paros), and finish up with an untouristy one like Folegandros. While it is true that feverish partying can overwhelm the young in summer, in other seasons the temptations are fewer, gentler, and more profound. If you move fast, you will see little, and the beauty is in the general impression of sea, sky, mountain, and village, and in the details that catch your eye: an ancient column used as a building block, an octopus hung to dry in the sun, a wedding or baptism in a small church you stopped by (welcome, stranger), a shepherd's mountain hut with a flagstone roof—they are endless. There are important sites such as Delos's ruins, but just enjoying the island rhythms often proves as soul-satisfying.

GETTING HERE AND AROUND

Transportation to the islands is constantly improving. Five of the Cyclades have airports, and high-speed ferry service between Athens and the islands and within the islands seems to increase with each season. But remember that boat schedules depend on Poseidon's weather whims, and service might be canceled when seas are rough. No matter how you travel, it's best to buy tickets well in advance of major spring and summer holidays.

AIR TRAVEL

Flight schedules change seasonally and are often revised; reservations are always a good idea. There are no airports on Tinos or Folegandros. Olympic Airways has one daily flight from Athens to Syros, four daily flights to Mykonos, three daily flights to Naxos, four daily flights to Paros, and five daily flights to Santorini; there may be more in peak season. Aegean Airlines has five daily flights to Mykonos and four to Santorini in summer, but the schedules are often subject to change. Many

GETTING THERE: BOAT VS. PLANE

To get to the Cyclades, you either fly or take a boat. Flights from Athens are short and convenient, but if you want to understand what it means to be in the Aegean archipelago, and why an island has a special feeling, take the boat— after all, these are islands in the fabled Aegean, inhabited 5,000 years before Homer. But flights cost three times the price of the slower ferries. Nevertheless, if you fly into Athens in time to make a flight connection (and especially if you don't want to visit the big city), it may be worth it. Seats are booked (sometimes overbooked) much in advance, and even in winter you need reservations. Single flights are much easier to get (even last-minute, owing to cancellations). High rollers can also hire a helicopter for €4,000, and you would be surprised how many travelers do this. Note that flights are often canceled owing to rough weather; the islands have small airports, and crosswinds (but not the prevailing north winds, which are fine, however strong) ground planes.

European airlines offer nonstop flights to both Mykonos and Santorini, and charter flights come from the Middle East, Turkey, and Poland.

Airport Contacts Mykonos Airport ✉ *4 km (2½ miles) southeast of Mykonos town, Mykonos* ☎ *22890/79000.* **Naxos Airport** ✉ *1 km (½ mile) south of Naxos town, Naxos* ☎ *22850/23969.* **Paros Airport** ✉ *Near Aliki village, 9 km (5½ miles) south of Paros town, Paros* ☎ *22840/92030.* **Santorini Airport** ✉ *On east coast, 6 km (3.5 miles) from Fira, Monolithos, Santorini* ☎ *22860/28400* ⊕ *www.santoriniairport.com.* **Syros Airport** ✉ *Syros* ☎ *22810/79545.*

BOAT AND FERRY TRAVEL

Greek boats in general are efficient, stable, fast, and comfortable. The new no-smoking law seems to be effective, and in summer they are all air-conditioned. There must be three times as many ferries connecting Athens with the Cyclades as there were a decade ago. Most boats leave from Athens's port of Piraeus and also from Rafina (accessible by KTEL bus from Athens); a few leave from Lavrio. The larger ferries are more stable, and islanders consider the various Blue Star Ferries their main connection to the mainland. Remember that some fast boats are small, and can roll uncomfortably in high seas. Also, high-speeds have little or no deck space; you are closed in. The Blue Star will give you a seat number for a small extra fee, and the fast boats have reserved seats only. In summer, you should always reserve seats in advance.

At Easter and around August 15, seats are hard to come by, and boat schedules change for the holidays. All ferries run much less frequently in winter, and many fast ferries don't run at all.

Off-season you don't need reservations, and you can purchase tickets just before departure at offices on the dock in Piraeus. Ferries can be canceled owing to gales, and then schedules go haywire and hundreds of people and cars have to fight for new tickets (in effect, the ferry companies never cancel boats; the harbor police decide, according to international regulations).

For schedules (not too far in advance, please), check ⊕ *www.openseas.gr* or ⊕ *www.gtp.gr*.

Contacts Piraeus boat departures/arrivals ☎ *14541, 14944.* **Piraeus Port Authority** ⊠ *Piraeus Port Authority, Akti Miaoúli 10, Piraeus* ☎ *210/455–0000 through 210/455–0100* ⊕ *www.olp.gr.* **Rafina KTEL Buses** ☎ *22940/23440 bus terminal* ⊕ *www.ktelattikis.gr.*

BUS TRAVEL

For information about Bus Travel, consult the Getting Here and Around sections listed under each island.

CAR AND SCOOTER TRAVEL

To take cars on ferries you must make reservations. Though there is bus service on all islands, you may find it more convenient to travel by car, especially on a larger island like Naxos. Although islanders tend to acknowledge rules, many roads on the islands are poorly maintained, and tourists sometimes lapse into vacation inattentiveness. Drive with caution, especially at night, when you may well be sharing the roads with motorists returning from an evening of drinking. All the major islands have car- and bike-rental agencies at the ports and in the business districts. Car rentals in summer cost about €40–€60 per day, with unlimited mileage and third-party liability insurance. Full insurance costs about €10 per day more. Many places now rent Smart Cars for about €60 a day: these two-seaters are way cool for getting around.

Often travelers opt for scooters or four-wheel semi-bikes (quads), but be careful—island hospitals are frequently filled with people with serious-looking injuries due to poor roads, slipshod maintenance, careless drivers, and excessive partying. Quads, which Greeks call *gourounia* (piggies), look safer than scooters but in fact turn over easily. Choose a dealer that offers 24-hour service and a change of vehicle in case of a breakdown. Most will take you from and to your plane or boat.

FOOT TRAVEL

The Cyclades are justly famous for their hiking. Ancient goat and donkey trails go everywhere—through fields, over mountains, along untrodden coasts. Since tourists crowd beaches, clubs, and town promenades, walking is uncrowded even in July and August. Prime walking months, though, are April and May, when temperatures are reasonable, wildflowers seem to cover every surface, and birds migrate. October is also excellent for hiking—plus, olive groves provide their own sort of spectacle when dozens of gatherers spread their cloths.

HOTELS

Overall, the quality of accommodations in the Cyclades is high, whether they be tiny pensions, private houses, or luxury hotels. The best rooms and service (and noticeably higher prices) are on Mykonos and Santorini, where luxury resort hotels now rank among the world's favorites. Wherever you stay in the Cyclades, make a room with a view and a balcony a priority. If you're not interested in staying at luxury hotels and unless you're traveling at the very height of the season (July 15–August 30), you're unlikely to need advance reservations on some islands. Sometimes the easiest way to find something, in fact, is to head for a tourist office and describe your needs and price range. And remember: few hotels have elevators, and even Santorini's best often have breathlessly picturesque cliff-side staircases (though many have porters to carry your bags).

RESTAURANTS

Eating is a lively social activity in the Cyclades, and the friendliness of most taverna owners compensates for the lack of formal service. Unless you order intermittently, the food comes all at once. Restaurant schedules on the Cyclades vary; some places close for lunch, most close for siesta, and all are open late. Reservations are not required unless otherwise noted, and casual dress is the rule. But luxury restaurants are a different kettle of fish in some respects.

Greek food used to have a bad international reputation, and you can certainly find bad food in Greece. This is often a result of restaurants trying to adapt to the tastes and wallets of the throngs of tourists. Greece produces top-quality tomatoes, lamb chops, melons, olive oil, and farmer's cheese. When Greeks go out to eat, they expect good, simple food culled from these elements, as should you. Do likewise, and you will dine with much pleasure.

Dishes are often wonderfully redolent of garlic and olive oil; as a simple, plain alternative, order grilled seafood or meat—grilled octopus with ouzo is a treat. A typical island lunch is fresh fried calamari with a salad of tomatoes, peppers, onions, feta, and olives. Lamb on a skewer and *keftedes* (spicy meatballs) are also favorites. Of course, nouvelle Greek has made great strides since it was first introduced in the early 2000s at the luxury hotels of the Cyclades. At the finer hotels, and at certain outstanding restaurants, you can taste the collision of centuries-old traditional dishes with newer-than-now-nouvelle spices and preparations. There are just so many times one can eat lamb-on-a-skewer, so go ahead and splurge at top restaurants—if you have a chubby wallet, that is.

Greek wines have tripled in quality in the last decade. The volcanic soil of Santorini is hospitable to the grape, and Greeks love the Santorini wines. Santorini and Paros now proudly produce officially recognized "origin" wines, which are sought throughout Greece. Barrel or farmer's wine is common, and except in late summer when it starts to taste a bit off, it's often good.

DINING AND LODGING PRICES IN EUROS			
$	**$$**	**$$$**	**$$$$**
Restaurants	Under €16	€16–€25	€26–€40	Over €40
Hotels	Under €126	€126–€225	€226–€275	Over €275

Restaurant prices are the average cost of a main course at dinner or, if dinner is not served, at lunch. Hotel prices are the lowest cost of a standard double room in high season.

SHOPPING

Mykonos is the best island in the Cyclades for shopping. You can buy anything from Greek folk items to Italian designer clothes, cowboy boots, and leather jackets from the United States. Although island prices are better than in the expensive shopping districts of Athens, there are many tourist traps in the resort towns, with high-pressure sales tactics and inflated prices for inferior goods. The Greeks have a word for a naive American shopper—*Americanaki*. It's a good sign if the owner of a shop selling traditional crafts or art lives on the island and is not a hot shot Athenian over for the summer to make a quick buck. Each island has a unique pottery style that reflects its individuality. Santorini potters like the bright shades of the setting sun, though the best pottery island is Paros. Island specialties are icons hand-painted after Byzantine originals; weavings and embroideries; local wines; and gold worked in ancient and Byzantine designs. Don't be surprised when the stores close between 2 and 5:30 in the afternoon and reopen in the evenings; even on the chic islands everybody takes a siesta.

VISITOR INFORMATION

For information about each island's tourist office (or travel agency) please consult the Visitor Information section listed under each island. General brochures and information about the Cyclades are also available through the website and offices of the Greek National Tourism Organization (*GNTO; EOT in Greece ⊕ www.gnto.gr*).

TINOS ΤΗΝΟΣ

Updated by Marissa Tejada

160 km (85 nautical miles) southeast of Piraeus harbor in Athens.

Tinos (or, as archaeologists spell it, Tenos) is among the most beautiful and most fascinating of the major Cyclades. The third-largest of the island group after Naxos and Andros, with an area of 195 square km (121 square miles), it is inhabited by nearly 10,000 people, many of whom still live the traditional life of farmers or craftspeople. Its long, mountainous spine, rearing between Andros and Mykonos, makes it seem forbidding, and in a way it is. It is not popular among tourists for a few reasons: the main village, Tinos town (Chora), lacks charm; the beaches are undeveloped; there is no airport; and the prevailing north winds are the Aegean's fiercest (passing mariners used to sacrifice a calf to Poseidon, ancient Tinos's chief deity, in hopes of avoiding shipwreck). On the other hand, Tinos is dotted with possibly the loveliest villages in the Cyclades.

Whether travelers head to Tinos or not, a visit here is essential for Greeks: its great Church of Panayia Evangelistria is the Greek Lourdes, a holy place of pilgrimage and miraculous cures; 799 other churches adorn the countryside. Encroaching development here is to accommodate those in search of their religious elixir and not, as on the other islands, the beach-and-bar crowd.

Tinos's magnificently rustic villages are, for some welcome reason, not being abandoned. The dark arcades of Arnados, the vine-shaded sea views of Isternia; the gleaming marble squares of Pirgos: these, finally,

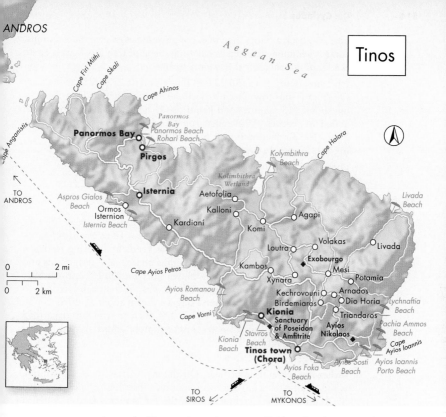

Tinos

Cape Firi Mithi
Cape Skali
Cape Ahinos

Panormos Bay
Panormos Bay
Panormos Beach
Rohari Beach

Pirgos

Kolymbithra Beach
Cape Halara

Cape Argonistis

TO ANDROS

Aspros Gialos Beach
Ormos Isternion
Isternia Beach

Isternia

Aetofolia

Kalloni

Kardiani
Komi

Kolimbithra Wetland

Agapi

Livada Beach

0   2 mi
0   2 km

Cape Ayios Petros

Ayios Romanou Beach

Cape Vorni

Kionia Beach

Stavros Beach

Loutra
Kambos
Xynara

Volakas
Exobourgo
Mesi

Livada

Potamia

Kechrovouni
Birdemiaros

Kionia
Sanctuary of Poseidon & Amfitrite

Arnados
Dio Horia
Triandaros

Ayios Nikolaos

Lychnaftia Beach
Pachia Ammos Beach
Cape Ayios Ioannis

Tinos town (Chora)

Ayios Foka Beach

Ayios Sosti Beach

Ayios Ioannis Porto Beach

TO SIROS

TO MYKONOS

are what make Tinos unique. A map, available at kiosks or rental agencies, will make touring these villages by car or bike somewhat less confusing, as there are nearly 50 of them. Of all the major islands, Tinos is the least developed for sports—the strong winds discourage water sports, and sports outfitters come and go.

GETTING HERE AND AROUND

In high season many boats stop at Tinos, since it is on the Mykonos line, and consequently Tinos becomes crowded with travelers. But Tinos, owing to the famous church, is also hugely popular with Greeks who arrive on Friday night and leave in time to get to work on Monday. The boats vary from big ferries to fast passengers-only boats, and it takes four to five hours, depending mostly on route and weather. Especially notice, as your boat rounds the point into the harbor, the high peak of Exambourgos with its acropolis and Venetian fort. For August weekends, reservations are recommended. For Easter and August 15 they are absolutely necessary, and the boats will be packed (the many cars in transit don't help). For these holidays, boat schedules do change; information much in advance is not trustworthy. Tinos has daily ferry connections with Andros, Mykonos, and Paros, less often with Naxos. Returning boats go either to Piraeus or to Rafina. When buying tickets at the quayside agencies, remember that not every office handles every boat, so check at more than one. For any queries or recommendations, contact Leonidas or Vangelis Kontonikolaou of Kalypso Travel. There is a lot of information at ⊕ *www.greeka.com.*

On Tinos, buses (☎ *22830/22440*) run several times daily from the quay of Chora (Tinos town) to nearly all the many villages in Tinos, including Kionia (15 minutes) and Panormos (1 hour); in summer buses are added for beaches. Prices range from €2 to €5 and service stops around 7 pm. The bus station is near the new dock.

VISITOR INFORMATION
Contacts Kalypso Travel ☎ *22830/22993* ⊕ *www.kalypso-travel.com.*

TINOS TOWN ΤΗΝΟΣ (ΧΩΡΑ)

14 km (9 miles) northwest of Mykonos town.

Civilization on Tinos is a millennium older than Tinos town, or Chora, founded in the 5th century BC. On weekends and during festivals, Chora is thronged with Greeks attending church, and restaurants and hotels cater to them. As the well-known story goes, in 1822, a year after the War of Independence began (Tinos was the first of the islands to join in), the Virgin sent the nun Pelagia a dream about a buried icon of the Annunciation. On January 30, 1823, such an icon was unearthed amid the foundations of a Byzantine church, and it started to heal people immediately.

EXPLORING

Archaeological Museum of Tinos. On the main street, near the church, is the small Archaeological Museum; its collection includes a sundial by Andronicus of Cyrrhus, who in the 1st century BC also designed Athens's Tower of the Winds. Here, too, are Tinos's famous huge, red storage vases, from the 8th century BC. ⊠ *Megalochari* ☎ *22830/22670* 🎫 *€2* ⊗ *Tues.–Fri. 9–4.*

Cultural Foundation of Tinos. Founded in 2002, the Cultural Foundation of Tinos, housed in a large and splendid neoclassic building at the south end of the quay, remains active in promoting the fantastic art, history, and culture of the island. The center revolves around a full schedule of traveling exhibitions, lectures, performances, and other events. It has a permanent exhibit of work by Tinian sculptor, Iannoulis Chalepas. There's also a café. ⊠ *Paralia Tinos* ☎ *22830/29070* ⊕ *www.itip.gr* 🎫 *€3* ⊗ *Wed.–Mon. 10–2 and 7–9 pm.*

Fodor'sChoice
★
Panayia Evangelistria. The Tinians, hardly unaware of the icon's potential, immediately built the splendid Panayia Evangelistria, or Church of the Annunciate Virgin, on the site, in 1823. Imposing and beautiful, framed in gleaming yellow and white, it stands atop the town's main hill ("hora"), which is linked to the harbor via Megalochari, a steeply inclined avenue lined with votive shops. Half Venetian, half Cypriot in style, the facade (illuminated at night) has a distinctive two-story arcade and bookend staircases. Lined with the most costly stones from Tinos, Paros, and Delos, the church's **marble courtyards** (note the green-veined Tinian stone) are paved with pebble mosaics and surrounded by offices, chapels, a health station, and **seven museums.** Inside the **upper**

three-aisle church dozens of bees-wax candles and precious tin- and silver-work votives—don't miss the golden orange tree near the door donated by a blind man who was granted sight—dazzle the eye. You must often wait in line to see the little icon, encrusted with jewels, which was donated as thanks for cures. To beseech the icon's aid, a sick person sends a young female relative or a mother brings her sick infant. As the pilgrim descends from the boat, she falls to her knees, with traffic indifferently whizzing about her, and crawls painfully up the faded red padded lane on the main street—1 km (½ mile)—to the

LOVEY-DOVEY MCMANSIONS

Tinos is renowned for its 1,300 dovecotes (*peristeriónes*), which, unlike those on Mykonos or Andros, are mostly well-maintained; in fact, new ones are being built. Two stories high, with intricate stonework, carved-dove finials, and thin schist slabs arranged in intricate patterns resembling traditional stitchery, the dovecotes have been much written about—and are much visited by doves.

church. In the church's courtyards, she and her family camp for several days, praying to the magical icon for a cure, which sometimes comes. This procedure is very similar to the ancient one observed in Tinos's temple of Poseidon. The **lower church,** called the Evresis, celebrates the finding of the icon; in one room a baptismal font is filled with silver and gold votives. The chapel to the left commemorates the torpedoing by the Italians, on Dormition Day, 1940, of the Greek ship *Helle*; in the early stages of the war, the roused Greeks amazingly overpowered the Italians. ⊠ *Evangelistria 1* ☎ *22830/22256* ⊕ *www.panagiatinou. gr* ⌧ *Free* ⊙ *Daily 8:30–3.*

OFF THE
BEATEN
PATH
Mountain Villages Above Chora. At night the lights of the hill villages surrounding Tinos's highest mountain, Mt. Tsiknias—2,200 feet high and the ancient home of Boreas (the wind god)—glitter over Chora like fireworks. By day they are worth visiting. Take the good road that runs through Dio Horia and Monastiri, which ascends and twists around switchbacks while passing fertile fields and a few of Tinos's most fanciful old dovecotes. After 9 km (5½ miles) you reach **Kechrovouni,** or Monastiri, which is a veritable city of nuns, founded in the 10th century. One cell contains the head of St. Pelagia in a wooden chest; another is a small icon museum. Though a nunnery, Kechrovouni is a lively place, since many of the church's pilgrims come here by bus. Out front, a nun sells huge garlic heads and braids to be used as charms against misfortune; the Greeks call these "California garlic." One km (½ mile) farther on, Tinos's telecommunications towers spike the sky, marking the entrance to **Arnados,** a strange village 1,600 feet up, overlooking Chora. Most of the streets here are vaulted, and thus cool and shady, if a bit claustrophobic; no medieval pirate ever penetrated this warren. In one alley is the **Ecclesiastical Museum,** which displays icons from local churches. Another 1½ km (¾ miles) farther on are the **Dio Horia** (Two Villages), with a marble fountain house, unusual in Tinos. The spreading plane tree in front of it, according to the marble plaque, was planted in 1885. Now the road starts winding down again, to reach **Triandaros,**

CLOSE UP

Traditional Festivals in the Cyclades

All over Greece, villages, towns, and cities have traditional celebrations that vary from joyous to deeply serious, and the Cyclades are no exception. In Tinos town, the healing icon from Panayia Evangelistria church is paraded with much pomp on Annunciation Day, March 25, and especially Dormition Day, August 15. As it is carried on poles over the heads of the faithful, cures are effected, and religious emotion runs high. On July 23, in honor of St. Pelagia, the icon is paraded from Kechrovouni Nunnery, and afterward the festivities continue long into the night, with music and fireworks. More down-to-earth is the Tinos International Literary Festival, bringing writers from around the world for three days of readings and performances in locations around the island at the end of July (⊕ www. tinoslitfestival.com).

If you're on Santorini on July 20, you can partake in the celebration of St. Elias's name day, when a traditional pea-and-onion soup is served, followed by walnut and honey desserts and folk dancing.

Naxos has its share of festivals to discover and enjoy. Naxos town celebrates the Dionysia festival during the first week of August, with concerts, costumed folk dancers, and free food and wine in the square. During Carnival, preceding Lent, "bell wearers" take to the streets in Apeiranthos and Filoti, running from house to house making as much noise as possible with strings of bells tied around their waists. They're a disconcerting sight in their hooded cloaks, as they escort a man dressed as a woman from house to house to collect eggs. In Apeiranthos, villagers square off in rhyming-verse contests: on the last Sunday of Lent, the *paliomaskari,* their faces blackened, challenge each other in improvising *kotsakia* (satirical couplets). On July 14, Ayios Nikodemos Day is celebrated in Chora with a procession of the patron saint's icon through town, but the Dormition of the Virgin on August 15 is, after Easter and Christmas, the festival most widely celebrated, especially in Sangri, Filoti (where festivities take place on August 4), and Apeiranthos.

On Paros each year on August 23, eight days after the huge festival in Parikia at the Church of a Hundred Doors, Naousa celebrates the heroic naval battle against the Turks, with children dressed in native costume, great feasts, and traditional dancing. The day ends with 100 boats illuminated by torches converging on the harbor. On June 2 there is much feasting in Lefkes for the Holy Trinity.

On Syros, the International Festival of the Aegean, which began in 2005, takes place every summer attracting those who simply love the arts. Ermopouli's historic neoclassical venues, including the Apollo Theater, is the elegant backdrop for opera, concerts, theater and cultural events featuring artists from around the world. Ermoupolis's two prominent churches, one Catholic and one Greek-Orthodox, means Christian holidays, like Easter, are celebrated twice. On October 26, the island celebrates its patron saint, St. Dimitrios, with feasts and events.

which has a good restaurant. Many of the pretty houses in this misty place are owned by Germans. Yannis Kyparinis, who made the three-story bell tower in Dio Horia, has his workshop and showroom here.

BEACHES

There is a series of beaches between Chora and Kionia (and beyond, for walkers).

Ayios Fokas Beach. This long sandy beach is the closest organized beach to Tinos town and it's also the island's largest beach overall. The coastline is marked with natural shade from tamarisk trees but

> ### CALLING ALL FAITHFUL
>
> Evangelistria, the street parallel to Panayia Evangelistria, the legendary church of Tinos town, is closed to traffic and is a kind of religious flea market, lined with shops hawking immense candles, chunks of incense, tacky souvenirs, tin votives, and sweets. There are several good jewelers' shops on the market street, where, as always on Tinos, the religious note is supreme.

beach chairs and umbrellas are readily available for rent during the summer. The main road behind the beach has a gathering of beach hotels, rooms, and tavernas. There's also a few beach bars and cafés along its 1.5 km (1 mile) stretch. **Amenities:** food and drink. **Best for:** walking; swimming. ⊠ *3 km (2 miles) from Tinos town, Ayios Fokas.*

Stavros Beach. Within walking distance of Tinos town, this beach is a peaceful little corner of Tinos. One or two tavernas are nearby but Stavros beach is really known for its fine sand and its beautiful surroundings. The turquoise waters remain clear and shady green trees dot the area surrounding Ayios Stavros, the pretty whitewashed church that gave the beach its name. ■ TIP→ **Come during sunset, as it makes for one of the most romantic settings on Tinos. Amenities:** food and drink. **Best for:** sunset; swimming. ⊠ *Stavros beach ⊹ 1 km (.5 mile) from Tinos town.*

WHERE TO EAT

$$

MEDITERRANEAN

Fodor's Choice

★

✗ **Itan Ena Mikro Karavi.** After entering off a main road in Tinos town, take a short walk down a pastel painted hallway to your open-air dining destination. This discreet entrance hides what's to come—an impressively ambient setting with hanging bougainvillea, decorated with lively yet warm colors. An outdoor dining room wall showcases artistic boat hangings, which coincides with its name that was inspired by a popular Greek kid's song, "It was a Small Boat." Chef Antonis Psaltis serves his "creative Mediterranean" with superb results. Excellent appetizers include a smooth split pea purée and an eggplant salad with sesame paste. Main dishes like fish soup and the pork, slowly cooked in a mustard and beer sauce, display the range of well-done dishes. Wines hail from the Cycladic islands. $ *Average main: €17* ⊠ *Trion Ierarchon* ☎ *22830/22818* ⊕ *www.mikrokaravi.gr* ☉ *Closed Nov.–Apr.*

$

GREEK

✗ **Metaxi Mas.** On a trellised lane by the harbor, Euripides and Marygo Tatsionas's restaurant, the best in Tinos, turns out to be no more expensive than a taverna. The name means "between us," and a friendly air prevails. The decor is traditional—pale stone walls and high stone arches—and the staff is welcoming. From starters to desserts, the food

11

is homemade, but with an haute-Athenian flair. For a starter, try local artichokes in vinegar sauce or hot eggplant slices wrapped around cheese, mint, and green pepper. Among the main dishes, the spicy lamb cooked in paper is especially succulent; the calimari stuffed with cheese, tomatoes, and peppers is also exceptional. For dessert daughter Argyro's mille-feuille is light and rich. With a fireplace in winter and an air-conditioner for summer, this place stays open year-round. $ *Average main: €10* ⊠ *Kontogiorgi alley* ☎ *22830/25945* ⊕ *www. metaximastinos.gr.*

$$
GREEK
✗ **Symposion.** Giorgos Vidalis's café and restaurant is situated in a sophisticated and well-preserved neoclassic building on a pedestrian-only street. Open all day you can eat breakfast, lunch or dinner on the second- and third-floor terraces that overlook the Turkish fountain and the passing scene. At night, it's interior is an ambient restaurant filled with pastel colors, elegant furnishings, and marble-topped tables. Try the Symposium salad, a delightful mix of French lettuce, avocado, grilled shrimp, and citrus vinaigrette. Main dishes include the sole fillet with parsley and basmati, and the Tinian veal fillet with peppercorns and roasted vegetables. The Greek wine list is impressive. $ *Average main: €16* ⊠ *Evangelistria 13* ☎ *22830/24368* ✉ *info@symposion. gr* ⊕ *www.symposion.gr* ☉ *Closed Nov.–Mar.*

$
GREEK
✗ **Zefki.** The Tsirou family cooks up delicious, homemade Greek classics with a Tinian touch. Try the Tinian omelet with sausage and fresh potatoes, or for a more hearty dish go for the savory roasted local goat. The desserts are homemade and change with the season. ■ **TIP →** Every Sunday during the summer you'll hear live Greek music along with your meal. It's open all year. $ *Average main: €10* ⊠ *Alex. Lagourou 6* ⊹ *Walk up Evangelistria street and take the second right* ☎ *22830/22231* ▬ *No credit cards.*

WHERE TO STAY

$
HOTEL
⊡ **Favie Suzanne Hotel.** Sleek, posh, and convenient, too: if you are willing to give up a sea view, this is the best place to stay in Tinos town, thanks, in good part, to the hotel's lovely decor, which, from fanlights to dovecotes, incorporates many Tinian details. **Pros:** set right in the heart of the busy town. **Cons:** Tinos town is a busy place. $ *Rooms from: €100* ⊠ *Antoniou Sochou 22* ☎ *22830/22693* ✉ *info@faviesuzanne.gr* ⊕ *www.faviesuzanne.gr* ⇲ *49 rooms* ☉ *Closed Nov.–Feb.* ¶◉¶ *Breakfast.*

$
B&B/INN
⊡ **Vincenzo Family Hotel.** Owner and manager Ioannis Vidalis has given Tinos just what it needs. **Pros:** a great budget choice if you want to be in town. **Cons:** town is busy. $ *Rooms from: €95* ⊠ *25th March 15* ☎ *22830/25888* ⊕ *www.vincenzo.gr* ⇲ *14 rooms* ¶◉¶ *Breakfast.*

NIGHTLIFE

Tinos has fewer bars and discos than the other big islands, but there's a lively late-night bar come summer. The action is behind the waterfront between the two boat docks.

Kaktos Bar. Jutting up next to a restored 16th century Cycladic windmill, Kaktos Cocktail Bar is an open-air terrace bar where locals and visitors alike can sit back and enjoy a cocktail while taking in the view of Tinos town and the Aegean sea. The stone walls, wall hangings, and artwork give off an Old West–style ambience complete with a few large cacti. The summer features a schedule of DJs that spin various house, mainstream, and dance beats. ☎ *22830/25930* ⊕ *www.kaktos-bar.gr* ⊗ *Closed Oct.–May.*

Koursaros Bar. Koursaros, which translates to pirate, gets its share of summer party crowds each year. Its decor is a soft mix of dark wood and stone with vintage maps and seafaring artifacts that play into the bar's nautical theme. It's location, at the very corner by the harbor, has made it one of the most visible landmark nightlife spots in Tinos since 1987. Café by day, a DJ turns up the music at night spinning rock, funk, or jazz. ⊠ *Akti Ellis 1* ☎ *22830/23963.*

Sivylla Club. Tinos town has a nightlife district, but it only comes to life in the heat of the summer. Sivylla, located on one of the district's alleyways, churns out both Greek pop and international mainstream dance hits. ⊠ *Taxiarchon 17* ☎ *22830/22511* ⊕ *www.sivylla.gr.*

Volto Club. Taxiarchon, Tinos town's nightlife alleyway, is home to Volto Club, which pumps live and loud Greek music accompanied by a dancing, happy crowd. ⊠ *Taxiarchon 24* ☎ *22830/21292.*

SHOPPING

Due to the island's landmark church, you'll find a wide variety of stores selling religious icons of every size and style, handmade from all types of material from gold, silver, and wood. Tinos is still a rural island in many ways, so locally produced honey, cheese, and foodstuffs are of top quality and simply delicious. Finally, the island is particularly known for its marble arts and sculptures. If you're looking for something that may not be found anywhere else, beautiful Tinian artwork may be just the thing.

CANDY

Halaris Sweet Shop. This sweet shop and bakery is the local go-to for anything traditional and sweet. It's known for Tinian specialties such as almond paste candies called *psarakia tinou,* and cheesecake bites made with Tinian cheese called *gliko tiropitaki tsibiti.* You'll find yourself walking away with little gift boxes filled with your favorites but before you go, try their homemade ice cream featuring flavors like Greek yogurt raspberry. ⊠ *Georgiou Plamari 3* ☎ *22830/23274.*

JEWELRY

Fodor's Choice
★
Anna Maria. By the small park next to the Cultural Center, the entrance to the small arts shop, Anna Maria, is draped with blue morning-glory vines. The boutique showcases jewelry by Greek craftsmen with ancient and Byzantine motifs and also marble pieces carved by owner Pavlos Kangas (a retired mathematics teacher) and other Tinian sculptors. The crowded shop is a delight. ⊠ *Alvanou St.* ☎ *22830/23456.*

Ostria. The selection here is especially good; in addition to delicate silver jewelry, it sells silver icon covers, silver plate, and 22-karat gold. ⊠ *Evangelistria 20* ☎ *22830/23893.*

MARKETS

Enosis (*Farmers' Cooperative*). Tinos produces a lot of milk. A short way up from the harbor, on the right, is the little store of the Enosis, which sells milk, butter, and cheeses, including sharp *kopanistí* made special in Tinos, perfect with ouzo; local jams and honeys are for sale, too. ⊠ *Main street up from harbor, Megalochari 16* ☎ *22830/23289.*

Farmers' Market. Tinos is a rich farming island, and every day but Sunday, farmers from all the far-flung villages fill the square with vegetables, herbs, and *kritamos* (pickled sea-plant leaves). ⊠ *Between two docks* ⏱ *Mon.–Sat. 7:30 am–4 pm.*

Fish Market. In a little square near the very center of town, local Tinian fishermen sell fresh seafood. Meanwhile, the local pelican (a rival to Mykonos's Petros) can often be found cadging snacks from them.

RELIGIOUS ICONS

Dia Cheros. The walls of Xenofon Varveris's colorful neoclassical shop are filled with detailed religious icons that may look similar at first glance, but once you look closer you'll see that each piece is unique since each one has been handmade and hand-painted in Greece. Besides a fantastic selection of the icon plaques, Dia Cheros features collections of handmade Greek jewelry as well as traditional glass lamps. ⊠ *Evangelistria 24.*

WEAVINGS

Biotechniki Scholi. The 100-year-old weaving school, or Biotechniki Scholi, sells traditional weavings—aprons, towels, spreads—made by its students, local girls. The largest of its three high-ceiling, wooden-floor rooms is filled with looms and spindles. ⊠ *Evangelistria, three-quarters of way up from sea* ☎ *22830/22894* ⏱ *Daily 9–2 and 6–9 pm.*

AYIOS IOANNIS BAY ΑΓΙΟΣ ΙΩΑΝΝΗΣ

7 km (4 miles) east of Tinos town.

Heading east from Tinos town, you'll travel on a winding road surrounded by bare, rocky Cycladic island landscape. It eventually slopes down into the Ayios Ioannis bay (O ormos tou Ayiou Ioanni in Greek). The quiet beaches here offer clear seas that curve into picturesque bays. Around Ayios Ioannis bay, several hotels, rooms for rent, and tavernas open each summer to cater to the season's travelers.

BEACHES

FAMILY **Ayios Sostis Beach.** Known for its shallow turquoise waters and excellent, clear view of Mykonos, the yellow sand-filled Ayios Sostis beach is said to be a continuation of Ayios Kyriaki beach. In the summer, beach chairs and umbrellas are available to rent. A few taverns and cafés are within walking distance for a meal break or refreshments. There are several ways to get to the beach including a few small roads lined with bougainvillea and tall reeds. **Amenities:** food and drink. **Best for:** swimming. ⊠ *Ayios Sostis.*

Ayios Ioannis Porto Beach. Since it's secluded from the summer's temperamental gusty island winds, the sands that fill up the pretty curved beach of Ayios Ioannis Porto beach stay put. Here you can spend the day under tamarisk trees for natural shade or rent beach chairs and umbrellas during peak season. Its shallow waters and calm nature make it a choice beach for families. Several beach hotels are in close proximity. A few tavernas are nearby for a beach break. **Amenities:** food and drink. **Best for:** swimming.

Pachia Ammos Beach. Secluded in a cove east of Tinos town, Pachia Ammos is named for its thick sand, which has a unique green hue that complements the surrounding short shrub hills that roll into the turquoise blue sea. Completely undeveloped, getting to the beach requires a 15–30 minute walk on an unmarked path that isn't ideal for flimsy flip-flops as you are balancing your beach necessities. Reaching it, however, means basking in one of the prettiest and most peaceful places on the island. To get there drive 10 km (6 miles) on the main road east towards Ayios Ioannis beach. Turn off when you see signs for Pachia Ammos. Park off the road and walk over the hill to your right; the beach isn't obvious right away but follow one of several trails and you'll see it before you. **Amenities:** none. **Best for:** solitude; swimming. ✉ *Past Porto, reached by a dirt road, Pachia Ammos.*

WHERE TO STAY

$ RESORT FAMILY

🏨 **Akti Aegeou.** The family that runs this little resort is lucky to own such a valuable piece of property as Akti Aegeou, or "Aegean Coast," right on the uncrowded beach at Laouti—a very pretty location. **Pros:** perfect for swimming in pool or beach; a sweet, quiet, and small beach hotel. **Cons:** far from town; too bad so many modern villas being built here. [$] *Rooms from: €90* ✉ *Laouti* ✣ *6 km (3.7 miles) east of Tinos town* ☎ *22830/24248* 🌐 *www.aktiaegeou.gr* 🛏 *19 studios, 14 apartments, 2 suites* 🕒 *Closed Nov.–Mar.* 🍴 *No meals.*

$ HOTEL FAMILY

🏨 **Porto Tango.** This ambitiously up-to-date and stylish resort-hotel strives for the best in decor and service—little wonder that Greece's late prime minister, Andreas Papandreou, stayed here during his last visit to Tinos. **Pros:** great for families. **Cons:** a bit out in the boonies. [$] *Rooms from: €110* ☎ *22830/24411* ✉ *portango@otenet.gr* 🌐 *www.portotango.gr* 🛏 *52 rooms, 5 suites* 🕒 *Closed Nov.–Mar.* 🍴 *Breakfast.*

KIONIA KIONIA

2½ km (1¼ miles) northwest of Tinos town.

The little seaside town of Kiona is a short scenic drive, bike ride, or hike west of Tinos town. A few simple tavernas and rooms are set off the main beach road, and on the main road the landmark Tinos Beach Hotel directly overlooks Kiona beach. Kiona's main attraction is the Sancutary of Poseidon, which dates back to the 4th century BC.

Sanctuary of Poseidon. The reason to come to this small community outside Tinos town is to visit the large, untended Sanctuary of Poseidon, also dedicated to the bearded sea god's sea-nymph consort, Amphitrite. The present remains are from the 4th century BC and later, though the sanctuary itself is much older. The sanctuary was a kind of hospital, where the ailing came to camp and solicit the god's help. The marble dolphins in the museum were discovered here. According to the Roman historian Pliny, Tinos was once infested with serpents (goddess symbols) and named Serpenttown (Ophiousa), until supermasculine Poseidon sent storks to clean them out. The sanctuary functioned well into Roman times. ✉ *Northwest of Tinos town.*

BEACHES

Kionia Beach. Just 3 km (2 miles) west of Tinos town, Kiona beach remains one of the island's most visited beaches. It's a combination of both pebbles and sand, but the long stretch of sandy coastline dominates. A section of it affronts an area where the archaeological site of the Sanctuary of Poseidon remains. The town of Kionia's beachfront road is lined with cafés, tavernas, rooms for rent, and the Tinos Beach Hotel *(⇨ below)*, which are all within walking distance of the beach. Beach chairs and umbrellas are available for rent during the summer season. **Amenities:** food and drink. **Best for:** swimming; walking.

WHERE TO EAT

$ GREEK 🍴 **Tsambia.** Abutting the Sanctuary of Poseidon and facing the sea, this multilevel taverna home makes traditional fare. For starters try the indigenous specialties: *louza* (smoked pork), local Tinian cheeses rarely sold in stores (especially fried local goat cheese), and homegrown vegetables. Fresh fish is available, depending on the weather. Tried-and-true are pork in red wine with lemon, or goat casserole with oregano. To get here, follow signs for "traditional taverna" before the Sanctuary of Poseidon. [$] *Average main: €10* ✉ *Epar. Od. Tinou-Kallonis* ☎ *22830/23142.*

WHERE TO STAY

$ HOTEL FAMILY 🏨 **Tinos Beach Hotel.** The winning points about this hotel is that it is big, comfortable, well-appointed, and fronts on Kionia's long beach. **Pros:** very well run. **Cons:** not walking distance from town. [$] *Rooms from: €65* ☎ *22830/22626* 🌐 *www.tinosbeach.gr* 🛏 *160 rooms* 🍽 *Breakfast.*

ISTERNIA ΙΣΤΕΡΝΙΑ

24 km (15 miles) northwest of Tinos town.

The village of Isternia (Cisterns) is verdant with lush gardens. Many of the marble plaques hung here over doorways—a specialty of Tinos—indicate the owner's profession, for example, a sailing ship for a fisherman or sea captain. A long, paved road winds down to a little port, Ayios Nikitas, with a beach and two fish tavernas; a small boat ferries people to Chora in good weather.

BEACHES

Isternia Beach. The beach, located right at the foot of the little fishing village of Isternia bay, is actually two beaches. There's one pebbled area and one sandy cove but both are known for their peaceful seclusion. For a beach break, two tavernas and a café are nearby. You can also take some time out to visit the inland village of Isternia about 5 km (3 miles) away.Whether you're lying on the beach or having a meal by the sea, you can look forward to enjoying one of the nicest sunset views in Tinos. **Amenities:** food and drink. **Best for:** solitude; swimming.

11

WHERE TO EAT

$$ ✕ **To Thalassaki.** The name means "the little sea" and this restaurant,
MEDITERRANEAN specializing in Mediterranean seafood, has one of the island's best
Fodor's Choice sea views. Set on a platform on Ormos Isternion bay, right up against
★ the Aegean sea with views of Syros, the restaurant's light blue and
gray decor matches the simple atmosphere. Chef and owner Antonia
Zarpa serves up innovative, well-thought-out dishes that capture the
local flavors from her beloved island. Excellent plates include the
Tinian cheese with garlic and poppy seeds; the oven-baked octopus
with olive oil and grape molasses; and the squid cooked with garlic,
onion, potatoes, and mint. Finish with a light and delightful lemon
meringue ice-cream custard. $ *Average main: €16* ⊠ *Ormos Isternion*
⊗ *Closed Nov.–Mar.*

PIRGOS ΠΥΡΓΟΣ

*32 km (20 miles) northwest of Tinos town, 8 km (5 miles) north of
Isternia.*

The village of Pirgos, second in importance to Chora, is inland and
up from the little harbor of Panormos. Tinos is famous for its marble
carving, and Pirgos, a prosperous town, is noted for its sculpture
school (the town's highest building) and marble workshops, where
craftsmen make fanlights, fountains, tomb monuments, and small
objects for tourists; they also take orders. The village's main square
is aptly crafted of all marble; the five cafés, noted for *galaktobou-
reko* (custard pastry), and one taverna are all shaded by an ancient
plane tree. The quarries for the green-vein marble are north of here,
reachable by car. The cemetery here is, appropriately, a showplace of
marble sculpture.

EXPLORING

Museum Iannoulis Chalepas. The marble-working tradition of Tinos sur-
vives here from the 19th century and is going strong, as seen in the two
adjacent museums Museum Iannoulis Chalepas and Museum of Tinos
Artists, which house the work of Pirgos's renowned sculptor, and other
works. ⊠ *1 block from bus stop* ☎ *22830/31262* ⊡ *€3* ⊗ *Daily 10–2
and 6–8 pm* ⊗ *Closed Oct.–Mar.*

Fodor's Choice **Museum of Marble Crafts.** In the highest building on Pirgos hill, the
★ Museum of Marble Crafts is part of the Piraeus Bank Cultural Foun-
dation's network of high-tech museums on the last century's traditional
industries. Inside the strikingly modern building exhibits on view show
the process of quarrying and carving and they are the best you'll ever
see. The master-artists's drawings for altarpieces and tomb sculpture
are also on display, as are some of their works. Open year-round.
✛ *Take the staircase up from the main square of Pirgos* ☎ *22830/31290*
⊕ *www.piop.gr/en* ⊡ *€3* ⊗ *Wed.–Mon. 10–6.*

SHOPPING

Lambros Diamantopoulos. A number of marble carvers are, appropri-
ately, found in Pirgos. You may visit the shop and view the work of
probably the island's best master carver, Lambros Diamantopoulos,

who accepts commissions for work to be done throughout Greece. He makes and sells traditional designs to other carvers, who may bring a portable slab home to copy, and to visitors. ⊠ *Near main square* ☎ *22830/31365.*

PANORMOS BAY ΟΡΜΟΣ ΠΑΝΟΡΜΟΥ

35 km (22 miles) northwest of Tinos town, 3 km (2 miles) north of Pirgos.

Panormos bay, an unpretentious port once used for marble export, has ducks and geese, a row of seafood restaurants, and a good beach with a collapsed sea cave. More coves with secluded swimming are beyond, as is the islet of Panormos. There are many rooms to rent.

BEACHES

Panormos Beach. The sandy beach affronts the lovely fishing village of Panormos, which at one point was the island's main harbor. Located north of Tinos town, most visitors also make it a point to visit the nearby inland village of Pirgos or beach hop to little beaches to the east and west of Panormos beach. When the island winds act up, windsurfers may take on the waters. **Amenities:** food and drink. **Best for:** windsurfing; swimming. ⊹ *34 km (21 miles) north of Tinos town.*

FAMILY **Rohari Beach.** Located in the next cove southeast from Panormos beach, Rohari remains just as popular in the summer as a favorite northern beach destination. Fully organized, the beachfront cantinas are the perfect spot for a cool drink; there are beach umbrellas and chairs for rent. It's within close proximity to the village of Panormos, which has a wide selection of tavernas and cafés for a beach-day break. **Amenities:** food and drink. **Best for:** swimming.

SYROS ΣΥΡΟΣ

Updated by Marissa Tejada

153 km (83 nautical miles) southeast of Piraeus.

The mercantile bustle of modern Ermoupoli—Syros's port, capital, and the archipelago's business hub since the 18th century—often makes people do a double take. Seen from a far distance out at sea, the city looks like a Cycladic village—one, however, raised to the nth dimension, with thousands of houses climbing their way up twin conical hills. The closer you get, the more impressive things look. As you pull up to the harbor, lined with big mansions and towering churches, you see that Hermesopolis—the city was originally named after Hermes, the god of trade—is a 19th-century neoclassic jewel. A palatial marble town hall, a grand city square that looks airlifted from Paris, an opera house modeled after La Scala, and a British-run gambling casino: these are just a few of the flourishes that announce Ermoupoli as the centuries-old administrative hub of the Cyclades. Partly colonized by one of Greece's largest Catholic populations, Syros is home to more than half the residents of the island chain.

Though it seems arid, Homer praised the island in Book XV of *The Odyssey*. Markos Vamvakaris, the great Syrian *rebetis* (performer of rembetika music), wrote a song celebrating the beauty of its women of Venetian and Frankish descent, the "Frankosyriani," perhaps the most popular of all *bouzouki* songs. Herman Melville, writing in 1856–57, gave the men equal time: "Lithe fellows tall with gold-shot eyes, Sunning themselves as leopards may."

Near the center of the Cyclades, due east of Kythnos and west of Mykonos, rocky Syros covers an area of 135 square km (52 square miles). Some might say that Ermoupoli is the only real reason for a stopover on Syros—but it is so architecturally rich that it should not be missed. Also, the island's untouristy urbanity and long, exciting history, much of it visible, make it worthwhile.

GETTING HERE AND AROUND

Olympic Airlines flies to Syros daily (40 minutes), and up to four ferries leave from Piraeus (4 hours), usually stopping at Tinos and/or Mykonos en route; seats book up fast during the summer season, so advance reservations are essential. And since Syros is the administrative hub for the Cyclades, you can find daily ferry connections back and forth to any of the islands in the chain, including Paros, Naxos, Tinos, and Mykonos. Several ferry companies schedule regular runs, including Blue Star Ferries, Nel Lines, and Hellenic Seaways. The Syros Port Authority can answer questions about ferry schedules.

Syros has an organized bus system that offers service every half hour from Ermopouli. Fares are less than €2 each way. The bus stops at the villages located on the ring road including Galissas, Finikas, Poseidonia, Megas Yialos, and Vari. Another bus line goes toward Kini. There are also taxi stands at the harbor, right where the ferries unload passengers. It costs about €5 to get from the port to Ano Syros.

Rental cars offer you more freedom to get to the beaches and other villages out of Ermopouli. Compact car rentals start at €40 a day, and motorbike rentals start at €15 per day.

Airport Contacts Syros Airport ✉ *Ermopouli, Syros* ☎ *22810/79545.*

Ferry Contacts Syros Port Authority ✉ *Ermopouli, Syros* ☎ *22810/88888.*

TOURS

Teamwork Travel. This full-service travel agency can help with any of your travel plans to the island and arrange tours while you're on shore. ✉ *Akti Papagou 18, Ermopouli, Syros* ⊕ *www.teamwork.gr.*

ERMOUPOLI ΕΡΜΟΥΠΟΛΗ

35 km (21 miles) west of Mykonos, 135 km (83 miles) northwest of Santorini, 154 km (95 miles) southeast of Athens.

Ermoupoli spills like multicolored lava from the twin colonial hills of Ano Syros and Vrodado, topped respectively by churches Roman Catholic (St. George, on the left-hand peak when viewed from the harbor) and Greek Orthodox (Resurrection, on the right). Capital not only of the island but of the entire Cycladic island group, Ermoupoli was the main port of Greece for half a century after its conception in 1822, during the War of Independence. During the struggle refugees fleeing from the Turkish massacres chose the site of the ancient "town of Hermes," god of travelers and merchants, on which to raise their new city, and crowned it with Vrodado's blue-dome Resurrection church. Following the war, Syros became so important it was seriously considered as a site for the fledgling nation's first capital. Starting at that time, waves of rich immigrants from Smyrna, Chios, Hydra, Psara, and Crete made the island into a cultural and commercial center.

EXPLORING

Apollo Theater. Built in 1861 as a small-scale version of Milan's La Scala, the Apollo Theater is another example of Syros's wealth. Severely damaged during WWII,

> **I LOVE THE NIGHTLIFE**
>
> Syros is known for its *rembetika* music—the noted songster Markos Vamvakaris was a native. The best places to hear traditional songs are the cafés way up on the Ano Syros hill (reservations needed) but you'll also find fine cafés down by the harbor, including To Rebetadio, a noted restaurant on Eptanisou street (one block up from the waterfront), where, late at night, the music begins to wail. Other nighttime options: the open-air Pallas Cinema (east of Miaoúli Square), concerts at Apollo Theater, or the elegant casino on the quay.

the theater was finally restored and reopened in 2000. Today, operas and other cultural events fill the summer schedule, including the world famous Festival of the Aegean, which takes place every July. ✉ *Miaoúli Sq., across from the Municipal Palace, Ermopouli, Syros* ⊕ *www. festivaloftheaegean.com.*

Archaeological Museum. Syros's Archaeological Museum is located on the left side of the Town Hall. The small space features artifacts from the island's rich history. The collection stretches back to the Neolithic era and includes artifacts taken from the prehistoric acropolis at Kastri to the north. Particularly illustrious are the Early Cycladic objects from Chalandriani (just south of Kastri), which indicate an advanced culture in the 3rd millennium BC. The museum, although not extensive, is one of the oldest in Greece. ✉ *Miaoúli Sq., Left side of Municipal Palace, separate entrance, Ermoupoli, Syros* ☎ 22860/88487 ☜ €5 ⊗ *Tues.– Sun. 9–3.*

Industrial Museum. Suitably housed in refurbished factories that helped establish the island's wealth and industrial supremacy in the 19th century, the Industrial Museum walks you through the commercial district's rise and fall. The three buildings once belonged to Katsimantis Paint, the Aneroussis Lead Factory, and the Kornilakis Tannery. A tour gives insight into how employees worked, who they worked for, and how their collective skills made Syros a bustling harbor and key European trading zone, all contributing to the island's prosperity and influence on Greece as a fledgling nation. Vintage photographs, various tools, and an exhibit of two-dozen large machines that were used until the mid-20th century also give insight into a thriving industrial center that once was. ✉ *Georgiou Papandreou 11, Ermoupoli, Syros* ☎ 22810/81243 ⊕ *www.ketepo.gr* ☜ €2 ⊗ *June–Sept., Wed.–Mon. 10–2 and 6–9 pm; Oct.–May, Wed. and Fri.–Mon. 10–2 and 6–9 pm.*

Miaoúli Square. Like the Municipal Palace behind it, this expansive palm-ringed marble square was designed by famed Bavarian architect Ernst Ziller and includes a grand statue of revolutionary war hero Admiral Andreas Miaoúlis. Families and couples fill the length of marbled pavement on summer evenings for their evening *volta* or walk as skateboarding children skid around them. The island's other architectural landmark, the Apollo Theater, is a short walk away. ✉ *Miaoúli Sq., Ermopouli, Syros.*

Municipal Palace/Town Hall. The Municipal Palace, also known as the Town Hall, was built in 1876 by Ernst Ziller whose credits include Athens's famous Grande Bretagne hotel and the nearby Miaoúli Square. The building is an impeccably maintained neoclassical landmark of Ermopoulis. During working hours, you can stroll in and take in the elegantly designed marble rooms. Local town officials still hold meetings here in the presence of grand oil paintings of King George I and Queen Olga. The building also houses the municipal courts, which deal with legal cases from all the Cycladic Islands, since Syros is the administrative capital. A traditional marble floor café, popular with the locals, is situated in the center, surrounded by high marble balconies. ✉ *Miaoúli Square, Ermopouli, Syros* ☎ *22810/86300.*

BEACHES

Although its beaches don't equal those of Mykonos, Paros, and Naxos, Syros has plenty of pleasant stretches of sand. Almost all of these are being developed, and villas, some truly hideous, are going up by the dozen.

Azolimnos Beach. As one of the closest organized beaches to Ermopoulis, Azolimnos attracts its share of crowds in the height of summer. The coast is a mixture of small rocks and sand with a picturesque little dock that juts out into the bay. Tamarisk trees offer natural shade, and lounge chairs and umbrellas are available for rent. The small road set in the background is lined with various options for food, coffee, drinks, and supplies. **Amenities:** food and drink. **Best for:** swimming. ✉ *Azolimnos, Syros.*

WHERE TO EAT

$ MEDITERRANEAN FAMILY

🍴 **Kouzina.** The colorful taverna-style restaurant is set in a bougainvillea-laced courtyard at the end of one of the prettiest streets in Ermoupoli, the proud reinvention of partners Mel Apostolidis and Anestis Paschalousis. Mel, the chef, is a Greek Canadian who is behind the Mediterranean fusion dishes influenced from his North American roots. Start off with homemade feta-filled spring rolls with a tangy tomato-ginger marmalade. Top main dishes include a grilled pork chop in a honey and balsamic glaze and a chicken breast fillet with mushrooms and red peppers in a white wine curry sauce. The menu also features a selection of gourmet beef burgers and rib-eye steaks, and a kid's menu with classic American favorites like chicken fingers. [$] *Average main: €10* ✉ *Androu 5, Ermoupoli, Syros* ☎ *22810/89150.*

$ GREEK

🍴 **To Kastri.** Located in the central market, To Kastri is run by the Women's Union of Syros, a group of 28 women who cook 10 dishes a day—home cooking so good that local housewives secretly buy food for their midday meals here. Open all year, this cafeteria often sells out by early afternoon. Beef stew, stuffed zucchini, stuffed cuttlefish, and beef in lemon sauce are what you would expect—but better. ⓢ *Average main: €5* ✉ *Parou 13, a small side street off Chiou, Ermopouli, Syros* ☎ *22810/83140* ⊕ *www.tokastri.blogspot.gr* ▭ *No credit cards* ⊙ *Daily 9–5.*

WHERE TO STAY

$ · HOTEL — **Diogenis Hotel.** Situated right where the ferries dock in Syros, the Diogenis Hotel took over a 19th century neoclassical building that was once used as a warehouse, lumber yard, and, during the Italian occupation, housed an Italian cabaret. **Pros:** centrally located. **Cons:** the port can be a busy place. ⓢ *Rooms from: €80* ✉ *Ermopouli, Syros* ☎ *22810/86301* ⊕ *www.diogenishotel.com* ⤴ *43 rooms* ⦿ *Multiple meal plans.*

$ · B&B/INN — **Hotel Omiros.** Perched on a steep hill just above Miaoúli Square, Omiros is set in a yellow-stucco neoclassic mansion that's a welcoming place to experience both modern comforts and old Syros. **Pros:** historic building; quiet location; friendly staff. **Cons:** no elevator; not centrally located; uphill walk from main town. ⓢ *Rooms from: €50* ✉ *Omirou Metamorfosi 43, Ermoupoli* ☎ *22810/84910* ⊕ *www.hotel-omiros.gr* ⤴ *11 rooms, 2 suites* ⊙ *Closed Oct.–Mar.* ⦿ *Breakfast.*

$$ · HOTEL — **Hotel Ploes.** Once a private 19th-century estate in the upscale district of Ermopoulis, Hotel Ploes has been completely renovated to luxury hotel status. **Pros:** direct access to the sea; centrally located; beautiful views. **Cons:** no swimming pool; on-site restaurant coming soon. ⓢ *Rooms from: €200* ✉ *Apollonos 2, Ermoupoli, Syros* ☎ *22810/9360* ⊕ *www.hotelploes.com* ⤴ *7 rooms; 1 suite* ⦿ *Breakfast.*

$ · HOTEL — **Nisaki.** Convenient and comfortable, this modern three-story building is set amid neoclassic buildings and is within walking distance of Ermopouli's most visited sites. **Pros:** centrally located. **Cons:** small bathrooms. ⓢ *Rooms from: €70* ✉ *E. Padadam 1, Ermoupoli, Syros* ☎ *22810/88200* ⊕ *www.hotelnisaki.gr* ⤴ *42 rooms* ⦿ *Breakfast.*

$ · HOTEL · Fodor's Choice ★ — **Syrou Melathron.** Located behind the St. Nicholas Cathedral and just a five-minute walk from Miaoúli Square, the neoclassical-style building, which was completed in 1857, sits off a paved sea road in the upscale neighborhood of Vaporia. **Pros:** centrally located; great service. **Cons:** rooms can be small. ⓢ *Rooms from: €80* ✉ *Babagiotou 5, Ermoupoli, Syros* ☎ *22810/86495* ✎ *info@syroumelathron.gr* ⊕ *www.syroumelathron.gr* ⤴ *21 rooms; 1 suite* ⊙ *Closed Nov.–Feb.* ⦿ *Breakfast.*

NIGHTLIFE

Baba Bar. A few steps away from the nightlife bustle of Petrou Ralli's row of music pumping bars, Baba Bar is still in the heart of the action, just slightly tucked away in a pretty little street that's lit by strings of soft white light bulbs. The bar's small, Cycladic-style interior can get packed with regulars that come back for their eclectic selection of cocktails with names like Pirate Martini, Rosemary Melon, Pina Rosa, and the signature Rum Baba. ✉ *Near Petrou Ralli, Ermoupoli, Syros.*

Liquid Music Bar. Located across the street from the quiet marbled Miaoúli Square, this corner dance club and bar gets busy and loud around midnight when the bouncer is securely in place and a line to get in may start forming. Liquid's clubby dark interior, strung with black and neon lights around a long dance floor, attracts a sexy younger crowd of both locals and visitors who are looking for a fun place to dance the night away to mainstream dance beats. ⊠ *El. Venizelou, across the street from Miaoúli Square, Ermopouli, Syros* ☎ *22810/83974.*

Mammo Wine and Food Bar. Nightlife in Syros revolves around the eastern part of the harbor, along Petrou Ralli, where you may find people dancing in the street; Mammo Wine Bar is at the center of it. Café and restaurant by day—serving bruschettas, gourmet salads, and a variety of international and Mediterranean plates—the energy heightens when the sun sets. Its sleek, dark and modern space gets packed and comes alive once a DJ is called in to play mainstream dance music, and colorful creative cocktails and shots make the rounds. The wine continues to flow and there are 100 to choose from. ⊠ *Akti Petrou Ralli 38, Ermopouli, Syros* ☎ *22810/76416* ⊕ *www.mammo-syros.gr.*

KINI KINI

7 km (4½ miles) west of Ermoupoli.

This small village on the island's west coast has a couple of good beaches, a selection of tavernas and cafés, and a few places to stay. Since it has one of the better beaches on the island, it's a popular stop for tourists.

BEACHES

Kini Beach. If you're looking for the best sunset on the island, head where the locals head—Kini. The beach, long and sandy, features a little picturesque port that's flanked by a line of shady trees and the lovely little whitewashed village it gets its name from. It's big enough to accommodate all beachgoing types including families, strolling couples, and water-sports lovers. The selection of taverns, restaurants, and cafés are plentiful and if you need a beach umbrella and chair rental, show up early during peak season. **Amenities:** food and drink. **Best for:** swimming; sunset; walking. ⊠ *Kini, Syros.*

Lotos Beach. Small, quiet, and secluded, this sand-and-pebble beach is flanked by shady tamarisk trees. There are no amenities here but it's within walking distance of the well-organized and popular Kini beach and Kini village where everything can be found. **Amenities:** none. **Best for:** solitude. ⊠ *Lotos beach, Syros.*

WHERE TO EAT

$$
GREEK
Fodor's Choice
★

✕**Allou Yialou.** Located right off the beach in Kini, on a raised whitewashed dining space lined with white curtains, Allou Yialou is known for its spectacular sunset dining. It's also where everyone goes for Greek dishes that take on a delightful and delicious gourmet twist. Chef Lina Fournistaki and her husband Yannis pay close attention to service and the presentation is impressive. Appetizers to savor include crab salad with couscous; local boiled greens with lemon and ginger;

and a beetroot salad with garlic yogurt. Their take on *strapatsada* (a traditional Greek egg dish similar to scrambled eggs) moves onto a new level to include fried potatoes, fresh tomatoes, and homemade sauce. Their seafood menu is complete with fresh fish selections and dishes like sea urchin spaghetti. Simply divine! $ *Average main: €20* ⊠ *Kini, Syros* ☎ *22810/71196* ⊘ *Closed Nov.–Apr.*

ANO SYROS ΑΝΩ ΣΥΡΟΣ

9 km (5½ miles) northwest of Ermoupoli.

One of the two towering peaks that rise over town, Ano Syros was greatly expanded by Venetians in the 13th century, who erected a walled town over the ancient acropolis to protect themselves from pirates. It's now the second city of Syros. From the Roman Catholic bishopric of the church of St. George crowning the hill, this lofty retreat maintains its 13th-century integrity. High atop the hill is the looming Capuchin Monastery (1633), where visitors on official religious business may enjoy a sojourn in the jasmine-scented garden overlooking all of Ermoupoli. Not far away is a belvedere—the town's high point—where a bronze bust of Pherekides commemorates that imaginative 6th-century BC Syrian philosopher, Pythagoras's teacher, who reputedly invented the sundial and was the first to write Greek prose. The bishopric, where bishops have presided since the time of Irenaios (343 AD), is downhill from the monastery. Farther down is the Jesuit Monastery, founded in 1747, and the adjacent church of the Virgin of Carmel. As you can see, the hill of Ano Syros remains mostly Catholic, but just across the townscape is the hill of Vrodado, which reminds us that Syros is now two-thirds Greek Orthodox (happily, relations remain cordial). The Catholic-flavored Venetian influence has given the island's culture and architecture a distinct flavor; having welcomed so many religious refugees to its shores, Syros came under the protection of Louis XIII in 1640, which accounts for the French-flavored influence. ■TIP➔ **Take a taxi up, but walk down so you can explore Omiros street, a handy thoroughfare through this picturesque quarter that's dotted with castle walls and stone alleyways.**

EXPLORING

Vamvakaris Museum. One of Greece's most prestigious *rembetika* (urban Greek folk music) artists, Markos Vamvakaris hails from Syros making this a fitting location for a museum in his honor. The composer is a legend in Greek folklore music hailing from the 1930s and is widely known for his rembetika songs, especially the Frangosyriani. In the little museum you'll see many of his personal items, vintage photographs, and a passport he never managed to use, all donated by his family. ⊠ *Agiou Sevastianou street, Ano Syros, Syros* ☎ *22813/60914* ⊘ *June–Aug., Tues.–Sun. 11–2 and 7–9 pm.*

11

GALISSAS ΓΑΛΗΣΣΑΣ

4 km (2½ miles) southwest of Ermoupoli.

The village of Galissas has a selection of tavernas and beach bar-cafés as well as room rentals and the Dolphin Bay Family Beach Resort. Since it has one of the island's longest sandy beaches, it's a popular destination for anyone stopping over on the island.

BEACHES

Galissas Beach. Competing with Kini for the most magical sunset, the long curve of sand and clear coastline of water at Galissas is a local favorite. It's also won the coveted EU Blue Flag award for being one of the cleanest in Europe. As one of the island's largest beaches, it's well-organized with beach umbrella and chair rentals available in peak season. When the island winds roar, windsurfers show up. ■ TIP→ There's a separate area for nudists. **Amenities:** food and drink. **Best for:** nudists; swimming; windsurfing. ⊠ *Galissas, Syros.*

WHERE TO EAT

$$ ✕ **Lilis Taverna.** This traditional taverna's stone terrace, which sits in
GREEK the old hilltop town of Ano Syros, offers one of the best panoramic sea views beyond Ermopouli and the port. The tavern has been in the Roussos family for three generations establishing it as a local favorite. Trained chef Leonardo Roussos has taken over and still believes in the simple beauty of local flavors, and it shows with classic flavorful dishes such as a caper dip and local sausage with anise. Try his homemade *kokkinisto*, a tomato beef stew. Below the restaurant the original enclosed tavern space, opened by his grandfather, is filled with memorabilia including a working jukebox and original tavern furniture. It's still in use and gives a glimpse of what original taverns and *rembetika* places were like in their heyday. $ *Average main: €17* ⊠ *Piatsa, Ano Syros, Syros* ☏ *22810/88087.*

POSEIDONIA ΠΟΣΕΙΔΩΝΙΑ

6½ km (4¼ miles) southwest of Ermoupoli.

This small village has a few whitewashed taverns, cafés, and churches, which serve as a backdrop to a popular beach. Other good beaches are to the north and south of the village.

BEACHES

FAMILY **Agathopes Beach.** Considered one of Syros's most beautiful beaches, Agathopes gets packed in peak season due to its shallow waters and fine sand. If you're there at the right time, you'll find a unique small islet where white sea lilies blossom. The sea view is also dotted with the uninhabited islands called Schinonissi and Stroggylo. Beachgoers can rent lounge chairs and umbrellas, and there's a local taverna within walking distance. **Amenities:** food and drink. **Best for:** swimming. ⊠ *Agathopes beach, Syros.*

Finikas Beach. Sheltered by the summer island winds, Finikas beach is the perfect spot for those seeking a calm beach day southwest of Ermopouli. Boasting the island's second largest port, yachts often dock here and there's typically a picturesque scene of fishing boats bobbing on the calm waters. Tamarisk trees dot the beach providing natural shade, although beach umbrella and chair rentals are available during peak season. There are plenty of eateries to choose from as well. **Amenities:** food and drink. **Best for:** swimming. ⊠ *Finikas, Syros.*

Poseidonia Beach (*Dellagrazia Beach*). This beach may have two names, but its known for one thing: being pretty. Located in the southwest part of Syros, it features smooth, yellow sand with scatterings of small pebbles. It shares the same views of Schinonissi and Stroggylo (the two small uninhabited islands) as neighboring Agathopes beach. Small boats and yachts often park here adding to the quaint views. **Amenities:** food and drink. **Best for:** swimming. ⊠ *Poseidonia, Syros.*

> ### MACHO GREEK FLAVORING
>
> When Athenians want *real* Greek food, they often head to Syros, which has long been known for its culinary brio. Not only was Greece's first cookbook published here in 1828, famed foodie Elizabeth David earned her toques in Mediterranean cooking here. Flavors are strong and accented with cheese, tomato, and fennel. Check out the lemon-and-anise-flavored *loukanika* sausages; the cured-pork *louza* tenderloin soaked in wine and cloves; the *marathopita*, lemon-herb and fennel bread; and the *kopanisti*, the island's tangy cheese.

MEGA YIALOS ΜΕΓΑ ΓΙΑΛΟ

9 km (5½ miles) south of Ermoupoli.

Mega Yialos has slowly grown into one of the island's more popular beach towns and is accessible by bus from Ermopouli. Its nearby beaches, including the popular Megas Yialos beach, are within easy walking distance for those staying at area hotels and rooms. Restaurants and cafés also cater to summer crowds.

BEACHES

Megas Yialos Beach. One of the largest beaches on Syros, Megas Yialos is also one of the most frequented and organized. Located on the island's southeast corner, the beach is known for its transparent waters and fine sand. The village is populated with room rentals and small hotels as well as restaurants and beach cafés. Some large shady trees dot the beach, but in peak season chairs and umbrellas are for rent. **Amenities:** food and drink. **Best for:** swimming. ⊠ *Megas Yialos, Syros.*

VARI ΒΑΡΗ

6 km (4 miles) southeast of Ermoupoli.

Vari is a small beach town on a sheltered bay on the south side of the island. Its location attracts visitors who seek the low-key, quiet calm of the nearby beaches.

BEACHES

Vari Beach. The small beach's fine sand is protected from the sometimes harsh summer Cycladic winds making its calm water a favorite with local families. Considered an organized beach, beach chair and umbrella rentals are available and a street lined with tavernas and cafés is within walking distance for any visitors that need a good meal after a day of beach lounging. **Amenities:** food and drink. **Best for:** sunsets; swimming. ⊠ *Vari, Syros.*

MYKONOS ΜΥΚΟΝΟΣ

Updated by Marissa Tejada

From backpackers to the superrich, from day-trippers to yachties, from regular people to celebrities (who head here by helicopter), Mykonos has become one of the most popular of the Aegean islands. Today's scene is a weird but attractive cocktail of tradition, beauty, and glitz, but travelers from all over the world have long been drawn to this dry, rugged island—at 16 km (10 miles) by 11 km (7 miles), one of the smaller Cyclades—thanks to its many stretches of sandy beach, its thatched windmills, and its picturesque port town. One thing is certain: Mykonos knows how to maintain its attractiveness, how to develop it, and how to sell it. Complain as you will that it is touristy, noisy, and overdeveloped; you'll be back.

In the 1950s a few tourists began trickling into Mykonos on their way to see the ancient marvels on the nearby islet of Delos, the sacred isle. For almost 1,000 years Delos was the religious and political center of the Aegean and host every four years to the Delian games, the region's greatest festival. The population of Delos actually reached 20,000 at the peak of its commercial period, and throughout antiquity Mykonos, eclipsed by its holy neighbor, depended on this proximity for income (it has been memorably described as Delos's "bordello"), as it partly does today. Anyone interested in antiquity should plan to spend at least one morning on Delos, which has some of the most striking sights preserved from antiquity, including the beautiful Avenue of the Lions or the startling, enormous stone phalli in the Sanctuary of Dionysus.

Today, the natives of Mykonos have happily fit cosmopolitan New Yorkers, Londoners, and Athenians gracefully into their way of life. You may see, for example, an old island woman leading a donkey laden with vegetables through the town's narrow streets, greeting the suntanned vacationers walking by. The truth is, Mykonians regard a good tourist season the way a fisherman inspects a calm morning's catch; for many, the money earned in July and August will support them for the rest of the year. Not long ago Mykonians had to rely on what they could scratch out of the island's arid land for sustenance, and some remember suffering from starvation under Axis occupation during World War II. How things have changed.

GETTING HERE AND AROUND

Mykonos is superpopular and easy to get to. It is totally jammed in season, in part thanks to 10 or more daily, 45-minute flights from Athens in summer (there are almost as many in winter); there are also direct flights from Europe and the Middle East. The trip by ferry takes from 2½ to 5 hours depending on your route, the boat, and Poseidon's weather ways. There are eight or more boats a day. For Easter and August 15, book early. In summer, reservations are necessary; off-season, you won't need one, but cars always need them. The boats usually pull in at the huge new dock area, from which you must take a bus or taxi, or get your hotel to pick you up (better hotels do this, and often charge you for it).

In Mykonos town the Ayios Loukas bus station in the Fabrica quarter at the south end of town has buses to Ornos, Ayios Ioannis, Platis Gialos, Psarou, Paradise beach, the airport, and Kalamopodi. Another station near the Archaeological Museum is for Ayios Stefanos, Tourlos, Ano Mera, Elia, Kalafatis, and Kalo Livadi. Schedules are posted (hotel concierges also should have this info); fares run from €2 to €10. Regular taxis line up at Mando Mavrogenous Square, while scooter-taxis greet new arrivals at the harbor; use them to get to your Mykonos town hotel, usually hidden away on a pedestrian (and scooter-only) street. Meters are not used on Mykonos; instead, standard fares for each destination are posted on a notice bulletin board; note there are only 13 regular cabs here even in August!

TOURS

Mykonos Accommodation Center. The Mykonos Accommodation Center has grown to offer just about every service a visitor may need on Mykonos, including a wide variety of group tours. A guide takes a group every morning for a day tour of Delos (€40). The company also has half-day guided tours of the Mykonos beach towns, with a stop in Ano Mera for the Panayia Tourliani Monastery (€35). You can also take an excursion to nearby Tinos (€60), arrange private tours of Delos and Mykonos and off-road Jeep trips (€60), charters yachts, and more. Owner John van Lerberghe is an expat who has lived on the island for decades, and he knows his stuff. ☒ *Enoplon Dynameon 10, in a picturesque old building, up a steep staircase, Mykonos town* ☎ *22890/23160* 🖶 *22890/24137* ⊕ *www.mykonos-accommodation.com.*

MYKONOS TOWN ΜΥΚΟΝΟΣ (ΧΩΡΑ)

177 km (95 nautical miles) southeast of Piraeus harbor in Athens.

Although the fishing boats still go out in good weather, Mykonos largely makes its living from tourism these days. The summer crowds have turned one of the poorest islands in Greece into one of the richest. Old Mykonians complain that their young, who have inherited stores where their grandfathers once sold eggs or wine, get so much rent that they have lost ambition, and in summer sit around pool bars at night with their friends, and hang out in Athens in winter when island life is less scintillating.

Put firmly on the map by Jackie O in the 1960s, Mykonos town—called Hora by the locals—remains the Saint-Tropez of the Greek islands. The scenery is memorable, with its whitewashed streets, Little Venice, the Kato Myli ridge of windmills, and Kastro, the town's medieval quarter. Its cubical two- or three-story houses and churches, with their red or blue doors and domes and wooden balconies, have been

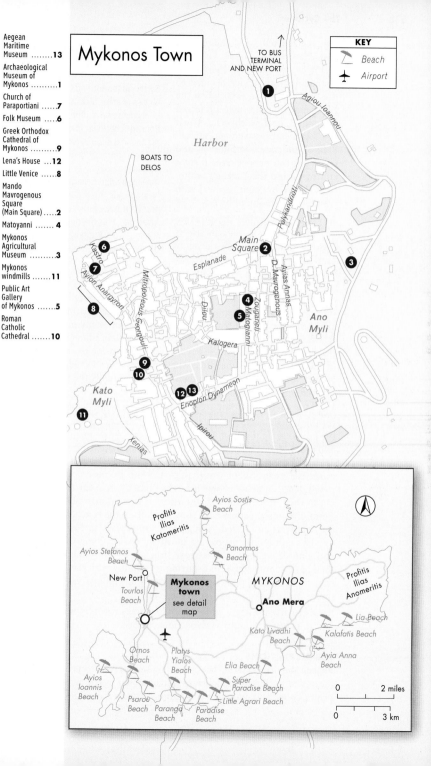

Mykonos Town

KEY

Beach

Airport

TO BUS TERMINAL AND NEW PORT

Harbor

BOATS TO DELOS

Kastro

Ayion Anargyron

Mitropoleous Georgouli

Main Square

Esplanade

Ayias Annas

D. Mavrogenous

Ano Myli

Polykandrioti

Agiou Ioannou

Zouganeli

Matoyanni

Dilou

Kalogera

Kato Myli

Enoplon Dynameon

Ipirou

Xenias

Ayios Sostis Beach

Profitis Ilias Katomeritis

Panormos Beach

Ayios Stefanos Beach

New Port

Tourlos Beach

Mykonos town see detail map

MYKONOS

Ano Mera

Profitis Ilias Anomeritis

Lia Beach

Kato Livadhi Beach

Kalafatis Beach

Ornos Beach

Platys Yialos Beach

Elia Beach

Ayia Anna Beach

Ayios Ioannis Beach

Psarou Beach

Paranga Beach

Paradise Beach

Super Paradise Beach

Little Agrari Beach

0   2 miles

0   3 km

long celebrated as some of the best examples of classic Cycladic architecture. Luckily, the Greek Archaeological Service decided to preserve the town, even when the Mykonians would have preferred to rebuild, and so the Old Town has been impressively preserved. Pink oleander, scarlet hibiscus, and trailing green pepper trees form a contrast amid the dazzling whiteness, whose frequent renewal with whitewash is required by law.

Any visitor who has the pleasure of getting lost in its narrow streets (made all the narrower by the many outdoor stone staircases, which maximize housing space in the crowded village) will appreciate how its confusing layout was designed to foil pirates—if it was designed at all. After Mykonos fell under Turkish rule in 1537, the Ottomans allowed the islanders to arm their vessels against pirates, which had a contradictory effect: many of them found that raiding other islands was more profitable than tilling arid land. At the height of Aegean piracy, Mykonos was the principal headquarters of the corsair fleets—the place where pirates met their fellows, found willing women, and filled out their crews. Eventually the illicit activity evolved into a legitimate and thriving trade network.

> ### THE PRANCE OF THE PELICAN
>
> By the time morning's open-air fish market picks up steam in Mykonos town, Petros the Pelican—the town mascot—preens and cadges eats. In the 1950s a group of migrating pelicans passed over Mykonos, leaving behind a single exhausted bird; Vassilis the fisherman nursed it back to health, and locals say that the pelican in the harbor is the original Petros (though there are several).

Morning on Mykonos town's main quay is busy with deliveries, visitors for the Delos boats, lazy breakfasters, and street cleaners dealing with the previous night's mess. In late morning the cruise-boat people arrive, and the shops are all open. In early afternoon, shaded outdoor tavernas are full of diners eating salads (Mykonos's produce is mostly imported); music is absent or kept low. In mid- and late afternoon, the town feels sleepy, since so many people are at the beach, on excursions, or sleeping in their air-conditioned rooms; even some tourist shops close for siesta. By sunset, people have come back from the beach, having taken their showers and rested. At night, the atmosphere in Mykonos ramps up. The cruise-boat people are mostly gone, coughing three-wheelers make no deliveries in the narrow streets, and everyone is dressed in their sexy summer best and starting to shimmy with the scene. Many shops stay open past midnight, the restaurants fill up, and the bars and discos make ice cubes as fast as they can.

Ready to dive in? Begin your tour of Mykonos town (Hora) by starting out at its heart: Mando Mavrogenous Square.

EXPLORING

TOP ATTRACTIONS

Aegean Maritime Museum. The charming Aegean Maritime Museum contains a collection of model ships, navigational instruments, old maps, prints, coins, and nautical memorabilia. The backyard garden displays some old anchors and ship wheels and a reconstructed 1890 lighthouse, once lighted by oil. ⊠ *10 Enoplon Dynameon* ☎ *22890/22700* 🖅 *€4* ⊙ *Daily 10:30–1 and 6:30–9.*

Archaeological Museum of Mykonos. Before setting out on the mandatory boat excursion to the isle of Delos, check out the Archaeological Museum, set at the northern edge of town. It affords insight into the intriguing history of its ancient shrines. The museum houses Delian funerary sculptures, many with scenes of mourning; most were moved to Rhenea when the Athenians cleansed Delos in the 6th century, during the sixth year of the Peloponnesian war, and, under instruction from the Delphic Oracle, the entire island was purged of all dead bodies. The most significant work from Mykonos is a 7th-century BC *pithos* (storage jar), showing the Greeks in the Trojan horse and the sack of the city. Open all year. ⊠ *Between the ferry port and downtown, Ayios Stefanos* ☎ *22890/22325* 🖅 *€2* ⊙ *Tues.–Sun. 9–4.*

Fodor's Choice
★
Church of Paraportiani (*Our Lady of the Postern Gate*). Mykonians claim that exactly 365 churches and chapels dot their landscape, one for each day of the year. The most famous of these is the Church of Paraportiani. The sloping, whitewashed conglomeration of four chapels, mixing Byzantine and vernacular idioms, looks fantastic. Solid and ultimately sober, its position on a promontory facing the sea sets off the unique architecture; it's said to be one of the most photographed churches in the world. ⊠ *Ayion Anargyron, near folk museum.*

Folk Museum. Housed in an 18th-century house originally built for Captain Nikolaos Malouchos, this museum exhibits a bedroom furnished and decorated in the fashion of that period. On display are looms and lace-making devices, Cycladic costumes, old photographs, and Mykonian musical instruments that are still played at festivals. ⊠ *South of boat dock, near Paraportiani church, Kastro* 🖅 *Free* ⊙ *May–Sept., daily 5–8 pm.*

Greek Orthodox Cathedral of Mykonos. This cathedral is dedicated to Virgin Mary the Great (as locals know it by) and is noted for its number of old icons of the post-Byzantine period. ⊠ *Alefkandra Sq., at the intersection of Anargyron and Odos Mitropolis.*

Lena's House. Take a peek into Lena's House, an annex of the local Folk Museum, and experience an accurate restoration of a middleclass Mykonos house from the 19th century. ⊠ *Enoplon Dynameon* ☎ *22890/22390* 🖅 *Free* ⊙ *Apr.–Oct., Mon.–Sat. 6:30–9:30 pm.*

Fodor's Choice
★
Little Venice. Many of the early ship's captains built distinguished houses directly on the sea here, with wooden balconies overlooking the water. Today this neighborhood, at the southwest end of the port, is called Little Venice. This area, architecturally unique and one of the most attractive in all the islands, is so called because its handsome houses, which once belonged to shipowners and aristocrats, rise from the edge of the sea, and their elaborate buttressed wooden balconies hang over the water—these are no Venetian marble palazzi reflected in still canals. Many of these fine old houses are now elegant bars specializing in sunset drinks, or cabarets, or shops, and crowds head to the cafés and clubs, many found a block inland from Little Venice. These are sometimes

soundproofed. Little Venice is waiting to be discovered and presents countless photo ops, especially at sunset. ⊠ *Mitropoleos Georgouli.*

Mando Mavrogenous Square. Start a tour of Mykonos town (Hora) on the main square, Mando Mavrogenous Square (sometimes called Taxi Square). Pride of place goes to a bust of Mando Mavrogenous, the island heroine, standing on a pedestal. In the 1821 War of Independence the Mykonians, known for their seafaring skills, volunteered

an armada of 24 ships, and in 1822, when the Ottomans landed a force on the island, Mando and her soldiers forced them back to their ships. After independence, a scandalous love affair caused the heroine's exile to Paros, where she died. An aristocratic beauty who becomes a great revolutionary war leader and then dies for love may seem unbelievably Hollywoodish, but it is true. ⊠ *Mando Mavrogenous Square.*

Matoyanni. The main shopping street, Matoyanni, is lined with jewelry stores, clothing boutiques, chic cafés, and candy shops. Owing to the many cruise ships that disgorge thousands of shoppers daily in season— some unload 3,000 jostling tourists—the rents here rival 5th Avenue's, and the more-interesting shops have skedaddled to less-prominent side streets. ⊠ *Perpendicular to harbor.*

Mykonos Windmills. Across the water from Little Venice, set on a high hill, are the famous Mykonos windmills, echoes of a time when wind power was used to grind the island's grain. The area from Little Venice to the windmills is called **Alefkandra,** which means "whitening": women once hung their laundry here. A little farther toward the windmills the bars chockablock on shoreside decks are barely above sea level, and when the north wind is up (often) surf splashes the tables. Farther on, the shore spreads into an unprepossessing beach, and tables are placed on sand or pebbles. After dinner (there are plenty of little tavernas here), the bars turn up their music, and knowing the beat thumps into the night, older tourists seek solace elsewhere. ⊠ *Alefkandra.*

WORTH NOTING

Mykonos Agricultural Museum. This museum displays a 16th-century windmill, traditional outdoor oven, waterwheel, dovecote, and more. ⊠ *Petassos, at top of Mykonos town* 🎟 *Free* ☉ *June–Sept., daily 5–9 pm.*

Public Art Gallery of Mykonos. Located on Mando Mavrogenous Square, the Public Art Gallery of Mykonos changes exhbitions every ten days giving Greek artitists and international artists a great place to showcase their work. ⊠ *Matoyanni* ☎ *22890/27190* ☉ *Daily 11 am–1 pm and 8–11 pm.*

Roman Catholic Cathedral. Next to the Greek Orthodox Cathedral is the Roman Catholic Cathedral, the Virgin of the Rosary, from the Venetian period. The name and coat of arms of the Ghisi family, which took over

Mykonos in 1207, are inscribed in the entrance hall. ✉ *Alefkandra Sq., at the intersection of Anargyron and Odos Mitropolis.*

BEACHES

Swimming in quiet Aegean bays with clean blue water enclosed by rugged hills cannot be overpraised—so it is little wonder some of Greece's finest strands of sand are found on Mykonos. Mostly protected from the prevailing north winds, they can be conveniently grouped. In general the beaches charge €5–€15 for an umbrella and chaise longue. Most of the island's beaches lie along Mykonos's southern coast; from Mykonos town, Ornos beach is about 10 minutes, Kalafati is less than an hour. Mykonos town does have a little beach that attracts local children or townies who just want a quick dip, but it's not going to be your beach of choice. All the others require transportation.

WHERE TO EAT

$$ INTERNATIONAL 🍴 **Avra.** Set in an ambient, open garden space shaded by colorful bougainvillea in the heart of Mykonos town, Avra offers mostly Mediterranean cuisine but Chef Nikos Iliopoulos also prides himself on a strong international selection which features good Asian and Italian dishes. Excellent appetizers include fried feta in pastry topped with sesame seeds, grapes, and rose petal jelly. For an impressive main course with Greek influences opt for a main dish like the oven-roasted lamb with rosemary. An excellent Asian plate is the Chicken Oriental seasoned with ginger, onion, cashews, and soy sauce. **■ TIP→ To find Avra, look for the sign for the cross street off Matoyianni.** [$] *Average main: €22* ✉ *Kalogera 27* ☎ *22890/22298* 🌐 *www.avra-mykonos.com* ✍ *Reservations essential* 🕒 *Closed Nov.–Apr.*

$$$ SEAFOOD 🍴 **Caprice Sea Satin Market.** If the wind is up, the waves sing at this magical spot, set on a far tip of land below the famous windmills of Mykonos. The preferred place for Greek shipowners, Caprice the restaurant (as opposed to the bar by the same name, which is nearby) sprawls out onto a seaside terrace and even onto the sand of the beach bordering Little Venice. When it comes to fish, prices vary according to weight. Shellfish is a specialty, and everything is beautifully presented. In summer, live music and dancing add to the liveliness. [$] *Average main: €35* ✉ *On seaside under windmills, Little Venice* ☎ *22890/24676* 🌐 *www.caprice.gr* ✍ *Reservations essential.*

$$ MEDITERRANEAN 🍴 **Funky Kitchen.** Tucked in a quiet corner of Mykonos town, on a picturesque whitewashed street lined with bougainvillea, you'll find chef Pavlos Grivas in his modern, open kitchen creating delicious Mediterranean fusion dishes with an innovative twist. He succeeds with starters like octopus carpaccio with oregano, capers, and olive oil; and a cool salad with smoked *louza* (pork sausage) in a sweet white wine and honey vinaigrette. His main dishes delight, including the fresh ravioli filled with Cypriot halloumi cheese in a light chicken and mint broth, as well as pork chops marinated in red wine and dry coriander with potato bravas. Finish with desserts like finger-shaped pastries filled with almonds and cinnamon in a rosewater syrup. Creative cocktails and excellent service round out the experience. [$] *Average main: €16* ✉ *40 Ignatiou Basoula* ☎ *22890/27272.*

$$ **Kounelas.** This long-established fresh-fish taverna is where many
GREEK   fishermen themselves eat, for solid, no-frills food; you can pick your
own fish. The menu depends on the weather—low winds means lots
of fish. ■**TIP→ Even in simple places such as Kounelas, fresh fish can
be expensive.** $ *Average main: €16* ⊠ *Off the port near Delos boats*
☎ *22890/28220.*

$$$$ **La Maison de Katrin.** This hidden restaurant features the best of both
FRENCH   Greek and French cuisine, which makes it worth the search through
the Dilou quarter of Mykonos. Outdoor tables are on a narrow street,
while the lovely interior features Cycladic arches and whitewash with
a faded 16th-century tapestry from Constantinople. Fine food and
excellent service keeps people coming, despite the prices. Start with
such delights as the zucchini flowers stuffed with rice, mint, and pine
nuts, or the spinach pie with leeks and feta cheese. Then move onto
the mussels in light cream sauce, white wine, and red peppercorns, or
try the chateaubriand with grilled vegetables. Finish with the apple
tartine with Calvados cream. Divine! $ *Average main: €50* ⊠ *Ayios
Gerasimos and Nikou, Dilou* ☎ *22890/22169* ⌂ *Reservations essen-
tial* ⊙ *Closed Nov.–Apr.*

$$ **Lotus.** For more than 30 years, Giorgos and Elsa Cambanis have
MEDITERRANEAN   lovingly run this tiny restaurant. Elsa is the cook, so compliment her
on the fine starter, the mushroom "Lotos" with cream and cheese.
The roast leg of lamb with oregano, lemon, and wine is succulent,
and the moussaka is almost too good to be traditional. For dessert,
have *pralina*, which resembles tiramisu. It's open year-round for dinner only: the porch is covered with bougainvillea in summer, and
there's a fireplace in winter. $ *Average main: €16* ⊠ *Matoyianni 47*
☎ *22890/22881* ⊙ *No lunch.*

$$$ **White Star.** Set in an elegant and modern outdoor dining area influ-
GREEK   enced by Cycladic architecture, Michelin-starred Chef Lefteris Lazarou
Fodor'sChoice   offers a menu that displays his creativity and expertise in Mediterranean
★   seafood and more. Appetizers like the quinoa salad with eggplant or the
sea bass carpaccio in olive oil and lemon are simply delightful. For the
next round, opt for the squid with basil pesto in a fried potato nest or
the risotto with cuttlefish. Finish with the refreshing and eclectic lemon
cube with lychee sorbet, raspberry, and candied roses. The wine list is
expansive and impressive, and so is the cocktail menu. You simply can't
go wrong. $ *Average main: €28* ⊠ *Lakka Sq.* ☎ *22890/77347* ✉ *info@
whitestar.gr* ⊕ *www.whitestar.gr* ⌂ *Reservations essential.*

WHERE TO STAY

$$$$ **Belvedere.** This is the hotel for lovers of style, who want to be with-it,
HOTEL   and like to see what they are paying for. **Pros:** this is Mykonos town's
most "in" hotel. **Cons:** you can pay plenty for a small room with no
view. $ *Rooms from: €500* ⊠ *Lakka Rohari, School of Fine Arts district*
☎ *22890/25122* ⊕ *www.belvederehotel.com* ⇆ *35 rooms, 8 suites, 1
villa* ⊙ *Closed: Dec.–Jan.* ⊠ *Breakfast.*

$$ **Hotel Mykonos Adonis.** Set on the edge of town not far from Little
HOTEL   Venice and overlooking the sea, this is not only Mykonos' friendli-
est hotel but is also both convenient and nicely out of the fray. **Pros:**
convenient to the scene, but not swamped by it. **Cons:** on a street with

DID YOU KNOW?

For the best overview of Little Venice—Mykonos town's most beautiful district—walk through the Alefkandra quarter and head to the famous hilltop windmills of Kata Myli.

traffic. $ *Rooms from: €200* ⊠ *Ayios Ioannis street* ☎ *22890/23433* ⊕ *www.mykonosadonis.gr* ⤢ *12 rooms, 12 suites* ☉ *Closed Nov.–Mar.* ⦿ *Breakfast.*

$
HOTEL
🏨 **Omiros.** Looking for an inexpensive, attractive, convenient, slightly out-of-town accommodation on a hill overlooking the bay? **Pros:** good value for the money. **Cons:** the walk from the town center is uphill. $ *Rooms from: €120* ⊠ *Chora* ☎ *22890/23328* ⊕ *www.omirosmykonos.com* ⤢ *10 rooms* ☉ *Closed Nov.–Mar.* ⦿ *No meals.*

$$
B&B/INN
🏨 **Philippi Hotel.** Of the inexpensive hotels scattered throughout town, this is the most attractive. **Pros:** inexpensive for Mykonos town; cleanliness; free Wi-fi. **Cons:** if you want to get away from it all, go elsewhere; no transfers; smallish rooms in need of updating. $ *Rooms from: €135* ⊠ *Kalogera 25* ☎ *22890/22294* ⊕ *www.philippihotel.com* ⤢ *14 rooms* ☉ *Closed Nov.–Mar.* ⦿ *No meals.*

$$$$
HOTEL
🏨 **Semeli.** Renovated in 2014, the Semeli hotel's architecture reflects the island's Cycladic minimalism with a perfect balance of whitewashed elements mixed with glass and stone. **Pros:** lounge areas are very inviting. **Cons:** stiff room rates. $ *Rooms from: €385* ⊠ *Below ring road* ☎ *22890/27471* ⊕ *www.semelihotel.gr* ⤢ *53 rooms, 3 suites* ☉ *Closed Dec. and Jan.* ⦿ *Breakfast.*

$$
B&B/INN
FAMILY
Fodor's Choice
★
🏨 **Villa Konstantin.** Styled in the traditional whitewashed Mykonian architecture with cozy lounging areas, Villa Konstantin is a set of apartments and studios that offers a quiet atmosphere away from the bustle of Mykonos town, but is still close enough to enjoy it. **Pros:** great pool area; inexpensive for what you get, which is a lot. **Cons:** the walk from town is uphill. $ *Rooms from: €160* ⊠ *Aghios Vassilios* ☎ *22890/26204* ⊕ *www.villakonstantin-mykonos.gr* ⤢ *19 apartments* ☉ *Closed Nov.–Mar.* ⦿ *Breakfast.*

NIGHTLIFE

Whether it's bouzouki, jazz, mainstream dance, or techno, the nightlife beats on Mykonos to an obsessive rhythm until undetermined hours—little wonder the world's gilded youth comes here *just* to enjoy the night scene. That scene centers around two places: Mykonos town and the southern beaches.

Nightlife begins in the late afternoon at beach bars that dot Paradise, Super Paradise, and Paranga. At 4 pm the music is pumping loudly as the hired, sexy dance crews top the tables, and cocktails flow freely. The beach scene dies down around 8 or 9, when the beach party animals rest up before the next round of nightlife.

The bars and clubs along Little Venice and throughout Mykonos town start to fill up after 11 pm, as patrons sip their first drinks of the night. The gay scene is still alive on Mykonos. Those who prefer a quieter lounge-type experience remain seated outside a sea-view café with a glass of wine, watching it all go by.

For the true night owls, much happens after midnight. You can either choose to club-hop around town or head south to the glamorous, outdoor arena-style clubs along Paradise and Super Paradise beaches. In the summer, posters and leaflets flung throughout Mykonos town advertise which of the hottest international DJs are booked to spin each night.

That and the promise of a packed, friendly, flirtatious young crowd gets the international partygoers ready for the beach well into the night. What is "the" place of the moment? The scene is ever-changing, so you'll need to track the buzz once you arrive. But there are some ever-popular options.

4711 Live Clubbing. If you want a taste of what real Greek nightlife is about and don't mind things sounding Greek to you, then head to 4711 Live Clubbing. Greek pop hits and Greek *bouzoukia* style music, including the classic Greek songs that all generations of Greeks know by heart, are sung live and pump out of the club into the early morning. If you last to the early morning hours, you'll be singing and dancing, too. It's dark and smoky, but best of all, lively. ⊠ *Behind Town Hall, Platia Agia Monis.*

Guzel. Ideally situated on the Mykonos town waterfront, you probably passed the club during the day without a second thought to its plain, unimpressive exterior that still shows its former name, 9 Muses, under its new name. At night the club comes alive and the best thing about it is the music. A loud, fun, crazy dance-making mix from their summer DJ lineup gets everyone inside moving on the floor and on chairs. Pastel neon lights fling around in the dark, bubbly crowd to the latest international and Greek pop beats. ⊠ *Waterfront.*

Interni. This whitewashed, modern Cycladic-style garden setting is flanked on all sides by lovely large trees. It's a Mediterranean restaurant (dinner) and event space but it really shines at night when it's lit up and the summer crowd gathers to its central bar for cocktails and to enjoy the open airy space. Gathering a calmer crowd that likes to be seen, it's a place you can have a good drink, listen to music, and hear a person speaking next to you in the heart of Mykonos town. ⊠ *Matoyianni* ☎ *22890/26333* ⊕ *www.interni-restaurant.gr.*

Kastro Bar. Kostas Karatzas's long-standing Kastro Bar with heavy beamed ceilings and island furnishings, creates an intimate environment for enjoying the evening sunset over the bay to classical music. ⊠ *Little Venice, Paraportiani* ☎ *22890/23072.*

Montparnasse/The Piano Bar. For more than 30 years, Montparnasse has been simply known as The Piano Bar. It's lively, lovely and gay-friendly with a longstanding tradition of supporting the island's local artists. Check out the latest artwork on its walls and then admire the gorgeous sunset views that precede energy-filled evenings of live cabaret and musicals. ⊠ *Ayion Anargyron 24, Little Venice* ☎ *22890/23719* ⊕ *www.thepianobar.com.*

Omega. Follow the loud, young crowd through the streets of Little Venice and you'll end up at Omega, where you'll join a hopping mass to dance and drink the night away. Fluorescent lights beam throughout the simple club, where the summer DJ roundup gets busy past 11 pm each night playing mainstream pop and dance. ⊠ *Little Venice* ☎ *22890/26505* ⊕ *www.omegaclub.gr.*

Rhapsody. Rubbing elbows with Montparnasse is Rhapsody, a cocktail bar open all year for Greek dancing. ⊠ *Little Venice* ☎ *22890/23412.*

Rock n Roll Mykonos. This simple whitewashed building gets cranking at night, when the music is loud and the drinks flow free. The crowd goes crazy for what the DJ is spinning—usually a great mix of mainstream dance and pop. Rock n Roll has added a new life to the space where Pierro's bar once stood, attracting a young, international party crowd looking to have a great time into the early morning hours. ⊠ *Andronikou* ⊕ *www.rocknrollmykonos.com.*

Skandinavian Bar. Toward the end of Mykonos town's main market street is the Skandinavian Bar, which spreads over two buildings, two floors (one for pub chats, one for dancing), and an outside seating area. The music in the three bars ranges from classic rock to pop to dance. ⊠ *K. Georgouli St.* ☎ *22890/22669* ⊕ *www.skandinavianbar.com.*

SPORTS AND THE OUTDOORS

WATER SPORTS

Water-sports facilities can be found at many beaches offering different types of equipment. The main hub for windsurfing in the southern part of the island is at Kalafati beach. The north side of the island is also a wind lover's haven; Panormos and Ftelia is where they all head.

SHOPPING

Most shops are to be found in Mykonos town, one right after the other among the warren of streets. In the peak of summer, many are open until midnight. The jet set is catered to quite well with an abundance of shops selling precious gems, fine jewelry, au courant fashion, swimwear, and shoes donning top international labels. Then, there are great local items that you'd only find in Greece—or in Mykonos—including handmade leather sandals, belts, and purses, and a selection of handicrafts and paintings created by local artists. Local food products and all-natural Greek cosmetics and soaps round out the best souvenirs options.

FASHION

Galatis. Designer Yiannis Galatis has outfitted such famous women as Elizabeth Taylor, Ingrid Bergman, and Jackie Onassis. He will probably greet you personally and show you some of his costumes and hostess gowns. His memoirs capture the old days on Mykonos, when Jackie O. was a customer. His new art gallery is adjacent. ⊠ *Mando Mavrogenous Sq., opposite Lalaounis* ☎ *22890/22255.*

Kalypso. Mother-and-daughter team Kalypso and Calliope Anastopoulou create their own collection of handmade leather sandals and women's clothing with colorful, island inspiration. Their shop, on busy Matoyianni street, also has a selection of handmade jewelry. ⊠ *Andronikou 17* ☎ *22890/77149.*

Kampanas. For a wide selection of handmade leather goods, head to Kampanas. It will be hard to choose from the array of sandals for both men and women that line the walls. There are also collections of handbags, belts, and sandals. The color choices are wide and the leather is top quality. ⊠ *Mitropoleos 3* ☎ *22890/22638* ⊕ *www.kampanas.gr* ☺ *Mon.–Sat. 9–6.*

Parthenis. Opened by Dimitris Parthenis in 1978, Parthenis now features designs by his daughter Orsalia, all showcased in a large Mykonian-style building on the up side of Alefkandra Square in Little Venice. The collection of cotton and silk garments (mostly in neutral colors) is very popular for their soft draping and clinging wrap effect. ⊠ *Alefkandra Sq.* ☎ *22890/22448* ⊕ *www.orsalia-parthenis.gr.*

Salachas. A small shop, Salachas is filled with linen and cotton garments of all Greek materials and manufacture. Grandfather Joseph Salachas was a tailor in the 1960s, and once made clothes for Christian Dior and various celebrities. Today, his grandchildren keep up the tradition. ⊠ *K. Georgouli 58* ☎ *22890/22710.*

The Workshop. Walking into The Workshop you'll immediately realize that the owner, Christos Xenitidis, loves two things: music and jewelry. His handiwork is responsible for the lovely gold and silver necklaces, rings, and earrings behind the simple glass displays. Look above his jewelry workbench to see a line of the guitar-like *bouzoukias* he fixes and collects. Sometimes, his musician Mykonian friends stop by and an impromptu concert will form before your eyes. ⊠ *Panahra 12* ☎ *22890/26455.*

Zonadiko. Head up the stairs off one of Mykonos's busiest pedestrian walkways to find Michalis Pavlos at work in his little leather workshop where he creates leather belts, sandals, and purses. Since the late 1980s, Pavlos has been making his own goods and distributing them all over Greece, but he opened his own shop in 2014 to show and sell his work directly on his favorite island. The quality of the leather he uses is second to none and he takes bespoke orders, too. ⊠ *Matoyianni* ☎ *22890/27833.*

FINE AND DECORATIVE ART

Anna Gelou. Anna Gelou's eponymous shop, started by her mother 50 years ago, carries authentic copies of traditional handmade embroideries, all using white Greek cotton, in clothing, tablecloths, curtains, and such. ⊠ *Ayion Anargyron 16, Little Venice* ☎ *22890/26825.*

Artists of Mykonos Studio. The Artists of Mykonos Studio features the work of several Mykonian artists including paintings by the expat artist Richard James North and pieces by Greek mosaicist Monika Derpapas. The collection is simply lovely, colorful, and expressive. ⊠ *Panachrantou 11* ☎ *22890/23527.*

Nikoletta. Mykonos used to be a weaver's island, where 500 looms clacked away. Only two active weavers remain today and Nikoletta Xidakis is one of them. She sells her skirts, shawls, and bedspreads made of local wool, as she has for 50 years. ⊠ *Little Venice, Skarpa* ☎ *22890/27503* ⊙ *Daily 4–11 pm.*

Ninemia. Maria Kouniou is a local artist and displays her own handmade and hand-painted woodcraft wall hangings in her little whitewashed shop. She's also proud to support other Greek artists and sells their fun, colorful jewelry and T-shirts that reflect the style and beauty of Greece. ⊠ *M. Axioti street 51* ☎ *22890/00073* ⊕ *www.ninemia.net.*

JEWELRY

Ilias Lalaounis. Known internationally, this fine jewelry collection is based on ancient Greek and other designs, but reinterpreted for the modern woman. With many of their earrings and necklaces as lovingly worked as art pieces, the shop is as elegant as a museum. New collections are introduced every year. ✉ *Polykandrioti 14, near taxis* ☎ *22890/22444* ✉ *lalaounismaykonos@lalaounis.gr* 🌐 *www.lalaounis.gr.*

AYIOS STEFANOS ΑΓΙΟΣ ΣΤΕΦΑΝΟΣ

6 km (4 miles) north of Mykonos town.

About a 45-minute walk north from Mykonos town, Ayios Stefanos has water sports, restaurants, and umbrellas and lounge chairs for rent; kids love it, and you can watch the yachts and enormous cruise ships slide by. The south coast's many beaches include this one fit for families.

BEACHES

Ayios Stefanos Beach. Like many beaches in Greece, Ayios Stefanos takes its name from the little chapel built on it. Just north of Mykonos town, this sandy stretch attracts its share of families for its shallow waters and array of eating, lodging, and café options within reach. Although it's unsheltered from northern winds it's always been an ideal beach to view the sunsets of Mykonos. **Amenities:** food and drink. **Best for:** sunset; swimming. ✉ *Less than 2 km (1 mile) north from Mykonos town.*

WHERE TO EAT

$$ MEDITERRANEAN 🍴 **Grace Restaurant.** The truly intimate feel of the Grace Restaurant is unique and appreciated on a bustling island like Mykonos. Located on the pool balcony of the Mykonos Grace Hotel, a calm nighttime ambience is owed to its beautiful lighting and minimalist environment that takes inspiration from Cycladic architecture. Dining here is a taste of Mediterranean cuisine with a creative sophisticated touch. Start with an octopus stew in a clay pot served with couscous; or opt for the *louza* (a smoked pork sausage unique to Mykonos), which is accompanied by a baby spinach salad with Gruyère shavings. For a main course, the sautéed sea bass fillet with ouzo and lemon verbena sauce is just as excellent as the rack of lamb with pistachio and honey crust served with a port reduction. **■ TIP→ A thoughtfully planned tasting menu is a simple option for those who want a diverse sample of Greece's traditional flavors.** [$] *Average main: €23* ✉ *Grace Mykonos* ☎ *22890/20000* 🌐 *www.gracehotels.com/mykonos.*

$$$ GREEK 🍴 **Tagoo.** High Mykonian style can be yours at the eatery of this noted hotel. It is a creation of Spondi, Athens's popular two-star restaurant. The haute cuisine is served up in either an all-white room or at outdoor tables, with Mykonos bay on one side and an infinity pool on the other. Start with slow-cooked octopus with fava pureé, caper chutney, and orange-infused oil. Fine entrées include rolled sea bass with basmati rice, coconut milk, and melon, and also veal medallions in sun-dried tomato crust. Fish is always fresh and delicately prepared. To top things off, try the chocolate sable with homemade coffee ice cream and

caramel. The sommelier helps with the large selection of wines. The restaurant is open May through October. $ *Average main: €40* ⊠ *Hotel Cavo Tagoo (12 mins by foot north of Mykonos town on sea road), Mykonos town* ☏ *22890/20100* ⊕ *www.cavotagoo.gr* ⚘ *Reservations essential* ⊘ *Closed Nov.–Apr.*

WHERE TO STAY

$$$$
HOTEL
Fodor'sChoice
★

Cavo Tagoo. Many consider this to be the top hotel in Mykonos for luxuriousness, service, and comfort. **Pros:** modulated luxury; beautiful view; alluring Mykonos style; ladies love the fancy spa. **Cons:** a 12-minute walk to town. $ *Rooms from: €490* ⊹ *Follow coast road, north of Old Port* ☏ *22890/20100* ⊕ *www.cavotagoo.gr* ⤳ *51 rooms, 18 suites, 11 villas* ⊘ *Closed Nov.–Apr.* ⦿ *Breakfast.*

$$$$
HOTEL
Fodor'sChoice
★

Grace Mykonos. Small, charming, luxurious, and set above the beach of Ayios Stefanos, the Mykonos Grace is graced with a truly impressive setting, replete with an encompassing view of Mykonos's harbor. **Pros:** impressive vistas; intimate atmosphere. **Cons:** not walking distance from town. $ *Rooms from: €400* ☏ *22890/20000* ⊕ *www.mykonosgrace. com* ⤳ *26 rooms, 5 suites* ⊘ *Closed Nov.–Mar.* ⦿ *Breakfast.*

ORNOS ΟΡΝΟΣ

3½ km (2¼ miles) south of Mykonos town.

Ornos has always been more popular with Mykonians than tourists. The locals like its relaxed atmosphere for a family swim and beachside dining. There are several good restaurants, two fine hotels above the bay, and several cheaper ones lower down, and chairs and umbrellas for rent. In calm weather, boats start here for the other southern beaches, so that they are all connected (45 minutes to the farthest southern beach, Elia), and you can beach hop easily.

BEACHES

FAMILY **Ayios Ioannis Beach.** One of the best places in Mykonos to catch the sunset is the pebble and sand beach of Ayios Ioannis. Divided into two sections by large rocks, the waters usually remain calm but the summer winds can take their hold. The shallow bay is popular with families, and dining and lodging options are plenty thanks to the whitewashed beach town that grew around it. ■TIP→ **The beach is also referred to as Shirley Valentine beach, because the 1989 British movie of the same name was filmed here.** **Amenities:** food and drink. **Best for:** sunset; swimming. ⊠ *Ornos bay, Ayios Ioannis.*

FAMILY **Ornos Beach.** A community has grown around this beach, which is now considered one of the most family-friendly on the island. It's pretty and sandy and there are umbrella and lounge chair rentals. A good selection of beach hotels, tavernas, restaurants, cafés, and shops make up Ornos bay and there's bus service from Mykonos town. It's also the launch point to take a boat to other beaches or to Delos. **Amenities:** food and drink. **Best for:** swimming.

WHERE TO EAT

$$ **GREEK** ✕ **Apaggio.** Tucked in a tranquil corner of Ornos bay, Apaggio is simply decorated and lined with large open windows for a perfect, unobstructed view of the sea. Beautifully presented tavern-style specialties include local fish and familiar Greek favorites such as Greek salad and moussaka. You'll also find local dishes including a Mykonian salad made with spicey *louza* sausage, bread crusts, and local cheese as well as zucchini stuffed with rice and seafood. The mussels sautéed with tomato sauce and feta is also excellent. Ⓢ *Average main: €16* ⊠ *Ornos beach, Ornos bay* ⊕ *www.apaggio.gr.*

WHERE TO STAY

$$$$ **HOTEL** 🏨 **Deliades.** If you like comfort, large rooms, friendly service, a sea-view, and quiet, Deliades is exactly for you. **Pros:** Ornos bay sea views; large rooms and baths; relaxed atmosphere. **Cons:** if you want to stay in the thick of the Mykonos scene, this isn't for you. Ⓢ *Rooms from: €310* ⊠ *Far end of Ornos beach, follow road up 30 yards, Ornos bay* ☎ *22890/79430, 22890/79470* ⊕ *www.deliades.com* ⤲ *30 rooms* ⊗ *Closed Oct.–Apr.* ⍩ *Breakfast.*

$$$$ **HOTEL** 🏨 **Kivotos Clubhotel.** The Kivotos Clubhotel is deluxe, architecturally ambitious, and stylishly arrayed around an impressive pool. **Pros:** exquisite design; quiet ambience. **Cons:** isolated; some rooms are small and lack views; those high room rates. Ⓢ *Rooms from: €580* ⊠ *Ornos bay* ⊹ *2 km (1 mile) from Mykonos town* ☎ *22890/24094* ⊕ *www.kivotosclubhotel.gr* ⤲ *10 rooms, 24 suites, 1 villa* ⊗ *Closed Nov.–Apr.* ⍩ *Breakfast.*

SOUTH COAST NOTIA AKTH

The first beach is Psarou, 4 km (2½ miles) southeast of Mykonos town; the last beach is Elia, 12 km (7½ miles) southeast of Mykonos town.

The popular south coast beaches stand on their own; hotels, restaurants, cafés, and beach bars have sprung up around them drawn to their turquoise seas. It's the home of Psarou beach, where yachts are always parked in the distance and expensive sun lounge beds are reserved in advance. Platis Gialos is popular with families and has its own little village behind it. But it's truly known for what the international party crowd loves: the beach bar and club scene that revolves around Paraga, Paradise, and Super Paradise beaches. Agrari and Elia are less developed, have more nudity, and are quieter.

BEACHES

The south coast is where you'll find the famous party beaches of Mykonos. Psarou draws the jet set while nearby Platis Yialos is popular with families. The young and sexy crowd heads to the Paraga, Paradise, and Super Paradise. While they used to be primarily nude beaches, that is not the case any longer, but they are still busy and popular and have parties starting almost every afternoon. Paradise draws the sexy straight crowd, Super Paradise the sexy gay crowd, though in truth there's a lot of overlap. The rocky path between Paradise and Super Paradise, an hour's rough walk, was once a sexual no-man's land, but it is no longer.

Farther along, Little Agrari and Elia are less developed, more nude, and quieter, though they too have not escaped the voyeur's wandering eye.

Agrari Beach. Agrari is a low-key beach with yellow pebble sand flanked by a low hill of small whitewashed buildings to the left and a rocky island hill to the right. Umbrellas and sun beds are available for rent. You can grab a snack, drinks, or a full meal at the beach's own bar and restaurant, but there are more options just a walk away. Boats leave from Platis Gialos and Ornos bay. It's also walkable via a footpath from neighboring Elia beach, attracting nudists who stay in certain areas. ■ TIP➡ **Driving east from Mykonos town, watch out for a stunning view of the turquoise blue as you make that final turn to the beach.** **Amenities:** food and drink; water sports. **Best for:** swimming. ✉ *Agrari.*

Elia Beach. Long, tranquil, and beautiful, Elia is a popular option for those who seek beach relaxation. Attracting a predominantly gay crowd, this southern beach is also popular with those who want to relax on a soft sand beach that's protected from the north winds that sweep through the island from time to time. Umbrellas and sun beds are for rent and water-sports facilities pop up during the peak summer months. Dining options are plentiful with several cafés and tavernas close by. **Amenities:** food and drink; showers; toilets. **Best for:** nudists; swimming. ✉ *Elia.*

Paradise Beach. Famous the world over for its party scene, young, fun, international crowds hop straight to Paradise beach. There's music, dancing, clubbing, and drinking at most hours of the day, but beach parties typically pick up around 4 pm and go on well into the next morning when everyone is dancing on tabletops, including sexy male and female models hired to get things moving. When partiers take a break, sun beds and umbrellas are available for lounging and a full line of restaurants and fast-food options provide nourishment. Scuba diving and water-sports rental shops are open for business. The bus from Mykonos town frequents the beach often and on time in the peak of summer. **Amenities:** food and drink; lifeguards; parking; showers; toilets; water sports. **Best for:** partiers. ✉ *Paradise.*

Paraga Beach. Small and stunning, and surrounded by a picturesque rocky coastline that juts out against a sparkling turquoise bay, Paraga beach is not only pretty, it's also one of Mykonos's liveliest party beaches. Several bars and beach clubs organize events every summer attracting a young, international crowd that gathers to mingle, dance, and drink. Hotels, rooms, and a large camping ground surround the beach. Umbrellas and chairs are available to rent at any of the beachside tavernas and cafés. A footpath to the east leads to neighboring party beach Paradise, or offers you another view of the sea; it's about a ten-minute walk. **Amenities:** food and drink; lifeguards; toilets. **Best for:** partiers. ✉ *Paraga* ✛ *6 km (4 miles) southeast of Mykonos town.*

FAMILY **Platis Gialos Beach.** Spacious, sandy, and pleasant, Platis Gialos is a calm southern beach getaway that's protected from the island's strong summer winds. Kids enjoy playing in the shallow waters, while adults head to deeper waters to try out the numerous water-sports rental options. The array of taverns, restaurants, and cafés is perfect for any food break. The beach is lined with rental umbrellas and chairs and getting to it is easy by Mykonos town beach boat and bus service. **■ TIP→ You can drive here too but parking spaces may be hard to find.** **Amenities:** food and drink; water sports. **Best for:** swimming. ✉ *Platis Gialos.*

Psarou Beach. With shiny yachts parked in its clear, pretty waters, sandy Psarou attracts vacationing international VIPs, Greek TV stars and singers, and the rich and/or famous. **■ TIP→ That oversized and high-priced beach bed and umbrella may be empty, but it may have been rented in advance by someone who doesn't want you to have it.** If you know someone, you can make reservations for one in advance, too. You might bump into someone's body guard; several may be casing the beach. Sophisticated yet lively restaurants are plentiful, and they host afternoon and evening parties that are fun but not crazy. If you drive from Mykonos town, a steep scenic road leads to the beach, but once you get there you'll notice parking options are slim. Many opt for valet parking run by private companies. You can also reach Psarou by taking a short walk from nearby Platis Gialos or hopping on a boat one stop away at Ornos bay. **Amenities:** food and drink; parking (paid). **Best for:** swimming; partiers. ✉ *Psarou* ✣ *4 km (2.5 miles) south of Mykonos town.*

Super Paradise Beach. Young and wild, gay and straight: All crowds head to Super Paradise to let loose. The stunning sandy beach is one plus, but the beach bars and clubs truly dominate the scene. Summer months mean daily late-afternoon beach parties, where drinks and dancing rule. Hired bikini-clad models move to the beat of the music to encourage a crazy party atmosphere that includes people dancing everywhere and anywhere they can. For those not in the party mood (yet), umbrellas and sun beds can be rented and dining options are available for a meal; Super Paradise Rooms is right on the beach for those who need a place to crash. **Amenities:** food and drink; toilets; showers; lifeguards; water sports. **Best for:** partiers. ✉ *Super Paradise* 🌐 *www.superparadise.com.gr.*

WHERE TO EAT

$$ MEDITERRANEAN

🍴 **Avli tou Thodori.** Overlooking pretty Platis Gialos beach, Avli tou Thodori offers beachfront dining in a minimalist Cycladic setting. The name translates to Thodori's Garden, a dedication to owner Thanassis Kousathanas's late father, a Mykonian fisherman whose black-and-white portraits are hung with pride. Cuisine presentation is excellent and the selection eclectic. To start try the feta cheese wrapped in phyllo pastry covered with a light sweet sauce made with *rakomelo* (a spicy liqueur) and sprinkled with sesame seeds. The watermelon salad with feta and ouzo dressing is refreshing and unique to Greece. Great main dishes include the prawns sautéed with eggplant and *katiki* cheese as well as the grilled sea bass fillet with avocado sauce. Finish off with a Greek yogurt and cheese cake with honey and walnuts—light, creamy, and wonderfully memorable. [$] *Average main: €18* ✉ *Platis Gialos* 🌐 *www.avlitouthodori.gr* ⏲ *Closed Nov.–Mar.*

$$$ MODERN GREEK

🍴 **Nammos.** This beach restaurant has become the in spot for well-to-do Athenians and for Mykonians who want to strut a bit on fashionable Psarou beach. All open-air, white wood, stone, bamboo, and palm trees, it serves up Mediterranean fusion cuisine (their words) and is especially popular for a late lunch. For appetizer try *louza* (Mykonian sun-dried pork fillet), or eggplant mille-feuille with feta and shrimp. Sea sounds will tempt you to order fresh fish or sushi, or dive into the great seared tuna tartare with white sauce or the homemade pasta with sea urchins. A non-svelte dessert is the chunky chocolate crème "guanajo" with blackberries and praline. $ *Average main: €30* ⊠ *Psarou beach, Psarou* ☎ *22890/22440* ⊕ *www.nammos.gr.*

NIGHTLIFE

Paradise Club. The international, young party people that flock to Mykonos pack this glamorous open-air club every summer season. It has three stages that are designed to feature the world's best DJs who fill its lineup each year. Paradise Club features a VIP area and a swimming pool. ⊠ *Paradise beach, Paradise* ⊕ *www.paradiseclubmykonos.com.*

Tropicana Beach Bar. One of the most popular beach bars in Mykonos is set on Paradise beach where the party starts every afternoon in the peak summer season. The international, young, and looking for fun head to the outdoor bar to dance in the sand, on tables, and by the sea. The music is loud, mainstream and fun, the people are happy, and the cocktail list is long. ⊠ *Southern beaches, Paradise* ☎ *22890/26990* ⊕ *www.tropicanamykonos.com.*

SPORTS AND THE OUTDOORS

DIVING

Mykonos Diving Center. Located in Paradise beach, the Mykonos Diving Center offers a range of excursions for certified divers, and training for all levels and experiences. ■ **TIP→ They lead excursions from 30 different points on the island.** ⊠ *Southern beaches, Paradise* ☎ *22890/24808* ⊕ *www.dive.gr.*

SOUTHEAST COAST ΝΟΤΙΟΑΝΑΤΟΛΙΚΗ ΑΚΤΗ

The first beach is Kalo Livadi, 11 km (6½ miles) southeast of Mykonos town; the last beach is Kalafatis beach, 12½ km (8 miles) southeast of Mykonos town.

The southeastern beaches, the farthest beaches from Mykonos town, are favorites for those looking for something calm, yet organized, such as Kalo Livadi. Water-sports lovers head to Kalafatis, which is well organized for any sport.

BEACHES

Ayia Anna Beach. Somewhat hidden in the shadow of Kalafatis beach, Ayia Anna is a low-key beach, named after a little whitewashed chapel built nearby. It's a place where you can observe windsurfers in the distance as fishing boats bob calmly in the wind-protected waters. Keep an eye out for the two hills that protect the bay—the locals lovingly call them *divounia* or Aphrodite's breasts. Summer beach chair and umbrella rentals are available and there is a handful of tavernas and cafés. There are also two easy hiking paths to neighboring Platis Gialos and Paraga beaches. **Amenities:** food and drink. **Best for:** swimming. ⊠ *Ayia Anna.*

Kalafatis Beach. This long stretch of picturesque beach with a line of shady trees is known for the water-sports and windsurfing crowds it attracts. The back road has an array of hotels, rooms-for-rent, tavernas and beach bars as well as a well-known windsurfing school and water-sports rental shop. A small dock to the left side of the beach houses a tavern, beach bar, and a diving center office that leads excursions out to nearby uninhabited islands. **Amenities:** food and drink; lifeguards; water sports. **Best for:** swimming; walking; windsurfing. ✉ *Kalafati.*

FAMILY **Kalo Livadi Beach.** Mykonos's characteristic rocky hills surround Kalo Livadi's long sandy beach, which is situated at the edge of an island valley for which it got its name, meaning "good valley." Families head here to spend the day playing with their kids in the shallow waters and take a break at one of the many restaurant options surrounding the beach. In summer the beach is divided into several areas that feature various styles of sun beds and umbrellas for rent. **Amenities:** food and drink. **Best for:** swimming. ✉ *Kalo Livadi.*

WHERE TO EAT

$$ MEDITERRANEAN FAMILY Fodor's Choice ★

🍴 **Nice n Easy.** Chef Christos Athanasiadis aims to keep things nice and easy, hence the name, and succeeds with farm-to-table Mediterranean cuisine using locally produced ingredients. The whitewashed Cycladic island style is infused with a bit of Hollywood by featuring artwork of 1950s icons, thanks to co-owner and former LA restaurateur Dimitris Christoforidis's influence. Enjoy Kalo Livadi's tranquil beach scene as you start with water buffalo meatballs with smoked tomato sauce. (They have an organic buffalo farm in northern Greece.) Main dishes to savor include the sautéed sea bass with flavored bulgur, Corinthian raisins, and basil oil and lemon; or the beef skirt *tagliata* with white truffle oil. Finish with a dream, a "white dream" that is: Greek brioche with white chocolate cream and strawberry consommé. The wine list is long and impressive, sushi is expertly made, and a kids' menu comes in handy. [$] *Average main: €20* ✉ *Kalo Livadi beach, Kalo Livadi* ☎ *22890/72315* 🌐 *www.niceneasy.gr.*

WHERE TO STAY

$$$ RESORT FAMILY

🏨 **Aphrodite Beach Hotel.** Water-sports lovers head here to combine their passion for sport with the upscale facilities of this resort located right off the wind-blessed beach of Kalafatis. **Pros:** fantastic location for water-sports lovers and families that want to be close to the beach. **Cons:** far from Mykonos town. [$] *Rooms from: €250* ✉ *Kalafati* ☎ *22890/71367* 📧 *reservations@aphrodite-mykonos.com* 🌐 *www.aphrodite-mykonos.gr* 🛏 *138 rooms; 10 suites* 🍽 *Breakfast.*

SPORTS AND THE OUTDOORS

SCUBA DIVING

Kalafati Dive Center. For twenty years, the Kalafati Dive Center has offered diving excursions with excellent visibility around Mykonos, including various wrecks. Courses are available for beginners and advanced divers and all those in between. Snorkeling trips are also available, as are equipment rental, children's courses, and private boat excursions. ✉ *Kalafati* ☎ *22890/71677* 🌐 *www.mykonos-diving.com.*

Lia Beach. By Mykonos standards, Lia beach is considered tranquil and quiet, perhaps because it's one of the farthest organized beaches from Mykonos town. You can drive to the beach or get off at the last stop on the Mykonos town boat that brings people to the beaches. Rows of beach chairs and umbrellas line the pebble and sand beach, which is surrounded on both sides by a rocky coastline and the typical bare yet beautiful hills of the island. Divers and snorkelers head here to explore the turquoise waters. ■TIP→ Once you're set up, see if you can spot Naxos and Paros in the distance. **Amenities:** food and drink. **Best for:** solitude; snorkeling; swimming. ⊠ *Lia beach ✛ 14 km (8 miles) east of Mykonos town.*

WATER SPORTS

Water-sports facilities can be found at many beaches offering different types of equipment. The main hub for windsurfing in the southern part of the island is at Kalafati beach.

Kalafati Watersports. All the water-sports rentals to enjoy Kalafati's famous water-loving conditions can be found at Kalafati Watersports. Water-ski, wakeboard, extreme tubes, and banana boat excursions are available as well as speedboat island tours. ■TIP→ **Book in advance during the peak summer season.** ⊠ *Kalafati* ☎ *69/4526–1242 mobile* ⊕ *www.mykonoswatersports.com.*

WINDSURFING

Pezi Huber Windsurfing. Located right on the famed water-sports beach of Kalafati, where the meltemi winds blow "loyal and faithful," Pezi Huber runs his own windsurfing shop. He offers individual and group lessons for beginners and rentals for windsurfing. Rentals for stand-up paddles and other surf gear are also available. ⊠ *Kalafati beach, Kalafati* ☎ *22890/72345* ⊕ *www.pezi-huber.com.*

ANO MERA ΑΝΩ ΜΕΡΑ

8 km (5 miles) east of Mykonos town.

Inland, the little town of Ano Mera has a couple of quiet tavernas and a monastery. The town only lights up during the monastery's festival day on August 15.

Monastery of the Panayia Tourliani. Monastery buffs should head to Ano Mera, a village in the central part of the island, where the Monastery of the Panayia Tourliani, founded in 1580 and dedicated to the protectress of Mykonos, stands in the central square. Its massive baroque iconostasis (altar screen), made in 1775 by Florentine artists, has small icons carefully placed amid the wooden structure's painted green, red, and gold-leaf flowers. At the top are carved figures of the apostles and large icons depicting New Testament scenes. The hanging incense holders with silver molded dragons holding red eggs in their mouths show an Eastern influence. In the hall of the monastery, an interesting **museum** displays embroideries, liturgical vestments, and wood carvings. A good taverna is across the street. The monastery's big festival—hundreds attend—is on August 15. ⊠ *On central square* ☎ *22890/71249* ☉ *By appointment only; call in advance.*

NORTH COAST BOPEIA AKTH

The first beach is Ftelia, 7 km (4 miles) southeast of Mykonos town; the last beach is Ayios Sostis, 8 km (5 miles) northeast of Mykonos town.

The beaches along the north coast are blessed with consistent winds suitable for windsurfing, and Ftelia is the island's center for that sport. But on calm days, Panormos and Ayios Sostis are worth a trip; both offer beautiful beach vistas without the crowds. If you are looking for uncrowded beaches (even in the busy summer season), these are your best bets.

BEACHES

Ayios Sostis Beach. All you'll find at Ayios Sostis is turquoise waters lapping against the sand and small pebble coast. Without natural shade, or any touristic development whatsoever, beachgoers who need shade should come prepared. This is a beach with hidden elements though, so be sure to go in search of the small unnamed beach tucked in between it and neighboring Panormos, which is accessible by footpath. Off another path that leads to the main road, you'll find the small church that this beach is named after. Next to the church, a crowd may gather outside nearby a garden tavern you might otherwise miss if it wasn't the peak summer season in July and August. **Amenities:** food and drink. **Best for:** solitude; swimming. ✉ *Ayios Sostis* ✣ *12 km (7.5 miles) north of Mykonos town.*

Ftelia Beach. Ftelia is famous for its winds, which attract windsurfers who love to test out the turquoise waters. The beach's smooth sand is free of any sun beds or umbrellas so when you approach it all you'll see is a wide open stretch of yellow sand—if the wind isn't blowing it all about. Several tavernas and rooms-for-rent dot the area but are not directly on the beach. **Amenities:** none. **Best for:** windsurfing. ✉ *Ftelia.*

FAMILY **Panormos Beach.** A fine-golden-sand beach with turquoise waters, Panormos caters to all kinds of beachgoers. Nudists head to the far right for peace and quiet, but there's an all-day beach bar and restaurant that offers music, food and drinks to the left; it's popular with families, couples, and singles. This is a great spot when the southern winds attack; otherwise it's positioned to get the full brunt of the northern island winds. Water-sports equipment, umbrellas, and chairs are available for rent. **Amenities:** food and drink. **Best for:** nudists; swimming. ✉ *Panormos beach.*

WHERE TO EAT

$$ GREEK 🍴 **Kiki's Taverna.** With no telephone number or signs, this simple little family-run garden taverna would likely be missed if there wasn't a constant line of people waiting to grab a table—in the summer, expect to wait up to an hour. The sea views of Ayios Sostis beach are relaxing and the perfect thing to gaze at as you wait for your meat and fish dishes that will be expertly grilled on a barbecue. The specialty is the pork cutlet but most traditional Greek tavern dishes are served with Greek salads and creamy dips. To find it, head down a few steps toward Ayios Sostis, but before the beach, off the paved walkway, follow the smell of barbecue and look for a line of hungry people. [$] *Average main: €21* ✉ *Ayios Sostis* 💳 *No credit cards.*

$$ INTERNATIONAL 🍴 **Panormos Beach Bar and Restaurant.** This bar and restaurant simply melts into its beautiful setting with earthy beachy shades and whitewashed furniture; this casual atmosphere doesn't lack in style though. This is a setting that encourages you to relax in the shade, with your toes in the sand and a drink in your hand while you gaze at the sea. Main plates are beautifully presented, with tastes to match; try the sea urchin spaghetti or mussels with ginger sauce; for dessert, the tartufo is also great. There's an impressive beach bar that offers creations like the Waka Waka (spiced rum with fresh lime, grapefruit and palm sugar), which goes perfectly with a sunny Mykonos beach day. [$] *Average main: €19* ✉ *Panormos beach.*

SPORTS AND THE OUTDOORS

The north side of the island is also a wind lover's haven; Panormos and Ftelia is where they all head.

DELOS ΔΗΛΟΣ

Updated by Marissa Tejada

10 km (6 miles) southwest of Mykonos.

Arrive at the mythical, magical, and magnificent site of Delos and you might wonder how this barren islet, which has virtually no natural resources, became the religious and political center of the Aegean. One answer is that Dhílos—to use the Modern Greek transliteration—provided the safest anchorage for vessels sailing between the mainland and the shores of Asia; another answer is that it had no other use. A third is provided if you climb Mt. Kynthos to see that the isle (which is not more than 5 km [3 miles] long and 1 km [½ mile] wide) is shielded on three sides by other islands. Indeed, this is how the Cyclades—the word means "circling ones"—got their name: they circle around the sacred island.

Delos's amazing saga begins back in the times of myth: Zeus fell in love with gentle Leto, the Titaness, who became pregnant. When Hera discovered this infidelity, she forbade Mother Earth to give Leto refuge and ordered the Python to pursue her. Finally Poseidon, taking pity on her, anchored the poor floating island of Delos with four diamond columns to give her a place to rest. Leto gave birth first to the virgin huntress Artemis on Rhenea and then, clasping a sacred palm on a slope of Delos's Mt. Kynthos, to Apollo, god of music and light.

By 1000 BC the Ionians, who inhabited the Cyclades, had made Delos their religious capital. Homeric Hymn 3 tells of the cult of Apollo in the 7th century BC. One can imagine the elegant Ionians, whose central festival was here, enjoying the choruses of temple girls—"Delian korai, who serve the Far-Shooter"—singing and dancing their hymn and displaying their graceful tunics and jewelry. But a difficult period began for the Delians when Athens rose to power and assumed Ionian leadership. In 543 BC an oracle at Delphi conveniently decreed that the Athenians purify the island by removing all the graves to Rhenea, a dictate designed to alienate the Delians from their past.

After the defeat of the Persians in 478 BC, the Athenians organized the Delian League, with its treasury and headquarters at Delos (in 454 BC the funds were transferred to the Acropolis in Athens). Delos had its

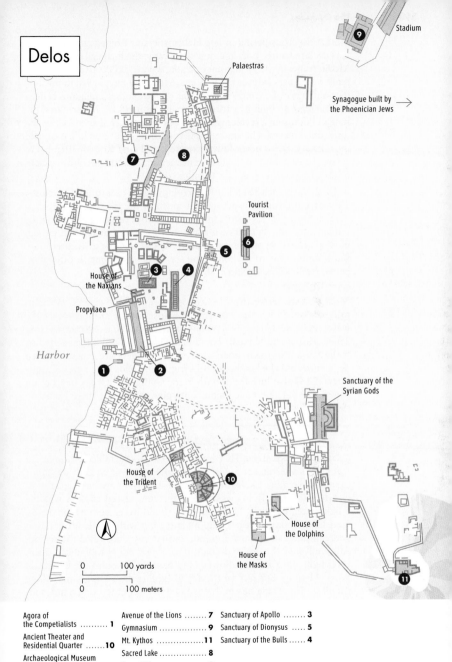

Delos

Palaestras

Synagogue built by
the Phoenician Jews →

Stadium

9

7 **8**

Tourist
Pavilion

6

5

House of
the Naxians **3** **4**

Propylaea

Harbor

1 **2**

Sanctuary of the
Syrian Gods

House of
the Trident **10**

House of
the Dolphins

House of
the Masks

11

0 100 yards

0 100 meters

most prosperous period in late Hellenistic and Roman times, when it was declared a free port and quickly became the financial center of the Mediterranean, the focal point of trade, where 10,000 slaves were sold daily. Foreigners from as far as Rome, Syria, and Egypt lived in this cosmopolitan port, in complete tolerance of one another's religious beliefs, and each group built its various shrines. But in 88 BC Mithridates, the king of Pontus, in a revolt against Roman rule, ordered an attack on the unfortified island. The entire population of 20,000 was killed or sold into slavery. Delos never fully recovered, and later Roman attempts to revive the island failed because of pirate raids. After a second attack in 69 BC, Delos was gradually abandoned.

In 1872, the French School of Archaeology began excavating on Delos— a massive project, considering that much of the island's 4 square km (2½ square miles) is covered in ruins. The work continues today. Delos remains dry and shadeless; off-season, the snack bar is often closed; most guards leave on the last boat to Mykonos in the early afternoon. But if on the way to Mykonos you see dolphins leaping (it often happens), you'll know Apollo is about and approves.

GETTING HERE

Most visitors arrive from Mykonos on one of the excursions helpfully organized by tour companies whose offices are located at the west end of the harbor in Mykonos town (tour boats also leave from Tinos, Paros, and Naxos). These boats leave around 9 am every day. If the sea is too rough, boats are cancelled. There are generally seven departures but the last boat returning from Delos is at 3 pm. Caïque boats (€15) also link Delos with Platis Gialos and Ornos beaches on Mykonos, but these excursions only give you about three hours on the sacred isle.

EXPLORING

Fodor'sChoice **Delos Archaeological Site.** This tiny, sacred place—the fabled birthplace of
★ Apollo—is a testament to Greece's glorious ancient civilization, home to one of the most fascinating and most important archaeological sites in Greece. When Delos was once a thriving sacred city—it was the religious center of the Cyclades—one could never be born or die on the island. Today the isle is unpopulated, but with a little imagination you can understand how a grand, ancient city once ruled the region. All you'll find is ruins and you'll have a few hours to explore them. Overnight stays are not allowed, and boats take you to the UNESCO World Heritage Site just for the day to explore the 5 km- (3 mile-) long island. ⚠ **The island has no shade, so don't forget to bring a hat, sunscreen, and plenty of water.** ⊠ *Accessible only by boat from Mykonos town* ☎ *22890/22259 archaeological museum, 22890/22218 Mykonos port (departures for Delos info)* ⊕ *www.culture.gr* ☎ *€8* ⊙ *Apr.–Oct., daily 8–8; Nov.–Mar., Tues.–Sun. 8–3.*

Agora of the Competialists. The first monument you'll see, from the left from the harbor, is the Agora of the Competialists (circa 150 BC). The competialists were members of Roman guilds, mostly freedmen and slaves from Sicily who worked for Italian traders. They worshipped the

As if posing for your camera, the ancient sculpted beasts of the Avenue of the Lions are Delos's most unforgettable photo op. They are copies; the originals are in Delos's museum.

Lares Competales, the Roman "crossroads" gods; in Greek they were known as *Hermaistai*, after the god Hermes, protector of merchants and the crossroads. ✉ *Just north of the Archaeological Museum of Delos.*

Ancient Theater and Residential Quarter. Beyond the path that leads to the southern part of the island is this ancient theater, built in the early 3rd century BC. It once sat 5,500 people. Near it was the elegant residential quarter inhabited by Roman bankers and Egyptian and Phoenician merchants. Their one- and two-story houses were typically built around a central courtyard, sometimes with columns on all sides. Floor mosaics of snakes, panthers, birds, dolphins, and Dionysus channeled rainwater into cisterns below; the best-preserved can be seen in the House of the Dolphins, the House of the Masks, and the House of the Trident.

Archaeological Museum of Delos. This museum is on the road south of the Gymnasium. It contains most of the antiquities found during excavations on the island: monumental statues of young men and women, stelae, reliefs, masks, mosaics, and ancient jewelry. ☎ *22890/22259.*

Avenue of the Lions. One of the most evocative and recognizable sights of Delos is the 164-foot-long Avenue of the Lions. The five marble beasts, which were carved in Naxos, crouch on their haunches, their forelegs stiffly upright, vigilant guardians of the Sacred Lake. They are the survivors of a line of at least nine lions that were erected in the second half of the 7th century BC by the Naxians. One statue, removed in the 17th century, now guards the Arsenal of Venice (though with a refurbished head); the remaining originals are in the Delos Archeological Museum on the island.

Gymnasium. Northeast of the palaestras is the Gymnasium, a square courtyard nearly 131 feet long on each side. "Gym" means naked in Greek, and here men and boys stayed in shape (and, in those heavily Platonic days, eyed each other) as they exercised in the nude. The long, narrow structure farther northeast is the stadium, the site of the athletic events of the Delian Games. East of the stadium site, by the seashore, are the remains of a synagogue built by Phoenician Jews in the 2nd century BC. A road south from the Gymnasium leads to the tourist pavilion, which has a meager restaurant and bar.

Mt. Kythnos. A dirt path leads up the base of Mt. Kynthos, which is the highest point on the island. Here lie the remains of many Middle Eastern shrines, including the Sanctuary of the Syrian Gods, which was built in 100 BC. A flight of steps goes up 368 feet to the summit of Mt. Kynthos (from which the name "Cynthia" was derived), where Greek mythology says Zeus watched the birth of his son, Apollo, on the slope. There are amazing views of Mykonos, Naxos, Paros, and Syros from the top of the mountain. The path is completely unshaded, so be prepared for the heat.

The Sacred Lake. A short distance north of the Sanctuary of the Bulls is an oval indentation in the earth where the Sacred Lake once sparkled. It is surrounded by a stone wall that reveals the original periphery. According to islanders, the lake was fed by the river Inopos from its source high on Mt. Kynthos until 1925, when the water stopped flowing and the lake dried up. Along the shores are two ancient *palaestras* (buildings for physical exercise and debate).

The Sacred Way. East of the Agora of the Competialists you'll find the entrance to the Sacred Way, which leads north to the Temple of Apollo. The Way was once bordered by beautiful marbled statues and monuments created by various kingdoms and city states of ancient Greece. It was also the route used by pilgrims during the holy Delian festival.

Sanctuary of Apollo. Beyond the Sacred Way is one of the most important sites on the island, the Sanctuary of Apollo. Three separate temples originally stood here flanked by altars, monuments, and statues, although not much remains of them. The main temple was grand, fittingly called the Great Temple of Apollo (circa 480 BC). Inside the sanctuary and to the right is the House of the Naxians, a 7th- to 6th-century BC structure with a central colonnade. Dedications to Apollo were stored in this shrine. Outside the north wall a massive rectangular pedestal once supported a colossal statue of Apollo (one of the hands is in Delos's Archaeological Museum, and a piece of a foot is in the British Museum). Near the pedestal a bronze palm tree was erected in 417 BC by the Athenians to commemorate the palm tree under which Leto gave birth. According to Plutarch, the palm tree toppled in a storm and brought the statue of Apollo down with it. In *The Odyssey*, Odysseus compares the Phaeacian princess Nausicaa to a palm he saw on Delos, when the island was wetter.

Sanctuary of the Bulls. Southeast of the Sanctuary of Apollo is the ruins of the Sanctuary of the Bulls, an extremely long and narrow structure built, it is thought, to display a *trireme* (an ancient boat with three banks of

11

oars) that was dedicated to Apollo by a Hellenistic leader thankful for a naval victory. Maritime symbols were found in the decorative relief of the main halls, and the head and shoulders of a pair of bulls were part of the design of an interior entrance.

Sanctuary of Dionysus. Immediately to the right of the Archaeological Museum is the small Sanctuary of Dionysus, which was erected about 300 BC. Outside the sanctuary you'll find one of the more-boggling sights of ancient Greece: several monuments dedicated to Apollo by the winners of the choral competitions of the Delian festivals, each decorated with a huge phallus, emblematic of the orgiastic rites that took place during the Dionysian festivals. Around the base of one of them is carved a lighthearted representation of a bride being carried to her new husband's home. A marble phallic bird, symbol of the body's immortality, also adorns this corner of the sanctuary.

PAROS AND ANTIPAROS
ΠΑΡΟΣ ΚΑΙ ΑΝΤΙΠΑΡΟΣ

Updated by Marissa Tejada

165 km (91 nautical miles) southeast of Piraeus harbor in Athens.

In the classical age, the great sculptor Praxiteles prized the incomparably snowy marble that came from the quarries at Paros; his chief rival was the Parian Scopas. Between them they developed the first true female nude, and gentle voluptuousness seems a good description of this historic island. Today, Paros is favored by people for its cafés by the sea, golden sandy beaches, and charming fishing villages. It may lack the chic of Mykonos and have fewer top-class hotels, but at the height of the season it often gets Mykonos's tired and detrending—Madonna (the singer, not Our Lady, who is always here) shows up every summer. The island is large enough to accommodate the traveler in search of peace and quiet, yet the lovely port towns of Paroikía (Paros town), the capital, and Naousa also have an active nightlife (overactive in August). Paros is a focal point of the Cyclades ferry network, and many people stay here for a night or two while waiting for a connection. Paros town has a good share of bars and discos, though Naousa has a more-chic island atmosphere. And none of the islands has a richer cultural life, with concerts, exhibitions, and readings, than does Paros. For this, check the English monthly, *Paros Life,* available everywhere (⊕ *www. paroslife.gr*).

Like all the bigger islands, Paros is developing too fast. Since the mid-1990s, more than 2,000 new homes have been built on the island, which has a population of 14,000. More are underway—and this equals the total number of homes ever built here. You'll understand why: you're likely to want to build a little house here yourself. The overflow of visitors is such that it has now washed up on Paros's sister, Antiparos: this island "forgetaway" still has an off-the-beaten-track vibe, even though the rich and famous—Tom Hanks is most prominent of them—have discovered it.

GETTING HERE AND AROUND

There are six Olympic Airlines flights a day to Athens in summer, three in winter. Early reservations are essential. If a dignitary wants a late flight, you may get bumped. Paros is well served by ferries—there are at least 15 of them daily—many connecting Paros to other islands. Five daily ferries out of Piraeus stop at Paros, and two from Rafina. In summer there are daily connections to Tinos, Mykonos, Naxos, and Santorini. There are also regular connections to Milos, Kimolos, Anafi Ios, Iraklia, Donousa, Koufonisi, Schinousa, Crete, Folegandros, Sikinos, Sifnos, Serifos, Kea, Kastelorizo, Kimolos, Astypalea, Kalymnos, Rhodes, Kos, Nisyros, and Astypalea. There is also a speedboat for hire, much used by lawyers. For boat schedules check ⊕ *www.openseas.gr*.

From the Paros town bus station, just west of the dock, there is service every hour to Naousa and less-frequent service to Aliki, Pounta (about 10 buses a day to this departure point for Antiparos), and the beaches at Piso Livadi, Chrissi Akti, and Drios. Schedules are posted. Buy tickets at the booth; fares run from €2.50 to €8. There is a taxi stand across from the windmill on the harbor (☎ *22840/21500*).

TOURS

Erkyna Travel. Erkyna Travel runs many excursions by boat, bus, and foot. ✉ *On main square, Naousa* ☎ *22840/22654, 22840/22655, 22840/53180* ⊕ *www.erkynatravel.com*.

Polos Tours. This agency handles all travel arrangments, from boat tickets to car rentals to excursions, with great efficiency. The company can also arrange boat tours to Antiparos. ✉ *Next to dockside OTE office, Paros town* ☎ *22840/22333* ⊕ *www.polostours.gr*.

Santorineos Travel Services. For yacht and other VIP services, check out Nikos Santorineos's office. ✉ *Opposite bus station, Paros town* ☎ *22840/24245* ⊕ *www.traveltoparos.gr*.

VISITOR INFORMATION

The most useful Paros website is ⊕ *www.parosweb.com*.

PAROS TOWN ΠΑΡΟΣ (ΠΑΡΟΙΚΙΑ)

168 km (91 miles) southeast of Piraeus, 35 km (22 miles) west of Naxos.

First impressions of Paroikía (Paros town), pretty as it is, may not necessarily be positive. The port flashes too much concrete, too many boats dock, and the traffic problem, now that Athenian families bring two cars and local families own two cars, is insoluble. The waterfront is lined with travel agencies, a multitude of car and motorbike rental agencies, and *fastfood-adika*—the Greek word means just what you think it does. Then, if you head east on the harbor road, you'll see a lineup of bars, tourist shops, and coffee shops—many, as elsewhere on the more-prosperous islands, operated by Athenians who come to Paros to capitalize on the huge summer influx. Past them are the fishing-boat dock, a partially excavated ancient graveyard, and the post office; then start the beaches (shaded and over-popular), with their hotels and tavernas.

Continued on page 569

Greece's Gods and Heroes

Superheroes, sex, adventure: it's no wonder Greek myths have reverberated throughout Western civilization. Today, as you wander ancient Greece's most sacred sites—such as Delos, island birthplace of the sun god Apollo—these ageless tales will come alive to thrill and perhaps haunt you.

Whether you are looking at 5th-century BC pedimental sculptures in Olympia or ancient red-figure vase paintings in Athens, whether you are reading the epics of Homer or the tragedies of Euripides, you are in the presence of the Greek mythopoetic mind. Peopled with emblems of hope, fear, yearning, and personifications of melting beauty or of petrifying ugliness, these ancient myths helped early Greeks make sense of a chaotic, primitive universe that yielded no secrets.

Frightened by the murder and mayhem that surrounded them, the Greeks set up gods in whom power, wisdom, and eternal youth could not perish. These gods lived, under the rule of Zeus, on Mount Olympus. Their rivalries and intrigues were a primeval, superhuman version of *Dynasty* and *Dallas*. These astounding collections of stories not only pervaded all ancient Greek society but have influenced the course of Western civilization: How could we imagine our culture—from Homer's *Iliad* to Joyce's *Ulysses*—without them?

Apollo, the sun god

ZEUS

Latin Name: Jupiter

God of: Sky, Supreme God

Attribute: Scepter, Thunder

Roving Eye: Zeus was the ruler of Mount Olympus but often went AWOL pursuing love affairs down on earth with nymphs and beautiful ladies; his children were legion, including Hercules.

HERA

Latin Name: Juno

Goddess of: Sky, Marriage

Attribute: Peacock

His Cheating Heart: Hera married her brother Zeus, wound up having a 300-year honeymoon with him on Samos, and was repaid for her fidelity to marriage by the many love affairs of her hubby.

APHRODITE

Latin Name: Venus

Goddess of: Love, Beauty

Attribute: Dove

And the Winner Is: Born out of the foam rising off of Cyprus, she was given the Golden Apple by Paris in the famous beauty contest between her, Athena, and Hera, and bestowed the love of Helen on him as thanks.

ATHENA

Latin Name: Minerva

Goddess of: Wisdom

Attribute: Owl, Olive

Top Billing: The goddess of reason, she gave the olive tree to the Greeks; her uncle was Poseidon, and the Parthenon in Athens was built in her honor.

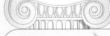

APOLLO

Latin Name: Phoebus

God of: Sun, Music, and Poetry

Attribute: Bow, Lyre

Confirmed Bachelor: Born at Delos, his main temple was at Delphi; his love affairs included Cassandra, to whom he gave the gift of prophecy; Calliope, with whom he had Orpheus; and Daphne, who, fleeing from his embrace, changed into a tree.

ARTEMIS

Latin Name: Diana

Goddess of: Chastity, Moon

Attribute: Stag

Early Feminist: Sister of Apollo, she enjoyed living in the forest with her court, frowned on marriage, and, most notoriously, had men torn apart by her hounds if they peeked at her bathing.

YE GODS!

WHO'S WHO IN GREEK MYTHOLOGY

The twelve chief gods formed the elite of Olympus. Each represented one of the forces of nature and also a human characteristic. They also had attributes by which they can often be identified. The Romans, influenced by the arts and letters of Greece, largely identified their own gods with those of Greece, with the result that Greek gods have Latin names as well. Here are the divine I.D.s of the Olympians.

DEMETER
Latin Name: Ceres
Goddess of: Earth, Fecundity
Attribute: Sheaf, Sickle
Most Dramatic Moment: After her daughter Persephone was kidnapped by Zeus, Demeter decided to make all plants of the earth wither and die.

HERMES
Latin Name: Mercury
God of: Trade, Eloquence
Attribute: Wings
Messenger Service: Father of Pan, Hermes was known as a luck-bringer, harbinger of dreams, and the messenger of Olympus; he was also worshipped as the god of commerce and music.

POSEIDON
Latin Name: Neptune
God of: Sea, Earthquakes
Attribute: Trident
Water Boy: To win the affection of Athenians, Poseidon and Athena were both charged with giving them the most useful gift, with his invention of the bubbling spring losing out to Athena's creation of the olive.

ARES
Latin Name: Mars
God of: Tumult, War
Attribute: Spear, Helmet
Antisocial: The most famous male progeny of Zeus and Hera, he was an irritable man; considering his violent temper, few temples were erected in his honor in Greece.

HESTIA
Latin Name: Vesta
Goddess of: Hearth, Domestic Values
Attribute: Eternal Fire
Hausfrau: A famous virgin, she was charged with maintaining the eternal flame atop Olympus; the Vestal Virgins of ancient Romans followed in her footsteps.

HEPHAESTOS
Latin Name: Vulcan
God of: Fire, Industry
Attribute: Hammer, Anvil
Pumping Iron: The best-preserved Doric style temple in Athens, the Hephaestaion, was erected to this god in the ancient agora marketplace; today, ironmongers still have shops in the district there.

HERCULES

THE FIRST ACTION HERO

Greece's most popular mythological personage was probably Heracles, a hero who became a god, and had to work hard to do it. This paragon of masculinity was so admired by the Romans that they vulgarized him as Hercules, and modern entrepreneurs have capitalized on his popularity in silly sandal epics and sillier Saturday morning cartoons. His name means "glory of Hera," although the goddess hated him because he was the son of Zeus and the Theban princess Alcmene. The Incredible Bulk proved his strength and courage while still in the cradle, and his sexual prowess when he impregnated King Thespius' fifty daughters in as many nights. But the twelve labors are his most famous achievement. To expiate the mad murder of his wife and his three children, he was ordered to:

1. Slay the Nemean Lion
2. Kill the Lernaean Hydra
3. Capture the Ceryneian Hind
4. Trap the Erymanthian Boar
5. Flush the Augean stables of manure
6. Kill the obnoxious Stymphalian Birds
7. Capture the Cretan Bull, a Minoan story
8. Steal the man-eating Mares of Diomedes
9. Abscond with the Amazon Hippolyta's girdle
10. Obtain six-armed Geryon's Cattle
11. Fetch the Golden Apples of the Hesperides, which bestowed immortality
12. Capture three-headed Cerberus, watchdog of Hades

In other words, he had to rid the world of primitive terrors and primeval horrors. Today, some revisionist Hellenistic historians considered him to be a historical king of Argos or Tiryns and his main stomping ground was the Argolid, basically the northern and southern Peloponnese. Travelers can today still trace his journeys through the region, including Lerna (near the modern village of Myli), not far from Nafplion, where the big guy battled the Hydra, now seen by some historians as a symbol for the malarial mosquitoes that once ravaged the area. Herc pops up in the myths of many other heroes, including Jason, who stole the Golden Fleece; Perseus, who killed Medusa; and Theseus, who established Athens' dominance. And his constellation is part of the regularly whirling Zodiac that is the mythological dome over all our actions and today's astrology.

Hercules fighting with the centaur Nessus, sculpted by Giambologna

But go the other way straight into town and you'll find it easy to get lost in the maze of narrow, stone-paved lanes that intersect with the streets of the quiet residential areas. The marble plaza at the town's entrance is full of strollers and playing children in the evening (during the day, you can fry eggs on this shadeless space). As you check your laptop (Paros town has Wi-Fi) along the market street chockablock with tourist shops, you'll begin to traverse the centuries: ahead of you looms the seaside Kastro, the ancient acropolis. In 1207 the Venetians conquered Paros, which joined the Duchy of Naxos, and built their huge marble castle wall out of blocks and columns from three temples. At the crest, next to the church of Saints Constantine and Helen (built in 1689), are the visible foundations of a late-Archaic temple to Athena—the area remains Paros's favorite sunset spot.

EXPLORING

Archaeological Museum of Paros. The Archaeological Museum contains a large chunk of the famed Parian Chronicle, which recorded cultural events in Greece from about 1500 BC until 260 BC (another chunk is in Oxford's Ashmolean Museum). It interests scholars that the historian inscribed detailed information about artists, poets, and playwrights, completely ignoring wars and shifts in government. Some primitive pieces from the Aegean's oldest settlement, Saliagos (an islet between Paros and Antiparos), are exhibited in the same room, on the left. A small room contains Archaic finds from the ongoing excavation at Despotiko—and they are finding a lot. In the large room to the right rests a marble slab depicting the poet Archilochus in a banquet scene, lying on a couch, his weapons nearby. The ancients ranked Archilochus, who invented iambic meter and wrote the first signed love lyric, second only to Homer. When he died in battle against the Naxians, his conqueror was cursed by the oracle of Apollo for putting to rest one of the faithful servants of the muse. Also there are a monumental Nike and three superb pieces found in the last decade: a waist-down kouros, a gorgon with intact wings, and a dancing-girl relief. ⌗ *Behind Hundred Doors Church* ☎ *22840/21231* ⌗*€2* ⊙ *Tues.–Sun. 8–3.*

OFF THE
BEATEN
PATH

Monastery of Longovarda. Halfway from Paros town to Naousa, on the right, the 17th-century Monastery of Longovarda shines on its mountainside. The monastic community farms the local land and makes honey, wine, and olive oil. Only men, dressed in conservative clothing, are allowed inside, where there are post-Byzantine icons, 17th-century frescoes depicting the Twelve Feasts in the Life of Christ, and a library of rare books; it is usually open mornings. ⌗ *3 km (5 miles) northeast of Paros town* ☎ *22840/21202.*

Fodor's Choice
★

Panayia Ekatontapyliani (*Hundred Doors Church*). The square above the port, to the northwest, was built to celebrate the church's 1,700th anniversary. From there note a white wall with two belfries, the front of the former monastic quarters that surround the magnificent Panayia Ekatontapyliani, the earliest remaining proto-Byzantine church in Greece and one of the oldest unaltered churches in the world. As such, it is of inestimable value to architecture buffs (such as Prince Charles, who has been spotted here).

The story began in 326, when St. Helen—the mother of Emperor Constantine the Great—set out on a ship for the Holy Land to find the True Cross. Stopping on Paros, she had a vision of success and vowed to build a church there. Though she died before it was built, her son built the church in 328 as a wooden-roof basilica. Two centuries later, Justinian the Great (who ruled the Byzantine Empire in 527–65) commissioned the splendid dome.

According to legend, 99 doors have been found in the church and the 100th will be discovered only after Constantinople is Greek again—but the name is actually older than the legend. Inside, the subdued light mixes with the dun, reddish, and green tufa (porous volcanic rock). The columns are classical and their capitals Byzantine. At the corners of the dome are two fading Byzantine frescoes depicting six-winged seraphim. The 4th-century iconostasis (with ornate later additions) is divided into five frames by marble columns. One panel contains the 14th-century icon of the Virgin, with a silver covering from 1777. The Virgin is carried in procession on the church's crowded feast day, August 15, the Dormition. During Easter services, thousands of rose petals are dropped from the dome upon the singing celebrant. The adjacent **Baptistery,** nearly unique in Greece, also built from the 4th to the 6th century, has a marble font and bits of mosaic floor. The church **museum,** at the right, contains post-Byzantine icons. ⊠ *750 feet east of dock* ☎ *22840/21243* ⊕ *www.ekatontapyliani.gr* ☉ *Daily 8 am–9 pm.*

PRIDE GOETH BEFORE A FALL

At one point, Justinian the Great (who ruled the Byzantine Empire in 527–65) had the Hundred Doors Church rebuilt. He appointed Isidorus, one of the two architects of Constantinople's famed Hagia Sophia, to design it, but Isidorus sent his apprentice, Ignatius, in his place. Upon inspection, Isidorus discovered the dome to be so magnificent that, consumed by jealousy, he pushed the apprentice off the roof. Ignatius grasped his master's foot and the two tumbled to their death together. Look for the folk sculpture at the sanctuary's closed left portal of the two men.

Scorpios Museum. The Scorpios Museum is set next to a garden full of large models of traditional Parian windmills, dovecotes, churches, and other such things, making for an utterly charming setting. It showcases the creations of fisherman Benetos Skiadas, who loves to make detailed models of ships, including his own, and his scrupulous craftsmanship is on view here; you can also order a model of your own design. ⊠ *On road to Aliki, just past airport* ☎ *22840/91129* 🖅 *€3* ☉ *Daily 9:30 am–2 pm* ☉ *Closed Oct.–Apr.*

BEACHES

From Paros town, boats leave throughout the day for beaches across the bay: to sandy Marcellos and Krios and the quieter Kaminia. Livadia, a five-minute walk, is very developed but has shade. In the other direction, Delfini has a beach bar with live music, and Parasporos has a few beach bars. Sun-lovers note: Paros is ringed with beaches.

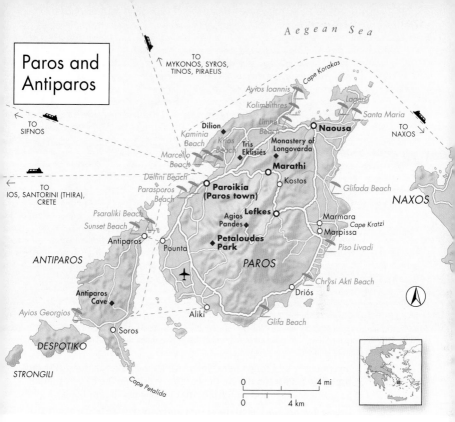

Paros and Antiparos

Aegean Sea

TO MYKONOS, SYROS, TINOS, PIRAEUS

Cape Korakas

Ayios Ioannis

Kolimbithres

Lageri

Santa Maria

TO SIFNOS

Dilion

Kaminia Beach

Limnes Beach

Naousa

TO NAXOS

Krios Beach

Tris Eklisiés

Monastery of Longovarda

Marcello Beach

Delfini Beach

Marathi

Parasporos Beach

Paroikia (Paros town)

Kostos

Glifada Beach

NAXOS

TO IOS, SANTORINI (THIRA), CRETE

Psaraliki Beach

Agios Pandes

Lefkes

Marmara

Cape Kratzi

Sunset Beach

Marpissa

Antiparos

Pounta

Petaloudes Park

Piso Livadi

ANTIPAROS

PAROS

Antiparos Cave

Chrysi Akti Beach

Ayios Georgios

Aliki

Driós

Soros

Glifa Beach

DESPOTIKO

STRONGILI

Cape Petalida

0   4 mi

0   4 km

Delfini/Souvlia Beach. This small beach is known for its pretty water and "chill" atmosphere. It's also known around the island for Magaya, a colorful beach bar set right in front of the beach; it's a popular meeting spot for the island's expats. In the summer, beach chairs and umbrellas are available for rent, so grab one and settle in to enjoy the view of Paros bay. ■ TIP→ There's a small rocky islet with an underwater cave in the near distance, popular for swimmers to head to, but it's often full of sea urchins. **Amenities:** food and drink. **Best for:** swimming.

Kaminia Beach. Sandy, long, and unorganized, Kaminia sits to the north of Paros bay. Beachgoers seeking more solitude can head here, even though its right next to the popular Krios beach. See if you can find the Cave of Archilochos, which is a small opening on the rock along the coast. The famous ancient Greek poet was said to visit the cave for inspiration and wrote poetry there. **Amenities:** none. **Best for:** solitude; swimming.

Krios Beach. Close to Paros town, this sandy beach is a popular summer destination. Cliffs jut into the sand line, parting the coastline and providing protection from the summer island winds. From under a rented umbrella you can watch the boats and ferries slowly sail into the harbor. If you need to take a break, there's a selection of nearby

Prince Charles (more than once) and many other architecture buffs have visited the great Church of Our Lady of the Hundred Doors, a proto-Byzantine landmark.

tavernas. ■TIP→ **To get here, you can hike the half-hour long cliff-top trail, take a small boat from the harbor, or drive to the nearby parking area. Amenities:** food and drink. **Best for:** swimming; walking.

Livadia Beach. Considered the closest authentic Parian beach near Paros town, Livadia is the first wide bay north of the harbor that's comprised of a series of smaller, white sand beaches. Some areas are organized with beach chair and umbrella rentals while others are untouched by tourism, and only trees provide shade. Just a ten-minute walk from the town and harbor and near camping grounds, it can get crowded. **Amenities:** food and drink. **Best for:** swimming.

Marcello Beach. Marcello's famously cool waters attract Parians on the hottest summer days. You can spend the entire day eating, drinking, swimming, or watching the calm water lap against this long, sandy stretch of coastline as the beach is well-equipped with beach bars and cafés, tavernas, and umbrella lounge chair rentals. Situated next Krios beach, it's accessible by car, ferry, or a 40-minute hike from Paros town. **Amenities:** food and drink. **Best for:** swimming; walking.

Parasporos Beach. This large sandy beach is surrounded by a few shady trees, but umbrellas (and chairs) are available for rent in the summer season. The clear turquoise water gets deep fast making it ideal for swimming. There are a few bars on-site that add a little beach-party fun. **Amenities:** food and drink. **Best for:** partiers; swimming.

WHERE TO EAT

$ ✕ **The Albatross.** You can expect great sunset views and well-prepared
SEAFOOD   traditional dishes at one of Paros's most popular seafood tavernas. For two decades, owner Maria Voularaki has never served a bad dish.

Properly it is an *ouzeri*, where one eats mezedes with wine or ouzo, so you'll find there are many small plates to choose from such as the shrimp *saganaki* (with cheese) in tomato sauce; skate salad; calamari salad with sun-dried tomatoes; various croquettes (the mushroom ones are very tasty); and grilled eggplant with three cheeses. Fresh fish is available according to weather. $ *Average main: €10* ✉ *Waterfront* ☎ *22840/21848* ⊘ *Closed Dec.–Mar.*

$ ✕ **Levantis.** Chef George Mavridis twists traditional Greek dishes with con-
GREEK FUSION temporary flavors creating a sophisticated menu that pays strict attention
Fodor'sChoice to presentation. Two intriguing starters are salt-cured mackerel with grilled
★ cauliflower, potato, caper, and dill salad; and thinly sliced herb-encrusted beef with greens, onion marmalade, and wasabi oil. Top entrées include yogurt-encrusted rabbit ragout with olive and eggplant; and linguine with roasted cherry tomatoes and sardines. For dessert indulge in the Greek thyme honey and *mizithra* (farmer's cheese) tart with grape pastry. A cool whitewashed indoor room expands the dining space, built to complement the cozy yet sophisticated garden dining area. $ *Average main: €14* ✉ *Central market street* ☎ *22840/23613* ✍ *levantisrestaurant@yahoo.gr* ⊕ *www. levantisrestaurant.com* ⊘ *Closed Nov.–Apr.*

WHERE TO STAY

$$ ⌂ **Bicycle House.** The name comes from the bicycle (of the noted late
B&B/INN dancer Vasilis Iakoumis) mounted to the front of this house, which contains three lovely units in a countryside-like complex with a pool and a view that overlooks the sea and sunset. **Pros:** small; attractive; friendly. **Cons:** only three rooms; walking distance from nowhere. $ *Rooms from: €100* ✛ *8 km (5 miles) from Paros town on airport road* ☎ *22840/92203* ⊕ *www.bicyclehouse.eu* ⟳ *3 apartments* ▭ *No credit cards* ⦿ *No meals.*

$ ⌂ **Pandrossos Hotel.** If you want a good night's sleep away from the
HOTEL pulse of Paros town but you don't want to give up shopping, nightlife, restaurants, and cafés, the Pandrossos—built on a hill with a splen-did view overlooking Paros bay—is the best choice. **Pros:** convenience; great views. **Cons:** some of the rooms are on the small side. $ *Rooms from: €80* ✉ *On hill at southwest edge of Paros town* ☎ *22840/22903* ⊕ *www.pandrossosparos.com* ⟳ *41 rooms, 5 suites* ⊘ *Closed Nov.– Mar.* ⦿ *Breakfast.*

$ ⌂ **Parian Village.** This shady, quiet hotel at the far edge of Livadia beach
HOTEL has small rooms, all with balconies or terraces, most with spectacular views over Paros bay. **Pros:** pretty place near the sea; good vistas. **Cons:** 15-minute walk to town past crowds in season. $ *Rooms from: €80* ✉ *25-min sea walk from center of Paros town* ☎ *22840/23187* ⊕ *www. parianvillage.gr* ⟳ *28 rooms* ⊘ *Closed Sept.–Apr.* ⦿ *Breakfast.*

NIGHTLIFE AND PERFORMING ARTS

BARS

Turn right along the waterfront from the port in Paros town to find the town's famous bars; then follow your ears. At the far end of the Paralia is the laser-light-and-disco section of town, which you may want to avoid. In the younger bars, cheap alcohol, as everywhere in tourist Greece, is often added to the more-colorful drinks.

Entropy Bar. Year-round, Entropy offers a casual, fun atmosphere with a creative shot menu that will probably peak your curiosity. Mandarin Jellybean, Disco Lemonball, or Shark Bite anyone? American expats Scott and Lisa Stavrou opened the bar just off the Paros town seafront to mix up their idea of perfect cocktails for locals and tourists alike. Their colorful selections include Watermelon Basil Smash, Aegean Blue Lagoon, and Tangerine Dream. ✉ *Market street, Paros town, Paros* ☎ *22840/27323* ✉ *info@entropybarparos.com* ⊕ *www. entropybarparos.com.*

Pirate Bar. Located in the Old Town, this cozy bar combines whitewashed walls with a stone and wood design and soft lighting. The result is a sophisticated crowd that loves its jazz and blues music as well as its cocktails. Some nights, live bands are featured. ✉ *Old Town, Paros town, Paros.*

PERFORMING ARTS

Of all the islands Paros has the liveliest art scene (check ⊕ *paroslife. parosweb.com* for openings and events), with dozens of galleries and public spaces presenting exhibitions. Many artists, Greek and foreign, live on the island or visit regularly—painters Jane Pack and Neva Bergmann, sculptor Richard King, photographers Stavros Niflis and Elizabeth Carson, portrait artist Angelika Vaxevanidou, filmmaker Ioannis Tritsibidas, and ceramist Stelios Ghikas are just a few—and the Aegean Center has proved a strong stimulant.

Fodor'sChoice ★ **The Aegean Center for the Fine Arts.** A small American arts college, the Aegean Center for the Fine Arts hosts readings, concerts, lectures, and exhibitions in its splendidly restored neoclassic mansion. Director John Pack, an American photographer, lives on the island with his family. Since 1966 the center has offered courses (two three-month semesters) in writing, painting, photography, and classical voice training. ✉ *Main cross street to market street* ☎ *22840/23287* ⊕ *www.aegeancenter.org.*

Holland Tunnel Gallery. Paulien Lethen's Holland Tunnel Gallery has its main space in Brooklyn, New York. The Paros space, open only in summer, is set in a whitewashed town house and has a fine stable of international artists with a Paros connection. ✉ *Market street* ☎ *22840/22195* ⊕ *www.hollandtunnelgallery.com.*

SPORTS AND THE OUTDOORS

WATER SPORTS

Many beaches offer water sports, especially windsurfing.

SHOPPING

CERAMICS

Yria Interiors. On the market street, look for the house with the beautifully carved Parian marble facade to find Paros's most elegantly designed shop. Here, Stelios Ghikas, Monique Mailloux, and daughter Ramona display their pottery from Studio Yria, as well as a carefully chosen range of stylish household items mostly from France. ✉ *Market street* ☎ *22840/24359* ⊕ *www.yriaparos.com* ☾ *Daily 9:30 am–2:30 pm, 6–11 pm.*

JEWELRY

Jewelry Workshop. Vangelis Skaramagas and Yannis Xenos, uncle and nephew, have been making their own delicate, precious jewelry at Jewelry Workshop for more than 20 years. ⊠ *End of market street* ☎ *22840/21008.*

Phaedra. Local Phaidra Apostolopoulou, who studied jewelry in Athens, has a tiny shop, Phaedra, where she shows her sophisticated silver and gold designs, and a line of lighthearted pieces for summer. ⊠ *Near Zoodochos Pyghi church, Paros town, Paros* ☎ *22840/23626* ⊕ *www. kosmimaphaedra.com* ⊙ *Daily 12:30–2, 6:30–9 pm.*

NAOUSA ΝΑΟΥΣΑ

10 km (6 miles) northeast of Paros town.

Naousa, impossibly pretty, long ago discovered the benefits of tourism. Its outskirts are mushrooming with villas and hotels that exploit it further. Along the harbor—which thankfully maintains its beauty and function as a fishing port—red and navy blue boats knock gently against one another as men repair their nets and foreigners relax in the ouzeri—Barbarossa being the traditional favorite—by the water's edge. From here the pirate Hugue Crevelliers operated in the 1570s, and Byron turned him into the corsair. Navies of the ancient Persians, flotillas from medieval Venice, and the imperial Russian fleet have anchored in this harbor. The half-submerged ruins of the Venetian fortifications still remain; they are a pretty sight when lit up at night. Compared to Paros town, the scene in Naousa is somewhat more chic, with a more-intimate array of shops, bars, and restaurants, but in winter the town shuts down. The island's unobtrusive gay scene is here, if it is anywhere.

EXPLORING

Folklore Museum. Naousa's small Folklore Museum, 150 yards from the main town square, is in a traditional house donated by Kanstantinos and Marouso Roussos. It's run by the Music, Dance and Theatre Group of Naousa and features folk costumes from Paros and the rest of Greece. The furniture and implements are also historic. ☎ *22840/52284* ⊠ *€1* ⊙ *Daily 7–9 pm* ⊙ *Closed Oct.–May.*

BEACHES

Ayios Ioannis. Served by the Kolimbithres boat, Ayios Ioannis's golden, sandy beach is peaceful, clean, and quiet. Protected by a rocky cove, the beach is attached to the Paros Eco Park, which offers a snack bar and numerous amenities. The blue-domed, whitewashed Ayios Ioannis Monastery sits to the right side of the beach, a short walk in the near distance. **Amenities:** food and drink; showers; toilets; water sports. **Best for:** swimming. ⊠ *In front of Paros Eco Park.*

FAMILY **Kolimbithres.** The beach, which is noted for its anfractuous rock formations, is also considered to be one of Paros's best, attracting its share of crowds to the small, sandy cove. The granite formations create shallow pools of water popular with the kids. It's within walking distance of two tavernas that overlook the region. Lounge chairs and umbrellas are available for rent from a seasonal café. Head to the top of nearby

Koukounaries hill to view the remains of an ancient site. You can get there by car, but there is no designated parking for the beach. People do park at area tavernas or along the road. Another way to reach the beach is by boat from Naousa bay. **■TIP→ A boat crosses the bay to Kolimbithres from Naousa bay.** **Amenities:** food and drink. **Best for:** swimming. ✉ *Directly across bay from Naousa.*

Lageri. A boat from Naousa regularly heads to Lageri, a long beach known for its fine sand, sand dunes, and calm, quiet atmosphere. Those are just a few of the reasons it attracts its share of nudists who prefer the less crowded Paros beaches. It's also accesible via a small foot path from the main road. **Amenities:** none. **Best for:** nudists; walking; solitude. ✉ *North of Naousa.*

FAMILY **Santa Maria.** Several sandy footpaths from the main road lead you to one of Paros's most popular family-friendly beaches; the boat that travels to nearby Lageri also makes a stop in Santa Maria. Little fishing boats dock in the distance from the sandy cove, which is filled with sand dunes and lined with green brush. There's no natural shade but in peak season it's well-equipped with beach chair and umbrella rentals from seasonal cafés. Several taverns are within walking distance. **Amenities:** food and drink. **Best for:** swimming. ✉ *Northeastern shore of Paros.*

WHERE TO EAT

$$ GREEK 🍴 **Mario.** Good food is enhanced here by the pretty location, a few feet from the fishing boats on Naousa's harbor. The taverna specializes in fresh fish (from the fisherman a few feet away), and also fine cuisine. Such starters as tuna carpaccio with aromatic oil and smoked salt, and grilled octopus with *bucovo* (crushed red pepper) and caper sauce segue to complex entrées like seafood pasta with diced asparagus and saffron, or fresh fish baked in a salt crust (order this in advance). For dessert, try the traditional spoon sweets made by Mario's mother. [$] *Average main: €20* ✉ *On fishing-boat harbor* ☎ *22840/51047* ✍ *Reservations essential.*

$$ GREEK 🍴 **Mediterraneo.** For a view of Naousa harbor and a taste of Greek seafood specialties head to Mediterraneo. Chef Giorgos Parousis stays true to traditional Greek taverna appetizers including fresh grilled octopus and marinated anchovies and dips like *taramosalata* (fish roe dip) and fava dip topped with caramelized onion. Main dishes also feature what he calls contemporary creativity including his specialty, a dark and delicious black risotto with cuttlefish. His marinated grilled squid, crisped to perfection with the right dash of Mediterranean spices, is also a top choice. [$] *Average main: €20* ✉ *On the dock* ☎ *22840/53176.*

$ GREEK 🍴 **Pervolaria.** "An enclosed garden" is the translation of this restaurant's Greek name and, indeed, this family tavern is found to be shady and quiet since it resides underneath a lush pergola. A good starter is fava with carmelized onions and capers. As for main dishes, Perivolaria is best known for its pork shank flavored with sage and roasted in a wood oven; another top choice would be the handmade tortellini stuffed with local cheese, spinach, and fresh tomatoes. The homemade *bougatsa* (custard in phyllo) is an exceptional desert. [$] *Average main: €15* ✉ *Liminaki* ☎ *22840/51721* 🌐 *www.pervolaria.gr.*

$$ × **Poseidon.** Eat here for elegant dining away from the fray, on a spa-
MEDITERRANEAN cious terrace with two pools, dozens of palm trees, and the bay of
Naousa in front of you. The vegetables are from their own garden, the
fish is fresh, and the food has a Mediterranean accent. Top starters?
Opt for the agnolotti, forest mushrooms, and prosciutto in a cream
sauce, or beef (fresh from France) carpaccio in a crush of herbs and
spices with arugula and Parmesan. An excellent main course would be
the rack of aromatic lamb with new potatoes and spinach in a Merlot-
mint sauce. If you can still manage dessert (you will want to sit here a
long time), try the chocolate indulgence cake. The lower terrace serves
Chinese food. $ *Average main: €25* ⊠ *Astir Hotel, Kolimbithres beach*
☎ *22840/51976* ⊕ *www.astirofparos.gr* ☉ *Closed Nov.–Apr.*

$$ × **Siparos.** Set along the coast of Naousa bay in the beach town of Santa
MEDITERRANEAN Maria, this seaside restaurant serves fresh seafood and meat dishes using
local products and traditional Greek recipes. Start off with their signature
appetizer, chickpeas with rosemary served in a hot pot. For a Siparos
signature dish opt for the orzo pasta with saffron, octopus and squid; or
try the slow-cooked veal in tomato, oregano, and anise sauce. Sunset and
sea views make the dining experience even more memorable. $ *Average
main: €20* ⊠ *Xifara, Santa Maria* ☎ *22840/52785* ⊕ *www.siparos.gr.*

WHERE TO STAY

$$$$ ⊞ **Astir of Paros.** Peaceful views of Naousa bay are part of the expe-
RESORT rience at this graceful and expensive deluxe resort hotel (expensive
Fodor's Choice for Paros, not for Mykonos). **Pros:** service is great, beautiful and ele-
★ gant. **Cons:** you need a vehicle to get anywhere. $ *Rooms from: €295*
⊠ *Take Kolimbithres road from Naousa* ☎ *22840/51976, 22840/51984*
✍ *astir@otenet.gr* ⊕ *www.astirofparos.gr* ✎ *11 rooms, 46 suites*
☉ *Closed Nov.–Mar.* ⊙│ *Breakfast.*

$ ⊞ **Svoronos Bungalows.** The best budget choice in Naousa, these bun-
B&B/INN galow apartments always seem to be fully occupied. **Pros:** convenient;
quiet; green. **Cons:** there is no air-conditioning, but it is cool. $ *Rooms
from: €70* ⊠ *Behind big church, 1 block in from Santa Maria Rd.*
☎ *22840/51211, 22840/51409* ✍ *svoronosbungalows@gmail.com*
⊕ *www.svoronosbungalows.wix.com/paros* ✎ *19 apartments* ☉ *Closed
Nov.–Apr.* ⊙│ *Breakfast.*

NIGHTLIFE AND PERFORMING ARTS

BARS

Agosta. Located in a pretty whitewashed building on the tip of the old harbor, Agosta is considered a local favorite for drinks and dancing the night
away. Depending where you stand you'll get a stunning view of Naousa
harbor or Agios Dimitrios beach. Past midnight this is the place where
everyone heads to boogie on one of two dance floors. ⊠ *At fishing harbor.*

Linardo. Housed in a whitewashed building that's more than 400 years
old, Linardo's interior is impeccably maintained and coolly decorated. It
has to be considering that it's one of Naousa's top hot spots where crowds
gather until the early morning. The bar features DJs that typically spin
progressive house music. The party may spill out into the street where
you'll catch a charming view of the Old Harbor. ⊠ *Liminaki.*

Fodor's Choice   **Sommaripa Consolato.** Located in a prime spot above idyllic Naousa har-
★   bor, Sommaripa Consolato infuses Paros tradition in its drinks. Instead of
a mojito, try their creation—a *sumito*, which replaces rum with the local
homemade island liquor called *suma*. Once the home of the Parian family,
the family's younger generation transformed it into a whitewashed, cool
open space with artwork and picture-perfect views of the bay. During
the day, stop by for a Greek coffee accompanied by one of Mama Sommaripa's homemade Greek cookies or slices of cake. ⊠ *Liminaki.*

DANCE PERFORMANCES
Music–Dance "Naousa Paros". The group Music–Dance "Naousa Paros",
formed in 1988 to preserve the traditional dances and music of Paros,
performs all summer long in Naousa in the costumes of the 16th century and has participated in dance competitions and festivals throughout Europe. Keep an eye out for posters; the schedule is online and
venues change. ☎ *22840/52284* ⊕ *www.users.otenet.gr/~parofolk/
index_en.html.*

Environmental and Cultural Park of Paros. Set on almost 200 acres of
the beautiful Agios Ioannis Detis peninsula, the Environmental and
Cultural Park of Paros offers a full summer program of concerts in
its outdoor theater. Locals, inspired to preserve the beautiful natural
landscapes of the island, organized themselves to restore and showcase
monuments. Lectures, festivals, ecological talks, marked and labled
pathways through the park's peninsula, a café, a beautiful church, and
a protected beach for swimming all contribute to the natural preserve's
splendor. ⊠ *Paros Park, Naousa* ☎ *22840/53573* ⊕ *www.parospark.gr.*

SPORTS AND THE OUTDOORS
WATER SPORTS
Santa Maria Surfing Beach. The Santa Maria Surfing Beach complex is
popular among sports lovers thanks to the fine facilities offered for
windsurfing,waterskiing, tubing, and diving. There's also a tennis court
and horseback riding excursions are available. Camping and accommodation services are also available. ⊠ *Santa Maria beach* ✥ *Approximately 4 km (2½ miles) north of Naousa* ☎ *22840/52491* ⊕ *www.
surfbeach.gr.*

SHOPPING
ART AND JEWELRY
Paros is an art colony and exhibits are everywhere in summer. It is also
home to quite a few creative jewelers.

Nid D'Or. A small shop, Nid D'Or showcases two lines: one is a collection by owner Aliki Meremetis, featuring rough-cut semiprecious
stones; the second is by another well-known and respected Greek jeweler, Katerina Kotsaki. ⊠ *On second street from harbor toward main
church* ☎ *22840/51775.*

FASHION
Tango. Kostas Mouzedakis's stylish shop has been selling classic sports-
wear for three decades. It sells its own Tangowear label, a men's line
that reflects a Cycladic island lifestyle in cream, white, coral, and blue
hues and various types of linen. ⊠ *On second street from harbor toward
main church* ☎ *22840/51014.*

MARATHI ΜΑΡΑΘΙ

10 km (6 miles) east of Paros town.

During the classical period the island of Paros had an estimated 150,000 residents, many of them slaves who worked the ancient marble quarries in Marathi. The island grew rich from the export of this white, granular marble known among ancient architects and sculptors for its ability to absorb light. They called it *lychnites* ("won by lamplight").

Three Caverns. Marked by a sign, three caverns are bored into the hillside, the largest of them 300 feet deep. Here is where the world-famed Parian marble was mined. The most recent quarrying done in these mines was in 1844, when a French company cut marble here for Napoléon's tomb. ⊠ *Short walk from main road.*

LEFKES ΛΕΥΚΕΣ

6 km (4 miles) south of Marathi, 10 km (6 miles) southeast of Paros town.

Rampant piracy in the 17th century forced thousands of people to move inland from the coastal regions; thus for many years the scenic village of Lefkes, built on a hillside in the protective mountains, was the island's capital. It remains the largest village in the interior and has maintained a peaceful, island feeling, with narrow streets fragrant of jasmine and honeysuckle. These days, the old houses are being restored, and in summer the town is full of people. Farming is the major source of income, as you can tell from the well-kept stone walls and olive groves. For one of the best walks on Paros, take the ancient Byzantine road from the main lower square to the lower villages.

Two **17th-century churches** of interest are **Ayia Varvara** (St. Barbara) and **Ayios Sotiris** (Holy Savior). The big 1830 neo-Renaissance **Ayia Triada** (Holy Trinity) is the pride of the village.

BEACHES

Beyond Lefkes, the road continues on to Piso Livadi and a string of popular beaches.

Golden Beach. Golden beach (or Chrysi Akti in Greek) is a series of tree-fringed sandy beaches that are well-organized and in close proximity to an array of taverns, restaurants, and cafés. The area is famous for its water-sports activities and several centers are based here offering diving excursions and kite and windsurfing lessons. The Windsurfing World Cup has held events here. **Amenities:** food and drink. **Best for:** water sports; windsurfing; swimming. ⊠ *Golden beach.*

Logaras Beach. Just around the bend from Piso Livadi is a long stretch of yellow sand called Logaras beach. A few tavernas are nearby and in the distance the little whitewashed church of Ayios Georgios Thalassites, or St. George of the Sea ,stands where it has since the 13th century. This quiet beach has chairs and umbrellas available for rent in the summer season. **Amenities:** food and drink. **Best for:** walking; swimming. ⊠ *Logaras beach.*

FAMILY **Piso Livadi Beach.** Piso Livadi beach is one of the most popular beaches on Paros's southeastern coast. There are trees offering natural shade but lounge chairs and umbrellas are also available to rent. Piso Livadi, once an ancient port for the marble quarries, surrounds the sandy stretch of well-developed beach. The small resort town is filled with lodging options, tavernas, restaurants, and cafés. Boats depart from this port for Mykonos, Naxos, Amorgos, Ios, and Santorini. **Amenities:** food and drink. **Best for:** swimming. ✉ *On road past Lefkes, Piso Livadi* 🌐 *www.pissolivadi.com.*

WHERE TO EAT

$ GREEK 🍴 **Taverna Klarinos.** You go to Nikos and Argiro Ragoussis's place for the real thing. Nikos grows the vegetables, raises the meat, makes the cheese (even the feta) from his own goats, and makes the wine from his own vineyards; Argiro cooks. Traditional dishes such as fried zucchini or beets with garlic sauce are the best you'll taste, and the grilled meats make the gods envious. [$] *Average main: €10* ✉ *Main entrance street, opposite square, on 2nd fl.* ☎ *22840/41608* 💳 *No credit cards* 🕓 *Closed Oct.– Apr.*

WHERE TO STAY

$ HOTEL 🏨 **Lefkes Village.** All the rooms in this elegant hotel are white, and the wooden furniture and fabrics are reproductions of traditional styles; all have balconies with magnificent views down the olive-tree valley and over the sea to Naxos. **Pros:** village style upgraded. **Cons:** Lefkes is far from the sea. [$] *Rooms from: €105* ✉ *East of Lefkes on main road* ☎ *22840/41827* ✍ *lefkesvl@otenet.gr* 🌐 *www.lefkesvillage.gr* 🛏 *20 rooms* 🕓 *Closed Oct.–Apr.* 🍽 *Breakfast.*

SPORTS AND THE OUTDOORS

Aegean Diving College. Offering scuba lessons that take you to reefs, shipwrecks, and caves, the Aegean Diving College is headed by director Peter Nicolaides, who discovered the oldest shipwreck known and is a marine biologist involved in many of Greece's ecological projects. It's located on the southeast corner of the island on Golden beach. ✉ *Golden beach* ☎ *22840/43347* 🌐 *www.aegeandiving.gr.*

SHOPPING

ART GALLERIES

Angelika Vaxevanidou Art Studio. A visit to the whitewashed studio and gallery of award-winning sculptor, mosaicist, and portrait artist Angelika Vaxevanidou is a glimpse into the world of a successful, internationally commissioned artist. The long-time local artist and resident is recognized internationally for her impressive, sensitive, and emotional large-scale colored pencil portraiture, and on display are works past and present. **TIP→ The studio is open year-round.** ☎ *22840/44076* 🌐 *www.angelikavaxevanidou.com* 🕓 *Mon.–Sat. 9–1:30 and 6–9 pm.*

POUNTA ΠΟΥΝΤΑ

4 km (2½ miles) south of Paros town.

Pounta is not even a village, just a few houses, three restaurants (one fine one), and a tiny harbor from which ferries leave for Antiparos. The road that turns left just before you get there continues on to many beaches.

And beyond—it is a beautiful drive—are the peaceful harbor towns of Aliki and Dryos, both with fine beaches and restaurants, especially Faragas, now overdeveloped.

EXPLORING

OFF THE BEATEN PATH

Christos sto Dasos (*Christ in the Wood*). A 15-minute walk or 2-minute drive back toward Paros town from the Valley of the Butterflies leads to the convent known as Christos sto Dasos, from where there's a marvelous view of the Aegean. The convent contains the tomb of St. Arsenios (1800–77), who was a schoolteacher, an abbot, and a prophet. He was also a rainmaker whose prayers were believed to have ended a long drought, saving Paros from starvation. The nuns are a bit leery of tourists. If you want to go in, be sure to wear long pants or skirt and a shirt that covers your shoulders, or the sisters will turn you away. ✉ *Between Valley of the Butterflies and Paros town.*

Petaloudes Park. The Jersey tiger moth returns year after year to mate in Petaloudes (Butterflies Valley), a lush oasis of greenery in the middle of this dry island. In May, June, and perhaps July, you can watch them as they lie dormant during the day, their chocolate-brown wings with yellow stripes still against the ivy leaves. In the evening they flutter upward to the cooler air, flashing the coral-red undersides of their wings as they rise. A notice at the entrance asks visitors not to disturb them by taking photographs or shaking the leaves. ✉ *Petaloudes, Petaloudes Park* ☎ *22840/91554* 🌐 *www.parosbutterflies.gr* 🎟 *€2; kids under 15 are free* 🕒 *Mid-May–Mid-Sept., daily 8–8.*

BEACHES

Pounta Beach. Pounta is Paros's party beach. A packed schedule of beach party events kicks off in the summer and continues daily. Mainstream pop music blares from the beach bars and cafés all day and all night. Dancing on the sand, and tabletops, is part of the scene. Greek pop stars hold concerts here too. Famous for its island winds, it's also an organized haven for windsurfers, kitesurfers, and extreme sport enthusiasts. **Amenities:** food and drink; toilets. **Best for:** partiers; windsurfing; surfing. ✉ *On road past Piso Livadi, Pounta* 🌐 *www.pundabeach.gr.*

WHERE TO EAT

$$ GREEK

🍴 **Thea.** From the terrace of this fine restaurant you can enjoy the view over the Antiparos strait and the little ferries that ply it. The interior is all of wood and hundreds of bottles of wine shelved from floor to high ceiling. Owner Nikos Kouroumlis is a wine fanatic, and Thea has the third most extensive wine list in all of Greece; his own wine is excellent. Nikos and family hail from northern Greece and Constantinople and so does their food: Caesaria pie, hot and spicy with cheeses, salted meat, and tomatoes; Cappodocian lamb, cooked with dried apricots; or one of their famous T-bone steaks. Save room for one of the traditional Greek sweets, especially the *ekmek* pastry served up with mastic ice cream. [$] *Average main: €20* ✉ *Pounta* ☎ *22840/91220* ✉ *nikostheaparos@yahoo.gr.*

SPORTS AND THE OUTDOORS

SCUBA DIVING

Eurodivers. A proud Professional Association of Scuba Instructors or PADI 5-Star Resort, Eurodivers offers courses from beginner to professional levels. ⊠ *On west side of Paros, Pounta* ☎ *22840/92071* ⊕ *www. eurodivers.gr.*

WINDSURFING

Paros Kite Pro Center. On the island's west coast, where turquoise waters meet windy conditions perfect for kitesurfing, the Paros Kite Pro Center offers International Kiteboarding Organization-certified lessons, equipment, and rentals. ⊠ *On the island's west coast, Pounta* ⊕ *www. paroskite-procenter.com* ⊗ *Daily 9–9.*

ANTIPAROS ΑΝΤΙΠΑΡΟΣ

5 km (3 miles) southwest of Paros town.

Fodor'sChoice ★ This smaller, sister isle of Paros may have once been the best little secret of the Cyclades but thanks to such gilt-edged visitors as Brad Pitt, Tom Hanks, and Sean Connery, everybody now knows about this pretty little "forgetaway." And let's not forget the fact that this green, inhabited islet belongs to the famously rich Goulandris family, benefactors of the Goulandris Cycladic Museum in Athens (and much else). As a result of all this glamour, Antiparos is developing all too rapidly. A great source of information about Antiparos, with a complete listing of hotels, can be found at ⊕ *www.antiparos-isl.gr.*

Twenty-five years ago you went to the Paros hamlet of Pounta, went to the church, opened its door (as a signal), and waited for a fishing caïque to chug over. Now, 30 car ferries ply the channel all day and a lovely seven-minute ride wafts you from Paros (from Pounta, that is; the ride from Paros town takes about 20 minutes) to Antiparos. A causeway once crossed the Antiparos Strait, which would be swimmable but for the current, and on one of its still emergent islets, Saliagos, habitations and objects have been found dating back almost to 5000 BC.

Antiparos's one town, also called Antiparos, has a main street and two centers of activity: the quay area and the main square, a block or two in. At both are restaurants and cafés. To the right of the square are houses and the Kastro's 15th-century wall. At the other end of the quay from the ferry dock a road goes to an idyllic sandy beach (it is 10 minutes by foot); you can wade across to the islet opposite, Fira, where sheep and goats graze.

It is pleasant to go around to the other side of Antiparos on the good road to Ayios Giorgios, where there are three excellent taverns, perfect after a swim. On request a boat will take you to the nearby islet of **Despotiko**, uninhabited except for seasonal archaeologists excavating a late-Archaic marble temple complex to Apollo. In autumn the hills are fragrant with purple flowering heather.

EXPLORING

Cave of Antiparos. In the 19th century the most famous sight in the Aegean was the Cave of Antiparos, and it still draws many visitors every year. Greece's oldest known cave sits on the southeastern part of Antiparos. It's filled with shapely stalactites and stalagmites of which the oldest is said to be 45 million years old. The natural wonder was first discovered by a French ambassador in the 16th century and myths, legends, and stories have been associated with it along the way. You'll need to take exactly 411 steps down into the cave's 100 meter deep core to explore. Look for Lord Byron's autograph. Outside is the church of Ayios Ioánnis Spiliótis, built in 1774. Audio tours are available. ⊠ *Agios Ioannis* ⌑ *€5* ⊘ *Daily 10–3:30 pm* ⊘ *Closed Nov.–Mar.*

Venetian Kastro. Close to the port you'll find yourself walking into the pedestrian paths of Antiparos town, lined with whitewashed shops, restaurants, and cafés. Up farther, the arched stonework entrance to the historical center, known as the *camara*, leads to the centuries-old Venetian *kastro*, or castle, of Antiparos. Like other Cycladic islands, this architecture reflects the construction of fortresses built between the 13th- and 16th-centuries when Venetian and Ottoman influences took over the islands. You can walk the whitewashed streets of this small village, where Antiparians still live in small homes built on top of each other as one continuous block construction within the stone walls. There are also four churches built within the settlement. ⊠ *Northern tip of the island, Antiparos town.*

BEACHES

Ayios Giorgios Beach. Head 11 km (7 miles) south of Antiparos town to the calm, southeastern beaches of Ayios Georgios. This series of small, fine sand coves has a view of the uninhabited island of Despotiko. Here, three small fish tavernas sit on the edge of the tiny village road, overlooking the sea. Otherwise, what you see is what you get—a serene untouched landscape. **Amenities:** food and drink. **Best for:** swimming; solitude; walking. ⊠ *11 km (7 miles) south of Antiparos town, Ayios Georgios.*

Camping Beach. This long, quiet sandy stretch of beach is located off a small path leading from the Antiparos Camping site and just north of Antiparos town. The view is peaceful: just the neighboring inlet of Diplos and a turquoise sea. One section of the beach rents out umbrellas and lounge chairs and another area is frequented by nudists—it's one of Greece's recognized naturist beaches. **Amenities:** food and drink. **Best for:** nudists; walking, solitude. ⊠ *Antiparos town.*

FAMILY **Psaraliki Beach.** Within walking distance of Antiparos town, this beach has two parts, referred to by locals as Psaraliki one and Psaraliki two. Yellow, soft sand fills both and each is dotted with natural shade trees; lounge chairs and umbrellas are available during the summer months. The shallow waters make it a favorite for families and its southeasterly placement on the island keeps it sheltered from gusty Cycladic winds. Several tavernas are closeby. **Amenities:** food and drink. **Best for:** walking; swimming. ⊠ *Antiparos town.*

Sunset Beach. As its name implies, this is where Antiparians head to watch their island's fantastic sunsets. Clear water and golden sand are guaranteed but ideal beach weather is not—located on the west coast, the beach isn't sheltered from the Cycladic winds that can stir things up. When the winds do die down, the conditions are ideal for snorkeling and swimming. **■ TIP→ The beach is also known as Sifneiko, because the neighboring island of Sifnos can be seen in the distance.** **Amenities:** food and drink. **Best for:** sunset; swimming; snorkeling. ✉ *Antiparos town.*

WHERE TO EAT

$ GREEK 🍴 **Akrogiali.** You can dine alfresco on Akrogiali's simple veranda and enjoy the view across the strait to the sacred isle of Despotiko. The restaurant is owned by the local Pipinos family. The bells you'll hear in the background belong to the goats of the Pipinos family (yes, they occasionally end up on the table here). Vegetables come from the garden. This is one of three good restaurants by the little dock. [$] *Average main: €15* ✉ *on the bay, Ayios Georgios* ☎ *22840/22107* 🌐 *www.akrogiali-antiparos.com* 💳 *No credit cards* 🕓 *Closed Oct.–Apr.*

$ SEAFOOD Fodor's Choice ★ 🍴 **Captain Pipinos.** Dining here happens on an elevated veranda right above the calm blue waters of Ayios Giorgios bay. The line of drying octopus may be out, evidence of Captain Pipinos pride in serving the freshest seafood on the island. Marcos Pipinos's family boats come in each day with fresh seafood and fish varieties. Try their grilled thornback ray appetizer marinated in olive oil and lemon, followed by the *psarasoupa* (fish soup speciality). [$] *Average main: €15* ✉ *Ayios Giorgios, Antiparos* 🌐 *www.captainpipinos.com.*

WHERE TO STAY

$ RESORT FAMILY 🏨 **Kastro.** Located on a small hill and within comfortable walking distance to town and Psaraliki beach, Antiparian couple Magda Kritsantoni and Markos Maouni have consistently upgraded and expanded their bright, open, whitewashed property over the last twenty years to accommodate more and more guests. **Pros:** walking distance to town and beach; sea views from its open spaces. **Cons:** breakfast not included; may be busy with kids if that bothers you. [$] *Rooms from: €85* ✉ *Antiparos* ☎ *22840/61011* 🌐 *www.antiparosgreece.com* 🛏 *2 studios; 4 rooms; 4 apartments* 🕓 *Closed Nov.–Apr.* 🍽 *No meals.*

$ HOTEL 🏨 **Kouros Village Hotel.** The hotels on Antiparos tend to be simple, pleasant places to stay near the beach, and this two-story building, which offers a series of rooms, apartments, and suites, most overlooking a pool and beautiful Antiparos bay, nicely fits the bill. **Pros:** attractive, convenient option; has all the usual amenities; balconies and terraces have fine sea views. **Cons:** you have to want to be in a busy port. [$] *Rooms from: €65* ✉ *Antiparos harbor* ☎ *22840/61084* 🌐 *www.kouros-village.gr* 🛏 *5 rooms, 5 studios, 15 apartments, 5 suites* 🕓 *Closed mid-Oct.–mid-Apr.* 🍽 *No meals.*

NAXOS ΝΑΞΟΣ

11

Updated
by Marissa
Tejada

190 km (100 nautical miles) southeast of Piraeus harbor in Athens.

"Great sweetness and tranquility" is how Nikos Kazantzakis, premier novelist of Greece, described Naxos, and indeed a tour of the island leaves you with an impression of abundance, prosperity, and serenity. The greenest, largest, and most fertile of the Cyclades, Naxos, with its many potato fields, its livestock and its thriving cheese industry, and its fruit and olive groves framed by the pyramid of Mt. Zas (3,295 feet, the Cyclades's highest), is practically self-sufficient. Inhabited for 6,000 years, the island has memorable landscapes—abrupt ravines, hidden valleys, long and sandy beaches—and towns that vary from a Cretan mountain stronghold to the seaside capital that strongly evokes its Venetian past.

Naxos is full of history and monuments—classical temples, medieval monasteries, Byzantine churches, Venetian towers—and its huge interior offers endless magnificent hikes, not much pursued by summer tourists, who cling to the lively capital and the developed western beaches, the best in the Cyclades.

GETTING HERE AND AROUND

Olympic flies three to five times a day from Athens to Naxos, and back; it take 35 minutes (in winter connections are much fewer). There are no other air connections. Summer flights fill up fast, so book well in advance. Ferries to Naxos, many of which follow the Paros/Naxos/Santorini route, take from four to seven hours depending on route, boat, and pelagic happenstance. In summer there are five a day, in winter fewer. There are also daily connections with Paros and Santorini, and regular connections with Mykonos, Amorgos, Kythnos, Kea, Ios, and sometimes others. The Naxos Port Authority can give you information on ferries.

On Naxos, the bus system is reliable and fairly extensive. Daily buses go from Naxos town, called Chora (near the boat dock), to Engares, Melanes, Sangri, Filoti, Apeiranthos, Koronida, and Apollonas. In summer there is added daily service to the beaches, including Ayia Anna, Pyrgaki, Ayiassos, Pachi Ammos, and Abram. Other villages have bus service but with much less frequency. Schedules are posted; hotel concierges also have this info, and schedules are posted online at ⊕ *www. naxosbeaches.gr* (under bus schedules). Fares run from €2.50 to €6. There is a taxi stand near the harbor.

Contacts Naxos Port Authority ☎ *22850/22300.*

TOURS

Zas Travel. This agency runs several one-day tours of the island sights with different itineraries, each costing about €45, and one-day trips to Delos and Mykonos as well as Santorini (about €60). ⊠ *At harbor, Naxos town* ☎ *22850/23330, 22850/23331.*

NAXOS TOWN ΝΑΞΟΣ (ΧΩΡΑ)

140 km (86 nautical miles) southeast of Piraeus, 33 km (21 miles) southeast of Mykonos, 35 km (22 miles) east of Paros.

As your ferry chugs into the harbor, you see before you the white houses of Naxos town (Chora) on a hill crowned by the one remaining tower of the Venetian castle, a reminder that Naxos was once the proud capital of the Venetian semi-independent Duchy of the Archipelago.

The most ancient settlements of Naxos were directly on the square in front of the Greek Orthodox cathedral. You'll note that several of the churches on this square, including the cathedral itself, hint at Naxos's venerable history, as they are made of ancient materials. In fact, this square was, in succession, the seat of a flourishing Mycenaean town (1300–1050 BC), a classical agora (when it was a 167-foot by 156-foot square closed on three sides by Doric stoas, so that it looked like the letter "G"; a shorter fourth stoa bordered the east side, leaving room at each end for an entrance), a Roman town, and early Christian church complex. City, cemetery, tumulus, hero shrine: no wonder the Early Christians built here. For more of ancient Naxos, explore the nearby precinct of Grotta.

TOP ATTRACTIONS

Domus Venetian Museum. Located in the 800-year-old Dellarocca-Barozzi house, the Domus Venetian Museum lets you, at last, into one of the historic Venetian residences. The house, enclosed within the soaring walls of Chora's castle, adjacent to the *Trani*, or Great Gate, was first erected in 1207. Inside, the house is like a Naxian attic filled with fascinating objects ranging from the Cycadic period to Victorian times. One is personally escorted through the house on a tour by the museum's entertaining director, Nikos Karavias, who will tell you all about the French, Greek, and Venetian roots of the Dellarocca and Barozzi clans. The house's idyllic garden, built into the Kastro wall, provides a regular venue in season for a concert series, from classical to jazz to island music. ⊠ *At Kastro north gate* ☎ *22850/22387* ⊕ *www.naxosfestival. com* ⊠ *€4, tour €6* ☉ *June–Aug., daily 10 am–11 pm.*

Kastro. You won't miss the gates of the castle. The south gate is called the **Paraporti** (side gate), but it's more interesting to enter through the northern gate, or **Trani** (strong), via Apollonos street. Note the vertical incision in the gate's marble column—it is the Venetian yard against which drapers measured the bolts of cloth they brought to the noblewomen. Step through the Trani into the citadel and enter another age, where sedate Venetian houses still stand around silent courtyards, their exteriors emblazoned with coats of arms and bedecked with flowers. Half are still owned by the original families; romantic Greeks and foreigners have bought up the rest.

The entire citadel was built in 1207 by Marco Sanudo, a Venetian who, three years after the fall of Constantinople, landed on Naxos as part of the Fourth Crusade. When in 1210 Venice refused to grant him independent status, Sanudo switched allegiance to the Latin emperor in Constantinople, becoming duke of the archipelago. Under the Byzantines, *archipelago* had meant "chief sea," but after Sanudo and his successors,

Naxos

Aegean Sea

TO
MYKONOS

TO
PAROS TOWN

PAROS

Cape Stavri

Ayia

Apollonas

Ormos Abram Beach

**Abram
Village**

Pachia Ammos Beach

Koronida/
Komiaki

Lionas

Galini

Engares

Koronos

**Naxos
town**

Ayios
Thaleleos

Kourounochori

Stavros tis Keramotis
Church

Ayios Georgios

*Ayios
Prokopios*

Miloi

Flerio

Moni

*Ayia
Anna*

Galanado

**Pano
Castle**

Chalki

Apeiranthos

Moutsouna

Ayia Anna

Plaka Beach

**Bellonia
Tower**

Potamia

**Ayios
Mamas**

Filoti

Sangri

TO
SANTORINI

M
O
U
N
T

Z
A
S

Mikri Vigla Beach

Mikri Vigla

**Temple of
Demeter**

Psili Ammos

Kastraki

Kastraki Beach

Pyrgaki

**Cheimarros
Pirgos**

Pyrgaki Beach

Panormos

KOUFONISI

Kalantos

Koufonisi Town

Askiti Cave

Kato Koufonisi Town

*KATO
KOUFONISI*

Cape Katomeri

KEROS

SHINOUSSA

0   2 mi

0   2 km

Aghios
Georgios

Shinoussa
Town

IRAKLIA

Naxos's most famous landmark is its "doorway to nowhere." The Portara is the sole remnant of a gigantic ancient Temple to Apollo.

it came to mean "group of islands," that is, the Cyclades. For three centuries Naxos was held by Venetian families, who resisted pirate attacks, introduced Roman Catholicism, and later rebuilt the castle in its present form. In 1564 Naxos came under Turkish rule but, even then, the Venetians still ran the island, while the Turks only collected taxes. The rust-color Glezos tower was home to the last dukes; it displays the coat of arms: a pen and sword crossed under a crown. ⊠ *Kastro*.

Metropolis Site Museum. Built in the square in front of the Metropolitan Cathedral is a small museum that showcases the history of Naxos beginning with the Mycenaean era. Displays include pottery, artifacts, and even a tomb from ancient times used to cover the graves of prosperous Naxians. ☎ *22850/24151* ⊡ *Free* ☉ *Tues.–Sun. 8–2:30.*

Naxos Archaeological Museum. Today the historic convent and school of the Ursulines houses the Naxos Archaeological Museum, best known for its Cycladic and Mycenaean finds. During the early Cycladic period (3200–2000 BC) there were settlements along Naxos's east coast and outside Naxos town at Grotta. The finds are from these settlements and graveyards scattered around the island. Many of the vessels exhibited are from the early Cycladic I period, hand-built of coarse-grain clay, sometimes decorated with a herringbone pattern. Though the museum has too many items in its glass cases to be appreciated in a short visit, you should try not to miss the white marble Cycladic statuettes, which range from the early "violin" shapes to the more-detailed female forms with their tilted flat heads, folded arms, and legs slightly bent at the knees. The male forms are simpler and often appear to be seated. The most common theory is that the female statuettes were both fertility and grave goddesses, and the males were servant figures. ⊠ *Kastro* ☎ *22850/22725* ⊠ *€3* ⊗ *Tues.–Sun. 8:30–3* ⊗ *Closed Nov.–Mar.*

Fodor'sChoice ★ **Old Town.** A bewildering maze of twisting cobblestone streets, arched porticoes, and towering doorways, the Old Town plunges you alternatively into cool darkness and then suddenly into pockets of dazzling sunshine. The Old Town is divided into the lower section, **Bourgos,** where the Greeks lived during Venetian times, and the upper part, called **Kastro** (castle), still inhabited by the Venetian Catholic nobility. ⊠ *Along quay, left at first big square.*

Portara. Although the capital town is primarily beloved for its Venetian elegance and picturesque blind alleys, Naxos's most famous landmark is ancient: the Portara, a massive doorway that leads to nowhere. The Portara stands on the islet of **Palatia,** which was once a hill (since antiquity the Mediterranean has risen quite a bit) and in the 3rd millennium BC was the acropolis for a nearby Cycladic settlement. The Portara, an entrance to an unfinished Temple of Apollo that faces exactly toward Delos, Apollo's birthplace, was begun about 530 BC by the tyrant Lygdamis, who said he would make Naxos's buildings the highest and most glorious in Greece. He was overthrown in 506 BC, and the temple was never completed; by the 5th and 6th centuries AD it had been converted into a church; and under Venetian and Turkish rule it was slowly dismembered, so the marble could be used to build the castle. The gate, built with four blocks of marble, each 16 feet long and weighing 20 tons, was so large it couldn't be demolished, so it remains today, along with the temple floor. Palatia itself has come to be associated with the tragic myth of Ariadne, princess of Crete:

Ariadne, daughter of Crete's King Minos, helped Theseus thread the labyrinth of Knossos and slay the monstrous Minotaur. In exchange, he promised to marry her. Sailing for Athens, the couple stopped in Naxos, where Theseus abandoned her. Jilted Ariadne's curse made Theseus forget to change the ship's sails from black to white, and so his grieving father Aegeus, believing his son dead, plunged into the Aegean. Seeing Ariadne's tears, smitten Dionysus descended in a leopard-drawn chariot to marry her, and set her bridal wreath, the Corona Borealis, in the sky, an eternal token of his love.

The myth inspired one of Titian's best-known paintings, as well as Strauss's opera *Ariadne auf Naxos.*

North of Palatia, **underwater remains of Cycladic buildings** are strewn along an area called **Grotta.** Here are a series of large worked stones, the remains of the waterfront quayside mole, and a few steps that locals say go to a tunnel leading to the islet of Palatia; these remains are Cycladic (before 2000 BC). ⊠ *At harbor's far edge.*

WORTH NOTING

OFF THE BEATEN PATH

Bazeos Tower. This 17th-century stonework tower, considered one of Naxos's most beautiful Venetian-era monuments, dominates the landscape as you approach the center of the island by car heading from Naxos town. It has been renovated as a museum and a cultural space where a full calendar of exhibitions, concerts, and educational seminars take place every summer. ⊠ *Between Naxos town and Agiassos* ⊕ *12* *km (18 miles) from Chora toward Chalki* ☎ *22850/31402* 🌐 *www.bazeostower.gr* 🕒 *Daily 10–5.*

Catholic Cathedral of Naxos. Built by Sanudo in the 13th century, this grand cathedral was restored by Catholic families in the 16th and 17th centuries. The marble floor is paved with tombstones bearing the coats of arms of the noble families. Venetian wealth is evident in the many gold and silver icon frames. The icons reflect a mix of Byzantine and Western influences: the one of the Virgin Mary is unusual because it shows a Byzantine Virgin and Child in the presence of a bishop, a cathedral benefactor. Another 17th-century icon shows the Virgin of the Rosary surrounded by members of the Sommaripa family, whose house is nearby. ✉ *At Kastro's center.*

Greek Orthodox Cathedral. The Greek Orthodox cathedral was built in 1789 on the site of a church called *Zoodochos Pigis* (Life-giving Source). The cathedral was built from the materials of ancient temples: the solid granite pillars are said to be from the ruins of Delos. Amid the gold and the carved wood, there is a vividly colored iconostasis painted by a well-known iconographer of the Cretan school, Dimitrios Valvis, and the Gospel Book is believed to be a gift from Catherine the Great of Russia. ✉ *Bourgos.*

Naxos Folklore Museum. This little museum shows costumes, ceramics, farming implements, and other items from Naxos's far-flung villages giving you insight into how life was on the island beginning in the 18th century. ✉ *Roubel Sq., Old market street* ☎ *22850/25531* 🌐 *www.naxosfolkmuseum.com* 🎟 *€3* 🕒 *July–Aug., daily 9–8; Sept.–Jun. by appointment only.*

BEACHES

The southwest coast of Naxos, facing Paros and the sunset, offers the Cyclades's longest stretches of sandy beaches. All the beaches have tavernas in case you get hungry or thirsty, and those directly on the beach may have chairs and umbrellas for rent.

FAMILY **Ayios Georgios Beach.** Essentially an extension of Naxos town, the easily accesible Ayios Georgios beach is a popular, developed destination that sees its throng of crowds during the peak summer months. Protected from summer winds, the sandy coastline edges up against shallow waters that make it ideal for kids. The bustle of the main town extends here; restaurants, tavernas and café bars are all within easy walking distance with views of the sea. It's also an ideal beach scene to take in the sunset. **Amenities:** food and drink. **Best for:** walking; swimming; sunset. ✉ *Ayios Georgios.*

WHERE TO EAT

$ MEDITERRANEAN 🍴 **Labyrinth.** Labyrinth's more-than-simple food, cozy flagstone garden, and good service are all praiseworthy. A good appetizer is the crunchy, sundried tomato and feta tart. Among the best main dishes are salmon fillet with fresh vegetables and orange sauce, and also the chicken fillet with shrimp, potatoes, and herbs. And don't miss out on the light and summery lemon mousse. The wine cellar is one of the island's most extensive. [$] *Average main: €15* ✉ *Old Town* ☎ *22850/22253* 💳 *No credit cards* 🕒 *Closed Oct.–Apr. No lunch.*

$$ GREEK 🍴 **Metaxi Mas.** Located in the winding alleys of the Palia Agora in Naxos town, Metaxi Mas is the local favorite for home-cooked taverna specialities year-round making the meaning of its name, "just between us," very appropriate. For more than a decade the Flerianos family has focused on the local flavors that Naxos has to offer including cheese and fresh seafood. Start off with their special feta *saganaki* sautéed with grilled tomatoes, peppers, and topped with oregano. Try the *makaraonada tou psara* (fisherman's pasta), which comes with shrimp, calamari, octopus, and mussels all mixed in a fantastic tomato sauce. [$] *Average main: €16* ✉ *Naxos town, Naxos* ☎ *22850/26425.*

$ GERMAN FAMILY 🍴 **Old Inn.** Berlin-trained chef Dieter von Ranizewski serves German food informed by Naxos. In a courtyard under a chinaberry tree, with rough whitewashed walls and ancient marbles, two of the old church's interior sides open into the wine cellar and gallery; on the fourth side, with beams and wood paneling, is a fireplace. The menu is extensive. For starters you might try sausages with beer sauce, smoked ham, or liver pâté—all homemade. For entrées, have the signature steak with tomatoes, olives, Roquefort, and bacon-flecked roast potatoes. For Dieter's famous schnitzel you get to choose one of 48 sauces. For dessert, the apple strudel—it is Grandma's recipe—is simply delicious. There is a children's menu and small playground. [$] *Average main: €15* ✣ *Naxos town; take car road off waterfront, turn right into 2nd alley* ☎ *22850/27013.*

$$ GREEK 🍴 **Palatia Island.** Located right under the island's famous ancient landmark, Apollo's Temple, Palatia Island's special location offers a beautiful summer dining experience. The open air, elegant dining space showcases a stunning view of Naxos harbor. As for the dishes, everything is fresh and local. Start with signature appetizers including anchovies marinated in oil and vinegar and the Naxian cheese wrap with honey and sesame. For mains, it's best to opt for local seafood plates like *gouna,* which is grilled sun-dried mackerel, or grilled squid stuffed with tomato, onion, peppers, and parsley. [$] *Average main: €20* ☎ *22850/26588* 🌐 *www.palatiarestaurant.com.*

$ GREEK Fodor's Choice ★ 🍴 **Popi's Grill.** The oldest family tavern in Naxos, established in 1948, remains true to the Margartis family traditions of cooking authentic Greek dishes with homegrown vegetables and local products. Order (and savor) the fried cheese appetizer, Naxian saganaki, while it's hot with a bit of lemon, or the chicken and pork souvlaki served with freshly cut fried Naxian potatoes. Save room for their famous complimentary dessert of creamy, thick Greek yogurt mixed with honey and lemon. The tavern also sells a range of Naxian liquor and fresh local cheese. Be sure to check out the historic black-and-white photos of Naxos town as it grew around the taverna over the decades. [$] *Average main: €10* ☎ *22850/23741* ⏲ *Closed Nov.–Mar.*

$ FAST FOOD 🍴 **Waffle House.** Offering a variety of creamy rich homemade ice cream, fresh waffles, and mini-sized "waffins," Waffle House has expanded since it opened in Naxos town to the country's capital in Athens. However, the Naxos original is a local favorite and tables get packed here and at the island's second location in Plaka beach. [$] *Average main: €6* ✉ *Pigadakia street, 500 meters up from harbor next to the Psari restaurant.*

WHERE TO STAY

$
B&B/INN

⬚ Apollon. In addition to being comfortable, charming, and quiet (it's a converted marble workshop), this hotel, set in the Fontana quarter, is easy walking distance to Naxos town and it even offers parking, which is a rarity. **Pros:** convenient; well done; low prices. **Cons:** rooms can be small. **$** *Rooms from: €70 ⊠ Behind Orthodox cathedral, car entrance on road out of town, Fontana ☎ 22850/22468 ⊕ www. apollonhotel-naxos.gr ⥅ 13 rooms, 1 suite ⓘ⦶ Breakfast.*

$
B&B/INN

⬚ Chateau Zevgoli. If you stay in Chora, try to settle in to Despina Kitini's fairy-tale pension, which is set in a comfortable Venetian house that offers distinctive guest rooms and a lovingly appointed living room. **Pros:** it is sweetly decorated; set in a fetching neighborhood. **Cons:** it is uphill and you must walk to it. **$** *Rooms from: €75 ⊠ Old Town ⊹ Follow the signs stenciled on walls ☎ 22850/22993, 22850/26143 ⊕ www.hotelzevgoli.gr ⥅ 10 rooms, 1 suite ⓘ⦶ Multiple meal plans.*

$$
HOTEL

⬚ Galaxy. All whitewash and stone, this hotel is perfect if you want to be on the beach (and don't mind the crowds at the seaside in summer). **Pros:** a full resort hotel. **Cons:** too far from town to walk. **$** *Rooms from: €190 ⊠ Ayios Georgios beach ☎ 22850/22422, 22850/22423 ⊕ www.hotel-galaxy.com ⥅ 43 studios, 11 rooms ☉ Closed Nov.–Mar. ⓘ⦶ Breakfast.*

$
HOTEL

⬚ Xenia Hotel. Conveniently located in the center of everything in Naxos town, Xenia Hotel's bright, clean and ambient spaces exude modern comfort. **Pros:** central in Naxos town; short walking distance to restaurants, harbor, and nightlife. **Cons:** crowds and noise during peak tourist season. **$** *Rooms from: €80 ⊠ Next to Waffle House, Pigadakia ☎ 22850/25068 ⊕ www.hotel-xenia.gr ⥅ 16 rooms, 2 suites ⓘ⦶ Multiple meal plans.*

NIGHTLIFE

During the busy summer season, there are numerous cultural events in Naxos town and also around the island. Important venues include the Catholic Cultural Center, the Domus Venetian Museum, and the Town Hall.

BARS

520. This cool, whitewashed, Cycladic-style space features a rooftop veranda perfect for sipping eclectic cocktails and traditional Greek liquors. Here's the place to try Greek vodka, yes it exists, and Greek liquors like *masticha*. A range of drinks are named after the letters of the Greek alphabet and if you opt for Omega, the last letter, you get the bartender's special surprise. Siblings Argiro and Manos Fotis named this spot 520 for the barcode automatically marked on any products that are made in Greece.

Meli and Kanela. The Kioulafis family paid attention to every detail when renovating this family treasure, a simple Cycladic dwelling built more than a century ago. Tucked in the walls of Old Town, Meli and Kanela's bright turquoise door beckons you into its bar lounge and café space that's been enhanced by soft lighting, creamy beige and white walls, and traditional charm. The name, which means honey and cinnamon in Greek, is a relaxing nightlife spot to chat over the family's own homemade *rakomolo* (Greek cocktail featuring honey and cinnamon) served with a large wedge of fresh orange. ☎ *22850/26565* ✉ *info@ melikaikanela.com* ⊕ *www.melikaikanela.com.*

Naxos Café. Tucked in the Old Town, this romantically lit little café-bar exudes the island's old-world charm and authenticity. It stays open late and sometimes the music is live. A few tables line the alleyways of the town. The Greek coffee is famous here when it's open during the day. Opt for the Greek honey liquor, *rakomolo*, at night. ⊠ *Bourgos* ☎ *22850/26343.*

Ocean Dance and Mojo. A lively chunk of Naxos nightlife is set on the south end of town where two happening bars, situated right next to each other, facing the waterfront, gather packed crowds of party people. Ocean Dance and Mojo, collectively known as OceanMojo, open at 11:30 pm pumping mainstream dance hits. Peak season, the party teeters to the edge of the street, right above the sea, where extra bars are set up to accommodate the happy crowds. ⊠ *Old Town* ☎ *22850/26766.*

SPORTS AND THE OUTDOORS

WATER SPORTS

Naxos-Surf Club. Located in Ayios Giorgios beach, just south of the Chora, the Naxos-Surf Club offers windsurfing lessons, equipment rentals, and other water-sports packages. Excursions to other prime windsurfing beaches, as well as mountain biking trips, are available. ⊠ *Ayios Giorgios* ✦ *15 min walk south from Naxos town* ☎ *22850/29170* ⊕ *www.naxos-surf.com.*

SHOPPING

The population of Naxos pours into Naxos town to get their shopping done, so visitors can be sure to find what they are looking for, whether it's fashionable clothing or antiques. Naxians are especially proud of what their land gives them, and many shops sell local products, including honey, liqueurs like citron, and more. Meanwhile, the streets are filled with myriad shops and galleries run by local artists who showcase local artwork including sculptures and handicrafts. Jewelry shops are also in abundance, selling traditional and more modern Greek designs in gold and silver.

ANTIQUES

Antico Veneziano. Eleni Dellarocca's shop, Antico Veneziano, is in the basement of her Venetian house, built 800 years ago. The columns inside come from Naxos's ancient acropolis. In addition to antiques, she has handmade embroideries, porcelain and glass, mirrors, old chandeliers, and vintage photographs of Naxos. One room is an art gallery, while the other is devoted to Greece's best CDs. ⊠ *In Kastro, down from museum* ☎ *22850/26206* ⊕ *www.anticoveneziano.com.*

BOOKS

Zoom. At Eleftherios Primikirios's bookstore Zoom, there's an excellent selection of English-language books about Naxos and much else. No other island bookstore is this well stocked. ⊠ *Chora waterfront* ☏ *22850/23675.*

CLOTHING

Loom. Vassilis and Kathy Koutelieris's Loom sells casual clothes made from organically grown Greek cotton including the Earth Collection, which comes in muted natural colors. The shop also features other Greek designers including Ioanna Kourbella. ⊠ *Dimitriou Kokkou 8, in old market* ✛ *Off main square, 3rd street on right* ☏ *22850/25531.*

JEWELRY

Nassos Papakonstantinou. The workshop of Nassos Papakonstantinou sells one-of-a-kind pieces both sculptural and delicate. His father was a wood-carver; Nassos has inherited his talent. ■ TIP→ **The shop has no sign—that is Nassos's style.** ⊠ *Ayiou Nikodemou St., on Old Town's main square* ☏ *22850/22607.*

TRADITIONAL CRAFTS

Argilos. Husband and wife, Grigoris and Zetta Argilos are also local Naxian artists who love the island they grew up on. They created a shop of their own to stylishly display their wares, which range from pottery to wall hangings and jewelry. The shop also promotes a diverse and colorful collection of art, jewelry, and ceramics handmade by Greek artists from Naxos and the Cycladic islands. ⊠ *Entrance to Old Town* ☏ *22850/25244.*

Pocket Gallery. Anglo-Australian expat Artist Tim Elkington's small craft and art shop showcases Greek artists and expat artists that are inspired by the beauty and culture of Greece. Elkington is a painter himself but sells pottery, cards, ceramics, drawings, jewelry, and clothing that have a connection to Greece. Located in the streets of the Old Town, his collection of art and gifts ranges from traditional to modern. ⊠ *Old Town, Dimitriou Kokkou and Alexinoros* ☏ *22850/27106.*

Techni. Techni translates to art in Greek and that's what the shop showcases—locally and traditionally inspired handmade arts and crafts. The collections include jewelry in traditional designs, as well as embroidery and knitted items created by the women in Greece's mountain villages. Handmade carpets and linens are also for sale. The family who runs Techni comes from a long line of goldsmiths and embroiderers. ⊠ *Old Market* ☏ *22850/24767* ⊕ *www.naxos-art.gr.*

WINE

Promponas Wines and Liquors. A large selection of their famous *kitro* (citron liqueur) and preserves, as well as Naxos wines and thyme honey, packed in attractive gift baskets, can be found at Promponas Wines and Liquors, located on the Naxos town waterfront. It has been around since 1915 and free glasses of kitro are offered. ⊠ *Dimitris Prombona 1* ☏ *22850/22258.*

AYIA ANNA ΑΓΙΑ ΑΝΝΑ

11

7 km (4 miles) south of Naxos town.

Ayia Anna is one of the island's ideal beach towns, where long stretches of sand front a main road lined with tavernas, restaurants, and cafés.

BEACHES

Ayia Anna Beach. Located south of Naxos town, Ayia Anna is a sandy smooth extension of Ayios Prokopios beach. A small port, with connections to Paros, often has picturesque little boats docked here. At one point it was considered a main commercial harbor of the island, today it's a popular beach for water-sports lovers and those that want to enjoy the simplicity of its turquoise waters. The small beach village behind it is filled with restaurants, cafés, and beach bars. Beach chair and umbrella rentals are abundant. **Amenities:** food and drink. **Best for:** windsurfing, swimming, walking.

Ayios Prokopios Beach. This is one of the most popular beaches on the island due to its close proximity to Naxos town and its long stretch of pure, fine, white sand. It features a small leeward harbor with a unique view of small lagoons where herons find refuge. Its position on the island protects it from island winds so swimming is a calm experience that you don't always find on neighboring beaches. The small village surrounding it is lined with taverns and cafés. Nudism is allowed in designated areas. **Amenities:** food and drink. **Best for:** nudists; walking; swimming. ⊠ *Ayios Prokopios.*

FAMILY **Plaka Beach.** South of town, Plaka beach is a natural extension of Ayia Anna beach. It's a gorgeous 2 -mile stretch of sand filled with sand dunes and bamboo groves. Most of the beach has been left undeveloped but you can still find sun beds to rent in organized areas. Come early to grab one in the peak season. There is a range of tavernas, restaurants, and café-bars all within walking distance. **Amenities:** food and drink; water sports. **Best for:** swimming; walking.

WHERE TO EAT

$ ✕ **Gorgona.** Bearded Dimitris and Koula Kapris's beachfront taverna GREEK is popular both with sun worshippers on Ayia Anna beach and locals from Naxos town, who come here winter and summer to get away and sometimes to dance until the late hours, often to live music. The menu is extensive and fresh daily—the fresh fish comes from the caïques that pull up at the dock right in front every morning. Two good appetizers are *kakavia* (fish stew) and shrimp *saganaki* (with cooked cheese), while spaghetti with crab is a fine entrée. The barrel wine is their own (they also bottle it). The small hotel next door is also theirs. Ⓢ *Average main: €14* ⊠ *Ayia Anna near dock* ☎ *22850/41007* ▭ *No credit cards.*

SPORTS AND THE OUTDOORS

WINDSURFING

Plaka Watersports. The paradisaical Plaka beach is the summer playground for Plaka Watersports. The well-equipped water ski, wakeboard, kneeboard, canoeing, and sailing outfitter also organizes beginner and expert bike riding tours throughout the most scenic areas of Naxos. ⊠ *Plaka* ☎ *22850/41264* ⊕ *www.plaka-watersports.com.*

MIKRI VIGLA ΜΙΚΡΗ ΒΙΓΛΑ

18 km (11 miles) south of Naxos town.

Mikri Vigla is a small village known for its nearby pristine beaches. Several small room rentals and a few cafés and beach bars dot the area. Windy days offer the ideal conditions for the windsurfing set.

BEACHES

South of Mikri Vigla are the two beaches farthest from Naxos town, Kastraki and Pyrgaki.

Kastraki Beach. Although close to the popular beach destinations, Kastraki beach has kept its tranquil, quiet, and low-key status in place. The sandy long stretch of beach is essentially a continuation of Mikri Vigla but attracts those that prefer the experience of undeveloped and untouched Greek island beaches. Several designated areas are popular with nudists. **Amenities:** none. **Best for:** nudists; swimming; walking; solitude. ⊠ *Kastraki.*

Mikri Vigla Beach. Mikri Vigla's pure white sand is beautifully offset by a rocky hill, turquoise waters, and large, gentle sand dunes. The beach itself is edged by cedar trees. Here, the fierce island winds are welcome to kitesurfers and windsurfers; Flisvos Kite Centre *(⇨ see the listing, below)* offers equipment rentals and lessons. Not as developed as other beaches, a scattering of tavernas and cafés that mostly service sports aficionados can be found nearby. **Amenities:** food and drink. **Best for:** windsurfing; walking; swimming; surfing.

Pyrgaki Beach. One of the island's quietest beaches is a stunning, wide cove of fine sand bordered by green cedar trees. Its name comes from a nearby hill that was used to scout for pirates back in the day. Today, its beauty remains untouched by development. Only a few tavernas and restaurants surround this corner of beach, which rarely gets crowded. **Amenities:** none. **Best for:** solitude; swimming. ⊠ *Pyrgaki* ✛ *17.7 km (11 miles) south of Naxos town on a developed main road, then turn onto a dirt road that will lead you to Pyrgaki.*

SPORTS AND THE OUTDOORS

WINDSURFING

Flisvos Kite Centre. Right behind Mikri Vigla beach, the Flisvos Kite Centre takes advantage of the reliable windy days that bless this beach. For a decade, Michele Gasbarro has offered International Kiteboarding Organzation certified lessons, windsurfing lessons, and equipment rentals. The center also runs the Orkos Beach Hotel, which is on-site along with a restaurant and café. ☏ *22850/75490* ⊕ *www.flisvos-kitecentre.com.*

GALANADO ΠΥΡΓΟΣ ΤΟΥ ΜΠΕΛΟΝΙΑ

5 km (3 miles) south of Naxos town.

On a hill, Galando's village streets offer a pretty view toward Naxos town. It's an agricultural village that is famous for the landmark Tower of Bellonia that faces the eastern side of the island.

EXPLORING

Bellonia Tower. The graceful Bellonia Tower (Pirgos Bellonia) belonged to the area's ruling Venetian family, and like other fortified houses, it was built as a refuge from pirates and as part of the island's alarm system. The towers were located strategically throughout the island; if there was an attack, a large fire would be lighted on the nearest tower's roof, setting off a chain reaction from tower to tower and alerting the islanders. Bellonia's thick stone walls, its Lion of St. Mark emblem, and flat roofs with zigzag chimneys are typical of these towers. ⊠ *Galanado, Naxos.*

"Double Church" of St. John. The unusual 13th-century "double church" of St. John exemplifies Venetian tolerance. On the left side is the Catholic chapel, on the right the Orthodox church, separated only by a double arch. A family lives in the tower, and the church is often open. From here, take a moment to gaze across the peaceful fields to Naxos town and imagine what the islanders must have felt when they saw pirate ships on the horizon. ⊠ *In front of Bellonia Tower, Galanado, Naxos.*

AYIOS MAMAS ΑΓΙΟΣ ΜΑΜΑΣ

3 km (2 miles) south of Bellonia Tower, 8 km (5 miles) south of Naxos town.

A kilometer (½ mile) past a valley with unsurpassed views is one of the island's oldest churches (9th century), Ayios Mamas.

Ayios Mamas. St. Mamas is the protector of shepherds and is regarded as a patron saint in Naxos, Cyprus, and Asia Minor. Built in the 8th century, the stone church was the island's cathedral under the Byzantines. Though it was converted into a Catholic church in 1207, it was neglected under the Venetians and is now falling apart. You can also get to it from the Potamia villages. ⊠ *Ayios Mamas, Naxos.*

SANGRI ΣΑΓΚΡΙ

3 km (2 miles) south of Ayios Mamas, 11 km (7 miles) south of Naxos town.

Sangri is the center of an area with so many monuments and ruins spanning the Archaic to the Venetian periods it is sometimes called little Mystras, a reference to the famous abandoned Byzantine city in the Peloponnese.

EXPLORING

Timios Stavros Monastery (*Holy Cross*). The name Sangri is a corruption of Sainte Croix, which is what the French called the town's 16th-century monastery of Timios Stavros. The town is actually three small villages spread across a plateau. During the Turkish occupation, the monastery served as an illegal school, where children met secretly to learn the Greek language and culture.

Kastro Apilarou. Above the village of Sangri, you can make out the ruins of Kastro Apilarou, which was the castle of the Italian conqueror, Marco Sanudo, who conquered Naxos after the 4th crusade. The castle was the defensive stronghold for the region but locals today still say its a bit of a mystery about who the Apilaros family really was before Sanudo came and took over. If you do make the tough climb up to view it up close, you'll be greeted with a fantastic view of the Naxian plains. ⊠ *On Mt. Profitis Ilias.*

Temple of Demeter. The Temple of Demeter, a marble Archaic temple circa 530 BC, was lovingly restored by German archaeologists during the 1990s. Demeter was a grain goddess, and it's not hard to see what she is doing in this beautiful spot. There is also a small museum here (admission is free). ■TIP→ **The 25-minute walk here is splendid.** ⊹ *Take the asphalt road right before the entrance to Sangri.*

CHALKI ΧΑΛΚΙ

6 km (4 miles) northeast of Sangri, 17 km (10½ miles) southeast of Naxos town.

Katharina Bolesch and Alexander Reichart, husband and wife, have lived in Naxos for decades. They've been credited with starting Chalki's beautiful revival, because they restored an old building near the main square here in 2006, which is now home to their beautiful Fish and Olive Creations gallery. The couple also runs the Axia music festival in August, which gets grander each year.

Frangopoulos Tower. Chalki itself is a pretty town, known for its neoclassic houses in shades of pink, yellow, and gray, which are oddly juxtaposed with the plain but stately 17th-century Frangopoulos Tower. Like other towers erected by the Venetians on the island, it was primarily used in its heyday for defense purposes. ⊠ *Main road, next to Panayia Protothrone* ⊡ *Free* ⊘ *Sometimes open in morning.*

EXPLORING

Panayia Protothrone (*First Enthroned Virgin Church*). You are now entering the heart of the lush Tragaia valley, where in spring the air is heavily scented with honeysuckle, roses, and lemon blossoms and many tiny Byzantine churches hide in the dense olive groves. In Chalki is one of the most important of these Byzantine churches: the white, red-roofed Panayia Protothrone. Restoration work has uncovered frescoes from the 6th through the 13th century, and the church has remained alive and functioning for 14 centuries. The oldest layers, in the apse, depict the Apostles. ⊠ *On main road* ⊘ *Mornings.*

Vallindras Distillery. In the back of their quaint neoclassical house, the Vallindras family has supplied Naxos and Greece with citron liqueur from their distillery since 1896. Before you take the free tour, sample various flavors and strengths of the Greek aperitif that is marked with a Protected Destination of Origin (PDO) status. In the distillery room, examine the more-than-100-year-old copper equipment, which continues to produce the island's strong, traditional aperitif. ☏ *22850/31220.*

SHOPPING

Era Products. Visit this little jam shop to sample natural jams and Greek fruit preserves known as spoon sweets handmade by Yannis Mandenakis; Mandenakis prides himself on only using three ingredients: fruit, sugar, and lemon. You may even catch him working his magic as he mixes, cans, and packages his in-season products right through the screened kitchen door located in the shop. ⊠ *Off the main street in town, Sakelliades Ioannis street* ☏ *22850/31009.*

Fish and Olive Creations. Katherina sells her masterful ceramics and Alexander sells his sensitive jewelry—all with fish or olive motifs. The back room is an impressive little art gallery. ⊠ *Central Platia ✛ 20 mins southeast of Naxos town* ☏ *22850/31771* ⊕ *www.fish-olive-creations.com.*

Handmade Textiles. Maria Maraki has been looming for decades, and if you're lucky, you may find her sitting at the wheel of her traditional silk and cotton weaving loom behind the shop window. Her creations— cotton table runners, curtains, placemats, and table covers—decorate every corner and wall of the shop. Maraki draws inspiration for her colorful designs from Greek history and her own imagination, but if she's in the shop, ask her to explain her designs. ⊠ *Sakelliades Ioannis street* ☏ *22850/32938.*

Phos Gallery. When he's not shooting for the acclaimed Greek film director, Theodore Aggelopoulos, photographer Dimitris Gavalas is busy at his own gallery, which he decided to build in his father's hometown of Chalki. His work includes landscapes, panoramics, and conceptual photography. ☏ *22850/31118* ⊕ *www.phosgallery.gr.*

MONI MONH

6 km (4 miles) north of Chalki, 23 km (14¼ miles) east of Naxos town.

Off the fine asphalt Chalkiou-Keramotis Road, Moni ("monastery") remains high in the mountains overlooking Naxos's greenest valley and has become a popular place for a meal or coffee on a hot afternoon. Local women make embroideries for Naxos town's shops.

Panayia Drosiani. Just below Moni is one of the Balkans' most important churches, Panayia Drosiani, which has faint, rare Byzantine frescoes from the 7th and 8th centuries. Its name means Our Lady of Refreshment, because once during a severe drought, when all the churches took their icons down to the sea to pray for rain, only the icon of this church got results. The fading frescoes are visible in layers: to the right when you enter are the oldest—one shows St. George the Dragon Slayer astride his horse, along with a small boy, an image one usually sees only in Cyprus and Crete. According to legend, the saint saved the child, who had fallen into a well, and there met and slew the giant dragon that had terrorized the town. Opposite him is St. Dimitrios, shown killing barbarians. The church is made up of three chapels—the middle one has a space for the faithful to worship at the altar rather than in the nave, as became common in later centuries. Next to that is a very small opening that housed a secret school during the revolution. It is open mornings and again after siesta; in deserted winter, ring the bell if it is not open. ⊠ *Off of Chalkiou-Keramotis Rd.* ☏ *22850/31003.*

FILOTI ΦΙΛΟΤΙ

6½ km (4 miles) south of Moni, 20 km (12½ miles) southeast of Naxos town.

Filoti, a peaceful village on the lower slopes of Mt. Zas, is the interior's largest. A three-day festival celebrating the Dormition starts on August 14. In the center of town is another Venetian tower that belonged to the Barozzi and the Church of Filotissa (Filoti's Virgin Mary) with its marble iconostasis and carved bell tower. There are places to eat and rooms to rent.

SPORTS AND THE OUTDOORS

HIKING

Zas Cave. Filoti is the starting place for several walks in the countryside, including the climb up to Zas Cave where obsidian tools and pottery fragments have been found; lots of bats live inside. Mt. Zas, or Zeus, is one of the god's birthplaces; on the path to the summit lies a block of unworked marble that reads *Oros Dios Milosiou*, or "Boundary of the Temple of Zeus Melosios." (Melosios, it is thought, is a word that has to do with sheep.) The islanders say that under the Turks the cave was used as a chapel, and two stalagmites are called the Priest and the Priest's Wife, who are said to have been petrified by God to save them from arrest. ⊠ *Southeast of town on small dirt track.*

APEIRANTHOS ΑΠΕΙΡΑΝΘΟΣ

12 km (7½ miles) northeast of Filoti, 32 km (20 miles) southeast of Naxos town.

Apeiranthos is very picturesque, with views and marble-paved streets running between the Venetian Bardani and Zevgoli towers. As you walk through the arcades and alleys, notice the unusual chimneys—no two are alike. The elders, whose ancestors came from Crete, sit in their doorsteps chatting, while packs of children shout "Hello, hello" at any passerby who looks foreign.

Archaeological Museum. A very small Archaeological Museum, established by a local mathematician, Michael Bardanis, displays Cycladic finds, including statues and earthen pots dug up from the east coast. The most important of the exhibits are unique dark gray marble plaques from the 3rd millennium BC with roughly hammered scenes of daily life: hunters and farmers and sailors going about their business. ⊠ *Off main square* 🖾 *€3* 🕾 *Daily 8:30–2:30.*

ABRAM VILLAGE ΧΩΡΙΟ ΑΜΠΡΑΜ

20 km (33 miles) northeast of Naxos town.

Tucked in a quiet, rocky northern part of the island, Abram is a small village built around a shore that curves into attractive bays and small beaches surrounding Abram bay. A few vineyards are scattered around the area as well as a few small tavernas and lodging options.

WHERE TO STAY

$ ⊞ **Abram Village.** If you love island nature and dislike crowds, this is
B&B/INN   your place—set on Naxos's northern coast. **Pros:** right on the sea; in
a beautiful area. **Cons:** isolated and far from town. $ *Rooms from:*
€35 ⊠ Abram ⊹ 20 km (33 miles) from Naxos town ☎ 22850/63244
⊕ www.abram.gr ⟿ 15 rooms, 8 apartments ⊘ Closed Oct.–Apr.
⏀ No meals.

FOLEGANDROS ΦΟΛΕΓΑΝΔΡΟΣ

Updated
by Stephen
Brewer

*180 km (96 nautical miles) southeast of Piraeus harbor in Athens, 86
km (53 miles) northwest of Santorini.*

If Santorini didn't exist, little, bare Folegandros would be world famous.
Its gorgeous Cycladic main town of Chora, built between the walls of
a Venetian fort, sits on the edge of a beetling precipice: this hilltop
setting represents, with the exception of Santorini, the finest cliff-side
scenery in the Cyclades. Beyond this, the island does not seem to have
much to offer on paper—but in person it certainly does. Beautiful and
authentic, it has become the secret island of Cyclades lovers, who find
here a pure dose of the magic essence of the Aegean. Only 31 square
km (12 square miles) in area and 64 km (40 miles) in circumference,
it lacks ruins, villages, green valleys, trees, country houses, and graceful cafés at the edge of the sea. But what the island does have—one of
the most stunning towns, deliberately downplayed touristic development, several good beaches, quiet evenings, traditional local food, and
respectful visitors—make it addictive. There are no discos, no bank,
but the sea is shining and, in spring, much of the island is redolent of
thyme and oregano.

Visitors to Folegandros—historians are divided on whether the name
immortalizes the Cretan explorer Pholegandrus or comes from the
Phoenician term for "rock-strewn"—mostly stay in or near the main
town, and hang around the town's three squares. A walk, a swim at
the beach, a visit to the little Folklore Museum at Ano Meria, meeting
other people who love the essence of the Greek islands: these require
few arrangements. Unless you want to stop on the side of the road to
look at views (the island does offer an array of interesting hiking trails),
the bus is adequate. There are a number of beaches—Angali and Ayios
Nikolaos are especially good. Because Folegandros is so small, it fills up
fast in August, and despite the absence of raucous nightlife, it somewhat
loses its special flavor.

GETTING HERE AND AROUND

Little islands like Folegandros used to get two or three boats a week.
Tourism, however, has changed all that, at least in summer, and Folegandros is firmly in the loop. There are no flights here, but two daily
boats from Piraeus in summer—fewer in winter—serve the island sufficiently. There are also regular connections to Anafi, Ios, Amorgos,
Kea, Kimolos, Koufonisi, Kythnos Milos, Naxos, Paros, Serifos, Sifnos, Sikinos, and Santorini. For schedules check ⊕ *www.openseas.gr*
or ⊕ *www.gtp.gr.* Faster boats are added on weekends but don't run in

winter. The trip from Piraeus takes from 4 to 11 hours.

Buses go from the little port to Chora every hour or so throughout the day; buses meet the boats. Buses go almost as often to the southern beaches and to Ano Meria (which has a separate Chora bus stop near the Sottovento tourist office). Fares run from €1.50 to €2.50. Taxis (☎ 22890/22400 or 22860/41048) meet boats and a stand is at the town entrance.

TOURS

Contacts Maraki Travel and Tours. This agency helpfully handles most travel arrangements. ✉ *Chora* ☎ *22860/41273*. **Sottovento.** The agency arranges travel and local boat trips and provides general information graciously. ✉ *Main square, Chora* ☎ *22860/41444* ⊕ *www.sottovento.eu*.

TOWERING VIEWS

The Cheimarros Pirgos (Tower of the Torrent), a cylindrical Hellenistic tower, can be reached from Filoti by a road that begins from the main road to Apeiranthos, outside town, or by a level, 3½-hour hike with excellent views. The walls, as tall as 45 feet, are intact, with marble blocks perfectly aligned. The tower, which also served as a lookout post for pirates, is often celebrated in the island's poetry: "O, my heart is like a bower/And Cheimarros's lofty tower!"

CHORA ΧΩΡΑ

42 km (27 miles) northwest of Santorini.

As the boat approaches the little port of Karavostasi, bare, sun-scoured cliffs—with a hint of relieving green in wet winter but only gray glare in summer—let you know where you are. Leaving the port immediately, since there is hardly anything here, visitors climb the road 3 km (2 miles) to Chora on buses (which meet all ferries). On the rugged way up, you'll see the spectacular, whitewashed **church of Koímisis tis Theotókou** (or Dormition of the Mother of God) dominating the town on the high cliff where the ancient settlement first stood. On Easter Sunday the chief icon is carried through the town.

After a steep ride, cliff-top Chora comes into view. Its sky-kissing perch is well out of sight of the port, an important consideration in the centuries when the seas here were plagued by pirate raiders. Today, Chora—small, white, old, and preserved lovingly by the islanders—is less hidden and is known as the main reason to visit the island. Its main street, starting at the bus stop (no cars in town) meanders through five little squares—the middle three are the main ones—each with a few restaurants and cafés shaded by bougainvillea and hibiscus. Some of the buildings are set into the walls of the Venetian fort, or Kastro, built by the Venetian duke of Naxos in the 13th century. The second street circles the Kastro and the precipice on which the town stands and is strikingly lined with two-story cube houses that form a wall atop the towering cliff. The glory days of Venice came to an end in 1715, when the ruling Turks sacked Folegandros and sold the captives as slaves. The old families go back to 1780, when the island was repopulated.

Perched at a nearly angelic height, the Church of the Dormition of the Mother of God lords it over Folegandros's main town.

WHERE TO EAT

$ ITALIAN 🍴 **Caffè dei Viaggiatori.** An Italian vibe lingers at this little place, where Flavio Facciolo and his wife offer a selection of good Italian wines, serve light snacks, pastas, and pizza, and make the best espresso on the island. [$] *Average main: €9* ✉ *On first bus square* ☎ *22860/41444* 🕒 *Closed Oct.–May.*

$ GREEK 🍴 **I Piazze.** This middle-square eatery has tables set out under trees. Specialties include *kalasouna* cheese pies and homemade noodles (called *matsata*) with pork or lamb. They also sell their own aromatic thyme honey. [$] *Average main: €8* ✉ *Middle square* ☎ *22860/41274* 💳 *No credit cards.*

$ GREEK 🍴 **O Kritikos.** Set under a tree and abutting a Byzantine church, this simple little taverna serves exclusively local meats and vegetables. Souroto, a local cheese, makes a fitting appetizer. *Kontosouli* is usually pork on the spit; here it is a mixture of lamb and pork, and delicious. [$] *Average main: €8* ✉ *Middle Sq.* ☎ *22860/41219* 💳 *No credit cards.*

WHERE TO STAY

$$$ HOTEL Fodor's Choice ★ 🏨 **Anemomilos Apartments.** Perched on the towering cliff overlooking the sea and set amid a series of small garden terraces (perfect for breakfast and drinks), this complex with truly breathtaking vistas of sea and sky, is the best place to stay in Folegandros. **Pros:** welcoming hospitality; beautiful pool; nice bar and restaurant. **Cons:** some apartments can feel closed in; quite expensive for the island. [$] *Rooms from: €230* ✉ *Edge of town* ☎ *22860/41309* 🌐 *www.anemomilosapartments.com* 🛏 *23 rooms* 🕒 *Closed mid-Oct.–Easter* 🍽 *Breakfast.*

A Water Sports Paradise

When it comes to the Cyclades, anyone who invests in a mask, snorkel, and flippers has entry to intense, serene beauty. But even without this underwater gear, this archipelago is a swimmer's paradise.

Most of the Cycladic islands gleam with beaches, from long blond stretches of sand to tiny pebbly coves. The best beaches are probably those on the southwest coast of Naxos. Beaches on Tinos tend to be less crowded than those on other islands in the Cyclades. The strands on Santorini, though strewn with plenty of bathers, are volcanic; you can bask on sands that are strikingly red and black.

As for water sports, there are many options to entice sunseekers. Waterskiing, parasailing, scuba diving, and especially windsurfing have become ever more popular. Note that many water-sports venues change from season to season.

$ **Meltemi Hotel.** Whitewashed and spotless, these good-size and sim-
HOTEL ply furnished rooms open to verandas and are at the edge of Chora, making this little inn convenient to restaurants and the bus stop for the port, beaches, and other points on the island. **Pros:** pleasant and convenient. **Cons:** no sea view; no pool or other amenities. $ *Rooms from: €80* ☎ *22860/41425* 🛏 *11 rooms* ▭ *No credit cards* ⊗ *Closed Nov.–Feb.* ⦿ *No meals.*

SHOPPING
JEWELRY
Creations Folegandros. Apostolos and Eleni have been creating their striking jewels, fashioned from silver and gold and often with Greek stones, for 20 years. They also sell some work by other artists. ✉ *Middle square* ☎ *22860/41524* ⊕ *www.creations-folegandros.gr* ⊗ *Closed mid-Sept.–mid-June.*

ANO MERIA ΑΝΩ ΜΕΡΙΑ

5 km (3 miles) northwest of Chora.

The paved road connects the port, the capital, and, after a short drive, Ano Meria. On the way there, you can see terraces where barley was coaxed seemingly from stone, though there is little farming now. The tiny town is a smaller version of Chora, and the cafés are perfect places for a drink.

Folklore Museum. Exhibits reconstruct traditional farming life. The adjacent church of Agios Panteliemon celebrates the feast day of Saint Panteliemon on July 27, and almost everyone goes. ☎ *22860/41069* 🎟 *€2* ⊗ *June–Sept., daily 10–6; Oct.–May, daily 10–3.*

SANTORINI (THIRA) ΣΑΝΤΟΡΙΝΗ (ΘΗΡΑ)

Updated
by Stephen
Brewer

235 km (128 nautical miles) southeast of Piraeus harbor in Athens.

Undoubtedly the most extraordinary island in the Aegean, crescent-shaped Santorini remains a mandatory stop on the Cycladic tourist route—even if you must enjoy the sensational sunsets from Ia, the fascinating excavations, and the dazzling white towns with a million other travelers. Called Kállisti (the "Loveliest") as long ago as ancient times, the island has now reverted officially to its subsequent name of Thira, after the 9th-century-BC Dorian colonizer Thiras. The place is better known these days, however, as Santorini, a name derived from its patroness, St. Irene of Thessaloniki, the Byzantine empress who restored icons to Orthodoxy and died in 802.

Flying to Santorini from Athens and many other cities is the most convenient way to get here, but to enjoy a true Santorini rite of passage, opt instead for the boat trip, which provides a spectacular introduction. After the boat sails between Sikinos and Ios, your deck-side perch approaches two close islands with a passage between them. The bigger one on the left is Santorini, and the smaller on the right is Thirassia. Passing between them, you see the village of Ia adorning Santorini's northernmost cliff like a white geometric beehive. You are in the caldera (volcanic crater), one of the world's truly breathtaking sights: a crescent of cliffs rising 1,100 feet, with the white clusters of the towns of Fira and Ia perched along the top. The bay, once the high center of the island, is 1,300 feet in some places, so deep that when boats dock in Santorini's shabby little port of Athinios, they do not drop anchor (as if placed there to emphasize the depths, a sunken ocean liner lies eerily submerged beneath the surface). The encircling cliffs are the ancient rim of a still-active volcano, and you are sailing east across its flooded caldera. On your right are the Burnt isles, the White isle, and other volcanic remnants, all lined up as if some outsize display in a geology museum. Hephaestus's subterranean fires smolder still—the volcano erupted in 198 BC, about 735, and there was an earthquake in 1956.

Indeed, Santorini and its four neighboring islets are the fragmentary remains of a larger landmass that exploded about 1600 BC: the volcano's core blew sky high, and the sea rushed into the abyss to create the great bay, which measures 10 km by 7 km (6 miles by 4½ miles) and is 1,292 feet deep. The other pieces of the rim, which broke off in later eruptions, are Thirassia, where a few hundred people live, and deserted little Aspronissi ("White isle"). In the center of the bay, black and uninhabited, two cones, the Burnt Isles of Palea Kameni and Nea Kameni, appeared between 1573 and 1925.

There has been too much speculation about the identification of Santorini with the mythical Atlantis, mentioned in Egyptian papyri and by Plato (who says it's in the Atlantic), but myths are hard to pin down. *(For the full scoop, see our special photo feature, "Santorini: The Lost Atlantis?" in this chapter.)* This is not true of old arguments about whether tidal waves from Santorini's cataclysmic explosion destroyed Minoan civilization on Crete, 113 km (70 miles) away. The latest carbon-dating evidence, which points to a few years before 1600 BC for the eruption, clearly indicates that the Minoans outlasted the eruption by a couple of hundred years, but most probably in a weakened state. In fact, the island still endures hardships: since antiquity, Santorini has depended on rain collected in cisterns for drinking and irrigating—the well water is often brackish—and the serious shortage is alleviated by the importation of water. Nevertheless, the volcanic soil also yields riches: small, intense tomatoes with tough skins used for tomato paste (good restaurants here serve them); the famous Santorini fava beans, which have a light, fresh taste; barley; wheat; and white-skin eggplants.

These days, unrestrained tourism has taken a heavy toll on Santorini. Fira, and now Ia, could almost be described as "a street with 40 jewelry shops"; many of the natives are completely burned out by the end of the peak season (the best times to come here are shoulder periods); and, increasingly, business and the loud ringing of cash registers have disrupted the normal flow of Greek life here. For example, if a cruise ship comes in during afternoon siesta, all shops immediately open. And you will have a pushy time walking down Fira's main street in August, so crowded is it. Still and all, if you look beneath the layers of gimcrack tourism, you'll find Greek splendor. No wonder Greece's two Nobel poets, George Seferis and Odysseus Elytis, wrote poems about it. For you, too, will be "watching the rising islands / watching the red islands sink" (Seferis) and consider, "With fire with lava with smoke / You found the great lines of your destiny" (Elytis).

GETTING HERE AND AROUND

The bay of Santorini is one of the world's great sights, and an incoming flight—45 minutes from Athens—gives a unique view of it. There are 12 daily flights, shared by Olympic Airlines, Athens Airways, and Aegean Airlines. There are also flights from Thessaloniki and from other European cities. Reservations, the earlier the better, are essential.

As many as six daily boats from Athens's port of Piraeus ply the wine-dark Aegean to Santorini. The trip takes from to four to 10 hours, depending on route, boat, and the weather. Try to make sure your boat enters the harbor before sunset (usually an early-morning departure from Piraeus), since this is a spectacular sight, one crucial to savoring Santorini's vibe. There are also daily connections to Paros, Naxos, and Anafi, and there are regular summer connections to Folegandros, Crete, Ios, Karpathos, Kasos, Amorgos, Kea, Kimolos, Kos, Koufonisi, Kythnos, Milos, Mykonos, and Rhodes. Reservations are needed in summer and at Easter, for cars all year. The port town, Ormos Athinios, is only that, and you must proceed by vehicle to your destination. Buses generally meet the boats, and the drive up the volcano-cut cliff is amazing.

Buses leave from the main station in central Fira just south of the town's main square. In high season, there are hourly buses for Akrotiri and buses on the half hour for Ia, Monolithos (airport), Kamari, and Perissa. Buses also connect with the main port of Athinios (at least a half-hour ride) as well as the popular Perissa and Kamari beaches. Schedules are posted; hotel concierges should also have this info. Fares run from €1.50

to €4. As might be expected, Santorini's buses can be as crowded as those of rush-hour Athens, so step lively! The main taxi station is near Fira's central square on Odos 25 Martiou. Connecting Fira with the harbor port of Fira Skala is the island's famed cable-car route, with its spectacular vistas. This is a must-do (a must-don't are the donkey treks up the cliff), even if you're not using the port facilities—but avoid times when cruise-ship passengers are trying to get back down to their tenders and lines can be impossibly long.

Contacts **Fira Bus Station** ✉ *Near main square, Fira* ☎ *22890/25404* ⊕ *ktel-santorini.gr.* **Fira Taxi Station** ✉ *Odos 25 Martiou, near main square, Fira* ☎ *22860/22555.* **Santorini Cable Car** ✉ *town center, Fira* ⊕ *scc.gr* 💳 *€5, plus €5 for luggage* ⊘ *daily 7 am–10 pm, departures every 20 minutes.* **Santorini Port Authority** ✉ *Ormos Athinios* ☎ *22860/22239* ⊕ *www.santorini-port.com.*

TOURS

Nomikos Travel. This agency has tours to the main sights along with some off-the-beaten-path attractions, including the island's wineries and the Monastery of Profitis Ilias. ✉ *Fira* ☎ *22860/23660.*

Pelican Travel. This popular agency runs bus tours, wine tastings, and visits to Ia; it also has daily boat trips to the volcano and Thirassia and arranges private tours. ✉ *Odus 25 Martiou, Fira* ☎ *22860/22220* ⊕ *www.pelican.gr.*

Santorini Wine Tours. Vaios Panagiotoulas, a professional somelier, is your guide on an informative and fun tour of some of the island's leading wineries. Vaios chooses wineries that produce a variety of wines, giving a wide-ranging introduction to many distinct varieties. The tour includes a look at the winemaking process and a drive through vineyards, but the emphasis is on tasting and lively, highly enlightening discussion. The tour includes hotel pickup in a comfortable minibus. ✉ *General Tourist Office, Vathonas* ☎ *22860/28358* ⊕ *www.santoriniwinetour.com.*

FIRA ΦHΡΑ

76 km (47 miles) southeast of Paros, 10 km (6 miles) west of the Santorini airport, 14 km (8½ miles) southeast of Ia.

Tourism is Santorini's major industry and adds more than 1 million visitors per year to a population of 7,000. As a result, Fira, the capital, midway along the west coast of the east rim, is no longer only a picturesque village but a major tourist center, overflowing with bars, shops, and restaurants. Many of its employees—often Eastern Europeans or young travelers extending their summer vacations—hardly speak Greek. To experience life here as it was until only a couple of decades ago, walk down the much-photographed, winding staircase that descends from town to the water's edge—walk (carefully, trying to avoid the many slippery mule droppings) or take the spectacular cable car ride back up, avoiding the drivers who will try to plant you on the sagging back of one of their bedraggled-looking mules. It soon becomes clear what brings the tourists here: with its white, cubical houses clinging to

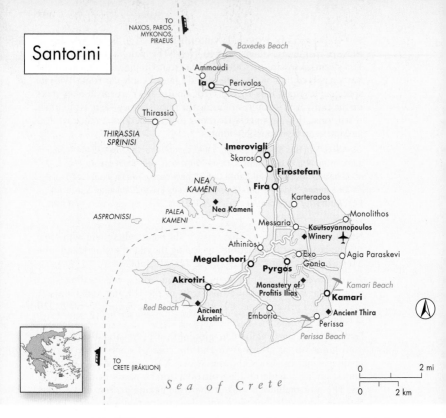

Santorini

TO NAXOS, PAROS, MYKONOS, PIRAEUS

Baxedes Beach

Ammoudi
Ia
Perivolos

Thirassia

THIRASSIA SPRINISI

Imerovigli
Skaros
Firostefani
NEA KAMENI
Fira
Karterados

ASPRONISSI
PALEA KAMENI
Nea Kameni
Messaria
Monolithos
Koutsoyannopoulos Winery

Athinios
Exo Gonia
Agia Paraskevi

Megalochori
Pyrgos

Akrotiri
Monastery of Profitis Ilias
Kamari Beach

Red Beach
Ancient Akrotiri
Emborio
Ancient Thira
Kamari
Perissa
Perissa Beach

TO CRETE (IRÁKLION)

Sea of Crete

0   2 mi
0   2 km

the cliff hundreds of feet above the caldera, Fira is a beautiful place, an exhilarating Greek extravaganza.

EXPLORING

Archaeological Museum. This dusty collection of bits and pieces from island's millenia of history includes pottery, statues, and grave artifacts found mosty at excavations in ancient Thira and Akrotiri, from the Minoan through the Byzantine periods. Should you have time or inclination for only one museum visit on Santorini, the Museum of Prehistoric Thira is far more riveting. ⊠ *Stavrou and Nomikos, Mitropoleos, behind big church* ☎ *22860/22217* ⊕ *www.culture.gr* ☞ *€3* ⊗ *Nov.–Mar., Tues.–Sun. 8–4; Apr.–Oct., Tues.–Sun. 9–4.*

Museum of Prehistoric Thera. This is the treasure house that displays frescoes and other artifacts from the famed excavations at Akrotiri. Many of the finds have been sent off to the Archaeological Museum in Athens, but the most charming fresco remains here: a colorful depiction of women in dresses gathering saffron from the stamens of crocuses. Also in this small collection are fresco fragments with the famous painted swallows, the island's favorite design motif, who still flock to Santorini to roost on the cliffs. The fossilized olive leaves from 60,000 BC prove the olive to be indigenous. ⊠ *Mitropoleos, behind big church*

☎ *22860/23217* ⊕ *www.culture.gr*
📠 *€3* 🕐 *Nov.–Mar., Wed.–Mon.*
8–3; Apr.–Oct., Wed.–Mon. 9–4.

AVOID THE MULES

Tourist touts still like to promote mules as a mode of transport to take you up the zigzag cliff path to the island capital of Fira. But animal-rights groups would prefer you didn't. And you should be aware of another reason: the mules on Santorini are piously believed to contain souls of the dead, who are thus doing their purgatory. It is an arduous ascent.

Nomikos Conference Center. Upper Fira's new exhibition hall, named for the famous ship owner, hosts many international conferences as well as concerts. Its permanent exhibition of fabulous photo replicas of the Akrotiri frescoes are beautiful and informative, with colorful depictions of sailing ships, leaping dolphins, fertile fields, and other aspects of life on the island 4,000 years ago. ✉ *Caldera path, just north of cable car* ☎ *22860/23016* ⊕ *www.santorini.gr-santorini.com/exhibitions/nomikos.htm* 📠 *€4* 🕐 *May–Oct., daily 10–8, Nov.–Apr., daily 10–6.*

Panayia Ypapantis. The modern Greek Orthodox cathedral is a major landmark; many businesses in Fira list their addresses simply as "near the cathedral." You'll quickly note how the local priests, with somber faces, long beards, and black robes, look strangely out of place in summertime, tourist-jammed Fira. ✉ *Southern part of town.*

OFF THE BEATEN PATH

Nea Kameni. To peer into a live, sometimes smoldering volcano, join one of the popular excursions to Nea Kameni, the larger of the two Burnt isles. After disembarking, you hike 430 feet to the top and walk around the edge of the crater, wondering if the volcano is ready for its fifth eruption during the last hundred years—after all, the last was in 1956. Some tours continue on to the island of Therassia, where there is a village. Many operators on the island offer volcano tours. ✉ *In caldera.*

WHERE TO EAT

$
GREEK

✕ **Naoussa.** It's nice to know that Santorini, and Fira especially, still offers a nice dining experience that emphasizes old-fashioned Greek fare made with care and served by a friendly and accommodating staff on a breezy balcony; tables at one end get a caldera view. Starters include tomato fritters and rich fava dip. A fisherman's spaghetti, with big chunks of lobster, is a seafood specialty, but many of the mainstays are meat oriented, including (what some say is the island's best) moussaka and a succulent veal *stifado*, simmered with fresh local vegetables. 💲 *Average main: €10* ✉ *On caldera, near cathedral* ☎ *22860/21277* ⊕ *www.naoussa-restaurant.com.*

$$$
INTERNATIONAL

✕ **Sphinx.** When Fira locals want more than a taverna, they come to this pretty vaulted room in a neoclassic mansion, which glows with spotlighted Cycladic sculptures and peach walls. As lush as this is, however, few can resist an outdoor terrace table, thanks to the striking caldera views in one direction and a vista of the giant cathedral in the other. Owner George Psichas is his own chef, and every dish is evidence of his loving care—even the bread and pasta are homemade. Starters include three-fish carpaccio with olive oil, lemon, and arugula, or the eggplant

Continued on page 614

SANTORINI
The Lost Atlantis?

Did Atlantis, "the island at the center of the earth," ever really exist? And if it did, where? Big-budget Hollywood films have placed it in the middle of the Atlantic Ocean. Several historians think it was located in the Bay of Naples; others that it was a Sumerian island in the Persian Gulf, or a sunken island in the Straits of Gibraltar. Nowadays, more and more experts are making a case for the island of Santorini—and therein lies a tale.

WHOLE LOTTA LAVA

Imagine: A land called Atlantis, with a vast, spectacular city adorned with hanging gardens, gigantic palaces, and marble colossi of Poseidon, ancient god of the sea. One fateful day, more than 3,500 years ago, an enormous earthquake triggers a cataclysmic volcano that destroys the capital. In the space of a few hours, a towering tidal wave washes all traces of this civilization into a fiery cauldron. All, that is, except for a rocky fragment framing a watery caldera. Historical detectives, archaeologists, and volcanologists have long wondered whether Greece's fabled isle of Santorini could be that last remnant of Atlantis. But is this theory more fable than fact?

For those who consider Atlantis merely a symbol or metaphor, the question is not important. Surfacing like a rising island in a deep bay, the notion of a Golden Age is ever-present in the human imagination, and the Atlantis story is among our most durable and poignant ideas of it. Reverberating

through Western culture and dazzling the mind, the name "Atlantis" glitters with glamour; it titles hotels, Web sites, towns, submarines, book and film companies, even a pop song by Donovan. But historians today remain divided on whether Atlantis was a funtastic shooting-star of history or just a legend with a moral lesson.

PLATO VERSUS THE VOLCANO

Plato (427–347 BC), the most fearless, and the most substantive writer, of all the ancient Greek philosophers, would have supported the latter option. He liked to end his famous Dialogues with a myth, and Atlantis shows up in both his "Timaeus" and his "Critias," as a parable (and history?) of good and bad government. Plato says that the great 6th-century lawgiver–poet of Athens, Solon (630–560 BC), went to Egypt, and there heard stories of Atlantis. They told him that 9,000 years ago Athens defeated the empire of Atlantis, a huge island in the Atlantic Ocean, in battle.

View of Santorini's caldera

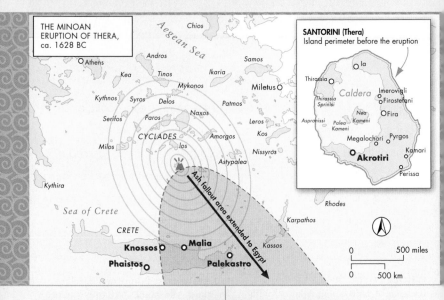

THE MINOAN
ERUPTION OF THERA,
ca. 1628 BC

Aegean Sea

Chios
Athens
Andros
Kea
Tinos
Ikaria
Kythnos
Syros
Delos
Mykonos
Patmos
Miletus
Samos
Serifos
Paros
Naxos
Leros
Kos
CYCLADES
Amorgos
Milos
Ios
Nissyros
Astypalea

Ash fallout area extended to Egypt

Kythira

Sea of Crete

CRETE
Knossos   Malia
Phaistos   Palekastro
Kassos
Karpathos
Rhodes

0   500 miles
0   500 km

SANTORINI (Thera)
Island perimeter before the eruption

Ia
Thirassia
Thirassia
Sprinisi
Caldera
Imerovigli
Firostefani
Aspronissi
Palea
Kameni
Nea
Kameni
Fira
Megalochori
Pyrgos
Akrotiri
Kamari
Perissa

Then a natural cataclysm destroyed the island in one day, "and Atlantis disappeared in the sea depths." Atlantis was created by and belonged to Poseidon, god of the sea and of earthquakes, and he made it a paradise ruled by his son, King Atlas, with the guidance of wise counselors. When later generations on the island abandoned his prudent ways, catastrophe struck: you mustn't love power more than you love the gods. The Bible had Sodom and Gomorrah; Plato had Atlantis.

Some authors claim the story of Atlantis is history, not fantasy. They believe that Solon misread 9,000 years as 900. If so, Atlantis would have flourished at the same time as Santorini, which, as we know and the classical Greeks suspected, was destroyed by earthquakes followed by a cataclysmic volcanic eruption, probably just before 1600 BC—some historians point to the date of 1628 BC.

THE MINOAN CONNECTION

In the late 1960s, when archaeologist Spyridon Marinatos's excavations of Santorini's caldera revealed the ruin of Akrotiri, preserved under 25 feet of volcanic ash, the island's claim to be Atlantis began to outweigh all others. The buried town had been large, comfortable, and attractive, the art beautiful and gentle, and its high Bronze Age civilization resembled Minoan Crete's, 47 miles south. Since a tsunami from the volcano must have devastated the larger island, it is not surprising that Crete, whose dimensions chime better with Plato's, is also called Atlantis.

Crete and its satellite, Santorini (don't call it this to a Santorini scholar, but it's true), were "feminine" civilizations. They worshipped the goddess of fertility; disliked depictions of war and weapons; kept their towns unwalled; loved magnificent jewelry; and their art eschews the monumental for spontaneous natural forms, such as swallows,

Imaginary view of Santorini's submerged volcano in eruption in 1866; (below) Akrotiri frescoes.

octopi, dolphins, and palm trees. They liked pretty people. The women's elaborate costumes exposed their breasts, and the men, nearly naked, wore gold jewelry and fancy hairstyles. They worshipped not in temples, but in caves, springs, and mountaintops. From our sparse evidence, it seems it was indeed a golden age, when "the earth bore freely all the aromatic substances it bears today, roots, herbs, bushes and gums exuded by flowers or fruit." Perfume was as popular here as in Egypt. A mural preserved in Athens from Akrotiri shows blue monkeys opening doors à la Wizard of Oz. Plato, the stern taskmaster, would probably have disapproved.

. . . ET TU, SANTORINI?

Today, archaeological excavation continues at Akrotiri, situated high—1,300 feet—over the whitecaps of the Aegean Sea. What was Santorini like when the great bay was terra firma, lush with olive trees and abundant harvests? Santorini's own Prehistoric Museum is studying the possibilities, as the writings of historians, poets, and philosophers provide food for thought. The fact remains that the evidence is not all in: there is a possibility that Santorini could, in fact, reawaken from its long slumber and once again erupt, and then subside again. The key to Atlantis's existence may lie in the once and future fury of this fascinating island.

with Santorini tomato sauce and mozzarella. George leans Italian, as the risotto with Santorini tomatoes, zucchini, and marscapone reveals. Fresh fish is usually available—try the fresh grouper steak with shellfish and white wine sauce. The fillet steak with foie gras, wild mushrooms, and Vin Santo sauce is superb. Desserts change day by day, but rich chocolate soufflé is always available. The wine list is long and Greek (and the "cave" is very much worth a look). $ *Average main: €30* ⊠ *Cliff-side walkway in front of Panayia Ypapantis* ☎ *22860/23823* ⊕ *www.sphinx-santorini.com* ⌂ *Reservations essential.*

$

GREEK

✕ **Taverna Nikolas.** It's nice to know that some old Santorini traditions live on, and this sparsely decorated taverna right in the center of Fira is one of them. It's been serving strictly traditional fare since the days when the only way to town was on foot or the back of a donkey. The moussaka is reputed to be some of the best on the island, and lamb with lemon sauce is a regualr special not to be missed. $ *Average main: €10* ⊠ *Near the main square* ⊟ *No credit cards.*

WHERE TO STAY

When you book a room, remember that many of Santorini's hotel cliff-side balconies elbow each other out of the way for the best view and, with footpaths often running above and beside them, privacy is often hard to come by.

$$$$

RENTAL

Fodor's Choice

★

Aigialos Hotel. A cluster of buildings from the 18th and 19th centuries composes the most comfortable and discreetly luxurious—as well as the most poetic and serenely quiet—place to stay in Fira. **Pros:** not a phony place set up for tourists; quiet elegance; friendly, discreet service. **Cons:** some steps, but fewer than elsewhere; the pool is tiny. $ *Rooms from: €350* ⊠ *South end of cliff-side walkway* ☎ *22860/25191* ⊕ *www.aigialos.gr* ⤳ *17 rooms and suites* ⊘ *Closed Nov.–Mar.* ⦿◉⦿ *Breakfast.*

$$

B&B/INN

Aroma Suites. Caldera views come at an especially good value in these small white cave-rooms with vaulted ceilings and the large cave suites, all nicely decorated with warm touches of color and sleek marble fixtures and sharing a common terrace overlooking the caldera. **Pros:** very attractive; small and friendly; perfect for guests who want a caldera view but aren't high rollers. **Cons:** those stairs; rooms are close together. $ *Rooms from: €185* ⊠ *Caldera walkway* ☎ *22860/24112* ⊕ *www.aromasuites.com* ⤳ *3 rooms, 3 suites, 2 apartments* ◉◉⦿ *No meals.*

$$$

HOTEL

Hotel Aressana. Though there's no view of the caldera, a slant of sea view is effulgently wonderful—add in the large freshwater pool, the spacious lobby with Italian design and wood-panel bar, excellent service, and location in central Fira, and the sum total makes these large, bright rooms a very popular option. **Pros:** drive to the door and avoid steps; stylish design in public areas; very comfortable and sparkling. **Cons:** no caldera view; few island touches; rather bland room decor. $ *Rooms from: €275* ⊠ *South end of cliff-side walkway* ☎ *22860/23900* ⊕ *www.aressana.gr* ⤳ *42 rooms, 8 suites* ⊘ *Closed Nov.–Mar.* ◉◉⦿ *Breakfast.*

$$

B&B/INN

Hotel Villa Renos. Huge terraces, shady porticos, and a small but dramatic cliff-hanging pool all take advantage of spectacular caldera views, while the large, elegantly furnished rooms are pleasant retreats from the madness of the crowded center of Fira, just a few steps away.

Pros: nice sense of quiet despite the central location; outstanding hospitality. **Cons:** steps, but fewer than there are at many other properties; small pool. $ *Rooms from: €220* ✉ *Off caldera walkway, near central square* ☎ *22860/22848* ⊕ *www.villarenos.com* ⇗ *9 rooms* ☉ *Closed Nov.–Mar.* ⍩ *Breakfast.*

$ ⛺ **Keti Hotel.** A stay in these traditional cave rooms puts you right in the center of Fira, but well below the bustle—a climb down a staircase leads to a quiet, intimate cliff-side aerie where the simple but charming vaulted rooms open to a welcoming veranda clinging to the cliff face above the Old Port. **Pros:** intimate little enclave with fantastic views; loaded with traditional charm; great rates for caldera view. **Cons:** lots of steps; no pool or other luxe amenities. $ *Rooms from: €110* ✉ *Off caldera walkway below central square* ☎ *22860/22324* ⊕ *www.hotelketi. gr* ⇗ *9 rooms* ⍩ *Breakfast.*

B&B/INN

$ ⛺ **Loizos Stylish Residences.** These extremely stylish accommodations lack a caldera view but they compensate with flair and lots of basic comforts. **Pros:** excellent value; excellently run; top neighborhood in Fira; accessible by car. **Cons:** no caldera view; comfortable but not for luxe-lovers. $ *Rooms from: €98* ✉ *On cobbled road up from main traffic street, near town hall* ☎ *22860/24046* ⊕ *www.loizos.gr* ⇗ *23 rooms* ☉ *Closed Nov.–Mar.* ⍩ *Breakfast.*

HOTEL

$$$ ⛺ **Panorama Boutique Hotel.** These very pleasant rooms combine traditional design with contemporary touches in the center of Fira, proving that it's possible to enjoy a caldera view without breaking the bank—and without dealing with steps. **Pros:** right on the caldera walkway in the center of town; convenient for taxis and buses; elevator makes access easy; nice design. **Cons:** some rooms are quite small; steps to the pool; busy surroundings. $ *Rooms from: €250* ✉ *On caldera, near central square* ☎ *22860/21760* ⊕ *www.panoramahotel.com.gr* ⇗ *30 rooms and suites* ☉ *Closed Dec.–Feb.* ⍩ *Breakfast.*

HOTEL

$ ⛺ **Pelican Hotel.** The neighborhood isn't pretty, but these rooms just down from the busy main (Theotokopoulou) square on Danezi street are decent and the cost can't be beat. **Pros:** very efficient and inexpensive; good restaurant next door. **Cons:** in a busy neighborhood away from the caldera; breakfast extra but served all day long. $ *Rooms from: €70* ✉ *On cobbled road up from main traffic street, near town hall* ☎ *22860/23113* ⊕ *www.pelicanhotel.gr* ⇗ *18 rooms* ⍩ *No meals.*

HOTEL

NIGHTLIFE AND PERFORMING ARTS

DANCING

Casablanca Soul. Santorini's "second" club, after the more popular Koo, offers a live music program on weekends and music played by DJs other nights, always accompanied by excellent cocktails. ✉ *Near the central square* ☎ *22860/27188* ⊕ *www.casablancasoul.com.*

Koo Club. For Fira, this is Disco Central and the township's most popular outdoor club by far. ✉ *North end of cliff-side walkway* ☎ *22860/22025* ⊕ *www.kooclub.gr.*

FESTIVALS

Santorini Music Festival. Thank pianist Athena Capodistria for September's Santorini Music Festival, which always includes internationally known musicians. ⊠ *Nomikos Conference Center, Firostefani* ☎ *22860/23166* ⊕ *www.santorinimusicfestival.com.*

MUSIC

Franco's Bar. Boasting a caldera view, the popular lounge with a terrace plays classical music and serves Champagne cocktails. ⊠ *Below cliff-side walkway* ☎ *22860/24428* ⊕ *www.francos.gr.*

SHOPPING

Despite the proliferation of shops displaying their wares on the street that can make Fira seem like a souk, you probably will not be too tempted by the goods on offers. T-shirts and cheap trinkets are, sadly, the norm, and shops selling fine jewelry and crafts for which the island was known in the early days of tourism are rare these days. With a little searching, however, you will come upon some treasures.

GALLERIES

Mati. There's a Greek exuberance to the work of Yorgos Kypris, accentuated by a bright, airy perch high above the caldera. In his sculptural creations in glass, clay, and other natural materials, seabirds flock and fish swirl in schools; some designs are also available as jewelry and bowls. ⊠ *Cathedral Sq.* ☎ *22860/23814* ⊕ *matiartgallery.com.*

Nikola's Art Gallery. Objets d'art are made from highly polished semi-precious stones and glow with color and form. Pantelis and Nikola Kaloteraki can also create jewelry in the stone of your choice. Vases, sculptures, and many other distinctive pieces also fill the shop, which has been a presence in Santorini for more than a quarter of a century. ⊠ *Town center* ☎ *22860/22283* ⊕ *www.nikolas-santorini.com.*

Phenomenon. Christoforos Asimis studied painting at Athens University and has had many exhibitions there and abroad. The nearby cathedral's murals are his. His paintings specialize in the light and landscape of his home island. His wife, Eleni Kollaitou, who also studied in Athens, creates some of Santorini's most elegant jewelry, bronze sculptures, and ceramics. ⊠ *Ypapantis walkway* ☎ *22860/23041* ⊕ *www.ak-galleries.com.*

JEWELRY

Fodor's Choice ★   **Bead Shop.** Marina Tsiagkouri's shop has expanded with worry beads and some ready-made trinkets, but beads are still the main reason to go. Marina's unique beads are made from Santorini's volcanic rock, wood, and other natural materials. ⊠ *Opposite entrance to Museum of Prehistoric Thera* ☎ *22860/25176.*

Kostas Antoniou Jewelry. Many of Kostas's exquisite gold necklaces and bracelets take their inspiration from the art of ancient Thera and Crete. The shop also sells excellent wines from the family's Antoniou vineyards just south of Fira around Megalochori. ⊠ *In Spiliotica shopping area, near Archaeological Museum* ☎ *22860/22633* ⊕ *antoniousantorini.com.*

Sophia's Art Jewelry. Easily above the standard glitter of Santorini, Sophia's sells gold jewelry from several Greek workshops. Letting her work speak for itself, Sophia Koutsogiannopoulou has no website or e-mail, nor does she stand at the doorway of her quiet shop (a block in from the cable-car) soliciting customers. ✉ *Near cable car* ☎ *22860/23587.*

FIROSTEFANI ΦΗΡΟΣΤΕΦΑΝΙ

1 km (½ mile) northwest of Fira.

Firostefani used to be a separate village, but now it comprises the quieter, more pleasant northern end of Fira. The 10-minute walk between central Fira and Firostefani, along the caldera, is one of Santorini's highlights. From Firostefani's single white cliff-side street, walkways descend to traditional vaulted cave houses, which are fast becoming pensions. Though close to the action, Firostefani feels calm and quiet.

WHERE TO EAT

$ GREEK 🍴 **Aktaion.** In his tiny taverna, Vangelis Roussos uses mostly recipes his family used when the place opened almost a hundred years ago. Outdoor tables overlook the caldera; inside, the paintings on the walls are Vangelis's own. Salad Santorini, his mother's recipe, has raw cod flakes, caper leaves, and seasonal ingredients. The moussaka, made with white eggplant, is incomparable. [$] *Average main: €14* ✉ *Main square* ☎ *22860/22336* 🌐 *www.aktaionsantorini.com.*

WHERE TO STAY

$$ RESORT 🏨 **Agali Houses.** Firostefani is a ten-minute walk north from the center of Fira but a world apart; a quiet enclave with handsomely furnished, arch-roofed houses dropping down the cliff side on a series of dramatic terraces. **Pros:** very attractive; lots of white curves and sumptuous sea views; large, well-appointed accommodations; privacy. **Cons:** many steps to reach the entrance and more once you're on the property. [$] *Rooms from: €210* ✉ *Off the main street* ☎ *22860/22811* 🌐 *www.agalihouses.gr* 🛏 *30 rooms and suites* 🕒 *Closed Nov.–mid-Apr.* 🍽 *Breakfast.*

$ B&B/INN 🏨 **Reverie Traditional Apartments.** Only a suite and the roof garden have caldera views, but everything about the whitewashed and tiled surroundings in this former family home make a charming and relaxing island getaway. **Pros:** friendly and inexpensive; nice neighborhood near the caldera; small but pleasant pool; no steps to reach. **Cons:** most units do not have sea views; breakfast is extra. [$] *Rooms from: €88* ✉ *Between Firostefani walkway and main traffic road* ☎ *22860/23322* 🌐 *www.reverie.gr* 🛏 *4 rooms, 11 studios, 2 suites* 🕒 *Closed Nov.–Mar.* 🍽 *No meals.*

$$$$ B&B/INN Fodor's Choice ★ 🏨 **Tsitouras Collection, Firostefani on Santorini.** *Architectural Digest*–worthy decor and earthy Cycladic charm blend together from what is truly Santorinian splendor; think sparkling white cubes with volcanic stone trimmings surrounding an 18th-century mansion. **Pros:** beautiful design; caldera views; lots of privacy. **Cons:** over-designed and museum-like to some tastes. [$] *Rooms from: €475* ✉ *Firostefani cliff face, next to St. Mark's* ☎ *22860/23747* 🌐 *www.tsitouras.com* 🛏 *5 suites* 🕒 *Closed Nov.–Mar.* 🍽 *Breakfast.*

IMEROVIGLI ΗΜΕΡΟΒΙΓΛΙ

3 km (2 miles) northwest of Fira, 2 km (1 miles) northwest of Firostefani.

Set on the highest point of the caldera's rim, Imerovigli (the name means "watchtower") is quiet, traditional, and less expensive than other places on the caldera. The 25-minute walk from Fira, with incredible views, should be on everyone's itinerary. The lodgments, some of them traditional cave houses, are mostly down stairways from the cliff-side walkway. The big rock backing the village was once crowned by Skaros Castle, whence Venetian overlords reigned after 1207. It collapsed in an earthquake, leaving only the rock. A trail descending from the church of Ayios Georgios crosses the isthmus and encircles Skaros; it's only 10 minutes to the castle top. After 1 km (½ mile) it reaches the small chapel of Theoskepasti with a memorable caldera view.

WHERE TO EAT

$$ GREEK 🍴 **Blue Note.** You can't go wrong with the location: a deck extended over the cliff, a panoramic caldera view, and a sunset. For a starter try Gruyère flambé. For a main dish, lamb *klephtiko* (stewed in wine and herbs in a ceramic dish) is a good choice, as is shrimp Blue Note (a secret recipe). [$] *Average main: €17* ✉ *On cliff-side walkway, behind church of Panaghia Maltesa, near parking and bus stop, Spiliotica Apartments* ☎ *22860/23771* 🌐 *www.spiliotica.com* 🕒 *Closed Nov.–Mar.*

WHERE TO STAY

$$$ B&B/INN Fodor's Choice ★ 🏨 **Aenaon Villas.** Set on one of the island's highest points, these seven sumptuous villas offer a 21st-century interpretation of the classic Greek-island hideaway, built in a traditional style with careful respect for Cycladic architecture, with smooth white walls standing out brilliantly against the surrounding dark volcanic stone and the deep blues of the Aegean sea. **Pros:** lovely private setting; owners make you feel like family. **Cons:** no restaurant on-site. [$] *Rooms from: €240* ☎ *22860/27014* 🌐 *www.aenaonvillas.gr* 🛏 *7 villas* 🍽 *Breakfast.*

$ B&B/INN 🏨 **Annio Furnished Flats.** Accommodations in this cliff-side lodgment are attractive and simple, with local furnishings both new and old. **Pros:** beautiful caldera view at a very good price. **Cons:** fairly basic; lots of stairs; no pool. [$] *Rooms from: €115* ☎ *22860/24714* 🌐 *www.annioflats.gr* 🛏 *11 rooms* 🕒 *Closed Nov.–Apr.* 🍽 *Breakfast.*

$$$$ RESORT Fodor's Choice ★ 🏨 **Astra Apartments.** Little cliff-side Imerovigli is a world apart from busy, nearby Fira, and this intimate enclave is an especially magical place to stay, with terraced, vaulted-ceilinged cave houses that are sophisticated and full of character. **Pros:** beautiful views and decor; personalized service. **Cons:** lots of steps, though porters are on hand to tote bags. [$] *Rooms from: €310* ✉ *Below caldera walkway* ☎ *22860/23641* 🌐 *www.astrasuites.com* 🛏 *27 rooms and suites* 🕒 *Closed Nov.–Mar.* 🍽 *Breakfast.*

$$ B&B/INN 🏨 **Heliades Apartments.** Four split-level cave houses, each white with blue-green accents, are on top of one of the higher cliff ridges, so the verandas all have really breathtaking (literally) caldera views. **Pros:** terraces with caldera views; few steps; kitchens included. **Cons:** on the simple side. [$] *Rooms from: €160* ✉ *On cliff-side walkway, behind church of Panaghia Maltesa, near parking and bus stop* ☎ *22860/24102* 🌐 *www.heliades-apts.gr* 🛏 *4 houses* 🕒 *Closed Nov.–Mar.* 🍽 *Breakfast.*

$$ Spiliotica Apartments and Suites. These individually themed cave houses
B&B/INN cascade steeply down the cliff side attracting everyone from families to celebrities. **Pros:** caldera view; nice array of conveniences; small but refreshing pool; discount at hotel's Blue Note restaurant. **Cons:** lots of steep steps. ⓢ *Rooms from: €180* ⊠ *On cliff-side walkway, behind church of Panaghia Maltesa, near parking and bus stop* ☎ *22860/22637* ⊕ *www.spiliotica.com* ↝ *21 houses* ☉ *Closed Nov.–Mar.* ⦿ *Breakfast.*

SPORTS AND THE OUTDOORS

SAILING

Santorini Sailing Center. This handy outfitter arranges charters and runs weekly two- to three-day sailing trips around the Cyclades for groups of up to 10. ☎ *22860/23891* ⊕ *www.sailingsantorini.com.*

IA OIA

14 km (8½ miles) northwest of Fira.

Fodor'sChoice At the tip of the northern horn of the island sits Ia (or Oia), Santorini's
★ second-largest town and the Aegean's most-photographed village. Ia is more tasteful than Fira (for one thing, no establishment here is allowed to play music that can be heard on the street), and the town's cubical white houses (some vaulted against earthquakes) stand out against the green-, brown-, and rust-color layers of rock, earth, and solid volcanic ash that rise from the sea. Every summer evening, travelers from all over the world congregate at the caldera's rim—sitting on whitewashed fences, staircases, beneath the town's windmill, on the old Kastro—each looking out to sea in anticipation of the performance: the Ia sunset. The three-hour rim-edge walk from Ia to Fira at this hour is unforgettable.

In the middle of the quiet caldera, the volcano smolders away eerily, adding an air of suspense to an already awe-inspiring scene. The 1956 earthquake (7.8 on the Richter scale) left 48 people dead (thankfully, most residents were working outdoors at the time), hundreds injured, and 2,000 houses toppled. Santorini's west side—especially Ia, until then the largest town—was hard hit, and many residents decided to emigrate to Athens, Australia, and America. Although Fira, also damaged, rebuilt rapidly, Ia proceeded slowly, sticking to the traditional architectural style. In 1900, Ia had nearly 9,000 inhabitants, mostly mariners who owned 164 seafaring vessels and seven shipyards. Now there are about 500 permanent residents, and more than 100 boats. Many of these mariners use the endless flight of stairs to descend down to the water and the small port of Armeni or take the road or steps to Ammoudi, where the pebble beach is home to some of the island's nicest fish tavernas and the port of embarkation for many excursion boats.

Ia is set up like the other three towns—Fira, Firostefani, and Imerovigli—that adorn the caldera's sinuous rim. There is a car road, which is new, and a cliff-side walkway (Nikolaos Nomikou), which is old. Shops and restaurants are all on the walkway, and hotel entrances mostly descend from it—something to check carefully if you cannot negotiate stairs easily. Short streets leading from the car road to the walkway have cheaper eateries and shops. There is a parking lot at either end,

Ia is world-famous for its magnificent sunsets. One evening there was immortalized by Jennifer Duc, Fodors. com member, in this lovely photo.

and the northern one marks the end of the road and the rim. Nothing is very far from anything else.

The main walkway of Ia can be thought of as a straight river, with a delta at the northern end, where the better shops and restaurants are. Many luxurious cave-house hotels are at the southern end, and a stroll by them is part of the extended evening promenade. Although Ia is not as crowded as Fira, where the tour boats deposit their thousands of hasty shoppers, relentless publicity about the town's beauty and tastefulness, accurate enough, are making the narrow lanes impassable in August. The sunset in Ia may not really be much more spectacular than in Fira, and certainly not better than in higher Imerovigli, but there is something tribally satisfying at the sight of so many people gathering in one spot to celebrate pure beauty. Happily, the night scene isn't as frantic as Fira's—most shop owners are content to sit out front and don't cotton to the few revelers' bars in operation. In winter, Ia feels pretty uninhabited.

EXPLORING

Fodor's Choice ★ **Naval Maritime Museum of Thera.** In an old neoclassical mansion, once destroyed in the big earthquake, the museum has an enticing collection. Pieces include ships' figureheads, seamen's chests, maritime equipment, and models which reveal the extensive nautical history of the island, Santorini's main trade until tourism took over. ⊠ *Town center* ☎ *22860/71156* ✉ *€4* ◷ *Wed.–Mon. 8:30–3.*

BEACH

Baxedes. The closest sand beach to Ia is handy when you don't feel like making a trip to more famous beaches on the south end of the island. It's not that there's anything second-rate about this beautiful spot: the cliff-backed strip of sand is rarely crowded; the sea floor is sandy, too, providing nice wading for kids and a pleasant experience when splashing around in the surf; and the cliffs provide welcome shade. A downside is the summertime meltemi winds, which churn up the surf and sand. Islanders used to grow fruits and vegetables down here, and the name comes from the Turkish word for garden, "baxes." **Amenities:** food and drink; parking (free). **Best for:** swimming; surfing (at times). ✉ *On coast below town* ✥ *Near Paradissos, about 2 km (1 mile) north of Ia.*

WHERE TO EAT

$$ INTERNATIONAL 🍴 **Kandouni.** An enticing front garden, candlelit at night, and memento-filled salons of a centuries-old sea captan's home in the back lanes of Ia are a charming setting for a menu that includes some island favorites as well as some international ones, which may reflect the time the Korkiantis family spent in Canada. Whatever the origin, the sea bass in a salt crust and pasta with salmon and caviar are the delicious centerpieces of a meal here, accompanied by a good selection of local wines. [$] *Average main: €16* ✉ *In back streets near bus station* ☎ *22860/71616* 🌐 *www.kandouni.com.*

$$ GREEK 🍴 **Kastro.** This is a popular perch from which to witness a famous Ia sunset, and at that magical hour the terrace is always filled. Happily, the food makes a fitting accompaniment. A good starter is olives stuffed with cream cheese dipped in beer dough and fried, served on arugula with a balsamic sauce. For a main dish try mussels with oil-pepper sauce. Lunch here is also popular. [$] *Average main: €20* ✉ *Near Venetian castle* ☎ *22860/71045* 🌐 *www.kastro-ia.gr* ✍ *Reservations essential.*

$$ GREEK Fodor's Choice ★ 🍴 **Red Bicycle.** This sophisticated café and restaurant is located at the north end of Ia's main walkway, just down the steps; its big terrace offers one of the town's finest caldera views. Owner Chara Kourti warmly touts her Santorini pureéd fava with onion chutney and *kafaifi* crust, and also her baked feta in a nacho crust with orange preserves and lemon balm. Among the fish choices are octopus with crabmeat, fresh coriander, potatoes, and truffle foam, and sea bass cooked in sea salt; a delicious slow-roasted lamb is served with fresh island greens. Desserts are a specialty; try mastic mousse with carmelized pistachios and rose-petal preserves. This popular spot is open from lunch until late. [$] *Average main: €25* ✉ *Off main walkway* ☎ *22860/71918* ⏲ *Closed Nov.–Mar.*

$ GREEK Fodor's Choice ★ 🍴 **Roka.** Regulars are more than willing to forgo a caldera view for a meal in these simple rooms and two terraces, where the menu focuses on old-fashioned favorites. The best way to dine here is to order several small plates for the table to share—fried eggplant with tomato; apple and feta pie; fava purée (the best on the island, according to many locals); fresh sardines baked in lemon; and even simple tzatziki, especialy good here because of the homegrown garlic and local yogurt. Whatever you order, wash it down with Assyrtiko, the island's dry white wine. [$] *Average main: €12* ✉ *In back streets near bus station* ☎ *22860/71896* 🌐 *www.roka.gr.*

$$ SEAFOOD Fodor's Choice ★ 🍴 **Sunset Taverna.** The first of the Ammoudi fish houses opened in the 1980s and is still a standout among the several excellent tavernas that line the quay in this tiny fishing port just below Ia—you can walk down and take a cab back to town. Lapping waves, bobbing fishing boats,

and tables so close to the water's edge that a clumsy move might add a swim to the evening's entertainment, testify to the freshness of the fish, which is simply grilled. Your choice is best served with a salad brimming with local produce, as are the tomato fritters, fava dip, and eggplant stuffed with feta. Most diners arrive in time to witness the sunset, but the meal steals the show. [$] *Average main: €16* ✉ *Waterfront, Ammoudi* ☎ *22860/71614* 🌐 *www.sunset-ammoudi.gr* ✍ *Reservations essential.*

WHERE TO STAY

$$$$ RESORT 🏨 **Canaves Hotel and Suites.** Two adjacent properties offer some of Santorini's most romantic accommodations, a collection of beautifully furnished rooms and suites, all done in crisp whites and handsome fabrics, meticulously maintained and enjoying stunning caldera views. **Pros:** extremely attractive; good dining poolside and in gourmet restaurant; elevator in suites section eliminates steps; sailing trips available. **Cons:** in the busy center of Ia; steps in hotel section; pricey. [$] *Rooms from: €600* ✉ *On caldera, center of town* ☎ *22860/71453* 🌐 *www.canaves.com* 🛏 *39 rooms and suites* ⏲ *Closed Nov.–Mar.* 🍴 *Breakfast.*

$$$ B&B/INN Fodor's Choice ★ 🏨 **Esperas Hotel.** At this welcoming collection of sparkling white, arch-roofed cave houses that spill down the side of the caldera, homey suites and studios all have cozy sitting areas, well-equipped bathrooms and kitchenettes, and a private, view-saturated terrace overlooking dark cliffs and turquoise seas. **Pros:** wonderful caldera location; excellent, attentive service; extremely appealing decor. **Cons:** lots of steps to reach the hotel and within the premises, though staff meets guests in parking area above to cart bags. [$] *Rooms from: €270* ☎ *22860/71501* 🌐 *esperas-santorini.com* 🛏 *20 studios and suites* ⏲ *Closed late Oct.–Apr.* 🍴 *Breakfast.*

$$$$ RESORT 🏨 **Ikies Traditional Houses.** A perch at the far eastern end of Ia provides wonderful views of the village as well as the caldera, which can be enjoyed from the private terraces of 11 handsomely furnished cave houses that were once used as workshops to repair and store fishing nets. **Pros:** nice sense of privacy in a small, off-the-beaten-track enclave; very attractive; low-key, attentive service. **Cons:** terraces are not entirely private; the inevitable steps. [$] *Rooms from: €290* ✉ *Off eastern end of caldera path* ☎ *22860/71311* 🌐 *www.ikies.com* 🛏 *11 suites* ⏲ *Closed Nov.–Mar.* 🍴 *Breakfast.*

$$$$ RESORT 🏨 **Katikies.** Sumptuously appointed, this immaculate white cliff-side complex layered on terraces offers ultimate luxury and sleek modern design, including Andy Warhol wall prints, stunning fabrics, and handsome furniture—chic as the surroundings are, the barrel-vaulted ceilings and other architectural details also lend a traditional air to the place. **Pros:** cliff-side infinity pool; all luxuries. **Cons:** many stairs; rather impersonal; located on crowded part of caldera. [$] *Rooms from: €940* ✉ *Ia cliff face, edge of main town* ☎ *22860/71401* 🌐 *www.katikies.com* 🛏 *5 rooms, 22 suites* ⏲ *Closed Nov.–Mar.* 🍴 *Breakfast.*

$$$$ RESORT 🏨 **Perivolas.** A cliff-hanging, much-photographed infinity pool that makes you feel you could easily swim off the edge into the caldera's blue bay 1,000 feet below is but one of the highlights at a luxury getaway that even the locals respect (big compliment). **Pros:** the original infinity

pool; attentive but relaxed service; beautiful and tranquil surroundings. **Cons:** lots of steps; a walk to town. [$] *Rooms from: €650* ✉ *Nomikou, Ia cliff face, east of center* ☎ *22860/71308* 🌐 *www.perivolas.gr* 🛏 *20 houses* 🕒 *Closed Nov.–Mar.* 🍴 *Breakfast.*

NIGHTLIFE

There are the usual cafés, bars, and pastry shops along the main street but a peaceful note is struck by the fact that establishments are forbidden to play loud music.

Skiza. A balcony overlooking the caldera is a prime spot in Ia for drinks and light snacks, and the pastries are considered the best on the island. ✉ *On caldera, near church* ☎ *22860/71569.*

SHOPPING

Ia mostly abjures the trinket madness of Fira, and instead offers a variety of handcrafted items. Since the shops are not so dependent on cruise ships, a certain sophistication reigns in the quiet streets. Art galleries, "objets" shops, crafts shops, and icon stores set the tone.

ANTIQUES AND COLLECTIBLES

Dimitris Koliousis Workshop. Steps from the main street lead down to arched cave rooms, a stark setting for exuberantly rich and colorful pieces on wood that replicate Byzantine and Russian icons. ✉ *Main street* ☎ *22860/71829.*

Loulaki. Manolis and Chara Kourtis sell antiques, ceramics, jewelry, and art in a delightful shop below their Red Bicycle restaurant; exploring their collection is a pleasure. Alexandra Solomos's painted plates are a favorite. ✉ *Main shopping street* ☎ *22860/71856.*

BOOKS

Fodor's Choice ★ **Atlantis Books.** A tiny English-language bookshop that would be at home in New York's Greenwich Village or London's Bloomsbury is an unexpected but wonderful treat in Ia. Only good literature makes it onto the shelves, and writers stop by to chat and give readings. ✉ *North end of main shopping street* ☎ *22860/72346* 🌐 *www.atlantisbooks.org.*

SPORTS AND THE OUTDOORS

SAILING

Sunset Oia. Five-hour morning and afternoon sailings from Ammoudi include stops at the hot springs around the volcano and two beaches for swimming, with stunning caldera-cliff views along the way; afternoon cruises coincide with sunset. Meals and drinks are served on board, and relatively small groups (especially in the company's "semi-private" offerings) ensure a genuinely memorable experience. ✉ *Ammoudi* ☎ *22860/72200* 🌐 *www.sailing-santorini.com.*

PYRGOS ΠΥΡΓΟΣ

5½ km (3½ miles) south of Fira.

Fodor's Choice ★ Though today Pyrgos has only 500 inhabitants, until the early 1800s it was the capital of the island. Medieval houses are stacked on top of one another and back-to-back for protection against pirates. Your reward for a climb up the picturesque streets ends at the ruined Venetian castle, where views extend across the vineyard-studded landscape to both coasts. In Pyrgos you are really in old Santorini—hardly anything has changed.

Monastery of Profitis Ilias. Standing on the highest point on Santorini, which spans to 1,856 feet at the summit, Santorini's largest monastery offers a Cineramic vista: from here you can see the surrounding islands and, on a clear day, the mountains of Crete, more than 100 km (66 miles) away. You may also be able to spot ancient Thira on the peak below Profitis Ilias. Unfortunately, radio towers and a NATO radar installation provide an ugly backdrop for the monastery's wonderful bell tower.

Founded in 1711 by two monks from Pyrgos, Profitis Ilias is cherished by islanders because here, in a secret school, the Greek language and culture were taught during the dark centuries of the Turkish occupation. A **museum** in the monastery contains a model of the secret school in a monk's cell, another model of a traditional carpentry and blacksmith shop, and a display of ecclesiastical items. ✉ *At highest point on Santorini* 🎫 *Free* ⏲ *No visiting hrs; caretaker is sometimes around.*

WHERE TO EAT

$ GREEK 🍴 **Franco's Cafe.** The hangout that is such a caldera-side hit in Fira also has a welcoming presence in Pyrgos, where cocktails and light snacks are served on breezy terraces overlooking the village, vineyards, and the sea. This spot is especially popular at sunset, but does a brisk business throughout the day, when the bar brews the island's best coffee well into the evening. [$] *Average main: €10* ✉ *Top of village near the fortress* ☎ *22860/33957.*

$ GREEK 🍴 **Metaxy Mas.** It seems that just about everyone in Santorini looks forward to a meal at this village taverna. Even though the name means "between us," the secret is out and the place is so popular that Greek customers will eat lunch at 5 pm or linger past midnight just to get a table in the colorful, stone-wall dining room or on one of the terraces. The key to success appears to be to keep it simple, and the kitchen sticks to traditional home-style cooking from Santorini and Crete—huge salads are made from garden-fresh vegetables, local white eggplants are oven roasted to perfection, and veal is sautéed with the local Vin Santo. You can only reach this rural outpost by car or taxi, though Fira is just a ten-minute ride away. [$] *Average main: €10* ✉ *Village center, just outside Pyrgos, Exo Gonia* ☎ *22860/31323* 🌐 *www.santorini-mataximas.gr.*

$$$$ GREEK Fodor's Choice ★ 🍴 **Selene.** Always a great restaurant, Selene is now probably the best in the Cyclades, with a beautiful location, elegant setting and service, and a deep love of island cuisine with local ingredients. The terrace of the old aristocratic house has two sea-views—south and caldera sunset—and overlooks vineyards spreading to the Aegean. Excellent starters include squid with smoked fava and cuttlefish ink flakes, or smoked quail *kouskousela* on crispy potatoes. Among the creative entreés are Aegean codfish with garlic-scented Jerusalem artichoke velouté and the lamb with vine shoots and lemon-scented potato croquette foam. Desserts are not neglected: the chocolate *mandolato* and the baklava with local pistachios are both supreme. The Greek wine list is extensive. On Selene's lower level there is a café-restaurant where you can sample Selene's dishes or even have a sandwich. Next to it is Selene's agricultural museum in

an old winery. Georgia Tsara, the maîtresse d', oversees all with grace, efficiency, and knowledge. In summer, owner George Hatziyianakis and his chefs give daylong cooking classes (be sure to check the website for details). $ *Average main: €35* ✉ *Village center* ☎ *22860/22249* ⊕ *www. selene.gr* ♨ *Reservations essential* ⊘ *Closed Nov.–Mar.*

WHERE TO STAY

$$$$

HOTEL

🏨 **Zannos Melathron.** A delightful walled garden is the setting for this magical hideaway set high above the island's medieval capital, where comfortable suites in two Cycladic-style manor houses sport stucco and stone walls, vaulted ceilings, antique furnishings, and flowery terraces that look out across the island to the sea. **Pros:** beautiful setting and surroundings; elegant yet comfortable and welcoming; surrounded by winding lanes of Pyrgos. **Cons:** in center of island away from sea; reached by steps (but porters carry bags, and donkeys are available for ride to and from hotel). $ *Rooms from: €350* ✉ *Village center* ☎ *22860/28220* ⊕ *www.zannos.gr* ⇥ *13 suites* ⊘ *Closed Nov.–Easter* ¶⊘ *Breakfast.*

MEGALOCHORI ΜΕΓΑΛΟΧΩΡΙ

4 km (2½ miles) east of Pyrgos, 9 km (5½ miles) southwest of Fira.

Megalochori is a picturesque, half-abandoned town. Many of the village's buildings were actually *canavas,* winemaking facilities. The tiny main square is still lively in the evening.

EXPLORING

Boutari Winery. The island's first winery open to the public puts on a big show, with a bright, view-filled tasting room surrounded by vineyards and the chance to see stainless steel tanks, pneumatic presses, oak barrels, and temperature control vats. A distinctly Santorini experience is a taste of Kallisti, a version of the ssyrtiko variety; the name, meaning "most beautiful," was given to the island in ancient times. ☎ *22860/81606* ⊕ *www. boutari.gr* ☕ *Tasting €7* ⊘ *Weekdays 10–6, Sat. 11–6.*

Gavalas Winery. This winery has been exporting its distinguished produce since the days when mules carted wine-filled goatskins to the port in Fira. Tastings in the atmospheric old storage and pressing rooms include Voudomato, a dry rosé, and Nykteri, a sophisticated white from the island's indigenous Assyrtiko grapes—the name means "working the night away," because the grapes have traditionally been harvested at night to avoid damage from the heat. ☎ *22860/82552* ⊕ *www. gavalaswines.gr* ☕ *Tasting €7* ⊘ *May–Oct., daily 10–7.*

WHERE TO STAY

$$$$

RESORT

🏨 **Vedema.** This distant and deluxe black-lava outpost is a world unto itself; 42 villas have been built around a beautiful 15th-century winery, almost like a gated community in Florida, all done in a minimalism-meets-Mediterranean leitmotif. **Pros:** Vedema is not cheap, but you'll get what you're paying for all the room, food, and service luxuries. **Cons:** isolated from island life, although a handy shuttle service ferries you to other parts of the island. $ *Rooms from: €425* ☎ *22860/81796* ⊕ *www.vedema.gr* ⇥ *35 rooms, 7 suites* ⊘ *Closed Nov.–Mar.* ¶⊘ *Breakfast.*

AKROTIRI ΑΚΡΩΤΗΡΙ

7 km (4½ miles) west of Pyrgos, 13 km (8 miles) south of Fira.

This village is most famous for its ancient ruins, but the little collection of houses surrounded by gardens and fields is a pleasant place in its own right, a pretty slice of rural Santorini. A stay here removes you from the hustle and bustle along the caldera and puts you within easy reach of sights, wineries, and the island's best beaches.

Fodor'sChoice ★ **Ancient Akrotiri.** If Santorini is known as the "Greek Pompeii" and is claimant to the title of the lost Atlantis, it is because of the archaeological site of ancient Akrotiri, near the tip of the southern horn of the island. The site re-opened in April 2012 after undergoing lengthy structural repairs of the protective roof spanning the entire enclosed site, which is in fact a whole ancient city buried under the volcanic ashes and much of it still waiting to be unearthed—almost intact.

In the 1860s, in the course of quarrying volcanic ash for use in the Suez Canal, workmen discovered the remains of an ancient town. The town was frozen in time by ash from an eruption 3,600 years ago, long before Pompeii's disaster. In 1967 Spyridon Marinatos of the University of Athens began excavations, which occasionally continue. It is thought that the 40 buildings that have been uncovered are only one-third of the huge site and that excavating the rest will probably take a century.

Marinatos's team discovered many well-preserved frescoes depicting aspects of Akrotiri life, some now displayed in the National Archaeological Museum in Athens; Santorini wants them back to join the small selection that are on view in the Museum of Prehistoric Thera in Fira. Meanwhile, postcard-size pictures of them are posted outside the houses where they were found. The antelopes, monkeys, and wildcats they portray suggest trade with Egypt.

Akrotiri was settled as early as 3000 BC, possibly as an outpost of Minoan Crete, and reached its peak after 2000 BC, when it developed trade and agriculture and settled the present town. The inhabitants cultivated olive trees and grain, and their advanced architecture—three-story frescoed houses faced with masonry (some with balconies) and public buildings of sophisticated construction—is evidence of an elaborate lifestyle. Remains of the inhabitants have never been found, possibly because they might have had advance warning of the eruptions and fled in boats—beds have been found outside the houses, suggesting the island was shaken with earthquakes that made it unwise to sleep indoors. ⊠ *South of modern Akrotiri, near tip of southern horn* ☎ *22860/81939* ⊕ *www.culture.gr* ⌸ *€5* ⊙ *Tues.–Sun. 8–8.*

WHERE TO EAT

$$
SEAFOOD
✕ **The Dolphins.** When the surf is rough, much of the outdoor dining room is surrounded by crashing waves, and on calm nights the moon playing off the water makes this quiet outpost on the southern end of the island one of the most romantic spots around. By day it's not unusual to see fresh fish being hauled into the kitchen fresh from the docks. Lobster spaghetti, a quick meal fishermen used to prepare in their boats, is the speciality, and the fresh catch kept on ice is nicely grilled

and served with generous salads. A meal is good enough, and the prices so reasonable, that you can almost forgive the sometimes sloppy service. $ *Average main: €17* ⊠ *On the beach* ☎ *22860/81151.*

WHERE TO STAY

$ ⌂ **Aura Marina Apartments.** A young
RESORT Italian architect came up with the design for this cluster of nine houses, keeping things simple with an emphasis on big terraces, private plunge pools, and nice, soothing interior spaces, some flowing over two or three levels. **Pros:** very attractive; quiet surroundings near beaches and sights on southern end of island; very helpful manager and staff. **Cons:** few hotel services; a bit of a distance from Fira (can be a plus); air-conditioning is extra. $ *Rooms from: €100* ⊠ *Off road to lighthouse* ☎ *22860/83101* ⊕ *www.aura-marina.com* ⇥ *9 apartments* ⊗ *Closed Nov.–Mar.* ⏛ *No meals.*

$ ⌂ **Hotel Goulielmos.** These very simple yet comfortable rooms, many
HOTEL with terraces, are among the island's unsung treasures, perched on the southern side of the caldera just outside Akrotiri, enjoying spectacular views up the rim to Fira and Ia. **Pros:** great views at bargain prices; nice grounds and sense of quiet. **Cons:** rooms need a bit of maintenance; few hotel amenities and services. $ *Rooms from: €80* ⊠ *On caldera off road into town* ⊕ *www.hotel-goulielmos.gr* ⇥ *17 rooms* ⊗ *Closed Nov.–Mar.* ⏛ *Breakfast.*

$ ⌂ **Best Western Paradise Hotel.** A cluster of houses surrounding a huge
HOTEL swimming pool and fragrant garden in the center of a pleasant village offers a different sort of Santorini experience, away from the caldera but within walking distance of ancient Akrotiri and Red beach. **Pros:** clean and comfortable; good base for exploring southern end of island; good value given quality of accommodations; big discounts for longer stays. **Cons:** no sea views; sometimes hosts groups. $ *Rooms from: €80* ⊠ *Village center* ☎ *22860/81277* ⊕ *www.hotelparadise.gr* ⇥ *30 rooms and suites* ⏛ *Breakfast.*

BEACH

Red Beach. A backdrop of red and black volcanic cliffs adds no small amount of drama to this strand of multicolored pebbles and red-hued sand, and the timelessness of the place is enhanced by the presence of nearby ancient Akrotiri. Crowds sometimes pile in during July and August, and a few too many lounges and umbrellas detract from the stunning scenery, but for the most part this is one of the quieter

SANTORINI WINE

The locals say that in Santorini there is more wine than water, and it may be true; Santorini produces more wine than any other Cyclades island. The volcanic soil, high daytime temperatures, and humidity at night are favorable to 36 varieties of grape, and these unique growing conditions are especially ideal for the production of distinctive white wine. Farmers twist the vines into a basketlike shape, in which the grapes grow, protected from the wind. A highlight of any Santorini trip is a visit to one of its many wineries—log on to ⊕ *www.santorini.org/wineries* for a helpful intro.

beaches on the south side of the island. **Amenities:** food and drink; parking (about €2, not always imposed; rough path from parking to beach). **Best for:** snorkeling; swimming. ⊠ *On southwest shore below Akrotiri.*

KAMARI KAMAPI

6½ km (4¼ miles) east of Akrotiri, 6 km (4 miles) south of Fira.

Santorini's most popular beach resort is just that—a long line of hotels and tavernas strung out along a stretch of red and black sand on the island's southeastern coast. Tourism has all but consumed the onetime quieter pursuits of fishing and farming, though many residents still depend on both, and sun lovers descend en masse in July and August. Still, backed by fields and dramatic cliffs and headlands, Kamari is fairly low-key and a pleasant place to hit the beach.

EXPLORING

Ancient Thira. A Dorian city—with 9th-century BC tombs, an engraved phallus, Hellenistic houses, and traces of Byzantine fortifications and churches—floats more than 650 meters (2,100 feet) above the island. At the Sanctuary of Apollo, graffiti dating to the 8th century BC record the names of some of the boys who danced naked at the god's festival (Satie's famed musical compositions, *Gymnopedies,* reimagine these). To get here, hike up from Perissa or Kamari or take a taxi up **Mesa Vouna.** On the summit are the scattered ruins, excavated by a German archaeology school around the turn of the 20th century; there's a fine view. ⊠ *On a switchback up mountain right before Kamari* ☎ *22860/23217* ⊕ *www.culture.gr* 🎟 *€2* ☉ *Tues.–Sun. 8:30–3.*

Fodor's Choice
★ **Koutsoyanopoulos Winery.** Founded in 1870, the Koutsoyanopoulos winery offers a tour of its old facility, now a multiroom museum that is picturesque, authentic, and mostly underground. Tools, techniques, and the original business office are from a world long gone—but the wines, as the ensuing tasting proves, are contemporary and refined. The *Wine Spectator* rated their Assyrtiko among the world's top 100 whites. To add your own kudos, note that this admired winery is open year-round. ⊠ *On the road to Kamari, Vothonas* ☎ *22860/31322* ⊕ *www. volcanwines.gr* 🎟 *Tasting €7* ☉ *April, May, and Nov., daily 10–5; June–Oct., daily 10–7; Dec.–Mar., Mon.–Sat., 9:30–2.*

BEACHES

Kamari Beach. Santorini's most popular beach, one of several excellent stretches of sand on the southern end of the island, manages to maintain its beauty despite an onslaught of sunseekers. The black sands are backed by dramatic cliffs, including the one topped by ancient Thira. A steep path from one end of the beach leads up to the ruins, past a refreshing and very welcome natural spring, but most beachgoers don't venture beyond their umbrella-shaded lounges or the long line of beach bars and tavernas. **Amenities:** food and drink; showers; toilets; water sports. **Best for:** snorkeling; swimming; walking. ✛ *8 km (5 miles) southeast of Fira.*

CRETE

WELCOME TO CRETE

TOP REASONS TO GO

★ **Palace of Knossos:** Get up close to the mysteries of the 3,500-year-old civilization of the Minoans.

★ **Beaches:** From palm-backed Vai to remote Elafonisi, some of the finest beaches in Greece are lapped by Crete's turquoise waters.

★ **Walking and Looking:** In Rethymnon and Chania, Venetian/Turkish quarters are threaded with narrow lanes leading to palazzos and shady squares.

★ **Hiking the Countryside:** With its snowcapped peaks and deep gorges, craggy Crete offers lots of escapes for those who want to get away from it all.

★ **Luxurious Resorts:** You can live like royalty in a Venetian palace or—at luxurious outposts like many of those in Elounda—sun worship the day away in your own private pool.

1 Eastern Crete. Knossos, the most spectacular of the Minoan palaces and Crete's most popular attraction, is here in the east. Just as this sprawling complex was the hub of island civilization 3,500 years ago, nearby Heraklion is Crete's bustling modern capital, and farther east along the coast is the Elounda peninsula, the island's epicenter of luxury, where some of the world's most sumptuous resort getaways are tucked along a stunning shoreline. The east isn't all hustle, bustle, and glitz, though—the beach at Vai is just one example of the natural beauty that abounds here in the east, and in mountain villages like those on the Lasithi plateau, old traditions continue to thrive.

12

GETTING ORIENTED

Crete is long and narrow, approximately 257 km (159 miles) long and only 60 km (37 miles) at its widest. The most development is present on the north shore; the southern coast largely remains blessedly unspoiled. The island's three major cities, Heraklion, Rethymnon, and Chania, are in the north and are connected by the island's major highway, an east–west route that traverses most of the north coast. Heraklion, Chania, Ayios Nikolaos, and Sitia are served by ferry from Piraeus, and Heraklion and Chania have international airports. By car or bus, it's easy to reach other parts of the island from these gateways.

2 Western Crete. The scenery gets more rugged as you head west, where the White mountains pierce the blue sky with snowcapped peaks and then plunge into the Libyan sea along dramatic, rocky shorelines. Mountain scenery and remote seacoast villages—some, like Loutro, accessible only on foot or by boat—attract many visitors to the west. Others come to enjoy the urban pleasures of Rethymnon and Chania, gracious cities that owe their harbors, architectural jewels, and exotic charms to Venetian and Turkish occupiers.

Updated
by Stephen
Brewer

To Greeks, Crete is the Megalonissi (Great Island), a hub of spectacular ancient art and architecture. Fabled as the land of King Minos, it is a unique world where civilization is counted by the millennium. From every point of view travelers discover landscapes of amazing variety. Mountains, split with deep gorges and honeycombed with caves, rise in sheer walls from the sea. Snowcapped peaks loom behind sandy shorelines, vineyards, and olive groves. Miles of beaches, some with a wealth of amenities and others isolated and unspoiled, fringe the coast. Yet despite the attractions of sea and mountains, it is still the mystery surrounding Europe's first civilization and empire that draws the great majority of visitors to Crete and its world-famous Minoan palaces.

Around 1500 BC, while the rest of Europe was still in the grip of primitive barbarity, one of the most brilliant civilizations the world was ever to know approached its final climax, one that was breathtakingly uncovered through the late 19th-century excavations of Sir Arthur Evans. He determined that the Minoans, prehistoric Cretans, had founded Europe's first urban culture as far back as the 3rd millennium BC, and the island's rich legacy of art and architecture strongly influenced both mainland Greece and the Aegean islands in the Bronze Age. From around 1900 BC the Minoan palaces at Knossos (near present-day Heraklion), Malia, Phaistos, and elsewhere were centers of political power, religious authority, and economic activity—all concentrated in one sprawling complex of buildings. Their administration seems to have had much in common with contemporary cultures in Egypt and Mesopotamia. What set the Minoans apart from the rest of the Bronze Age world was their art. It was lively and naturalistic, and they excelled in miniature techniques. From the scenes illustrated on their frescoes, stone vases, seal stones, and signet rings, it is possible to build a picture of a productive, well-regulated society. Yet new research suggests that prehistoric Crete was not a peaceful place; there may have been years of warfare before Knossos became the island's dominant power, in around 1600 BC. It is now thought that political upheaval, rather than the devastating volcanic eruption on the island of Santorini, triggered the violent downfall of the palace civilization around 1450 BC.

But there are many memorable places in Crete that belong to a more recent past, one measured in centuries and not millennia. Other invaders and occupiers—Roman colonists, the Byzantines, Arab invaders, Venetian colonists, and Ottoman pashas—have all left their mark on Heraklion, Chania, Rethymnon, and other towns and villages throughout the island. Today Crete welcomes outsiders who delight in its splendid beaches, charming Old Town quarters, and array of splendid landscapes. Openly inviting to guests who want to experience the real Greece, Cretans remain family oriented and rooted in tradition, and you'll find that one of the greatest pleasures on Crete is immersing yourself in the island's lifestyle.

PLANNING

WHEN TO GO

The best times to visit Crete are May, when every outcrop of rock is ablaze with brilliant wildflowers and the sea is warm enough for a brisk dip, or September and October, when the sea is still warm and the light golden but piercingly clear. A spring visit comes with the advantage of long days.

Most of Crete, outside the major cities, is really only noticeably busy from mid-July through August, when the main Minoan sights and towns on the north coast come close to overflowing with tourists. Take special care at these times to avoid such places as Malia and Limin Hersonissos, hideously overdeveloped towns where bars and pizzerias fill up with heavy-drinking northern Europeans on summertime package tours.

Even in the height of summer, though, you can enjoy many parts of the west and south coasts without feeling too oppressed by crowds. Crete can also be a pleasure in winter, when you can visit the museums and archaeological sites and enjoy the island's delightful towns without the crush of crowds. Remember, though, that rainfall can be heavy in January and February, and note that many hotels and restaurants, especially resorts, close from late October or November through mid-April or May.

PLANNING YOUR TIME

Enticing as Crete's beaches are, there is much more to the island than sand and surf. Archaeological sites in Crete open at 8 or 8:30 in summer, so get an early start to wander through the ruins before the sun is blazing. You'll also want to visit some of the folklife museums that pay homage to the island's traditional past. One of the finest collections is in Vori, southwest of Heraklion; there are also excellent folk collections at the Historical and Folk Art Museum in Rethymnon and the Historical Museum of Crete in Heraklion. An evening should begin with a stroll around the shady squares that grace every Cretan town and village, or along a waterfront promenade—those in Chania, Ayios Nikolaos, and Sitia are especially picturesque and jammed with locals. Most evenings are spent over a long meal, almost always eaten outdoors in the warm weather. For entertainment, seek out a *kentron* (a taverna that hosts traditional Cretan music and dancing). The star performer is the *lyra* player, who can extract a surprisingly subtle sound from the small pear-shaped instrument, held upright on the thigh and played with a bow. Ask at your hotel where lyra players are performing—hearing the enchanting serenade could prove to be a treasured Cretan memory.

GETTING HERE AND AROUND

AIR TRAVEL

Olympic Airways connects Athens, and other islands, with Heraklion, Chania, and Sitia.

Aegean Airlines flies between Athens and Heraklion and Chania. Sky Express flies to both Heraklion and Sitia. Fares are highest in the summer (about double the cost of a ferry).

The principal arrival point on Crete is Heraklion Airport, where up to 16 flights daily arrive from Athens and daily flights arrive from throughout Greece. Heraklion is also serviced directly by flights from other European cities. (Plans are afoot to relocate the airport, currently on the seafront just outside town, to the site of an air force base outside the nearby village of Kastelli as early as 2018. Skeptics doubt that timetable will be met.)

There are several daily flights from Athens and (in summer) other European cities to Chania Airport, and several per week from Athens to Sitia, which is also connected to Rhodes with a few weekly flights in summer.

A municipal bus just outside Heraklion Airport can take you to Platia Eleftherias in the Heraklion town center. Tickets are sold from a kiosk next to the bus stop; the fare is €1.10. From Chania Airport, Olympic Airlines buses take you to the airline office in the center for €3, but these run infrequently. Cabs line up outside all airports to meet flights; the fare into the respective towns is about €5 for Heraklion, €7 for Chania, and €4 for Sitia.

Airport Contacts Chania Airport (*CHQ*). ⊠ *Souda Bay* ✛ *15 km (9 mile) northeast of Chania, off the road to Sterne* ☎ *28210/83800* ⊕ *www.chania-airport. com.* **Heraklion Airport (Kazantzakis International Airport)** (*HER*). ⊠ *Heraklion* ✛ *5 km (3 miles) east of town, off the road to Gournia* ☎ *28103/97800.* **Sitia Airport** (*JSH*). ⊠ *Sitia* ✛ *1 km (½ mile) northwest of town, off the main coast road* ☎ *28430/24424.*

BIKE AND MOPED TRAVEL

Be cautious: motorbike accidents account for numerous injuries among tourists every year. Reliable rentals can be arranged through Blue Sea Rentals in Heraklion, but you'll find rentals in just about any town on the tourist trail. Expect to pay about €20 a day for a 50cc moped, for which you will need to present only a valid driver's license; law requires a motorcycle license to rent larger bikes. Fees usually cover insurance, but only for repairs to the bike, and usually with a deductible of at least €500. The law mandates that you wear a helmet.

Contacts Blue Sea Rentals ⊠ *Kosmo Zoutou 5–7, Heraklion* ☎ *28102/41097* ⊕ *www.bluesearentals.com.*

BUS TRAVEL

You can find schedules and book seats in advance at bus stations, and tourist offices are also well equipped with schedules and information about service. As efficient as the bus network is, you might have a hard time getting out of Heraklion, what with its confusing multitude of stations. You'll find the bus station for western Crete, Bus Station A, opposite the port; this station also serves places on the north coast east of Heraklion, such as Hersonissos, Archanes, Sitia, Ayios Niko-laos, and the Lasithi plateau. The station for the south, Bus Station B, is outside the Chania Gate to the right of the Archaeological Museum; this is where you get buses for such places as Matala and Phaestos. Ask someone at the tourist information office to tell you exactly where to find your bus and to show you the spot on a map. You'll need to make reservations in advance for all buses. An excellent source for informa-tion on bus travel in Crete, as well as on all other things Cretan, is Crete Travel *(see Tour Options).*

BOAT AND FERRY TRAVEL

Heraklion and Souda Bay (5 km/3 miles east of Chania) are the island's main ports, but there is regular service as well to Sitia and several-times-a-week service to Rethymnon. Most ferries are overnight, but there are daytime ferries from Piraeus to Heraklion and Chania in the summer. Ferries also connect Crete with other islands, mostly those in the Cyclades and Dodecanese. Service includes fast-ferries between Santorini and Heraklion (cutting travel time to just under two hours) and a ferry linking Sitia with the Dodecanese islands of Kassos, Kar-pathos, and Rhodes. There is also weekly service from Kalamata and Gythion in the Peloponnese to Kissamos (Kastelli) in the far west of the island. Ships also sail from Heraklion to Limassol, in Cyprus, and to Haifa, Israel. On the overnight runs, you can book either a berth or an airplane-style seat, and there are usually cafeterias, dining rooms, shops, and other services on board. The most economical berth accom-modations are in four-berth cabins, which are relatively spacious and comfortable and are equipped with bathrooms.

A one-way fare from Piraeus to Heraklion, Rethymnon, or Chania without accommodations costs about €38, and from about €55 with accommodations. A small discount is given for round-trip tickets. Car fares are about €65 each way, depending on vehicle size. In July and August, a boat service around the Samaria Gorge operates along the southwest coast from Hora Sfakion to Loutro, Ayia Roumeli, Souyia, Lissos, and Paleochora, the main resort on the southwest coast. Ferries also sail from Paleochora to Ghavdos, an island south of Crete, and from Ierapetra to Krissi, an island also to the south. Most travel agen-cies sell tickets for all ferries and hydrofoils. Make reservations several days in advance during the July to August high season.

Ferry routes change often, but at this writing, among the lines that serve Crete are Anek (Piraeus to Herklion and Chania), Blue Star Ferries (Piraeus to Heraklion), Cretan Lines (Piraeus to Rethymnon), Hellenic Seaways (Heraklion to Santorini, Paros, and Mykonos), and Minoan Lines (Piraeus to Heraklion). Ferry schedules are best checked at ⊕ *www.ferries.gr.*

Contacts Cretan Lines. Piraeus to Rethymnon ⊠ *Sof. Venizelou 15, Rethymnon* ☎ *28310/21013.*

CAR TRAVEL

Roads on Crete are not too congested, yet the accident rate is high compared to other parts of Europe. Driving in the main towns can be nerve-racking, to say the least. Most road signs are in Greek and English, though signage is often nonexistent or inadequate. Be sure to carry a road map (or GPS) at all times, and to stop and ask directions when the need arises—otherwise, you may drive miles out of your way. Gas stations are not plentiful outside the big towns, and gasoline is more expensive in Crete than it is in the United States and on par with prices elsewhere in Europe—expect to pay about €1.70 a liter (about €6.45 a gallon).

Drive defensively wherever you are, as Cretan drivers are aggressive and liable to ignore the rules of the road. Sheep and goats frequently stray onto the roads, with or without their shepherd or sheepdog. In July and August, tourists on motor scooters can be a hazard. Night driving is not advisable.

As for car rentals, you can arrange beforehand with a major agency in the United States or in Athens to pick up a car on arrival in Crete, or work through one of the many local car-rental agencies that have offices in the airports and in the cities, as well as in some resort villages. For the most part, these local agencies are extremely reliable, provide excellent service, and charge very low rates. Many, such as the excellent Crete Car Rental, will meet your ship or plane and drop you off again at no extra charge.

Even without advance reservations, expect to pay about €40 or less a day in high season for a medium-size car with unlimited mileage. Weekly prices are negotiable, but with unlimited mileage rentals start at about €200 in summer. At many agencies, you are responsible for a €500 deductible for any damage, regardless of your insurance coverage.

Big international agencies, including Avis and Sixt, are well represented on Crete *(see Car Travel in Travel Smart for contact information).*

Contacts Crete Car Rental ⊠ *Kallipoleos 11, Heraklion* ☎ *28102/13445* ⊕ *www.crete-car-rental.com.*

HOTELS

Some of Greece's finest resorts line the shores of Elounda peninsula, offering sumptuous surroundings and exquisite service. Although the atmosphere at these resorts is more international than Greek, in other places you'll find authentic surroundings in the Venetian palaces and old mansions that are being sensitively restored as small hotels, especially in Chania and Rethymnon. Many of the better hotels on Crete offer special rates and packages through their websites, and it's always worthwhile to

12

check out what discounts might be available during your stay—special rates often bring even a luxurious hotel into affordable range, especially outside of high season. For a more rustic yet authentic experience on Crete, opt for simple, whitewashed, tile-floor rooms with rustic pine furniture in the ubiquitous "room to rent" establishments in mountain and seaside villages. Another common term is "studio," which implies the presence of a kitchen or basic cooking facilities. Standards of cleanliness are high in Crete, and service is almost always friendly.

RESTAURANTS

Cretans tend to take their meals seriously, and like to sit down in a taverna to a full meal. Family-run tavernas take pride in serving Cretan cooking, and a number of the better restaurants in cities now also stress Cretan produce and traditional dishes. One way to dine casually is to sample the *mezedes* served at some bars and tavernas. These often include such Cretan specialties as *trypopita* (cheese-filled pastry), and a selection of cheeses: Cretan *graviera*, a hard, smooth cheese, is a blend of pasteurized sheep's and goat's milk that resembles Emmentaler in flavor and texture—not too sharp, but with a strong, distinctive flavor; and *mizythra* (a creamy white cheese). As main courses, Cretans enjoy grilled meat, generally lamb and pork, but there is also plenty of fresh fish. Mezedes and main courses are usually shared from large platters placed in the center of the table.

Cretan olive oil is famous throughout Greece; it's heavier and richer than other varieties. The island's wines are special: look for Boutari Kritikos, a crisp white; and Minos Palace, a smooth red. Make sure you try the *tsikouthia* (also known as *raki*), the Cretan firewater made from fermented grape skins, which is drunk at any hour, often accompanied by a dish of raisins or walnuts drenched in honey. Restaurants often offer raki, along with a sweet, free of charge at the end of a meal.

Lunch is generally served from 1 to 3 or so. Dinner is an event here, as it is elsewhere in Greece, and is usually served late; in fact, when non-Greeks are finishing up around 10:30 or so, locals usually begin arriving.

DINING AND LODGING PRICES IN EUROS			
	$	$$	$$$	$$$$
Restaurants	Under €16	€16–€25	€26–€40	Over €40
Hotels	Under €126	€126–€225	€226–€275	Over €275

Restaurant prices are the average cost of a main course at dinner or, if dinner is not served, at lunch. Hotel prices are the lowest cost of a standard double room in high season.

TOUR OPTIONS

Most travel agents can arrange for personal guides.

BUS TOURS

Resort hotels and large agents organize guided tours in air-conditioned buses to the main Minoan sites; excursions to spectacular beaches such as Vai in the northeast and Elafonisi in the southwest; and trips to

Santorini and to closer islands such as Spinalonga, a former leper colony off Ayios Nikolaos.

Crete Travel. The Crete Travel website is an excellent source for tour information, with insights into many of the island's more worthwhile sights and tours including hiking excursions and visits to out-of-the-way monasteries. A tour of Knossos and the Archaeological Museum in Heraklion costs about €40; a tour of Phaistos and Gortyna plus a swim at Matala costs about €20; a trip to the Samaria Gorge costs about €25. ⊠ *Kallipoleos 11, Heraklion* ☎ *2810/1021–3445* ⊕ *www.cretetravel.com.*

HIKING TOURS
Crete is excellent hiking terrain, and many trails crisscross the mountains and gorges, especially in the southwest. The Greek National Tourism Organization (GNTO or EOT) is a source of information.

Alpine Travel. This outfitter offers one-day, one-week, and two-week hiking tours throughout western Crete and makes transportation and accommodation arrangements for individual trekkers as well. ⊠ *2nd Pass. Akrotiriou street, Chania* ☎ *28210/50939* ⊕ *www.alpine.gr.*

Greek Mountaining Club of Chania. This association operates overnight refuges in the White mountains and on Mt. Ida and operates expeditions into the mountains of western Crete and other wilderness regions. ⊠ *Tzanakaki 90, Chania* ☎ *28210/44647* ⊕ *www.eoshanion.gr.*

VISITOR INFORMATION
Tourist offices are more plentiful, and more helpful, on Crete than they are in many other parts of Greece. Offices of the Greek National Tourism Organization (GNTO or EOT), in the major towns, are open daily 8–2 and 3–8:30. The municipalities of Ayios Nikolaos, Sitia, and Ierapetra operate their own tourist offices, and these provide a wealth of information on the towns and surrounding regions, as well as help with accommodations and local tours; most keep long summer hours, open daily 8:30 am–9 pm.

EASTERN CRETE ΑΝΑΤΟΛΙΚΗ ΚΡΗΤΗ

Eastern Crete includes the towns and cities of Heraklion, Ayios Nikolaos, Sitia, and Ierapetra, as well as the archaeological sites of Knossos and Gournia. Natural wonders lie amid these man-made places, including the palm-fringed beach at Vai, and the Lasithi plateau and other inland plains and highlands are studded with villages where life goes on untouched by the hedonism of the coastal resorts. You may well make first landfall in Heraklion, the island's major port. You'll want to spend time here to visit the excellent Archaeological Museum and Knossos, but you're likely to have a more relaxing Cretan experience in Ayios Nikolaos, a charming and animated port town; in the resorts on the stunning Elounda peninsula; or on the beautiful and undeveloped eastern end of the island, around Palaikastro.

HERAKLION ΗΡΑΚΛΕΙΟ

175 km (109 miles) south of Piraeus harbor in Athens, 69 km (43 miles) west of Ayios Nikolaos, 78 km (49 miles) east of Rethymnon.

In Minoan times, Crete's largest city—the fifth-largest city in Greece—was a harbor for Knossos, the largest palace and effective power center of prehistoric Crete. The Bronze Age remains were built over long ago, and now Heraklion (also known as Iraklion), with more than 130,000 inhabitants, stretches far beyond even the Venetian walls. Heraklion is not immediately appealing: it's a sprawling and untidy collection of apartment blocks and busy roadways. Many travelers looking for Crete's more rugged pleasures bypass the island's capital altogether, but the city's renowned Archaeological Museum and the nearby Palace of Knossos make Heraklion a mandatory stop for anyone even remotely interested in ancient civilizations.

Besides, at closer look, Heraklion is not without its charms. A walk down Daidalou and the other pedestrians-only streets provides plenty of amusements, and the city has more than its share of outdoor cafés where you can sit and watch life unfold. Seaside promenades and narrow lanes that run off them can be quite animated, thanks to ongoing restoration, and the inner harbor dominated by the Koules, a sturdy Venetian fortress, is richly evocative of the island's storied past.

GETTING HERE AND AROUND

Heraklion is Crete's major air hub, and Kazantzakis Airport has been greatly expanded in recent years. Flights on Olympic and Aegean airlines arrive almost hourly from Athens, and many flights from other European cities use the airport; Aegean and other airlines have regularly scheduled flights to Rome and a few other European cities. The airport is only about 5 km (3 miles) east of the city, easy to reach on public bus (€1.10) or taxi (about €10).

Frequent ferries connect Heraklion to Piraeus (at least five daily, including daytime ferries from May through August), Thessaloniki (three times weekly in the high season), and the Cyclades (Santorini, Mykonos, and others). Operators and schedules change frequently; for the latest info, check on your route at ⊕ *www.ferries.gr*, or stop by one of the travel agencies that operate near all Greek ports.

Heraklion is Crete's hub for bus travel, and you can get just about anywhere on the island from any of the city's bus terminals. Service to the main towns—Ayios Nikolaos, Rethymnon, and Chania—runs hourly. Buses to all these towns arrive at and leave from the two adjacent terminals on the harbor, just east of the city center.

EXPLORING

If you have just a day in Heraklion, your time will be tight. Get an early start and spend a couple of hours in the morning walking around the city, stepping into the churches if they're open and poking around the lively market. Save most of your energy for the Archaeological Museum. Of course, nearby Knossos could easily occupy most of a day. If you're staying overnight in or near Heraklion, take an evening stroll in the busy area around Ta Leontaria and Kornarou Square; half the population seems to converge here.

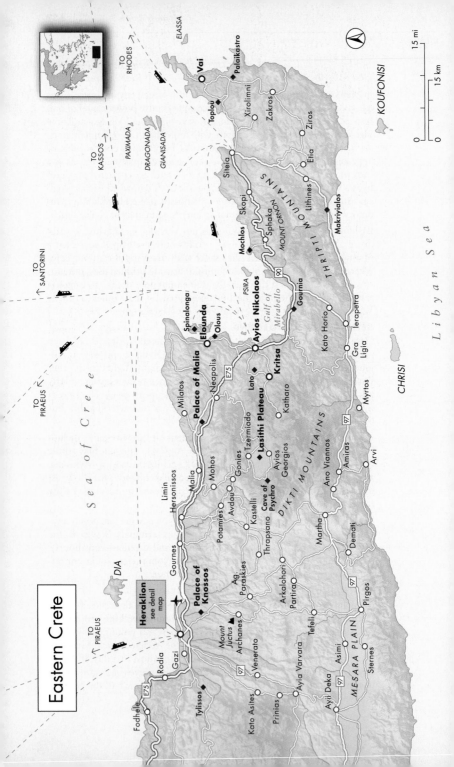

Eastern Crete

TO PIRAEUS

TO SANTORINI

TO PIRAEUS

TO KASSOS

TO RHODES

ELASSA

KOUFONISI

Sea of Crete

Libyan Sea

DIA

PAXIMADA
DRAGONADA
GIANISADA

PSIRA

CHRISI

Gulf of Mirabello

MOUNT ORNON
MOUNTAINS

THRIPTI
MOUNTAINS

DIKTI MOUNTAINS

MESARA PLAIN

0   15 mi
0   15 km

Fodhele
Rodia
Gazi
Heraklion *see detail map*
Gournes
Gournia
Limin
Hersonissos
Malia
Milatos
Palace of Malia
Neopolis
Elounda
Spinalonga
Olous
Ayios Nikolaos
Kritsa
Lato
Mochlos
Skopi
Siteia
Toplou
Vai
Palaikastro
Xirolimni
Zakros
Ziros
Efia
Lithines
Makriyialos
Goumia
Sphaka
E75
90
Mohos
Gonies
Avdou
Kastelli
Potamies
Thrapsano
Cave of Psychro
Lasithi Plateau
Tzermiado
Ayios Georgios
Katharo
Kato Horio
Ierapetra
Gra Ligia
Myrtos
Ano Viannos
Amiras
Arvi
Demati
Martha
Pirgos
97
97
97
Ag. Paraskies
Palace of Knossos
Mount Juctus
Archanes
Venerato
Kato Asites
Prinias
Ayia Varvara
Ayii Deka
Sternes
Asimi
Tefeli
Partira
Arkalohori
Tylissos
E75

Heraklion's ever-improving road network is making it easier to avoid the all but impassable city center; note that if you're spending any time at all in Heraklion, it's best to wait until you are leaving the city to pick up a rental car.

TOP ATTRACTIONS

12

Heraklion Archaeological Museum. Standing in a class of its own, this museum guards practically all of the Minoan treasures uncovered in the legendary excavations of the Palace of Knossos and other monuments of Minoan civilization. These amazing artifacts, many 3,000 years old, were brought to light in 20th-century excavations by famed British archaeologist Sir Arthur Evans and are shown off in handsome, newly renovated galleries. It's best to visit the museum first thing in the morning, before the tour buses arrive, or in late afternoon, once they pull away. Top treasures include the famous seal stones, many inscribed with Linear B script, discovered and deciphered by Evans around the turn of the 20th century. The most stunning and mysterious seal stone is the so-called Phaistos Disk, found at Phaistos Palace in the south, its purpose unknown. (Linear B script is now recognized as an early form of Greek, but the earlier Linear A script that appears on clay tablets and that of the Phaistos Disk have yet to be deciphered.)

But perhaps the most arresting exhibits are the sophisticated frescoes, restored fragments found in Knossos. They depict broad-shouldered, slim-waisted youths, their large eyes fixed with an enigmatic expression on the Prince of the Lilies; ritual processions and scenes from the bullring, with young men and women somersaulting over the back of a charging bull; and groups of court ladies, whose flounced skirts led a French archaeologist to exclaim in surprise, "*Des Parisiennes!*", a name still applied to this striking fresco.

Even before great palaces with frescoes were being built around 1900 BC, the prehistoric Cretans excelled at metalworking and carving stone vases, and they were also skilled at producing pottery, such as the eggshell-thin Kamares ware decorated in delicate abstract designs. Other specialties were miniature work such as the superbly crafted jewelry and the colored seal stones that are carved with lively scenes of people and animals. Though naturalism and an air of informality distinguish much Minoan art from that of contemporary Bronze Age cultures elsewhere in the eastern Mediterranean, you can also see a number of heavy, rococo set pieces, such as the fruit stand with a toothed rim and the punch bowl with appliquéd flowers.

The Minoans' talents at modeling in stone, ivory, and a kind of glass paste known as faience peaked in the later palace period (1700–1450 BC). A famous rhyton, a vase for pouring libations, carved from dark serpentine in the shape of a bull's head, has eyes made of red jasper and clear rock crystal with horns of gilded wood. An ivory acrobat—perhaps a bull-leaper—and two bare-breasted faience goddesses in flounced skirts holding wriggling snakes were among a group of treasures hidden beneath the floor of a storeroom at Knossos. Bull-leaping, whether a religious rite or a favorite sport, inspired some of the most memorable images in Minoan art. Note, also, the three vases, probably originally

The Koules harbor fortress is a mighty reminder of the age when Venetians ruled Crete from their outpost in Heraklion.

covered in gold leaf, from Ayia Triada that are carved with scenes of Minoan life thought to be rendered by artists from Knossos: boxing matches, a harvest-home ceremony, and a Minoan official taking delivery of a consignment of hides. The most stunning rhyton of all, from Zakro, is made of rock crystal. ⊠ *Platia Eleftherias* ☎ *28102/24630* ⊕ *odysseus.culture.gr* ✉ *€6; combined ticket for museum and Palace of Knossos €10* ☉ *Apr.–mid-Oct., daily 8–8; mid-Oct.–Mar., Mon. 11–5, Tues.–Sun. 8–3.*

Fodor'sChoice
★

Historical Museum of Crete. An imposing mansion houses a varied collection of early Christian and Byzantine sculptures, Venetian and Ottoman stonework, artifacts of war, and rustic folklife items. The museum provides a wonderful introduction to Cretan culture, and is the only place in Crete to display the work of famed native son El Greco (Domenikos Theotocopoulos), who left the island—then part of the Venetian Republic—for Italy and, then, Spain around 1567; his *Baptism of Christ* and *View of Mount Sinai and the Monastery of St. Catherine* hang amid frescoes, icons, and other Byzantine pieces. Upon entering, look out for the *Lion of St. Mark* sculpture, with an inscription that says in Latin "I protect the kingdom of Crete." Left of the entrance is a room stuffed with memorabilia from Crete's bloody revolutionary past: weapons, portraits of mustachioed warrior chieftains, and the flag of the short-lived independent Cretan state set up in 1898. The 19th-century banner in front of the staircase sums up the spirit of Cretan rebellion against the Turks: *eleftheria o thanatos* ("Freedom or Death"). Upstairs, look in on a room arranged as the study of Crete's most famous writer, Nikos Kazantzakis (1883–1957), the author of *Zorba the Greek* and an epic poem, *The Odyssey, a Modern Sequel*; he was born in Heraklion and is buried here, just inside the section of the walls known as the Martinengo. The top floor contains a stunning collection of Cretan textiles, including the brilliant scarlet weavings typical of the island's traditional handiwork, and another room arranged as a domestic interior of the early 1900s. ⊠ *Sofokli Venizelou 27* ☎ *28102/83219* ⊕ *www.historical-museum.gr* ⌫ *€5* ⊗ *Apr.–Oct., Mon.–Sat. 9–5; Nov.–Mar., Mon.–Sat. 9–3:30.*

Koules. Heraklion's inner harbor, where fishing boats land their catch and yachts are moored, is dominated by this massive fortress so named by the Turks but, in fact, built by the Venetians as the Castello del Molo in the 16th century and decorated with three stone lions of St. Mark, symbol of Venetian imperialism. On the east side of the fortress is the vaulted arsenal; here Venetian galleys were repaired and refitted, and timber, cheeses, and sweet Malmsey wine were loaded for the three-week voyage to Venice. The view from the battlements takes in the inner as well as the outer harbor, where freighters and passenger ferries drop anchor, and the sprawling labyrinth of concrete apartment blocks that is modern Heraklion. To the south rises Mt. Iuktas and, to the west, the pointed peak of Mt. Stromboli. ⊠ *Inner harbor* ☎ *28102/88484* ⌫ *€2* ⊗ *Apr.–Oct., Tues.–Sun. 8:30–7; Nov.–Mar., daily 8:30–3.*

Loggia. A gathering place for the island's Venetian nobility, this open-air arcade (with a meeting hall above) was built in the early 17th century by Francesco Basilicata, an Italian architect. Now restored to its original Palladian elegance, it adjoins the old Venetian Armory, now the City Hall. ⊠ *25 Augoustou.*

<table>
<tr><td>

**NEED A
BREAK?**

</td><td>

Kir-Kor. Stop into this venerable old *bougatsa* shop for an envelope of flaky pastry that's either filled with a sweet, creamy filling and dusted with cinnamon and sugar, or stuffed with soft white cheese. A double portion served warm with Greek coffee is a nice treat. Thick Cretan yogurt and ice cream are other indulgences on offer. Kir-Kor is a popular place to hang out after getting off the night boat from Piraeus and waiting for museums and businesses to open. ⊠ *Platia Eleftherias*

</td></tr>
</table>

Martinengo Bastion. Six bastions shaped like arrowheads jut out from the well-preserved Venetian walls. Martinengo is the largest, designed by Micheli Sanmicheli in the 16th century to keep out Barbary pirates and Turkish invaders. When the Turks overran Crete in 1648, the garrison at Heraklion held out for another 21 years in one of the longest sieges in European history. General Francesco Morosini finally surrendered the city to the Turkish Grand Vizier in September 1669. He was allowed to sail home to Venice with the city's archives and such precious relics as the skull of Ayios Titos—which was not returned until 1966. Literary pilgrims come to the Martinengo to visit the **burial place of writer Nikos Kazantzakis.** The grave is a plain stone slab marked by a weathered wooden cross. The inscription, from his writings, says: "I fear nothing, I hope for nothing, I am free." ⊠ *In walls south of city center, off Plastira.*

Beaches in Crete

With hundreds of miles of dramatic coastline, Crete serves up an almost endless supply of beaches. Many are soft and powdery, some are action-packed with water sports, and others are blissfully untrammeled. The very best bookend the island: palm-shaded Vai to the east and Elafonisi to the west, where white sands ring an islet just offshore.

Lovers of sand and surf quickly discover that there are really two distinct types of beaches on Crete: the highly developed strands on the north coast and the rugged getaway beaches on the south coast. Northern beaches stretch along the flat, sandy coastal plain between the island's major cities and are easily reached by the east–west national highway, as well as by an extensive bus network. Most are packed with umbrellas and sun beds and backed by hotels, including some of Greece's most luxurious resorts. In fact, all you need to bring for beachgoing on the north coast is a bathing suit, towel, and sunscreen—everything else, from beach lounges to umbrellas and snorkeling gear, are available for rent at many.

Beaches on the south coast are tucked into coves and bays, often at the end of poor roads; a rental car is a must to explore the south coast beaches. You should also equip yourself with a good map to find tucked away coves and remote beaches.

Platia Eleftherias. The city's biggest square is paved in marble and dot-ted with fountains. The Archaeological Museum is off the north end of the square; at the west side is the beginning of Daidalou, the main thoroughfare, which follows the line of an early fortification wall and is now a pedestrian walkway lined with tavernas, boutiques, jewelers, and souvenir shops. ⊠ *Southeast end of Daidalou.*

Ta Leontaria. "The Lions," a stately marble Renaissance fountain, remains a beloved town landmark. It's the heart of Heraklion's town center—Platia Eleftherias, a triangular pedestrian zone filled with cafés and named after the Cretan statesman who united the island with Greece in 1913. The square is also known simply as Ta Leontaria and was the center of the colony founded in the 13th century, when Venice colonized Crete, and Heraklion became an important port of call on the trade routes to the Middle East. The city, and often the whole island (known then as Candia), was ruled by the Duke of Crete, a Venetian administrator. ⊠ *Daidalou and 25 Augoustou.*

WORTH NOTING

Ayia Aikaterina. Nestled in the shadow of the Ayios Minas cathedral is one of Crete's most attractive small churches, named for St. Kath-erine and built in 1555. The church now houses a museum of icons by Cretan artists, who often traveled to Venice to study with Ital-ian Renaissance painters. Look for six icons (Nos. 2, 5, 8, 9, 12, and 15) by Michael Damaskinos, who worked in both Byzantine and Renaissance styles during the 16th century. Crete's most famous art-ist, Domenikos Theotocopoulos, better known as El Greco, studied at

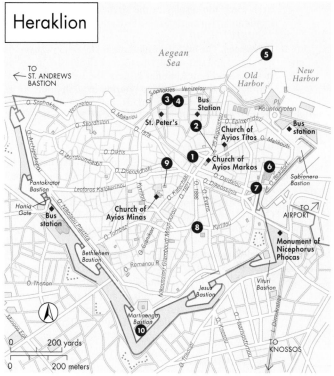

Heraklion

the monastery school attached to the church in the mid-16th century. ✉ *Kyrillou Loukareos* 🎟 *€4* 🕙 *Mon. and Wed. 9:30–1, Thurs. and Sat. 9–1 and 5–7, Fri. 9–1.*

Monastery of St. Peter and St. Paul. One of Heraklion's oldest monuments, dating from the 13th century, has been been rebuilt many times over the years and has done duty as a church, monastery, mosque, and cinema. After recent refurbishments, St. Peter's is now an exhibition hall and its 15th-century frescoes, the oldest in the city, have been beautifully restored. ✉ *West of harbor along seashore road.*

WHERE TO EAT

$　✕ **Erganos.** One of Heraklion's most traditional restaurants—just out-
GREEK　side the old city walls south of Platia Eleftherias—takes its name from one of the cities of ancient Crete and serves authentic local fare, served as small plates that include mouthwatering little pies (*pitarakia*) filled with cheese and honey, wild herbs from the mountains, and ground meats. Lunch and dinner both are often accompanied by Cretan music, sometimes provided by a fellow patron. 💲 *Average main: €10* ✉ *Georgiadi 5* ☎ *28102/85629.*

$　✕ **Ippokambos.** This seafront institution, always busy and lively with
SEAFOOD　a local crowd, is one of the most popular spots in town for fresh fish. Service is attentive no matter how busy, and simple preparations of the

fresh catch (on display in the kitchen) are accompanied by delicious salads and crisp house wines. $ *Average main: €12* ⊠ *Sofokli Venizelou 3* ☎ *28102/80240.*

$
GREEK ✕ **Pantheon.** The liveliest restaurant in Heraklion's covered meat market has grilled and spit-roasted meats, as well as hearty tripe soup, rich lamb stew, and other traditional dishes. The surroundings are simple, but that doesn't stop locals from pouring in at all hours for a meal, which is nicely accompanied by salads made from the freshest Cretan produce. $ *Average main: €11* ⊠ *Market off Kornarou Sq.* ☎ *28102/41652* ⊟ *No credit cards.*

WHERE TO STAY

$
HOTEL El Greco. Basic, comfortable, and smack-dab in the city center, these pleasantly furnished rooms don't offer much more than wooden beds and desks, but they're a good-value base for visiting the Archaeological Museum and Knossos. **Pros:** central location; excellent value. **Cons:** a little faded; street noise in some rooms. $ *Rooms from: €53* ⊠ *4 Odos 1821* ☎ *28102/81071* ⊕ *www.elgrecohotel.gr* ⇱ *90 rooms* ⦶ *Breakfast.*

$$
B&B/INN
Fodor'sChoice
★ **Kalimera Archanes Village.** An especially appealing base for exploring Knossos and Heraklion is the well-kept wine village of Archanes, where three 19th-century stone houses tucked into a garden are fitted out with beautiful traditional furnishings and all the modern comforts. **Pros:** highly atmospheric and very comfortable; near many sights but provides a nice dose of Greek village life; beautiful interiors and outdoor spaces. **Cons:** beaches are 15 minutes away. $ *Rooms from: €140* ⊠ *Theotokopoulou, Archanes* ☎ *69/7746–0555 mobile* ⊕ *kalimera-village.gr* ⇱ *4 houses* ⦶ *Breakfast.*

$
HOTEL Marin Dream Hotel. Sleek, contemporary decor and furnishings in the public spaces and guest rooms make this perch just above the harbor especially soothing and restful. **Pros:** central location but on a quiet side street; a welcome oasis in busy Heraklion; nearby parking for €3 a day. **Cons:** somewhat generic furnishings. $ *Rooms from: €80* ⊠ *Doukos Bofor 12* ☎ *28103/00018* ⊕ *www.marinhotel.gr* ⇱ *44 rooms* ⦶ *Breakfast.*

$
HOTEL GDM Megaron. A 1920s office building that for decades stood derelict above the harbor now houses an unusually luxurious and restful hotel, by far the best in town, with a real plus for an in-town lodging— a top-floor terrace where a swimming pool is perched dramatically at the edge of the roof. **Pros:** central location; most rooms with water views; wonderful rooftop pool and restaurant. **Cons:** rather formal surroundings; expensive for Heraklion, but special Internet rates are often lower than those at other hotels in this class. $ *Rooms from: €120* ⊠ *D. Beaufort 9* ☎ *28103/05300* ⊕ *www.gdmmegaron.gr* ⇱ *38 rooms, 8 suites* ⦶ *Breakfast.*

KNOSSOS ΚΝΩΣΟΥ

5 km (3 miles) south of Heraklion.

Paintings of bull-leapers, sculptures of bare-breasted snake charmers, myths of minotaurs, and the oldest throne in Europe are just a few of the wonders that the British archaeologist Arthur Evans brought up from the earth at Knossos at the close of the 19th century, to the astonishment of newspapers around the world. They proved telling evidence of the great elegance of King Minos's court (Evans chose the king's name to christen this culture), as the evocative ruins continue to do today.

GETTING HERE

Municipal buses No. 2 and No. 4 head to the fabled Palace of Knossos every 10 minutes or so from Heraklion, where the main stops include Platia Eleftherias.

EXPLORING

Fodor'sChoice ★ **Palace of Knossos.** This most amazing of archaeological sites once lay hidden beneath a huge mound hemmed in by low hills. Heinrich Schliemann, father of archaeology and discoverer of Troy, knew it was here, but Turkish obstruction prevented him from exploring his last discovery. Cretan independence from the Ottoman Turks made it possible for Sir Arthur Evans, a British archaeologist, to start excavations in 1899. A forgotten and sublime civilization thus came again to light with the uncovering of the great Palace of Knossos.

The magnificent Minoans flourished on Crete from around 2700 to 1450 BC, and their palaces and cities at Knossos, Phaistos, and Gournia were centers of political power and luxury—they traded in tin, saffron, gold, and spices as far afield as Spain—when the rest of Europe was a place of primitive barbarity. They loved art, farmed bees, and worshipped many goddesses. But what caused their demise? Some say political upheaval, but others point to an eruption on Thera (Santorini), about 100 km (60 miles) north in the Aegean, that caused tsunamis and earthquakes and brought about the end of this sophisticated civilization.

The Palace of Knossos site was occupied from Neolithic times, and the population spread to the surrounding land. Around 1900 BC, the hilltop was leveled and the first palace constructed; around 1700 BC, after an earthquake destroyed the original structure, the later palace was built, surrounded by houses and other buildings. Around 1450 BC, another widespread disaster occurred, perhaps an invasion: palaces and country villas were razed by fire and abandoned, but Knossos remained inhabited even though the palace suffered some damage. But around 1380 BC the palace and its outlying buildings were destroyed by fire, and around 1100 BC the site was abandoned. Still later, Knossos became a Greek city-state.

You enter the palace from the west, passing a bust of Sir Arthur Evans, who excavated at Knossos on and off for more than 20 years. A path leads you around to the monumental **south gateway**. The **west wing** encases lines of long, narrow storerooms where the true wealth

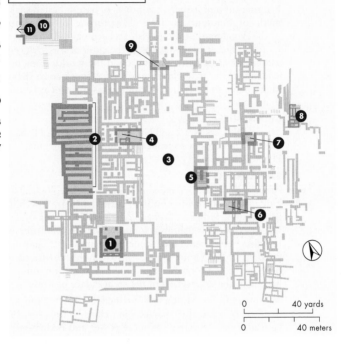

Palace of Knossos

of Knossos was kept in tall clay jars: oil, wine, grains, and honey. The **central court** is about 164 feet by 82 feet long. The cool, dark **throne-room complex** has a griffin fresco and a tall, wavy-back gypsum throne, the oldest in Europe. The most spectacular piece of palace architecture is the **grand staircase,** on the east side of the court, leading to the domestic apartments. Four flights of shallow gypsum stairs survive, lighted by a deep light well. Here you get a sense of how noble Minoans lived; rooms were divided by sets of double doors, giving privacy and warmth when closed, coolness and communication when open. The **queen's megaron** (apartment or hall) is decorated with a colorful dolphin fresco and furnished with stone benches. Beside it is a bathroom, complete with a clay tub, and next door a toilet, whose drainage system permitted flushing into a channel flowing into the Kairatos stream far below. The east side of the palace also contained **workshops.** Beside the staircase leading down to the **east bastion** is a stone water channel made up of parabolic curves and settling basins: a Minoan storm drain. Northwest of the east bastion is the **north entrance,** guarded by a relief fresco of a charging bull. Beyond is the **theatrical area,** shaded by pines and overlooking a shallow flight of steps, which lead down to the **royal road.** This, perhaps, was the ceremonial entrance to the palace.

For a complete education in Minoan architecture and civilization, consider touring Knossos and, of course, the Archaeological Museum in Heraklion (where many of the treasures from the palace are on view), then traveling south to the Palace of Phaistos, another great Minoan site that has not been reconstructed. To reach Knossos by bus, take No. 2 (departing every 15 minutes) from Odos Evans, close to the market, in Heraklion. ⊠ *Knossos* ☎ *28102/31940* ⊕ *www.culture. gr* ✍ *€6; combined ticket for Knossos and Archaeological Museum in Heraklion €10* ☾ *Apr.–Oct., daily 8:30–8; Nov.–Mar., Mon.–Sat. 8–6, Sun. 8:30–3.*

12

LASITHI PLATEAU ΟΡΟΠΕΔΙΟ ΛΑΣΙΘΙΟΥ

47 km (29 miles) southeast of the Palace of Knossos, 52 km (32 miles) southeast of Heraklion.

The Lasithi plateau, 2,800 feet high and the biggest of the upland plains of Crete, lies behind a wall of barren mountains. Windmills for pumping water rise above fields of potatoes and the apple and almond orchards that are a pale haze of blossom in early spring (the process has been supplanted with electric pumps in recent years, though the windmills still stand, quite photogenically). The plateau is remote and breathtakingly beautiful, and ringed by small villages where shops sell local weaving and embroidery.

EXPLORING

Cave of Psychro. This impressive, stalactite-rich cavern is one of a few places in Crete that claim to be the birthplace of Zeus, king of the gods, and where he was reared in secret, out of reach of his vengeful father, Kronos. Approach the cave, once a Minoan sanctuary and now the plateau's most popular tourist attraction, on a short path from the large parking lot on foot or by donkey (a rather uncomfortable experience). ⊠ *Near village of Psychro, Lasithi* ✍ *€5* ☾ *July and Aug., daily 8–7; Sept.–June, daily 8:30–3.*

Cretan Folklore Museum. An old village house in Ayios Georgios stands as it was when generations of farmers lived here. The living quarters and stables, along with the delightful assemblage of simple furnishings, embroidery, tools, provide a chance to see domestic life as it was, and indeed still is, for many residents of the plateau. ⊠ *Ayios Georgios* ☎ *28440/31460* ✍ *€3* ☾ *Mid-Apr.–late Oct., daily 10–4.*

WHERE TO EAT

$

GREEK

✕ **Kronio.** The promise of a meal in this cozy, family-run establishment is alone worth the trip up to the plateau. Delicious meat and vegetable pies as well as homemade casseroles and lamb dishes emerge from the kitchen, to be accompanied by fresh-baked bread and the house wine and followed up with homemade desserts. The charming proprietors, Vassilis and Christine, encourage you to linger over your wine or raki, and are a mine of knowledge about the Lasithi plateau. ■ TIP➔ **They also offer comfortable accommodations surrounding a welcoming terrace and pool just down the road.** $ *Average main: €7* ⊠ *Tzermiado* ☎ *28440/22375* ☾ *Closed Nov.–Mar.*

A rewarding detour as you travel east from Heraklion toward the Lasithi plateau and Malia takes you south to Kastelli, about 15 km (9 miles) southeast of Heraklion, where the lovely Byzantine church of Ayios Pandeleimon is decorated with elaborate frescoes. Interspersing the landscape here and there are segments of an aqueduct that served the nearby ancient Greek city of Lyttos, yet to be excavated. Thrapsano, about 7 km (4½ miles) farther southwest, is a famous pottery center, where workshops turn out earthenware jugs, pots, and decorative items for sale in the main square and at shops throughout town.

Palace of Malia. Like the palaces of Knossos and Phaistos, the Palace of Malia was built around 1900 BC; it was less sophisticated both in architecture and decoration, but the layout is similar. The palace appears to have been destroyed by an earthquake around 1700 BC, and rebuilt 50 years later. Across the west court, along one of the paved raised walkways, is a double row of **round granaries** sunk into the ground, which were almost certainly roofed. East of the granaries is the **south doorway,** beyond which is the large, circular limestone table, or *kernos* (on which were placed offerings to a Minoan deity), with a large hollow at its center and 34 smaller ones around the edge. The **central court** has a shallow pit at its center, perhaps the location of an altar. To the west of the central court are the remains of an imposing staircase leading up to a second floor, and a terrace, most likely used for religious ceremonies; behind is a long corridor with **storerooms** to the side. In the north wing is a large **pillared hall,** part of a set of public rooms. The **domestic apartments** appear to have been in the northwest corner of the palace, entered through a narrow dogleg passage. They are connected by a smaller **northern court,** through which you can leave the palace by the **north entrance,** passing two giant old *pithoi* (large earthenware jars for storage of wine or oil). Excavation at the site continues, which is revealing a sizable town surrounding the palace. ✛ *3 km (2 miles) northeast of Malia town* ☎ *28970/31597* ⊕ *www.culture.gr* 🎫 *€4* ⊗ *Nov.–Mar., Tues.–Sun. 8:30–3; Apr.–Oct., Mon. 1–7:30, Tues.–Sun. 8–7:30.*

> ### MINOS AND THE MINOTAUR
>
> As you tour Knossos, you are stepping into the pages of Greek mythology. As myth has it, Minos coveted the Minoan throne and prayed to Poseidon to send a white bull he would sacrifice in thanksgiving. His wife became smitten and, seducing the animal, gave birth to the Minotaur. Minos ordered the architect Daedalus to build a labyrinthine prison for the monster, who was half man and half bull. The Minotaur was ultimately killed by Theseus, son of the King of Athens, who successfully maneuvered his way through the labyrinth by unwinding a ball of string.

Although some critics claim that Sir Arthur Evans's restoration "Disneyfied" the Palace of Knossos, no one can deny the results are spectacular.

AYIOS NIKOLAOS ΑΓΙΟΣ ΝΙΚΟΛΑΟΣ

30 km (19 miles) east of the Lasithi plateau, 69 km (43 miles) east of Heraklion.

Ayios Nikolaos is clustered on a peninsula alongside the gulf of Mirabello, a dramatic composition of bare mountains, islets, and deep blue sea. Behind the crowded harbor lies a natural curiosity, tiny lake Voulismeni, linked to the sea by a narrow channel. Hilly, with narrow, steep streets that provide sea views, the town is a welcoming and animated place, far more pleasant than Malia and the other resort centers in this part of Crete: you can stroll along waterside promenades, cafés line the lakeshore, and many streets are open only to pedestrians. Ayios Nikolaos and the nearby Elounda peninsula provide an excellent base for exploring eastern Crete.

GETTING HERE AND AROUND

By ferry, the best option is to take it to and from Heraklion, less than an hour away by bus service that runs at least every hour, and often more frequently during the day. Like other major towns on the north coast, Ayios Nikolaos is on the national highway. Parking in the town center is difficult, though you'll often find spaces along the seafront on Akti Koundourou; look at signs carefully to make sure you are not in a space reserved for residents. The bus station is just south of the town center, near the sea on Akti Atlantidos (off Platia Venizelou at the end of Venizelou street).

VISITOR INFORMATION

Contacts Ayios Nikolaos Visitor Information ✉ *Koundourou 21A* ☎ *28410/22357* ⊕ *www.aighosnikolaos.gr* ⊘ *Daily 8:30–9:30.*

EXPLORING

Folk Museum. This excellent museum showcases exquisite weavings and embroidered pieces, along with walking sticks, tools, and other artifacts from everyday rural life in Crete. ✉ *Odos Palaiologou 2* ☎ *28410/25093* ✎ *€3* ⊘ *Tues.–Sun. 10–2.*

Kritsa. The village on a mountainside above Ayios Nikolaos is renowned for its weaving tradition and its narrow lanes—wide enough for only a donkey to pass—that surround a large, shady town square filled with café tables that afford views down green valleys planted with olive trees to the sea. The woven tablecloths and other wares are hard to miss—villagers drape them over every usable service and hang them from storefronts and even trees. The lovely Byzantine church here, the whitewashed **Panayia Kera,** has an unusual shape, with three naves supported by heavy triangular buttresses. Built in the early years of Venetian occupation, it contains some of the liveliest and best-preserved medieval frescoes on the island, painted in the 13th century. ✉ *Kritsa* ✛ *11 km (7 miles) west of Ayios Nikolaos* ⊘ *Church, Sat.–Thurs. 9–3.*

BEACHES

You can dip into the clean waters that surround Ayios Nikolaos from several good beaches right in town. Kitroplatia and Ammos are both only about a five- to 10-minute walk from the center. You can rent lounges and umbrellas at both.

WHERE TO EAT

$$
MEDITERRANEAN
✗ **Migomis.** Dress well (no shorts), ask for a seat by the windows, and partake of an excellent meal accompanied by airy views of the town and the sea. At one of the best restaurants in town, the menu embraces both Greece and Italy, with some excellent pastas and Tuscan steaks and the freshest fish and seafood. $ *Average main: €20* ✉ *20 Nikou Plastira* ☎ *28410/24353* ⊕ *migomis.com* ✎ *Reservations essential* ⊘ *Closed Nov.–Mar.*

$
SEAFOOD
✗ **Pelagos.** An enchanting garden and the high-ceilinged parlors of an elegant neoclassic mansion are the setting for what many locals consider to be the best seafood tavern in Ayios Nikolaos. *Simple* is the key word here: fresh catches from the fleet bobbing in the harbor just beyond are grilled and accompanied by local vegetables and Cretan wines. $ *Average main: €14* ✉ *Stratigou Koraka 11* ☎ *28410/25737.*

$
GREEK
✗ **Stavrakakis Rakadiko.** Enhance the short trip out to Kritsa and Lato with a stop in the nearby village of Exo Lakonia to enjoy a meal at the homey *kafenion* of Manolis and Katerina Stavrakakis. Dishes are based on family recipes, and most are made from ingredients the couple grow themselves. Dolmades are made with zucchini flowers instead of vine leaves, wild mountain greens are boiled or appear in salads dressed with local olive oil, and even such staples as *tzatziki* are outstanding. $ *Average main: €6* ✉ *Exo Lakonia* ✛ *about 8 km (5 miles) west of Ayios Nikolaos* ☎ *28410/22478.*

WHERE TO STAY

$ HOTEL 🏨 **Hotel Du Lac.** Airy and spacious guest rooms right on the lake in the center of town are nicely done with simple, contemporary furnishings; studios, with kitchens and large baths, are enormous. **Pros:** studios are especially good value; nice lakeside restaurant downstairs. **Cons:** large differential in size between rooms and studios. [$] *Rooms from: €65* ✉ *28th October 17* ☎ *28410/22711* 🌐 *www.dulachotel.gr* 🛏 *18 rooms, 6 studios* 🍴 *Breakfast.*

$$$$ RESORT Fodor's Choice ★ 🏨 **St. Nicolas Bay.** Lovely and luxurious, this marble-floored resort is set within verdant gardens overlooking the sea at the edge of Ayios Nikolaos, within easy reach of the busy town center; chic and comfortable surroundings—teak woods, blue-and-white-striped cottons, bouquets of bougainvillea, rough-hewn stone walls, multiple pools, and a sandy beach—have turned this into a delightful Cretan cocoon. **Pros:** convenient yet set apart on a quiet beach; high taste level; personable service; attractive decor and setting; good discounts for longer stays. **Cons:** away from the town center; not inexpensive. [$] *Rooms from: €408* ✉ *Thessi Nissi* ☎ *28410/25041* 🌐 *www.stnicolasbay.gr* 🛏 *102 rooms* 🕒 *Closed Nov.–late Apr.* 🍴 *Breakfast.*

SHOPPING

Chez Sonia. An appealing array of beads, quartz and silver jewelry, woven tablecloths and scarves, and carved bowls and other handicrafts fills Chez Sonia. ✉ *28th October* ☎ *28410/28475.*

Elixir. You can get a very nice taste of the island to take home with you from a huge selection of Cretan olive oils and wines and locally harvested honey and spices. The shop also sells a wide variety of sponges, some from Greek waters. ✉ *Koundourou 15* ☎ *28410/82593.*

ELOUNDA ΕΛΟΥΝΤΑ

11 km (7 miles) north of Ayios Nikolaos, 80 km (50 miles) east of Heraklion.

Traversing a steep hillside, a road with spectacular sea views runs north from Ayios Nikolaos around the gulf of Mirabello to the village of Elounda and the stark peninsula that surrounds it. The beaches tend to be narrow and pebbly, but the water is crystal clear and sheltered from the *meltemi* (the fierce north wind that blows in July and August). Elounda village is a full-scale resort destination: dozens of villas and hotels dot the surrounding hillsides, and the shore of the gulf south of Elounda is crowded with some of the most luxurious hotels in Greece. Don't come here in search of Authentic Greece; expect to meet fellow international travelers.

EXPLORING

Olous. A sunken, ancient city is visible just beneath the turquoise waters off a causeway that leads to the Spinalonga peninsula (not to be confused with the island of the same name), an undeveloped headland. The combination of warm waters and the promise of seeing the outlines of a Roman settlement on the seabed are alluring to snorkelers and swimmers. A few scant remains, including a mosaic floor, can be seen on dry land (fenced and marked with a sign). ✉ *Elounda* ✣ *3 km (2 miles) east of Elounda.*

OFF THE BEATEN PATH

Spinalonga. The Venetians built a huge, forbidding fortress on this small, narrow island in the center of the gulf of Mirabello in the 17th century. In the early 1900s the island became a leper colony, serving this purpose with cruelly primitive conditions for more than 50 years. Travel agents in Ayios Nikolaos and Elounda can arrange boat excursions to the island, some complete with a midday beach barbecue and a swim on a deserted islet; you can also just sign up with any of the many outfitters that leave from the docks in both towns (expect to pay about €15 from Ayios Nikolas, €10 from Elounda). The real treat is cruising on these azure waters, and as you sail past the islet of Ayioi Pantes, a goat reserve, you're likely to see the *kri-kri* (Cretan wild goat), with its impressive curling horns. ✉ *Gulf of Mirabello, Spinalonga* 🎟 *Fortress €2* ⏲ *Daily 8–7.*

WHERE TO EAT

$ GREEK

🍴 **Marilena.** In good weather, meals are served in the large rear garden, or you can choose a table in the cavernous dining room or on a sidewalk terrace facing the harbor. The kitchen sends out excellent fresh, grilled fish, and a rich fish soup, as well as grilled steaks and chops; any meal here should begin with a platter of the house's assorted appetizers, a meal in themselves. [$] *Average main: €11* ✉ *Harborside, main square* ☎ *28410/41322* 🌐 *www.marilenarestaurant.gr* ⏲ *Late Oct.–early Mar.*

$ GREEK

🍴 **Pefko.** Despite the presence of an enormous new resort at the edge of town, Plaka remains a delightful fishing village and Pefko (the Pine Tree) a pleasant place to take in village life and sea views. The menu offers a nice assortment of appetizers, salads, and such basics as moussaka and lamb, to be enjoyed on a shady terrace or in a cozy dining room where music is played some evenings. [$] *Average main: €7* ✉ *Near beach in center of town, Plaka* ☎ *28410/42510* 💳 *No credit cards.*

WHERE TO STAY

$ HOTEL

🏨 **Akti Olous.** A waterfront perch on the edge of the gulf of Mirabello outside Elounda and near the sunken city of Olous is not as luxurious as some of its neighbors, but the bright rooms, all with balconies, are a step away from a strip of sandy beach and provide sweeping views of the sea and peninsula. **Pros:** seaside location within walking distance of town; beautiful views from rooms. **Cons:** some rooms are a bit small; groups can be noisy. [$] *Rooms from: €80* ✉ *Waterfront road* ☎ *28410/41270* 🌐 *www.eloundaaktiolous.gr* 🛏 *70 rooms* ⏲ *Closed Nov.–mid-Apr.* 🍽 *Breakfast.*

$$$$ HOTEL Fodor's Choice ★

🏨 **Elounda Beach Hotel & Villas.** One of Greece's most renowned and luxurious resort hotels, on 40 acres of gardens next to the gulf of Mirabello, offers a dazzling array of delights: five restaurants; soothing whitewashed walls, shady porches, and cool flagstone floors; and a guest-friendly variety of accommodations, from villas with James Bond–like electronic gadgetry and their own swimming pools to large, gracious doubles in a hotel block. **Pros:** beautiful, comfortable accommodations; lovely gardens and seashore; attentive service; one of the world's finest hotels. **Cons:** self-contained resort a distance from town and other services; room rates are steep (but check hotel for deals); too many rooms? [$] *Rooms from: €675 ✛ 3 km (2 miles) south of village ☎ 28410/41412 ⊕ www.eloundabeach.gr ⤳ 215 rooms, 78 suites ⊘ Closed Nov.–Mar.* ⫶⊘⫶ *Breakfast.*

$$$$
RESORT

⊞ **Elounda Gulf Villas.** From private infinity pools to gyms and saunas en suite, luxury seems to know no bounds in these beautiful villas and suites tucked into verdant hillside gardens above the gulf of Mirabello, yet a comfortable, homey atmosphere prevails. **Pros:** beautiful accommodations in an intimate setting; private pools in some units; hotel offers transport to a private beach. **Cons:** not beachfront. [$] *Rooms from: €330 ✛ 3 km (2 miles) south of village ☎ 28102/27721 ⊕ www.eloundavillas.com ⤳ 18 villas, 10 suites* ⫶⊘⫶ *Breakfast.*

$$$$
HOTEL
Fodor'sChoice
★

⊞ **Elounda Mare.** This extraordinary Relais & Châteaux property on the gulf of Mirabello blends luxury, sophistication, and a comfortably relaxed atmosphere accompanied by attentive service—more than half the rooms, all bathed in cool marble and stunningly decorated in a soothing blend of traditional Cretan and contemporary furnishings, are in villas set in their own gardens, many with private pools. **Pros:** gorgeous setting; attractive accommodation; excellent service; sense of being on a private seaside estate. **Cons:** interior stairs and stepped walkways on the grounds may pose a difficulty for travelers with mobility issues. [$] *Rooms from: €350 ✛ 3 km (2 miles) south of village ☎ 28410/68200 ⊕ www.eloundamare.gr ⤳ 24 rooms, 20 suites, 36 bungalows ⊘ Closed Nov.–mid-Apr.* ⫶⊘⫶ *Breakfast.*

VAI ΒΑΪ

170 km (104 miles) east of Heraklion.

The appeal of the surrounding, fertile coastal plain was not lost on the ancient Minoans, who left behind ruins that are not as grand as those on the center of the island but are evocative nonetheless.

EXPLORING

Palaikastro. A sprawling Minoan town currently being excavated by archaeologists, Palaikastro is missing any Knossos-type drama here (for instance, there is no large palace structure), but you get a strong sense of everyday life here amid the stony ruins of streets, squares, and shops. ✉ *Palaikastro ✛ 2 km (1 mile) outside modern Palaikastro ☎ 28410/22462 ⊕ www.culture.gr* ✉ *Free.*

BEACHES

Palm Beach at Vai. Even the classical Greeks recognized the beauty of this palm grove at the eastern end of the island, which is unique in Europe. The sandy stretch with nearby islets in clear turquoise water is such a stunner that many bus tours come all the way east just to show off the sand and palms, so Vai can get jammed in the summer. If the sand in front of the grove of 5,000 palms is too crowded, follow the path south over the headland to a slightly less crowded cove. **Amenities:** food and drink; parking (free); showers; toilets; water sports. **Best for:** snorkeling; swimming.

WHERE TO STAY

$ ⚏ **Hotel Hellas.** Sparkling clean and comfortable, each of the simple rooms
HOTEL here overlooks Palaikastro and the sea from a balcony. **Pros:** in pleasant
town center; near beaches. **Cons:** front rooms can be a bit noisy. Ⓢ *Rooms
from: €37 ⊠ Main Sq., Palaikastro ☎ 28430/61240 ⊕ www.palaikastro.
com/hotelhellas ⇦ 17 rooms ▭ No credit cards ⦿ Breakfast.*

WESTERN CRETE ΔΥΤΙΚΗ ΚΡΗΤΗ

Much of western Crete's landscape—soaring mountains, deep gorges,
and rolling green lowlands—remains largely untouched by mass tourism. Only the north coast is developed, leaving many interesting byways
to be explored. This region is abundant in Minoan sites—including
the palace at Phaistos—as well as Byzantine churches and Venetian
monasteries. Two of Greece's more-appealing cities are here: Chania
and Rethymnon, both crammed with the houses, narrow lanes, and
minarets that hark back to Venetian and Turkish occupation. Friendly
villages dot the uplands, and there are some outstanding beaches on
the ruggedly beautiful and remote west and south coasts. Immediately
southwest of Heraklion lies the traditional agricultural heartland of
Crete: long, narrow valleys where olive groves alternate with vineyards
of sultana grapes for export.

VORI ΒΟΡΙΟΝ

*65 km (40½ miles) southwest of Heraklion, 5 km (3 miles) north of
Palace of Phaistos.*

Vori, the closest town to Phaistos and Ayia Triada, is a pleasant farming
community of whitewashed houses on narrow lanes; you might enjoy
stopping here for some refreshment at one of the cafés on the lively
main square and to visit the excellent folk museum.

Fodor'sChoice **Foundation Museum of Cretan Ethnology.** A rich collection of Cretan folk
★   items showcases exquisite weavings and pottery, basketry, farm implements, household furnishings, and clothing, all beautifully displayed
and descriptively labeled in a well-designed building. ⊠ *Edge of village center ☎ 28/9209–1112 ⊕ www.cretanethnologymuseum.gr ⊠ €3
⊗ Daily 10–6.*

PALACE OF PHAISTOS ΑΝΑΚΤΟΡΟ ΤΗΣ ΦΑΙΣΤΟΥ

50 km (31 miles) southwest of Heraklion, 11 km (7 miles) south of Vori.

On a steep hill overlooking olive groves and the sea on one side, and
high mountain peaks on the other, the second-largest (and also second-
greatest) Minoan palace was the center of Minoan culture in southern
Crete. Unlike Knossos, Phaistos has not been reconstructed, though the
copious ruins are richly evocative. Nearby is another palace, Ayia Triada.

Fodor'sChoice **Palace of Phaistos.** The palace of Phaistos was built around 1900 BC and
★   rebuilt after a disastrous earthquake around 1650 BC. It was burned
and abandoned in the wave of destruction that swept across the island

12

around 1450 BC, though Greeks continued to inhabit the city until the 2nd century BC, when it was eclipsed by Roman Gortyna.

You enter the site by descending a flight of steps leading into the west court, then climb a grand staircase. From here you pass through the **Propylon porch** into a light well and descend a narrow staircase into the **central court.** Much of the southern and eastern sections of the palace have eroded away. But there are large pithoi still in place in the old **storerooms.** On the north side of the court the recesses of an elaborate doorway bear a rare trace: red paint in a diamond pattern on a white ground. A passage from the doorway leads to the **north court** and the **northern domestic apartments,** now roofed and fenced off. The **Phaistos Disk** was found in 1903 in a chest made of mud brick at the northeast edge of the site and is now on display at the Archaeological Museum in Heraklion. East of the central court are the **palace workshops,** with a metalworking furnace fenced off. South of the workshops lie the **southern domestic apartments,** including a clay bath. From there, you have a memorable view across the Messara plain. ⊠ *Phaistos* ✣ *Follow signs and ascend hill off Ayii Deka–Mires–Timbaki Rd.* ☎ *28920/27100* ⊕ *www.culture.gr* 🎫 *€4; combined ticket with Ayia Triada €6* ⊙ *Apr.–Oct., daily 8–7:30; Nov.–Mar., daily 8:30–3.*

Ayia Triada. Another Minoan settlement was destroyed at the same time as Phaistos, which is only a few miles away on the other side of the same hill. Ayia Triada was once thought to have been a summer palace for the rulers of Phaistos but is now believed to have consisted of a group of villas for nobility and a warehouse complex. Rooms in the villas were once paneled with gypsum slabs and decorated with frescoes: the two now hanging in the Archaeological Museum in Heraklion show a woman in a garden and a cat hunting a pheasant. Several other lovely pieces, including finely crafted vases, also come from Ayia Triada and are now also on display in Heraklion. Though the complex was at one time just above the seashore, the view now looks across the extensive Messara plain to the Lybian sea in the distance. ⊠ *Phaistos* ✣ *Follow signs 3 km (2 mi) west from Phaistos* ☎ *28920/91360* ⊕ *www.culture. gr* 🎫 *€4; combined ticket with Phaistos €6* ⊙ *May–Sept., daily 8–7:30; Oct.–Apr., daily 8:30–3.*

EN ROUTE
The quickest route from Phaistos, Matala, and other places on the Messara plain to the north coast is the Heraklion road, a small section of which is four lanes. But a very pleasant alternative leads northwest through Ayia Galini (the largest resort in this part of the southern coast) and the mountain town of Spili to Rethymnon. The route shows off the beauty of rural Crete as it traverses deep valleys and gorges and climbs the flanks of the interior mountain ranges. Just beyond Spili, follow signs to Moni Preveli, a stunningly situated monastery perched high above the sea. A monument honors the monks here who sheltered Allied soldiers after the Battle of Crete and helped them escape the Nazi-occupied island via submarine. Below the monastery is lovely Palm beach, where golden sands are shaded by a palm grove watered by a mountain stream. But avoid this patch of paradise at midday during high season, when it is packed with day-trippers who arrive by tour boat from Ayia Galini.

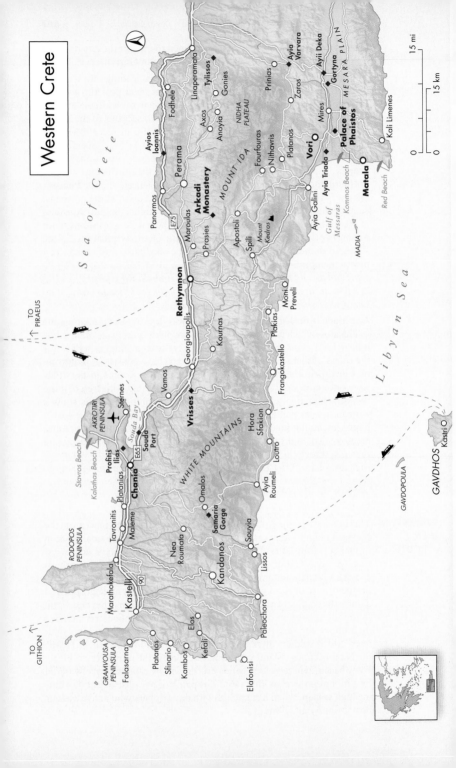

MATALA ΜΑΤΑΛΑ

10 km (6 miles) southwest of Vori, 70 km (42 miles) southwest of Heraklion.

Renowned in the 1960s as a stopover on the hippie trail across the eastern Mediterranean, Matala today is a small, low-key beach resort. The 2nd-century AD Roman tombs cut in the cliff side attract day-trippers from Heraklion and make an impressive vista from the pleasant town beach.

BEACHES

Red Beach. This beautiful crescent of sand is accessible only by a 20-minute walk across a rocky promontory on a path from Matala. The trek includes a scramble up and over a headland and some steep climbs and descents, though grades are manageable with moderate exertion. Your reward is a lovely, unspoiled crescent of golden sand washed by clear waters and especially popular with nudists. Surf in the small bay can be rough, with riptides. Shade is scarce, though a small concession sometimes rents umbrellas and simple snacks. **Amenities:** food and drink (only sometimes available). **Best for:** solitude; nudists; swimming; walking. ✥ *1 km (½ mile) west of town.*

Kommos Beach. Fabulous, pine-and palm-fringed Kommos lies below the site of a Minoan harbor where excavations are ongoing. At its far northern end lies the scrappy little resort of Kalamaki, where a few modest hotels and tavernas back the sand (some rent out umbrellas and lounges) and a simple taverna and a lounge-chair concession operates on the north end. But for the most part the beach is an unspoiled stretch of white sand washed by clear waters and backed by hills shaded with tamarac trees. Kommos is especially popular with nudists, and it's a nesting ground for the loggerhead sea turtle (*Caretta caretta*). **Amenities:** food and drink; parking (free); showers and toilets. **Best for:** solitude; nudists; sunset; swimming; walking. ✉ *Near Pitsidia, off Mires–Matala road* ✥ *2 km (1 mile) from signposted turnoff.*

WHERE TO EAT

$ GREEK 🍴 **Taverna Sigelakis.** Residents from villages for miles around come to the town of Sivas to enjoy a meal of *briam* (baked vegetables), moussaka, and other specialties, including delicious roasted lamb and chicken, all served on the front terrace in warm seasons or in the stone-wall, hearth-warmed dining room when the weather's cold. A meal comes with friendly service, a visit from proprietor Giorgios, and a free glass of raki and a sweet. [$] *Average main: €9* ✉ *Sivas* ✥ *6 km (4 miles) northeast of Matala* ☎ *69/7481–0905 mobile.*

WHERE TO STAY

$ RENTAL 🏨 **Studios Sigelakis.** Located on a hillside in the little farming village of Sivas, about 5 km (3 miles) from the beach, these "studios" (think simple apartments) have basic kitchens, and are some the of the most comfortable and tastefully decorated around. **Pros:** attractive units and terraces; excellent value for the quality; beaches, Phaistos, and other attractions are nearby; available by day or week. **Cons:** no daily housekeeping, reception, or other hotel amenities. $ *Rooms from: €50* ⊠ *Sivas ✣ 6 km (4 miles) northeast of Matala* ☎ *69/7481–0905* ⊕ *www. sigelakis-studios.gr* ⥄ *8 apartments* ⦿❘ *No meals.*

$ ⛱ **Thalori.** To enjoy a remote Cretan retreat without sacrificing comfort,
RESORT   it's hard to beat these beautifully renovated stone houses in an ages-old village that clings to a mountainside high above the Libyan sea. **Pros:** beautiful surroundings; ideal for those who want to get away from it all and enjoy nature; very comfortable accommodations. **Cons:** at least a half-hour drive from the nearest village or beach and far from other south coast attractions. $ *Rooms from: €70* ⊠ *Kapetaniana* ☎ *28930/41762* ⊕ *www.thalori.com* ⥄ *14 apartments* ⦿❘ *Breakfast.*

ARKADI MONH

18 km (11 miles) southwest of Fodhele, 30 km (19 miles) southwest of Heraklion.

As you approach Arkadi from the north, through the rolling lands at the base of Mt. Ida (one of the contenders in the dispute over the alleged Cretan birthplace of Zeus), you'll follow a gorge inland before emerging onto the flat pastureland that surrounds one of Crete's most beautiful and important monasteries. The approach is even more dramatic from the south, as you traverse the uplands of the beautiful Amari valley before dropping into the mountain plateau that the monastery and its vast holdings occupy.

Arkadi Monastery. A place of pilgrimage for Cretans, Arkadi is also one of the most stunning pieces of Renaissance architecture on the island. The ornate facade, decorated with Corinthian columns and an elegant belfry above, was built in the 16th century of a local, honey-color stone. In 1866 the monastery came under siege during a major rebellion against the Turks, and Abbot Gabriel and several hundred rebels, together with their wives and children, refused to surrender. When the Turkish forces broke through the gate, the defenders set the gunpowder store afire, killing themselves together with hundreds of Turks. The monastery was again a center of resistance when Nazis occupied Crete during World War II. ⊠ *South of old Heraklion–Hania road, Arkadi* ☎ *28310/83135* ⛭ *€2* ⊘ *June–Aug., daily 9–8; Sept.–Oct. and Apr.–May, daily 9–7; Nov., daily 9–5; Dec.–Mar., daily 9–4.*

WHERE TO STAY

$$ ⛱ **Kapsaliana Village Hotel.** A 300-year-old hamlet set amid vast olive
HOTEL   groves has been converted to one of Crete's most distinctive and relaxing
Fodor's Choice   lodgings with luxurious, stylishly appointed rooms, welcoming lounges,
★   and an excellent dining room—all fashioned out of beautiful, ancient stone houses that were once part of the Arkadi Monastery holdings. **Pros:** former village-turned-hotel; a welcome break from anonymous resorts; atmospheric surroundings; extremely attractive accommodations; casual yet attentive service; unique history; reasonable rates. **Cons:** remote location makes a rental car a necessity; some distance from beaches. $ *Rooms from: €140* ⊠ *Arkadi* ☎ *28310/83400* ⊕ *www. kapsalianavillage.gr* ⥄ *11 suites, 6 rooms* ⦿❘ *Breakfast.*

RETHYMNON ΡΕΘΥΜΝΟ

25 km (15 miles) west of Arkadi Monastery, 78 km (48½ miles) west of Heraklion.

Rethymnon is Crete's third-largest town, after Heraklion and Chania. The population (about 30,000) steadily increases as the town expands—a new quarter follows the coast to the east of the Old Town, where the beachfront has been tastelessly developed with large hotels and other resort facilities catering to tourists on package vacations. Nevertheless, much of Rethymnon's charm perseveres in the old Venetian quarter, which is crowded onto a compact peninsula dominated by the huge, fortified Venetian castle known as the Fortezza. Wandering through the narrow alleyways, you come across handsome carved-stone Renaissance doorways belonging to vanished mansions, fountains, archways, and wooden Turkish houses with latticework screens on the balconies to protect the women of the house from prying eyes.

GETTING HERE AND AROUND

At this writing, a several-times-a-week ferry connects Rethymnon with Pireaus, though service has a way of changing in frequency and disappearing altogether. If a boat is not operating when you wish to make the trip, a good option is to use the ferry terminal or airport at Chania, about 45 minutes and €55 away by taxi. Rethymon is also served by hourly bus service from Chania and Heraklion, each about an hour away, and the fare to either is about €8 each way. Rethymon's bus terminal is on the west side of town, on the sea near the Venetian fortress, at Atki Kefaloyianithon. Rethymon is on Crete's national highway, which runs along the north coast, and there is public parking on the seaside road around the Venetian fortress, next to the old harbor, and elsewhere around town.

EXPLORING

Archaeological Museum. Here's even more evidence of just how long Crete has cradled civilizations: a collection of bone tools from a Neolithic site at Yerani (west of Rethymnon); Minoan pottery; and an unfinished statue of Aphrodite, the goddess of love, from the Roman occupation (look for the ancient chisel marks). The museum building used to be a Turkish guardhouse and prison. ✉ *Chimaras, next to entrance of Fortezza* ☎ *28310/54668* 🖅 *€3* ⊘ *Nov.–Mar, Tues.–Sun. 9–3; Apr.–Oct. Tues.–Sun. 9–4.*

Fortessa. The west side of the peninsula on which Rethymnon sits is taken up almost entirely with this massive fortress, strategically surrounded by the sea and thick ramparts. Entering the fortress is a bit of a letdown, because the high, well-preserved walls enclose not much more than a vast empty space occupied by a few scattered buildings—a mosque, two churches, and abandoned barracks that once housed the town brothels and are surrounded by fields of wildflowers in spring. After a small fortress on the site failed to thwart a 1571 attack of 40 pirate galleys, Venetians conscripted 100,000 forced laborers from the town and surrounding villages to build the huge compound. It didn't fulfill its purpose of keeping out the Turks: Rethymnon surrendered after a three-week siege in 1646. ✉ *West end of town* ☎ *28310/341337* 🖅 *€3* ⊘ *Daily 8–10.*

Historical and Folk Art Museum. A restored Venetian palazzo almost in the shadow of the Neratze minaret houses a delightful collection of rustic furnishings, tools, and exquisite weavings that provide a charming and vivid picture of what life on Crete was like until well into the 20th century. ✉ *Vernardou 28* ☎ *28310/23398* 🎫 *€4* ⏲ *Mon.–Sat. 10 am–2:30 pm.*

Neratze. The most visible sign of the Turkish occupation of Rethymnon is the graceful minaret, one of the few to survive in Greece, that rises above the Neratze. This large stone structure looming over the narrow lanes of the city center was a monastery, then church, under the Venetians, and was subsequently converted to a mosque under the Ottomans before being transformed into today's concert hall. ✉ *Odos Verna and Odos Ethnikis Adistaseos.*

Venetian Loggia. The carefully restored clubhouse of the local nobility is now enclosed in glass and houses the Archaeological Museum's shop. This remnant of Venetian rule is enhanced by the nearby Rimondi Fountain, just down the street at the end of Platanos Square and is one of the town's most welcoming sights, spilling refreshing streams from several lions' heads. You'll come upon several other fountains as you wander through the labyrinth of narrow streets. ✉ *Arkadiou.*

Venetian Harbor. Rethymnon's small inner harbor, with its restored 13th-century lighthouse, comes to life in warm weather, when restaurant tables clutter the quayside. Fishing craft and pleasure boats are crammed chockablock into the minute space. ✉ *Waterfront.*

WHERE TO EAT

$$ GREEK

🍴 **Avli.** This stone, barrel-vaulted dining room and a multitiered garden are part of the gorgeous Avli hotel (*see below*) and are attractive settings for creative interpretations of Cretan cuisine: in addition, the grass-fed lamb, fresh-caught fish, and garden vegetables are all organic and natural. Even a simple *horiatiki* (Greek salad) and grilled lamb chop can be transporting here, as is the excellent selection of the island's finest wines. Meals are also served in the narrow lane in front of the hotel, a transporting experience as well. **TIP→ Reservations are a good idea in summer.** [$] *Average main: €22* ✉ *Paleologou 22* ☎ *28310/26213* 🌐 *www.avli.gr.*

$ GREEK

🍴 **Kyria Maria.** At this simple, family-run taverna in the center of the Old Town, good home cooking of the moussaka and pastitsio variety is served from a small menu of traditional Greek specialties. Neighborhood life buzzes around the tables set beneath an arbor and cages of chirping birds in a narrow lane behind the Rimondi Fountain. This place is open from breakfast through late-night dinners daily. [$] *Average main: €9* ✉ *Moschovitou 20* ☎ *28310/29078.*

$ SEAFOOD

🍴 **Prima Plora.** The name means "bow and stern" and it's hard to find a better seaside setting in Rethymnon, with tables set so close to the water that your dinner could swim right onto your plate (in bad weather meals are served in an airy, glass and white-beam pavilion). The kitchen makes the most of the setting with such innovative creations as octopus and fava salad, mussels served dozens of ways, and *kritharoto*, with grilled shrimp on a bed of beautifully seasoned orzo, accompanied

Continued on page 666

NECTAR OF THE GODS

The roots of Greek wine run deep: Naughty Dionysus partied his way through mythology as the God of Wine and became a symbol for celebration in Greece. During the ancient festivities called Dionysia, husbands and wives alike let loose and drank themselves into a heady joy. Now that you're in the land of the god, be sure to enjoy some liquid Dionysian delights. Greece's wine is flavorful and original, so much so that some of the wines here you won't find anywhere else.

This is one reason why few can resist taking some bottles home (a bottle of excellent Greek wine will cost at least €15 to €20, but good varieties can be found for around €10). Remember to ask the clerk to pad them with bubble wrap so they won't break in your suitcase on the journey back. Following are some tips about vintners who are leading the Greek winemaking renaissance, along with a rundown of the grape varietals that Greek wineries specialize in.

Hillside vineyard, Samos Island

THE GREEK WINES TO LOOK FOR

Former Yugoslav Republic of Macedonia
BULGARIA
MACEDONIA
ALBANIA
Assyrtiko
Athiri
Roditis
Xinomavro
TURKEY
THE SPORADES
Limnos
EPIRUS
THESSALIA
Roditis
Lesbos
CENTRAL GREECE
Assyrtiko
Athiri
Roditis
Savatiano
Rombola
Achaia
ATTICA
White Muscat
Athens
Samos
THE CYCLADES
DODECANESE
Agiorgitiko
Mavrodaphne
Moschofilero
Roditis
White Muscat
PELOPONNESE
IONIAN ISLANDS
Assyrtiko
Athiri
Rhodes
Santorini
Athiri
Mandilaria
CRETE
Kotsifali
Mandilaria

REDS

Agiorgitiko. The name means St. George and it's mainly found in the Nemea region of the Peloponnese. Richly colored and scented, with aromas of sour cherries and pomegranate, it goes well with red meat and yellow soft cheeses.

Kotsifali. Grown mainly in Crete, it is rich and aromatic, with hints of raisins, prunes, and sage. Pair with red meat, light red sauces, and yellow cheeses.

Mandilaria. Mainly cultivated in Rhodes and Crete, it is rich and intense, with hints of pomegranate. Pair with grilled and stewed meats with spicy sauces and mild cheeses.

Mavrodaphne. Found in the Peloponnese regions of Achaia and Ilia and the Ionian Islands, it is a lovely dessert wine. Drink alone or with a light dessert.

Xinomavro. Found in Macedonia, it is rich, acidic, and bursting with aromas such as gooseberry with hints of olives and spices. Pair with grilled meats, casseroles, and yellow spicy cheeses.

WHITES

Assyrtiko. One of Greece's finest white wines and found mainly in Santorini, Attica, and Macedonia, it is rich and dry with honeysuckle and citrus aromas and an earthy aftertaste. Pair with grilled fish, poultry, or pork and feta.

Athiri. An ancient variety found mainly in Santorini, Macedonia, Attica, and Rhodes, it is vibrant and fruity with tropical fruit and honey tones. Pair with poultry or pork, pasta, grilled fish, or white cheeses.

Moschofilero. Originating in the Peloponnese, it is vivid and has rich fruity and floral aromas. Pair with poultry, pasta, and seafood.

Roditis. Popular in Attica, Macedonia, Thessaly, and Peloponnese, it is light and has vibrant scents of pineapple, pear, melon, and jasmine. Pair with poultry, fish, and mild cheeses.

Rombola. Grown in the Ionian island of Cephalonia, it is scented with citrus and peach and has a lemony aftertaste. Pair with fish or poultry.

Savatiano. Grown in Attica, it is full-bodied with fruity tones of apple, pear, and peach. Pair with poultry, pork, or fish as well as soft white cheeses.

White Muscat. Cultivated on the Aegean island of Samos and in the northern Peloponnese city of Patras, it is sweet and intense. Pair with desserts and ice cream.

PICK OF THE VINE

(left) Dionysos Kantharos, God of wine; (right) a toast with Santorini wine.

Wherever you head in Greece, wine-makers are perfecting the millennia-old traditions of Greek wine, with high-class estates such as Gaia, Boutari, and Porto Carras leading the way. These wineries can all be visited by appointment. A good introductory Web site is ⊕ *www.allaboutgreekwine.com.*

Peloponnese, Tetramythos Vineyards. While vineyards throughout the region produce Agiorgitiko, an aromatic and deeply colored red, those from Tetrmythos (⊕ *www.tetramythos.com*) on the northern slopes of Mt. Helmos, rising 7,775 feet above the Gulf of Corinth, are especially velvety and rich.

Cyclades, Haridimos Hatzidakis. On Santorini, his winery (⊕ *www.hatzidakiswines. gr*) near Pyrgos Kallistis comprises a celebrated set of organic vineyards. One of his top organic wines is the Aidani Assyritiko, a dry, fruity white.

Macedonia, Yiannis Boutaris. Up north, in Naoussa, Imathia wine lovers make a beeline to Yiannis's Ktima Kir-Yianni winery (⊕ *www.kiryianni.gr*). He split from his family's estate ten years ago to concentrate on producing standout dry reds.

DRINK LIKE A CRETAN

While Crete's viticultural history goes back 3,500 years, the island's wines are becoming newly popular. Vidiano, a complex, fruity, and full-bodied white, is quickly emerging from obscurity as a favorite of connoisseurs. Nikolaos Douloufakis is gaining attention with his bottlings of Vidiano and Vilana, a white grape with spicy aromas and notes of banana and clementine, and he also is known for his dry-red and sweet versions of Liatiko, another ages-old Cretan varietal. He comes from an established, nearly 80-years-old winemaking family in Dafnes (⊕ www.cretanwines.gr), a village near the island capital of Heraklion, which is well known among wine enthusiasts. Dafnes and nearby Archanes are surrounded by vineyards, and tasting rooms in and around both villages provide a satisfying introduction to Cretan wines.

by garden-fresh salads and vegetables. There's a nice selection of Cretan wines, and even some locally brewed beers. Note: Prima Plore is not in the Old Town, but on the seafront a 15-minute walk or short taxi ride west of the fortress. [$] *Average main: €14* ✉ *4 Akrotiriou* ☎ *28310/56990* 🌐 *www.primaplora.gr.*

$ GREEK 🍴 **Thalassographia.** The name means "seascape," a poetic notion for this romantic gathering spot that spreads across a series of terraces wedged between the Fortessa and the azure waters below. This is the best place in town for a cocktail, and if you want to stay to enjoy the sunset, you can dine lightly on such delicious mezedes as *hohlioi* (snails fried in rosemary-infused butter) and fresh salads. [$] *Average main: €8* ✉ *Kefalogianhidou 33* ☎ *28310/52569.*

WHERE TO STAY

$$ HOTEL Fodor's Choice ★ 🏨 **Avli.** Some of the most beautiful accommodations in town are arranged around a garden and in surrounding old houses, where rooms could merit the cover of the *World of Interiors* with their sumptuous mix of baroque gilt frames, rough whitewashed stone walls, glittering chandeliers, rich textiles, Greek antiques, and massive wood beams. **Pros:** some of the most fanciful and commodious rooms in Greece; pleasant roof terrace; steep discounts for longer stays. **Cons:** stairs to rooms; rooms facing restaurant garden can be noisy at times; service can be a bit casual. [$] *Rooms from: €150* ✉ *Xanthodidou 22* ☎ *28310/58250* 🌐 *www.avli.gr* 🛏 *12 rooms* 🍽 *Breakfast.*

$ HOTEL 🏨 **Leo Hotel.** Eleni Christonaki oversees this lovely little inn that occupies the 600-year-old house in which she was raised and where large, beautifully decorated guest rooms are embellished with stone walls and beamed ceilings and filled with handsome contemporary furnishings that include supremely comfortable beds. **Pros:** attractive, comfortable surroundings; friendly service; central location on a quiet street in the Old Town. **Cons:** steep stairs may pose a problem for some guests; breakfast is extra. [$] *Rooms from: €102* ✉ *Arkadiou 2–4* ☎ *28310/261967* 🌐 *www.leohotel.gr* 🛏 *8 rooms* 🍽 *No meals.*

$$ HOTEL 🏨 **Palazzino di Corina.** Rethymnon has several hotels occupying old palaces, but Corina is the most pleasant, with luxurious and stylish surroundings that include a nicely planted courtyard surrounding a small pool. **Pros:** beautiful courtyard is a perfect place to relax; most rooms are extremely quiet. **Cons:** some rooms on upper floors require a climb. [$] *Rooms from: €140* ✉ *Damvergi and Diakou* ☎ *28310/21205* 🌐 *www.corina.gr* 🛏 *29 rooms and suites* 🍽 *Breakfast.*

$ B&B/INN 🏨 **Vetera Suites.** A Venetian-Ottoman house evokes the rich ambience of old Rethymnon, with atmospheric and comfortable rooms and two-level suites embellished with exposed beams, chimneys, stonework, and other original details and furnished with picturesque antiques. **Pros:** distinctive surroundings; quiet location at edge of old town. **Cons:** rooms are reached by steep stairs; breakfast is extra. [$] *Rooms from: €98* ✉ *Kastrinoyannaki 39* ☎ *28310/23844* 🌐 *www.vetera.gr* 🛏 *4 suites* 🍽 *No meals.*

SPORTS AND THE OUTDOORS

Fodor's Choice
★
Happy Walker. This outfitter arranges easy day hikes in the mountains and gorges near Rethymnon, adding a welcome stop for a village lunch to each walk. Each walk costs €30. The outfit also leads multi-day treks through the remote regions of Crete and other islands. ⊠ *Tombazi 56* ☎ *28310/52920* ⊕ *www.happywalker.com* ☼ *Closed late Oct.–Mar.*

SHOPPING

Rethymnon's narrow lanes may remind you of a Middle Eastern souk— or a tacky shopping mall, depending on your frame of mind. If you are looking for something a bit more substantial than, say, playing cards with erotic images of gods and goddesses, you can also find some small shops selling some genuinely high-quality goods, whether it's Cretan olive oil or the work of island craftspeople.

Archaeological Museum Shop. Handsomely housed in the Venetian loggia, this store has an excellent selection of books, as well as reproductions of artifacts from its collections and from other sites in Crete and throughout Greece. ⊠ *Arkadiou* ☎ *28310/54668* ☼ *Mon.–Fri. 8–3.*

Agora—Avli Raw Materials. The popular shop sells many of the herbs, spices, oils, and other ingredients that flavor the cuisine it serves just around the corner at is eponymously named restaurant, as well as fine Greek wines and other products. ⊠ *Xanthoudidou 22* ☎ *28310/26213* ⊕ *www.avli.gr/agora/.*

Kalymnos. For a souvenir that will be light to carry, stop in and browse shelves brimming with sponges harvested off the eponymous island and in other Greek waters. ⊠ *Arampatzouglou 26* ☎ *28310/50802.*

Omodamos Clayart. Charming ceramic pieces are made by artisans throughout Greece, whose creations range from hand-thrown pots to whimsical figurines. ⊠ *5 Souliou* ☎ *28310/58763* ⊕ *www.rethymnoguide.com/omodamos.*

VRISSES ΒΡΥΣΕΣ

26 km (14 miles) west of Rethymnon, 105 km (65 miles) west of Heraklion.

This appealing old village is famous throughout Crete for its thick, creamy yogurt—best eaten with a large spoonful of honey on top— that is served in the cafés beneath the plane trees at the center of town. Georgioupolis, on the coast about 7 km (4½ miles) due west, is another shady, lovely old town, where the Almiros river flows into the sea. Some of the coast here is undergoing rather unattractive development, but inland walks—including one through a eucalyptus-scented valley that links Vrisses and Georgioupolis—make it easy to get away from the fray.

CHANIA XANIA

52 km (33 miles) west of Vrisses, 78 km (48 miles) west of Rethymnon.

Fodor'sChoice
★

Chania surrendered its role as capital of Crete to Heraklion in 1971, but this elegant city of eucalyptus-lined avenues, miles of waterfront promenades, and shady, cobbled alleyways lined with Venetian and Ottoman houses is still close to the heart of all Cretans. It was here that the Greek flag was raised in 1913 to mark Crete's unification with Greece, and the place is simply one of the most beautiful of all Greek cities.

GETTING HERE AND AROUND

Daily ferry service connects Chania with Pireaus, arriving at the harbor on Souda bay every morning at about 6 am and departing around 9 pm. The crossing takes roughly eight hours. During summer, ferries also provide daytime service between Pireaus and Chania, and crossings take six hours. Souda is a 20-minute taxi ride from the town center (€15), and municipal buses also run from Souda to Chania (€1.10). Chania's airport, also on Souda bay, has daily service from Athens, as well as flights from many European cities, mostly charters, during high season. Buses run from the airport infrequently, so plan on taking a taxi or picking up your rental car at the airport. Hourly buses connect Chania with Rethymnon, about €8, and Heraklion, about €13. Less frequent bus service connects Chania with Kissamos, Paleohora, and many other places in western Crete. The well-organized bus station, with a helpful information desk, is at Kidonias 25, just off Halidon. The city center is well marked from the national road. For parking, drive to the center and make your way, following well-posted parking signs, to the west side of the Old City, where you'll find free parking near the sea. Be careful where you park, as some places are open only to residents, and violators are fined.

TRAVEL AGENTS

Contacts Diktynna Travel ✉ *Archontaki 6* ☎ *28210/41458* ⊕ *www.diktynna-travel.gr.*

EXPLORING

The sizable Old Town is strung along the harbor (divided by a centuries-old seawall into outer and inner harbors), where tall Venetian houses face a pedestrians-only, taverna-lined waterside walkway, and fishing boats moor beside a long stretch of Venetian arsenals and warehouses. Well-preserved Venetian and Turkish quarters surround the harbors and a covered food and spice market, a remnant of Venetian trade and Turkish bazaars, is set amid a maze of narrow streets.

TOP ATTRACTIONS

Archaeological Museum. The former Venetian church of St. Francis, surrounding a lovely garden in the shadow of the Venetian walls, displays artifacts from all over western Crete and the collection bears witness to the presence of Minoans, ancient Greeks, Romans, Venetians, and Ottomans. The painted Minoan clay coffins and elegant late-Minoan pottery indicate that the region was as wealthy as the center of the island under the Minoans, though no palace has yet been located. ✉ *25 Chalidron* ☎ *28210/90334* ⊕ *odysseus.culture.gr* ✉ *€2; combined*

12

admission with Byzantine and Post-Byzantine Collection €3 ☉ Daily 9–4 (reduced hours in winter).

Ayia Triada. Lands at the northeast corner of the Akrotiri peninsula, which extends into the sea from the east side of Chania, are the holdings of several monasteries, including Ayia Triada (Holy Trinity). The olive groves that surround and finance the monastery yield excellent oils, and the shop is stocked with some of the island's finest. Ayia Triada is a delightful place, where you can visit the flower-filled cloisters and the ornately decorated chapel, which dates from the monastery's founding in 1611 (by two brothers of a Venetian-Cretan family). ⊠ *Akrotiri ✛ 16 km (10 miles) north of Hania, follow road from Chordaki* ☎ *28210/63572* ⊕ *www.agiatriada-chania.gr ☉ Summer: daily 8–sunset; winter: daily 8–2 and 4–sunset.*

Byzantine and Post-Byzantine Collection of Chania. You'll get some insight into the Venetian occupation *and* the Christian centuries that preceded it at this small museum housed in the charming 15th-century church of San Salvadore alongside the city walls just behind the Firka. Mosaics, icons, coins, and other artifacts bring to life Cretan civilization as it was after the Roman Empire colonized the island and Christianity took root as early as the 1st century. ⊠ *Theotokopoulou 82* ☎ *28210/96046* ⊕ *odysseus.culture.gr* 🎫 *€2; combined ticket with Archaeological Museum €3 ☉ Tues.–Sun. 8:30–3.*

Fodor's Choice ★ **Firka.** Just across the narrow channel from the lighthouse and marking the west entrance to the harbor is the old Turkish prison, which now houses the **Nautical Museum of Crete.** Exhibits, more riveting than might be expected, trace the island's seafaring history from the time of the Minoans, with a reproduction of an Athenian *trireme*, amphora from Roman shipwrecks, Ottoman weaponry, and other relics. Look for the photos and mementos from the World War II Battle of Crete, when Allied forces moved across the island and, with the help of Cretans, ousted the German occupiers. Much of the fighting centered on Chania, and great swaths of the city were destroyed during the war. Almost worth the price of admission alone is the opportunity to walk along the Firka's ramparts for bracing views of the city, sea, and mountains. ⊠ *Waterfront at far west end of port* ☎ *28210/91875* ⊕ *odysseus.culture.gr* 🎫 *€2.50 ☉ Apr.–Oct., daily 9–4; Nov.–Mar., daily 9–2.*

Gouvernetou. This 16th-century, Venetian-era monastery on the north end of the Akrotiri peninsula is said to be one of the oldest and largest remaining religious communities on Crete. Delightful frescoes cover the wall of the courtyard chapel, while a path leads down the flanks of a seaside ravine past several caves used as hermitages and churches to the remote, 11th-century Katholiko, the monastery of St. John the Hermit, who persued his solitary life in a nearby cave. Follow the path down to the sea along a riverbank for another mile or so to a secluded cove that is the perfect place for a refreshing dip. The return walk requires a steep uphill climb. ⊠ *Stavros ✛ Northern end of Akrotiri peninsula, 4 km (2.5 miles) north of Ayia Triada; 19 km (12 miles) north of Chania, follow road north from Chordaki* ☎ *28430/63319* 🎫 *Free ☉ Mon., Tues., Thurs. 9–11 and 5–7 pm, Sat.–Sun. 5–8 pm.*

Venetian Arsenali. As you follow the harbor front east from the mosque, you come to a long line of Venetian *arsenali* (warehouses) from the 16th and 17th centuries, used to store wares and repair craft. The seawalls swing around to enclose the harbor and end at the **old lighthouse** that stands at the east side of the harbor entrance; from here you get a magnificent view of the town, with the imposing White mountains looming behind the animated harbor. ⊠ *Akti Enoseos, east end of old harbor.*

WORTH NOTING

Cretan House. Chania's colorful folklife museum is bursting at the seams with farm equipment, tools, household items, wedding garb, and a wealth of other material reflecting the island's traditional heritage. Packed to the rafters as the stuffy house is, the collection is charming though not of the same high quality as those in folk and history museums in Heraklion, Vori, and Rethymnon. ⊠ *Chalidron 46, off the church courtyard* ☎ *28/2109–0816* ⌧ *€2* ⊙ *Mon.–Sat. 9:30–3 pm and 6–9 pm.*

Etz Hayyim Synagogue. This ancient landmark is tucked away in what was once the Jewish ghetto, a warren of narrow lanes known as Evraki, just off the harbor south of the Firka. The building was formerly the Venetian church of St. Catherine, became a synagogue under the Ottomans in the 16th century, and was sorely neglected and near collapse by the end of the 20th century. Venetian Gothic arches, a *mikveh* (ritual bath), tombs of three rabbis, and other architectural features have been beautifully restored and are a stirring memorial to Crete's once sizable Jewish population, obliterated during World War II; many Cretan jews drowned when a British torpedo sunk the ship carrying them toward Auschwitz in 1944. ⊠ *Parodos Kondylaki* ☎ *28210/86286* ⊕ *www. etz-hayyim-hania.org* ⌧ *Free* ⊙ *May–mid-Oct., weekdays 10–6; mid-Oct.–Apr., weekdays 9–5.*

Janissaries Mosque. Kastelli hill creates a backdrop to the Janissaries Mosque, built at the water's edge when Turks captured the town in 1645 after a two-month siege. You can enter the building only when the town uses it to host temporary art and trade exhibitions, but the presence of the domed structure at the edge of the shimmering sea lends Chania part of its exotic aura. Hours vary from show to show; the place is most often closed. ⊠ *East side of inner harbor.*

Kastelli hill. The hill where the Venetians first settled rises above the east end of the harbor and it became the quarter of the local nobility. Their palaces, now partially in ruin from neglect and World War II bombings, still line the ridge above the harbor. Kastelli had been occupied much earlier: parts of what may be a Minoan palace have been excavated at the base of the hill. ⊠ *Above harbor.*

**OFF THE
BEATEN
PATH**

Samaria Gorge. South of Chania a deep, verdant crevice extends 10 km (6 miles) from near the village of Xyloskalo to the Libyan sea. The landscape—of forest, sheer rock faces, and running streams and inhabited by the elusive and endangered *kri-kri* (wild goat)—is magnificent. The Samaria, protected as a national park, is the most traveled of the dozens of gorges that cut through Crete's mountains and emerge at the sea, but the walk through the canyon—in places only a few feet wide and almost 2,000 feet deep—is thrilling nonetheless. Buses depart the central

DID YOU KNOW?

Hiking the Samaria gorge—
Europe's longest—you'll
encounter wildflowers,
streams (which can close
the gorge in early spring),
vultures, and maybe even the
kri-kri, the Cretan wild goat.

bus station in Hania at 7:30 and 8:30 am for Xyloskalo. Boats leave in the afternoon from the mouth of the gorge (most people don't hike back up) at Ayia Roumeli for Hora Sfakion, from where buses return to Hania. Travel agents also arrange day trips to the gorge. Also from Chania a couple of extremely scenic routes head south across the craggy White mountains to the isolated Libyan sea villages of **Paleochora**, the main resort of the southwest coast, and **Souyia**, a pleasant collection of whitewashed houses facing a long beach. Much of this section of the coast, including the village of **Loutro**, is accessible only by boat or by a seaside path. ⊠ *Xyloskalo* ✛ *35 km (21 miles) south of Chania, entrance near Omalos* ☎ *28/2104–5570* ⊕ *www.samariagorge.eu* ✉ *€5.*

BEACHES

A string of beaches extends west from the city center, and you can easily reach them on foot by following the sea past the old olive-oil factory just west of the walls and the Byzantine Museum. They are not idyllic, but the water is clean. Locals who want to spend a day at the beach often head out to some of the best beaches on Crete along the surrounding coastline.

Elafonissi. A peninsula on the western end of the island, about 75 km (45 miles) west of Chania, extends into turquoise waters, with a lagoon on one side and isolated sands and coves on the other. The pink-sands, rock formations, and colorful waters evoke the Caribbean or South Seas. In places, the peninsula is broken by narrow channels, requiring beachgoers to wade through the warm, shallow waters, adding to the remote aura. The eastern, lagoon side of the peninsula has facilities and is popular with families (the water is never more than a few feet deep) while other parts, especially the western, ocean-facing side, are relatively isolated and frequented by nudists. **Amenities:** food and drink; lifeguards; showers; parking (free); showers; toilets. **Best for:** solitude (western end); nudists; snorkeling; sunset; swimming; walking. ⊠ *Elafonissi.*

Falassarna. What many Cretans consider to be the best beach on the island stretches along the western edge of the island, about 60 km (38 miles) west of Chania. The long expanse of sand is broken into several coves and has a little bit of everything—facilities on the main section, Pacheia Amos; plenty of isolation in other parts; a much attended beach party the first weekend of August; and even ancient ruins—the Roman city of Flansarna—behind the northern end. One drawback is a steady wind from the west, which can make the water choppy (but is a boon for windsurfers). **Amenities:** food and drink; lifeguards; parking (free); showers; toilets, water sports. **Best for:** solitude; partiers; nudists; sunset; swimming; walking; windsurfing. ⊠ *Falassarna.*

Stavros. If this cove at the northen end of the Akrotiri peninsula, about 15 km (9 miles) east of Chania, looks familiar, you may be recongnizing it as the location of the 1964 film *Zorba the Greek*. The onetime fishing village has grown a bit since then but it's still a charming place, especialy with this white-sand beach on a lagoon backed by a steep mountain (it was here that Zorba did his Sirtaki dance); a slightly wilder, less crowded beach is just to the west. **Amenities:** food and drink; parking (free); showers; toilets; water sports. **Best for:** snorkeling; swimming. ⊠ *Stavros.*

WHERE TO EAT

$ SEAFOOD 🍴 **Apostolis.** What many Chania residents consider to be the freshest and best-prepared fish in town is served on a lively terrace toward the east end of the Old Harbor, near the Venetian arsenals. Choose your fish from the bed of ice and decide how you would like it prepared, or opt for the calamari stuffed with feta, rich fish soup, or even one of the expertly grilled and seasoned chops. [$] *Average main: €12* ✉ *Akti Enoseos 10* ☎ *28210/43470.*

$ GREEK 🍴 **Portes.** Irish-born Susanna Koutoulaki shows a great flare for hospitality as well as a knack for traditional Greek cooking, while an out-of-the-way corner of the Old Town next to the city walls adds a dash of romantic atmosphere to a meal. Eggplant simmered with walnuts, fennel pies, and onion fritters are great preludes to such main courses as oven-baked lamb and a memorable moussaka. [$] *Average main: €12* ✉ *Portou 48* ☎ *28210/76261.*

$ MEDITERRANEAN 🍴 **Tamam.** An ancient Turkish bath has been converted to one of the most atmospheric restaurants in Chania's Old Town. Specialties served up in the tiled dining room, and on the narrow lane outside, show a nice influence from the premise's Ottoman roots and include peppers with grilled feta cheese and eggplant stuffed with chicken. [$] *Average main: €9* ✉ *Zambeliou 49* ☎ *28210/96080.*

$ MEDITERRANEAN 🍴 **Well of the Turk.** It's an adventure just finding this restaurant with a lovely terrace: ask passersby for help, because everyone in the neighborhood knows the place. Behind the Venetian warehouses on the harbor, it stands in a narrow alley near the minaret in the old Arab quarter. The food ranges from simple Greek fare (a prerequisite is the wonderful, large appetizer platter) to some Continental dishes, such as sautéed chicken in a wine sauce, while Middle Eastern influences show up in a memorable confit of lamb and other dishes. [$] *Average main: €10* ✉ *Kalinikou Sarpaki 1–3, Splantiza* ☎ *28210/54547* 🌐 *www.welloftheturk.com* 💳 *No credit cards* 🕘 *No lunch. Closed Tues.*

WHERE TO STAY

$$ RESORT FAMILY 🏨 **Ammos Hotel.** Everything about this small retreat suggests fun and relaxation, with airy, brightly colored public spaces, beautiful terraces and gardens facing a golden beach, and pleasant, contemporary-style rooms and suites with kitchenettes and outdoor space and done in soothing tones with bursts of color. **Pros:** extremely attractive surroundings; friendly and hospitable staff; kid-oriented activities; good food. **Cons:** outside the city center, but easily reached by frequent bus service; in an uninspiring beach strip. [$] *Rooms from: €150* ✉ *Irakli Avgoula, Glaros Beach* ☎ *28210/33003* 🌐 *ammoshotel.com* 🛏 *30 rooms, 3 suites* 🕘 *Closed Nov.–early Apr.* 🍽 *Breakfast.*

$$ HOTEL 🏨 **Casa Delfino.** A Venetian Renaissance palace that was once home to Italian merchant Pedro Delfino is now in the hands of his descendants, who have created one of the island's most distinctive and luxurious hotels, with dramatically decorated guest rooms entered through graceful stone archways surrounding a courtyard paved in pebble mosaic. **Pros:** character-filled surroundings in the heart of the Old Town; large, handsomely appointed rooms; attentive and professional service; excellent breakfast buffet with many homemade specialties. **Cons:** can only

be reached on foot from streets at the edge of the Old Town. [$] *Rooms from: €200* ✉ *Theofanous 9, Palio Limani* ☎ *28210/87400* 🌐 *www.casadelfino.com* 🛏 *24 suites* 🍴 *Breakfast.*

$ HOTEL 🏨 **Doma.** A 19th-century seaside mansion on the eastern edge of town, about a 20-minute walk along the water from the Venetian harbor, is an outpost of old Cretan taste and refinement. **Pros:** lovely atmosphere; shady rear garden; gracious service. **Cons:** front, sea-facing rooms can be noisy when the windows are open. [$] *Rooms from: €80* ✉ *Eleftheriou Venizelou street 124* ☎ *28210/51772* 🌐 *www.hotel-doma.gr* 🛏 *20 rooms, 4 suites* 🕒 *Closed Nov.–Mar.* 🍴 *Breakfast.*

$ HOTEL 🏨 **Hotel Amphora.** In this character-filled 14th-century Venetian mansion on a lane above the inner harbor, rooms are large and many have sea views, as well as such extras as beamed ceilings, fireplaces, private balconies, old-style Cretan furnishings, and kitchenettes. **Pros:** wonderful harbor views from the beautiful rooftop terrace and many rooms; distinctly Cretan surroundings. **Cons:** some rooms can be noisy from crowds at surrounding bars; can only be reached on foot. [$] *Rooms from: €110* ✉ *50 Akti Kountourioti* ☎ *28210/93224* 🌐 *www.amphora.gr* 🛏 *20 rooms* 🍴 *No meals.*

$ HOTEL 🏨 **Porto Veneziano.** Bright, airy, and stylish accommodations in a modern building are perched over the harbor at the edge of the Old Town, providing expansive sea views and a sense of being away from the fray but just an easy walk to the city's sights and attractions. **Pros:** excellent location; sea views come with most rooms (and can be enjoyed on balconies); lovely rear garden; open year-round, making this an excellent base for an off-season visit. **Cons:** not all rooms have sea views, though those without overlook a quiet garden. [$] *Rooms from: €110* ✉ *Old Venetian Harbor* ☎ *28210/27100* 🌐 *www.portoveneziano.gr* 🛏 *51 rooms, 6 suites* 🍴 *Breakfast.*

SHOPPING

One or two souvenir stores on the waterfront sell English-language books and newspapers. The most exotic shopping experience in town is a stroll through Chania's covered market to see local merchants selling rounds of Cretan cheese, jars of golden honey, lengths of salami, salt fish, lentils, and herbs.

Carmela. This enticing shop just off the harbor sells the work of contemporary jewelers and other craftspeople from Crete and throughout Greece, as well as the work of owner Carmela Iatropoulou. ✉ *Odos Anghelou 7* ☎ *28210/90487.*

Cretan Rugs and Blankets. Many of these antique blankets and rugs were made for dowries from homespun wool and natural dyes. ✉ *Odos Anghelou 3* ☎ *28/2109–8571.*

RHODES AND THE DODECANESE

Rhodes, Symi, Kos, Patmos

WELCOME TO RHODES AND THE DODECANESE

TOP REASONS TO GO

★ **The Old Town of Rhodes:**
The monuments built by the Knights of St. John some 700 years ago draw as many visitors to Rhodes as the beaches do; Rhodes's Old Town is a remarkably well-preserved and photogenic testimony to its Crusader past.

★ **The Asklepieion:** Kos's site of ancient healing, the Asklepieion, was the renowned medical school founded by Hippocrates, father of Western medicine.

★ **Natural Wonders:**
The terrain yields butterflies (Rhodes), hot sea springs (Kos), countless coves (Patmos), and mountain paths (Symi).

★ **St. John's Patmos:**
Called the "Jerusalem of the Aegean," Patmos is as peaceful as it was when the Apostle John glimpsed the Apocalypse in his cave here—the spiritual mystique of this little island is still strong.

1 Rhodes. Start, like the crusading Knights of St. John did, with the walled city of Rhodes's Old Town with its monuments, shops, and restaurants. Heading south around the island, discover the moth-mecca of the Valley of the Butterflies in Petaloudes, then take the island's mountainous western road to ancient Kameiros city and medieval Monolithos fortress. The eastern road leads to lovely, car-free Lindos and many, many beaches.

TURKEY

Datca
Yialos
Symi
Choria
SYMI Palaiachora
Rhodes
Ialyssos
Kameiros Petaloudes
Epta Piges
HALKI
Siana RHODES
Monolithos Lindos
Gennadi

0   20 mi
0   20 km

2 Symi. *Picturesque* is the word for both Yialos harbor, with its restaurants and shops, and Chorio located just above it. The inner island is littered with small churches. The impressive and popular Panormitis Monastery is serviced by boats.

3 Kos. The port town is an appealing blend of ancient stones and northern European partying teens. A short drive out of town, Asklepieion was once the greatest healing site of the ancient era. Large swaths of coast are perfect for swimming.

4 Patmos. Make your pilgrimage to Chora to see the cave and the surrounding Monastery of the Apocalypse, hallowed by the presence of St. John. Towering over Chora's skyline is the imposing, fortified Monastery of St. John the Theologian, and far below is Skala, Patmos's pleasant main town and harbor.

GETTING ORIENTED

13

The Dodecanese (Twelve Islands) are the easternmost holdings of Greece and are set around the shores of Turkey and Asia Minor. Here, classic, Byzantine, and Ottoman architectures blend, and multiculturalism is an old idea. Romans, Crusaders, Turks, and Venetians have all left their marks on Rhodes, in the south of the archipelago and the busiest, most populated, and most visited of the 12 islands. Just to the north is tiny, craggy Symi, sparsely inhabited and ringed by enticing coves. Kos, with its lush fields and sandy beaches, lies between Symi and Patmos, the northernmost island of the group, where arid hillsides are occasionally clad in great stands of cypress.

Updated by Stephen Brewer

Wrapped enticingly around the shores of Turkey and Asia Minor, the southernmost group of Greek islands called the Dodecanese (Twelve Islands) lies at the eastern edge of the Aegean sea. The Dodecanese archipelago first grabbed the spotlight when Rhodes was colonized by the crusading Knights of the Order of St. John in the 14th century. Today, of course, the Order of the Holy Holiday Maker now besieges its famed capital, Rhodes town (and the island's overbuilt beach resorts), but happily Kos's native Hippocrates—father of Western medicine—seems to have immunized many of the inland landscapes of blissfully peaceful Symi and Patmos against tourists.

These islands have long shared a common history: Romans, Crusaders, Turks, and Venetians all built picturesque temples, castles, and fortresses in exotic towns of shady lanes and tall houses. Strategically located Rhodes has by far the most important place in history thanks to its starring role during the Crusades. Kos comes in second in popularity and has vestiges of antiquity; the Sanctuary of Asklepios, a center of healing, drew people from all over the ancient world. Today, parts of the coast have been transformed into an endless line of shops and restaurants. Retreat inland, however, to find hillsides crowded only with bleating goats.

Symi is a virtual museum of 19th-century neoclassic architecture almost untouched by modern development, while Patmos, where St. John wrote his Book of Revelation, became a renowned monastic center during the Byzantine period. Sometimes called the Jerusalem of the Aegean, this little island is as peaceful as it must have been when St. John lived here. It continues as a significant focal point of the Greek Orthodox faith, and today has become a favorite getaway for both Greeks as well as an elite international crowd. Symi and Patmos both offer a sense of peace and quiet that in large part has been lost on much of overdeveloped Rhodes and Kos. But despite the invasion of sunseekers, there are still delightful pockets of local color on these islands, too.

PLANNING

WHEN TO GO

To avoid crowds, just before and after peak seasons (May, June, and September) are good times to visit. August is the busiest season on all these islands, when hotel reservations and even spots on interisland ferries can be hard to come by. Patmos and Rhodes are popular Easter getaways for Greeks, and celebrations include candlelight processions and fireworks late Saturday around midnight; island bakeries serve *tsoureki* (sweet braided bread). From October to May, most archaeological sites remain open, but many hotels, restaurants, and shops are closed, and boat travel is limited by curtailed schedules and the weather's whims.

PLANNING YOUR TIME

Rhodes and Kos are two of Greece's most popular resort islands, and for good reason: they offer not only some magnificent sandy beaches but also some real historical dazzlers and some rich, off-the-beach experiences. On Rhodes, cultural must-dos include visits to the Palace of the Grand Master and other sights in Rhodes's Old Town, as well as the Acropolis of Lindos. Kos's great archaeological treasure is the Asklepieion, the great healing center of antiquity. All open as early as 8 am in the summer and stay open well into the evening, and on an early or late visit you will avoid the heat and crowds.

On these busy islands it's also easy to wander off the beaten path to enjoy mountainous hinterlands carpeted in pine forests, vineyards, and groves of olives and oranges. A visit to either island should include a country drive (or bus excursion) and lunch in a village taverna; good stops are Siana in Rhodes and Kefalos or Zia on Kos. Symi and Patmos are geared to travelers looking for low-key retreats and a glimpse of authentic island life. It's easy to slip away to uncrowded beaches and coves on either, but also join islanders for their time-honored ritual of an evening stroll. On Symi, you can amble around the harbor in Yialos, then walk up the Kali Strata (Good Steps) to Chorio. In Patmos, the gathering spots are the main waterfront promenade and narrow lanes of Skala, which come alive in the evening.

GETTING HERE AND AROUND

AIR TRAVEL

Though you can get to the hubs of Rhodes or Kos in under 10 hours nowadays on the faster ferries, if you have limited time it's best to fly to these two islands. Aegean and Olympic airlines fly between Athens and Rhodes, as do a number of other carriers, and Olympic and Aegean also run several daily flights between Athens and Kos. Flying time is about 45 minutes to either island. Aegean and Olympic also connect Rhodes and Kos with several other Greek islands, as does Sky Express.

Finally, it's possible to fly directly to Rhodes and Kos from a number of European capitals on Aegean and several European carriers, especially during the summer. Neither Patmos nor Symi has an airport.

AIRPORTS

Rhodes Diogoras Airport is in Paradissi, 15 km (12 miles) southwest of Rhodes town and well connected by public bus (6 am–11 pm, €3) and taxi (approximately €15 for the half-hour drive). Parts of the Old Town are inaccessible to cars, so hotels will usually arrange to have a porter meet you near one of the gates.

Kos Airport is located 26 km (16 miles) southwest of Kos town. There is bus (€3) and taxi service from there to Kos town and to some beach resorts; expect to pay about €35 for the taxi fare to Kos town and about that to the beach resorts.

Contacts Kos Airport ⊠ *Antimahia, Kos* ☎ *22420/56000* ⊕ *www.kos-airport. com.* **Rhodes Airport** ⊠ *Diagoras, Paradissi, Rhodes* ☎ *22410/88700* ⊕ *w ww.rhodes-airport.info.*

BOAT AND FERRY TRAVEL

In August, for good rates and an assured spot, it is essential that you book as far as possible (at least two weeks) in advance. Boats at this time can be uncomfortably crowded, with deck-class passengers claiming key spots on the floor, in the lounge areas, and even—in peak season—on the metal deck under the stars. If you're taking an overnight boat in August, book a berth so you'll be assured a comfortable place to lay your head. If you are traveling to and around the Dodecanese islands outside the summer season, you'll find that service is curtailed.

When traveling from Piraeus to Rhodes by ferry (12–18 hours), you first make several stops, including at Patmos (6–10 hours) and Kos (10–16 hours). Bringing a car aboard can quadruple costs. Of the several ferry lines serving the Dodecanese, Blue Star Ferries has the largest boats and the most frequent service, sailing several times a week out of Piraeus. The Athens–Dodecanese ferry schedule changes seasonally, and ferries to Patmos do not run daily out of season, so contact ferry lines, the Greek National Tourism Organization (GNTO or EOT) in Athens, or a travel agency for details. An excellent source for ferry schedules is the Web-based tourist site, the Greek Travel Pages (GTP).

The easiest way to travel among the Dodecanese islands is by high-speed craft operated by Dodekanisos Seaways during the summer. Times and fares: Rhodes to/from Symi takes 50 minutes (€14); Rhodes to/from Kos takes 2¼ hours (€28); Rhodes to/from Patmos takes 5 hours (€43).

Contacts Dodekanisos Seaways ⊠ *Thalassini Pili, Kolona port, Rhodes town, Rhodes* ☎ *22410/70590* ⊕ *www.12ne.gr.* **Rhodes Port Authority** ⊠ *26 Lohagou Fanouraki, Rhodes town, Rhodes* ☎ *22410/27242.*

BUS TRAVEL

There is a decent bus network on all the islands, though there are more-infrequent routes on smaller islands. Buses from Rhodes town leave from two different points on Averoff street for the island's east and west sides. Symi's and Patmos's bus stations are located on the harbor. Kos town is served by a city bus while KTEL buses service the rest of the island.

Contacts Kos KTEL Bus Station ✉ *Cleopatras 7, Kos town, Kos* ☎ *22420/22292* ⊕ *www.ktel-kos.gr.* **Kos Town Bus Station** ✉ *Akti Koundouriotou (main harbor), Kos town, Kos* ☎ *22420/26276.* **Rhodes East-Side Bus Station** ✉ *Averoff, near the end of Rimini Sq., Rhodes town, Rhodes* ☎ *22410/27706.* **Rhodes West-Side Bus Station** ✉ *Averof, next to the market, Rhodes town, Rhodes* ☎ *22410/26300.*

13

CAR TRAVEL

A car is useful for exploring Rhodes or Kos, or to hop between Patmos's many beaches. In Symi, with its few roads, a car is of little use, and you should opt for the vans that serve as the island buses, make use of the island taxis, or walk along the paths that connect most places on the island.

You may take a car to the Dodecanese on one of the large ferries that sail daily from Piraeus to Rhodes and less frequently to the smaller islands. The relatively small network of roads on Rhodes is well maintained and detailed maps are available; traffic is likely to be heavy only from Rhodes town to Lindos. In Kos, a car makes it easy to skirt the coast and make stops at the many sandy beaches, though resorts are serviced by bus. In Patmos, a car or motorbike makes it easy to tour the island, while sights and outlying restaurants are easily reached by bus or taxi, and a few beaches can be reached by either bus or boat. Symi, which has only one road suitable for cars, is best explored on foot or by bus or boat. Expect to pay at least €30–€40 a day to rent a car on one of the islands.

TAXI TRAVEL

Taxis are available throughout most of Rhodes. All taxi stands have a sign listing set fares to destinations around the island. Expect a delay when calling radio taxis in high season. Patmos taxi drivers move at breakneck speed on twisty roads.

Contacts Kos Taxi ☎ *22420/23333.* **Rhodes Radio Taxi** ☎ *22410/69800.* **Patmos Radio Taxi** ☎ *22470/31225.*

HOTELS

Rhodes has more hotels per capita than anywhere else in Greece (except for Athens). Most of them are resort or tourist hotels, with sea views and easy access to beaches. Many old houses in Rhodes's Old Town have been converted to hotels, some modest and others quite luxurious. Mass tourist accommodations are also plentiful on Kos, but as in Rhodes, most lodging isn't especially Greek in style. Hotels on Symi are small and usually charming, since the island never encouraged the development of mammoth caravansaries. Similarly, Patmos has attractive, high-quality lodgings that tend to be both more elegant and traditional than its resort-magnet neighbors. High season can prove extremely crowded and you may have difficulty finding a room on any of these islands if you don't book well in advance. Many hotels throughout the Dodecanese are closed from November through April. Lodgings in water-poor Symi and Patmos may remind you to limit water use.

RESTAURANTS

Throughout the Dodecanese, you can find sophisticated restaurants, as well as simple tavernas serving excellent food. On Rhodes and Kos, beware many completely mediocre eateries catering to tourists with fast food. It is sometimes best to wait until after 9 pm to see where the Greeks are eating. Because Rhodes and Kos produce most of their own foodstuffs, in better restaurants you can count on fresh fruit and vegetables. Fish, of course, is readily available on all islands. Large fish goes by the kilo, so confirm the exact amount you'd like when ordering. Tiny, tender Symi shrimp, found only in the waters around this island, have such soft shells they can be easily popped in the mouth whole. They are used in dozens of local dishes. Wherever you dine, ask about the specialty of the day, and check the food on display in the kitchen of tavernas. Rhodes produces some excellent wines that appear on tables throughout the Dodecanese, and vintages from throughout Greece also show up on wine lists. With the exception of a few very high-end spots, dress on all the islands is casual; reservations are not necessary unless specified.

DINING AND LODGING PRICES IN EUROS			
	$	$$	$$$	$$$$
Restaurants	Under €16	€16–€25	€26–€40	Over €40
Hotels	Under €126	€126–€225	€226–€275	Over €275

Restaurant prices are the average cost of a main course at dinner or, if dinner is not served, at lunch. Hotel prices are the lowest cost of a standard double room in high season.

TOUR OPTIONS

From April to October, local island boat tours take you to area sights and may include a picnic on a remote beach or even a visit to the shores of Turkey.

A1 Yacht Trade Consortium. This brokerage, rental agency, and outfitter organizes sailing tours around the Greek islands near the Turkish coast. ⊠ *Commercial harbor, Rhodes town, Rhodes* ☎ *22410/01000* ⊕ *www. a1yachting.com.*

Astoria Travel. On Patmos, Astoria Travel provides day bus trips to Patmos's St. John the Theologian Monastery and the Monastery of the Apocalypse (€20). ⊠ *Skala harbor, Skala, Patmos* ☎ *22470/31205* ⊕ *www.astoriatravel.com.*

Kalodoukas Tours. On Symi, Kalodoukas Tours runs boat trips to the Monastery of Panormitis, as well as to secluded beaches and islets, which include swimming and a barbecue lunch. And George Kalodoukas leads wonderful guided hiking tours around the island and does an excursion to his Marathoudas beach–area organic farm. ⊠ *Harbor front, Yialos, Symi* ☎ *22460/71077* ⊕ *www.kalodoukas.gr.*

Symi Tours. The island's venerable tour organizer arranges boat excursions around the island and can help tourists book accommodations. ⊠ *Harbor front, Yialos, Symi* ☎ *22460/71307* ⊕ *www.symitours.com.*

Triton Holidays. A caïque leaves Mandraki harbor in Rhodes town in the morning, deposits you in Lindos for a day of sightseeing and beachgoing, and returns you in the evening for €25. If you're not renting a car on Rhodes, it can be worth it to take a bus tour to its southern points and interior. Triton Holidays has, among other trips, a guided bus tour to Thermes Kallitheas, Epta Piges, and Lindos (€30); a bus tour to Kameiros, Filerimos, and Petaloudes (€30); and a full-day trip through several points in the interior and south (€35). ⊠ *Plastira 9, Rhodes town, Rhodes* ☎ *22410/21690* ⊕ *www.tritondmc.gr.*

RHODES ΡΟΔΟΣ

Rhodes (1,400 square km [540 square miles]) is the fourth-largest Greek island and, along with Sicily, Crete, and Cyprus, is one of the great islands of the Mediterranean. It lies almost exactly halfway between Piraeus and Cyprus, 18 km (11 miles) off the coast of Asia Minor, and it was long considered a bridge between Europe and the East. Geologically similar to the Turkish mainland, it was probably once part of Asia Minor, separated by one of the frequent volcanic upheavals this volatile region has experienced.

Today Rhodes retains its role as the center of Dodecanese trade, politics, and culture. Its diversity ensures it remains a polestar of tourism as well: Rhodes town brings together fascinating artifacts, medieval architecture, an active nightlife, and is reputedly the sunniest spot in all of Europe. Like a gigantic historical pop-up book, Rhodes offers layers upon layers of sights: Romans, Crusaders, Turks, and Venetians built a remarkable array of temples, castles, and fortresses in exotic quarters of shady lanes and tall houses. But if you head out to the island's east coast you'll find it blessed with white-sand beaches and dotted with copses of trees, interspersed with fertile valleys full of figs and olives. And though some of the shore is beset by vast resort hotels and holiday villages, there are still some wonderfully unsullied sections of beach to be found all around the island; if you look for it, you'll even find a taste of rural life.

The island's history unfolds as an especially rich pageant. Rhodes saw successive waves of settlement, including the arrival of the Dorian Greeks from Argos and Laconia early in the 1st millennium BC. From the 8th to the 6th century BC, Rhodian cities established settlements in Italy, France, Spain, and Egypt and actively traded with mainland Greece, exporting pottery, oil, wine, and figs. Independence and expansion came to a halt when the Persians took over the island at the end of the 6th century BC and forced Rhodians to provide ships and men for King Xerxes's failed attack on the mainland (480 BC). A league of city-states rose under Athenian leadership. In 408 BC the united city of Rhodes was created on the site of the modern town; much of the populace moved there, and the history of the island and the town became synonymous. As the new city grew and flourished, its political organization became the model for the city of Alexandria in Egypt.

The Colossus of Rhodes may be long gone, but the Palace of the Grand Masters remains a colossal landmark of the Old Town quarter.

In 42 BC, Rhodes came under the hegemony of Rome, and through the years of the empire it was fabled as a beautiful city where straight roads were lined with porticoes, houses, and gardens. According to Pliny, who described the city in the 1st century AD, the town possessed some 2,000 statues, at least 100 of them of colossal scale. One of the most famous examples of the island's sculptural school is the world-famous *Laocöon*—probably executed in the 1st century BC—which showed the priest who warned the Trojans to beware Greeks bearing gifts (it stands in the Vatican today). Sadly, the ancient glory of Rhodes has few visible remnants. The city was ravaged by Arab invaders in AD 654 and 807, and only with the expulsion of the Arabs and the reconquest of Rhodes by the Byzantine emperors did the city begin to revive—gloriously. Rhodes was a crucial stop on the road to the Holy Land during the Crusades. It came briefly under Venetian influence, then Byzantine, then Genoese. In 1309, when the Knights of St. John took the city from its Genoese masters, the island's most important modern era began.

The Knights of St. John, an order of Hospitalers, were organized to protect and care for Christian pilgrims. By the beginning of the 12th century the order had become military in nature, and after the fall of Acre in 1291, the Knights fled from Palestine, withdrawing first to Cyprus and then to Rhodes. In 1312 the Knights inherited the immense wealth of the Templars (another religious military order, which had just been outlawed by the pope) and used it to fortify Rhodes. But for all their power and the strength of their walls, moats, and artillery, the Knights could not hold back the Turks. In 1522 the Ottomans, with 300 ships and 100,000 men under Süleyman the Magnificent, began what was to be the final siege, taking the city after six months.

During the Turkish occupation, Rhodes became a possession of the Grand Admiral, who collected taxes but left the Rhodians to pursue a generally peaceful and prosperous existence. They continued to build ships and trade with Greece, Constantinople (later Istanbul), Syria, and Egypt. The Greek mainland was liberated by the War of Independence in 1821, but Rhodes and the Dodecanese remained part of the Ottoman Empire until 1912, when the Italians took over. After World War II, the Dodecanese were formally united with Greece in 1947.

GETTING HERE AND AROUND

Rhodes is well served by regularly scheduled flights from Athens and Thessaloniki as well as both scheduled and charter flights from London, Rome, and other major European cities. Two daily ferries leave from Piraeus bound for Rhodes and the Dodecanese, a 15-hour overnight trip. You will find schedules and booking information for ferry service to and from Rhodes and other islands in the Dodecanese at ⊕ *www. ferries.gr or www.gtp.gr*.

Regional ferries connect Rhodes and Kos and Symi. Smaller boats, including those to other islands in the Dodecanese, dock at Rhodes town's 2,500-year-old Mandraki harbor; the larger overnight ferries use the adjacent new harbor.

Diogoras Airport is in Paradissi, 15 km (12 miles) southwest of Rhodes town and well connected by public bus (running from 6 am to 11 pm, €3) and taxi, about €15 for the half-hour drive.

Rhodes town's two bus terminals are hubs for service throughout the island—points on the western side of the island are served by buses from the West Side Station, near the shopping district of the New Town on Averof; most places on the eastern side are served from the East Side Station on Platia Rimini (Rimini Square), just down the street from the West Station next to the market on Mandraki harbor. Bus service is excellent, with, for example, buses to and from Lindos running almost hourly from the East Side Station; €3.70 each way, €25 by taxi.

VISITOR INFORMATION

The central Rhodes Municipal Tourism Office, near the bus station, is open May–October, daily 7:30 am–11 pm. The Rodos Tourism Promotion Organization maintains a helpful English website.

Contacts Rhodes Municipal Tourism Office ⊠ *Averof 3, Rhodes town* ☎ *22410/35240* ⊕ *www.rhodes.gr.* **Rodos Tourism Promotion Organization** ⊠ *Plotarchou Blessa 3, Rhodes town* ☎ *0241/74555* ⊕ *www.rodosisland.gr.*

RHODES TOWN ΡΟΔΟΣ (ΠΟΛΗ)

463 km (287 miles) east of Piraeus harbor in Athens by ferry.

Fodor'sChoice
★
Early travelers described Rhodes as a town of two parts: a castle or high town (Collachium) and a lower city. Today Rhodes town—sometimes referred to as Ródos town—is still a city of two parts: the Old Town, a UNESCO World Heritage Site that incorporates the high town and lower city, and the modern metropolis, or New Town, spreading away from the walls that encircle the Old Town. The

narrow streets of the Old Town are for the most part closed to cars and are lined with Orthodox and Catholic churches, Turkish houses (some of which follow the ancient orthogonal plan), and medieval public buildings with exterior staircases and facades elegantly constructed of well-cut limestone from Lindos. Careful reconstruction in recent years has enhanced the harmonious effect.

Spreading out in all directions from the original city walls, the New Town is "new" only in relative terms—islanders began settling outside the walls of the Old Town with the arrival of the Turks in 1522. Italians added a great deal of flair in the first part of the 20th century, adding the art deco administrative buildings clustered near the harbor. Later growth has also been relatively kind to New Town, and the streets of low-rise modern apartment blocks are tree-lined and many commercial streets are attractive pedestrian walkways.

TOP ATTRACTIONS

Archaeological Museum of Rhodes. The Hospital of the Knights (now the island's archaeological museum), completed in 1489, surrounds a Byzantine courtyard, off which are the refectory and wards where the wealthy institution once administered to the knights and towns-people. These wonderful surroundings are enhanced with findings from around Rhodes and nearby islands, among them two well-known representations of Aphrodite: the *Aphrodite of Rhodes,* who, while bathing, pushes aside her hair as if she's listening; and a standing figure, known as *Aphrodite Thalassia,* or "of the sea," as she was discovered in the water off the northern city beach. Two 6th-century BC *kouros* (statues of idealized male youth) were found in the nearby ancient city of Kameiros, and in a beautiful 5th-century BC funerary stela, a young woman named Crito, hair cut short in mourning, gives a farewell embrace to her mother, Timarista, who is already moving outside the frame, as she leaves the world. Another stela of three-year-old Ploutos is inscribed, "loosening the support of a cart which had upon it a heavy load of stakes I passed over the threshold of Hades." ⊠ *Mouseou Sq.* ☏ *22410/75674* ⊕ *odysseus.culture.gr* 🖃 *€6* ⊙ *Apr.–Oct., Mon. 9–4, Tues.–Fri. 8:30–8, weekends 8–3; Nov.–Mar., Tues.–Sun. 8–3.*

Inn of France. The most elaborate of the striking inns on this famously historic street today houses a French languge institute (appropriately enough). The facade is ornately carved with the fleur-de-lis and heraldic patterns and bears an inscription that dates the building between 1492 and 1509. ⊠ *About halfway down Street of Knights from Loggia of St. John.*

Loggia of St. John. This 19th-century neo-Gothic structure stands on the site of the 14th-century church of St. John, patron of the Knights of St. John and the final resting place of many members of the order. Used as an ammunition storehouse during Turkish occupation, the church was reduced to rubble in an explosion sparked by lightning in 1856. ⊠ *Next to Palace of Grand Masters.*

Continued on page 695

THE MARCH OF GREEK HISTORY

The 21st-century Greeks are one of the oldest peoples on the face of the earth: they have seen *everything*. While Greeks are now subjected to an annual full-scale invasion by an army of camera-toting legions, their ancestors were conquered by numberless encroachers for the past four millennia. During this epic time span, Greece was forged, torn asunder, and remade into the vital nation it is today.

Paradox is a Greek word and highly applicable to Greek history. Since the rehabilitation of Homer by Hermann Schliemann's excavations, Agamemnon, Great King of Mycenae, and the earliest heroes of ancient Greece have moved from legend into history. Today, the remote 13th century BC sometimes appears more familiar than most Greek events in better documented later periods. Not that subsequent ages were any duller—the one epithet that is utterly unsuitable in Greece—but they lacked the master touch of the great epic poet.

However, while ancient temples still evoke Homer, Sophocles, Plato, and the rest, today's Greeks are not just the watered-down descendants of a noble people living in the ruined halls of their ancestors. From time immemorial the Greeks have been piling the present on top of the past, blithely building, layering, and overlapping their more than 30 centuries of history to create the amazing fabric that is modern Greece.

(top) Gerald Butler as King Leonidas
in the 2006 Warner Bros. film *300*

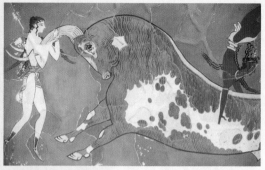

(top) Cycladic female figure; (top right) Bull fresco from Minoan ruins on Crete; (bottom) Fresco of ladies from Minoan ruins on Crete

3000 BC–1900 BC

Cycladic Origins

Greece is far older than the glory days of the Classical age—the 5th century BC—which gave us the Parthenon. It has been inhabited almost continuously for the past 13,000 years. Tools made on the island of Milos around 11,000 BC have been found in a cave in the Peloponnese, suggesting that even in those long-ago reaches of history Greeks were sailing across the sparkling Aegean between islands and mainland shores. Around 3000 BC, about the time cultures were flourishing in Egypt and Mesopotamia, small cities were springing up throughout the Cycladic islands—the first major

Greek settlements, today known as the Keros-Syros culture. These early Cycladic people lived by sea and, as the need for protection from invaders intensified, in fortified towns in the uplands. Objects found in mass graves tell us they made tools, crockery, and jewelry. The most remarkable remnants of Cycladic civilization are flat, two-dimensional female idols, strikingly modern in appearance.

■ Sights to see:
Museum of Cycladic Art (Goulandris Foundation), Athens.

2000 BC–1150 BC

Minoan Bronze Age

By 2000 BC, a great culture—Europe's oldest state (as opposed to mere tribal groupings)—had taken root on the island of Crete. What these inhabitants of Greece's southernmost island actually called themselves is not known; archaeologist Sir Arthur Evans named the civilization Minoan after Minos, the legendary king of the famous labyrinth who probably ruled from the magnificent palace of Knossos. Their warehouses were filled with spices traded throughout the Mediterranean, and royal chambers were decorated with sophisticated art—statuary, delicate rythons,

Presumed Minoan eruption of Thera	Hellenic tribes (Achaeans, Aeolian, Ionians, Dorians) appear		The Trojan War
1500 BC	1300 BC	1100 BC	900 BC

13

IN FOCUS THE MARCH OF GREEK HISTORY

(top) Replica of Trojan Horse; (top, right) Lion Gate at Mycenae; (bottom) Mycenean gold funeral mask

and, most evocative of all, alluring frescoes depicting fanciful secular scenes as well as the goddesses who dominated the matriarchal Minoan religion. A system of writing, known as Linear A and Linear B script, appears on seal stones. The cause of the downfall of the Minoans remains a mystery—political unrest, invasions from the mainland, a volcano on nearby Santorini and subsequent earthquakes? Enter the mainland Mycenaeans.

■ Sights to see:
Palace of Knossos, Crete. Archaeological Museum, Heraklion.

1600 BC–1100 BC

The Mycenaeans

By the 14th century BC, the Mycenaeans wielded power throughout mainland Greece and much of the rest of the known world, from Sicily to Asia Minor. Their capital, Mycenae (in the Peloponnese), was one of several great cities they built around palaces filled with art and stories of the new Olympian gods and heavily fortified. As civilized as the Mycenaeans were, they were also warlike. Their exploits inspired the *Iliad* and *Odyssey*, and Agamemnon, legendary hero of the 12th-century Trojan Wars—the starting point in the endless ping-pong match between Europe and Asia—is said to have ruled from

Mycenae. For all their might, the Mycenaeans fell into decline sometime around 1100 BC. Soon the Dorians, from northern Greece, moved south, pushing the Mycenaeans into a dark age during which art and writing were lost. But Greeks who sailed across the Aegean to flee the Dorians established Ephesus, Smyrna, and other so-called Ionian cities in Asia Minor, where a rich culture soon flourished.

■ Sights to see:
Lion Gate, Mycenae, the Argolid. Cyclopean Walls, Tiryns. Nestor's Palace, Messinia.

First Pan-Hellenic
Olympics held

800 BC   700 BC   600 BC   500 BC

(top) Ancient vase depicting Olympic athletes; (left) Bust of Homer; (right) Statue of King Leonidas

The Age of Homer

1000 BC–800 BC

By the 8th century BC, Greeks were living in hundreds of *poleis*, city-states that usually comprised a walled city that governed the surrounding country-side. Most poleis were built around a raised acropolis and an agora (a market-place), as well temples and often a gymnasium; limited power lay with a group of elite citizens—the first inklings of democracy. As the need for resources grew, Greeks began to establish colonies in Sicily and Gaul and on the Black Sea, and with this expansion came contact with the written word that laid the foundations of the Greek alphabet.

Two essential elements of Greek culture led the new Greek renaissance that forged a nation's identity: Homeric legends began circulating, recounting the deeds of heroes and gods, and athletes showed off their strength and valor at the Olympic Games, first staged in 776 BC. Participation in these games meant support of Hellenism—the concept of a united Greece.

■ Sights to see: Greek colonies set up in Asia Minor, Sicily (Agrigento, Syracuse), and southern Italy (Paestum).

Persian Invasions

499 BC–449 BC

The most powerful poleis, Athens and Sparta, would soon become two of history's most famous rivals—but for a brief time in the fifth century, they were allies united against a common foe, the Persians, who, in 490 BC, launched an attack against Athens. Though far outnumbered, the Athenians dealt the Persians a crippling blow on the Marathon plain. Ten years later, the Persians attacked again, this time with a massive army and navy commanded by King Xerxes. The Spartan King Leonidas and his "300"— the men of his royal guard (along with an unknown

(top) Still from Warner Brothers' movie *300*; (top right) Bust of Pericles; (right) Relief sculpture fragment depicting the king of Persia; (bottom) Greek helmet

number of slaves, or Helots)—sacrificed their lives to hold the Persians off at Thermopylae, allowing the Athenians time to muster ships and sink much of the Persian fleet. Xerxes returned the following year, in the summer of 479 BC, to sack Athens, but an army drawn from city-states throughout Greece and under the command of Pausanias, a Spartan general, defeated the Persians and brought the Persian Wars to an end.

■ Sights to see: Marathon Tomb, Marathon, Attica.

460 BC–431 BC
Pericles' Golden Age

Athens thrived for much of the fifth century BC under the leadership of Pericles. The city became the center of the Hellenic world—and the cradle of Western civilization. The Parthenon was built; Socrates engaged in the dialogues that, recorded by Plato, became the basis of European philosophy; Aeschylus, Aristophanes, Euripides, and Sophocles wrote dramas; Praxiteles sculpted his masterpieces; and Herodotus became the "father of history."

■ Sights to see: The Parthenon, Athens. Sanctuary of Apollo, Delphi.

431 BC–404 BC
Peloponnesian War

Athens was leader of the Delian League, a confederation of 140 Greek city-states, and Sparta headed the Peloponnesian League, a formidable alliance of city-states of southern and central Greece. From 431 to 404 BC these two powers engaged in battles that plunged much of Greece into bloodshed. Sparta emerged the victor after Athens suffered two devastating defeats: the destruction of a massive force sent to attack Syracuse, a Spartan ally in Sicily, and the sinking of the Athenian fleet.

■ Sights to see: Archaeological Museum, Sparta, Laconia.

(top) Alexander the Great listening to his tutor Aristotle; (top right) Byzantine basilica; (bottom) Alexander the Great on horseback

Alexander the Great

338 BC– AD 323

In the years following the Peloponnesian War, Sparta, Athens, and an emerging power, Thebes, battled for control of Greece. Eventually, the victors came from the north: Macedonians led by Philip II defeated Athens in the Battle of Chaeronea in 338 BC. Philip's son, Alexander the Great, who had been tutored by Aristotle, quickly unified Greece and conquered Persia, most of the rest of the Middle East, and Egypt. In the ensuing 11 years of unparalleled triumphs he spread Greek culture from the Nile to the Indus. Alexander died in Babylon of a mysterious illness in 323 BC and the great empire he amassed soon fell asunder. Roman armies began moving toward Athens, Greece became the Roman province of Achaia in 27 BC, and for the next 300 years of peace Rome readily adapted Greek art, architecture, and thought. This cultural influence during the Pax Romana compensated for the loss of a much-abused independence.

■ Sights to see: Birthplace, Pella, Central Macedonia. Royal Tombs, Vergina, Central Macedonia. Roman Agora, Athens. Archaeological Museum, Marathon, Attica.

Byzantine Greece

324–1204

With the division of the Roman Empire into East and West, Greece came under the control of the Eastern Empire, administered from the Greek city of Byzantium (later Constantinople), where Emperor Constantine moved the capital in 324. The empire had embraced Christianity as its official religion, and Byzantium became the seat of the Eastern Orthodox Church, which led to the Great Christian Schism of 1094. Byzantium's Greek culture evolved into a distinct architectural style and religious art forms best represented by mosaics and icon paintings. For centuries Byzantine

841 Parthenon transformed
into cathedral

Fourth Crusade
invades Greece

800   1000   1200   1400

13

IN FOCUS THE MARCH OF GREEK HISTORY

(top) Gold-leaf mosaics;
(left) Palace of the
Grand Masters, Rhodes;
(right) Portrait of
Mehmet II

Greece fended off invasions from Visigoths, Vandals, Slavs, Muslims, Bulgars, and Normans. As an ally of the empire, the Republic of Venice developed trading strongholds in Greece in the 11th century. Interested in the control of maritime routes, the Venetians built a network of fortresses and fortified towns along the Ionian coast of Greece. Venice later extended its possessions over several Aegean islands and Crete, which it held until 1669.

■ Sights to see:
Little Mitropolis, Athens.
Byzantine Museum, Rhodes.

1204–1453 Crusaders and Feudal Greece

The Byzantine Empire, and Greece with it, finally succumbed to Crusaders who pillaged Constantinople in 1204. Frankish knights created vassal feudal states in Thessalonica, the Peloponnese, and Rhodes, while other short-lived kingdoms in Epirus and on the shores of the Black Sea became the refuge of Byzantine Greek populations. Soon, however, a new threat loomed as Ottoman Turks under Sultan Mehmet II began marching into Byzantine lands, occupying most of Asia Minor, Macedonia, and Thessaly.

■ Sights to see:
Palace of the Grand Masters, Rhodes.

1453–1821 Ottoman Age

Constantinople fell to the Ottomans in 1453, and by the 16th century Sultan Suleyman the Magnificent had expanded his Empire from Vienna through the Middle East. Greece was the stage of many battles between East and West. In 1687, Athens was besieged and the Parthenon heavily damaged by Venetian bombardments. Only in 1718 all of Greece was conceded to the Ottoman Empire, just in time for a resurgence of Hellenist culture in Europe, Neoclassicism in the arts, and a brand-new interest in Greek archaeology.

■ Sights to see:
Old Town, Rethymnon.

| 1522 Knights of St. John surrender Rhodes to the Attomans | Lord Elgin removes marbles | Olympic Games in Athens |
| | Greeks drive Turks out | |

1600   1800   2000

(top) 2004 Olympic Stadium, Athens; (far left) Portrait of Eleftherios Venizelos; (left) Portrait of Lord Byron

A Greek Nation

1821–1935

Ottoman rulers allowed a degree of autonomy to Greece, yet uprisings became increasingly fierce. In 1821 the bloody War of Independence, which started as a successful rebellion in the Peloponnese, spread across the land. Western Europeans, including the Romantic poet Lord Byron, rushed to the Greek cause. After years of setbacks and civil wars, Britain, France, and Russia mediated with the Ottomans to establish Greece as an autonomous region. Otto of Bavaria, only 17, was named sovereign of Greece in 1831, the first of the often-unpopular monarchs who reigned intermittently

until 1974. Public favor soon rested with prime ministers like Eleftherios Venizelos, who colonized Crete in 1908. In 1919 Venizelos, a proponent of a "Greater Greece," sought to conquer ethnic Greek regions of the new Turkish nation, but his forces were defeated and hundreds of thousands, on both sides, were massacred. The subsequent peace decreed the massive population exchange of two million people between the two countries, resulting in the complete expulsion of Greeks from Asia Minor, after 3,000 years of history.

■ Sights to see:
Achilleion Palace, Corfu. National Garden, Athens.

A New Republic

1936–PRESENT

Greece emerged from the savagery of Axis occupation during World War II in the grip of civil war, with the Communist party battling right-wing forces. The right controlled the Greek government until 1963, when Georgios Papandreou became prime minister and proposed democratic reforms that were soon put down by a repressive colonels' junta led by Georgios Papadopoulos. A new republic was proclaimed in 1973, and a new constitution replaced the monarchy with an elective government—democratic ideals born in Greece more than 2,000 years earlier.

■ Sights to see:
2004 Olympic Stadium, Athens.

Palace of the Grand Master of the Knights of Rhodes. This massive affair with fairy-tale towers, crenellated ramparts, and more than 150 rooms crowns the top of the Street of Knights and is the place to begin a tour. Unscathed during the Turkish siege of Rhodes in 1522, the palace was destroyed in 1856 by an explosion of ammunition stored nearby in the cellars of the Church of St. John. The present structure—a Mussolini-era Italian reconstruction—was rebuilt in a storybook, pseudo-medieval style all the rage in the early 20th century and was later used as a holiday abode for King Vittorio Emmanuele III of Italy. Today, the palace's collection of antiques and antiquities includes Hellenistic and Roman mosaic floors from Italian excavations in Kos, and in the permanent exhibition downstairs, extensive displays, maps, and plans showing the layout of the city will help you get oriented before wandering through the labyrinthine Old Town. ⊠ *Ippoton, Old Town* ☏ *22410/23359* ⊕ *odysseus.culture.gr* 🎟 *€6* ☉ *May–Oct., daily 8–7:45; Nov.–Apr., Tues.–Sun. 8–3.*

Street of Knights. The Knights of St. John built most of their monuments along this cobbled lane, also known as Ippoton, which descends from the Palace of the Grand Masters—at the highest spot of the medieval city—toward the commercial port. The lane is a little more than a third of a mile long and follows the route that once connected the ancient acropolis to the harbor. It is bordered on both sides by the Inns of the Tongues, where the Knights supped and held their meetings. ⊠ *Ippoton, Old Town.*

Turkish Library. A rare collection of Turkish, Persian, and Arab manuscripts, including many rare Korans, founded in 1794, is a striking reminder of the Ottoman presence. The collection and the adjacent Mosque of Suleiman are still used by those members of Rhodes's Turkish community who stayed in Rhodes after the 1923 population exchange, a mass repatriation of Greek and Turkish migrants. ⊠ *Sokratous, opposite Mosque of Suleiman* ☎ *22410/74090* 🎫 *Free* ۞ *Mon.–Sat. 9:30–4.*

> ### SEE MORE AND SAVE
>
> Plan on hitting all of Rhodes's Old Town attractions? Purchase a multisight ticket (€10), which gets you admission to the Palace of the Grand Masters, Archaeological Museum, Museum of Decorative Arts, and Byzantine Museum. It's available at any of the sights.

Walls of Rhodes. One of the great medieval monuments in the Mediterranean, the walls of Rhodes are wonderfully restored and illustrate the engineering capabilities as well as the financial and human resources available to the Knights of St. John. For 200 years the Knights strengthened the walls by thickening them, up to 40 feet in places, and curving them so as to deflect cannonballs. The moat between the inner and outer walls never contained water; it was a device to prevent invaders from constructing siege towers. You can get a sense of the enclosed city's massive scale by walking inside the moat.

Parts of the walkway that runs the 4 km (2½ miles) along the top of the walls is sometimes accessible for an extra fee to visitors to the Archaeological Museum and to the Palace of the Grand Masters; access is through the Palace of the Grand Master. Hours vary, so check with one of the sights or the tourist office. ⊠ *Old Town* 🎫 *Moat free; tours €3.*

WORTH NOTING

Byzantine Museum. Icons and frescoes from churches throughout Rhodes town (most of them long since destroyed) are displayed within the 11th-century Lady of the Castle church, once the Byzantine cathedral and, under the Turks, a mosque. ⊠ *Off Mouseou Sq.* ☎ *22410/25500* 🎫 *€3* ۞ *Apr.–Oct., Tues.–Sun. 8:30–7; Nov.–Mar., Tues.–Sun. 8:30–3.*

Commercial Harbor. Rhodes's port for traffic to and from Pireaus and some boats to other islands in the Dodecanese (others leave from smaller Mandraki harbor, just north) is at the eastern edge of the Old Town. The port authority and customs offices are found here.

Decorative Arts Collection. Housed in a stone-vaulted warehouse of the Knights, the town's museum of decorative arts today exhibits finely made ceramics, wooden tools and utensils, and costumes and textiles from the various regions of the Dodecanese. ⊠ *Argyrokastrou Sq.* ☎ *22410/72674* ⊕ *odysseus.culture.gr* 🎫 *€3* ۞ *Apr.–Oct., Tues.–Sun. 8:30–7; Nov.–Mar., Tues.–Sun. 8:30–3.*

Evangelismos Church. The town's cathedral is a 1920s Italian-built replica of the Knights Church of St. John in the Old Town and rises next to the harbor. ⊠ *Near Mandraki harbor* ☎ *22410/77916* ۞ *Daily 7–noon and 5–7:30.*

Mighty fortifications, like this Palace of the Grand Master of the Knights of Rhodes, remind us that the Crusaders dominated Rhodes until the Ottoman era.

Fort Ayios Nikolas. This circular fortress, built by the Knights in the 15th century, guards the entrance to Mandraki harbor, near a row of picturesque but disused windmills. ✉ *North of Old Town walls, bordering Mandraki harbor.*

Mandraki Harbor. What was once the main harbor, in use since the 5th century BC, adjoins the commercial harbor on the east side of Old Town and is home to the city's municipal buildings and an open-air bazaar.

Mosque of Suleiman. This magnificent, pin-domed landmark was built circa 1522 to commemorate Sultan Suleiman's conquest of Rhodes and rebuilt in 1808, with distinctive pink and white stripes. ✉ *At top of Sokratous* ☎ *22410/24918* ⌕ *Closed for renovation.*

Mt. Smith. A road climbs to the top of the mountain, about 2 km (1 mile) to the west of Rhodes's town center, where many of the villas and gardens dotting the slopes have been torn down to make way for modern apartment buildings. For a dramatic view, make your way to the westernmost edge of the summit, which drops via a sharp and almost inaccessible cliff to the shore below, now lined with enormous hotels.

Atop Mt. Smith are the freely accessible ruins of the Acropolis, a fine example of the stately sanctuaries that the ancient Greeks situated atop many of their cities. The complex includes a theater that the Italians restored in the early 20th century; a stadium; the three restored columns of the Temple of Apollo Pythios, and the scrappy remains of the Temple of Athena Polias; a Nymphaia; and an Odeon. ✉ *New Town* ⊕ *www.culture.gr.*

CLOSE UP

The Great Colussus

At the end of the 4th century BC the Rhodians commissioned the sculptor Chares, from Lindos, to create the famous Colossus, a huge bronze statue of the sun god, Helios, and one of the Seven Wonders of the Ancient World. Two bronze deer statues mark the spot where legend says the Colossus once straddled the Mandraki harbor entrance. The 110-foot-high statue only stood for half a century. In 227 BC, when an earthquake razed the city and toppled the Colossus, help poured in from all quarters of the eastern Mediterranean. After the calamity the Delphic oracle advised the Rhodians to let the great Colossus remain where it had fallen. So there it rested for some eight centuries, until AD 654 when it was sold as scrap metal and carted off to Syria, allegedly by a caravan of 900 camels. After that, nothing is known of its fate.

Our Lady of the Bourg. Soaring vaults are all that remains of what was once a magnificent Gothic church, completed by the Knights in 1456. The Knights believed that Mary, the mother of Jesus, provided them and Rhodes special protection against the ever-present threat of a Muslim invasion. ⊠ *Inside remains of walls, access through Gate of the Virgin, Old Town.*

OFF THE BEATEN PATH

Thermes Kallitheas. As you travel south along the east coast, a strange sight meets you: an assemblage of buildings that look as if they have been transplanted from Morocco. In fact, this spectacular mosaic-tile bath complex was built in 1929 by the Italians. As far back as the early 2nd century BC, area mineral springs were prized; the great physician Hippocrates of Kos extolled these springs for alleviating liver, kidney, and rheumatic ailments. Though the baths are no longer in use, the ornate Rotunda has been restored (art exhibitions are often on view), as have peristyles and pergolas, and you can wander through the beautifully landscaped grounds—note the pebble mosaics, an ancient folk tradition come alive again, with mosaics of fish, deer, and other images—and have a drink or snack in the attractive café. A pretty beach rings a nearby cove. ⊠ *Kalithea ✛ 10 km (6 miles) south of Rhodes town* ☎ *22410/65691* ⊕ *www.kallitheasprings.gr* ⤳ *€3* ☉ *Apr.–Oct., daily 8–8; Nov.–Mar., daily 8–5.*

BEACHES

Elli Beach. Though the beach is pebbly rather than sandy, a handy location right at the edge of Old Town makes this seaside strip immensely popular, and it's lined with chairs and umbrellas. An offshore diving platform is a huge hit with kids and what seems to be most of the teenage population of Rhodes. What you won't find here is solitude, and what semblance of peace and quiet you might find will likely be interrupted by an endless stream of hawkers selling everything from trinkets to cold drinks. Among the most popular offerings are massages, administered by wandering masseuses. **Amenities:** food and drink; lifeguards; toilets; showers; water sports. **Best for:** swimming; walking. ⊠ *North of Old Town, near Rhodes Yacht Club.*

Faliraki Beach. The most popular beach in Rhodes will be your idea of paradise or hell, depending on what you think of crowded sands backed by fun parks, supermarkets, all-inclusive resorts, and fast-food joints. Stretches of the 5 km (3 miles) of fine sand are a little less cramped than others, the southern end part especially, officially designated as a naturalist beach. Buses run between Rhodes town and Faliraki throughout the day and late into the evening. **Amenities:** food and drink; lifeguards; parking (free); showers; toilets; water sports. **Best for:** partiers; nudists; swimming; walking. ✉ *Faliraki* ✥ *14 km (8.5 miles) south of Rhodes town.*

WHERE TO EAT

$$$ SEAFOOD Fodor's Choice ★ 🍴 **Alexis 4 Seasons.** Yiannis Katsimprakis serves the very best seafood on Rhodes and speaks passionately of eating fish as though it's a lost art. He established his reputation at nearby Alexis, founded by his father in 1954, but these days the better and less expensive place to experience his skills is in these handsome old rooms, beautiful walled garden, and roof terrace. Mussels in wine, scallops in vodka sauce, simply grilled fish—a bounty culled fresh from the port every day—fills the menu. A side dish might be sautéed squash with wild *glistrida* (purslane), grown in the restaurant's own gardens. [$] *Average main: €30* ✉ *Aristotelous 33* ☎ *22410/70522* 🌐 *www.alexis4seasons.com.*

$$$ SEAFOOD 🍴 **Dinoris.** The great hall that holds Dinoris was built in AD 310 as a hospital and then converted into a stable for the Knights in 1530. The fish specialties and the spacious, classy setting lure appreciative and demanding clients, from visiting celebs to Middle Eastern sheikhs. For appetizers, try the variety platter, which includes *psarokeftedakia* (fish balls made from a secret recipe) as well as mussels, shrimp, and lobster. Other special dishes are sea urchin salad and grilled calamari stuffed with cheese. In warm months, cool sea air drifts through the outdoor garden area enclosed by part of the city's walls. [$] *Average main: €30* ✉ *Mouseou Sq. 14a* ☎ *22410/25824* ✍ *Reservations essential* ⏲ *Closed Jan.*

$$ MODERN GREEK 🍴 **Marco Polo Cafe.** One of the most enchanting places to dine in all of Rhodes is found in the garden of a little guest house, where you'll want to linger amid the foliage and flowers for an entire evening. Efie, the exuberant host, wanders from table to table to extend a warm welcome and announce the nightly offerings, often a rich lamb souvlaki and a delectable seasame-encrusted tuna. Fava with caramelized onions is the not-to-miss starter, while desserts lean toward Italy, including a masterful *semifreddo.* [$] *Average main: €20* ✉ *Agiou Fanouriou 42, Old Town* ☎ *22410/25562* 🌐 *www.marcopolomansion.gr* ⏲ *No lunch. Closed Nov.–Feb.*

$ GREEK 🍴 **To Steno.** When Rhodians want a traditional meal, they head to this simple little taverna on a residential street in the New Town. Dining is in a plain room and on a sparkling white terrace in warmer months, where you can compose a meal of such delicious mezedes as *baccala* (salted cod) in garlic sauce, pumpkin fritters, and zucchini flowers filled with feta cheese. [$] *Average main: €7* ✉ *Agion Anargiron 29* ☎ *22410/35914* ⏲ *No lunch.*

WHERE TO STAY

$$$ B&B/INN **Avalon Boutique Hotel.** Each accommodations in this old house near the Street of the Knights is a suite, with a large, comfortable sitting room and terrace overlooking the Old Town—all are decorated in a pleasing mix of contemporary and traditional style, and four have fireplaces. **Pros:** excellent location in the center of the Old Town; atmospheric surroundings; extremely spacious accommodations. **Cons:** a walk is required to reach the hotel. [$] *Rooms from: €240* ✉ *Haritos 9, Old Town* ☎ *22410/31438* 🌐 *www.avalonrhodes.gr* 🛏 *6 rooms* 🕒 *Closed Nov.–Mar.* 🍴 *Breakfast.*

$$$$ B&B/INN **Kokkini Porta Rossa.** As befits Rhodes's muticultural heritage, the opulent, intriguing rooms of this hotel surround a garden, beautifully blending Ottoman and Greek heritage with sumptuous antiques, rich fabrics, fine woods, and contemporary fittings to provide warm surroundings that seem like a posh private home. **Pros:** superbly designed; large and comfortable accommodations; feel of a private home with excellent service. **Cons:** most easily reached on foot, but just inside gates; not for those looking for low-key casual surroundings. [$] *Rooms from: €300* ✉ *Next to Gate of St. John* ☎ *22410/75114* 🌐 *kokkiniporta.com* 🛏 *5 suites* 🍴 *Breakfast.*

$ HOTEL Fodor's Choice ★ **Marco Polo Mansion.** Entering this renovated 15th-century Ottoman mansion in the maze of the Old Town's colorful Turkish section is like stepping into another world. **Pros:** exotic ambience; warm hospitality; the courtyard restaurant is wonderful. **Cons:** rooms are reached via several sets of stairs; hotel can only be reached on foot; come here to live like a pasha, not to indulge in modern amenities. [$] *Rooms from: €100* ✉ *Aghiou Fanouriou 40–42* ☎ *22410/25562* 🌐 *www.marcopolomansion.gr* 🛏 *17 rooms* 🕒 *Closed Nov.–Feb.* 🍴 *Breakfast.*

$ B&B/INN **Medieval Inn.** These simple, whitewashed lodgings with bright accents are sparkling clean and surround a flowery courtyard. **Pros:** excellent location; very clean and comfortable; friendly service; bargain priced. **Cons:** basic comforts; some bathrooms, while private, are outside the room; can only be reached on foot. [$] *Rooms from: €60* ✉ *Timachida 9, Old Town* ☎ *22410/22469* 🌐 *www.medievalinn.com* 🛏 *12 rooms* 🍴 *No meals.*

$ HOTEL Fodor's Choice ★ **S. Nikolis Hotel.** All the atmospheric magic of Rhodes's medieval Old Town is captured here at this charmingly restored house from the year 1300. **Pros:** atmospheric rooms and surroundings; beautiful garden; warm hospitality. **Cons:** some rooms are small. [$] *Rooms from: €100* ✉ *Odos Ippodamou 61* ☎ *22410/34561* 🌐 *www.s-nikolis.gr* 🛏 *10 rooms, 8 suites* 🍴 *Breakfast.*

$$$$ HOTEL Fodor's Choice ★ **Spirit of the Knights.** A restored Ottoman house on the quiet back lanes of the Old Town is one of Rhodes's most distinctive getaways: it's stylish, exotic, and extremely comfortable. **Pros:** beautiful and exotic surroundings; lovely courtyard with plunge pool; quiet location; excellent breakfast and service; free bicycles for guest use. **Cons:** can only be reached on foot; no elevator. [$] *Rooms from: €200* ✉ *Alexandridou 14* ☎ *22410/39765* 🌐 *www.rhodesluxuryhotel.com* 🛏 *1 room, 5 suites* 🍴 *Breakfast.*

NIGHTLIFE AND PERFORMING ARTS

BARS AND DISCOS

A stylish nightlife has sprung up amid the medieval buildings and flower-filled courtyards of the Old Town. Some bars and cafés here are open all day for drinks, and many—often those with beautiful medieval interiors—stay open most of the year. Nighttime-only spots in the Old Town open up around 10 pm and close around 3 or 4 am. The action centers on narrow, pebble-paved Miltiadou street, where seats spill out from trendy bars set in stone buildings. Another hot spot is Arionos Square. Those wanting to venture to the New Town's throbbing discos should head to Orfanidou street, where bronzed, scantily clad tourists gyrate till dawn at massive clubs.

13

Colorado. The biggest disco on the island is a three-stage complex with live rock, as well as dance hits and R&B. ⊠ *Orfanidou 57, New Town* ☎ *22410/75120* ⊕ *colorado.com.gr.*

Hammam. Located in a 14th-century bathhouse, this atmospheric, candlelit spot occasionally hosts live Greek bands and is a good place to stop for a drink at any time. ⊠ *Aischylou 26, Old Town* ☎ *22410/33242.*

Macao. A haven for grown-up lounge lizards is all about dark, moody lighting, a romantic terrace, mellow music, and worldly cocktails. ⊠ *Archelaou 5* ☎ *69364/00305.*

CASINOS

Casino Rodos. Housed in a 1920s, Italian-built faux-palace of Byzantine and Arabesque design, Rhodes's municipal casino evokes the island's mid-20th century heyday as a gathering spot for the international elite. Aside from gaming, the casino also offers concerts and other events. To enter, you must be at least 21 years old and present a passport. Also, respectable casual attire is required. ⊠ *Hotel Grande Albergo Delle Rose, Papanikolaou 4, New Town* ☎ *22410/97500* ⊕ *www.casinorodos.gr* 🎫 *€6* ☉ *Daily noon–5 am; live games, Mon.–Thurs. 5 pm–3 am, Fri. 4 pm–4 am, Sat. 2 pm–4 am, Sun. noon–3 am.*

DANCE PERFORMANCES

Nelly Dimoglou Folk Dance Theatre. This company is often on tour, but during the summer it performs around Rhodes town. Its performances have kept alive the tradition of Greek dance since 1971, with strict adherence to authentic detail in costume and performance. ⊠ *Andronikou 7, behind Turkish baths, Old Town* ☎ *22410/20157.*

FESTIVALS

Medieval Rose Festival. You can get a glimpse of life in medieval Rhodes in late May when jesters, jugglers, and fire-eaters parade through the cobblestone streets of Old Town. ⊕ *www.medievalfestival.gr.*

SPORTS AND THE OUTDOORS

Dive Med College. A "Discover Scuba" program includes a 30-minute theory lesson and practice in shallow water, then a 20-minute descent. Longer, open-water dive training sessions are also available. ⊠ *45 Kritika* ☎ *22410/61115* ⊕ *www.divemedcollege.com.*

SHOPPING

In Rhodes town you can buy good copies of Lindos ware, a delicate pottery decorated with green and red floral motifs. The Old Town's shopping area, on Sokratous, is lined with boutiques, some of which sell furs, jewelry, and other high-ticket items.

Astero Antiques. Owner Mahalis Hatziz travels throughout Greece each winter to fill his shop with some of the most enticing goods on offer on the island. ⊠ *Ayiou Fanouriou 4, off Sokratous* ☎ *22410/34753.*

EPTA PIGES ΕΠΤΑ ΠΗΓΕΣ

30 km (19 miles) south of Rhodes town.

Epta Piges. A deeply shaded glen watered by seven mountain springs (*epta piges* in Greek) is made all the more photogenic thanks to the imported peacocks that flaunt their plumage in the woods around the pools. The waters are channeled through a 164-yard-long tunnel, which you can walk through, emerging at the edge of a cascading dam and a small man-made lake where you can swim. Here an enterprising local shepherd began serving simple fare in 1945, and his sideline turned into the busy waterside taverna and tourist site of today. Despite its many visitors, the beauty of the springs remains unspoiled. ⊠ *Archangelos* ✛ *To get here, turn right on the inland road near Kolymbia and follow signs.* ☎ *22410/56259* ⊕ *eptapiges.com* ✉ *Free* ☉ *Daily, always open.*

LINDOS ΛΙΝΔΟΣ

19 km (12 miles) southwest of Epta Piges, 48 km (30 miles) southwest of Rhodes town.

Lindos, cradled between two harbors and dominated by its massive hilltop acropolis, is incredibly scenic and remarkably well preserved. Many 15th-century houses are still in use, and the Crusader architecture you see in Rhodes town is everywhere: substantial houses of finely cut Lindos limestone, with windows crowned by elaborate arches. Many floors are paved with black-and-white pebble mosaics. Intermixed with these Crusader-era buildings are whitewashed Cycladic-style houses with square, blue-shuttered windows.

Before the existence of Rhodes town, Lindos was the island's principal maritime center, possessing a revered sanctuary, consecrated to Athena, whose cult probably succeeded that of a pre-Hellenic divinity named Lindia; the sanctuary was dedicated to Athena Lindia. By the 6th century BC, an impressive temple dominated the settlement, and after the foundation of Rhodes, the Lindians set up a *propylaia* (monumental entrance gate) on the model of that in Athens. In the mid-4th century BC, the temple was destroyed by fire and almost immediately rebuilt, with a new wooden statue of the goddess covered by gold leaf, and

One of the most magnificent examples of Crusader era architecture is the great fortress at Lindos.

with arms, head, and legs of marble or ivory. Lindos prospered into Roman times, during the Middle Ages, and under the Knights of St. John. Only at the beginning of the 19th century did the age-old shipping activity cease.

Like Rhodes town, Lindos is enchanting off-season but can get unbearably crowded when summertime pilgrims make the trek from Rhodes town daily, and passage through narrow streets lined with shops selling clothes and trinkets slows to a snail's pace. At these times, an overnight visit allows you to enjoy the town's beauties after the day-trippers leave. Only pedestrians and donkeys are allowed in Lindos because the town's narrow alleys are not wide enough for vehicles. If you're arriving by car, park in the lot above town and walk the 10 minutes down (about 1,200 feet) to town.

EXPLORING

FAMILY

Fodor's Choice

★

Acropolis of Lindos. A 15-minute climb (on the back of a donkey if you prefer) from the village center up to the acropolis of Lindos leads past a gauntlet of Lindian women who spread out their lace and embroidery like fresh laundry over the rocks. The final approach ascends a steep flight of stairs, past a marvelous 2nd-century BC relief of the prow of a Lindian ship, carved into the rock.

The entrance takes you through the medieval castle built by the Knights of St. John, then to the Byzantine Chapel of St. John on the next level. The Romans, too, left their mark on the acropolis, with a temple dedicated to Diocletian. On the upper terraces, begun by classical Greeks around 300 BC, are the remains of elaborate porticoes and stoas, commanding an immense sweep of sea and making a powerful statement on behalf of Athena and the Lydians (who dedicated the monuments on the Acropolis to her); the lofty white columns of the temple and stoa on the summit must have presented a magnificent picture. The main portico of the stoa had 42 Doric columns, at the center of which an opening led to the staircase up to the Propylaia (or sanctuary). The Temple of Athena Lindia at the very top is surprisingly modest, given the drama of the approach. As was common in the 4th century BC, both the front and the rear are flanked by four Doric columns. Numerous inscribed statue bases were found all over the summit, attesting in many cases to the work of Lindian sculptors, who were clearly second to none. ⊠ *Above the village* ☎ *22440/31258* ⊕ *www.culture.gr* 🎫 *€6* ⊙ *May–Oct., Tues.–Sun. 8–8, Mon. 8–3; Nov.–Apr., Tues.–Fri. 8–sunset Mon., Sat.–Sun. 8–3.*

Tomb of Kleoboulos. Escape the crowds by trekking to the Tomb of Kleoboulos, which is incorrectly named after Lindos's 6th-century BC tyrant Kleoboulos; it's actually the final resting place of a wealthy family of the 1st to 2nd century BC. After about 3 km (2 miles), a 30-minute scenic walk on a stony path across the headland (on the north side of Lindos bay), you encounter the small, rounded stone tomb. You can peer inside and see the candle marks, which testify to its later use as the church of St. Emilianos. ⊹ *Look for sign at parking lot near beach above main square. Follow the dirt path along the hill on opposite side of bay from acropolis.*

Church of the Panayia. A graceful building with a beautiful bell tower probably antedates the Knights, though the bell tower bears the arms of Grand Master d'Aubusson with the dates 1484–90. Frescoes in the elaborate interior were painted in 1779 by Gregory of Symi, and the black-and-white pebble floor is a popular Byzantine design. ⊠ *Off main square* ⊙ *May–Oct., daily 9–2 and 5–9; Nov.–Apr., call number posted on church to have door unlocked.*

WHERE TO EAT

$$
GREEK

✕ **Mavrikos.** The secret of this longtime favorite, with a large terrace overlooking the sea and main village square, is an elegant, perfect simplicity. Seemingly straightforward dishes, such as sea-urchin salad, fried *manouri* cheese with basil and pine nuts, swordfish in caper sauce, and lobster risotto, become transcendent with the magic touch of third-generation chef Dimitris Mavrikos, who now owns this family-run institution, which has been in business since the 1930s, with his brother, Michalis. He combines the freshest ingredients with classical training and an abiding love for the best of Greek village cuisine. The meat dishes, including oven-baked lamb, are also sublime. $ *Average main: €20* ⊠ *Main Sq.* ☎ *22440/31232* ⊙ *Closed Nov.–Mar.*

WHERE TO STAY

$
B&B/INN

🏨 **Electra Studios.** Linger on the spacious terrace, with views of the town and sea, or down in the blossoming garden of this simple decades-old pension, where many of the high-celinged, simply furnished rooms have sea views. **Pros:** sea views; pleasant atmosphere; friendly staff; nice location on pedestrian lanes of Old Town. **Cons:** comforts are basic; a bit of a trek from bus or parking with luggage. $ *Rooms from: €50* ☎ *22440/31266* ⊕ *www.electra-studios.gr* 🛏 *7 rooms, 1 with bath in hall* ▭ *No credit cards* ⊙ *Closed Nov.–May* ⦿ *No meals.*

$$ | RESORT | 🖼 **Lindos Blu Hotel.** Sea views seem to fill every inch of this small, sun-drenched, adults-only resort, where many of the stylishly contemporary guest rooms and suites have their own pools tucked onto terraces. **Pros:** attentive, personalized service; resort amenities in an initmate atmosphere. **Cons:** decor is a bit generic. $ *Rooms from: €200 ⊠ Vlicha Lindos, 2 km (1 mile) outside village center* ☎ *22440/32110 ⊕ www.lindosblu.gr ↜ 55 rooms, 15 suites ⊗ Closed Nov.–Mar.* ◯ *Breakfast.*

$$$$ | HOTEL | Fodor's Choice | ★ | 🖼 **Melenos Hotel.** Michalis Melenos worked for years to make this stone villa set into gardens overlooking Lindos bay into a truly special retreat, filling rooms with traditional Lindian village beds, hand-carved woodwork, Turkish tiles, and antique furnishings brought from throughout Greece and Turkey. **Pros:** atmospheric surroundings; beautiful garden; terraces with sea views; exquisite service. **Cons:** quite expensive (though high-season discounts are available on the hotel website). $ *Rooms from: €310 ⊠ At edge of Lindos, on path to Acropolis* ☎ *22440/32222 ⊕ www.melenoslindos.com ↜ 12 suites ⊗ Closed Nov.–Mar.* ◯ *Breakfast.*

NIGHTLIFE

Most of Lindos's bars cater to a young, hard-drinking crowd; few are without a television showing soccer. Many are open year-round to serve the locals.

Gelo Blu. The most popular hangout in town serves homemade ice cream by day and drinks day and night in the cool, blue-cushioned interior and pebbled courtyard and on the rooftop terrace of a sea captain's house. ⊠ *Near Theotokou Church* ☎ *22440/31761.*

Rainbird. Coffee and drinks are served all day, but the views from the romantic terrace make this spot especially popular around sunset. ⊠ *On lane to acropolis* ☎ *22440/32169 ⊕ www.rainbirdbar.com.*

GENNADI AND THE SOUTH COAST
ΓΕΝΝΑΔΙ ΚΑΙ ΝΟΤΙΑ ΠΑΡΑΛΙΑ

20 km (12½ miles) south of Lindos, 68 km (42 miles) south of Rhodes town.

The area south of Lindos, with fewer beaches and less fertile soil, is less traveled than the stretch to its north. Though development is increasing, the still pretty and inexpensive coastal village of Gennadi has pensions, rooms for rent, and a handful of tavernas, nightclubs, and DJ-hosted beach parties.

BEACHES

Lachania Beach. Stretching uninterrupted for several miles, Lachania beach lies below unspoiled, whitewashed village of the same name, one of the most picturesque in Rhodes. Though stretches of the sand are lined with sun beds, it's easy to find a fairly secluded spot backed by scrub-covered dunes. **Amenities:** food and drink; water sports. **Best for:** solitude; swimming; walking. ⊠ *Lachania ✤ 9 km (6 miles) south of Gennadi.*

Plimiri Beach. A lovely bay is ringed by soft and quiet sands, where it's easy to find a relatively secluded spot. The clear, calm waters are ideal for swimming, though winds tend to pick up in the afternoon, a boon for windsurfers. A few tavernas prepare delightfully simple seafood meals. **Amenities:** food and drink. **Best for:** nudists; solitude; swimming; windsurfing. ⊠ *Plimiri.*

MONOLITHOS TO KAMEIROS ΜΟΝΟΛΙΘΟΣ ΠΡΟΣ ΚΑΜΕΙΡΟΣ

28 km (17 miles) northwest of Gennadi, 74 km (46 miles) southwest of Rhodes town.

Rhodes's west coast is more forested, with fewer good beaches than its east coast—but if you're looking to get away from the hordes, you'll find peace and quiet among the sylvan scenery, august ruins, and vineyards.

EXPLORING

Kameiros. One of the three ancient cities of Rhodes, excavated by the Italians in 1929, lies on three levels on a slope above the sea. Most of the city, apparently never fortified, that is visible today dates to the classical period and later, and include an acropolis, a large reservoir, a gridlike pattern of streets lined with houses and shops, and several temples. The hill hides many more ruins, yet to be unearthed. ⊠ *Kameiros* ✥ *Off main Rhodes road, 23 km (14 miles) northeast of Siana; turn at sign for "Ancient Kameiros"* ☎ *22413/65200* ⊕ *www.culture. gr* ⊠ *€4* ☉ *Apr.–Oct., Mon. 8–3, Tues.–Sun. Nov.–Mar., Tues.–Sun. 8:30–3.*

Kastello. This ruined-yet-still impressive fortress built by the Knights in the late 15th century rises high above the sea on the coast just north of Mt. Avrios, with good views in every direction. ⊠ *Kritinia* ✥ *13 km (8 miles) northeast of Siana* ⊠ *Free.*

Fodor'sChoice
★   **Monolithos.** A medieval fortress of Monolithos—so named for the jutting, 750-foot monolith on which it is built—rises above a fairy-tale landscape of deep-green forests and sharp cliffs plunging into the sea. Inside the Venetian stronghold (acessible only by a steep path and series of stone steps) there is a chapel, and the ramparts provide magnificent views of Rhodes's emerald inland and the island of Halki. The small pebble beach of Fourni beneath the castle is a delightful place for a swim. ⊠ *Monolithos* ✥ *Take western road from middle of Monolithos village; near hairpin turn there's a path up to fortress* ⊠ *Free* ☉ *Daily at all hours.*

Siana. This small town perches on the wooded slopes of Mt. Acramitis above a vast, fertile valley. A popular stop on the tourist trail, Siana is known for its fragrant honey and for Souma (a very strong, sweet wine that resembles a grape-flavor schnapps); look for stands selling both. Or make a stop at Manos (closed mid-Nov.–Jan.), a little taverna/shop past town church on main road, or one of several other shops along the street that sell Siana's renowned honey and walnuts, as well as Souma, a potent firewater made from figs. ⊠ *Siana* ✥ *5 km (3 miles) northeast of Monolithos.*

EN ROUTE Beyond Siana, the road continues on a high ridge through thick pine forests, which carpet the precipitous slopes dropping toward the sea. To the east looms the bare, stony massif of Mt. Ataviros, Rhodes's highest peak, at 3,986 feet. If you follow the road inland rather than continue north along the coast toward Kritinia, you'll climb the flanks of the mountains to the traditional, arbor-filled village of Embonas in Rhodes's richest wine country *(see "Nectar of the Gods" in Chapter 8).*

PETALOUDES ΠΕΤΑΛΟΥΔΕΣ ΚΑΙ ΙΑΛΥΣΟΣ

22 km (14 miles) east of Kameiros, 25 km (16 miles) southwest of Rhodes town.

Petaloudes. The "Valley of the Butterflies" lives up to its name, especially in July and August. In summer the *callimorpha quadripunctaria,* actually a moth species, cluster by the thousands around the low bushes of the pungent storax plant, which grows all over the area. Through the years the numbers have diminished, partly owing to busloads of tourists clapping hands to see them fly up in dense clouds—an antic that causes the moths to deplete their scant energy reserves and is strongly discouraged. Access to the valley involves an easy walk up an idyllic yet crowded trail through a pretty wood past a stream and ponds. ⊠ *Theologos* ✛ *Turn off coastal road south and follow signs leading to the site with its own parking lot.* ☎ *22410/81801* 💰*€4* ⊙ *Late Apr.–Oct., daily 8–7.*

SYMI ΣΥΜΗ

45 km (27 miles) north of Rhodes by ferry.

The island of Symi is an enchanting place, where island life centers around sparkling Yialos harbor, and Chorio, a 19th-century town of neoclassical mansions, crowns a hillside above. The island has few beaches and almost no flat land, so it is not attractive to developers. As a result, quiet Symi provides a peaceful retreat for travelers, who tend to fall in love with the island on their first visit and return year after year.

GETTING HERE AND AROUND

Little Symi is well served by boats, either on one-day excursion trips from Mandraki harbor in Rhodes town (check with any travel agent like Triton Holidays *(see Tour Options)* or one of the shills on the harbor; the trip takes less than an hour. All boats arrive in Yialos, Symi's main harbor, and catamarans also make a stop in Panormitis or Pedi, though these remote places are of most interest to day-trippers who just want a day at a remote beach.

A sturdy bus makes the hourly trip from Yialos harbor up to Chorio and on to Pedi bay, €0.80. But once on Symi, you'll learn that the easiest way to get around is by foot, as roads are few and many of those are quite rough. If you are staying in Nimborios or another outlying place, make arrangements in advance for your hotel to pick you up, as taxis refuse to make the trip on unimproved roads.

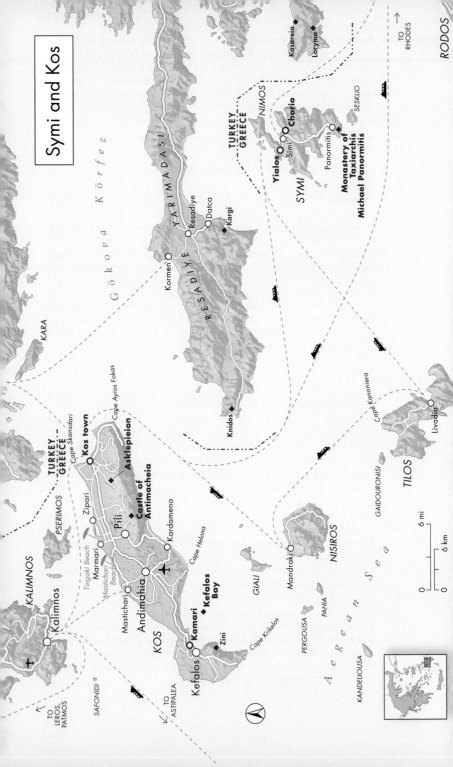

Symi and Kos

VISITOR INFORMATION

The region's only English-language newspaper is found on Symi. The *Symi Visitor* (⊕ *www.symivisitor.com*), available at tourist spots, is full of information on events, news, and activities, plus has an overview of the sites, and bus and ferry schedules; the website has accommodations listings and weather updates.

EXPLORING

Nireus, the ancient king of Symi noted for his looks, sailed with three vessels to assist the Greeks at Troy, as mentioned by Homer. Symi was later part of the Dorian Hexapolis dominated by Rhodes, and it remained under Rhodian dominance throughout the Roman and Byzantine periods. The island has good natural harbors, and the nearby coast of Asia Minor provided plentiful timber for the Symiotes, who were shipbuilders, fearless seafarers and sponge divers, and rich and successful merchants. Under the Ottomans their harbor was proclaimed a free port and attracted the trade of the entire region. The Symiotes' continuous travel and trade and their frequent contact with Europe led them to incorporate foreign elements in their furnishings, clothes, and cultural life. At first they lived in Chorio, high on the hillside above the port, and in the second half of the 19th century spread down to the seaside at Yialos.

Proof of their prosperity are the neoclassic mansions that line the narrow streets of Chorio and the main harbor in Yialos. There were some 20,000 inhabitants at this acme, but under the Italian occupation at the end of the Italo-Turkish war in 1912, the island declined; the Symiotes lost their holdings in Asia Minor and were unable to convert their fleets to steam. Many emigrated to work elsewhere, and now there are just a few thousand inhabitants in Chorio and Yialos.

YIALOS ΓΙΑΛΟΣ

45 km (27 miles) north of Rhodes town.

As the boat from Rhodes to Symi rounds the last of many rocky barren spurs, the port of Yialos, at the back of a deep, narrow harbor, comes into view. The shore is lined with mansions whose ground floors have been converted to cafés with waterside terraces perfect for whiling away lazy hours.

Church of Ayhios Ioannis. This church built in 1838 incorporates in its walls fragments of ancient blocks from a temple that apparently stood on this site and is surrounded by a plaza paved in an intricate mosaic, fashioned from inlaid pebbles. ⊠ *Near center of Yialos village.*

FAMILY **Symi Nautical Museum.** Sponge-diving tools, model ships, antique navigation tools, and vintage anchors give a good taste of life in Symi in the 19th and early 20th centuries. It's hard to miss the ornamental blue-and-yellow building—a landmark on Yialos harbor, it was once one of the world's great sponge-diving centers. ⊠ *Yialos waterfront* ⌨ *€2* ☽ *Tues.–Sun. 10–2.*

WHERE TO EAT

$
SEAFOOD
✕ **Manos Fish Restaurant.** Many people think this outdoor harborside eatery serves the best fish on Symi, and you may agree as you try the succulent mussels steamed in white wine, followed by a mixed grill of octopus, squid, prawns, and locally caught fish, all done to perfection over a wood fire. Specialities like rock lobster and shot glasses filled with sea urchin eggs cater to local seafood lovers. Manos, an enterprising Athenian who married a local woman, doesn't let a single tourist pass without inviting them to sit down. $ *Average main: €15* ✉ *Yialos harbor front* ☎ *22460/72429* ۞ *Closed Nov.–Apr.*

$$$
CONTEMPORARY
Fodor's Choice
★
✕ **Mylopetra.** A delightfully converted old flour mill, Mylopetra is a feast for the eyes, with rich stone work accented with island antiques, rich fabrics, and an ancient tomb embedded in glass beneath the floor. German couple Hans and Eva Sworoski painstakingly oversee this extraordinary restaurant, ensuring gracious service and a daily menu that always includes inventive sauces made with wild herbs gathered on the island, homemade pasta married with anything from spinach to rabbit to salmon, and abundant seafood and meat (often game) options. $ *Average main: €40* ✉ *Behind church on backstreet* ☎ *22460/72333* ⊕ *www.mylopetra.com* ☜ *Reservations essential* ۞ *Closed late-Oct.– Apr. No lunch.*

$$
GREEK
✕ **Tholos.** A seaside perch at the end of Yialos harbor is the picturesque setting for an excellent meal, which often begins with such traditional appetizers as stuffed zucchini or boiled greens (the *taramasalta* here might just be among the best in Greece) and includes fresh grilled fish and other daily home-cooked offerings. You may want to arrive early enough to enjoy sunset views of the harbor. $ *Average main: €20* ✉ *Waterfront* ☎ *22460/72033* ☜ *Reservations essential* ۞ *Closed mid-Oct.–Apr.*

WHERE TO STAY

$$
HOTEL
Fodor's Choice
★
🏠 **Aliki Hotel.** At this three-story, 1895 mansion on the waterfront, guest rooms are furnished with a tasteful mix of antiques and newer pieces—the best, of course, are those that face the water. **Pros:** lovely old house with plenty of atmosphere; waterfront location. **Cons:** rooms are reached by a climb up steep stairs. $ *Rooms from: €130* ✉ *Yialos waterfront* ☎ *22460/71665* ⊕ *www.hotelaliki.gr* ☜ *12 rooms, 3 suites* ❑ *Breakfast.*

$
B&B/INN
🏠 **Niriides.** A little fishing village of Nimborios, about a mile from Yialos, is the setting for a get-away-from-it-all retreat in these pleasant apartments overlooking the sea and the coast of Turkey and surrounded by gardens. **Pros:** wonderful relaxing atmosphere; great hospitality; spacious, attractive accommodations; beautiful rural location. **Cons:** remote location. $ *Rooms from: €70* ✉ *Nimborios* ☎ *22460/71784* ⊕ *www.niriideshotel.com* ☜ *11 rooms* ۞ *Closed Nov.–Apr.* ❑ *Breakfast.*

$$
HOTEL
🏠 **The Old Markets.** Symi's historic sponge trading halls—one of many landmarks that surround the Old Harbor—have been restored as an intimate and atmospheric inn where centuries-old surroundings are accented by stone walls, painted ceilings, exquisite antiques, and such 21st century touches as high-tech lighting and supremely comfortable

beds. **Pros:** extremely comfortable accommodations, including a lavish suite. **Cons:** harbor location puts you amidst the one busy spot on the island. ⓢ *Rooms from: €220* ✉ *Kali Strata* ☎ *22460/71440* ⊕ *theold-markets.com* ⇄ *5 rooms* ⊘ *Nov.–Apr.* ⏐⊙⏐ *Breakfast.*

BEACHES

One reason Symi's beaches are so pristine is that almost none are reachable by car. From the main harbor at Yialos, boats leave every half-hour between 10:30 am and 12:30 pm to the beautiful beaches of **Aghia Marina, Aghios Nikolas, Aghios Giorgos,** and **Nanou** bay. Return trips run from 4 to 6 pm. The round-trips cost €5 to €10. In summer, there are also small boats for hire from the clock tower.

For a swim near Yialos, you can go to the little strip of beach beyond the **Yialos** harbor—follow the road past the bell tower and the Aliki Hotel and you come to a seaside taverna that rents umbrellas and beach chairs for €5 a day. If you continue walking on the same road for about 2 km (1 mile), you come to the pine-shaded beach at Nimborios bay, where there is another taverna.

Aghios Giorgos. The half-hour boat trip down the rugged east coast of the island from Pedi bay is part of the pleasure of an excursion to this beautiful strip of sand, backed by sheer cliffs. The absence of facilities requires a bit of preparation—bring water, food, and an umbrella, as there are few shade-providing trees. Aghios Giorgos is a favorite destination for yachters, who drop anchor for a swim and a picnic, though you'll often feel as if you have this remote strand to yourself. **Amenities:** none. **Best for:** solitude; nudists; snorkeling; swimming. ✉ *Pedi bay.*

FAMILY **Aghios Nikolas.** Accessible only by water taxi from Pedi bay or a half-hour walk along a rough path, this sandy beach along a little bay slopes gently, providing shallow waters that are excellent for children, and is backed by a grove of shade-giving trees. Despite the relative isolation, the beach attracts summertime crowds and is well-equipped with food vendors and other facilities. **Amenities:** food and drink; toilets; water sports. **Best for:** snorkling; swimming. ✉ *3km (2 miles) east of Pedi bay.*

FESTIVALS

Symi Festival. The Symi Festival brings free dance, music, theater performances, and cinema screenings to the island every year from June through September. Most events take place in the main harbor square in Yialos, but some are scheduled in the Monastery of Taxiarchis Michael Panormitis and other historic places around the island. A schedule of events is posted at the square, and programs can be found at local shops, travel agents, and the town hall. ⊕ *www.symi.gr.*

CHORIO ΧΩΡΙΟ

1 km (½ mile) east of Yialos.

Fodor'sChoice It's a 10-minute walk from the main harbor of Yialos up to the hilltop
★ town of Chorio, along a staircase of some 400 steps, known as Kali Strata (Good Steps). There is also a road that can be traveled in one

of the island's few taxis or by bus, which makes a circuit with stops at the harbor in Yialos, Chorio, and the seaside community of Pedi. The Kali Strata are flanked by elegant neoclassic houses with elaborate stonework, lavish pediments, and intricate wrought-iron balconies. Just before the top of the stairs (and the welcome little Kali Strata bar), a line of windmills crowns the hill of Noulia. Most of Chorio's many churches date to the 18th and 19th centuries, and many are ornamented with richly decorated iconostases and ornate bell towers. Donkeys are often used to carry materials through the narrow streets for the town's steady construction and renovation work.

EXPLORING

Archaeological Museum of Symi. The collection at the Archaeological Museum, housed in a neoclassical dwelling amid the maze of Chorio's lanes, displays Hellenistic and Roman sculptures and inscriptions as well as more recent carvings, icons, costumes, and handicrafts; the re-creation of a simple Symi dwelling is especially charming. ✥ *Follow signs from central square to Lieni neighborhood* ☎ *22460/71114* 🎫 *€2* ⏲ *Tues.–Sun. 8–2:30.*

Kastro (*Castle*). Incorporating fragments of an ancient acropolis within its walls, the castle was built by the Knights of St. John in a short-lived attempt to expand their holdings in Rhodes. A church and several chapels dot the sparse hillside around the remnants of its walls. The hilltop view takes in both sides of the narrow peninsula that Chorio crowns, with the villages of Yialos and Pedi (and their sparkling harbors) far below. ✉ *At top of town, in the ancient acropolis.*

WHERE TO EAT

$ GREEK ✕ **Georgio and Maria's Taverna.** Meals at this simple Chorio taverna, which is as popular with locals as it is with tourists, are served in a high-ceilinged, whitewashed dining room or on a terrace that is partially shaded by a grape arbor and affords wonderful views over the sea and surrounding hills. Fish is a specialty, and simply prepared *mezedes* (small dishes), such as roasted peppers topped with feta cheese and fried zucchini, can constitute a delicious meal in themselves. If you're lucky, one of the neighbors will stroll in with instrument in hand to provide an impromptu serenade, and live Greek music usually accompanies Friday night dinners. $ *Average main: €10* ✉ *Off the main square at top of the Kali Strata* ☎ *22460/71984.*

WHERE TO STAY

$ B&B/INN **Hotel Fiona.** At this bright, cheerful perch on the hillside in Chorio, just about all of the large, white-tile-floored rooms have a sea-facing balcony. **Pros:** friendly service; excellent views over the harbor far below. **Cons:** on foot, the nearby Yialos waterfront and beaches are reached by an atmospheric yet strenuous climb down and back up 400 steps. $ *Rooms from: €60* ✉ *Near main square* ☎ *22460/72088* 🌐 *www.fionahotel.com* 🛏 *14 rooms, 3 studios* ⏲ *Closed Nov.–Apr.* 🍽 *Breakfast.*

MONASTERY OF TAXIARCHIS MICHAEL PANORMITIS
ΜΟΝΗ ΤΑΞΙΑΡΧΗ ΜΙΧΑΗΛ ΠΑΝΟΡΜΙΤΗ

7 km (4½ miles) south of Chorio.

The tiny hamlet of Panormitis on the south end of the island is a remote and idyllic setting for this holy assemblage, a popular place of pilgrimage and a pleasure to visit simply for the scenery. A trip to the monastery can be accompanied by a refreshing swim at the designated edges of the deep-blue harbor. There's bus service twice a day from Yialos, which passes through Chorio, or you can take one of the daily boats from Yialos or Rhodes. Several tour companies organize day trips to the monastery, with time for a swim and a hike in the surrounding countryside, for about €15, including lunch. *(See Tour Options for more information.)*

Fodor's Choice   **Monastery of Taxiarchis Michael Panormitis.** The main reason to venture ★   to the atypically green, pine-covered hills surrounding the little gulf of Panormitis is to visit this unexpectedly grand monastery dedicated to Symi's patron saint, the protector of sailors. The site's entrance is surmounted by an elaborate **bell tower,** of the multilevel wedding-cake variety on display in Yialos and Chorio. A black-and-white pebble mosaic adorns the floor of the **courtyard,** which is surrounded by a vaulted stoa. The interior of the **church,** entirely frescoed in the 18th century, contains a marvelously ornate wooden iconostasis, which is flanked by a heroic-size 18th-century representation of Michael, all but his face covered with silver. There are two small **museums** devoted to Byzantine and folk art. The Byzantine includes a collection of votive offerings, including an enchanting collection of wooden ship models and bottles with notes containing wishes and money in them, which, according to local lore, travel to Symi on their own after having been thrown into the sea. A trip to the monastery can be accompanied by a refreshing swim at the designated edges of the deep-blue harbor. There's bus service twice a day from Yialos, which passes through Chorio, and boats from Yialos and Rhodes daily. You can also hike to the monastery along a well-marked route from Chorio; the distance is about 10 km (6 miles) but can certainly seem longer if you don't set out early enough to avoid the heat of the day. Several tour companies organize day trips to the monastery, with time for a swim and a hike and lunch in the surrounding countryside.

If a day trip isn't enough for you, the monastery rents 60 spartan rooms (☎ 22460/72414) with kitchens and private baths. Though the price doesn't include a towel or air-conditioning and there are insects (some rather large), the spiritual aspect makes for an enriching experience. A nursing home as well as a market, bakery, restaurant, and a few other business make up the rest of the settlement. The monastery is at its busiest for the week leading up to November 8, Michael's feast day, an event that draws the faithful from throughout the Dodecanese and beyond. ✉ *Symi's south side, at harbor* ☎ *22460/71581 museums, 22460/72414 rooms* ⊕ *www.imsymis.org* 🖃 *Monastery free; museums €1.50* ⊗ *Monastery: daily 7–8; museums: Apr.–Oct. 8:30–1 and 3–4; Nov.–Apr. by appointment.*

KOS ΚΩΣ

92 km (57 miles) north of Rhodes.

Aglow with flowering oleanders and hibiscus, the island of Kos is the third-largest in the Dodecanese. It certainly remains one of the most verdant in the otherwise arid archipelago, with lush fields and tree-clad mountains, surrounded by miles of sandy beach. Its highest peak, part of a small mountain range in the northeast, is a respectable 2,800 feet. All this beauty has not gone unnoticed, of course, and Kos undeniably suffers from the effects of mass tourism: its beaches are often crowded, most of its seaside towns have been recklessly overdeveloped, and the main town is noisy and busy between June and September.

In Mycenaean times and during the Archaic period, the island prospered. In the 6th century BC it was conquered by the Persians but later joined the Delian League, supporting Athens against Sparta in the Peloponnesian War. Kos was invaded and destroyed by the Spartan fleet, ruled by Alexander and his various successors, and was twice devastated by earthquakes. Nevertheless, the city and the economy flourished, as did the arts and sciences. The painter Apelles, the Michelangelo of his time, came from Kos, as did Hippocrates, father of modern medicine. Under the Roman Empire, the island's Asklepieion and its renowned healing center drew emperors and ordinary citizens alike. The Knights of St. John arrived in 1315 and ruled for the next two centuries, until the Ottomans replaced them. In 1912 the Italians took over, and in 1947 the island was united with Greece.

GETTING HERE AND AROUND

Kos is a major air hub, with regular service from Athens and during high season from many other European cities. The airport is about 25 km (15 miles) outside Kos town, about an hour by bus (€5) and half-hour by taxi (€30), so keep the time and taxi-cost factors in mind when booking an early morning outgoing flight.

Kos is also well-served by ferries, with at least two boats arriving from Pireaus daily in high season (10 hours) and at least two arriving from Rhodes (about 2½ hours). Boats also arrive from Mykonos, Paros, and other islands in the Cyclades about twice a week. Schedules change all the time, so check with ⊕ *www.ferries.gr, www.gtp.gr,* or with any of the many travel agencies along the waterfront in Kos town for the latest info on boat service. Kos harbor is adjacent to the city center, so convenient to services and bus connections.

An excellent bus network serves most of the island, putting most resort towns around the island within easy reach of Kos town by public transportation; as many as six buses a day connect Kos town in the north and Kefalos in the south, for example, and the trip takes about an hour and costs €3.

VISITOR INFORMATION

Contacts Kos Municipal Tourism Office ⊠ *Vasileos Georgiou 1, Kos town* ☎ *22420/28724* ⊕ *www.kos.gr* ⊗ *Mon.–Fri. 8–2:30 and 3–10; also Sat. 9–2 May–Oct.*

KOS TOWN ΚΩΣ ΠΟΛΗ

92 km (57 miles) north of Rhodes.

The modern town lies on a flat plain encircling spacious Mandraki harbor and is a pleasant assemblage of low-lying buildings and shady lanes, with a skyline pierced by minarets and palm trees. The fortress, which crowns the west side of town, is a good place to begin your exploration of Kos town. Hippocrates is supposed to have taught near here, in the shade of a plane tree that is said to have grown on one side of little Platanou Square—but this is merely legend, as the Koan capital, called Astypalaia, was at the far, western end of the island and Thucydides recounts its destruction by an earthquake. A loggia, actually a mosque built in 1786, now graces the square.

EXPLORING

Agora and Harbor Ruins. Excavations by Italian and Greek archaeologists have revealed ancient agora and harbor ruins that date from the 4th century BC through Roman times. Remnants include parts of the walls of the old city, of a Hellenistic stoa, and of temples dedicated to Aphrodite and Hercules. The ruins are not fenced and, laced with pine-shaded paths, are a pleasant retreat in the modern city. In spring the site is covered with brightly colored flowers, which nicely frame the ancient gray-and-white marble blocks tumbled in every direction. ⊠ *Over bridge from Platanou Sq., behind Castle of the Knights.*

FAMILY **Casa Romana** (*Roman House*). The Roman House is a lavish restoration of a 3rd-century Roman mansion, with 36 rooms grouped around three atriums. The house provides a look at what everyday life of the well-to-do residents of the Roman town might have been like, and also houses some beautiful frescoes and mosaics. But the Greek and Roman ruins that surround the house are freely accessible and are just as evocative. ⊠ *Pavlou and Grigoriou* ☎ *22420/23234* ⊡ *€3* ☉ *Tues.–Sun. 8:30–3.*

Castle of the Knights. Built by the Knights of St. John in the 15th century and taken by the Turks in 1522 (with the rest of the knights' Dodecanese holdings), the castle/fortress is an imposing presence on the harbor. It's best to let that remain the impression you have of this massive structure: Little remains inside the walls but a field littered with fragments of ancient funerary monuments and other sculptural material from the island's Greek and Roman inhabitants. ⊠ *Over bridge from Platanou Sq.* ☎ *22420/27927* ⊡ *€3* ☉ *Tues.–Sun. 8:30–2:30.*

West Excavations. These excavations laced through a quiet residential district have uncovered a portion of one of the main Roman streets with many houses, including the **House of the Europa Mosaic**, and part of the **Roman baths** (near main Roman street) that was later converted into a basilica. The **gymnasium** is distinguished by its partly reconstructed colonnade, and the so-called **Nymphaion** is a lavish public latrine that has been restored. In the **Odeon**, 18 rows of stone seats remain intact. The West Excavations are always open, with free access, and significant finds are labeled. ⊠ *Southwest of agora and harbor ruins.*

BEACHES

If you must get wet but can't leave Kos town, try the narrow pebble strip of beach immediately south of the main harbor.

WHERE TO EAT

$

MODERN GREEK

✕ **Petrino.** Three brothers have created a calm oasis a few streets in from the hustle and bustle of Kos harbor. A 150-year-old stone house provides cozy dining in cool months, and in summer, tables pepper a garden full of private nooks, fountains, and gentle music. The enormous menu lists Greek recipes, like zucchini pancakes and liver with oregano, side-by-side with much-heralded house creations that include figs wrapped in prosciutto and stuffed with blue cheese, or the shrimp sautéed with mushrooms in ouzo. Servings are generous, and the service tends to be informal yet gracious. $ *Average main: €15* ✉ *Ioannou Theologou Sq.* ☎ *22420/27251* ⊕ *www.petrino-kos.gr.*

$$

GREEK

✕ **Platanos.** The setting, on the shady square where Hippocrates once taught, is the most storied place in Kos, and this island institution maintains its high standards for excellent cooking and topnotch service year after year. Occupying an early-20th-century Italian club, the surroundings may be elaborate (with dining in arched, elaborately tiled rooms or on a candlelit balcony) but the cuisine here is simply prepared and delicious—try the beautifully spiced grilled lamb chops or chicken stuffed with dates. Live music accompanies meals as the evenings wear on. $ *Average main: €20* ✉ *Platia Platanos* ☎ *22420/28991* ⊕ *www.platanoskos.gr* ⌂ *Reservations essential* ⊘ *Closed Nov.–Mar.*

WHERE TO STAY

$$$

RESORT

Fodor'sChoice

★

🏨 **Aqua Blu.** Who says chic can't be supremely comfortable—as these truly exciting lodgings prove, with sea views, private pools, fireplaces, hardwood floors, handsome built-ins, and all sorts of other extras. **Pros:** outstanding design; small and intimate yet extremely luxurious; polished and friendly service; excellent food. **Cons:** outside town; not a full-scale resort (can be a plus); no kids allowed. $ *Rooms from: €250* ✉ *Ephelondon Paleon Polemiston, Lambi beach* ☎ *22420/30011* ⊕ *www.aquabluhotel.gr* ⤳ *51 suites* ⊘ *Closed Nov.–Mar.* ⭐ *Breakfast.*

$$

HOTEL

🏨 **Aktis Art Hotel.** With a perch right on the beach at the edge of the Old Town, these modernist guest rooms seem to be afloat in the Aegean, whose azure waters fill the floor-to-ceiling windows and glass-fronted balconies. **Pros:** excellent location on the sea near all in-town attractions; relaxing and stylish decor and ambience. **Cons:** full-range of resort amenities is not available; hotel doesn't have its own pool. $ *Rooms from: €190* ✉ *Vasileos Georgiou 7* ☎ *22420/47200* ⊕ *www.kosaktis.gr* ⤳ *36 rooms, 6 suites* ⭐ *Breakfast.*

$$$

RESORT

🏨 **Grecotel Kos Imperial.** The grounds of this huge resort, covering a gentle slope next to an idyllic Aegean beach, comprise a water world, laced with seawater and freshwater pools, artificial rivers and lagoons, glimmering glass-tile hydrotherapy pools, and dozens of spa treatment basins—and set amid them are airy and beautifully designed guest rooms. **Pros:** finest of the big resorts on Kos; excellent facilities; attractive and comfortable guest rooms. **Cons:** big resort feel; a distance from

13

Kos town (but easily accessible by bus or taxi). $ *Rooms from: €250* ✉ *Psalidi ✛ 4 km (2½ miles) east of Kos town* ☎ *22420/58000* ⊕ *www. grecotel.com* ↪ *330 rooms, 55 suites* ⏶ *Breakfast.*

$ 🛏 **Hotel Afendoulis.** Plain, whitewashed rooms with dark-wood furni-
HOTEL ture are spotless, attractive, and of far better quality than most in this price range (the best open to little balconies with sea views), and the genuinely warm, attentive service far exceeds the norm. **Pros:** pleas-ant, quiet surroundings; in-town location; excellent hospitality includes laundry service. **Cons:** no pool or other resort amenities. $ *Rooms from: €40* ✉ *Evripilou 1* ☎ *22420/25321* ⊕ *www.afendoulishotel.com* ↪ *23 rooms* ⏶ *No meals.*

NIGHTLIFE

Things start cooking before 7 pm and in many cases roar on past 7 am on Akti Koundourioti and in the nearby Exarhia area, which includes rowdy Nafklirou and Plessa streets. Competing bars try to lure in bar-hoppers with ads for cheap beer and neon-colored drinks.

X Club. Massive surroundings off Delphinia Square offer an outdoor bar, happy hour, a throbbing indoor dance floor, and guest DJs, who seek to provide young, international travelers the kind of club music they'd hear back home. ✉ *Odos Kanari 2* ☎ *22420/22592.*

H20. This loungey seaside club has a small, sleek interior as well as outdoor seating, and excellent meals are served in the adjoining res-taurant of the same name. ✉ *Aktis Art Hotel, Vasileos Georgiou 7, on the beach* ☎ *22420/47207.*

FESTIVALS

Hippocrates Festival. Every summer from July through mid-September Kos hosts a much-attended festival when music, dance, movie screen-ings, and theater performances enliven venues such as the Castle of the Knights and the Odeon. The festival also includes exhibits around town and activities for children. ☎ *22420/48222* ✐ *www.kosinfo.gr.*

SPORTS AND THE OUTDOORS

BIKING

Kos, particularly the area around the town, is good for bicycle riding. Ride to the Asklepieion for a picnic, or visit the Castle of Antimacheia. Note: be aware of hazards such as cistern openings, for very few have security fences around them. You can rent bicycles everywhere—in Kos town and at the more-popular resorts. Try the many shops along Elefthe-riou Venizelou street in town. Renting a bike costs about €6 per day.

ASKLEPIEION ΑΣΚΛΗΠΙΕΙΟΝ

4 km (2½ miles) west of Kos town.

Fodor'sChoice **Asklepieion.** Hippocrates began to teach the art of healing on Kos in
★ the 5th century BC, attracting health seekers to the island almost up to the time of his death, allegedly at age 103, in 357 BC. This elabo-rate, mutitiered complex dedicated to the god of medicine, Asklepios, was begun shortly after Hippocrates's death and flourished until the decline of the Roman Empire as the most renowned medical facility in the Western world. The lower terrace probably held the Asklepieion

Festivals, famed drama and dance contests held in honor of the god of healing. On the middle terrace is an **Ionic temple,** once decorated with works by the legendary 4th-century BC painter Apelles, including his renowned depiction of Aphrodite (much celebrated in antiquity, it was said the artist used a mistress of Alexander the Great as a model). On the uppermost terrace is the **Doric Temple of Asklepios,** once surrounded by colonnaded porticoes. ✉ *Platani* ✥ *Take the local bus from Kos town to the hamlet of Platani and walk to the ruins from there* ☎ *22420/28326* 🌐 *odysseus.culture.gr* 🎟 *€4* 🕒 *Apr.–Oct., daily 8–8; Nov.–Mar., Tues.–Sun. 8–3.*

EN ROUTE

Leaving the main road southwest of the Asklepieion (turnoff is at Zipari, 9 km [5½ miles] southwest of Kos town), you can explore an enchanting landscape of cypress and pine trees on a route that climbs to a handful of lovely, whitewashed rural villages that cling to the craggy slopes of the island's central mountains, including Asfendiou, Zia, and Lagoudi. The busiest of them is Zia, with an appealing smattering of churches; crafts shops selling local honey, weavings, and handmade soaps; and open-air tavernas where you can enjoy the views over the surrounding forests and fields toward the sea.

WHERE TO EAT

$ GREEK Fodor's Choice ★

🍴 **Taverna Ampavris.** The surroundings and the food are both delightful at this charming, rustic taverna, outside Kos town on a lane leading to the village of Platani. Meals are served in the courtyard of an old farmhouse, and the kitchen's emphasis is on local country food—including wonderful stews and grilled meats, accompanied by vegetables from nearby gardens. The owners wait on you, steering you toward tasty meals (you can't go wrong with the zucchini blossoms stuffed with rice), or offering detailed advice on sightseeing. [$] *Average main: €8* ✉ *on way from Kos town to Platani, Ampavris* ☎ *22420/25696* 🌐 *www.ampavris.gr* 💳 *No credit cards* 🕒 *No lunch.*

MARMARI ΜΑΡΜΑΡΙ

10 km (6 miles) west of Asklepieion, 14 km (9 miles) west of Kos town.

You won't find much that's authentically Greek in this unattractively overbuilt resort town surrounded by holiday villages. Even so, the surrounding beaches are beautiful, and without too much effort you can find a deserted strip of sand to call your own.

BEACHES

Mastichari Beach. In this north coast resort 32 km (20 miles) west of Kos town, the wide sand beaches backed by shade-providing pines are much discovered, backed by tavernas, rooms for rent, and luxurious all-inclusive resorts. The beach is lined with chairs and umbrellas and the lauching pad for pedal boats and jet skis. Mastichari is also a fishing pier where boats set sail on day trips to the uncrowded islet of Pserimos. **Amenities:** food and drink; toilets; showers; water sports. **Best for:** snorkeling; swimming; walking. ✉ *Mastichari.*

Tigaki Beach. One of the lower key and more appealing beach towns on overbuilt Kos, on the north coast 13 km (8 miles) west of Kos town, faces a pretty, sandy beach that stretches for miles. Though some resort hotels and other attractions line the sands, much of the inland terrain just behind the beach dunes remains rural, with fields and salts marshes spreading out across the plain around a large lake that attracts huge flocks of egrets. Beachgoers can enjoy the amenities of some of the more built-up sections then hike through grasslands to the lakeshore. The more isolated, western edge of the beach is popular with gay men. **Amenities:** food and drink; showers; toilets; water sports. **Best for:** solitude; nudists; swimming; walking. ⊠ *Tigaki.*

CASTLE OF ANTIMACHEIA ΚΑΣΤΡΟ ΑΝΤΙΜΑΧΕΙΑΣ

11 km (7 miles) southwest of Marmari, 25 km (15 miles) southwest of Kos town.

This proud fortress standing high above the sea is not just a symbol of the former might of the Knights of St. John. These days it also reminds us that overbuilt, tourist-oriented Kos has a proud past and had some historical clout. Plus, the cool stone interiors and views over verdant hillsides to the sparkling sea are a refreshing tonic and nice break from the beach.

Castle of Antimacheia. The thick, well-preserved walls of this 14th-century fortress look out over the sweeping Aegean and Kos's green interior. Antimacheia was another stronghold of the Knights of St. John, whose coat of arms hangs above the entrance gate. Within the walls, little of the original complex remains, with the exception of two stark churches; in one of them, Ayios Nikolaos, you can make out a primitve fresco of St. Christopher carrying the infant Jesus. ⊠ *Antimacheia.*

KAMARI ΚΑΜΑΡΙ

10 km (6 miles) south of the Castle of Antimacheia, 35 km (22 miles) southwest of Kos town.

On Kefalos bay, the little beach community of Kamari is pleasant and less frantic than the island's other seaside resorts. On a summit above is the lovely Old Town of Kefalos, a pleasant place to wander for its views and quintessential Greekness. Close offshore is a little rock formation holding a chapel to St. Nicholas. Opposite are the ruins of a magnificent 5th-century Christian basilica.

BEACHES

Ayios Stefanos Beach. A chunk of beautiful Ayios Stefanos beach, just north of Kefalos, is now occupied by a Club Med; the rest belongs to beach clubs renting umbrellas and chairs and offering activities that include waterskiing and jet-skiing. Expect to pay about €35 for a water-skiing session, €50 for jet skiing. Two early Christian basilicas crown a promontory at the southern end of the beach, adding to the allure of this lovely spot. **Amenities:** food and drink; parking (no fee); showers; water sports. **Best for:** snorkeling; swimming. ⊠ *Kefalos.*

Polemi Beach. This long stretch of lovely sand is about 10 km (6 miles) north of Kefalos, just far enough away to remain wonderfully undeveloped. Backed by scrub-covered dunes, the sands offer little except some sun bed concessions (expect to pay about €7 for a bed and umbrella) and are washed by calm, crystal clear waters. Polemi, also known as Exotic and Magic, is considered to be the best nudist beach on the island. **Amenities:** parking (free). **Best for:** solitude; nudists; swimming; walking. ✉ *Kefalos.*

WHERE TO STAY

$ HOTEL **Hotel Kokalakis Beach.** Many guests return annually to this simple hotel to enjoy the peaceful proximity to pebble and sand beaches and the hospitality of the Kokalakis family. **Pros:** close to beach; nice pool area; extremely welcoming hosts. **Cons:** fairly basic accommodations. [$] *Rooms from: €40* ✉ *Behind waterfront, Kefalos* ☎ *22420/71466* 🛏 *32 rooms* 💳 *No credit cards* ⏲ *Closed Oct.–Apr.* 🍴 *No meals.*

PATMOS ΠΑΤΜΟΣ

161 km (100 miles) north of Kos.

For better or worse, it can be difficult to reach Patmos—for many travelers, this lack of access is definitely for the better, since the island retains the air of an unspoiled retreat. Rocky and barren, the small, 34-square-km (21-square-mile) island lies beyond the islands of Kalymnos and Leros, northwest of Kos. Here on a hillside is the Monastery of the Apocalypse, which enshrines the cave where St. John received the "revelation" in AD 95. Scattered evidence of Mycenaean presence remains on Patmos, and walls of the classical period indicate the existence of a town near Skala. Most of the island's approximately 2,800 people live in three villages: Skala, medieval Chora, and the small rural settlement of Kambos. The island is popular among the faithful, who make pilgrimages to the monastery, as well as among vacationing Athenians and stylish international vacationers, who have bought homes in Chora and elsewhere around the island. Happily, administrators have carefully contained development, and as a result, Patmos retains its charm and natural beauty—even in the busy month of August.

GETTING HERE AND AROUND

Patmos has no airport, and outside of July and August, ferries wending through the Dodecanese from Athens call only every other day or so, with daily service in high season; the trip from Athens takes only seven hours, but boats arrive at the ungodly hour of 2 am. It's much easier to fly to Kos and board one of some four daily boats for the two-hour trip up to Patmos. On days when ferries do not call at Patmos, the boat to Kos with a transfer to Patmos is also an option. A convenient way to reach beaches around the island is to board a water taxi from Skala harbor.

The island's limited bus route provides regular service from Skala to Chora, Kambos, and other popular spots. It's easy to move around by taxi—and fairly inexpensive since distances are short.

VISITOR INFORMATION
Contacts **Patmos Municipal Tourism Office** ⊠ *Near ferry dock, Skala*
☎ *22470/31666* ⊕ *www.patmosweb.gr.*

SKALA ΣΚΑΛΑ

161 km (100 miles) north of Kos.

Skala, the island's small but sophisticated main town, is where almost all the shops and restaurants are located. It's a popular port of call for cruise ships, and in summer the huge liners often loom over the rooftops. There's not much to see in the town, but it is lively and very attractive. Most of the town center is closed to cars and, since strict building codes have been enforced, even new buildings have traditional architectural detail. The medieval town of Chora and the island's legendary monasteries are perched above Skala on a nearby hill. Take a 20-minute hike up to Kastelli, on a hill overlooking Skala, to see the stone remains of the city's 6th- to 4th-century BC town and acropolis.

BEACHES

The small island is endowed with at least 24 beaches. Although most of them, which tend to be coarse shingle, are accessible by land, sun worshippers can sail to a few (as well as to the nearby islet cluster of Arkoi) on the caïques that make regular runs from Skala, leaving in the morning. Prices vary with the number of people making the trip (or with the boat); transport to and from a beach for a family for a day may cost around €35.

FAMILY   **Kambos Beach.** The most popular beach on the island stretches for a mile or so along Kambos bay, with a gently sloping sea floor that's ideal for young waders and swimmers. Sun beds line the strand of fine pebbles and sand, while a nice grove of pines behind the beach provides plenty of shade for those who wish to spread out a blanket. The many amenities include windsurfing, waterskiing, and pedal-boat rentals, while several nearby tavernas serve snacks and simple meals. Regular bus service connects Kambos with Skala, about 6 km (4 miles) away. **Amenities:** food and drink; parking (free); showers; water sports. **Best for:** snorkeling; swimming; wind surfing. ⊠ *Kambos.*

Psili Amos. It's well worth the effort required to reach the most beautiful (and remote) beach on the island, a lovely scallop of sand backed by pines and rough, goat-filled hills. Getting there requires a 45-minute caïque ride (€10) from Skala or a 20-minute walk on a footpath from Diakofti (the narrowest point on the island), where visitors can park their cars. While nudism is not officially allowed on Patmos, this is one beach where nude bathing is tolerated and common, at the far edges. An extremely basic taverna sometimes serves light fare, but you'll want to bring water and snacks for an outing to this pristine spot. **Amenities:** food and drink; parking (free); toilets. **Best for:** solitude; nudists; snorkeling; swimming. ⊠ *Diakofti.*

WHERE TO EAT

$$ MEDITERRANEAN Fodor's Choice ★ 🍴 **Benetos.** A native Patmian, Benetos Matthaiou, and his American wife, Susan, operate this lovely restaurant abutting a seaside garden that supplies the kitchen with fresh herbs and vegetables. These homegrown ingredients find their way into a selection of Mediterranean-style dishes that are influenced by the couple's travels and include phyllo parcels stuffed with spinach and cheese, the island's freshest Greek salad, and a juicy grilled swordfish in citrus sauce. Accompany your meal with a selection from the eclectic Greek wine list. Service is gracious and friendly, and an evening on the terrace here is one of the island's nicest experiences. [$] *Average main: €18* ✉ *On harborside road between Skala and Grikos, Sapsila* ☎ *22470/33089* 🌐 *www.benetosrestaurant.com* 🕒 *No lunch. Closed Mon. and mid-Oct.–May.*

$ GREEK 🍴 **Tzivaeri.** The excellent island cooking here is spiced up by the sea views, which you can savor from a seaside balcony table or right on the beach below. The *mezedes* menu includes such traditional favorites as leek pie, fried eggplant, and smoked pork. Grilled lamb chops and other main courses are served as well. Live music (*Tzivaeri*, which roughly translates as "my beloved," is also the name of a popular Greek folk song) is performed many nights, usually not earlier than around midnight. [$] *Average main: €8* ✉ *Harborside road* ☎ *22470/31170* 💳 *No credit cards* 🕒 *No lunch.*

$$ GREEK 🍴 **Vegghera.** A handsome mansion overlooking the harbor is the setting for an exquisite meal that combines traditional Greek and international influences. Fresh seafood tops the menu, but pastas, herb-flavored chops, and the lavish creations fashioned by vegetables chef George Grillis from his own garden are a delight as well. Summertime dining is on a terrace overlooking the marina. [$] *Average main: €25* ✉ *Marina* ☎ *22470/32988* ✍ *Reservations essential* 🕒 *Closed Nov.–Easter. No lunch.*

WHERE TO STAY

$$$$ HOTEL Fodor's Choice ★ 🏨 **Hotel Petra.** One of Greece's truly special retreats sits high above Grikos bay south of Skala and provides a luxurious yet informal getaway, with large and sumptuous guest quarters, delightful outdoor lounges, a welcoming pool, and soothing sea views. **Pros:** attractive and comfortable surroundings; wonderful outdoor spaces; superb service and hospitality; beach is just steps away. **Cons:** the hotel climbs a series of terraces reached only by steps. [$] *Rooms from: €320* ✉ *Grikos* ☎ *22470/34020* 🌐 *www.petrahotel-patmos.com* 🛏 *13 rooms* 🕒 *Closed Nov.–mid-Apr.* 🍽 *Breakfast.*

$$ HOTEL 🏨 **Hotel Skala.** Skala's best in-town option places you in the center of the action, steps from the municipal beach yet removed from the harbor noise and offering simple but comfortable guest rooms that surround a bougainvillea-filled garden. **Pros:** top location; attractive terrace and pool. **Cons:** the hotel occasionally hosts large groups; high-season rates are high, given quality of accommodations. [$] *Rooms from: €130* ✉ *Harbor front* ☎ *22470/31343* 🌐 *www.skalahotel.gr* 🛏 *78 rooms* 🕒 *Closed Nov.–Mar.* 🍽 *Breakfast.*

13

$$ HOTEL Fodor's Choice ★ **Porto Scoutari.** It seems only fitting that Patmos should have a hotel that reflects the architectural beauty of the island while providing luxurious accommodations. **Pros:** large, very attractive rooms with sleeping and sitting areas; beautiful grounds; near beach; excellent service; extremely attractive rates available for longer stays. **Cons:** only ground-floor rooms would be suitable for travelers with mobility issues. [$] *Rooms from: €140* ✉ *1 km (½ mile) northeast of Skala center* ☎ *22470/33123* 🌐 *www.portoscoutari.com* 🛏 *30 rooms, 4 suites* 🕓 *Closed Nov.–Apr.* 🍴 *Breakfast.*

SHOPPING

Patmos has some elegant boutiques selling jewelry and crafts, including antiques, mainly from the island.

FOOD

DeSantis. This shop dispenses gelato that many fans claim is not just the best in Greece but could hold its own against the finest in Italy. ✉ *Off central square* ☎ *69/4714–5533.*

CRAFTS

Katoi. Head here to explore a wide selection of ceramics, icons, and silver jewelry of traditional design. ✉ *Skala–Chora Rd.* ☎ *22470/31487.*

Parousia. This is a top place to purchase Byzantine-style icons, wooden children's toys, and small religious items. ✉ *Past square at beginning of road to Chora* ☎ *22470/32549.*

Selene. Whether made of ceramic, glass, silver, or wood, each work—by one of 40 different Greek artists—displayed in a former boat-building shop is unique. ✉ *Harbor front* ☎ *22470/31742.*

CHORA ΧΩΡΑ

5 km (3 miles) south of Skala.

Atop a hill due south of Skala, the village of Chora, clustered around the walls of the Monastery of St. John the Theologian, has become a preserve of international wealth even as the whitewashed houses, Byzantine mansions, and quiet, twisting lanes retain a great deal of dignity and charm. Though the short distance from Skala may make walking seem attractive, a steep incline can make this challenging. A taxi ride is not expensive, about €6, and there is frequent bus service (€1) from Skala and other points on the island.

EXPLORING

Monastery of the Apocalypse. In AD 95, during the emperor Domitian's persecution of Christians, St. John the Theologian was banished to Patmos, where he lived until his reprieve two years later. He writes that it was on Patmos that he "heard . . . a great voice, as of a trumpet," commanding him to write a book and "send it unto the seven churches." According to tradition, St. John wrote the text of the Book of Revelation in the little cave, the Sacred Grotto, now built into the Monastery of the Apocalypse. The voice of God spoke through a threefold crack in the rock, and the saint dictated to his follower Prochorus. A slope in the wall is pointed to as the desk where Prochorus

The luckiest monks on Patmos—famed for its vibrant community of monks—get to call the Monastery of St. John the Theologian home.

wrote, and a silver halo is set on the stone that was the apostle's pillow. The grotto is decorated with wall paintings from the 12th century and icons from the 16th.

The monastery, which is accessible via several flights of outdoor stairs, was constructed in the 17th century from architectural fragments of earlier buildings, and further embellished in later years; the complex also contains chapels to St. Artemios and St. Nicholas. ⊠ *2 km (1 mile) south of Chora on Skala–Chora Rd.* ☎ *22470/31276 monastery* ⌨ *Free* ⊙ *May–Aug., daily 8–1:30 (also 2–6 on Sun., Tues., and Thurs.); Sept.– Apr., hours vary.*

Fodor's Choice ★ **Monastery of St. John the Theologian.** On its high perch at the top of Chora, the Monastery of St. John the Theologian is one of the world's best-preserved fortified medieval monastic complexes, a center of learning since the 11th century, and today recognized as a UNESCO World Heritage Site. Hosios Christodoulos, a man of education, energy, devotion, and vision, established the monastery in 1088, and the complex soon became an intellectual center, with a rich library and a tradition of teaching. Monks of education and social standing ornamented the monastery with the best sculpture, carvings, and paintings and, by the end of the 12th century, the community owned land on Leros, Limnos, Crete, and Asia Minor, as well as ships, which carried on trade exempt from taxes.

A broad staircase leads to the entrance, which is fortified by towers and buttresses.

The complex consists of buildings from a number of periods: in front of the entrance is the 17th-century **Chapel of the Holy Apostles**; the

main Church dates from the 11th century, the time of Christodoulos (whose skull, along with that of Apostle Thomas, is encased in a silver sarcophagus here); the **Chapel of the Virgin** is 12th century.

The **Treasury** contains relics, icons, silver, and vestments, most dating from 1600 to 1800. An 11th-century icon of St. Nicholas is executed in fine mosaic work and encased in a silver frame. Another icon is allegedly the work of El Greco. On display, too, are some of the library's oldest codices, dating to the late 5th and the 8th centuries, such as pages from the Gospel of St. Mark and the Book of Job. For the most part, however, the **Library** is not open to the public and special permission is required to research its extensive treasures: illuminated manuscripts, approximately 1,000 codices, and more than 3,000 printed volumes. The collection was first cataloged in 1200; of the 267 works of that time, the library still has 111. The archives preserve a near-continuous record, down to the present, of the history of the monastery as well as the political and economic history of the region. ☎ *22470/20800* 🌐 *www.patmosmonastery.gr* 🎟 *Church and chapels free, treasury €6* 🕓 *Daily 8–1:30 (also 2–6 on Sun., Tues., and Thurs.); Dec.–Mar., call to arrange a treasury visit, as hrs are irregular.*

WHERE TO EAT

$ GREEK 🍴 **Vagelis.** Choose between a table on the main square (perfect for people-watching) or the raised terrace out back with stunning views of the sea. Fresh grilled fish and lemon-and-oregano-flavor goat are specialties of the traditional kitchen, and other simple dishes such as mint-flavored *dolmades* (stuffed grape leaves) and *tzatziki* (yogurt and cucumber dip) are the way to go. Want traditional lodging to go with that meal? The management is happy to help find rooms in private homes in Chora. [$] *Average main: €8* ✉ *Main square* ☎ *22470/31967* 💳 *No credit cards.*

FESTIVALS

Patmos Festival of Sacred Music. In late August or early September, the Monastery of the Apocalypse hosts the **Festival of Sacred Music of Patmos,** with world-class Byzantine and ecclesiastical music performances in an outdoor performance space. ✉ *Monastery of the Apocalypse* ☎ *22470/31666* 🌐 *patmosfestival.gr.*

THE NORTHERN
AEGEAN ISLANDS

Lesvos, Chios, and Samos

WELCOME TO
THE NORTHERN AEGEAN ISLANDS

TOP REASONS
TO GO

★ **Samos Block Party:**
Math genius Pythagoras,
freedom-loving Epicurus,
and the fabled Aesop were
just a few of this island's
brightest stars, and their
spirits probably still haunt
the ancient Heraion temple.

★ **Mesmerizing Mastic
Villages:** Pirgi in Chios
is known for the resin
it produces, but with its
Genoese houses patterned
in black and white, it's the
Escher-like landscape that's
likely to draw you in.

★ **Sappho's Island:** If it's
poetic truth you seek,
head to one of Lesvos's
oldest towns, Molyvos—a
haven for artists and
an aesthete's dream.

★ **Sailing to Byzantium:**
Colorful Byzantine mosaics
make Chios's 11th-century
Nea Moni monastery an
important piece of history—
and a marvel to behold.

★ **Dizzyingly Good Ouzo:**
Though you can get this
potent potable anywhere
in Greece, Lesvos's is
reputedly the best—enjoy
it with famed salt-baked
Kalloni sardines.

1 Samos. This famously
fertile island, in classical
antiquity a center of Ionian
culture and luxury, is still
renowned for its fruitful land
and the delectable Muscat
wines it produces. The
island attracts active archaeology fanatics and lazy
beach lovers alike, leaving
visitors spoiled for choice
among a plethora of ancient
sights (such as the Temple
at Heraion—once four times
larger than the Parthenon)
and long sandy beaches
with crystal waters.

2 Lesvos. Often called
Mytilini after its historic (but
today somewhat boisterous)
capital, Lesvos is the third-
largest island in Greece.
Known as the "sweet home"
of lesbians from around the
world, this was the land of
origin of the ancient poetess
Sappho, whose romantic
lyrical poetry was said to
be addressed to women.
Sapphic followers who flock
to the island mostly stay in

Skala Eressou, but Lesvos
has something for everyone:
exquisite cuisine and ouzo,
beautiful beaches, monas-
teries with miraculous icons,
and lush landscapes.

3 Chios. You'll find
something of authentic
Greece here. Go beyond the
architecturally unappeal-
ing main town to discover
the lush countryside and
quaint village squares. The
11th-century monastery of
Nea Moni is celebrated for
its Byzantine art. Chios is
the "mastic island," producing the highly beneficial
resin that is used in chewing
gum and cosmetic products;
the most noted mastic
village is Pirgi, famed for the
geometric patterns on its
house facades.

GETTING ORIENTED

About the only thing the islands of Samos, Chios, and Lesvos share is their proximity to Turkey: from their shores, reaching from Macedonia down to the Dodecanese along the coast of Asia Minor, you can see the very fields of Greece's age-old rival. No matter that these three islands may be a long haul from Athens: few parts of the Aegean have greater variety and beauty of landscape—a stunning blend of pristine shores and craggy (Homer's word) mountains.

14

Updated by Adrian Vrettos and Alexia Amvrazi

Quirky, seductive, fertile, sensual, faded, sunny, worldly, ravishing, long-suffering, hedonistic, luscious, mysterious, legendary—these adjectives only begin to describe the islands of the northeastern Aegean. This startling and rather arbitrary archipelago includes a sizeable number of islands, such as Ikaria, Samothraki, and Thassos, but in this chapter we focus only on the three largest—Lesvos, Chios, and Samos. Closer to Turkey's coast than to mainland Greece, and quite separate from one another, these islands are hilly, sometimes mountainous, with dramatic coastlines and uncrowded beaches, brilliant architecture, and unforgettable historic sites.

Lesvos, Greece's third-largest island and birthplace of legendary artists and writers, is dense with gnarled olive groves and dappled with mineral springs. Chios, though ravaged by fire in 2012, retains an eerie beauty and has fortified villages, old mansions, Byzantine monasteries, and stenciled-wall houses. Samos, the lush, mountainous land of wine and honey, whispers of the classical wonders of antiquity.

Despite their proximity to Asia Minor, the Northern Aegean islands are the essence of Greece, the result of 4,000 years of Hellenic influence. Lesvos, Chios, and Samos prospered gloriously in the ancient world as important commercial and religious centers, though their significance waned under the Ottoman Empire. They also were cultural hothouses, producing such geniuses as Pythagoras, Sappho, and (probably) Homer.

These are not strictly sun-and-fun islands with the extensive tourist infrastructure of, say, the Cyclades. Many young backpackers and partiers bypass the Northern Aegean. You can still carve out plenty of beach time by day and wander into lively restaurants and bars at night, but these islands reveal a deeper character, tracing histories that date back to ancient, Byzantine, and post-Byzantine times, and offer landscapes that are both serene and unspoiled. Visitors to the northern islands should expect to find history, culture, beauty, and hospitality. These islands offer commodities that are valued ever more highly by travelers—a sense of discovery and the chance to interact with rich, enduring cultures.

PLANNING

WHEN TO GO

Like everywhere else in the world, Greece has been affected by climate change, which guarantees unpredictable weather; sometimes periods that are expected to be sizzling hot will suffer rainfall and wind and vice versa.

Nevertheless, in general from early May to early June, the weather is sunny and warm and the sea is still a bit chilly for swimming. From mid-June until the end of August, the weather goes through quite a sweeping change and can become very hot, although the waters of the Aegean can prove sufficiently refreshing. In September the weather begins to mellow considerably, and by mid-October is usually at its warmth limit for swimming, although sunshine can continue throughout the year on and off. Between November and March these islands can make for an enjoyable trip; unlike the holiday-oriented islands there are enough restaurants, museums, and sites open to keep visitors happy, though the weather can make ferries unreliable.

PLANNING YOUR TIME

If you have a week to devote to this region, try to visit two islands. Start by exploring Mytilini, the capital of Lesvos, a bustling center of commerce and learning, with its grand old mansions overlooking the harbor. From there, head to the countryside to the northern destinations: Molyvos, a medieval town sprawling under the impressive Molyvos Castle; Skala Eressou with its fine beach and bars; and the hilltop Agiassos, immersed in verdant forests. For your second stop, take a ferry to Chios, where you can enjoy the nightlife in the main town, and don't miss the old quarter. Travel via Lithi—derived from *Alithis limin*, meaning "true haven," which is rather apt for this beautiful fishing village—to enjoy a good fish lunch. Next, go to Pirgi (famous for its unique mosaics) and Mesta, part of the "masticohoria" or mastic villages, world renowned for their cultivation of mastic trees, which preserve a Greece of centuries past.

If you have less time and want to visit just one island, take the ferry from Piraeus directly to Samos. Circle the island, stopping at its lovely beaches and at Pythagorio, the ancient capital, or the temple at Heraion, one of the Wonders of the Ancient World. Consider visiting the popular traditional fishing village of Kokkari, which has managed to keep its architectural authenticity, then head for the beaches Tsamadou and Lemonaki, where the green pine slopes meet the cobalt blue waters of the Mediterranean. If you're drawn to the shores of Turkey, Samos makes a convenient stopover, as there's a daily ferry service to Kusadasi.

14

GETTING HERE AND AROUND

AIR TRAVEL

Even if they have the time, many people avoid the 8- to 10-hour ferry ride from Athens and fly, which takes less than an hour. Olympic Air (now a subsidiary of Aegean Airways) has at least a dozen flights a week (3 to 4 daily) from Athens to Lesvos and Chios in summer and at least four daily flights to Samos. Aegean Airlines flies once per day from Athens to Chios. There are several Olympic Air flights a week from Chios to Lesvos, Limnos, Rhodes, and Thessaloniki; and several a week from Lesvos to Chios, Limnos, and Thessaloniki. From Samos there are several weekly Olympic flights to Limnos, Rhodes, and Thessaloniki; there are few flights (usually only one per week) between Samos and the other northern islands. Overbooking is not uncommon; if you have a reservation, you should be entitled to a free flight if you get bumped. *For airline contact information, see Air Travel in Travel Smart.*

AIRPORTS

Lesvos Airport is 7 km (4½ miles) south of Mytilini. Chios Airport is 4½ km (3 miles) south of Chios town. The busiest airport in the region is on Samos, 17 km (10½ miles) southwest of Samos town. More than 40 international charters arrive every week in midsummer.

Contacts Chios National Airport ⊠ *Chios town, Chios* ☎ *22710/81400.*
Odysseas Elitis Airport ⊠ *Mytilini, Lesvos* ☎ *22510/38700.*
Samos International Airport ⊠ *Pythagorio, Samos* ☎ *22730/87800.*

BUS TRAVEL

The public (KTEL) bus system on the Northern Aegean islands is generally reliable, cheap (a few euros one-way), and obliging. Nevertheless, especially on Lesvos, buses can leave something to be desired.

BOAT AND FERRY TRAVEL

Owing to sudden changes, it's difficult to get advance information on ferry schedules. Port Authority offices have the most recent ferry schedule information, and the Greek Travel Pages website (⊕ *www.gtp.gr*) and Ferries.gr (⊕ *www.ferries.gr*) are also helpful.

Ferries between any of the Northern Aegean islands and Piraeus, Athens's port, take 8 to 11 hours (Piraeus–Samos, approximately €45).

There is one daily overnight ferry from Piraeus to Lesvos, except Saturday (€43, 10–11 hrs); there is only one weekly ferry from Thessaloniki to Lesvos (€38, 16 hrs). These ferries call at Chios first (€38, 8–9 hrs).

Five to nine ferries travel each week from Piraeus to Samos (€39, 15 hrs), arriving in either Samos town or Karlovassi (28 km [17 miles] northwest of Samos town), some stopping at Syros, Mykonos, and Evdilos/Ikaria.

Ferries and hydrofoils to Kusadasi, on the Turkish coast, leave from Samos town.

As for service between the various Northern Aegean islands, there is daily service between Lesvos and Chios. The regular ferry costs €19.50 and takes 2½ hours. There can be as many as three ferries per week between Lesvos or Chios and Samos (7 hours from Lesvos, €18; 3 hours from Chios, €13).

Contacts Chios Port Authority ☎ *22710/44433, 22710/44434 in Chios town.* **Mytilini Port Authority** ☎ *22510/40827 in Mytilini, 22510/37447, 22510/24115.* **Piraeus Port Authority** ☎ *210/455–0000, 210/455–0100* ⊕ *www.olp.gr.* **Samos Port Authority** ☎ *22730/27318 in Samos town, 22730/30888 in Karlovassi, 22730/61225 in Pythagorio.*

CAR TRAVEL

Lesvos and Chios are large, so a car can be useful on either island. You might also want to rent a car on Samos, where mountain roads are steep; motorbikes are a popular mode of transport along the coast. Expect to spend about €35 to €80 per day for a compact car with insurance and unlimited mileage. An international driving permit (available at your local AAA office) is required to rent a car in Greece, and this rule is strictly enforced on Chios; although some agencies on other islands may allow you to rent with your national license, if you are stopped by the police or get into an accident and cannot produce an international or EU license, you might have problems. Budget, at Lesvos Airport, has newer cars and is cheaper than other agencies. Vassilakis on Chios has reliable, well-priced vehicles. Aramis Rent-a-Car, part of Sixt, has fair rates and reliable service on Samos.

Contacts Action Cars ✉ *Near port, Karlovasis, Samos* ☎ *22730/30360, 22730/37177.* **Aramis Rent-A-Car** ✉ *Directly across from port, Samos town, Samos* ☎ *22730/23253* ⊕ *samos-rentacar.com* ✉ *Town center, opposite Commercial Bank, Kokkari, Samos* ☎ *22730/92385.* **Budget** ✉ *Airport, Mytilini, Lesvos* ☎ *22510/61665 airport, 22510/29600 at the port* ⊕ *www.budget.com.* **Vassilakis** ✉ *92 El.Venizelou, Chios town, Chios* ☎ *22710/43880* ⊕ *www.rentacarinchios.com.*

CRUISE TRAVEL TO LESVOS

Mytilini is a popular destination for cruise ships. The island's capital has more than enough attractions for those stopping over for a day and not wishing to hurriedly rush around the rest of the island. The main town is a five-minute walk from the port.

Pandora Travel offers custom-made tours for the independent-minded cruise passenger *(see Tour Options)*. Those wishing to go it on their own can take a taxi to the Teriade Museum and back for about €40, or to Gera Hot Springs for about €50. *See Taxi Travel for more information.*

TAXI TRAVEL

On some islands you'll find special taxi phones at the port or main bus stops. Due to the small number of taxis, prices are high: expect to shell out around double what you'd pay in Athens, but always check the rates in advance. If you do spring for a ride, it's a good idea to ask for a card with the driver's number in case you need a lift later in your trip. On Lesvos, Michalis Parmakelis is a recommended driver, who speaks fluent English.

Contacts Michalis Parmakelis ✉ *Lesvos* ☎ *69744/63299.*

HOTELS

Restored mansions, village houses, sophisticated hotels, and budget accommodations are all options. Reserve early in high season for better-category hotels, especially in Pythagorio on Samos and Molyvos on Lesvos. Off-season you can usually bargain down the official prices and you may be able to avoid paying for a compulsory breakfast. Lodging in general is cheaper here than elsewhere in Greece, but many hotel rooms are basic, with simple pine furniture and sparse, locally built furnishings. Happily, islanders are extremely friendly hosts, and while they may become more standoffish when the multitudes descend in August, they treat you as a guest rather than a billfold. On Lesvos, stay in Mytilini if you like a busy, city-like ambience, in Molyvos for its dramatic medieval beauty, or in Skala Eressou for its laid-back beach style. On Chios avoid staying in the main town unless you're just stopping over briefly, as it lacks in beauty and style, and opt to stay in the picturesque mastic village of Mesta instead. Vathi (Samos town), the main town, is a good central option in Samos, but even more ideal is the atmospheric Pythagorio.

RESTAURANTS

Although waterfront restaurants in the touristed areas can be mediocre, you can most often find delightful meals, especially in the villages. Unless noted, reservations are unnecessary, and casual dress is always acceptable. Go to the kitchen and point to what you want (the Greek names for fish can be tricky to decipher), or be adventurous and let the waiter choose for you (although you may wind up with enough food to feed a village). Remember, however, that fresh fish is very expensive across the islands, €50 and up per kilo, with a typical individual portion measured at about half a kilo. The price for fish is not factored into the price categories below (and lobster is even more expensive). Many restaurants close from October to May.

On Lesvos, sardines—the tastiest in the Mediterranean, traditionally left in sea salt for a few hours and eaten at a sushi-like consistency—from the gulf of Kalloni are famous nationwide, as is the island's impressive ouzo variety. Apart from classic salads and vegetable dishes like seasonal *briam* (a kind of ratatouille), and oven-baked or stewed Greek-Turkish dishes, meat dishes may reflect more of a Turkish influence. Try *soutzoukakia* (meatballs spiced with cumin and cinnamon), or *keskek* (chopped meat mixed with wheat, served most often at festivals).

Local figs, almonds, and sun-ripened raisins are delicious; a Lesvos dessert incorporating one of those native treats is *baleze* (almond pudding). Besides being recognized for its mastic products, Chios is also known for mandarins—try the "mandarini" ice cream or juice in the main town. You'll also find a great variety of mastic-flavor sweets as well as savory foods.

Thyme-scented honey, *yiorti* (the local version of keskek), and *revithokeftedes* (chickpea patties), are Samos's edible claims to fame.

DINING AND LODGING PRICES IN EUROS				
	$	$$	$$$	$$$$
Restaurants	Under €16	€16–€25	€26–€40	Over €40
Hotels	Under €126	€126–€225	€226–€275	Over €275

Restaurant prices are the average cost of a main course at dinner or, if dinner is not served, at lunch. Hotel prices are the lowest cost of a standard double room in high season.

TOUR OPTIONS

Chios Tours. This full-service travel agency can help you make all arrangements for travel in Greece or even Turkey, including in Chios, where you can book accommodations, car rentals, and tours. ✉ *Aigeou, waterfront, Kokkali 4, Chios town, Chios* ☎ *22710/29444* ⊕ *www.chiostours.gr.*

Masticulture. Masticulture in Chios orients visitors to a hearty perspective of local traditional life; organizing everything from walking tours, cooking classes, tending mastic trees, grape pressing, and offering original accommodations to suit every taste, they are happy to provide plugged-in tips on what to see and do locally. They stand out among other travel agencies for nicely providing what eclectic travelers are looking for today. ✉ *Mesta, Chios* ☎ *22710/76084* ⊕ *www.masticulture.com.*

Pandora Travel Lesbos. Pandora is a reliable tour operator on Lesvos, catering to both the cruise-ship crowd on the island for a few hours as well as to other tourists who may be on the island for a longer time. ✉ *Agora, Lisvori, Lesvos* ☎ *22520/42080, 69/8672–9992* ⊕ *www.pandoralesvos.com.*

Petra Tours. Petra Tours, located in Petra, just south of Molyvos, plans bird-watching, botanical, walking, and scuba-diving excursions. ✉ *Petra, Lesvos* ☎ *22530/41390, 22530/42011* ⊕ *www.petratours-lesvos.com.*

Pure Samos. "Don't just visit—experience!" That's what this travel agency, created by locals, lets visitors to Samos do, thanks to their wide array of experiential vacations: from yoga workshops to wine tours, from horseback-riding to spear-fishing and scuba diving, visitors can experience a memorable tailor-made holiday (which can include unique accommodations such as country cottages). ✉ *Iras 2, Pythagorio, Samos* ☎ *22730/62760, 69/3874–4978* ⊕ *www.puresamos.gr.*

Travel Services Lesvos. This company is a full-service tour and travel agency that can sell you a guided tour as well as make other travel arrangements, including accommodations, car rentals, and ferry tickets. ✉ *Kountouriotou 69, Mytilini, Lesvos* ☎ *22510/21966, 22510/41464* ⊕ *www.travelservices-lesvos.com.*

VISITOR INFORMATION

Please see the Visitor Information listing in the pages devoted to each island for Lesvos and Chios.

14

LESVOS ΛΕΣΒΟΣ

The Turks called Lesvos the "garden of the empire" for its fertility: in the east and center of the island, about 12 million olive trees line the hills in seemingly endless, undulating groves. The western landscape is filled with oak trees, sheep pastures, rocky outcrops, and mountains. Wildflowers and grain cover the valleys, and the higher peaks are wreathed in dark green pines. This third-largest island in Greece is filled with beauty, but its real treasures are the creative artists and thinkers it has produced and inspired through the ages.

Lesvos was once a major cultural center known for its Philosophical Academy, where Epicurus and Aristotle taught. It was also the birthplace of the philosopher Theophrastus, who presided over the Academy in Athens; of the great lyric poet Sappho; of Terpander, the "father of Greek music"; and of Arion, who influenced the later playwrights Sophocles and Alcaeus, inventors of the dithyramb (a short poem with an erratic strain). Even in modernity, artists have emerged from Lesvos: Theophilos, a poor villager who earned his ouzo by painting some of the finest native modern art Greece has produced; novelists Stratis Myrivilis and Argyris Eftaliotis; and the 1979 Nobel Prize–winning poet Odysseus Elytis.

The island's history stretches back to the 6th century BC, when its two mightiest cities, Mytilini and Mythimna (now Molyvos), settled their squabbles under the tyrant Pittacus, considered one of Greece's Seven Sages. Thus began the creative era, but later times brought forth the same pillaging and conquest that overturned other Greek islands. In 527 BC the Persians conquered Lesvos, and the Athenians, Romans, Byzantines, Venetians, Genoese, and Turks took turns adding their influences. After the Turkish conquest, from 1462 to 1912, much of the population was sent to Turkey, and traces of past civilizations that weren't already destroyed by earthquakes were wiped out by the conquerors. Greece gained sovereignty over the island in 1923. This led to the breaking of trade ties with Asia Minor, diminishing the island's wealth, and limiting the economy to agriculture, making this one of the greener islands of Greece.

Lesvos has more inhabitants than either Corfu or Rhodes with only a fraction of the tourists, so here you can get a good idea of real island life in Greece. Many Byzantine and post-Byzantine sites dot the island's landscape, including castles and archaeological monuments, churches, and monasteries. The traditional architecture of stone and wood, inspired by Asia Minor, adorns the mansions, tower houses, and other homes of the villages. Beach composition varies throughout the island from pebble to sand. Some of the most spectacular sandy beaches and coves are in the southwest.

GETTING HERE AND AROUND

From Athens there are four direct flights every day, which take 40 minutes and cost between €70 and €130 one-way.

There are one or two ferries that leave from Piraeus daily and take between 9 and 11 hours and cost €42–€43. These also stop at Chios

in both directions so there are regular links to this neighboring island
(€14–€20, 2½ hours). Once a week there is a ferry from Thessaloniki
to Lesvos (€42–€43, 16 hours).

Lesvos's buses are infrequent, though there are a couple a day from
Mytilini to Molyvos (€6.90 one way) via Kalloni. The main bus station
is at Aghias Eirinis 2 in central Mytilini.

VISITOR INFORMATION

Contacts Lesvos Municipal Tourist Office ✉ *Harbor front, James Aristarchou
6, Mytilini* ☎ *22510/42511, 22510/44165* ⊕ *www.lesvos.gr.*

MYTILINI ΜΥΤΙΛΗΝΗ

*350 km (217 miles) northeast of Piraeus by ferry, 218 km (135 miles)
southeast of Thessaloniki by ferry.*

Built on the ruins of an ancient city, Mytilini (so important through
history that many call Lesvos by the port's name alone) is, like Lesvos,
sculpted by two bays, making its coast resemble a jigsaw-puzzle piece.
This busy main town and port, with stretches of grand waterfront
mansions and a busy old bazaar area, was once the scene of a dramatic
moment in Greek history. Early in the Peloponnesian War, Mytilini
revolted against Athens but surrendered in 428 BC. As punishment,

the Athens assembly decided to put to death all men in Lesvos and enslave the women and children, so a trireme set sail to issue the order. The next day a less vengeful mood prevailed in Athens; the assembly repealed its brutal decision and sent a double-manned trireme after the first one. The second trireme pulled into the harbor just as the commander of the first ship finished reading out the death sentence. Just in time, Mytilini was saved.

EXPLORING

The bustling waterfront just south of the headland between the town's two bays is where most of the town's sights are clustered.

Ancient Theater. The only vestige of ancient Mytilini is the freely accessible ruin of an ancient theater, one of the largest in ancient Greece, from the Hellenistic period; it seated an estimated audience of 10,000. Pompey admired it so much that he copied it for his theater in Rome. Though the marbles are gone, the shape, carved into the mountain, remains beautifully intact. ⊠ *In pine forest northeast of town, Mytilini, Lesvos.*

Archaeological Museum of Mytilene. In a 1912 neoclassical mansion, this island's archaeological museum displays finds from the Neolithic through the Roman eras, a period of some 5,000 years. A garden in the back displays the famous 6th-century Aeolian capitals from the columns of Klopedi's temples. The museum's modern "wing" (on the corner of Noemvriou and Melinas Merkouri), contains finds from prehistoric Thermi, mosaics from Hellenistic houses, reliefs of comic scenes from the 3rd-century Roman house of Menander, and temporary exhibits. ⊠ *Mansion, Argiri Eftaliotis 7, behind ferry dock, Mytilini, Lesvos* ☏ *22510/28032* ⊕ *odysseus.culture.gr* 🎫 *€3* ⊙ *Tues.–Sun. 8–3.*

Ayios Therapon. The enormous five-domed post-baroque church of Ayios Therapon was designed by architect Argyris Adalis and was completed in 1935. The church is dedicated to St. Therapon, whose name means healer, and it's been visited by many people who came to Lesvos to recuperate from illness. It has an ornate interior, a frescoed dome, and there's a Byzantine Museum in the courtyard that's filled with religious icons. ⊠ *Southern waterfront, Mytilini, Lesvos* ☏ *22510/22561* 🎫 *Museum €2 (free on 1st Sun. of month)* ⊙ *Mon.–Sat. 9–1.*

Ermou. Stroll the main bazaar street, Ermou, which goes from port to port. Walk past the fish market on the southern end, where men haul in their sardines, mullet, and octopus. Narrow lanes are filled with antiques shops and grand old mansions. Head toward the sea to find the elegant suburb of Varia, once home to the modern "naive" artist Theophilos; Stratis Elefteriadis "Tériade", famous publisher of modern art journals; and the poet Odysseus Elytis. ⊠ *Ermou, Mytilini, Lesvos.*

Kastro. The pine-covered headland between the bays—a nice spot for a picnic—supports a Kastro, a stone fortress with intact walls that seem to protect the town even today. Built by the Byzantines on a 600 BC Temple of Apollo, it was repaired with available material (note the ancient pillars crammed between the stones) by Francesco Gateluzzi of the famous Genoese family. Look above the gates for the two-headed eagle of the Palaiologos emperors, the horseshoe arms of the Gateluzzi family, and inscriptions made by Turks, who enlarged it; today it is a **military bastion.** Inside the castle there's only a crumbling prison and a Roman cistern, but you should make the visit for the fine view. ⊠ *On hill, northeast of port, Mytilini, Lesvos* ⊕ *odysseus.culture.gr* ▧ €2 ⊙ *Tues.–Sun. 8–2:30.*

Musée–Bibliothèque Tériade. The Musée–Bibliothèque Tériade was the home of Stratis Eleftheriadis, better known by his French name, Tériade. His Paris publications *Minotaure* and *Verve* helped promote modern art. Among the works on display are lithographs done for him by Picasso, Matisse, Chagall, Rouault, Giacometti, and Miró. The museum is set among the olive trees of Varia, near the Museum of Theophilos. ■ TIP➔ **Best to call ahead to make sure it's open.** ⊠ *Varia, Lesvos* ✛ *4 km (2½ miles) southeast of Mytilini* ☎ *22510/23372* ⊕ *www. museumteriade.gr* ▧ €3.50 ⊙ *Tues.–Sun. 9–2 and 5–8.*

Museum of Theophilos. This museum houses a large number of the eponymous artist's "naive", precise neo-Hellenic works, detailing the everyday life of local folk such as fishermen and farmers, and polytheistic fantasies of another age. Theophilos lived in poverty but painted airplanes and cities he had never seen. He painted in bakeries for bread, and in cafés for ouzo, and walked around in ancient dress. ■ TIP➔ **The museum, freshly renovated in 2013, sits within an olive grove and exhibits only 50 artworks, as the rest are being restored to their original state in Athens and will be returned to the museum as they are completed.** ⊠ *Varia, Lesvos* ✛ *4 km (2½ miles) southeast of Mytilini, next to the Tériade Museum* ☎ *22510/41644* ▧ €3.50 ⊙ *Mon.–Fri. 9–3.*

WHERE TO EAT

$ ✕ **Antonis Ouzeri.** Popular with locals and tourists, this family-run spot
GREEK is found in the hill village of Kagiani, which is just up Varia south of Mytilini, and has wonderful views of Mytilini town, the Aegean sea, and Asia Minor beyond. The menu includes all the local meat and fish favorites, and in traditional Lesvos style most are served as *mezedes* to accompany ouzo. Of course grilled octopus is a must as is the perfectly fried crispy red mullet. ■ TIP➔ **Best to make a reservation, as it can get busy in the summer months.** $ *Average main: €8* ⊠ *Up the hill from Taxiarhes, Varia, Lesvos* ☎ *22510/61951* ⊕ *antonis-kagiani.gr* ◪ *Reservations essential* ⊙ *Daily noon–1am.*

$ ✕ **Ermis Ouzeri.** Lesvos is famed for its ouzo, so visitors must go to an
GREEK *ouzeri* (ouzo bar) at least once—if not thrice—and there are few bet-
Fodor's Choice ter than this centuries-old landmark located on the main thorough-
★ fare between the Old and New harbors. This old-school ouzeri, which dates back to Ottoman times, is where local and visiting artists, poets, and politicians prefer to sip their ouzo on a vine-shaded terrace, with marble-top tables. There's a selection of 15 types of ouzo, whose distinctive island tastes are nicely accompanied by some delicious "aperitif" mezedes such as *tsoutsoukakia* (spiced meatballs in tomato sauce), octopus in wine sauce, long-cooked chickpeas, or homemade sausages. The long-standing hangout has similarly long hours: from 6 am until the last person leaves at night. $ *Average main: €6* ⊠ *Ermou 2, toward the north end of the street, Mytilini, Lesvos* ☎ *22510/26232* ▭ *No credit cards.*

$ ✕**Kalnterimi.** An ouzeri-come-grill, Kalnterimi is centrally located on
GREEK   shady Thassou street in the Old Town and is a favorite of townsfolk. Lovely fresh grilled baby calamari, lightly fried courgette flowers stuffed with goat cheese and a cool *tzatziki* yogurt dip on the side make for enticing bites to accompany a glass of ouzo, of which they stock a generous selection. Some evenings local musicians come and play *rembetika* music (Greek folk music), which for some strange reason makes the ouzo taste even better. $ *Average main: €7* ⊠ *Thassou 2, Mytilini, Lesvos* ☎ *22/5104–6557.*

$ ✕**Polytechnos.** Locals and visiting Athenians pack the outdoor tables—
GREEK   a solid indication this restaurant has earned its reputation. Some folks choose from the impressive fish selection; others order simple, traditional, Greek dishes like souvlaki or succulent pork medallions, and get a small salad of tomatoes and cucumbers to go with it. This casual restaurant lies across from the municipal building on the waterfront, and is the first along the quay. $ *Average main: €15* ⊠ *Fanari quay, Mytilini, Lesvos* ☎ *22510/44128* ▭ *No credit cards.*

WHERE TO STAY

$$ ⬚ **Loriet Hotel.** The most exclusive digs in the area may be in the Loriet's
HOTEL   1880 stone mansion, where high frescoed ceilings, friezes, and antique
FAMILY   furniture set the mood—little wonder you'll sometimes find visiting dig-
Fodor's Choice   nitaries booking the fancy "suites" here (these start at €550 in high sea-
★   son). **Pros:** beautifully restored mansion transports you to the wealthy mercantile era of the 19th century. **Cons:** the long stretch of beach in front is distinctly average. $ *Rooms from: €150* ⊠ *Varia, Lesvos* ⌖ *2 km (1 mile) south of Mytilini* ☎ *22510/43111* ⊕ *www.loriet-hotel.com* ⇱ *35 rooms* ⍾ *Breakfast.*

$ ⬚ **Porto Lesvos I.** If you want to stay in the center of Mytilini, this old,
HOTEL   carefully renovated building a block inland from the harbor is a solid moderately priced choice—the guest rooms all have exposed stonework and some have sea views; the breakfast room is nicely done in wood and stone. **Pros:** you can feel the Papadakis family touch in the furnishings and service. **Cons:** some rooms do not face the harbor. $ *Rooms from: €65* ⊠ *Komninaki 21, Mytilini, Lesvos* ☎ *22510/41771* ⊕ *www. portolesvos.gr* ⇱ *12 rooms* ⍾ *Breakfast.*

$ ⬚ **Pyrgos of Mytilene.** A restored 1916 mansion in the ornate Sec-
HOTEL   ond Empire style, replete with amazing white-and-Grecian-blue tile work, fuses modern-day amenities and 19th-century nostalgia, with the emphasis on the latter in the frilly guest rooms, thanks to their period furniture, chandeliers, and stucco moldings, each room coming with its own style and color scheme (pistachio green to Venetian red). **Pros:** adorable exterior looking out onto the sea; excellent restaurant. **Cons:** room decor verges on kitsch, with too much Trump-y gilt and gold. $ *Rooms from: €98* ⊠ *Eleftherios Venizelou 49, Mytilini, Lesvos* ☎ *22510/27977, 22510/25069* ⊕ *www.pyrgoshotel.gr* ⇱ *12 rooms* ⍾ *Breakfast.*

NIGHTLIFE

The cafés along the harbor turn into bars after sunset, generally closing at 3 am.

Hacienda. For a relaxed Caribbean-style start to your night, start with a cocktail at Hacienda. ⊠ *East end of port, Mytilini, Lesvos* ☎ *22510/46850.*

Kohilia. You need transportation (best to take a taxi) to reach Kohilia, an outdoor beach bar with an upscale, artistic vibe. ⊠ *Aeorodromio-Kratigos, Mytilini, Lesvos* ✛ *7 km (4½ miles) south of Mytilini, on beach past Mytilini Airport* ☎ *69/5558–6412, 22510/63104.*

SHOPPING

Much of the best shopping is along the Ermou street bazaar. Here you can buy a little of everything, from food (especially olive oil and ouzo) to pottery, wood carvings, and embroidery.

Veto. Lesvos produces 50 brands of ouzo, and George Spentzas's shop, Veto, right on the main harbor, has made its own varietals on the premises since 1948. It also sells local food products such as olive oil, olives, dried fruit, and *hilopites* (pasta). It's open Monday through Saturday, 7 am to 10 pm. ⊠ *J. Aristarchou 1, Mytilini, Lesvos* ☎ *22510/24660.*

MORIA ΜΟΡΙΑ

7 km (4½ miles) northwest of Varia, 6 km (4 miles) northwest of Mytilini.

On the coast as you head north from Mytilini, Moria is best known for its Roman aqueduct. But the town is also famed for its annual Feast of Ayios Dimitrios. The celebrations begin the night of October 25 and continue well into the next day, with the killing and all-night cooking of a bull, accompanied by the entire village singing, dancing, and participating in daylong horse races.

Roman aqueduct. Moria's Roman aqueduct dates back to the 2nd century, and all that remains are these 17 arches. Constructed from gray Lesviot marble, the aqueduct stretched 26 km (16 miles) from Olympos mountain at Tsingos to Mytilini. It was in Lesvos that Julius Caesar first made his mark. Sent to Bythinia to drum up a fleet, he hung around so long at King Nicodemus's court that he was rumored to be having an affair with the king, but he finally distinguished himself by saving a soldier's life.

PAMFILA ΠΑΜΦΙΛΑ

4 km (2½ miles) north of Moria, 8 km (5 miles) north of Mytilini.

In the 19th century, Pamfila's traditional tower mansions were used by wealthy families as summer homes. The views across the straits to Turkey are wonderful. Equally beautiful are the old stone factories in this area, some of which are still in use.

14

PIRGI THERMIS ΠΥΡΓΟΙ ΘΕΡΜΗΣ

8 km (5 miles) northwest of Mytilini.

Pirgi Thermis is known for its tower mansions and for its 12th-century church, Panayia Tourlot, near the outskirts of town.

WHERE TO STAY

$ **Votsala Hotel.** Bravely attempting to break out of the traditional hotel
HOTEL mold, Votsala prides itself on offering a gracefully refined, family-like ambience that allows you to feel like a local, not a guest. **Pros:** friendly, "you're a local" atmosphere. **Cons:** no TVs in rooms; beach nice but basic. **$** *Rooms from: €95* ✉ *Pirgi Thermis, Lesvos* ☎ *22510/71231* 🖷 *22510/71179* ⊕ *www.votsalahotel.com* ⇆ *45 rooms* ☾ *Nov.–Mar.* �ⵙ *Breakfast.*

MANDAMADOS ΜΑΝΤΑΜΑΔΟΣ

7 km (4½ miles) northwest of Pirgi Thermis, 36 km (22½ miles) northwest of Mytilini.

Pretty Mandamados has stone houses, wood carvings, and the ruins of a medieval castle. The village is famous for its pottery, *koumari* urns (they keep water cool even in scorching heat), and an icon.

Taxiarchis Michail. The black icon of Archangel Michael is in the 17th-century monastery dedicated to the island's patron saint, Taxiarchis Michail. The gruesome legend has it that the icon was carved by a monk who used mud and the blood of his comrades, slain in an Ottoman attack, to darken it. Believers used to make a wish and press a coin to the archangel's forehead; if it stuck, the wish would be granted. Owing to wear and tear on the icon, the practice is now forbidden. ✉ *North end of village, Mandamados, Lesvos* ☾ *Daily 8–1 and 6–8.*

SKALA SIKAMINIAS ΣΚΑΛΑ ΣΥΚΑΜΙΝΙΑΣ

35 km (22 miles) northwest of Mytilini.

At the northernmost point of Lesvos, past Pelopi, is the exceptionally lovely fishing port of Skala Sikaminias, a miniature gem—serene and real, with several good fish tavernas on the edge of the dock. The novelist Stratis Myrivilis used the village as the setting for his *Mermaid Madonna*. Those who have read the book will recognize the tiny chapel at the base of the jetty. The author's birthplace and childhood home are in Sikaminia, the village overlooking Skala Sikaminias—and the Turkish coast—from its perch high above the sea.

WHERE TO EAT

$ **Skamnia.** Sit at a table of Skala Sikaminias's oldest taverna, under
GREEK the same spreading mulberry tree where Myrivilis wrote, to sip a glass of ouzo and watch the fishing boats bob. Stuffed zucchini blossoms or cucumbers and tomatoes tossed with local olive oil are food for thought: light, tasty, and ideal for picking at. Other tempting dishes on the extensive menu include delights such as chicken in grape leaves, but being a stone's throw from the sea, we suggest you stick to the wonderfully fresh fish and seafood. **$** *Average main: €12* ✉ *On waterfront, Skala Sikaminias, Lesvos* ☎ *22530/55319, 22530/55419* ⊕ *www.skamnia.net.gr.*

MOLYVOS ΜΟΛΥΒΟΣ

17 km (10½ miles) southwest of Skala Sikaminias, 61 km (38 miles) west of Mytilini.

Fodor's Choice ★ Molyvos, also known by its ancient name, Mythimna, is a place that has attracted people since antiquity. Legend says that Achilles besieged the town until the king's daughter fell for him and opened the gates; then Achilles killed her. Before 1923 the Turks made up about a third of the population, living in many of the best stone houses. Today these balconied buildings with center staircases are weighed down by roses and geraniums; the red-tile roofs and cobblestone streets are required by law. Attracted by the town's charms, many artists live here. Don't miss a walk down to the picture-perfect harbor front.

Fodor's Choice ★ **Kastro.** Come before high season and walk or drive up to the Kastro, a 13th-century Byzantine-Genoese fortified castle, for a hypnotic view down the tiers of red-tile roofs to the glittering sea. At dawn the sky begins to light up from behind the mountains of Asia Minor, casting silver streaks through the placid water as weary night fishermen come in. Purple wisteria vines shelter the lanes that descend from the castle and pass numerous Turkish fountains, some still in use. ✉ *Above town, Molyvos, Lesvos* ☎ *22530/71803* 🎟 *€2* 🕓 *Tues.–Sun. 8–8.*

OFF THE BEATEN PATH

Leimonos Monastery. The stunning 16th-century Leimonos Monastery houses 40 chapels and an impressive collection of precious objects. Founded by St. Ignatios Agalianos on the ruins of an older Byzantine monastery, it earned its name from the "flowering meadow of souls" surrounding it. The intimate St. Ignatios Church is filled with colorful frescoes and is patrolled by peacocks. A folk-art museum with historic and religious works is accompanied by a treasury of 450 Byzantine manuscripts. Women are not allowed inside the main church. ✉ *Kalloni, Lesvos* ✣ *Up a marked road 5 km (3 miles) northwest of Kalloni, 15 km (9 miles) southwest of Molyvos* ☎ *22530/22289* 🌐 *84.205.233.134/index_en.php* 🎟 *Museum and treasury €2* 🕓 *Daily 9:30–sunset.*

WHERE TO EAT

$ GREEK 🍴 **Gatos.** Gaze over the island and harbor from the veranda of this yellow-and-green-dressed charmer, or sit inside and watch the cooks chop and grind in the open kitchen: Gatos is known for its grilled meats. The beef fillet is tender, the lamb chops nicely spiced, and the salads fresh. You might also consider ordering the *kokkinisto* (beef in tomato sauce) with garlic and savory onion. ■ TIP→ **This is also a lovely spot to enjoy a morning or afternoon coffee.** [$] *Average main: €9* ✉ *Center of old market, Molyvos, Lesvos* ☎ *22530/71661* 🌐 *www.gatos-restaurant.gr.*

$ GREEK 🍴 **Panorama.** High over the town, this terraced restaurant cooks terrific Greek food and, as the name suggests, it has a spectacular view. Good appetizers include spicy cheese salad, and fried stuffed peppers; among the main courses are moussaka and other lovely home-style dishes, meat on the grill, and fresh fish. Patrons are encouraged to pop into the kitchen to choose some of their dishes; among the precooked options are moussaka and *magirefta*; other dishes (grilled fish and meats) are always cooked to order. ■ TIP→ **It's worth coming here** just for a sunset drink, to see the sun illuminate the red roofs of Molyvos and the sea beyond. $ *Average main: €9* ⊠ *Under kastro, Molyvos, Lesvos* ☎ *22530/71848* ▭ *No credit cards.*

$$
GREEK FUSION

✗ **Sansibal Restaurant.** One of the flock of tavernas roosting under Molyvos Castle, Sansibal features a modern Greek menu that contrasts nicely with its medieval souroundings. From each of the three terraces one can enjoy dishes such as the fresh garden salad or seafood risotto while taking in the stunning views of the Lepetymno mountain range and the Aegean sea. $ *Average main: €16* ⊠ *Molyvos, Lesvos* ☎ *22530/71329* ⊗ *No lunch.*

WHERE TO STAY

$
HOTEL

▦ **Belvedere Hotel.** A little away from the buzz of Molyvos, this cluster of traditional red-roof buildings offers ample chance to relax, thanks to deep-seated sofas, an airy lounge, and a swimming pool—hard to find in Molyvos proper—not to mention the poolside Jacuzzi. **Pros:** hotel shuttle service runs up to town, as does the local bus. **Cons:** nearby beach is rather mediocre; unexceptional hotel decor. $ *Rooms from: €100* ⊠ *On road to Eftalou, Molyvos, Lesvos* ☎ *22530/71772* ⇥ *74 rooms* ⊗ *Closed Nov.–Mar.* ⏍ *Breakfast.*

$
HOTEL
FAMILY

▦ **Clara Hotel.** Laid out in "village style," the Clara weaves its way down an amphitheatrical hill, allowing its red-roofed bungalows to share in grand bayside views of Petra and Molyvos—you'll be drinking in this vista from your own veranda but you'll also love just chilling out in the guest rooms, many of which are symphonies of lovely Greek accents, such as the blue-on-blue palettes (each room has its own color scheme), the cathedral ceilings, and the traditional wood wainscoting. **Pros:** plush, great facilities; aesthetically pleasing, some would say gorgeous, room decor. **Cons:** beach nearest to hotel clean but has seaweed; no elevator $ *Rooms from: €125* ⊠ *South of Petra, Avlaki, Petra, Lesvos* ☎ *22530/41532* ⊕ *www.clarahotel.gr* ⇥ *51 rooms* ⊗ *Closed Nov.–Mar.* ⏍ *Breakfast.*

$
HOTEL

▦ **Sea Horse Hotel.** This delightful stone-front hotel on Molyvos harbor overlooks the eateries on the photogenic quay; the lobby even extends into a waterfront café. **Pros:** port setting gives you a real Greek fishing-village experience; enchanting bay views. **Cons:** even though small, hotel attracts group bookings. $ *Rooms from: €80* ⊠ *Molyvos quay, Molyvos, Lesvos* ☎ *22530/71320, 22530/71630, 69/4633–4935 during annual closure* ⊕ *www.seahorse-hotel.com* ⇥ *16 rooms* ⊗ *Closed mid-Oct.–mid-Apr.* ⏍ *Breakfast.*

NIGHTLIFE

Congas Bar. The breezy Congas bar, a few steps from the water's edge, has been a favorite hangout for some time, filling with locals and tourists alike who dance the night away. Cool grooves, great cocktails, and colorful sunsets are the beach bar's signature features. ⊠ *Molyvos, Lesvos* ☎ *22530/72181* ⊕ *www.congas.gr.*

Molly's Bar. Two-story Molly's Bar plays music to unwind to in a friendly environment graced with waterside views (Molly is open from 6 pm until the early hours). ⊠ *On street above harbor, Molyvos, Lesvos* ☎ *22530/71772.*

Music Cafe Del Mar. This popular spot hosts live acoustic *bouzouki* music and has a cocktail terrace with a fetching sea view. ⊠ *Harbor front, Molyvos, Lesvos* ☏ *22530/71588.*

SHOPPING

Earth Collection. Go "green" by shopping here for organic clothes made exclusively of natural products. It's open daily from 10 to 10. ⊠ *Molyvos quay, Molyvos, Lesvos* ☏ *22530/72094.*

Elleni's Workshop. Stop by Elleni's workshop on the way to Efthalou hot springs for handmade olive wood artworks and ergonomic utensils. You'll find gifts of all shapes and sizes, for all budgets. ⊠ *On the road to Efthalou, Molyvos, Lesvos* ☏ *22530/72004.*

Evelyn. A wide variety of local goods is available here, including ceramics, pastas, olive oil, wines, ouzo, sauces, and marmalades. It's open daily from 10 am to midnight. ⊠ *Kyriakou Sq., Molyvos, Lesvos* ☏ *22530/72197.*

SKALOHORI ΣΚΑΛΟΧΩΡΙ

58 km (36 miles) west of Mytilini.

Skalohori is set beautifully in a valley, with tiered houses facing west toward the Aegean sunsets. Until recently, wild horses roamed the volcanic northwestern part of Lesvos around Skalohori and Andissa; they were believed to be the last link with the horse-breeding culture of the Troad, mentioned by Homer.

Monastery of Ayios Ioannis Theologos. The monastery of Ayios Ioannis Theologos, or Moni Ipsilou, was founded in 800 and rebuilt in the 12th century. Of special note are the small collection of 12th-century manuscripts, icons, and textiles; the tiles embedded in the facade; and the outstanding wood-lattice ceiling. ⊠ *On summit of extinct volcano, Skalohori, Lesvos* ⊙ *Daily 9–1 and 6–8.*

SIGRI ΣΙΓΡΙ

13 km (8 miles) southwest of Molyvos, 93 km (58 miles) west of Mytilini.

Sigri is built around a lovely cove with exceptional dark-sand beaches nearby.

FAMILY

Fodor's Choice ★

Natural History Museum of the Lesvos Petrified Forest. Don't miss the spacious, unique Natural History Museum, where you can learn about how trees were petrified and where petrified tree trunks can be touched; the exhibits are scrupulously labeled and laid out. There are also some unique and amazing fossils of animals like the *Deinotherium*, an early ancestor of the elephants, and vegetation preserved like delicate Zen art on volcanic rock. ⊠ *Main road, Sigri, Lesvos* ☏ *22530/54434* ⊕ *www.lesvosmuseum.gr* ☏ *€5* ⊙ *Daily 9 am–6 pm (call in advance due to variable hrs).*

Petrified Forest. A much-touted petrified forest consists of conifer trees fossilized by volcanic ash up to 20 million years ago. If you expect thick woods, this seemingly barren site at first appears like a bunch of stumps leaning every which way among shrubs and rock and even sea.

But a closer look reveals delicate colors and a stark, strange beauty. You can also study the specimens at Ipsilou, a large monastery on the highest peak in this wild, moonscape-like volcanic landscape, overlooking western Lesbos and Asia Minor across the Aegean. ⊠ *Between Sigri and Eressou, Sigri, Lesvos* ☎ *22510/54434* ⊕ *www.lesvosmuseum.gr* ⌨ *€2* ⊙ *Tues.–Sun. 9–5.*

SKALA ERESSOU ΣΚΑΛΑ ΕΡΕΣΟΥ

40 km (25 miles) southwest of Molyvos, 89 km (55 miles) west of Mytilini.

The poet Sappho, according to unreliable late biographies, was born here circa 612 BC. Dubbed the Tenth Muse by Plato because of her skill and sensitivity, she perhaps presided over a finishing school for marriageable young women. She was married herself and had a daughter. Some of her songs erotically praise these girls and celebrate their marriages. Sappho's works, proper and popular in their time, were burned by Christians, so that mostly fragments survive; one is "and I yearn, and I desire." Sapphic meter was in great favor in Roman and medieval times; both Catullus and Gregory the Great used it, and in the 19th century, so did Tennyson. Since the 1970s and until today, many gay women have come to Skala Eressou to celebrate Sappho (the word "lesbian" derives from Lesvos), although the welcoming town is also filled with plenty of heterosexual couples.

EXPLORING

Acropolis of Eresos. On the acropolis of ancient Eresos, overlooking the coastal area and beach, are remains of Archaic pre-classical walls, medieval castle ruins, and the AD 5th-century church, Ayios Andreas. The church has a mosaic floor and a tiny adjacent museum housing local finds from tombs in the ancient cemetery. ⊠ *Skala Eressou, Lesvos* ✛ *1 km (½ mile) north of Skala Eressou* ☎ *22530/53332, 22530/53037* ⊕ *odysseus.culture.gr* ⌨ *Free* ⊙ *Tues.–Sun. 7:30–3:30.*

Eresos. The old village of Eresos, separated from the coast by a large plain, was developed to protect its inhabitants from pirate raids. Along the mulberry tree–lined road leading from the beach you might encounter a villager wearing a traditional head scarf (*mandila*), plodding by on her donkey. This village of two-story, 19th-century stone and shingle houses is filled with superb architectural details. Note the huge wooden doors decorated with nails and elaborate door knockers, loophole windows in thick stone walls, elegant pediments topping imposing mansions, and fountains spilling under Gothic arches. ⊠ *Skala Eressou, Lesvos* ✛ *11 km (7 miles) inland, north of Skala Eressou.*

BEACHES

Some of the island's best beaches are in this area, which has been built up rapidly—and not always tastefully.

Skala Eressou Beach. Especially popular is the 4-km-long (2½-mile-long) town beach at Skala Eressou, where the wide stretch of dark sand is lined with tamarisk trees. A small island is within swimming distance, and northerly winds lure windsurfers as well as swimmers and sunbathers. There are many rooms to rent within walking distance of the beach. **Amenities:** food and drink; showers; toilets; water sports; parking (free). **Best for:** sunset; swimming; snorkeling; walking; partiers; windsurfing. ✉ *Skala Eressou, Lesvos.*

WHERE TO EAT

$ CAFÉ 🍴 **Parasol.** Totem poles, colored coconut lamps, and other knickknacks from exotic travels make this beach bar endearing. The owner and his wife serve omelets, fruits, yogurt, and sweet Greek coffee for breakfast, and simple dishes like pizzas, veggie spring rolls, and cheese platters the rest of the day. But the most obvious reason to come here is to relax after sundown with one of the bar's creative drinks, such as the signature green cocktail, the Wooloomooloo Wonder, made with vodka and fresh melon. The music might be characterized as sophisticated lounge; the owner calls it "intellectual." [$] *Average main: €10* ✉ *Beachfront, Skala Eressou, Lesvos* 💳 *No credit cards* 🕒 *Closed Nov.–Apr.*

$ SEAFOOD 🍴 **Soulatso.** The enormous anchor outside is a sign that you're in for some seriously good seafood. On a wooden deck, tables are set just a skipping-stone's throw from the break of the waves. Owner Sarandos Tzinieris serves, and his mother cooks. Fresh grilled squid is mellifluous, and the fish are carefully chosen every morning. [$] *Average main: €15* ✉ *At beach center, Skala Eressou, Lesvos* ☎ *22530/52078* 💳 *No credit cards.*

WHERE TO STAY

$ HOTEL 🏨 **Heliotopos.** Less than 300 meters from the beachfront "action," this lovely option is set in a delightfully peaceful and lovingly maintained large garden, cared for by delightful hosts Patrick and Debbie. **Pros:** peaceful setting; lush garden; delightful hominess. **Cons:** no breakfast served. [$] *Rooms from: €65* ✉ *Skala Eressou, Lesvos* ☎ *69/7714–6229* 🌐 *www.heliotoposeressos.com* 🛏 *5 studios, 3 apartments* 🕒 *Closed mid-Nov.–Feb.* 🍽 *No meals.*

AGIASSOS ΑΓΙΑΣΟΣ

87 km (53 miles) northwest of Skala Eressou, 28 km (17½ miles) southwest of Mytilini.

Agiassos village, the prettiest hill town on Lesvos, sits in an isolated valley amid thousands of olive trees, near the foot of Mt. Olympus, the highest peak. (In case you're confused, 19 mountains in the Mediterranean are named Olympus, almost all of them peaks sacred to the local sky god, who eventually became associated with Zeus.) Exempted from taxes by the Turks, the town thrived. The age-old charm of Agiassos can be seen in its gray stone houses, cobblestone lanes, medieval castle, and local handicrafts, particularly pottery and woodwork.

Panayia Vrefokratousa (*Madonna Holding the Infant*). The church of Panayia Vrefokratousa was founded in the 12th century to house an icon of the Virgin Mary, believed to be the work of St. Luke, and remains a popular place of pilgrimage. Built into its foundation are shops whose revenues support the church, as they have through the ages. The church museum has a little Bible from AD 500, with legible, elegant calligraphy. ✉ *Central Sq., Agiassos, Lesvos* 🎟 *€0.80* 🕒 *Daily 8–1 and 5:30–8:30.*

WHERE TO EAT

$ ✕**Dagielles.** Stop here for a coffee made by owner Stavritsa and served
GREEK by her no-nonsense staff. You might also try the *kolokitholouloudo*
(stuffed squash blossoms) and the dishes that entice throughout winter:
kritharaki (orzo pasta) and *varkoules* ("little boats" of eggplant slices
with minced meat). For a few short weeks in spring, the air is laden
with the scent of overhanging wisteria. $ *Average main: €7* ⊠ *Near bus
stop, Agiassos, Lesvos* ☎ *22520/22241* ▭ *No credit cards.*

$ ✕**To Stavri.** Up the hill toward the top of the village you will find the
GREEK taverna To Stavri with its tables straddling the bridge that crosses the
main thoroughfare. The menu consists of local favorites and most of
the delicious produce is homegrown. You can't go wrong with a simple
Greek salad and a plate of locally made *touloumotiri* (a cheese left to
mature in a goat's skin). $ *Average main: €8* ⊠ *Top of the village, Agi-
assos, Lesvos* ☎ *22520/22936* ▭ *No credit cards.*

PLOMARI ΠΛΩΜΑΡΙ

*20 km (12½ miles) south of Agiassos, 42 km (26 miles) southwest of
Mytilini.*

Plomari, the second-largest town on Lesvos, is dramatically set in a cliff
face overlooking a wide harbor and Aegean sunsets. This was once a
major maritime area but today is a cheerful mix of resorts and quiet
fishing village with narrow, cobbled lanes and houses spilling down to
the sea. The town is famous throughout Greece for its ouzo, and there's
a lively night scene on the harbor, where visitors gather after a long day
at the beach. There's a good sand-and-pebble beach at Ayios Isidoros,
2 km (1 mile) east of Plomari. The best beach in the area, Melinta, is
located 6 km (4 miles) north of Plomari.

WHERE TO STAY

$ ⌂ **Aegean Sun.** Near the beach of Ayios Isidoros and built around two
HOTEL small pools, this charming, family-run hotel has the feel of a tradi-
FAMILY tional seaside village and offers a host of services and facilities for
the demanding holiday-maker. **Pros:** services for people with special
needs. **Cons:** some rooms can feel a little boxy. $ *Rooms from: €65*
⊠ *On beachfront, Plomari (10 km/6 miles south of Agiassos), Lesvos*
☎ *22520/31830* ⊕ *www.aegeansun.gr* ⇆ *94 rooms* ⦿❙ *Breakfast.*

VATERA ΒΑΤΕΡΑ

6 km (4 miles) west of Plomari, 53 km (33 miles) east of Mytilini.

The village of Vatera is all about its 9-km-long (5½-mile-long) sandy
strip of sparkling water, lined with tamarisk trees and framed by green
hills. You can sit and enjoy the view of the cape of Ayios Fokas, with
its excavated Temple of Dionysus. As is often the case in succeeding
cultures, the temple's marble fragments were recycled, built into the
center aisle of a Christian basilica.

BEACHES

Gera bay is made up of half a dozen or so beaches including the much favored Tarti. Tsilia, Ligonari, Tsafi, Fara and Yialiotissa are more secluded and trickier to reach. And then there's Gera beach itself, with a sandy shore and clean waters, located southeast in Gera bay. The Vatera town beach, with its curving, southern exposure, is idyllic.

WHERE TO STAY

$ ⊞ **Vatera Beach Hotel.** This low-key but well-designed hotel has all
HOTEL   the makings of a more-expensive lodging. **Pros:** excellent location
FAMILY   right on the beach; warm and friendly service. **Cons:** not all rooms have a sea view. $ *Rooms from: €80* ✉ *Vatera beach, Vatera, Lesvos* ☎ *22520/61212, 22520/61165* ⊕ *www.vaterabeach.gr* ↝ *24 rooms, 16 with bath* ☽ *Closed Nov.–Mar.* ¡◎¡ *Breakfast.*

14

CHIOS ΧΙΟΣ

"Craggy Chios" is what local boy Homer, its first publicist, so to speak, called this starkly beautiful island, which almost touches Turkey's coast and shares its topography. The island may not appear overly charming when you first see its principal city and capital, Chios town, but consider its misfortunes: the bloody Turkish massacre of 1822 during the fight for Greek independence; major earthquakes, including one in 1881 that killed almost 6,000 Chiotes; severe fires, which in the 1980s burned two-thirds of its pine trees; and, through the ages, the steady stripping of forests to ax-wielding boat builders. Yet despite these disadvantages, the island remains a wonderful destination, with friendly inhabitants, and villages so rare and captivating that even having just one of them on this island would make it a gem.

The name Chios comes from the Phoenician word for "mastic," the resin of the *Pistacia lentisca,* evergreen shrubs that with few exceptions thrive only here, in the southern part of the island. Every August, incisions are made in the bark of the shrubs; the sap leaks out, permeating the air with a sweet fragrance, and in September it is harvested. This aromatic resin, which brought huge revenues until the introduction of petroleum products, is still used in cosmetics and chewing gum sold on the island today. Pirgi, Mesta, and other villages where the mastic is grown and processed are quite enchanting. In these towns you can wind your way through narrow, labyrinthine Byzantine streets protected by medieval gates and lined with homes that date back half a millennium.

Chios is also home to the elite families that control Greece's private shipping empires: Livanos, Karas, Chandris; even Onassis came here from Smyrna. The island has never seemed to need tourists, nor to draw them. Yet Chios intrigues, with its deep valleys, uncrowded sandy and black-pebble beaches, fields of wild tulips, Byzantine monasteries, and haunting villages—all remnants of a poignant history.

GETTING HERE AND AROUND

From Athens, both Olympic Air and Aegean offer four flights daily to Chios (50 minutes; from €69 to €128 one-way). There are also daily Astra Airlines flights from Thessaloniki (1 hour, €37.60 to €87.60). Chios Airport is 4½ km (3 miles) south of Chios town; a taxi ride runs around €6 to €10.

There are one to two ferries that leave from Piraeus daily (8 hours; €38 to €39); these daily ferries go on to Lesvos (3 hours; €14 to €20). Several times a week there is a ferry from Thessaloniki (up to 20 hours, €38). For schedule information, see ⊕ *www.gtp.gr*.

BUS TRAVEL ON CHIOS

Blue and Green Bus System buses leave the town of Chios several times per day for Mesta and Pirgi. The main bus station is in Chios town at Vlatarias 13, north of the park by Platia Plastira. A second bus station, which services the long-distance Green KTEL buses, is found to the south of the park adjacent to the main taxi stand on the central square. Bus fares run €1.50 to €5. KTEL also offers island tours daily at 9:30 and 10 am, finishing at 5 pm for €8 to €15 depending on the route.

VISITOR INFORMATION

Contacts Chios Municipal Tourist Office ⊠ *Kanari 18, Chios town* ☎ *22710/44389, 22710/44344* ⊕ *www.chios.gr.*

CHIOS TOWN ΧΙΟΣ ΠΟΛΗ

285 km (177 miles) northeast of Piraeus, 55 km (34 miles) south of Mytilini.

The main port and capital, Chios town, or Chora (which refers to the main "town" of Chios), is a busy commercial settlement on the east coast, across from Turkey. This is the best base from which to explore the island, and you don't need to venture far from the port to discover the beautiful mansions of Kambos or the captivating orange groves just south of town. The daytime charm of the port area is limited, in part because no buildings predate the 1881 earthquake but also because it badly needs a face-lift. But in the evening when the lights twinkle on the water and the scene is softened by a mingling of blue hues, the cafés begin to overflow with ouzo and good cheer and locals proudly promenade along the bayside.

EXPLORING

TOP ATTRACTIONS

Byzantine Museum. The only intact mosque in this part of the Aegean, complete with a slender minaret, houses the Byzantine Museum, which has been under renovation for years. It holds a *tugra* (the swirling monogram of the sultan that indicated royal possession), rarely seen outside Istanbul; its presence indicated the favor Chios once enjoyed under the sultan. Housed inside are the Jewish, Turkish, and Armenian gravestones leaning with age in the courtyard. ⊠ *Vounakiou Sq.* ☎ *22710/26866* 💰 €2 ☉ *Tues.–Sun 8–3.*

Chios Archaeological Museum. A collection that ranges from proto-Helladic pottery dug up in Emborio to a letter, on stone, from Alexander

Many of the churches on the Northern Aegean islands are picture-perfect, thanks to their beautiful frescoes.

the Great addressed to the Chiotes and dated 332 BC, this museum also displays beautiful Ionian sculptures crafted by Chiotes. ⊠ *Michalon 8* ☎ *22710/44239* 🖃 *€2* ⊘ *Tues.–Sun. 9–4.*

Citrus Museum. The Kambos district is famed as one of the most superlatively fertile orchard regions of Greece—orange and lemon groves here are given the status of museums and landmarks, so it is only fitting that the owners of the Perleas Mansion hotel have now opened this beautifully fragrant estate, known officially as the Citrus Museum, to showcase the history of citrus products on the island, and, oh yes, also entice visitors with a shop and café selling citrus-inspired sweets. Happily, the estate buildings are gorgeous, centered on a terra-cotta-hue farm, set with hunter-green window shutters and replete with folkloric-painted watermill. Nearby is an exceedingly picturesque arbor. In Greek, they call this museum "the aroma of memories" and this title may be more fitting. ■ TIP → **Call in advance to check visiting hours as they can vary, sometimes dramatically.** ⊠ *Artgenti St. 9-11, Kambos* ☎ *22710/31513* ⊕ *www.citrus-chios.gr* ⊘ *Tues.–Sun. 10–10.*

Fodor's Choice
★

Old Quarter. The Old Quarter is inside the **Kastro** (castle) fortifications, built in the 10th century by the Byzantines and enlarged in the 14th century by the Genoese Giustiniani family. Under Turkish rule, the Greeks lived outside the wall; the gate was closed daily at sundown. A deep dry moat remains on the western side. Note the old wood-and-plaster houses on the narrow backstreets, typically decorated with latticework and jutting balconies. An air of mystery pervades this old Muslim and Jewish neighborhood, full of decaying monuments, fountains, baths, and mosques.

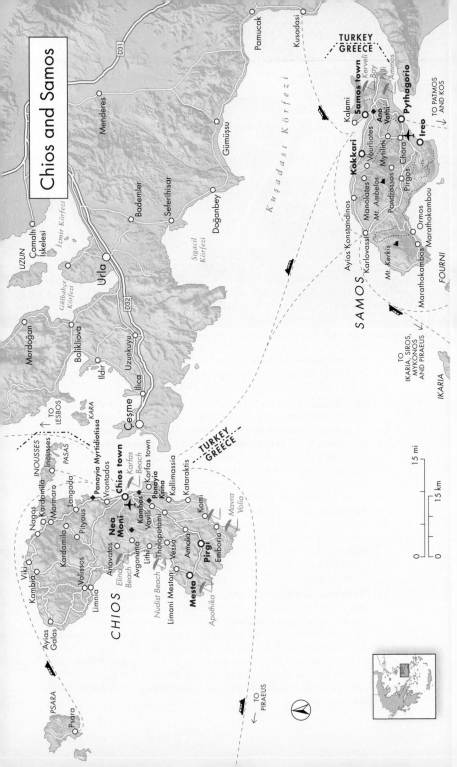

WORTH NOTING

Bazaar District. The capital is crowded with half the island's population, but its fascinating heart is the sprawling Bazaar District. Merchants hawk everything from local mastic gum and fresh dark bread to kitchen utensils in the morning, but typically it closes in the afternoon. ⊠ *South and east of Vounakiou Sq. (the main square).*

Chios Maritime Museum. Livanos, Karas, Chandris, Onassis: many of the world-famous shipping families were based or born on Chios. In celebration of the sea-based heritage of the island, this museum showcases exquisite ship models and portraits of vessels that have belonged to Chios owners over time. One exhibit highlights the Liberty ships and others constructed during World War II that contributed to the beginning of Greece's postwar shipping industry. ⊠ *Stefanou Tsouri 20* ☎ *22710/44139* ⊕ *www.chiosnauticalmuseum.gr* ⊡ *Free (with donation box)* ⊘ *Mon.–Sat. 9–1 pm.*

Chios Prison. In 1822, in the tiny prison, 75 leading Chiotes were jailed as hostages before they were hanged by the Turks, part of the worst massacre committed during the War of Independence. The Turks drove out the Genoese in 1566, and Chios, spurred by Samians who had fled to the island, joined the rest of Greece in rebellion in the early 19th century. The revolt failed, and the sultan retaliated: the Turks killed 30,000 Chiotes and enslaved 45,000, an event written about by Victor Hugo and depicted by Eugène Delacroix in *The Massacre of Chios.* The painting, now in the Louvre, shocked western Europe and increased support for Greek independence. Copies of *The Massacre of Chios* hang in many places on Chios. ⊠ *Inside main gate of castle, near Giustiniani Museum.*

OFF THE BEATEN PATH

Daskalopetra (*Teacher's Rock*). Daskalopetra, where Homer is said to have taught his pupils, stands just above the port of Vrontados, 4 km (2½ miles) north of Chios town. Archaeologists think this rocky outcrop above the sea is part of an ancient altar to Cybele; you can sit on it and muse about how the blind storyteller might have spoken here of the fall of Troy in *The Iliad.* ⊠ *Vrontados.*

Frouriou Square. In Frouriou Square, look for the **Turkish cemetery** and the large **marble tomb** (with the fringed hat) of Kara Ali, chief of the Turkish flagship in 1822. ⊠ *At fort, Old Quarter.*

Giustiniani Museum. Housed inside a 15th-century building that may have acted as the headquarters of the Genoese, the Giustiniani Museum exhibits Byzantine murals and sculptures, post-Byzantine icons, and other small Genoese and Byzantine works of art. ⊠ *Just inside Old Quarter* ☎ *22710/22819* ⊕ *www.culture.gr* ⊡ *€2* ⊘ *Tues.–Sun. 8–7.*

Kambos District. Mastodon bones were found in the Kambos district, a fertile plain of tangerine, lemon, and orange groves just south of Chios town. In medieval times and later, wealthy Genoese and Greek merchants built ornate, earth-color, three-story mansions here. Behind forbidding stone walls adorned with coats of arms, each is a world of its own, with multicolor sandstone patterns, arched doorways, and pebble-mosaic courtyards. Some houses have crumbled and some still stand, reminders of the wealth, power, and eventual downfall of an earlier time. These suburbs of Chios town are exceptional, but the unmarked lanes can be confusing, so leave time to get lost and to peek behind the walls into another world. ✥ *4 km (2½ miles) south of Chios town.*

Kronos Ice Cream Parlor. This spot has been making the best-selling Kronos Praline ice cream since 1930. ✉ *Philipos Argenti 2* ☎ *22710/22311* 🌐 *www.pagotakronos.gr.*

Main Street. Along the Main Street are the elegant **Ayios Georgios** church (closed most of the time), which has icons from Asia Minor; houses from the Genoese period; and the **remains of Turkish baths** (north corner of fort).

Philip Argenti Museum. This historic and folkloric collection sits on the second floor above the Korais Library, Greece's third largest. The museum displays meticulously designed costumes, embroidery, pastoral wood carvings, and furniture of a village home. ✉ *Korais 2, near the cathedral* ☎ *22710/44246* 🌐 *www.koraeslibrary.gr* 🎫 €2 🕒 *Sun.–Thurs. 8–3, Fri. 8, Sat. 9–2.*

BEACHES

Karfas Beach. This beach fronts a shallow bay, and its golden brown sands and warm waters make it a good spot for young families. Tavernas are in the area, and in summer there's transportation to and from town. Farther south, Komi has a fine, sandy beach. **Amenities:** food and drink; showers; toilets; water sports; parking (free). **Best for:** swimming; snorkeling; sunrise ✥ *8 km (5 miles) south of Chios town.*

WHERE TO EAT

$ GREEK

🍴 **O Hotzas.** Family portraits and brass implements hang below a wood-beam ceiling at this spacious taverna with a medieval interior. In addition to deep-fried dishes, there's also succulent lamb with lemon sauce and several vegetable choices. The squid is always reliable, and it's delicious with the homemade retsina or ouzo. For dessert, order yogurt with homemade cherry or quince preserves. [$] *Average main: €8* ✉ *Yioryiou Kondili 3* ☎ *22710/42787* ✍ *Reservations essential* 🕒 *Closed Sun. No lunch.*

$$ MEDITERRANEAN Fodor's Choice ★

🍴 **O Mpakses.** This lovely new restaurant in Kambos is set in the garden of a traditional farmhouse. Its rural setting matches the food's rustic Greek and Mediterranean tastes. Try the hearty braised beef in a rich tomato sauce, the pork stewed with apple and plum, or for those more adventurous, the garlic snails. The breads are freshly baked and all the produce is either home grown or locally sourced. [$] *Average main: €16* ✉ *Kalvokoresi 80, Kambos* ☎ *69/7202–7947* 🕒 *Closed Mon.–Tues. No lunch Wed.–Fri.*

$ MEDITERRANEAN

🍴 **Pirgos.** Attentive service, fine food, and pretty surroundings characterize a meal at the poolside garden restaurant of the Grecian Castle hotel. Beef carpaccio and spinach salad are excellent starters, followed by beef *pagiar,* a fillet stuffed with *mastello* (the local goat cheese), sun-dried tomatoes, and pesto-olive sauce. Or try the pork with prunes, mushrooms, and *Vin Santo* (a sweet wine) sauce. The extensive menu also includes crepes, pastas, and seafood. Mastic ice cream with rose syrup closes a meal on a richly local note. [$] *Average main: €14* ✥ *Leoforos Enosseos, 1 km (½ mile) south toward airport* ☎ *22710/44740* ✍ *Reservations essential.*

$ ✕**Taverna tou Tassou.** Dependably delicious traditional food is why so
GREEK many locals eat here in a garden courtyard beneath a canopy of trees.
FAMILY Fresh fish and seafood, lamb chops and other meats, stuffed peppers
and cooked greens—you can't go wrong. Expect Greek owner Dimitrius
Doulos and his son, the chef, to warmly welcome you. The taverna is
at the south edge of town toward the airport, and there's a playground
nearby for kids. $ *Average main: €8* ⊠ *Livanou 8, south toward airport*
☎ *22710/27542* ☻ *Closed Nov.*

WHERE TO STAY

$$ 🏨**Chios Chandris.** It may take a bit of a hike from the town center, but
HOTEL once you're at Chios Chandris you can enjoy the best location of any
hotel in and around Chios town: it looks out at both the sea and the
harbor. **Pros:** not too far from town hubbub with lovely countryside
setting. **Cons:** exterior a bit worn. $ *Rooms from: €140* ⊠ *Between
port and beach, 2nd Eugenia's Chandris St.* ☎ *22710/44401 through
22710/44410* ⊕ *www.chandris.gr* ⤺ *129 rooms, 10 suites* ⎟⊙⎟ *Breakfast.*

$ 🏨**Chios Rooms.** A budget option, the Chios Rooms are sweetly set in a
B&B/INN 19th-century neoclassical building located on the southern corner of
Chios's harbor, with casual rooms inside that quickly make guests feel
welcome. **Pros:** very friendly management makes you feel right at home.
Cons: noisy at night due to street traffic out front. $ *Rooms from: €40*
⊠ *Leoforos Aigaiou 110* ☎ *22710/20198* ⊕ *www.chiosrooms.gr* ⤺ *10
rooms* ⊟ *No credit cards* ⎟⊙⎟ *No meals.*

$$ 🏨**Grecian Castle Hotel.** With spacious guest rooms, a pretty pool, and
HOTEL carefully landscaped grounds this sophisticated hotel sets a high stan-
Fodor's Choice dard for Chios, as you'll see once you pass the impressive stone gateway
★ and head up a regal avenue to arrive at the main building—a grandly
proportioned building whose stone facade is echoic of Chios's medieval
castle. **Pros:** urbane ambience; gorgeous stone building; lovely grounds
and pool. **Cons:** a few not-so-spacious rooms. $ *Rooms from: €138*
⊠ *Leoforos Enosseos, 1 km (½ mile) south toward airport* ☎ *22/7104–
4740* ⊕ *www.greciancastle.gr* ⤺ *51 rooms, 4 suites* ⎟⊙⎟ *Breakfast.*

$ 🏨**Kyma Hotel.** Begun in 1917 for a shipping magnate, this rather odd
HOTEL neoclassic villa on the waterfront was completed in 1922, when it served
as Colonel Plastiras's headquarters after the Greek defeat in Asia Minor
(Plastiras went on to become a general and prime minister of Greece).
Pros: friendly, professional staff; good location. **Cons:** not all rooms
have a sea view. $ *Rooms from: €80* ⊠ *Chandris 1* ☎ *22710/44500*
✎ *kyma@chi.forthnet.gr* ⊕ *hotelkyma.com* ⤺ *59 rooms* ⎟⊙⎟ *Breakfast.*

$ 🏨**Perleas Mansion.** With its start back as an estate constructed by rich
B&B/INN Genoese merchants in the 16th century, this house is a tough cousin
Fodor's Choice to a "mansion," but today it is a striking blend of rough hewn stone,
★ dramatic steel beams, and lovely medieval touches—including a Gothic-
style stone water cistern—all surrounded by lovely gardens fragrant
with orange blossom. **Pros:** simple exclusive beauty with wonderful
homegrown food; the real deal. **Cons:** 10-minute drive from nearest beach. $ *Rooms from: €120* ⊠ *Kambos district, 4 km (2½ miles)
south of center, Vitiadou street* ☎ *22710/32217, 22710/32962* ⊕ *www.
perleas.gr* ⤺ *7 rooms* ⎟⊙⎟ *Breakfast.*

14

NIGHTLIFE

Design-centered nightspots along the harbor are trendier than those on most of the other Northern Aegean islands, and many of the clubs are filled with well-off young tourists and locals. You can just walk along, listen to the music, and size up the crowd; most clubs are open to the harbor and dramatically lighted.

Cosmo. This spot stands out as an inviting cocktail lounge playing international and Greek music. ⊠ *Aigaiou 100* ☎ *69/3684–2868.*

Metropolis Lounge Cafe Bar. This is one of the new cool hangouts of Chios town. Stop by for cold coffee and chill music during the day, but return at night for exotic mixed spirits and high-tempo beats. ⊠ *Aigaiou 92* ☎ *22710/43883.*

Odyssey Wine Bar. This new wine bar is where fun-loving and creative Chiotes like to hang out. Accompanying the generous wine list is the occasional live blues and jazz night as well as avant-garde Greek music preformed by local talent. ⊠ *Aigaiou 102, Chios town, Chios* ☎ *22710/20585.*

SHOPPING

The resinous gum made from the sap of the mastic tree is a best buy in Chios. It makes a fun and notoriously healthy souvenir and conversation piece; the brand is Elma. You can also find mastic (digestif) liquor called *mastiha,* and *gliko koutaliou,* sugar-preserved fruit served with a spoon in small portions. Stores are typically closed Sunday, and open mornings only Monday, Wednesday, and Saturday.

Mastic Spa. At the elegant shop of Mastic Spa, all the beauty and health products contain the local balm. ⊠ *Aigaiou 74, on waterfront close to the dock* ☎ *22710/40223.*

Moutafis. Try this place for its fine array of mastiha, fruit preserves, and other sweets and spirits. ⊠ *Venizelou 7* ☎ *22710/25330.*

Zaharoplasteion Avgoustakis. A traditional candy store, this spot specializes in *masourakia* (crispy rolled pastries dripping in syrup and nuts) and *rodinia* (melt-in-your-mouth cookies stuffed with almond cream). ⊠ *Psychari 4* ☎ *22710/44480.*

VOLISSOS ΒΟΛΙΣΣΟΣ

42 km (26 miles) northwest of Chios town.

Homer's birthplace is thought to be here at Volissos, though Smyrna, Colophon, Salamis, Rhodes, Argos, and Athens also claim this honor. Once a bustling market town, this pretty village is today half empty, with only a few hundred inhabitants. There are few services for tourists, save a casual restaurant here and there in the village and on the beach. Solid stone houses march up the mountainside to the Genoese fort, where Byzantine nobles were once exiled. Atop the hill is the place for sunset lovers.

BEACHES

Limia. Some of the best beaches on the island are in the vicinity, including Limia, with calm, turquoise waters. **Amenities:** none. **Best for:** sunset; swimming; solitude; snorkeling. ✛ *2 km (1 mile) south of Volissos.*

WHERE TO STAY

$

RENTAL

Volissos Travel Houses. Energetic Stella Tsakiri has overseen the transformation of three traditional, stone houses into the nine apartments of Volissos Travel Houses, preserving where possible such vernacular touches as tree trunks supporting a sleeping loft. **Pros:** good price; great location. **Cons:** rooms need to be cleaned more regularly; no elevator. $ *Rooms from: €70* ☎ *22740/21421* ⊕ *www.volissostravel.gr* ↴ *4 apartments* ⊗ *Closed Nov.–Mar.* ⦿ *No meals.*

14

NEA MONI NEA MONH

17 km (10½ miles) west of Chios town.

Almost hidden among the olive groves, the island's most important monastery—with one of the finest examples of mosaic art anywhere—is the 11th-century Nea Moni. Emperor Constantine IX Monomachos ("the Dueler") ordered the monastery built where three monks found an icon of the Virgin Mary in a myrtle bush. The octagonal *katholikon* (medieval church) is the only surviving example of 11th-century court art—none survives in Constantinople.

Fodor's Choice ★

Nea Moni. The monastry has been renovated a number of times: the dome was completely rebuilt following an earthquake in 1881, and a great deal of effort has gone into the restoration and preservation of the mosaics over the years. The distinctive three-part vaulted sanctuary has a double narthex, with no buttresses supporting the dome. This design, a single square space covered by a dome, is rarely seen in Greece. Blazing with color, the church's interior gleams with marble slabs and mosaics of Christ's life, austere yet sumptuous, with azure blue, ruby red, velvet green, and skillful applications of gold. The saints' expressiveness comes from their vigorous poses and severe gazes, with heavy shadows under the eyes. On the iconostasis hangs the icon—a small Virgin and Child facing left. Also inside the grounds are an ancient refectory, a vaulted cistern, a chapel filled with victims' bones from the massacre at Chios, and a large clock still keeping Byzantine time, with the sunrise reckoned as 12 o'clock. ✉ *In mountains west of Chios town on road towards Karies* ☎ *22710/79391* ⊕ *www.neamoni.gr* ▨ *Donations accepted* ⊗ *Tues.–Sun. 8–1 and 4–8.*

PIRGI ΠΥΡΓΙ

25 km (15½ miles) south of Nea Moni, 20 km (12½ miles) south of Chios town.

Beginning in the 14th century, the Genoese founded 20 or so fortified inland villages in southern Chios. These villages shared a defensive design with double-thick walls, a maze of narrow streets, and a square tower, or *pyrgos,* in the middle—a last resort to hold the residents in case of pirate attack. The villages prospered on the sales of mastic gum and were spared by the Turks because of the industry. Today they depend on mastic production, unique to the island—and tourists.

Pirgi is the largest of these mastic villages, and aesthetically, the most wondrous. It could be a graphic designer's model, a set of a mad moviemaker, or a still town from another planet. Many of the buildings along the tiny arched streets are adorned with *xysta* (like Italian *sgraffito*); they are coated with a mix of cement and volcanic sand from nearby beaches, then whitewashed and stenciled, often top to bottom, in patterns of animals, flowers, and geometric designs. The effect is both delicate and dazzling. This exuberant village has more than 50 churches.

> **DID A GREEK DISCOVER AMERICA?**
>
> About 50 people named Kolomvos live in Pirgi, claiming kinship with Christopher Columbus, known to have been from Genoa, the city-state that built the town. Some renegade historians claim Columbus, like Homer, was really born on Chios.

EXPLORING

Armolia. In the small mastic village of Armolia, 5 km (3 miles) north of Pirgi, pottery is a specialty. In fact, the Greek word *armolousis* ("man from Armola") is synonymous with potter. To the west, above the village there is an impressive Byzantine castle that was built in 1446, and to the east is the wonderful 18th century baroque-styled Vrettou Monastery. ⊠ *Armolia.*

Ayioi Apostoli (*Holy Apostles*). Check out the fresco-embellished 12th-century church Ayioi Apostoli, a very small replica of the katholikon at the Nea Moni Monastery. The 17th-century frescoes that completely cover the interior, the work of the Cretan artist Antonios Domestichos, have a distinct folk-art leaning. ⊠ *Northwest of main square* ⊗ *Tues.– Sun. 8–3.*

Kimisis tis Theotokou church (*Dormition of the Virgin church*). Look for especially lavish *xysta* on buildings near the main square, including the Kimisis tis Theotokou church, built in 1694. ⊠ *Off main square* ⊗ *Daily 9–1 and 4–8.*

BEACHES

Mavra Volia (*Black Pebbles*). Known by locals as Mavra Volia, this glittering volcanic black, pebbled beach is near Emborio. The cove comprises three beaches, which are backed by jutting volcanic cliffs and fronted by calm dark blue water colored by the deeply tinted seabed. Here, perhaps, was an inspiration for the "wine-dark sea" that Homer wrote about. **Amenities:** parking (free). **Best for:** swimming; solitude; sunrise; walking. ⊠ *Emborio* ✛ *8 km (5 miles) southeast of Pirgi.*

SHOPPING

Lagini. At this ceramics studio and shop you can see the potter ply her trade, as well as buy the traditional handmade pottery. ⊠ *Armolia–Pirgi Road* ☎ *22/7107–2634* ⊕ *www.chiosceramics.gr.*

MESTA ΜΕΣΤΑ

11 km (7 miles) west of Pirgi, 30 km (18½ miles) southwest of Chios town.

Fodor's Choice
★

Pirgi may be the most unusual of the mastic villages, but Mesta is the island's best preserved: a labyrinth of twisting vaulted streets link two-story stone-and-mortar houses that are supported by buttresses against earthquakes. The enchanted village sits inside a system of 3-foot-thick walls, and the outer row of houses also doubles as protection. In fact, the village homes were built next to each other to form a castle, reinforced with towers. Most of the narrow streets, free of cars and motorbikes, lead to blind alleys; the rest lead to the six gates. The one in the northeast retains an iron grate. Artists and craftspeople are attracted to this ancient area, so you'll unearth art galleries and craft boutiques with a little hunting here.

14

EXPLORING

Megas Taxiarchis (*Great Archangel*). One of the largest and wealthiest churches in Greece, the 18th-century church of Megas Taxiarchis commands the main square; its vernacular baroque is combined with the late-folk-art style of Chios. The church was built on the ruins of the central refuge tower. ■**TIP→ If the church is closed, ask at the square and someone may come and open up for you.** ⊠ *Central square.*

BEACHES

Escape to the string of secluded coves, between Elatas and Trahiliou bays, for good swimming.

Apothika. Apothika beach, just 100 meters down from the end of the road at Mesta, is one of the best on Chios. The clear waters lap against the sand and pebbles that make up this small stretch of coastline. There's a canteen up near the road that looks down upon the unspoiled beach. **Amenities:** food and drink; showers; toilets; water sports; parking (free). **Best for:** sunset; swimming; solitude; snorkeling; walking; windsurfing.

Nudist Beach. This beach is noted for its fine white pebbles—and also for drawing a nude clientele. **Amenities:** none. **Best for:** nudists; swimming; solitude; snorkeling; walking. ✛ *2 km (1 mile) north of Lithi.*

WHERE TO EAT

$
SEAFOOD
✕**Limani Meston.** The fishing boats bobbing in the water only a few feet away supply Limani Meston with a rich daily fish selection. The friendly, gracious owner may well persuade you to munch on some of his smaller catches, such as sardines served with onions and pita, accompanied by calamari and cheese balls. Meats served at the simple taverna include homemade sausage, and lamb or beef on the spit. You can sit outside among the ivy and blossoms, where Mesta's working harbor unfolds before you. On colder days, enjoy the fireplace with the locals. The owner rents studio apartments within walking distance. $ *Average main: €8* ⊠ *Mesta harbor, 3 km (2 miles) north of Mesta village* ☎ *22710/76389* ▭ *No credit cards.*

$
GREEK
✕**Restaurant Café Mesconas.** A traditional Greek kitchen turns out the delicious food served on outdoor tables in the small village square, adjacent to Megas Taxiarchis. You dine surrounded by medieval homes and magical lights at night, but the setting is lovely even for a daytime

On Chios, you'll often find imposing medieval structures side by side with charming villages. Here is a view of Nea Moni Monastery.

coffee and relaxed conversation. The best dishes include rabbit *stifado* (stew), made with shallots, tomatoes, and olive oil; and *pastitsio,* a meat pie with macaroni and béchamel sauce. All the recipes use local ingredients, with herbs and spices gathered from the vicinity. *Soyma* is the local equivalent of ouzo but made from figs—it can be blindingly potent, up to 70% alcohol. [$] *Average main: €8* ✉ *Main square* ☎ *22710/76050.*

WHERE TO STAY

$ HOTEL **Fodor's Choice** ★ 🏨 **Lida Mary Hotel.** Stay in the lovingly restored complex that makes up Lida Mary Hotel, set in the maze-y lanes of the Genovese fortified village of Mesta. **Pros:** priceless experience and quality one would expect from a top boutique hotel for surprisingly good prices. **Cons:** afraid of ghosts? [$] *Rooms from: €78* ☎ *22710/76217* 🌐 *www.lidamary.gr* 🛏 *3 rooms, 3 studios, 2 suites* 🍴 *Breakfast.*

NIGHTLIFE

Maona. The nightlife in Mesta is not exactly rocking, but this café and bar offers some relief to the restless souls who want to extend their night. ✉ *Main square.*

SPORTS AND THE OUTDOORS

FAMILY **Fodor's Choice** ★ **Masticulture.** Masticulture, the ecotourist specialists on Chios, lead all kinds of tours throughout the week. Trek through the mastic tree groves, where local farmers show you how they gather mastic through grooves carved into the trees' bark. Learn how wine, *Souma* (a type of ouzo made from distilled figs), and olive oil are produced, and go on fascinating custom-designed walks discovering the unique flora and fauna of Chios. Greek cooking courses are also available, which focus on seasonal foods in accordance with the Mediterranean diet. Check the website for dates, times, and prices. The nature of the mastic villages is such that finding lodgings is a bit of a lottery so the best option, if you wish to stay in these mesmerizing medieval communities, is to book through Masticulture. ✉ *Main square* ☎ *22710/76084* ⊕ *www.masticulture.com.*

Tortuga Diving School. Based at the stunning beach of Apothika, Tortuga Diving School offers scuba diving excursions, free diving and snorkeling courses, and sea kayak rentals. ✉ *Apothika beach* ☎ *69/7472–5459 mobile.*

SAMOS ΣΑΜΟΣ

The southernmost of this group of three north Aegean islands, Samos lies the closest to Turkey of any Greek island, separated by only 3 km (2 miles). It was, in fact, a part of Asia Minor until it split off during the Ice Age. Samos means "high" in Phoenician, and its abrupt volcanic mountains soaring dramatically like huge hunched shoulders from the rock surface of the island are among the tallest in the Aegean, geologically part of the great spur that runs across western Turkey. As you approach from the west, Mt. Kerkis seems to spin out of the sea, and in the distance Mt. Ambelos guards the terraced vineyards that produce the famous Samian wine. The felicitous landscape has surprising twists, with lacy coasts and mountain villages perched on ravines carpeted in pink oleander, red poppy, and purple sage.

When Athens was young, in the 7th century BC, Samos was already a political, economic, and naval power. In the next century, during Polycrates's reign, it was noted for its arts and sciences and was the expanded site of the vast Temple of Hera, one of the Seven Wonders of the Ancient World. The Persian Wars led to the decline of Samos, however, which fell first under Persian rule, and then became subordinate to the expanding power of Athens. Samos was defeated by Pericles in 439 BC and forced to pay tribute to Athens.

Pirates controlled this deserted island after the fall of the Byzantine Empire, but in 1562 an Ottoman admiral repopulated Samos with expatriates and Orthodox believers. It languished under the sun for hundreds of years until tobacco and shipping revived the economy in the 19th century.

Small though it may be, Samos has a formidable list of great citizens stretching through the ages. The fabled Aesop, the philosopher Epicurus, and Aristarchos (first in history to place the sun at the center of the solar system) all lived on Samos. The mathematician Pythagoras was born in Samos's ancient capital in 580 BC; in his honor, it was renamed Pythagorio in AD 1955 (it only took a couple of millennia). Plutarch wrote that in Roman times Anthony and Cleopatra took a long holiday on Samos, "giving themselves over to the feasting," and that artists came from afar to entertain them.

Since the late 1990s Samos has become popular with European package tourists, particularly in July and August. Thankfully the curving terrain allows you to escape the crowds easily and feel as if you are still in an undiscovered Eden.

GETTING HERE AND AROUND

Olympic Airways has four flights daily to Samos (55 minutes, €69 to €121). Astra Airlines has daily flights to Samos from Thessaloniki (1 hour, €40 to €90). The Samos airport is 3 km (2 miles) from Pithagorio; taxis from the airport cost €15 to Vathi (the main town, also known as "Samos") or €9 to Pithagorio.

The main port of Samos is Vathi. Ferries from the Piraeus and the Cyclades usually stop at both Vathi and Karlovassi (Samos's second port). During high season, there are usually seven weekly ferries from Pireaus (8 hours, €38); two to Chios (4 hours, €12); three to Syros and Mykonos (5½ hours, €48), with transfers available for Santorini and Naxos. There is usually a service most days to Patmos from Pythagorio.

BUS TRAVEL ON SAMOS

Samos has reliable bus service, with frequent trips (as many as eight daily) between Pythagorio, Samos town (Vathi), and Kokkari. Samos town is home to the island's main bus station ⊕ *www.samospublicbusses. gr*), located at Ioannou Lekati and Kanari in central Samos town. Fares range from €1.50 to €3. Taxis can be hailed on Platia Pithagora.

TOURS

Pure Samos. "Don't just visit—experience!" That's what this travel agency, created by locals, lets visitors to Samos do, thanks to their wide array of experiential vacations: from yoga workshops to wine tours, from horseback-riding to spear-fishing and scuba diving, visitors can experience a memorable tailor-made holiday (which can include unique accommodations such as country cottages). ⊠ *Iras 2, Pythagorio* ☎ *22730/62760, 69/3874–4978* ⊕ *www.puresamos.gr.*

SAMOS TOWN ΣΑΜΟΣ ΠΟΛΗ

278 km (174 miles) east of Piraeus, 111 km (69 miles) southeast of Mytilini.

On the northeast coast at the head of a sharply deep bay is the capital, Samos town, also known as Vathi (which actually refers to the old settlement just above the port). Red-tile roofs sweep around the arc of the bay and reach toward the top of red-earth hills. In the morning at the sheltered port, fishermen still grapple with their nets, spreading them to dry in the sun, and in the early afternoon everything shuts down. Slow summer sunsets over the sparkling harbor match the relaxed pace of locals.

EXPLORING

Ano Vathi. In the quaint 17th-century enclave of Ano Vathi, wood-and-plaster houses with pastel facades and red-tile roofs are clustered together, their balconies protruding over cobbled paths so narrow that the street's water channel takes up most of the space. From here savor a beautiful view of the gulf. ⊠ *Southern edge of Samos town, beyond museum, to right.*

Archaeological Museum of Vathi of Samos. The stepped streets ascend from the shopping thoroughfare, which meanders from the port to the city park next to the Archaeological Museum, the town's most important sight. Samian sculptures from past millennia were considered among the best in Greece, and examples here show why. The newest wing holds the impressive **kouros from Heraion,** a colossal statue of a male youth, built as an offering to the goddess Hera and the largest freestanding sculpture surviving from ancient Greece, dating from 580 BC. The work of a Samian artist, this statue was made of the typical Samian gray-and-white-band marble. Pieces of the kouros were discovered in various peculiar locations: its thigh was being used as part of a Hellenistic house wall, and its left forearm was being used as a step for a Roman cistern. The statue is so large (16½ feet tall) that the wing had to be rebuilt specifically to house it. The museum's older section has a collection of pottery and cast-bronze griffin heads (the symbol of Samos). An exceptional collection of tributary gifts from ancient cities far and wide, including bronzes and ivory miniatures, affirms the importance of the shrine to Hera. ⊠ *Dimarhiou Sq.* ☎ *22730/27469* ⊕ *www.culture.gr* ⊠ *€3* ⊗ *Tues.–Sun. 8–3.*

14

Museum of Samos Wines. Samos is famous for its (internationally awarded) wines, particularly its delectable Vin Doux wine or other sweet wines such as Nectar and Anthemis, and more recently its dry whites such as Phyllas, made with organic Muscat grapes. All wines produced on Samos are by law made by the Union of Vinicultural Cooperatives, who in 2005 created this museum on the winery's grounds in tribute to the island's winemaking past and present. Start by looking at the photo exhibition of local winemaking over the last century and proceed to see large and small the tools used in production, as well as early 20th-century casks, and finally the French oak barrels used today, before proceeding to the main hall to indulge in a wine tasting of the union's wines, which are also sold at the museum shop (in some cases at a higher price than you will find in other local shops). ⊠ *Opposite side of bay from port, Malagari* ☎ *22730/87551* ⊕ *www.samoswine.gr.*

OFF THE BEATEN PATH

Fancy an excursion to Turkey? From Samos town (as well as from Pythagorio and from Ormos Marathokambos), you can easily take a ferry to Turkey. Once you're there, it's a 13-km (8-mile) drive from the Kusadasi Port on the Turkish coast, where the boats dock, to Ephesus, one of the great archaeological sites and a major city of the ancient world. (Note that the Temple of Artemis in Ephesus is a copy of the Temple of Hera in Heraion, which now lies in ruins.) Many travel agencies have guided round-trip full-day tours to the site (€120), although you can take an unguided ferry trip for €55 with same-day return. You leave your passport with the agency, and it is returned when you come back from Turkey.

BEACHES

Kerveli Bay. The beach at Kerveli bay has an enticing pebble-to-sand beach with calm, turquoise waters, and shade from pine trees. It's a quiet escape from the beaches near the more populated centers, and getting here involves a pleasurable final stretch through some of the loveliest forested parts in eastern Samos. Tavernas on the beach dish out light summer salads, fresh seafood, and heartier *magirefta* (cooked dish) of the day, like *pastititchio* (a rich pasta bake). Unfortunately, there are no equipment rentals of any kind. **Amenities:** food and drink; showers; toilets; parking (free). **Best for:** swimming; snorkeling; sunrise; walking. ⊠ *On coast east of Samos town, Kerveli.*

Psili Ammos. One of the island's more popular beaches is Psili Ammos—a pristine, sandy beach protected from the wind by cliffs. There are two tavernas here, and it can get extremely busy during high season. **Amenities:** food and drink; showers; toilets; parking (free). **Best for:** swimming; sunrise. ✉ *Southeast of Samos town, near Mesokambos.*

WHERE TO EAT AND STAY

$ GREEK 🍴 **Ta Kotopoula.** Chicken is the star on the menu of this affordable grill restaurant, which serves simple yet delicious, seasonal dishes throughout the day in a laid-back ambience. [$] *Average main: €10* ✉ *Vlamaris, Prosfigika* ☎ *22730/28415* 💳 *No credit cards.*

$ SEAFOOD 🍴 **Zen.** Vathy (Samos town) is sadly not known for its good restaurants and Zen is yet one more unremarkable dining option; however, it is good enough for a pleasant, affordable meal. Open at lunch and dinner, the restaurant's focus is on fresh fish, while it also serves home-style dishes based on local recipes, grilled meat, and seasonal salads. [$] *Average main: €10* ✉ *Kefalopoulou 6* ☎ *22730/80983.*

$ HOTEL 🏨 **Hotel Samos.** Sleek modern rooms come equipped with amenities uncommon in this price range, like soundproof windows (the hotel faces the sometimes noisy harbor front), hair dryers, and wireless Internet. **Pros:** more luxurious than it may seem at first sight; given a rooftop pool, hot tub, and garden, the prices are relatively low. **Cons:** no parking; could do with a touch up. [$] *Rooms from: €80* ✉ *Them. Soufouli 11* ☎ *22/7302–8377* 🌐 *www.samoshotel.gr* 🛏 *98 rooms, 2 suites* 🍽 *Breakfast.*

$ HOTEL Fodor's Choice ★ 🏨 **Ino Village Hotel.** Set in a tranquil setting that makes you feel you're in the more peaceful outskirts of Vathy, the Ino Village is ideal for friends or families that enjoy lounging around the pool or enjoying a satisfying meal on the refreshing terrace (plugged into Wi-Fi)—drink in the vista here or request guest rooms in the 800 block for a spectacular view of Samos bay and the mountains beyond. **Pros:** friendly, clued-in staff; great quality for the price; fine kitchen. **Cons:** you have to walk 15 minutes uphill from the town center, but you can call the hotel to arrange for transport back up (a car is best here). [$] *Rooms from: €75* ✉ *1 km (½ mile) north of Samos town center, Kalami* ☎ *22/7302–3241* 🌐 *www.inovillagehotel.com* 🛏 *65 rooms* 🍽 *Breakfast.*

NIGHTLIFE

Bars generally are open May to September from about 8 or 10 pm to 3 am.

Escape. Begin your evening at Escape, a popular gathering place, with a sunset cocktail on the spacious patio just above the water, or end up there for partying until the early hours. The music in this hip spot picks up later, and so does the dancing. Friday is theme night and there are full-moon parties. ✢ *Past port police station, on main road out of town, near hospital* ☎ *22730/28345.*

PYTHAGORIO ΠΥΘΑΓΟΡΕΙΟ

14 km (8½ miles) southwest of Samos town.

Samos was a democratic state until 535 BC, when the town now called Pythagorio (formerly Tigani, or "frying pan") fell to the tyrant Polycrates (540–22 BC). Polycrates used his fleet of 100 ships to make profitable raids around the Aegean, until he was caught by the Persians and crucified in 522 BC. His rule produced what Herodotus described as "three of the greatest building and engineering feats in the Greek world." One is the Heraion, west of Pythagorio, the largest temple ever built in Greece and one of the Seven Wonders of the Ancient World. Another is the ancient mole protecting the harbor on the southeast coast, on which the present 1,400-foot jetty rests. The third is the Efpalinio tunnel, built to guarantee that water flowing from mountain streams would be available even to besieged Samians. Pythagorio remains a picturesque little port, with red-tile-roof houses and a curving harbor filled with fishing boats, but it is popular with tourists. There are more busy restaurants and cafés here than elsewhere on the island.

14

EXPLORING

Archaia Polis (*ancient city*). Among acres of excavations, little remains from the Archaia Polis, or ancient city, except a few pieces of the Polycrates wall and the ancient theater a few hundred yards above the tunnel. ✉ *Bordering small harbor and hill.*

Kastro (*castle, or fortress*). At the east corner of Pythagorio lie the crumbling ruins of the Kastro, probably built on top of the ruins of the acropolis. Revolutionary hero Lykourgou Logotheti built this 19th-century edifice; his statue is next door, in the **courtyard** of the church built to honor the victory. He held back the Turks on Transfiguration Day, and a sign on the church announces in Greek: "Christ saved Samos 6 August 1824." On some nights the villagers light votive candles in the church cemetery, a moving sight with the ghostly silhouette of the fortress and the moonlit sea in the background.

Panayia Spiliani Church. Enter this spacious cave and descend sharply downward to the tiny church of Panayia Spiliani (Virgin of the Grotto). Half-church, half-cavern, this most unique landmark, located northwest of Pythagorio, is also called *Kaliarmenissa* ("for good travels"), and features an antique icon of the Virgin Mary as well as a pool of what is considered to be holy water. ✉ *Above the town.*

Archaeological Museum of Pythagoreion. This tiny but impressive museum contains local finds, including headless statues, grave markers with epigrams to the dead, human and animal figurines, in addition to some notably beautiful portrait busts of the Roman emperors Claudius, Caesar, and Augustus. ✉ *Pythagora Sq., in municipal bldg.* ☎ 22730/62811 ⊕ *www.culture.gr* 🎟 €4 ☉ *Tues.–Sun. 8–3.*

Fodor's Choice ★ **To Efpalinio Hydragogeio.** Considered by Herodotus as the world's Eighth Wonder, this famed underground aqueduct, the To Efpalinio Hydragogeio (or Efpalinio tunnel), was completed in 524 BC with archaic tools and without measuring instruments. Polycrates, not a man who liked to leave himself vulnerable, ordered the construction of the tunnel to ensure that Samos's water supply could never be cut off during an attack. Efpalinos of Megara, a hydraulics engineer, set perhaps 1,000 slaves into two teams, one digging on each side of Mt. Kastri. Fifteen years later, they met in the middle with just a tiny difference in the elevation between the two halves. The tunnel is about 3,340 feet long, and it remained in use as an aqueduct for almost 1,000 years.

More than a mile of (long-gone) ceramic water pipe once filled the space, which was also used as a hiding place during pirate raids in the 7th century. Today the tunnel is exclusively a tourist attraction, and though some spaces are tight and slippery, you can walk the first 1,000 feet—also a wonderful way to enjoy natural coolness on sweltering hot days. Unfortunately the tunnel is closed for renovations until April 2016, but once these are complete visitors will be able to traverse the whole tunnel. ⊠ *Just north of town* ☎ *22/7306–2811* ⌨ *€4* ⏱ *Tues.–Sun. 8:45–2:45.*

WHERE TO EAT

$

MODERN GREEK

✕ **Elia.** If you're tired of the usual views and culinary suspects found along the harbor front, stroll past its row of cafés, bars, and tavernas to Elia for a nice change in ambience and style. The chef here is Swedish, and his menu offers a refreshingly eclectic take on Greek cuisine. Prawns sautéed in ouzo; chicken stuffed with spinach, feta, and topped with a tarragon sauce; and the pork cooked with Samos wine all tempt with their engaging flavors. Results are not always spectacular but the menu keeps evolving and improving. As one would expect, the wine list is full of sumptuous Samian wines as well as a few of the best from the rest of Greece. ⌨ *Average main: €14* ⊠ *Far end of the harbor front* ☎ *22730/61436* ⊕ *www.eliarestaurant-samos.gr* ⌕ *Reservations essential.*

$

GREEK

✕ **Maritsa.** A regular Pythagorio clientele frequents Maritsa, a simple fish taverna in a garden courtyard on a quiet, tree-lined side street. You might try shrimp souvlaki, red mullet, octopus, or squid garnished with garlicky *skordalia* (a thick lemony sauce with puréed potatoes, vinegar, and parsley). The usual appetizers include a sharp *tzatziki* (tangy garlic-yogurt dip with cucumber) and a large *horiatiki* ("village" or "country" salad) piled high with tomatoes, olives, onion, and feta cheese. Additional recommendations include lamb on the spit, the mixed grill, and stuffed tomatoes. ⌨ *Average main: €12* ⊠ *Off Lykourgou Logotheti, 1 block from waterfront* ☎ *22730/61957.*

WHERE TO STAY

$$

RESORT

FAMILY

⌂ **Doryssa Bay Hotel-Village.** "A true village!" **Pros:** hotel is a world within a world; lots of delightful amenities; enchanting "village" stage-set. **Cons:** lots of tour groups in summer. ⌨ *Rooms from: €200* ⊠ *Pythagorio beach, near road to airport* ☎ *22730/88300, 22730/88400* ⊕ *www.doryssa-bay.gr* ⌫ *172 rooms, 125 bungalows, 5 suites* ⏱ *Closed Nov.–Mar.* ⎮⊙⎮ *Breakfast.*

$

HOTEL

⌂ **Fito Bay Bungalows.** A complex of individual white bungalows all aglisten with terra-cotta roofs set neatly around a sparkling long pool and next to winding paths lined with roses and lavender: the first impression here can be a little generic and cold but everything quickly warms up thanks to the welcome of the friendly staff who do their best to make you feel at ease at this economical and family-friendly place just steps from Pythagorio beach. **Pros:** close to beach and town; nice view over the lovely garden; beautifully kept grounds. **Cons:** bare corridors; no sea view. ⌨ *Rooms from: €95* ⊠ *Pythagorio beach, on road to airport* ☎ *22730/61314* ⊕ *www.fitobay.gr* ⌫ *87 rooms, 1 suite* ⏱ *Closed Oct.–Apr.* ⎮⊙⎮ *Breakfast.*

$$$ RESORT FAMILY 🏨 **Proteas Blu Resort.** With a village-like layout, this resort hotel is designed in a fresh, contemporary style with large, airy spaces, gardens planted with local flowers, an Olympic-size pool, a beautiful secluded-cove beach, and guest rooms that offer balconies that open out to a sparkling sea view: the blue sea and sky and mountains of Turkey rising up from the water. **Pros:** great place for quiet and pampered stay; disability-friendly. **Cons:** some of the rooms are boxy. [$] *Rooms from: €266* ✉ *Pythagorio Rd., Samos town* ☎ *22/7306–2144, 22/7306–2146* 🌐 *www.proteasbluresort.gr* 🛏 *20 rooms, 72 suites* 🕒 *Closed Oct.–May* 🍴 *Breakfast.*

NIGHTLIFE

Beyond. Run by Michael, the Beyond martini lounge is a showcase for his cultivated taste in bar decor, superb skill in cocktails, and elegant finger food, refined delights mostly exported from Boston back to his local Samos. Try his tantalizing Beyond Basil Bliss—a play on mojito that replaces mint with basil and rum with tequila—as you sit at the space-age white and neon bar or perch over the waterfront on the second-floor terrace. ☎ *69/9416–3663* 🌐 *beyondsamos.com.*

SPORTS AND THE OUTDOORS

Samosail. Based in Pythagorio, this local yacht charter has a modern fleet of sailboats for rent, for one- or two-week trips, with or without a captain. They can also tailor trips to suit any needs. ☎ *22730/61739* 🌐 *www.samosail.com.*

14

IREO ΗΡΑΙΟ

6 km (4 miles) southwest of Pythagorio, 20 km (12½ miles) southwest of Samos town.

Heraion of Samos. The early Samians worshipped the goddess Hera, believing she was born here beneath a bush near the stream Imbrassos and that there she also lay with Zeus. Several temples were subsequently built on the site in her honor, the earliest dating back to the 8th century BC. Polycrates rebuilt the **To Hraio**, or Temple of Hera, around 540 BC, making it four times larger than the Parthenon and the largest Greek temple ever conceived, with two rows of columns (155 in all). The temple was damaged by fire in 525 BC and never completed, owing to Polycrates's untimely death. In the intervening years, masons recycled the stones to create other buildings, including a basilica (foundations remain at the site) to the Virgin Mary. Today you can only imagine the To Hraio's massive glory; of its forest of columns only one remains standing, slightly askew and only half its original height, amid acres of marble remnants in marshy ground thick with poppies.

At the ancient celebrations to honor Hera, the faithful approached from the sea along the **Sacred Road,** which is still visible at the site's northeast corner. Nearby are replicas of a 6th-century BC sculpture depicting an aristocratic family; its chiseled signature reads "Genelaos made me." The kouros from Heraion was found here, and now is in the Archaeological Museum in Samos town. Hours may be shortened in winter. ✉ *Near Imvisos river, Ireo* ☎ *22730/62811* 🌐 *www.culture.gr* 🎟 *€4* 🕒 *Apr.–Oct., daily 9–4.*

KOKKARI KOKKAPI

5 km (3 miles) southwest of Samos town.

Beyond the popular beaches of Tsabou, Tsamadou, and Lemonakia, the spectacular stretch of coast road lined with olive groves and vineyards ends in the fishing village of Kokkari, one of the most-lively spots on the island. Until 1980, not much was here except for a few dozen houses between two headlands, and tracts of onion fields, which gave the town its name. Though now there are a score of hotels, and many European tourists, you can still traipse along the rocky, windswept beach and spy fishermen mending trawling nets on the paved quay. Cross the spit to the eastern side of the headland and watch the moon rise over the lights of Vathi (Samos town) in the next bay. East of Kokkari you pass by Malagari, the winery where farmers hawk their harvested grapes every September.

BEACHES

Acclaimed coves of the north coast with small pebbly beaches and gorgeous blue-green waters include **Lemonakia, Tsamadou,** and **Tsabou**; all are just a few minutes' drive from one another—but they're to be avoided when the *meltemi* (northern winds) blow unless you're a windsurfer.

WHERE TO EAT

$ ✕**Ammos Plaz.** Ammos Plaz serves what many locals consider the best
GREEK   traditional Greek food in Kokkari, and in an ideal location—smack on the beach. Expect the dishes to change daily, but you may find choices like lamb fricassee and stuffed *kalamaria* (calamari). The owner's father is a fisherman, and he brings his haul to the restaurant daily. Octopus in a sweet Samos wine sauce and grilled lobster are two favorites (but considerably more expensive than many selections on the menu). $ *Average main: €15 ⊠ Kokkari promenade ☎ 22730/92463 ⊘ Closed Nov.–Mar.*

WHERE TO STAY

$ ⛱ **Olympia Beach/Olympia Village.** Set in a big flowery garden, this bright-
HOTEL   white hotel has been designed to look like a traditional Greek village, with flowery Samian ceramics decorating the spare, immaculate guest rooms that flaunt sea views from their balconies and houses draped with electric-pink bougainvillea. **Pros:** Olympia is virtually on the beach; great views over the sea. **Cons:** can be hard to find a room during high season. $ *Rooms from: €95 ⊠ Northwest Beach Rd. ☎ 22730/92420, 22730/92324 ⊕ www.olympiabeach.gr ⇆ 12 rooms, 22 apartments ⊘ Closed Nov.–Apr. ⦿ Breakfast.*

SPORTS AND THE OUTDOORS

FAMILY   **Kokkari Surf and Bike Center.** A professional and well-equipped windsurfing center, this outfitter rents windsurfing equipment, sea kayaks, and mountain bikes during the summer months. They also provide windsurfing instruction and run treks for hikers. Windsurfing courses are offered for all, from absolute beginners to advanced freestyle levels. ⊠ *On road to Lemonakia ☎ 22730/92102 ⊕ www.samoswindsurfing.gr.*

GREEK VOCABULARY

THE GREEK ABC'S

The proper names in this book are transliterated versions of the Greek name, so when you come upon signs written in the Greek alphabet, use this list to decipher them.

GREEK	ROMAN	GREEK	ROMAN
A, α	a	N, ν	n
B, β	v	Ξ, ξ	x or ks
Γ, γ	g or y	O, o	o
Δ, δ	th, dh, or d	Π, π	p
E, ε	e	P, ρ	r
Z, ζ	z	Σ, σ, ς	s
H, η	i	T, τ	t
Θ, θ	th	Y, υ	i
I, ι	i	Φ, φ	f
K, κ	k	X, χ	h or ch
Λ, λ	l	Ψ, ψ	ps
M, μ	m	Ω, ω	o

The phonetic spelling used in English differs somewhat from the internationalized form of Greek place names. There are no long and short vowels in Greek; the pronunciation never changes. Note, also, that the accent is a stress mark, showing where the stress is placed in pronunciation.

BASICS

Do you speak English?	Miláte angliká?
Yes, no	Málista or Né, óchi
Impossible	Adínato
Good morning, Good day	Kaliméra
Good evening, Good night	Kalispéra, Kaliníchta
Good-bye	Yá sas
Mister, Madam, Miss	Kírie, kiría, despiní
Please	Parakaló
Excuse me	Me sinchórite or signómi
How are you?	Ti kánete or pós íste
How do you do (Pleased to meet you)	Chéro polí

I don't understand.	Dén katalavéno.
To your health!	Giá sas!
Thank you	Efcharistó

NUMBERS

one	éna
two	dío
three	tría
four	téssera
five	pénde
six	éxi
seven	eptá
eight	októ
nine	enéa
ten	déka
twenty	íkossi
thirty	triánda
forty	saránda
fifty	penínda
sixty	exínda
seventy	evdomínda
eighty	ogdónda
ninety	enenínda
one hundred	ekató
two hundred	diakóssia
three hundred	triakóssia
one thousand	hília
two thousand	dió hiliádes
three thousand	trís hiliádes

DAYS OF THE WEEK

Monday	Deftéra
Tuesday	Tríti

Wednesday	Tetárti
Thursday	Pémpti
Friday	Paraskeví
Saturday	Sávato
Sunday	Kyriakí

MONTHS

January	Ianouários
February	Fevrouários
March	Mártios
April	Aprílios
May	Maíos
June	Ióunios
July	Ióulios
August	Ávgoustos
September	Septémvrios
October	Októvrios
November	Noémvrios
December	Dekémvrios

TRAVELING

I am traveling by car . . .	Taxidévo mé aftokínito . . . me
train . . . plane . . . boat.	tréno . . . me aeropláno . . .me vapóri.
Taxi, to the station . . .	Taxí, stó stathmó . . .
harbor . . . airport	limáni . . . aerodrómio
Porter, take the luggage.	Akthofóre, pare aftá táprámata.
Where is the filling station?	Pou íne tó vensinádiko?
When does the train leave for . . . ?	Tí óra thá fíyi to tréno ya . . . ?
Which is the train for . . . ?	Pío íne to tréno gía . . . ?
Which is the road to . . . ?	Piós íne o drómos giá . . . ?
A first-class ticket	Éna isitírio prótis táxis
Smoking is forbidden.	Apagorévete to kápnisma.

Where is the toilet?	Póu íne í toaléta?
Ladies, men	Ginekón, andrón
Where? When?	Póu? Póte?
Sleeping car, dining car	Wagonlí, wagonrestorán
Compartment	Vagóni
Entrance, exit	Íssodos, éxodos
Nothing to declare	Den écho típota na dilósso
I am coming for my vacation.	Érchome giá tis diakopés mou.
Nothing	Típota
Personal use	Prossopikí chríssi
How much?	Pósso?
I want to eat, to drink, to sleep.	Thélo na fáo, na pió, na kimithó.
Sunrise, sunset	Anatolí, díssi
Sun, moon	Ílios, fengári
Day, night	Méra, níchta
Morning, afternoon	Proí, mesiméri, or apóyevma
The weather is good, bad.	Ó kerós íne kalós, kakós.

ON THE ROAD

Straight ahead	Kat efthían
To the right, to the left	Dexiá, aristerá
Show me the way to . . .	Díxte mou to drómo . . .
Please.	Parakaló.
Where is . . . ?	Pou íne . . . ?
Crossroad	Diastávrosi
Danger	Kíndinos

IN TOWN

Will you lead me? take me?	Thélete na me odigíste? Me pérnete mazí sas?
Street, square	Drómos, platía
Where is the bank?	Pou íne i trápeza?
Far	Makriá

Police station	Astinomikó tmíma
Consulate (American, British)	Proxenío (Amerikániko, Anglikó)
Theater, cinema	Théatro, cinemá
At what time does the film start?	Tí óra archízi ee tenía?
Where is the travel office?	Pou íne to touristikó grafío?
Where are the tourist police?	Pou íne i touristikí astinomía?

SHOPPING

I would like to buy	Tha íthela na agorásso
Show me, please.	Díxte mou, parakaló.
May I look around?	Boró na ríxo miá matyá?
How much is it?	Pósso káni? (or kostízi)
It is too expensive.	Íne polí akrivó.
Have you any sandals?	Échete pédila?
Have you foreign newspapers?	Échete xénes efimerídes?
Show me that blouse, please.	Díxte mou aftí tí blouza.
Show me that suitcase.	Díxte mou aftí tí valítza.
Envelopes, writing paper	Fakélous, hartí íli
Roll of film	Film
Map of the city	Hárti tis póleos
Something handmade	Hiropíito
Wrap it up, please.	Tilixteto, parakaló.
Cigarettes, matches, please.	Tsigára, spírta, parakaló.
Ham	Zambón
Sausage, salami	Loukániko, salami
Sugar, salt, pepper	Záchari, aláti, pipéri
Grapes, cherries	Stafília, kerássia
Apple, pear, orange	Mílo, achládi, portokáli
Bread, butter	Psomí, voútiro
Peach, figs	Rodákino, síka

AT THE HOTEL

A good hotel	Éna kaló xenodochío
Have you a room?	Échete domátio?
Where can I find a furnished room?	Pou boró na vró epiploméno domátio?
A single room, double room	Éna monóklino, éna díklino
With bathroom	Me bánio
How much is it per day?	Pósso kostízi tin iméra?
A room overlooking the sea	Éna domátio prós ti thálassa
For one day, for two days	Giá miá méra, giá dió méres
For a week	Giá miá evdomáda
My name is . . .	Onomázome . . .
My passport	Tó diavatirió mou
What is the number of my room?	Piós íne o arithmós tou domatíou mou?
The key, please.	To klidí, parakaló.
Breakfast, lunch, supper	Proinó, messimergianó, vradinó
The bill, please.	To logariasmó, parakaló.
I am leaving tomorrow.	Févgo ávrio.

AT THE RESTAURANT

Waiter	Garsón
Where is the restaurant?	Pou íne to estiatório?
I would like to eat.	Tha íthela na fáo.
The menu, please.	To katálogo, parakaló.
Fixed-price menu	Menú
Soup	Soúpa
Bread	Psomí
Hors d'oeuvre	Mezédes, orektiká
Ham omelet	Omelétta zambón
Chicken	Kotópoulo
Roast pork	Psitó hirinó
Beef	Moschári

Potatoes (fried)	Patátes (tiganités)
Tomato salad	Domatosaláta
Vegetables	Lachaniká
Watermelon, melon	Karpoúzi, pepóni
Desserts, pastry	Gliká or pástes
Fruit, cheese, ice cream	Fróuta, tirí, pagotó
Fish, eggs	Psári, avgá
Serve me on the terrace.	Na mou servírete sti tarátza.
Where can I wash my hands?	Pou boró na plíno ta héria mou?
Red wine, white wine	Kokivó krasí, áspro krasí
Unresinated wine	Krasí aretsínato
Beer, soda water, water, milk	Bíra, sóda, neró, gála
Greek coffee	Ellenikó kafé
Coffee with milk, without	Kafé gallikó me, gála skéto
sugar, medium, sweet	métrio, glikó

AT THE BANK, AT THE POST OFFICE

Where is the bank?	Pou íne i trápeza?
post office	to tachidromío
I would like to cash a check.	Thélo ná xargiróso mía epitagí.
Stamps	Grammatóssima
By airmail	Aëroporikós
Postcard, letter	Kárta, grámma
Letterbox	Tachidromikó koutí
I would like to telephone.	Thélo na tilephonísso.

AT THE GARAGE

Garage, gas (petrol)	Garáz, venzíni
Oil	Ládi
Change the oil.	Aláksete to ládi.
Look at the tires.	Rixte mia matiá sta lástika.
Wash the car.	Plínete to aftokínito.
Breakdown	Vlávi

Tow the car.	Rimúlkiste tó aftokínito.
Spark plugs	Buzí
Brakes	Fréna
Gearbox	Kivótio tachitíton
Carburetor	Karbiratér
Headlight	Provoléfs
Starter	Míza
Axle	Áksonas
Shock absorber	Amortisér
Spare part	Antalaktikó

TRAVEL SMART
GREECE

GETTING HERE AND AROUND

▌ AIR TRAVEL

Flying time to Athens is 3½ hours from London, 10½ hours from New York, 12 hours from Chicago, 16½ hours from Los Angeles, and 19 hours from Sydney.

There are only two nonstop flights from the United States to Athens, on Delta (from New York–JFK) and US Airways (from Philadelphia). Therefore, most U.S. travelers will need to connect in an airport in Europe; further, most travelers originating in the United States will need to transfer in Athens to reach any other destination in Greece. There are a large number of charter flights, especially from northern Europe, that fly directly to resort destinations in Greece during the high season, but since most of these must be booked through travel agents in Europe, they will be irrelevant to the vast number of U.S. travelers. Nevertheless, many discount carriers fly from (mostly) secondary airports in Europe nonstop to Greece, and these flights may be relevant, particularly for those travelers who plan to visit another country in addition to Greece.

Strikes, either for several hours or days, can be a sporadic problem in Greece, so it's always a good idea to keep your eyes on the local headlines while traveling. Athens International Airport (Eleftherios Venizelos) posts real-time flight information on its website (*see Airports, below*). You can contact the Hellenic Civil Aviation Authority at the main Athens airport if you have complaints or concerns about flight cancellations, flight delays, or denied boarding.

Airline Security Issues Transportation Security Administration ⊕ *www.tsa.gov.*

Air Travel Resources in Greece Hellenic Civil Aviation Authority ✉ *Athens International Airport–Eleftherios Venizelos, Level 3, Room 607, main terminal bldg., Spata* ☎ *210/353–4158 weekdays 9–2, 210/353–4147 2 pm–9 am, 210/353–4148 2 pm–9 am* ✐ *hcaa9@athensairport.gr* ⊕ *www.hcaa.gr.*

AIRPORTS

Athens International Airport at Spata, 33 km (20 miles) southeast of the city center, opened in 2001 as the country's main airport. Officially named Eleftherios Venizelos, after Greece's first prime minister, the airport is modern and quite user-friendly (there's also a very nice Sofitel if you need to stay over). The main terminal building has two levels: upper for departures, ground level for arrivals. Unless you are flying directly to one of the islands, you'll likely pass through the Athens airport during your trip to Greece. It's quite easy to switch from international to domestic flights or get to Greece's main harbor, Piraeus, about a one-hour train ride south of the airport. Greece's second-largest city has another busy international airport: Thessaloniki Makedonia airport, which handles both international and domestic flights. So does the airport on Rhodes (in the Dodecanese islands). Two other airports, in Heraklion and Corfu, also have a large number of international flights. Airports on many smaller islands (Santorini, Syros, Mykonos, Karpathos, Kos, and Paros among them) receive international charter flights during the busier summer months.

Contacts Athens International Airport– Eleftherios Venizelos (*ATH*). ✉ *Spata* ☎ *210/353–0000 flight information and customer service, 210/353–0515 lost and found* ⊕ *www.aia.gr.* **Heraklion International Airport–Nikos Kazantzakis** (*HER*). ✉ *Heraklion, Crete* ☎ *2810/397800.* **Kerkyra Airport–Ioannis Kapodistrias** (*CFU*). ✉ *Corfu town, Corfu* ☎ *26610/89600.* **Rhodes International Airport Diagoras** (*RHO*). ✉ *Rhodes* ☎ *22410/88700.* **Thessaloniki International Airport–Makedonia** (*SKG*). ✉ *Kalamaria* ☎ *2310/985000* ⊕ *www.thessalonikiairport. com.*

GROUND TRANSPORTATION

See the respective destination chapters for detailed information on airport transfers. While both Athens and Thessaloniki have public transportation, other places in Greece, especially the islands, do not.

FLIGHTS

In addition to Delta and US Airways, many carriers offer one-stop connections to major destinations in Greece (but particularly Athens) from the United States. And most of the larger airlines, including Air France, British Airways, KLM, and Lufthansa, also offer codeshare flights with their U.S. partners. Some European budget carriers, including EasyJet and Ryanair offer flights to a wide range of destinations throughout Greece.

FLIGHTS WITHIN GREECE

In Greece, when faced with a boat journey of six hours or more, consider flying since domestic flights have good prices for many destinations. The frequency of flights varies according to the time of year (with an increase between Greek Easter and November), and it is essential to book well in advance for summer or for festivals and holidays, especially on three-day weekends. There is usually a fee to check bags; only hand luggage (with strictly enforced limits) is free.

Scheduled domestic air travel in Greece is provided by Aegean Airlines and its subsidiary Olympic Air (both of which operate out of Athens International Airport in Spata), Astra Airlines (which flies from Thessaloniki), and Sky Express (which has a more diffuse network of flights around Greece). Aegean Airlines and Olympic Air have the largest route network around Greece, with flights to virtually every destination you might need, with the best connections through Athens. If you fly into Athens, you'll be able to transfer quite easily to a domestic flight.

Contacts Aegean Airlines ✉ *Viltanioti 31, Kifissia, Athens* ☎ *801/112–0000 toll-free in Greece, 210/353–0101 in Athens airport, 210/626–1000 from abroad/mobile*

phones ⊕ *www.aegeanair.com.* **Air Canada.** Flights from Montreal and Toronto to Athens. ☎ *888/247–2262* ⊕ *www.aircanada.com.* **Air France.** Flights from Paris (CDG), Toulouse, Nice, and Marseille to Athens. ☎ *800/992–3932* ⊕ *www.airfrance.us.* **Air One.** Flights from Rome and Naples to Athens ☎ *(39) 091/255–1047 in Italy* ⊕ *www.flyairone.com.* **Air Transat.** Flights from Montreal and Toronto to Athens ☎ *866/847–1112* ⊕ *www.airtransat. ca.* **Alitalia.** Flights to Athens, Thessaloniki, Mykonos, Rhodes, and Heraklion from Rome (FCO). Flights to Athens, Thessaloniki, and Heraklion from Milan (LIN). Flights to Rhodes from Milan (MXP). ☎ *800/223–5730* ⊕ *www. alitalia.com.* **Astra Airlines** ☎ *23104/89390* ⊕ *www.astra-airlines.gr.* **British Airways.** Flights to Athens, Mykonos, Heraklion, Rhodes, Santorini, and Salonica (summer only). ☎ *800/247–9297* ⊕ *www.britishairways.com.* **Delta Airlines.** Flights to Athens from JFK. ☎ *800/241–4141 International Reservations, 14654 Greek office, 210/353–0116 Greek office* ⊕ *www.delta.com.* **easyJet.** Flights to Athens, Chania, Corfu, Heraklion, Kalamata, Kefalonia, Kos, Mykonos, Rhodes, Salonica, Santorini, and Zakynthos.* ☎ *0870/600–0000 in the U.K., 210/353–0300 in Athens* ⊕ *www. easyjet.com.* **Iberia Airlines.** Flights to Athens. ☎ *800/772–4642, 210/353—3441 in Athens* ⊕ *www.iberia.com.* **Jet2.com** ⊕ *www.jet2. com.* **KLM Royal Dutch Airlines.** Flights to Athens. ☎ *800/618–0104, 210/353–3436 in Athens* ⊕ *www.klm.com.* **LOT.** Flights from Warsaw to Athens. ☎ *210/327–4920 in Athens, 212/789–0970 in U.S.* ⊕ *www.lot.com.* **Lufthansa.** Flights to Athens, Chania, Heraklion, Rhodes, and Thessaloniki. ☎ *800/645–3880, 210/617–5200 in Athens* ⊕ *www. lufthansa.com.* **Monarch Airlines.** Flights from the U.K. to Chania, Corfu, Heraklion, Kefalonia, Rhodes, Skiathos, Volos, and Zakynthos. ☎ *0333/003–0700 in the U.K.* ⊕ *www.monarch. co.uk.* **Norwegian.** Flights from Oslo to Athens. ☎ *800/357–4159 in the U.S.* ⊕ *www. norwegian.com.* **Olympic Air** ☎ *210/355–0500 in Athens, 801/80110101 toll-free within Greece, 855/359–6200 in the U.S.* ⊕ *www. olympicair.com.* **Qatar Airways.** Flights from Doha, Qatar, to Athens. ☎ *210/950–8700* in Athens ⊕ www.qatarairways.com. **Royal Jordanian.** Flights from Amman, Jordan to Athens. ☎ 210/924–2600 in Athens ⊕ www.rj.com. **Ryanair.** Flights to Athens, Chania, Corfu, Kalamata, Kefalonia, Kos, Patras, Rhodes, Thessaloniki, Volos, and Zakynthos. ☎ (44) 871/246–0002 in the U.K. (fee per minute) ⊕ www.ryanair.com. **SAS Scandanavian Airlines.** Flights from Oslo to Athens. ☎ 210/961–8411 Greek office ⊕ www.flysas.com. **Sky Express** ☎ 28102/23800 ⊕ www.skyexpress.gr. **Swiss International Airlines.** Flights from Zurich to Athens, Corfu, Heraklion, and Thessaloniki. ☎ 877/359–7947, 210/617–5320 in Athens, 210/353–0382 in Athens airport ⊕ www.swiss.com. **Tarom.** Flights from Bucharest to Athens ☎ (40) 21/204–6464 in Romania ⊕ www.tarom.ro.

▌ BOAT AND FERRY TRAVEL

Ferries, catamarans, and hydrofoils make up an essential part of the national transport system of Greece, reaching every inhabited island. There are fast and slow boats and ferries that are more modern than others. When choosing a ferry, take into account the number of stops and the estimated arrival time. Sometimes a ferry that leaves an hour later gets you there faster.

With so many private companies operating, so many islands to choose from, and complicated timetables—and with departures changing not just by season but also by day of the week—the most sensible way to arrange island-hopping is to select the islands you would like to visit, then consult a travel agent to ask how your journey can be put together. Dolphin Hellas, a full-service tour and travel company based in Athens (see Travel Agents), has a unique online portal to view various schedules and purchase ferry tickets.

If the boat journey will be more than a couple of hours, it's a good idea to take along water and snacks. Greek fast-food franchises operate on most ferries, charging high prices. On longer trips ferries have both cafeteria-style and full-service restaurants.

Ferries may be delayed by weather conditions, especially when the northern winds called *meltemi* hit in August, so stay flexible—one advantage of not buying a ticket in advance. If your ship's departure is delayed for any reason (with the exception of force majeure), you have the right to stay on board in the class indicated on your ticket or, in case of prolonged delay, to cancel your ticket for a full refund. If you miss your ship, you forfeit your ticket; if you cancel in advance, you receive a partial or full refund, depending on how far in advance you cancel.

Two websites (⊕ www.ferries.gr and ⊕ www.greekferries.gr) are also quite helpful to check schedules and book tickets.

MAJOR FERRY PORTS

Of the major ferry ports in Greece, Piraeus, Rafina, and Lavrion are fairly well connected to Athens by bus, and the latter two are close enough to the Athens airport in Spata to be reached by taxi. For the Cycladic, Dodecanese, and Ionian islands, small ferry companies operate local routes that are not published nationally; passage can be booked through travel agents on the islands served.

PIRAEUS

Greece's largest and busiest port is Piraeus, which lies 10 km (6 miles) south of Central Athens, at the end of Metro Line 1, which is close to gates E5 and E6. The train ride from Central Athens takes about 25 minutes, and you can board at Thisseion, Monastiraki, or Omonia; change at Monastiraki if you get on or want to go to Syntagma.

A taxi can take longer than the metro and will cost around €25, plus baggage and port surcharges. Often, drivers wait until they fill their taxi with debarking passengers headed in roughly the same direction, which leads to a longer, more circuitous route to accommodate everyone's destination. It's often faster to walk to the main street and hail a passing cab.

From Piraeus you can reach the Saronic islands (Aegina, Hydra, Poros, Angistri, and Spetses); Peloponnesian ports (Hermioni and Porto Heli); the Cyclades (Amorgos, Folegandros, Anafi Ios, Milos, Mykonos, Naxos, Paros, Santorini, Serifos, Sifnos, Syros, and Tinos); and the northern Aegean islands (Samos, Ikaria, Mytileni, and Chios).

Be aware that Piraeus port is so vast that you may need to walk some distance to your gate (quay) of departure once you arrive, so be sure to arrive with plenty of time to spare. Changes may occur at the last moment. Just confirm at an information kiosk. Usually, the gates serve the following destinations:

E1   the Dodecanese

E2   Crete, Chios, Mytilini (Lesvos), Ikaria, Samos

E3   Crete, Kithira

E4   Kithira

E5   Main pedestrian entrance

E6   Cyclades, Rethymnon (Crete)

E7   Cyclades, Rethymnon (Crete)

E8   Saronic islands

E9   Cyclades, Samos, Ikaria

E10   Cyclades, Samos, Ikaria

RAFINA

From Greece's second-busiest port, which is 35 km (22 miles) northeast of Athens, you can reach Evia (Euboea) daily, as well as some of the Cyclades (Mykonos, Paros, Tinos, and Andros). Ferry timetables change in winter and summer, and special sailings are often added around holiday weekends in summer when demand is high.

To get to Attica's second port, Rafina, take a KTEL bus, which leaves approximately every half-hour (or every 15 minutes during rush hour; inquire about their schedule before your departure). Usually KTEL buses run from 5:30 am to 9:30 pm from Aigyptou Square near Pedion Areos Park, which is within walking distance from the Viktoria (green line) station. The KTEL bus takes about an hour to get to Rafina; the port is slightly downhill from the bus station.

It's also possible to take a taxi (a 40-minute trip), but it is fairly expensive.

LAVRION

From the port of Lavrion, 61 km (38 miles) southeast of Athens and close to Sounion, you can reach Kea (Tzia) and Kythnos, and (less regularly) Syros, Mykonos, Paros, Naxos, Anafi Ios, Sikinos, Folegandros, Kimolos, Milos, Tinos, Andros, Ag. Efstratios, Limnos, and Alexandroupolis. There are hourly buses from the Athens airport directly to Lavrion, or it's about 35 to 40 minutes by taxi.

PATRAS

From Patras, on the western coast of the Peloponnese, 210 km (130 miles) west of Athens, you can reach Italy (Ancona, Bari, Brindisi, Ravenna, Trieste, and Venice) as well as the Ionian islands (Corfu, Ithaki, and Kefalonia). The drive from Athens takes about 3 hours.

KILLINI

From Killini, 73 km (45 miles) south of Patras, you can reach the Ionian islands of Kefalonia and Zakynthos.

IGOUMENITSA

From Igoumenitsa, on Greece's northwest coast 482 km (300 miles), you can reach Italy (Ancona, Bari, Brindisi, Ravenna, Trieste, and Venice) and Corfu (several ferries daily). Given its distance from Athens, it is generally more realistic to fly.

OTHER PORTS

From northern mainland towns of **Kavala** and **Alexandroupolis** you can reach the Dodecanese islands of Limnos, Samothrace (Samothraki), and Thassos.

From **Agios Konstantinos, Volos,** or **Thessaloniki** you can reach the Sporades islands of Alonissos, Skiathos, and Skopelos.

From **Kimi,** on the east coast of Evia, you can reach Skyros.

From **Heraklion** you can reach the Cyclades islands of Mykonos, Paros, and Santorini (summer only).

Contacts Agios Konstantinos Port Authority ☎ 22350/31759. **Igoumenitsa Port Authority** ☎ 26650/99400. **Kimi Port Authority** ☎ 22220/22606. **Lavrion Port Authority** ☎ 22920/25249, 22920/26859 ⊕ www.oll.gr. **Patras Port Authority** ☎ 2613/615400. **Piraeus Port Authority** ☎ 210/417–2675. **Rafina Port Authority** ☎ 22940/23605, 22940/22840 ⊕ www.rafinaport.gr. **Thessaloniki Port Authority** ☎ 2313/325821, 2313/325822 ⊕ www.thpa.gr. **Volos Port Authority** ☎ 24210/28888, 2410/38888.

BUYING FERRY TICKETS

It's best to buy your ticket at least two or three days ahead if you are traveling between July 15 and August 30, when most Greeks vacation, if you need a cabin (good for long trips), or if you are taking a car. If possible, don't travel by boat around August 15, when most ferries are very crowded. The ferry schedule systems are not organized well in advance, so booking tickets more than a month ahead of time is usually not possible.

You can buy tickets from a travel agency or *praktoreio* at the port, online through travel websites (popular sites include ⊕ *www.directferries.gr* ⊕ *www.greekferries.gr* and ⊕ *www.ferries.gr*). Although you can also buy tickets directly from the ferry company offices and websites, it's usually easier to use a travel agent. Last-minute tickets can always be purchased from a ferry company kiosk at every port. Always book your return upon arrival if you are pressed for time.

Generally you can pay by either credit card or cash, though the latter is often preferred if you don't use a travel agent. On islands the local office of each shipping line posts a board with departure times.

FERRY TYPES

Greek ferries can be both slow and fast. On longer trips, the experience is a bit like a minicruise. You can relax on board, enjoy the sea views, snap photos from the deck at ports of call (there may be multiple calls on some routes) and as you approach your destination. Slow ferries from Piraeus to Lesvos, Rhodes, Crete, and Santorini can last eight hours or more, so there's also the option to rent a cabin for the journey that may run overnight.

If boat rides equal boredom for you, high-speed ferries, catamarans, and hydrofoils—or in Greek *iptamena delphinia* (flying dolphins)—are a pricier option that cuts travel time in half. Catamarans are the larger of these fast ferries, with more space to move around, although passengers are not allowed outside when the boat is not docked. If the sea is choppy, these boats often cannot travel. Although they are faster, they lack the flavor of the older ferries with the open decks.

Schedules vary between both the slower and faster boats. It's best to check what fits your time frame and budget.

INTERNATIONAL FERRIES

From Greece you can opt to travel to neighboring Italy and Turkey. Travel time to Turkey from most destinations in Greece is relatively short, usually less than 90 minutes. Travel to various stops in Italy can take from 9 to 21 hours.

TRAVEL TO TURKEY

You can cross to Turkey from the northeastern Aegean islands. The journey takes anywhere from one hour to 90 minutes, depending on the destination. Ferries sail between the Greek islands of Rhodes, Kos, Samos, Simi, Chios, and Lesvos to the Turkish destinations of Bodrum, Marmaris, Kusadasi, and Cesmi.

Note that British, Australian and American passport holders must have $20 or €14 with them (in cash) to purchase a visa on landing in Turkey. New Zealanders don't need a visa. Canadian citizens need $60 or €42.

Ferry lines that sail between Greece and Turkey include the following: Erturk, Marmaris Ferries, Meander Ferries, NEL Lines, SeaDreams, and Yesil Marmaris Lines.

TRAVEL TO ITALY

There are also frequent ferries between Greece and Italy. From Igoumenitsa, Patras, and Corfu you can find ferries that head to Ancona, Bari, Brindisi, and Venice.

The most respected and competitively priced is Minoan Lines. Its modern, well-maintained vessels are outfitted with bars, a self-service restaurant, a pool, a spa, a gym, an Internet café, a casino, shops, and even a conference center.

Prices depend on the season and your class of service (deck, seat, or cabin). High season runs from late July to late August; prices drop considerably in low and middle season. Some companies offer special family or group discounts, while others charge extra for pets or offer deep discounts on return tickets, so comparing rates does pay. When booking, also consider when you will be traveling; an overnight trip can be offset against hotel costs, and you will spend more on incidentals like food and drink when traveling during the day.

Ferry lines that sail between Greece and Italy include the following: Anek, Blue Star Ferries, Endeavor, European Sealines, Minoan Lines, Superfast Ferries, and Ventouris.

Ferry Lines Aegean Flying Dolphins ☎ 210/422-1766 in Athens ⊕ www. aegeanflyingdolphins.gr. **Aegean Speed Lines.** Greek islands: the Cyclades. ☎ 210/969-0950 in Athens ⊕ www.aegeanspeedlines.gr. **Alpha Ferries.** Greek islands: the Cyclades ☎ 210/428-4001 in Athens ⊕ www.ferries.gr/ alpha-ferries. **Anek Lines.** Ferries to Italy and Greek islands. ☎ 210/419-7400 ticket info in Athens, 210/419-7470 customer service in Athens, 210/419-7420 reservations in Athens ⊕ www.anek.gr. **ANEM Ferries.** Greek islands: the Dodecanese ☎ 22420/59124. **ANEN Lines.** The Peloponnese and Greek islands: Crete, Ionian islands ☎ 28210/20345 ⊕ www.ferries. gr/anen-lines. **Anes Ferries.** Greek islands ☎ 210/422-5625 in Athens ⊕ www.anes.gr. **Blue Star Ferries.** Italy and the Greek islands ☎ 210/891-9800 in Athens, 18130 Reservation (within Greece), 210/891-9810 Customer

Service in Athens ⊕ www.bluestarferries. gr. **Dodekanisos Seaways.** Greek islands ☎ 22410/70590 ⊕ www.12ne.gr. **Endeavor Lines.** Italy and Greek islands: Ionian islands ☎ 210/940-5222 in Athens ⊕ www.endeavor-lines.com. **Erturk Lines.** Turkey: Chios to Cesmi ☎ (90) 232/712-6768 in Turkey ⊕ www. erturk.com.tr. **European Sealines.** Italy and Greek islands: Ionian islands ☎ 210/956-1630 in Athens ⊕ www.europeansealines.com. **Fast Ferries.** Greek islands: the Cyclades ☎ 210/418-2163 in Athens ⊕ www.fastferries. com.gr. **Golden Star Ferries.** Greek islands: the Cyclades ☎ 80122/24000 in Greece ⊕ www.goldenstarferries.gr. **Hellenic Seaways.** Greek islands ☎ 210/419-9000 Ticket information in Athens ⊕ www. hellenicseaways.gr. **Ionian Ferries.** Greek islands: Ionian islands ☎ 210/324-9997 in Athens ⊕ www.ionianferries.gr. **Kallisti Ferries.** Greek islands: northern Aegean islands and Cyclades ☎ 80111/77700 in Greece ⊕ www.ferries.gr/kallisti-ferries. **Lane Ferries.** Peloponnese and Greek islands: Crete, Dodecanese, Cyclades, Ionian islands ☎ 210/427-4011 in Athens ⊕ www.ferries. gr/lane. **Marmaris Ferries.** Turkey: Rhodes to Marmaris ☎ (90) 252/413-0230 in Turkey ⊕ www.marmarisferry.com. **Meander Ferries.** Samos to Kusadasi ☎ (90) 256/612-8888 in Turkey ⊕ www.meandertravel.com. **Minoan Lines.** Italy and Greek islands ☎ 210/337-6910 in Athens, 210/414-5700 Reservations in Athens ⊕ www.minoan.gr. **NEL Lines.** Turkey and Greek islands ☎ 210/412-5888 in Athens, 210/411-5015 in Athens ⊕ www.nel. gr. **Nova Ferries.** Greek islands: Argosaronic islands ☎ 210/412-6181 in Athens ⊕ www. novaferries.gr. **SAOS Ferries.** Greek islands: northern Aegean islands ☎ 22510/38503 ⊕ www.saos.gr. **Saronic Ferries.** Greek islands: Saronic gulf islands ☎ 210/411-7341 in Athens ⊕ www.saronicferries.gr. **Sea Dreams–Aegean Shipping Company.** Turkey and Greek islands ☎ 22410/76535 in Rhodes ⊕ www.seadreams.gr. **Seajets.** Greek islands: the Cyclades ☎ 210/412-0001 in Athens, 210/412-1901 in Athens ⊕ www. seajets.gr. **Skyros Shipping Company.** Greek islands: the Sporades ☎ 22220/92164

⊕ *www.sne.gr.* **Strinzis Ferries.** Greek islands: Ionian islands ☏ *210/422–5000 in Athens* ⊕ *www.strintzisferries.gr.* **Superfast Ferries.** Italy and Greek islands ☏ *210/891–9130 in Athens* ⊕ *www.superfast.com.* **2 Way Ferries.** Greek islands: Ionian islands ☏ *26610/30190* ⊕ *www.2wayferries.gr.* **Tilos 21 Century.** Greek islands: Dodecanese islands ☏ *22640/44000* ⊕ *www.tilosferries. gr.* **Ventouris Ferries.** Italy and Greek islands ☏ *210/482–8001 through 210/482–8004 in Athens* ⊕ *www.ventouris.gr.* **Yesil Marmaris Lines.** Turkey: Rhodes to Bodrum and Marmaris ☏ *(90) 252/412–1033 in Turkey* ⊕ *www. rhodesferry.com.*

CRUISES

For full information about the top cruise lines sailing Greek waters and their best itineraries, see Chapter 2, Cruising the Greek islands.

∎ BUS TRAVEL

For information on guided bus tours, see Tour Options in the Planning section of individual chapters.

Greece's nationwide bus network is extensive, with routes to even the most far-flung villages. It's divided into a fairly reliable regional bus system (KTEL) made up of local operators. Buses from Athens travel throughout the country, and other Greek cities have connections to towns and villages in their own regions. Routes are listed on KTEL's website, but unless you speak Greek or know someone who does, it won't make sense. If you plan to visit Thessaloniki, you can visit the Greek tourist agency site ⊕ *www.viva.gr,* which has an English-language version that will enable you to plan your bus trip and purchase the tickets online. If you prefer to buy your ticket in person, you can always head to the main KTEL terminal in any Greek city to inquire about schedules and rates.

BUYING TICKETS

There is no central website in English to buy KTEL tickets in advance, though there is an information website that could be helpful. It's easiest to purchase your bus tickets in person at the KTEL station or on the bus. Reservations are unnecessary on most routes, especially those with several round-trips a day. If you are traveling on holiday weekends, it's best to go to the station and buy your ticket a couple of days in advance. To give you a sense of costs and schedules, the bus from Athens to Corinth costs €10 and takes about 1 hour; to Nafplion, €15, 2½ hours; to Patras, €25, 2½–3 hours; and to Thessaloniki, €50, 6½ hours.

CATCH YOUR BUS

Athens has three bus stations. In Athens, KTEL's Terminal A is the arrival and departure point for bus lines to northern Greece, including Thessaloniki, and to the Peloponnese destinations of Epidauros, Mycenae, Nafplion, and Corinth. Terminal B serves Evia, most of Thrace, and central Greece, including Delphi. Most KTEL buses to the east Attica coast— including those for Sounion, Marathon, and the ports of Lavrion and Rafina— leave from the downtown KTEL terminal near Pedion Areos park.

The buses, which are punctual, span the range from slightly dilapidated to luxurious and air-conditioned with upholstered seats. There is just one class of ticket. Board early, because Greeks have a loose attitude about assigned seating, and ownership counts here. Although smoking is forbidden on KTEL buses, the driver will stop every two hours or so at a roadside establishment; smokers can light up then.

PUBLIC TRANSPORTATION BUSES

In large cities, you can buy individual tickets for urban buses at terminal booths, convenience stores, or at selected *periptera* (street kiosks). *See our Athens chapter Getting Here and Around section for information on the city's convenient multiday transportation passes (good for buses, trolleys, and the metro).*

Bus Information KTEL ⊕ *www.ktelbus.gr.*

Athens Bus Stations Downtown Athens KTEL terminal ✉ *Aigyptou Sq., Mavromateon and Leoforos Alexandras, near Pedion Areos park, Athens* ☎ *210/880–8080, 210/818–0221* ⊕ *www.ktelattikis.gr.* **Terminal A - KTEL Kifissou** ✉ *Kifissou 100, Kolonos, Athens* ☎ *210/801–11440.* **Terminal B - KTEL Liosson** ✉ *Liosion 260, Kato Patissia, Athens* ☎ *210/880–8000.*

▌ CAR TRAVEL

Road conditions in Greece have improved in the last decade, yet driving in Greece still presents certain challenges. In Athens, traffic is mind-boggling most of the time and parking is scarce, so public transportation or taxis are much better options than a rental car. If you are traveling by ferry, taking along a car will increase your ticket costs substantially and limit your ease in hopping onto any ferry (fast ferries do not accommodate cars). On islands, you can always rent a taxi or a car for the day if you want to see something distant, and domestic flights are fairly cheap, especially if you book well in advance. The only real reason to drive is if it's your passion, if you are a large party with many suitcases and many out-of-the-way places to see, or if you need the freedom to change routes and make unexpected stops not permitted on public transportation.

DOCUMENTS

International driving permits (IDPs), required for drivers who are not citizens of an EU country, are available from the American, Australian, Canadian, and New Zealand automobile associations. These international permits, valid only in conjunction with your regular driver's license, are universally recognized; having one may save you a problem with local authorities.

Regular registration papers and insurance contracted in any EU country or a green card are required, in addition to a driver's license (EU or international). EU members can travel freely without paying any additional taxes.

GASOLINE

Gas pumps and service stations are everywhere, and lead-free gas is widely available. Nevertheless, away from the main towns, especially at night, open gas stations can be very far apart (⇨ *Hours of Operation, below*). Don't let your gas supply drop to less than a quarter tank when driving through rural areas. Gas costs about €1.80 a liter for unleaded ("ah-*mo*-lee-vdee"), €1.40 a liter for diesel ("*dee*-zel"). Prices may vary by as much as €0.50 per liter from one region to another, but a price ceiling has been imposed on gas prices during the busy summer months in popular tourist destinations. You aren't usually allowed to pump your own gas, though you can do everything else yourself. If you ask the attendant to give you extra service (check oil, air, and water or clean the windows), leave a small tip. Gas stations are now required by law to issue receipts, so make sure you pick up yours from the attendant. The word is *apodiksi.* Credit cards are usually accepted at big gas stations (BP, Shell, Elinoil, EKO, Avin, Aegean, Revoil, etc.), less so at stations found in remote areas.

INSURANCE

In general, auto insurance is not as expensive as in other countries. You must have third-party car insurance to drive in Greece. If possible, get an insurance "green card" valid for Greece from your insurance company before arriving. You can also buy a policy with local companies; keep the papers in a plastic pocket on the inside right front windshield. To get more information, or to locate a local representative for your insurance company, call the Hellenic Union of Insurance Firms/Motor Insurance Bureau.

Contacts Hellenic Union of Insurance Firms/Motor Insurance Bureau ✉ *Xenofontos 10, Athens* ☎ *210/333–41000* ⊕ *www. eaee.gr.*

PARKING

The scarcity of parking spaces in Athens is one good reason not to drive in the city. Although a number of car parks operate in the city center and near suburban metro stations, these aren't enough to accommodate demand. They can also be quite expensive, with prices starting at €10 for an hour. Pedestrians are often frustrated by cars parked on sidewalks, and police have become stricter about ticketing. "Controlled parking" zones in some downtown districts like Kolonaki have introduced some order to the chaotic system; a one-hour card costs €2, with a maximum of three hours permitted (for a total cost of €6). Buy a parking card from the kiosk or meter and display it inside your windshield. Be careful not to park in the spots reserved for residents, even if you have a parking card, as you may find your license plates mischievously gone when you return!

Outside Athens, the situation is slightly better. Many villages, towns, and islands have designated free parking areas just outside the center where you can leave your car.

ROAD CONDITIONS

Driving defensively is the key to safety in Greece, one of the most hazardous European countries for motorists. In the cities and on the highways, the streets can be riddled with potholes; motorcyclists seem to come out of nowhere, often passing on the right; and cars may even go the wrong way down a one-way street. In the countryside and on islands, you must watch for livestock crossing the road, as well as for tourists shakily learning to use rented motorcycles.

The many motorcycles and scooters weaving through traffic and the aggressive attitude of fellow motorists can make driving in Greece's large cities unpleasant—and the life of a pedestrian dangerous. Greeks often run red lights or ignore stop signs on side streets, or round corners fast without stopping. It's a good idea at night at city intersections and at any time on curvy country lanes to beep your horn to warn errant drivers.

In cities, you will find pedestrians have no qualms about standing in the middle of a busy boulevard, waiting to dart between cars. Make eye contact so you can both determine who's going to slow. Rush hour in the cities runs from 7 to 10 am and 1:30 to 3:30 pm on weekdays, plus 8 to 10 pm on Tuesday, Thursday, and Friday. Saturday morning brings bumper-to-bumper traffic in shopping districts, and weekend nights guarantee crowding around nightlife hubs. In Athens, the only time you won't find traffic is very early morning and most of Sunday (unless you're foolish enough to stay at a local beach until evening in summer, which means heavy end-of-weekend traffic when you return). Finally, perhaps because they are untrained, drivers seldom pull over for wailing ambulances; the most they'll do is slow down and slightly move over in different directions.

Highways are color-coded: green for the new, toll roads and blue for old, National Roads. Tolls are usually €2.50–€4. The older routes are slower and somewhat longer, but they follow more-scenic routes, so driving is more enjoyable. The National Roads can be very slick in places when wet—avoid driving in rain and on the days preceding or following major holidays, when traffic is at its worst as urban dwellers leave for villages.

ROADSIDE EMERGENCIES

You must put out a triangular danger sign if you have a breakdown. Roving repair trucks, owned by the major road assistance companies, such as ELPA, patrol the major highways, except the Attiki Odos, which has its own contracted road assistance company. They assist tourists with breakdowns for free if they belong to an auto club, such as AAA or ELPA; otherwise, there is a charge. The Greek National Tourism Organization, in cooperation with ELPA, the tourist police, and Greek scouts, provides an emergency telephone line for those who spot a dead or wounded animal on the National Road.

Contacts Automobile Touring Club of Greece - ELPA *(ELPA).* ☎ *10400 for break-downs, 171 for a dead or hurt animal, 210/606–8800 head office.*

RULES OF THE ROAD

Remember to always buckle your seat belt when driving in Greece, as fines are very costly if you don't. Children 10 years old or younger are required to sit in the backseat. You have to be at least 18 to be able to drive in Greece. Motorcycle helmets are compulsory, though Greeks tend to ignore these rules, or comply with them by "wearing" the helmet strapped to their arms.

International road signs are in use throughout Greece. You drive on the right, pass on the left, and yield right-of-way to all vehicles approaching from the right (except on posted main highways). Cars may not make a right turn on a red light. The speed limits are 120 kph (74 mph) on a National Road, 90 kph (56 mph) outside urban areas, and 50 kph (31 mph) in cities, unless lower limits are posted. But limits are often not posted, and signs indicating a lower limit may not always be visible, so if you see Greek drivers slowing down, take the cue to avoid speed traps in rural areas.

In central Athens there is an odd-even rule to avoid traffic congestion. This rule does not apply to rental cars, provided the renter has a foreign passport. If you are renting a car, ask the rental agency about any special parking or circulation regulations in force. Although sidewalk parking is illegal, it is common. And although it's tempting as a visitor to ignore parking tickets, keep in mind that if you've surrendered your ID to the rental agency, you won't get it back until you clear up the matter. You can pay your ticket at the rental agency or local police station. Under a driving code aimed at cracking down on violations, fines start at €50 (for illegal parking in places reserved for the disabled) and can go as high as €1,200, if you fail an alcohol test; fines for running a red light or speeding are now €700, plus you have your license revoked for 60 days and your plates revoked for 20 days. If fines are paid in cash within ten days, there is a 50% discount in the amount that you actually pay.

If you are involved in an accident, don't drive away. Accidents must be reported (something Greek motorists often fail to do) before the insurance companies consider claims. Try to get the other driver's details as soon as possible; hit-and-run is all too common in Greece. If the police take you in (they can hold you for 24 hours if there is a fatality, regardless of fault), you have the right to call your local embassy or consulate for help getting a lawyer.

DRIVING IN AND OUT OF ATHENS

Greece's two main highways, Athens–Corinth and Athens–Thessaloniki (Ethniki Odos and the Attiki Odos), circulate traffic around the metropolis. Avoid using them during periods of mass exodus, such as Friday afternoon or Sunday evening. These highways and the Egnatia Odos, which goes east to west across northern Greece, along with the secondary roads, cover most of the mainland, but on islands, some areas (beaches, for example) are accessible via dirt or gravel paths. With the exception of main highways and a few flat areas like the Thessalian plain, you will average about 60 km (37 miles) an hour: expect some badly paved or disintegrating roads; stray flocks of goats; slow farm vehicles; detours; curves; and, near Athens and Thessaloniki, traffic jams. At the Athens city limits, signs in English mark the way to Syntagma and Omonia squares in the center. When you exit Athens, signs are well marked for the National Road, usually naming Lamia and Thessaloniki for the north and Corinth or Patras for the southwest.

CAR RENTAL

When you reserve a car, ask about cancellation penalties, taxes, drop-off charges (if you're planning to pick up the car in one city and leave it in another), and surcharges (for being under or over a certain age, for additional drivers, or for driving across state or country borders or beyond a specific distance from your point of rental). Don't forget to check if the rental price includes unlimited mileage. All these things can add substantially to your costs. Request car seats and extras such as GPS when you book.

Rates are sometimes—but not always— better if you book in advance or reserve through a rental agency's or an airline's website. There are other reasons to book ahead, though: for popular destinations, during busy times of the year, or to ensure that you get certain types of cars (vans, SUVs, exotic sports cars).

■TIP➜ Make sure that a confirmed reservation guarantees you a car. Agencies sometimes overbook, particularly for busy weekends and holiday periods.

Because driving in Greece can be harrowing, car rental prices can be higher than in the United States, and transporting a car by ferry hikes up the fare substantially. The exception is on large islands where the distance between towns is greater and taxi fares are higher; you may want to rent a car or a moped for the day for concentrated bouts of sightseeing. Official rates in Greece during high season (July–September) are much cheaper if you rent through local agents rather than the large international companies.

In summer, renting a small car with standard transmission will cost you about €275 to €375 for a week's rental (including tax, insurance, and unlimited mileage). Four-wheel-drives can cost anywhere from €100 to €180 a day, depending on availability and the season. Luxury cars are available at some agencies, such as Europcar, but renting a BMW or a Mercedes can fetch a hefty price—anywhere from €120 per day in low season to €550 a day in high season. This does not include the 23% V.A.T. Convertibles ("open" cars) and minibuses are also available. Probably the most difficult car to rent, unless you reserve from abroad, is an automatic. Note that car rental fees really follow laws of supply/demand so there can be huge fluctuations and, in low season, lots of room for bargaining. Off-season, rental agencies are often closed on islands and in less-populated areas.

If you're considering moped or motorcycle rental, which is cheaper than a car, especially for getting around on the islands, try Motorent or Easy Moto Rent, both in Athens. On the islands, independent moped rentals are available through local agents.

You can usually reduce prices by reserving a car through a major rental agency before you leave. Or opt for a midsize Greek agency and bargain for a price; you should discuss when kilometers become free. These agencies provide good service, and prices are at the owner's discretion. It helps if you have shopped around and can mention another agency's offer. If you're visiting several islands or destinations, larger agencies may be able to negotiate a better total package through their local offices or franchises. Some hotels or airlines may also have partner agencies that offer discounts to guests.

In Greece your own driver's license is not acceptable unless you are a citizen of the European Union. For non-EU citizens an international driver's permit (IDP) is necessary (➪ Car Travel, above). To rent, you must have had your driver's license for one year and be at least 21 years old if you use a credit card (sometimes you must be 23 if you pay cash); for some car categories and for some agencies, you must be 25. You need the agency's permission to ferry the car or cross the border (Europcar does not allow across-the-border rentals). A valid driver's license is usually acceptable for renting a moped, but you will need a motorcycle driver's license if you want to rent a larger bike.

Most major car-rental agencies have several offices in Athens and also at the Athens airport, in major cities like Thessaloniki, and often throughout the country.

Contacts Avis ☎ *210/322–4951 in Athens* ⊕ *www.avis.gr.* **Budget Rent a Car** ☎ *213/021–3120 in Athens* ⊕ *www. budgetrentacar.gr.* **Enterprise Rent a Car** ☎ *210/349–9030 in Athens* ⊕ *www. enterpriserentacar.gr.* **Europcar Car Rental** ✉ *Syngrou Avenue 25* ☎ *210/921 1444* ⊕ *www.europcar-greece.gr.* **Hertz** ☎ *210/922–0102 in Athens* ⊕ *www.hertz.gr.* **Sixt Car Rental** ☎ *210/922–0171 in Athens* ⊕ *www.sixt.gr.*

▌TAXI TRAVEL

In Greece, as everywhere, unscrupulous taxi drivers sometimes try to take advantage of out-of-towners. All taxis must display the rate card; it's usually on the dashboard, though taxis outside the big cities don't bother. Ask your hotel concierge or owner before engaging a taxi what the fare to your destination ought to be. It should cost between €35 and €50 from the airport (depending on whether you are traveling with Rate 1 or Rate 2 taxi charges) to the Athens city center (this includes tolls) and about €15 to €25 from Piraeus port to the center. It does not matter how many are in your party (the driver isn't supposed to squeeze in more than four); the metered price remains the same. Taxis must give passengers a receipt (*apodiksi*) if requested.

Make sure that the driver turns on the meter to Rate (Tarifa) 1 (€0.68), unless it's between midnight and 5 am, when Rate (Tarifa) 2 (€1.19) applies. Remember that the meter starts at €1.19 and the minimum is €3.16 in Athens and Thessaloniki (€3.40 for the rest of the country). A surcharge applieswhen taking a taxi to and from the airport (€3.84) and from (but not to) ports, bus and train stations

(€1.07). There is also a surcharge of €0.40 for each item of baggage that's over 10 kilograms (22 pounds). If you suspect a driver is overcharging, demand to be taken to the police station; this usually brings them around. Complaints about service or overcharging should be directed to the tourist police; at the Athens airport, contact the Taxi Syndicate information desk. When calling to complain, be sure to report the driver's license number.

Taxi rates are inexpensive compared to fares in most other European countries, mainly because they operate on the jitney system, indicating willingness to pick up others by blinking their headlights or slowing down. Would-be passengers shout their destination as the driver cruises past. Don't be alarmed if your driver picks up other passengers (although he should ask your permission first). Drivers rarely pick up additional passengers if you are a woman traveling alone at night. Each new party pays full fare for the distance he or she has traveled.

A taxi is available when a white-and-red sign (*elefthero*) is up or the light is on at night. Once the driver indicates he is free, he cannot refuse your destination, so get in the taxi before you give an address. He also must wait for you up to 15 minutes, if requested, although most drivers would be unhappy with such a demand. Drivers are familiar with the major hotels, but it's good to know a landmark near your hotel and to have the address and phone number written in Greek.

You can download the TaxiBeat app from home, an app that lets you order a nearby taxi that is equipped with GPS (to easily find your destination), and choose your taxi driver based on languages spoken and customer rating. The driver will come right to your destination, recognizable by his license plates. The service is at no extra cost.

On islands and in the countryside, the meter may often be on Rate (Tarifa) 2 (outside city limits). Do not assume taxis will be waiting at smaller island airports when your flight lands; often, they have all been booked by arriving locals. If you get stuck, try to join a passenger going in your direction, or call your hotel to arrange transportation.

When you're taking an early-morning flight, it's a good idea to reserve a radio taxi the night before, for an additional charge of €3.39 to €5.65 (depending on whether it is daytime or night tariff). These taxis are usually quite reliable and punctual; if you're not staying in a hotel, the local tourist police can give you some phone numbers for companies. Taxis charge €10.85 per hour of waiting.

Taxi Complaints in Athens Taxi Syndicate ☎ 210/523–6904 for Greece, 210/523–9524 for Attica, 210/522–1123 for Athens. **Tourist police** ☎ 1571.

❚ TRAIN TRAVEL

Traveling by train is a convenient, cost-effective, and scenic way to reach certain destinations in Greece and to connect to other European countries. The Greek Railway Organization (TrainOSE) runs the national train network and the *proastiakos* light-rail line is part of the network (⊕ *www.trainose.gr*). In Athens, the main train station is Larissis Station, off Diliyianni street west of Omonia Square (⇨ *Athens Getting Here and Around in Chapter 3 for more information*). In Thessaloniki the station is located on Monastiriou avenue, which is a 15-minute drive from Aristotle Square. Besides Athens, there are also intercity light-rail and train networks in Thessalonki and Patras.

ABOUT TRAVEL IN GREECE

Trains are generally on time. At smaller stations, allow about 15–20 minutes for changing trains; on some routes, connecting routes are coordinated with the main line.

All trains have both first- and second-class seating. On any train, it is best during high season, around holidays, or for long distances to travel first-class, with a reserved seat, as the difference between the first- and second-class coaches can be significant: the cars are cleaner, the seats are wider and plusher, and, most important, the cars are emptier.

The assigned seating of first class (*proti thesi*) is a good idea in July and August, for example, when many trains are packed with tourists. Many travelers assume that rail passes guarantee them seats on the trains they wish to ride: Not so. You need to book seats ahead even if you are using a rail pass *(see Rail Passes, below)*; seat reservations are required on some European trains, particularly high-speed trains, and are a good idea on trains that may be crowded—particularly in summer on popular routes. You also need a reservation if you purchase sleeping accommodations. On high-speed (IC) trains, you pay a surcharge.

You can pay for all train tickets purchased in Greece with cash (euros) or with credit cards (Visa and MasterCard only). Note that any ticket issued on the train costs 50% more. You can get train schedules from TrainOSE offices.

POPULAR TRAIN ROUTES

The main line running north from Athens divides into three lines at Thessaloniki, continuing on to Skopje and Belgrade; the Turkish border and Istanbul; and Sofia, Bucharest, and Budapest.

Within Greece, some popular routes include Athens to Thessaloniki, Alexandroupoli (Dikaia), Florina Kalambaka, Volos, and Chalkida. There is also an InterCity Express service from Athens to Thessaloniki that takes four hours instead of six. At this writing, the IC train costs €39 for A class, versus €29 for B class. In Athens, the light-rail also runs regularly from the airport connecting to the Doukissis Plakentias station, where you can change trains and continue to the city center (Metro Line 3 to Egaleo), using the same ticket. The service can also take you to Kiato, east of Corinth.

A few historic train lines have been kept up and continue to be popular with travelers. The one- hour journey from Diakofto to Kalavryta in the northern Peloponnese travels up a pine-crested gorge in the Peloponnese mountains. It is one of the oldest rail lines in Greece, assigned by PM Harilaos Trikoupis in 1889. The 90-minute trip aboard the steam train of Pelion departs from Ano Lehonia, stops in Ano Gatzea and arrives in Milies, crossing breathtaking landscapes in central and northern Greece. Finally, the 45-minute journey from Katakolo to Ancient Olympia passes through Pirgos.

BUYING TICKETS

You can head to the TrainOSE website to view train schedules in English as well as to book tickets online. You can also purchase tickets in person at any OSE station. Light-rail tickets are available at stations and cost €1.40 for a basic ticket and €8 one-way for the airport. Validating machines are on the platform, not on board.

Some sample train fares for longer trips include: €12 Athens to Chalkida, and €37 Athens to Thessaloniki (on TrainOSE, B-class). First-class costs about 30% more than second-class (*thefteri thesi*).

Contacts TrainOSE Customer Service
✉ *Karolou 1–3, Omonia Sq., Athens*
☎ *210/522-3478 in Athens, 1110 customer service (7 am–10 pm).*

RAIL PASSES

Greece is one of 25 countries in which you can use Eurail passes, which provide unlimited first-class rail travel, in all of the participating countries, for the duration of the pass. Please note that the Greek National Organization has suspended circulation of international trains indefinitely (i.e., trains connecting Greece to Bulgaria, Fyrom, or Turkey), though you will still be able to use your pass within the country, or to travel from Italy to Greece. If you plan to rack up the miles in several countries, get a standard Eurail Global Pass. These are available for 15 days of travel ($798), 21 days ($1,031), one month ($1,269), two months ($1,793), and three months ($2,210).

In addition to standard Eurail passes, ask about special rail-pass plans. Among these are the Eurail Pass Youth (for those under age 26), the Eurail Saver Pass (which gives a discount for two or more people traveling together), and the Eurail Flexi Pass (which allows a certain number of travel days within a set period). Among those passes you might want to consider: the Greece Pass allows first-class rail travel throughout Greece; the standard three days' unlimited travel in a month costs $158, and the rate rises per day of travel added. The Greece–Italy Pass gives you four days' travel time over a span of two months; the cost is $395 for first class, $314 for second. Youths (18–25 years of age) pay about 50% less, and there are special rates for groups and families.

Passes can be shipped to anywhere you are in Europe, as well as worldwide, but can't be shipped to a particular train station. Shipping is by registered mail. Residents of Canada must purchase their tickets from the Rail Europe's Canadian site at ⊕ *www.raileurope.ca.*

Rail Passes Rail Europe ☎ *800/622-8600 in the U.S., 800/361-7245 in Canada* ⊕ *www.raileurope.com.*

ESSENTIALS

▌ ADDRESSES

To make finding your way around as easy as possible, it's wise to learn to recognize letters in the Greek alphabet. Most areas have few road signs in English, and even those that *are* in English don't necessarily follow the official standardized transliteration code (⊕ *www.elot.gr*), resulting in odd spellings of foreign names. Sometimes there are several spelling variations in English for the same place: Agios, Aghios, or Ayios; Georgios or Yiorgos. Also, the English version may be quite different from the Greek, or even what locals use informally: Corfu is known as Kerkyra; island capitals are often just called Chora (town), no matter what their formal title; and Panepistimiou, a main Athens boulevard, is officially named Eleftheriou Venizelou, but if you ask for that, no one will know what you're talking about. A long street may change names several times, and a city may have more than one street by the same name, so know the district you're headed for, or a major landmark nearby, especially if you're taking a taxi. In this guide, street numbers appear after the street name. Finally, there are odd- and even-numbered sides of the streets, but No. 124 could be several blocks from No. 125.

▌ ACCOMMODATIONS

When it comes to making reservations, it is wise to book several months in advance for the high season, from June through August, especially when booking top-end hotels in high-profile destinations like Santorini and Hydra. Accommodations may be hard to find in smaller summer resort towns in winter (when many hotels close for repairs) and at the beginning of spring.

Many hotels have reduced their prices to remain competitive in the face of the country's ongoing economic crisis. Sometimes during off-season you can bargain down the official prices even further (rumor has it to as much as a quarter of the officially quoted price). So be sure to ask if there are any additional discounts for the off-season. The response you get will depend largely on the length of your stay, the hotel's policy, and the season in question. You can also reduce the price by eliminating breakfast or by going through a local travel agency, particularly for larger hotels on major islands and in Athens and Thessaloniki. (In Greece, travel agencies still make a lot of the hotel bookings and often offer preferred rates.) A 6.5% government Value-Added Tax and 0.5% municipality tax are added to all hotel bills, though usually the rate quoted includes the tax; be sure to ask. When booking, it's worth asking whether or not the hotel provides transportation from the airport/port as part of their services.

Plumbing in rooms and most low-end hotels (and restaurants, shops, and other public places) is delicate enough to require that toilet paper and other detritus be put in the wastebasket and not flushed.

The lodgings we list are the cream of the crop in each price category. When pricing accommodations, always ask what's included and what's not. Common items that may add to your basic room rate are breakfast, parking, use of certain facilities such as tennis courts, the spa, or gym, Wi-Fi, etc.

Note that some resort hotels also offer half- and full-board arrangements for part of the year. And all-inclusive resorts are mushrooming. Inquire about your options when booking.

For price charts detailing our array of hotel price categories, see Planning in every regional chapter.

HOTELS

The EOT (GNTO) authorizes the construction and classification of hotels throughout Greece. It classifies them into five categories, A–E, which govern the rates that can be charged. Ratings are based on considerations such as room size, hotel services, and amenities including the furnishing of the room. Within each category, quality varies greatly, but prices don't. Still, you may come across an A-category hotel that charges less than a B-class. The classifications can be misleading—a C-rated hotel in one town might qualify as a B in another.

For category A expect the equivalent of a 5-star hotel in the United States, although the room will probably be somewhat smaller. A room in a C-class hotel can be perfectly acceptable; with a D the bathroom may or may not be shared. Ask to see the room before checking in. You can sometimes find a bargain if a hotel has just renovated but has not yet been reclassified. A great hotel may never move up to a better category just because its lobby isn't the required size.

Official prices are posted in each room, usually on the back of the door or inside the wardrobe. The room charge varies over the course of the year, peaking in the high season when breakfast or half-board (at hotel complexes) may also be obligatory.

A hotel may ask for a deposit of the first night's stay or up to 25% of the room rate. If you cancel your reservations at least 21 days in advance, you are entitled to a full refund of your deposit.

Unless otherwise noted, in this guide, hotels have air-conditioning (*climatismo*), room TVs, and private bathrooms (*banio*). Bathrooms mostly contain showers, though some older or more luxurious hotels may have tubs. Beds are usually twins (*diklina*). If you want a double bed, ask for a *diplo krevati*. In upper-end hotels, the mattresses are full- or queen-size.

Use the following as a guide to making accommodations inquiries: to reserve a double room, *thelo na kleiso ena diklino*; with a bath, *me banio*; without a bath, *horis banio*; or a room with a view, *domatio me thea*. If you need a quiet room (*isiho domatio*), get one with double-glazed windows (*dipla parathyra*) and air-conditioning, away from the elevator and public areas, as high up (*psila*) as possible, and off the street.

RENTAL ROOMS

For low-cost accommodations, consider Greece's ubiquitous "rooms to rent": bed-and-breakfasts without the breakfast. You can count on a clean room, often with such amenities as a terrace, air-conditioning, and a private bath, at a very reasonable price, in the range of €40–€50 for two. Look for signs in any Greek town or village; or, let the proprietors find you—they have a knack for spotting strangers who look like they might need a bed for the night. When renting a room, take a good look first and be sure to check the bathroom before you commit. If there are extra beds in the room, clarify in advance that the amount agreed on is for the entire room—owners occasionally try to put another person in the same room.

When approached by one of the touts who meet the island ferries, make sure he or she tells you the location of the rooms being pushed, and look before you commit. Avoid places on main roads or near all-night discos. Around August 15 (an important religious holiday of the Greek Orthodox Church, commemorating the Assumption of the Virgin Mary), when it seems all Greeks go on vacation, even the most-basic rooms are almost impossible to locate, although you can query the tourist police or the municipal tourist office. On some islands, the local rental room owners' association sets up an information booth.

▌ COMMUNICATIONS

INTERNET

Major hotels have high-speed Internet connections in rooms, and most smaller ones have at least a terminal in the lounge for guests' use. Telecom privatization has helped Greece close the Internet gap with other European countries and, especially on touristed islands, you'll find most cafés offer Wi-Fi, often for free.

The City of Athens offers free Wi-Fi access in Syntagma Square, Thissio, Gazi-Karameikos, and Platia Kotzia (Kotzia Square), and a number of rural towns also have free Wi-Fi in public areas. If your cell phone works in Greece and you have a connection kit for your laptop, then you can buy a mobile connect card to get online. Head to the national electronic store chains Plaisio, Multirama, and Germanos to purchase mobile Internet access within Greece by the day, week, or month.

Computer parts, batteries, and adaptors of any brand are expensive in Greece and may not be in stock when you need them, so carry spares for your laptop. Also note that many upscale hotels will rent you a laptop.

Contacts City of Athens Wi-Fi Spots. This has a list of Wi-Fi hook-up spots and cafés in Athens. ⊕ www.athenswifi.gr. **Cybercafes.** The website lists more than 4,200 Internet cafés in 141 countries around the world. ⊕ www.cybercafes.com. **Free Wi-Fi in Greece.** This website lists free Wi-Fi Internet hotspots in Greece, according to region. ⊕ www.free-wifi.gr.

PHONES

Greece's phone system has improved markedly. You can direct dial in most better hotels, but there is usually a huge surcharge, so use your calling card or a card telephone in the lobby or on the street. You can make calls from most large establishments, kiosks, card phones (which are everywhere), and from the local office of Greece's major telephone company, known as OTE ("oh-*teh*").

Establishments may have several phone numbers rather than a central switchboard. Also, many now use mobile phones, indicated by an area code that begins with 69.

Doing business over the phone in Greece can be frustrating—the lines always seem to be busy, and English-speaking operators and clerks are few. You may also find people too busy to address your problem—the independent-minded Greeks are *not* service-conscious. It is far better to develop a relationship with someone, for example a travel agent, to get information about ferry schedules and the like, or to go in person and ask for information face-to-face. Though OTE has updated its phone system in recent years, it may still take you several attempts to get through when calling from an island or the countryside.

The country code for Greece is 30. When dialing Greece from the United States, Canada, or Australia, first dial 011, then 30, the country code, before punching in the area code and local number. From continental Europe, the United Kingdom, or New Zealand, start with 0030.

CALLING WITHIN GREECE

For Greek directory information, dial 11888; many operators speak English. In most cases you must give the surname of the shop or restaurant proprietor to be able to get the phone number of the establishment; tourist police are more helpful for tracking down the numbers of such establishments.

Pronunciations for the numbers in Greek are: one ("*eh*-na"); two ("*dthee*-oh"); three ("*tree*-a"); four ("*tess*-ehr-a"); five ("*pen*-de"); six ("*eh*-ksee"); seven ("ef-*ta*"); eight ("och-*toh*"); nine ("eh-*nay*-ah"); ten ("*dtheh*-ka").

All telephone numbers in Greece have 10 digits. Area codes now have to be dialed even when you are dialing locally. For cell phones, dial both the cell prefix (a four-digit number beginning with 69) and the telephone number from anywhere in Greece.

CUSTOMS OF THE COUNTRY

Greeks are friendly and openly affectionate. It is not uncommon, for example, to see women strolling arm in arm, or men two-cheek kissing and hugging each other. Displays of anger are also quite common. To the person who doesn't understand Greek, the loud, intense conversations may all sound angry—but they're not. But there's a negative side to Greeks' outgoing nature. Eager to engage in conversation over any topic, they won't shy away from launching into political discussions about the state of the economy or foreign policy (best politely avoided) or asking personal questions like how much money you earn. The latter isn't considered rude in Greece, but don't feel like you need to respond. Visitors are sometimes taken aback by Greeks' gestures or the ease in which they touch the person to whom they're speaking—take it all in stride. If a pat on the hand becomes a bit too intimate, just shift politely and the other person will take a hint. On the other hand, kissing someone you've just met good-bye on the cheek is quite acceptable—even between men.

GREETINGS AND GESTURES

When you meet someone for the first time, it is customary to shake hands, but with acquaintances the usual is a two-cheek kiss hello and good-bye. One thing that may disconcert foreigners is that when they run into a Greek with another person, he or she usually doesn't introduce the other party, even if there is a long verbal exchange. If you can't stand it anymore, just introduce yourself. Greeks tend to stand closer to people than North Americans and northern Europeans, and they rely more on gestures when communicating. One gesture you should never use is the open palm, fingers slightly spread, shoved toward someone's face. The *moutza* is a serious insult. Another gesture you should remember, especially if trying to catch a taxi, is the Greek "no," which looks like "yes": a slight or exaggerated (depending on the sentiment) tipping back of the head, sometimes with the eyes closed and eyebrows raised. When you wave with your palm toward people, they may interpret it as "come here" instead of "good-bye"; and Greeks often wave good-bye with the palm facing them, which looks like "come here" to English speakers.

OUT ON THE TOWN

Greeks often eat out of communal serving plates, so it's considered normal in informal settings to spear your tomato out of the salad bowl rather than securing an individual portion. Sometimes in tavernas you don't even get your own plate. Note that it is considered *tsigounia*, stinginess, to run separate tabs, especially because much of the meal is to be shared. Greeks either divide the bill equally among the party, no matter who ate what, or one person magnanimously treats. A good host insists that you eat or drink more, and only when you have refused a number of times will you get a reprieve; be charmingly persistent in your "No." Always keep in mind that Greeks have a loose sense of time! They may be punctual if meeting you to go to a movie, but if they say they'll come by your hotel at 7 pm, they may show up at 8 pm.

You can make local calls from the public OTE phones using phone cards, not coins.

Keep in mind since there are more cell phone users than ever, OTE hasn't bothered to repair or replace broken phone booths. Some kiosks may also have metered telephones, which allow you to make local or international calls.

CALLING OUTSIDE GREECE

To place an international call from Greece, dial 00 to connect to an international network, then dial the country code (for the United States and Canada, it's 1), and then the area code and number. If you need assistance, call 134 to be connected to an international operator. You can use AT&T, Sprint, and MCI services from public phones as well as from hotels.

Long-Distance Carriers AT&T ☎ *800/225-5288*. **MCI-Verizon** ☎ *800/888-8000, 800/444-3333*. **Sprint** ☎ *1-800/877-7746*.

Access Codes AT&T Direct ☎ *00/800-1311 for Greece, 1-800/225-5288 in U.S.* **MCI-Verizon WorldPhone** ☎ *00/800-1211 for Greece, 1-800/888-8000 in U.S.* **Sprint International Access** ☎ *00/800-1411 in Greece, 800/877-4646 in the U.S.*

CALLING CARDS

Phone cards worth €4 or €10 can be purchased at kiosks, convenience stores, or the local OTE office and are the easiest way to make calls from anywhere in Greece. These phone cards can be used for domestic and international calls (the Chronocarta phone card especially costs €6 and allows one to talk for up to 290 minutes to U.S. and Canadian land lines and mobile phones). Once you insert the phone card, the number of units on the card will appear; as you begin talking, the units will go down. Once all the units have been used, the card does not get recharged—you must purchase another.

MOBILE PHONES

If you have a multiband phone (some countries use different frequencies from what's used in the United States) and your service provider uses the world-standard GSM network (as do T-Mobile, AT&T, and Verizon), you can probably use your phone abroad. Roaming fees can be steep, however: 99¢ a minute is considered reasonable. And overseas you normally pay the toll charges for incoming calls. It's almost always cheaper to send a text message than to make a call, since text messages have a very low set fee (often less than 5¢). In Greek mobile phone contracts, only the caller and not the person receiving the call can be charged for local phone calls (both are charged for international calls, however).

If you just want to make local calls, consider buying a new SIM card (note that your provider may have to unlock your phone for you to use a different SIM card) and a prepaid service plan in the destination. You'll then have a local number and can make local calls at local rates. If your trip is extensive, you could also simply buy a new cell phone in your destination, as the initial cost will be offset over time.

■ TIP→ **If you travel internationally frequently, save one of your old mobile phones or buy a cheap one on the Internet; ask your cell phone company to unlock it for you, and take it with you as a travel phone, buying a new SIM card with pay-as-you-go service in each destination.**

If you take your cell phone with you, call your provider in advance and ask if it has a connection agreement with a Greek mobile carrier. If so, manually switch your phone to that network's settings as soon as you arrive. To do this, go to the Settings menu, then look for the Network settings and follow the prompts.

If you're traveling with a companion or group of friends and plan to use your cell phones to communicate with each other, buying a local prepaid connection kit is far cheaper for voice calls or sending text messages than using your regular provider. The most popular local prepaid connection kits are Cosmote's What's Up, Vodafone's Unlimited and CU, or Wind's

F2G or Card To All—these carriers all have branded stores, but you can also buy cell phones and cell phone packages from the Germanos and Plaisio chain stores as well as large supermarkets like Carrefour.

Contacts Cellular Abroad. This company rents and sells cell phones and sells SIM cards that work in many countries. ☎ 800/287–5072, 310/862–7100 ⊕ www.cellularabroad.com. **Mobal.** This company rents mobiles and sells GSM cell phones (starting at $29) that will operate in more than 170 countries. Per-call rates are charged per minute, there are no monthly or annual service charges and vary throughout the world. ☎ 888/888–9162 ⊕ www.mobal.com. **Planet Fone.** This company rents cell phones, but the per-minute rates are expensive. ☎ 888/988–4777 ⊕ www. planetfone.com.

▌ CUSTOMS AND DUTIES

For non-EU citizens, foreign banknotes amounting to more than $2,500 must be declared for re-export.

Only one per person of such expensive portable items as cameras, camcorders, computers, and the like is permitted into Greece. You should register these with Greek Customs upon arrival to avoid any problems when taking them out of the country again. Sports equipment, such as bicycles and skis, is also limited to one (or one pair) per person. One windsurf board per person may be imported/exported duty-free.

To bring in a dog or a cat, they must have a pet passport and be identified by the electronic identification system (microchip) according to ISO standard 11794 or 11785. They must also have been vaccinated against rabies. Traveling pets must also be accompanied by a health certificate for noncommercial movement of pets (regulation EC No. 998/2003) endorsed by a USDA state veterinarian.

For more information on Greek Customs, check with your local Greek Consulate or the Greek Ministry of Finance in Athens, which has more-detailed information on customs and import/export regulations.

Finally, there are also limits to the amount of goods you can bring back to the United States duty-free. The U.S. Customs and Border Protection department maintains accurate information on those limits.

Contacts in Greece Ministry of Finance - Customs Office ☎ 210/354–2138 Foreign exchange declaration, 210/354–2122 Information ⊕ www.gsis.gr.

Contacts in the United States U.S. Customs and Border Protection ⊕ www.cbp.gov.

▌ EATING OUT

MEALS AND MEALTIMES

Greeks don't really sit down for breakfast, so with the exception of hotels, few places serve that meal. You can pick up a cheese pie, a baguette sandwich, and rolls at a bakery or a sesame-coated bread ring called a *koulouri* sold by city vendors; order a *tost* ("toast"), a sort of dry grilled sandwich, usually with cheese or paper-thin ham slices, at a café; or dig into a plate of yogurt with honey. Local bakeries may offer fresh doughnuts in the morning. On the islands in summer, cafés serve breakfast, from Continental to combinations that might include Spanish omelets and French coffee. Caffeine junkies can get a cup of coffee practically anywhere.

Greeks eat their main meal at either lunch or dinner, so the offerings are the same. For lunch, heavyweight meat-and-potato dishes can be had, but you might prefer a real Greek salad (no lettuce, a slice of feta with a pinch of oregano, and ripe tomatoes, cucumber, onions, and green peppers) or souvlaki or grilled chicken from a taverna. For a light bite you can also try one of the popular Greek chain eateries such as Everest or Grigori's for grilled sandwiches or spanakopita and *tiropita* (cheese pie); or Goody's, the local equivalent of McDonald's, where you'll find good-quality burgers, pasta dishes, and salads.

Coffee and pastries are eaten in the afternoon, usually at a café or *zaharoplastio* (pastry shop). The hour or so before restaurants open for dinner—around 7—is a pleasant time to have an ouzo or glass of wine and try Greek hors d'oeuvres, called *mezedes,* in a bar, *ouzeri,* or *mezedopoleio* (Greek tapas place). Dinner is often the main meal of the day, and there's plenty of food. Starters include dips such as *taramosalata* (made from fish roe), *melitzanosalata* (made from smoked eggplant, lemon, oil, and garlic), and the well-known yogurt, cucumber, and garlic *tzatziki.* A typical dinner for a couple might be two to three appetizers, an entrée, a salad, and wine. Diners can order as little or as much as they like, except at very expensive establishments. If a Greek eats dessert at all, it will be fruit or a modest wedge of a syrup-drenched cake like *ravani* or semolina halvah, often shared between two or three diners. Only in fancier restaurants might diners order a tiramisu or crème brûleé with an espresso. One option for those who want a lighter, shared meal is the mezedopoleio.

In most places, the menu is broken down into appetizers (*orektika*) and entrées (*kiria piata*), with additional headings for salads (Greek salad or *horta,* boiled wild greens; this also includes dips like tzatziki) and vegetable side plates. But this doesn't mean there is any sense of a first or second "course," as in France. Often the food arrives all at the same time, or as it becomes ready.

Breakfast is usually available until 10:30 or 11 at many hotels and until early afternoon in beach cafés. Lunch is between 1:00 and 6 (especially during summer months), and dinner is served from about 8:00 to midnight, or even later in the big cities and resort islands. Most Greeks dine very late, around 10 or 11 pm. Unless otherwise noted, the restaurants listed in this guide are open daily for lunch and dinner.

PAYING

For restaurant price categories, see the Planning section in every regional chapter. For guidelines on tipping see Tipping, below.

RESERVATIONS AND DRESS

Regardless of where you are, it's a good idea to make a reservation if you can. In some places (especially the more upmarket restaurants), it's expected. We only mention them specifically when reservations are essential (there's no other way you'll ever get a table) or when they are not accepted. For popular restaurants, book as far ahead as you can and reconfirm on the day of your reservation. (Large parties should always call ahead to check the reservations policy.) We mention dress only when men are required to wear a jacket or a jacket and tie.

▌ ELECTRICITY

The electrical current in Greece is 220 volts, 50 cycles AC. Wall outlets take Continental-type plugs with two round oversize prongs. If your appliances are dual-voltage, you'll need only an adapter; if not, you'll also need a step-down converter/transformer (United States and Canada).

Consider making a small investment in a universal adapter, which has several types of plugs in one lightweight, compact unit. Most laptops and mobile phone chargers are dual voltage (i.e., they operate equally well on 110 and 220 volts) so require only an adapter. These days the same is true of small appliances such as hair dryers. Always check labels and manufacturer instructions to be sure. Don't use 110-volt outlets marked "for shavers only" for high-wattage appliances such as hair dryers.

Contacts Steve Kropla's Help for World Travelers. This website has information on electrical and telephone plugs around the world. ⊕ *www.kropla.com.* **Walkabout Travel Gear.** This website has a good coverage of electricity under "adapters." ⊕ *www. walkabouttravelgear.com.*

▌ EMERGENCIES

Regrettably, vacations are sometimes marred by emergencies, so it's good to know where you should turn for help. In Athens and other cities, hospitals treat emergencies on a rotating basis; an ambulance driver will know where to take you. Or, since waving down a taxi can be faster than waiting for an ambulance, ask a cab driver to take you to the closest "*e-phee-me-re-von*" (duty) hospital. Large islands and rural towns have small medical centers (*iatreio*) that can treat minor illnesses or arrange for transport to another facility.

Medications are only sold at pharmacies, which are by law staffed by licensed pharmacists who can treat minor cuts, take blood pressure, and recommend cold medication. Pharmacies are marked with a green-and-white cross and there's one every few city blocks. Outside standard trading hours, there are duty pharmacies offering 24-hour coverage. These are posted in the window of every pharmacy. The tourist police throughout Greece can provide general information and help in emergencies and can mediate in disputes.

Foreign Embassy Embassy of the United States of America ✉ *Vasilissis Sofias 91, Mavili Sq., Athens* ☎ *210/721–2951 Switchboard* ⊕ *athens.usembassy.gov.*

▌ HEALTH

Greece's strong summer sun and low humidity can lead to sunburn or sunstroke if you're not careful. A hat, a light-color long-sleeve shirt, and long pants or a sarong are advised for spending a day at the beach or visiting archaeological sites. Sunglasses, a hat, and sunscreen are necessities, and be sure to drink plenty of water. Most beaches present few dangers, but keep a lookout for the occasional jellyfish and, on rocky coves, sea urchins. Should you step on one, don't break off the embedded spines, which may lead to infection, but instead remove them with heated olive oil and a needle. Food is seldom a problem, but the liberal amounts of olive oil used in Greek cooking may be indigestible for some. Tap water in Greece is fine in most urban areas, and bottled spring water is readily available. Avoid drinking tap water in many rural areas.

In greener, wetter areas, mosquitoes may be a problem. In addition to wearing insect repellent, you can burn coils ("*spee-rahl*") or buy plug-in devices that burn medicated tabs ("pah-*steel*-ya"). Hotels usually provide these. Citronella candles are usually an effective and more natural way to keep insects away. The only poisonous snakes in Greece are the adder and the sand viper, which are brown or red, with dark zigzags. The adder has a V or X behind its head, and the sand viper sports a small horn on its nose. When hiking, wear high tops and hiking socks and don't put your feet or hands in crevices without looking first. If bitten, try to slow the spread of the venom until a doctor comes. Lie still with the affected limb lower than the rest of your body. Apply a tourniquet, releasing it every few minutes, and cut the wound a bit in case the venom can bleed out. Do NOT suck on the bite. Whereas snakes like to lie in the sun, the scorpion (rare) likes cool, wet places, in woodpiles and under stones. Apply Benadryl or Phenergan to minor stings, but if you have nausea or fever, see a doctor at once.

For minor ailments, go to a local pharmacy first, where the licensed staff can make recommendations for over-the-counter drugs. Most pharmacies are closed in the evenings and on weekends, but each posts the name of the nearest pharmacy open off-hours. Most state hospitals and rural clinics won't charge you for tending to minor ailments, even if you're not an EU citizen; at most, you'll pay a minimal fee. For a doctor or dentist, check with your hotel, embassy, or the tourist police.

Do not fly within 24 hours of scuba diving.

▎HOURS OF OPERATION

Most business and retail stores are open weekdays 6 am–9 pm, Saturday 6 am–8 pm, and are closed on Sunday (some more traditional shop owners close for a few hours on Monday, Wednesday, and Saturday afternoons). But each establishment is at the discretion of establishing its own particular timetable within those limits, and establishments in tourist resorts may remain open longer, even after midnight. In 2014, a controversial law was passed for retail businesses in certain areas of Greece, frequented by tourists, to remain open on Sunday. They include Athens, Rafina, Thessaloniki, Chalkidiki, and the islands of Rhodes, Kos, Syros, Mykonos, and Santorini.

For certain categories such as pharmacies, banks, and government offices, hours have always been standardized, but again there are some establishments in tourist resorts that follow extended hours.

Many small businesses and shops in main urban hubs close for at least a week around mid-August, and most tourist establishments, including hotels, shut down on the islands and northern Greece from November until mid-spring. Restaurants, especially tavernas, often stay open on holidays; some close in summer or move to cooler locations. Christmas, New Year's, Orthodox Easter, and August 15 are the days everything shuts down, although, for example, bars work full force on Christmas Eve, since it's a social occasion and not particularly family-oriented. Orthodox Easter changes dates every year, so check your calendar. On Orthodox Easter Week, most shops follow a different schedule while on Good Friday, shops open after church services, around 1 pm.

Banks are normally open Monday through Thursday 8–2:30, Friday 8–2, but a few branches of Alpha and Eurobank are open until 7 pm weekdays and on Saturday morning. Hotels also cash traveler's checks on weekends, and the banks at the Athens airport have longer hours.

Government offices are open weekdays from 8 to 2. For commercial offices, the hours depend on the business, although most private companies have by now adopted the 9–5 schedule.

All gas stations are open daily 6–9 (some close Sunday). These hours are extended during the high season (usually from May 1 to September 30) from 6 am to 10:30 pm and some stations pump all night in the major cities and along the National road and Attica highway. They do not close for lunch.

Pharmacies are open Monday, Wednesday, and Friday from about 8 to 2:30 and Tuesday, Thursday, and Friday from 8 to 2 and 5:30 until 8:30 at night. The pharmacy at Athens International Airport operates 24 hours. According to a rotation system, there is always at least one pharmacy open in any area (⇨ *Emergencies, above*).

If it's late in the evening and you need an aspirin, a soft drink, cigarettes, a newspaper, or a pen, look for the nearest open kiosk, called a *periptero*; these kiosks on street corners everywhere brim with all kinds of necessities. Owners stagger their hours, and many towns have at least one kiosk that stays open late, occasionally through the night. Neighborhood mini-markets also stay open late.

NATIONAL HOLIDAYS

January 1 (New Year's Day); January 6 (Epiphany); Clean Monday (first day of Lent); March 25 (Feast of the Annunciation and Independence Day); Good Friday; Greek Easter Sunday; Greek Easter Monday; May 1 (Labor Day); Pentecost; August 15 (Assumption of the Holy Virgin); October 28 (Ochi Day); December 25–26 (Christmas Day and Boxing Day).

Only on Orthodox Easter and August 15 do you find that just about *everything* shuts down. It's harder getting a room at the last minute on these days (especially the latter), and traveling requires stamina if you want to survive on the ferries and the highways. On the other hand, the local rituals and rites associated with these two celebrations are interesting and occasionally moving (like the Epitaphios procession on Good Friday).

▌MAIL

Letters and postcards take about five days to reach the United States. That's airmail. It takes even longer in August, when postal staff is reduced; and during Christmas and Easter holidays. If what you're mailing is important, send it registered, which costs about €3.40 in Greece. For about €2.35 for a 20-gram envelope or postcard (with the cost increasing depending on the weight), you can send your letter "express"; this earns you a red sticker and faster local delivery. The ELTA post office also operates a courier service, EMS Express (otherwise known as ELTA courier). Delivery to the continental United States takes about two to four days, and costs €40. Packages take three to five days and cost depends on the weight. If you're planning on writing several letters, prepaid envelopes are convenient and cost €0.95 each.

Post offices are open weekdays 7:30–2, although in city centers they may stay open in the evenings and on weekends. The main post offices in Athens and Piraeus are open weekdays 7:30 am–8 pm, Saturday 7:30–2, and Sunday 9–1:30.

The post offices at Athens International Airport and the Acropolis are open weekends, too. Throughout the country, mailboxes are yellow and sometimes divided into domestic and international containers; express boxes are red.

At this writing, airmail letters and postcards to destinations other than Europe and weighing up to 20 grams cost €0.90, and €1.45 for 50 grams (€0.90 and €1.30, respectively, to other European countries, including the United Kingdom).

Contacts Hellenic Post (ELTA) ☎ *800/118–2000 Toll-free, 210/335-3777* ⊕ *www.elta.gr.*

▌MONEY

Although costs have risen astronomically since Greece switched to the euro currency in 2002, the country will seem reasonably priced to travelers from the United States and Great Britain. Popular tourist resorts (including some of the islands) and the larger cities are markedly more expensive than the countryside. Though the price of eating in a restaurant has increased, you can still get a bargain. Hotels are generally moderately priced outside the major cities, and the extra cost of accommodations in a luxury hotel, compared to in an average hotel, often seems unwarranted.

ITEM	AVERAGE COST
Cup of Coffee	€2.50–€5 (in a central-city café; Greek coffee is a bit cheaper)
Glass of Wine	€5–€8
Glass of Beer	€3.5; €5–€9 in a bar
Sandwich	€2.80–€4
1-mile (½-km) Taxi Ride in Capital City	€3.50
Archaeological Site Admission	€2–€12

Other typical costs: soft drink (can) €1.50, in a café €2.5; spinach pie, €2.20; souvlaki, €2.50; local bus, €1.20; foreign newspaper, €3–€5.30.

Prices throughout this guide are given for adults. Discounts are almost always available for children, students, and senior citizens.

ATMS AND BANKS

Your own bank will probably charge a fee for using ATMs abroad; the foreign bank you use may also charge a fee. Nevertheless, you'll usually get a better rate of exchange at an ATM than you will at a currency-exchange office or even when changing money in a bank. And extracting funds as you need them is a safer option than carrying around a large amount of cash.

■TIP➜ **PIN numbers with more than four digits are not recognized at ATMs in Greece. If yours has five or more, remember to change it before you leave. Letters do not generally appear on Greek ATM keypads.**

ATMs are widely available throughout the country. Virtually all banks, including the National Bank of Greece (known as Ethniki), have machines that dispense money to Cirrus or Plus cardholders. You may find bank-sponsored ATMs at harbors and in airports as well. Other systems accepted include Visa, Master-Card, American Express, Diners Club, and Eurocard, but exchange and withdrawal rates vary, so shop around and check fees with your bank before leaving home. The word for PIN is pronounced "peen," and ATMs are called *alpha taf mi*, after the letters, or just *to mihanima*, "the machine." Machines usually let you complete the transaction in English, French, or German and seldom create problems, except Sunday night, when they sometimes run out of cash. For most machines, the minimum amount dispensed is €20. Sometimes an ATM may refuse to "read" your card. Don't panic; it's probably the machine. Try another bank.

■TIP➜ **At some ATMs in Greece you may not have a choice of drawing from a specific account. If you have linked savings and checking accounts, make sure there's money in both before you depart.**

CREDIT CARDS

It's a good idea to inform your credit-card company before you travel, especially if you don't travel internationally very often. Otherwise, the credit-card company might put a hold on your card owing to unusual activity—not a good thing halfway through your trip. Record all your credit-card numbers—as well as the phone numbers to call if your cards are lost or stolen—in a safe place, so you're prepared should something go wrong. Both MasterCard and Visa have general numbers you can call (collect if you're abroad) if your card is lost, but you're better off calling the number of your issuing bank, since MasterCard and Visa usually just transfer you to your bank; your bank's number is usually printed on your card.

If you plan to use your credit card for cash advances, you'll need to apply for a PIN at least two weeks before your trip. Although it's usually cheaper (and safer) to use a credit card abroad for large purchases (so you can cancel payments or be reimbursed if there's a problem), note that some credit-card companies *and* the banks that issue them add substantial percentages to all foreign transactions, whether they're in a foreign currency or not. Check on these fees before leaving home, so there won't be any surprises when you get the bill.

■TIP➜ **Before you charge something, ask the merchant whether or not he or she plans to do a dynamic currency conversion (DCC). In such a transaction the credit-card *processor* (shop, restaurant, or hotel, not Visa or MasterCard) converts the currency and charges you in dollars. In most cases you'll pay the merchant a 3% fee for this service in addition to any credit-card company and issuing-bank foreign-transaction surcharges.**

Dynamic currency conversion programs are becoming increasingly widespread.

Merchants who participate in them are supposed to ask whether you want to be charged in dollars or the local currency, but they don't always do so. And even if they do offer you a choice, they may well avoid mentioning the additional surcharges. The good news is that you *do* have a choice. And if this practice really gets your goat, you can avoid it entirely thanks to American Express; with its cards, DCC simply isn't an option.

Should you use a credit card or a debit card when traveling? Both have benefits. A credit card allows you to delay payment and gives you certain rights as a consumer. A debit card, also known as a check card, deducts funds directly from your checking account and helps you stay within your budget. When you want to rent a car, though, you may still need an old-fashioned credit card.

Both types of plastic get you cash advances at ATMs worldwide if your card is properly programmed with your personal identification number (PIN). Both offer excellent, wholesale exchange rates. And both protect you against unauthorized use if the card is lost or stolen. Your liability is limited to $50, as long as you report the card missing. But shop owners often give you a lower price if you pay with cash rather than credit, because they want to avoid the credit-card bank fees. Note that the Discover card is not widely accepted in Greece.

Reporting Lost Cards American Express ☎ 800/528–4800 in U.S., 715/343–7977 collect from abroad ⊕ www.americanexpress. com. **Diners Club** ☎ 800/234–6377 in U.S., 303/799–1504 collect from abroad ⊕ www. dinersclub.com. **Discover** ☎ 800/347–2683 in U.S., 801/902–3100 collect from abroad ⊕ www.discovercard.com. **MasterCard** ☎ 800/627–8372 in U.S., 636/722–7111 collect from abroad, 800–11/887–0303 in Greece, toll free ⊕ www.mastercard.com. **Visa** ☎ 800/847–2911 in U.S., 1–303/967–1096 collect from abroad, 800–11/638–0304 toll-free in Greece ⊕ www.visa.com.

CURRENCY AND EXCHANGE

Greece uses the euro. Under the euro system, there are eight coins: 1 and 2 euros, plus 1, 2, 5, 10, 20, and 50 euro cents. Euros are pronounced "evros" in Greek; cents are known as "lepta." All coins have the euro value on one side; the other side has each country's unique national symbol. Greece's images range from triremes to a depiction of the mythological Europa being abducted by Zeus transformed as a bull. Bills (banknotes) come in seven denominations: 5, 10, 20, 50, 100, 200, and 500 euros. Bills are the same for all EU countries.

Off Syntagma Square in Athens, the National Bank of Greece, Alpha Bank, and Pireos Bank have automated machines that change your foreign currency into euros. When you shop, remember that it's always easier to bargain on prices when paying in cash instead of by credit card.

If you do use an exchange service, good options are American Express and Eurochange. Watch daily fluctuations and shop around. Daily exchange rates are prominently displayed in banks and listed in the *International New York Times*. In Athens, around Syntagma Square is the best place to look. In some tourist resorts you might be able to change money at the post office, where commissions may be lower than at banks. To avoid lines at airport exchange booths, get a bit of local currency before you leave home.

▓**TIP→ Even if a currency-exchange booth has a sign promising no commission, rest assured that there's some kind of substantial, hidden fee. (Oh . . . that's right. The sign didn't say no fee.) And as for rates, you're almost always better off getting foreign currency at an ATM or exchanging money at a bank.**

Eurochange ✉ *Karageorgi Servias 2, Syntagma, Athens* ☎ *210/331–2462* ⊕ *www. eurochange.gr* ⊗ *9-9 daily.*

Kapa Change ✉ *Filellinon 1, Syntagma, Athens* ☎ *210/331–3830* ⊕ *www.kapachange. gr* ⊗ *Mon.–Sat. 8:30–8:30, Sun. 8:30–5.*

Bank of Greece. Greece's Central Bank offers foreign exchange at competitive rates. ✉ *21 Panepistimiou (El. Venizelou) ave., Syntagma, Athens* ☎ *210/320–1111* ⊗ *Mon.–Thurs. 8–2:30, Fri. 8–2.*

National Bank of Greece. This offers extended foreign exchange. ✉ *Karageorgi Servias 2, Syntagma, Athens* ☎ *210/334–8015* ⊗ *Mon.–Thurs. 8–2:30, Fri. 8–2.*

▌ PASSPORTS AND VISAS

All citizens (even infants) of the United States, Canada, Australia, and New Zealand need only a valid passport to enter Greece for stays of up to 90 days. Your passport should be valid for at least three months beyond the period of your stay. If you leave after 90 days and don't have a visa extension, you will be fined anywhere from €600 to €1,300 (depending on how long you overstay) by Greek airport officials, who are not flexible on this issue. Even worse perhaps, you must provide *hartosima* (revenue stamps) for the documents, which you don't want to have to run around and find as your flight is boarding. If you want to extend your stay beyond 90 days, there is heavy bureaucracy involved but eventually you will be able to do it for a cost of about €150. Inquire at your local police station for details.

If you are going to visit Greece, you can enroll to the Smart Traveler Enrollment Program of the U.S. Embassy in Greece. Then, you can be kept up-to-date with important safety and security announcements. Enrolling also will help your friends and family get in touch with you in an emergency.

▌TIP→ Before your trip, make two copies of your passport's data page (one for someone at home and another for you to carry separately). Or scan the page and email it to someone at home and/or yourself.

VISAS

U.S. citizens traveling to Greece do not need visas. Greece is a party to the Schengen Agreement. As such, U.S. citizens may enter Greece for up to 90 days for tourist or business purposes without a visa. Your passport should be valid for at least three months beyond the period of your stay. You may also need to demonstrate at the port of entry that you have sufficient funds for your trip and that you have a return airline ticket.

U.S. Passport Information U.S. Department of State ☎ *877/487–2778* ⊕ *travel.state.gov/passport.*

▌ TAXES

Taxes are typically included in all quoted prices.

Value-Added Tax, 6.5% for books and 23% (V.A.T. is 15% on some remote Aegean islands) for almost everything else, called FPA (pronounced "fee-pee-ah") by Greeks, is included in the cost of most consumer goods and services, including most groceries. If you are a citizen of a non-EU country, you may get a V.A.T. refund on products (except alcohol, cigarettes, or toiletries) worth €120 or more bought in Greece in one shopping spree from licensed stores that usually display a Tax-Free Shopping sticker in their window. Ask the shop to complete a refund form called a Tax-Free Check receipt for you, which you show at Greek customs.

Have the form stamped like any customs form by customs officials when you leave the country or, if you're visiting several European Union countries, when you leave the EU. Be ready to show customs officials what you've bought (pack purchases together, in your carry-on luggage); budget extra time for this. After you're through passport control, take the form to a refund-service counter for an on-the-spot refund, or mail it back in the pre-addressed envelope given to you at the store. You receive the total refund stated on the form, but the processing time can be long, especially if you request a credit-card adjustment. Note that there are no cash refunds issued in the United States anymore.

If you are leaving from the Eleftherios Venizelos airport for a country outside the EU, after your Tax-Free Check form has been stamped, you can go directly to the Eurochange bureau de change (extra-Schengen area, Gates 1–4) and get your refund cash.

A refund service can save you some hassle, for a fee. Global Blue is a Europe-wide service with 300,000 affiliated stores and more than 200 international tax refund offices at major airports and border crossings. The service issues refunds in the form of cash, check, or credit-card adjustment, minus a processing fee. If you don't have time to wait at the refund counter, you can mail in the form instead.

V.A.T. Refunds Global Blue ☎ *+421/232–111111* ⊕ *www.global-blue.com.*

▌ TIME

Greek time is Greenwich Mean Time (GMT) plus two hours. To estimate the time back home, subtract 7 hours from the local time for New York and Washington, 8 hours for Chicago, 9 for Denver, and 10 for Los Angeles. Londoners subtract two hours. Those living in Sydney or Melbourne, add eight hours. Greek Daylight Saving Time starts on the last Sunday in March and ends the last Sunday in October. Stay alert—newspapers barely publicize the change.

▌ TIPPING

How much to tip in Greece, especially at restaurants, is confusing and is usually up to the discretion of the individual.

TIPPING GUIDELINES FOR GREECE	
Bartender	10% maximum
Bellhop	€1 per bag
Hotel Concierge	€3–€5, if he or she performs a service for you
Hotel Maid	Up to €10 per stay
Hotel Room-Service Waiter	€2–€3 per delivery, even if a service charge has been added
Porter at Airport or Train Station	€1 per bag
WSW Skycap Services at Airport	€1–€3 per bag checked
Taxi Driver	Round up the fare to the nearest €0.50 or €1
Tour Guide	10% of fee
Waiter	By law a 13% service charge is figured into the price of a meal; however, it is customary to round up the bill if the service was satisfactory. During the Christmas and Greek Easter holiday periods, restaurants tack on an obligatory 18% holiday bonus to your bill for the waiters.
Others	For restroom attendants €1–2 is appropriate. People dispensing programs at theaters get about €2.

■ TRAVEL AGENTS

Many travel arrangements in Greece are still made (and indeed better made) through travel agencies. There are countless travel agents in Greece, and as is the case anywhere, the service you get makes a difference. Some agents simply want to confirm as many bookings as possible then move on, but when you find an agent who understands that bespoke personalized attention is great for you and for future business, you'll find no more helpful professional. Greek travel agents who do the job right can take the headache out of figuring out the logistics behind your dream Greek itinerary. They know the ins and outs of the ferry systems from timetables to schedules, they can suggest which accommodations suit your style, and they can propose tours that interest you. And they can often get you better prices than you can find on your own, even through popular discounters.

If you are traveling in July and August, travel agencies can come to the rescue with pre-set packages for the islands you want to visit or suggest other options from archeological sites, mountain trips, or coastal villages. *See the individual destination chapters for more local recommendations.*

Dolphin Hellas Travel. Dolphin Hellas has been working with travelers worldwide since 1970. They pride themselves on tailor-made trip planning. They specialize in group, honeymoon, and individual travel that includes hotel and villa rentals, cruises, and transportation services. Through their website clients can check online ferry schedules and make reservations. If you are planning a trip to Greece, contact this agency in advance, especially before booking your hotels, to see if their prices are better than what you can find on your own. ⊠ *Syngrou 16, Athens* ☎ *210/922–7772 in Athens* ⊕ *www. dolphin-hellas.gr.*

Fantasy Travel. Since 1983, Fantasy Travel's agents aim to offer personalized service when planning travel for their clients that visit Greece. They specialize in cruises, tours, island-hopping itineraries, bespoke vacation packages, and more. ⊠ *Filillenon 19, Athens* ☎ *210/331–0530* ⊕ *www.fantasytravelofgreece.com.*

Navigator. If you are looking for a Greece-based travel agency through which to book a cruise, you can do no better than Navigator. With decades of experience in the travel agency business, the agency specializes in Greek island cruises. ⊠ *Athens* ☎ *210/360–9801 in Athens* ⊕ *www. navigator.gr.*

■ VISITOR INFORMATION

Tourist police, stationed near the most-popular tourist sites, can answer questions in English about transportation, steer you to an open pharmacy or doctor, and locate phone numbers of hotels, rooms, and restaurants. You can download maps, brochures, and guides from the Greek National Tourism Organization website. The complete *Greek Travel Pages* is available online and is a valuable resource for all travel in Greece.

Contacts Greek National Tourism Organization (*GNTO*). ⊠ *305 East 47th St., New York, New York, USA* ☎ *212/421–5777* ⊕ *www. visitgreece.gr.* **Greek Travel Pages** ⊠ *International Publications Ltd., Psylla 6, Athens* ☎ *210/324–7511* ⊕ *www.gtp.gr.*

INDEX

PHOTO CREDITS

Front cover: Anastasios71/Shutterstock. [Description: Caryatids in Erechtheum from Athenian Acropolis]. 1, T. Papageorgiou/age fotostock. 2, MomofZeus, Fodors.com member. 5, Ciprian Dumitrescu/ iStockphoto. Chapter 1: Experience Greece: 8-9, Johanna Huber/simephoto/eStock Photo. 10, aggsPanorama, Fodors.com member. 11 (left), Evy73, Fodors.com member. 11 (right), Pascal Arseneau, Fodors.com member. 12, Pierdelune/Shutterstock. 13 (left), Natalia Pavlova/iStockphoto. 13 (right), Georgios Alexandris/Shutterstock. 14, Greek National Tourism Organization. 15 (left), Meredith, Fodors.com member. 15 (right), Saso Novoselic/iStockphoto. 20 (left), Marc C. Johnson/Shutterstock. 20 (top center), Mr.checker/wikipedia.org. 20 (bottom center), Betsy Bobo, Fodors.com member. 20 (right), Karel Gallas/Shutterstock. 21 (left), Krishna.Wu/Shutterstock. 21 (top center), PixAchi/Shutterstock. 21 (bottom center), Panos Karapanagiotis/Shutterstock. 21 (right), BlueOrange Studio/Shutterstock. 22, Ken Russell Salvador/wikipedia.org. 23 (left), Netfalls/Shutterstock. 23 (right), Cheryl Jenkins, Fodors.com member. 24, Kristie's/Flickr. 32, Wolfgang Staudt/Flickr. 38, Kreder Katja/age fotostock. 40 (top), Andreas G. Karelias/Shutterstock. 40 (bottom), Wolfgang Staudt/Flickr. 41 (top), Juergen Richter/age fotostock. 41 (bottom), Netfalls/Shutterstock. 42 (left), Milos Jokic/iStockphoto. 42 (top right), Anders Ljungberg/Flickr. 42 (bottom right), Alfred Rijnders/iStockphoto. 43, Vandelizer/ Flickr. 44, Eric James/Alamy. Chapter 2: Cruising the Greek Islands: 45, Princess Cruises. 46, Sidell Chase/iStockphoto. Chapter 3: Athens: 83, SuperStock/age fotostock. 86, Andreas Trepte/wikipedia. org. 98-99, SIME s.a.s/eStock Photo. 100, Vidler/age fotostock. 101, Kord.com/age fotostock. 104, Juha-Pekka Kervinen/Shutterstock. 105, Green Bear/Shutterstock. 106 (top left), Javier Larrea/age fotostock. 106 (bottom left and bottom right), Visual Arts Library (London)/Alamy. 106 (top right), wikipedia.org. 107 (top left), Mary Evans Picture Library/Alamy. 107 (top right), Picture History/Newscom. 107 (bottom), POPPERFOTO/Alamy. 116, George Kavallierakis/age fotostock. 121, P. Narayan/age fotostock. 129, bobthenavigator, Fodors.com member. 135, Stefan Obermeier/age fotostock. 168, Alvaro Leiva/age fotostock. 187, vittorio sciosia/age fotostock. 188 (top left), Elpis Ioannidis/Shutterstock. 188 (bottom left), Bridget McGill/iStockphoto. 188 (right), Charles Stirling (Travel)/Alamy. 189 (left), Amal Sajdak/iStockphoto. 189 (top right), Inger Anne Hulbækdal/Shutterstock. 189 (bottom right), Rene Mattes/age fotostock. Chapter 4: Attica and Delphi: 191, Krishna.Wu/Shutterstock. 192, byrdiegyrl/Flickr. 194, Andreykr | Dreamstime.com. 201, Hercules Milas / Alamy. 211, stefano lunardi/age fotostock. 227, Wojtek Buss/age fotostock. 237, Wojtek Buss/age fotostock. Chapter 5: The Saronic Gulf Islands: 241, Andreas Karelias / Alamy. 252, SMG/age Fotostock. 257, Natalia Pavlova/iStockphoto. 265, vlas2000/Shutterstock. 266 (top), LOOK Die Bildagentur der Fotografen GmbH/Alamy. 266 (bottom), franco pizzochero/age fotostock. 267 (top), Alvaro Leiva/age fotostock. 267 (bottom), Ingolf Pompe/Aurora Photos. 268 (top), foodfolio/Alamy. 268 (2nd from top), Liv friislarsen/Shutterstock. 268 (3rd from top), imagebroker/Alamy. 268 (4th from top), Colin Dutton/SIME s.a.s/eStock Photo. 268 (bottom), IML Image Group Ltd/Alamy. 269 (left), Roberto Meazza/IML Image Group/Aurora Photos. 269 (top right), Christopher Leggett/age fotostock. 269 (center right), IML Image Group Ltd/Alamy. 269 (bottom right), Ingolf Pompe/Aurora Photos. 281, Vaggelis Vlahos/CC by 3.0. 283, IML Image Group Ltd/Alamy. Chapter 6: The Sporades: 285, SIME s.a.s/eStock Photo. 286, Milos Jokic/iStockphoto. 287 (top), iStockphoto. 287 (bottom left), David Newton/iStockphoto. 287 (bottom right), Paul Phillips/iStockphoto. 288, philos from Athens/Flickr. 297, nevio doz/age fotostock. 309, 312, and 317, Robert Harding Produc/age fotostock. 325, Genetzakis/IML/age fotostock. Chapter 7: Epirus and Thessaly: 327, MATTES Renée/age fotostock. 328, Netfalls/Shutterstock. 329 (top), ollirg/Shutterstock. 329 (bottom), Konstantinos Stampoulis/wikipedia.org. 330, Tal Naveh/Shutterstock. 340, Meazza/IML/age fotostock. 343, giulio andreini/age fotostock. 349, DEA PICTURE LIBRARY/age fotostock. 354, R. Matina/age fotostock. 356 (top), cod_gabriel/Flickr. 356 (bottom), Ralf Siemieniec/Shutterstock. 357 (top), Petr Svarc/Alamy. 357 (bottom), R. Matina/age fotostock. 358, José Fuste Raga/age fotostock. 359, Ciprian Dumitrescu/iStockphoto. 360, Walter Zerla/age fotostock. Chapter 8: Thessaloniki and Central Macedonia: 363, SIME s.a.s/eStock Photo. 365 (top), Mircea BEZERGHEANU/Shutterstock. 365 (bottom), PANAGIOTIS KARAPANAGIOTIS/iStockphoto. 366, Mircea BEZERGHEANU/Shutterstock. 373, JTB Photo/age fotostock. 385, giulio andreini/age fotostock. 395, DEA/G DAGLI ORTI /age fotostock. 402, Detsis/IML/age fotostock. 404, Hapsis/IML/age fotostock. Chapter 9: Corfu: 407, PCL/Alamy. 408 (top), sanderovski & linda/Flickr. 408 (bottom), Philippe Teuwen/wikipedia.org. 409 (top), Ljupco Smokovski/Shutterstock. 409 (bottom), Netfalls/ Shutterstock. 410, Betsy Bobo, Fodors.com member. 419, Ellen Rooney/age fotostock. 427, Werner Otto/age fotostock. 438, Ljupco Smokovski/Shutterstock. Chapter 10: The Peloponnese: 441, Johanna Huber/simephoto/eStockphoto. 442, ollirg/Shutterstock. 443 (top), Steve Maehl/Shutterstock. 443 (bottom), Robert Ranson/Shutterstock. 444, ollirg/Shutterstock. 457, Tuul/age fotostock. 462, Greece/ Alamy. 468, DEA/A VERGANI/age fotostock. 477, Moustafellou/IML/ age fotostock. 480, Public

Domain. 481, J.D. Dallet/age fotostock. 482, Mary Evans Picture Library/Alamy. 483 (top left, bottom left, top right, and center right), J.D. Dallet/age fotostock. 483 (bottom right), Daniel Mühlethaler/ iStockphoto. 484-85, ACE STOCK LIMITED/Alamy. 492-93, Richard Bowden/shutterstock. 502, J.D. Dallet/age fotostock. Chapter 11: The Cyclades: 505, Barry Fishman, Fodors.com member. 506, Petros Tsonis/Shutterstock. 507, byrdiegyrl/Flickr. 508, Barry Fishman, Fodors.com member. 543, San Rostro/ age fotostock. 556, Willine Thoe, Fodors.com member. 561, Marco Simoni/age fotostock. 565, volk65/ Shutterstock. 568, Danilo Ascione/Shutterstock. 572, Spyropoulos/IML/age fotostock. 588, Cheryl Jenkins, Fodors.com member. 603, Constantineas/IML/age fotostock. 610, Apollofoto/Shutterstock. 612, Wolfgang Amri/Shutterstock. 613 (top), The Print Collector/Alamy. 613 (bottom), Wojtek Buss/age fotostock. 620, Jennifer Duc, Fodors.com member. Chapter 12: Crete: 629, Giovanni Simeone/SIME-4Corners Images/eStock Photo. 630 (top), robertpaulyoung/Flickr. 630 (bottom), Shadowgate/Flickr. 631 (top and bottom), Irina Korshunova/Shutterstock. 632, Alvaro Leiva/age fotostock. 640, Vladimir Dolgov / Shutterstock. 642, Doug Pearson/age fotostock. 651, Yiannis Papadimitriou/Shutterstock. 663, Walter Bibikow/age fotostock. 664, liv friis-larsen/iStockphoto. 665 (top left), Jastrow/wikipedia. org. 665 (top right), San Rostro/age fotostock. 665 (bottom), blickwinkel/Alamy. 671, GUIZIOU Franck/age fotostock. Chapter 13: Rhodes & the Dodecanese: 675, Ellen Rooney/age fotostock. 676, Jozsef Szasz-Fabian/Shutterstock. 677 (top), Khirman Vladimir/Shutterstock. 677 (bottom), Olga Lipatova/Shutterstock. 678, Barry Fishman, Fodors.com member. 684, Vladimir Dolgov/Shutterstock. 687, Warner Bros/ Everett Collection. 688 (left), wikipedia.org. 688 (top right), Walter Bibikow/age fotostock. 688 (bottom right), SLATER Eliott/age fotostock. 689 (left), Terence Waeland/Alamy. 689 (top right), giulio andreini/age fotostock. 689 (bottom right), Image Asset Management/age fotostock. 690 (top left), ACE STOCK LIMITED/Alamy. 690 (bottom left), wikipedia.org. 690 (right), Rene Mattes/ age fotostock. 691 (top left), Warner Bros/ Everett Collection. 691 (center left and right), Peter Horree/ Alamy. 691 (bottom left), Keith Binns/iStockphoto. 692 (top left), Image Asset Management/age fotostock. 692 (bottom left), wikipedia.org. 692 (right), T. Papageorgiou/age fotostock. 693 (top left), ALIKI SAPOUNTZI/aliki image library/Alamy. 693 (bottom left), terry harris just greece photo library/ Alamy. 693 (right) and 694 (top and bottom left), wikipedia.org. 694 (bottom right), Web Gallery of Art. 697, Voutsas/IML/age fotostock. 703, P. Narayan/age fotostock. 712, Jon Arnold Images Ltd/ Alamy. 725, giulio andreini/age fotostock. Chapter 14: The Northern Aegean Islands: 727, Reiner Harscher/laif/Aurora Photos. 728 (top), Pe-sa/wikipedia.org. 728 (bottom), Greek National Tourist Organization. 729, Saso Novoselic/iStockphoto. 730, Kostisl/wikipedia.org. 751, Walter Bibikow/age fotostock. 760, Unknown Spectrum phot/age fotostock. Back cover (from left to right): Gosiek-B/ iStockphoto; Steve Maehl/Shutterstock; David H.Seymour/Shutterstock. Spine: ivanmateev/iStock-photo.

About Our Writers: All photos are courtesy of the writers.

NOTES

NOTES

NOTES

NOTES

NOTES

NOTES

NOTES

NOTES